author index and bibliography, *Method and Theory in Experimental Psychology* is enhanced by numerous graphs and illustrations, many appearing for the first time. Its penetrating theoretical insights, wealth of experimental evidence and complete clarity of style make it a major contribution to its field.

the author . . .

Charles E. Osgood is Professor of Psychology and Director of the Institute of Communications Research, University of Illinois. He previously taught at the University of Connecticut and at Yale University where he received his Ph.D.

METHOD AND THEORY IN EXPERIMENTAL PSYCHOLOGY

METHOD AND THEORY
IN
EXPERIMENTAL PSYCHOLOGY

CHARLES E. OSGOOD

PROFESSOR OF PSYCHOLOGY
UNIVERSITY OF ILLINOIS

NEW YORK ■ OXFORD UNIVERSITY PRESS

Preface

My principal purpose in writing this book was to provide undergraduate majors and graduate students in psychology with a text that evaluates experimental literature in close relation to critical theoretical issues. In my opinion, most advanced texts have failed to demonstrate this close interrelatedness of fact and theory. I have covered the major portion of what is called experimental psychology, including sections on sensory processes, perception, learning, and symbolic processes. Rather than simply laying out a series of separate studies, however, I have attempted to provide an interpretive framework that both brings out the significance of existing research and directs the reader's thinking toward as yet unsolved problems that need further research.

As my aim has been to provide a carefully organized and extensive textbook coverage of the experimental literature, a more detailed description of critical experiments has been given than is usual. Moreover, largely neglected material on such questions as synesthesia, human problem-solving, and language behavior has been brought into relation with standard content. The book's usefulness as a reference work is enhanced by a combined author index and bibliography, and use has been made of numerous graphs and figures, many of them appearing here for the first time.

Although the coverage is extensive, it is also selective. I have tried to maintain throughout a certain continuity of approach, stressing those studies most pertinent to the theoretical issues. This, I believe, is the greatest benefit deriving from single authorship of such a book.

I have tried to overcome the potential disadvantage of single authorship by submitting the many chapters that lay outside my own fields of special competence to one or more experimentalists who are experts in the fields concerned. Thus Professors Alphonse Chapanis of Johns Hopkins University, Lorrin Riggs of Brown University, and Vernor Wulff of Syracuse University (physiology) have read the chapter on vision; Professors Grant Fairbanks of the University of Illinois and Dewey Neff of the University of Chicago have read the chapter on audition; many physiological sections were read by Professor Lawrence O'Kelly of the University of Illinois; the first three chapters on learning (basic phenomena, theories, and critical issues) were read by Professors G. Robert Grice and O. Hobart Mowrer of the University of Illinois, and the final two chapters in this section (human learning), by Professor Carl Hovland of Yale University; Dr. Davis Howes of Wright Field Aero-Medical Laboratory and Professor

v

George Miller of the Massachusetts Institute of Technology read the chapters on audition and language, Professor Theodore Karwoski of Dartmouth College, those on vision and language, and Professor Weston Bousfield of the University of Connecticut, those on human learning and language, while Professor Ross Stagner of the University of Illinois read the entire section on symbolic processes. These readers contributed suggestions and criticisms which were of incalculable help to me.

I should also like to express my gratitude to Professor Kenneth W. Spence of the University of Iowa; Professor D. O. Hebb of McGill University in Canada; Professor E. G. Wever of Princeton University; and Professor Harry Helson of the University of Texas, who read and commented on portions of the manuscript at the request of the publishers. In addition, a number of graduate students have read the entire manuscript as part of their preparation for Preliminary Examinations, and their comments have been most useful.

In the last analysis, however, the point of view which gives unity to this book is my own. It will become evident that I favor the 'full' as contrasted with the 'empty' organism position, and that I am eager to use whatever physiological information is available on each problem and willing to employ hypothetical and intervening variables where the facts seem to require them. The phenomena of learning and symbolic processes are organized and interpreted in terms of what is called a mediation hypothesis, which provides a consistent picture of behavior, from simple conditioning and maze running in the white rat, to complex language performances in the human. This stresses once again the importance of meaning in the science of psychology, and a serious attempt is made to anchor this central variable to observable phenomena. Finally, the pervasive theoretical issue between gestalt and behavioristic positions has been made explicit in the many areas where it appears—in perception, in learning, in remembering, and in problem-solving and thinking—and it is felt that some progress has been made toward its resolution.

These and the other points of view which shape this book are part of a large but indefinite debt I owe to the many teachers, friends, and students from whose active minds I have borrowed, at Dartmouth, Yale, Connecticut, and Illinois. I take this opportunity to thank my mother for her constant support; without her sacrifices I could not have received the training which made this book possible. To my wife I also owe a special word of gratitude; during a decade while all my energies have been going into my work, she has managed more or less single-handedly to keep our family life on an even keel, and has still found time to help with the preparation of this book for publication.

C. E. O.

Champaign, Illinois
July 1953

Contents

Part I   **SENSORY PROCESSES, 1**

1. Sensory Quality, 3
2. Sensory Intensity, 42
3. Audition, 84
4. Vision, 128

Part II   **PERCEPTUAL PROCESSES, 191**

5. The Nature of Perceptual Organization, 193
6. Projection Dynamics in Perception, 229
7. Central Dynamics in Perception, 261

Part III   **LEARNING, 299**

8. Fundamental Operations in Learning, 301
9. Theories of Learning, 362
10. Certain Controversial Issues in Learning Theory, 413
11. Neurophysiology of Learning, 474
12. Serial and Transfer Phenomena, 495
13. Retention, 549

Part IV   **SYMBOLIC PROCESSES, 601**

14. Problem-solving and Insight, 603
15. Thinking, 638
16. Language Behavior, 680

BIBLIOGRAPHY AND AUTHOR INDEX, 729

SUBJECT INDEX, 781

Part I

SENSORY PROCESSES

Where is the environment? The answer to this question comes promptly enough—the environment is 'out there.' It is this book, the walls of this room, the people passing to and fro; it is everything that is outside of us. This answer is, of course, a rational one, but it is founded upon an elaborate system of inferences developed through a lifetime of experiencing. If a forefinger is placed along the lower ridge of the eye socket so that its tip is against the nose and the other eye is covered, pressing the eyeball gently and moving it up and down will cause the environment to jump back and forth. Now this is manifestly unreasonable! Any force sufficient to shake the room would also have been felt as vibration. But what, then, is the explanation of this phenomenon? When the visual image shifts *without* synchronous innervation of the muscles, we normally interpret the change as owing to movement in the environment—we have been motionless and hence the environment must have moved. In the present demonstration the eye is moved passively, without innervation of eye or neck muscles, and we therefore make the perceptual inference that the environment moved—in keeping with all previous experience.

This is an illusion and, as is true with most illusions, it serves to reveal a basic fact about the nature of awareness. The only 'environment' of which we are directly aware as sensate organisms is the pattern of physical energies that directly affects our receptors. The seen environment is a changing pattern of radiant energies upon the retina. A friend's voice is a changing pattern of vibrations transmitted to the auditory receptors. It is not the rose that smells, but a kind of chemical action taking place on the olfactory epithelium within our own nose. In other words, all of the environment of which we are directly aware is quite literally plastered upon our body surface, for within this surface are located the specialized receptors that react to various forms of energy abounding in the physical world. Without these specialized receptors we should be like insensate blocks of wood—no environment would exist for us.

But we can internalize the environment still further. Here is another demonstration: select a fairly rough surface, such as the cover of this book; aim the forefinger at it and, closing your eyes, weave the finger slowly toward the surface, waiting expectantly for the sensation of contact.

Where does the sensation of contact seem to be localized? Obviously it is felt at the tip of the finger, yet this too is an inference. The awareness of sensation is not at the finger tip but rather somewhere in the cutaneous areas of the brain. How do we know this? For one thing, electrical stimulation of the sensory cortex produces sensations which the subject feels as if they were at various points on the periphery. If your own sensory cortex were bared for investigation by removal of part of the skull and protective membrane, painstaking exploration might possibly reproduce a sensation equivalent to 'touching the surface of a book,' and you would feel it as if it were at your finger tip. Furthermore, people who have had arms or legs amputated sometimes experience 'phantom limbs.' Owing possibly to irritation of sensory fibers in the stump, sensations are produced which the patient refers to a twisted ankle or an itching toe—and it is most uncomfortable to have an itch in a nonexistent toe!

Behaviorally, the environment is a pattern of neural energies in the central nervous system. This is to be construed as a statement about the relation of the organism to its environment, not as a philosophical position denying the existence of the material world. Indeed, it is the physical energies in the material world that presumably set into action those neural processes that eventuate in awareness. Our problem in the chapters that constitute this section will be to trace this process of stimulation: what are the specialized receptors which react to physical energies of various types? how sensitive are they? what demonstrable correlations exist between physical stimulus and psychological sensation? how does the structure and function of the sensory nervous system mediate between stimulus and sensation? In the first two chapters we shall survey sensitivity in general, first *sensory quality* and then *sensory intensity*. The information available on both *audition* and *vision* merit—indeed, require—separate treatment, and separate chapters in this section will be devoted to a study of these modalities.

Chapter 1

SENSORY QUALITY

The organism is surrounded by a pressing, vibrating, radiating, chemically reacting manifold of physical energies. Into this maelstrom of forces, like a sensitive antenna, extends the nervous system. The physical energies to which it reacts originate both in the external and the internal environments; movements of muscles and changes in blood chemistry, to the extent that receptors are excited, are as much a part of the environment as are flashes of light or sound waves. As the science of behavior, psychology is chiefly concerned with end results of nervous activity.

The nervous system, however, is limited in its receptivity. It is limited first by the design of its *specialized receptors*. In vision, for example, receptors are selectively sensitive to a narrow band of wave lengths of radiant energy; on both sides of this narrow band extend wave lengths for which we have no direct awareness. The general picture one gets is that human and other organisms have forms and ranges of sensitivity that match biologically significant variations in environmental energies. They are maximally sensitive to sounds produced by grossly moving objects, to odors produced by putrid flesh and flowering plants. Darwinian principles have undoubtedly played their part in molding our sensory equipment as well as in forming other bodily structures. The nervous system is also limited in its *intensive sensitivity;* this will be studied in the next chapter.

METHODS OF INVESTIGATION

The irrationality of erecting arbitrary barriers between the sciences is clearly demonstrated in the study of sensory processes. Progress here has come from the combined efforts of many specialists—physicists, ophthalmologists, chemists, physiologists, and neurologists, to call only part of the roll, as well as psychologists. Methods vary from the thoughtfully phenomenological approach of the introspective psychologist to the precisely quantitative approach of the mathematical physiochemist. Three major relations may be studied: (1) that between physical stimulus and reportable psychological sensation; (2) that between physical stimulus and afferent neural activity; and (3) that between afferent neural activity and reportable psychological sensation. The first relation is patently psychological and has

3

historical priority. The second lies within the province of neurophysiology. The third relation—that between measurable activity in the sensory nerves and reportable sensations—is virtually unexplored. The reason is that only human subjects can describe their private sensations, and they are not willing to undergo the extreme sacrifices which physiological analysis usually demands. Although we shall draw upon illustrations from the skin senses in this survey of methods, it should be kept in mind that the same procedures have been applied in all modalities.

Localization of Differentially Sensitive Points

The strictly psychological method of identifying different sensations with different loci on the receptive surface is usually a first step. This procedure demands introspections from human subjects. These subjective reports are usually the only connection between structural, electrical, and other characteristics of the sensory system and the qualitatively discriminable sensations of conscious humans. The earliest scientific explorers of the skin used this method. In the 1880's three different investigators, Blix (a Swede), Goldscheider (a German), and Donaldson (an American), independently reported the discovery that the skin, rather than being the continuously sensitive surface it appears to casual introspection, showed *punctate receptivity*. It is a mosaic of points yielding different qualities of experience. Blix, for example, used faradic stimulation—when the surface of the skin was explored with the single electrode from an induction coil, different loci gave rise to sensations of pressure, of pain, of cold, and of warmth. Note that the same form of stimulus is producing different sensations, depending on the place stimulated. Von Frey (1896), whose work contributed heavily to the classic theory in this field, also used this method.

Exploration of the surface of the skin, a standard project in the psychological laboratory, is carried on in somewhat the same way a mineralogist explores the surface of the earth for precious ores. Like an explorer of the earth, we need both a map and specialized tools. A map is readily provided by a rubber stamp that etches a square centimeter of skin, say on the volar surface of the forearm, into 100 millimeter squares. Von Frey provided appropriate tools for studying *touch sensitivity*—he used both human and horse hairs as stimulators, fastening them to short sticks with sealing wax. The advantage of using hairs for this purpose is that maximum pressure is reached almost at the moment of application, and pressure remains constant as long as the bending point of the hair is perpendicular to the stimulation point. By using such a tool and pressing systematically over the mapped area, certain points are found to yield a clear pressure sensation, and these are marked with indelible ink. If a thicker, stiffer stimulator is used (i.e. greater intensity), the number of touch spots is found to increase. We also observe that every hair growing on the skin has a pressure spot associated with it, the hair serving as a tiny lever to magnify small energies. Pressure spots occur, however, where there are no hairs.

A sharp needle may be used to test for *pain sensitivity*. If the needle is pressed lightly into previously located touch spots, the subject usually reports pressure, not pain—provided the intensity of stimulation is not too great. Further exploration reveals that this small area is richly and irregularly supplied with points which do give rise to prickly pain. An instrument that will apply a stimulus of known temperature and constant pressure to a small area is required to localize *warmth and cold sensitivity*. Dallenbach (1927) devised a commonly used thermal stimulator: a projecting copper stimulus point is kept at a given temperature by circulating water through a tubular system which surrounds the copper point; the handle of the instrument is affixed to a scaled spring which makes it possible to equate pressure. Superficial exploration with such an instrument makes it appear as though cold spots were much more numerous than warm spots; it turns out that this is only because warm spots tend to be clustered more closely.

Are these sensory 'spots' stable? The reports of early investigators often made it appear that this was the case, yet students in every psychological laboratory find these 'spots' to be rather fickle—plots on day 1 are seldom accurately duplicated on day 2. There are really two questions here: (a) Do 'spots' change in the quality they yield from time to time? The answer here seems to be 'no,' provided intensity is constant. (b) Do 'spots' that initially yield a given sensation sometimes fail to respond? The answer here is 'yes,' unequivocally. Dallenbach (1927) has attributed much of the variation in localization to looseness in experimental technique—a map impressed on skin is bound to be inexact; changes in the temperature of the stimulator by as little as one degree can change the plot; pressure inequalities may 'paradoxically' stimulate thermal receptors, and so on. Observing his own strictures, Dallenbach then proceeded to plot and replot cold and warm spots in the same regions. His results showed that the localizations on successive plottings correspond better to what would be expected on the hypothesis of definite, punctate spots than on the hypothesis of chance. Why is there any variation? It is probable that the 'spots' located by this method represent clusters or concentrations of many individual receptors which vary from time to time in their sensitivity (cf. Jenkins's concentration theory below).

Occasionally, when exploring with a warm stimulus (approximately 45° C.), a spot is touched that yields a clear-cut cold sensation. This experience is known as *paradoxical cold*—paradoxical because it is elicited by a warm stimulus. This is part of a large body of evidence supporting a famous law in sensory psychology, the 'law of specific energies of nerve fibers,' announced by Johannes Müller in 1826: *The quality of sensation depends upon the type of fiber excited, not upon the form of physical energy which initiates the process.* The mere fact that the skin shows punctate sensitivity favors this law.

Whether or not Müller's Law has general validity is a question we must bear in mind throughout this and the following chapters in this section. Von Frey, on the basis of his own extensive exploration of the skin surface, linked each of the four cutaneous modalities (touch, pain, warmth, and cold) with a different type of end organ. It was perhaps because this view fitted hand in hand with Müller's law of specific nerve energies that it became the classic theory in the field. We shall see, however, that the association of different modalities with different kinds of end organs has not stood up under the constant barrage of experimentation. It is interesting, when viewed in historical perspective, that Von Frey formulated his specific receptor theory without any reference to the earlier work of Blix, Goldscheider, and Donaldson. Both Goldscheider and Donaldson had excised sensitive spots for various modalities and found nothing but free nerve endings of apparently identical type (cf. Boring, 1942). This leads us to consider another method.

Histological Analysis

Once differentially sensitive spots have been localized in terms of introspective reports, the next logical step is to excise the skin directly below the

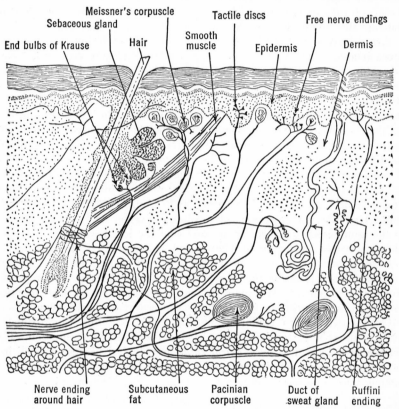

FIGURE 1. Schematic drawing of a cross section of the human skin. In the classic view, touch sensitivity is associated with basket cells about hair follicles and with Meissner's corpuscles, pain with free nerve endings, cold with Krause's end bulbs, and warmth with Ruffini endings. Not all of the structures shown in the diagram are to be found in any one area of skin. Heavy lines denote myelinated fibers and light lines unmyelinated ones. After Woolard *et al.* From E. Gardner, *Fundamentals of Neurology*. Philadelphia: Saunders, 1947, p. 111.

spots and examine it microscopically. It would seem to be a very simple matter—all we have to do is note the kind of nervous end organ always found below a given kind of spot. It is not as simple as this: (a) the skin is a remarkably complicated structure. Figure 1 presents a typical thin section of skin after it has been excised and stained with methylene blue or silver preparations, and some idea can be gathered of the complexity of the nerve supply. (b) We know that the effects of stimulation—mechanical distortion of the skin surface, a change in temperature, or something else— irradiate through the skin. How are we ever to be sure that the receptor responsible for a particular sensation is located directly beneath a given spot? (c) There is no necessary reason to assume that the nerve endings associated with different modalities must necessarily 'look different.' The legend of Fig. 1 follows Von Frey's classic picture, in essence: pressure is attributed to basket cells about the hair follicles and, where no hairs are present, to Meissner's corpuscles; pain is attributed to free nerve endings; cold to Krause's end bulbs; warmth to the Ruffini cylinders. Although these structures may be receptors for the qualities given, it is doubtful whether they are the only organs responsible.

Careful inspection of sections of skin like that shown in Fig. 1 reveals three general types of neural structures: free nerve endings, interfiltrating nerve plexi, and specialized endings of various sorts. As one ascends the phylogenetic series there is increasing complexity and variety of end organs. Branches of single fibers, however, are found to bear endings of only one type—branches of a single nerve may innervate basket cells over as wide an area as 1 sq. cm., but not Krause end bulbs. Similarly, nerve nets arising from a single fiber spread over a considerable area, the regions subserved by different fibers overlapping. When a single cutaneous nerve is severed, a small area is rendered completely anesthetic, this being surrounded by a wider band of reduced sensitivity (cf. Weddell, Gutmann, and Gutmann, 1941). The region of reduced sensitivity is being supplied in part by surrounding fibers.

A less direct histological method correlates, within given areas, the number of sensitive spots of each quality with the number of endings of each type subsequently observed (cf. Bazett, McGlone, Williams, and Lufkin, 1932). Thus, if there is correspondence in frequency of Krause end bulbs in various regions of the skin with the number of cold spots in the same regions, identification between the two is indicated. Irradiation of stimulation, variation in receptor thresholds, and the likely possibility that free nerve endings are involved in all modalities cast doubt on the validity of this method. In general, in so far as the critical issue is identification of particular endings with particular forms of skin sensitivity, histological methods have not been too successful.

Electrophysiological Methods

Probably no single technological development has given more impetus to biological research than the introduction of electronic devices, particularly the vacuum tube which makes it possible to amplify infinitesimally small electrical currents to the point where they can be recorded. Since repeated reference to these electrophysiological techniques will be made throughout this section on sensory processes, it will be well to become familiar with their nature at the beginning. Electrical systems, like other methods of recording action (cf. Wendt, 1938), may be described in terms of four stages: pickup or coupling systems, transmitting systems, amplifying systems, and recording systems. (Specific details of application, which vary from problem to problem and modality to modality, will be considered in context—only a general description is offered here.)

The *pickup system* couples the apparatus to the organism. With electrical devices a pair of electrodes usually serves this purpose. In monopolar recording, one electrode, the active or grid electrode, is placed near the location of the energy exchange one wishes to measure and the other, the ground electrode, is placed some distance away on inactive tissue. This is the technique employed in obtaining electroencephalograms (EEG's) from the brain: one or more active electrodes are fastened to the skull with collodion and the ground electrode is usually attached to the ear lobe. Similar methods are used in recording action currents in nerve trunks and muscle. In bipolar recording, both electrodes are placed near the site of the energy exchange. In recording from single fibers, for example, both electrodes may be placed at different points on the same nerve. In either case potential differences between the two electrodes are measured. A more recent development is the coaxial electrode. A very fine silver wire, to serve as the grid electrode, is inserted within the small tube of a syringe needle, the outer shell of which serves as the ground electrode. Insulating cement is put in the tube around the wire to shield one electrode from the other. This tiny instrument is then carefully ground and tested for 'battery effect' (producing its own current between the two electrodes). This battery effect is one of the distortions that may arise at the point of coupling with electrical devices. Another source of distortion is an inconstant electrical contact with the tissue— spurious changes in potential are introduced. A special electrode paste is generally used to insure constant contact.

The *transmission system* conveys the energy picked up at the point of coupling to the place where it is transformed into intelligible information. Unlike mechanical and pneumatic systems—which, owing to inertia and friction factors, always produce distortions that can only be minimized— most electrical systems transmit without distortion to the recording device. They share this advantage with optical systems, where the movements of a beam of light (or shadow) transmit the desired energy changes directly to the photographic recording paper.

In studying nerve potentials we are dealing with energy transformations in the order of one millionth of a volt. How can such almost inconceivably small magnitudes be rendered observable? It was to this problem that the *vacuum tube amplifier* provided a satisfactory answer. The basic principle is extremely simple: a small potential change is used to control and modulate the flow of a much larger current. The English term 'valve' is much more descriptive than ours, for this is precisely the function of the small input current in the vacuum tube. Figure 2 shows the basic design. Potential differences between the grid electrode and ground electrode (B) constitute the input to the system. These changes in potential vary the resistance which the grid (G) in the vacuum tube offers to the flow of a much larger current from the filament (F) to the plate (P). The large current output thus reflects potential changes in the small current input. The output leads of this first amplification unit are simultaneously the input leads for a further amplification stage, and so on, until initial electrical magnitudes as small as a millionth of a volt can be magnified to the point where they are sufficient to operate a recording system. Amplification in such a system is limited only by the background action under the electrodes and within the transmission system, i.e. the 'noise' in the system. Another advantage of this apparatus is that there is no 'back action'—it takes no current from the organism and delivers none to it.

Finally, the *recording system* transforms the information to a record which is readily inspected by the experimenter and, ideally, is capable of being permanently stored. The smoked-paper kymograph was a standard, if crude, recording device in psychological laboratories: smoked paper was wrapped around the cylindrical kymograph which turned at a steady rate; curl-pointed styli, as termini of mechanical or pneumatic transmission systems, moved up and down against this sooty surface, wiping it away and leaving a trace; after the record had been secured, the smoked paper was dipped in a special shellac which, when dried, preserved the record from smudging—all in all a very messy procedure that many of us have nevertheless suffered through! Obviously in this recording system we have to

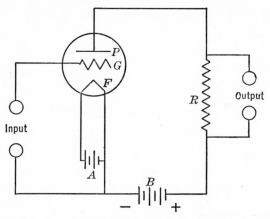

FIGURE 2. Circuit diagram illustrating the principle of the vacuum tube amplifier.

worry about the friction created at the point of contact with the recording surface. Most modern recording systems eliminate such friction almost entirely. In spark-gap recordographs, for example, an electrical spark leaps repeatedly between two points (moved mechanically as the terminus of the transmission system) and passes through the moving recording paper, burning a path through this paper but not impeding its motion. When waxed paper and heated styli are used, again friction is largely eliminated, the pathway in the melted wax revealing the darker paper beneath and thus providing a graphic record of the response. Most commonly used today are *ink-writing polygraphs*. Very light capillary pens, which also serve as the termini of transmission via mechanical, pneumatic, or electrical means, write upon continuous graph paper that moves under the writing surface at a constant rate. The only resistance here is the surface tension of the ink itself, since the pens do not touch the paper.

One of the most useful recording devices in electrical work is the *cathode-ray oscillograph*. Its function is to translate an electrical wave into a visual pattern which may be photographed and analyzed in detail; its main advantages are that it requires a minimum of signal input to operate, has (practically speaking) no inertia, friction or 'bounce,' and can therefore follow responses of any speed without distortion. It is invaluable for recording bursts of impulses in nerve fibers (with frequencies up to 500 or more per second), analyzing sound waves (with frequencies up to many thousand cycles per second), and so on. Figure 3 describes the essential elements. A vacuum tube of the shape illustrated contains a filament (cathode) that, when heated, emits a stream of electrons; these electrons are drawn rapidly toward the positively charged plate (anode) which contains a small hole through which some of the electrons shoot, striking against the broad end of the tube. Since this end of the tube is coated with a fluorescent material, the stream of electrons creates a fine point of light. The sweep circuit charges the vertical plates through a condenser system, drawing the stream of electrons more and more toward one side, then releasing them, and so on, and the point of light moves successively, in one direction, across the face of the tube at a rate that can be varied. The potential changes representing the amplified signal (impulses in nerve, electrical waves in a microphone, etc.) are now impressed on the horizontal plates, thus causing the

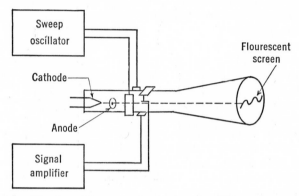

FIGURE 3. Diagram of cathode-ray oscillograph.

bright spot to move up and down. By appropriate adjustments in the timing of the sweep circuit, a burst of impulses in a nerve fiber may be made to appear as a series of spikes on the surface of the tube. Similarly, the potential changes characteristic of a single impulse may be traced.

These electrical techniques seemed to open a direct attack on the law of specific energies. Could it be shown that the fibers subserving different cutaneous modalities had different transmission characteristics? The specific method here is to stimulate a sensory nerve at one point and record action currents from electrodes attached some distance away (cf. Gasser, 1935; Erlanger and Gasser, 1937). Recordings taken from large numbers of fibers yield what is known as a 'spectrum' of conduction rates. Although classificatory systems are not standardized, the general picture can be presented as follows (see Jenkins and Stone, 1941, and Sanders, 1947):

FIBER TYPE	MYELINATION	SIZE	CONDUCTION RATE
A	heavily	large	fast (30 m./sec. plus)
B	lightly	medium	medium (5 to 15 m./sec.)
C	not	small	slow (1 to 2 m./sec.)

The large, heavily myelinated fibers tend to have the fastest conduction rates; the small unmyelinated fibers, the slowest. Two words of caution must be mentioned: (a) nerve fibers are not literally divided into 'types'; rather there is fairly continuous variation in size, myelination, and conduction rate,

A type verging into B type and so on; (b) there is as yet no *direct* correlation between fiber type and sensory quality—precise records of nerve fiber action are obtained from animal preparations, whereas the quality of sensations can only be reported by conscious human subjects.

Although direct correlation between nerve action and reported sensory quality is difficult to obtain, highly suggestive indirect evidence is gained in the following fashion: with conscious human subjects, application of various drugs to the cutaneous nerves, or shutting off their blood supply (asphyxiation), causes sensitivity to disappear in definite orders; similar treatment with animal preparations checks the order of disappearance of various types of action currents in cutaneous nerve trunks. The implicit assumption here is that the sensory nervous systems of animals like the cat, rabbit, and dog function like that of the human—probably a quite justifiable expectation when dealing with peripheral nervous structures. So, we measure sensations in humans, nerve fiber activity in animals, and draw inferences from the correlation.

When a cutaneous nerve trunk in the human subject is blocked by cocaine and continuous exploration of skin sensitivity is made while the drug is taking effect, sensitivity to dull pain diminishes first, followed by cold and warmth, then bright pain, and finally light pressure. Correlated animal studies show that the slow impulses associated with small, unmyelinated fibers disappear first in the record, followed by impulses of medium speed, and finally by the large, fast impulses associated with the heavily myelinated fibers. Presumably, the resistance of nerve to the effects of a narcotic depends upon the thickness of its myelin sheath. One can also trace the course of *recovery* from injection; Lanier (1935) has done this following injection of alcohol and Bishop (1944) following injection of Novocain. Here again dissociation between sensory modalities in their rates of recovery is evidence for specificity. When a cuff is placed about the arm of the human subject and tightened, thus cutting off circulation, continuous testing shows a pattern of sensitivity loss quite different from that produced by drugs: light pressure disappears first, followed by cold and dull pressure, then warmth, and finally pain. This is a fairly accurate description of what happens when one's arm or leg 'goes to sleep.' The oscillograph records from animals subjected to local asphyxiation show a correlated elimination of fiber types: here impulses in A fibers disappear first, then B fibers, and finally C fibers. Presumably the resistance of a nerve fiber to asphyxiation varies inversely with the energy used up in firing it—large A-type fibers exhaust their local oxygen supply more rapidly.

From these correlations one is tempted to identify light-pressure sensitivity with A-type fibers, warmth and cold with B-type, and dull pain with the more primitive C-type fibers. That so-called bright pain (under the fingernails) is associated with A-type fibers and so-called dull pain (toothache) with C-type is suggested by Lewis (1942). But this attractive solution is somewhat superficial. It is possible that bright pain may be mediated by either A or B fibers, or both; it is not even clear from the evidence that the 'brightness' of bright pain can be dissociated from pressure (Bishop, 1946). Although cold seems to be identifiable with B-type fibers, between the fast A-type touch fibers and the slow C-type dull-pain fibers, warmth appears to include fibers both faster and slower in their conduction rates than cold, overlapping both A- and C-type distributions (cf. Morgan, 1943). Finally, as far as direct substantiation of Müller's Law is concerned, the evidence is in some respects flatly contradictory: A-type fibers appear to subserve both pressure and pain, and possibly warmth; B-type fibers include cold and possibly both warmth and pain; and C-type fibers may mediate warmth as well as dull pain. It is quite likely that this situation will be clarified by future research.

In some cases it is possible *to record from isolated sensory fibers.* Using delicate surgical techniques and animal subjects, single afferent fibers are teased out from nerve bundles and placed in contact with electrodes. Impulse characteristics may then be recorded as various stimuli are applied to the attached end organs. This method has been applied to the skin senses by Adrian and his co-workers (cf. Adrian, 1928), but the results are more relevant to problems of intensive sensitivity. The method has also been used fruitfully in studying both vision and hearing and will be described in some detail in those places.

CUTANEOUS PRESSURE SENSITIVITY

One of the first questions that arise with respect to any sensory modality is, What are the *receptors* which 'couple' the organism to a particular source of environmental energy exchange? What are the receptors for pressure against the skin? There is no question but that the *basket cells* about the bases of hair follicles mediate light pressure. This has been evident from all the methods surveyed. This form of sensitivity, however, also exists where no hair follicles are found, and it is likely that both *Meissner corpuscles* and *Merkel disks* also subserve this modality. There is further evidence that *undifferentiated free nerve endings* are involved here as well. When the superficial epidermis, containing only free nerve endings, is removed, the large, fast impulses associated with light pressure are eliminated (Erlanger and Gasser, 1937). Gilmer (1942) has added the *glomus bodies,* associated with the vascular system of the skin, to the specialized structures subserving this sense. That the various qualities of touch—light pressure, deep pressure, vibratory sensitivity—may be distributed selectively among these different end organs is certainly a possibility, but there is little direct evidence.

A second question with respect to any modality is, What is the *adequate stimulus?* Receptors in the skin can be activated by numerous stimulus-objects, such as fine hairs, heated copper points and needles. But these objects are not stimuli; they are the agents by which receptors are stimulated. One might also call the experimenter an agent in this sense, but he is certainly not the stimulus. *A stimulus may be defined as that form of physical energy that activates a receptor.* What is the form of physical energy exchange that sets up impulses in pressure receptors, in basket cells, Merkel disks, and so on?

The obvious explanation—that the 'pressure' experience is caused by pressure against the skin—was effectively dismissed by Von Frey when he demonstrated that an identical experience could be produced by *lifting* an object attached to the skin, i.e. decreasing pressure. Another familiar contradiction is the fact that, when one's arm is immersed in water, pressure is felt only at the water line. Observations of this sort led to the gradient theory. Receptors in the skin are mechanically stimulated by distortion or stretching its surface, the magnitude of stimulation varying with the pressure gradient set up at a given point. This leads to the expectation that pressure experience should vary with the perimeter of a stimulating object rather than the area stimulated, i.e. with the amount of skin subjected to a sharp-pressure gradient. Holway and Crozier (1937 *a, b*) have questioned this explanation. They placed solid and annular glass vessels on the skin and added water at a gradual rate until a just noticeable difference in pressure was reported. They found differential sensitivity to vary with weight per unit area, independent of the shape of the stimulator; when objects of the same area but different perimeters were employed, differential sensitivity was constant. Jenkins and Stone (1941) have criticized this method. They offer evidence for a chemical mode of stimulation of touch receptors, mainly that touch adaptation rates can be varied by chemical treatment of the skin. Even were this the case, however, the chemical release mechanism would presumably be linked to mechanical distortion.

PAIN SENSITIVITY

There is no question but that the free nerve endings associated with small C-type fibers are receptors for *dull pain*. When cutaneous nerves are blocked by asphyxiation to the point where only the small unmyelinated fibers are functioning, only dull pain survives. It seems likely from the evidence cited earlier that *bright pain* is mediated by large A-type free nerve endings. The central areas of the cornea of the eye yield only bright pain when stimulated and only free nerve endings are present. Lewis and his collaborators (cf. Sanders, 1947) have established the reality of a double pain experience to pin prick—an initial bright-prick sensation and a secondary, longer lasting ache. These two experiences are separable by both asphyxiation and co-cainization, reaction times, and the like and have been identified with A and C fibers, respectively.

The glib textbook stimulus for pain is 'injury to the free nerve endings,' although by what strange alchemy the word 'injury' becomes a form of physical energy is not apparent. We are faced with a technical difficulty at the outset: there is no stimulus-object specific for pain. A sharp needle excites not only pain but pressure. The same duality of stimulation applies to heating or freezing the skin. It has been suggested that rupture of the membrane of the free nerve endings may set up an *osmotic gradient* that serves as the physical stimulus. Stone and Jenkins (1940) review evidence in favor of a chemical basis for pain. For example, hyperalgesia (a state of the skin in which pain may be relatively intense) is caused by light burns, scratches, or other injuries, this state lasting for several days and being accentuated by heat and relieved by cold treatment—presumably the chemical surround of the pain receptors has been modified. However, the nature of this chemical substance remains to be identified.

Will any receptor, if stimulated with sufficient intensity, yield a pain sensation? This is a problem of ancient vintage and the evidence as a whole is negative. Goldscheider, in his controversy with Von Frey (cf. Stone and Jenkins, 1940, p. 286), had claimed that the end effect of adapting to pain was a sensation of pressure. He argued therefrom that the initial pain was due to intense firing of pressure receptors. More recent investigators have substantiated Goldscheider's result but have disagreed with his interpretation—the agent that produces the pain (needle) is also an adequate stimulator for pressure. A crucial experiment was contributed by Stone and Dallenbach (1934), who used radiant heat as a stimulator to avoid contamination with pressure reception; under these conditions the painful sensation merely faded away without qualitative change. Adrian (1932) stimulated a single hair basket cell by means of a rod vibrating at high frequencies, and no painful sensations could be obtained. Similarly, if a Meissner (touch) corpuscle is isolated surgically, thereby making possible discrete stimulation, a needle may be stuck right into it without producing anything other than touch quality (Woolard, Weddell, and Harpman, 1940). Individuals who are analgesic (insensitive to pain because of neural disorder) can be plied with hot rods to the skin and yet report only warmth, not pain (cf. Morgan, 1943). In fact, all of the evidence cited earlier which showed differential effects of drugs and asphyxiation upon A, B, and C fiber types points to the existence of a separate pain sense. For presentation of the other point of view, see Nafe (1934).

THERMAL SENSITIVITY

Thermal experiences do not depend directly upon external molecular energies (physical heat) but rather upon changes in the temperature of the skin itself. Heat is normally flowing out from the skin at a constant rate; if this rate is decreased, warmth is experienced; if the rate is increased, cold is experienced. Stimulation with a metallic object, which conducts heat away from the skin, gives rise to the sensation of cold; stimulation with a woolen cloth, which is a poor conductor of heat and hence checks the normal rate of flow, gives rise to a warmth sensation. This lack of direct dependence upon external physical temperature is further shown by the phenomenon of thermal adaptation: after one's hand has been kept in warm water for a time, a physically warm thermal stimulus which previously would have elicited sensation now fails to do so. The *gradient theory* of thermal stimulation holds that the intensity of thermal experience depends upon the sharpness of the change in rate of flow of heat from the skin. This, however, does not tell us the adequate stimulus for cold or warmth. What physical energy transformations initiate impulses in cold and warmth fibers? One's answer depends on which of three theories is sponsored.

Von Frey's Specific Receptor Theory

Von Frey's view is the classic one in the field. In keeping with his general assumption that different sensations are initiated in different types of end organs, he identified Krause end bulbs as the receptors for cold and Ruffini cylinders as the receptors for warmth. For one thing, the average depth of these encapsulated end organs corresponds roughly with the reaction times for the two sensations; for another, certain areas of the body (nipples of the breast, genitalia, and margins of the cornea) having high thermal sensitivity are found to be richly supplied with these receptors. Mere correlation of numbers of end organs of a given type with a certain kind of sensation is, however, only partial evidence. More recent histological studies have revealed numerous cold and warmth spots that are associated with neither Krause end bulbs nor Ruffini cylinders. Most critically, capsulated end organs are not found throughout the skin generally (Stone and Jenkins, 1940), but cold and warmth sensitivity is. The evidence as a whole supports this conclusion: Krause end bulbs and Ruffini cylinders may be specialized receptors for cold and warmth, respectively, but they are not the only endings serving this modality.

Nafe's Vascular Theory

The skin as a whole is richly supplied with blood vessels, these having walls of smooth muscle which are innervated by both motor and sensory fibers. As part of the homeostatic mechanism controlling blood temperature, efferent impulses from the central nervous system produce vasoconstriction and vasodilation, and these muscle movements in turn activate sensory endings. Critical to Nafe's theory is the fact that smooth muscle is also responsive to external changes in temperature (Lewis, 1927); the reaction of smooth muscle to thermal stimulation shows a very neat parallel with thermal experience, increases in temperature causing relaxation and decreases causing contraction. According to the theory, these muscle reactions stimulate receptors imbedded in the muscle walls of the vascular system, and the impulses they set up are experienced as cold and warmth. Nafe (1934) speaks of the quality of sensation as being determined by the spatial and temporal 'patterns' of discharges but does not elaborate on this point. Although it may seem strange that sensations produced by muscle movements should 'feel' cold or warm, there is no essential reason why this should not be; it is no more strange than the fact that impulses in other fibers 'feel' red. The adequate stimulus for thermal experience, according to Nafe's theory, is *mechanical*—contraction or dilation of the smooth muscle walls of the blood vessels causing impulses in sensory endings.

Jenkins's Concentration Theory

Evidence indicating that free nerve endings mediate both pressure and pain has already been offered; W. L. Jenkins completes the load by adding cold and warmth to the list. He assumes that such free nerve endings, although undifferentiated anatomically, are somehow differentiated functionally into cold and warmth receptors. These endings are assumed to be widespread throughout the skin and to vary in both their concentration and their individual thresholds. Given these characteristics, certain well-authenticated observations become predictable: (a) When extremely fine thermal stimulators are used, 'spots' are found to occur in clusters of varying size, i.e. 'hills' and 'valleys' of concentration. (b) The number of reported 'spots' varies with both the size and intensity of the stimulator. (c) Degree of sensitivity varies directly with the number of measured 'spots,' since the more concentrated the receptors, the more probable the presence of some with low thresholds. Evidence for these statements may be found in a series of papers by Jenkins (1939 a, b, c, d). He has proposed a *chemical* mode of stimulation of the thermal receptors (Jenkins, 1938 b). A pseudoreversible chemical reaction, $A \rightleftharpoons B$, is suggested for the cold receptors, with a third substance, C, necessary for the recovery phase. The change in skin temperature about a cold receptor causes a breakdown of A into B, this chemical reaction setting up impulses in the nerve fiber; rebuilding of A from B involves chemical C, which is assumed to be supplied by the blood stream. A similar chemical system (X, Y, and Z) is proposed for warmth stimulation.

Jenkins regards this theory of thermal stimulation as merely a working hypothesis. There are several lines of evidence, however, which favor it. (a) Bazett and McGlone (1932) demonstrated that intense warmth can be experienced upon the release of asphyxial blood back into the arm, while the arm is immersed in a bath kept at constant blood temperature. Since skin temperature is constant, the experience of thermal sensation must be based upon some other source of stimulation, possibly chemical. Note that this would also cause vasodilation, in keeping with Nafe's theory. (b) A series of researches on thermal adaptation by Jenkins himself (1937, 1938 *a, b, c*) offers further evidence. He finds, for example, a relation between the initial strength of sensation in an isolated cold spot and the time required for adaptation—presumably the more C available, the stronger will be the initial sensation and the longer A substance can be replenished. Since the C substance can be partially replenished by blood flow from surrounding areas, one would expect adaptation time to be slower with larger areas and with annular as compared with solid stimulators—which generally proves to be the case. (c) A similar chemical system has been worked out in great detail for the visual sense (see pp. 68-9). Although this does not mean that such a system must hold for thermal sensitivity, it does make the possibility more attractive.

Evaluation of Vascular and Concentration Theories

A vigorous controversy has been waged by proponents of vascular and concentration theories (see especially Jenkins, 1938 *d,* and Nafe, 1938). Let us look first at some of the physiological and anatomical evidence that has been brought to bear. (1) Crucial to Nafe's theory is the fact that *smooth muscle is responsive to external changes in skin temperature* (Lewis, 1927). Temperatures above 52° C. and below 3° C. are felt as painful and produce spastic contraction in smooth muscle; temperatures between 33° (physiological zero, normal skin temperature) and 45° C. are 'warm' and cause vasodilation. Between 45° and 52° C. constricting elements are found within generally dilating muscles, and this is paralleled by 'heat'; between 33° and 12° C. the experience is 'cold' and vasoconstriction is produced; and between 12° and 3° C. an experience much like 'heat' is also produced, being paralleled by severely constricting elements within generally contracted muscle (cf. Nafe, 1934; Nafe and Wagoner, 1936 *a*). Although not in itself conclusive, this parallelism certainly makes the vascular theory feasible—Jenkins would consider such smooth muscle reactions to temperature epiphenomenal, as far as sensory experience is concerned. (2) There is also the anatomical fact that *thermal spots seem to be clustered about masses of blood vessels.* This might mean merely that specific receptors are drawn to such locations in the process of development—and Jenkins's complete theory does involve the replenishment of certain chemicals from the blood supply. (3) *Only the margins of the cornea are thermally sensitive.* Nafe and Wagoner (1936 *b*) point out that only these margins are vascular. Again, however, blood supply is essential to Jenkins's theory as well. (4) *Screeching tones and fever can produce chills and warmth flashes without changes in skin temperature.* Although Nafe interprets this as owing to reflexive stimulation of the vascular system, Jenkins believes it is due to changes in blood chemistry.

There is also some physiological evidence contrary to a vascular interpretation. (5) *Asphyxiation affects cold and warmth differentially.* As discussed earlier, when the blood supply to the arm is cut off and nerve fibers are affected according to their size, cold sensitivity is eliminated prior to warmth. This suggests that these sensations are mediated by different types of fibers. (6) Hergert, Granath, and Hardy (1941 *a*) have plied a small area of the forehead with flickering radiant heat and found that *alternations in sensation as rapid as 10 per second* (5 radiations per second) *can be obtained.* This means a latency at least as small as one-tenth of a second, which is well below the reaction time of smooth muscle (said to be 'sluggish'). How can changes in sensation be more rapid than the muscular reactions upon which Nafe assumes them to depend? (7) This brings up the question of *differential sensitivity.* In the region of maximal sensitivity (around 33° C.), changes in temperature as small as one-twentieth of a degree can be detected (cf. Nafe, 1934). Are contractile and dilatory changes in the smooth muscle walls of blood vessels finely enough graded to provide this degree of discrimination?

There is also evidence more psychological in nature. (8) Several facts point to *spatial segregation of cold and warmth spots.* Under ordinary conditions of exploration, the loci of cold spots are not identical with those of warm spots, and there are some regions that yield only cold or warmth sensations, not both. Although these facts fit Jenkins's specific receptor kind of theory, they are difficult to interpret in terms of a vascular theory: Why should the smooth muscle in some locations give rise to impulses only when dilating? (9) *The phenomena of paradoxical cold and warmth* are also hard to adjust to a vascular theory. Why should certain blood vessels contract under thermal conditions for dilation, or vice versa? Nafe points out (1934) that mechanical stimulation can occasionally produce contraction in generally dilating smooth muscle (or vice versa), and it is only fair to add that these paradoxical phenomena are ephemeral in nature. (10) A large number of investigators (cf. Nafe, 1934) have found *reaction time to cold stimuli to be faster than to warm.* Specific receptor theorists have interpreted this to mean that warm receptors are more deeply imbedded in the skin than cold. Nafe, however, points out that smooth muscle shows this same variation in reaction time to cold and warm stimuli. But Schriever (1926, as reported in Woodworth, 1938), using the electrosmotic methods of cocainizing the skin in which a solution of cocaine is applied directly to the skin and carried in gradually by electricity, found the cold sense to be impaired after only 3 minutes of treatment, whereas the warmth sense persisted for about 8 minutes. This long delay could not be due to differences in latency, as Nafe maintains.

Certain psychological facts, however, tend to favor the vascular view. (11) Nafe and Wagoner (1936 *c*) have shown experimentally that *stimulation of one hand can produce reflexive adaptation in the other.* Thresholds for warmth and cold in the contralateral member shift without concomitant changes in skin temperature but with demonstrable vasodilation or constriction. (12) The distinctive characteristics of *ordinary thermal adaptation* clearly fit Nafe's vascular theory better than Jenkins's concentration theory. Application of a temperature change to a large area of skin produces a general shift in the physiological zero level. Stimuli at 36° C. normally do not feel cold, yet after the skin has been adapted to 40° C. (and this level now produces no thermal experience), the 36° C. stimulus produces a cold sensation. How can lack of excitation of cold receptors result in a change in their sensitivity? Jenkins is again forced to postulate chemical changes in the surround of cold receptors.

Finally, (13) we may note that *whereas Jenkins's theory, postulating independent fibers for cold and warmth, is compatible with the law of specific energies, Nafe's theory is not.* If all the varieties of thermal experience are initiated by movements of the muscular walls of blood vessels, then the sensory fibers innervating these muscles must carry several different messages. It is conceivable, of course, that the vascular system is innervated by several types of sensory fibers (although there seems to be no evidence for this), and we should remember that the 'law' of specific energies itself is really an hypothesis.

How does this evidence add up? Most critically opposed to Jenkins's concentration theory seem to be the facts of reflexive adaptation and shifts in physiological zero during ordinary adaptation—both require postulation of rather obscure chemical effects. Critically contrary to Nafe's vascular theory are the facts that cold and warmth sensitivity can be spatially independent of one another and that flicker discrimination of radiant heat seems to be faster than the reaction time of smooth muscle. Nafe's theory is in flat contradiction to the law of specific energies, but how one evaluates this fact depends upon his opinion of this 'law.' Nafe has talked about the 'patterning' of thermal impulses in higher centers, but it is not clear how these patterns are resolved into the various qualities. Crucial test of either theory requires that one mechanism (neural or vascular) be innervated without synchronous activation of the other, and existing techniques do not make this possible with a conscious human being who can report his thermal experiences.

The Sensory Nature of 'Heat'

Another interesting controversy in this area has concerned changes in experience as temperature is gradually raised. Subjects first report 'warmth,' then at about 45° C. 'heat,' and at about 50° C. 'burning pain.' The role of pain receptors in the final quality has never been seriously questioned (at least in this connection), but what is responsible for the intervening experience of 'heat'? If we adhere to a specific energies theory, a change in the quality of sensation presumes a change in the sensory fibers active. From the fact that *paradoxical cold* can be produced by thermal stimulation around 45° C., it seems likely that the new quality that fuses with 'warmth' to yield 'heat' is 'cold.' This was the way Alrutz (1897) concluded, and Von Frey (1904) was happy to accept this view which fitted so well with his own. As shown in Fig. 4, warmth fibers are first excited alone, are joined by cold fibers at about 45° C. to yield 'heat,' and are compounded with pain fibers at about 50° C. to yield 'burning hot.' Why Alrutz failed to insert a border sensation between 'cold' and 'burning cold,' when paradoxical warmth has also been demonstrated (although not so definitely), is not clear.

One of the criticisms brought against this view illustrates a drawback in the introspective method itself. In the 'heat' experience many investigators reported that although a new quality was added, 'cold,' it did not produce a sensory fusion but remained introspectively separable into cold and warmth. Other investigators claimed that 'heat' could not be experienced until pain was introduced. Another line of criticism has come more recently from Jenkins (1938 e). Using 126 *untrained* college students as subjects

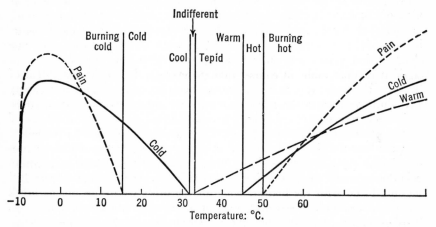

FIGURE 4. Excitation of several cutaneous senses as a function of temperature, as inferred from introspective data (Alrutz, 1897; Von Frey, 1904). E. G. Boring, *Sensation and Perception in the History of Experimental Psychology*, Appleton-Century-Crofts, Inc., New York, 1942, p. 505.

and stimulating them with simultaneous cold and warmth by means of interlacing grills, he found the term 'heat' to be used only rarely; apparently, he argues, the concept 'heat' as used by sophisticated introspectionists does not refer to the same quality labeled thus by ordinary individuals. On the other hand, the combination of warm stimulation with electric shock regularly gives rise to the report of 'heat' or 'burning hot' in the naïve subject.

It is apparent that we are dealing in part with a semantic problem: certain individuals in our society (introspective psychologists), by virtue of their training, have come to label a certain sensory experience 'heat,' an experience called 'very warm' perhaps by the ordinary individual—who is oriented toward the properties of the object rather than the qualities of the sensation per se. But this is not the real problem. The crucial question is whether or not *three* changes in quality (warmth, *X*, and pain) or only *two* (warmth and pain) occur as temperature is raised, regardless of how these changes are discriminated in our general language or its specialized argots. Most convincing evidence favoring Alrutz's view comes from the Hergert, Granath, and Hardy experiment (1941 a) cited earlier. Using the radiant-heat method on a circumscribed area of the forehead, they found that difference thresholds as a function of progressive increases in absolute thermal level showed three distinct plateaus (cf. Fig. 20, and accompanying discussion). These plateaus corresponded to three reported changes in quality, 'warmth' to 'heat' to 'pain.' Since pressure is ruled out by the radiation method, cold fibers remain the only likely contender for the second plateau.

Other Cutaneous Blends

The experience of 'heat' is only one of many sensory fusions. As a matter of fact, in ordinary experience the skin senses are more often aroused in complex blends than in isolation. A friend's handclasp presents sensations of light and deep pressure, warmth, and perhaps even pain, depending on his body build. Moving the fingers over a flower petal yields a complex of light pressure plus a rapid rate of vibration (smoothness), along with coolness. One of the contributions of the introspective method has been the classification and clarification of these tactual perceptions, for the problem is an introspective one. The general method has been to determine what combinations of stimulation are essential to any given perception.

What sensory stimulation, for example, is essential to the perception of 'wetness'? Bentley at Cornell, in 1900, undertook to synthesize this quality (cf. Boring, 1942, p. 510) from the primary cutaneous modalities. When trained observers were asked to describe the sensory content of 'wetness,' they generally reported combinations of pressure and coldness. But where was the 'wetness' itself? It turned out that this perception could be produced with *dry* cold liquids—by covering the finger with a tight-fitting, thin rubber membrane and immersing it in cold water. The physical wetness had nothing to do with the matter. Some of the other cutaneous blends break down as follows: 'soft'—warm, uneven pressure having a poor boundary; 'hard'—cold, even pressure having a clear-cut boundary; 'sticky'—variable pressure accompanied by movement of the stimulation and having a poor boundary.

SUMMARY ON THE CUTANEOUS SENSES

Free nerve endings have definitely been identified as the receptors for pain, are probably receptors for touch, and may be receptors for cold and warmth as well. Besides these undifferentiated endings there are basket cells (touch), Meissner corpuscles and Merkel disks (touch), Krause end bulbs (cold), and Ruffini cylinders (warmth) as structurally specialized endings. The role of the vascular system in cutaneous sensation remains a moot question. The picture as a whole fits an evolutionary point of view. With undifferentiated C-type fibers, having slow conduction rates and low amplitude impulses, as the most 'primitive' form of sensitivity, it appears that evolution of cutaneous receptors has proceeded along two lines: (1) *More effective transmission*. A- and B-type fibers, with heavier myelination and faster conduction rates, are developed to subserve light pressure, bright pain (A-type), and possibly cold and warmth (B-type), and yet retain their undifferentiated endings. (2) *Specialized encapsulated end organs*. Various structural refinements of the sensory nerve endings are developed to react selectively to specify forms of physical energy. A similar design is apparent in other sense departments.

Less is known about the adequate stimuli for the cutaneous senses. Despite voluminous research, covering many decades, little definite information exists regarding precisely what transformations in physical energy initiate impulses in the cutaneous fibers. Changes in the surface tension of the skin through distortion is generally favored for pressure sensitivity, the stimulus thus being mechanical. Pain is difficult to study because it cannot be roused without simultaneous arousal of other qualities. The hypothetical stimulus for thermal sensitivity depends upon the theory sponsored. One may observe, however, that chemical mediation has been suggested for all the skin senses.

THE CHEMICAL SENSES

Psychological parlance generally specifies three modalities as chemical: common chemical reception, gustation (taste), and olfaction (smell). Comparatively little is known about these forms of sensitivity. Boring, in his *Sensation and Perception in the History of Experimental Psychology* (1942), devotes only 25 of his 613 pages to this topic. The real difficulty lies in *technique*. Receptors for both taste and smell are clustered in relatively inaccessible places, and most of the refined methods developed in connection with the skin senses cannot be used for studying these modalities. We cannot localize a roasted coffee 'spot' in the olfactory epithelium, stain it, and then dig beneath it to isolate a roasted coffee receptor. We never know what happens neurally when a given odor is introduced. Is one receptor activated? All receptors at different rates? Only 'fragrant' receptors?

The term 'descriptive osmics' refers to a comprehensive survey of the behavior, both objectively and introspectively noted, associated with use of the olfactory receptors. The behavior of the perfume chemist, from whom much of our descriptive information comes (cf. Beck, 1949), merely accentuates and refines the odor discriminations, judgments, and memories of the housewife, gardener, and traveler. The perfume chemist must make fine discriminations on the similarities and dissimilarities of odors—the essential oils, coming from natural sources, vary considerably and must be accepted or rejected in terms of their equivalence to the standard samples maintained by his firm. The perfume chemist's nose must also be a qualitative and quantitative analyzer and compounder of odors—should his house wish to duplicate a costly floral extract with more easily procurable synthetic ingredients, he must first 'sniff out' the molecular components of the extract in their approximate proportions and then proceed to compound the synthetic.

The perfume chemist may compose odors creatively, striving to compound an effluvium he has in mind. And to communicate his experiences with other perfume chemists, he has developed a rough classification of odors, these being, in the main, object and function names, like 'leathery' and 'grassy.' Since, however, language is a poor substitute for the intimate knowledge of the nose, communication among perfumers is usually accomplished by means of strips of bibulous paper saturated with the odorants. One might think of the professional taster as fulfilling for gustation the same role the perfume chemist fulfills for olfaction, but such is not the case. Most of the richness we ordinarily ascribe to flavor is actually due to smell. The simple procedure of holding the nostrils while tasting various foods is completely convincing on this point: roast turkey becomes just so much 'stuff' in the mouth; a dry wine turns to vinegar. Pressure and thermal modalities also contribute to the flavor complex—think of the touch contrasts that are encountered as one moves through a plate of chow mein.

The Receptors

Common chemical sensitivity. As the term suggests, this form of sensitivity is found quite generally throughout the tissues of the body. It could be counted as a fifth skin sense, although it is by no means restricted to this surface, being found in conjunction with most moist, mucous-covered surfaces of the body. That this common chemical awareness is carried in its own specific fibers is shown by experiments reported by Crozier (1934) : an area of the skin was cocainized to the point where neither pain nor touch remained, yet sensitivity to the application of an acid was still present. It appears that this form of sensitivity is mediated by deeply imbedded, small-sized free nerve endings of the same general class we have already encountered. Morgan (1943) refers to the primitive nature of this modality, and it is conceivable that the more highly specialized receptive systems for smell and taste have evolved in restricted areas from these primitive, undifferentiated fibers.

Gustation. Specialization of receptors for taste has been along the line of evolving accessory cells rather than of elaborating the neural end organs themselves. The gustatory nerves terminate in *taste cells,* up to a dozen of which may be clustered into a *taste bud* that is provided with a pore through which various solutions on the tongue surface may enter and stimulate the receptors. Each taste cell terminates in a hair which protrudes into the pore, and it is likely that the energy transformations which result in stimulation occur through the membranes of these hairs. These structures may be seen in Fig. 5*A*. The tongue surface can be mapped in much the same manner as that followed on the skin. Individual taste buds (but *not* individual cells) can then be stimulated in isolation. When this is done, it is found that many buds are sensitive to nearly all flavors. Some, however, react to only a single type of stimulus, and this makes it possible to estimate the number of different forms of taste sensitivity. After a history of confusing classifications of multiple tastes, the field has finally settled down to the standard four: salt, sweet, bitter, and sour. The fact that some individual taste buds respond to only one form of stimulation has another important implication, gustatory fibers follow the same law of specific energies evinced in other modalities we have studied.

This conclusion may have to be limited in the light of recent research by Pfaffman (1941) on the cat, especially if the same receptive structure is found to be duplicated in man. Individual fibers from the gustatory nerve were ingeniously teased out, electrodes placed on them, and impulses recorded when the tongue was stimulated with acid, salt, quinine, or sugar. Three distinct types of fiber were found to be present: one type fired only to acid stimulation; another type fired to *both* acid and salt; a third type fired to *both* acid and quinine. Sugar seemed to excite few if any impulses in any fibers (is the cat sensitive to variations in sweetness?). It would appear that a given fiber in the gustatory tract can mediate salt (or quinine) and also, in collaboration with all other fibers, mediate acid experiences. This would be in clear contradiction to the law of specific energies of nerve fibers, at least as applied to peripheral nerves.

Olfaction. Whereas the course of specialization in taste has been in terms of developing accessory cells, in smell it has taken the form of evolving the nerve cells themselves. The *olfactory nerve endings* (see Fig. 5B) are imbedded in the *olfactory epithelium,* which is a small yellowish or brownish

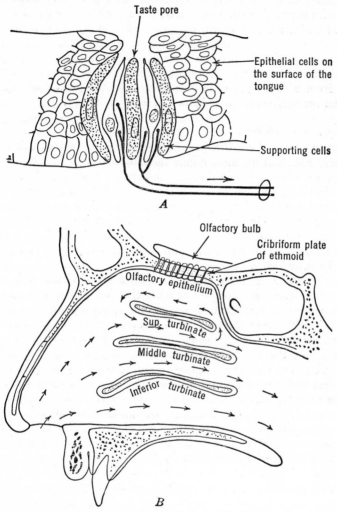

FIGURE 5. *A.* Schematic representation of taste bud with taste-sensitive cells. E. Gardner, *Fundamentals of Neurology,* 2nd ed., W. B. Saunders and Co., Philadelphia, 1952, p. 204. *B.* Antero-posterior section through the nasal fossae showing location of olfactory receptors. Starling, *Human Physiology,* 11th ed., J. and A. Churchill, Ltd., London, 1952, p. 492.

patch about 500 sq. mm. in extent in man, located in the alcove at the roof of each nasal cavity. Odorous air is reflected up into these alcoves by striking small bony folds (*conchae*) which project into the nasal cavity, and the act of 'sniffing,' by which animals and man investigate odorous materials, increases the surge of air over the sensitive area. The ovoid cell bodies of the olfactory fibers are imbedded in the inner face of the *cribiform plate,* which also serves as part of the basal support of the brain, and their axones extend upward a very short distance through the many perforations in this plate into the olfactory bulb. (The brief course and inaccessibility of the primary olfactory neurons is one of the reasons why investigation of this sense is so difficult.) The olfactory cells are interspaced with supporting columnar cells; there are also free nerve endings in this area which mediate touch, common chemical sensitivity, and possibly pain—certain of the qualities associated with olfaction, such as stinging pungency, are probably borne on these fibers. Extending into the surface of the epithelium from the olfactory cell bodies are fine, cilialike protoplasmic 'hairs,' from 2 to 12 per cell; it is likely that the process of stimulation occurs on the surfaces of these hairs (cf. Crozier, 1934).

The Adequate Stimuli

Common chemical sensitivity. The free nerve endings of this sense are apparently not stimulated directly by chemical changes in the mucous-covered surfaces beneath which they lie; rather they are affected mediately by changes in the epithelium in which they are imbedded. Adequate chemical substances for stimulation seem to be those which ionize well or dehydrate tissues. This primitive form of chemical reception is also found to have a much higher threshold, requiring more concentrated solutions, than either taste or smell. The most effective stimuli are moderately dilute solutions of acids, alkalis, and salts.

Gustation. The adequate stimuli for taste are obviously substances in solution, but precise specification of what chemical groups yield what taste experiences, or how stimulation is accomplished, remains for future research. Sourness is exclusively excited by acid solutions and is thus attributable to the hydrogen ion; saltiness is generally excited by the presence of inorganic salts, especially the halides of sodium; bitterness is usually produced by the alkaloids, but may also be elicited by certain of the inorganic salts and other substances; sweetness, of course, is associated with the sugars, but this relationship is not exclusive. One reason for complications here is that stimulation may result from *interaction* between the substances brought to the cells and substances which the taste cells themselves contain. It has been suggested that sensitivity can be varied by inducing specific deprivation states, e.g. increasing sensitivity for sugar by reducing this constituent in the diet of animals and insects (cf. Crozier, 1934). Direct injection of decholin in solution into the blood stream has been followed by a sudden bitter taste of extraordinary sharpness, which fades rapidly, however. (Hartridge, 1945 *b*.) Then, too, individuals differ from one another in their sensitivities to various substances, and in many cases (e.g. 'taste-blindness') these differences appear to be due to inheritance (cf. Crozier, 1934).

With such evidence as this, Lasareff (1928) has developed a general theory for taste stimulation. The fundamental assumptions are these: (1) Taste cells, whose reactions result in different taste experiences, contain different chemical substances capable of being decomposed by combination with certain classes of chemicals. (2) The decomposition products, which excite the neurons, are steadily diffused from the area of excitation or rebuilt into the primary receptive substance. (3) The rate of excitation (and therefore the intensity of the experience) is a function of the rate of decomposition of the sensitive substance, which depends upon its concentration and the intensity of stimulation. Since the initial stage in stimulation would involve a faster rate of breakdown of the sensitive substance than removal of the exciting end product, the intensity of a taste experience should first increase—which is the common observation. Since all of the decomposition products are not rebuilt into the primary substance, prolonged stimulation should result in progressive exhaustion of the sensitive substance and hence gradual reduction in rate of excitation—this is observed as taste adaptation. This theory, it should be noted, is closely analogous to Jenkins's conception of thermal stimulation, which we have already considered, and Hecht's conception of visual stimulation, which will be described in a later chapter.

Olfaction. In 1887 Zwaardemaker, 'a cultivated and erudite Dutch physiologist, who really created an interest in the psychology of smell' (Boring, 1942), designed the best known *olfactometer*. A narrow glass tube was inserted into the forward part of the nostril, curving downward and then outward and passing through a screen which separated subject and experimenter; the experimenter's end of this tube was graduated in linear units and inserted into a slightly larger tube whose sides were lined with an odorous substance. By varying the size of the odorous surface over which the inhaled air passed, intensity of the smell experience could be varied and thresholds thereby determined. As an arbitrary unit for smell, Zwaardemaker selected 1.76 sq. cm. of ordinary India rubber (commonly used for laboratory tubing), since this amount exposed in his olfactometer yielded a just perceptible odor, and he called this unit 1 *olfactie*. It is clear that the size of the olfactie—the area of a substance yielding a threshold sensation—will vary markedly from substance to substance.

Detailed description and evaluation of various methods for controlling and administering the olfactory stimulus may be found in a recent article by Wenzel (1948). Most of the earlier techniques, including Zwaardemaker's, were inadequate on several grounds: (a) adsorption, or adhesion of the odorous substance to the walls of containers, was often possible; (b) repeated testing of subjects from the same container permitted dilution; (c) although nonvolatile substances were susceptible to contamination with the substances in which they had to be dissolved, volatile substances were prone to diffusion in the process of being measured for concentration; (d) fluctuations in temperature are known to modify olfactory reception and this was often not taken into account; (e) finally, and perhaps most important, no control was exercised over the actual amount of odorous stimulus reaching the receptors—just how much of an inhalation is meant by a 'sniff' cannot be clear. Two of the best recent methods, one described by Elsberg and Levy (1935) and the other by Wenzel (1948), utilize a 'blast injection technique' in which a known volume of odorous air under pressure is released into a tube leading to the subject's nostrils. Wenzel's apparatus has the additional advantages that the pressure, which has been found to be an important variable in threshold determinations (cf. Jerome, 1942), is kept constant through the duration of stimulation, and the number of molecules present in the stimulus can be directly computed.

What is the mode of olfactory stimulation? The *chemical view* requires that the odorant be soluble in the mucous surround of the receptors; reactivity between the substance of the odorant and some constituent within the receptors is specified by some, and others specify reactivity between two or more constituents released in the receptors by the odorant. Is solubility of the odorant essential? Some early students attempted to answer the question by the unappealing and painful method of pouring an odorous liquid into the nostrils while the head was inverted, but inconclusive results were obtained. Although it is clear that the stimuli for olfaction must be capable of existing in gaseous form at ordinary temperatures, it remains an unsolved question whether or not they must also be soluble. Indirect evidence that the chemical states of the receptors (or their surrounds) are critically involved is available: Elsberg (1935) reports that olfactory sensitivity varies cyclically with the menstrual period in women, and it is known that this cycle involves hormonal changes in blood chemistry. About the only distinctive characteristic of perfume chemists is that they have dark pigmentation—of a group of thirty studied, all had dark hair, dark eyes, or dark skin, and none were pure blond (Beck, 1949).

The *physical view* of olfactory stimulation holds that the initial event is physical. Some theorists have specified mechanical effects (such as bending of the olfactory hairs), and others have specified some radiation principle— the latter possibility is bolstered by the fact that the olfactory epithelium is pigmented like the retina. Although most theories have assumed that radiation occurs from the molecules of the odorant to the receptor, a recent hypothesis has been described by Beck and Miles (1947) and Beck (1949) that reverses this relationship. According to these investigators, the olfactory receptors radiate differentially within the infrared region of the spectrum (between 8,000 and 14,000 millimicrons or mμ). The selective adsorption of this radiation by the molecules of an odorous substance produces transient cooling of certain receptors and thus gives rise to impulses in the sensory fibers. The fact that vapors in the lower nasal cavity are quite cool relative to the temperature of the olfactory epithelium (which is the point of highest temperature in the body) would facilitate this type of energy exchange.

Several experiments on insects whose olfactory receptors are on the external body surface, on the antennae, seemed to bear out this simple radiation hypothesis. In one study cockroaches were placed in a hermetically sealed inner chamber with windows at both ends; by a system of filters, radiant energy in the infrared band could pass through one window but not through the other, and odorous air could be pumped into either external chamber, no trace being present in the inner chamber. When air impregnated with oil of cloves was pumped into the control chamber, no behavioral signs of reception by the roaches could be observed, but when pumped into the chamber passing infrared radiation, 24 per cent of the subjects responded with usual antennae movements, this number being approximately equal to the number responding to direct stimulation with oil of cloves in the air. In another experiment two honey-containing chambers were set out in a garden near a beehive, one chamber again passing infrared radiation and the other not; six times as many bees clustered on the infrared passing window as on the control window.

The direct-radiation hypothesis is questioned, however, in a recent experiment on human subjects, by Beck (1949) who compared the olfactory effects of optical isomers. These substances are composed of identical elements and have identical radiation spectra, yet they differ slightly in their chemical structure. According to the radiation hypothesis, such substances should be identical in olfactory quality. Using three sets of pure optical isomers (*d*- and *l*-citronellol, *d*- and *l*-limonene, and *d*- and *l*-carvone), 15 naïve subjects sniffed and made comparative judgments: *d*- and *l*-citronellol, in keeping with the theory, seemed to differ only in intensity and pungency, but *d*- and *l*-limonene were easily distinguished qualitatively by all 15 subjects, the former smelling like freshly crushed lemon rind and the latter like moldy lemon; and *d*- and *l*-carvone were readily distinguished by 9 of the 15 subjects, the former being reported to smell like spearmint and the latter more like dillseed or caraway.

Beck's present hypothesis, stemming from the findings cited above and accounting for the differential odors of optical isomers, is that an odorant is adsorbed as a monomolecular film onto the surface of the olfactory sense cells, the receptors cooling off selectively by radiating through this film. The pattern of cells that cool off, and hence give rise to neural excitation, depends upon the molecular structure of the odorant. One advantage of this hypothesis is that it can easily explain the speed with which one smell sensation can be replaced by another, since the deposition of one odorant would promptly disrupt the film previously deposited. How are the bee and roach experiments to be explained? According to Beck, 'Any odors already adsorbed onto the surface of the antennae would be exaggerated by the cold cavity behind the infra-red transmitting window.' This cold cavity, created by inserting carbon-dioxide snow, was used to maximize radiation energy transfers.

Regardless of one's theory of the mode of olfactory stimulation, the quest for adequate chemical stimuli can proceed on a strictly empirical basis. Not all substances that appear in gaseous state at normal temperatures are odorous (e.g. oxygen, nitrogen, and carbon monoxide). What chemical characteristics seem to be responsible for odorousness? The first step in answering such a question lies within the special area of the chemist; he must identify the elements that make up various odorous substances and determine their structures and proportions. It turns out that only a few of the 90-odd chemical elements enter into odorous substances, and only the halogens are odorous as elements. Most odorous materials contain carbon, i.e. are organic compounds. These make up living materials and are usually complex in structure.

Do similarities and differences among olfactory experiences depend on similarities and differences among the chemical substances that give rise to them? One would certainly expect this to be the case. Homologous series of compounds, which are similar chemically except for the number of carbon atoms arranged in chains, are often similar in odor, with degree of similarity depending on nearness in the series. Sensory quality may also vary widely within the same homologous series, and the converse may be true— dissimilar chemical compounds can give rise to highly similar olfactory experiences.

Any satisfactory answer to this question presupposes that odors, in all their complexities, can be classified psychologically and arranged into a coherent system. There have been a number of attempts to work out an introspective systematization of odor experiences, the best known being

Henning's 'smell prism' (1915). On the basis of judgments of qualitative similarities and differences, several observers first arranged odors in a single, continuous series, such as that from 'fragrant' to 'spicy,' and then, since these subjects were able to specify certain odors as outstanding or striking, the corners were assembled. Woodworth (1938), who describes Henning's procedure here in as much detail as the original apparently made possible, states that in successively sniffing odors in a series running through a salient odor 'it was like turning a corner and heading for a new landmark.' A number of other workers have tried to check the validity and reliability of Henning's classification (Dimmick, 1927; MacDonald, 1922; Findley, 1924) with generally negative results. Variability of judgments, both from

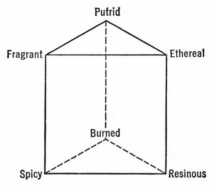

FIGURE 6. Henning's smell prism. Three dimensional model representing the six salient odorous experiences. After Henning, *Der Geruch,* 1924.

observer to observer and within the same observer from time to time, was always high; most of the samples studied seemed to fall somewhere within the prism rather than along its edges, since they were simultaneously related to three or more corners. Even had the prismatic arrangement been verified by subsequent investigators, one would have to ask—*what* is verified? A subtle implication in this classification is that six primary odors, having their own specialized receptors and fibers, have been isolated physiologically, the intermediary odors depending on fusions or mixing of the six primaries. But this is in no sense the case. Upon what does the judgment of similarity of two odors depend? It may be to some extent physiological, of course, but the cultural loading is undoubtedly heavy. Odors do not have abstract names but rather refer to specific objects, and the observer may be unconsciously comparing objects rather than odors (i.e. rose and violet may be judged similar because they are recognized as 'flower smells'). It is indeed possible that Henning's prism is nothing other than a neat demonstration of cultural standardization.

A method of classification that seems largely to eliminate this language and cultural difficulty, as well as absolute odor memory (i.e. recalling the context or object associated with a given odor), has been developed by Crocker and Henderson (cf. Crocker and Henderson, 1927; Boring, 1928; Ross and Harriman, 1949) in connection with the concrete problems of perfume chemistry. A set of psychophysically scaled odor standards is sniffed comparatively with the unknown odor; the subject does not feel forced to label the unknown from absolute memory but is able to classify it from immediate memory of the various standards. This set of standards includes four different qualities, *fragrant, acid, burned,* and *caprylic* (goaty), with each graduated into an intensity scale from 0 to 8. The reference kit thus includes 32 standards. In classifying the odor of a rose, for example, this effluvium might be judged most equivalent to 6 on the fragrant scale, 4 on the acid scale, 2 on the burned scale, and 3 on the caprylic scale—the odor of this rose, then, would be definable as 6423.

This is a component or factor method of classification; the four-receptor system which is implied, however, may or may not be a necessary assumption. Boring (1928 *a*), on request of the originators, checked the feasibility of this system with favorable results as to its reliability. Similarly, Beck (1949) has compared the classic 'naming' method with the Crocker and Henderson method of 'matching,' and found the latter far more satisfactory. On the other hand, Ross and Harriman (1949) report unfavorable results: subjects instructed to arrange the 32 standards in terms of qualitative similarities often came out with many more than four classes; with subjects instructed to rank the eight odors of each class in an intensive series, gross inconsistencies appeared. Nevertheless, this seems to be the most promising development to date.

The subjective effects of mixing odors are extremely puzzling. Some odors do fuse well, but in other mixtures only one 'dominant' is sensed; some odorous stimuli may effectively cancel one another to sensory nil, and one odor may effectively cancel out several apparently unrelated ones. A mixture may even appear subjectively as a pattern, analogous to a chord of musical tones. Another unusual phenomenon of smell concerns adaptation: in most sense departments adaptation is a simple decrease in the intensity of a sensation with persistent application of the physical stimulus; in the case of smell it may be accompanied by *modulation* (change in the quality of the experience). Ionone, for example, resembles cedarwood at high intensities but shifts toward violet as adaptation proceeds; cheap perfume shifts from flowery to putrid. Another characteristic of olfactory adaptation is its *mutuality*. Adaptation to one odorous substance frequently diminishes or abolishes sensitivity to other substances. This would seem to offer an excellent method for classifying odors in terms of their physiological similarities, but nothing has come of it.

KINESTHESIS

The term 'kinesthesis,' which refers quite literally to sensations of movement introspectively determined, has been largely replaced by the term 'proprioception,' which emphasizes receptor and sensory nerve action neurophysiologically determined—this as part of a general shift in psychological orientation during the past half century. These points of view were both foreshadowed in the philosophical and physiological antecedents of psychology (cf. Boring, 1942, Chap. 14). Both Descartes (1637) and Berkeley (1709), for example, had stressed the role of sensations from the eye muscles in perceiving depth and distance. Charles Bell (1826), in a paper before the Royal Society entitled 'On the Nervous Circle Which Connects the Voluntary Muscles with the Brain,' directly anticipated present-day emphasis on the reflex circle. And it is worth noting that both classic and contemporary theorists have used this earthy muscle sense to explain the highest mental processes: whereas 'kinesthesis' underlaid the structuralist's motor theory of thought and conscious attitude, 'proprioception' is the basis for the behaviorist's 'pure-stimulus-acts' (Hull) and 'movement-produced-cues' (Guthrie) with which the same higher level events are explicated.

(1) *Proprioception.* By means of sensitivity in the muscles, tendons, and joints, the organism is able to orient its various members, make finely graduated motor reactions, and generally integrate sequences of movements. The first receptors for this modality to be isolated and identified were the *Pacinian corpuscles,* which are encapsulated end organs found commonly in tendons, joints, and muscle sheaths and also in the subcutaneous tissue (where they are probably responsible in large part for sensations of deep pressure). A second type of receptor-organ to be discovered was the *muscle spindle,* shown in Fig. 7. The muscle spindle is innervated by two types of sensory fibers, the *annulospiral* and *flower-spray endings,* the former being associated with large, more heavily myelinated fibers. Since these receptors are activated when the muscle fibers are being stretched (i.e. when the antagonistic muscle is being contracted), they are known as *stretch afferents.* This was shown conclusively by Matthews (1931), who used a single muscle fiber and spindle from the muscle of a frog. Working in reciprocal relation to the stretch afferents are the *Golgi tendon organs,* which are found at the junctures of muscles and their tendons; these receptors are also associated with heavily myelinated nerve fibers and appear to be *tension recorders.* Also concerned with the muscular system, although probably not ending directly upon muscle fibers, are numerous free nerve endings mediating pain and (possibly) common chemical sensitivity. These receptors are probably responsible for the sensations of fatigue which accompany extended muscular work.

The demonstrable existence of an extensive receptor system for proprioception, with numerous large and heavily myelinated fibers capable of returning rapid and discriminative 'messages' to the brain, makes those contemporary theories that place a heavy burden upon the proprioceptive system more feasible. It does not, of course, confirm them. Early experiments by Goldscheider (1889; in Boring, 1942) made it clear that the discrimination of limb movements is very fine, perhaps even finer than cutaneous spatial discrimination. But an interesting problem appears: a number of studies indicate that this fine discrimination of limb position depends not upon the highly developed receptor system in the muscles and tendons but rather upon receptors in the joints. What, then, is the role of the muscle sense proper? We have here a great deal of theory but little fact. There is no question but that the proprioceptive system can deliver a richly diversified and graded pattern of activity to the cortex, but there the information ends. To date, most studies on the experimental interruption of proprioceptive pathways (cf. Ruch, 1935; Ruch, Fulton, and German, 1938) have been limited to the effect upon simple weight discrimination.

(2) *Labyrinthine mechanisms.* Two other kinesthetic senses, those of bodily movement and bodily position, are provided by specialized receptors within the bony canals of the inner ear and mediated by nonauditory seg-

ments of the VIIIth nerve. The three semicircular canals in each ear are arranged in opposing planes so that acceleration of the head movement in any direction will give rise to a different pattern of movement of the fluids within the canals. Each canal has, near its entrance, an enlargement containing a *crista,* which is a pliable gelatinous body into which the hairlike

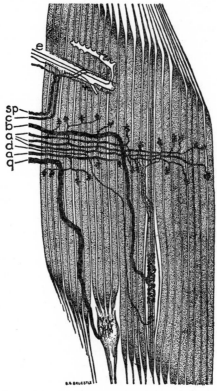

FIGURE 7. Denny-Brown's diagram illustrating the sensory and motor innervation of a group of 23 mammalian muscle fibers. The motor innervation comes from 4 fibers, *a, a, a, a;* the muscle spindle is made up of 3 intrafusal fibers, each one innervated by branches of motor nerve fibers *a, a, a, a.* The spindle has one large annulospiral ending, *b,* and a single flower spray ending connected with the nervous system by a fiber of relatively small diameter, *d.* There is a single Golgi tendon organ, *g,* and a sympathetic plexus, *sp,* accompanied by a small myelinated pain fiber, *c,* from the blood vessel, *e.* Creed, Denny-Brown, *et al. Reflex Activity of the Spinal Cord,* Oxford University Press, 1932.

endings of the sensory fibers extend. Endolymphatic fluid within the canals surges one way or the other depending upon the direction of rotation of the head, bending the crista, and thus mechanically exciting these fibers. It is now known that these cristae are moved only during acceleration or deceleration of head movement and hence contribute to the sense of *change* in bodily position. In the *saccule* and *utricle,* the other nonauditory labyrinths of the inner ear, are groups of hair cells termed *maculae.* These receptors are mechanically stimulated by changing pressures within the saccular or utricular sacs and provide for the *static* sense of bodily position.

As early as 1801 Erasmus Darwin had described certain of the sensory phenomena associated with the labyrinthine mechanisms—that the environment seems to revolve in the opposite direction while one is spun about, that this backward direction of apparent movement gradually slows down during rotation and even reverses itself when one is suddenly stopped, and that vertigo and nausea follow such treatment. Somewhat later, in the 1820's, Purkinje gave more analytic description of these phenomena: he suggested that perhaps the brain, being a soft mass, might lag behind the bony skull and thus give rise to these experiences. At about the same time Pierre Flourens, one of the first to use the ablation technique to determine the functions of various parts of the brain, was coming closer to the real explanation in certain studies on pigeons. After the two corresponding semicircular canals on both sides of the head were sectioned, the bird became incapable of co-ordinated bodily movements, especially in the plane of the sectioned canals. Cutting all six canals resulted in convulsions. Much later Breuer (1875, as reported by Dusser de Barenne, 1934) demonstrated that receptors in the cristae are responsible for rotational effects, whereas those in the saccule and utricle are responsible for what he called 'positional' reflexes. Interesting confirmation of this view was provided by William James in one of his few experiments. Since deaf-mutes often have involvement of the semicircular canals, it might be expected that they would not become dizzy when spun about with their eyes closed; of 200 Harvard students and faculty spun about in a swing, all but one reported dizziness, but 186 deaf-mutes out of a total of 519 reported no dizziness whatsoever.

Several rather intriguing problems arise in connection with these movement senses. For one thing, both the secondary effects of rotation (nausea, circulatory changes, and so on) and even the primary visual effects (perception of reversed movement and optical nystagmus) show habituation—witness the whirling dervish or the figure skater. Since it is extremely unlikely that the fluids in the inner ear 'learn' not to surge or that the receptors 'learn' not to be stimulated, this must represent some central process. Another puzzle concerns the law of specific energies: since movements of the fluids in the semicircular canals press the cristae in both directions, how can the same receptors carry two specific energies and yield cues about the direction of rotation? One suggestion is that the receptors in a semicircular canal in one ear are 'silent' when those in the contralateral canal are stimulated, i.e. canals in the same plane work as reciprocal teams. There seems to be no direct evidence on this matter.

Most interesting is the fact that these movement and positional systems are *senses without sensations*. The experiences that accompany rotation and disequilibrium arise from other modalities, excited in reflexive fashion—this applies to the visual effects of rotation as well as to the visceral components. The impulses set up in the cristae and maculae do not yield conscious experience of any sort. This makes neurophysiological sense when we consider that these fibers make juncture only with reflex centers in the brain stem and cerebellum; Dusser de Barenne (1934) gives a detailed description of these labyrinthine reflexes. The proprioceptive muscle sense also seems to lack the sharp sensory quality of other modalities. When we move the tongue about within the mouth, being careful not to touch the sides, or when we move fingers held out in space, a clear and detailed awareness of the positions of these members is present, yet the experience lacks the specific character of a pattern of colored lights. Apropos of the motor theory of thinking (cf. Chap. 15), one is certainly aware of thoughts and meanings but, like proprioception, this is also awareness without obvious sensory quality.

THE NEURAL BASIS OF SENSORY QUALITY

Contemporary writers in psychology have been happy to let the philosopher tussle with the problem of the nature of awareness, as if by carefully planned omission they themselves could imply acceptance of the only obviously tenable position. A notable exception is Boring's searching analysis in *The Physical Dimensions of Consciousness* (1933). This issue is part of the hoary 'mind-body' problem in which psychology has its origin and Janus-like existence, and the solution is by no means obvious. In fact, it is not an issue that can be decided on evidence—one can only assert the reasonableness and fruitfulness of a point of view. Is this justification for omission? From the point of view of this writer, empirical facts lose much of their excitement when divorced from the ultimate questions that lead men to establish them.

The Problem

Two sets of observations must somehow be related. On the one hand we have *psychological variables* which are most readily defined by introspection. The human observer can make discriminative reports in terms of sensory *quality*. Now I am aware of an odor like that of violets, now pressure at my finger tip, now prickly pain. And qualitative discrimination proceeds within modalities: color experiences are richly diversified as are pitches and odors. Awareness also varies in terms of sensory *intensity*. With quality constant, pressure experience may be 'heavy' or 'light,' redness may vary in 'brightness,' a sound in 'loudness,' and so on throughout sense departments. To these psychological dimensions, Boring (1933) would add *extensity* and *protensity* (duration). Whether these should be considered as sensory or as perceptual variables—or whether sensation and perception are separable for analysis, as Boring seems to deny—are difficult questions. In any case, we shall consider extensity and protensity as derivative phenomena, quality and intensity being the major 'mental' variables.

On the other hand, we have 'material' or *physiological variables* which are most adequately defined by the methods of neurophysiology. Possible variations in the neural 'message'—an unfortunate term since it implies a non-neural recipient—are limited by certain generally accepted laws: (1) *The all-or-none law.* If a stimulus is sufficient to excite nervous tissue, the response of this tissue is an all-or-nothing affair, each impulse utilizing to the fullest the available materials in the portion of the fiber it is traversing. Impulses in any single nerve cannot be graded as to magnitude. (2) *The essential identity law.* We are here coining a label for another well-accepted law of neurophysiology, namely, that impulses are all the same in kind (cf. Le Gros Clark, 1947). Impulses traveling in optic fibers seem to differ qualitatively in no way from impulses in cutaneous fibers; activity in the visual areas of the cortex does not appear to differ qualitatively from activity in the somesthetic areas—nor, for that matter, from that in motor areas. This principle, of course, is itself limited by available techniques; existing observations fail to reveal any qualitative variations in nerve impulses, and neurophysiologists seem to agree that none will be found. (3) *The refractory law.* Nervous tissue is limited in the rate at which it can react, recover, and react again. A brief interval follows each impulse during which the nerve is absolutely refractory, this being followed by a period of relative refractoriness through which decreasing intensities of stimulus are able to excite the nerve (cf. pp. 66-7). This law both places an ultimate limit on the impulse frequency any fiber can carry and underlies the fact that, within limits, increasing intensities of stimulation are accompanied by increasing frequencies of response in nerve.

Within these limitations, then, how may the neural 'message' vary? There may be variations in 'what' fibers are active, 'how often' they fire, and 'how many' fibers are synchronized—and this seems to be the end of it. Since activity in all nerve tissue is essentially identical in kind, 'what' fibers must come down to 'where.' But where, in the nervous system, is this 'where'? Of course, speaking generally, we know that awareness takes place in the brain. More specifically, we know that sensory cortical areas, and perhaps the so-called 'associational' areas, are critically involved. Direct stimulation of the bared cortex gives rise to sensations (cf. Penfield and Rasmussen, 1950). While the conscious human reports these experiences to be of an 'as if' nature—'as if' his forearm were being pricked, 'as if' a tiny flare of light had briefly shown over there—the monkey, in his lack of sophistication into experimental matters, busily scratches for the 'real' tormentors in his hide when appropriate areas of the somesthetic cortex are stimulated. Specifically, the precise quality of awareness appears to depend upon the precise locus of neural activity in the sensory cortex—by 'depend' here we mean that certain areas are essential for certain experiences, not that these experiences are 'localized' in these places. Before detailing any evidence, however, let us look further at the underlying problem.

Man has generally localized consciousness in his head, right behind his eyes—which may only reflect the importance of vision in primate behavior. But even though we may agree that the correlation between nerve impulses and conscious sensations occurs in the brain, just what is the nature of this correlation? (1) *Dualism.* At some point in the material sequence between physical stimulus and physical response, at some place in the material brain, nervous impulses 'give rise to,' 'cause,' or 'parallel' sensations in the mind, which consist of entirely different, nonmaterial 'stuff.' This is the classical view in psychology, and it had its philosophical origin with Descartes (who specified the pineal gland as the locus of this material-to-mental transfer). (2) *Idealistic monism.* There is only one 'stuff' and that is mental. The physical world, in all its details, is an egoistic creation of mind—which of course may follow rigid laws in its creative activity. This view, irrefutable though it may be as a philosophical position, has never been attractive to psychologists or to other natural scientists. (3) *Materialistic monism.* There is only one 'stuff' and that is material. Mental events, in the final analysis, are compounded of the same materials-in-movement as physical events and are subject to the same laws, the laws of natural science. With regard to the nature of awareness, the materialistic monist says that any momentary state of consciousness 'is,' 'equals,' 'is identical with' the momentary pattern of activity existing in the sensory cortex. We may measure this neural activity by the effects it produces on imbedded electrodes; we may also measure this neural activity by the effects it produces on vocal muscles (introspective reports). The observations made in both cases are equally physical.

The problem for science per se is not to decide among these philosophical positions. It can only search for a system of *invariant correlates* between what may be measured electrophysiologically as nerve impulses and what may be measured introspectively as sensations. At best it can merely show that whenever there is *this* quality and intensity of sensation reported, there must invariably be *this* specific locus and type of activity recorded in the brain. How such invariant correlations are interpreted is another matter entirely: those with monistic orientations may interpret the correlation as evidence for identity (the sensation *is* the neural activity, as it eventuates in verbal behavior). Those with dualistic orientations may interpret the correlation as evidence for perfect parallelism or interdependence of material and mental universes (the sensation invariably *parallels* or *is caused by* the neural activity). Idealistic monists are not really concerned with correlations of this order.

Psychophysical dualism is certainly the easiest interpretation to make, since this is part of the natural philosophy of the layman—'natural' because it evolves directly from the connotations of our language. Words like 'thought,' 'idea,' and 'sensation' *mean* some formless, nonmaterial stuff. If there are words for such things, then (so the unconscious reasoning goes) they must exist, and if they exist, an adequate philosophy must take them into account. The scientist and the philosopher are also bedeviled by the dualism implicit in language. It is difficult to describe the monistic position, to say nothing of trying to think it out, without continually falling into linguistic booby traps—the mere statement that 'a sensation *is* a pattern of activity in nerve fibers' acts as a semantic blockade. The attempt is very much like trying to build an electrical circuit with tools designed for plumbing. A new language is needed to describe a monistic philosophy.

The Correlate of Sensory Quality

What can be shown to vary consistently and inevitably with the quality of sensation? This is really the problem of specificity approached from a slightly different angle. Does the specificity (quality) of sensation depend directly upon the physical stimulus? The evidence here is certainly negative: impulses in optic nerves may be initiated by many different forms of physical energy (light, pressure, chemical, electrical, and so on), but once stimulated the sensation is always visual in quality; a cold receptor may be 'paradoxically' stimulated by a warm stimulus, by the pressure of a metallic point, and so on, but the sensation is always cold in quality. This was the real point of Müller's law of specific energies of nerve fibers—not that the quality of sensation is dependent upon the specific character of individual nerve fibers but that it is *independent* of the character of the stimulus.

Is there any basis at all for applying Müller's law of specific energies to nerve fibers? There appears to be none: within the limitations of available neurophysiological technique, there are no differences among nerve fibers in either their structure or the kind of impulses they carry. It is true that, depending upon size and degree of myelination, individual fibers will vary in both the rate and magnitude of impulses they carry (viz. A-, B-, and C-type fibers), but sensory quality is not covariant with this spectrum of fiber types. Fibers do vary in the *frequency* of impulses they carry. Could sensory quality depend upon the frequency of impulses within the same set of fibers? The only modality for which this relation has been seriously suggested is audition (cf. the volley theory, Chap. 3), and the evidence against this proposal is considerable. In any case, frequency is generally found to be a correlate of sensory intensity.

This leaves us with 'where' (the locus of neural activity) as the only apparent contender for the correlate of sensory quality. Does the anatomy of the sensory nervous system give credence to this view? As for *between modality* discrimination, there is no question but that visual, auditory, olfactory, gustatory, proprioceptive, and cutaneous fibers, via systems of synaptic junctures in lower centers, are projected to different areas of the cortex. In a sense, then, *this* sensation is visual because impulses are mediated through the striate portions of the occipital lobes, and *that* sensation is auditory because impulses are mediated through the superior temporal convolution of the cerebral cortex. This, of course, is more than a little naïve since, for one thing, there is always spontaneous activity present in the cortex and it does not eventuate in sensory experience. Little is known at present about interactions between peripheral and cortical mechanisms in the process of stimulation, or, for that matter, about the neural basis for the selective process of attention, but vagueness here does not deny the anatomical fact of spatial segregation of sensory fibers in the cortex.

Is there anatomical basis for spatial organization *within modalities?* The evidence for *audition* is clearly positive. Ever since Helmholtz, about a century ago, pointed to the basilar membrane in the inner ear as the peripheral (spatial) analyzer of sound frequency and implied that this spatial organization was preserved by projection up to the auditory cortex, observations favoring this view have been accumulating. Recent electrical recordings from the auditory cortex have demonstrated spatial arrangement of fibers mediating pitch quality, from high tones at one point progressively to low tones at another (cf. Chap. 3). Yet all auditory fibers appear to be essentially identical in structure and function.

The situation for *vision* is necessarily more complicated, since discrimination includes not only quality and intensity but also spatial organization of the visual field. It is now known conclusively that spatial organization of the retina is preserved faithfully by a precise system of projection up to the striate areas of the occipital cortex. If cortical 'where' is thus used up by visual local-sign, how can visual quality be represented? It is obvious that 'redness' cannot be discriminated from 'greenness' on the basis of cortical locus in any simple way—both qualities can be experienced at the same loci in the field. Detailed anatomical studies by Le Gros Clark (cf. 1947) indicate that three optic fibers pass back to the higher centers from each retinal local spot, these three fiber types being unsegregated in the optic tract and becoming disentangled only within the geniculate body. Here they fall into three layers, termed *a, b,* and *c,* and there is suggestive evidence that this segregation is made on the basis of three primary color receptors. Fibers from the two retinas are joined here as well. The geniculates thus serve as a sorting center and as a binocular integrating center. Since the three-unit system is relayed to each local point in the visual cortex, it is possible that color quality depends upon the relative rates of excitation in the three fiber types at each cortical locus.

If the specific receptors we have found subserving the *cutaneous modalities* (touch, pain, cold, and warmth) are to form the basis for sensory discrimination, then there must also be some 'sorting out' of their innervating fibers in the higher centers. The cutaneous senses are strictly equivalent to vision, however, in that spatial localization must also be represented, i.e. pressure at the tip of the finger can be discriminated from pressure at the first joint, and the same localizability is evident for pain and thermal sensations. According to Clark (1947, p. 8), 'On reaching the cord . . . [the various cutaneous nerves] become sorted out so that impulses of each specific type are conveyed up to the brain in separate discrete tracts of nerve fibers. The segregation proceeds even farther, for *within* each tract there is a grouping of fibers in relation to the segmental origin of the impulses which they carry, and the terminations of the tracts within the thalamus show a clear-cut spatial organization depending on the segmental origin.' Thus, for the cutaneous senses, we have spatial segregation both between groups of fibers according to modality and within these groups according to the point of origin on the body surface. With regard to cortical representation the evidence is unclear: although the spatial organization of the body surface is preserved in spatial organization of the cutaneous areas, it remains to be determined whether spatial segregation among the modalities is preserved— electrical stimulation of the cortex seldom elicits sensations of pain, cold, or warmth.

Very little can be said about *olfactory and gustatory sensitivity* since the anatomical picture remains to be worked out—the technical difficulties in the way of direct neurophysiological analysis have already been discussed. Does the apparently infinite variety of odor discriminations depend upon richly diversified spatial organization? Upon some modulation principle such as may apply to color vision? Since partial excision of the olfactory bulb leads to a general thinning out of olfactory receptors and not to a sharply restricted local patch of atrophy (Clark, 1947), it seems probable that there is a sorting out of olfactory fibers in the incredibly complex plexuses between receptors and the olfactory bulb—segregation presumably proceeding according to specific receptor types. Beyond this we are at present unable to go.

What is the case, then, for correlating sensory quality with the locus of neural activity in the higher centers? Differences between modalities are clearly shown to depend upon locus. It is probable that differences in quality within modalities also depend on spatial organization. Anatomical segregation of fibers mediating different qualities can be demonstrated right up to the cortex in the auditory system and at least through lower centers in visual and cutaneous systems. It is possible that each visual 'local-point' in cortical representation is fed by three or more types of fibers, the quality depending upon the ratio of impulses in the types. This, however, would be a 'what fiber' basis for specificity rather than 'where,' and it would seem to require qualitative differences in the three or more fibers involved. Perhaps there are qualitative differences among fibers that will be revealed only when sensitive measures other than electrical are devised.

Even were locus conclusively shown to be the invariant correlate of sensory quality, would this be sufficient specificity? No—there must also be stimulus selection at the periphery. A moment's thought will indicate why this is so. Suppose all receptors were absolutely identical in structure and function: this would mean that any form of stimulus energy, a light, a sound, a pressure, would excite *all* receptors equally, and, regardless of anatomical segregation within the nervous system, all possible sensations would result—a sound wave would produce all pitches, all colors, all pressures and pains, and so on. The fact is that receptors are located and designed so as to be excited by limited forms and ranges of physical energy. Visual receptors are enclosed in a mechanism (the eye) which enhances the probability of radiant energies being present but which largely eliminates other energies; the visual receptors themselves are designed so as to react to minute radiant energies but only extreme intensities of energy in other forms. Gustatory fibers terminate in taste cells which are located where chemicals in solution are present, and the fibers themselves are selectively activated by this type of stimulus. In all sensory systems there are similar provisions for peripheral analysis.

A Final Problem for the Philosopher

A materialistic monist might summarize and interpret existing evidence as follows: *any momentary quality of awareness is the activity of nerve fibers at a specific locus in the material brain.* Such a statement, although insufficient in detail, is in keeping with empirical observations. But another observation poses a truly difficult question: what was here termed 'the law of essential identity of neural action' expressed the fact that existing techniques fail to reveal any qualitative differences in the structure or function of nerve fibers (and neurophysiologists seem to agree that none will be found). Why, then, do different sensory modalities have palpably different quality? If 'redness' is merely the activity of nerve fibers at locus *a* and 'tingling at the left elbow' is merely the activity of essentially identical nerve fibers at locus *b,* how can 'redness' and 'tingling' be different in quality? Why should the same kind of energy exchange *feel* different merely because it occurs at a different place? What is it that gives the essential 'redness' to the experience, the essential 'tingling'? This is the fundamental criticism that has always been aimed at the materialistic philosopher by his nonmaterialistic brethren.

There are really two questions here. The first is how impulses in nerve, as physiochemical energy exchanges having characteristic magnitudes, rates, and durations, can resemble any psychological quality whatsoever. The two things seem entirely different in nature. The simplest answer to this question is—*why not?* To be a little less cryptic, there is no more reason why impulses in the sensory cortex should *not* be 'redness' than that an electric bulb should not light because we cannot see radiant energy streaming along the conducting wires. When we ask for an introspective description of 'redness,' we receive nothing more than a set of metaphors ('rough,' 'warm,' 'agitated,' and so on), or better, a statement of objective correlation (this experience occurs when certain specifiable conditions are met, such as placing an object which radiates within a certain wave-length band before the eyes). Primary sensory experiences are unanalyzable, and being unanalyzable there seems no a priori reason why they should not be impulses in nerve fibers. The basis for confusion here may be that all observations on the effects of nervous activity, other than immediate awareness as it eventuates in introspective vocalization, are mediate in nature. To be sure, action spikes seen on the surface of a cathode tube do not look 'red' or 'tingly' or 'cold,' nor is there any reason one should expect them to.

The other question is this: How can essentially identical nerve impulses be different in quality merely because they occur in different loci? Let us see how Boring (1933) handles this question. Using a hypothetical situation in which Berkeley, the good Bishop of Cloyne, sees a coach approaching, Boring asks (p. 156) how Berkeley would have known he was seeing the coach rather than hearing it. 'He would have known that he was seeing and not hearing (if he was seeing) because the visual path, before its merger with the auditory, would arouse the visual qualitative sign in the way of a contextual process. . . The Bishop knows when he sees because he knows that he is using his visual apparatus, including the projection paths that still belong peculiarly to vision. . . This theory of modality is frankly relativistic. It asserts that the peculiar quality of vision is our capacity to distinguish vision from other modalities. A being with only one sense would have no way in which he could become aware of the peculiar quality of that sense, because he would have no other sense-qualities from which to distinguish his one possession.' And later (p. 158), in discussing the inadequacy of a mere correlation between quality and locus, Boring writes: 'However, right there the theory stopped. It said nothing more than: If you stimulate this part, you'll see, or that part, you'll hear. It was a mere correlation and ever so unsatisfactory as a theory. Why should you see for this part and hear for that? But if, on the other hand, this part and its systematic connections innervate the process which is the first term in the knowledge that the visual system is in use, then at once the localization of function becomes meaningful, and we see why an anatomically or functionally distinct system is the sort of system to provide the ground for the judgment of modality. . . The difference between a sight and a sound is that you know they are different.' *

It would seem that in trying to circumvent the inadequacy of a mere correlation between locus and quality, Boring steps outside the bounds of the materialistic monism to which he so rigidly hews elsewhere. What is the nature of this process of 'knowing' that a sight and a sound are different? What is the nature of 'the visual qualitative sign' which accompanies activation of visual pathways? The essence of Boring's contribution, however, would seem to be his statement that consciousness is 'relativistic'—*that the central nervous system is designed so as to provide differences in excitation, differences upon which discriminatory behavior can be established.* Let us explore this possibility further. Accepting the fact that nerves are essentially identical in their function, it nevertheless follows from anatomical structure that physical stimuli of a given kind will eventuate in nervous action at a given, specifiable locus, whereas physical stimuli of a different kind will eventuate in nervous action at a different but equally specifiable locus. This is the anatomical basis for the innumerable correlations between external stimulus situations and otherwise unanalyzable sensations; it is simultane-

* Boring, E. G., *Dimensions of Consciousness,* Appleton-Century-Crofts, Inc., New York, 1933.

ously the basis for the richly diversified discriminatory behaviors by which the organism maintains its adjustment to the environment. The difference in quality *is* this demonstrable difference in the locus of neural events, and it is only the persistence of a latent dualism (implicit in the very word 'quality' which we must use for communication) that makes this statement seem inadequate.

Is it possible that differences in sensory quality are elaborated by the same process of *inference* by which a touch sensation comes to be localized at the finger tip? We have already seen that differences in sensory quality are unanalyzable—they are different, and that is all. Yet, given the structure and function of his nervous system, there has always been and must always be a fairly constant system of relations between external situations, neural mediation, and the acts and words used by the individual human and others of his race and culture. The sensations that arise when the finger tip is pressed can be made to exist or not exist by moving certain muscles; the sensations that arise when a light is shone in the opened eyes can be made to exist or not exist by moving other muscles. As the organism develops, the movements by which a tremendous variety of sensations can be manipulated, modulated in quality and intensity, become more and more diversified. Social communication extends still further the complex system of correlations. Does the apparent difference in sensory quality gradually accrue to these invariant correlations through inferences as to the initiating external events?

Apropos of this problem, it is instructive to note the names by which we describe qualitative sensory differences. Many qualities, to be sure, have completely abstract labels, such as 'red,' 'cold,' 'bitter,' and so on. But in olfaction all quality labels refer to concrete objects or situations; 'flowery,' 'spicy,' 'burned,' 'putrid,' and 'odor of tar' obviously point to objects that give rise to different—but unanalyzably different—experiences. Touch and pain qualities also usually refer to the acts or objects that produce them— witness 'tickle,' 'squeezing,' 'penetrating,' 'pricking,' 'itching,' 'stabbing,' and 'stinging.' And what does 'saline' mean other than saltlike? One also notes that recently coined color names, such as 'turquoise,' 'indigo,' 'ivory,' and 'ebony,' derive from the objects in which these visual experiences originate. Is it possible that what are now abstract color terms had their origins, too, in the names of concrete objects? In the remote time of language origins, did the progenitors of 'red' often concretely mean fresh-flowing blood? And did 'red' thence, by extension, come to refer to objects bloodlike in color, and eventually lose its concrete reference and become the abstract color term it is today? The use of metaphor in describing sensory qualities—at which psychologists of the introspective school were most prolific—is also suggestive as to the basis of inferred quality. Since the quality of pitch is ultimately unanalyzable, one may speak of 'high' and 'low' tones with no feeling of inappropriateness. In the same way one may refer to 'bright' and 'dull' pain. Comparative study of the origins of sense-quality words in our own and other languages could prove a rewarding enterprise.

The position of the materialistic monist has been stressed throughout these pages—it is a faith, a belief, a credo, and as such it is incapable of either proof or disproof by the methods of science. The position of the dualist has not been elaborated since it is the point of view at which one arrives by simply letting the connotations of his language 'have their head.' The monistic position has been shown to be compatible with existing knowledge. Is it a fruitful view? The fruitfulness of any position really comes down to one's primitive assumptions and techniques. Accepting the fundamental assumptions and methods of natural science, materialistic monism is the *only* fruitful position. If nonmaterial, mental 'stuff' exists, as well it may, it cannot be observed, measured, and analyzed by the techniques of objective science. It is therefore not fruitful for the natural scientist to postulate it.

Chapter 2

SENSORY INTENSITY

Just as the nervous system is limited in its qualitative coverage of physical energies abounding in the environment, so is it limited in its intensive coverage. In the first place, all sensory systems have *absolute thresholds*—physical energies, even though adequate in form, must have a certain minimal magnitude or they do not exist as far as the organism is concerned. If you hold your wrist watch close to your ear and then gradually move it away, its audibility will decrease; a point will be reached where the ticking sound can be barely heard, coming and fading irregularly—at this distance the intensity of the sound stimulus is approximately at threshold level. Another characteristic of all sensory systems is that they have *difference thresholds*— if any change in the environment is to be perceived, the increment or decrement in physical energy applied to the receptor must be greater than a certain minimal amount. When hefted one after the other, a 100-gram weight cannot be distinguished from a 101-gram weight; the illumination of a room is constantly varying by small amounts, but these changes go unnoticed by the occupant. A third limitation on intensive sensitivity is seen in the phenomenon of *adaptation*. Although energy of a constant magnitude may be applied continuously to a receptor, its sensory effect nevertheless varies. If one's hand is immersed in cold water, the quality of coldness slowly gives way to thermal neutrality. A tight-fitting ski-cap is at first an extremely irritating pressure about the ear line, but within a few minutes all consciousness of it disappears.

These observations make it apparent that the nervous system is not a perfectly valid and reliable measuring instrument. Changes in awareness do not parallel changes in physical energy in any one-to-one fashion. Viewed within a dualistic philosophical framework, this is exactly what would be expected: physical events follow one set of laws and have their own natural units of magnitude; mental events follow other laws and have different units. Indeed, nearly a century ago a German philosopher of empirical bent by the name of Fechner tried to discover the quantitative relationships between physical stimuli and psychological sensations, believing that he was thereby establishing the fundamental laws that relate mental and material universes. Before detailing data on sizes of thresholds and the like, we shall carefully study the methods by which these facts are obtained. Contrary to popular opinion, the rationale of these methods sets some profoundly exciting problems.

THE PSYCHOPHYSICAL METHODS

The notion that psychological experience varies quantitatively goes deep into the philosophical origins of the science. Leibnitz, and Herbart thereafter, had utilized the idea of a limen; sensations and ideas had to be above a certain limiting strength to be conscious. Yet neither of these men believed that mental phenomena were actually measurable. It remained for Fechner, in his *Elemente der Psychophysik* (1860), to establish firmly a quantitative attitude toward mental phenomena. He devised several methods of measurement, presented sample data obtained therewith, and gave the new approach a name, *psychophysics*. Although the metaphysical connotations of the term— measuring relations between the 'psyche' (mental events) and the 'physical' (material events)—have not persisted, the methods themselves have become an integral part of psychological technique.

Is It Possible To Measure Sensations?

In the International Bureau of Standards in Paris resides the international meter, as carefully guarded as any hoard of gold or precious gems. This standard meter is the distance between two scratches on a platinum bar, which is kept at constant temperature and humidity and protected from accidental disturbance. This is *the* meter, and all others are directly or indirectly equated with this standard. There are many other standard units of measurement in the International Bureau, but search as we might, we would find no standard AL (absolute limen) and no standard DL (difference limen). Why not?

To answer this question, we may first observe how a physical dimension such as length comes to be measured. A first step· is the establishment of units. Primitive units were often literally the hand, the foot, the finger— commonly available objects having a roughly constant extensity. A horse could be described as being so many 'hands' high from ground to shoulder; the amount of liquid in a glass could be described as so many 'fingers.' The measuring procedure, then, is to determine how many times the unit fits into the extensity being described. This is still the essence of measurement, but—since science progresses with the accuracy of its descriptions— more refined units must be devised. Rough-hewn, variable units like a man's hand or foot are replaced by arbitrary, invariant units like the meter, and scientific operations thereby become more precise and more readily duplicated.

But what about measuring sensations? How much loudness is there in this tone? How much louder is it than another tone? Working from analogy with the measurement of length, we should like to select some arbitrary unit and see how many times it is fitted into the 'loudness' of a given tone. And for accurate measurement and precise communication we should like a rigidly constant unit; we should like a sensory 'meter' rather than a sensory 'hand.' What about the absolute limen and the difference limen? When different individuals are studied, these values are not found to have the same magnitude; even when the same individual is studied at different times, values show considerable variability. *As sensory units the AL and DL are highly variable,* and that is one reason why we do not find one in the Bureau of Standards.

There is another critical difference between physical and psychological measures. Standard physical units are arbitrary segments of the dimension being measured. A meter is itself an arbitrary portion of the dimension we call length; a gram is itself an arbitrary portion of the dimension we call weight. In other words, most physical units are defined in terms of operations inherent in the dimension being measured. This is not true of sensory dimensions: *psychological units, such as the AL and DL, are defined in terms of physical units.* Thus the *DL* for brightness at a given level of illumination may be defined as so many foot-candles or photons, these being physical units of radiant intensity. The *DL* for loudness is defined as so many decibels, a physical unit of sound intensity. This is not particularly disturbing to materialistically inclined investigators.

Can sensations themselves be measured? Once a vital question and the focal point of considerable verbosity, this problem has now been shelved—which does not mean that it has been solved to anyone's satisfaction. Are sensations being measured in psychophysical experiments or far more complex behavioral processes? Are psychological events being measured in terms of physical units or, perhaps, are we merely re-scaling physical dimensions with the human nervous system as an instrument? We shall return to these fundamental questions after the methods themselves have been surveyed.

The Methods

(1) *Adjustment Methods.* Most of the psychophysical methods include both a constant, standard stimulus (S_c) and a variable, comparison stimulus (S_v). The adjustment methods are characterized by the fact that the observer himself manipulates the variable stimulus. Figure 8 diagrams a *wedge photometer* that might be used to measure differential sensitivity to brightness changes. One half of this mirror wedge is illuminated by one source (S_c) which, for any given set of determinations, is kept constant; the other half is illuminated by another source light (S_v) whose intensity can be smoothly varied by the observer, who moves a marker, turns a wheel, and so on. When illumination is the same on both sides, the observer sees an undifferentiated rectangle of light. When illumination is sufficiently different on the two sides, the observer can perceive a break between them. The general purpose of this method, as of all others, is to find out how small a difference in stimulation can be sensed by an observer.

Adjustment 1. The most common technique is to start with a gross difference between S_c and S_v, established by the experimenter, and require the observer to adjust the variable until the two stimuli are perceptibly equated. This is also known as the *method of average error,* because the subjective equation is reached before an actual physical equation. The observer thus starts with a perceptible difference and adjusts the variable to a point of perceptible sameness. As shown by the figure under Adjustment 1 in Fig. 8, a large number of these approximations yield a normal curve of error, and the mean of these errors, as an average deviation from the standard stimulus, represents the j.n.d., that is, the *just noticeable difference* or average point at which the observer just perceives a difference between two stimuli. American behaviorists took kindly to this method because it seemed to measure

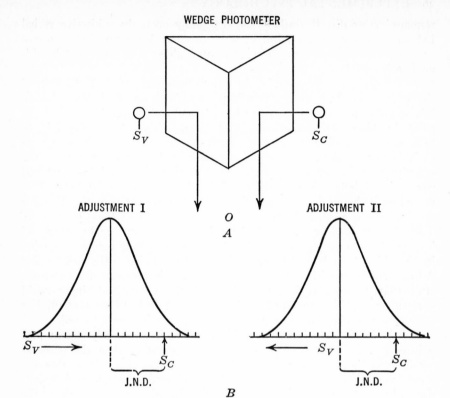

WEDGE PHOTOMETER

S_V S_C

ADJUSTMENT I O ADJUSTMENT II

A

$S_V \longrightarrow$ S_C $\longleftarrow S_V$ S_C

J.N.D.   J.N.D.

B

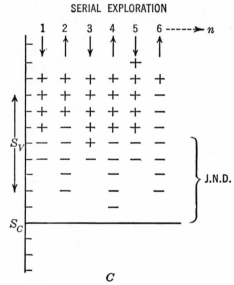

SERIAL EXPLORATION

FIGURE 8. Diagrammatic representation of *A*, a wedge photometer, *B*, determination of threshold by two varieties of *adjustment method*, and *C*, determination of threshold by the *serial exploration method.*

45

response errors directly rather than depending upon the subjective verbal judgments of the observer. But by what precious distillation judgments of sameness and difference on the part of the subject are eliminated by this method is not clear.

Adjustment II. Although in the above-mentioned method the critical change in judgment is from 'different' to 'same,' it is equally feasible, though less common, to record the change from 'same' to 'different' as the critical point. In this case the experimenter sets S_v approximately equal physically to S_c at the beginning of each estimation, and the observer must adjust the variable to the point where he can just notice a difference. Here again the magnitude of the adjustment varies from trial to trial, yielding a normal curve of variability, the mean of which is taken to represent the *DL*. This procedure is shown diagrammatically under Adjustment II in Fig. 8. Some tendency to 'overshoot the mark' is present in both of these procedures. The observer is changing the variable in one direction or the other and is more likely to go beyond the critical point than to stop before he reaches it. For this reason it would seem advisable to combine Adjustment I and Adjustment II, requiring the observer to approach sameness and difference alternately. Presumably the errors inherent in the two methods singly would tend to cancel. This combined method may be called *Adjustment* III. For some reason this combination of procedures has rarely been followed.

(2) *Serial Exploration.* This method differs from the adjustment procedures mainly in that here the experimenter rather than the observer manipulates the variable stimulus. A further minor difference is that the comparison stimulus is varied in small but discrete steps rather than continuously. Here, interestingly enough, the direction of approaching the critical point is nearly always randomized; on one trial the experimenter starts within the 'sameness' range and works out to the point where the judgment changes to 'different,' whereas on another trial he starts well beyond the 'difference' point and works in toward the standard until the observer's judgment changes. In many cases the experimenter starts with S_v clearly different from S_c (either greater or smaller), works through 'same,' and continues through 'different' again, in this way obtaining data for both upper and lower limens on each trial. The same wedge photometer diagrammed in Fig. 8 could be used with this method as well, and a sample of serial explorations is shown on the right. Notice that here again the magnitude of the just noticeable difference (j.n.d.) varies from trial to trial, yielding a distribution of values whose mean, as a deviation from the standard, is usually taken to be the difference threshold.

Both this method and the adjustment procedures are highly susceptible to unconscious suggestion and outright malingering. The fact that the variable stimulus changes consistently in one direction on a given trial may lead the observer to report a difference some time before or after it exists perceptually. It is also possible for an unco-operative subject (or one who is trying too hard to co-operate) to outwit the controls and consciously withhold (while approaching sameness) or anticipate (while approaching difference) his judgment so as to facsimilize a smaller threshold. Several devices are used to eliminate these sources of error: the point at which different trials begin is randomly varied; the experimenter may repeat the same magnitude several times; or he may reverse direction within one series. Ultimately we depend upon a serious regard for scientific methodology on the part of the subject and upon the care with which we train him to make judgments.

(3) *Comparison Methods (Methods of Constant Stimuli).* Although both the adjustment and serial exploration methods may be termed *direct* methods, in the sense that thresholds are directly apparent in the behavior of the subject, the comparison methods are *indirect,* in the sense that

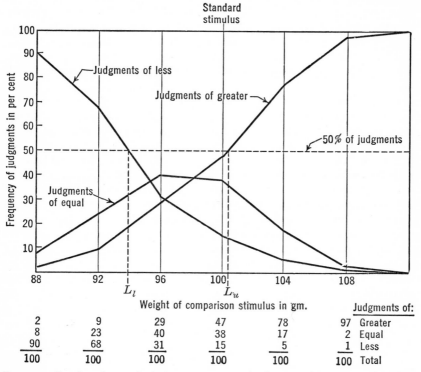

2	9	29	47	78	97	Greater
8	23	40	38	17	2	Equal
90	68	31	15	5	1	Less
100	100	100	100	100	100	Total

FIGURE 9. Results of a typical three-category paired comparison study of weight discrimination. After Boring, Langfeld, and Weld, *Psychology,* John Wiley and Sons, Inc., New York, 1935, p. 55.

thresholds appear only in the final statistical treatment of the data. To illustrate these methods, we may take the classic problem of determining the difference threshold for lifted weights. Figure 9 and the accompanying data represent results that might be obtained when the standard stimulus is 100 grams. The general procedure is as follows: for each comparison the subject lifts first the standard weight (100 gm.) and then one of the comparison weights. He judges the second stimulus to be heavier, lighter, or equal to the first, the order of presenting the comparison stimuli being randomly varied. This procedure is continued until a certain number of judgments (e.g. 100) have been made for each comparison. In this method the comparison stimuli are of discrete, constant magnitude, hence the term 'method of constant stimuli.' Weights *between* 92 and 96 are never judged, even though the lower limen is found to fall within this range. This limen, then, is a statistical product, not an observed limit to the subject's discriminatory capacity. Notice the 'time error' here—the point of subjective equality is not the same as the point of objective equality.

The stimuli for comparison may be presented either simultaneously or successively, the latter being the more common procedure. When, for example, the weights are presented *simultaneously,* the subject must use both hands, and different sets of receptors are involved; when presented *successively,* he uses the same hand, and the same receptors are involved. In the successive situation, therefore, adaptation effects may be expected—the after-effects of hefting the standard presumably affect judgment of the comparison stimulus. Although adaptation effects are avoided in the simultaneous situation, we are now dealing with different receptor populations and have no guarantee that their sensitivity levels are equivalent. Comparison methods also vary in terms of the number of categories of judgment allowed.

Comparison method 1. *Three categories.* This is the method described in Fig. 9. It can be seen that the 92-gram comparison stimulus was judged 'heavier than' the standard 100-gram stimulus only 9 times, was judged 'equal to' the standard 23 times, and 'lighter than' the standard 68 times, in the total 100 comparisons made. The curves represent the frequencies of each kind of judgment for each of the comparison stimuli used. The point where the 'lighter than' curve crosses the 50 per cent line is taken to represent the lower limen and that where the 'heavier than' curve crosses the 50 per cent line the upper limen (i.e. those magnitudes of comparison stimuli which *would be* judged 'lighter' or 'heavier' than the standard 50 per cent of the time). We must say 'would be judged' rather than 'are judged' because these liminal magnitudes have never actually been presented to the subject. The DL is equal to $(L_u - L_l)/2$. In other words, the difference threshold is assumed to be equal to half the interval of uncertainty lying between the upper and lower limens. Details of statistical treatment for this and other psychophysical methods may be found in many sources (cf. Guilford, 1936; Woodworth, 1938).

Since we have obtained the difference limen without any use of the 'equal to' judgments, why not just leave them out entirely? Actually, it is the presence of 'equal to' judgments that makes it possible to obtain a threshold with the three-category method. If no equal judgments are made (as sometimes happens with observers who guess one way or the other on all comparisons), the point of 50 per cent 'heavier than' judgments becomes equal to the point of 50 per cent 'lighter than' judgments, the interval of uncertainty disappears entirely, and the DL becomes zero. This is obviously nonsense—we certainly do not conclude that this observer's differential sensitivity is perfect simply because he fails to use the 'equal to' category.

This calls into question the validity of the three-category procedure. Fernberger (1931), for example, varied the instructions given to observers using the three-category procedure, some being told to say 'equal' only after they had tried to find a difference and failed, some being given 'normal' instructions, and some being told to say 'equal' whenever they were uncertain. The DL was 1.06 grams with instructions to minimize the equals category, 2.17 grams with normal instructions, and 4.90 grams with instructions designed to inflate the equal category. Clearly the DL obtained by the three-category method reflects the extent to which the observer uses the 'equal to' category and not his differential sensitivity. Nor can it be assumed that giving 'normal' instructions makes the method valid—we do not know how much use of the 'equal to' category should be allowed to approximate actual threshold values.

On the other side, Boring (1920) has argued that the equal category should be included, but not confounded with 'doubtful' judgments. When observers apply rigid standards, however, and say 'equal' only when no difference can be noted, this category is rarely used (Warner Brown, 1910). Culler (1926 *b*), while admitting that the *DL* derived from the three-category procedure is a poor measure of sensitivity, has demonstrated that the *precision* of judgments (an index like the standard deviation—see below) is greater when three categories are allowed. All this means is that the transition from 0 per cent to 100 per cent (in either 'lighter' or 'heavier' judgments) is more rapid when equal judgments are allowed—which follows automatically from the absorption of borderline heavier and lighter judgments into the equal category.

Comparison method II. *Two categories.* When judgments are restricted to 'heavier' and 'lighter,' the middle category drops out and no direct measurement of the difference limen is possible. But how can we obtain some estimation of the observer's sensitivity if no limens are measured? Looking back at Fig. 9, and specifically at the curve for 'heavier' judgments, it may be seen that the curve is roughly sigmoidal in form, i.e. a normal or Gaussian distribution in cumulative form. The most common index of the variability of such a distribution is the *SD* or sigma (σ), which represents one half the distance between the two points of inflexion in the curve. Now if an observer has extremely fine sensitivity, his range of uncertainty will be small (i.e. the shift from 0 per cent 'heavier' to 100 per cent 'heavier' judgments will occur within a few steps) and therefore the *SD* will be small. If another observer has poor sensitivity, his range of uncertainty will be large and the *SD* therefore large. It is clear, then, that the *SD* can be used to index relative differential sensitivity, since its magnitude varies directly with the range of uncertainty (cf. Thomson, 1920; Kellogg, 1930). In practice two sigmas are computed, one for 'heavier,' and another for 'lighter' judgments, and their average value is used to represent the observer's sensitivity.

But does this method yield any measure of the *size* of the difference threshold? The *DL* is usually defined as the increment in physical stimulus necessary to produce a just noticeable difference in sensation, and some writers do speak of the *SD* obtained in this method as if it were a measure of this increment. Woodworth (1938, p. 425), for example, concludes that 'the *SD* is a true measure of differential sensitivity, as can be seen clearly in the two-category experiment.' This statement may be valid, but it is misleading. The *SD* is an index of an observer's differential sensitivity in the sense that its magnitude varies directly with his discriminatory capacity under the two-category procedure, *but the SD does not measure the actual size of the difference threshold*. The *SD* itself is nothing more than a measure of the variability in judgments. To the extent that variability in judgments (uncertainty) is correlated with fineness of discriminative capacity, the *SD* serves as an index of observers' *relative* sensitivity. If an *SD* of 7.20 is computed for one observer and an *SD* of 5.20 for another, the latter presumably has finer differential sensitivity within that modality, but neither value represents the increment (in grams) necessary for a detectable difference (cf. Kellogg, 1930)—in fact, differences considerably smaller than this may be perceived.

(4) *Absolute Comparison (Method of Single Stimuli)*. The methods considered so far have all required the observer to judge the sameness of or difference between two stimuli, the standard and a variable. In the method of absolute comparison a series of *single* stimuli is presented and the observer is asked merely to classify each as 'heavy' or 'light.' More finely divided subjective scales, including a 'medium' classification, may also be used. The objective magnitudes of the single stimuli are randomly varied, and the data are handled in essentially the same manner as in the preceding comparison methods. The proportions of 'heavy' and 'light' judgments for each of the constant stimuli are plotted and the SD computed. If three categories are allowed, either the SD or the DL may be obtained, as cited above. The chief advantage of this method is that it reduces by half the total number of stimuli that must be presented.

Does the omission of an objective standard mean that none is employed by the subject? Not at all. As any series of judgments proceeds, a subjective standard is gradually evolved. The observer establishes a frame of reference determined in part by previous experiences with weights and in part by preceding stimuli in the experiment. S_1 appears in a context established by pre-experimental weight lifting, and it becomes part of the context determining judgment of S_2; both S_1 and S_2 serve as 'standards' for S_3, and so on. That this is the case has been demonstrated in a number of studies on the 'anchoring' of absolute judgments, both in classic psychophysical situations (cf. Hunt and Volkmann, 1937; Hunt, 1941; Rogers, 1941) and in many social evaluative situations (cf. McGarvey, 1943). If, for example, a very light weight (say, 50 grams in relation to the series we have been using for illustrative purposes) is presented first and indicated as 'light,' judgments of all weights about 100 grams will cluster more closely as 'heavy.' It should also be pointed out that, just as was the case with two- and three-category comparison methods, this absolute-judgment method gives no direct measure of the *size* of the difference threshold.

(5) *Flicker-fusion Method*. When a subject is stimulated alternately with two different stimuli and the rate of fluctuation is rapid enough, fusion occurs and the subject becomes aware of a continuous, unvarying sensation. At some critical value a slight flicker is just barely perceptible. It has been amply demonstrated in visual brightness studies that this critical fusion frequency (CFF) is a valid index of the differential sensitivity of the receptors involved (cf. Chap. 4). The method has also been applied in audition where it is known as the 'warble technique,' in studying thermal sensitivity by means of flickering radiant heat, and even in studying pressure sensitivity by using a paleoesthesiometer which 'flickers' a small stylus against the skin. The method has generally been used, however, to determine *relative* sensitivity (i.e. the fact that cone vision yields finer discriminability than rod vision is indicated by the higher CFF in the former case). The chief advantage of this method is that it provides a very simple judgmental situation, the subject having merely to report the existence or nonexistence of sensory sameness.

(6) *Reaction-time Method.* Rather than making verbal judgments of perceived sameness or difference, the subject may be required to make a differential manual reaction in a suitably designed apparatus. He may have to press a key on that side corresponding to the brighter (louder, heavier, etc.) stimulus. Most often the latency of reaction is measured. When two categories (i.e. 'greater' and 'less') are employed, latency is found to vary inversely with magnitude of the stimulus difference (Kellogg, 1931); reaction times were found to be faster for two-category procedures than for three, the 'equal' reactions being especially slow. It has also been shown (Cartwright, 1941) that reaction times increase about the borders between categories, suggesting that latency is in part a function of the subject's confidence in his judgments. In any case, it is hard to see how changing the form of reaction from verbal to motor has any advantage; implicit judgmental processes are undoubtedly involved in both cases. Furthermore, reaction time (just like the SD) does not give any estimation of the size of the difference threshold. At what point does a 'slow' reaction to a barely perceptible difference become a 'slower' reaction to a nonperceptible difference?

(7) *Discrimination-learning Method.* This is the only method directly applicable to animal subjects. It may, of course, be combined with flicker-fusion and reaction-time measures, but some overt response on the part of the animal must index the presence or absence of discrimination. The subject is trained to make some response (jumping, pressing a lever, etc.) to the standard stimulus and to inhibit this response to any other stimulus. The threshold value is generally assumed to be reached when 75 per cent correct reactions are made, i.e. halfway between 100 per cent discriminability and chance. Of course, the human subject is also making discriminatory reactions in any of the psychophysical methods. Although his 'training' is largely encompassed in the instructions given him by the experimenter, learning probably does enter the picture to some extent. It is commonly observed that there is a practice effect on psychophysical judgments, the variability of judgments, and sometimes even the size of thresholds, decreasing with training. Knowledge of results (i.e. of the correctness of one's judgments) facilitates performance. Performance improves with the attention and motivation of the observer, yet, in a situation inherently boring and frustrating, usually little is done to maximize these subjective factors.

Evaluation of Some Implicit Assumptions

As is true of all scientific methods, psychophysical techniques are founded on certain assumptions. Some of these are explicitly verbalized, but others tend to remain unexpressed or even unconsidered. The latter are like skeletons in the family closet, and, like family skeletons, they need to be periodically drawn forth and inspected—they often reveal unsuspected weaknesses in the family methodological.

(1) *That 'the same thing' is variously estimated by different methods.* It is often naïvely assumed that the various psychophysical methods are merely alternative ways of measuring the same thing—the difference threshold. Nothing could be farther from the truth. It will be recalled that the DL is defined as the smallest variation in physical energy necessary to produce a just perceptible difference in sensation. Some methods do yield an estimation of the *size* of this 'just perceptible difference,' namely, the adjustment

and serial exploration procedures. The discrimination and flicker-fusion methods may also yield such a value. Other methods provide an *index of variability*. In some cases, especially with the *SD* obtained in the two-category and absolute-comparison techniques, this index of variability is also an index of relative differential sensitivity, but the value of the *SD* itself does not represent threshold size. In other cases the *SD* measures variability and nothing more. In the method of average error, for example, although the *mean* of the individual errors, as a deviation from the standard, represents the size of the *DL* directly, the *SD* of this distribution of errors represents the precision with which judgments were made, reflecting the training, motivation, and painstaking attention of the subject. Since the *SD* obtained with two-category and absolute-comparison methods is also affected by these attitudinal and training factors, we must conclude that it is a valid index of relative sensitivity only when these factors are constant among observers and conditions. Finally, with regard to the *DL* obtained in the three-category comparison procedure, we conclude that it yields neither a valid estimate of the size of the difference threshold nor any index of variability— rather, it reflects an observer's readiness to use the equal category. It is clear that the various psychophysical methods are not merely different ways of measuring the same thing.

(2) *That there is a 'true' limen.* It is usually assumed that there is a real limit to absolute and differential sensitivity, that there is actually a true minimum intensity (*AL*) and minimal change (*DL*) in physical energy below which no sensory effect can be initiated. The values obtained in experiments are assumed to be approximations to this 'true' value. But what do our measurements actually give us? They yield nothing more than statistical abstractions, inconstant magnitudes that no psychologist would accept as necessarily being the same thing as the 'true' threshold. And we have seen that with some methods the values obtained may be pure artifacts of methodology. Yet, on the other hand, common sense tells us that there must be some limit to human sensitivity; there must be low intensities and small changes of which we are never aware. The assumption that there is a 'true' limen of finite magnitude, then, rests largely upon evidence other than that provided by the psychophysical methods themselves. This assumption is bolstered, of course, by the repeated reports of 'no difference' by observers when objective differences of small magnitude are presented in psychophysical experiments, but the methods do not make it possible to state that *this* is *the* limen—which leads us to the next assumption.

(3) *That the limen is inherently variable.* There is no question but that the statistical abstractions we call thresholds do vary from time to time within the same individual. But does this mean that the threshold—defined as the minimum change in physical energy necessary to produce a just noticeable change in sensation—is itself varying? In a sense, by defining the threshold in this manner, we have forced a negative conclusion: if the threshold is the *minimum* change, then it follows that it can be nothing other than the smallest value. But more is involved here than that. The real underlying assumption is that the capacity of the sensory nervous system to mediate between physical energy and sensation does change 'spontaneously' from time to time. We know of many factors external to the sensory nervous system, however, which affect the size of the measured threshold,

such as fluctuations in attention, changes in motivation, and practice at making judgments. Although there is considerable evidence that the general level of the threshold for a given subject may change from day to day, must we attribute this shift to 'spontaneous' changes in sensory capacity? Look at the problem this way: How much variation in sensory capacity would be found if identical, optimal conditions were repeated from day to day? This question cannot be answered empirically at present. It seems likely, nevertheless, that a large proportion of the variability in *measured* thresholds is attributable to disturbing factors that are not intrinsic to the sensory nervous system. This problem will be discussed in more detail in relation to the quantal hypothesis.

(4) *That measured threshold values are normally distributed about the 'true' threshold value.* In adjustment and serial exploration methods, for example, the *mean* of a series of estimations, as a deviation from the standard stimulus, is taken as the size of the *DL*. Individual estimations on successive trials are, to be sure, distributed roughly according to a normal curve, but does this necessarily imply that they are symmetrical about the 'true' threshold value? Does the limen necessarily fall precisely at the mean of the distribution? Keep in mind that variability in successive estimations is attributable to a multitude of independent factors extrinsic and (possibly) intrinsic to the nervous system. Now if we take the position that the *mean* is the best estimate of the 'true' threshold, then we are assuming that there are just as many independent factors tending to lessen the measured threshold as there are factors tending to increase its size. But from what has gone before concerning the causes of threshold variability, it seems more probable that *most factors tend to increase the size of the measured threshold.* Although the spontaneous variability intrinsic to the nervous system (assuming it exists) might be symmetrically distributed about a 'true' limen, it seems probable that most extrinsic factors, such as distractions, fatigue, momentary fluctuations in attention, and the like, would tend to inflate the measured threshold.

From this analysis it would follow that the mean gives too large an estimation of the *DL*. But what other estimate can be used? The smallest obtained value cannot be used since there are some factors that would produce errors in this direction (such as ordinary carelessness), and, furthermore, some of the obtained values go beyond the standard! If a point one *SD* from the obtained mean, in the direction of the standard, were used, it would be on the assumption that 84 per cent of the measured values are larger than the 'true' limen, i.e. on the assumption that 84 per cent of the factors causing variability tend toward inflation. To determine the best value to employ, it would be necessary to see what proportion of manipulatable factors actually do cause an increase in the measured threshold, but we are far from this level of experimental finesse.

(5) *That the standard stimulus is constant.* Fluctuations in the size of both absolute and difference limens are usually attributed to changes in the sensory value of the comparison stimulus. This takes for granted that the standard *is* standard. But by the very same token that the sensory effects of the comparison stimulus vary, must not an equal mutability be attributed to the effects of the standard stimulus? It seems likely that most of the intrinsic and extrinsic factors that produce variability in the size of the

threshold apply equally to both. In those procedures where the standard is present at the time the comparison stimulus is evaluated (e.g. adjustment methods, serial exploration, and so forth), the problem of the validity of usual statistical procedures is posed again. Use of the objective value of the standard as the point from which to compute the threshold implies that variations in the standard are normally distributed about this value as their mean. And this assumes that the sensory effect of the standard is not influenced in any manner by the simultaneous presence of the comparison stimulus—an assumption very difficult to accept in view of demonstrable *areal interaction* in vision and other modalities. Whereas this type of interaction seems to have escaped the notice of psychophysicists, they have considered at great length the problem of interaction between standard and comparison stimuli over time. What is called a *time error* is usually found, and this is a clear case where the sensory effect of the standard stimulus does vary. In a moment we shall concentrate our attention on this phenomenon.

(6) *That sensations are being measured.* Thresholds are usually defined as changes in physical energy necessary to produce just noticeable differences in sensation—which is all very well, except that sensations are never measured. The measures made actually relate physical stimuli and recorded judgments of an observer (or their equivalents). When the psychophysicist talks about relations between physical stimuli and *sensations,* on the basis of such data, he is making the implicit assumption that the complex behavioral processes that mediate between 'sensations' and verbal judgments are constant. Is this justifiable? Do the increased precision and frequent lowering of the threshold through practice mean that the observer's *sensory* discriminatory capacity is becoming greater? In some methods the difficulty of making judgments is greater than in others. Does this mean that *sensory* capacity changes with the method of measuring it? The psychophysical methods do not measure the relation for which they were designed. They do measure a relation that is perhaps more important—that between variations in the physical environment and the capacity of organisms to make discriminatory reactions.

The Time Error

Fechner observed that the point of subjective equality between standard and variable weights is not identical with the point of objective equality; rather, the second weight has to be somewhat lighter than the first if it is to be judged equal. Apparently the observer's impression of the first weight changes during the $S-V$ interval. This leads one to wonder just what the process of successive comparison may be. The original stimulation is no longer present. With what, then, is the variable compared? Early investigators believed observers used an image of the first stimulus as a basis for comparisons, but workers in the Würzburg School (cf. Martin and Müller, 1899), unable to specify introspectively any kinesthetic or other imagery, concluded that some absolute impression of the variable stimulus must be formed. This 'absolute' impression, however, was based upon a subjective scale established in the course of the experiment—a weight was 'heavy' in terms of the range of previously presented weights—and this was the forerunner of present-day emphasis upon the role of a context in determining judgments.

The time error poses a number of intriguing problems of this sort, but first some clarification of terminology is in order. Time errors may be either positive or negative, the latter being more commonly obtained. 'Positive' and 'negative' refer to the changes presumably taking place in the impression of the standard stimulus. When one's impression of the standard has presumably weakened during the $S-V$ interval (and an objectively weaker V is therefore judged equal to S), we speak of a *negative time error*. When one's impression of the standard has presumably augmented during the interval (and an objectively stronger V is therefore judged equal to S), we speak of a *positive time error*. To specify the conditions under which time errors of given directions and magnitudes are obtained is the empirical problem; to explain these relations is the problem of theory.

Physiological trace explanation. Gestalt theorists, such as Köhler (1923) and Koffka (1935), postulate a physiological trace of the standard stimulus, this brain trace being 'silent' itself (not conscious) yet providing the basis on which the comparison stimulus is judged. Since this brain trace is assumed to disintegrate through time, the gradient between the intensity of the trace and the intensity of the present excitation from the variable stimulus becomes steeper, yielding the typical increasingly negative time error. With 12 naïve subjects and using pairs of sharp clicks varying in loudness as stimuli, Köhler obtained the following results: for very brief $S-V$ intervals, up to 1.5 seconds, the error was positive, the second click having to be louder to appear equal (effects of temporary receptor fatigue?); but for longer intervals, up to 12 seconds, the error was increasingly negative, the second click having to be softer to appear equal. Although this result has been duplicated essentially by others (Wada, 1932; Needham, 1935 *a*), McClelland (1943 *b*) has recently suggested that these findings may have been due to the fading of the standard stimulus itself rather than to any trace dynamics. Using visual stimuli (lines varying in length), he found that when the standard was allowed to fade gradually, negative time errors were produced: 'In nearly every instance [negative time errors] may be attributed more parsimoniously to a fading in the sensation itself, caused either by a fading stimulus source or by receptor-adjustments following stimulation' (p. 94).

In any case, the conception of a fading physiological trace will not account for cases where positive time errors are obtained. Lauenstein (1933) broadened the applicability of the trace notion by postulating that the trace of the standard, as a dynamic process, tended to *assimilate* with, or be attracted toward, other processes simultaneously active in the brain field. He supported this view by demonstrating that either positive or negative time errors could be induced by interpolating loud or soft background noises during the $S-V$ interval—in both cases the magnitude of the error increased with the length of the interval. In other words, if the trace of S is attracted toward a loud background, the impression of the standard is augmented during the interval and louder comparison stimuli will appear equal, yielding a positive time error. If the interval between S and V is 'blank,' the trace of S tends to assimilate with this low intensity background, yielding the usual negative time error. Guilford and Park (1931) had obtained similar results by interpolating relatively heavy or light weights. This explanation, however, runs into one major difficulty: the negative time error produced by interpolating a soft background noise is of greater magnitude than that produced by interpolated 'silence' (Pratt, 1933). It might be said that 'no noise' is less similar to the standard stimulus than 'soft noise,' and hence has less assimilative effect, but this argument tends toward circularity.

Context explanation. Another type of explanation emphasizes the context or frame of reference within which successive judgments are made. This view had its origins in the concept of 'set' applied especially to judging weights (Müller and Schumann, 1889). After lifting the standard weight, the observer adjusts the force of his next lifting movement accordingly: if the comparison weight rises easily, it is judged 'light'; if the force is insufficient, it is judged 'heavy.' Although such a set is undoubtedly a part of the total context in all successive comparisons, the concept loses much of its significance when applied to judgments of brightness, loudness, and the like. The general nature of the context explanation runs as follows: The pair of stimuli compared do not exist in a vacuum. By the same token that evaluation of V is affected by the after-effects of S, it is also affected by the after-effects of other previous stimuli. If I have just been lifting a number of books of varying weight, my subjective scale at any moment depends upon (a) the immediately preceding object, (b) the general average of books used in the experiment, and (c) an 'absolute' scale of weight-meaning proscribed by general experience. However, the actual nature and mode of operation of 'context' has never, as we shall see, been explicated, and the difference between 'trace' and 'context' views may be largely semantic.

Evidence for the operation of contextual factors comes most clearly in experiments employing a series of standards. Time errors are typically positive for weak standards and negative for strong standards, yielding what is known as a *central tendency effect.* In other words, changes in the impression of any standard during the S–V interval tend toward the average magnitude of stimuli previously encountered, weak standards augmenting and strong standards fading. Data demonstrating the central tendency effect have been obtained for judgments of the extent of arm movement (Hollingworth, 1909), judgments of visual extents (Ipsen, 1926), lifted weights (Woodrow, 1933), and the loudness of sounds (Lauenstein, 1933; Needham, 1935 *b*). Recent data showing the central tendency for judgments of the pitch of tones are shown in Fig. 10. Another important aspect of context is also shown in these data of Koester and Schoenfeld (1946): the effect of the immediately preceding stimulus S upon the judgment of V decreases as the interval between them increases, allowing the averaging effect (central tendency) of the total context to become more apparent. Thus the central tendency effect is more marked when the interval between standard and variable stimuli is 6 seconds than when it is only 1 second.

A disturbing note is contributed by Marchetti (1942) working with visual extents. Observers were presented with black lines drawn upon white cards, the standard line being 100 mm. in length, and a *positive* time error was obtained. This result certainly doesn't fit what one would predict from the fading trace conception, nor does it superficially seem to agree with the context view. McClelland (1943 *b*) has suggested that under these conditions the standard stimulus line assimilated with the longer contours of the cards upon which they were drawn. Testing this hypothesis experimentally, he found that although presence or absence of extensive room contours (i.e. judgments made in light or dark) had little effect upon the time error, introducing a rectangular frame about either S or both S and V reliably shifted the time error in the positive direction. By way of confirmation, Tresselt (1944) finds no evidence for positive error when bright lines are projected in a dark room. The essential similarity of assimilation and context explanations is apparent in this work: one can say that the standard stimulus line 'assimilates' with the longer lines of the cards upon which they are drawn, or one can say that the longer contour lines are part of the simultaneous 'context' in which judgments are made. It should also be

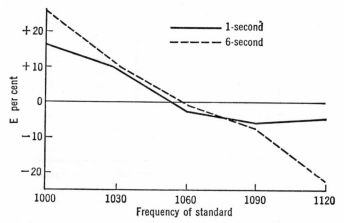

FIGURE 10. The constant error (E—per cent) for pitch judgments made by seven subjects at five frequency levels and at one- and six-second intervals between standard and comparison stimuli. Koester and Schoenfeld, *Journal of Experimental Psychology,* 1946, 36:420.

emphasized, as McClelland (p. 94) points out, that time error phenomena are intimately connected with those of transfer and retroaction in human learning and memory (see Chap. 12); the effect of S upon the judgment of V depends upon the retention of $S,$ as variably affected by interpolated activities. These relations remain to be worked out in detail.

Adaptation explanation. Perhaps the simplest explanation of the time error is in terms of sensory adaptation. Thus positive time errors are found in brightness discrimination, the second field appearing less bright than the first because of partial adaptation; and the second of two hefted weights seems to be heavier because of the slight fatigue left by the first lifting. Not only is this explanation limited to cases of positive time error (where it may often play a part) but it does not explain the fact that both positive and negative errors typically *increase* as the S–V interval is lengthened. Progressive recovery from the effects of adaptation should yield the opposite result.

Summary. Although one cannot feel that either the nature or the cause of the time error has been satisfactorily explained to date, several relevant conclusions may be drawn: (a) The assumption that the sensory effect of the standard stimulus is necessarily constant through time is clearly invalid. This limits the usefulness of successive comparison as a technique for measuring difference thresholds. (b) The evidence as a whole reveals the process of judgment in successive comparison to be remarkably complicated—another count against it as a psychophysical method. (c) Assimilation and context explanations of the time error are probably different only in the language used to describe temporal and spatial interactions within the total stimulating field.

Which Is the Best Psychophysical Method?

To answer this question, we must first counter with another: best method for what? If the purpose is to measure the absolute threshold, then we are limited to either adjustment or serial exploration, for with these methods the 'standard' can be set at zero and the increment needed for any sensation determined. These methods, along with flicker-fusion, are also the only ones that can yield a direct estimate of the *size* of the difference threshold. The general advantages of adjustment and serial exploration methods are that they provide three useful measures, the AL, the DL, and the SD, the latter serving here merely as a measure of precision.

But often we are not so much concerned with the actual size of the threshold as we are with comparing individuals, procedures, parts of the sensory apparatus, and so forth, in terms of their differential sensitivity. Although adjustment and serial exploration methods could be used for this purpose, it has been more common to use two-category and absolute-comparison procedures. The SD in these cases indexes *relative* sensitivity and has been found to be a stable measure. It was affected little, for example, by the changes in instruction given in Fernberger's study (1931).

Returning now to the question of the actual size of difference limens— which is an important empirical problem—of the several feasible methods, which is best? The answer is simple enough logically: *the best method is the one that yields the smallest threshold.* In other words, assuming that judgments are limited to the modality being studied (i.e. that there are no extraneous cues), then if an observer using one method can consistently perceive differences smaller in magnitude than those he can perceive with another method, the former is automatically the better method. The 'true' limen must be at least as small as the smallest difference he can reliably report. But, compelling though this logic may be, little comparative evidence is available. Kellogg (1929) compared the methods of average error (adjustment) and constant stimuli (comparison), finding the former to yield the finest thresholds but the latter to be most reliable; he also reviewed the meager literature up to the date of his writing. The main reason it is difficult to evaluate methods in terms of these studies is that investigators differ in their operational definitions of methods—the detailed procedures of 'serial exploration,' for example, vary considerably from investigator to investigator.

The psychophysical methods have as long a history as any field in experimental psychology, yet several of the most basic methodological problems remain to be resolved. (1) *Investigation of comparative sensitivity obtained with various methods, using the same subjects.* We have already seen some of the difficulties here; ingenuity in experimental design and almost infinite persistence will be required of the investigator who tackles the problem. The answer may well come down to determining which methods provide the easiest judgmental situations for observers. (2) *Study of the susceptibility of various methods to 'enlarging' factors.* Fernberger's experiment on the effects of varied instructions was a step in this direction, but which methods are most susceptible to changes in motivation, attention, fatigue, and so on? (3) *Study of the stability of values obtained by different methods under constant, optimal conditions.* Whereas the research suggested under (2) intentionally manipulates known sources of error, that suggested here attempts to get at the effects of unspecifiable sources. The final test of comparative reliability is thus to measure inherent stability under objectively constant and optimal conditions.

THE QUANTAL HYPOTHESIS

Casual introspection affirms the continuity of experience. Smoothly graduated changes in environmental energy are paralleled by smoothly graduated changes in awareness. Yet we know that sensory mechanisms are composed of discrete neural units which follow the all-or-none law. This is a paradoxical state of affairs. Either (a) a basis for continuity in sensory nerve action must be demonstrated or (b) precise investigation must show that the apparently continuous nature of experience is really step-wise. The classic view assumes the former position, since the psychometric functions between 0 per cent and 100 per cent judgments of difference between two stimuli are typically found to be smoothly sigmoidal in form. A number of recent workers, starting with Békésy in 1930, have taken the other position, claiming that changes in sensation are essentially quantal or discrete in nature.

Extrinsic vs. Intrinsic Variability

The normal or chance variability found in psychophysical measurement presumably reflects the complex interaction of numerous small and independent factors. As we have already seen, many of these factors are extrinsic to the limited part of the sensory nervous system critically involved in making discriminations in a given experiment—changes in the criteria of judgment, in attention, and in the functioning of laboratory equipment are examples. It is also possible that the sensitivity of nervous elements fluctuates with the physicochemical state of their medium. The critical question is this: *Is the intrinsic variability of the sensory nervous system continuous or does it vary by discrete steps?* Békésy (1930), after prolonged effort to eliminate extrinsic variability and hence increase the precision of his observations, obtained results implying all-or-none discreteness for human discrimination. This and several more recent studies suggest that in most psychophysical work the presence of extrinsic factors has masked the true *quantal* nature of sensory function.

Quantum theorists attribute momentary variations in over-all sensitivity to what we have termed extrinsic factors (cf. Stevens, Morgan, and Volkmann, 1941). The absolute threshold for hearing, for example, fluctuates randomly from moment to moment, presumably because of breathing movements, heart beat, attention, and so on. These extrinsic variations are assumed to be large in relation to the size of the single quantum. That intrinsic variations in the sensory capacity itself also occur is accepted, but it is believed that these fluctuations have a longer period. If over-all sensitivity does vary momentarily because of extrinsic factors, test of the quantal hypothesis demands that 'we must add ΔI instantaneously, and remove it before the organism is able to change in sensitivity by more than a negligible amount' (Stevens, Morgan, and Volkmann, p. 319), and all data to be combined should be obtained in as brief a period as possible.

The Hypothesis

Since individual neural units function according to an all-or-none principle, the simplest possible assumption we can make is that an organism will perceive a change in stimulation when, and only when, an increment is large enough to excite one additional 'neural unit' (Stevens and Davis, 1938). As shown in Fig. 11, the standard stimulus is adequate to excite the neural units (NU) shaded. The residual or surplus energy in the stimulus, although

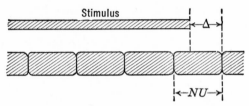

FIGURE 11. Schematic representation of the quantal hypothesis as applied to differential sensitivity. Stevens and Davis, *Hearing: Its Psychology and Physiology*, John Wiley and Sons, Inc., New York, 1938, p. 146. After Békésy.

not adequate to excite an additional unit, is available for summation with the increment (Δ) in energy provided by the comparison stimulus. How much surplus energy will there be at any moment? Since over-all sensitivity fluctuates momentarily and randomly through magnitudes considerably larger than a single quantum, surplus energies of all amounts between zero and that necessary to excite the next neural unit are equally probable. It follows therefore that *the probability of a given increment exciting an additional neural unit, and hence being perceived, will vary linearly with the size of the increment.* In other words, while a relatively large increment will have a high probability of pairing with a momentary surplus sufficient to set off another neural unit, a small increment will happen to pair with a momentary surplus of sufficient magnitude only rarely.

If we let the symbol Su represent the amount of the momentary surplus energy at the time ΔI is given, and Q equal the size of the quantal unit, then the ΔI that will *always* just succeed in exciting the additional unit is given by the equation

$$\Delta I = Q - Su$$

and it may be seen that the necessary increment varies inversely with the momentarily available surplus. Since the value of Su is assumed to fluctuate randomly, the proportion of time that a given ΔI actually does succeed in exciting an additional neural unit will be given by the equation

$$p = \frac{\Delta I}{Q}$$

where p equals the probability that a given increment will elicit an additional unit. It will be seen that p can vary between 0.00 and 1.00. When the size of the increment is equal to the size of the quantum ($\Delta I = Q$), of course the difference is always perceived. Furthermore, p becomes a linear function of ΔI. Under conditions where both standard and variable stimuli (tones) were of extremely brief duration and followed one another immediately, Békésy (1930) was occasionally able to obtain results fitting this equation.

The equations cited above assume that the standard stimulus is itself constant. But in most experiments where the quantum notion has been tested, the standard stimulus has been of such duration that fluctuations in sensitivity can take place during its presentation. In this case it is impossible for the subject to distinguish fluctuations brought about by increments in the comparison stimulus from those occurring spontaneously in the standard. Here the subject must adopt a 'two-quantum criterion,' responding only when the change excited by the increment is greater than the spontaneous changes perceived in the standard. Under these conditions the equation above becomes

$$p = \frac{\Delta I}{Q} - 1$$

where any increment of 1 quantal unit or less has zero probability of being perceived and any increment 2 quantal units in size has 100 per cent probability of registering. The function is still linear between $Q1$ and $Q2$. The results described in Fig. 13 fit this equation and are typical of those obtained under optimal conditions.

Certain Predictions and Their Experimental Test

(1) *The proportions of presentations discriminated will be distributed rectilinearly rather than sigmoidally between 0% and 100%.* In other words, p is a linear function of ΔI. The classic view, on the other hand, predicts a sigmoidal probability function between 0% and 100% perceived differences. Suppose the data shown by open circles in Fig. 12 had been obtained from a single, well-trained subject at a single sitting. Which of the two hypotheses, sigmoidal or quantal, better fits these data points? We must first construct best fitting sigmoidal and rectilinear curves. Now, inspecting the two theoretical curves, we can see that neither one gives a perfect fit— neither curve runs through all points. By applying the *Chi-square* test, however, one may determine the probability that these data could have been obtained by chance when the 'true' function was either rectilinear or sigmoidal in nature. If the obtained values would occur as chance deviations from a 'true' sigmoidal curve only 1% of the time, but 50% or more of the time as chance deviations from a 'true' rectilinear curve, then they obviously fit the rectilinear hypothesis better.

Stevens, Morgan, and Volkmann (1941) found the rectilinear hypothesis to fit their data better than the sigmoidal one, both for loudness discrimination results and also for pitch discrimination (see Fig. 13). Flynn (1943) has substantiated these results for pitch, and the quantal hypothesis has also been satisfied by data for olfactory thresholds (Jerome, 1943) and tactual movement thresholds (DeCillis, 1944). There is one difficulty with this curve-fitting criterion. As may be seen by inspection of Fig. 12, it is only near the 20% and 80% levels that differences of any magnitude would be expected from the two hypotheses. Many sets of data are found to fit both hypotheses reasonably well, and the 'goodness-of-fit' criterion can be applied only when a number of data plots are available. In the typical experiment ten sets of data may fit the quantal hypothesis better, whereas four fit the sigmoidal one better (cf. Flynn, 1943).

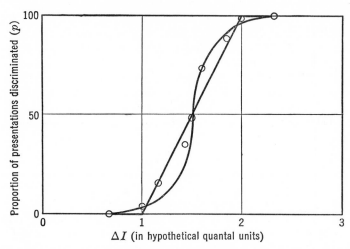

FIGURE 12. Proportion of presentations discriminated (p) described as either a linear or a sigmoidal function of ΔI, based on hypothetical data (open circles). Modified from Stevens, Morgan, and Volkmann, *American Journal of Psychology,* 1941, 54:319.

(2) *The largest difference which is perceived* 0% *of the time will be exactly one half as large as that which is perceived* 100% *of the time.* This holds when a 'two-quantum' criterion of judgment is used, i.e. when the standard is of sufficient duration to vary itself within the limits of a single quantum. In other words, not until the increment equals 1 quantum should the observer begin occasionally to perceive differences, but when the increment equals 2 quanta he should always perceive the difference. And since quanta are assumed to be equal in size, the magnitude of the increment at 0% discrimination (1 quantum) should be exactly one half that at 100% discrimination (2 quanta). Stevens, Morgan, and Volkmann obtained data clearly fitting this prediction, as may be seen by inspection of the set of curves for pitch discrimination in Fig. 13. Notice that although individual observers differed in the absolute sizes of their quantal units, the 100% points were consistently double the 0% points. Subject J. V. perceived no difference in pitch when the increment was 2.5 cycles or less, but he always responded for increments 5.0 cycles or more. Subject M. J.'s 0% point was only 1 cycle and his 100% point was exactly double, 2 cycles. Not all investigators have been successful in meeting this criterion. Flynn, for example, obtained data that do not conform to the 2 to 1 ratio, and he was also working with pitch discrimination. Jerome's data for olfaction and DeCillis's on tactual movement both fail to meet this criterion. In both of these studies,

however, *absolute* rather than difference thresholds were measured, and it may be that quanta behave differently near the absolute threshold of sensitivity.

(3) *Variability of judgments should increase and decrease cyclically as the magnitude of the standard is changed.* If sensory discrimination varies in step-wise fashion as a function of stimulus magnitude, stimuli falling

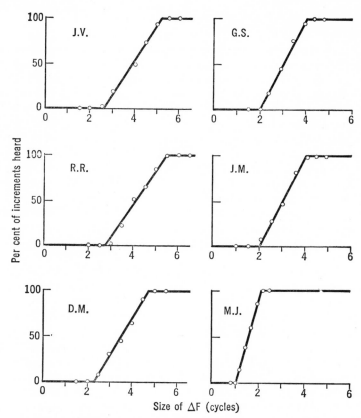

FIGURE 13. Frequency discrimination functions for six subjects. Standard tone 1000 c.p.s., 54 db above threshold. Stevens, Morgan, and Volkmann, *American Journal of Psychology*, 1941, **54**:325.

near the middle of a quantal unit should produce less variability in judgment than stimuli falling near the transition point between one neural unit and another. In the latter case, given the continuous fluctuations in energy surplus, the stimulus will sometimes excite N quanta and sometimes $N + 1$ quanta. Increasing the magnitude of the stimulus by small, sub-quantal steps should therefore result in cyclic changes in variability of judgments. Only one test of this prediction is available to date. Volkmann (1946) exposed tachistoscopically the same-sized black rectangle twenty-six times in succession in each series; the subjects, who were given no reason to believe the size was constant within each series, were told to judge each succeeding presentation as larger, smaller, or equal to the immediately preceding presentation as the standard. The size of rectangles was varied by very small amounts from series to series. Indexing variability by the relative frequency of 'greater' plus 'smaller' judgments as compared with 'equal' judgments, cyclical increases and decreases were obtained, definite for some observers but evident in the data for all. This technique would seem to be applicable to any dimension of stimulus variation, and it is probable that other investigations are under way.

Why Have Classical Psychophysical Data Failed to Meet Quantal Criteria?

Most investigations of both absolute and differential sensitivity have failed to reveal such quantal characteristics as these—even studies explicitly designed to explore the interval of uncertainty with finely graded stimuli (cf. Warner Brown, 1910, 1914). One possible reason for this is the (1) *averaging of data*. In trying to get at the 'best estimate' of the threshold, and following the assumption of normal or chance variability, investigators have often combined data from various sessions and even from different subjects. From our present vantage point it can be seen that quantal functions could never be revealed by such procedures: the *intrinsic* sources of variability, such as differences between subjects in their sensory capacity and differences within the same subject over periods of time, would obscure such functions. Miller and Garner (1944) have shown that two sets of data obtained from the same subject under procedurally identical but spaced conditions—and each yielding a rectilinear plot separately—will average into a sigmoidal distribution.

Another reason classic data have yielded nonquantal distributions is that (2) *the criteria for judgment have been allowed to shift within a single session.* This may happen when poorly trained observers are employed or when the size of the variable increment is shifted randomly within a series of judgments (the usual procedure in psychophysical experiments). Miller and Garner have shown that a random order of presenting increments of different sizes prevents even the well-trained observer from adopting a stable criterion. Stevens and Volkmann (1940 *a*) report that a shift in quantal function can result in tests made before and after drinking a cup of coffee. Ideally, the observer maintains either a 'one-quantum' or a 'two-quantum' criterion, depending upon the conditions of the experiment, but this is probably a difficult thing to do.

The 'standard' procedure in experiments designed to get at quantal functions, at least where difference thresholds are concerned, has been to present 20 or so 'warbles' of exactly the same increment in a series lasting about 1¼ minutes; the size of the increment is then shifted to another value (cf. Stevens, Morgan and Volkmann, 1941). Although this provides perhaps the simplest task for the observer, it calls up a serious methodological problem: if the subject knows that all increments in a given series are going to be identical, is it not possible for him to set up a *subjective standard* on the basis of which he graduates the frequency of his responses? To illustrate, suppose that on the third 'warble' of the series the subject barely notices a change; he knows that all subsequent changes will be of the same minimal character. Is it possible then that his judgments will be influenced by this so that he 'responds' by striking the key only rarely, say 20 per cent of the time? In this case the rectilinearity of the function would describe the stability of the observer's subjective, frequency-of-response scale in relation to his judgment of the size of the increment on those occasions when he does perceive it.

A disturbing note which seems to justify the above possibility is to be found in the Stevens, Morgan, and Volkmann article: '. . . most O's report that some of the increments they perceive are larger and plainer than others. Increments heard 80% of the time tend to be subjectively larger than increments heard only 20% of the time' (p. 334). And these authors go on to speculate that the perception of magnitude, as separate from the perception of presence or absence, may also be a quantal phenomenon, involving units of smaller size. This may be true, but it may also serve to invalidate the whole quantal conception. Going back to the essential nature of the theory, discrimination depends upon the addition of another neural unit to those already in operation. How can the *same* additional quantal unit seem smaller when it is added only 20 per cent of the time as compared with its being added 80 per cent of the time? This seems to be a crucial issue for the quantal theory, but it is not clear how it can be disentangled from the subjective frame of reference established in the standard procedure.

What Is the Nature of the Quantum?

The simplest assumption identifies the quantal unit with the smallest neural unit, the individual nerve fiber, and this was Békésy's (1930) inference. Stevens, Morgan, and Volkmann have seriously questioned this view, specifying three difficulties with it: (a) the quantum is of no fixed magnitude for the individual subject, changes in its value being occasionally observed; (b) there are more auditory nerve fibers, for example, than there are quanta for any given sensory attribute; (c) the binaural quantum is regularly somewhat smaller (approximately two-thirds) than the monaural quantum, which certainly doesn't fit any single fiber identification. On the basis of such evidence as this, these authors suggest that the quantal, 'all-or-none' function appears at some central locus, involves a number of fibers, and is functional rather than anatomical. 'The organism behaves as though a definite increment of excitation, or potential, or chemical concentration, is needed at some central locus in order to enlist a "final common path" and thereby produce "key-pressing" ' (p. 333). The quantal hypothesis has certain advantages over the classic view: it draws a clear distinction between extrinsic and intrinsic sources of variability; it offers a rational conception of the nature of sensory discrimination which is compatible with existing knowledge of the nervous system.

THE NEURAL BASIS OF SENSORY INTENSITY

Although the quantal hypothesis concerns a fundamental relation between psychological experience and nervous functioning, it does nothing to specify how the nervous system actually mediates intensive awareness—the 'neural units' referred to are hypothetical constructs. What is the neural correlate of sensory intensity? What variations in the neural 'message' signal changes in intensity? Before the development of electrical methods of studying nerve action it was generally assumed that sensory intensity was correlated with the 'size' of impulses in fibers. The overwhelming evidence upon which the 'all-or-none' law is based rules this possibility out today. The two remaining possibilities—frequency of impulses in individual fibers and total number of fibers excited—are both supported by considerable evidence.

Frequency of Impulses in Individual Fibers

Although Keith Lucas (1917), Forbes and his associates (1915, 1924), and others had laid the methodological and factual groundwork for a frequency theory of sensory intensity, it remained for Adrian and his coworkers to describe this relation in convincing detail. The story is told with simplicity and clarity in *The Basis of Sensation* (1928). Adrian employed improved vacuum tube amplification and worked with preparations in which

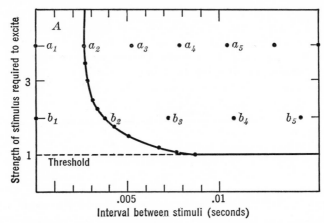

FIGURE 14. Recovery curve of frog's sciatic nerve. Values indicate the intensity of the second of two stimulations necessary to excite activity in the nerve. E. D. Adrian, *The Basis of Sensation,* Christophers, London, 1928, p. 63.

the activity of individual sensory fibers could be distinguished. He was able to show conclusively that sensory fibers follow the all-or-none law as rigidly as do motor fibers (for which this law had been demonstrated previously by Forbes and Gregg, 1915), and, more importantly for our present interest, he showed that changes in stimulus intensity are reflected in changes in the *frequency* of nerve impulses. Working with the sterno-cutaneous preparation (a small muscle in the frog containing only 15 to 25 sensory fibers that can be pared down by sectioning small strips of the muscle), he found that frequency of discharge in individual fibers increased as the pull on the muscle was increased. The same relation held when the toe-pad of the cat was stimulated by deep pressure, light touch and pricking with a needle, appropriate nerves having been isolated; when three or four hairs on the external surface of the cat's ear were moved and impulses recorded from a small cutaneous nerve in the ear; and when the eye of the conger eel was stimulated by light and impulses led off the optic nerve.

There is a good reason why frequency of impulses in nerve should increase with intensity of stimulation—all nerve fibers have *refractory periods.* Figure 14 shows the strength of the *second* of two stimuli necessary to excite the sciatic nerve of a frog as a function of the interval between the two stimuli. For approximately .002 seconds following the first impulse, the nerve is absolutely refractory, and infinite intensity of stimulus would be required to set up another impulse. Between .002 and .009 seconds the nerve is relatively refractory, and decreasingly intense stimuli can excite another impulse. By approximately .009 seconds the nerve has fully recovered its normal excitability. Now let us suppose that a *continuous* stimulus of extremely high intensity is applied to the receptor: the nerve will be excited deep in its relative refractory period (a_2), when it has only partially recovered from the initial impulse (a_1), and will continue to be set off successively at this level (a_3, a_4 $\cdots$ a_n), yielding a rapid rate of impulses. A somewhat less intense stimulus will excite the nerve later in its refractory period (b_2) and, in the same manner, will set off a series of impulses (b_3, b_4 $\cdots$ b_n), but the rate will be less rapid than in the case above.

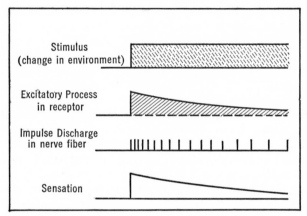

FIGURE 15. Relation between stimulus, sensory message, and sensation. Adrian, *The Basis of Sensation,* Christophers, London, 1928, p. 119.

This picture of repetitive action in the frog's sciatic nerve is typical of all nerve conduction, and thus it shows that the refractory period is *not* a sufficient explanation of intensity mediation. Were this the only controlling factor, impulse frequency could vary only between about 100 and 500 per second. Since fibers may carry much slower rates than 100 impulses per second, it appears that some concentration process in the receptor (chemical, electrical) must also determine the rate of firing. In other words, the nerve will respond at a rate below its own threshold if the rate of concentration of the stimulus (and its utilization for each impulse) is sufficiently slow. The phenomenon of temporal summation (cf. pp. 75, 166) illustrates concentration of the stimulus, and sensory adaptation illustrates the reverse. With regard to the latter, Adrian has shown how the sensory experience of smoothly decreasing intensity which accompanies a constant stimulus could be mediated by a gradually reducing rate of nerve fiber discharge. As shown in Fig. 15, he attributes adaptation to a gradual reduction in the excitatory state of the receptor.

Number of Excited Fibers

Although there is no evidence that the frequency principle is erroneous, there is evidence that it is insufficient. Sensory intensity may vary without any change in the frequency of impulses in individual fibers if the total number of fibers contributing to a given experience is increased. The apparent brightness of an illuminated patch can be augmented by increasing its size; the apparent intensity of a warmth stimulus can be augmented by increasing the area stimulated (Herget, Granath, and Hardy, 1941 *b*) ; two pressures on neighboring skin areas, individually subthreshold, can be felt if applied simultaneously (Brükner, 1901, after Boring, 1933)—these are all cases of *areal summation*. That an increasing area is actually accompanied by an increase in the total number of impulses has been demonstrated, for vision at least, by Adrian and Matthews (1927) using the excised eye of the conger eel.

Integration of Frequency and Number Principles

It seems likely that both frequency and number principles will be found to apply to all modalities. Both sets of observations are made at the periphery, however, and experienced intensity must ultimately depend upon what happens in higher centers. Do frequency and number principles function as alternate mediators of experienced intensity, or do they become integrated into a single variable at some point along the projection pathways? There are at least two feasible integrations that can be suggested: (1) *Sensory intensity depends upon the total frequency of impulses delivered per unit time at some higher center.* According to this view, it is quite irrelevant whether variations in total frequency are produced by changing frequency within a limited number of fibers or by changing the number of fibers contributing a constant frequency. In both cases the total number of impulses per unit time (fn/t) is varied. (2) *Sensory intensity depends upon the frequency of impulses in individual fibers* (i.e. delivered at a specific locus in some higher center). In what sense can this be construed as an integration when the number principle is left out entirely? It is quite possible that, via bombardment of common synaptic junctures, number of excited fibers at the periphery becomes translated into frequency in second- or third-order neurons. In other words, the frequency of impulses in a higher order neuron may depend upon the number of peripheral elements delivering energy to its synapse as well as the frequency borne by these elements. If we accept provisionally a conclusion reached at the end of the preceding chapter—that sensory quality depends upon the locus of activity in higher centers—then the second alternative is certainly the more attractive. Otherwise, increasing intensity (and hence the number of different fibers) should regularly cause a broadening or 'fuzzing' of sensory quality.

The Receptor Excitatory Process

Although the exact process of stimulation—the energy exchange that initiates impulses in sensory nerve—is quite obscure in most modalities, a chemical mechanism has been suggested as the initial step in all cases. It will be reasonable, therefore, to describe *Hecht's chemical theory* of visual stimulation (where a chemical basis is definite) as a model for the excitatory process in general, provided we keep in mind that it is only a rough approximation. The general model must be adapted to the peculiarities of each sense department: Jenkins's chemical theory of thermal stimulation and Lasareff's chemical theory of gustatory stimulation are examples. Readers interested in chemical and mathematical details of Hecht's theory may consult original sources (cf. Hecht, 1934, 1935).

The visual receptors contain a photosensitive substance, S, which is decomposed by incident light into a number of by-products $(P + A)$. The velocity of this initial photochemical reaction, called the 'light reaction' $(S \rightarrow P + A)$, varies directly with the intensity of light and the mass or concentration of the sensitive substance—a familiar chemical law. The photosensitive substance, S, itself is not capable of eliciting impulses in nerve tissue, but certain of its decomposition products have this exciting capacity. It must also be assumed that the primary decomposition product, P, is removed as it is formed; otherwise infinite duration of stimulation would render any light visible, no matter how weak—and we shall see that temporal summation is limited in the time over which it operates. Furthermore, since sensitivity is known to increase in the dark (and reach a state of equilibrium under constant stimulation), the photosensitive substance, S, must constantly be in the process of being replenished. Existing evidence indicates that S is constantly being resynthesized from its own end products $(S \leftarrow P + A)$ *plus* a third substance which is present in excess—a pseudo-reversible chemical reaction:

$$S \xrightarrow{\text{light}} P + A + B$$
$$S \xleftarrow[\text{dark}]{} P + A + C$$

where B is the substance which carries on the effects of the primary light reaction and C is the additional substance required for resynthesis of S. The resynthesizing process is referred to as the 'primary dark reaction,' and its velocity is also a function of the concentration of the reacting substances.

It can be seen that light and dark reactions act like a balance system: the more rapid the light reaction (under intense stimulation), the greater the mass of $P + A$, and hence the more rapid will be their combination with C to resynthesize S. Since time is required for equilibrium to be reached between the two reactions, and since velocity varies with concentration, adaptation to changes in intensity level will follow negatively accelerated functions (e.g. bright and dark adaptation), being rapid at first and approaching an asymptote. The process whereby impulses are set up in nerve is termed the 'secondary dark reaction'; its magnitude is assumed to be a direct function of the rate at which the initial light reaction proceeds. The adequacy with which this model will fit other modalities remains to be seen.

Sensory Neural Mediation

The most general statement of how the sensory nervous system handles intensive changes has been given by Crozier. Unfortunately, Crozier's own theorizing has appeared in extremely condensed form as parts of his many research reports (cf. 1940 *a, b,* and particularly 1940 *c*). The following account places emphasis on his underlying assumptions. Let us take the case in which a limited area of sensitive surface (the retina, the skin) is plied with increasingly intense stimulation. In accordance with the quantal hypothesis, Crozier assumes that any change in intensive awareness must be based upon the addition or subtraction of one 'neural unit' to those already present. It seems most likely, on the basis of all that has gone before, that this 'neural unit' is a constant increment or decrement in the *frequency* of impulses in the fibers subserving this region. A first assumption may therefore be phrased as follows:

> *All equally perceptible changes in intensive awareness represent the addition or subtraction of a constant impulse frequency in the set of fibers utilized by the stimulus.*

The assumption that all just discriminable increments or decrements represent a constant number of impulses, regardless of the absolute level of intensity, is based on the fact that all just perceptible changes (j.n.d.'s) are subjectively equal.

Since all nerves have refractory periods, it follows that (a) there must be some finite maximum impulse frequency which a limited number of fibers can carry (set by their absolute refractory periods), and (b) that below this limit individual fibers will fire at rates dependent on the intensity of stimulation (set by their relative refractory periods). Nerve fibers, however, also show equilibration (or accommodation, as Crozier calls it), their excitability decreasing during continuous stimulation at a rate and to a degree determined by the initial rate of response—which in turn is dependent upon the prevailing intensity level. This means that stimulus intensity must be increased *disproportionately* in order to maintain a constant rate of increase in impulse frequency. The size of any just perceptible increment in intensity therefore depends upon the absolute intensity level, i.e. the necessary increment in intensity (ΔI) is some function of intensity (I). It has long been assumed that this is a *logarithmic* function, and the fact that impulse frequency is roughly proportional to the log of the stimulus has been verified empirically in a number of neurophysiological studies (cf. Hoagland, 1930, for an analysis of Adrian and Zotterman's data; Matthews, 1931, for data on impulse frequency in an isolated muscle receptor). But since it has already been assumed that the necessary increment in impulse frequency required to yield a just perceptible difference is *constant,* regardless of the intensity level, it must follow that:

> *The increment in intensity necessary to yield the critical increment in impulse frequency* (and hence a perceptible change in intensive awareness) *will increase as the logarithm of the intensity level.*

This, it should be noted, is merely a recasting of the Weber-Fechner Law—that sensation increases as the log of the stimulus—into terms compatible with present-day neural conceptions.

But the Weber-Fechner Law does not fit empirical observations, except through limited ranges of $I,$ and there only roughly. In order to obtain a better fit with these observations, there is another assumption, also in keeping with available information, which must be made: it must be assumed that because of a multitude of independent factors the excitability of individual neural units varies from unit to unit and within the same unit from moment to moment. In other words, Crozier assumes variability in excitability among any population of sensory units to be distributed according to a normal or Gaussian curve. This is the critical aspect of his theory. The import of the argument is that the mathematical properties of the normal curve must be added to the simple logarithmic relation between threshold and intensity. Letting the symbol P stand for the probability integral (and thus greatly simplifying the mathematical statement), the equation becomes $\Delta I = (P) \log I$, and the function becomes sigmoidal rather than linear. Applying this correction:

> *The size of the increment in intensity necessary to yield the critical increment in impulse frequency* (and hence a perceptible change in intensive awareness) *will increase as a sigmoidal function of the logarithm of the intensity level.*

This means that plotting just discriminable increments (ΔI's) against successive values of $\log I$ will yield an S-shaped curve, nearly linear through its middle range where the Weber-Fechner function is approximated.

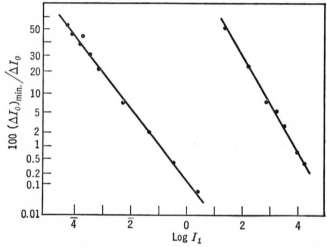

FIGURE 16. Brightness thresholds for rod (left) and cone (right) populations expressed as proportions of maximal $1/\Delta I_0$ ratio on probability grid, where I_0 is the absolute threshold and I_1 is the intensity level to which the eye is adapted. Crozier, *Proceedings of the National Academy of Science*, Washington, 1940, **26**:383.

In practice, Crozier usually plots the *reciprocal* of the threshold ($1/\Delta I$) as a function of $\log I$. There appear to be two reasons for this, one logical and the other practical. The logical reason is that this reciprocal can be shown to be an index of 'differential excitability': given a finite limit to the total number of impulses any group of fibers can carry, Crozier explains that if the proportion 'used up' by the standard stimulus increases with the intensity level ($\log I$), as we have seen, then the proportion left 'available' for the comparison stimulus must vary with the reciprocal of $\log I$, i.e. the number of potential impulses that can mediate a change in intensity decreases as the intensity level is raised and more impulses are 'used up.' Since ΔI is proportional to $\log I$ (cf. above), $1/\Delta I$ must be proportional to $1/\log I$; therefore, $1/\Delta I$ is proportional to the 'available' impulses or potential excitability. As Crozier puts it, this means that the reciprocal of the difference threshold is a measure of the remaining excitability at any given intensity level.

The practical reason is that use of the reciprocal of the threshold makes it possible to plot functions directly on probability grids where truly sigmoidal functions become linear plots. Such a plot is shown as Fig. 16, for threshold data obtained by Blanchard (1918). The ordinate gives $1/\Delta I_o$ (threshold increment) as a percentage of the maximum of this fraction (the absolute threshold). The absolute threshold value is arbitrarily set at a value of 1.0 (ΔI_o min.), and subsequent increases in absolute size of the threshold with log I, by increasing the value of the denominator (ΔI_o), will decrease the magnitude of the fraction. Obtaining such linear distributions on probability grid paper serves to substantiate the underlying hypotheses. Although Crozier does not seem to have elaborated on *how* the sensory nervous system generates such sigmoidal functions, it is likely that the departures from linearity are due to the bringing in of new elements according to their thresholds (low intensities) and the dropping out of elements according to their absolute refractory periods (high intensities).

INCORPORATION OF CERTAIN THRESHOLD AND ADAPTATION PHENOMENA

Having discussed psychophysical methods for data gathering and some general principles about sensory nervous functioning, the logical next question is, Do the facts about intensive awareness fit our present theoretical conceptions? Actually, psychophysical data have not proved as useful in testing principles as one might hope. Not only do the details of methods, samples of receptors, and other conditions vary considerably from experiment to experiment—and one cannot simply average results—but it is difficult to make comparisons across modalities because the physical units in which threshold data are reported vary from sense to sense. Although visual and auditory data may be described in equivalent energy units (ergs per sec.), olfactory and gustatory thresholds are usually expressed as per cent concentrations of a given substance, pressure and pain in terms of mechanical force (grams per sq. mm.), and thermal sensitivity in temperature units. Although the excitatory process in every sense department is an energy exchange and hence is theoretically expressible in common energy units, to actually execute this transformation would require greater knowledge of the process of stimulation than we now have. Admitting these limitations, we shall nevertheless try to formulate certain empirical generalizations that seem warranted by the evidence and relate them to the principles of sensory excitation and neural mediation already covered.

Absolute and Difference Thresholds

The minimum energy required to elicit a just reportable sensory experience is small indeed for all modalities. It has been estimated that a single visual 'rod' cell is capable of being excited by a single quantum of radiant energy. The auditory mechanism closely rivals vision: it has been said that if the absolute threshold for hearing were only a little finer, the ear would be able to detect the movements of the molecules in the air. Although data for olfaction and gustation cannot be directly compared with those for vision and hearing, they can be compared with one another, and smell thresholds prove to be several thousand times finer than those for taste. Boring (1935) has estimated that the threshold concentration for putrid-smelling mercaptan contains only about 0.000,000,000,002.2 grams of the substance, which is one-thirtieth of the smallest amount of matter (sodium) that can be detected by the spectroscope. Threshold values as small as .033° have been observed for cold and warmth, and rough estimates of the minimal energy for pressure give a value of about .0001 erg, which is some 10,000 times larger than that for vision.

(1) *Magnitudes of absolute and difference thresholds are correlated.* Where comparable units of measurement make this hypothesis testable *between* modalities, it seems to be substantiated fairly well by the data. Absolute thresholds for vision are somewhat smaller than those for hearing, and the same relation holds for the sizes of difference thresholds. The same statement can be made for smell versus taste. As for comparisons *within* modalities, it is unfortunate that the data have not been collected with this hypothesis in mind. In the skin senses, for example, AL's and DL's are not usually reported by the same investigator, using the same subjects and methods, and testing the same series of skin positions. Absolute and difference thresholds are correlated in hearing, however, both varying concomitantly as functions of frequency. A relation of this sort would be expected, since receptors capable of reacting to minute absolute energies should be similarly sensitive to minute changes in energy level. The absolute threshold is merely the first of a series of discriminable steps, all equally dependent upon the same receptor characteristics. Superficially the visual receptors appear to refute this generalization—cones (day vision) have finer differential sensitivity but much larger absolute thresholds than rods (night vision). It must be noted, however, that cones display the smallest difference thresholds in terms of the *ratio* of increment to standard intensity level ($\Delta I/I$), not in terms of absolute magnitude of the increment.

(2) *Both absolute and difference thresholds vary inversely with the number of receptors per unit area of the stimulus.* Visual, auditory, and olfactory receptors are densely concentrated as compared with skin and taste receptors, and threshold sizes have been shown to vary accordingly—the more dense the receptors, the more elements are available per unit area of the stimulus. Within each cutaneous sense, according to this hypothesis, threshold size should vary inversely with the number of sensitive 'spots' per unit area, but again data have not been collected with this relationship in mind. Reported frequencies of 'spots' and reported threshold values seldom overlap in the skin area sampled, and the observations of different investigators cannot be combined since number of 'spots' per square centimeter varies with stimulus intensity and thresholds vary with the method employed. Nevertheless, the data for both pressure and pain in Table 1 give rough substantiation to this hypothesis: lips and fingers have heavy concentrations of touch 'spots' as compared with other parts of the body, and their thresholds are very much smaller; eyelid, inner joint of knee, and back of hand are richly supplied with pain 'spots' and have equivalently small absolute thresholds.

Why should thresholds become finer as receptor density increases? For one thing, if individual receptors vary randomly in sensitivity, the more elements involved by the stimulus, the greater the probability of contacting

TABLE 1. ABSOLUTE THRESHOLDS FOR PRESSURE AND PAIN AS FUNCTIONS OF LOCUS OF STIMULATION AND NUMBERS OF SENSITIVE SPOTS FOR SAME LOCI

	PRESSURE			PAIN	
Locus	*AL (gm./mm.^{2})*	*Spots/cm.^{2}*	*Locus*	*AL (gms.)*	*Spots/cm.^{2}*
lips	0.50	100+	eyelid	0.18	172
finger tip	0.57	100+	knee (inner jt.)	0.30	232
back of hand	1.27	28	back of hand	0.66	188
elbow	1.33	12	tip of nose	1.00	44
upper arm	1.44	9	ball of thumb	2.50	60
lower leg	2.16	6	sole of foot	3.00	48
chest	2.70	22			
back	4.00	26			

Data from Dallenbach in Boring, Langfeld, and Weld, *Psychology*, John Wiley and Sons, Inc., New York, 1935, ch. 7.

some with low thresholds. More importantly, since the frequency of impulses necessary for sensing a change in intensity is assumed to be a constant, the size of the threshold intensity must go down as the supply of available impulses increases. One obvious way to increase the number of available impulses while keeping area constant is to pack the receptor elements more densely—which is exactly what has happened in vision, hearing, and smell. This relation between threshold and receptor density thus follows directly from Crozier's theory.

(3) *Within certain critical limits, both absolute and difference thresholds vary inversely with stimulus area (receptor density constant).* This is the well-known reciprocal relation between intensity and area:

$$I \times A = C$$

where I is intensity of stimulation, A is area stimulated, and C is some constant level of discrimination (usually the absolute or difference threshold). This means that a constant, threshold level of sensation can be maintained despite reductions in the intensity of stimulation as long as the area over which the stimulus acts is increased. If, on the other hand, we keep intensity constant and increase area, the magnitude of sensation increases; this is known as *areal summation,* and the phenomenon is best substantiated in vision (cf. Chap. 4). It has also been demonstrated for the warmth sense by Herget, Granath, and Hardy (1941 *b*), who used flickering radiant heat against the forehead, and analogous data could be drawn from other sense departments. In terms of Crozier's theory again, if the number of impulses that must be added to produce a perceptible difference is a constant, increasing the area will increase the potential supply of impulses and hence reduce the necessary increment in intensity. But why should the area over which this reciprocal relation holds be limited? The area over which summation occurs (and hence over which number of elements is equivalent to frequency within elements) depends upon the anatomy of the sensory projection system—specifically, upon the density of lateral connections. Areal summation comes down to a facilitation of excitation in more centrally located neurons when they receive near-synchronous inputs from more peripherally located, disparate neurons. This anatomical correlate will become clearer when we study summation in vision.

(4) *Within certain critical limits, both absolute and difference thresholds vary inversely with stimulus duration.* The eye and the ear, and perhaps all other receptive mechanisms, are integrative systems in the sense that energies distributed through time summate. Again, we have a reciprocal relation:

$$I \times T = C$$

in which I refers to intensity, T to duration of stimulation, and C to some constant level of discrimination (again, usually the absolute or difference threshold). A constant threshold value of sensation can be maintained despite reductions in intensity as long as the time over which the stimulus is applied is sufficiently increased. Here, too, there is a limit to the duration over which integration can occur. Temporal summation has also been most adequately studied in vision.

Crozier handles time and intensity as equivalents, often substituting one for the other in his equations—and his equations conform well with observed data. But it is not at all clear how this reciprocal relation is derived from his theory. It is apparent that if number of available impulses increases with duration of stimulation, thresholds will decrease in size. But why should availability of impulses increase with duration? Hecht's chemical theory provides a ready answer: with continued stimulation at subthreshold intensity, the concentration of excitatory substance in the receptors accumulates until, with sufficient duration for a given intensity level, threshold concentrations are reached and impulses generated. Why is there a limit to the duration over which temporal summation can occur? According to the chemical theory, the end products of the light reaction must be utilized for neural excitation within a brief critical period or they are either removed or resynthesized (Hecht, 1934).

(5) *The fraction by which a stimulus must be increased (or decreased) in order for the change to be just perceptible is constant regardless of the absolute magnitude of the stimulus* (Weber's Law). Working mainly on the discrimination of hefted weights, E. H. Weber in 1834 observed that one stimulus could be judged different from another if it were approximately one-thirtieth greater or less than the standard—and this ratio appeared to be independent of the absolute magnitude for which discriminations were obtained. He phrased a statement roughly equivalent to that given above as an empirical generalization from his observations, but it remained for the more philosophically inclined Fechner to elevate the proposition to the status of a fundamental law governing the mind-body relation. And indeed—were this law found to be immutable for all modalities—it would seem that one was getting at least a glimpse of some Grand Design. It is not necessary to delve into laboratory reports to discover the gross functioning of such a law of proportionality: a one-half inch added to the side of a postage stamp is immediately discernible, but a one-half inch added to the side of a billboard is completely imperceptible.

Is this law actually valid? It would require that for all magnitudes of S,

$$\frac{\Delta S}{S} = \text{a constant,}$$

a constant, that is, for a given dimension within a given modality. The term S (stimulus) is used here rather than I (intensity) since this law has been applied to qualitative as well as quantitative dimensions. In graphic terms, as shown in Fig. 17, the fraction $\Delta S/S$ should have the same value throughout the scale of absolute magnitudes of S, i.e. should generate the line parallel to the base. The other curve in this figure describes typical results obtained in most modalities. In no modality is the law completely satisfied; rather, continuously curvilinear functions are found. The just perceptible increment is therefore not a constant fraction of S but rather a constantly

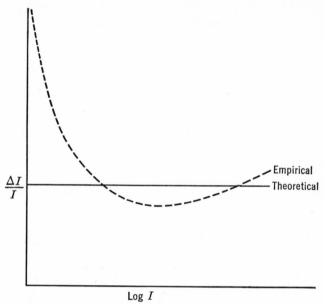

FIGURE 17. Comparison of typical Weber ratios ($\Delta I/I$) as a function of intensity (log I) with the theoretical constant ratio.

varying fraction of S. The discrepancy between fact and theory is greatest for low values of S (as shown in this diagram), and most observations also indicate an increase in the fraction for extremely high values.

Weber's Law is not precisely valid for any modality—which may be the reason space devoted to it in psychological texts has been steadily decreasing, decade by decade. Yet to dismiss this law because it does not hold over the entire range would be to obscure a fundamental fact about sensory mechanisms. In actual practice empirical curves of the type illustrated in Fig. 17 are expressed in logarithmic units. This, in effect, *assumes* the validity of Weber's Law, since equal ratios rather than equal units then form the base line. The practical reason for doing this is that the wide range of sensitivity, from the minimal energy required at threshold to the limiting values which may be many million times the threshold energy, may be manipulated within the confines of an ordinary graph. The effect of this procedure is, however, to exaggerate the narrow, low intensity segment and to minimize the great range over which the law is essentially valid.

Fechner accepted Weber's Law and made one additional assumption— that all just noticeable differences, being equally 'just noticeable,' must be of equal subjective magnitude. Then he proceeded to cast Weber's Law into the form of an integrative equation:

$$n = C \log S$$

in which S refers to the intensity of the stimulus measured in appropriate physical units, C is a constant including the appropriate Weber fraction, and n is the number of equal-appearing subjective steps above threshold ($1n$ being the value of the absolute threshold). This has come to be known as *Fechner's Law,* and it states in effect that sensory intensity increases arithmetically as stimulus intensity increases geometrically. When Fechner, pursuing philosophical implications, substituted the term 'sensation' for n, making the formula read

$$\text{sensation} = C \log \text{stimulus}$$

a wholly irrelevant controversy arose over whether sensations could actually be measured (cf. Boring, 1929). This controversy was irrelevant because 'sensation' merely refers to n, number of equal-appearing intervals, which are themselves expressed in physical units.

But why is it that 'sensation plods along step by step while the stimulus leaps ahead by ratios,' as Woodworth (1938) so neatly puts it? The practical consequence of the arrangement is clear enough: immense variations in physical energy are telescoped into a relatively small number of psychological steps—the environment is 'cut down to size,' so to speak. But why should this particular relation hold? Why should equal ratios rather than equal magnitudes appear equal psychologically? Fechner thought this represented a 'lag' in the psychic sphere, but this would hardly satisfy a materialistic monist. That the relation *is* of this sort, regardless of why, reflects the manner in which the sensory nervous system functions. As was noted earlier in relation to Crozier's theory, sensory nerves show *equilibration,* a decrement in excitability as a function of rate of fire (which in turn depends upon intensity of stimulation)—and this means that the intensity of stimulation must be increased disproportionately if a constant rate of increase in impulse frequency is to be maintained. Crozier's statistical theory also takes into account the discrepancy between Weber's Law and empirical facts by assuming normal or Gaussian variability in the thresholds and refractory periods of individual neural elements. The bringing in of additional elements near the absolute threshold and the dropping out of elements near the limits of intensity registration shifts the function from a linear logarithmic relation to a sigmoidal one. Weber's Law holds only for the middle range of intensities where all fibers are involved, at least minimally, and where ΔI is therefore a strict logarithmic function of I.

Sensory Adaptation

Sensitivity may vary spontaneously under conditions of constant stimulation. The temporal course and degree of this process can be gauged in several ways, all varieties of the psychophysical methods we have studied. Progressive changes in absolute or difference limens can be measured—here as functions of the duration of unvarying stimulation. Critical fusion frequency for fresh receptor elements can be compared with that for the same elements after periods of stimulation, reduced CFF serving to index lessened differential sensitivity. Especially well designed for measuring the temporal course of sensory adaptation is the equating method (simultaneous comparison): a constant fatiguing stimulus is applied to one set of receptors and, at intervals, a variable comparison stimulus is applied to fresh receptors; by adjusting intensity of the variable until both stimuli seem equal, adaptation at the test point is measured.

There are numerous sources of error in studying sensory adaptation. It is necessary that the adapting stimulus be constant in both intensity and quality, but this is extremely hard to achieve in some sense departments—for example, taste solutions are continuously being diluted by the flow of saliva (cf. Abrahams, Krakauer, and Dallenbach, 1937). It is also essential that the same receptor elements be stimulated throughout the course of adaptation, for if the stimulus is allowed to shift about on the sensory surface, fresh receptors are brought into play and the adaptation picture is obscured. Slight tongue movements, bringing fresh taste buds into action, produce sudden increases in the intensity of taste sensations. Variations in what subjects attend to also cause trouble. Culler (1926 a) reports that untrained subjects have difficulty restricting their attention to thermal sensations, for example, while judging thermal adaptation, often relying on tactual (numb, smooth, glowing) or pain (tingling, prickly, burning) criteria.

Considerable confusion arises from the fact that the meaning of adaptation varies remarkably from modality to modality. For the skin and chemical senses it means progressive decrease in the intensity of sensation with continued and unvarying stimulation—this is the most general meaning of the term. But the process termed 'visual dark adaptation' is actually a case of *increasing* sensitivity accompanying *lack* of stimulation, i.e. the eye becomes more sensitive to light (absolute threshold becomes smaller) as time in the dark increases. Perhaps this should be called 'dark sensitization' to avoid confusion. For both visual and thermal sense departments the adaptation concept includes the 'range-setting' character of the process; in both, the region of finest discrimination shifts along the absolute intensity scale. But whereas the level adjusted to in the thermal sense is always a neutral zone in which neither cold nor warm sensations are experienced—called 'physiological zero,' for some reason—no such neutral zone of 'zero' brightness accompanies visual range setting. In audition, it is doubtful whether any process strictly equivalent to adaptation occurs.

Four fairly general laws characterize sensory adaptation. (1) *The temporal course of adaptation is negatively accelerated,* proceeding rapidly at first and gradually slowing in rate. Typical data for visual dark adaptation, shown as Fig. 56 in Chap. 4, clearly fit this generalization. Data on the temporal course of visual bright adaptation are hard come by since the process occurs with extreme rapidity, but Hecht's (1934) analysis of the process in the fresh-water clam, Mya, indicates it to be negatively accelerated. That data for pressure and cold fit the law is apparent in Fig. 18, *A* and *B*. Although no quantitative information has been located for the pain sense, numerous casual observations indicate that the same function holds. For both smell and taste (Fig. 18, *C* and *D*), adaptation seems to be a linear function of time, but the data are of dubious validity. In neither case can the intensity of the adapting stimulus be kept constant with any

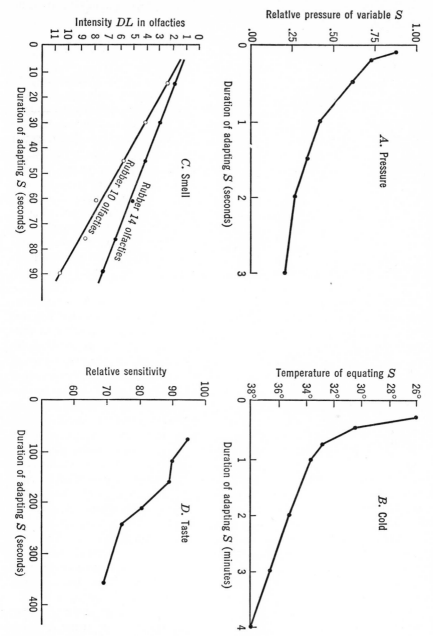

FIGURE 18. Typical curves for various modalities showing adaptation as a function of the duration of the constant adapting stimulus (S). A. Pressure (data of Von Frey and Goldman, 1915). B. Cold (data of Hahn, 1930). C. Smell (data of Zwaardemaker, 1895). D. Taste (data of Lasareff, 1928).

assurance. Crozier (1934), in discussing Lasareff's results, has expressed the opinion that taste adaptation will eventually be found to fit the negatively accelerated model.

Adrian (1928), it will be recalled, has shown that adaptation is accompanied by a slowing of the rate of impulses in sensory nerves. In terms of Hecht's formulation, the rate of utilization of the excitatory substance is rapid initially while its concentration is large, slowing and approaching an asymptote as utilization and regeneration reach equilibrium. In those modalities where adaptation is complete, we assume that the rate of regeneration of the excitatory substance is sufficiently slow so that equilibrium is established at a concentration below that necessary for threshold stimulation. In those modalities where adaptation is to a changed 'range setting,' we assume that equilibrium is established at a concentration above threshold.

(2) *The time required for adaptation increases with the intensity of the adapting stimulus.* Although complete adaptation, in the sense of a final lack of sensation, never occurs in vision, Craik and Vernon (1941) have shown that the time required to reach a constant level of dark adaptation varies directly with the intensity of a preadapting, fatiguing light. Zigler's (1932) data for the pressure sense, based on averages from eight subjects, fit the hypothesis (Fig. 19A). Both Stone and Dallenbach (1936), using areal pain, and Strauss and Uhlman (1919), using punctiform stimulation of marked pain spots (data shown as Fig. 19B), obtained data fitting the hypothesis, but Burns and Dallenbach (1933) found only a slight correlation between intensity of stimulus and adaptation time, using punctiform stimulation. As for the thermal modality, time for complete adaptation increases with divergence of the adapting stimulus from initial skin temperature (Culler, 1926 a) and with the initially reported intensity of sensation from isolated warmth (Aronoff and Dallenbach, 1936) and cold (Levine and Dallenbach, 1936) spots. Data obtained by Holm (1903, reported in Culler, 1926 a) are shown as Fig. 19C. When, however, the temperature of the surround of isolated cold spots is kept constant, Jenkins (1937) finds all times so short that 'it is impossible to say whether there is a definite relation between adapting temperature and the time needed to reach complete thermal indifference.' Implicit in the data already shown for olfaction in Fig. 18C is the fact that the *rate* of adaptation is faster for more intense odors (compare rubber 14 olfacties with rubber 10 olfacties), yet it is reported (cf. Henning, in Woodworth, 1938) that the time to reach complete adaptation is longer for more intense stimuli, if indeed it is ever attained. Recent data for taste adaptation clearly fit the law (Fig. 19D). The various curves in Fig. 19 have no consistent form; whether this is due to intrinsic differences among receptor systems or to methodological differences among experiments cannot be decided on present evidence.

This relation between time required for adaptation and intensity of stimulation seems to pose serious difficulties for both chemical and statistical theories. With respect to the former, the higher the intensity of stimulation, the more rapid should be the utilization of excitatory substances, and one would therefore expect adaptation time to *decrease* as intensity is raised. If the writer understands Crozier's theory, the same problem is present—since increased intensity results in a more rapid equilibration in rate of fire, the change to a steady state representing adaptation should be quicker. Of

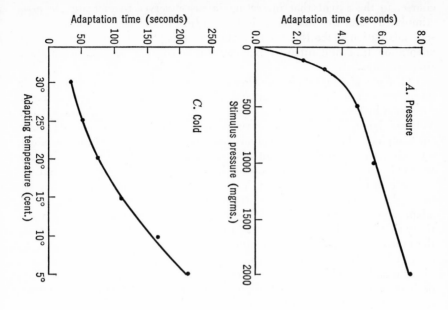

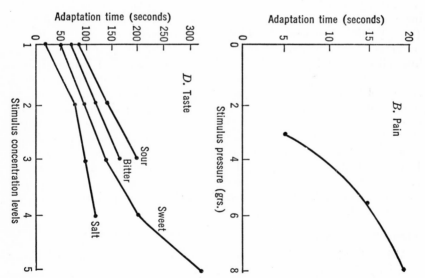

FIGURE 19. Typical curves for various modalities showing adaptation time as a function of the intensity of the constant adapting stimulus. *A.* Pressure (data of Zigler, 1932). *B.* Pain (data of Straus and Uhlman, 1919). *C.* Cold (data of Holm, 1903, as reported by Culler, 1926 *a*). *D.* Taste (adapted from Abrahams, Krakauer, and Dallenbach, *American Journal of Psychology,* 1937, **49**:466; Krakauer and Dallenbach, *American Journal of Psychology,* 1937, **49**:473).

course, to the extent that increasing intensity serves to increase the *area* stimulated—and the methodological difficulties in the way of studying sensory adaptation make this interpretation reasonable—the relation between adaptation time and intensity may become a relation between adaptation time and area.

(3) *Rate of adaptation decreases as the area stimulated increases.* Such an inverse relation between adaptation rate and area has been demonstrated for vision by Craik and Vernon (1941). It also holds for the thermal sense. Whereas large areas of skin (e.g. the entire hand) require considerable time for complete adaptation, individual cold spots adapt with extreme rapidity (Jenkins, 1937). Although control over the area stimulated is difficult with both pain and taste, this law probably holds there as well. The relation cannot be tested at all for olfaction. The only contrary evidence is contributed by Zigler (1932), who, when studying the pressure sense, found faster adaptation with larger stimuli. Working with a theory of thermal sensitivity that bears close resemblances to Hecht's, Jenkins (1937) assumes that the materials needed for regeneration of the excitatory substance from its own end products can be drawn from a considerable area since they are distributed by the blood stream. A more extensive stimulus, having a greater perimeter, would have a larger potential supply, and excitation could be maintained for a longer time.

(4) *Reflexive enhancement of sensitivity during adaptation.* Allen and his collaborators, in using the flicker-fusion method, have reported some puzzling findings. Allen (1923) found that bright adaptation of one eye was accompanied by increased sensitivity of the other eye, as indicated by increased *CFF*. Working with the pressure sense, Allen and Hollenberg (1924) tightly bandaged the *third* finger of an observer's hand to produce continuous adaptation and then made repeated tests of fusion frequency for intermittent stimulation applied to the *index* finger. *CFF* increased, indicating 'reflexive enhancement' at one locus owing to adaptation at another. Allen and Weinberg (1925) report the same phenomenon for taste adaptation. Adaptation to either salt or sour at one locus on the tongue produced increased sensitivity to sweet stimuli, as measured by fusion of intermittent electrolytic stimulation, at another locus. Reciprocal enhancement during taste adaptation has also been observed by earlier workers (Zuntz and Heymans, both cited by Troland, 1930), so Allen's findings cannot be a specious effect of the flicker-fusion method. Facts like these indicate that sensory adaptation is a far more complicated phenomenon than has generally been assumed.

Integration of Intensive and Qualitative Mediation Principles

Although it is convenient for analysis to separate intensive and qualitative sensitivity, in ordinary experiences the two dimensions are tightly interwoven. The same neurons provide information about both intensity and quality of stimulation, and this simultaneously. Data obtained by Herget, Granath, and Hardy (1941 *a*) on thermal discrimination are admirably suited to illustrate this sort of integration. Flickering radiant heat against the forehead was used as a stimulus. The size of the *DL* for a small patch of skin was measured as absolute thermal intensity was increased progressively from the level of normal skin temperature. In Fig. 20 the threshold data are expressed in arbitrary caloric units: the abscissa gives the absolute intensity values used (note that this is I, not $log\ I$); the ordinate gives the size of the just discriminable increments (ΔI) in the same units for each level of intensity tested. The subjects in this experiment also reported their subjective qualitative experiences at each level of threshold determination—changes in intensive discrimination may therefore be correlated with changes in experienced quality.

The size of the difference threshold is shown to increase in a complex but systematic fashion. If we section the total curve on the basis of changes in reported quality, it can be seen that the three plateaus correspond to the

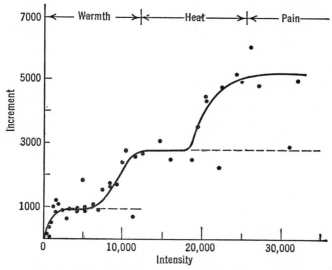

FIGURE 20. Difference thresholds and experienced qualities as functions of the intensity of thermal stimulation. Herget, Granath, and Hardy, *American Journal of Physiology*, 1941 a, **134**:649.

arousal of three successive qualities, warmth, 'heat,' and pain. Investigation was halted soon after the pain threshold was reached, so the complete sigmoidal function for this quality is not shown. What do these plateaus mean? They represent portions of the total curve where ΔI remains constant even though absolute intensity is still being increased, i.e. regions through which Weber's Law does not hold. In terms of Crozier's statistical theory, such divergences from the law of proportionality between I and ΔI are due to the bringing in or the taking out of new neural elements. The second plateau presumably represents the coming in of 'cold' fibers, according to the Gaussian variability in their thresholds, the fused cold and warmth being sensed as 'heat.' The third plateau presumably represents the coming in of pain fibers, also according to the variability in their thresholds, the fused warmth, cold, and pain being sensed as 'burning hot.' Here we have strikingly clear evidence for the fundamental psychophysical correlates described in these chapters: sensed quality is shown to be a function of 'what' fibers are delivering impulses, and sensed intensity is shown to be a function of 'how often' they fire. These are the two kinds of information our sensory nervous systems are able to provide.

Chapter 3

AUDITION

THE PHYSICS OF SOUND

When a tuning fork like that shown in Fig. 21 is struck with a felt-covered hammer, it vibrates back and forth, displacing air molecules on either side. The air is an elastic medium; these particles in turn displace neighboring ones and a *pressure wave* is propagated. Although one usually thinks of air as the medium through which sounds are transmitted, nearly any material— water, wood, metal—will carry pressure waves at a velocity dependent upon its physical structure. Many hearing aids make use of the fact that the bones of the skull can transmit pressure waves to the auditory receptors when injuries prevent normal transmission.

Certain Characteristics of Pressure Waves

As the tuning fork vibrates back and forth, air particles are displaced from their momentary resting positions, first in one direction and then in the other. If vibration of the sound generator is not maintained, the *amplitude* of these back-and-forth movements gradually decreases until the air particles regain their resting position—the hearer experiencing a tone that gradually decreases in loudness. When several generators that vibrate at different rates are struck in sequence, air particles are jostled first at one *frequency* and then at another—the hearer experiencing a succession of differently pitched tones. The spatial and temporal aspects of the movement of a single hypothetical particle can be described graphically as in Fig. 21. The periodic oscillations shown are known as *sine waves*. Spatial displacement away from (+) and back toward (−) the emitting object is shown on the vertical axis and is labeled *amplitude*. The temporal course of the particle is shown along the horizontal axis and is measured in thousandths of a second. Wave *a* completes one cycle in .001 seconds, makes 1000 such cycles in a second, and is referred to as a 1000 c.p.s. (cycles per sec.) tone. Wave *b* completes one cycle in .0005 seconds, makes 2000 such cycles in each second, and is called a 2000 c.p.s. tone.

Pure sine waves occur rarely in nature, most sound generators producing *complex sounds*. If the component frequencies are in the ratio 1:2:3:4, etc., to each other, we refer to the complex as a *harmonic* series. The exact selection and emphasis on overtones is a function of the sound-emitting object. A trumpet, a violin, and a clarinet, all sounding the same fundamental tone, will be clearly differentiated to the trained ear in terms of their distinctive overtone patterns, e.g. the *timbre* of the instruments. So far we have referred only to *tones* which have recognizable pitch. A *noise* is a complex of fre-

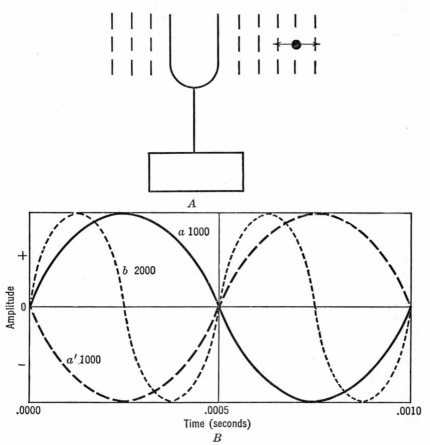

FIGURE 21. *A*. Oscillation of hypothetical air particle in neighborhood of vibrating tuning fork. *B*. Sine waves generated by particle oscillating at 1000 c.p.s. (*a*), at 2000 c.p.s. (*b*), and at 1000 c.p.s., 180° out of phase with *a* (*a′*).

quencies assembled more or less at random and having no recognizable pitch. When a sound complex includes all audible frequencies in equal energy ratios, it is called 'white noise,' analogous to the production of white light in vision through mixture of all wave lengths of light. The difference between 'noise' and 'tone,' as psychological experience, is to some extent modifiable by experience—Chinese music sounds like 'noise' to most occidentally trained ears.

Now suppose we have two sound generators that produce waves of the same frequency (i.e. two identical tuning forks). If the outputs of these two generators are synchronized in time, the result is maximum *summation of amplitude*. The hypothetical particle is acted upon simultaneously by forces in parallel; its displacement is increased equivalently (and hence the intensity of the sound). If the outputs of the two generators are so timed that the peaks in one correspond exactly to the troughs in the other (i.e. so that they are in opposite phase), the result is maximum *cancellation of amplitude*. The hypothetical particle is simultaneously acted upon by equal and opposed forces and it remains stationary. This situation may be seen graphically by comparing waves *a* and *a′* in Fig. 21. Two sound waves of different frequency summate and cancel their combined amplitude when sounded together (compare waves *a* and *b* in Fig. 21). If the outputs of two generators differ in frequency by small amounts, say 2 c.p.s., the sound waves summate through part of the time and cancel through the remainder, and the listener hears the tone wax and wane in loudness twice every second—such periodic changes in loudness are called *beats*. When a steady tone is generated in any ordinary room, reflection of sounds from various surfaces results in a pattern of *standing waves,* these representing a system of summations and cancellations in intensity. If the listening ear, or a microphone, is moved about the room, variations in intensity are readily noted. When exact control over the intensity of sounds is required, as in the laboratory, these effects may be minimized either by the use of earphones or by covering the walls of the room with sound-absorbent materials.

If the loud pedal of a piano is pressed down, thus allowing the strings to vibrate freely, and one then sings a loud, brief note, a soft echo of the voice may be heard coming from the instrument. This is a striking demonstration of *resonance*. Those strings whose natural frequencies match the harmonics of the human voice are forced into vibration and a replica of the original sound is created. Whenever a vibrating body is coupled to another body, either directly or by way of some medium such as the air, the motion of the first body is communicated to the second. The more closely the impressed frequency matches the natural vibration rate of the forced body, the greater the transmitted effect. The resonant body does not immediately take up the impressed frequency, however; rather, it runs through a series of *transient tones* before the steady state is reached, and the same effect occurs when the external driving force is removed. The time required for these transient tones to die away varies with the extent to which the receiving system is *damped;* in an ideally damped system, the steady state would be achieved immediately. The ear as a receiving system depends upon forced vibrations, as we shall see, and its damping is large but by no means perfect.

Apparatus for Producing and Recording Sounds

The rapid advances that have been made in recent years by researchers in audition are largely attributable to the development of electronic devices, especially the vacuum tube. A general description has already been given. The brief discussion of apparatus which follows is based upon that in Stevens and Davis, *Hearing* (1938, pp. 35-41). The block diagrams in Fig. 22 trace stages in the production of pure tonal stimuli (*A*) and the recording and analysis of sounds (*B*); the systems shown represent ideal arrangements for the investigation of psychophysiological acoustics, not necessarily any particular laboratory setup. In producing measurable auditory stimuli, we may begin with the beat-frequency oscillator or some recorded signal and end with a loudspeaker or headset; in recording sounds we begin with a microphone and end with a wave analyzer or cathode-ray oscillograph.

An *oscillator* is essentially a special type of vacuum tube amplifier in which a small part of the output current is led back to the grid circuit at such a rate that a particular frequency of amplified impulses is set up. Beat-frequency oscillators contain two such oscillators having natural frequencies of the order of 100,000 c.p.s., the outputs of both leading to a single mixer-tube where they interact to produce beats. With one oscillator constant at 100,000 cycles, the output of the other is varied, and the frequency of beats is equal to the difference in frequency between them—if the

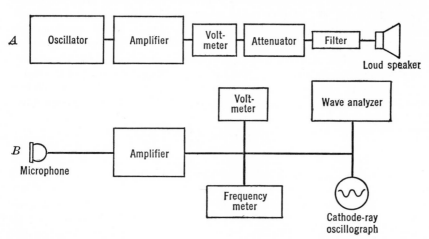

FIGURE 22. Experimental setups for producing (*A*) and recording (*B*) sounds. Stevens and Davis, *Hearing: Its Psychology and Physiology,* John Wiley and Sons, Inc., New York, 1938, p. 35.

variable is set at 101,000, for example, the beat-frequency output will be 1000 c.p.s.

The *voltmeter* measures the oscillator output. The *filter,* by a system of inductances and capacitances, selectively impedes certain frequencies and allows others to pass, eliminating undesired harmonics. The intensity of sound is varied by means of the *attenuator,* which is a network of resistances designed to reduce all frequencies equally. Ideally, as a generator of sound, the *loudspeaker* should respond equally to currents of all frequencies within the audible range; further, the intensity of the sound wave generated should be proportional to the impressed voltage, so that sound intensity can be directly indexed by measuring voltage. Some expensive loudspeakers approximate these requirements.

Turning now to the recording system, a *microphone* is essentially a loudspeaker in reverse; whereas the loudspeaker transforms electrical impulses into mechanical vibrations (and hence sound), the microphone transforms mechanical vibrations into electrical energy. The electrical output of the microphone is amplified and then may be led into any or all of the instruments shown in the lower portion of Fig. 22. If one knows the gain of the *amplifier* and the response contour of the microphone, the intensity of a sound picked up by the microphone can be calculated directly from the *voltmeter* reading. The frequency of a sine wave can be determined by the *frequency meter,* and if the sound is complex, its wave composition can be determined by the *wave analyzer.* The *cathode-ray oscillograph,* one of the most useful instruments in auditory research as in most other areas of psychophysiology, has already been described. In this case the input potentials (signal) originate in the microphone.

Measurement of Sound

Pressure waves vary mainly in two dimensions, their frequency and their intensity—in dealing with complex sounds we should have to add a third dimension, their composition. The *frequency* of a sound wave is defined quite simply as the number of pressure changes per second (cycles per second). There are several instruments used to record this characteristic. The *intensity* of a sound wave is not so easily specified. Intensity is measured in such absolute units as the watt and ergs per second. It is proportional to the square of the pressure, the latter being described in dynes per square centimeter. In practice, however, relative rather than absolute measures are used. The fundamental concept here is the *bel,* which is defined as follows:

$$N \text{ (bels)} = \log_{10} \frac{P^2}{P_r{}^2}$$

in which N refers to the number of bels, P to the sound pressure of the tone being measured, and P_r to the sound pressure of some standard reference tone. The reference pressure most commonly employed is 0.0002 dyne per square centimeter—for a 1000 c.p.s. tone, this intensity is just about at the absolute threshold for hearing. In order to have a smaller unit that discriminates in the range of sound intensities through which experimentalists and acoustical engineers are interested, the *decibel* (1/10 bel) is used:

$$N \text{ (decibels)} = 10 \log_{10} \frac{P^2}{P_r{}^2}$$

The decibel (db) offers a number of advantages: it becomes unnecessary to make cumbersome physical measurements of sound pressures or energies directly; the great range of auditory sensitivity is compressed into manageable units (the most intense sound the ear can support is about a million-million times the intensity of the minimum audible). Some idea of the meaning of the decibel as a measure of sound intensity will be gained from the following equations: a whisper has an intensity of about 18 db above the auditory threshold; the noisiness of the average office is about 40 db; the intensity of a near-by pneumatic drill is equal to about 80 db. This brief presentation of the physics of sound is intended for orientation; interested readers will want to consult more specialized sources.

MECHANICAL AND ELECTRICAL CHARACTERISTICS OF THE EAR

The ear is one of the most remarkable mechanical devices in the human body. It makes possible the reception of energies which, at threshold, produce displacements of the eardrum smaller than the diameter of a single molecule, and it can carry energies which, at the threshold of painfulness, are a million-million times the minimum audible. As an analyzer of sounds it is capable of resolving complex sound waves into their frequency components. For descriptive purposes the ear is commonly divided into three parts, the outer, the middle, and the inner ears. We shall trace the course of stimulation through the auditory mechanism, and constant reference to Fig. 23 will facilitate understanding.

The Outer Ear

In ordinary language the 'ear' refers to one of the two irregularly shaped appendages that adorn the sides of our heads. This elastic, skin-covered plate of cartilage is legitimately known as the *pinna*. Although many lower animals are able to 'point' their pinnas in the direction of sound-producing objects, and thus increase the total energy received, man has lost this skill for the most part (a few members of the species retain rudiments of the skill but use it for entertaining their fellows rather than for magnifying sounds). It would appear that removal of this appendage in man has little practical effect upon hearing. Sound waves travel down the *external meatus,* the 'hole' in the ear, and strike the *tympanic membrane* at its end. This tube is lined with stiff hairs and glands which secrete a bitter wax; these serve to discourage the entrance of foreign bodies. The tympanic membrane is a taut band of skin which separates the outer and middle ears. Being suspended between two bodies of air at roughly equal pressures, this membrane vibrates freely so as to give a faithful picture of the frequency and amplitude of sound waves, unless the intensity is too great and its vibrations are protectively damped.

The Middle Ear

Firmly attached to one side of the inner surface of the tympanic membrane is the handle of the *malleus,* one of a series of three small bones which transmit vibrations from the tympanic membrane to the oval window of the inner ear. Back-and-forth movements of the malleus cause a corresponding movement of the *incus,* into whose socketlike end fits the head of the *stapes.* The footplate of this third bone fits securely over the oval window. The stapes moves in a rocking motion rather than in and out as one might expect. These three bones are commonly called the hammer, anvil, and stirrup. Attached to the malleus is one muscle, the *tensor tympani,* and to the stapes another, the *stapedius.* When both muscles contract reflexively, the tympanic membrane is made more taut and the footplate of the stapes is pushed inward. Both of these effects play a protective role: as the intensity of stimulation increases beyond certain limits, these muscles contract and the amplitude of vibration of the membranes is effectively damped. This is most pronounced with tones of low frequency. If, however, the rising time of an intense stimulus is too rapid—faster than the 14-16 msec. reaction time for these muscles—they fail to serve their protective function and the eardrum is often ruptured and other damages are incurred within the inner ear. This type of damage may be suffered by unprotected ears in battle, i.e. explosion deafness. Equalization of air pressure between the middle ear and the outside is accomplished by opening the *Eustachian tube* during swallowing or yawning. The lower end of this tube opens into the nasopharynx. The 'cracking' in our ears experienced when driving up or down steep hills is produced by sudden changes in pressure within the middle ear.

Transmission over the three bones of the middle ear is an extremely efficient process. Although fairly extensive punctures in the tympanic membrane cause only slight loss in hearing, disarticulating the three bones by removing a small piece of the incus results in an elevation of threshold by 60 db on the average (Wever and Bray, 1936). Distortions in the middle

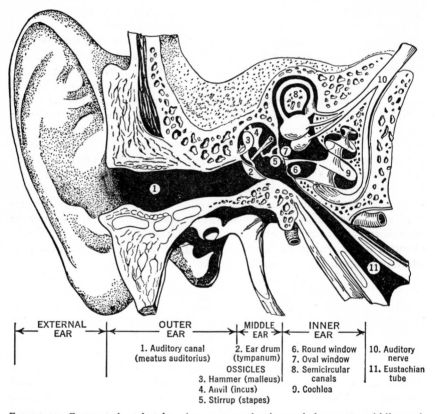

EXTERNAL EAR	OUTER EAR	MIDDLE EAR	INNER EAR	
	1. Auditory canal (meatus auditorius)	2. Ear drum (tympanum) OSSICLES 3. Hammer (malleus) 4. Anvil (incus) 5. Stirrup (stapes)	6. Round window 7. Oval window 8. Semicircular canals 9. Cochlea	10. Auditory nerve 11. Eustachian tube

FIGURE. 23. Cross section showing the gross mechanisms of the outer, middle, and inner ear. By permission of the Otarion Co., Inc., Chicago.

ear, however, can arise. The intra-aural muscles serve to attenuate the loudness of intense tones by reducing the amplitude of vibration. Direct transmission of pressure waves through the air from the tympanic membrane to the round window (the other opening of the inner ear onto the middle ear) may occur and, since these vibrations are in opposite phase to those delivered to the oval window via the bone system, hearing may be impaired.

The Inner Ear

Now we come to structures that are of the greatest importance for hearing but whose precise functions are not too well understood. The oval and round windows communicate with the *labyrinth,* a series of interconnecting cavities that consist of an outer bony wall and an enclosed membranous tube. Between the bony wall and the inner membrane is *perilymph* and within the membranous tube is *endolymph,* chemically constituted like the cerebrospinal fluid. The labyrinth consists of three parts, the *vestibule,* the *semicircular canals,* and the *cochlea,* the only part involved in hearing. The cochlea, which is shaped like a snail shell, broad at base and tapering toward its apex, consists of a divided canal which makes 2¾ turns about its axis. Most diagrams of the auditory mechanism are misleading about the size of the cochlea because they magnify its apparent size in keeping with its functional importance; actually, the cochlea measures approximately 5 mm. from

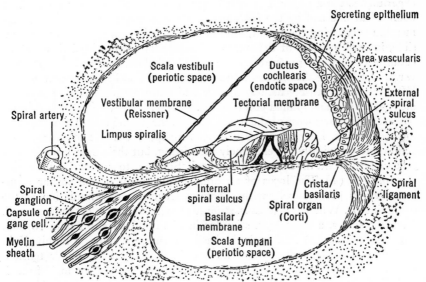

FIGURE 24. Diagrammatic cross section of the cochlear canal. A. T. Rasmussen, *Outlines of Neuro-anatomy,* Brown and Co., Dubuque, Iowa, 1943.

tip to base and 9 mm. across the base. The detailed structure of the cochlear canal and its membranes is shown in cross section in Fig. 24. Dividing the canals and suspended on ligaments is the *basilar membrane.* This tough, flexible membrane stretches from its point of attachment between the oval and round windows almost to the apex of the cochlea. A small passageway at the tip of the cochlea, the *helicotrema,* permits the perilymph in the two major canals, the *scala vestibuli* and the *scala tympani,* to communicate. Between these two canals and separated from them by the basilar membrane and *Reissner's membrane* is the *scala media* or cochlear duct, which contains endolymph. The delicate *organs of Corti,* which contain the ultimate sensory receptors for hearing, the hair cells, are within this duct and are supported on the basilar membrane. The hair cells are so-named because they have tiny cilia which project into the cochlear duct.

The basilar membrane is narrowest at the base of the cochlea and widest at the apex, in contradistinction to the changing size of the structure in which it is extended, and this, as we shall see, has certain theoretical significance. The hair cells, on the other hand, are quite evenly sized and spaced throughout the extent of the basilar membrane, there being approximately 3500 inner hair cells and about 20,000 outer hair cells arranged in three columns. Although each inner hair cell is innervated by only one or two fibers, the outer hair cells have multiple innervation (Lorente de Nó, 1933), and a single auditory fiber may gather impulses from cells distributed over as wide an area as half a turn in the cochlear canal. The auditory nerve fibers have their cell bodies imbedded in the *spiral ganglia,* located in the inner walls of the cochlea; their axones are gathered together along the central axis of the cochlea and pass out of the bottom of the cochlea as part of the VIIIth cranial nerve.

The functioning of the cochlear mechanism has become clearer in recent experiments. As a physical system it acts like an enclosed column of fluid bounded at one end by the footplate of the stapes and at the other by the membrane covering the round window. Since fluid is practically incompressible, inward pressure of the stapes is immediately transmitted through the column as outward pressure on the round window, setting up a pressure wave. But how do these pressure waves affect the flaccid basilar membrane? Working first with mechanical models and more recently with fresh specimens of human and animal cochleas (cf. Békésy, 1947), Békésy has directly observed the movements of the basilar membrane during stimulation at varying frequencies. His techniques of preparing specimens and observing their action microscopically are extremely interesting, but their description would take us far beyond the bounds of this book. Suffice it to summarize his major conclusions: (1) The locus of maximal displacement of the basilar membrane varies progressively with changing frequency of stimulation at the oval window. Whereas a 50 c.p.s. stimulus has a maximal effect some 32 mm. from the stapes, a 1600 c.p.s. stimulus has its maximal effect only 18 mm. from the stapes. (2) Although the basilar membrane shows a hundredfold variation in stiffness throughout its length, it is not itself under tension. (3) Vortex movements in the cochlear fluids appear about the loci of maximal displacement, and Békésy believes that these eddies in the fluids contribute to stimulation of the hair cells, thus restricting the region excited.

The Wever-Bray Effect

In 1930 Wever and Bray reported observations of considerable theoretical significance. They had attached an electrode to the auditory nerve of an anesthetized cat and led the amplified potentials recorded there to a telephone receiver. The cat and one experimenter were in one room and the receiver and the other experimenter were in another, completely shielded from the first. When the cat's ear was stimulated by sounds, not only were tonal frequencies up to 5000 c.p.s. clearly audible coming from the telephone receiver, but the detailed characteristics of human speech could also be heard. Was the pattern of impulses in the auditory nerve bundle so faithfully reproducing the physical characteristics of the stimulus that it could reflect precisely the qualities of sound? Wever and Bray sought to rule out an obvious artifact—that the effect was produced by some type of microphonic action, the direct translation of mechanical (sound) energy into electrical form in some part of their apparatus. But when a number of controls were run and the preparation was shielded in various ways, and the phenomenon persisted, they concluded that the auditory nerve trunk must literally duplicate in the amplitude and frequency of its action the physical characteristics of complex sounds. As it turns out, their records were confounded with a purely physical, nonneural electrical phenomenon which has come to be known as the *cochlear microphonic* (Davis and Saul, 1931; Davis, Derbyshire, Lurie, and Saul, 1934), but since the implications they drew about the necessary functioning of the auditory nerve have been justified by subsequent research (Derbyshire and Davis, 1935; Stevens and Davis, 1936, and others), we may continue the argument as they saw it.

This phenomenon clearly called for some revision in auditory theory. Since there was good reason to believe that individual sensory fibers cannot fire at anything like 5000 impulses per second, how could a 5000 c.p.s. tone be 'heard' through a cat's auditory nerve? Wever and Bray therefore postulated a *volley principle*. When the frequency of the stimulus rises above that which can be borne by individual fibers, they fall into 'squads' which first fire alternately, then at every third peak in stimulus energy, then at every fourth, and so on—the rate of bursts in the *auditory nerve trunk as a whole* keeping pace with the frequency of the stimulus. Although, as is usually the case in science, the methodological groundwork was prepared for this discovery—electrical methods of recording were already in use on neurophysiological problems (the early studies by Adrian, for example) and some work had even been done on audition (Buytendijk, 1910; Forbes, Miller, and O'Connor, 1927)—the Wever and Bray phenomenon set fire to the imagination and certainly posed a significant problem for theory.

The major differences between the two types of potential, the cochlear microphonic and actual auditory nerve potentials, may be summarized as follows: (1) *Localization.* The cochlear microphonic is most readily picked up when electrodes are placed on the round window membrane. Auditory nerve potentials, as might be expected, are best obtained when the electrode is placed in direct contact with the VIIIth nerve trunk and is shielded to avoid contamination with the cochlear microphonic (presumably the explanation of the original Wever-Bray effect). (2) *Anesthesia.* Removal of oxygen promptly eliminates activity in the auditory nerve but does not impair the cochlear microphonic. (3) *Blood supply.* Interruption of the circulation supplying the cochlear region quickly eliminates the nerve potentials; the effect of this treatment upon the microphonic is usually to gradually reduce the magnitude of the effect but not destroy it. (4) *Death.* Impulses in the auditory nerve are eliminated almost immediately after death, but the cochlear microphonic may persist, though diminishing, through several hours. (5) *Sectioning.* Cutting through the VIIIth nerve does not affect the cochlear microphonic as long as the blood supply to the cochlea is maintained. (6) *Latency and threshold.* Although auditory nerve potentials show latencies and thresholds typical of other sensory fibers, the cochlear microphonic has a latency at least as brief as 0.1 msec., and probably less, and no measurable threshold.

Nature of the Cochlear Microphonic

It is clear from the foregoing that the cochlear microphonic is not the result of neural energy transformations. The energy recorded from nerve fibers in action is produced in the cells themselves; the energy recorded as the microphonic appears as a direct transformation of mechanical pressure changes within the cochlea into equivalent electrical potential changes, the energy here deriving directly from the stimulus. We have already seen that the cochlear microphonic (1) has a minimal latency and an unmeasurable threshold. What are its other significant characteristics? (2) *Frequency limits.* The cochlear microphonic has been recorded for frequencies far below the limits of tonal hearing, for example, in guinea pigs to sinusoidal waves as low as 5 c.p.s. (Wever, Bray, and Willey, 1937); the upper limit is difficult to estimate because of instrumental problems, but it also extends probably beyond the limits of hearing (Wever and Bray, 1937 a). (3) *Relations to intensity.* The voltage of the cochlear potential increases as a continuous function of the intensity of the stimulating sound, linearly until extremely high intensities are reached, and there is no evidence of the stepwise increments characteristic of nervous processes (cf. Wever, 1949, p. 147). (4) *Wave form.* The fidelity with which the potential changes in the microphonic reproduce the wave form of the stimulating sound is indicated by the fact that one can recognize a speaker by the quality of his voice when mediated via the microphonic. Fidelity is greatest for moderate intensities (Wever, 1939).

Where, in the cochlea, do these electrical potentials originate? What structures serve as transducers of mechanical into electrical energy? The generally accepted view today is that cochlear potentials are produced in the *hair cells* in a manner analogous to the behavior of piezoelectric crystals. When lateral mechanical pressure changes are applied to such a crystal (or hair cell here), vertical electrical polarization occurs, which alternates in direction with the changes in pressure—i.e. the crystal (and the hair cell) functions as an electromechanical transducer. The chief evidence favoring the hair-cell theory comes from the study of congenitally deaf animals, especially albino cats and waltzing guinea pigs (Howe and Guild, 1932-3; Howe, 1935); in such cases the membranes may be apparently normal, yet the organs of Corti and their hair cells are absent as is the cochlear potential.

THEORIES OF HEARING

Although the mechanism whereby the physical characteristics of sound waves become translated into patterns of impulses in the auditory nerve has not been satisfactorily worked out as yet, adequate methods are available and the matter is being pressed empirically. On the other hand, we have very few facts concerning the relation between auditory nervous activity and reportable psychological experiences, and we do not have adequate techniques to gather them. Action potentials are recorded in animal subjects, who could not describe their experiences even were they not under anesthesia. It is not surprising, therefore, that it is here that theories apply, being designed to answer the question, How does the auditory nervous system mediate between physical stimulus and psychological experience? How is auditory quality (pitch) mediated? How is auditory intensity (loudness) mediated?

Speculation is naturally limited by the general laws of nerve action. Ultimately the auditory message comes down to patterns of impulses in the auditory cortex, which may vary in terms of what fibers are excited (locus), the impulse frequency they bear, and the total number of fibers involved. Within these limitations the theorist must account for all char-

acteristics of hearing—pitch, loudness, timbre, complexity, threshold phenomena, and so on. Although most theorists have agreed that loudness depends somehow upon total frequency, they have disagreed heartily on the
determination of pitch. The 'place' theorists relegate pitch to the *locus* of
neural activity in the auditory system; the 'frequency' theorists (and 'volley'
theorists in part) relegate pitch to the *frequency* of impulses in the auditory
system. In the history of this problem there have also been many intermediate and compromise positions (cf. Boring, 1942; Wever, 1949).

Resonance Place Theory

The theory of hearing which Helmholtz proposed in 1863 represented a
remarkable integration of the information existing at his time. That the
relationships he drew seem obvious today is in no way to his discredit—
brilliant integrations always appear simple and obvious in retrospect. And
Helmholtz's theory was in essence an 'obvious' extension of Müller's doctrine of specific energies. Whereas Müller had merely indicated specificity
for fibers subserving the different modalities, Helmholtz applied the notion
to fibers subserving different qualities within the same modality. Pitch
discrimination thus depended on the particular fibers activated by a given
tone—but what mechanism accomplished the initial analysis of sound frequency? How were different stimulus frequencies distributed to their appropriate nerves? Helmholtz was familiar with the fact that the ear analyzes
sounds much as a large set of resonators might, and the problem seemed to
come down to specifying some structures in the inner ear that could serve
as resonators. Observations on the microscopic anatomy of the inner ear by
Corti and others were available at this time, and Helmholtz first specified
the *rods of Corti* as resonators since these structures were longer at the tip
of the cochlea than at the base. Later, influenced by Hensen's description
of the *basilar membrane* in men and animals as being made up of transverse
fibers graduated in length and hence suitable as resonators, he shifted to this
structure as the mechanism. This membrane is known to vibrate under
stimulation, and it is in intimate association with the hair cells on which
terminate the auditory nerve fibers—it is much as if there were a tiny harp
in each ear which, when 'sung into' by the stimulus, responds with sympathetic vibrations to match its frequency characteristics.

Of course this resonance theory has encountered numerous criticisms, their
nature varying with the tenor of the times. Some thinkers, cognizant of the
reduction of visual quality to three or four specific fiber types, were reluc-
tant to accept some five or ten thousand specific fibers for hearing—they
forgot that the visual nerves also carry a multiplicity of spatial 'local signs.'
Another criticism arose from the fact that the ratio of the longest to the
shortest fibers along the basilar membrane is only about 12 to 1, enough to
account for only a three-octave range. How could a frequency range from
20 to 20,000 cycles—roughly ten octaves—be accommodated? Much later
it was noted that the shorter fibers could be under relatively greater tension,
whereas the longer fibers, being most heavily laden with lymph columns,
would be slowed in their rate of vibration. Most recently, however, Békésy
has demonstrated by direct observation that the basilar membrane is not
under tension.

Another criticism of this theory has been that, given the interconnectedness of the fibers along the basilar membrane, a *band* of fibers must be stimulated by any tone. Yet the auditory experience elicited by a pure tone is pure, not fuzzy. Gray (1900) offered an explanation of this difficulty with what he termed 'the principle of maximal stimulation.' Although a considerable range of nerve fibers will be delivering impulses toward the higher centers, the frequency of their action will vary with their nearness to the locus of maximal resonance; by some unexplained mechanism, the less intensely excited, bordering elements are inhibited and only the pitch corresponding to the locus of maximal activity is experienced. There have been a number of attempts to explain how such lateral inhibition might take place (cf. Wever, 1949, pp. 112-15), but none of them rings very true. This is a very significant problem: we shall meet with it again in connection with auditory masking and subsequently in studying visual summation, contrast, and contour formation. In discussion of the latter, a possible explanation will be suggested (cf. particularly pp. 168, 233). The resonance place theory has weathered nearly a century of buffeting and is still a widely held view, but the recently accruing evidence on the mechanical and electrical activity in the ear seems to be toppling the House that Helmholtz built.

Nonresonance Place Theory

Place and resonance conceptions are not necessarily synonymous, although they have often been treated as if they were. The determination of pitch on the basis of what fibers are active, which is the essence of a place conception, may be accomplished by mechanisms other than a graded system of resonators in the inner ear. Stevens and Davis, Békésy, and others have adopted the view that the cochlea is a hydraulic system contained in a vessel with elastic walls. Appropriate analysis demonstrates that the locus of maximal displacement along the basilar membrane will vary with the frequency of the stimulating tone, being toward the helicotrema for low frequencies and near the oval window for high. We have here another feasible mechanism whereby different sets of fibers can be stimulated as a function of sound frequency. Again, since a band of fibers is always stimulated, some principle of 'focusing' is required to explain 'single hearing.' Loudness becomes a function of the total frequency of impulses delivered per unit time. Diagrammatical description of this nonresonance place theory is given in Fig. 25. Tones of frequencies *a* and *b* are shown to produce vibrations at different loci along the basilar membrane, eliciting impulses in bands of fibers that overlap but yet have different maxima. Increasing the intensity of either tone is shown to increase the width of the excited neural band as well as the total frequency of impulses.

Actually, one may hold to a place theory of hearing without postulating *any* spatial arrangement in the peripheral organ. The only requirement is that different auditory fibers be selectively excited by tones of different frequencies. The resonance principle provides one feasible mechanism whereby such selection could take place and the traveling-wave conception provides another. But if selectively tuned resonators were scattered at random through the cochlea, specific fibers associated with certain resonators would still yield a frequency analysis of sounds—indeed, Hensen (1863) is credited with suggesting that the hair cells themselves are the resonators. As pseudo crystals, they could vary in the frequency to which they maximally respond. This would also be a resonance view, but it requires no strict spatial distribution within the cochlea.

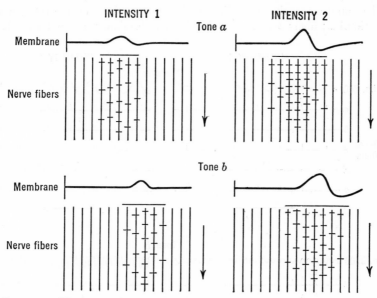

FIGURE 25. Diagrammatic representation of a nonresonance place principle.

Frequency Theories

A number of frequency theories have been propounded, such as Rutherford's 'telephone theory' (1886), Max Meyer's 'leather chair-seat' theory (1907)—according to which the basilar membrane did not vibrate but was drawn flaccidly up and down by movements of the stapes—and Troland's combined place and frequency theory (1929), which anticipated the contemporary 'volley' notion. Although the electrophysiological fact that individual auditory fibers cannot fire at a more rapid rate than 800 or so impulses per second seemed to deliver the *coup de grâce* to these theories, another electrophysiological fact revitalized them. This was the demonstration by Wever and Bray that stimulus frequencies above the limit of individual fibers are reproduced faithfully by volleying in the auditory nerve as a whole—at least up to about 4000 c.p.s. This, it should be noted, is simply a statement of fact. Present-day volley theorists believe that the *pitch* characteristics of tones below certain frequencies are determined by the frequency of impulses set up in the auditory nerve as a whole. Successive energy peaks in the pressure wave excite all available fibers; if the *frequency* of these energy changes is slow enough, all auditory fibers are excited on each peak. As the frequency rises and the refractory periods of different fibers are reached, the fibers are assumed to fall automatically into 'squads' or 'platoons' which fire at every other wave peak, at every third peak, and so on. Since it is known that fibers can be made to fire within their relative refractory periods if the stimulus is sufficiently intense, it follows that the total number of fibers firing at each peak will increase as the intensity of stimulation is increased. Thus loudness becomes a function of the total number of impulses per unit time.

Diagrammatic summary of the *volley principle* is given in Fig. 26. A low intensity tone of 800 c.p.s. is shown as exciting fibers *a, c,* and *e* at each peak of the sound wave, thus matching in the total nerve trunk the frequency of the stimulus; fibers *b* and *d,* having higher thresholds, are not stimulated.

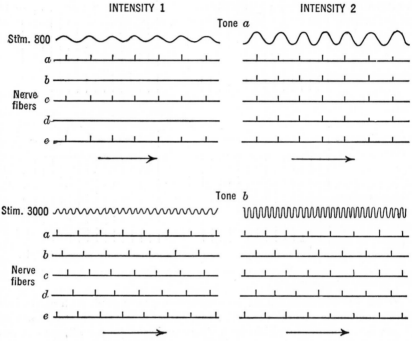

FIGURE 26. Diagrammatic representation of a volley principle.

The more intense 800 c.p.s. tone brings in fibers *b* and *d,* impulse rate remaining unchanged, and a louder tone is experienced. The second tone produces waves at 3000 c.p.s. and all five hypothetical fibers are excited, but in a staggered manner: fibers *a* and *e* are shown as part of one 'platoon,' firing at every fourth peak in the sound wave (i.e. after firing at one peak, they cannot recover until three cycles have elapsed) ; the other fibers fire at the same rate but at different times, the frequency in the auditory nerve as a whole, however, matching the frequency of the sound stimulus. When the second tone is made more intense, each fiber is activated at a more rapid rate, being set off within its relative refractory period, and the total number of impulses per unit time is increased without changing the frequency in the auditory nerve.

The essential notion underlying any volley theory—that the pitch quality one experiences is based upon the frequency of impulses being delivered to the auditory centers—has also come in for its share of criticism. The fact that no measurable volleys can be observed in the auditory nerve trunk when the frequency of the stimulating tone is above 4000 c.p.s. puts a definite limitation on the generality of such a notion. As a matter of fact, even more stringent limitations on 'volleying' are encountered when we record neural activity in higher levels of the auditory pathways (cf. pp. 110-11). Wonderment is sometimes expressed about how two or more low-pitched tones could be experienced simultaneously, i.e. how different frequency rates can be borne simultaneously by the same bundle of fibers and yet yield discriminable experiences. This is possible through variations in the amplitude of volleys; while carrying a base rate of 800 c.p.s., for example, a frequency of 200 c.p.s. will appear as periodic variations in amplitude (on every fourth burst) of the volleys. This means, however, that complex sounds are represented by temporal patterns of impulses that must be 'interpreted' at some higher level in the nervous system.

Resonance-volley Theory

Perhaps the most widely accepted theory of hearing today is a compromise between place and volley conceptions. In the sections on research results that follow we shall find ample evidence favoring a place conception, particularly for the mediation of high frequencies; we shall also find incontrovertible evidence that volleying does occur, particularly in the mediation of low frequencies. Wever himself accepts such a dual theory: 'Pitch therefore has a two-fold representation, in terms of place on the basilar membrane and hence of particularity of nerve fibers, and in terms of composite impulse frequency. Frequency serves for the low tones, place for the high tones, and both perform in the broader ground between' (1949, pp. 189-90). He suggests that place representation joins frequency representation around 400 c.p.s. and takes over entirely around 5000 c.p.s., these transitions necessarily being gradual. And there are signs of compromise in the 'place' camp. Davis, in a recent article reporting research in which 'sound pips' were used to stimulate human ears at varying frequencies, writes: 'It now seems clear that either place or frequency or both may be the physiological correlate(s) of physical frequency. We therefore do not regard pitch as a single attribute, but as a composite of "buzz" (the correlate of physiological frequency) and "body" (the correlate of physiological place or channel). . . The theory that emerges incorporates much of the frequency theory as stated by Wever, but more observations are needed (Davis, Silverman, and McAuliffe, 1951).'

NEUROPHYSIOLOGICAL INFORMATION

Evidence from Cochlear Destruction

A direct implication of both resonance and nonresonance place theories is that localized destruction of the cochlear mechanism should result in limited hearing loss. The volley theory, on the other hand, would predict over-all hearing loss regardless of the locus of destruction. Since the cochlea is only accessible by surgery, and human subjects are naturally unco-operative, research of this type has been restricted to animal preparations. The general experimental procedure is first to determine the normal, pre-experimental thresholds of the animal ears used, either by measuring cochlear microphonics or by conditioning the animal to make certain reactions when tones are heard. Following destruction of some part of the receptor mechanism, by some one of a number of methods to be described, postexperimental thresholds are determined; ideally the animals are then sacrificed and post-mortem examination of the cochlear structures is made to determine pre-cisely the location and extent of damage.

(1) *Stimulational deafness.* Finch and Culler (1934 *a*) trained a dog to flex its leg whenever a tone was heard and then used this response as a basis for measuring the animal's normal threshold. After 18 hours of con-tinuous exposure to a 3000 c.p.s. tone, a general rise in threshold of from 40 to 50 db was observed throughout the range from 200 to 5000 cycles. Davis, Derbyshire, Kemp, Lurie, and Upton (1935) used change in the

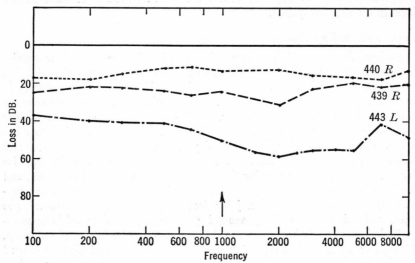

FIGURE 27. Sensitivity losses in guinea pig subjects (*R*—right ear; *L*—left ear) resulting from 4-minute exposure to an intense 1000 cycle tone. Wever and Smith, *Journal of Experimental Psychology*, 1944, 34:241.

intensity threshold of the cochlear microphonic as a measure of loss in sensi-tivity and employed guinea pig subjects. Regardless of the frequency of the deafening tone, decrements in sensitivity tended to center about 1200 cycles. Magnitude of decrement was found to agree moderately well with degree of damage histologically. A more recent investigation by Wever and Smith (1944), also using guinea pig subjects and the cochlear microphonic as a measure, substantiates these findings. Sample data from this study, for a 1000 c.p.s. exposure tone, are shown in Fig. 27, the numbers on the curves serving merely to identify the ears reported.

In the Wever and Smith study the average magnitude of loss in db was roughly equal for 300-, 1000-, and 5000-cycle exposure tones. This appears strange in the extreme when considered in connection with the histological analysis made of these same ears and reported by Smith (1947). Damage to the organ of Corti and tympanic lamella incurred by the 300 c.p.s. tone, although largely restricted to the apical end of the cochlea, was extreme; damage to both structures was less for the 1000 c.p.s. tone and centered about two-thirds of the way along the basilar membrane toward the helico-trema; with the 5000 c.p.s. tone, however, damage was very slight and localized approximately halfway along the membrane. For no exposure tone did the magnitude of sensitivity decrement (as indexed by the cochlear microphonic) correlate with the histologically estimated cochlear damage. One possible explanation of this discrepancy is that the cochlear microphonic obtained with test tones of varying frequency is not a valid index of sensitivity loss. It is also possible that histological observations did not give a valid index of destruction under these conditions.

(2) *Microdestruction.* The technique of producing cochlear damage by prolonged or intense stimulation is of dubious value in testing the place hypothesis since it is impossible to restrict the spatial effects of an intense stimulus. More direct evidence would be anticipated from restricted and specifiable lesions in the cochlear structure. This approach has been tried. Hughson, Thompson, and Witting (1935) drilled small holes through the bony casing of the cochlea and scorched the base of the hole by high-frequency cautery. Although lesions in the apical region produced little measurable effect, those elsewhere affected mainly high tones. The most precise correlation between the locus of damage and loss in sensitivity has been reported by Stevens, Davis, and Lurie (1935). They also drilled tiny holes into the cochlea and produced local mechanical disruptions in the organs of Corti. Thresholds for the cochlear microphonic were measured, and although there was a general loss in sensitivity in some cases, usually there was a fairly abrupt elevation of threshold for certain frequencies. Subsequent histological analysis revealed a progressive shift of the point of maximal destruction along the basilar membrane toward the round window as the frequency entailing maximal sensitivity loss increased.

(3) *Related evidence.* The cochlear microphonic can be impaired by the application of many drugs as well as by mechanical disturbance. Drugs, such as cocaine and chloroform, and strong saline solutions may be injected through the round window membrane or merely placed upon this membrane (cf. Wever, 1939). Using the latter method with the cat as subject, Fowler and Forbes (1936) noted a progressive decrease in cochlear response, high tones being affected earlier and to a more marked degree than low tones, and interpreted it as evidence in favor of the place theory. Wever and Bray (1937 *b*), however, found the series of changes produced by the application of sodium chloride solution to be more complicated, the systematic relation of impairment to frequency appearing only after an interval. Although not actually destroying receptor mechanisms, Hallpike and Rawdon-Smith (1934 *a, b*) have obtained evidence that high and low tones have different localization within the cochlea. Into small holes drilled into the base and apex of the cochlea were placed drops of mercury, and with an active electrode contacting the mercury, cochlear potentials were recorded. Responses to low tones were three times as strong when led from the apical electrode as when led from the basal one, whereas responses to high tones were four times as strong when led from the basal electrode.

Culler (1935) has extended this technique—which has the advantage that the cochlear structures are not damaged—with the guinea pig as subject, recording microphonics from 25 different points on the external surface of the cochlea in response to tones of various frequencies. For any given frequency, a point on the cochlea could be located yielding maximal effect, the magnitude of response decreasing in both directions from this point.

Systematic exploration made it possible for Culler to plot a 'frequency map' of the guinea pig cochlea, as shown in Fig. 28. A more recent repetition of this procedure with similar guinea pig subjects yielded essentially the same results (Culler, Coakley, Lowy, and Gross, 1943).

To this evidence should be added the observations of Békésy, cited earlier, on the locus of maximal vibration of the basilar membrane for tones of varying frequency. A progressive shift of this locus from the helicotrema toward

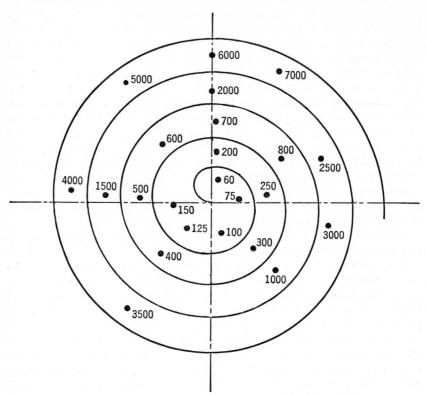

FIGURE 28. Frequency map of the guinea pig cochlea. Culler *et al. American Journal of Psychology,* 1943, 56:495.

the stapes with increasing frequency of stimulation was found. With regard to the place-theory implications of this sort of evidence, Wever (1949, p. 68) has pointed out that when stimulation is via bone conduction, the energy is applied not only at the stapes but all over the cochlear structure, yet hearing is normal. How then could traveling waves of the sort described by Békésy be responsible for pitch discrimination? It is possible, of course, that even in bone conduction of sounds the chief effect is upon mechanisms in the usual pathway. It is also possible that these traveling waves, and the electrical effects they produce, are epiphenomena, quite irrelevant of the process of auditory stimulation. Finally, in fairness to the frequency theorists, it must be emphasized that the Stevens, Davis, and Lurie experiment and those by Culler and his associates used the cochlear microphonic as an index of aural sensitivity. Keeping in mind Smith's (1947) evidence for discrepancy between localization of damage and measured sensitivity changes, the case for a 'place' interpretation of these data would be stronger if the same results could be obtained with the conditioning procedure.

Evidence from the Study of Isolated Auditory Fibers

Study of the response of isolated auditory nerve fibers to stimulation at various frequencies should yield a definitive answer to the major theoretical issue. If individual fibers are found to respond indiscriminately to all or nearly all frequencies, then only some form of frequency theory is feasible. If individual fibers respond selectively to a very limited range of frequencies, then only some form of place theory is feasible. If firing to low tones is indiscriminate, while only certain fibers fire to various high tones, then the resonance-volley theory proposed as a compromise by Wever would be up-held. The theoretical implications would be clear enough, but there is very little evidence. A moment's thought shows why this is the case: in order to record selectively from isolated fibers, specially devised and insulated micro-electrodes must be employed; the auditory nerve trunk must be laid bare at some accessible point, and the electrodes inserted; more or less ubiquitous cochlear microphonics must be eliminated from the records; once an elec-trode is set in position, painstaking exploration within the stimulus frequency range must be made—and this details only a few of the technical difficulties. Such research was completely impossible, of course, before the development of electronic methods of recording.

If impulses in different fibers arrived at a given measuring point at dif-ferent times, either because of varying transmission rates or for some other reason, a method of studying the characteristics of various *types* of fibers, at least, would be provided. Studies by Derbyshire and Davis (1935), Kemp and Coppee (1936), and Kemp, Coppee, and Robinson (1937) have demon-strated just such staggering of activity in the auditory tracts. A triphasic reaction is usually observed in response to a brief click, the three more or less discrete waves being arbitrarily labeled F, G, and H in order of in-creasing latency. That these three components are somehow functions of sound frequency can be demonstrated by partially masking the click stimulus with various pure sine waves. The F-wave is preferentially masked by high tones and the slowest H-wave by low tones. Since there is no evidence that fibers making up the auditory nerve vary in size, it appears unlikely that this phenomenon represents differences in conduction rates (cf. A, B, and C fibers in the cutaneous senses). Stevens and Davis (1938) consider this evi-dence for a place theory: traveling waves along the basilar membrane first excite activity near the round window (high-tone components) and progres-sively move toward the helicotrema (low-tone components).

The most direct attempt to study the action of individual auditory fibers has been made by Galambos and Davis (1943, 1944). A method was devised for inserting micro-electrodes into the auditory nerve bundle intracranially where it passes into the medulla oblongata. Originally believing that they had actually obtained records from individual auditory nerve fibers, these investigators now have conceded that they were recording from second-order nerve cells in the cochlear nucleus. Nevertheless, their findings are important, since activity in the first-order neurons must be at least as dis-criminative as that in second-order neurons. Most significant was their observation that the elements recorded showed selectivity with respect to frequency. At threshold intensity, a given element might respond *only* to a very narrow frequency band about 2000 c.p.s. (e.g. a '2000 c.p.s. fiber') ; as intensity was raised, this same fiber would respond to a broader range of frequencies, typically lower than that to which this particular element was maximally sensitive. Another placement gave a minimum threshold at 3700 c.p.s., and so on. With regard to basilar mechanics, it seems plausible that the elements being measured had their endings in that portion of the membrane most easily vibrated by the sound frequency representing their minimum threshold. Increasing the intensity of the stimulus, and hence the extent of the basilar membrane involved, meant that a wider range of frequencies was capable of minimally exciting the same endings. This evidence favors a place theory since, for frequencies well within the range presumably covered by the volley principle, different elements showed preferential sensitivity, but it must be noted that of the 43 fibers for which data were obtained only four had maxima below 1000 cycles.

Activity in the VIIIth Nerve Trunk

There is more evidence available here, but the problem is one of interpretation. (1) *Limit of synchronization.* As noted earlier, impulses in the auditory nerve occur in bursts which 'follow' the frequency of the stimulus up to about 3000 or 4000 c.p.s. as an upper limit. (2) *Equilibration.* An amply demonstrated characteristic of sensory fibers in general (cf. Adrian, 1928) is that impulse rate decreases rapidly under continuous stimulation to a comparatively steady state representing a balance between catabolic and anabolic processes in the fiber. When measurements are taken of the nerve trunk as a whole, this process appears as a sharp drop in amplitude of response, the number of fibers contributing to each burst decreasing. This phenomenon is known as equilibration, and it is significant that no noticeable variation in auditory experience accompanies it. Since both the specific fibers excited and the number of bursts per second remain constant, no change in pitch would be anticipated from either theory under consideration, but both would seem to require a change in loudness based on the reduction in total number of impulses delivered per unit time. Since both rate and final degree of equilibration depend upon the rapidity with which fibers are excited (i.e. the rate at which available reserve materials are utilized), it follows that equilibration should vary with stimulus frequency— and this is the observed fact.

(3) *Amplitude as a function of frequency.* A direct implication of the volley principle is that amplitude of response in the nerve trunk as a whole should decrease as stimulus frequency is increased. When fibers fall into squads that fire at every alternate wave of the stimulus, only half as many are contributing to the trunk response at any given moment; each further division means still fewer fibers firing, and measured amplitude (voltage) depends upon the total number of fibers momentarily active. Derbyshire and Davis (1935) have measured amplitude as a function of frequency in the auditory nerve of a cat. Amplitude remained high and constant up to about 900 c.p.s., whereupon a sudden drop to approximately half the initial value occurred; between 900 and about 1800 c.p.s. amplitude again remained constant, another sudden drop appearing at 1800; amplitude beyond 3000

c.p.s. was too small for accurate measurement. It is apparent that this phenomenon must be related to equilibration: the degree of equilibration should increase regularly with increasing frequency up to the point where the fibers fall into alternating squads; at this point, since each fiber goes back to a slower rate of response, equilibration should return to its initial level. Figure 29 describes this relation schematically. Each sudden drop in amplitude is shown as being paralleled by an abrupt decrease in equilibration. It should be kept in mind that these two measures would actually be taken

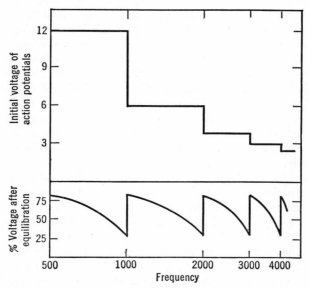

FIGURE 29. Schematic diagram showing the initial voltage of action potentials and the course of their equilibration for an ideal nerve in which the refractory period of all fibers is 1 msec. Stevens and Davis, *Hearing: Its Psychology and Physiology,* John Wiley and Sons, Inc., New York, 1938, p. 400.

separately and under somewhat different conditions: initial voltage or amplitude in the nerve trunk is recorded immediately after onset of the stimulus to avoid equilibration effects; degree of equilibration is recorded as the difference between this initial level of response and that found after a constant period (at least 2 sec.) of continuous stimulation. The two phenomena are related by the fact that they both display correlated functions of stimulus frequency.

This clearly substantiates the volley principle, in that we have here bona fide evidence that fibers in the nerve trunk do in fact fall into squads as stimulus frequency is raised above their individual refractory limitations. There is no explanation here of how such organization of the auditory neural system takes place—nor indeed does there seem to be any answer at present. Why is it that approximately half of the available fibers suddenly begin to fire in alternation with the other half? Although it is clear that all fibers would have to fire at every other energy peak once their absolute refractory period is reached, it is not clear why they should fall nicely into alternating squads. What 'tells' *these* fibers to fire at the odd-numbered peaks and *those* fibers to fire at the even-numbered peaks? This question is especially relevant because the above evidence implies, by the abrupt drop in amplitude, that all auditory fibers have equal refractory periods (approx. .001 sec.). Wever discusses this problem in his recent book (1949) on theories of hearing.

How would present-day place theorists interpret these data? Stevens and Davis (1938) are signally reticent on this point. If they agree that the measured volleying involves fibers along the entire membrane, then they would have to accept the dual resonance-volley theory proposed by Wever in which a volley principle holds for low frequencies and a place principle for high. In other words, if *all* fibers are firing for tones between 20 and about 3000 c.p.s., one cannot say that pitch depends upon 'what' fibers are activated. But the evidence does not *require* this interpretation: the measurement of amplitude does not specify what fibers are contributing, and different groups of fibers may be substituted for one another and yet maintain the same amplitude. Let us assume that as frequency changes, different parts of the basilar membrane are maximally excited and different sets of fibers are brought into play. Given a constant intensity, the total number of fibers excited within a given region could be constant even though 'what' fibers changed continuously. When the stimulus reached a region along the membrane less liberally supplied with fibers, the total amplitude could drop quite abruptly.

(4) *Partial sectioning of the VIIIth nerve.* Of special interest are the results of experiments in which the auditory nerve is partially severed. A pure place theory would predict selective hearing loss, its extent depending on magnitude of lesion and its character depending upon what fibers were sectioned. A pure volley theory would predict generalized hearing loss. The resonance-volley theory would predict selective loss for high tones but little if any loss for low tones. The data, as we shall see, fit none of these positions precisely but seem to require a more elaborate conception. In one of the rare cases in which human subjects provide evidence on this sort of problem, Dandy (1934) partially sectioned the VIIIth nerve to relieve symptoms of a disease that involves a dizziness and nausea due to disturbance of the vestibular system. In some cases moderate lesions resulted in selective loss of sensitivity to high tones; in others, loss over a broad range, with greatest effect for high tones, but in no case was loss for low tones reported without concomitant loss at all higher frequencies.

The most recent and extensive study, using cats as subjects, is offered by Neff (1947). The procedures were ideally adapted to this type of problem and deserve somewhat detailed description: (1) The cochlea of one ear was destroyed in order to restrict hearing to a single experimental ear. (2) Each animal was trained to react to loud tones by running forward in a revolving cage, shock serving as the unconditioned stimulus. After the running habit was well established, the frequency of the tones was varied and the intensity gradually reduced. (3) The method of limits was used to determine absolute thresholds for tones of 125, 250, 500, 1000, 2000, 4000, and 8000 c.p.s., these threshold values serving as a zero base line against which to estimate experimentally induced changes. (4) Through an opening made surgically in the skull, lesions of varying extent were made in the VIIIth nerve. (5) Recovery from surgery was rapid, and thresholds were redetermined within two or three days. Tests were continued, however, for at least a month and in some cases longer for double assurance against surgical artifacts. (6) Approximately two months after the last hearing tests (by the conditioned response method), cochlear microphonics were recorded from five of the experimental animals, and then all animals were sacrificed and their cochleas examined histologically. The cochlear microphonic and histological data are reported in a companion paper (Wever and Neff,

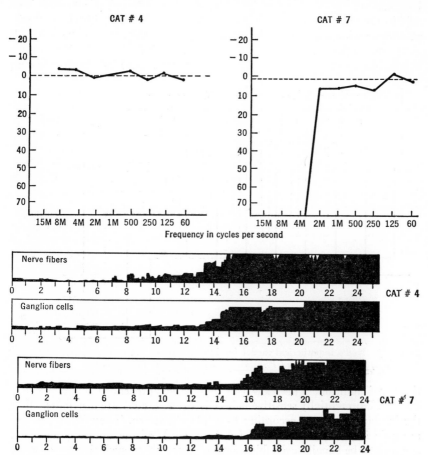

FIGURE 30. Hearing losses and histological destruction data for two cats following partial sectioning of the VIIIth nerve. Notice the normal hearing of cat #4, despite extensive destruction; observe also that loss is restricted to high tones in cat #7. After Neff, 1947, and Wever and Neff, 1947, *Journal of Comparative Physiological Psychology,* 40:208, 223.

1947). (7) As a control for possible nonauditory cues in the conditioning tests, one cat had both cochleas destroyed.

The first observation of note was that for lesions involving up to approximately half of the fibers of the VIIIth nerve, no significant losses in hearing anywhere in the frequency range were found. This must mean that there is a high degree of functional replication among the auditory fibers. Hearing and histological data for cat #4 are shown in Fig. 30 and illustrate this result. With more extensive lesions, hearing loss moved progressively down the frequency scale from high to low tones, loss involving all frequencies higher than the lowest for which there was any significant reduction. Cat #7 in Fig. 30 illustrates this finding: it may be seen that all frequencies above 4000 c.p.s. are completely inaudible, yet nearly normal sensitivity is found below this level. Only when all or nearly all fibers were severed did hearing loss extend below 1000 c.p.s., and in these cases the loss tended to be complete for all frequencies. The cochlear microphonic records were within the normal range for all of the animals studied, with the exception of one for whom there was clear evidence for degeneration of the hair cells.

In interpreting these findings Neff has devised a scheme for the innervation of the cochlear hair cells which is in effect a combined place-frequency

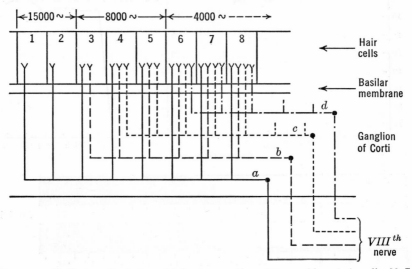

FIGURE 31. Neff's hypothetical model for innervation of the cochlear hair cells. Neff, *Journal of Comparative and Physiological Psychology*, 1947, 40:210.

theory of audition. This view can best be comprehended by reference to Fig. 31. Differentially sensitive hair cells (1, 2, 3, etc.) are distributed along the basilar membrane according to a 'place' pattern. These receptors have multiple innervation by fibers (*a, b, c,* etc.) of the auditory nerve, all assumed to be equally excitable: some of these fibers, such as fiber *a,* collect from broad regions that include the high-tone hair cells; others, such as fiber *d,* collect from narrower regions that include only lower tone hair cells. If hair cells 3, 4, and 5 were destroyed, for example, restricted loss of hearing, observed as 'tonal gaps' in the human audiogram, would be expected. But sectioning of the nerve trunk could only produce progressive loss of high tones, as was observed in this experiment. If only fiber *a* is destroyed, loss will extend only down to 8000 c.p.s. since the other fibers also innervate the lower tone regions; to produce loss of hearing for all tones above 4000 c.p.s., on the other hand, it would be necessary to section fibers *a, b,* and *c.* Neff does not make this point clear, but if we are to avoid direct conflict with the law of specific energies of nerve fibers, then pitch discrimination must depend upon frequency of impulses rather than upon 'what' fibers, for each fiber is assumed to be responsive to a range of frequencies. This is apparent in the following quotation: 'However, if we destroy just fibers *b* and *c,* leaving *a* intact, we do not find a loss of hearing for frequencies in the 8000 cycle range with normal hearing for 15,000 cycles. Instead, we have no hearing loss since fiber *a* is stimulated by the lower frequencies as well as by 15,000 cycles' (p. 211). And by the same token one and the same fiber, *a,* is carrying and delivering more than one pitch quality.

It would seem quite possible to retain the advantages of Neff's multiple innervation hypothesis and yet hold to the 'what fiber' conception, which is the essence of a place theory. Figure 32 represents a very slight but significant modification in Neff's scheme. Fiber *a,* here as in Neff's hypothesis, gathers from a wide range of the basilar membrane, but it is assumed to

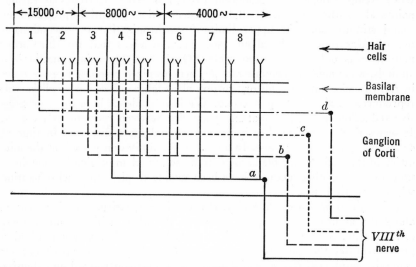

FIGURE 32. Alternative to Neff's scheme which does not contradict either the law of specific energies or a place theory of pitch reception.

yield *only* a specific low-pitched quality. Fibers *b* and *c* gather from progressively narrower regions and yield progressively *higher* tones. Fiber *d* gathers only from an even more limited region and yields a yet higher tone experience. It is further assumed that the number of functionally equivalent (for pitch quality) fibers decreases from apex to base of the membrane, i.e. there are fewer high-pitch fibers than low-pitch ones.

This hypothesis would seem to fit as large a swath of evidence as Neff's view. Direct destruction of hair cells will again result in comparatively limited losses in sensitivity, but because of the wider receptive field of the low-pitch fibers, elimination of low-tone sensitivity will be harder to obtain by either loud sound or micro-needle destruction of the cochlea. A high degree of replication of pitch-specific fibers is postulated, and it is therefore necessary to sever up to one half of the VIIIth nerve before any losses in hearing become apparent; but since the extent of replication is assumed to increase from high- to low-frequency fibers, further amounts of sectioning yield a progressive loss from high to low pitch, i.e. the fewer the number of fibers mediating a given quality, the more probable the loss of this quality by a given lesion. It should be possible by chance, however, to leave 'islands' of high-tone reception after partial sectioning of the VIIIth nerve according to this hypothesis—according to Neff's view such 'islands' cannot be produced by this method. The number of animals used here (11) was too small to provide a satisfactory test, although one animal (cat #9) did show evidence of just such an 'island' of retained sensitivity.

Evidence concerning the Role of the Higher Auditory Centers

(1) *Further limitations on synchronization.* We have already seen that 'following' the frequency of the stimulus by impulses in the VIIIth nerve (first-order neurons) is not higher than 4000 c.p.s. How faithfully is the frequency of the stimulus duplicated in the higher levels of the auditory pathway? Kemp, Coppee, and Robinson (1937) inserted electrodes at various points along these pathways and recorded action potentials produced by sound stimulation. The upper limit of synchronization for second-order neurons was found to be about 2500 c.p.s., whereas that for third-order neurons was only about 1000 cycles. Davis (1935), using anesthetized animals, was unable to demonstrate any synchronized response to pure tones in records taken in the auditory cortex, although a succession of clicks was reproduced to about 100 per second. We have evidence here for a progressive reduction in synchronization of activity between receptor and cortex. It seems likely that impulses become more and more dispersed in time as successive synapses are passed. In any case, the limitation placed on the adequacy of the volley principle becomes more serious than originally thought— unless our recording methods have been unable to pick up synchronization which actually exists.

(2) *Effects of gross extirpation.* It is possible to extirpate various centers along the auditory pathways or to sever the fibers which connect these centers. Cats usually serve as subjects in these studies, and conditioning procedures like those described in connection with the Neff experiment are generally employed. Kryter and Ades (1943) have contributed an extensive study of the role of the higher centers in hearing. No significant losses in sensitivity were observed as a result of bilateral extirpation of auditory cortex; however, subsequent bilateral removal of the inferior colliculi (subcortical auditory centers) produced significant losses in acuity. Kryter and Ades conclude that the inferior colliculus is the primary subcortical auditory reflex center and that it is capable of maintaining approximately normal absolute intensity thresholds in the absence of auditory cortex. With animals reduced to only brain-stem auditory centers (below inferior colliculi), conditioned reactions to tones could be elicited, but only by relatively intense tones some 40 db above threshold. These authors theorize that the response in this case was mediated by proprioceptive pathways, i.e. the loud tone elicited a reflexive head-and-neck orienting response, the proprioceptive stimuli produced thereby mediating the running reaction. This serves again to illustrate the complexities involved in studying the role of higher sensory centers in animal subjects.

(3) *Effects of limited lesions.* Of greater import for auditory theory are the effects produced by limited lesions in the higher centers. Is there the selective loss of sensitivity demanded by place theory or is there general loss? In the experiment by Kryter and Ades cited above incomplete removal of the inferior colliculi occurred in some cases, and the loci along the frequency scale of decrements were found to vary from animal to animal, de-

pending upon the locus of the lesions. This suggests that portions of the inferior colliculi mediate specific frequencies. In an earlier study Ades, Mettler, and Culler (1938) were able to make small, localized lesions in the medial geniculate body (a relay station in the auditory system just before the cortex) without also destroying superficial cortex, using the Horsley-Clarke stereotaxic instrument. Losses in sensitivity were as great as 20 db, but tests were made within a few days after surgery and thus did not take into account any gradient of spontaneous recovery. Of interest, however, was the fact that losses were fairly well restricted in terms of frequency; these authors were able to specify different foci for tones between 125 and 8000 cycles within the geniculates.

(4) *Action potentials in the higher centers.* It is possible to record electrical activity as a result of stimulation all along the auditory pathways, but the records obtained in the cortex—where the impulses attributable to peripheral stimulation become enmeshed in the spontaneous activity of the cortex itself—are difficult to interpret. Licklider (1942) and Licklider and Kryter (1942) studied frequency localization in the auditory cortex of the cat and the monkey, respectively, and obtained fairly clear localization. Lipman (1940) reported similar findings on the dog. Woolsey and Walzl (1942) stimulated small groups of fibers in the operatively exposed cochlea of the cat and obtained action potentials over restricted portions of the auditory cortex. The points of maximal response in the cortex had a systematic arrangement, from fibers at one end of the cochlea to those at the other, but there was considerable dispersion of cortical response, particularly for activity originating in the apical portions (low-tone region) of the cochlea. Tunturi (1944, 1945, 1946) has contributed the most extensive information here: it was shown that spread of activity in the cortex varied directly with the intensity of stimuli. Although localization for weak tonal stimuli was demonstrable, it was of a complicated sort—there appear to be several foci of action within the auditory cortex for the same frequency according to the results obtained by this investigator.

PSYCHOLOGICAL INFORMATION

Only the experienced observer draws a clear distinction between sensations and the physical conditions that give rise to them. One speaks casually of the 'loudness of that whistle' and the 'pitch of that tone' as if these were attributes of sound itself. Pressure waves have neither pitch nor loudness. These are sensory attributes mediated by the nervous system. Pitch depends upon frequency and loudness upon intensity, but these relations are neither one-to-one nor exclusive. The problem of auditory psychophysics is, in fact, to determine these relations. Considerable difficulty has been met in *scaling* such psychological attributes as pitch and loudness. Ideally a psychological scale should have numerical significance, in the sense that mathematical manipulations (adding, dividing, etc.) yield verifiable results which bear a reasonable relation to the experience of observers (Stevens and Davis, 1938).

Pitch as a Function of Frequency

Stevens, Volkmann, and Newman (1937) have used the *method of fractionation* to establish a numerical scale of pitch. With an arbitrary loudness·

level of 60 db for all tones, subjects were given the task of setting the frequency of a variable so as to appear half as 'high' in pitch as a standard frequency, 10 different standards distributed along the frequency dimension being used. These 'half as high in pitch' judgments proved easier to make than might be thought, especially if the subject paid no attention to traditional musical intervals. A pitch scale was constructed on the basis of these data, the number 1000 being assigned arbitrarily as the pitch of a 1000 c.p.s. tone. With this anchorage point, a value of 500 was necessarily assigned to that tone judged half as high in pitch and a value of 2000 was necessarily assigned to that tone for which 1000 c.p.s. was judged half as high. Extension of this procedure yielded a numerical scale of pitch, linear and composed of equal-appearing intervals in so far as the psychological operations on which it was based were concerned.

As a name for the unit of this new scale the authors chose the term 'mel' (root of the word 'melody'); a tone of 2000 mels sounds half as high in pitch as a tone of 4000 mels and twice as high as a tone of 1000 mels. The fractionation procedure upon which this scale is based meets one of the requirements of a numerical scale—a magnitude represented by the number N does appear half as great as that represented by the number $2N$. Validation of such a scale demands that *other* mathematical operations with these new units yield results compatible with the experience of observers. When an observer is presented with two tones, one at 4000 mels and the other at 2000 mels, and is asked to adjust a third variable tone so that it is halfway between the standards, will his adjustment fall at 3000 mels? This is known as the *method of bisection,* and the results checked with those obtained by fractionation.

How is this psychological scale of pitch related to the physical scale of frequency? This is a fundamental question for psychophysics. If sensory processes bore a one-to-one relation with changes in physical energy, having established an anchorage-point at 1000 c.p.s. for a pitch of 1000 mels, the two scales would display perfect parallelism, a 4000 c.p.s. tone having a pitch of 4000 mels, and so on. Inspection of Fig. 33, which gives pitch (in mels) as a function of frequency (in cycles per sec.), shows this not to be the case. Although mels keep step with cycles-per-second fairly well (but not exactly) up to 1000 c.p.s., the deviation increases regularly beyond this point—a tone of 4000 c.p.s., for example, has a pitch of only about 2300 mels. In other words, the pitch of a high-frequency tone is not as high as it 'should' be if we were in perfect rapport with our physical environment. Stevens, Volkmann, and Newman have demonstrated that the size of standard musical intervals, like the octave and the fifth, varies throughout the frequency range when measured in mels—which means that octaves are not equal-appearing intervals psychologically any more than they are equal frequency units physically.

An abnormality of hearing known as *diplacusis* is interesting in relation to the determination of pitch. When listening to a single tone with both ears, some individuals hear two slightly disharmonious tones, one in each ear. Perhaps this phenomenon should not be considered an abnormality, except in extreme cases, for Stevens and Egan (1941) have found it to be present in some degree in most normal observers. It is also possible to produce temporary diplacusis as large as an octave by intense stimulation of one ear

(Davis, *et al.*, 1946). Since the same sound wave frequency is delivered to both ears during tests, and since fibers are known to fire to successive energy peaks, it is difficult to see how any frequency or volley theory can incorporate this phenomenon (however, cf. Wever, 1949, pp. 356-61). If we assume slight variations in the vibratory characteristics of the basilar membranes, or in the thresholds of individual fibers, in the two ears, the place theory can interpret diplacusis. Stevens and Egan report diplacusis for tones

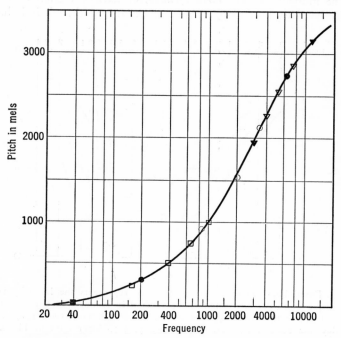

FIGURE 33. Functional relation between subjective pitch (in mels) and frequency of stimulus, based on judgments of equal-appearing intervals. Stevens and Volkmann, *American Journal of Psychology*, 1940 *b*, 53 : 336.

as low as 400 cycles in some observers, which is well within the region presumably utilizing the volley principle in the resonance-volley theory.

Loudness as a Function of Frequency

Loudness also varies with frequency. If a 1000 c.p.s. tone and a 100 c.p.s. tone of the same physical intensity are presented to the ear, the former sounds louder. To determine the precise manner in which loudness varies with frequency, it is necessary to use the intensity of a tone of some standard frequency as a reference level. Subjects then vary the intensities of tones of other frequencies and make loudness equations. A 1000 c.p.s. tone is the commonly accepted standard. The curves shown in Fig. 34 are called *equal loudness contours*. The loudness of each contour is indicated by loudness-level in decibels. Taking the contour for a loudness-level of 40 db as an example, each point on the contour represents the intensity that a tone of any given frequency must be to sound as loud as a 1000 c.p.s. tone at 40 db intensity. The contour for zero loudness-level represents the threshold of audibility as a function of frequency, and it may be seen that the ear is most sensitive to frequencies in the middle range. We may also observe that the degree to which loudness depends upon frequency decreases as the absolute level of intensity rises. The contour at 100 db, for example, is nearly level between 100 and 4000 cycles.

In certain abnormalities of hearing the relation of loudness to frequency is distorted. Of chief concern to the theorist are cases of *selective hearing loss.* Some individuals have *tonal lacunae,* or narrow regions of lowered sensitivity bounded by regions of normal hearing. Although it is hard to

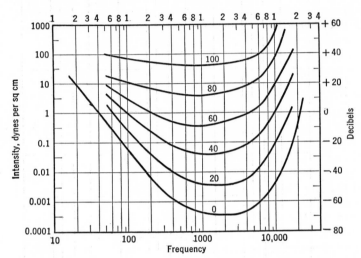

FIGURE 34. Equal loudness contours. Each curve represents the intensity required at each frequency to produce a tone judged equal in loudness to a 1000 c.p.s. tone whose level above threshold appears on the curve. Wever, *Theory of Hearing,* John Wiley and Sons, Inc., New York, 1949, p. 307. After data of Fletcher and Munson, 1933.

think of any transmission impedance that would interfere with frequencies limited to a narrow region, selective impairment of small regions of the basilar membrane, through fixation, loss of hair cells, or nerve degeneration, is quite feasible. In fact, the guinea pig subjects used by Stevens, Davis, and Lurie (1935) in experiments on microdestruction of cochlear regions might have reported just such limited deficiencies—had they had any way to report.

A more familiar example of selective hearing loss is the progressive impairment in hearing high tones that accompanies aging. Progressive atrophy of the auditory nerve supplying the basal turn of the cochlea has been correlated with these age changes (Crowe, Guild, and Polvogt, 1934). These data also provide an interesting parallel with experimental findings, specifically Neff's observations (1947) on the effects of partial sectioning of the VIIIth nerve in cats. Most forms of *transmission deafness* appear as selective loss of acuity for low tones, and they exaggerate the normal effects of tension on those muscles that damp action of the ossicles. Selective losses in hearing for specific frequencies are more compatible with a place theory than with any form of frequency theory.

Loudness as a Function of Intensity

Dynes per square centimeter do not measure loudness any more than cycles per second measure pitch. Loudness is also an attribute of auditory experience and must be measured in terms of some recordable aspect of the behavior of listening organisms. A number of different methods for establishing a loudness scale have been tried. (1) *Fractionation*. Just as in scaling pitch, the subject may be asked to adjust the physical intensity of a variable tone until it appears half as loud as a standard tone, this procedure being followed over many segments of the loudness continuum until sufficient data from which to construct a scale have been obtained. (2) *Monaural-binaural equations*. A tone introduced simultaneously to both ears is said to sound twice as loud as the same tone led into a single ear. Therefore, if an observer adjusts the intensity of a variable tone led into one ear until it seems *equal* in loudness to a tone of the same frequency led into both ears, we have a method of fractionation comparatively free of judgmental errors. Although there is no question but that binaural summation occurs (cf. Hirsh, 1948 *a*), whether it is necessarily in the ratio of 2 to 1 for all individuals is still a debated issue. Békésy (1929) and Fletcher and Munson (1933) have presented evidence for this ratio, and Stevens and Davis (1938) and Woodworth (1938) both accept the 2 to 1 ratio as fact, but recent data obtained by Causse and Chavasse (1942, as reported in Hirsh, 1948 *a*) indicate that the ratio changes with the absolute intensity used.

As was the case with setting up a scale for pitch, a scale for loudness established by operations that satisfy one mathematical requirement (e.g. fractionation) should also satisfy other mathematical requirements stemming from the same set of primitive assumptions about the numbers on the scale. (3) *Bisection*. If an observer adjusts a variable tone until it seems to fall halfway between two fixed tones in loudness, the scale value of the variable should bisect the interval between the standards, i.e. if the fixed tones have values of 2 and 4, the adjusted variable should be found to have a value of 3 on the loudness scale established by other methods. Newman, Volkmann, and Stevens (1937) found the method of bisection to be internally consistent, but the scale values for loudness did not agree with those obtained by fractionation. (4) *Equal-appearing intervals*. If an interval covering a certain number of units of the loudness scale established by fractionation is presented to an observer as a standard, the interval along another part of the scale which he sets as being equal in size should cover the same number of units. Wolff (1935, reported in Stevens and Davis, 1938) obtained results with this method which fit fairly well with a loudness scale established by the method of fractionation.

We may now consider how loudness varies as a function of intensity. Utilizing data obtained by the method of fractionation, and giving special weight to the monaural-binaural procedure, Churcher (1935) determined this relation. The arbitrary number 1 is assigned to the loudness of a 1000 c.p.s. tone 40 db above threshold, this unit being called a *sone*. The intensity of a 1000 c.p.s. tone which sounds half as loud must now be 0.5 sones. By extending this process throughout the obtained data, and extrapolating, loudness of a 1000 c.p.s. tone (in sones) as a function of intensity (in decibels) is determined. Figure 35 shows the function for this and other frequencies. The curve for 1000 c.p.s. is quite accurate for frequencies between about 700 and 4000 cycles. The less sensitive the ear to a given frequency (i.e. both high and low tones), the more rapidly loudness grows with increasing intensity. This is especially marked for very low frequencies for which a small change in db will bring the tone from inaudibility to maximum loudness.

The question of how the auditory nervous system mediates loudness is a thorny one. Auditory fibers are known to fire at every peak in sound wave

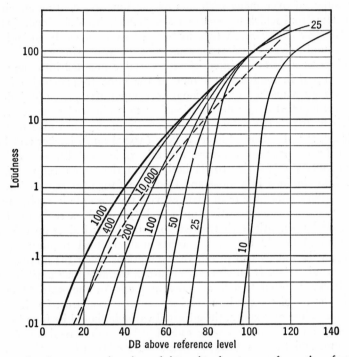

FIGURE 35. Loudness as a function of intensity for tones of varying frequency. Stevens and Davis, *Hearing: Its Psychology and Physiology,* John Wiley and Sons, Inc., New York, 1938, p. 118.

energy, so loudness cannot depend simply upon frequency of impulses in individual fibers, at least not at the periphery—a 1000 c.p.s. tone does not sound twice as loud as a 500 c.p.s. tone. Both place and volley theorists relate loudness to *total frequency of impulses per unit time,* regardless of what particular fibers are contributing the input. If this is the case, one wonders how it is possible to distinguish which of two differently pitched tones is the one being shifted in intensity when both are sounding simultaneously, yet this is easily done. The question of loudness is very closely related to the phenomenon of *masking,* to which we must now turn our attention.

Masking

Listeners are naturally more concerned with sounds they hear than with sounds they fail to hear. Yet under most conditions hearing includes the elimination of sounds through masking, and this phenomenon has considerable theoretical significance. Masking may be defined as a rise in the absolute threshold of a test sound owing to the simultaneous presentation of another sound. This definition implies a direct method of measurement: after determining the absolute threshold for a given test sound under conditions of quiet, the threshold is redetermined in the presence of a masking sound, which may be varied in terms of its frequency, intensity, and composition. Sample data for a pure 800 c.p.s. masking tone are shown in Fig. 36.

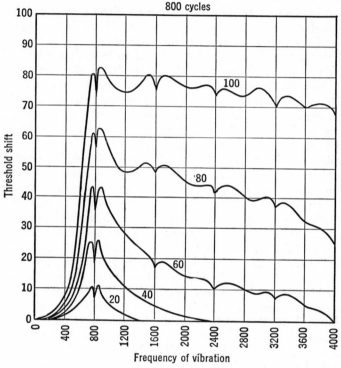

FIGURE 36. Masking effects of an 800 c.p.s. tone observed along the frequency continuum. Curves given are for varying intensities (db) of the masking tone. Fletcher, *Speech and Hearing,* D. Van Nostrand Co., Inc., New York, 1929, p. 169.

Each curve represents the rise in threshold (ordinate) for the various test tones distributed along the abscissa occasioned by the masking tone at each of the intensities shown.

Several characteristics of the phenomenon are apparent in these curves. (a) The range of frequencies affected increases with the intensity of the masking tone. (b) the magnitude of masking varies, in the main, with the nearness of test and masking sounds. (c) Tones higher in frequency than the masking tone are affected more than tones lower in frequency. (d) Sharp dips are found about those frequency points representing the overtones of the masking tone—the aural beats which occur about these points before the test tone is actually heard serve to lower the detection threshold. To these characteristics several others must be added: (e) The lower the frequency of the masking sound, the more widely spread is its effect. (f)

When test and masking tones are presented to opposite ears, a masking effect may be observed, but it is small in magnitude and is probably due to bone conduction (Wegel and Lane, 1924). This suggests a peripheral origin of the phenomenon. (g) Significantly, masking is not, however, evident in the cochlear microphonic, i.e. it is a neural, not a mechanical, phenomenon.

The audiogram obtained in the presence of a masking tone may be viewed as a picture of the excitation pattern of the masking tone itself along the basilar membrane, e.g. the masking tone can only raise the thresholds of neighboring tones to the extent that it utilizes some of their pathways. Looked at in this way, masking data become a direct correlate of the neurophysiological data obtained by Galambos and Davis (1943, 1944) when recording from individual elements in the auditory pathways. It will be recalled that a '2000 c.p.s. fiber' was found to be excitable by an increasingly wide range of frequencies as the intensity of these stimuli was increased; similarly, the masking effect of a 1000 c.p.s. tone upon a 2000 c.p.s. tone is found to increase as the intensity of the masking tone increases. Measurements at these two levels, neurological and psychological, are also related by the fact that spread of low-frequency effects toward higher frequencies is greater than the reverse in both cases.

How does masking relate to loudness? Considerable evidence (cf. Fletcher and Munson, 1933; Churcher, 1935) indicates that simultaneously sounded tones summate in loudness, provided they are far enough apart in frequency to avoid masking effects. More recently Howes (1950) has studied these relations, using psychological units for pitch (mels) and loudness (sones). As the number of component tones in a complex was increased from 1 to 11 (either 250 or 500 mels apart), loudness increased in simple additive fashion, as determined by equal-loudness judgments with a pure 1000 c.p.s. tone as standard. This was true up to fairly high intensities, when masking effects began to appear. With differences in pitch between component tones equal, as in this case, the masking effect per component is a constant depending solely upon the loudness-level of the components. When masking is present, therefore, the loudness of multicomponent sounds is found to deviate cumulatively and linearly from the simple additive function obtained when masking is absent.

Since overlapping excitations *subtract* from the total loudness experienced rather than summate, the notion that masking involves some kind of inhibitory process is suggested (cf. below). But why should non-overlapping tones (i.e. those which do not mask one another) summate in loudness at all? Summation in the nervous system usually indicates channeling upon common loci. As Howes points out (p. 29), no satisfactory physiological correlate of loudness has been demonstrated as yet. Perhaps the subtractive effects of masking take place peripherally (in the cochlear nuclei?), but additive effects upon loudness take place higher in the auditory pathways through some channeling process. The mediation of loudness remains a thorny problem.

The usual explanation of masking itself has been on a 'line busy' basis (cf. Fletcher, 1929). Fibers within the influence of the masking tone are excited by it and are thus rendered relatively refractory to their 'normal' stimuli. But if impulses are generated in such fibers by the masking tone, why does this activity fail to be represented in experience? To be sure, the

'line' may be 'busy,' but busy lines in the nervous system generally eventuate in sensory experience. This is the real problem here, and it recalls the
entire question of 'single hearing'—a band of excitation, very broad with
intense stimuli, is somehow resolved into a tone of precise quality. The
same mechanism that eliminates hearing tones corresponding to the submaximally excited portions of the band (and allows 'single hearing') presumably eliminates hearing test tones that fall within the envelope of a
masking sound. In both cases submaximally excited elements contribute only
to the loudness of the experience characteristic of the maximally excited
region. Some principle of *inhibition,* such as has been applied fruitfully to
the understanding of lateral effects in vision, would seem to be required
here as well. Harris (1948), studying pitch discrimination, and Hirsh
(1948 *b*), studying binaural hearing—both under conditions of masking—
felt it necessary to postulate inhibitory mechanisms.

Pitch as a Function of Intensity

Although pitch varies mainly with frequency of the stimulus, it can also
be shown to vary with intensity, but the dependence here is neither marked

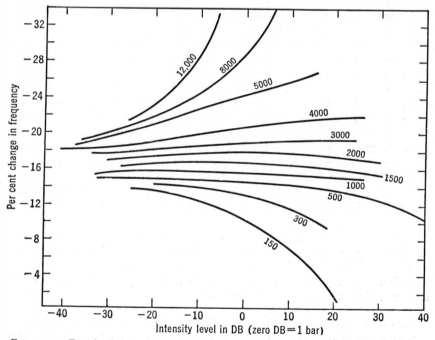

FIGURE 37. Equal pitch contours for tones of various frequencies, as functions of
intensity. Stevens, *Journal of the Acoustical Society of America*, 1935, **6**:152.

nor precisely determined. Only recently has this relation been studied quantitatively. Stevens (1935), using a single, trained observer, obtained the
results shown in Fig. 37. These curves might be termed *equal-pitch contours.* As intensity is increased, the frequency of a tone must be either increased or decreased by some amount if a constant pitch is to be maintained.
The numbers on the contours represent the 11 frequencies studied. The

import of these curves is that the apparent pitch of high-frequency tones gets higher and that of low-frequency tones gets lower with increasing intensity, tones in the middle-frequency range to which the ear is most sensitive showing little variation. More recent experiments by Galambos and Morgan (cited in Morgan, 1943) have failed to find the rise in pitch for high-frequency tones, and the downward shift in pitch for low tones was less marked than in Stevens's data.

Accepting some such relation as shown in Fig. 37, why should it be, according to a place theory? The shift in pitch is always away from the region of greatest sensitivity (near 2000 c.p.s.), high tones becoming higher and low tones lower with increased intensity. If one assumes that there is a limit on the maximum impulse rate for any given set of fibers, further increases in intensity could only be reflected in changing locus. If such dispersion of excitation were not symmetrical along the membrane, a change in pitch would occur. Assuming the asymptote to be reached more rapidly where sensitivity is greatest (i.e. around 2000 c.p.s.), shifts in pitch would necessarily be away from this region. The resonance-volley theory proposed by Wever would have to predict that sufficiently low tones would fail to shift with increased intensity, the point on the frequency scale where this first occurred being the shift-over point from place to volley principles of action. Existing evidence (Snow, 1936) indicates that the magnitude of pitch change with a constant intensity increment *increases* progressively down to about 100 cycles. Here, to be sure, the trend reverses, but whether this means a shift-over to a volley principle or merely that the end of the basilar membrane (helicotrema) is being reached is not known.

Thurlow (1943) has called the place explanation of this phenomenon into question by demonstrating that the same changes in the perceived pitch of a tone sounded in one ear can be produced by simultaneously sounding a tone in the *other* ear, thus increasing total intensity. Since this was done under conditions where peripheral interaction via air or bone conduction could be ruled out, it would appear that a change in pitch may occur without any shift in the position of maximal stimulation along the basilar membrane. Thurlow argues against any explanation in terms of central overloading and resultant displacement of the impulse pattern, since there seems no a priori reason that such dispersion should be more in one direction than another. He offers no alternative explanation, however, and a volley theory seems incapable of explaining the mere fact that pitch does change with intensity. Wever (1949, pp. 344-6) dismisses the phenomenon as an illusion, a confusion of volley and place cues.

Pitch and Loudness Discrimination as Functions of Frequency

The measurement of difference thresholds in audition is made difficult because of the transient tones, i.e. spread of energy along the frequency continuum, which occur whenever one tone (standard S) is terminated and another (comparison S) is substituted. In an attempt to circumvent this difficulty while measuring *loudness thresholds,* Riesz (1928) utilized the phenomenon of *beats:* to the standard tone he added another, 3 cycles away in frequency, which was increased in intensity until just perceptible 'beating' of the standard tone became apparent. This increment in db, while presumably not equal in size to the minimal threshold (owing to masking), is probably proportional to the loudness *DL*. At moderate intensity levels, he found ΔI to decrease rapidly in size as frequency was raised to about 100 c.p.s., then to decrease more gradually to 4000 c.p.s. where the smallest thresholds obtain, and thence to increase in size with yet higher frequencies. To measure *pitch thresholds,* Shower and Biddulph (1931) smoothly modulated a continuous tone back and forth between two frequency points, noting the average frequency separation at which an observer could just detect variations in pitch. The difference threshold for pitch, ΔF, was shown to be roughly constant and minimal to about 2000 c.p.s., increasing rapidly in size for frequencies above this point. These are the facts—what implications do they have for theory?

Stevens (1939) has distinguished between additive and substitutive changes in excitation as bases for loudness and pitch discrimination, respectively. Excitation of different sets of fibers along the basilar membrane (substitutive) causes pitch to vary, whereas increasing or decreasing the total number of fibers active (additive) causes loudness to vary. The fact that the *time error* for successive comparison of tones varying in pitch is much smaller than it is for tones varying in loudness checks with this view (cf. Postman, 1946; Koester and Schoenfeld, 1946). Pushing this line of inquiry further, it will be recalled that Crozier has argued that the size of the difference threshold varies with the number of impulses *available* to reflect the effects of the stimulus increment. Now, since *rate* of fire in auditory fibers is determined by stimulus frequency, the additional impulses for loudness discrimination must come from the recruitment of new fibers on an additive basis. The additional impulses for pitch discrimination must also come from new fibers, but on a substitutive basis. In both cases, therefore, if the logic is correct, the sizes of *DL*'s should vary with the *density* of auditory nerve fibers subserving the region within which the stimulus acts, i.e. the more dense the neural supply, the more impulses become available. Is there any evidence for systematic variation in the density of fibers along the basilar membrane?

Direct histological studies on human ears have been made available by the Otological Research Laboratory of Johns Hopkins University (cf. Guild, Crowe, Bunch, and Polvogt, 1931; Wever, 1949, pp. 290-94). The general technique is to count the numbers of ganglion cells in samples taken from those portions of the *modiolus* (central core of the cochlea) that correspond to various portions of the basilar membrane. Figure 38 describes average density data in millimeters for a considerable number of human ears as a function of distance along the membrane. The important question is this: How is this distribution of receptor density related to the approximate distribution of frequency reception along the basilar membrane? The frequency localization data added to Fig. 38 are estimates based upon experiments of several sorts: position of maximal vibration on the basilar membrane as observed in human ears and mechanical models (Békésy, 1949); position of maximal microphonic response as observed in the guinea pig (Culler, *et al.,* 1943); decrement in sensitivity produced by localized lesions in the guinea pig (Stevens, Davis, and Lurie, 1935); and degeneration observed histologically in cases of localized deafness (Crowe, Guild, and Polvogt, 1934). One thing is immediately apparent from this comparison— the lower 40 per cent of the frequency range (up to 8000 c.p.s.) utilizes well over 80 per cent of the basilar membrane and an equivalent proportion of the available fibers. It is not surprising, therefore, that both loudness and pitch *DL's* increase rapidly in size as we move upward in frequency from 8000 c.p.s.

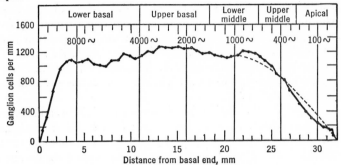

FIGURE 38. Variation in density of innervation of the human cochlea. Based on observation of 23 ears by members of the Otological Research Laboratory, Johns Hopkins University. Wever, *Theory of Hearing,* John Wiley and Sons, Inc., New York, 1949, p. 292. Approximate frequency localization data added by the writer.

What about the relation between difference thresholds and receptor densities *below* 8000 c.p.s.? Knowing the basilar distances subtended by various frequencies (at least, roughly) and knowing the average density of auditory nerve fibers within these regions, one can estimate fiber density per cycle of the stimulus frequency. Such estimations are shown in Table 2, and they

TABLE 2. INNERVATION DENSITY AND THRESHOLD DATA COMPARED

Frequency Range	*N mm. Subtended*	*Av. N fibers per mm.*	*Av. Density per Cycle*	*Approx. ΔI*	*Approx. ΔF*
0–400	9	400	9 fibers	1.0 db	2.5 c.p.s.
400–1000	5	1000	8 fibers	0.8 db	2.5 c.p.s.
1000–4000	10	1200	4 fibers	0.5 db	5.0 c.p.s.
4000–8000	7	1100	2 fibers	0.6 db	14.0 c.p.s.

are related to approximate sizes of loudness thresholds (Riesz's data, at 40 db intensity level) and pitch thresholds (Shower and Biddulph's data, 40 db intensity level) within the same frequency regions. According to Crozier's availability hypothesis, size of threshold should vary inversely with density of fibers in the region utilized by the stimulus. This definitely does *not* hold for loudness discrimination—Δ*I* gets progressively smaller between 20 and 4000 c.p.s., but the average density of neural elements also gets smaller. On the other hand, it definitely does hold for pitch discrimination— as the average density of fibers decreases, pitch discrimination becomes poorer. There is another interesting thing about these data: according to Crozier, the added number of impulses necessary for a just perceptible change in sensation is a *constant.* In the present case this means that average density of fibers per cycle in frequency multiplied by the size of the threshold in cycles should be a constant. Performing this operation we obtain 22.5, 20.0, 20.0, and 28.0 for the number of fibers required to mediate a just perceptible difference in pitch at the four frequency ranges above.

Given the admittedly approximate nature of these data, the deviations from constancy are not very great.

Pitch and Loudness Discrimination as Functions of Duration

The ear is an integrative system in the sense that energies distributed in time summate. Tones of extremely short duration (under 4-5 msec.) are experienced as clicks having little or no pitch quality, this experience presumably being caused by the rapid series of transient frequencies produced as the ear overcomes its inertia. With somewhat longer duration (10-15 msec.) the click experience becomes more tonal, apparent pitch varying with the frequency of the stimulus but not being equivalent to that produced by tones of longer duration. We may refer to this as *click-pitch* in contrast with usual *tone-pitch*. Duration thresholds (i.e. the minimum duration at which any given type of experience can be reported) for both click-pitch and tone-pitch reach a minimum at about 1000 cycles when stimulus frequency is varied; shortened durations of stimulation can be compensated, to some extent, by increasing intensity (Doughty and Garner, 1947), this being the reciprocal relation found in other modalities. As tonal duration is decreased from 100 msec., *pitch discrimination* gradually becomes poorer (Turnbull, 1944); below 17 msec. (i.e. within the click-pitch range for the tones used here) the size of the difference threshold rises sharply toward infinity. Turnbull was also able to demonstrate a reciprocal relation between duration and intensity in maintaining a constant pitch-difference threshold.

With regard to *loudness,* Garner and Miller (1947) have found the relationship between threshold intensity and duration of stimulus to be linear and reciprocal up to a certain critical duration of about 200 msec., this, incidentally, being typical of values for visual brightness summation. With regard to *difference thresholds for loudness,* both Békésy and Lifshitz (1929, 1936, as reported in Stevens and Davis) and Garner and Miller more recently (1944) find a reciprocal relation between intensity and duration to hold. Researchers in vision have demonstrated that two subthreshold stimuli may summate to yield a visible result if they occur close enough together in time and retinal space. Garner (1947), using varying rates of repetition of short tones, has obtained the same type of summation among temporally discrete auditory stimuli.

Certain 'Subjective' Auditory Experiences

When a pure sine wave is led into the ear, the subjective experience may be impure if intensity is sufficiently high. With a 1000 cycle stimulus, for example, *overtones* at 2000, 3000, 4000 cycles, and so on, are detectable, their loudness decreasing with their order. Overtones of insufficient intensity to be heard can be detected by the phenomenon of beats: although the 4000 harmonic in the present case may be inaudible, exploration with another stimulus will yield beats—a 4008 c.p.s. tone beating eight times per second, for example. When two sine waves are presented simultaneously, the situation becomes tremendously complicated; not only does each tone produce its own system of harmonics, but a complicated array of intertones, difference tones, and summation tones is also generated. Newman, Stevens, and Davis (1937) were able to record some 66 distinct tones in the cochlear microphonic of a cat stimulated by 700- and 1200-cycle sine waves at 90 db intensity. Of course the intensity of these secondary responses was much less than that of the primary ones, being generally less than 5 per cent.

As the frequency separation of two tones is gradually increased, a series of auditory experiences can be described (Wever, 1929). When the frequency difference is very slight (under 7 cycles), a single *intertone* having a pitch between the two primaries is heard, waxing and waning at a slow rate dependent upon the cycle difference. With a larger frequency difference the two primaries are also heard; they seem to lie on both sides of the intertone, which beats with a definite, throbbing quality. With yet further frequency differences the intertone becomes roughened in quality, lower in loudness, and finally disappears. If the ear is stimulated with two fairly intense tones, well separated in frequency, the listener will hear a *difference* tone, i.e. a 4000 c.p.s. and a 4500 c.p.s. tone will be accompanied by a low-pitched 500 c.p.s. difference tone.

These phenomena are subjective only if the sound wave is considered the stimulus. Actually, many theorists (cf. Stevens and Davis) attribute overtones and difference tones to mechanical distortions during transmission through the middle ear, and intertones and beats to incomplete damping of the basilar membrane. Since these effects occur before stimulation of auditory fibers, they are characteristics of the stimulus and are not subjective. The fact that all of these phenomena can be recorded in the cochlear microphonic substantiates this view. Lewis and Reger (1933), however, have reported such phenomena in the hearing of subjects lacking both tympanic membrane and ossicles, so the matter is certainly not settled.

Other Attributes of Tones

Loudness and pitch are two psychological attributes of tones. Are there any others? Three qualities have commonly been suggested: volume, density, and brightness. Let us first consider in general terms the criteria that must be applied to any proposed attribute of sensation. (1) *Any attribute of sensation must display a specifiable dependency upon physical variables of the stimulus.* There is no requirement that this dependency relation be linear or be associated with a single stimulus variable. Pitch and loudness are different functions of *both* frequency and intensity. (2) *Any attribute of sensation must be referable to differential activity of the sensory nerves within the modality to which the attribute applies.* Both pitch and loudness depend upon auditory receptor action, the precise type of action depending upon one's theory of the matter. The tactual and painful sensations that appear at extremely high intensities are not considered attributes of auditory experience because they involve modalities other than hearing. In a broader sense, we may refer to sounds as being 'light,' 'pear-shaped,' or even 'red-hot' (see discussion of synesthesia on pp. 642-5), yet we would not consider these attributes of tones since these descriptions obviously stem from meaningful associations. (3) *Any attribute of sensation must be independent of other attributes within the same modality.* If volume, for example, were to be considered an attribute, it would have to be shown to be independent of both pitch and loudness—this is usually the only criterion that has been applied.

Volume. Both Carl Stumpf and William James insisted that sounds were discriminable on the basis of this spatial characteristic. Early experiments (Rich, 1916; Halverson, 1924; Zoll, 1934) yielded contradictory results. Stevens (1934 *a, b*) applied essentially the same methods as were used to study pitch and loudness: given tones of slightly different frequency in rapid alternation (40 per minute), the subject varied the *intensity* of one until it seemed to be equal in volume to the standard. In each case the intensity of the higher frequency tone would be raised to make the equation, so it appeared that volume increased with intensity and decreased with frequency.

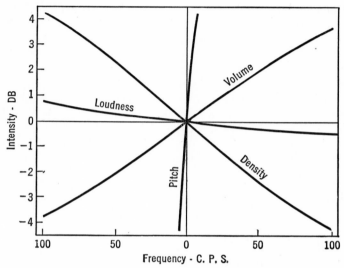

FIGURE 39. Intensity and frequency characteristics (expressed as deviations) of tones judged equal in pitch, loudness, volume, or density to a standard tone of 500 c.p.s. and 60 db, i.e. contours of subjective equivalence for these qualities. Stevens, *Proceedings of the National Academy of Science,* Washington, 1934, 20:458.

Sample results are shown in Fig. 39. Each contour represents the combinations of frequency and intensity required to maintain each attribute constant in experience. To keep the attribute of loudness constant as frequency is changed from 400 to 600 cycles, intensity must be lowered slightly (i.e. this is a short segment of one of the equal loudness contours shown in Fig. 34). To keep judged volume constant as frequency is increased, intensity must be increased considerably. Since, with a 500-cycle tone at 60 db intensity as a standard, the volume of a comparison tone may be judged equal despite changes in both pitch and loudness, Stevens concludes that this is an independent attribute of auditory sensation.

Density. Observers may differentiate tones in terms of their 'hardness' or 'compactness.' Using the same method described above for volume, Stevens (1934 *c*) determined the equal-density curve shown in Fig. 39. 'The meaning of the concept was illustrated to the uninitiated observers by presenting them with a high tone (4000 cycles), followed by a low tone (200 cycles). The observers quickly recognized the dense compactness of the high tone as contrasted with the diffuseness of the low tone' (Stevens and Davis, 1938, p. 163). Again, since judgments of equal density could be made despite marked variations in both pitch and loudness, density was considered to be another independent dimension. But are density and volume independent of one another? Is 'diffuseness' (cf. quotation above) anything other than voluminousness? If subjects were asked to equate the diffuseness of tones as their intensity and frequency were varied, would the results fall elsewhere than along the curve for 'volume' in Fig. 39? Although Stevens defends the independence of density and volume, it seems quite possible that these dimensions are really mirror images of one another—that in judging volume one is also judging nondensity; whereas in judging density, one is also judging nonvoluminousness, so we might better refer to the single dimension of 'spatiality' just as we refer to the 'height' of pitch.

With regard to *brightness* as an attribute, some investigators (Rich, 1919) have found it inseparable from pitch, and others (Boring and Stevens, 1936) have found it inseparable from density. Even were there such an attribute, the term 'brightness' would be a gross misnomer, reflecting inadequacies in our descriptive language, for this is clearly a visual term that is applicable to auditory experience only through metaphor. It seems likely that the brightness 'attribute' is actually nothing other than a verbal analogy. If one were to speak of 'white-black' tones or of 'lively-dead' tones, the meaningful (as opposed to sensory) nature of the reference would only be more obvious.

This leads us to consider once more the proposed attributes of density and volume. Stevens and others appear to have based their conclusion that these are genuine attributes of auditory sensation mainly upon the criterion that they can be shown to vary independently of either pitch or loudness. Also used, but less obviously, is the criterion that they display a specifiable dependency upon the physical variables of sound—as intensity increases and frequency decreases, the experience is *consistently* judged to become more voluminous. But there is a third criterion—the attribute must be referable to activity of the sensory fibers within the modality to which it applies. When it is applied to tones, 'brightness' is probably referable to complex meaningful associations rather than to variable activity of the auditory fibers. Would the same statement be applicable to 'volume' and 'density'? Are these verbal metaphors? The consistency with which subjects can make judgments as to the degree of these 'qualities' is no guarantee that they are auditory attributes. Some complex and well-practiced synesthetes can make highly consistent judgments as to the hue that is appropriate to instruments having various timbres, but this does not mean that color is an attribute of tones. And the fact that different subjects may agree fairly well in volume judgments may merely reflect consistencies in our language. If, for example, one were told to call loud tones 'white' and soft tones 'black,' he could then proceed to select shades of gray to parallel variations in loudness with considerable consistency. This argument is offered as a warning that such sensory attributes as these should be very carefully scrutinized, not as proof that they are invalid. Stevens offers—but not boldly—the suggestion that density may depend upon the density of nervous excitation at the cortex (vertically?) and volume may depend upon the spread of this excitation (horizontally?); this is an attempt to satisfy the requirements of the second criterion.

A FINAL WORD ON THEORIES OF HEARING

The most widely accepted theory of hearing today is a compromise between place and volley positions. We are now able to see why this has come about. There is ample experimental evidence for a place theory of frequency reception—for high tones certainly but not so clearly for low tones. On the other hand, there is equally sound evidence that volleying or synchronization in the auditory nerve as a whole does occur—certainly for low tones but not for high tones. There is, however, considerable evidence that a volley principle is not sufficient in itself: (1) not only does synchronization of impulses disappear above 4000 c.p.s. in the auditory nerve itself, but the limitation becomes more and more stringent as successive levels in the neural transmission system are passed. (2) Diplacusis has been observed for frequencies well below 1000 c.p.s. and pitch varies with intensity to below 100 c.p.s.—neither of these phenomena seems to be compatible with a volley theory. (3) Although Galambos and Davis were recording from second-order neurons in the cochlear nucleus, their finding that individual elements are selectively responsive to stimuli of varying frequency—some having minima below 1000 c.p.s.—is nevertheless contrary to a pure volley theory. And much additional evidence, on selective hearing losses and so forth, could be adduced.

Is the sufficiency of a place theory ruled out by existing evidence? The simple fact that volleying does occur in the VIIIth nerve is one major stumbling block, since if *all* fibers are involved in this volleying, we certainly cannot claim that pitch depends upon 'what fibers' are active. But, as was pointed out, volleying does not require this interpretation. It is at least conceivable that *differently placed* fibers contribute to the volleying as frequency is raised, the drops in total amplitude occurring when regions less densely supplied are reached. That density of available fibers per frequency unit does decrease as we go from low- to high-frequency sounds is certainly suggested by the existing evidence; pitch discrimination functions clearly fit this interpretation, but loudness discrimination functions do not. It is also possible that the fibers subserving extremely low tones gather from wider regions of the cochlea. Neff's finding that low tones are extremely hard to eliminate by making lesions in the VIIIth nerve, together with evidence that losses of hearing with age and through both gross and particularized cochlear destruction generally preserve low frequency reception, fits this view. This excursion into guesswork is made solely to point out that the sufficiency of a place theory is not definitely ruled out by present evidence.

Chapter 4

VISION

The subjective visual field is a three-dimensional and complexly patterned affair, all parts of it being simultaneously represented in consciousness. Just as life experiences are oriented about the momentary 'now' of consciousness, visual experiences are organized about a subjective anchorage, the *fixation point*. When I 'look at' a lamp across the room, that becomes subjective zero and all other objects are perceived as 'nearer,' 'farther,' 'above,' or 'below' this fixation point. If this spatial organization of the field be called its *form,* then its substance is *color*. Form and color characteristics of the visual field, however, are not independent of one another. In fact, it is the dishomogeneities of color within the field which give rise to spatial organization. There is no form nor spatiality in a perfectly homogeneous visual field, such as an unblemished blue sky—there is nothing on which to fixate.

Such interaction between substance and spatial cues can be shown to underlie what are called the 'phenomenal varieties of color experience' (cf. Katz, 1911, 1935). When there are no cues for spatial orientation available, we experience *film color*—like the blue sky, it seems to float indefinitely in space. When sufficient cues are available for accurate fixation (accommodation and convergence of the eyes), we experience *surface color*—the color appears as part of, to be lying on, the visually identified surface. The color of an apple seems to be localized on the skin of that object, to be a part of it. When cues for spatial depth are present, *bulky color* is experienced. The world as seen through rose-colored glasses is composed of bulky rose-colored masses, varying only in brightness. The other varieties of color experience are equally dependent upon spatial cues: *transparent color* describes the experience we have when fixating a point *behind* a transparent-colored medium (e.g. looking through a piece of colored cellophane) ; *lustrous color* is what we experience when points of higher brightness are reflected from tiny mirrorlike reflectors on a colored surface (e.g. the polished metal surface of a new automobile) ; *luminous color* is produced when bulky translucent objects are illuminated from within or behind. Film colors rather than surface colors are generally used for research purposes because they are not object-tied and their meaningful reference is therefore minimized.

One of the first tasks in any primitive science is to organize the phe-nomena in its field. This resolves itself into the psychological process of noting similarities and differences among events and classifying them in the simplest yet most inclusive system possible. Suppose you are given a box full of colored paper chips, several hundred of them varying in all con-ceivable ways, and are told to arrange them in a natural system. Having spread them out on a large table, your first rough categorization would probably be in terms of *hue;* you would collect piles of 'red ones,' 'blue ones,' and so on. Is this 'natural,' or is it because certain segments of the dimen-

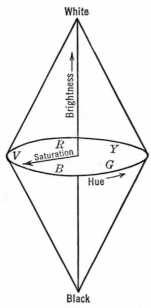

FIGURE 40. Typical color solid. Brightness variations are represented along the vertical dimension, hue variations around the horizontal circumference, and varia-tions in saturation as distance from the axis.

sion of hue have been associated with verbal labels, the names of the so-called 'primary' colors? Do the red ones stand out merely because they have been conceptualized? Having gone this far, you notice certain inade-quacies with your system. One whole set of chips is 'colorless,' a series of shades of gray ranging from jet black to brilliant white. This forms another dimension, that of *brightness,* and you would observe that similar grada-tions could be made within each hue classification—there are 'light' reds and 'dark' reds. But this two-dimensional classification is not sufficient: for any given hue and brightness set there are several paper chips discriminably different from one another. Here is a set of moderately bright reds—some of them are rich, full colors, some are paler, and yet others have just the barest trace of redness to distinguish them from equivalently bright grays. This is the third dimension of color experience which we call *saturation.*

Phenomenological analysis of this sort produces a *color solid,* such as that shown in Fig. 40. Following along the circumference, one moves through a series of hues; a line drawn through the vertical dimension, from white to black, represents changes in brightness; moving outward from the core in any direction, one moves progressively toward more and more saturated colors. One would expect these psychological dimensions of color experience to be correlated with physical variables, and this is the case—hue depends upon the wave length of light, brightness upon the intensity of light, and saturation upon the admixture of wave lengths—but, as was found with audition, these relations are neither exclusive nor one-to-one. The tapering shape of this solid reflects the fact that maximal saturation is possible only at moderate brightnesses of color. Some phenomenologists (viz. Ebbinghaus, 1902) have tried to show the introspective primacy of red, yellow, green, and blue by placing them at the corners of a double pyramid, but whether this is a sensory or a conceptual matter is a moot question. At best, models of this kind serve only as pedagogical devices. They are inevitably inaccurate in detail, the relations among hue, saturation, and brightness being far more complex than they are shown, and they tell us nothing about underlying processes.

Most hues we experience in everyday life are liberally desaturated, because the surfaces they originate from are heterogeneous in their reflectance characteristics. This is actually a form of *color mixture,* but it is capricious. Methods for deliberately composing color mixtures are as old as history itself. Primitives blended pigments derived from soils and plants and layered them upon cave walls, wood carvings, and themselves. Mixing pigments is a *subtractive* process: as all daubers know, yellow and blue pigments mix to make green. The yellow pigment reflects light in red, yellow, and green regions of the spectrum, absorbing (or subtracting) all else; blue pigment reflects in green, blue, and violet regions, absorbing all else. When the two pigments are mixed, the only region of light still reflected is green. In general, as would be expected, mixing pigments reduces brightness—zinc white cannot be mixed on the palette, it has to be carried about in a tube.

The artists have also given us an *additive* method of color mixture. If a heterogeneous color is analyzed into its components, e.g. yellow into green and red, and these components are interspersed on a surface in the form of small dots, the original compound is perceived, provided the observer is far enough from the surface. This was precisely the technique used by the French Impressionist Seurat in his 'A Sunday Afternoon on the Grande Jatte.' The standard laboratory procedure for demonstrating color mixture also makes use of an additive principle, but here it is addition over time rather than over space. If disks of differently colored paper, slit so that they can be interlaced, are placed on an ordinary electric fan motor and rotated rapidly, the succeeding color impressions fuse into a perfectly uniform mixture of the components. When yellow and blue papers are mixed in this additive fashion, we get, not green, but neutral gray—a summation of the two regions of the spectrum represented by yellow and blue. Since duration of stimulation is equivalent to intensity under these conditions, making one color segment larger than the other with which it is mixed on the wheel increases the weight of this component in the mixture. If three-fourths of the disk is red and only one-fourth yellow, the fused mixture is a decidedly reddish orange.

The laws of additive color mixture are actually rather simple. (1) *Every hue has its complementary, a color which when mixed with the standard in appropriate ratio yields the experience of neutral gray.* Complementary hues are opposite each other on the color circle, red with blue-green, yellow with blue, and so on. Varying the ratio between complementary colors simply gives a saturation series between the two colors—mixing a little blue with yellow decreases the saturation of the yellow but does not change the hue. (2) *Mixture of noncomplementary colors yields intermediary hues whose saturations depend upon* (a) *the nearness of the components on the color circle and* (b) *the saturation of the components.* Figure 41 provides a simple scheme for determining the approximate result of mixing any two colors. Saturation increases in all directions from the center of the circle, marked

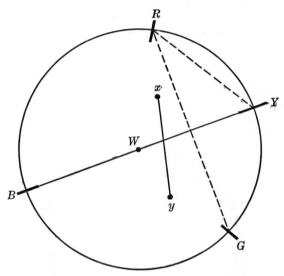

FIGURE 41. Convenient diagram for representing the results of mixing any two hues of given saturation.

W (white or neutral gray). Suppose we mix *Y* and *B*—all resultants must fall along a line between *Y* and *B*, and one ratio will yield completely desaturated white, i.e. all complementary colors connect through *W*. If we mix *R* with *Y* the resultant is a reddish orange that is more nearly saturated than the yellow resultant of mixing *R* and *G,* since the latter are farther apart on the color circle, and the line connecting them therefore passes nearer the center, *W*. Going beyond the complementary point for *R* (e.g. blue-green), mixing *R* with *B* yields a relatively desaturated purple, *R* with violet a more saturated reddish violet, and so on. If a desaturated red is mixed with a desaturated green (e.g. points *x* and *y*), the resultant is less saturated than when *R* and *G* are mixed. Two points of general significance should be mentioned: (a) Any mixture falls nearer the center than the components which make it up, i.e. it is less saturated. (b) There are practically infinite ways a particular color can be produced—for example, think of all the lines that could be passed through point *y*. (3) *All hues experienced by the human observer, including white, can be matched by appropriate mixtures of only three colors.* As we shall see, this fact about color mixture has had far-reaching implications for theory. It should be noted that no particular colors are specified here—the only requirement is that the three primaries be as far apart as possible on the color circle without being complementaries.

Although the color wheel has served long and faithfully in the psychological laboratory, it leaves much to be desired for precise measurement. For one thing, it is difficult to specify with accuracy the physical compositions of the colored papers used for stimulation. For another, the papers used as standards are already quite desaturated by the reflection of much heterogeneous light—and this limits severely the possible saturation of mixtures. For these and other reasons, quantitative work in recent years has usually been done with a *colorimeter*. Here lights of specifiable wave length and intensity are mixed directly through prisms and lenses and cast onto any desired area of the eye (cf. pp. 139-41).

THE EYE AND THE VISUAL RECEPTORS

The eye is an intricately specialized mechanism for conveying radiant energies to the light-sensitive elements. It can be likened to a pocket-sized,

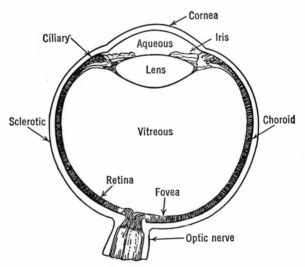

FIGURE 42. Cross section of the human eye showing its gross structure. Troland, *The Principles of Psycho-Physiology,* D. Van Nostrand Co., Inc., New York, 1930, 2:98.

automatically adjustable camera. By means of the ocular muscles and the oculomotor reflex system, both eyes can be fixated upon stationary objectives in the environment, can follow approaching and receding objectives by convergent or divergent movements, can pursue objectives that travel across the field, and can rapidly scan or inspect the environment with conjugate movements. The eye itself is equipped to control the amount of light entering its interior and to facilitate the formation of a clear image upon the sensitive elements. Its interior is filled with transparent substances surrounded by a shell having three concentric layers. The outer layer, the *sclerotic coat,* is a tough protective membrane (see Fig. 42). Within this is a darkly pigmented *choroid layer* which serves to make a dark box of the human camera. The innermost layer is the *retina* which contains the light-sensitive elements.

Radiant energies first strike the *cornea.* This tough transparent frontal portion of the scleroid coat serves as the 'window' of the eye, and its curved outer surface is responsible for most optic refraction. Light then passes through the *aqueous humor* and the *lens.* The black spot we see in the center of the eye is the opening into the inner dark-box, and its size depends upon the degree of tension in the muscles that control the *iris.* The iris is the colored part of the eye, actually the frontal portion of the choroid layer. It controls the light entering the eye just as the circular shutter in a camera— but it is automatic, closing in bright light and opening to its maximum in the dark. The *lens* is equivalent to the lens in a camera, but again it is more flexible. It makes possible the focusing of images of external objects upon the retina and accomplishes this by changing the curvature of its outer surface. The lens, an inherently elastic, crystalline material, tends to bulge when tension on its suspensory ligaments is reduced through contraction of the ciliary muscles. Contraction of these muscles while striving to *accommodate* to near objects is sensed as ocular strain. Following the principles of geo-metrical optics, a relatively flat lens serves to throw a clear image of distant objects upon the retina, whereas a more bulging lens is necessary to produce a clear image of an object close to the eyes.

Transparent, semigelatinous *vitreous humor* constitutes the inner mass of the eye, and light passes through this medium to impinge on the retina. The inner dark-box of the eye is not perfectly light-occlusive. Entoptic stray light arises from diffraction (which causes scatter within the vitreous humor itself), from reflection of the image to all other parts of the retina, and from passage of some light through the sclerotic coat near the cornea. This scattering of light within the ocular media produces some blurring of the retinal image. 'An homogeneously bright object with sharp contours will not produce an image with identical characteristics. The transition from illumination in the image to darkness outside of it is not abrupt, but gradual' (Bartley, 1941, p. 67). The retina itself is comparable to the chemically sensitive film that 'takes' a picture in the camera, but it has the truly re-markable capacity of recovering its photographic qualities in very brief intervals of time, sending a rapid series of 'pictures' to the brain.

Gross Anatomy of the Retina

Contrary to what one might expect, the visual receptors are not extended toward the source of light. Rather than being on the surface of the retina, they are on the bottom with their light-sensitive endings impinging on the choroid, pigmented layer. The reason for this may be that retinal chemistry requires interaction with the substances in this pigmented layer. In terms of the retinal cross section shown in Fig. 43, light should be thought of as traveling from bottom to top, pigmented and scleroid protective layers being at the top of the diagram in that order. Light therefore must pene-trate several layers of translucent cells before striking sensitive elements, and here we have another source of image distortion.

The retina can be divided conceptually into three major levels: (1) Near-est the pigmented choroid, the receptor level is composed of densely packed *rods and cones,* shown in their typical forms in Fig. 43 (levels 2-5). (2) An intermediary level is composed of short *bipolar cells,* which collect impulses from the receptors and relay them, and *horizontal and amacrine cells,* which provide for lateral interaction within the retina (levels 5-7). (3) A final

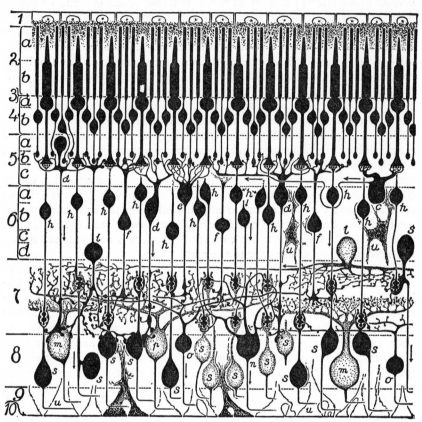

FIGURE 43. Schematic diagram showing the neural microstructure of the retina. Diagram of nervous elements of retina in a monkey, based on Golgi impregnations. The scheme shows chief characteristics of retinal nerve cells and their position. Layers are: (1) pigment epithelium; (2a) outer segment of rods and cones; (2b) the inner segment of rods and cones; (3) outer limiting membrane; (4) outer nuclear layer; (5) outer plexiform layer (cone-pedicles and rod-spherules); (6) inner nuclear layer; (7) inner plexiform layers; (8) ganglion cells (origin of primary visual projections); (9) layer of optic nerve fibers; (10) inner limiting membrane; *c,* horizontal cells; *d, e, f, h,* bipolar cells; *i, l,* 'amacrine cells'; *m, n, o, p, r, s,* ganglion cells. S. Polyak, *The Retina,* University of Chicago Press, Chicago, 1941.

level is made up of *ganglion cells,* whose axons converge to form the visual nerve (levels 7-9). Although Fig. 43 does give some idea of the complexity of retinal structure, it is actually greatly oversimplified. Whereas rods are always associated with diffuse-type bipolar cells, cones may have synaptic association with either diffuse or individual bipolars, the latter relation being characteristic of the macular region (a yellow pigmented area near the center of the retina). Some bipolar cells gather from both rods and cones, an anatomical fact which decidedly complicates the functional picture. There is a considerable degree of reciprocal overlap—cells collecting activity from regions that overlap one another—even at this level. Reciprocal overlap is even more extensive among the ganglion cells, as can be seen in Fig. 43. Although the 'giant' ganglion cells (*m* and *n* in the figure) show extensive reciprocal overlap and receive impulses from both rod and cone processes, the 'midget' ganglion cells (*s* in figure) may receive impulses from single bipolars which in turn are specifically associated with single cones. Horizontal and amacrine cells are most numerous in the macular region.

The *fovea* is a small depression in the surface of the retina located at the terminus of the optic axis. Its area is about equal to the angle subtended by a penny held at arm's length. It is characterized by the presence of extremely close-packed cones and the absence of rods, hence the subtitle, 'rod-free area.' Measurement of retinal distances and areas of stimulation are made in terms of *visual angles,* expressed as degrees (°), minutes ('), and seconds (") of arc and are computed from the exact center of the fovea as a reference point (0°). In these terms the fovea is found to extend for only 1° in any direction from its center, although the entire sensitive surface of the retina covers about 207° (Polyak, 1941). It is common to speak of the area about the fovea as the *central retina* and the outlying areas as the *peripheral retina;* these are, however, not clearly defined concepts. If one imagines a line drawn vertically through the fovea, the half toward the nose is termed the *nasal retina* and the outer half is the *temporal retina.*

Some 18° from the fovea toward the nasal side of each eye is the *blind spot* (or optic disk), a region approximately 5° by 7° in extent, where axones from ganglion cells all over the retina converge to form the optic nerve and leave the eye toward the higher centers. There is no blind spot in the subjective visual field, however, even under monocular conditions. The visual field usually appears complete and continuous, even though exploration with one small point of light when the eye is fixated upon another will reveal an irregular area in which the test point is invisible—the location and area of the blind spot is plotted in this manner. The actual 'blind' spot is nothing more than a larger-than-usual gap between receptor units on the retina, and since the gap does not exist in the visual cortex, none is apparent in the subjective visual field. The fact that fairly intense stimulation of the blind spot yields both visual sensations and a vague idea of the shape of the stimulus is probably to be explained by the scattering of light by the ocular media, thus stimulating receptors on the rim of the blind spot (cf. Bartley, 1941). Some investigators believe, however, that the blind spot itself is sensitive in some manner (cf. Helson, 1929, 1934). If this is so, it must be due to the presence of a few scattered receptors rather than to direct stimulation of optic fibers since the latter would result in diffuse, nonlocalized visual experience.

The Rods and Cones

The human retina is duplex, having two histologically and functionally discrete receptor mechanisms. There are numerous lines of evidence for this dichotomy into rod and cone vision. (1) *Anatomical evidence.* Cones usually have a conical outer segment, whereas rods are longer and cylindrical; again cones usually have dendritic endings, whereas rods have knoblike endings. The chemical substance, *visual purple* (of which we shall have more to say later), is associated with rods but not with cones. The foveal area is rod-free, an anatomical fact neatly correlated with certain functional characteristics. Whereas, in the foveal area at least, cones display a one-to-one relation with their bipolar and ganglion cells, as many as 80 peripheral rods may converge their impulses upon the same ganglion cell. Cones are most dense in the fovea and their number per unit area decreases regularly toward the periphery. Rods, on the other hand, increase to a maximal density about 20° from the foveal center, decreasing regularly thenceforth out toward the periphery (Østerberg, 1935). The ratio of rods to cones becomes progressively larger from center to periphery. Estimates of the actual numbers of rods and cones provide interesting information, but it is hard come by histologically, particularly in the fovea (cf. Walls, 1934). There are about 125 million rods and about 6½ million cones in a single retina. Since only about 800,000 optic nerve fibers convey impulses to the higher centers, the great amount of convergence in the visual pathways is evident. These numbers also impress on one the minute size of these retinal elements.

(2) *Functional differences.* The identification of cones with human vision at daylight levels of illumination and of rods with human vision at nighttime levels is inescapable in view of the evidence. For daylight vision highest acuity (fineness of form discrimination) is within the small foveal area, as would be expected from the density of cones here and their individual connections with optic fibers. Daylight vision is also unique in being colored. Night vision is achromatic or colorless, and highest sensitivity to light is found about 20° from the foveal center (Sloan, 1947), corresponding to the density of rod elements in this region. Whereas cones are most sensitive to light in the yellow-green region of the spectrum, rods are most sensitive to light in the blue-green region. Correlated with this experimental evidence is the Purkinje Phenomenon: if a red and a blue paper of equated brightness in ordinary daylight are viewed at twilight, the blue paper appears brighter. This phenomenon also indicates that the transition from cone to rod vision is not abrupt but gradual, the difference in color being perceptible at both levels of illumination.

(3) *Comparative and pathological evidence.* Nocturnal vertebrates have mostly rods, but those that forage by day, mostly cones. In many fish, amphibians, and birds, possessing duplex retinas, some cells lengthen in the light and shorten in the dark, but others do the reverse—the former are classed as cones and the latter as rods. Occasionally we find individuals who are totally color blind; they are also photophobic, suffering pain under high illuminations, and usually completely blind in the foveal region (Ladd-Franklin, 1929). There are also some who are 'night blind'—although they function adequately with daylight illumination, they are unable to adapt to dim light. None of these individuals, whether day or night blind, show the Purkinje effect.

Although the duplexity law certainly holds for human vision, it cannot be generalized to other species. For one thing, there is sufficient variation among both rods and cones to lead some recent investigators to regard them as variants of a single photoreceptor (cf. Bartley, 1941, p. 82). Diurnal birds, for example, have rods with dendritic rather than knoblike endings. Actually, foveal cones in the human retina, being long rodlike cells, are considered cones largely on a functional basis. For another thing, animals that have pure rod or pure cone vision, on an anatomical basis, do not necessarily have corresponding visual characteristics. The 'rod' retina of the gecko (a nocturnal reptile) and the 'cone' retina of the turtle display essentially equivalent ranges of brightness sensitivity (Crozier and Wolf, 1938). Electrophysiological responses considered typical of cone elements may be obtained from animals with pure rod retinas (Adrian, 1946).

There is accumulating indirect evidence that human rods (as well as cones) must be subdivided into at least two types. Gordon (1947) found *form* acuity at rod levels of illumination to be finest about 7° from the fovea rather than at 20° coincident with the region of maximal rod density. Similarly, Chapanis (1945) summarizes evidence showing that the retinal locus of the smallest absolute thresholds for sheer awareness of light at night does not correspond to the locus of clearest recognition for forms in night observing. Since degree of convergence of rod cells upon optic nerve ganglia (and hence reduced acuity) increases regularly out to the periphery (cf. Østerberg, 1935), this discrepancy cannot be explained in terms of differential discreteness of receptor hookups. It therefore suggests the existence of a separate receptor mechanism—a 'conelike' rod (or a 'rodlike' white cone) having maximal density between 7° and 10° from the fovea and a more nearly one-to-one neural hookup (cf. Granit, 1947).

PSYCHOPHYSICAL RESEARCH METHODS

A recent Committee on Colorimetry (1944) defined *light* as 'the aspects of radiant energy of which a human observer is aware through the visual sensations which arise from the stimulation of the retina of the eye' (p. 245). Light is thus not identified with either radiant energy or with sensations, but is rather a relational concept. Since most experimentation in vision requires precise specification of the stimulus, our main interest here will lie with the measurement of light, in regard to both its luminous and chromatic aspects. In keeping with the definitions adopted by this committee, we shall use the term *luminance* to refer to the intensity or energy of light and the term *brightness* to refer to the intensive aspects of visual awareness. The *chromaticity* of light refers to its physical composition, specified in terms of its *dominant wave length* and *purity,* these corresponding to the psychological dimensions of hue and saturation.

Light waves are infinitesimally small, being measured in millimicrons ($m\mu$)—one micron equals a millionth of a meter, and a millimicron is one-thousandth of this minute magnitude. The human visual apparatus reacts differentially to wave lengths between 400 $m\mu$ (blue-violet) and 700 $m\mu$ (deep red). This visible spectrum can be observed through any glass prism or naturally in the rainbow. Of course, there is no 'color' in the light itself; color is experience that depends on the functioning of the sensory nervous system.

Lighting engineers are concerned with the *illumination* of various surfaces. How much illumination will be cast by a 100-watt bulb on a table in a library cubicle? How many watts will be required to illuminate a runway at the airport? *The illumination of a uniformly lighted surface is the density of light per unit surface area, and it varies inversely with the square of the distance from a point source.* It may be expressed in a number of different units: a *foot-candle* is the illumination produced on a perfectly spherical surface one foot distant from a one candle-power point source. Researchers in the psychology of vision are not so much concerned with illumination per se as with the luminosity of either emitted or reflected (as from a paper disk) light. *Luminance is the candle power* (intensity) *per unit surface area of an emitter or reflector of light.* The distance of the source from the eye is immaterial: although the total energy entering the eye decreases with distance from the object, so equally does the area of the retinal image of the object, both as inverse squares of the distance—luminance of the source thus remains constant.

Luminance of a surface depends not only upon its illumination but also upon its *reflectance*. Reflectance of a surface, in turn, depends upon a number of factors, chiefly *diffusion* of light at the surface and selective *absorption* of various wave lengths. A perfectly diffusing surface would be one whose microstructure reflects light waves equally in all directions; highly polished steel or mirror glass, on the other hand, shows minimal diffusion, reflecting light waves in the same direction. Certain materials we call 'white' reflect all wave lengths of light uniformly, absorbing none; other materials we call 'black' absorb nearly all wave lengths; and those materials we call 'blue,' 'red,' and so on absorb different wave lengths selectively according to their composition.

The difference between illumination and luminosity can perhaps best be understood in an example: imagine a white piece of paper on a dark walnut table in a uniformly lighted room. Both white paper and dark table top are equally illuminated (i.e. the density of light received per unit area is the same for both), but the white paper is much more luminous than the table top because its reflectance is higher. The difference in reflectance here is due mainly to the difference in absorptive capacity of the two materials.

Photometry

The most common method of determining the intensity of light employs the human organism as a measuring instrument. Two brightnesses are compared and equated, one (V) being the light to be measured and the other (S) being a calibrated lamp of standard output. The essential principle of a typical *photometer* is shown diagrammatically in Fig. 44. Two finely ground prisms are placed in contact as shown. Light from one source (V) enters one prism and is deflected everywhere except at the point of contact, where it passes through and forms the inner circle of light in the target viewed by the observer. Light from the standard source (S) enters the other prism and is reflected to form the outer circle of light, except at the places of contact where it continues through the other prism. The intensity of the standard can be varied through known magnitudes by varying the distance between the standard source light and the prism, making use of the inverse square law.

In practice, the photometer is directed at a test surface, and the observer repeatedly records the setting of the standard light at which the border between inner and outer areas disappears, i.e. where the subjective brightness is equated. The use of a photometer is thus nothing other than the psychophysical method of limits under conditions designed to set the observer the simplest possible judgmental task. As might be expected, the accuracy of photometric measurement depends upon the difference threshold of the human observer. It is often necessary in experimental work to measure the luminosities of colored light sources. This is called *heterochromatic photometry,* and it is a much more difficult process. The observer has to make a judgment of equal brightness while ignoring the sharp difference in hue.

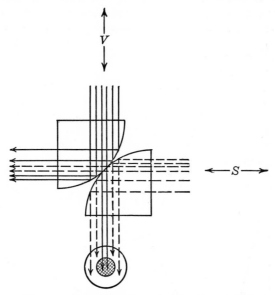

FIGURE 44. Diagram illustrating the principle of a typical photometer.

Colorimetry

Color may be specified in terms of (1) its appropriate photometric quality (luminosity), (2) its dominant wave length, and (3) its purity (admixture of other wave lengths). White light is a color, but one having zero purity and an indeterminate dominant wave length. In this sense, photometry is included within the general science of colorimetry. Measurements of color are based upon adjusting both chromatic and photometric magnitudes of a known standard light until all visibly apparent differences between it and an unknown test light are eliminated. There are many instruments, *colorimeters,* designed to simplify and quantify this process. Through an optical system three spectrally homogeneous lights, sufficiently far apart in the spectrum (usually from red, green, and blue regions) are combined into a single standard light spot. By varying the *relative* luminous intensities of these three lights (hue and saturation) and the *total* luminous intensity of all three combined (brightness), the characteristics of a test-light spot can be matched. Once a match has been made, the ratios of the intensities of the three fixed wave lengths—*trichromatic coefficients*—provide a standardized language for specifying the character of the test light.

The chroma and purity of a test light are not obtained directly in the process of matching but must be computed from a tri-stimulus graph, as shown in Fig. 45. Point C represents that mixture of red, green, and blue (here, 700 mμ, 525 mμ, and 450 mμ, respectively) that yields a satisfactory match for ordinary daylight. This point does not necessarily represent an equal (.33, .33, .33) mixture since it depends upon the exact chromatic values of the three primaries used. Any test patch (*x*) will fall at some point within the parameters of the color-space. Suppose we pass ordinary daylight through a green filter before it enters the system as the test patch: since some of the energy in the red and blue regions is absorbed by this filter, smaller amounts of these components are needed to match the test sample and the match for this test light might fall at *x* in Fig. 45. By

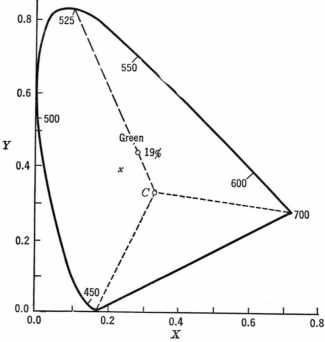

FIGURE 45. Chromaticity diagram, illustrating graphic determination of dominant wave length and purity. After Committee on Colorimetry, *Journal of the Optical Society of America*, 1944, 34:263.

drawing a straight line from *C* through *x*, the place where it intersects the spectrum locus represents its dominant wave length, and the proportion of the distance between *C* and the spectrum locus at which *x* falls indicates the colorimetric purity of the test color. In the present example the test color is 'green, 525 mµ, 19 per cent purity.'

One of the important uses of the colorimeter is to determine precisely what proportions of three arbitrary primaries are required to match various points along the spectrum. With an unmixed spectral light of some given wave length and intensity presented in one half of a bipartite field, the observer adjusts the proportions of three primaries which are fused on the other half of this field until a match is made. When this is done throughout the spectrum, data like that shown in Fig. 46 are obtained. As primaries Wright (1928-9) used *R* 650 mµ, *G* 530 mµ, and *B* 460 mµ. A satisfactory match for spectral yellow (585 mµ) is made with approximately equal parts of *R* and *G,* for example; the violet hues of the spectrum require a slight admixture of R with a great deal of B. At the three points in the spectrum representing the primaries, of course, 100 per cent of each particular primary, unmixed with other wave lengths, matches the test patch.

What is the significance of the negative values at nearly all points along the spectrum? Operationally the observer finds he can match any spectral light in *hue* by using only *two* of the three primaries, but the *saturation* of his match is nearly always too low. As we shall see later in connection with color theories, each primary is assumed to excite all color receptors, but in varying degree. In the present instance the two primaries used to match the hue of the test patch also excite a third quality so much that it de-

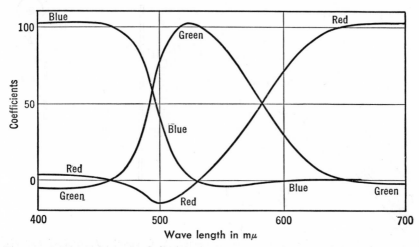

FIGURE 46. Direct data of color mixture, based on 10 observers. The three curves give the proportions of each of the three primaries required to match each region of the spectrum. Hecht, *Journal of the Optical Society of America*, 1930, **20**:239. After data of Wright, 1928-9.

saturates the experience. The only way a match can be made is to *reduce the saturation of the spectral test patch itself by adding some of the third primary to it*. An example will make this clear: approximately 60 per cent G 530 and 40 per cent B 460 provide a satisfactory match in hue for spectral 500 mμ, but this mixture is clearly paler than the spectral patch. We therefore add some R 650 *to the spectral patch,* reducing its saturation, and obtain a match. The amount of R 650 added to the spectral patch is indicated by the negative value for R at this point. Since adding light to the spectral patch in this manner increases its intensity, the intensities of the two hue-producing components must be increased equivalently—this explains why components rise above 100 per cent at some points. In this fashion the three components always sum to 1.00. But what does this signify? It means that the visual spectrum cannot be matched by the simple *addition* of three primaries—some inhibitory processes seem to be operative—and, as we shall see, most color theories do not take this into account.

Spectral Systems as Research Instruments in Visual Psychophysics

Human visual experience varies within three dimensions: brightness, hue, and saturation. An adequate research tool must make it possible to vary the physical correlates of these dimensions—luminance, wave length, and purity—by specifiable amounts. Many research instruments are designed to accomplish this end, but they vary greatly in design and in the generality of purposes they satisfy. Recent developments in the design of such systems are described by W. D. Wright (1947) and by Cohen (1953). The system illustrated in Fig. 47, designed by Chapanis (1944), serves admirably to clarify the basic apparatus and manipulations. It is a *double monochrometer,* with certain accessory equipment. White light from the *source* (L_1) is projected upon a flint-glass *prism* by means of a lens. This prism is the

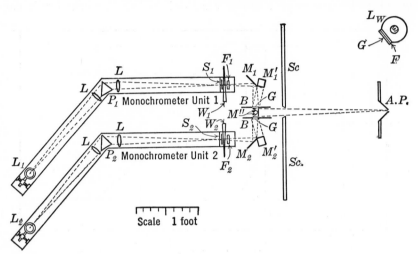

FIGURE 47. Diagram of a double monochrometer. A. Chapanis, *Journal of Experimental Psychology,* 1944, 34:26.

core of the spectral system; it breaks white light up into its component wave lengths, a phenomenon first demonstrated by Sir Isaac Newton and now a cornerstone of modern physics. The spectrum is focused upon a *slit* (S_1) which passes only a narrow band of wave lengths. Narrowing the spectral beam results in a loss in intensity, which sets practical limits on how fine a spectral band can be selected out in the system. Selection among wave lengths may be accomplished by moving the selector slit, turning the prism, or moving the source light in relation to a stationary prism, the latter method being used in the present instance. These adjustments must be calibrated against a millimicron scale. The monochromatic light now passes through a series of *neutral tint filters* which make it possible to vary the luminous intensity of the light without affecting its wave-length composition. By moving in the *wedge filter* (W_1) luminosity can be changed by small degrees (i.e. as a function of the amount of gelatinous material through which the beam must pass). The monochromatic light is reflected 90° from a mirror (M_1) through a uniformly *diffusing glass* (G) and finally onto half of a *wedge mirror* (M''), which is seen by the subject as the test patch. The second spectral system illuminates the other half of this wedge mirror. Two accessory systems eventuate in M'_1 and M'_2 and flood the two diffusing glasses with uniform white light; by varying the proportions of this white light and the monochromatic light contributing to the illumination of each half of the mirror wedge, the *purity* of the light can be varied. The subject looks through an *artificial pupil* (*A.P.*) at a *screen* (*Sc*), painted with a dull white paint of high reflectance, the test patch appearing as a circular spot divided by a thin vertical line. The screen can be illuminated or darkened, before or during observations, depending upon the conditions desired. The uses of such a system in exploring various psycho-physical relations may now be described.

(1) *Absolute brightness thresholds as a function of wave length.* By using only a single monochromer and restricting the test patch to a size that falls well within the fovea, we may determine the minimum luminosity

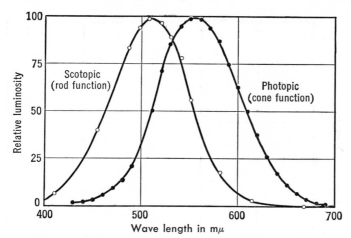

FIGURE 48. Relative luminosity curves for human rod and cone vision. Chapanis, *Human Factors in Undersea Warfare,* National Research Council, Washington, 1949, p. 10. After photopic data of Gibson and Tyndall and scotopic data of Hecht and Williams.

that is just visible in pure cone vision for various settings of the wave-length scale. By having a dark-adapted subject fixate his eye on a point so that the test patch falls about 20° from the fovea, and using intensities well below cone-sensitivity levels, similar data can be obtained for the rods. Known as *relative luminosity functions,* the curves in Fig. 48 indicate the relative amounts of energy required to make various portions of the spectrum appear equally bright. The points here are *reciprocals* of threshold values, i.e. the minimum threshold is taken as 1.0 and all other values represent increasing amounts of energy required to be just visible, .0 being infinite intensity. This method makes it possible to place both rod and cone functions on the same graph despite the gross differences between them in absolute sensitivity. As we have already seen, rods are most sensitive to light in the blue-green region (approx. 510 mμ) and cones to light in the yellow-green region (approx. 554 mμ).

(2) *Wave-length discrimination.* How great a change in the wave length of light is necessary for a human observer to notice a change in hue? Does the size of this difference threshold vary with the portion of the spectrum being studied? In order to answer these questions, one half of the mirror wedge may be illuminated with monochromatic light of a selected wave length (the standard stimulus), while the other system, illuminating the

other half of the mirror wedge, is varied in wave-length setting (the variable stimulus) from an identical setting to a point where the subject reports a just noticeable difference between the two halves of the test patch. It is necessary, of course, that brightness be equated for both sides of the test patch and that saturation be maximal. Data obtained by Steindler (1906) are shown in Fig. 49. Differential sensitivity varies through the spectrum, four regions of maximal sensitivity being shown, centering on 440 (blue-violet), 485 (blue), 575 (yellow), and 640 (red) mμ. Such a complex function presumably reflects the simultaneous action of a number of differently constituted cone mechanisms—*how* many will be considered later.

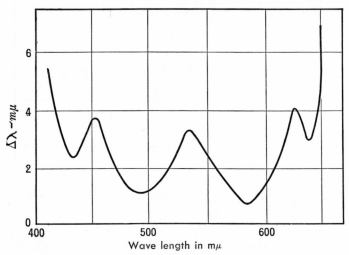

FIGURE 49. Wave length discrimination. Minimum increment in mμ necessary for a just discernible difference in hue for various regions of the spectrum. (Hecht, using data of Steindler, 1906.) Murchison, *Handbook of Experimental Psychology,* Clark University Press, Worcester, Mass., 1934, p. 802.

More recent studies (Jones, 1917; Laurens and Hamilton, 1923) have revealed the same general function, although the precise relations differ somewhat from individual to individual even under identical conditions (Hecht, 1934).

(3) *Absolute thresholds for saturation.* The amount of any pure spectral wave length that must be mixed with white light to produce a just perceptible hue experience represents the absolute threshold for saturation in that portion of the spectrum. The double monochrometer described in Fig. 47 is ideally suited for such measurements—indeed, it was designed for that purpose (Chapanis, 1944). With both halves equated in amount of white light from the accessory systems, light of a given wave length (i.e. blue, 480 mμ) is added gradually to one side of the mirror wedge until the subject just notices a difference. In practice, additional white light must be added to the other side of the wedge in order to maintain an equation in brightness; otherwise one would not know the basis for discrimination. The curves for two observers shown in Fig. 50 indicate that whereas only .001% blue light will perceptibly saturate white and only .005% red is necessary, approximately .05% yellow light is required. Put in another way, if physical

colorimetric purity were equal throughout the spectrum, the yellow region would *appear* desaturated relative to the red and blue regions. Saturation and brightness, it may be noted, are roughly inverse as functions of wave length—the portion of the spectrum that seems brightest is the least well saturated.

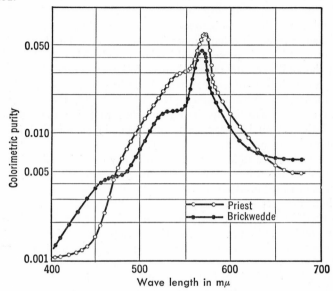

FIGURE 50. Saturation threshold for two observers. Minimum proportion of homogeneous spectral light which must be added to heterogeneous white light in order to give it just perceptible hue (Hecht, using data of Priest and Brickwedde, 1926). Murchison, *Handbook of Experimental Psychology*, Clark University Press, Worcester, Mass., 1934, p. 801.

The Flicker-Fusion Method

The eye may be stimulated intermittently by either rotating a black-and-white sectored disk or interrupting a source of light with an episcotister, the latter providing for more accurate measurement of the stimulus. At very low rates a simple alternation of light and dark phases is perceived, the experience changing to coarse and then to fine flicker as the rate is increased and finally to a uniform brightness experience at a certain critical rate (critical fusion frequency or *CFF*). The brightness of the fused field corresponds to the original illumination of the lighted sector multiplied by the fraction of time it is operative. In other words, with a light-dark ratio of one to one, the fused field will appear one-half as bright as the illuminated sector; with a ratio of two to one the fused field will be two-thirds as bright as the illuminated sector. This relation is known as the Talbot-Plateau Law, having been described independently and almost simultaneously by these two men more than a century ago. As long as flicker persists, it is apparent that the sensory system is capable of resolving (or discriminating) stimulation in time.

The subjective rate of flicker does not, however, necessarily bear a one-to-one relation to the objective rate of alternation. Bartley (1938) has shown that the rate of 'marginal flicker' (i.e. that perceived just before fusion) is roughly constant while the *CFF* varies from a minimum of 4 per second to 40 per second. Further evidence on the complex nature of the flicker phenomenon comes from a recent series of experiments by Knox (1945 *a, b, c, d*). *CFF* could be raised or lowered considerably when originally naïve subjects practiced trying to perceive either the flicker or fusion. Although simultaneous *auditory* flicker would not produce visual flicker in a fused field, it was found to increase the pronouncedness of visual flicker if it was already present. Perhaps most interesting was the observation that when auditory flicker is present, subjective visual flicker tends to keep in step with the auditory rate rather than to follow the rate of visual stimulation. At a certain rate of presentation the light sector appears subjectively brighter than when it is uninterrupted. Significantly, the rate at which brightness enhancement is maximum matches that for the stable alpha rhythm of the occipital cortex (8-10 per second) as revealed in electroencephalographic records (Bartley, 1938).

All these facts serve to indicate the complexity of flicker phenomena, but they do not deny the primary role of the visual receptors in setting limits on discrimination. Later processes in the visual pathways cannot create a differential where none exists in receptor action. This primacy of the retinal events is established by the fact that both retinal action potentials in the cat (Creed and Granit, 1933) and optic nerve potentials in the excised eye of the conger eel (Adrian and Matthews, 1928) show fusion at approximately the same flash rates as reported fusion occurs for human observers; they also display nearly identical functions of intensity and area of stimulation. Although central factors can influence *CFF* and certainly are involved in subjective flicker, brightness enhancement, and the like, maximum possible *CFF* reflects chiefly the resolving power of the retina itself.

Keeping in mind that *CFF* is an index of the discriminatory power of the visual system, its major determinants may be listed. (1) *CFF increases with the intensity of the light phase.* This relation will be studied in some detail at a later point in this chapter. (2) *CFF is higher for cones than for rods.* This reflects the greater differential sensitivity of the photopic mechanism. (3) *CFF, intensity, and the light-dark ratio are interrelated.* With low intensities a ratio of one to one yields maximum *CFF;* with higher intensities maximum *CFF* is obtained with progressively smaller light sectors (Bartley, 1941), indicating that the after-effects of intense stimulation are more prolonged. Other facts about *CFF* will be added in appropriate contexts.

NEUROPHYSIOLOGICAL RESEARCH METHODS

In most highly developed sensory organs at least two mechanisms can be distinguished: a primary one designed to translate the appropriate physical energies into a form that excites sensory neurons and a secondary mechanism that sets up activity in the attached nerve. The primary mechanism in vision is photochemical; energy in the incident light initiates reactions in certain chemical substances in the receptor cells and starts the sequence of events that results in sensation. The secondary mechanism is probably electrical in nature. Records of electrical activity can be taken at several points along the visual pathways, each locus of investigation yielding its own characteristic picture and demanding its own specialized techniques. The general nature of electrical recording methods has already been discussed.

Photochemistry of the Retina

Vision is a chemical sense. This statement is as unquestionably valid for rod vision as any scientific hypothesis can be and is probably valid for cone vision as well. *Rhodopsin* (visual purple) has been identified as the photosensitive substance utilized in rod vision. As early as 1876 Kühne had discovered that the dark red color of the retina is bleached by light and regenerated in darkness. Boll reported the same phenomenon for the retina

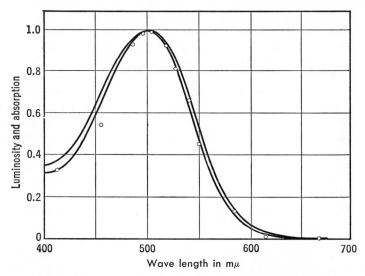

FIGURE 51. Comparison of scotopic luminosity function with absorption spectrum for rhodopsin. For ease of comparison, both functions have been made equal to 1.0 at maxima, 500 mμ. Hecht, *The American Scientist,* 1944, 32:171.

of the frog, and it was soon found to be associated with the rod mechanism in the retinas of many species. By using excised retinas of dark-adapted eyes, rhodopsin can be extracted into aqueous solution, purified, and its absorption spectrum determined, i.e. the sensitivity of this substance to radiation of different wave lengths measured. When the relative sensitivity of human rods to various wave lengths of light is plotted in conjunction with the absorption spectrum for rhodopsin (curves in Fig. 51), a remarkable agreement is shown. Both distributions have precisely the same maximum, near 500 mμ, and approximately the same course as functions of wave length. And this is only a small part of the impressive evidence for dependence of rod vision upon the photosynthesis of visual purple.

The *sequence of chemical events* underlying the decomposition and regeneration of visual purple is not completely understood. Radiant energy initiates the sequence, changing the chemical constitution of the rhodopsin it strikes. This change follows Einstein's Law of Photochemical Equivalence, namely, that each quantum of energy is absorbed by a single molecule of rhodopsin which is then changed chemically (cf. Hecht, 1944). But what are the end products of this decomposition of rhodopsin? It has been known for some time that the retina appears yellow after a brief period of illumination, and this 'visual yellow' has been identified (Wald, 1935) as a yellow carotinoid, *retinene*. This substance is the first end product of the decomposition of visual purple that is stable enough to be easily observed, but it has low photosensitivity and is itself probably not involved in initiating light sensations. As part of an extensive series of researches on retinal chemistry, Lythgoe (1937) isolated 'transient orange' as an intermediary step in the formation of retinene, and transient orange does have photosensitivity with a maximum at about 460 mμ. Under continued or intense stimulation, visual yellow breaks down into what is known as visual white, another insensitive substance (cf. Wald, 1950).

Persistent vision demands that the primary photosensitive substance, visual purple, be regenerated—in fact, that a balance be established between the rate of decomposition and the rate of regeneration. What are the *mechanisms of regeneration?* At least three have been demonstrated. (1) An extremely rapid regeneration of rhodopsin from its own end product, transient orange. (2) A somewhat slower, but still very rapid, synthesis from retinene. (3) A gradual regeneration from visual white. The chemical decomposition and regeneration of rhodopsin is a pseudoreversible reaction—certain additional substances are necessary to maintain it. One of these substances is undoubtedly Vitamin A, although the actual part it plays is still somewhat obscure (Granit, 1947). It is known that oxygen is another substance involved in regeneration of visual purple. The regeneration of visual purple from its own end products must require the addition of energy to the system from some external source, perhaps by the absorption of light itself (Chase, 1937) or a chemical process utilizing oxygen (Lythgoe, 1940).

The firm establishment of chemical mediation for rod vision makes it overwhelmingly probable that cone or color vision is subserved by a similar mechanism, but here the technical difficulties are much greater. Cones do not display any visible pigmentation. Furthermore, since cone thresholds are some thousand times larger than rod thresholds, one would expect low concentrations of photosensitive substances and hence more difficulty in demonstrating their presence. The evidence is confused (see the review by Bliss, 1946). The most probable photosensitive substance in cone vision is *iodopsin*. In 1937 Wald reported extraction of this substance from the retina of the chick, which was found to be sensitive to red, bleaching to a yellow end product. Significantly, its absorption spectrum bore a rough resemblance to the luminosity curve for the light-adapted chicken. Bliss (1946) found it impossible to obtain pure solutions of iodopsin from the chick retina for analysis because solutions were contaminated with rhodopsin. With a species of diurnal lizard, whose eye comes closer to the ideal of a pure cone retina than the chicken's, he could demonstrate no photosensitive pigments. When the absorption spectrum for iodopsin is deduced by correction for impurities, however, a fairly good match with the luminosity curve for human cone vision is found.

Just before his untimely death, Lythgoe (1940) suggested another possible mechanism for the chemical mediation of cone vision. He had found that the chemical properties of the kind of visual purple regenerated directly from transient orange were slightly different from those of the parent substance. For one thing, the absorption curve was modified. It seemed possible that bright light decomposes *primary* visual purple into transient orange from which *secondary* visual purple is immediately formed, this secondary substance being utilized by the cones. In this connection it may be noted that Vitamin A deficiency, which lowers rod sensitivity, has also been shown to lower cone sensitivity (Hecht and Mandelbaum, 1938). Furthermore, certain fish whose rod mechanism utilizes a slightly different type of visual purple from that in humans (having its maximum absorption in a somewhat longer wave-length region) *also* have an equivalently displaced cone sensitivity (cf. Granit, 1947).

The Electroretinogram (ERG)

When one electrode is placed on the cornea and the other at the back of the excised eye, close to the exit of the nerve, a flash of light will produce

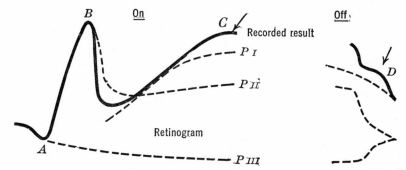

FIGURE 52. *On* and *off* responses in the *ERG*. Components isolated by Granit (*P*I, *P*II, *P*III) also shown. Bartley, *Psychological Review*, 1939, **46**: 347.

a succession of potential changes like those shown by the solid line in Fig. 52. There is first a slight negative deflection (*a*-wave), followed by a large positive deflection (*b*-wave), whose falling course meets a third and more gradual positive sweep (*c*-wave). When the illumination is terminated abruptly, the potential falls back to the base line, but is accompanied by a hump (*d*-wave). Although it is true that such a complex wave form as this might be produced in a single nervous source, the evidence indicates that several component activities are involved. For one thing, various portions of the wave are independently variable. Granit (1933), by having a decerebrate cat inhale ether, was able to demonstrate that the three major components of the retinogram are eliminated in a regular order. The three components are indicated in Fig. 52 as *P*I, *P*II, and *P*III, the order in which they are removed by ether treatment.

Although it is too early to identify the source of these three components with complete assurance, there are significant implications in the available evidence. [For a detailed presentation the reader may consult Granit's recent book, *Sensory Mechanisms of the Retina* (1947).] *P*I (*C-wave*). The *C*-wave is absent in the pure cone retinas of certain reptiles. In the duplex retina of the frog it may be eliminated by using extreme red light stimulation. These facts point to an identification of *P*I with *rod* function. *P*II (*B-wave*). The *B*-wave varies with the intensity of stimulation, the positive deflection increasing with increased intensity. Monochromatic stimulation both at 430 mμ (violet) and at 630 mμ (red) affects the *B*-wave, the former showing a long latent period, the latter a short latent period. These facts suggest that *both rod and cone* functions may be reflected in the P_{II} component. P_{III} (*A-wave*). The *A*-wave is by all odds the most puzzling component in the retinogram. For one thing, it is associated with the upswing in the *D*-wave which constitutes the 'off-effect' (an actual increase in frequency of impulses when stimulation is abruptly removed). Granit relates P_{III} to inhibitory processes in the retina, the release from this inhibition at the end of stimulation being largely responsible for the off-effect. Both the magnitude of the *A*-wave and the size of the off-effect increase with either the intensity or duration of stimulation. The *A*-wave is more prominent in pure cone retinas and in duplex retinas that are first light adapted. Further suggestion of an association between the *A*-wave and *cone* function is the fact that the *A*-wave is of very small size at low intensities.

The *ERG* is spatially gross, reflecting events taking place over the retina as a whole. It is a method for tracing the *temporal* course of stimulation, but even here there is considerable confusion as to interpretation. P_{III} is certainly the first event in time and, although the dashed curve in Fig. 52 does not show it, P_I probably arises prior to P_{II}. It is possible that P_{II} depends upon neural processes intermediate between receptors and ganglion cells—the ganglion cells themselves are ruled out since direct stimulation of their axons (and hence depolarization) does not eliminate P_{II}. Finally, certain relations between *ERG* and *CFF* measurements should be mentioned: fluctuations in P_{III}, and in the off-effect to which it is related, are rapid enough to subserve fine flicker at high flash rates; measurable fluctuations in P_{II}, on the other hand, disappear at flash rates above 4 or 5 per second (Bartley, 1941). This makes it appear that fine flicker is attributable to the burst of impulses associated with the off-effect, whereas the steady underlying illumination is attributable to fused P_{II}. The fact that *CFF*, P_{III}, and the off-effect are all known to diminish as intensity is lowered further substantiates this view.

Optic Nerve Discharge

To pick up electrical impulses in the optic nerve it is necessary to lay bare a portion of the nerve trunk and attach two electrodes along its course, changes in potential being recorded as impulses pass along the fiber bundle. In an early study Adrian and Matthews (1927) utilized the excised eye and attendant optic nerve of the eel, but loss of blood supply in warm-blooded animals injures the eye and prevents the use of this method. Recently Bartley and Bishop (1940) have gotten at the optic nerve of the rabbit *in situ* by removing a large portion of the skull and superficial gray matter of the anesthetized animal, revealing the optic chiasma. One electrode is inserted into the optic nerve where it emerges into the brain case and the other into the chiasma itself. Potential changes are amplified and led into a cathode-ray oscillograph whose surface is photographed to provide a permanent record.

When normal stimulation via the retina is compared with direct stimulation of the nerve by electrical shock, the former is found to set up a prolonged series of impulses, whereas the latter usually results in a single volley. This indicates that the staggering of activity in the optic nerve is established in the retina, as would be anticipated from an analysis of the electroretinogram. Adrian and Matthews (1927) were able to show that the frequency of impulses in the optic nerve, under normal stimulating conditions, varies directly with both the intensity and the area of the light, paralleling variation in the *B*-wave (*P*II) of the *ERG*. Sample records of the activity of the optic nerve obtained by Bartley and Bishop (1940) with the duplex retina of the rabbit are shown in Fig. 53. Certain characteristics of the optic nerve discharge are shown here: (a) If the stimulation is long

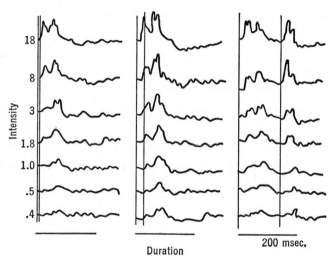

FIGURE 53. Optic nerve discharge records. Each column represents a sample for which the *duration* of the light flash was constant (left, 8 msec., center, 30 msec., right, 135 msec., as shown by vertical lines). Bartley, *Vision: A Study of Its Basis,* D. Van Nostrand Co., Inc., New York, 1941, p. 286. After Bartley and Bishop, 1940.

enough (e.g. in 135 msec. records), the optic nerve displays both an 'on-effect' and an 'off-effect,' that is, the frequency of impulses increases immediately after onset of the stimulus and also immediately following its removal. When too short a flash is used, the two effects merge. (b) The on-response is usually duplex, the first large wave having a short latency and the second wave a longer one. (c) As intensity of stimulation is reduced, the first wave of the on-response is sharply reduced but the second, slower wave is relatively unaffected; lowering intensity also reduces the off-response.

We know that the optic nerve bundle carries messages originating in both rod and cone receptors (at least here, in the case of the rabbit), and one might expect differences on this basis. The fact that the first component of the on-response has a short latency, shows parallel variation with the off-response, and is diminished by lowering the intensity immediately suggests that cone-instigated activity is being recorded. The fact that the second, slower wave is relatively unaffected by intensity variations might suggest rod functioning. But investigators using this technique have been vary careful not to make this identification (cf. Bartley, 1941). For one thing, although animals of different species and with different types of retinas do show distinctive optic discharge patterns, these patterns are not clearly correlated with rod and cone divisions (cf. Adrian, 1946). The guinea pig, for example, which has a pure rod retina, displays the same dual wave form in its on-response that is typical of the duplex retina of the cat or pigeon.

Recording from Isolated Fibers of the Optic Nerve

The patterns of activity obtained from the optic nerve bundle are as indiscriminate spatially as the electroretinogram. Recently techniques have been devised for isolating individual visual fibers. The eye of Limulus, the horseshoe crab, is ideal for this purpose since its optic nerve fibers are the

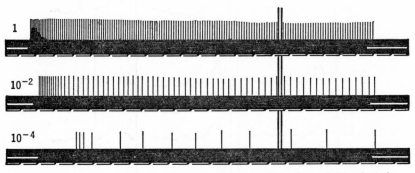

FIGURE 54. Discharge of impulses in an optic nerve fiber (eye of Limulus) in response to illumination of the eye at three different intensities (relative values given at left). Eye partially light adapted. Signal of exposure to light blackens out white line above time marker. Time marked in ⅕ sec. Hartline, *Harvey Lectures,* The Harvey Society, The Academic Press, Inc., New York, 1941, p. 41.

axones of the visual receptors themselves, i.e. there are no mediating bipolar and ganglion cells. Hartline and Graham (1932), using this organism, were able to demonstrate how the simple receptor mechanism responds to stimulation. Figure 54 describes some of their results. As the intensity of stimulation is increased, the frequency of impulses in the fiber increases and latency decreases. A typical on-effect appears as a rapid burst of impulses at the onset of stimulation, being followed by a process of equilibration. Any change in illumination of sufficient magnitude produces another brief burst of impulses before the nerve settles down to a new constant rate of response. The on-effect is probably reflected in human experience by the momentarily enhanced brilliance that accompanies the turning on of a light or the flickering brightness effect produced by moving the eyes over a field of alternating black and white lines, thus bringing fresh receptors into play. Hartline (1941) makes the point that all sensory endings studied by these methods show the same relations to intensity of stimulation.

The task of isolating individual fibers in the optic nerve of the vertebrate is much more difficult. Hartline (1938) accomplished it by means of his exquisite microdissection technique. Following removal of the eye of a cold-blooded vertebrate and exposure of the retina, small bundles of optic fibers, which form a thin layer on the surface of the retina, are split and dissected under a microscope until only a single fiber remains active. This is placed on electrodes and its activity is recorded while a small spot of light is used to explore the retinal surface to determine the region the fiber serves. High variability in the responses of different individual fibers (of the frog) was found: about 20% of the fibers tested showed the maintained type of response to continued illumination characteristic of the receptor cells of Limulus, these being termed 'on' type fibers; about 50% responded to both the onset and termination of stimulation, 'on-off' type fibers; and about 30% fired only to the removal of illumination, 'off' type fibers. These fiber types are not segregated spatially in the frog's retina.

Granit and his co-workers (cf. 1947) have developed a method for recording impulses from optic fibers *in situ,* which makes it possible to study warm-blooded as well as cold-blooded animals. A micro-electrode is inserted into the opened eye of an anesthetized animal after the cornea and other superficial structures have been removed, and impulses are recorded from fibers somewhere between the ganglion cells and the optic disk. Not all retinas yielded the results cited above for the frog. Mammalian retinas were found to be constituted mainly of only two types of fibers, those responding to *continuous* illumination ('on' type) and those responding to *changes* in illumination ('on-off' type). The guinea pig, with its pure rod retina, has a high proportion of 'on' type fibers; the cat, with a large proportion of cones, has many 'on-off' fibers as well. Recalling that the P_{III} component of the *ERG* is associated with the off-effect and cone functioning, whereas the P_I component is associated with rod functioning, this evidence on response characteristics of individual fibers in the optic nerve suggests that firing to both the onset and cessation of light is characteristic of the cone mechanism, but firing continuously to persistent illumination is characteristic of the rod mechanism. This is by no means demonstrated conclusively.

The Cortical Response

Cortical potentials may be recorded from the scalp of the intact organism. This is known as electroencephalography and is extensively used with human subjects. Records may also be taken from needle electrodes inserted into the gray matter, using animal subjects, of course. Stimulation may be applied directly to the optic nerve via electric shock or mediately via illumination of the retina. Although shock stimulation is spatially indiscriminate (selection of fibers being solely on the basis of their thresholds), illumination of the retina includes all of the temporal complexities of its functioning.

The visual cortex is not 'silent' when unstimulated. Part of its spontaneous activity is rhythmic in nature, both large, slow *alpha* waves (8-12 per second in man) and smaller, more rapid *beta* waves (30-50 per second) being discernible. Since any stimulation effects are imposed upon this spontaneous activity, the cortical response is found to vary markedly even when the characteristics of the stimulus are held constant. This severely complicates the investigator's task. When strychnine is applied directly to the surface of the cortex or injected intravenously, however, spontaneous activity is inhibited and the effects of stimulation are enhanced (Bartley, 1933). The train of waves matching the *alpha* rhythm, which normally follows the initial spike because of stimulation, is inhibited, and the initial spike itself becomes as much as ten times its former size. This serves as evidence that under normal conditions incoming stimulation to the visual cortex is enmeshed in and graded by its on-going activity. Using the peak of the first cortical spike as a reference point, Bartley (1934, 1935) has been able to show that the *latency* of the cortical response decreases with intensity of illumination, duration of the light flash, and the area of stimulation. Similar relations have been found for the optic nerve discharge, as would necessarily be the case.

On both anatomical and experimental grounds two groups of fibers can be distinguished on the basis of their size, threshold, and conduction rates (Bishop and O'Leary, 1938). Large, fast fibers with low thresholds (cf. A-type cutaneous fibers) deliver their impulses chiefly to the cortex. It is also known that in man and other primates, at least, the central areas of the retina, especially the fovea, have relatively much more representation on the visual cortex than do the peripheral areas—and the fovea is a pure cone mechanism. Following this reasoning, it seems possible that the large, fast fibers, which deliver their messages chiefly to the cortex and perhaps give rise to the large initial spike, originate in cone receptors. Using the monkey as subject, Adrian (1946) found that a flash of blue light often produced no detectable cortical response (although a large potential was simultaneously recorded from the eyeball), but red light readily yielded positive results. He points out that this may have been due merely to the location of his electrodes (i.e. in the cone projection areas), for we are certainly aware of blue light and of colorless, rod-determined sensations.

Summary on the Process of Visual Stimulation

The eye is designed in such a manner that light waves fall upon the retina where their energy is translated into electrical form, presumably by means of photochemical substances in the rods and cones. Impulses generated in this manner in the receptors appear in the electroretinogram, probably as the P_{III} (cone) and P_I (rod) components. The second stage in retinal transmission is the activation of the bipolar and transverse amacrine cells by bombardment from the receptors, and this activity is most probably represented in the electroretinogram by the P_{II} component which, it will be recalled, is highly correlated with impulses in the optic nerve itself. We assume therefore that bipolar axones bombard the cells of the optic nerve across their synapses, giving rise to impulses here as the third neural step in visual stimulation. Activity in the optic nerve is finally projected to the various levels of the occipital cortex.

The sharp distinction in human vision between rod and cone functions naturally directed neurophysiologists to inquire whether this distinction was evident in their own records. Much indirect evidence implies that the P_I component in the *ERG* reflects rod activity, whereas P_{III} reflects cone activity—reducing intensity, for example, minimizes P_{III}, whereas previous light adaptation eliminates P_I. For the human eye Adrian (1945) has shown that a fast, abrupt component of the retinogram is produced by red light, a slow, more gradual component by blue light, and both components by orange light. Later studies on various subhuman species (Adrian, 1946) have not been so successful in segregating rod and cone processes. This may indicate either high variability in rod and cone functions or, possibly, inadequate anatomical characterization of these receptor mechanisms.

VISUAL INTENSITY

Drama in science is seldom experienced by the casual student, but he may catch a bit of it in the answer to this question: What is the smallest amount of radiant energy sufficient to produce a visual sensation? Recent studies by Hecht (1944) and his co-workers indicate that it is a very small amount of energy indeed. Subjects were first dark-adapted for an hour. The test patch was of optimal size (10' of arc) and was applied to the most sensitive part of the retina (20° from the fovea); it was of an optimal wave length for rod vision (510 mμ) and lasted for one-thousandth of a second. Using a spectral system similar to the one described earlier, absolute thresholds for several observers were repeatedly obtained and radiometric equivalents were measured by substituting a thermopyle in the apparatus for the human eye. When translated into quantal energy terms, threshold values were found to range from 54 to 148 quanta, individuals differing from one another and from themselves from time to time.

But not all the light that strikes the cornea is utilized by the receptors. Hecht estimates that in his experiment only about 50 per cent of the light entering the eye actually reaches the retina, some being reflected from the cornea and some being lost through refraction within the ocular media, leaving only 26 of the original 54 quanta. As he puts it, 'It seems profane to be so free with these few precious quanta, yet this is not the end.' Visual purple does not absorb all the light that contacts it. A number of independent studies have shown that absorption is in the order of 10 per cent. This means that of the 26 quanta falling on the retina, only a few are actually utilized. Taking the threshold range of 54 to 148 quanta striking the cornea, we may convert to a range of 5 to 14 effective, absorbed quanta, and these are distributed over an area containing roughly 500 rods!

The conclusion seems inescapable that *a single quantum must be sufficient to activate a single rod.* The simultaneous firing of 5 to 14 rods is presumably necessary to be distinguished from spontaneous retinal activity. 'It is therefore a tribute to the power of natural selection that because of it animals became more and more sensitive until they reached the limit set up by the physical structure of light. One quantum is the smallest unit of energy, and when a retinal rod cell is capable of being brought into action by one quantum of light, the end has been reached and nothing more can be done in this direction.'

Absolute Thresholds for Brightness

Hecht was interested in finding the limit of visual sensitivity and he purposely employed optimal conditions. These conditions, however, are themselves variables which determine the absolute threshold at any moment, and their study yields further insights into the nature of the visual apparatus.

(1) *As a function of area of stimulation.* The retina displays areal summation within certain critical limits. For rather small visual angles, a con-

stant threshold response can be maintained despite lowering of intensity if the area stimulated is increased concomitantly. The area over which such brightness summation works is much larger in the periphery than in the fovea. Letting C equal a constant threshold value, then

$$I \times A = C$$

within areal summation limits. This is known as Ricco's Law. Piper's Law states that the product of intensity and the *square root* of the area yields a constant threshold value. Elsberg and Spotnitz (1937, 1938) have suggested, however, that the *cube root* of the area must be used, implying that threshold discriminations are based upon volume reactions in the nervous system. In one of the most extensive empirical studies on the problem, Graham, Brown, and Mote (1939) obtained the results shown in Fig. 55 for both fovea and periphery. None of the so-called laws fits the data over the entire range. Rather, each fits the restricted range within which it was first applied. The precise nature of the areal function is thus indeterminate at present, although the fact that area and intensity bear a reciprocal relation to one another is indisputable. It is also clear that areal summation is greater in the periphery than in the fovea, and both of these facts point to lateral interactions within the retina.

(2) *As a function of duration of stimulation.* The retina also displays temporal summation within critical limits. Threshold excitation can be maintained while intensity is lowered if the time through which the illumination persists is increased. There are obviously limitations to this relationship—infinite time will not render *any* light visible. Again letting C equal a constant threshold value,

$$I \times T = C$$

which is known as the Bunsen-Roscoe Law. Strict reciprocity, however, holds only for very short durations (approx. 50 msec.). The same relationship between intensity and duration has been demonstrated in many subhuman species as well as in man, including both vertebrates and invertebrates, and Hecht (1934) cites the intriguing bit of information that the phototropic response of oat seedlings show the $IT = C$ relation over an exposure range from .001 seconds to 43 hours, a range never approached by animals. The degree to which increased duration can compensate for reduced intensity is also limited by the area stimulated. Graham and Margaria (1935) have shown that the critical duration through which I and T are reciprocal is shorter for small areas than for large; this suggests that temporal summation depends upon neural interaction as well as upon more obvious receptor chemistry.

(3) *As a function of retinal locus.* Not only are the peripheral rods more numerous in their ratio to bipolar and optic nerve cells than the foveal cones, but they also are associated with highly photosensitive visual purple. It is not surprising, therefore, that with maximum dark adaptation the periphery is a thousand times more sensitive to the presence of light than the central region. Within the periphery itself sensitivity increases regularly as the locus of stimulation is moved from 4° to 20° eccentricity. It

will be recalled that the rod population is most dense 20° from the center of the eye. Troland (1934, p. 670) cites early experiments by Pertz and by Wolfflin as demonstrating that the threshold rises again beyond the 20° locus, presumably as the rod population thins.

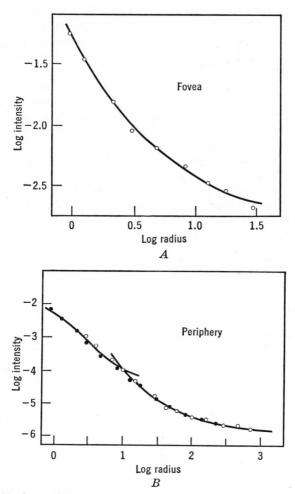

FIGURE 55. Absolute brightness threshold as a reciprocal function of stimulus intensity and area. *A*. Foveal measurements. *B*. Peripheral measurements. Graham, Brown, and Mote, *Journal of Experimental Psychology*, 1939, **24**:562.

The absolute threshold for brightness is also a function of the *wave length* of the light employed. The relative luminosity curves discussed earlier (see Fig. 48) are essentially inversions of absolute threshold functions, and from them it can be seen that the peripheral (rod) threshold is smallest near 510 mμ, but the foveal (cone) threshold is smallest near 554 mμ. The absolute threshold depends as well upon the *degree of light or dark adaptation* preceding measurement; adaptation to bright light causes the threshold to rise, whereas adaptation in the dark produces the opposite effect. But the literature here is sufficiently extensive to merit separate treatment.

Light and Dark Adaptation

In order to cover both light and dark adjustments visual adaptation must be defined as the *gradual improvement in visual performance* attendant upon shifts in the level of illumination. When entering a darkened theater, one is at first functionally blind, the audience is a formless mass; but gradually as dark adaptation occurs it becomes possible to distinguish individuals and to find available seats. Conversely, on stepping back into the brilliantly sunlit street, a brief period of uncomfortable dazzle is experienced until one becomes adapted to the higher level of illumination. These adjustments are accomplished in part by changes in the size of the pupils, narrowing in bright light to reduce the amount entering the eyes and widening in the dark to admit more light. Pupillary adjustments, however, account for only a minute fraction of total adaptation, most of the process being due to changes within the retina.

(1) *Light adaptation.* Measurements on both human and Mya (freshwater clam) show this process to be completed within 10 minutes at the outside, most of the change occurring within the first few minutes (cf. Cook, 1934; Hecht, 1934; Wald and Clark, 1937). By using test patches restricted to the fovea, Wright (1934) was able to show that light adapta-

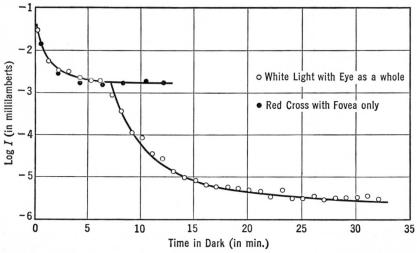

FIGURE 56. Dark adaptation of the eye as a whole, showing separable functions for cones and rods (Hecht). Murchison, *Handbook of Experimental Psychology*, Clark University Press, Worcester, Mass., 1934, p. 727.

tion in this pure cone region is practically complete at the end of one minute. This implies that the gradual (10-minute) adjustment and accompanying dazzle is a peripheral rod effect. In other words, utilizing visual purple that has been stored during previous dark conditions, the rods continue to fire until their photosensitive substance is reduced below a critical level.

(2) *Dark adaptation.* When the total course of dark adaptation, from normal daylight levels of illumination to the minimum threshold, is plotted,

both cone and rod components are apparent in the resultant curve. In Fig. 56, the open circles show measurements on the eye as a whole. Each datum represents the momentary absolute threshold for white light after a given amount of time in complete darkness. The solid circles show data obtained with a red stimulus restricted to the fovea. The fact that the solid points duplicate precisely the upper limb of the curve for the whole eye proves, if such proof be necessary, that the initial stage in total dark adaptation is due to cone sensitization. Cone adjustments are nearly complete in 10 minutes, the increase in sensitivity being approximately in the order of ten

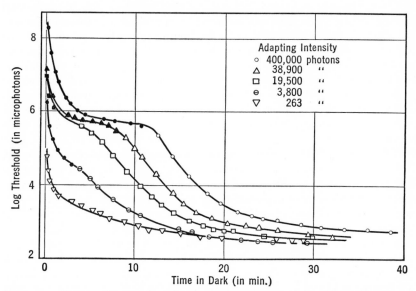

FIGURE 57. Course of dark adaptation as measured with violet light following different degrees of light adaptation. Filled-in symbols indicate that a violet color was apparent at the threshold, while the empty symbols indicate that the threshold was colorless. Hecht, Haig, and Chase, *Journal of General Physiology*, 1937, **20**:837.

times; rod adjustments, appearing as the sharp break in the curve, are nearly complete in 30 minutes (although slight changes can be recorded over periods as long as 24 hours), and represent an increase in sensitivity in the order of 10,000 times.

Keeping in mind that points on the curve for the whole eye represent absolute thresholds for white light at successive moments, the sharp break poses a problem. Why are the rod adjustments delayed for nearly 7 or 8 minutes? A plausible answer is supplied in recent work by Granit and his collaborators (cf. Granit, 1947). The amplitude of the *B*-wave of the electroretinogram was used as an index of rod action after varying degrees of dark adaptation, and this was correlated with actual measurements of amounts of extracted visual purple (from analogous eyes) following similar dark intervals. It was found that significant increments in the *B*-wave appear only after roughly 50 per cent of the maximal visual purple concentration has been regenerated. It appears that this photosensitive substance must reach a certain critical mass before the rod mechanisms can respond, thus explaining the 'kink' in the curve for the total eye.

(a) *As a function of the brightness and duration of the pre-adapting light.*
The shape of the dark adaptation curve and the time required to reach any
given level depend upon the degree of illumination that precedes measurement. The family of curves in Fig. 57 shows the results obtained by Hecht,
Haig, and Chase (1937) who varied the intensity of the pre-adapting white
light. Here thresholds for a violet test light were determined in the usual
manner, the solid circles indicating that the subject could perceive the color
of the stimulus and the open circles indicating that the stimulus appeared
colorless. Similar curves were found when the intensity of the pre-adapting
light was constant but the duration of its application varied. It can be seen
that the degree of dark adaptation reached in a given amount of time (say
10 minutes) varies inversely with pre-adapting intensity. The onset of the
rod limb of the curve is progressively delayed as the intensity of the pre-
adapting light is increased, although the level of illumination at which it
appears is approximately constant. This last fact is obviously related to the
findings of Granit cited above. The critical mass of rod photosensitive substance is roughly constant, but previous light adaptation reduces its quantity
to different extents and hence delays the time required to reattain the critical level.

(b) *As a function of the wave length of test and pre-adapting lights.*
Testing with extreme monochromatic red light yields a pure cone adaptation curve, but testing with an extreme violet light minimizes the cone component and speeds up appearance of the rod component. Intermediary wave
lengths yield compromise curves between these extremes. Similar findings
have been obtained for the wave length of the pre-adapting light. Pre-
adapting with extreme monochromatic red light is nearly as effective preparation for night vision work as being in complete darkness. Hecht and Hsia
(1945) have recently estimated that extreme red light (wave lengths below
600 filtered out) can be thirty times as intense as heterogeneous white light
and yield the same degree of dark adaptation in the same time. One of
the practical consequences of this finding has been the use of red goggles
by the armed forces before going out on night duty (Miles, 1943). A naval
observer can read maps and books and attend to most normal duties while
wearing red goggles (and hence using cone vision), and yet he can step out
onto the darkened bridge, remove his goggles, and see nearly as well as if
he had spent the same amount of time in absolute darkness.

(c) *As a function of retinal locus.* The differences between foveal and
peripheral adaptation curves, shown in Fig. 56, are further testimony to the
duplexity of the human retina. Varying the location of the test patch from
4° to 20° within the periphery itself would be expected to increase the rate
and lower the final level of dark adaptation, and this has been demonstrated (Hecht, Haig, and Wald, 1935). This applies to sheer sensitivity
to light. Research cited earlier (Chapanis, 1945; Gordon, 1947) indicates
that *form* perception in the completely dark-adapted eye is most efficient
between 4° and 12°. Low (1946) has found that accuracy of form perception in the periphery develops gradually for several minutes after the
test object (Landolt ring) can be sensed as an illuminant. When the test
object is placed 30° or 45° eccentric from the fovea, only half as much time
is required to achieve maximum acuity as when it is placed at a visual angle
of 15°, *but* the final level of discrimination achieved is not as great.

(d) *Individual differences in dark adaptation.* Even under standard test conditions, normal individuals vary by as much as 1 log unit in the final level of dark adaptation they can achieve. This means that a man near the upper limit of the normal range requires about ten times more illumination of the test object than a man near the lower limit. A number of conditions, such as retinal pigmentation, ocular transparency, density of rod population, and the like, produce these differences. Interestingly enough, the correlation between rod thresholds and form discrimination at night (i.e. actual field performance) is low. Complex factors such as intelligence, familiarity with landscapes, and motivation are also important determinants of performance in the field.

(3) *Neurophysiological correlates of adaptation.* A number of physiological conditions are known to affect the level of dark adaptation that can be reached by the normal individual. Anoxia, experienced by fliers at high elevations, causes a decrease in sensitivity, the rod threshold being raised as much as 50 per cent at 12,000 feet. Carbon-monoxide poisoning has similar effects. Saturation of the blood with 5 per cent CO is equivalent to an altitude of 8,000 to 10,000 feet in raising the rod threshold—and the chain smoking of three cigarettes takes a man up 8000 feet in terms of his visual sensitivity! Even bright sunlight has a cumulative and adverse effect on the capacity for dark adaptation, making it necessary for personnel who work at night to wear dense glasses in daylight (Hecht, 1945). Because Vitamin A is involved in the regeneration of visual purple, it would be expected that its removal from the diet would have a deleterious effect upon dark adaptation. Hecht and Mandelbaum (1938) demonstrated a progressive loss of sensitivity for 35 days in human subjects under these conditions.

The processes of light and dark adaptation can be tapped by common neurophysiological techniques. Light adaptation in Limulus appears as a rapidly falling rate of discharge in the optic nerve during continuous stimulation (Riggs and Graham, 1940), and similar results have been found for isolated retinal elements in the cat (Granit, 1947). Typical dark adaptation curves have been obtained from the intact eye of the frog by measuring the latency and height of the B-wave of the ERG as functions of time in the dark (Riggs, 1937). These findings localize the processes of visual adaptation in the retina rather than in the higher centers.

From results obtained with isolated fibers during dark adaptation in both cat and guinea pig, Granit (1947, p. 253) concludes that 'there must be two different types of rod, one reacting like cones so far as adaptation is concerned, the other like an "ideal" rod reflecting, fairly accurately, the course of visual purple regeneration.' We have seen other evidence suggesting the existence of 'conelike' rods, notably the fact that maximum visual acuity at scotopic levels has a different locus (nearer the fovea) than maximum sensitivity to light per se. Granit suggests that the conelike rods can function at cone levels of illumination as well as at rod levels but that they have much higher dark adaptation thresholds than the 'ideal' rods.

Differential Thresholds for Brightness

What variables determine the smallest *change* in illumination that can be perceived by an observer? The classic method of answering this question was to measure the subject's DL or *brightness discrimination* by one of the several psychophysical methods. When the method of simultaneous comparison between two adjacent fields of differing intensity is used, and adjustments of the variable made until the entire field becomes uniform, we have the practical photometer, described earlier. When the smallest space between two lines or the smallest object discriminable is measured, we are studying *visual acuity,* and again the essential method is that of simultaneous comparison of two visual areas of differing brightness (i.e. a fine black line on a white field). When two fields of different intensity are presented in such rapid alternation that they just fuse, we have the *flicker-fusion* method of studying differential sensitivity.

(1) *As a function of intensity (Weber function).* Weber's Law states that the amount by which the intensity of stimulation must be increased to be just perceptible is a constant fraction of the absolute intensity level, i.e. that $\Delta I/I = C$. The failure of this law to describe experimental data in general has been discussed earlier, and its failure with visual data is no less abject, as seen in the curves in Fig. 58. None of the three methods, brightness discrimination A, flicker fusion B, or visual acuity C, shows $\Delta I/I$ to be constant as a function of intensity. Rather, all methods agree that this ratio decreases as the intensity is increased. The flicker-fusion curve has been inverted from its usual manner of presentation in order to show its essential similarity to data obtained directly in j.n.d. experiments. In common-sense terms, these curves show that as the intensity of illumination becomes greater, visual processes become more and more finely discriminative, in terms of comparing the brightness of gross surfaces, resolving brief flashes in time, or resolving fine extents in space. Notice, however, that it is the *relative,* not the absolute, ΔI that decreases as I is raised.

The duplex character of the retina is reflected in all three curves. The upper limb of each represents rod vision (i.e. at low intensities), whereas the lower limb, which displays the expected finer discrimination, represents cone vision. The fact that none of these curves shows any inversion at even the highest intensities is somewhat puzzling. One might expect a point to be reached somewhere along the line where, in order to notice a change in brightness, larger and larger increments would be required. It may be that a 'discomfort threshold' is reached before the human visual system is pushed to its limit.

(2) *As functions of time and area.* In common with the absolute threshold (and presumably for the same reasons) the difference threshold reveals a reciprocal relation between intensity and both area and time. Graham and Kemp (1938) have shown that the intensity of an increment can be decreased if the time through which it operates is lengthened—this relation again holding only within certain critical limits. Identical results are found when the area of the stimulus patch is varied (Lasareff, 1911; Steinhardt, 1936; Graham and Bartlett, 1940). A similar areal effect would be expected, and has been demonstrated, in flicker-fusion work. Granit and Harper (1930), working with test patches falling within 10° of the foveal center, and Brown (1945), working well out into the periphery (25°, 50°, 70°, and 90° eccentricities), both find *CFF* to increase with the area of the flickering stimulus. Comparison of these two studies indicates that summation holds for larger areas in the periphery than near the fovea, as would be predicted from the differences in neural organization. With regard to the

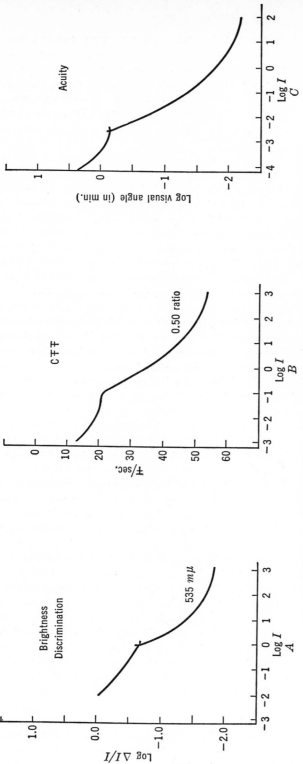

FIGURE 58. Three measures of differential sensitivity to brightness. *A.* Brightness discrimination (Hecht *et al. Journal of General Physiology,* 1938, 22:15). *B.* Critical fusion frequency (after data of Crozier and Wolf, *Journal of General Physiology,* 1941, 24:639). *C.* Visual acuity (Hecht and Mintz, *Journal of General Physiology,* 1939, 22:597). Upper limbs of curves represent rod vision, lower limbs cone vision. Observe the essential similarity of these functions.

163

visual acuity method, it has been shown that the visibility of a fine line depends upon its length (Anderson and Weymouth, 1923), and one would expect to find a reciprocal relation between length (i.e. area) and intensity for a constant acuity level. Such a relation is implicit in the results of a number of recent researches (cf. Hecht and Mintz, 1939; Hecht, Ross, and Mueller, 1947). The duration factor has been studied by Graham and Cook (1937), the expected reciprocality between duration and intensity for constant acuity being demonstrated.

(3) *Certain paradoxes concerning visual acuity.* The fact that *visual acuity does vary with illumination* is somewhat paradoxical in itself. The resolving power of the retina, composed as it is of a mosaic of sensitive cells, depends in part upon the separation of its receiving elements. Since retinal elements are permanently fixed in space, and therefore the separation between them cannot become narrower as illumination is increased, why should acuity increase? One answer was suggested by Hecht (1934, p. 775). Assuming that individual visual receptors vary randomly in their absolute thresholds, fewer and fewer receptors will be excited as intensity is lowered. Therefore the *functional* distance between the elements will increase, thus lowering acuity. This argument also assumes that the range in threshold variations equals the entire intensity range over which visual acuity varies, since some receptors must be added for every discriminable change in acuity. Despite the critical nature of these assumptions, there is no direct experimental evidence on them as far as this writer is aware.

Another problem is that *visual acuity is finer than the units of the retinal mosaic.* Using thin lines against an illuminated field, Hecht and Mintz (1939) have found threshold acuity to be roughly one-sixtieth the width of a single foveal cone. How can this be? These investigators felt that the answer lay in the diffraction of light passing through the ocular media. The image of a line, as it affects the retina, is not sharp; rather it is spread over a considerable number of elements. Even the finest wire (indicated in the lower portion of Fig. 59) delivers a diffraction pattern to several elements (shown as blocks in the upper portion of the figure). But the intensity applied to particular elements varies normally about the center of the image. Hecht and Mintz calculated the intensity difference between adjacent cones at threshold acuity to be precisely that just discernible in ordinary j.n.d. measurements. Although this indicates the close relation between visual acuity and brightness discrimination, it is now becoming clear that both processes depend upon the *distribution* of frequency patterns in overlapping systems. A statistical theory of discrimination functions in terms of populations of neural elements has been given in greatest detail by Marshall and Talbot (1942). Optical diffraction and rapid oscillation of the eyes (physiological nystagmus) contribute initially to a distribution of excitation on the retina; within the projection system, lateral reciprocal overlap of dendritic processes at the several synaptic levels and vertical summation between levels serve to modify further the input to higher centers. The image of a hairline on the comparatively gross mosaic of the retina is transformed into a Gaussian distribution of excitation in the finer mosaic of the visual cortex, the steepness of this gradient determining the fineness of acuity. This story is told in more detail in Chap. 5, where it is related to various perceptual phenomena (cf. also a recent review by Senders, 1948).

Another puzzle for the theorist is posed by the fact that *fine visual acuity and areal summation exist simultaneously*. Granit and Harper (1930) arranged two bright semicircles so that the distance between them could be varied; flicker-fusion frequencies were then determined, both in the foveal region and in the periphery. Measurements were taken for each patch alone and for both together. Summation—shown by an increase in *CFF* for the two patches together—was found to increase regularly with the nearness of the two semicircles. Yet at a distance where such interaction was maximal, subjects could still discriminate the fine dark line between the patches. How can neural interaction occur through the very interspace that is dis-

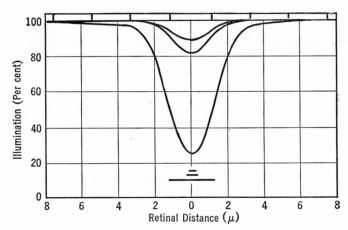

FIGURE 59. Light intensity distribution in diffracted retinal images produced by the fine wires whose geometrical images are shown as three lines in the lower part of the figure. The pupil is taken as 3 mm. Scale on top of the figure represents the retinal mosaic, consisting of cones whose diameters are 2.3 μ, this being the average size of the cones in the exact center of the fovea. Hecht and Mintz, *Journal of General Physiology*, 1939, **22**:601.

criminated? The coexistence of fine acuity and areal summation seems to require the operation of a minimum of two processes, excitation and inhibition, but further inquiry into the nature of these processes leads us to the next topic.

The Retina as an Integrative Neural Center

The sheet of nerve cells that makes up the retina behaves more nearly like a neural center than a simple collection of receptor units. This is not at all surprising when one considers that, embryologically, it is an outgrowth of the brain itself. The preceding survey of brightness sensitivity created a number of questions whose answers most probably lie in the integrative action of the retina—if we only knew more about its integrative action!

One is tempted to explain *temporal summation* in the retina purely on a photochemical basis. This form of integrative action has been demonstrated in the nonsynaptic receptor units of Limulus, for example, where areal factors are largely eliminated (Hartline, 1934). Figure 60 (on p. 166) indicates with striking clarity that both the frequency of impulses in isolated optic nerve fibers and their latency can be varied by increasing either the intensity or the duration of the light flash, i.e. that intensity and duration are reciprocally related. It appears that the chemical end products of the light reaction must be utilized for neural excitation within a certain critical period of time or they are either removed or resynthesized (cf. Hecht, 1934). At threshold the chemical light reaction is just sufficient to initiate impulses in nerve; up to a point, increased duration of the light will permit decrease in intensity since the effective end products accumulate through time. Beyond a critical duration, however, the rate of removal or resynthesis of these chemical end products will just match the rate of their formation in

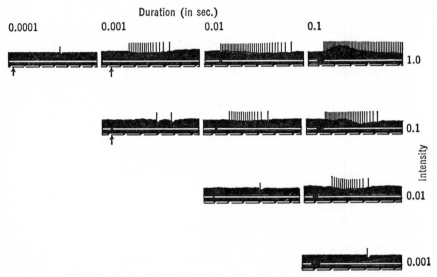

FIGURE 60. Reciprocal relation between intensity and duration of stimulus as demonstrated in a single optic nerve fiber of Limulus. Hartline, *Journal of Cellular and Comparative Physiology*, 1934, 5:237.

the light reaction, hence the critical amount necessary for excitation will not be reached.

But photochemistry cannot be the entire answer to temporal summation in the vertebrate retina. Graham and Margaria (1935), it will be remembered, found that the degree to which increased duration permits reductions in intensity is limited by the *area* stimulated. Granit and Davis (1931) found that if one subliminal flash is followed by another, also subthreshold, the two summate to yield a reportable light sensation. The excitatory capacity of the second flash presumably adds to the changes already initiated by the first. The authors point out, however, that this cannot be due solely to photochemical summation. They were able to show that temporal summation of subliminal stimuli could occur (especially in the peripheral retina) when the two stimuli were separated in locus by as much as 30 minutes of arc, although the temporal duration under these conditions was sharply reduced. Such lateral spread in the effects of subliminal excitation suggests the role of neural connections.

The classic study on *areal summation* was that by Adrian and Matthews (1927), using the excised eye of the conger eel. They found that the response to four small disks had a shorter latency than the response to any one of them. We note that in such a preparation the retina itself must be the locus of interaction. That *lateral connections* in the retina are involved is implied by Graham's (1932) failure to obtain areal summation in Limulus. The regular finding that areal effects are more widespread in the periphery than in the fovea also speaks for neural structures as the basis. One may wonder how areal summation within the fovea is possible at all, given the point-for-point projection in this region. Recent histological investigations have shown that amacrine cells make possible horizontal effects, each foveal cone being supplied with at least one such cell (cf. Polyak, 1941).

Granit (1930) adapted the Adrian and Matthews four-spot procedure to the human retina, using CFF as a measure of summation. Summation— indexed by increased CFF for the four spots as compared with any one of them—was clearly evident in the periphery but not in the fovea. Summation increased with both nearness and intensity of the spots. Beitel (1934) has demonstrated summation into a visible result for spatially separated subthreshold stimuli, just as it has been demonstrated for temporally separated subthreshold stimuli. Summation in the periphery decreased rapidly out to 20′ angular separation, then more gradually out to some 70′ where the drop in summation again became steep. This complex function suggests the existence of several bases for areal interaction. Similar results were obtained for the fovea, but the total area covered was only one-fifteenth as great. The anatomical feasibility of areal summation has been neatly demonstrated by Hartline (1940). Recording from single optic fibers of the frog and exploring the retina with a microilluminator, he was able to plot the 'receptive fields' of individual neurons. Within the relatively small area of approximately one-half degree, a fiber responds to stimuli of threshold intensities; a considerably wider area of about 4° is found to feed this fiber when high intensities are applied. Reciprocality between intensity and area holds within the receptive field of a single fiber. The similarity of these findings to those of Galambos and Davis in hearing (cf. pp. 103-4) should be observed.

It seems likely that these lateral connections in the retina also contribute to the *synchronization of impulses* observed in vertebrate eyes. Adrian and Matthews (1928) found synchronization of discharge to appear spontaneously in the eel's optic nerve when a large area was stimulated. Graham and Granit (1931) found CFF for a test patch to be higher (i.e. more summation) when a second patch was flickered at the same rate than when it was held steady at an equated luminosity. Brown (1945) obtained evidence for areal summation within a single flickering patch which was varied in size when the entire surrounding region was kept at the same level of illumination as the fused brightness of the flickering stimulus. These results indicate that total amplitude of excitation (and hence visual brightness) can be increased both by enlarging the area stimulated and by 'impressing' synchronization of impulses in separate loci. The only reasonable mechanisms in the retina for such synchronization between disparate loci are its lateral connections.

There remain the *inhibitory processes* in the retina to be considered. Granit and Harper (1930), it will be recalled, demonstrated that fine acuity for the dark space between two flickering semicircles could exist simultaneously with areal summation between them. Graham and Granit (1931) changed the conditions of this experiment in one particular—the intensities of the two flickering semicircles were varied independently. They found that the *CFF* of the *brighter* patch was relatively enhanced (as compared with its *CFF* when presented alone), but that of the *darker* patch was relatively damped. This effect was demonstrable in the fovea but not in the periphery. Along similar lines, Beitel (1936) has found that the absolute threshold for one small foveal patch is *raised* (rather than lowered, as is usually the case in areal summation studies) by illuminating a near-by area, *if* the intensity of the second patch is some hundredfold greater. It is interesting that although the same phenomenon can be obtained in the periphery, the intensity difference must be much larger.

One interpretation of retinal inhibition might take the following form: Let us assume that a second- or third-order neuron (bipolar or optic nerve cell) can be kept in a state of relative refractoriness to the passage of normally intense stimuli by receiving a lateral bombardment of subliminal impulses. Accepting as fact the lateral spread of impulses in the retina from one area to another (e.g. from *a* to *b*) and assuming further that the frequency of lateral impulses received at *b* must equal the frequency set up in the area stimulated, *a,* then two conclusions follow: (1) If the rate of stimulation set up at *b* is equal to or greater than that received laterally from *a,* facilitation in the form of increased response in the *b* neurons will result. This is the situation in ordinary areal summation and in the case when the brighter of two patches is enhanced in brightness; it also applies to the case when two flickering patches have the same flash rate and intensity. (2) If the rate of stimulation set up at locus *b* is slower than that received laterally from locus *a,* inhibition in the form of reduced response in *b* neurons will result. This would apply to the case when one bright spot lowers sensitivity in a near-by area; it would also fit the case when the brighter of two flickering patches inhibits the *CFF* of another. Although this hypothesis is entirely conjectural at the present time, there seems to be nothing in the neurophysiological literature to deny the possibility (cf. Creed, Denny-Brown, Sherrington, Eccles, Liddell, 1932; Fulton, 1949).

VISUAL QUALITY

The psychology of vision is replete with conflicting theories, designed as explanations of how the nervous system mediates the known relations between physical light stimulus and psychological color experience. Theories are limited only by existing knowledge of how, in general, the sensory nervous system works and by an accumulated mass of indirect evidence, but they tend to stray beyond even these boundaries. Impetus to theory building came from the discovery that all hue experiences could be duplicated by appropriate mixtures of only three primaries; this seemed to limit the complexity of the problem—perhaps only three receptor types were sufficient to explain color vision.

Could it be done with less than three? At the extreme we would have a *single receptor theory,* with hue dependent upon the frequency of impulses in the visual nerve tract (in a manner analogous to the volley theory of pitch) and brightness dependent upon total frequency per unit time. This has seldom been seriously proposed (however, see Troland, 1921; Fry, 1945) : the notion runs into flat contradiction of the law of specific energies (a difficulty shared with respectable theories, by the way), fails to provide a ready explanation of color mixture and saturation, and certainly doesn't explain how we can have different types of color blindness. Is the other extreme, an *N-receptor theory,* feasible? This notion, like the place theory of hearing, would require as many different types of receptors as there are discriminable hues, and there are some 128 of them (cf. Troland, 1934). This would seem to place an impossible burden upon retinal chemistry; it is difficult to conceive of anything approaching this number of different light-sensitive substances. Furthermore, since vision (unlike audition) includes a spatial dimension, each small area of the retina yielding full color discrimination would have to include full replication of all cone types.

All contemporary theories represent a compromise between these extremes, specifying some *limited* number of receptor types that vary in their rate of discharge with the wave length of light. The classic Young-Helmholtz theory, deriving its *raison d'être* from the facts of color mixture, specifies three types of cones. Despite numerous weaknesses, this is still the dominant point of view. Other theories have appeared from time to time, but they are chiefly criticisms of the Young-Helmholtz position. We shall first describe the classic theory and then evaluate it against many kinds of experimental evidence, taking cognizance of competing theories.

The Young-Helmholtz Theory

By the time Thomas Young (1801) was mulling over these problems, a century after Newton, it was well established that light is infinitely divisible. Young, like present-day theorists, found it difficult to conceive of each sensitive point in the retina containing 'an infinite number of particles, each capable of vibrating in perfect unison with every possible undulation.' His ingenious suggestion was that there are only three kinds of fibers corresponding to three primary colors. Although Young never made the implications of this theory explicit, it follows that if anything other than the primaries are to be sensed (a) each fiber must respond in varying degrees to all wave lengths and (b) the messages carried by the three types of fibers must be fused or interpreted, presumably in the brain. After reposing quietly in the Philosophical Transactions of the Royal Society for nearly fifty years, these ideas were discovered, more or less simultaneously, by both Maxwell and Helmholtz, who brought them into close alignment with the facts of color mixture.

The Young-Helmholtz theory postulates three types of cones, *R, G,* and *B,* each containing a slightly variant substance (chemistry) so that it is maximally sensitive in a different region of the spectrum. Following the law of specific energies—in a rough statement of which, incidentally, Young had anticipated Johannes Müller, as is evident in this color theory—*R* cones, if stimulated in isolation, would yield a red sensation, *G* cones a green sensation, and so on. The rate of firing for each type of cone, its excitability, depends upon the wave length of the stimulating light. *Hue* thus depends on the relative frequencies of impulses set up in the three types of fibers, *brightness* on the total frequency of impulses in all three fibers, and *saturation* on the amount of white produced in any fusion, i.e. if a given stimulus elicits

3 *R*, 8 *G*, and 12 *B*, three units of each will go into the production of white, leaving 5 *G* and 9 *B* to fuse into a somewhat desaturated greenish blue.

The determination of excitability curves for the three types of cones seemed a direct enough matter to early investigators: they had merely to determine by *color mixture* what proportions of the three primary wave lengths are required to match each portion of the visible spectrum—i.e. the facts of color mixture were assumed to provide a faithful picture of the composite action of the three kinds of cones. König and Dieterici (1892) were the first to make such colorimetric measurements with sufficient accuracy, and their *Grundempfindungen*—basic sensation curves—are shown in Fig. 61*A*. These curves are several steps removed from direct color-mixture data, however. In the first place, direct colorimetric matching of the spectrum shows that at most points one of the primaries has a *negative value* (cf. Wright's data in Fig. 46). Since it did not seem reasonable that receptors could respond at *less* than zero frequencies, König and Dieterici (and other subsequent workers) shifted their curves to a level where all values became positive. Secondly, since König assumed that the three primaries contribute equally to the experience of white, the *areas* under the three curves were arbitrarily made equal. Despite these transformations and the mediate character of the data, of which König himself was well aware, these *Grundempfindungen* have often been treated as if they represented direct measurements of the relative rates of the firing of the three types of cones.

If these curves did reflect faithfully the composite action of three types of cones, then other major facts of color vision should also be derivable from them. This is not the case (cf. Hecht, 1930). (a) Since cone responses determine brightness as well as color experience, *adding together excitation curves for the three cone mechanisms should generate the general luminosity curve for cone vision* (i.e. the unimodal curve shown in Fig. 48). A glance at König's basic sensation curves shows that the blue portion of the spectrum would be made disproportionately bright, and the total luminosity function derived in this manner would certainly not be unimodal. To approximate the actual luminosity function for cone vision, the 'blue' excitation curve must be multiplied by a factor of only 0.006, the 'green' curve by 0.426, and the 'red' curve by 0.568 (Ives, 1923). In other words, the contribution of 'blue' to color experience is all out of proportion to its contribution to brightness. (b) Since, according to the Young-Helmholtz theory, white is produced by the combined activity of all three components, *the least well-saturated portions of the spectrum should be those in which the greatest overlap occurs among the three excitation curves*. Since yellow is the least saturated spectral color, overlap should be maximal near 585 mμ, but it is actually greatest about 500 mμ. (c) It will be recalled that the data for *hue discrimination* (see Fig. 49) revealed four regions of maximal differential sensitivity to change in wave length. Helmholtz himself (1891, trans. 1924) was the first to suggest that wave-length discrimination should vary directly with the rate at which spectral sensitivity of the three cone components was changing along the spectrum. For example, if frequency of response for the green cones was changing rapidly between 500 and 510 mμ, differential sensitivity should be fine in this region. This means that *hue discrimination data should be predictable from basic excitation curves*. When Helmholtz tried to derive König and Dieterici's hue discrimination data from their own *Grundempfindungen,* however, he found it impossible and therefore derived a new set, shown as Fig. 61*B*. It is certain that the excitation ratios of *R*, *G,* and *B* cones as a function of wave length cannot be faithfully represented by *both* sets of *Grundempfindungen.*

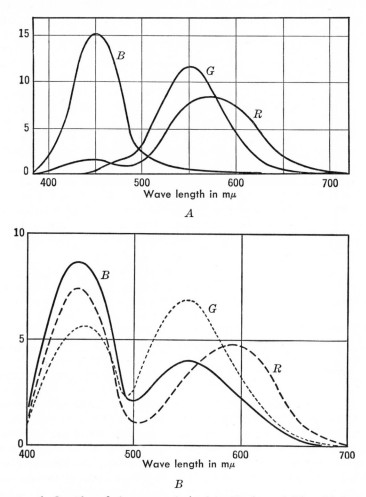

FIGURE 61. *A*. Grundempfindungen as derived by König and Dieterici from color mixture data. *B*. Grundempfindungen which Helmholtz constructed in order to account for the data of König and Dieterici on hue discrimination. Hecht, *Journal of the Optical Society of America,* 1930, 20:238, 248.

In a brilliant theoretical analysis, Hecht (1930) has greatly enhanced the tenability of the Young-Helmholtz theory by describing quantitative functions for a three-cone mechanism from which not only the data of color mixture can be derived but also those of brightness, saturation, and hue discrimination. His excitation curves are shown in Fig. 62, violet (*V*) being used as the third primary rather than blue for reasons we shall consider later. (a) Hecht's excitation curves are given such values that they summate directly to give the *photopic visibility curve,* i.e. the relative brightness of various portions of the spectrum can be derived from them. (b) Within this limitation, these theoretical curves are further made to intersect in those ways required to account for complementary equations and *the general facts of color mixture;* R and G curves, for example, cross at 585 mμ to account for yellow. The large amount of overlap among these similar curves, rather than producing white (as in the classic view), is assumed to contribute to

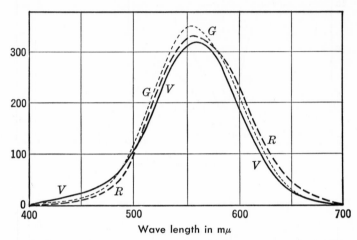

FIGURE 62. Basic sensation curves proposed by Hecht to account for brightness, hue discrimination, and saturation thresholds, as well as color mixture data. Hecht, *Journal of the Optical Society of America,* 1930, 20:252.

the total brightness of experience. (c) For the portion of the spectrum between 400 mμ and 500 mμ, S (saturation) $= \dfrac{V + G - 2R}{V + G + R}$, and between 500 mμ and 700 mμ, $\dfrac{G + R - 2V}{V + G + R}$. Where the three components are equal, S equals zero, or pure white; the greater the dominance of the two hue-producing components over the third white or brightness-producing component, the greater the saturation. Hecht made further slight adjustments in his curves until application of these formulas to them would generate data on *saturation thresholds* obtained by Priest and Brickwedde (1926). (d) Similar minor adjustments made it possible to incorporate data on *hue discrimination* obtained by Laurens and Hamilton (1923).

The reader must also be cautioned that *Hecht's excitation curves do not represent actual measurements of R, G, and V cone-excitation ratios.* Rather, they represent *inferred* characteristics of three postulated cone types, just as did König's *Grundempfindungen.* They are founded on a broader empirical base, however, the insight being that luminosity as well as wave-length functions must be included if such curves are to have any generality. The fact that they yield a precise derivation of several different sets of empirical observations is inconsequential—as Hecht himself repeatedly points out, they were constructed to do exactly this. This in no way detracts from Hecht's contribution; the tenability of any hypothesis varies with the number of relevant phenomena incorporated. The impressiveness of the demonstration lies in the fact that functions for only three-cone mechanisms *can* integrate such a large number of interlocking visual phenomena.

The Phenomenological Primacy of Yellow

Phenomenologists have generally agreed that there are four primary hues, red, *yellow,* green, and blue. Furthermore, although the components can be distinguished in many color mixtures, yellow cannot be analyzed into its red and green components. The same unitary character holds for sensations of white and black. To provide a hypothetical neurological base for such a 'natural' color system, Hering (1920, or see Boring, 1942) postulated three chemical substances in three types of cones, a white-black substance, a yellow-blue substance, and a red-green substance. Breaking down (catabolism) these substances was supposed to yield one type of sensation (e.g. white, yellow, and red), but building up (anabolism) the same substances was supposed to yield the antagonistic sensations (e.g. black, blue, and green). *All* light was necessarily assumed to excite both catabolic and anabolic activities in the white-black substance, yielding a gray whose brightness was a function of the ratio between these processes; otherwise the antagonism between complementary colors, such as yellow and blue, would produce 'nil' rather than neutral gray.

The main reason Hering's theory has not survived is that it runs into such obvious conflict with the law of specific energies. Each cone is asked to distinguish (through the quality of its impulses) between the anabolic and catabolic changes in its chemical substance. In other words, the same fibers must carry both 'yellow impulses' and 'blue impulses,' but according to present-day views sensory fibers are incapable of distinguishing between the stimuli that give rise to them. Since the law of specific energies is by no means certain—as we shall become increasingly aware—Hering's theory is still a possibility. And the existence of independent Y receptors proves to be a popular notion.

Color Blindness and Perimetry Measurements

Christine Ladd-Franklin, in 1892 (cf. 1929), proposed a theory of color vision that was, in a sense, a compromise between the Young-Helmholtz and the Hering positions. Keeping the phenomenological advantages of Hering's theory, she postulated four primaries $(R, G, Y,$ and $B)$; to avoid collision with the law of specific energies, she postulated separate cone mechanisms for each primary. She was undoubtedly motivated by two often observed difficulties with the Young-Helmholtz view: (1) in the two most common forms of *color blindness* red and green cannot be discriminated but yellow, supposedly produced by the combined action of red and green, is experienced; (2) in *perimeter studies* it has been found that as small patches of either red or green are directed more and more toward the periphery, they turn into *yellow.* How can yellow be experienced at a retinal locus where neither of its presumed components can be? Yellow and blue patches retain their own hues until quite far out toward the periphery, changing finally into achromatic gray. It seems reasonable to suppose that these two sets of facts are related—one might say that the normal eye is red-green blind somewhat peripherally, becoming totally color blind in the extreme periphery.

Color blindness and its implications have long been matters of special interest not only to the layman, because it seems strange that everyday objects may not look the same to others as to him, but also to the philosopher-scientist, because here the 'obvious' relation between stimulus and sensation breaks down. Superficially the Young-Helmholtz theory requires that functional loss of one type of cone will eliminate that component from vision, i.e. a 'green-blind' subject should experience only red-blue hues, a 'red-blind' subject only green-blue hues, and so on. What do the color blind actually experience? Obviously a color-blind person cannot describe for us what he experiences in a language based on sensations he cannot have, but there are rare cases where color blindness is confined to one eye and such individuals can tell us how vision with the color-blind eye differs from that with the normal eye. We find that what appears white to the normal eye also appears white to both red-blind and green-blind eyes; for both red-blind and green-blind eyes the visible spectrum is divided at a neutral point into two hues, *yellow* and blue. Neither of these facts makes sense in an unextended Young-Helmholtz theory.

Let us look briefly at the *varieties of color defect*. Normal color vision is referred to as *trichromatism*, specifying the fact that ordinary individuals require three primaries to match all the spectral hues they can experience. Those who are *protanomalous trichromats* and *deuteranomalous trichromats* also require three primaries, but the former use more red in their mixtures and the latter more green. Actually, there is considerable variability within the normal range, and these anomalous trichromats are merely on the extremes of the continuum. The *protanopic dichromat* (red-blind) and the *deuteranopic dichromat* (green-blind) require only two primaries to match all the hues they can experience. The protanope is relatively insensitive to wave lengths in the 'red' region but relatively more sensitive in the 'blue' region. The deuteranope, on the other hand, is *not* less sensitive than normal to wave lengths in the 'green' region—the term 'green-blind' for this defect is clearly a misnomer. For both protanopes and deuteranopes the spectrum appears blue in the short wave-length portion and yellow in the long wave-length portion, these two bands being divided by a hueless region called the *neutral point,* saturation increasing in both direction from this division. Both protanopes and deuteranopes have difficulty in discriminating reds and greens (or mixtures in which these components serve as differentials to the normal eye). Red-green blindness of one form or the other, by all odds the most common defect, is known to be inherited. It appears some ten times more often in men than in women. *Tritanopia,* a form of dichromatism in which the eye is insensitive to yellow and blue, is a very rare defect associated with diseases of the eye. The *monochromat* is totally color blind, matching all spectral hues solely on the basis of brightness. This is also a very rare defect, representing complete lack of cone vision.

Mrs. Ladd-Franklin linked her four-receptor theory to certain evolutionary facts and was able to give a convincing account of both color blindness and perimetry data. Achromatic rod vision was assumed to be the most primitive form of the light sense (in vertebrates, at any rate). The rod structures evolve into primitive yellow and blue cones, differentially sensitive to long and short wave lengths of the spectrum, respectively. The third evolutionary step is the modification of some of the yellow cones into still further specialized mechanisms, the red and green cones whose chemistries selectively split the spectral region originally spanned by yellow. Note that red and green light combine to yield the sensation characteristic of the parent yellow cone, and yellow and blue light combine to yield the sensation characteristic of achromatic rods. Color blindness represents a throwback to a more primitive condition; since it is well known that the most recently acquired characteristics are the most readily eliminated in such cases, red and green blindness is the most common defect—an *inherited* defect, we recall. And visual experience for these people, appropriately enough, *is* yellow-blue. The final assumption, also buttressed by comparative studies, is that evolution has been most rapid in the foveal area of the eye, itself an advanced structure, slowing down toward the periphery. In other words, various portions of the retina 'recapitulate' the course of evolution—all four types of color receptors are present near the fovea (and red and green patches are discriminated in perimetry experiments); farther out, the yellow cones have not differentiated (and both red and green patches can only excite yellow cones); and still farther out in the most primitive periphery, the rods have not differentiated (and all colored patches are perceived as gray).

What about the Young-Helmholtz theory? Obviously it is incapable of handling these facts in its classic form. An ingenious suggestion, however, originally offered by Fick (1879) and elaborated by Hecht (1930, 1934), solves the problem neatly. Let us assume that protanopes, rather than lacking red cones, have cones in which the photosensitive substance is changed so that their absorption spectrum becomes identical with that for green cones (or vice versa, for deuteranopes). Since the rest of the (neural) mechanism remains unchanged, stimulation of these modified 'red' cones will still yield *red* sensations, but response frequencies to various wave lengths of light will be identical with those for 'green' cones. In such a case any wave length between 500 mμ and 700 mμ would necessarily yield yellow experience (e.g. equal excitation of R and G), desaturated to the extent that the blue mechanism is excited. Any wave length between 400 mμ and 500 mμ would necessarily yield blue experience, desaturated to the extent that fused R and G are excited. But such an eye would be incapable of discriminations on the basis of R and G mixtures, as is the case. The same kind of argument could be given for perimetry data—for some reason, R and G cone chemistries are identical in the medial retina. It should be pointed out, however, that this chemistry shift is a sheer *ad hoc* notion (and it is just as much an additional postulate for the Young-Helmholtz theory as Ladd-Franklin's Y receptor). Furthermore, it offers no ready explanation of the rarity of blue-yellow blindness (tritanopia) or its noninherited origin.

Ladd-Franklin's evolutionary theory has much to recommend it, yet it has never been as popular as the Young-Helmholtz view. The reason is *not* that there exists crucial evidence favoring the latter. There are at least three quite different reasons: in the first place, the immense prestige of Helmholtz as a scientist has undoubtedly weighted the scales in favor of the theory he sponsored. Secondly, Hecht's relatively recent demonstration that a three-cone hypothesis can be made to fit a wide swath of relevant data has greatly increased the theory's tenability—although a similar feat would presumably be feasible for a four-cone hypothesis. Thirdly, many students, following the law of parsimony, have concluded that if a three-cone hypothesis can accomplish as much as a four-cone hypothesis, there is no need for the extra (yellow) entity, but it should be kept in mind that the 'law' of parsimony is at best a rough guide, not a scalpel.

Information as to Receptor Types

If we had direct information about the nature and number of color receptors—in regard to the existence of an independent Y cone, for example—there would certainly be fewer competing theories in the field. Unfortunately such information is hard to obtain. Cone types do not label themselves histologically; their small size and comparative inaccessibility make direct neurophysiological study difficult—particularly with the human, who alone can tell us what sensations result from the stimulation of certain receptors. And indirect attacks are usually open to several interpretations. Nevertheless, tremendous ingenuity has gone into the search for receptor types, which, after all, is the critical theoretical issue.

(1) *Differential absolute thresholds.* Taking advantage of the fact that there is an achromatic gray interval at low intensities before light is perceived as colored, Göthlin (1944) has made a direct experimental determination of the short wave-length primary in man's color sense. Both Young and Helmholtz had specified violet as the short wave-length fundamental because blue could be obtained by mixing green and violet. Maxwell, on the other hand, had specified blue because it is psychologically a more unitary experience than violet. Using violet hues between 430 and 455 mμ, Göthlin gradually increased intensity from subthreshold levels and noted the points at which both blue and red components of the violet sensation appeared. In all cases the first color experience to arise was *blue,* the sensation becoming violet (e.g. the red component added) at much higher intensities. This would seem to clinch the fact that B is a fundamental, having its own receptors, and violet a compound, unless there is some unknown factor operating here. This method would seem to be applicable to other points along the spectrum as a determinant of fundamentals, but for some reason no further information is available.

(2) *Neutral points of the color blind.* König (1897) thought that the neutral points of the color blind held the answer to cone types. With one type of receptor nonfunctional, the crossing of the *Grundempfindungen* for the other two should yield a white or gray neutral point (assuming the chemical shift discussed above). The fact that the protanopes have a neutral point at 495 mμ, the crossing of G and B functions (see Fig. 46), certainly fits this assumption. But if the third primary be called *blue,* then the R and G functions must cross twice in order to account for the reddish blue of the violet end of the spectrum (refer again to Fig. 46). By this logic, then, a *tritanopic* individual who is presumably deficient in the blue mechanism should show *two* neutral points, one about 460 mμ and the other about 570 mμ. Since König found only one neutral point about 570 mμ, he decided in favor of *violet* as the short wave-length component. Hecht (1930) follows this reasoning in choosing V rather than B for his functions, but he also cites more recent evidence obtained by Dieter in 1927 as showing the predicted second neutral point for tritanopes. To explain the dilemma of a V curve and a B psychological primacy, Hecht sug-

gests that some, say 10 per cent, of the R cones have taken on the spectral characteristics of the substance in the B cones. Light sufficient to excite the B mechanism therefore excites R minimally. In other words, Hecht assumes that all normal eyes are slightly red blind.

(3) *Binocular fusion of yellow*. Hecht (1930) has argued thus: '. . . if red light falls on the retina of one eye, and green light falls on the corresponding portion of the retina of the other eye, and the result is a yellow sensation, then only Young's idea is tenable' (p. 235). He reasons that if the yellow experience can be manufactured binocularly in this fashion, there is no need to postulate any Y cone. This reasoning is actually quite faulty. Ladd-Franklin, for example, could agree with the binocular mixture of Y from R and G, and still postulate a separate Y cone for other reasons. The important point is that were binocular production of yellow not possible, then the Young-Helmholtz theory would not be tenable; successful demonstration of the phenomenon does not mean it is the 'only' tenable theory.

After a confusing history of claims and counterclaims (e.g. between Helmholtz, who couldn't get it, and Hering, who could—which is an interesting reversal), it is gradually becoming clear that central fusion of red and green into yellow can occur. Although Hecht's own demonstration (1928) was soundly criticized by Murray (1939), Prentice (1948) has obtained the phenomenon under conditions that leave little room for doubt. What is probably more puzzling than the fact that binocular fusion of complementaries like red and green can occur is the fact that it is so difficult. In a rather extensive study on binocular mixtures, Pickford (1947) found that although similar colors (e.g. neighboring on the color circle) readily fused, complementaries did so only with great difficulty. In fact, the usual result of such attempts is binocular *rivalry,* not fusion, i.e. first one hue and then the other is centrally 'suppressed.' But why? We know that when intermingled red and green dots are presented to *one* eye, they easily fuse to yellow; we also know that two slightly different visual patterns presented to the *two* eyes fuse to a single contour experience, as in the perception of depth (cf. Chap. 6)—in fact, it is unusual under ordinary conditions that anything other than single vision with the two eyes occurs. What is the difference when corresponding retinal points of the two eyes are stimulated separately with red and green lights? One would expect that *only* binocular fusion could occur.

(4) *Microstimulation of the retina*. Hartridge (1946 *a, b, c*) has devised an instrument, essentially a microscope used in reverse, which will cast an extremely small image on the retina. He estimates that areas as small as the distance between the centers of adjacent foveal cones can be stimulated in this manner. It is not clear, however, to what extent diffraction in the ocular media and involuntary eye movements would obscure the results here. When such a stimulator is moved slowly across the fovea, hue changes are perceived although the wave-length composition of the stimulus is constant. Monochromatic orange (620 mμ) appears red in some loci and pale orange in others; monochromatic green (540 mμ) appears green, pale green, or even white. An achromatic white light may appear as red, as green or as blue, or as paler intermediaries, depending upon locus. Hartridge was also able to show that the fixation points for the various primary hues were in slightly different places in his own fovea, suggesting

a clustering of cones of the same type. The evidence up to this point seems quite compatible with the Young-Helmholtz conception of three-cone types. When a *foveal* luminosity curve was determined with this stimulator, however, two regions of reduced sensitivity appeared, one corresponding to blue and the other to *yellow*. Hartridge considers this evidence for the existence of an independent yellow mechanism, which would be compatible with the Ladd-Franklin hypothesis. Actually, given the extreme amount of overlap among R, G, and V sensation curves as developed by Hecht for the Young-Helmholtz theory (cf. Fig. 62), one would expect nearly any stimulating light to elicit nearly any color experience, depending on what particular receptors happened to be contacted. But this was not the case—for example, monochromatic oranges and yellows never appeared blue.

(5) *Electrophysiological analysis.* Hartridge was trying to obtain the ideal of separately exciting individual receptor elements. Can this be accomplished with electrophysiological techniques? Granit and his various col-

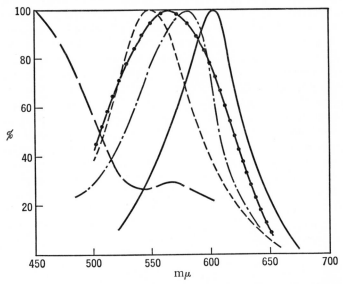

FIGURE 63. Sample of modulator curves for light adapted eye of a frog. Granit, *Journal of the Optical Society of America*, 1941, 31 : 575.

laborators (summarized in 1947) have devised a technique for use with animal subjects that also approaches this ideal. With the cornea and lens removed, a very fine micro-electrode is inserted into the retina. Electrical activity in one or more *optic fibers* (not receptors, unfortunately) which lie on the retinal surface can then be recorded while the characteristics of the visual stimulus are experimentally varied. The eyes of many different species have been studied in this manner. For a single reading, with the electrode in a stable locus and after appropriate pre-adaptation of the eye, the minimum intensity of light of a given wave length required to produce a just recordable response is determined; by varying the wave length of the stimulus on successive tests, the sensitivity curve for that particular locus is obtained.

When an eye was sufficiently dark-adapted, almost any locus was found to yield a *scotopic dominator curve*. This sensitivity curve has its maximum near 500 mμ and closely matches the absorption spectrum for visual purple, i.e. it is the typical rod function. After an eye containing both rods and cones had been sufficiently light-adapted, a *photopic dominator curve* could be obtained from most any locus. It has its maximum near 560 mμ, thus demonstrating the Purkinje shift, and is similar to the cone visibility curve for human observers. Occasionally, after light-adaptation, certain placements of the electrode would yield curves having *narrow* sensitivity ranges. Granit has termed these *photopic modulator curves*. These narrow curves are quite variable in their maxima, but tend to cluster in certain regions of the spectrum—*R* modulators (maxima about 600 mμ), rarer *Y* modulators (about 580 mμ), *G* modulators (about 530 mμ), and *B* modulators (about 450 mμ). Figure 63 describes a set of modulator curves for the frog's eye, which is similar to man's in its photopic spectrum, along with the commonly appearing photopic dominator curve.

On the basis of these and other observations Granit (1947, Chaps. 18-22) has developed a theory which is also a kind of compromise between the classic Young-Helmholtz and the Hering positions. Although, like Young, he postulates a limited number of receptors yielding unique sensations (the modulators), he does not restrict himself to three, being quite open to the possibility that there may be more than the four (*R, Y, G, B*) modulator mechanisms already evident in the data. Like Hering, however, he separates the color and brightness aspects of sensation, attributing the former to modulator action and the latter to dominator action. This separation of color and brightness into two neural mechanisms has certain advantages, as we shall see. Granit's hypothetical excitation curves are shown in Fig. 64. As was the case with Hecht's curves, these functions are so constructed as to summate into the luminosity curve for human day vision. Unlike Hecht's analysis, however, Granit has made no rigorous attempt to integrate the phenomena of color mixture, hue discrimination, spectral saturation, and so on with his hypothetical functions. These curves are chiefly a graphic summary of his electrophysiological findings.

Certain of Granit's observations lead to serious problems. He reports, for example, that 'in a mixed eye a great majority of the units tested will, sooner or later, give a sensitivity curve determined by visual purple. This . . . is evidence that both rods and cones can activate the same nerve fiber' (p. 305). Polyak (1941) has offered histological evidence that cone endings do overlap on bipolar cells, as well as cone and rod endings merging the same way. In fact, Polyak has theorized that the cones must give qualitatively different responses to wave lengths which are 'analyzed' by the bipolar cells. But what will the *sensation* be in such cases? Will one and the same fiber convey 'red' information while its response is being determined by an *R*-cone modulator and then turn about and convey 'white' information when its response is being determined by the rod-dominators? If so, we must discard the law of specific energies of nerve fibers—and, indeed, we may have to do just that. But let us look more closely at Granit's method. He frankly admits there is no guarantee that his micro-electrodes were recording from only a single fiber. Suppose that the electrodes were actually picking up activity from a small *group* of fibers, and keep in mind that his method (noting just-recordable response) was one that selects the most sensitive elements for a given condition: under conditions of bright-adaptation the fiber for a 'red' modulator under the electrode would determine the sensitivity function but, as the eye became dark-adapted, fibers for rod dominators would come to determine the function. In such a case, the Purkinje shift obtained at a single locus would not necessarily refute the specific energies law.

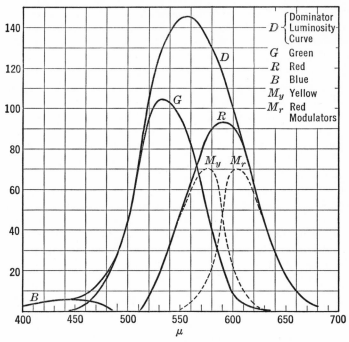

FIGURE 64. Basic sensation curves proposed by Granit. The photopic dominator curve (D) is a synthesis of modulator functions. Granit, *Sensory Mechanisms of the Retina,* Oxford University Press, Inc., New York, 1947, p. 332.

But what about the modulator curves themselves? These relatively narrow and widely separated sensitivity functions bear no resemblance to Hecht's fundamental curves for *R, G,* and *V* cones, and, whereas Hecht's functions are purely hypothetical, these modulator curves at least approximate recordings from individual fibers. *If Granit's observations on modulator functions prove to be valid as indicators of the spectral sensitivities of different types of cones, then Hecht's analysis and the theory it supports must go by the board.* But again we must look into the method. Threshold observations are tricky matters, requiring extremely rigid control over both the degree of pre-adaptation and the length of time following at which observations are made. The fact that individual curves for the same modulator in the same species often showed considerable variation in maxima suggests the existence of considerable errors in measurement. It doesn't seem at all likely that receptor chemistries for the same modulator mechanism could vary sufficiently to account for these differences. On the other hand, although we have no guarantee that single fibers were being measured here, it would be difficult to explain the *narrow* sensitivity curves on this basis. Observations of this order constitute a serious challenge to the adequacy of the Young-Helmholtz theory.

Brightness and Color Vision

As was noted earlier in this chapter, *saturation varies with intensity.* If the intensity of monochromatic light is raised above or lowered below the optimal level, the saturation of the color experience decreases. And even with strictly foveal stimuli, all wave lengths of light except extreme spectral red evoke colorless, gray experience if the intensity is lowered sufficiently (Purdy, as reported in Troland, 1930, pp. 167-8). The intensity range through which chromatic stimuli yield colorless experience is called the *photochromatic interval* (a better term would be the *achromatic interval*), and it has been shown to be widest for short wave lengths and narrowest for long ones, wider in the periphery than in the fovea. A special case of the relation between saturation and intensity is *chromatic summation:* as the area of a stimulus is reduced to very small size, saturation decreases toward gray (i.e. areal summation holds for color as well as for brightness). Color theorists have paid little attention to these well-known facts, yet they pose serious problems for views of the Young-Helmholtz and Ladd-Franklin types. Why should the quality of sensation correlated with activity in 'green' fibers change from green to gray merely because the frequency of impulses in them is reduced? The change from green to gray implies a shift in 'what' fibers are delivering impulses, but neither of these theories puts 'white' receptors in the fovea. Granit has no difficulty here: since the white dominators have a wider sensitivity range than the more specialized modulators, increasing or decreasing intensity from the optimum shifts the population of receptors excited in favor of the dominators; reducing the area of stimulation decreases the probability of contacting the less numerous modulators and hence 'whitens' the sensation.

The study of *chromatic adaptation* has had an extensive but mottled history (cf. Cohen, 1946 *b*). The general procedure is to expose a part of the retina to a constant 'fatiguing' stimulus and measure changes in saturation, hue, and brightness as a function of time, using a fresh region of the retina as a basis for comparison. All investigators agree that there is loss of saturation under continued stimulation. This would be expected in terms of all the theories we have considered, since the more intensely excited receptors should adapt most rapidly, balancing the color equation and 'whitening' the experience. All theories would also predict a loss in brightness, owing to a total reduction in impulse frequency. Although it is true that many investigators have obtained this result, the most recent and carefully executed experiment in the area (Cohen, 1946 *a*) describes an actual *increase* in brightness. This implies an increase in the total impulse frequency during chromatic adaptation—as if reduction in rate of fire in the dominant mechanism were releasing other mechanisms from inhibition. We shall return to this matter of inhibitory mechanisms at a later point. Finally, these theories would predict a shift in hue during the course of adaptation, a shift toward certain 'basic colors' as stable points: suppose R and G cones (or modulators) are firing in the ratio of 2 to 1 for an orange stimulus; the more rapid reduction in R impulses will produce not only a loss in saturation but also a shift in hue toward the green region. Again, most investigators report this phenomenon, but Cohen found no consistent shifts in hue during adaptation. Unless Cohen's results can be explained away as the results of some artifact (which this reviewer, at least, is unable to discover), they constitute negative evidence for existing theories.

What about brightness functions for the color blind—do they offer any information for an evaluation of color theories? Figure 65 combines the

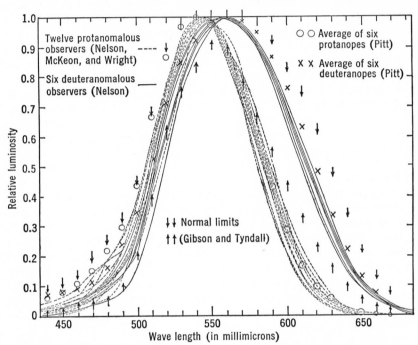

FIGURE 65. Relative luminosity functions of anomalous trichromats (six deuteranomalous, twelve protanomalous) compared with averages for dichromats and with limits for normal trichromats. Judd, *Journal of the Optical Society of America,* 1943, 33:303.

data of several studies, showing *luminosity functions* for several types of color blindness as well as the range considered normal. Protanopes, to be sure, have reduced sensitivity in the red region, but they have also relatively increased sensitivity to light in the blue region. Deuteranopes, who presumably should show reduced sensitivity in the green region, actually return a luminosity curve that falls well within the normal range. Another interesting point in these data is that protanomalous trichromats show nearly as much deviancy in sensitivity to red light as do the protanopic dichromats, yet the former vary from normal behavior only in the proportions of their color mixtures. The *saturation of the spectrum* for color defectives has been studied by Chapanis (1944), using absolute saturation thresholds at nineteen spectral points as a measure. All types of color blindness were shown to suffer loss in saturation throughout the spectrum, as compared with normal controls. For the deuteranope this means that a marked loss in saturation of the spectrum can occur without any concurrent abnormality in brightness sensitivity. Chapanis (1946, 1947) has also studied *dark adaptation* in the color deficient. Whereas both protanopes and deuteranopes returned normal dark-adaptation functions when a *violet* test light was used, and deuteranopes were also normal with a *red* test light, the adaptation curves of *protanopes* to *red* light revealed a novel and previously unreported effect: after about 12 minutes in the dark, during which time little adaptation occurs, the protanopic retina suddenly begins to adapt further to red light, reaching a final level that is essentially normal. Since this effect fails to appear when the red stimulus is restricted to the foveal, rod-free area, Chapanis concludes that 'the rods are sensitive to red light, but . . . this cannot be observed in the color normal individual because his cones are at least equally as sensitive to red as are his rods.'

Even in its contemporary form, the Young-Helmholtz theory has trouble with these data. From the close overlap of Hecht's sensation curves, it can be seen that the mere shift in cone chemistry (R cones to G or vice versa) should cause little change in luminosity functions. This fits the deuteranope but not the protanope—Hecht (1934) frankly admits the inadequacy of the three-cone hypothesis on this point. Chapanis finds no support in his saturation data for either the classic or the contemporary version of the Young-Helmholtz theory. Since basic sensation curves for the Ladd-Franklin view have never been worked out rigorously, it cannot be said whether it would cover these data or not. By virtue of its dissociation of hue and brightness mechanisms, Granit's dominator-modulator theory is in a better position. The deuteranope lacks the 'green' modulator, but his photopic dominator system is normal; the protanope lacks the 'red' modulator and his photopic dominator system is also deficient. The deuteranope's marked loss in saturation without concomitant reduction in brightness sensitivity also becomes understandable. But why should protanopia alone be associated with malfunctioning dominators and why should the curve have the form it does? Jahn (1946) suggests that dominator functions are recorded from giant ganglion cells which have multisynaptic connections with both rods and all types of cones, whereas modulator functions are recorded from midget ganglion cells (cf. Polyak, 1941) which are associated with single cones via single bipolar cells. In deuteranopia it is the 'green' midget ganglia that are nonfunctional, but since the 'green' cones still contribute to dominator channels via the giant multisynaptic ganglia, the luminosity curve is unaffected. In protanopia it is the 'red' cones that are nonfunctional, and hence both 'red' modulator activity and luminosity in the red region are affected.

Do the Rods Play Any Role in Color Vision?

Although it is generally agreed that at least three mechanisms must participate in color vision, it is not necessary that all three be cones in the usual sense. Several writers have toyed with the idea that the rods may contribute to color vision. The most detailed development of this notion has been made by Willmer (1946). Noting the lack of anatomical evidence for different types of cones, he specifies a single type of cone which contributes the R component. Ordinary dark-adapting rods are assumed to contribute a B component and a class of nonadapting day rods contributes the third component. Since the central fovea is supposed to have only cones and nonadapting rods (i.e. is diplodic), it is relatively blue-blind and prone to hue-discrimination confusions when intensity is varied. How these three mechanisms combine in the production of white is not entirely clear.

There is considerable indirect evidence suggesting an identification of the *B* component of color vision with a rodlike mechanism. In the first place, Pieron (1932, as reported in Granit, 1947) has shown that the 'rising time' (reaction latency) for perceiving stimulation is longest for blue light and shortest for red light; it will be recalled that in the *ERG*,

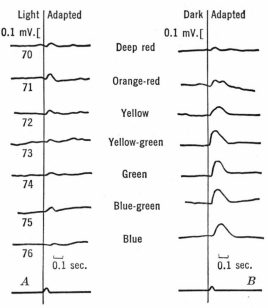

FIGURE 66. *ERG*'s for various wave lengths in (*A*) light-adapted and (*B*) dark-adapted human eye. Adrian, *Journal of Physiology*, 1945, **104**:89.

as well as in the electrical response of the optic nerve, activity attributable to rods showed a longer latency than that attributable to cones. Adrian (1945) has recorded *ERG*'s from his own eye. When stimulating the peripheral retina, he found a brief diphasic response to characterize the cone mechanism (e.g. after bright adaptation) and a monophasic response to characterize the rod mechanism (e.g. after dark adaptation). Using color filters of known transmission values, the response to deep red was then found to be a pure cone affair, as would be predicted, and that to blue revealed *only* the rod component, which would not be predicted from most theories. Intermediary stimuli displayed the effects of both mechanisms. These results are shown in Fig. 66. Granit (1947, p. 341) adds this bit of evidence: a blue modulator function is prominent in the pure rod retina of the guinea pig but absent in the pure cone retina of the snake. Whether the foveal area is in fact 'blue-blind' or tritanopic is very much a matter of controversy in the recent literature (cf. Craik, 1943; Willmer, 1944; Willmer and Wright, 1945; Hartridge, 1944, 1945 *a*).

Some facts about *after-images* are germane to this discussion. If a black-and-white figure is fixated for a few seconds under high illumination and one then looks at a neutral gray paper, a negative after-image will be seen, the brightness relations of the original now being reversed. If a colored patch is used as a stimulus, the after-image is typically in the complementary hue. Both of these phenomena point to selective adaptation of the visual receptors. Depending on their excitation characteristics, different receptor types respond at different rates to the original stimulus and hence adapt to different degrees; when a uniform field is then substituted, these receptors fire at *different* rates depending on their states of adaptation, and yield a reversed (brightness and/or hue) image. Furthermore, as might be expected from Pieron's latency data above, the after-effects of a brief flash of white light are not achromatic, but rather appear as a 'flight of colors'—which, for some unknown reason, do not have any regular order of appearance (cf. Woodworth, 1938).

The after-effects above depend upon prolonged or intense stimulation and are persistent enough to be easily observed. Following any retinal stimulation, however, there is a very rapid series of after-effects which are of considerable theoretical interest but are difficult to study. Normally we are unaware of them. These fleeting events can be disentangled by *moving the light stimulus across the retina,* thus translating temporal effects into spatial terms. Bidwell (1898), one of the first to use this method, reported that pale, bluish semicircles seemed to float along behind a circular, white stimulus, these coming to be known as 'Bidwell's Ghosts.' Investigators using this method (McDougall, 1904; Fröhlich, 1921, 1922; Karwoski and Crook, 1937; Karwoski and Warrener, 1942) describe the following sequence of events following a brief stimulus: (1) a very fleeting positive after-image of the same hue as the original, called the *Hering image,* with a latency of about one-twentieth of a second; (2) following a dark interval, a second positive image appears which is called the *Purkinje image,* sometimes complementary in hue but usually bluish, with a latency of about one-fifth of a second; (3) further oscillations of longer phase and reduced intensity occur. The Purkinje after-image has a long latency, becomes increasingly prominent as illumination is lowered, is predominantly blue in hue, and is difficult to obtain with extreme red light or on the fovea—all these facts suggest involvement of the rod mechanism. It is true that Karwoski and Warrener (1942) report obtaining this image with red light, and unbrokenly when a slit is moved across the foveal region, but the red stimulus was somewhat orange and the image had a 'bulge' (e.g. even longer latency) when crossing the fovea. If the fovea be considered a 'blind spot' with respect to rod vision, this bulge may represent a filling in of the form at some higher level in the projection system where the foveal 'gap' is eliminated.

The biggest single stumbling block for Willmer's position is that he specifies the dark-adapting rods as contributing the B component. It will be recalled that Granit has shown a correlation between the regeneration of about 50 per cent maximum visual purple and the appearance of the rod component in the ERG; the ways in which the 'hump' in the dark-adaptation curve can be shifted in latency by manipulating the wave length and intensity of pre-adapting and test lights also fits the view that the 'ideal' rods are not functional in day vision. We might also note that the onset of the rod 'limb' of the dark-adaptation curve is accompanied by simple desaturation of the hue of a colored stimulus patch, not a progressive 'bluing' before turning white, which Willmer's theory should demand.

There is, however, another way a rodlike mechanism can be brought into the picture. Suppose we relegate Granit's 'ideal,' dark-adapting rods to simple night-vision functions, but identify his 'conelike' rods with the B component in color vision. We should then have to postulate two types of cones, R and $G,$ as a minimum. If we further assume that these rodlike receptors are present in the fovea yet have their maximum density some $7°$ to $10°$ eccentric (rather than $20°,$ as the 'ideal' rods), then certain other facts fall in line. Optimum form perception in the dark-adapted eye has a higher threshold as well as a more central locus on the retina than sheer brightness perception. Even in the fovea, saturation decreases as intensity is lowered below an optimum, and there is an achromatic interval, widest in the blue region of the spectrum and narrowest in the red region, where experience is neutral gray. We also have to assume here that these conelike rods have a wider intensity range than cones proper. In Ladd-Franklin's evolutionary scheme, the conelike rods (or rodlike cones) would be the first step in the development of true cones, more specialized in their intensity coverage and neural connections than primitive rods but retaining the spectral characteristics of rods and their slower latency. Why should these mechanisms yield achromatic experience rather than blue experience when stimulated alone (e.g. at low intensities)? Actually, all color vision theories agree that hue depends upon the *ratio* of rates of fire in several mechanisms, quite independent of the quality mediated by any mechanism alone. These conelike rods could yield achromatic experience when firing alone and yet *modulate* a complex experience toward 'blue' when fused with the excitation of R and G cones.

Inhibitory Processes in Color Vision?

We have already uncovered some evidence for inhibitory mechanisms in color vision. Cohen's (1946 *a*) demonstration that adaptation to monochromatic light was accompanied by an over-all increase in total brightness suggested the release of certain mechanisms from inhibition. The fact that protanopes apparently have somewhat heightened sensitivity in the blue region of the spectrum, as compared with normals (Hecht, 1930), has similar implications. And most significantly, it will be recalled that the direct data of colorimetric matching of the spectrum indicate something other than simple addition of excitation is involved. At nearly all loci along the spectrum except those representing the wave lengths of the primaries themselves, some one component must have a *negative value* (i.e. must be added to the spectral test patch) if saturation is to be equated.

Basing his argument chiefly on the occurrence of these negative values in colorimetric equations, Göthlin (1943) has developed a theory which, like the Young-Helmholtz view, utilizes $R, G,$ and B receptors but which also includes inhibitory processes. As shown in Fig. 67, excitatory and inhibitory effects are conceived as a system of balances: R and G are mutually inhibitory, their cancellation or balance yielding the yellow sensation; R and G together are mutually inhibitory with $B,$ the total balance yielding the white sensation. Complementary after-images are cited as evidence. Strong green light, for example, excites the G receptors maximally, simultaneously inhibiting R (first balance) and B (total balance); upon removal of the green light and consequent release from inhibition of both R and B components, a complementary purple after-image is seen. In ordinary color vision, impulses from R and G, in varying proportions, account for all sensations between red and green, their equality yielding yellow; impulses in B interact with those in the first balance, yielding violets and purples if the first balance is weighted toward R and yielding blue-greens if the first balance

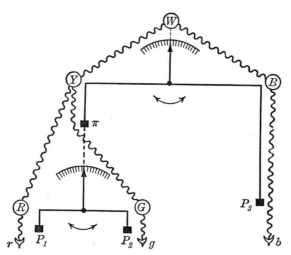

FIGURE 67. Diagrammatic representation of Göthlin's inhibitory process theory as a system of interlocking balances—here as arranged in the production of white sensory quality. Göthlin, *American Journal of Psychology*, 1943, 56:546.

is weighted toward G. This is an attractively simple theory, but its assumption that R/G and B are *mutually* inhibitory runs into difficulty.

Close inspection of Wright's colorimetric matching data (cf. Fig. 46) indicates that while B is successfully inhibited by R and possibly by G, R *is inhibited by neither G nor B*. In interpreting these curves it must be realized that the negative values for a component actually indicate *lack* of inhibition, i.e. this component was excited in mixing the other two wave lengths and hence is present to desaturate the experience. Near 500 mμ, for example, both G and B are vigorously excited in the production of blue-green, but R must be added to the spectral patch in order to match saturation, i.e. R mechanisms were *not* inhibited in this mixture. To this we may add some highly relevant neurophysiological information. Granit (1947, pp. 113-14) definitely considers P_{III} in the ERG to represent retinal inhibitory processes, and this component of the ERG has been identified with cone pathways. Adrian (1945) has shown that the negative component of the ERG is most pronounced for red stimulation, decreasing as wave length of the stimulus is shifted toward blue. Secondly, we have evidence that fibers in the optic nerve vary in diameter (Bishop, 1933), larger fibers being generally associated with a more rapid rate of impulses, and we found in the preceding section that the B mechanism displays the long latency characteristic of small-fiber systems. Finally, it has been shown (Bishop and O'Leary, 1938) that the large, fast-rate fibers deliver their impulses chiefly to the optic cortex; Adrian (1946) reports that although red light readily yields a large cortical response, blue light produced no detectable effect here.

This admittedly sketchy information suggests a modification of Göthlin's view which is more nearly in accord with evidence for a rodlike mechanism as the *B* component. In connection with an earlier analysis of brightness summation, inhibition, and acuity, it was shown that these phenomena could be incorporated by the simple assumption that inhibition of locus *a* upon locus *b* occurs when the frequency of impulses received laterally at *b* is more rapid than that received directly through its projection pathways. If we assume that lateral connections exist between the different color-producing mechanisms, which seems most likely, then the same hypothesis would apply here: *B activity would be inhibited to the extent that R activity is present because of the latter's more rapid impulse rate.* By the same token, any factor that diminishes the rate of fire in *R* fibers should 'release' the *B* component. At the neurophysiological level the 'off-effect' in the *ERG* represents such a 'release'—it is prominent in the response to red light but absent in the response to blue. The increased total brightness during adaptation found by Cohen might represent a similar effect. The fact that protanopia is accompanied by both a decided shift in luminosity of the spectrum and relatively enhanced brightness in the *blue* region, while deuteranopia is not, also becomes more understandable if we assume that an elimination of *R* impulses has 'released' the *B* mechanism from inhibition. All this is very hypothetical, but then, color vision is still the happy hunting ground for theorists.*

Summary

The Young-Helmholtz theory of color vision is the most widely accepted view among psychologists today. It has the twin advantages of simplicity and Hecht's quantification. It runs into a number of difficulties, however. In order to account for the experiences of the color blind, it must postulate a variety of shifts in cone chemistries on an *ad hoc* basis. Ladd-Franklin's theory, which adds a yellow cone and an evolutionary rationale, does better here. But both of these views have trouble with brightness functions of both normals and color blind: why should color experiences become less saturated (a change of quality toward 'white') as intensity is lowered? why should protanopes have a markedly distorted luminosity curve but deuteranopes a normal one? Granit's dominator-modulator theory works much better here because of its separation of color and brightness functions. And if Granit's basic observations on the luminosity functions of individual optic nerve fibers (?) prove valid, Hecht's theoretical sensation curves and the theory they support must be discarded. Finally, there is considerable evidence that the *B* component in color vision has quite different properties than either *R* or *G* components, in fact, properties decidedly rodlike in

---

* Unexpected confirmation of this interpretation has recently been found in an as yet unpublished study by J. Cohen and W. A. Gibson. Analysis of the color space by the theory of invariants showed, among other things, that one receptor must be completely an inhibitor while the other two are completely excitors, or vice versa—in either case, some inhibitory process is required.

nature. Willmer has developed a theory on this basis which postulates only one kind of cone interacting with two types of rods, adapting and nonadapting. A similar possibility was suggested here: namely, that there are only two types of cones, R and G, with the B component being contributed by a 'conelike' nonadapting rod.

All of these theories relegate the actual determination of hue sensations to some process of fusion in the higher centers, probably the visual cortex. When, for example, we look at a patchwork quilt of many colors, a different ratio of impulses in several fiber types is produced within each patch as subjectively represented. We speak glibly about central 'interpretation' of color at this point, but this is merely a confession of complete ignorance in regard to mechanism—there is no 'little man' up there busily noting down incoming frequencies at all loci and judging their ratios. It must be a remarkable mechanism, however, unlike anything we know of in other modalities (except, possibly, olfaction). According to Le Gros Clark (1947), in the course of projection from retina to brain three fiber types coming from corresponding points of the two eyes are segregated in bands in the geniculates and passed up to each cortical locus having unique spatial reference. Somehow, at each one of these cortical loci, ratios of impulse rates channeling upon common synapses become a variety of experienced hues.

Part II

PERCEPTUAL PROCESSES

In the classic view of structuralism, sensations were the elements with which percepts are compounded. It seemed proper, therefore, to have a section on sensory processes followed by one on perception. Today the linkage between sensation and perception is not so close. As part of an increasing recognition of the role that central determinants play in behavior, there has been a growing tendency to think of perception in relation to phenomena such as concept formation and meaning. In keeping with this trend, the following chapters were originally planned to introduce a final section on Symbolic Processes, which includes chapters on problem-solving, thinking, and language—and perhaps they belong in that context. But in the course of writing about perception it became increasingly evident that most of our information in this area lies on the sensory side. This is probably owing in part to the classic tradition and its effect upon the directions of research, but it is certainly owing as well to the paucity of techniques for investigating central events.

As a matter of fact, this dilemma will serve as a basis for organizing this section on perception. In the first chapter we shall consider three theoretical points of view toward perception—physiological, behavioristic, and gestalt—and their application to the basic problem of perceptual organization. In the second chapter we shall try to segregate those phenomena, usually considered perceptual, that can be shown to depend largely upon mechanisms inherent in the projection systems. These will include contour and contrast effects, figural after-effects, perception of movement, and certain aspects of space perception—all of which are found to represent, in one way or another, the dynamics of contour processes. In the third and final chapter of this section we shall study those phenomena, also considered perceptual, that clearly *cannot* be explained in terms of known projection mechanisms. Certain aspects of distance perception, the perceptual constancies, and the effects of motivational and attitudinal determinants upon perception require the operation of mechanisms beyond the projection system, which may be termed 'central dynamics.' As to the nature of the latter we know just about nothing, but this does not preclude interest in these processes.

Chapter 5

THE NATURE OF PERCEPTUAL ORGANIZATION

MEANING OF 'PERCEPTION'

Can one ever experience a 'pure' sensation? It is doubtful that even the most arduously trained introspectionists achieved this degree of abstraction, although many of them learned to talk as if they had. True, one may pay attention to a pressure stimulation on his forearm and describe his sensations exhaustively, but it still appears as a 'figure' against the background of other sensations; it is still *perceived* relative to a meaningful frame of reference. Perhaps for the newborn infant, as William James insisted, the world is a blooming, buzzing confusion of pure sensations sans organization, but by the time the infant is able to communicate its experiences to us, perceptual organization has become an integration of many unconscious skills. Anything even approaching a pure sensation is a traumatic experience to the adult: sometimes the slight movements of one's ear against the pillow produce a roaring sound, like coal sliding down into the cellar or a flight of bombers approaching. Until, by immediate experiment, the source of this experience is localized—and the sensation 'put in its place' so to speak—one feels a mounting anxiety. This datum fits into no frame of reference.

What are the characteristics of the phenomena most people term 'perceptual'? The following six characteristics may help us understand what the term means to them. (1) These phenomena involve *organization* of peripheral, sensory events—looking about us we see patterned objects in space, not mere conglomerations of color points. (2) They manifest *holistic,* all-or-nothing properties, i.e. a pattern of dots or lines may give rise to a complete percept of a square or a cube. (3) They display *constancy* to a high degree—a white house seems to remain so despite immense variations in luminance as high noon revolves into evening, but they are (4) also broadly *transposable*—a triangular stimulus can be directed to many different parts of the retina without disturbing response. (5) They operate *selectively*— for the hungry organism, food-related objects assume figure qualities. Finally, (6) they are very *flexible* processes—the regular black-and-white pattern of a tile floor assumes a bewildering variety of temporary organizations as we watch it.

What do all these characteristics taken together imply in regard to the meaning of 'perception'? The term seems to be applied (a) whenever experience varies despite constancy of underlying sensory events or (b) whenever experience is constant despite variations in sensory events. In other words, *the term 'perception' refers to a set of variables that intervene between sensory stimulation and awareness,* as the latter state is indexed by verbal or other modes of response. Since 'sensory stimulation' usually refers to receptor input (in vision, the physical distribution of radiant energies upon the retina), modifications introduced in the course of projection onto the higher centers contribute part of this intervening variability. But there are other sources of variability as well. A large part of our problem in these chapters will be to distinguish between those intervening variables for which fairly well-known neurological mechanisms can be specified and those for which dynamisms of unknown nature must be postulated. We shall refer to the latter, for convenience' sake, as 'central perceptual determinants.'

Are these central perceptual determinants anything other than habits? If we conceive of habit as a single-stage affair (S–R), then the notion is insufficient. The other extreme position—that perceptions are patterns of forces in a field independent of central anatomy—is no more adequate. Hebb (1949, pp. 12-16) has aptly brought out this dilemma: 'Köhler . . . starts out with the facts of perceptual generalization, in his theory of cerebral fields of force, and then cannot deal with learning. . . The theory elaborated by Hull, on the other hand, is to be regarded as providing first of all for the stability of learning. It then has persistent difficulty with perception' (p. 15). Hebb then proposes as a resolution of the dilemma what is in essence a two-stage learning theory having much in common with the *mediation hypothesis* to be described later in this book (cf. pp. 392ff.). He also offers a feasible neurological mechanism for it which we shall consider in a moment.

Many thinkers of materialistic bent believe that the 'something added' in perceptual behavior is nothing other than stimulation from the organism's own responsive activities. Depending on how the external stimulus is responded to, and thus on an added pattern of proprioceptive stimulation playing back from the muscles, the total experience will vary. Many casual observations certainly point to motor contribution in perceiving: if, while coasting down an incline in an automobile with the motor off, one steps on the accelerator—a movement normally followed by the perceptual complex of acceleration—he now becomes definitely aware of being *held back.* This illusion is so clear the writer required assurance by a mechanic that this operation cannot possibly affect the movement of a car when it is out of gear and the engine is turned off! Obviously the responses that contribute to perceiving, if they do contribute, do not need to be overt. One's perception of a situation can change abruptly without any observable movement (as in reversible figures, for example). Motor theories are, however, prevalent and persistent; we shall find them cropping up at various points in these chapters on perception and later in connection with thought and meaning.

Finally, a word is in order concerning the relation between perception and *meaning.* One would be hard put to draw a defensible distinction between the two. The faces of a group of men on the picket line during a serious strike are caught by a news photographer: 'grim determination to defend their rights as individuals' is seen by one percipient; 'savage aggression at society' is seen by another less favorably disposed toward unions.

One could remark with equal appropriateness that the facial expressions are *perceived* differently by these two men of opposed attitude or that these expressions *mean* different things to them. Similarly, one may say that a Rorschach blot means such and such to a subject or that the subject perceives it in this or that manner. True, perception is usually thought of as being on the input side of the behavioral equation, whereas meaning is thought of as being on the output side. But perception is certainly at the termination of input and meaning is certainly at the initiation of output— together they occupy the no man's land of central mediation.

THREE POINTS OF VIEW TOWARD PERCEPTUAL PHENOMENA

The three attitudes toward perceptual phenomena we shall discuss— physiological, gestalt, and behavioristic—are merely attitudes; they are not theories in any rigorous sense, nor are they mutually exclusive. The physiological point of view reflects a parsimonious attempt to reduce all perceptual phenomena to known neurophysiological mechanisms, motivated usually by an abhorrence of hypothetical, explanatory constructs. The gestalt viewpoint makes full use of hypothetical central forces and, by doing so, is able to cover the wide range of perceptual phenomena more fully. The behavioristic position, least adequately formulated in this area, stresses the learned nature of perceptual behavior. All three views will contribute to any final understanding of the problem.

Physiological Point of View

Traditionally this has come down to an attempt to explain all perceptual phenomena in terms of known *peripheral* mechanisms. In the case of vision, with a retinal structure as complicated neurologically as many higher centers, this has often proved fruitful—so fruitful, in fact, that we should always look first at the retina before postulating central processes. There are many perceptual phenomena, however, which cannot be explained at the periphery. Does this mean we must assume 'forces' and 'fields' in the brain? Not necessarily. In recent years the neurophysiologist has been pushing the 'known' back from the retina toward the cortex, and he has carried his point of view right along—only the point of view now is to explain perceptual phenomena in terms of known *central* mechanisms rather than postulating hypothetical forces. This is certainly a healthy point of view and one that eventually must prove valid (providing fruitful hypotheses are suggested to direct the lines of neurophysiological experimentation).

So that we may be able to make use of this point of view wherever fruitful, let us gather some of the more pertinent information regarding the visual pathways. First, the *general plan* of the system: The impulses that eventuate in visual experience start as an 'irregular screen-plate reproduction' (Troland, 1930) of the incident radiant energies on the sensitive surface of the *retina,* i.e. the retinal image. The possibilities for modification in the layers of the retina, including summative, inhibitory, and adaptative effects, have been described earlier (cf. Chap. 4). Once these impulses are channeled into *optic nerve fibers,* there is little chance for modification of the image; although at the *optic chiasma* projections from the left visual field of both retinas are merged in course to the right hemisphere and vice versa, there are no possibilities of synaptic interaction. Synaptic junctures in the *geniculates* do provide some possibilities for interaction. From this point the image fans out in the *optic radians* and is projected onto the lowest level of the *optic cortex*. Here, in Brodmann's area 17, easily recognized by its striate appearance, there are several levels of densely packed neurons and rather unlimited possibilities for modification in the image, especially in the matwork of tangential 'association' fibers in the upper levels of the visual cortex. At this point the story becomes rather vague. Troland, for example, spoke of 'neurograms,' which were assumed to be learned organizations called forth on some similarity basis by the patterns of incoming peripheral impulses, degree of coherence between aroused neurogram and incoming pattern determining the stability of perception. Relations of this view to certain gestalt notions will become apparent.

Today we have more information on how the visual system works. (1) *Spontaneous activity.* Many cells in the brain are set so as to fire periodically and independently of afferent stimulation, although afferent stimulation of such cells can serve to modulate or control their spontaneous activity. The *EEG* is assumed to be correlated with synchronization of this spontaneous activity. (2) *Reciprocal overlap.* 'The principle of reciprocal overlap has long been recognized, but only recently has direct evidence become available. . . In the cat, optic tract endings in the geniculate divide into several branches and as many as 40 ring-shaped boutons have been seen on single radiation cells which may come from as many as 10 optic tract fibers. Each fiber also divides to form synapses with several radiation cells' (Marshall and Talbot, 1942, pp. 121-2). This provides for multiplication of pathway and summation of activities. There is also accumulating evidence that the firing of cells typically requires the summated (in both time and place) stimulations from several afferent endings. Further, the greater the area of contact, i.e. number of specific boutons (knobs) or free axon-type junctures between two cells, the greater the probability that the firing of one will be decisive in determining the firing of the other.

Now let us look at the projection system more carefully. The traditional view implies both a point-for-point *spatial* correspondence between retina and cortex and a *temporal* synchrony of impulses, so that the 'retinal image' can be faithfully transformed into a 'cortical image.' (3) *Temporal dispersion.* As we have already seen in studying the electroretinogram, the retinal image is somewhat dispersed in time within the optic tract. Further dispersion occurs in the higher centers. Bartley and Bishop (1940) have shown that a single short flash produces a multiple response extending over appreciable portions of a second. Closed circuits among interneurons at various levels can add to the dispersion of the image through time (Lorente de Nó, 1938). (4) *Spatial dispersion.* The evidence for reciprocal overlap disrupts the pretty picture of a retinal mosaic simply projected onto a cortical mosaic. And although there is greater overlap in the peripheral than in the foveal projection systems, the difference is one of degree. Another extended quotation from Marshall and Talbot will be useful at this point. 'The anatomical conception of one-to-one projection of the retina onto the cortex then, may be regarded as functionally correct in so far as the maintenance of spatial relations is concerned. But quantitatively the unit paths near central vision should now be conceived, not as lines, but as expanding cylinders whose ends bear a ratio of 1:10,000, and a cellular ratio of perhaps 1:100. These unit paths then are related at each synaptic level by reciprocal dendritic overlap of increasing extent. . . We must conclude that there is one primary cortical locus for each foveal cone. But multiplication of path makes that locus a group . . . of cortical cells, which would all have nearly equivalent connections to the retinal cone. . . If synaptic effect is proportional to the number of knobs excited, then our cylindrical unit-path would be changed by reciprocal overlap to, say, a "gaussian distribution of connections" symmetrical about its axis' * (1942, pp. 134-5). Binocular corresponding retinal points are found to project to the same cortical areas.

The end of complication is not yet. (5) *Eye movements.* It is usually assumed that, for the purposes of the theorist, the eyes remain stationary and in perfect fixation during experimental observations. As a matter of fact, the eyeballs are in constant fluttering motion, called *physiological nystagmus* (cf. Marshall and Talbot, pp. 136-9). Between ten and a hundred times per second there are tremors falling within 2' (4 cones); about five times per second fluctuations within 4' (8 cones) occur; and about one time per second it reaches 30' (60 cones). Unless the visual field is perfectly homogeneous (a rare situation), this means that there are continuous changes in excitation level, especially for cells near the borders of intensity differentials in the field. Under normal conditions of observation, therefore, the 'retinal image' is itself a shifting, fluctuating pattern of intensity gradients.

Does this revised picture of the projection system make impossible a neurophysiological interpretation of visual phenomena? Not at all. It does require that a dynamic *statistical conception* be substituted for the classic geometrical one, but this actually gives the physiological point of view added potentialities. It becomes possible to demonstrate how details and regularities, never feasible with the geometrical model, can be obtained. Consider the simple matter of sharp contour (whether the edge of two contrasting areas of stimulation or a fine line against an otherwise homogeneous field). It is known that very fine 'hair lines,' as small as one-sixtieth the diameter of a single cone, can be perceived if their length covers about 150 cones and if they are projected on a bright, uniform background. How is this possible? According to Marshall and Talbot, 'the neural "image" plays continuously over the projection area at every synaptic level, building gradients and peaks of activation at every edge and line. . . Multiplication of path both increases the reciprocal overlap and refines the mosaic in proportion to the sharper gradients and peaks produced, as sand forms sharper peaks than bricks. . . A fine line oscillating over 4 or 5 rows of receptors . . . [produces] a center of gravity of excitation which is further peaked at the center through the action of partially shifted overlapping connections' (p. 139). Particularly interesting to theorists of perception are the following implications: (1) a broken line (peripherally) will tend to be filled in along its own axis by this overlapping action; (2) unconnected figures will tend to be completed in the same fashion; (3) the borders of figures (e.g. bright bars against black backgrounds) will tend to be given

---

* Marshall and Talbot, *Biological Symposia,* ed. Heinrich Klüver, copyright 1942 by the Ronald Press Company.

emphasis because of the sharp gradients of activity established in these regions. By way of caution, it will be well to keep in mind that the mechanisms described here will operate only over relatively small areas of the visual field.

What about phenomena that display interactions over wide areas of the field? What about constancy? What about the fact that three dots, no matter how placed, may look like a 'triangle'? Hebb (1949) has developed a feasible neurological basis for perceptual phenomena of this order. Being convinced that most perceptual organizations are learned (evidence for which will be presented later), he starts with a 'conditioning' postulate much like Kapper's Law of Neurobiotaxis: 'When an axon of cell *A* is near enough to excite a cell *B* and repeatedly or persistently takes part in

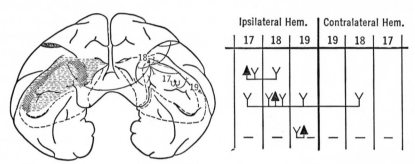

FIGURE 68. Experimental analysis of cortical pathways. Areas found by physiological neuronography (left) and firing diagram (right). Solid triangles indicate the areas stimulated with strychnine, the *Y*-symbols other areas excited, and the minus-symbols areas suppressed. Bonin, Garol, and McCulloch, *Biological Symposia*, Heinrich Klüver, ed., The Ronald Press Co., New York, 1942, 7:188.

firing it, some growth process or metabolic change takes place in one or both cells such that *A*'s efficiency, as one of the cells firing *B,* is increased' (p. 62). More specifically, it is suggested that activity of neighboring cells in the densely packed cortical tissues causes the development of boutons on the receiving cell, which effectively enlarge the area of contact between them.

Hebb next draws on evidence obtained by Von Bonin, Garol, and McCulloch (1942). By applying strychnine locally to portions of the visual cortex of primates, association pathways were traced by means of electrodes placed in various other positions. Figure 68 summarizes their results. Localized excitation in area 17 (projection area) resulted in restricted activity within area 17 and in a band of firing in that portion of area 18 bordering on 17, but there was no point-for-point correspondence. This shows that topographical organization breaks down beyond area 17. Excitation within area 18, on the other hand, results in a widely dispersed pattern of action to all parts of area 18 itself (both ipsilaterally and contralaterally), back into neighboring areas of 17, into area 19 (anterior to 18), and even into area 20 (in the lower portions of the temporal lobes). Some such widespread activity as this must underlie the 'cohesive' phenomena to be described subsequently. Finally, excitation within area 19 may result in equally widespread *suppression* of activity in areas 17 and 18 (both ipsilaterally and contralaterally) and contralateral 19. There is a suggestive mechanism here for the 'attentional' properties of perception, its selectivity and flexibility.

Hebb interprets this evidence as justifying the notion that reverberatory circuits of varying complexity may be set up within area 18, and between cells in this area and cells in 17, 19, and 20. Repetitive activity of this sort theoretically serves to develop boutons and thus leads to more and more stable organization of brain action (cell assemblies). Given the complexity of actual neural connections—as many as 1300 boutons having been observed on a single cell and the ramification from one tiny cortical point in area 18 having been traced to the entire area—the development of such 'cell assemblies' must be thought of in statistical terms.

But perceiving is not a static process; the integrations that result in form perception and the like involve behavior of the organism, especially eye

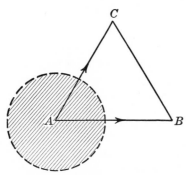

FIGURE 69. Triangle *ABC* is seen with fixation on point *A*. The macular field represented by hatched circle, so that points *B* and *C* fall in peripheral vision. Arrows represent the direction and strength of eye movement tendencies aroused by stimulation from *B* and *C*. D. O. Hebb, *The Organization of Behavior*, John Wiley and Sons, Inc., 1949, p. 85.

movements. Hebb has described a possible mechanism whereby the sequential cell assemblies set up by eye movements could be integrated. Let us consider the system of organization that eventuates in 'perception' of any triangular shape. From the work of Marshall and Talbot reviewed earlier, it can be predicted that there will be a dominant visual tendency to fixate the corners of figures like that shown in Fig. 69. The macular area (shaded) is richly represented cortically and is an area of high acuity (and presumably largely responsible for establishment of 'form' cell assemblies); the peripheral retina has been shown more effective in directing eye movements, these preceding typically along continuous lines in the field. In this case movement tendencies would be equal between *AB* and *AC*. Letting *a* represent the 'cell assembly' set up by fixating *A*, *b* that set up in fixating *B*, and so on, and assuming that in repeated experiencing of triangles successive fixations of corners occur (*ACBABCBA*, etc.), it could be predicted that *a*, *b*, and *c*, as already established cell assemblies, would become integrated with systems of eye movements in such a manner that looking at any triangle will always result in localized activity at some point *t* in areas 18 or 20, for example. Activity at *t*, then, *is* the perception of a triangle as a whole; it is also the 'concept' of a triangle. This higher level organization with its focal point at *t* is a perceptual 'habit.'

How are we to evaluate this sort of neurologizing? It certainly goes far beyond Marshall and Talbot in the inferences made, and Hebb himself is careful to point this out: 'A conceptual system has been elaborated which relates the individual nerve cell to psychological phenomena. A bridge has been thrown across the great gap between the details of neurophysiology and the molar conceptions of psychology. The bridge is definitely shaky in the middle . . .' (p. 101). The bridge is shaky because there are so many possibilities, so many schemes of action for the complex higher centers, and Hebb has merely elaborated one. Nevertheless, as a stimulus for research this type of theorizing is valuable. This specific type of scheme has additional advantages in solving a fundamental psychological dilemma: the *transposability* of perceptions is made compatible with their *constancy,* in that multiple locations of similar activity in area 17 can channel onto common and specific loci in area 18.

Gestalt Point of View

The following attempt to distil the essentials of the gestalt view is based mainly on the writings of Koffka (1935), Köhler (1938, 1940), and Brown and Voth (1937). The theory concerns events that transpire within the *visual field,* this being a dynamic distribution of energy whose parts are interdependent through their participation in the whole. The field is *structured* to the extent that there exist intensive or qualitative differences within it; to the extent that it is structured the field contains potential energy, capable of doing (perceptual) work. The standard analogy of the energy field about a magnet is probably the simplest to grasp: throughout the space about the two poles of the magnet there exists a force field, intensity and direction of the force varying continuously from place to place. The realignment of the cluster of iron filings that occurs when the field of the magnet is introduced demonstrates not only that these energy differentials are capable of doing work but also that the work done serves to describe the nature of the force field. In precisely the same manner the phenomenal aspects of perceptions (e.g. work done) will be employed by gestalt theorists to characterize the forces in the visual field.

At this point the question naturally arises, Where (in the material nervous system) is this visual field located? Brown and Voth state: 'By the *visual field* we mean a *spatial construct* to which the phenomena of visual experience may be ordered.' It is true that the field may be handled in theory as a purely hypothetical construct. This is probably the safest procedure, but gestalt theorists generally postulate physiological processes to account for their psychological 'field' phenomena. As Koffka (1935) puts it: '. . . let us think of the physiological processes not as molecular, but as molar phenomena. If we do that, all the difficulties of the old theory disappear. For if they are molar, their molar properties will be the same as those of the conscious processes which they are supposed to underlie' (p. 56). And later he writes: '. . . where the local processes are not *completely* insulated they will no longer be completely independent, and therefore what happens in one place will depend upon what happens in all the others . . . there are innumerable cross connections which probably connect every nerve cell with every other . . . [and therefore] the events in this network of nervous tissue can no longer form a mere geometrical pattern . . . the processes that take place within them can no longer be independent and we must consider them as molar distributions with a degree of interdependence varying inversely with the actual operative resistances' (p. 60). This still does not tell us *where* (e.g. area 17, area 18, or so on in the material brain) these dynamic forces operate, and indeed we are never told by the gestalt theorists.

With regard to *how* the known properties of the material nervous system can be manipulated so as to account for field processes, Köhler has been the most explicit (cf. Köhler, 1940; Köhler and Wallach, 1944). He points out (1940, pp. 73-82) that perceptual processes behave in a manner analogous to currents in electrolytes and then asks if it is possible that percepts are actually associated with electrical currents in the nervous system. His physiological rationale may be summarized as follows: Drawing upon evidence that chemical neurohumors are liberated at the termini of fibers (cf. Cannon and Rosenblueth, 1937), it is assumed that in the visual brain '. . . when nerve impulses arrive at the end branches of sensory fibers, chemicals penetrate from the fibers into the common medium which here surrounds those branches' (p. 75). With large numbers of fibers in a given region firing in repeated waves and presumably releasing neurohumor, it is assumed that a steady state of chemical concentration will be achieved. This concentration, representing in its spatial distribution the figure, will be different from the concentration representing the ground. Since these regions of different concentration of the chemical have a common and continuous boundary, ions will diffuse from the region of higher concentration into that of lower concentration, thus establishing an electromotive force which will drive a current about the contours of the figure. This current flow will be independent of anatomical conduction pathways as such. 'Since it is the presence of the figure which causes this current we are justified in saying that its flow constitutes a functional halo or *field* of the figure' (p. 80). Köhler believes that a great deal of psychological evidence requires some theory such as this.

Both Koffka's notion of molar physiological processes paralleling psychological processes and Köhler's urge to uncover fieldlike brain functions are predicated on the principle of *isomorphism.* This means, literally, 'equality of form.' To borrow an illustration from Boring (1942, p. 84): 'If a system of points is marked on a flat rubber membrane and the membrane is then stretched tightly over some irregular surface, then the points in the stretched membrane are isomorphic with the points in the flat membrane.' Notice that there is no requirement that distances be identical in magnitude, only that the points correspond in their orders. Spatial and temporal orderings of experience will correspond to spatial and temporal orderings of physiological processes; to a context experienced as 'one thing,' there will correspond a unit or whole in the underlying physiological process. As a resolution of the mind-body problem, this is a variant of psychophysical parallelism, a parallelism of molar mental events with molar physiological events. Projection of the sensory surface upon the cortex makes such a view feasible—certainly looking at a white square is accompanied by a (roughly) squarelike region of excitation in area 17—but isomorphism in gestalt theorizing goes beyond this. It holds that a *consciously perceived* square must be paralleled by a corresponding squarelike excitation pattern at some place in the visual brain, i.e. if a pattern of four dots is perceived as a 'square,' some squarelike physiological process must have been operative. If this principle is valid, then one can use conscious experience directly as a means of studying molar physiological functions, as the gestalt theorists maintain. This, in a way, is the essence of phenomenology. These theorists take isomorphism as a fundamental 'given'—it is axiomatic. They cannot conceive of localized, specific pathways of association since such physiological events have, isomorphically, no corresponding conscious representations.

What are the forces operative within the visual field? There is one fundamental dynamism, one source of energy for perceptual work: *like processes in the visual field attract one another* (cf. Köhler, 1930). This attraction between similar processes is the basis for the *cohesive forces* in the visual field, these being central in origin, integrative (organizing, simplifying) in function, and 'perceptual' in nature. 'We suppose that between all objects in the visual field there exist *cohesive field-forces* having the nature of vectors. . . The visual field must further be thought of as a four-dimensional *manifold,* having a temporal as well as three spatial dimensions' (Brown and Voth, p. 544). The nearer like processes are in space or time, the greater this cohesive tendency between them. Köhler (1940, p. 55ff.) offers numerous illustrations of this in visual and other modalities: the tendency for two points on the skin to seem nearer together when touched near-simultaneously than is the case objectively, the same phenomenon in hearing, the fusion of slightly disparate points in depth perception. Now it is obvious that if there were no restriction upon these cohesive tendencies, all objects in the field would simply flow together into a perfectly spherical globule. We must, therefore, postulate an opposing set of forces, *restraining forces,* these being peripheral in origin, segregative (disintegrative, autonomous) in function, and 'sensory' in nature. According to Koffka (pp. 138-9) '. . . we have two kinds of forces, those which exist within the process in distribution itself and which will tend to impress on this distribution the simplest possible shape, and those between this distribution and the stimulus pattern, which constrain this stress toward simplification.'

As implied above, the strength of the cohesive force between processes varies in accordance with certain quasi-quantitative laws. (1) *The greater the qualitative similarity between processes in the visual field, the greater the cohesive force between them.* If certain letters in a page of ordinary print are red in hue, the total shape they make (say, an X) is readily apparent—the similar red processes cohere. The same letters in black would form no shape, since they would cohere equally with all other black marks on the page. (2) *The greater the intensive similarity between processes, the greater the cohesive force between them.* One of the neatest demonstrations of this is the *Liebmann effect* (cf. Koffka, p. 126). If the luminosity of a colored figure is made equal to that of the neutral gray ground on which it is viewed, the shape of the colored figure becomes obscure. The strong cohesive forces between processes of like intensity are working *between* figure and ground, obscuring the segregating effect of qualitative dissimilarity and hence blurring the contours. This effect is most marked with blue figures. (3) *The less the distance between like processes, the greater the cohesive force between them.* (4) *The less the time interval between like processes, the greater the cohesive force between them.* Both of these laws are best illustrated in the phi phenomenon. Two lights flashing in alternation can be perceived as a single light moving back and forth, under appropriate conditions. If the time interval is optimum, increasing the spatial distance between the lights reduces the impression of movement. Animated cartoonists have learned that to reduce jerkiness of movement in their creations the differences between successive drawings (e.g. distance) must be slight. And, in general, the smaller the time interval between alternating flashes, the better the apparent movement.

We may now turn to the perceptual work done by these cohesive and restraining forces. Koffka (p. 139) states that '. . . we should expect very stable organizations whenever the two kinds of forces act in the same direction, if e.g. our spot has a circular shape. Conversely, if the forces are in strong conflict, the resulting organization should be less stable.' We may generalize in this way: *the greater the discrepancy between cohesive and restraining forces, the greater the energy in the visual field capable of doing perceptual work.* This perceptual work can assume many forms: closure of incompleted figures, distortions (illusions), grouping of visual objects, apparent movement, and so on. If, following the Brown and Voth analysis, we represent the sum of all cohesive forces acting on a given point as ΣC and the sum of all restraining forces acting on the same point as ΣR, then the following relations are conceivable: (1) $\Sigma C = \Sigma R$; (2) $\Sigma C > \Sigma R$; (3) $\Sigma C < \Sigma R$. If the first condition exists, there is no energy for perceptual work—it is the stable, resting state. In the second case, where cohesive forces outweigh restraining forces, modifications (perceptual work) are predicted. The third case, with restraining forces stronger than cohesive forces, also represents instability in the visual field, but exactly what phenomenal changes should take place is not clear. Brown and Voth suggest that this is the condition for autokinetic movement.

As a matter of fact, little is said in the theory about restraining forces. The cohesive forces acting on a given point represent the attractions exerted by all like processes elsewhere in the visual field (the strength of the vectors being proportional to the similarity, nearness, and so on of the other processes). But what are the restraining forces? Their sole function appears to be that of keeping the apparent localization of a point precisely coincident with the locus of maximal impulse rate in the excitation distribution representing the stimulus. Therefore, presumably, as cohesive forces displace objects in the visual field from their 'true' position, restraining forces are created, increasing until ΣR equals ΣC. If this argument is valid, then equation (3) cited above can never exist, i.e. restraining forces come into existence only when displacements in the visual field are produced by cohesive forces, and they can never become greater than the cohesive forces that create them. This argument appears in a paper by Orbison (1939) reporting research done under J. F. Brown's aegis. 'If two objects are seen as a stable configuration, by definition the $\Sigma R = \Sigma C$. This does not, however, mean that the two objects have not been attracted toward each other. Rather, it means that the two objects have been attracted toward each other until $\Sigma R = \Sigma C$. Such an interpretation demands that the restraining field-forces increase as the object is displaced from its position' (p. 33).

It is apparent then that *all visual fields will tend toward a minimization of tension,* i.e. toward the condition in which $\Sigma C = \Sigma R$. In fact, what is experienced as a stable perception is always the end result of this resolution of forces, the pre-existence and direction of the cohesive forces being indexed by the fact that what is perceived is not identical with what would have been predicted solely on the basis of retinal stimulation. What are the directions that resolution will take (i.e. what are the directions of cohesive forces) ? We have already seen that, unhindered, all processes in the visual field would cohere into a perfectly balanced sphere extended into the fourth (temporal) dimension. Actual coherence will be as great as existing (retinal) conditions allow. Koffka (p. 107) gives the soap bubble analogy: 'Why has it the shape of a sphere? Of all solids the sphere is that whose surface is smallest for a given volume, or whose volume is largest for a given surface . . . The soap particles attract each other, they tend to take up as

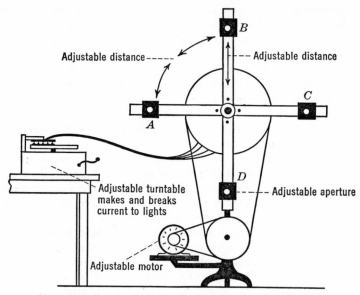

FIGURE 70. Apparatus for studying both real and apparent movement. Radial separation of lights, their size, flash rate, duration, intensity, and sequence, as well as the rate of real movement, can be varied independently. Brown and Voth, *American Journal of Psychology*, 1937, 49:546.

little space as possible, but the pressure of the air inside forces them to stay on the outside, forming the surface membrane of this air volume . . . the final time-independent distribution contains a minimum of energy capable of doing work.' The final time-independent state is always a function of existing conditions (here, the given retinal pattern): although a raindrop in a medium of equal density would assume a spherical shape, it would assume a flattened form on a solid support. Koffka concludes that cohesive forces will tend toward regularity, symmetry, and simplicity—hence, the *law of prägnanz*, according to which 'psychological organization will always be as "good" as prevailing conditions allow' (p. 110).

Certainly the most compelling application of this general gestalt theory of perception has appeared in Brown and Voth's own studies of apparent movement (1937). Using the flexible apparatus shown in Fig. 70, lights *A, B, C,* and *D* are flashed in rotation at a rate that can be controlled by the experimenter. If the time interval between flashes is long enough, no apparent movement of a single light about the square will be perceived—

the time intervals between *A–B, B–C,* and so on, are such that cohesive forces are minimal and four separate lights are seen going on and off. When the time interval is shortened, pure phi movement is first to appear—a single light seems to leap about the corners of a square. In this case *B* occurs sufficiently close in time to *A* to affect it cohesively, as does *B* with *C,* and so on, but *C* is too long delayed to exert any affect on *A.* With further reductions in the time interval, however, the path of apparent movement must first become a bowed curve along the sides of the square and then describe a circle whose circumference falls well *within* the actual loci of the flashing lights. Analysis of this latter stage is shown graphically in Fig. 71. Stimulations *B, C,* and *D* will fall close enough in time to influence

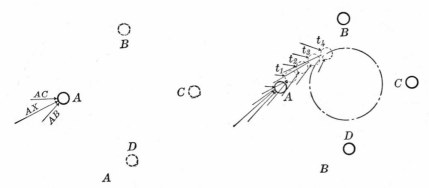

FIGURE 71. *A.* Vector field when *AB = AC* at a particular moment in time. *AX =* resolution of forces. *B.* Vector field at four discrete time moments in close succession. Broken line indicates resultant path of apparent movement. Brown and Voth, *American Journal of Psychology,* 1937, **49**:550.

point *A,* but in the decreasing amounts of cohesive force indicated by the lengths of the vectors applied to *A* in Fig. 71*A.* Since the comparative strengths of these vectors will vary smoothly and continuously with each change in the apparent position of *A,* as shown in Fig. 71*B* (with vector *A–D* omitted for simplicity), the apparent movement of the single light will be about the arc of a circle well within the points of stimulation. The same analysis applies to each of the four points. Careful measurements fully substantiated these predictions from theory as well as many others that could be made for modified conditions (distances of lights, intensity of lights, and so on).

With further reductions in the time interval the size of the circular path of movement reversed and became larger until all four lights were seen simultaneously (when only 50 msec. actually separated them); Brown and Voth assume that the strength of cohesive forces as a function of time interval at first increases and then decreases. No reason for this reversal of function is offered. Another possibility is that restraining forces, as reflections of retinally determined neural events, have a more rapid and negatively accelerated decay function following elimination of the stimulus than cohesive forces. With very short intervals, the differential favoring *C* forces would be slight; with somewhat longer intervals (given rapid decay of retinally determined stability), the differential favoring *C* forces would become maximal; with further increase in interval, decay of cohesive tendencies themselves would produce reduced effects.

Another striking demonstration of the applicability of this theory is offered by Orbison (1939). In this case stable configurations (where $\Sigma C = \Sigma R$) are used rather than those in which instability gives rise to apparent movement. The technique was to introduce various objectively symmetrical figures into fields structured so as to have certain dominant cohesive directions. The general hypothesis would be substantiated if these objectively symmetrical figures were distorted in the direction of the positions of cohesive equilibrium (i.e. the positions that would be occupied were it not for restraining forces) within such fields. Treating cohesive forces

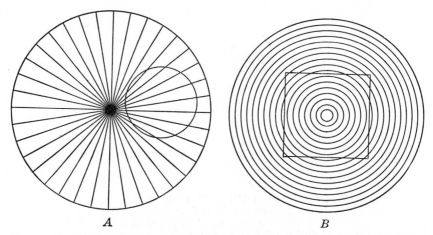

FIGURE 72. *A.* Distortion of a circle superimposed on a field of radiating lines. *B.* Distortion of a square superimposed on a field of concentric circles. Orbison, *American Journal of Psychology*, 1939, 52 : 39, 42.

solely as functions of the spatial separations between like processes, Orbison determined theoretically these positions of cohesive equilibrium for each of the fields used (details may be found in the original article). The circle on field *A* and the square on field *B* are clearly distorted—so much, in fact, that one finds it hard to believe that these figures are objectively regular (see Fig. 72).

A final postulate of the gestalt theory of perception *might* be phrased as follows: *existing organizations of the field tend to resist modification.* We say 'might' because, although much perceptual evidence fits this statement and the same notion will be encountered in gestalt theorizing about insight and problem-solving, there is another mass of evidence supporting the diametrically opposite statement—*that existing organizations of the field tend to block their own persistence* (cf. Köhler, 1940, pp. 67-73). Let us look at evidence for the first statement: The difficulty in seeing the 'hidden face' in the leaves of the tree in a puzzle picture is commonly laid to the dominance of an earlier perceptual organization. Some persons experience difficulty in perceiving *both* of two possible organizations in ambiguous figures; for example, who are the *two* ladies in Fig. 73? Some readily perceive the young 'wife,' but then can't see the 'mother-in-law.' An example of a more experimental character can also be cited: if, using apparatus like that of Brown and Voth (see Fig. 70), lights *AD* are flashed simultaneously in alternation with the simultaneous flashing of lights *BC,* the apparent movement will give the impression of either a vertically tilting bar (if the distances *AB* and *CD* are made smaller than the distances *BC* and *DA*) or a horizontal teetering bar (if distances *AB* and *CD* are larger than *BC* and *DA*). Now suppose we start with the adjustable arms in the position shown as (2) in Fig. 74, where the vertical tilting motion is always perceived, and gradually increase the distance between *A* and *B*. When the point where *B* is equidistant from both *A* and *C* is reached, there is no shift in the direction of apparent movement. In fact, the vertical tilt-

FIGURE 73. An ambiguous figure. Boring, *American Journal of Psychology,* 1930, 42:444.

ing movement persists to a point where distance *AB* is much greater than distance *AC,* in flat contradiction to the law of nearness as it applies to cohesive forces. A point is finally reached (5) where the stress is too great, and the pattern suddenly shifts to a horizontal seesaw movement. Obviously the existing organization of the field, resisting modification, tended to persist. Psychologists of another generation would have considered this an illustration of 'set,' which it is.

What is the evidence for the opposite statement: that existing organizations of the field create forces that tend toward their own disintegration? Köhler (1940, p. 68), using the reversible figure-ground pattern shown as Fig. 81, found that the frequency of reversals (seeing either the narrow segments or the wide segments as figure) increased in frequency with the time spent in observation. If, after prolonged observation, the stimulus was rotated so that the contours fell upon relatively 'fresh' regions, an increase in stability was noted. He concludes that persistence of a figure process in a given region of the visual medium weakens the organizing forces that maintain it. Another example cited is the figural after-effect (cf. Chap. 6). Following prolonged inspection of one figure, subsequent test figures tend to be displaced from the region presumably 'satiated' by the preceding process. That both increased resistance and decreased resistance to modification can accompany figural processes seems evident, but how the two functions are related is not so clear.

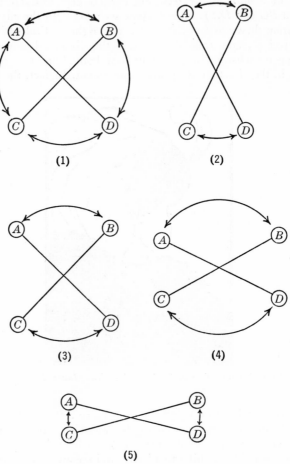

FIGURE 74. Setup for demonstrating persistence of a given perceptual organization. Shift in direction of apparent movement appears between stages (4) and (5) rather than between (3) and (4).

Behavioristic Point of View

In marked contrast to their contributions in the areas of learning and motivation, the behaviorists (as theorists) have not contributed significantly to our understanding of perceptual processes. When perceptual phenomena are treated in behavioristic texts, it is usually from a strictly descriptive point of view, with little or no attempt at integration or interpretation. The fact that triangular forms are perceived as such, that the colors of recognized objects show constancy, that objects are seen as three dimensional, is vaguely attributed to 'learning,' but there the matter usually ends. It is assumed that, since perceptions are learned behaviors, they must follow the same principles as other responses—they must display habit formation, generalization, inhibition, and so on—but no attempt has been made to apply these principles to perceptual phenomena in any detail. The reason for this is certainly not elusive: almost by definition, perceptual events are neither exclusively dependent upon manipulatable stimulus variables nor reflected in readily recorded overt movements—they are mediation processes. How is the theorist to fit these events to his mold when they cannot be identified in terms of the major constructs (S's and R's) defining his equations? And to make the matter even more difficult, most perceptual habits, if such they are, are well established long before the behaviorist (as experimentalist) can subject them to analysis. It will not surprise the reader, then, that we give only a brief discussion of the behaviorist's position.

The most comprehensive attempt to handle perception from within a behavioristic framework appears in Hull's systematic theory, and even here it is largely programmatic. Like other molar theorists (e.g. Köhler), Hull selects molecular neurophysiological evidence that seems to justify his principles. The *stimulus trace* (cf. pp. 375-6) assumes that the after-effects of receptor stimulation continue in the central nervous system for a brief period following termination of the physical stimulus, following a negatively accelerated function; evidence obtained by Lorente de Nó on reverberatory circuits is cited as substantiation. Hull then goes on to postulate, as a fundamental principle of his system (1943, p. 47), that *all afferent neural impulses active in the nervous system at any given instant interact and change each other into something partially different in a manner that varies with every concurrent, associated afferent impulse or combination of such impulses.* The phenomenon of simultaneous contrast is given as an illustration: the afferent impulses arising in the area of the visual system affected by the gray paper interact with those arising from the blue surround in such a way as to change their quality (i.e. the gray patch now appears yellowish). This is a case of *spatial interaction*. Since the *traces* of stimuli may interact to the extent that they are simultaneously present in the nervous system, we may also have *temporal interaction*—the meaning of a speech-sound is modified by the preceding verbal context.

How does this principle relate to problems of perception? Essentially it means that all afferent processes are potentially interactive with all others that are simultaneously present, i.e. the local process at *a* can be modified by local processes at *b, c ⋯ n*. Since anatomical possibilities for interaction in the higher centers are practically unlimited, this becomes a vague field principle. Depending on *how* afferent impulses are modified through interaction, the perceived color of a house can remain 'white' despite changes in illumination, a certain pattern of lines drawn on a plane surface may appear as a three-dimensional cube, and so on. Hull considers such a principle as this 'plausible,' some of his critics consider it 'meaningless' (Leeper, 1944), and to the present writer it seems 'inevitable,' for just the neurological reasons Hull describes. In other words, if interaction among the traces of stimulus events is a fundamental law of the nervous system, it must *always* happen—it is not only to be drawn forth when other explanatory devices prove insufficient. Hull is aware of this, but he has not re-examined his other principles with ubiquitous interaction in mind.

The principal use Hull has made of this principle is to make possible certain deductions concerning *patterning of stimulus compounds.* The general deduction may be phrased as follows: *particular spatial and temporal patterns of stimuli may become associated with reactions that are distinct from those elicited by the component stimuli occurring in any other patterns.* The basis for this deduction is very simple. Since s_a in conjunction with s_b is qualitatively different from s_a in conjunction with s_c, in accordance with the interaction principle, we have in reality s_{a_1} and s_{a_2} as qualitatively different stimuli, and the degree to which distinctive reactions can become associated with them depends upon ordinary discrimination processes. This reaffirms the notion that all stimulus situations as they affect organisms are essentially unique. The child may learn to react positively both to daddy's

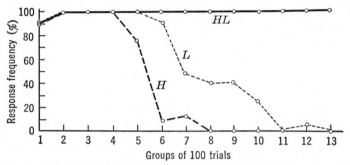

FIGURE 75. Stimulus patterning. Dog 'Dick' learns to inhibit reaction to either high (H) or low (L) pitched buzzers while maintaining reaction to the compound (HL). Woodbury, *Journal of Comparative Psychology,* 1943, 35:29-40. As presented in Hull, *Principles of Behavior,* Appleton-Century-Crofts, Inc., New York, 1943, p. 352.

face and to daddy's hat, yet burst into cries of fear when the two appear as a particular compound. Conversely, subjects may be trained by shock conditioning to raise their hands only at the sound of a specific tone (e.g. G above middle C), yet they will not respond at all when this note appears fourteen times in the course of listening to 'Home Sweet Home' in the key of C. This latter effect is known as Humphrey's Arpeggio paradox (cf. Humphrey, 1933, p. 237), and it is typical of many perceptual and meaningful phenomena in which the nature of reaction depends upon context.

An illustration of patterning has been provided by Woodbury (1943). One dog named Dick was trained to nose a bar in a wooden stall in order to obtain pellets of appetizing food. Conditions were arranged so that food would be forthcoming only when the animal made this reaction immediately following the sounding, simultaneously, of a high-pitched buzzer and a low-pitched buzzer (HL). If the dog reacted to either of the components when presented alone, no reinforcement was given. That patterning did occur under these conditions is indicated in Fig. 75. The slower discrimination of the low-pitched buzzer is probably to be explained by its having a more 'raucous' tone quality and thus dominating the auditory character of the compound. Another dog, Chuck, was trained with the components positive and the compound negative, and this type of patterning was also demonstrated. Using the same apparatus and procedures, and dogs Ted and Bengt, Woodbury carried out tests of temporal patterning. In this case a particular

sequence of buzzer tones (H, L) given one second apart was either reinforced (Ted) or nonreinforced (Bengt), but other temporal orders were
treated in the opposite fashion. Here again, patterning was obtained, although many more trials than had been the case with simultaneous presentation were required.

But this, it will be objected, has nothing to do with perception. This is
merely discrimination learning. In fact, if one accepts the interaction hypothesis, all learning must involve discrimination of this sort. Even in
ordinary conditioning the animal must discriminate between compounds
including the critical cue and compounds in which it is absent. This objection is valid. Woodbury's experiment has nothing to do directly with perception. It does, however, demonstrate that organisms can learn to respond
differentially in terms of consistently repeated patterns or configurations of
stimuli, and this type of discrimination is probably basic in the establishment
of many perceptual habits.

Why is it that perceptual processes per se do not appear as a significant
variable in these experiments? As was pointed out earlier in this chapter,
perceptual processes refer to those events that *mediate* between initial afferent and final efferent pathways, i.e. they presume a two-stage transmission process. But Woodbury's experimental design precludes independent
manipulation of mediating activities, and Hull's theoretical analysis of the
work is restricted to a single-stage $(S-R)$ interpretation. In other words,
we have no way here of studying what or how these dogs *perceive* when
stimulated by component or compounded auditory cues; we merely learn
that they can discriminate among them (which is useful, if not too surprising, information). It seems to the writer that the experimental designs
employed by Krechevsky (1938 *b*) and Lawrence (1950) in studying discrimination learning in animals (cf. pp. 449-53) offer the most promising
leads for behavioristic investigations of perception. In these cases *previous*
training was given so as to get the animals to 'perceive the stimulus situations in certain ways,' and exactly how they were perceiving them was then
determined in *subsequent* instrumental discrimination tests. This is one
way to investigate mediation processes in nonverbal organisms, and for
this reason it is promising for the study of perception.

Hull's interaction hypothesis has really pleased no one. Other behaviorists look upon it as a concession to the enemy, throwing wide the gates to
mysterious and unquantifiable 'field-forces'; gestaltists, on the other hand,
see it either as a grossly mechanistic encroachment on their domain or as a
booby trap to ensnare the unwary. In any case, no good can come of it.
Yet Hull is right. We have enough evidence on both neurological and
behavioral levels to prove conclusively that interactions of exceedingly
complex nature do take place—not occasionally, but regularly. The trouble
with Hull's formulation is that it is too gross. To state merely that 'all
afferent impulses . . . interact' explains nothing. The laws governing the
degrees of such interaction and the effects (perceptual as well as behavioral)
of such interaction must be formulated. Hull is aware of this insufficiency
and has suggested (1945) a method whereby quantitative characteristics of
interaction could be investigated. Essentially the method is to insert a new
stimulus element in a previously conditioned compound and note the amount
of external inhibition created, i.e. the greater the interaction of the new

element with those associated with the reaction, the greater the qualitative change in them and hence the greater the change in effective habit strength. Although the formulation of functions will not be as simple as this, the general results can perhaps be anticipated. When the students of Hull work out the quantitative aspects of afferent interaction to the extent that it becomes a usable principle, the quantitative laws will probably be essentially the same as those described by gestalt theorists as governing the strengths of cohesive forces between processes in the perceptual field: qualitative and intensive similarity, nearness in space and nearness in time. The particular inclinations of theorists, semantic and otherwise, do not dictate natural arrangements.

PERCEPTUAL ORGANIZATION

How is the phenomenal world organized in perceiving? As we look about us, we see, not James's confusion of sensations, but an environment neatly partitioned into conceptualized objects. Here is a 'pencil' (yellow) lying on a 'book' (green), not merely a blob of yellow inserted in a green field; there is 'Samuel Jones's face,' not a chaotic conglomeration of red, white, and brown sensations. It may well be, as the empiricist claims, that, previous to perceptual *learning,* experience *is* chaotic in character, but certainly by the time young individuals have developed sufficiently in motor capacity to be experimented upon, they have also subjected sensory chaos to perceptual order. What is the nature of this perceptual order? What kinds of organization are imposed? Under what stimulus and central conditions? And 'why,' in terms of physiological, gestalt, and behavioristic theories, does perceptual organization have its particular characteristics?

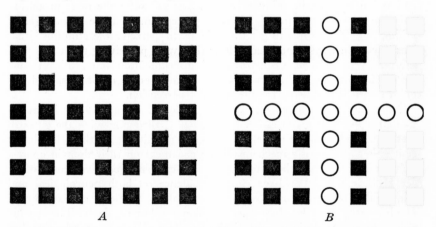

A B

FIGURE 76. *A.* Arrangement of forms which permits alternate organizations while being observed (after Schumann, 1900). *B.* Arrangement in which one dominant organization resists modification.

Phenomenal Laws of Grouping

Observe the pattern of little black squares in Fig. 76*A* fixedly for a while: you will note the swift flow of alternative organizations—now vertical lines and now horizontal, now clusters of subsquares of four dots each, now a central cross. We have here an ambiguous situation in which various peripheral (stimulus) factors and various central ('set,' meaning, etc.) factors are all competing to determine what is perceived. This 'checker-board pattern' was first discussed by Schumann (1900), who ascribed fluctuating organizations to the vagaries of attention. In Fig. 76B we have introduced a dominant stimulus factor—a group of open circles arranged in a familiar pattern—and it completely overrides attentional processes. Try as we may to direct our attention to horizontal or vertical rows, try as we

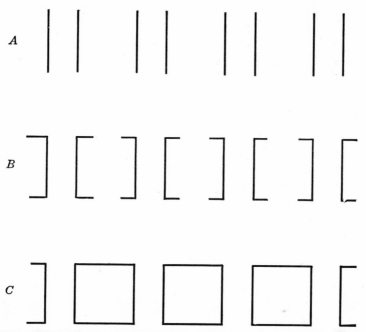

FIGURE 77. *A*. The nearness factor predisposes the observer to organize the lines in groups according to proximity. *B*. The continuity factor counterbalances nearness, favoring grouping of less proximal lines. *C*. Closure eliminates the possibility of grouping near parts of separate figures.

may to perceive an X shape (necessarily composed of both black and white figures of differing shape), these particular organizations resist our efforts. Wertheimer (1923) made the first comprehensive study of factors contributing to perceptual grouping of elements in the visual field. The following discussion originates in his classification of factors, but does not exactly correspond to it.

(1) *Nearness*. Other things being equal, the nearer objects are to one another in the visual field, the more likely they are to be organized into single, unified percepts. The pairs of lines in Fig. 77*A* are easily organized on this basis, each two neighboring lines forming a unit. It is nearly impossible to perceive the spaced lines as belonging together, i.e. to break up the units based on nearness. It is not mere nearness, however, but nearness of processes of similar kind. (2) *Similarity*. The greater the similarity among objects in the visual field, the more likely they are to be organized into single, unified percepts. The fact that the cross in Fig. 76*B* is imme-

diately and persistently perceived illustrates the operation of this stimulus factor—it is composed of qualitatively identical elements. (3) *Continuity*. The more that elements in the visual field fall in locations corresponding to continuous, regular sequence—i.e. function as parts of familiar contours—the more likely they are to be organized into single, unified percepts. In Fig. 77*B* the nearness and similarity factors are as they were in *A*, but in this case more distant elements have the characteristic of continuing into one another as parts of simple wholes. Hence one can easily organize the relatively distant bent lines into single units, despite the nearness factor. (4) *Closure*. The more elements of the visual field form continuous wholes, the more readily they will be organized into single percepts. This is merely the logical extension of the continuity principle. In Fig. 77*C* the bent lines are continued to closure in the form of squares; such closed contours have high priority in visual organization.

These are objective, stimulus variables. There are also central (meaningful, attitudinal) factors at work to determine how we organize the visual field. The line of letters given below readily breaks up into units according to the meaning of the individual words.

THEDOGATEMEAT

Present the same statement in an unknown language, of course, and no such organization arises. Evidently we impose an organization upon sensory data in terms of meanings, and this is a matter of learning, not innate perceptual organization. Meaningful organization is not limited to verbal

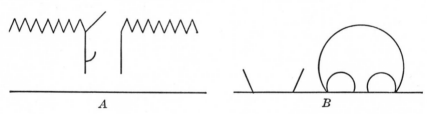

FIGURE 78. Two figures illustrating the influence of meaning upon perceptual organization. See discussion in text.

materials. The diagrams in Fig. 78 probably mean little to most readers—just jumbles of unrelated lines and forms. But as soon as you are told that the first represents 'A Soldier and His Dog Passing by a Hole in a Picket Fence' and the second 'A Washerwoman Cleaning the Floor,' they suddenly snap into intelligible organization. And notice this: once having associated these particular meanings with the diagrams (and hence perceiving them in this particular fashion), it becomes very difficult to reconstruct them and perceive them as anything else.

At this time the physiological point of view has little to contribute to our understanding of these laws of grouping. It is true, of course, that contour formation is a prerequisite for all types of perceptual organization, and the statistical mechanisms described by Marshall and Talbot are undoubtedly involved. The gestalt point of view, on the other hand, offers nearly complete coverage—which is not surprising since the gestalt theory developed largely within the framework of perception experiments. Similarity and nearness in perceptual organization are direct expressions of the ways in which cohesive forces vary in strength. Continuity and closure can be considered expressions of the *law of prägnanz*. The role of meaning as an organizing force escapes the classic gestalt theory, which lays so much stress upon the innate character of perceptual processes.

Surprisingly enough, the behavioristic position has more to say about these organizing characteristics than about other perceptual phenomena. According to Hull's patterning deduction, organisms are able to establish differential reactions to patterns of stimuli that are repeatedly presented, reactions different from those made to the component stimuli in other compounds. Since it is a physical fact that most objects cohere, it follows that the stimuli arising from them will repeatedly affect the organism as interactive patterns. The young infant learns to make distinctive reactions to its own hand, to its bottle, and to its mother's face as discriminated 'wholes,' and subsequent application of specific verbal labels facilitates further behavioral organization of the stimulus manifold. The cohesive factors of similarity and nearness in grouping stimulus elements become *generalized perceptual habits*. Since manipulated objects do have the physical nature of cohesion, stimuli near in sensory space will be associated with interactive patterns more often than those far apart. This generalized tendency to respond to neighboring parts as 'belonging' leads to many perceptual errors on the child's part—he will grasp the top block on a piled column and appear surprised that only this one comes up when he tugs. Likewise, for many objects handled in infancy (spoons, clothespins, and crib bars, for example), the interacting parts are highly similar in sensory quality, and this leads to the generalized tendency to perceive similar elements as 'belonging.' The child makes industrious attempts to pick the pretty red flower from his mother's print dress; he has difficulty perceiving a slender piece of brown twine as connected to a bright red toy he is striving to draw toward himself (cf. Richardson's insight experiments, p. 625).

Transposition

Perceptual patterns, as integrated wholes, are transposable despite gross changes in the sensory elements that compose them. A familiar illustration is the melodic theme. The temporal pattern of tones we recognize as 'Sweet Adeline' can be passed from strings to brass to voice, from one key to another, even changed in rhythm, yet it retains its 'whole character.' This character is lost, however, when the melody is played in reverse—a point to which gestalt theorists have not given sufficient attention. Similarly, a circle or square retains its 'whole character' despite gross changes in size, color, angle of regard, and so on. This phenomenon is closely related to both perceptual constancy and concept formation.

Hebb's neurophysiological hypotheses, while admittedly speculative in nature, have application here. Despite the variation in stimulus character of triangles of different sizes, i.e. despite the variation in the locus of activity in area 17, these cell assemblies can come to channel upon specific loci in area 18, for example, excitation at this place representing the 'form' triangularity. Similar argument would be applied to 'form' in other modalities, e.g. melodic structures that vary in key. For the gestalt theorist, transposability follows easily from the notion of isomorphism: sensory patterns having the same *molar* physiological organization or structure must be paralleled by the same perceived form in the psychological field. Hull has discussed transposition phenomena, particularly Humphrey's Arpeggio paradox, in connection with his interaction hypothesis, but the argument is neither detailed nor convincing.

Unum and Duo

Central to the gestalt view of perceptual organization is the *principle of prägnanz,* according to which our perceptions will tend to be as simple and 'good' as prevailing stimulus conditions allow. Koffka (1935, pp. 153-9)

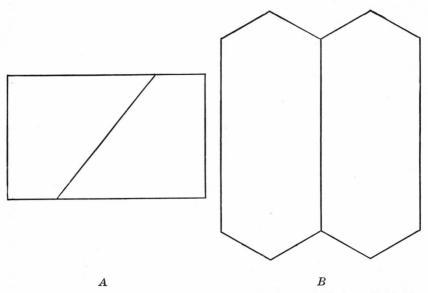

A   B

FIGURE 79. *Unum* and *duo:* an example. *A* is perceived as a single form divided by an interior line; *B* is perceived as two independent forms placed side by side. After Koffka, *Principles of Gestalt Psychology,* Harcourt, Brace and Company, Inc., New York, 1935, p. 153. Routledge and Kegan Paul, Ltd., London.

poses this question: When will an outline figure be seen as one, with lines in its interior, and when as two? Figure 79*A* is perceived as 'one,' as a rectangle divided by an included line. Figure 79*B,* on the other hand, is perceived as 'two,' as two separable units placed side by side. Why should this be? 'The reason is clear: in the first the total figure is a better figure than either of the two part figures, whereas the opposite is true in the second.' Koffka dismisses the empiricist's explanation—that 'better' figures become so through behavioral manipulations (familiarity)—by reference to an experiment by Gottschaldt (1926). This investigator gave subjects repeated experience with simple line figures like that in Fig. 80*A*. Then they were shown patterns like that in Fig. 80*B* and asked to report what they observed. Although the familiar figure was always imbedded in the new one, only rarely did any subject notice it. In fact, it is difficult to find the famil-

iar shape when one deliberately searches for it. By using these results as an
argument against the learning of form perceptions, Koffka assumes that the
empiricist is also necessarily an elementarist. Almost any contemporary behaviorist would agree that adding one stimulus pattern to another is more
than simple summation—interaction serves to modify the entire situation.
In the present instance it should be noticed that the additions that most
successfully obscure simple shapes are those that extend their contours in
the same direction and induce erroneous eye movements (and hence, according to the physiological view, call forth incompatible cell-assemblies). The
added lines in Fig. 80C do not interfere with seeing the original form one
whit since the added contours all cross the original ones at approximately
right angles.

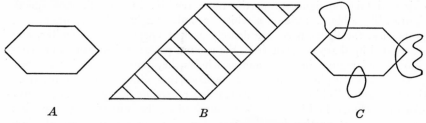

A   B   C

FIGURE 80. Perceptual misdirection. The simple form shown as *A* is included in both
B and *C*. It is very difficult to isolate perceptually in *B*, whereas in *C* it is readily
discernible. Koffka, *Principles of Gestalt Psychology*, Harcourt, Brace and Company, Inc., New York, 1935, p. 156. Routledge and Kegan Paul, Ltd., London. After
Gottschaldt, 1926.

Figure and Ground Articulation

Why, as Koffka so artfully puts it, do we see things and not the holes
between them? It is certain that when I hold out my hand with fingers
spread and look at it, the hand appears as a *figure,* as a 'thing,' and the
various other objects in the field of view become for the nonce amalgamated
into a formless, featureless mass we call the *ground.* Under exceptional circumstances we may see 'holes' as if they were figures—when, for example,
a sharp piece of blue sky is seen through a dark mass of rocks—but in such
cases we suspect that many of the factors normally associated with figures
have been transferred to what is usually ground. In ordinary vision, in our
three-dimensional world, a number of purely physiological factors contribute to the articulation of what is fixated: the thing looked at is seen as
single, whereas objects in the field both nearer and farther are seen as obscure double images; accommodation is adjusted to the texture of the thing
looked at, which makes this object visually clear at the expense of other
objects in the field. But there are many other forces at work to produce
figure-ground differentiation, and most of them are best illustrated with
reference to *two-dimensional* forms (perhaps because communication of scientific ideas in our culture has been largely via the plane surfaces of book
pages).

In the first place, the *phenomenal laws of grouping* we have already
studied find integrated expression in the process of figure formation. The
nearer to each other the elements to be included as a figure, the more easily
it can be isolated—witness the fact that the systems of stars which have

acquired names are close together and uninterrupted by intruding stars that are not part of the configuration. Likewise, the greater the *similarity* among the elements making up a figure, the more easily it is perceived as such. Another stimulus variable, not included in our discussion of unit formation, is *contrast:* other things being equal, the greater the contrast between figure elements and ground elements (whether this be in brightness, color, or form), the more easily will figures be formed. The same applies to both *continuity* and *closure:* the more elements making up a figure follow a regular and visually predictable direction, and the more they form closed spaces, the more easily figures will arise. Meaning is also a determinant. If the etched patch of sky between the rocky masses has the character of forming a familiar form—a profile, an animal, a standard geometrical shape —it will take on figure properties more readily. In general, most 'good' figures, like a black circle on a white ground, combine all these organizing properties: the figure parts are densely packed (near), highly similar, and segregated by sharp contrast from the ground parts; their contours are continuous and regular in form, and as wholes they represent familiar shapes.

What are the phenomenal characteristics that differentiate figures from their grounds? Rubin (1915, 1921), using reversible figure-ground patterns like those shown in Figs. 81 and 82, arrived at the following distinctions: (1) The figure portion has the *character of an object* or 'thing' (*Dingcharakter*), but the ground is relatively formless and has the character of a material or substance (*Stoffcharakter*). (2) The figure portion seems *phenomenally nearer in space* than the ground; although this spatial effect is not extreme in magnitude, it is definite, and the figure appears to lie on top of the ground. In fact, when reversible figures reverse, one often gets the impression of movement back and forth in the third dimension. (3) In keeping with this spatial effect, *the ground appears to extend continuously behind the figure,* giving rise to what Koffka (1935, p. 178) has called 'double representation'—the portion of the geographical field representing the figure is represented doubly in the psychological field, once as figure surface and once as (inferred) ground surface. (4) The *contours are perceived as belonging to the figure,* not the ground. This is another very distinct subjective impression one gets when observing reversible figures (see Fig. 81). Although each included contour is common to both potential figures, it 'clings,' as it were, to the portion of the field that is functioning as figure at the moment. Koffka (pp. 181-4) makes much of this characteristic of figures, expressing the opinion that this 'one-sidedness' of contours is a significant aspect of the shape-producing processes in perception.

Wever (1927) substantiated and extended Rubin's conclusions. Using black figures on a white ground and graduated exposure times (Dodge tachistoscope), he added that (5) whereas the *figure has definite localization in space and has surface texture,* the ground is poorly localized and has filmy texture. Wever also found that with gradual increases in the length of exposure the various characteristics of figures (contour, shape, protrusion, etc.) developed at different rates. The formation of contours seemed a prerequisite for any figural experience. It has also been reported that 'goodness' of shape and meaningfulness facilitate figure perception (Ehrenstein, 1930). A particularly interesting observation of Rubin's (1921) was that subjects show poor recognition for stimulus configurations when figure-ground relations have been reversed. Exchanging the land and water masses in a familiar map or looking at photographic negatives would be common illustrations of this observation.

Koffka believes that since figural organization is a dynamic process, since energy is expended in maintaining a particular perception, the density of energy should be greater within the figure than within the ground. This has a number of testable implications. (1) When colored sectors are used for reversible figures, the portion functioning momentarily as figure should have more color than the portion functioning as ground. He reports (1935, p. 186) that when a pattern like Fig. 81 is made of alternating gray and green patches, the green loses saturation when it shifts from figure to

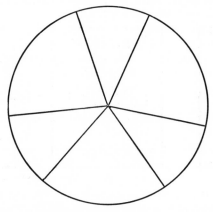

FIGURE 81. Illustration of ambiguous figure-ground pattern. Köhler, *Dynamics in Psychology,* Liveright Publishing Corp., New York, 1940, p. 68. Faber and Faber, Ltd., London.

ground and the gray gains contrast-red as it becomes figure. (2) Since energy-density within a figure is higher than within the ground, *CFF* for the former should be higher. Koffka reports data of L. Hartmann (1923) showing that *CFF* for the white portion of a black-white reversible figure was higher when it was perceived as figure than when perceived as ground. (3) Since simple 'good' figures require less energy to maintain themselves as perceptual entities, however, they should fuse at a lower flicker rate than complex figures. Hartmann's data also support this hypothesis; for example, a square had a lower *CFF* than a triangle. (Is a square a simpler figure than a triangle?) Hartmann's work was done at a time when little was known about *CFF:* to attribute these differences to form, it would be necessary to demonstrate that total brightness and area had been kept constant. Knox (1945 *b*) has reported that stability of forms has no effect upon *CFF*. More evidence is needed on the matter.

Another prediction is that (4) perception of sub-regions within a figure should require a greater intensity difference than perception of subregions within the ground. The reason is that the cohesive forces within the figure tend to 'iron out' differences. Experiments by Gelb and Granit (1923) are cited by Koffka as substantiating this expectation. Under conditions where regions of the same brightness could be made to function as either figure or ground, a small spot of light was added and the minimum intensity for perceptibility determined. The necessary increment was larger when added to a figure region than when added to a ground region. More recent work by Craik and Zangwill (1939) suggests, however, that the differences in brightness threshold are not due to figural processes as such: the same threshold changes could be produced simply by having a line in the field near one test patch but not near the other. In the following chapter, where we shall study contour mechanisms in some detail, similar 'ironing out' processes within bounded contours will be found.

Fluidity of Perceptual Organizations

The order and stability impressed upon sensory data by perceptual processes is at best a temporary affair. Any sensory field, if inspected for a long

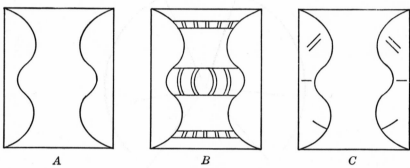

A	B	C

FIGURE 82. Manipulation of figure-ground relations. *A.* Uninfluenced field, 'vase' and 'faces' nearly equal in probability of occurrence. *B.* 'Vase' figure made more probable. *C.* 'Faces' figure made more probable.

enough period, will begin to shift and flow beneath our eyes, revealing its truly ambiguous character. When the sensory information is deliberately made ambiguous, as in reversible figure-ground patterns, this tendency merely becomes more pronounced. We may look upon any sensory pattern as potentially capable of inducing multiple perceptual organizations. In most 'normal' cases of perception, one mode of organization is decidedly dominant over other possibilities, owing to either innate or learned mechanisms, or both. When I look at the picture of Grandfather on the wall, there is extremely high probability that a particular perceptual organization will occur and, by virtue of its high probability, will persist unmodified for a prolonged period. Yet, even Grandfather's face, after being stared at for several minutes, begins to undergo surprising transformations.

Now stare at Fig. 82*A* for a while: Unlike Grandfather's face, this pattern is initially ambiguous; at first you see a vaselike figure, then something that looks rather like two buxom ladies engaged in face-to-face social exchange, then a vase again, and so on. As sensory information, this visual pattern is associated with these two alternative organizations to nearly equal degrees. We can deliberately modify the probability relations in this situation. If, as shown in Fig. 82*B,* we give the vaselike region distinctive markings that further enhance its 'thing-character,' reversals to the other mode of organization are diminished. If, as shown in Fig. 82*C,* we make meaningful faces out of the two outer regions, a pair of identical twins takes precedence over the vase. These manipulations were performed on the sensory information itself. We can also modify perceptual probabilities by changing the attitudes, meanings, and values of the observer. Schafer and Murphy (1943), for example, have shown that reward and punishment can reliably modify which of two reversible profiles will be perceived.

Nor is ambiguity restricted to alternation between only two competing organizations. Visual situations can be designed that may call out a large number of different perceptual organizations with about equal probability. Miles (1931) has devised what he calls a *kinephantoscope:* the sharply etched shadow of a rotating horizontal metal strip is cast upon a screen, the visual sequence shown in Fig. 83 repeating itself indefinitely. The observer may see 'two arms flapping toward me,' then suddenly it becomes 'two arms flapping behind or away from me,' then 'twirling around clockwise,' then

FIGURE 83. Miles's kinephantoscope. Rotation of a metal vane behind an illuminated screen produces a continuously varying shadow form which goes repeatedly through cycle shown above. Many alternate modes of perception are possible (Walter Miles, 1931).

'a bar stretching and shortening,' then 'flapping toward me again,' then 'a hole in a white sheet opening and closing,' and so on. These multiple possibilities are easily influenced by suggestion: if the observer chants 'flapping in . . . in . . . in, flapping out . . . out . . . out' and so on, the character of the perceived movement usually adjusts itself to the autosuggestion. Harrower (1939) has shown that individuals with cerebral lesions are less flexible in general and less affected by deliberate stimulus weighing of the probabilities. She used plane reversible figures like that given as Fig. 82. The implications here for rigidity in social perceptions deserve detailed experimental exploration.

What factors influence stability of perception? One, as we have already seen, is the *relative strength of competing perceptual organizations,* and this can be modified both by manipulating stimulus characteristics and by manipulating attitudes. Another factor is *fatigue.* In general, the longer one looks at a stimulus pattern, the more liable the dominant organization is to modification and, with initially reversible figures, the more rapid become the alternations. This has been demonstrated by Köhler (cf. above) and Philip and Fisichelli (1945) report similar observations. Using *Lissajous figures* (revolving abstract designs, reversible in direction of apparent movement, that are produced on the surface of a cathode-ray oscillograph), the frequency of reversals was found to increase significantly for the second half of a one-minute inspection period as compared with the first half. These authors stress fatigue of individual neurons in the visual projection system as an explanation. Fisichelli (1947) summarizes a number of other variables that affect fluctuation of Lissajous figures: reversals increase with *complexity of form* and with *speed of rotation* but decrease with the *size* of the form. All of these effects are interpreted as owing to increased susceptibility to reversal as the rate of excitation of given sets of fibers is increased. It should be remembered that with Lissajous figures we have a constantly moving pattern of excitation.

Köhler has interpreted the increasing reversal of stationary ambiguous figures under continued inspection as owing to a process of 'satiation' of the neural medium in which these figures have their representation. This explanation runs into the paradox that *both* potential figures utilize the same contours, i.e. are located in the same brain regions. Hebb might explain this phenomenon as relative fatigue in two or more particular loci in area 18, these loci being equivalently associated with the pattern of activity in area 17. As for the behaviorists' position, it would be interesting if, on a shorter time scale, these observations on reversible figure ground were found to parallel those on extinction and spontaneous recovery in ordinary learning.

Maximizing Form-producing Forces

Although, in a sense, any phenomenon is a measure of the forces that produce it—as the bending of objectively straight lines in certain illusions is evidence of the forces at work—certain phenomena provide more sensitive measures than others. What manipulations of sensory events should be most favorable for the measurement of form-producing forces? The answer comes readily enough, at least from gestalt theory. Since cohesive forces persist in the direction of their operation until they reach a balance with existing restraining forces, *anything that reduces the strength of restraining forces in the field will maximize the effects of cohesive forces and thus reveal their nature more clearly.* Restraining forces are presumed to be peripheral in origin; therefore, we must reduce the impact or clarity of the sensory input while arranging the structure of the field so as to vary the directions and magnitudes of cohesive forces induced. Of the several ways this can be accomplished, all come down to decreasing the intensity of stimulation.

The *visual after-image* is one such method. Activity in the visual pathways persists after peripheral stimulation has been withdrawn, but is less intense. Rothschild (1923) observed the after-images produced by various contour figures, such as those shown in Fig. 84. Regular 'good' figures tended to produce stable after-images, e.g. a perfect circle or square would appear undistorted in the after-image, fading and returning as a whole. An incomplete figure, such as the broken circle in Fig. 84*A*, tended to be completed in the after-image, i.e. closure. Subordinate details were less likely to survive in the after-image and, if they appeared at all, came and went independently of the major, unified figure. Such was the fate of the 'tail' attached to the square in Fig. 84*B*. Symmetry and balance were achieved to a greater degree in after-images than in original perceptions; the displaced parallel lines *C* moved closer together horizontally in the after-image. Perhaps the most striking of Rothschild's demonstrations is illustrated in *D:* in relation to the fixation point, the chaotic lines in the second figure precisely duplicate some of the lines making up the star-shape in the first figure; the after-image of the complete star functioned as a unified whole, whereas the after-images of the chaotic lines came and went in complete disregard for one another.

Directly *reducing the intensity* of presented stimuli does not seem to have been used often as a method for studying perceptual forces. Koffka (1935,

p. 143) reports an experiment by Hempstead conducted in Titchener's laboratory in 1900. After figures were projected on a moderately illuminated screen, an episcotister was used to vary their intensity relative to the ground illumination. At low intensities the presented figures were 'strongly deformed, being simpler, more symmetrical, with rounded instead of pointed corners, gaps closed, and even lines which were demanded by the general shape but absent in the stimulus filled in.' Experiments by Wohlfahrt are also reported in which reducing the size of figures produced the same types of effects.

Using a technique devised by Karwoski (cf. Karwoski and Warrener, 1942), in which a large, black-felt covered wheel is rotated slowly with

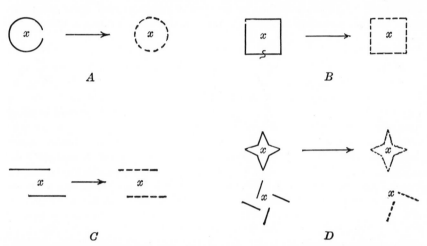

FIGURE 84. Original form stimuli (solid lines) and typical after-images (dashed lines) for various conditions reflecting the operation of gestalt dynamisms in perception. After Rothschild, 1923.

various stimulus forms attached to it, and exploring some of the problems originally discussed with him, the writer has observed certain rather interesting field effects. With small circular disks of white cardboard against the black ground as stimuli and fixation maintained on a small reflecting surface in the center of the rotating field, white filmy 'stuff' can be seen connecting the stimulus disks when intensity is such that the disks are barely visible. Several examples of this effect are shown in Fig. 85. When the illumination is suddenly increased to normal daylight levels, this 'filling in' effect can still be observed, but now it appears as black pathways between the stimulus points, blacker than the black-felt wheel on which they are projected.

Notice that this 'filling in' effect has none of the characteristics of after-images. Rather than following each stimulus form at an interval determined by latencies of nerve action, this effect takes place along the pathways *between* stimulated points, outlining forms suggested by the arrangements of the points. Just as the ordinary after-image is the projection of differences in activity within the visual system onto the field (where the effects can be measured), so this 'filling in' may be the projection of integrative processes within the higher visual centers. Its characteristics suggest that the neural processes essential for *form perception* are represented. The same phenomenon can be observed in many everyday situations. If the eyes are moved slowly over a bright surface on which a line or pattern of darker dots is placed (e.g. a line of nailheads holding white ceiling board in place), a 'filling in' of lines connecting the discrete points can usually be observed. Penciled dots on a circular piece of white or gray cardboard which is rotated irregularly about its center serve equally well.

Under ordinary conditions, and with ordinary individuals, these 'filling in' phenomena are very ephemeral. If we were able to discover a pathological individual in whom, for some reason, cohesive forces were abnormally strengthened relative to restraining forces, would he report readily and confidently phenomena which for most of us are obscure? Purdy (1936) describes what appears to be just such a case. C. displayed a number of

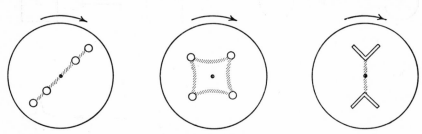

FIGURE 85. Examples of the 'filling in' phenomenon. When white stimuli (shown by open circles, angles) are placed on a black felt wheel and rotated slowly, pale connective materials (indicated by cross-hatching) appear.

visual abnormalities, among which was a singular instability of the visual field. 'Visual patterns, when continuously fixated by this subject, tended very rapidly to lose their internal differentiation and appear monotonous in structure. . . Thus, geometrical figures often approached a circular shape as they blurred. . . If C. looks at two black dots side by side, and regards them as "belonging together" (i.e. as members of a coherent "pair"), *the dots may appear to become joined together by a very distinct gray band or line.** If he "thinks of the dots as two separate things," this line fails to appear. . . If the contours of the objects are too sharp, confluence does not take place until they have been rendered slightly diffuse by a brief period of fixation . . . a sharp contour seems to be a place of resistance towards the spreading of color' (pp. 66-73). Purdy points out that C. possesses an unusual ability to maintain steady fixation upon one object and at the same time attend to another object in the peripheral field, i.e. he is able to become 'visually dissociated' to a greater degree than most persons.

The *tachistoscope* is an apparatus for presenting visual stimuli of brief duration. There are many kinds of tachistoscopes, but the best provide for accurate measurement of both exposure time and intensity of illumination. Since intensity and duration bear a reciprocal relation to one another, presenting visual stimuli tachistoscopically becomes another way of reducing the intensity of peripheral stimulation and thus, in theory, of reducing the strength of restraining forces. Koffka (1935, p. 143) reports experimental work by Lindemann which showed that complex and irregular figures are

* Italics mine.

simplified and regularized under tachistoscopic presentation. Granit (1921) obtained similar results. Ehrenstein (1930) found that 'good' forms (symmetrical, simple, etc.) and meaningful forms required less exposure time to be perceived.

Movement of objects in the visual field is another important way of enhancing integrative, cohesive forces. It has long been recognized by investigators in this area that movement—jiggling the stereoscope, for example, when an impression of depth has been lost—can strengthen perceptual organizing forces. We have already seen, in connection with the Brown and Voth study, that the phenomenon of *apparent* movement can be used to bring out perceptual dynamics; the same authors conclude that *real* movement can also be used to describe the operation of cohesive forces. Similarly, the present writer's observations of the 'filling in' phenomenon were obtained best when the entire field was in movement. Why does movement facilitate the operation of cohesive forces? It probably comes down to another case of weakening restraining forces by reduction in the intensity of sensory input. Stimulation which either actually shifts its location on the retina (real movement) or alternates rapidly between two or more separated points (apparent movement) is being applied to any particular set of receptors only very briefly—and this is equivalent to a reduction in intensity. This is intended as a possible explanation of the way movement facilitates cohesive forces, not as an explanation of movement perception.

Is Perceptual Organization Innate or Acquired?

Gestaltists, taking isomorphism for granted, are prone to attribute all characteristics of perceiving to innate fieldlike properties of the central nervous system. Behaviorists, following some notion of parsimony, try to find evidence for learning in all these behaviors. This is part of the continuing, and probably necessary, argument between nativism and empiricism. As usual, however, the answer gradually reveals itself as a compromise—certain aspects of perceptual organization are innately determined and others are the products of experience. What conditions are demanded for 'answers' on this problem? Since perceptual organization, in the normal course of things, develops along with the instrumental behaviors one must use as measures—probably *ahead* of these instrumental behaviors in the case of primates—it becomes necessary to prevent perceptual development during the period when other capacities are forming. With animals, this means rearing subjects from birth in complete darkness (assuming it is visual perception we wish to study); with humans, we must trust to happenstance—occasionally, individuals congenitally blind have their sight restored by surgery.

Hebb (1949) gives the most adequate account of the evidence bearing on this problem, and the reader desiring to press further should consult his book and the sources he cites (particularly Senden's (1932) survey of cases in which sight has been restored to people blind from birth and Riesen's (1947) study of chimpanzees reared in darkness). Hebb's thesis is that although certain characteristics of perceptual organization are innately determined (especially the processes which segregate figure from ground), other characteristics can be shown to be the results of long periods of learning. It is to the latter forms of organization that he applies his neurophysiological hypotheses (integration of cell-assemblies, etc.).

(1) *Primitive sensory segregation.* Upon first recovering sight, the person blind from birth does respond to objects as wholes, can detect differences between objects when simultaneously presented (implying figure-ground differentiation), and is able to learn color names and retain them. Rats reared in complete darkness also show articulation of figures from their grounds—trained to thread a white pathway against a black ground, they transfer readily to a black pathway on a white ground (Hebb, 1937 *a*). Upon what kinds of processes do these activities depend? Probably they represent the segregative functions of area 17 and antecedent sections of the visual projection system. These include *contour formation* on the basis of differential rates of excitation, *contrast* in terms of both brightness and color, which further segregates figure from ground, and presumably *certain selective, attentional mechanisms* of an innate nature, such as the reflex that drives the infant's eyes to fixate bright points in the field.

Riesen (1947) reared two chimpanzees in total darkness up to the age of 16 months. The first tests of visual reactions showed good pupillary reflexes to change in illumination, a pronounced startle reaction to sudden increases in illumination (accompanied by head and eye movements toward the source), pursuit movements of low accuracy after a moving light (which implies some figure-ground segregation), and characteristic nystagmus. Yet, aside from such adjustments, these animals appeared to be functionally blind. For a long time there was no blinking to an object suddenly brought up before the eyes (i.e. no innate perception of size as a cue for distance?), no adequate fixation of objects, and only a gradual development of visual recognition of familiar objects, such as the feeding bottle (the first sign of recognition of this object, interestingly enough, was an anticipatory pursing of the lips). Guidance of movements by vision was grossly inaccurate. Riesen notes that there is much more rapid organization of vision in both chicks (cf. Cruze, 1935) and rats, and he concludes that, for more highly developed species, beyond the maturation factor generally emphasized, 'the long period is also essential for the organization of perceptual processes through learning.'

Our judgments about what is 'complex' and 'high level' behavior may not correspond to nature's judgment. Consider the matter of transposition: Hebb (1937 *b*) reared rats to maturity in complete darkness and, after training them to discriminate two stimuli on the basis of either brightness or size, tested them for transposition to other stimuli along these continua. The preponderance of relative choices led to the conclusion that 'an innate property of visual perception is the organization of gradations in intensity or size into ordered and directed series. . .' An earlier experiment by Lashley and Russell (1934) on the organization of distance perception can probably be interpreted as another demonstration of transposition. They studied the 'distance perception' of rats brought up in complete darkness for the first hundred days of life by having them jump from a platform at a target. Both the distance leaped and the force applied by the animal in leaping could be measured. The results indicated an immediate adjustment of force to distance and a very rapid improvement in accuracy. This is interpreted as evidence for an innate organization of relative distance perception in the rat; it may equally well be another case of transposition in terms of either (or both) size or brightness cues, when the force of jumping is the criterion measure. In this particular experiment food rewards were placed on the landing-platform, and one wonders if olfactory distance cues could have been operative—no controls on this are discussed.

(2) *Acquired, nonsensory organization.* There are many figural organizations in perceiving that depend not at all upon sensory segregation per se (although this is a prerequisite, of course). Look back at Fig. 73: without changing your fixation (and therefore without changing the spatial arrangement of contours), you can perceive 'the Wife' and then 'the Mother-in-law.' Similarly, one may look at 'the middle' of a length of rope or 'the corner' of a room, even though these conceptualized entities have no sensory contours that segregate them from other parts of the field. An experiment by Leeper (1935 *a*), using Boring's 'wife' and 'mother-in-law' and other ambiguous figures, indicates that these nonsensory figures are amenable to both verbal suggestion and learning. In the latter case subjects first looked for 30 seconds at a figure in which either the 'old' or the 'young' woman was dominant (and the other obscured), and then at the usual figure in which both organizations are about equally probable. They were not equally probable after training.

(3) *Identity in perceiving.* One mass of lines, spaces, and colors in the field may have coherence and stand out as a figure, yet not be recognized as any particular object; another conglomeration is immediately identified as 'a man riding a bicycle' or 'an outline cube.' This is not entirely a matter of discriminability. One may place two unrecognizable patterns side by side and readily observe differences in color, shape, pattern, and so on. The difference lies in the implications of the term 'recognition': certain perceptual organizations have been associated with distinctive reactions, and it is these reactions that give the recognized patterns meaning, or 'identity.' The specific visual pattern is referred to a class of events (i.e. is conceptualized)—'this is a circle,' 'this is a man's face,' and so forth. Recognizing or identifying objects is obviously a result of learning, and since the concrete instances of visual 'circle' or 'face' are quite variable, the form of learning must have much in common with *concept formation* (cf. pp. 666ff.).

Senden (1932) reports that even highly motivated patients who have recently recovered sight have to look painstakingly for corners in order to tell whether a presented form is a circle or a triangle—the difference is not immediately self-evident as it appears to be with normal adults. This difficulty persists for many weeks but is ultimately overcome. Equally significant is the fact that these patients are unable to transpose recognition of forms when conditions are changed even slightly. Having learned to name correctly a square made of white cardboard, a patient could not recognize it when its color was changed to yellow, yet this patient (and others) had little trouble learning or retaining color names (cf. Hebb, pp. 28-9). With one patient, eleven months after operation and after repeated experience with common objects, an egg, a potato, and a cube of sugar were not recognized when placed in colored light (ibid. p. 32). Substantiating data has been obtained for chimpanzees raised in complete darkness (Riesen, 1947). Although the normal chimpanzee is unaffected by brightness reversals of figure and ground or by rotations of simple figures (e.g. from an upright to an inverted triangle), the chimpanzee raised in complete darkness makes discriminative transfers on the basis of form only after prolonged training.

By way of general conclusions, it would appear that simple sensory segregation of the visual field, in terms of contour formation, contrast, and certain reflexive attentional mechanisms, is an innate property of the visual nervous system—for both rat and human. From this evidence, then, we must conclude that the gestalt view, according to which qualitative and intensive similarity and nearness in the visual field innately set up cohesive tendencies, is more nearly correct than the behavioristic view, according to which these grouping tendencies are learned as generalized habits. On the other hand, those organizational characteristics of perceiving we call 'nonsensory figure perception' and 'recognition' are clearly shown to be the results of learning, slow and arduous learning at that. 'It is possible then that the normal human infant goes through the same process, and that we are able to see a square as such in a single glance only as the result of complex learning. The notion seems unlikely, because of the utter simplicity of such a perception to the normal adult. But . . . subjective simplicity and immediacy may be very deceptive as an index of physiological simplicity' (Hebb, 1949, p. 33).

Chapter 6

PROJECTION DYNAMICS IN PERCEPTION

The preceding chapter was orientative with respect to the two that follow. It attempted first to sketch in the relationships which the concept 'perception' bears to other major psychological categories. Then three general points of view toward perception—physiological, gestalt, and behavioristic—were described, and it was stressed that these points of view are by no means exclusive of one another. This will become increasingly evident throughout this and the following chapter where, in order to achieve even the crudest beginnings of an understanding of perceptual phenomena, we shall need the characteristic contributions of each point of view. Our general approach to each phenomenon will be to first seek understanding in terms of comparatively well-known physiological mechanisms—particularly those which have been described as characterizing the projective system up to and including Brodmann's area 17—and then to draw upon more speculative central mechanisms, reluctantly and gingerly, as they seem to be necessitated by the facts.

CONTOUR AND CONTRAST EFFECTS

The first phenomenon we shall study is contour formation, a process, in part at least, simply dependent upon quite well-known principles of neural activity in the visual projection system. Contours arise from intensity differentials in the objective field, these being represented neurologically by gradients of impulse rate in the fine mosaic of cells in area 17. The greater the intensity differences between adjacent portions of the field, the sharper become impulse-frequency gradients and the clearer perceived contours. Lateral reciprocal overlap in the visual pathways and statistical 'peaking' of excitation through vertical facilitation serve to enhance differentials in regions of contrasting brightness. Inhibition about the borders of such excitation ridges has been established neurologically as depression in impulse frequency (cf. Marshall and Talbot, 1942) and this presumably further enhances the formation of sharp subjective contours. Since black lines on white and white lines on black serve equally well in contour formation, it seems probable that *'on-off' retinal mechanisms* and their central connections are chiefly concerned. Only such mechanisms, kept active by continuous physiological nystagmus, could prevent adaptation to brightness differences and consequent fading of contours.

The experimental work on contour formation is reviewed by Bartley (1941, Chap. 10), and an intimate relation with retinal summation and inhibition is suggested. Suppose that with regions B and C in Fig. 86 equal in brightness, the heavy contour between them is varied in its distance from disk A. What will be the effect upon the threshold visibility of the disk (i.e. upon the contour between A and B)? The experimental result is that the A/B contour is progressively weakened as the B/C contour is moved closer to it (Fry and Bartley, 1935). Interaction of this sort between contours seems to be limited to a retinal distance of about four degrees near

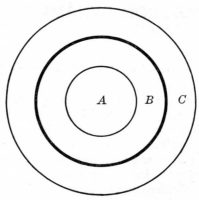

FIGURE 86. Pattern for studying the effect of one contour upon another within its region of influence. Bartley, *Vision: A Study of Its Basis,* D. Van Nostrand Co., Inc., New York, 1941, p. 230. After Fry and Bartley, 1935.

the fovea. This and other similar evidence leads to the generalization that *formed contours exert an inhibitory influence upon similar processes in their immediate surround.* It is apparent that this effect is related to both lateral inhibition at retinal levels and to depression in impulse rate at higher levels, but the exact mechanisms remain to be worked out. Another characteristic is that *contours prevent activity from spreading within the visual system.* Bartley (p. 231) gives evidence for this, and we shall find additional evidence in studying contrast phenomena. Conversely, *the existence of common contours about, or connecting, regions of the visual field serves to equate processes within them.* If we make disk A different in brightness from region B (e.g. a light gray), the objective brightness difference is minimized by contour B/C just as contour A/B is inhibited—both effects are fundamentally the same thing. Another illustration of this comes from the study of after-images. Creed and Granit (1928) have shown that the latency with which an after-image follows original stimulation varies with distance from the fovea. As one increases the size of a centrally fixated stimulus, however, latency varies with distance of the outer contour from the fovea *but the entire image appears simultaneously,* i.e. latency differences *within* the common contour seem to be ironed out in some unknown manner. Although the after-image latencies of two small and separate circles will vary independently with their retinal locus, linking them with a common, inclusive contour minimizes their independent action.

Contour formation is a process that requires time. This has been demonstrated in studies by Werner (1935). Under stroboscopic conditions, one figure (a_1 in Fig. 87) was followed after an interval of about 150 msec. by another (b_1) which was centered at the same point and which formed a frame about the first. For most subjects the small black circle (a_1) disappeared entirely. By preventing the formation of its contours, the entire figure was eliminated as well as the brightness difference from the background.

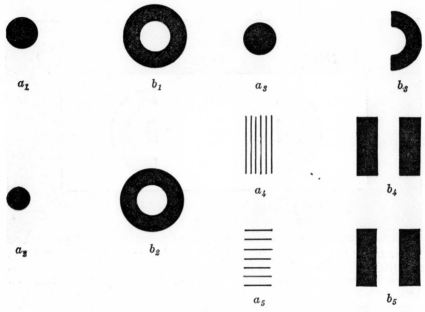

FIGURE 87. Forms used in studying contour processes: a figures are presented slightly prior to b figures. After Werner, 1935.

It would be interesting to see for how large an area this effect would hold. Since destruction of contour entirely obliterates appreciation of the brightness a surface would otherwise have, this means that the presence or absence of a distant contour can completely change the perceived quality of local stimulation. This probably indicates the role of mechanisms beyond area 17. If the presentation order is reversed, so that the annular disk precedes the solid disk, both are seen, i.e. formation of the ring contours is not interfered with by the subsequent contour formation of the solid disk. Why this should be so is not clear in Werner's report. He explains the original phenomenon (elimination of the disk) as follows: 'The process of forming the contour of the disk will, therefore, be utilized in the building up of the ring. A specific, separate perception of the contour of the disk, in consequence of this fact, is absent' (pp. 42-3). Another of Werner's demonstrations (a_2 and b_2) indicates that the distance over which this inhibitory effect extends is limited. In this case the contour of solid disk falls well within the inner contour of the ring, and the disk does not disappear at any rate of presentation. Another interesting fact deserves mention: the optimum rate of succession for this effect turns out to be that which is optimal for perception of apparent movement.

Werner presents many demonstrations of this sort. Some of them seem readily explicable from known neurological principles related to contour formation—a partial ring, for example (a_3 and b_3), obliterates roughly those portions of the solid disk it impinges on. Others seem to require additional principles: contours that parallel the dominant (inhibiting) contours are more strongly affected than contours that run at right angles to them (a_4/b_4 vs. a_5/b_5). Substantiating evidence is reported by Fry and Bartley

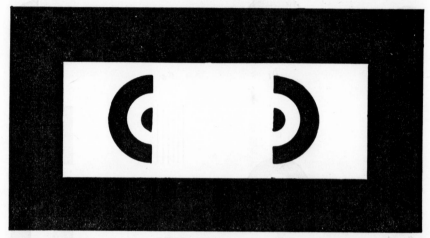

FIGURE 88. Subjective contour. The broken edges of the black rings are sufficient to give rise to the impression of an included white square (Schumann, 1904). As described in Woodworth, *Experimental Psychology,* Henry Holt and Co., Inc., New York, 1938, p. 637.

(1935). Another phenomenon that defies explanation in terms of existing neurological principles is 'subjective contour.' In the pattern shown as Fig. 88, for example, most people readily perceive a white square in the center, bounded by intermittent black-white on left and right. The fact that the black forms end abruptly along a vertical plane seems sufficient to establish a subjective contour. This, it should be noted, is very similar to the 'filling in' phenomenon discussed in the preceding chapter—here, also, like processes in the field, although separated, seemed to give rise to activities which unite them.

Contour formation is fundamental to all perceptual activity. Forms, objects, 'things' in the visual field exist only to the extent that there are energy differentials of sufficient abruptness in the medium. Organization of the visual field is further enhanced by *contrast,* brightness and color differences between regions being maximized in this way. Let us refer to the region in which the effects of contrast are observed as the *test patch* and to that which produces these effects as the *inducing area.* Actually, the effects are reciprocal. The usual procedure is to surround a relatively small test patch with a relatively large inducing area, which maximizes the effect upon the test patch and minimizes the effect in the opposite direction. *Brightness contrast* may be observed when two objectively identical small gray squares are placed so that one appears against a bright white background and the other appears against a jet-black background—the former is perceived as definitely darker than the latter. *Color contrast* can be produced in several ways: if our identical gray test patches are placed on red and blue inducing areas, respectively, the former gray appears tinged with blue-green (the complementary of red) and the latter appears tinged with yellow (the complementary of blue); or we may place a red test patch on a blue ground, and the test patch turns toward orange (i.e. the red combines with the complementary of blue, yellow, which yields orange); or we may place a pale, desaturated yellow against a deeply saturated blue, and the test patch becomes a more richly saturated yellow. Observe that in every case, whether for brightness or for color contrast, the direction of the effect is such as to maximize the perceived difference between the two regions of stimulation and hence increase their discriminability. In the case of color, the test patch is always shifted toward the complementary of the inducing area.

Again we are dealing with lateral interactions, and it will be profitable at this point to recast a hypothesis developed to account for summation and inhibition in the retina (cf. Chap. 4, p. 168). Letting b represent the test patch and a the inducing area from which lateral impulses are received, the following hypothesis may be phrased: *When the impulse rate at a is less than or equal to that at b, the lateral effects upon b summate with those being delivered directly on this area, increasing the frequency of excitation of b; when the impulse rate at a is greater than that at b, the lateral effects upon b are inhibitory and decrease the frequency of excitation of b*. No definite neurological basis for this inhibitory notion is available, but the entire question of inhibition in neural transmission is very much up in the air at this time (cf. Fulton, 1949, pp. 97-103). Nerve cells typically have large numbers of boutons upon which the exciting action of other fibers is received. Although relatively few boutons on receiving cells in b cited above might be affected by lateral inputs as compared with direct inputs along the projection system, it is conceivable that a rapid rate of subliminal excitation at these points could 'drain off' the electrical excitability of these cells, raising their thresholds to stimulation along the direct pathways. To incorporate *color* contrast phenomena, one further assumption must be made; namely, that *the density of lateral connections is greater between cells mediating the same quality* (e.g. R with R mechanisms, B with B, etc.) *than between cells mediating different quality*. In other words, the effects of R activity in the inducing area will be chiefly upon R activity within the test patch.

How do these hypotheses apply to contrast phenomena? First, with regard to *brightness contrast*, this effect is eliminated when illumination of test and inducing regions is equal. Although summation is maximal, no differentiation is produced (and there are no contours). Brightness contrast increases with illumination difference between test and inducing regions. The more rapid lateral excitation from the bright region depresses activity in the dimmer region, whereas the slower lateral effects from the dim region facilitate activity in the bright region (and contours become stronger). What about *color contrast?* When a gray test patch is placed on a well-saturated blue inducing area, the gray becomes yellowish. The frequency of impulses received laterally by B cells in the gray patch is more rapid than the frequency set up directly by the gray light, and subtraction of B in this region enhances $R–G$, hence the yellowish tinge. A pale yellow test patch against blue becomes more saturated for the same reasons. Since density of lateral connections decreases with distance, it can be predicted that contrast effects will be (1) greatest about the margins of large test patches, (2) greater for small as compared with large test patches, and (3) decrease with the distance between test and inducing areas. All of these phenomena are well known.

Relations between contrast and *contour* processes also give rise to certain effects. We have seen that one of the characteristics of contours is that *they prevent activity from spreading in the visual system*. This is irrelevant as far as simple brightness contrast is concerned, since the same stimulus properties give rise to both phenomena. (Indeed, the lateral inhibition of one contour upon a neighboring one is probably nothing other than the inhibition between like processes of unequal intensity which underlies contrast.) But this limiting effect of contours is highly significant with respect to color contrast. Since the contrast phenomenon depends upon lateral interactions, any barrier between test and inducing regions will minimize it. Since, as we have seen, brightness differences between adjacent regions set up contours, it follows that color contrast should be diminished to the extent that there are brightness differences between test and inducing regions. This is decidedly the case—the most vivid color contrasts are obtained when total brightness is equal for test and inducing regions. A common trick to enhance contrast is to cover both regions with thin tissue paper; this makes the contour between test and inducing regions less abrupt.

These hypotheses also predict a phenomenon that, to this writer's knowledge, has not been reported previously. Just as both brightness summation and brightness inhibition have been demonstrated, so *color summation,* as well as color contrast, should be observable under appropriate conditions. What are these conditions? In theory, all that is required is the excitation of a particular quality greater in the test region than in the inducing region, but this is difficult to accomplish in practice. The fact that an inducing area has a given dominant hue means that, relative to other components, this component has a high excitation rate. How are we to give this component a faster rate in the test patch? If we use a deeply saturated and *dark* blue for the inducing area and a *bright* white for the test patch, it is probable that the rate of fire for the blue mechanisms in the bright white patch will actually be more rapid than in the blue surround, even though the test patch appears white because of equal excitation of other mechanisms. Theoretically, the blue in the surround should summate with the blue in the test patch to give a bluish tinge to the central patch. But if the test patch is a sharply cut white circle, the effect is very slight. Why? Because the over-all brightness difference between bright patch and dark ground sets up a strong contour which inhibits lateral effects. The writer has found, however, that a definite bluing (or pinking, or greening, depending on the hue of the dark inducing area) can be obtained under these conditions *if the abruptness of the contour is broken down* by using an irregular test patch with fuzzy edges. Notice that this is the direct opposite of color contrast— the central patch becomes tinged with the *same* hue as the surround, not the complementary—and the phenomenon is predictable from the hypotheses stated.

So far no facts about contrast phenomena have been described that require any perceptual forces per se. Lateral interactions along anatomically established pathways in area 17 (the projection area), to say nothing of the retina itself, seem sufficient. There are at least two sets of facts that deny such a conclusion: (1) Although contrast effects are most prominent about the borders of interacting areas (as the anatomical conception would demand), they do affect entire test regions as wholes, i.e. regions well beyond

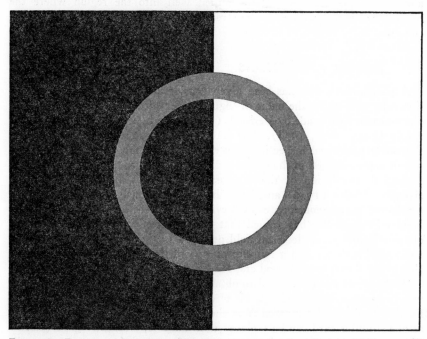

FIGURE 89. Demonstration of simultaneous contrast (as described by Koffka, 1935). Contrast is brought out by bisecting the gray circle with a pencil or thread. Moving this pencil slowly to left and then right will 'draw' the contrast into regions when the effect would not be expected. The author thanks Dr. Jozef Cohen of the University of Illinois for preparing this figure.

the distances over which lateral summation and inhibition effects operate are modified in accordance with what transpires at the borders. This fact is strictly equivalent to what we found for contour formation and its effect on form perception—obliteration of the contour of a black figure could completely eliminate the figure. (2) The demonstration shown by Fig. 89 is attributed by Koffka (1935, p. 134) to Wertheimer and Benussi, although Wundt apparently used a form of it in lecture demonstrations much earlier. The neutral gray ring is half against a black ground and half against a white ground, yet little if any brightness contrast can be seen. Now if the reader will take a narrow object, perhaps his pen or pencil, and neatly divide the ring along the line separating black from white, the double contrast will suddenly and vividly appear. Why was it lacking before? The gestalt theorist speaks of the cohesive forces exerted on all the part-processes of a good figure by the whole. Being perceived as a whole, the ring attains a uniform gray throughout. Or we might speak of the 'ironing out' process that functions within contours—which adds no more to our understanding of it. When the ring is divided, it becomes 'two half-rings on different backgrounds' perceptually, and a strong contrast effect occurs. The new contour prevents activity in one half-ring from affecting the visual activity in the other half-ring. Another unusual effect can be obtained by slowly moving the vertical divider across the figure: the dark tinge characteristic of the portion of the gray ring upon the white background can be literally pulled along with the moving contour, pulled well into the region where the background is black. Such is the strength of the leveling processes within contours.

FIGURAL AFTER-EFFECTS

A phenomenon that has been given considerable attention in the recent literature goes under the name of 'figural after-effect.' Early reports on the phenomenon were made by Verhoeff (1925) and by Gibson and his collaborators (1933, 1937, 1938). The latter investigators, for example, noted that after prolonged inspection of a curved line a subsequent straight line would appear curved in the opposite direction. The most elaborate phenomenological description of the various forms of this after-effect has been given by Köhler (1940) and by Köhler and Wallach (1944), who have considered the phenomenon critical evidence in favor of a field-type theory. Köhler in particular has argued that these after-effects require postulation of certain nonneural electrical field processes in the visual cortex. An evaluation of his theory and a reinterpretation of the evidence is already available in the literature (Osgood and Heyer, 1951).

The general procedure used to obtain after-effects is as follows: One figure (inspection or I-figure) is observed for several minutes with constant fixation (on the point marked X in the following diagrams). Then, as soon as one stimulus card can be replaced with another, a second figure (test or T-figure) is observed and its phenomenal characteristics reported immediately. Figure 90 gives a typical example. Objectively the two T-squares are identical in size, brightness, distance from X, and so on, but both are somewhat smaller than the I-square. The left-hand T-square is arranged to fall within the contours of the previously inspected I-square and slightly nearer its right contour. Phenomenally the left-hand T-square appears *smaller* than the right-hand one, it seems *displaced* away from X, its borders appear *paler,* and it may seem to be *further back* in three-dimensional space. Not all of these characteristics need appear to a given subject at a given time, suggesting that attitudinal factors play some part in such observations. Indeed, several investigators have had trouble verifying certain after-effects (Weitz and Post, 1948; Marks, 1949; Weitz and Compton, 1950), possibly because relatively naïve subjects were used. The judgments about the comparative size, nearness, brightness, and so on of test and control figures are difficult to make, especially since the critical regions are usually distant from the fixation point.

Some mention has already been made of Köhler's electrical field theory. Let us now see how it applies to figural after-effects. Some unspecified region of the central visual system must be conceived as a quasihomogeneous volume of tissue through which electrical currents can flow without regard to anatomical arrangements. These currents are presumed to follow paths of least resistance. But the very flow of current through tissues, through polarization of membranes, increases resistance to further passage of current. When the I-figure is presented, equilibrium in this region is disrupted and a flow of current is set up along the paths of least resistance, in this case along the contours of the I-figure. This current flow, however, gradually increases the resistance of the tissues through which it passes, and thus forces the current to detour into neighboring regions. This process results in a gradient of increased resistance, 'satiation,' about the contour of the I-figure. Analogous to the heating of conductors and their increased resistance, tissues do not immediately become depolarized. Therefore, these satiation

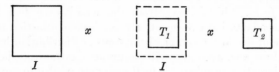

FIGURE 90. Procedure for observing figural after-effects. Observer first fixates X when only the inspection figure (I) is in the field. When the point between the two smaller figures (T_1, T_2) is later fixated, the left hand square falls within the region previously surrounded by the contours of the inspection figure. Various distortions are produced in this fashion. Osgood and Heyer, *Psychological Review*, 1952, 59:99.

effects persist after the I-figure has been removed and can be measured by observing distortions in subsequent T-figures. In other words, the flow of current representing subsequent T-figures will necessarily detour about heavily satiated regions, giving rise to size and displacement phenomena and (not so clearly) brightness and distance effects.

Numerous questions are raised by a theory of this sort. One wonders how such nonneural electrical effects can eventuate in behavior, i.e. in the initiation of impulses in motor fibers. At some point along the line we must transfer from direct currents in a field to impulses in nerve, since this is the way muscles are innervated. And why is the elaborate differentiation of sensory cortical tissues necessary? The Köhler theory would apply just as well were the peripheral projection system to terminate on a field of simple cell membranes enclosing electrolytic fluids—the fact that the field is composed of *nerve* tissues is superfluous. And there are several other detailed criticisms from the viewpoint of neurophysiology. The critical issue is this: Is it necessary to postulate an entirely novel set of nonneural electrical forces in the brain? Köhler and Wallach believe the phenomena of visual perception, particularly these after-effects, force some such extension of theory. If, however, these phenomena can be attributed to the functioning of comparatively well-known projection mechanisms, postulation of electrical fields becomes unnecessary and the interests of parsimony are served.

Drawing directly on the work of Marshall and Talbot (1942), we may assume that the representation of a contour in the projection cortex is a normal distribution of excitation, symmetrical about its own axis transversely and extending as a 'ridge' throughout the longitudinal extent of the contour. It is also reasonable to assume that 'on-off' type fibers and their central connections are chiefly involved in contour formation—white figures on black or black on white will thus be equivalent, as proved in the case with figural after-effects. Accepting the fact that contours are represented by a distribution of excitation in area 17, it follows that rate of fire at any given locus will vary both with nearness to the 'peak' of such a contour process and with the sharpness (intensity difference) of the contour. Coming now to after-effects themselves, *under constant fixation of a figure, the cells in area 17 mediating the 'on-off' activity will become differentially adapted as negatively accelerated functions of (a) the rate of their excitation and (b) the time through which they are excited.* Equilibration of firing under conditions of continued stimulation is a common characteristic of nerve tissues. Since, under the conditions of Köhler's observations, there is a brief interval between *I*- and *T*-figures, it follows *that in the time following inspection such gradients of differential adaptation will become flattened in form.* This follows from the well-known fact that rate of recovery from adaptation is a negatively accelerated function of its degree. Since the rate of fire in the center of the contour distribution has been more rapid than elsewhere, recovery will occur at a faster rate here and thus flatten the adaptation gradient. A final assumption, also in agreement with Marshall and Talbot, must be made, namely, *that the apparent localization of a contour in subjective space coincides with the location of maximal excitation in area 17.* The statistical distribution of excitations is not perceived as a graduated 'blur' but as a fine point or line.

For present purposes it is necessary to show that apparent localization can be shifted predictably for 'test' contours following prolonged observation of 'inspection' contours, provided these contours fall close enough to each other in space. Figure 91 illustrates how the locus of maximal rate of fire in the distribution representing a *T*-contour can be shifted because of the differentially adapted region on which it falls. Curve I_a represents the hypothetical distribution of excitation in 'on-off' processes in area 17 resulting from inspection of one contour, *I*. In the interval before the *T*-contour can be presented and fixated, differential recovery from fatigue flattens out this distribution to the form of curve I_b. When the subsequent *T*-contour falls objectively somewhat to one side or the other of the previously inspected *I*-contour, the bilaterally symmetrical distribution of excitation it would normally produce, curve T_a, is modified by the differential excitability of the region into curve T_b. Since apparent localization of a contour depends upon the locus of maximal excitation, the apparent location of the *T*-contour must shift from *T* to *T'*. With appropriate pairs of *T*-figures (to make possible simultaneous comparison), this shift in apparent localization of a contour may appear simply as that—*displacement*—or, if the *I*-contour completely surrounds the *T*-contour, the *size* of the included figure will appear to shrink. And if an observer is 'set' to make distance judgments, the same size effects are interpretable as increased *distance* from the observer. Since contrast depends upon the difference in amplitude of response between two regions, and since total amplitude is reduced within the region of relative adaptation, the borders of an affected *T*-figure will appear *paler* than those of the comparison *T*-figure. These are the major characteristics of figural after-effects, as reported by Köhler and Wallach.

We may now apply this analysis to certain interesting figural after-effects. (1) *The distance paradox.* Superficial application of either Köhler's theory or the 'statistical theory,' as we may term the interpretation offered here, would imply that the magnitude of the after-effect should increase regularly as the *T*-contour is made to lie closer and closer to the locus of a previous *I*-contour. This is not the case. Köhler and Wallach present qualitative and quantitative data to show that *as the objective locus of the T-contour is moved progressively toward the I-contour by small amounts, the magnitude of the displacement at first increases and then decreases, reaching zero when the T-contour coincides with the I-contour.* The final *de-*

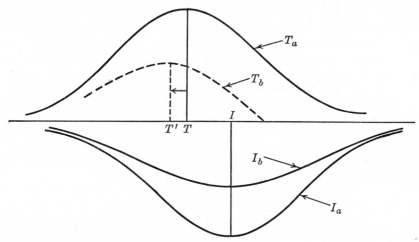

FIGURE 91. Interpretation of figural after-effects in terms of 'statistical theory.' I_a. Hypothetical excitation distribution produced by inspection contour. I_b. Relative adaptation function following removal of inspection contour. T_a. Hypothetical excitation distribution normally produced by test contour. T_b. Excitation distribution obtained by subtracting I_b from T_a. T' represents the displacement of contour T resulting from previous inspection of I. Osgood and Heyer, *Psychological Review*, 1952, 59:105.

crease in after-effect as *T*- and *I*-contours approach coincidence is explained by Köhler and Wallach (p. 338) as follows: '. . . as we bring the *T*-line nearer and nearer, the satiated *I*-region will gradually extend *beyond* the place of the *T*-line. The more this is the case the less will the *T*-current be deflected, and the less therefore will the line be displaced, because the position of the *T*-line within the satiated *I*-region begins to be progressively more symmetrical. This development will continue until the resistance on one side of the *T*-line is just as great as it is on the other side.' That the same prediction follows from the 'statistical theory' is demonstrated in Fig. 92, which describes hypothetical excitation distributions for four degrees of contour approach as well as complete coincidence. When the central peak of the *T*-distribution falls beyond the range of *I*-adaptation (a), or if it precisely coincides with the distribution of *I*-adaptation (e), there can be no displacement in the locus of maximal excitation for the actual *T*-distribution—and hence no displacement in apparent localization in space. Between these two extremes, however (b, c, d), displacement must first increase and then decrease, given the assumption of a Gaussian distribution of excitation. Köhler and Wallach do report that the *paling* of contours increases regularly to a maximum at coincidence; notice that in Fig. 92 the amplitude of excitation for T' is progressively reduced from (a) to (e).

(2) *After-effects in the third dimension.* In a more recent communication, Köhler and Emery (1947) have described a large number of after-effects in the third dimension. It is their general contention that depth is

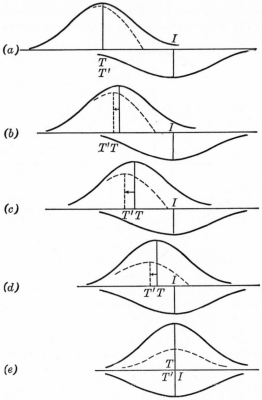

FIGURE 92. 'Statistical theory' interpretation of the distance paradox in figural after-effects. Amount of predicted displacement of the test contour (T to T') is shown to first increase and then decrease as I and T contours approach juxtaposition. Osgood and Heyer, *Psychological Review,* 1952, 59:107.

a sensory fact, that objects can be 'pushed' forward or backward in subjective visual space by appropriate after-effects, and they toy with the notion of a solid or 'layered' topography in the visual cortex. These effects are readily explained, however, as the same kind of *size* changes we have already been discussing, except that here the observer is 'set' for distance judgments and hence interprets size changes as 'nearer' or 'farther.' There is space here for only one illustration (see Osgood and Heyer, 1951, for further details). In the situation diagrammed as Fig. 93*A,* the solid lines represent white squares of identical size which are viewed against a large black screen. Following prolonged fixation of a point on the same plane as the I-square, either T_1 and T_2 (nearer to the observer) or T_3 and T_4 (farther from the observer) are substituted. In the former case the affected T-square seems nearer than its companion, but in the latter case it seems farther away. This is interpreted as an after-effect in the third dimension, and it certainly is in a phenomenal sense. As shown in Fig. 93B, however, these effects are easily explained as size changes, interpreted as changes in distance when observers are properly disposed. The I-square and T_1 are equal in objective size; consequently when T_1 is placed nearer in space, its contours must fall *out-side* the location of the previous I-contours on the retina—it will therefore be expanded in apparent size and judged relatively nearer. T_3 must fall *within* the contours of the previous I-square, and it will therefore shrink in

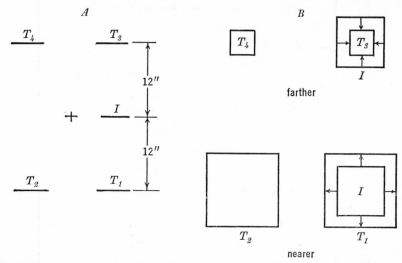

FIGURE 93. A. Setup for demonstrating third dimensional after-effects. B. Interpretation in terms of contour displacement dynamics. Osgood and Heyer, *Psychological Review*, 1952, 59:112.

apparent size and be judged relatively further away. Köhler and Emery give quantitative data showing that the same 'distance paradox' characteristic of two-dimensional after-effects is found here as well.

There is great need for quantitative study of figural after-effects, particularly with reference to the ways in which they vary as functions of angular displacement of I- and T-contours, intensity gradients, inspection time, time following inspection, location on the retina, and so on. Köhler and his collaborators have usually been content with acute demonstrations rather than quantitative data. One investigation on temporal factors has recently been reported by Hammer (1949), and other quantitative studies are no doubt under way. In the Hammer study vertical lines served as I- and T-figures and the angular distance between them of 2.2 mm. was kept constant. The I-line was sometimes to the left and sometimes to the right of the affected T-line; the affected T-line was 5 mm. below the fixation point and the comparison T-line an equal distance above it. Displacement of the lower T-line as a result of previous inspection of the I-line was determined by the amount the subject had to shift the upper T-line in order to make the two of them fall on a single vertical plane again. Figure 94A shows how magnitude of displacement varies as the *inspection period* is lengthened from 0 to 150 seconds—the displacing process ('satiation' or differential adaptation in area 17) builds up rapidly within the first 60 seconds and approaches asymptotic values by 150 seconds. In both *A* and *B*

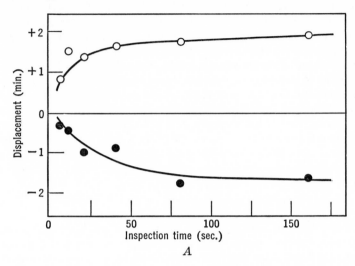

A

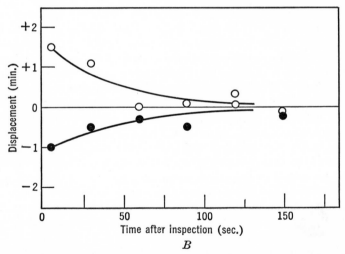

B

FIGURE 94. *A*. Test-contour displacement as a function of inspection time. *B*. Test-contour displacement as a function of the time after inspection. Hammer, *American Journal of Psychology*, 1949, **62**:350, 348.

figures, the upper curves and lower curves merely refer to the location of the *I*-line, to the left or to the right of the affected *T*-line. Figure 94*B* shows how magnitude of displacement varies as *the period following inspection* is lengthened from 0 to 150 seconds—the displacing process weakens rapidly according to a negatively accelerated function, becoming unmeasurable after 100 seconds. In this case the inspection period was constant at 60 seconds. Notice that these negatively accelerated curves are typical of those obtained for the course of adaptation and for recovery following adaptation.

Köhler has argued lengthily and ably that perceptual facts require a field theory for their understanding. This may be true, since there are many phenomena in this area that do not follow easily from known neural mechanisms, some of which we have already encountered. He has laid heavy emphasis upon figural after-effects, however, as phenomena that particularly demand such an interpretation, and with this we must disagree. There are no characteristics of these after-effects that do not follow directly from known neurological mechanisms of the visual projection system. None of these mechanisms include any 'field' principle as such. Indeed, there seems to be nothing 'figural' about them—they are merely one of several phenomena deriving from the lateral spread of contour processes. In themselves, then, figural after-effects do not require the postulation of novel electrical fields in the brain.

PERCEPTION OF MOVEMENT

It did not occur to psychologists that there was any problem for them in the perception of motion until, in the mid-nineteenth century, a number of illusions of motion were made common property. It had seemed perfectly obvious that movement of excitation across the retina should be perceived as movement in space of the object responsible. But this doesn't explain *stroboscopic movement*, in which a series of a stationary but disparate pictures presented at a fast enough rate may give rise to an impression of movement that is quite indistinguishable from the 'real thing.' And it certainly doesn't explain the numerous *after-images of movement*. For example, after one observes a continuously plunging fall in the 'waterfall illusion,' or a downward moving band of alternating black-and-white stripes in the laboratory, stationary objects then appear to move in the opposite direction. A striking illusion of contracting or expanding can be obtained in the following fashion: observe a spiral line that is rotating slowly, so that it appears to be contracting in on itself; then suddenly shift your gaze to a friend's face; the face will seem to expand in space. In these cases we have perceived movements when there is obviously no equivalent movement of excitation patterns on the retina, and the normal parallelism between stimulus and experience breaks down. In attempting to understand these illusory phenomena, psychologists began to question the 'obvious' explanation of ordinary movement perception.

Stroboscopic movement underscores the fact that a succession of discrete stimulations can somehow be perceived as a smooth continuity. How is this possible? Earlier theorists, probably under the influence of Helmholtz, assumed that the continuity of experience was an 'unconscious inference.' It was Wertheimer (1912) who argued most strenuously against this kind of theorizing and, in doing so, gave birth to the Gestalt School of Psychology. In exploring the temporal conditions determining stroboscopic movements, he discovered what was called 'pure phi'—at an interval somewhat longer than that necessary for optimal stroboscopic movement; one sees only the two objects at their terminal positions, yet there is a clear impression of movement from one place to the other. This effect can be produced by holding a finger close enough to the eyes that double images are seen and then alternately opening and closing the two eyes—the finger definitely seems to leap from one place to another, but no image moves across the space. For Wertheimer this meant that movement is just as immediate and direct a datum of experience as color or brightness; it can be perceived under appropriate conditions in a pure form, analyzable no further—an experience of sheer, objectless movement.

Before delving further into the problem of explanation, let us gather some general facts. The most accurate experimental work has been contributed by Neuhaus (1930; see Neff's comprehensive review, 1936), although Korte's work is probably better known since certain of the stimulus conditions have been dubbed 'Korte's Laws.' The typical conditions for observation are that one visual object, usually a bright circle or line, appears briefly at one point in the field and is followed after a short interval by another object at another point in the field; movement (when it appears) is from the first object to the second. The *time interval* between stimulations is the fundamental variable. If the interval is too long (more than about 200 msec.), the two objects are seen in succession without apparent movement between them; at a somewhat shortened interval, 'pure phi' movement can be obtained; with a still shorter interval, dual movements appear, both objects usually moving partially along the path. At some optimal interval (Wertheimer reported 60 msec., but it is actually variable with numerous conditions), the clearest stroboscopic movement can be observed, the two objects becoming one that visibly moves through space. With intervals below the optimum, independent flickering and oscillating of the two objects is seen; and with an interval of about 30 msec., both objects are seen simultaneously. Variations in *exposure time, distance,* and *intensity* are complexly related to time interval in affecting the phenomenon. In general, the greater the distance between objects, the more difficult it is to obtain movement. With exposure time constant, increased distance requires increased temporal interval for optimal movement. Korte and Neuhaus obtained conflicting results when intensity was varied; the exact relationships remain to be worked out.

Numerous other factors may affect stroboscopic movement, some of which are of considerable theoretical interest. When lights of different color are used, the 'single' moving object usually appears to change hue in course. Familiar objects show greater tolerance ranges for other stimulus variables, i.e. facilitate the impression of movement. The phenomenon is apparently susceptible to both training and attitude. Zeitz and Werner (1927; cf. Neff, p. 28) found that when slower-than-optimum rates of presenting the visual objects were combined with a faster rate of auditory or kinesthetic stimulation, the visual apparent movement could be made more nearly optimal. When an obstructing visual stimulus is located between the two alternating lights, the path of the apparent movement may curve around it rather than follow the shortest distance (Benussi, 1916, as reported by Boring, 1942, p. 597). It is reported (DeSilva, 1929, 1935) that continuous optimal movement cannot be obtained with angular separations greater than 4.5°—this distance, interestingly enough, is just about that over which one contour can exert inhibitory influence on another (see p. 230).

Taking a cue from the last-mentioned fact, let us look first at the explanatory possibilities within comparatively well-known projection mechanisms. Whether real or apparent, perceived movement is a change in the localization of contours. Contours, as we have already seen, arise from differential rates of fire in area 17, the 'ridge' of the distribution of impulse frequencies determining apparent localization. Now in the work of Fry and Bartley (1935) it has been shown that the presence of one contour may inhibit the formation of another within 4° *distance,* and in the work of Werner (1935) we have seen that at a certain critical *interval* a subsequent contour may prevent the formation in experience of an earlier one. Werner found this critical interval to be approximately that at which apparent movement is optimal. In the previous section on the figural after-effect, the Marshall and Talbot type of 'statistical analysis' was applied fruitfully to an understanding of how the apparent localization of one contour can be shifted following prolonged inspection of another. Will the same type of analysis aid our understanding of how real and apparent movement are perceived?

First, with respect to real movement, it is clear that as a sufficiently sharp intensity gradient is moved across the retina, the peak of the impulse distribution in area 17 must shift and, with it, apparent localization. What about *stroboscopic* movement? We already know that smooth, continuous apparent movement can only be obtained from discrete, disparate stimulations when they fall within the same region over which lateral contour effects are obtainable. This suggests the hypothesis that apparent movement arises when two contours interact in such a manner that their excitation peaks are mutually shifted. Since stimulus *a* precedes stimulus *b* by a brief interval, it follows that the distribution representing *a* will be in the process of decay (decreasing rate of discharge) while that representing *b* is in the process of development (increasing rate of discharge). The necessary condition for smooth, continuous apparent movement—optimal movement— would be that in which the summated distributions produce a single 'peak' that *continuously* shifts from *a* to *b.* Time interval, duration of stimuli, distance, and intensity would be expected to interact so as to modify the particular combinations under which this progressive shift of the contour could be experienced. Figure 95 illustrates how such a continuous shift could be produced in the interaction of two contour processes, one fading and the other augmenting. The arrow indicates the shifting position of the single perceived contour.

Partial or dual apparent movement also seems interpretable in this fashion. In this case with a greater time interval between the two contour processes, the onset of *b* would first partially shift the peak of the decaying *a* distribution, producing a partial movement toward the direction of *b;* but as soon as the *b* distribution surpassed *a* in amplitude of excitation rate, the apparent contour would jump suddenly to a locus near *b*—*suddenly* because of the lateral inhibition exerted by the dominant contour on other like processes in its vicinity, and *near b,* rather than at *b,* because of summation with the *a* distribution. The experience would be that of an interrupted movement between the two loci. The role of lateral inhibitory mechanisms is to insure that only one contour is seen at a time, at the locus of most intense activity within this 4° region. When the interval is shorter than that for optimal apparent movement, approaching that in which both contours are perceived simultaneously, chance variations in impulse frequencies could both alternate the direction of relative inhibition and slightly modify the location of distribution maxima, thereby producing the independent flickering and oscillating reported for such brief intervals.

This discussion in terms of contour processes is not considered an entirely satisfactory analysis of the phenomenon of perceived movement. For one

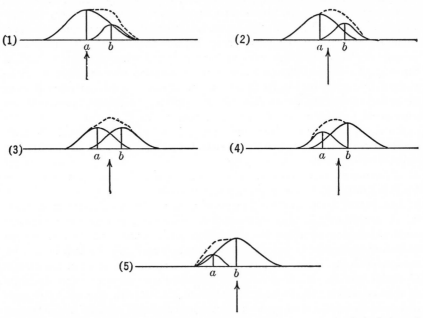

FIGURE 95. Interpretation of optimum apparent movement by a 'statistical theory' of projection mechanisms. The decay of the excitation distribution associated with one contour (*a*) is accompanied by augmentation of that associated with the second contour (*b*), the maximum of the summated distributions (broken line) moving smoothly from location *a* to location *b*.

thing, this analysis is only a sketchy outline of possibilities which, though rather exciting, will remain only possibilities until detailed analysis is made by investigators more familiar with neurological mechanisms. Secondly, as was true in the case of contour and contrast phenomena themselves, projection mechanisms provide only part of the answer here. Many characteristics of perceived movement require 'perceptual' processes working over greater angular distances than is presumably possible in area 17. Most significant is the experience of 'pure phi.' At intervals long enough that not even partial object movement occurs (i.e. no shift in contour localization), there is nevertheless a distinct *perception* of pure movement between the two objects. And this variety of perceived motion is by no means limited to 4° retinal distance. There are other facts not readily met by a peripheral theory: Brown and Voth (1937) were able to obtain a circular path of apparent movement well *within* the loci of the disparate stimulations; known mechanisms in the projection system do not explain why familiar objects facilitate apparent movement or how it can be influenced by auditory or kinesthetic impulses or how the path of movement can bend around visual obstructions in the field.

It is really to the phenomenon of 'pure phi' that the gestalt type of explanation was most applicable. Hewing closely to the line of isomorphism, Wertheimer's original interpretation (1912) was that since there is a psychological experience of movement between places a and b, there must be a dynamic process somewhere in the material visual brain which connects these places. In other words, continuity in experience must mean continuity in the physiological substratum. The Brown and Voth analysis in terms of vectors in a dynamic field, while more sophisticated as theory, does not help us locate the path through the visual brain which must (isomorphically) parallel the experienced movement. Certain other facts need to be kept in mind in this connection: for one thing, it is impossible to arrange conditions that will yield a slow 'pure phi' movement, as can be done in real perceived movement or stroboscopic movement. This swift impression of movement always occurs in an all-or-nothing leap. For another thing, the pathways in the neural substratum, if such they be, must be visually 'silent,' since no visual experience proceeds from a to b. This would imply that the impression of movement, if it represents a pathway in the nervous system at all, utilizes structures well beyond area 17, yet we know that all point-for-point ordering breaks down beyond area 17.

The gestalt view runs into experimental as well as logical difficulties. K. R. Smith (1948) has obtained clear evidence for apparent movement with alternating stimulation of the two nasal retinas, where it is pretty certain that no neural interaction corresponding to the horizontal path of movement exists. The two stimulus lights were carried in a harness placed on the subject's head, and they were so placed that two small luminous disks at the opposite ends of the horizontal meridian of his normal field were perceived in alternation. Since the neural paths from opposite nasal retinas project to contralateral occipital lobes, 'the hypothetical field would have involved the meningeal layers and the cerebro-spinal fluid which separates the two points of primary stimulation.' Gengerelli (1948) has shown that 'pure phi' is obtained more readily between stimulations in the same hemisphere than between stimulations in contralateral hemispheres. With four stimulus lights, $A, B, C, D,$ arranged in a square and with AD alternating with BC—the same type of setup described earlier in connection with the Brown-Voth work—apparent movement either in the vertical plane (see-sawing) or in the horizontal plane (tilting) should be equally probable. When fixation was on a central dot, however, movement in the vertical plane was reported much more frequently. As a control condition, fixation was held on a dot either to the left or the right of the entire square, so that all four stimulations would be projected to the same hemisphere—here there was no significant difference in frequency of vertical versus horizontal apparent movement. This study demonstrates a dependence of apparent movement upon anatomical arrangements, and it therefore also argues against a pure field interpretation.

We still know nothing whatsoever about the neural mechanisms involved in the 'pure phi' experience. From the modicum of evidence at hand, it seems unlikely that this impression of movement depends either upon neural pathways between points or, as Köhler would have us believe, upon electrical forces flowing through a quasihomogeneous medium. A point of view stressed long ago by a German investigator, Linke (1907; see Neff's review), is apropos at this juncture: generalizing from his own experimental work, Linke stated that such movement will only be perceived *when the subject identifies the two phases seen as referring to the same object.* Disparate stimulations of the visual system are continually occurring, yet they are not interpreted as movement. It is only when the disparate stimulations are highly similar in their various attributes (size, brightness, shape, hue, etc.)—when they actually duplicate the visual conditions of one and the same objects shifting in space—that the impression of movement is gained. And this seems to bring us back once more to Helmholtz: when the 'same' object is perceived near-simultaneously at two places, a long history of perceptual learning gives rise to the 'unconscious inference' of movement. And perhaps, like the concept of triangularity, this fleeting impression of objectless movement depends upon a localized excitation somewhere in area 18, *à la* Hebb's analysis, rather than upon a path through a neural field, abhorrent as this notion may be to those who take isomorphism for granted.

SPACE PERCEPTION: I. DEPTH AND SOLIDITY

'The subject of distance perception has been the battle-ground of theorists and the despair of experimentalists for many a long year.' It is thus that one modern investigator (Vernon, 1937-8) introduces the problem. Of course the theorists and the experimenters have usually been the same individuals. A list of discussants on space perception reads like an honor roll of science: Euclid, in 300 B.C., noted the fact that the two eyes present different images. Galen and Leonardo da Vinci also observed this and drew certain implications. Ptolemy, in A.D. 150, began the controversy over the real and apparent size of the moon, a controversy which has been continued down the centuries by such men as Kepler, Descartes, Lambert, and Helmholtz—and which is brought up in modern times by Boring (1943). Philosophers like Berkeley and Kant have made paradoxical assertions about space perception which have needled complacency as to explanation, and for psychologists 'experimental investigations of space perception . . . have served as touchstones for general theories, expressing fundamental convictions about the nature of our perceptive processes' (Koffka, 1930).

Paradox of Three-dimensional Perception

The fact that we can perceive objects in three dimensions at all is puzzling. Since the distribution of radiant energies on the retina is two-dimensional, how can we perceive depth and distance? It is true, of course, that as an object is moved further away, the angle it subtends on the retina must become objectively smaller. It is also true that since our eyes are separated in space, the two-dimensional images of the 'same' object will be slightly different. But why should these two-dimensional effects be *perceived* as distinctive attributes of a third dimension? Here, again, Berkeley talked about 'acts of judgment' and Helmholtz about 'unconscious inferences,' but perceptions of depth and distance in the visual field are just as immediate and compelling as color attributes. Since there must be *some* sensory differential, our problem becomes this: What additional cues or what dynamic properties of two-dimensional images give rise to three-dimensional experiences?

Let us look for a moment at the sensory basis of certain spatial inferences (cf. Carr, 1935). We are concerned with three sets of cues: (a) 'figural' visual cues, the objects attended and fixated; (b) 'background' visual cues, the remainder of the field; and (c) 'movement' cues, sensations arising from our own eye, head, and body movements. What inference is made when the shifting of both figural and background visual cues is accompanied by sensations of movement from one's own eye muscles? 'I am moving my eyes in relation to a stationary environment.' Suppose the figural pattern is stationary with respect to the retina while the background pattern moves, and that this visual situation is also accompanied by sensations of eye movement—inference? 'I am pursuing a moving target with my eyes.' Suppose the figural pattern changes location on the retina while the background is stationary, there being *no* sensations of eye movement—inference? 'It (the object of attention) is moving, but I am not following it.' Now both figural and background sets of visual cues shift across the retina, but there are no sensations of eye or body movements—what inference now? Unless I have additional reasons to know that my body as a whole is moving (e.g. knowledge that I am in a moving train), then movement is attributed to the environment.

All of the situations cited above are 'normal' in that the inferences can be checked by other means and found valid. Certain common *illusions of orientation* arise when the same inferences are made from exactly the same combinations of retinal and motor cues, but we have additional evidence that the inferences are erroneous. The train on the next track seems to start moving backward, but this inference is corrected when we become aware of the sounds and pressures that accompany acceleration of our own train. Another illusion of this type was described at the beginning of this book: when the eyeball is *passively* moved by pressing with a finger in the eye socket, objects 'out there' seem to jump up and down. What is the combination of cues in this case? Shifting of both figural and background visual cues is *not* accompanied by innervation of the eye muscles, which is the 'normal' combination for inferring movement 'out there.' This is an illusion only because we have exterior reasons to believe the world about us is not jumping up and down. The after-effects of being spun about provide another instructive, if unpleasant, example of the way in which visual and motor cues interact. The subject's eyes can be seen to drift and whip back following such treatment (postrotation nystagmus), but he is unaware that his eyes are moving. This situation seems to reproduce all the necessary conditions for the inference 'I am moving my eyes in relation to a stationary environment,' yet here it is the *environment* that seems to whirl about— movement is inferred to be 'out there.' The only apparent difference is that in the former case eye movements are voluntary, whereas here they are involuntary. This may mean that it is the interaction between voluntary innervation of eye muscles and the retinal pattern that determines these orientational inferences (cf. Purdy, 1935 *a, b;* 1936).

Problem of Fixation

Despite its critical bearing on space perception, fixation has received very little attention. The momentary fixation point is the reference about which the entire visual framework is oriented. As we move through the environment, there are continual, largely unconscious leaps in fixation which serve as guides for our movements and for judgments of 'nearer,' 'farther,' 'above,' and 'below.' Although no one seems to have studied the matter systematically, it is likely that these progressive fixations have a tolerance distance at which they fall and a preference for the types of binocular configurations which excite them. A fundamental fallacy about fixation is this: 'I fixate (look at) something intentionally by an act of will.' This implies that the fine eye movements causing the binocular images of the same object to fall upon corresponding retinal points, and hence be seen as single, are both voluntary and guided by the conscious motivations of the observer. Although it is true that gross hunting movements of the eyes may be voluntarily conditioned, the precise alignments that guarantee single vision depend chiefly on involuntary mechanisms. In fact, one cannot, by 'an act of will,' direct synchronous fixation of the two eyes unless there are appropriate visual stimuli presented. This can be demonstrated very easily: hold one finger quite close to the eyes and another at arm's distance; either finger may be easily fixated (seen singly) by simple shifts in degree of convergence; but now try to maintain stable fixation upon some point in space *between* these two fingers—it is impossible.

What are the involuntary visuomotor controls that govern binocular fixation? Some unpublished research by the writer will perhaps cast some light on the problem. Figure 96 describes the simple apparatus used and some of the tests made. The subject looks down a long dark box through a pair of opposed-angle polaroid lenses at a pair of stimulus objects cut out of black paper and lighted from behind. Another pair of polaroid lenses is set before the two stimulus-objects, angled in such a way that the subject can see only O_R with his left eye and only O_L with his right eye (i.e. crossed images). When the two stimulus objects are identical, the subject sees a single object floating before him in space at a locus determined by the crossing of the lines of regard. By means of flexible black cloth backing and sliding holders for the stimulus cards, the angle of convergence of the eyes can be varied through any degree and at any rate desired. A rough measure of the fusional properties of the stimuli is obtained by determining the rate of change in convergence which can be maintained without diplopia. Simple 'good' figures of identical contour, such as circles (#1 below), show the highest resistance to fusional breakdown. Complex, irregular, or meaningless shapes, even if identical in contour, seem harder to maintain in fusion (#2). Size differences in the images presented to the two eyes (#3) are tolerated within limited degrees, i.e. fusion is maintained and a single object seen, but diplopia occurs more and more readily as the size difference (contour disparity) increases. When the size difference is such that two circles are seen, the smaller usually floats about *within* the contour of the larger. Crossing lines (#4) do not fuse at all, drifting across one another unstably despite conscious efforts to hold them in the form of an X. Crossed circles (#5), on the other hand, give momentarily stable fusion, but the fusional conflict is shown by the rapid alternation between fusion of the upper and then of the lower circles. Interestingly enough, the displacement at which this involuntary alternation is most rapid (i.e. the retinal distance between the unfused circles) is within 4° retinal angle—the area over

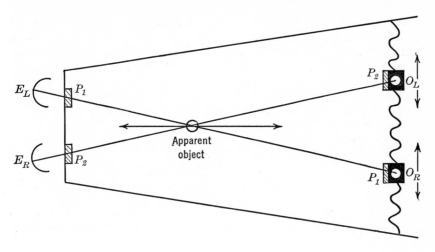

STIMULUS OBJECTS

FIGURE 96. Apparatus for demonstrating binocular fusional phenomena. Sample stimulus objects that have been observed, and typical results, shown below.

which the inhibition of one contour by another can be measured. For displacements less than this, simultaneous fusion occurs with a pronounced depth effect.

It is apparent that in binocular fusion we are dealing, neurologically, with summated activity arising from contour processes in the two retinas. The preceding evidence makes it appear that *near* correspondence in location of extensive contours gives rise to an imperative physiological 'urge' toward fusion. This urge is either absent or, more likely, balanced in the case of crossed oblique lines in the two monocular systems; in the case of identical circles (or other monocular images having extensive corresponding contours), however, this fusional urge is very definite. When the two separately seen, monocular images are brought within the critical area, there is a sudden 'flowing together' and subsequent cohesion into single vision which thenceforth vigorously resists diplopia. When field conditions are arranged so that two or more monocular contours *simultaneously* fall within the critical region (as in #5 above), conflict in fusional tendencies occurs. The Marshall and Talbot type of analysis is presumably applicable here. As suggested in Fig. 97, once the statistical distributions representing the two monocular contours overlap sufficiently to produce a single peak of excitation, no matter how slight the differential, lateral inhibitory processes come into play, which erase secondary contours and elicit reflexive, centering eye movements. Keep in mind that, anatomically, activity from corresponding retinal regions of the two eyes is projected to the same regions of area 17. The hypothesis suggested here is that the 'urge' toward fusion is nothing other than these reflexive, centering tendencies elicited when, in experience, the double monocular contours falling within the critical region of separation are erased and a single binocular contour is substituted.

An experiment by Burian (1939) illustrates a technique whereby the fusional power of any part of the retina may be measured. Two horizontal lines are thrown on a screen through polaroid material and viewed through polaroid lenses so that each is seen monocularly, e.g. —— ——, in the foveal region. Another lantern projects a small square of light to any part of the retina; this stimulus is seen by both eyes and can be made to fall on slightly disparate points vertically by a split-beam device. Fusional movements are measured by vertical displacements of the singly seen horizontal lines. Burian was able to show that strictly *peripheral* disparate images produce strong fusional movements, even though the observer may be unable to decide whether or not they are fused because of their indistinctness. Using a slight modification of this technique, he demonstrated that in certain conditions peripheral disparateness can override central fusion. A fused square was fixated between the horizontal (polarized) lines. When a large circle of slightly disparate printed material was presented peripherally, diplopia of the centrally fixated square was produced. Why doesn't this happen regularly in ordinary seeing, when the preponderance of peripheral stimuli must be somewhat disparate? We fall back on some interest or attention factor, unsatisfactory an explanation as this is. In this connection, may we observe that peripheral double images are seldom noticed in ordinary seeing unless they are directly looked for.

As we have already seen in contrast and movement phenomena, projective mechanisms like those producing contour resolution tell only part of the story. Attitudinal, interest, and meaningful factors also play a part in producing and maintaining fusional tendencies. We observe, for example, that familiar and meaningful stimulus materials are more resistant to fusional breakdown during convergent and divergent movements of the eyes. Direct substantiation is given in an earlier experiment by Sander (1928). When diplopia was produced by rotating one of a pair of stereoscopic slides, it was found that 'meaningless' stimuli, like fused horizontal lines, broke apart at smaller angles of rotation than 'meaningful' stimuli,

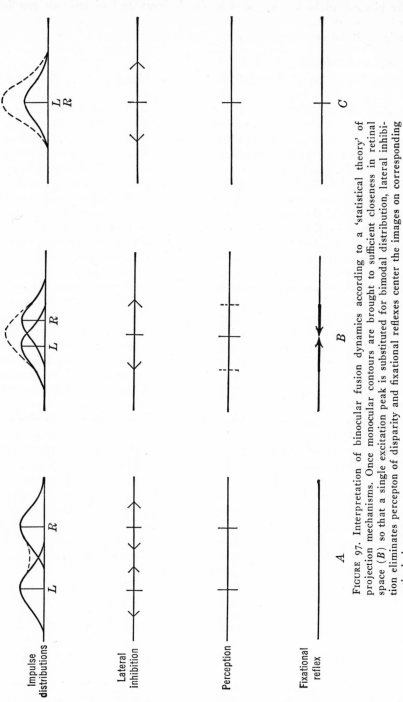

FIGURE 97. Interpretation of binocular fusion dynamics according to a 'statistical theory' of projection mechanisms. Once monocular contours are brought to sufficient closeness in retinal space (B) so that a single excitation peak is substituted for bimodal distribution, lateral inhibition eliminates percepton of disparity and fixational reflexes center the images on corresponding retinal elements.

like pictures of buildings and animals. A great deal of research remains to be done on the determinants of binocular fusion, particularly on how peripheral and central determinants interact.

Depth and Solidity

The impression of depthfulness in objects about us is an immediate, unintellectualized characteristic of perceiving. It is to Leonardo da Vinci that we owe the first clear statements concerning the nature of many of the cues that contribute to this impression. The great Renaissance painter was striving to duplicate as closely as possible what is actually presented to the eyes when looking at a scene rather than things as they are known intellectually. He noted that perception of depth in a picture can be emphasized by *shading*. He distinguished between cast and attached shadow. The shadow one object casts on another indicates relative distance between them; attached shadow, in the eye sockets and muscle furrows of a face, contributes to the depth impression. Leonardo also discussed *binocular parallax*. Because our eyes are in different positions in space, we are able to see partially around objects, but less so as their distance from us increases. *Head movement parallax* further increases the difference in views of the same object. When one is standing still in a thick woods, it is impossible to distinguish in the maze of foliage and branches what belongs to one tree and what to others. As soon as we begin to move our heads about, especially from side to side, things become disentangled.

Now students of depth perception had known for a long time that the two eyes receive slightly different images of the same solid object (binocular parallax). They had also known about the *horopter:* with a given fixation, only those points in space falling upon a limited surface (the horopter) affect corresponding retinal points and hence should give rise to single vision; all other points affect disparate elements and hence should give rise to double images. It was perfectly obvious, therefore, that when one point on the surface of a solid object (say, a round marble) is binocularly fixated, other portions of the object must fall upon disparate points. Yet not until Wheatstone, in 1838, invented the stereoscope and proved that fused, plane line drawings can give rise to definite impressions of depthfulness was it realized that disparity between monocular images is itself a major depth cue. A standard illustration is the truncated cone shown as Fig. 98. Each plane figure is drawn as it appears to each eye. This requires that there be disparities in the horizontal dimension—our eyes are separated horizontally, not vertically. When these two monocular images are fused with the aid of a stereoscope, a solid cone, smaller end upward, is perceived. When fused by simply crossing the eyes, the reverse depth effect is achieved—one seems to be looking *into* a cone whose narrow end is farther away. Wheatstone's mirror device has gone through many modifications in the hands of subsequent investigators; perhaps the best for research purposes is that designed by Carr and his associates (see Fig. 102 where it is described in connection with its experimental uses).

Wheatstone's demonstrations proved that binocular disparity is a sufficient condition for perceiving depth—not a necessary condition, of course, since some depth in objects is appreciable monocularly as well. But *why* should slight spatial disparities in the images derived from the two retinas give rise to the unique perceptual quality of solidity? One searches in vain through the literature for a positive answer to this question. There have been numerous negative answers to the effect that geometrical disparity does not in itself explain the phenomenon. The traditional view merely states that single, nondepthful vision results from stimulation of corresponding points on the two retinas, the impression of depth from slight disparity,

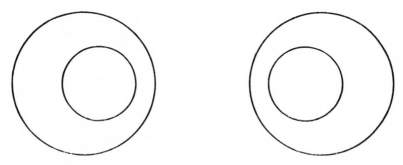

FIGURE 98. Plane figures which, when fused binocularly (either by use of stereoscope or by crossing eyes), yield depthful experience.

and double images or diplopia from still greater noncorrespondence of stimulation. This is an unsubtle description of the geometrics of the situation.

Does nondepthful experience necessarily result when corresponding points are stimulated? Koffka's spirited discussion (1930, pp. 163-7) of the Necker cube and related plane figures is an apt denial of this position. All three line drawings shown in Fig. 99 are objectively two-dimensional, yet *B* (the Necker cube) and *C* (another 'solid' figure) are inevitably perceived as

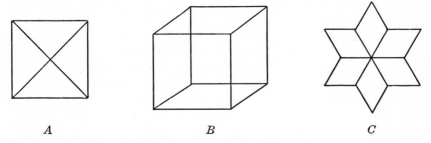

A   B   C

FIGURE 99. Certain two-dimensional forms yield depthful, three-dimensional experience (*B* and *C*) while others do not (*A*).

depthful—the depth is 'felt' to be either protruding from or extending below the surface of the paper. Is this simply due to 'past experience' with cubes and the like? Koffka points out, reasonably enough, that our past experiences have not been with transparent cubes constructed of lines of wire. But his own interpretation is no more satisfactory: 'This more radical hypothesis explains the tridimensional shape of our figure as the result of spontaneous organization of the visual field . . . when simple symmetry is achievable in two dimensions, we shall see a plane figure; if it requires three dimensions, then we shall see a solid . . . We have explained the appearance of the Necker cube not by experience but on the ground of principles of organization.' The argument is entirely circular. Figures that happen to be readily perceived as solid are said to exhibit three-dimensional symmetry, i.e. they are 'good' in three dimensions; figures that happen to be perceived as plane exhibit two-dimensional symmetry. But why? The break in circularity lies in the principles of organization, which should be specific in regard to the conditions under which one or the other kind of symmetry will be dominant. In any case, it is clear that depthful experiences can occur without retinal disparity.

The traditional statement is that depthfulness arises from 'slight' disparity? How much is 'slight'? Stimulations originating on the horopter affect corresponding retinal loci, i.e. presumably retinal loci equidistant from the two foveae and in the same direction. But how large are such loci? They are certainly not 'points,' as given in the geometric model. In fact, as one pursues this matter, he finds that the production of the empirical horopter—that surface in visual space from which stimulations affect 'corresponding points'—depends upon observer reports of singleness versus doubleness of vision. Now this is very interesting: unless one assumes that the observer's binocular *fixation* is rigidly constant, single vision might have resulted from stimulations that were not 'corresponding' at all in terms of retinal geometry. There is considerable evidence that conditions for single vision are much more pliable than the geometric model allows. Ames, Ogle, and Gliddon (1932) have demonstrated that, although mathematical formulas can be derived to indicate the location of the empirical horopter, they are so dependent upon known variables (such as size and shape of retinal images) and unknown variables that precise prediction of single vision is impossible. Glanville (1933) also failed completely to find any fixed region within which objects were seen as single and outside of which they were seen as double. Peckham (1936), using stereoscopic conditions, found that although the degree of horizontal disparity which could be tolerated without diplopia was fairly constant for individual subjects, it varied considerably from subject to subject. This study had the advantage that eye movements were recorded. Correlating these movements with actual shifts of one stimulus, he found that fusion was reported in some cases with retinal disparity as great as 10°. Doubtful as this figure may be—particularly since we know the foveal area to be a region, not a point—it nevertheless adds to the disruption of any simple geometric view.

One more 'negative answer': Koffka (1930, 1935) points out that the entire notion of disparate stimulation is geometrical rather than psychological. Under normal conditions of seeing, geometrically corresponding points are *always* being stimulated, though not necessarily by the *same* kind of stimulation. In other words, the job of the theorist here is not to explain why stimulation of noncorresponding points gives rise to the perception of depth but rather how *like* processes or kinds of stimulation at slightly disparate loci become related in the depth experience. This is an important point and deserves illustration for the sake of clarity: two pairs of black lines, so spaced that when one pair is fused stereoscopically the other pair must affect disparate points, are viewed—the lines in Fig. 100 may be fused by crossing the eyes. With respect to the disparate lines, black stimulation on one retina corresponds to white stimulation on the other. Why are the similar figural stimulations, the two black lines, perceived as such and related? As Koffka puts it (1930, pp. 179) : 'We should be obliged to explain physiologically why equal processes correspond to each other instead of mere locations.' Just what are these 'like' or 'equal' processes about which Koffka is talking? They are *not,* as his argument seems to imply, stimulations of similar quality (such as black lines with black lines, white patches with white patches) ; rather, *the like processes which become related over disparate loci are contour processes.* Koffka himself (1935, p. 271) cites a

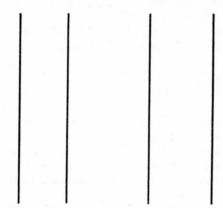

FIGURE 100. Slight horizontal disparities between adjacent contours yield depthful experience. The pairs of lines in this figure are so drawn that when fused binocularly (by crossing the eyes) two lines are seen at different distances from the observer.

critical demonstration by Helmholtz: if the figure presented to one eye in the stereoscope is a black outline on a white ground and the figure presented to the other eye is a slightly disparate but identical *white* outline on a black ground, a perfectly satisfactory depth impression is gained. In other words, it is the 'on-off' neural activity set up about two closely neighboring contours that is in some manner related or fused.

This suggests the beginnings of a positive answer to our question. As we have already argued in connection with the fusional tendencies that underlie binocular fixation, when the displacement of two monocular contours is reduced to well within 4°, the overlapping excitation distributions in area 17 summate to a single peak, lateral inhibitory processes erase awareness of two contours, substituting one, and reflexive 'centering' eye movements complete the fixational response. But what happens when two or more sets of fusable contours at different disparities exist in the field? This is the stereoscopic situation described in its essence in Fig. 100. It is also the situation in ordinary seeing when one fixates binocularly some 'near' point on a solid object, such as a marble—the back-lying contours of the solid object must excite somewhat disparate regions of the two retinas. In such cases accurate fixation of one set of related contours necessarily sets up the neural conditions for strong fusional attraction of the other contours;

therefore we have continuous fluctuation in the peaks of both pairs of summated excitation distributions. Just as a *progressive* shift in excitation peak
from one locus to another may be perceived as optimum apparent movement (see Fig. 95), so it is suggested here that a rapidly and randomly
oscillating excitation peak may be the neural basis for perceiving solidity.
In a real sense, perhaps, these rapid oscillations in apparent localization of a
contour serve to 'fill in,' and hence make solid and depthful, the lateral
region within which they occur.

Heinz Werner (1937) arrived at a similar conclusion, but from a gestalt
configurational rather than a neurological point of view. Earlier Koffka
(1930, p. 179) had postulated that 'these forces must be forces of attraction between the monocular processes . . . lines close together in the visual
field attract each other; if each is given to one eye, this attraction will
result in an eye movement of fusion which unites the lines. . .' Werner
provided experimental verification of this hunch: the observer fixates on one
thread and sees a further thread as uncrossed double images. Beyond the
second thread is an indicator which may be varied in angular direction.
When the observer lines up one of the double images with this indicator,
its visual direction is shown. Werner found that with binocular vision the
image of each eye was displaced toward that of the other, thus differing
from its visual direction in monocular vision. There is, therefore, a measurable attraction between like processes (contours) in the two eyes, an
'induced displacement,' as Werner calls it. He also reported that the
strength of this attraction increased with nearness of the two half-images
to one another.

This theory of Werner's runs into a very serious difficulty, one which
highlights a discrepancy between anatomical and functional data. When
one thread is fixated binocularly and another, either nearer or further in
space, is seen as double, *the monocular half-images necessarily fall upon
nonhomonymous hemiretinas*. If the second thread is further in space than
the fixation point, the (uncrossed) monocular images fall on the *nasal*
halves of both retinas; if the second thread is nearer in space, the (crossed)
monocular images fall on the *temporal* halves of both retinas. Now projection in the primate visual system involves decussation at the optic chiasma.
Fibers from the temporal half of each retina remain on the same side and
terminate in the ipsilateral hemisphere, whereas fibers from the nasal half
cross at the chiasma and terminate in the contralateral hemisphere. This
system guarantees that corresponding retinal points shall project to identical
cortical points, thus providing for singleness of vision. In the present instance this means that the cortical representations of the two monocular
half-images must be located in opposite cerebral hemispheres.

How, then, can the attracting, cohesive forces that Werner postulates
work to induce 'displacement' of the two half-images toward one another
in subjective space? Assuming that Werner's gestalt theory is also based
upon the notion of isomorphism, spatial phenomena in the subjective field
must be paralleled by equivalent spatial processes in the material, brain
field. But there are no direct anatomical connections between contralateral
areas 17, and although there are such connections between contralateral

areas 18, via the *corpus callosum,* the firing of cells in 17 into area 18 is known to be *diffuse,* and the point-for-point projection necessary for iso-morphism breaks down. The Marshall and Talbot type of theory is no better off: for exactly the same reasons as those cited above, there seems to be no way in which the distributions of excitation representing the two monocular images could be fused when they are projected to different hemi-spheres. Notice that this limitation on both theories applies only when we are dealing with interactions across the vertical meridian of the visual field.

Since this is a significant problem, let us look more closely at the anatomy of the situation. Fibers from the two halves of each retina, including the two halves of the fovea, have been shown to go to opposite hemispheres. That the dividing line follows the vertical meridian is indicated experi-mentally in the monkey by cutting one optic tract beyond the chiasma and studying subsequent retrograde degeneration of the ganglion cells—degen-eration is quite sharply limited to the homonymous halves of both retinas, temporal side of one and nasal of the other (cf. Polyak, 1941, p. 438). Furthermore, when action potentials are recorded at the striate cortex (area 17) and restricted regions of the retina are stimulated with light (Talbot and Marshall, 1941), and a 'cortical map' is obtained thereby, the hemi-foveae and borders of the vertical meridian are shown to project to distinct but homologous regions of the two hemispheres, in fact, to widely separated regions. An interesting point here is that representation of the vertical meridian, including the fovea, is arranged about the *edge* of area 17 so that it is in intimate association with area 18.

What is the paradox here? The existence of the optic chiasma and the partial decussation that takes place there in animals with overlapping binocu-lar fields is mute testimony to the elaborate provisions that have been made to insure single vision over most of the field. Yet the regions that provide the sharpest single vision functionally—the vertical meridian and particu-larly the foveal centers—deliver their excitations to widely separated cor-tical loci. And what about functional evidence? Despite the oscillations of physiological nystagmus, a fine vertical line, centrally fixated, is not seen as double; the phi phenomenon can occur across the vertical meridian (cf. Gengerelli, 1948, and Smith, 1948); and all other transverse processes (contour formation, brightness and color summation and contrast, *and* depth effects) seem to proceed across the vertical meridian as well as else-where in the field. In other words, the great anatomical gulf between the two halves of the visual field, established at the vertical meridian, does not appear in visual functions.

What do neurophysiologists say about this? Marshall and Talbot admit that 'more experiments are needed to reveal visual relationships affected by this division.' Polyak merely states the paradox: 'Dynamically, the entire primate visual system, essentially cyclopic in its character, is organized about the common binocular fixation-point. The same is true also of the "cerebral eye," except that the single fixation-point is here split in two, one in each pole of the two occipital lobes, although even so, functionally, the two cerebral fixation points may be regarded as a single point, always work-ing as a unit' (p. 442). *But how can these two anatomically separated fixa-*

tion points 'work as a unit' when there are no provisions for such teamwork?
There is considerable evidence (Curtis, 1940; Bonin, Garol, and McCulloch, 1942; LeGros Clark, 1942) that no neural pathways connect contralateral areas 17 via the *corpus callosum,* and the diffuseness of transmission
from 17 to 18 would seem to limit binocular integrations via this medium.
No way of resolving the problem is evident at this time; it is worthy of
concentrated study by both neurologists and psychologists.

Chapter 7

CENTRAL DYNAMICS IN PERCEPTION

It may be that in some more sophisticated age we shall bring our descriptive language about perception more into line with underlying mechanisms than with superficial similarities. Although it is true that *phenotypically* 'optimum' apparent movement and 'pure phi' apparent movement belong together, as do color contrasts at the borders of patches with the 'ironing out' effect within such patches, nevertheless *genotypically* 'optimum' movement and border contrast are both projection phenomena, whereas pure phi and the ironing out process within contours seem to be central phenomena. Similarly, the depth or solidity aspect of space perception seems to depend mainly on projection mechanisms (and was therefore included in the preceding chapter), whereas distance perception seems to require mechanisms well beyond the projection system (and hence is taken up in the present chapter).

SPACE PERCEPTION: II. RELATIVE AND ABSOLUTE DISTANCE

Relative Distance

Many of the cues for judging the relative distance of objects in the field are matters of knowledge about the world—secondary cues, as experimentalists are inclined to disdainfully call them. But this does not deny their effectiveness. Consider *masking,* for example: when the foliage of a tree blots out a large portion of a house, there is little doubt that the tree is nearer than the house. Or consider *aerial perspective:* when, owing to imperfect transmission of light through the air medium (and the granular nature of the retina), a range of mountains becomes more bluish in tinge and less detailed in articulation, there is little doubt that we are receding from it. A more immediate cue for relative distance has been said to be *double images.* When one fixates the nearer of two objects (e.g. the threads in Werner's experiment described in the preceding chapter), the further must appear as *uncrossed* double images; when the further object is fixated, the nearer one must now appear as *crossed* double images. Geometrically valid it may be, but this writer always has to alternately shut one eye and then the other while observing in order to recall on which side of the horopter crossed and uncrossed images lie.

A very important factor in judging relative distance is *size,* but it is a complicated one. We may distinguish (1) *physiological size,* which is the variation in visual angle on the retina subtended by an object as it is moved nearer and farther; (2) *apparent size,* which is the absolute magnitude attributed to an object when cues for its distance are available; (3) *visual texture,* which is the cyclic variation in stimulation when one looks at any surface having microstructure or pattern—i.e. a complex of size cues; and (4) *visual density,* which is the graduated variation in texture with distance of a surface from the observer. The values of all size cues in perceiving relative distance come down to interactions between visual angle and other cues. Visual angle itself is always an ambiguous indicator of distance. Let us take the simplest case: standing in the dark we see a globule of light which grows larger and then smaller as we watch it. Is this 'object' coming nearer and farther in space or is it merely expanding and contracting in real size? Now, of course, if we *know* that this is a concrete, immutable object—an illuminated jack-o'-lantern, for example—then we can confidently interpret the change in visual angle as a change in distance.

The interdependence of size and distance judgments is revealed in many experiments, such as those by Woodburne (1934), Martin and Pickford (1938), and Holway and Boring (1941). In the latter study two circular light areas were viewed along an extended, dark hallway. One, the standard stimulus, was kept at a constant *retinal* size of 1° visual angle but its distance from the observer was varied (i.e. it was made larger in actual size as distance increased). The comparison light area remained at a constant distance but was varied in size by the observer to match apparent sizes of the former. With various distance cues available, size of the standard stimulus seemed to increase as distance increased, i.e. an object which is known to be farther away, yet cuts the same retinal angle, must be something that is actually growing larger. With distance cues largely eliminated, on the other hand, apparent size was nearly independent of distance, i.e. the magnitude of the adjustable circle was always set at about 1° regardless of where the standard stimulus was located.

Similarly, visual texture can serve as a cue for distance when the pattern of the surface being viewed is known—the greater the density of size elements, the greater the distance from the eye. Even without knowledge of the actual size of the elements making up a patterned surface, variations in density of visual texture give rise to perceptions of *slant* (i.e. relative distance). While standing on a broad rug or lawn, for example, the angle of tilt or slant to the surface is gleaned from the progressive change in density of visual texture, i.e. the visual angles subtended by the repetitious elements in the surface become smaller with increasing distance. Observe the unconscious assumption here that the elements making up the surface are replications of identical real size. Geometrical perspective is a specific instance of varying texture-density: the successive ties in a railroad bed become progressively shorter (visually) as the track extends toward the horizon. Texture factors have been studied most extensively by J. J. Gibson (1950). He finds that when patterned surfaces are photographed from various angles and these pictures are later viewed by subjects through a reduction-screen setup, definite impressions of slant are obtained, the denser portions of the pattern appearing farther away.

Unquestionably the most effective demonstrations of interaction among various cues, such as brightness, size, and binocular parallax, in determining distance perceptions are those developed by Adelbert Ames, Jr. at the Dartmouth Eye Institute during the past decade. Many of these demonstrations have been described in our national magazines and the physical setups for displaying them, including distorted rooms, are now available in a number of universities. All that can be done here is to describe and discuss some of the more relevant demonstrations and suggest that the reader take advantage of one of the demonstrations in his area.

Let us look first at some examples of how size, brightness, and distance interrelate. (*Demonstration* 5, p. 5, *Preliminary Manual*, 1949.) Two star-points of light are at the same distance but of different brightnesses; viewed with the head stationary, the brighter point seems nearer. Why is it that we do not perceive points of differing brightness at the *same* distance (the actual case)? The answer, according to Ames, is as follows: *given sufficient cues of similarity between two objects, we leap to the inference of complete identity;* if the two star-points *were* identical objectively, one would look brighter than the other only when nearer in space. (*Demonstration* 18, p. 14.) Two balloons at an equal, fixed distance from the observer may be made to vary independently in either size or brightness. As one balloon is made brighter (size constant), it seems to move nearer; as one balloon is made larger (brightness constant), it seems to move nearer. *Apparently we give more weight in perceptual judgments to dynamic, changing factors than to static ones.* If one balloon is simultaneously made both larger and brighter, the amount to which it comes nearer is much greater than before. It appears, therefore, that static brightness or static size in these cases did not mean that these cues were eliminated—they had negative value. If size and brightness indicators are put in conflict, distance changes are barely perceptible, but they are present and follow size rather than brightness. Why should size be more effective than brightness in determining distance judgments? According to Ames, in ordinary experience the correlation between visual angle and distance is more constant than that between brightness and distance (owing to wide and random fluctuations in illumination). There is, therefore, greater probability for the adapting organism that reaction to size will be correct than reaction to brightness.

We have already mentioned the importance of masking, or overlay, in perceptions of relative distance. Another of Ames's demonstrations shows how this factor can override size cues, even for well-known objects. The plain cards in the left-hand row of Fig. 101*A* are of such absolute sizes that the visual angles they subtend for the observer are equal. Nevertheless, the way in which one overlays the other yields a definite impression of varying distance. Because of faked masking (segments are cut out of cards that are actually nearer the observer), the middle row looks just like the first row, even though it is now the *nearest* card (objectively) which looks the farthest away. In the right-hand row, again through faked masking, the farthest playing card (6 of clubs) is made to appear nearest, whereas the nearest playing card (king of clubs) is made to appear farthest. And notice that apparent size is adjusted accordingly, despite the fact that these are objects of known size. In other words, the observer 'gives up' his assumption of identity of kind with respect to the playing cards in order to

FIGURE 101. *A.* Illusion of size differences created by partial masking. *B.* How this illusion was created. *Life,* 1950, **28**, #3:61.

make his perception of the situation consistent with the dominant cues. *Such phenomena as these point to a remarkable integrating and balancing mechanism in perception.* We shall encounter more evidence for this in studying constancy. Figure 101*B* shows how the masking effects were produced in the Ames demonstration.

Absolute Distance

Spatial orientation also involves perceptions of absolute distance. The telephone is perceived as being 'there' in space—not merely so much nearer or farther than something else, but at such and such a definite distance from us. This does not mean that we perceive distance in terms of so many feet or inches when we look at objects in space. Judgments are in terms of what Ames (1949, p. 20) calls 'functional units'—how far one would have to reach to touch the object, how many strides would have to be taken, and so on. This implies that the spatial significance of various visual cues has been *learned* in the course of a lifetime of behaving in relation to recognized objects—reaching for the bottle and Mother's face, running over to pick up the kitten, and graduating the force with which a stone is thrown to hit a distant object.

Many of the cues for absolute 'thereness' are obviously dependent upon knowledge about objects. This applies particularly to *size*. If we recognize a standard object (such as a playing card), the visual angle it subtends at the moment is an accurate cue in regard to its distance from us. Further demonstrations from the Dartmouth Eye Institute are relevant here. (*Demonstrations* 29-36, pp. 20-22.) Two artificially illuminated fields, one binocular and one uniocular, are set up in such a way that one can be shifted immediately to the other by a simple change in lighting. The binocular field is liberally supplied with indicators of distance, disparity, overlay, shadows, etc., and, for convenience in designating distance, it also contains a series of uprights, evenly spaced and numbered 1 to 5. In the uniocular field only the 'thing' which is to be assigned a specific distance is visible. The procedure is as follows: an object is put in the uniocular field opposite the #3 upright, and it is seen floating in complete blackness; after a short time in which the subject gains his impression of absolute distance, the binocular field is suddenly illuminated and the apparent distance is specifiable by the point at which the object now appears in the metricized binocular field. Two significant results are obtained: (1) All objects, whether abstract (star-points, lines) or concrete (playing cards, cigarette packages), seem to have a definite 'thereness' attribute, even though the apparent distance in the uniocular field may be quite inaccurate with respect to that given by the binocular field. (2) Concrete objects, such as cigarette packages, are accurately localized by size alone, whereas abstract objects, such as geometrical designs, are not. It appears to be experience with known objects of culturally standardized sizes that gives size its value as an absolute distance cue. An oak leaf, which is a concrete but relatively *unfamiliar* object for most people, was judged with confidence to be at a great variety of distances. On the other hand, a concrete but *familiar* (and culturally standardized) object, like a pack of cigarettes, was judged to be near #3, where it was actually placed, by all observers.

The following demonstrations show convincingly that *it is the assumed stability and constancy of known objects that is the basis for absolute distance impressions in the cases cited above.* (*Demonstrations* 41-50, pp. 27-32.) Although it is very difficult to vary the objective sizes of most things without manufacturing oversized or undersized replicas (which is probably the reason why size is such a high-priority cue), it is a simple matter to project *images* of objects on a screen and vary either their size or brightness. In this case, in the uniocular field, a screen is placed opposite upright #3, the middle distance in the binocular field. If the image of a playing card is made small, it is judged near #4 or #5; if it is made larger than 'normal,' it is judged opposite #2 or even #1. If an actual playing card is held at the distance judged in any particular case, the visual angle it subtends is found to be nearly identical with that being projected on the screen.

In other words, the observer is 'carrying about in his head' a constant value for the normal size of a playing card. Where did this 'normal' size come from? Presumably it was learned in the course of behavioral manipulations—but this remains to be demonstrated. The following experiment is suggested: With a screen at a constant but unknown distance from the observer, allow *him* to vary the projected size of various objects until they seem normal to him. If the behavioral hypothesis is valid, the visual angle subtended by the normal size should closely approximate that given at the distance each object is typically inspected, a few inches for needles and tacks, crooked-arm's length for a pack of cigarettes, twenty-odd feet for automobiles, and so on. This applies to objects of culturally standardized magnitude. Ames reports that 'normal' varies markedly for abstract or unfamiliar objects, like white rectangles and oak leaves. When the same operations are made with brightness variable (and size of the projected image constant), distance effects are less apparent and, interestingly enough, greater for nonstandardized objects. As Ames notes, size is more intimately tied up with the unique 'thatness' or 'thingness' of objects than is brightness.

From all the foregoing it is perfectly clear that although size and, to a lesser extent, brightness normally serve as indicators of absolute distance, these cues are dependent upon knowledge about the 'real' characteristics of things. Are there any cues comparatively independent of experience which arise more directly from the structure and function of the organism? The ocular mechanisms of accommodation and convergence fit the requirements ideally, at least for distances within 25 feet. As an object is moved nearer the eyes, contraction of the ciliary muscles (accommodation) and the internal recti (convergence) increases, and it is generally assumed that the degree of contraction is fairly constant for any given distance of fixation. Both muscle systems are associated with proprioceptive mechanisms; the sensory 'playback' can be felt when one rapidly shifts his fixation from far to near. Theorists have always favored such 'innate' factors, since they could be the bases on which the significance of size changes, brightness changes, and so on are learned.

As early as 1637 Descartes roughly specified the accommodation mechanism and had the following to say about convergence: '. . . we perceive distance by the relation which the two eyes bear to each other. . . When our eyes are converged upon a point, [we] know the distance of that point by the length of the interocular line and the magnitude of the angles formed at the points of intersection of the interocular line and the visual axes.' Bishop Berkeley, in 1709, pointed out the fallacy in this argument: 'I appeal to any one's experience, whether, upon sight of an object, he computes its distance by the bigness of the angle made by the meeting of the two optic axes?' He nevertheless emphasized the importance of convergence in distance perception. '. . . it is certain by experience, that when we look at a near object with both eyes, according as it approaches or recedes from us, we alter the disposition of our eyes by lessening or widening the interval between the pupils. This disposition or turn of the eyes is attended with a sensation, which seems to me to be that which in this case brings the idea of greater or lesser distance into mind' (p. 9). There is no doubt that accommodation and convergence *could* serve as important, primary cues for distance perception—the real question is whether or not they do. Both are motor responses and as such they do not occur *in vacuo* but as a result of visual stimulation. Since there cannot be any finer motor discrimination than the visual discrimination by which these movements are elicited, why, we ask, are not the visual cues sufficient? Why wait for the kinesthetic playback?

The experimental history of this problem is a series of tests, each believed by its author to be the crucial demonstration, but each in its turn providing the methodological flaws that fathered the next 'crucial' test. We begin with Wundt's 'hanging threads' experiment. The observer looked through a tube at the central portion of a black thread hanging in an otherwise bare, illuminated room; after seeing one position, the observer turned his head aside while the distance was changed, making a judgment of nearer or farther when looking into the tube again. Wundt (1862) concluded that both accommodation and convergence were effective as cues, the latter being the more effective since significantly smaller discrimination thresholds were obtained. Criticisms? (1) Convergence is not ruled out when an observer uses one eye—close one eye, holding the finger lightly against the ball, and follow a rapidly moving finger in and out from the nose; you will feel the closed eye moving as well. (2) To the extent that fixation was not perfect at the moment of looking back in the tube, visual displacement of the contour from the fovea, double images (binocular condition), and other visual factors could operate. After all, what are the *visual* stimuli that excite accommodative and convergent movements?

Hillebrand (1894) tried to rule out visual factors by using, in place of Wundt's thread, a smooth straight-edge which formed the edge of a rectangle whose other three sides were too near the observer to be accurately focused. He also eliminated the binocular condition entirely. He found that when changes in the distance of the test edge were gradual, judgment was very poor; with abrupt changes in distance, accuracy was fairly high. Dixon (1895), Arrer (1898), and finally Baird (1903) repeated Hillebrand's procedure in all essentials and obtained the same results. Criticisms? (1) In the abrupt condition, one straight-edge is swung out of view and replaced with another at a different distance. If the observer's eye does not remain stationary during the shift, the angular displacement will be a cue for distance. (2) The subject gets perfect accommodation on the first edge, another is substituted, and it is accommodated upon—again, the only cue for this motor adjustment is some visual texture, either of the cardboard surface or of slight imperfections in its edge. Which is the critical cue, the *visual* 'blurring' which guides accommodative movements or the *kinesthetic* tensions from the ciliary muscle? (3) In any case, it was generally agreed that a straight-edge of this sort was an extremely uncomfortable thing to perch upon visually.

Bourdon's 'bright spot' experiment (1902) was much more satisfactory from the observer's point of view. Lanterns with paper-covered diaphragm apertures of variable size were placed at varying distances from the observer along a black hallway, visual angle being held constant. Results were discouraging: using one eye, subjects couldn't even be sure which was nearer, a light at 20 meters or one at only 1 or 2 meters; even with both eyes, in a locality entirely unfamiliar a single bright spot 10 meters distant might be judged to be as far as 100 meters away. Criticisms? (1) Since results were negative, there is no guarantee that visual differentia were sufficient to guide accommodation. (2) The distances used were generally beyond the effective range of the motor mechanisms. Peter (1915) and Bappert (1923), also using the 'bright spot' technique, have corrected this deficiency in Bourdon's experiment, working within the 1-meter distance. Again results were negative—Bappert's subjects did significantly *poorer* than chance! (3) This indicates another difficulty, the 'abstraction fallacy': keeping extraneous cues constant does not eliminate their influence; rather, in this case, constant size and brightness is an indication of *no* change in distance.

This problem has also been attacked with stereoscopic techniques. In the 1930's Harvey Carr and his students designed the research mirror stereoscope described in Fig. 102. Essentially it made possible varying accommodation and convergence without varying size, brightness, and (it was thought) texture, double images or displacement. Using this apparatus, Swenson (1932) compared the effectiveness of accommodation and convergence—notice that the apparatus makes it possible to manipulate the two factors (distance of milk glass and angle of rotation) independently. When both factors were set for equal distances, 'all subjects showed a high degree of accuracy. . . These results prove that the associated factors of convergence and accommodation are highly effective in mediating judgments of distance within the range of 25 to 40 cm.' (p. 373). When the two factors were dissociated, the apparent localization was nearer the point determined by convergence than that for accommodation, but always between them. Swenson concludes that '. . . accommodation possesses only about ⅓ of the effectiveness of convergence for the distance limits we investigated' (p. 378).

Even accepting Swenson's conclusion that the total stimulus complex associated with convergence is more effective for distance perception than the total complex associated with accommodation, does this necessarily show that either of these discriminations is based upon kinesthetic cues? Swenson apparently forgets that both accommodation and convergence require visual guidance for their operation. Changes in the microtexture of the milk glass provide visual cues for the former and synchronous retinal displacements, either during rotation of the targets or in re-establishing fusion following such rotation, provide visual cues for the latter. A more recent investigator, Grant (1942), was certainly aware of this problem. After obtaining results similar to Swenson's, except that accommodation and convergence were found to have more nearly equal effectiveness (Grant's apparatus provided a better visual stimulus for accommodation), he remarks, with regard to double images (retinal displacements): 'Nevertheless their presence, since they cannot be eliminated, must apparently be accepted as an inevitable limitation of this type of study, rather than as a defect in the control of visual factors. If double images are literally inseparable from convergence

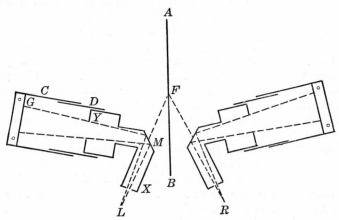

FIGURE 102. Cross section of an improved mirror stereoscope. Centers of rotation of the eyes are at L and R. Mirror M reflects image from milk glass G. By rotating the two tubes, the angle of convergence can be changed without changing the brightness or size of the image. The observer moves a metal rod along AB to indicate apparent distance of the image (which he sees as a single object directly in front of him); these estimations are made with fair accuracy. By telescoping the tubes, the distance of the milk glass surface can be varied from 25 to 40 cm. without changing either area or brightness of the image—area is set by the aperture Y and brightness decreases proportionately with the square of the area of G included. Carr, *An Introduction to Space Perception,* Longmans, Green and Co., New York, 1935, p. 248.

the matter of their relative influence on space impressions is hardly a vital issue' (p. 101).

It is true that one would have to search far for an issue more completely devoid of practical significance. But the *theoretical* significance is considerable. This problem of kinesthetic cues in distance perception is a specific instance of the controversy over the nature of meanings and perceptions in general. One group of theorists contends that kinesthetic playbacks from the musculature are important determinants of meanings, attitudes, and so on. If it could be demonstrated conclusively that the specific playback from the ocular muscles *does* contribute to the perception of distance, this would be evidence in favor of their view. But is it possible? Can one, for experimental purposes, dissociate the motor responses of convergence or accommodation from the visual stimulations that normally elicit them? Contrary to Grant's implied negative conclusion, it would seem that there are at least two ways in which this can be accomplished, one has been tried and the other, although equally feasible, has escaped attention.

The tried method derives from the fact that *the ocular muscles cannot simultaneously induce movements in opposed directions*. Early investigators, using spark-gap illumination, had shown that depth could be perceived in stereoscopic slides when the illumination time was well below that required for muscular response (Dove, 1841; Von Karpinska, 1910). This, however, is not crucial evidence against a motor theory, since there is nothing to inhibit appropriate contractions in the interval between illumination and report. Stevenson Smith (1946, 1949) arranged conditions so that *three* pairs of points could be simultaneously flashed. These three pairs of points were presented at different disparities so that, when maintained for a period, the observer would see three diagonal fused points, each at a different distance. In the experiment proper, a one-sixtieth-second flash was used and relative distances of the fused points (e.g. upper, nearest; middle, farthest; and lower, intermediate) were randomly varied. All subjects did much better than chance, some achieving perfect scores. As Smith says, 'Certainly no eye movements occur until after the stimulation has ended, and there is no reason to suppose that three separate degrees of convergence could be induced by a stimulus pattern that has ceased to operate before the first convergence has occurred' (p. 394). We conclude that the kinesthetic sensations resulting from ocular movements are not *necessary* for stereoscopic depth perception. Whether or not they would be sufficient, in the absence of concomitant visual cues, is not answerable from this study.

The method that remains to be tried arises from the fact that *the retinal and kinesthetic cues normally associated with distance perception can be put in conflict*. This can be understood most readily from inspection of Fig. 103, in which the necessary experimental conditions are described. First, it must be recalled that even though only one eye may be viewing the movement of a point in space, *both* eyes tend to follow the movement (this may be checked by closing one eye and touching it lightly while the other eye follows a moving finger). As far as the retinal displacement factor is concerned when one eye is used, however, a small shift in *direction* (P_1 to P_{2a}) is completely indistinguishable from a large shift *inward* (P_1 to P_{2b}), or convergence. This is true as long as one uses point sources of light in a completely dark room, i.e. as long as there are no other cues available. In the apparatus shown in Fig. 103, only the left eye sees the stimuli in the dark box; the right eye looks into a mirror, and the observer *thinks* he sees the points of light with both eyes. Actual movements of the nonstimulated eye can be observed directly or recorded by means of a camera set at C.

Three sets of measures are required in this experiment: (1) the objective changes in position of the point source (randomized from P_1 to P_{2a} or to P_{2b}); (2) the actual movements of the observer's right eye (his left eye will simply repeat an identical rotation); and (3) the subjective report of the observer about whether he perceives a light 'going in and out' *or* 'going from left to right.' Now if there is a significant correlation between (1) and (3), it indicates something wrong with the setup—i.e. the observer *is* able to identify correctly the direction of movement, which should be impossible if conditions are adequately controlled. If the movement of the right eye correlates with judgments of direction and distance (i.e. if convergent with the left eye, 'nearer,' and if conjugate with the left eye, 'to the right'), then it would appear that kinesthetic sensations are sufficient for spatial perceptions. If, on the other hand, actual eye movements bear no relation to what is perceived, it would appear that kinesthetic sensations are irrelevant in themselves.

What are the results? At the present time it must be reported that we do not know. A preliminary investigation by this writer failed because there actually was correlation between (1) and (3), between objective changes in the point source and observer judgments. Owing to lack of accommodation, the point source developed irradiation rings in the near position, and these served as a cue for 'nearer.' Judging from the findings of Smith cited above, the results will be negative because no correlation will appear between eye movements and distance perception. And this is perhaps the most

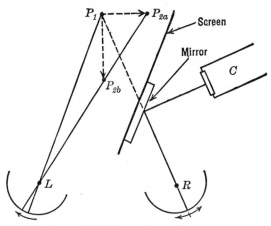

FIGURE 103. Apparatus for studying the role of motor cues in distance perception. See discussion in text.

reasonable expectation: since, in normal seeing, retinal cues must precede and guide eye movements, it seems unnecessary that distance perception should require an additional (and certainly no more discriminative) input from the proprioceptors in the eye muscles.

PERCEPTUAL CONSTANCY

When a piece of black paper is brought from a dark corner of the room into the direct sunlight by a window, the intensity of the radiant energy being reflected from its surface increases manyfold, yet the paper still appears 'black.' This is but one of many forms of constancy—brightness, shape, size, color—that have been known to psychologists for generations. Katz, summarizing his work in *The World of Color* (1935), was the first to emphasize that it is *surface colors,* perceived as object-tied, which show constancy. Notice how well this fits in with Ames's demonstrations, in which size served as a stable cue for distance only when referable to a concrete object. Constancy has fundamental biological significance: it is to particular objects (foods, enemies, implements, possessions) that the organism must react, not to momentary stimulus qualities, and to the extent that constancy is shown, it is objects that are being perceived.

Measurement of Constancy Effects

Demonstrations of constancy are not the same as measurement. White paper looks 'white,' not gray, in dim light; this demonstrates constancy but tells us nothing about the magnitude of the effect. Measurement requires comparison, judgments of sameness and difference, and thus the application of psychophysical methods. What is compared? *The 'same' object* (with sufficient cues to infer identity) *is shown under different conditions of observation* (with sufficient cues that the conditions are different), *and the observer adjusts its appearance under the two conditions to phenomenal equality.* In everyday living such judgments are usually made under *successive* presentations—the paper is seen now under one illumination and then under another. In the laboratory, to obtain more precise judgments, *simultaneous* comparison is generally used—one white paper is viewed under one illumination and another physically identical paper is seen simultaneously under different illumination. If the observer shows perfect constancy, the 'same' paper will always appear equally bright phenomenally regardless of illumination conditions; if the observer shows complete lack of constancy, phenomenal brightness will depend solely upon the physical luminosity of the paper. The usual result is a compromise between these two extremes.

The diagrams in the upper portion of Fig. 104 describe one of the earliest experimental setups for studying constancy (Katz, 1911) and one which is still a standard in the psychological laboratory. The left-hand diagram shows the normal condition in which illumination cues are available. The light from the window (*W*) falls full upon test surface *B,* but, owing to the interposition of the screen (*S*), test surface *A* is in shadow. Both *A* and *B* are color wheels on which the segments of black and white can be varied. Suppose disk *A,* in the shadow, is 360° white, i.e. as bright as the prevailing conditions allow. The subject's task is to adjust the proportions of black on disk *B* until the two surfaces appear identical in brightness—he is usually told merely 'to make them look alike.' Now if constancy were perfect, disk *B* would be made 360° white, like disk *A ;* to the extent that the observer is affected by the physical luminosity differences, he will add black to disk *B.* How are we to know what proportion of white on disk *B* represents 0 per cent constancy? One way would be to measure the luminosities of the two disks with an illuminometer. A simpler way is to eliminate illumination cues with a *reduction screen,* a screen with two holes so placed that the observer sees only segments of each disk as if they were bits of film color. When our observer makes another brightness match with this screen, we obtain a good approximation of 0 per cent constancy, i.e. a physical luminosity match. The right-hand diagram describes this condition. Now a camera doesn't *perceive*—its film is bleached in strict accordance with physical intensities. If, therefore, we substitute a camera for the human eye after the observer has made his equations in both above-mentioned conditions, we should be able to demonstrate how far away from objective equality the observer was when, under the normal condition, he got what appeared to him as two equally bright surfaces.

So far we have merely discussed procedures. In what units do we indicate 'how much'? An ideal white object reflects all the incident light, but an ideal black object reflects none. The *albedo* of the object is simply the ratio of the reflected to the incident light. An object's albedo is completely independent of the degree of illumination, i.e. the same ratio of reflectance holds whether the illumination is weak or intense. It is this which we perceive when we show perfect constancy. The *luminosity* of an object, as we already

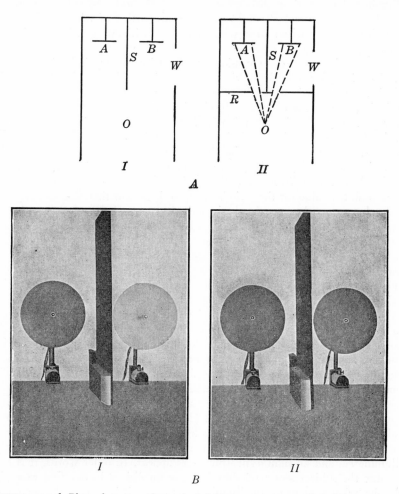

FIGURE 104. *A*. Plan of an experiment in brightness constancy, viewed from above. *B*. Photographs showing the match made (*I*) without a reduction screen and (*II*) with a reduction screen. D. Katz, *Die Erscheinungsweisen der Farben*, Barth, Leipzig, 1911, p. 181. After Boring, Langfeld, and Weld, *Psychology*, John Wiley, 1935.

know, refers to the total energy being reflected from it, and it will vary continuously with the illumination. It is this characteristic of the stimulation we approximate when using a reduction screen or an illuminometer. What quantities do we need for our measurement? Using standard notations, we need numerical values for *A* (the albedo of the standard object or surface); *S* (the luminosity of the standard object or surface); and *R* (the albedo of the comparison object or surface, i.e. the actual match made by the observer). When color wheels are used, stimulus values can be expressed in proportions (e.g. angular degrees of white), and all of these quantities are made equivalent. In the setup we have described, for example, A would equal the proportion of white in the standard, shadowed disk (here, 360°); S would equal the proportion of white in the well-illuminated comparison disk *when matched through the reduction screen* (perhaps, 260°); and R would equal the proportion of white in the well-illuminated comparison disk when matched without a reduction screen (possibly, 320°).

A convenient way of expressing amount of constancy in a single value has been introduced by Brunswik (1929). It is readily seen that if R equals A (i.e. the comparison disk has the same proportion of white as the standard disk, despite the differing illuminations), the observer is showing perfect constancy. On the other hand, if R equals S (i.e. the proportion of white in the comparison disk is the same with or without a reduction screen), then the observer is showing perfect *lack* of constancy. What we want is an expression of the proportion or per cent of perfect constancy actually shown. The *Brunswik ratio* equals $(R-S)/(A-S)$. When R and A are equal, the value for the ratio is 1.00; to the extent that R is less than A, the value approaches .00. In the hypothetical example given above, A was 360°, R was 320°, and S was 260°. The Brunswik ratio in this case equals .60. Had another subject, perhaps more analytic in his approach, shown an R value of 280°, his Brunswik ratio would have been .20. Thouless (1931) has criticized this ratio on the ground that, since the sensory effects of light vary according to the logarithm of the intensity (Fechner's Law), the values for A, S, and R should first be transformed into a log scale.

In the sample experimental setup given above, cast shadow was employed to produce differential illumination of the test surfaces. This condition is not essential. There are many possible designs whereby constancy can be studied. Rather than shadowing the standard disk, *additional* illumination may be cast upon it. As long as the observer is given cues that this additional illumination exists, and it falls on the surround of the test surface as well, this situation is much like the first described. Nor is it necessary to have a *prevailing* room illumination. Hsia (1943) has compared constancy values for conditions in which a prevailing illumination is present with those in which each test surface (and immediate surround) is independently illuminated, and no significant differences appear. In other words, it is not because the subject sees a window lighting up disk B in our first example that he 'takes account of' the illumination; rather it is because the surround of one surface is perceived as being differently illuminated from the surround of the other.

What if the observer does *not* have cues for the special illumination? A striking demonstration by Gelb (1929) shows what can happen in this case. With several objects dimly lit by a ceiling light, a *black* disk was shown in the foreground and illuminated by an intense, but concealed, lantern. The beam of this lantern was adjusted so that it exactly fit the area of the black disk, no additional light being cast upon the surround. Observers reported a *white* disk standing in dim light. Then a bit of 'real' (high albedo) white paper was held within the beam of the concealed lantern for a moment—the 'white' disk somersaulted into a 'black' disk seen in bright light! As soon as this cue for the special illumination was removed, the disk flipped back into its 'white' appearance again. This is a very significant observation: notice that, despite 'knowledge' of the special illumination—having seen the bit of real white paper—when that cue is not palpably present, the existing visual conditions determine what is perceived.

Generality of the Constancy Phenomenon

All stimulus characteristics that have been studied with this phenomenon in mind reveal the constancy effect. (1) *Brightness constancy.* This is the form most extensively studied, and its general nature has already been discussed. (2) *Color constancy.* When a blue paper is placed in yellow illumination of the right intensity and observed through a reduction screen, it appears neutral gray—this is simply what would be predicted from the laws of color mixture. When observed *without* the screen, however, it appears as a blue paper in a yellow illumination. Cramer (1923; cited by Woodworth, 1938) has shown that well-known objects projected onto an obviously colored screen retain their object colors; whereas an abstract blue square appeared gray when projected on a yellow screen, a child's blue dress retained its blueness. Experiments on color constancy are often confounded by color adaptation. Helson and Judd (1932) have shown that complete color adaptation occurs (and objects again appear in their normal hues) when weakly colored glasses are worn.

(3) *Size constancy.* A large number of experiments on size constancy are available in the literature. Most comparable, in terms of the procedures followed, to studies of brightness constancy was an early investigation by Martius (1889, reported in Boring, 1942, p. 293), and a more recent one by Brunswik (1940). Martius suspended wooden rods, 20, 50, and 100 cm. in length, one at a time, at a distance of 50 cm. from the observer. With these as standards, the observer was then to select a rod equal in length from a set of comparison rods at either 300-cm. distance or 575-cm. distance. Martius himself, as an observer, showed almost perfect constancy: the 20-cm. rod, as a standard at 50-cm. distance, was equated with one of 20.6 cm. at 300 cm. and with one of 21.7 cm. at 575-cm. distance. (Observe that equated visual angles at these distances would have been 120 and 230 cm., respectively.) As Boring suggests, this looks more nearly like judgment than immediate perception. Brunswik's study seems to justify this verdict. A series of 13 cubical blocks was lined up 12 m. from the observer, varying in size from 30 mm. to 90 mm. on a side. The standard blocks (50, 55, 60, 65, and 70 mm.), one at a time, were placed at varying distances from the observer, but always nearer to him than the comparison series. Again the technique was to have the observer select the block that appeared equal in apparent size to the standard. Although considerable constancy was shown, there was a more obvious compromise between perfect object reference (100 per cent constancy) and equation of visual angles.

(4) *Shape constancy.* This phenomenon is so prevalent in ordinary experience, so much taken for granted, that instructors in introductory courses often have difficulty convincing students there is any problem here. Hold a book so that its flat surface is horizontal and somewhat below your eye level. What is the shape of that surface? Why, it certainly *looks* rectangular, as we know it actually is. But now take a piece of paper and *draw* a rectangular shape to represent the book surface at this angle of regard—

you can't! In order to duplicate the correct appearance, you must draw a trapezoid. This approximates the shape as it was impressed on the retina. One reason for unreality in the artistic creations of children and primitives is that they draw things as they know them to be, i.e. as they would appear if normal (perpendicular) to the plane of regard. By way of experimentation, Thouless (1931) used a circular shape as the standard stimulus, inclining it obliquely to the observer's line of sight so that its retinal image would be elliptical to varying degrees. A series of true ellipses, normal to the line of regard, were used as comparison stimuli. Observers invariably chose shapes intermediate between true circles and those that matched the retinal image of the standard, thus showing shape constancy. It seems likely that all characteristics of objects could be shown to maintain their constancy in perception, provided adequate conditions of measurement were devised. Is there such a thing as *odor* constancy? *Taste* constancy? *Pitch* constancy? Apparently no one has as yet explored these possibilities.

Empirical Generalizations regarding Constancy

(1) *What is perceived represents a compromise between sensory data and object reference.* Neither perfect stimulus matching nor perfect constancy is obtained in experiments. What looks like an equation to the observer is a balance between these two extremes, even though it is unconsciously rather than deliberately arrived at. This statement is amply justified in the extensive literature. Thouless (1931), for example, reports constancy ratios for brightness, color, shape, and size characteristics obtained under roughly comparable conditions; in all cases there was a compromise between sensory and perceptual determinants, ratios sometimes approaching, but never reaching, .oo or 1.00. Nevertheless, the *degree* of compromise varies considerably from subject to subject and from condition to condition. What are the factors that determine how much constancy is shown?

(2) *Degree of constancy increases with the absolute stimulus difference between standard and comparison objects.* Hsia (1943) has summarized evidence for this statement. In his own experiments on brightness constancy, standard and comparison disks appeared against a distant dark background which was unaffected by differential field illuminations; these disks were set in open-end compartments lined with neutral gray paper; they were independently lighted and thus gave the observer cues as to special illumination. Hsia found that constancy ratios regularly increased as the absolute difference in the illumination of the two fields increased—i.e. the greater the difference in brightness of the two gray compartments, the more constancy the observer showed in matching test and comparison disks. Brunswik's (1940) data on size constancy reveal the same relationship: the farther apart the standard and comparison objects were (and hence the greater the discrepancy in visual angle), the more constancy was shown. For example, with a standard block 50 mm. in size, a Brunswik ratio of .50 was obtained when only 2 m. distant from the comparison series; a ratio of .78 when 6 m. distant, and a ratio of .96 when 10 m. intervened between standard and comparison blocks. Similar data have been assembled by Hsia for Thouless's (1931) results on shape constancy.

On the face of it, this is a very puzzling business. Why should an observer show *more* constancy as the objects to be compared deviate more and more from one another in absolute stimulus values? Hsia offers little by way of explanation, except to say in his conclusions: 'In the adjustment to a changing situation, possibly greater effort is dispensed to overcome a greater change of conditions. Therefore the greater the illumination difference, the higher the constancy, and parallel statements can be made, perhaps, of the other "thing-constancies" ' (p. 60). Is it possible to look at this problem from the stimulus-matching side rather than the constancy side? Let us suppose that observers do have some tendency to make analytic stimulus matches—only to the extent that they can *compare* two objects or surfaces can this end be achieved. And the greater the physical difference between things to be compared, the more difficult this becomes. Whereas slight differences in general illumination permit one to observe small discrepancies in the brightness of test and standard surfaces, gross differences in illumination obscure comparisons between particular surfaces and make the entire task quite frustrating. It is the common report that although observers find it easy to make satisfactory brightness matches with a reduction screen, it is extremely difficult in the open view.

(3) *The more cues identifying standard and comparison objects as being 'the same,' the more pronounced the constancy effect.* It is when the observer thinks he is looking at the same object, albeit under different conditions, that he reacts in the fashion we term constancy. Suppose we casually show someone a wooden block—no experimental atmosphere created—and simply ask him to point to 'the one just like it' in size in a line of blocks across the room. If (3) is valid (and we suspect it is), near-perfect constancy should be shown in this 'natural' condition. Suppose we show this person an ellipsoid surface, holding it in such a way that the retinal image must be approximately circular, and then ask him to select 'one just like it' from a set pinned on the wall *at right angles to his line of regard.* Again, we should expect him to show near-perfect constancy. In both of these real-life situations there are liberal cues about the 'real' character of the object (its distance in the first case and its angle of regard in the second), and further, there are sufficient reasons for the observer to assume identity between the objects seen under different conditions. At the other extreme we have the use of a reduction screen, where cues for object identification are entirely eliminated and the constancy effect disappears.

Burzlaff (1931) has come close to creating 'natural' conditions like those cited above. Two sets of 48 small gray papers, one in regular order from white to black and the other in random order, were mounted on large, medium-gray cardboards. The irregular set was put near a window and the regular set was put far back in the room where the illumination was only one-twentieth of that by the window. Using both adults and children of varying ages as subjects, Burzlaff would point to a particular gray paper on the near chart and have the subject indicate which of the far papers seemed the same. *Nearly perfect constancy was shown by both adults and children of all ages,* and there were no significant differences on the basis of age. In another experiment by the same investigator, the charts were replaced by two color wheels with variable black-and-white segments. One wheel was placed where it received one-twentieth the illumination of the other, as in the first experiment, and the usual constancy procedures were followed. In this case much less constancy was shown by both adults and children, but adults more closely approached object constancy. Why the children should show a greater tendency toward stimulus matching than the adults is puzzling, particularly in view of certain comparative data we shall take up in a moment. It is possible that instructions were differently interpreted by people of different ages, giving rise to different attitudes toward the task.

(4) *Maintaining an everyday object-oriented attitude toward the task increases the constancy effect.* Individual observers vary widely in the per cent constancy they show, despite identical instructions. This is usually blamed on differences in attitude toward the task, some observers adopting a 'critical' stimulus-oriented attitude and others adopting a 'naïve' object-oriented attitude. The subject who pays attention to, and makes allowance for, the total illumination, the angle of regard, the actual distance, and so on shows the greatest constancy. Is this being more naïve? If so, Martius (p. 275) was so 'naïve' an observer that he achieved near-perfect size constancy and Boring accused him of making intellectual judgments rather than perceiving! And, by the same criterion, Burzlaff's younger children were the most 'critical' and his adults the most 'naïve'! We think of object-orientation as more naïve simply because this is the normal, adjustive re-action to sensory data. Now the artist *wants* to depict objects as they actually affect the senses, not as they are known to be. To do this, he must adopt—is it a more naïve or a more analytic attitude? Do professional artists show less constancy? Thouless (1932) finds that they do, although they can never completely eliminate the tendency toward constancy. He also finds that artists have learned various techniques of observing which help them get back to the sensory data. One such trick of the trade is to nearly close the eyelids while observing, thus blurring contours and minimizing the object-character of things. This is being critical in the sense that the observer is deliberately playing down cues that serve to identify objects as conceptualized classes.

Surprisingly there are few studies in which attitude has been deliberately manipulated and the effect on constancy determined. Henneman (1935) gave observers who originally showed low ratios instructions to pay attention to the illumination, and he gave those originally showing high ratios instructions to disregard illumination cues. That these instructions were effective is indicated by the following results: those having an original average Thouless ratio of only .221 subsequently yielded a value of .721; those having an original ratio of .575 subsequently gave a value of .474. Apparently it is easier to deliberately adopt the natural, object-oriented attitude than the artist's stimulus-oriented attitude. Thouless (1931) makes the point that the tendency toward constancy cannot be entirely eliminated by adopting an analytic attitude. The following demonstration is completely convincing on this point: from a set of chinaware, select a large dinner plate and a smaller salad plate, both having identical shapes and patterns. Place the larger plate on the floor and, holding the smaller in your hand, adjust its distance so that the sizes seem identical *monocularly* (this will approximate equal visual angles). Now open both eyes. Immediately the dinner plate looks much larger than the nearer salad plate, and nothing one can do about his attitude eliminates this impression (cf. Thouless, 1931, p. 24).

Considerable interest has attached to the *age* variable. It is certainly reasonable to believe that the young must learn to perceive objects as such, must learn to take account of the continuous variations in sensory data. Certainly the mother's face appears in many illuminations, the baby's dish appears at many angles, and his block is seen at many distances—and the growing child presumably must learn to react adjustively in terms of the *objects* represented. Results obtained by Beyrl (1926) on size constancy using children as young as 2 years, Burzlaff (1931) on brightness constancy using children as young as 4 years, and Thouless (1932) on shape, size, and brightness constancy using adults varying in age from 20 to 50 years, agree in showing that constancy increases with age. Yet Burzlaff found no differences between his youngest children and his adults in degree of brightness constancy when using the more 'natural' situation of picking identical gray papers from samples under different illuminations. If these age differences are due to the attitudes engendered by instructions, it is hard to understand why the younger individuals should be led to deliberately avoid illumination, distance, and other cues about the 'real' nature of the object. This whole question is very much up in the air at this time.

(5) *Comparative data.* If the reason younger individuals show less constancy is that they are not sophisticated enough to take account of conditions, then one should certainly expect lower animals than the human to display less constancy as well. But this is definitely not the case. Early experiments by Köhler (1918) and Götz (1926) have indicated a high degree of brightness constancy and size constancy, respectively, in the chicken. Katz and Révész (1921) obtained the same result for color constancy with this species: having trained chickens to select white rice grains and leave those stained yellow, tests were then made under strong yellow light and the birds still chose the white grains. Locke (1935) compared four rhesus monkeys and five human adults under essentially the same conditions for measuring brightness constancy and found that the monkeys showed *more* constancy than the humans! The same investigator (1937) compared monkeys, human children, and human adults in a size-constancy situation and although the monkeys did not show more constancy, at least there were no significant differences. Going much further down the vertebrate scale, Burkamp (1923) trained aquarium fish (*Cyprinides*) to get their food from metal trays with aprons of a certain color from among 24 variously colored trays. When illumination values were changed by moving the aquarium nearer a window or by passing light through colored filters, very little change in behavior resulted, i.e. a high degree of both brightness and color constancy was demonstrated.

What are the implications of these comparative data? Although they do not *prove* that constancy in perceiving is unlearned, they do suggest an innate neural organization of such behavior in lower species—neither hens nor fish are particularly notable for their learning capacity. Since all species tested have shown fully as much perceptual constancy as humans, if not more, it certainly indicates that the process by which organisms 'take account of' the conditions of observation cannot be a highly intellectualized one—Helmholtz's 'inferences' are surely unconscious in the aquarium fish. On the other hand, of course, these animals would have had a great deal of practice if learning were involved. Finally, with regard to the performance of children, these comparative data suggest an attitudinal basis for their relative lack of object constancy—Burzlaff's youngest children *could* respond with nearly perfect constancy under natural conditions.

Why Constancy in Perceiving?

There is no harm asking this question, even though we shall not get far trying to answer it. There is no doubt that constancy is the adaptive way of behaving. But this doesn't explain *how* humans (and fish) are able to behave this way—it might also be adaptive to communicate telepathically, but our nervous systems are not built that way. Apparently we *are* wired for constancy. How and where is this 'constancy circuit' built in?

In the interest of parsimony, we should first look for explanation in *peripheral and projective mechanisms*. Hering (cf. Vernon, 1937, p. 123) had thought the answer lay in retinal adaptation and pupillary functions. The simplest rebuttal to any retinal explanation is an after-image demonstration (Thouless, 1931, p. 9). In the standard constancy situation, adjust the albedos of two gray disks standing in different illuminations to the point where they seem equally bright (to the extent that constancy is present, they will *not* be equal in luminosity); fixate a point between the disks steadily for a minute or so and then, looking at some uniform surface, observe the after-images of the two disks—they do not appear equally bright. The after-images reflect differences in luminosity which were present when, owing to perceptual constancy, the two disks seemed equally bright; this indicates that the processes responsible for constancy had not occurred in the peripheral mechanism.

The idea that brightness and color constancy are nothing more than *contrast* phenomena in a special setting has appeared repeatedly in the literature. Jaensch and Müller (1920, cf., Vernon, 1937) tried to show that constancy could be explained this way and, most recently, Wallach has described a number of cases in which both phenomena clearly follow identical functions. What is the relationship here? A neutral gray test surface viewed against a black surround appears brighter than when viewed against a white surround—this is brightness contrast. When the surround of a test surface is obviously in shadow, the test surface appears relatively brighter than when the surround is obviously illuminated—this is known as constancy and we refer to 'taking account of' the field illumination. Similarly, surrounding a gray surface with red makes it appear bluish-green (color contrast). Uniformly illuminating a blue-green surface *and* its neutral surround with red light leaves the surface bluish-green in appearance even though mixture of blue-green and red should produce gray (color constancy). According to the contrast explanation, the surround which is now red induces its complementary in the mixed central gray. If we ignore the illumination and deal directly with differential stimulation of retinal regions, aren't the laws of contrast sufficient?

In one of their demonstrations of the equivalence of color contrast and constancy, Wallach and Galloway (1946) arranged two color wheels against a uniform neutral screen as shown in Fig. 105. One color wheel (*G*) was neutral gray and the other (*R*) was red with a small segment of blue. The entire background *and* the red color wheel were flooded with green light from one projection lantern (*A*). The green projection slide had a circular spot in it which precisely shielded the neutral gray color wheel from the green illumination. Another projection lantern (*B*) was fitted with an opaque slide which would emit only neutral light through a round hole, this beam precisely fitting the gray color wheel and making it possible to vary its brightness. As a preliminary step, the gray produced by the mixture of blue-tinged red with green illumination on wheel *R* was matched for brightness with the natural gray on wheel *G* by varying the latter's special illumination—this was accomplished by a reduction-screen technique. When the reduction screen was removed, the red appearing on wheel *R* in green illumination (constancy) looked exactly like the red appearing on wheel *G* (contrast). Equivalence persisted when the brightness

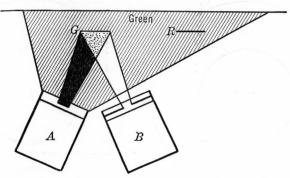

FIGURE 105. Experimental setup for studying relations between color constancy and color contrast. Constructed from description by Wallach and Galloway, 1946. See discussion in text.

of the background screen was varied and when other color combinations were used.

In the second study Wallach (1948) first demonstrated that the occurrence of surface color and its whiteness depends on the intensity relations between two bordering regions. If, on a screen in a perfectly dark room, a disk of light is projected and surrounded by a ring of light, the perceived whiteness of the included disk can be shifted from 'white' to 'black' by progressively increasing the luminosity of the ring from low to high levels. When both disk and ring are seen in relation to one another, they have the appearance of surface colors; when either is projected alone, it has the shimmering, luminous quality of film color, even when at low intensity. Now brightness *constancy* is attained in perceiving when an observer maintains a constant *ratio* between test surface and surround. Can the same response to ratios be demonstrated in this contrast situation? A *pair* of disk-ring combinations was projected as shown in Fig. 106. Four 500-watt projectors, fitted with variable episcotisters to control intensity, were used to vary independently the intensity of each ring and each disk. The episcotister of the standard ring was set at 360° (full intensity) and that of its included disk was set at 180°, i.e. an intensity ratio of one half. Then the episcotister governing the intensity of the comparison ring was set at 45°. At what intensity must the included comparison *disk* be set in order to appear equal in whiteness to the standard disk? The mean setting for several observers was 24.2°, which is approximately the same ratio as that given in the standard pair. The same proportionality held for several intensity settings and for several variations in procedure.

These are very impressive demonstrations. Wallach's discussion of them agrees rather well with the analysis of brightness and color contrast previously given here in terms of lateral summation and inhibition within the projection system. Wallach agrees that differentially excited regions must be neighboring if interactions are to occur. He also shows that the darkening, inhibitory effect on the disk increases as the brighter ring is increased in size, but only up to a point. (Increasing the size of the ring beyond the point where lateral connections are available can have no further effect.) His discovery of a law of proportionality may open up possibilities

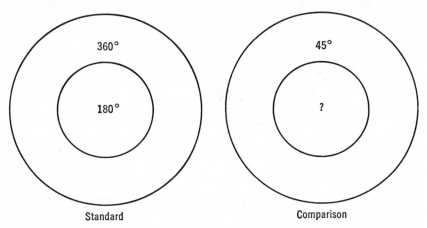

FIGURE 106. Experimental setup for studying relations between brightness constancy and brightness contrast. Constructed from description by Wallach, 1948. See discussion in text.

for quantifying these lateral processes in the projection system. As a whole, it would seem a step forward to explain constancy phenomena along these lines. We could forget many disturbing questions, such as how the organism 'takes account of' the illumination—which would be particularly gratifying when dealing with the hen or the fish! In fact, we could eliminate the concept of constancy entirely in so far as it applies to the perception of brightness and color.

But can constancy be accounted for in this fashion? (1) Wallach himself stresses the fact that the inducing color or brightness surround must border on the test surface. This is a necessary condition for contrast, as we have already seen, but is it necessary for constancy? Hsia (1943) presented his standard and variable disks against distant dark curtains which were unaffected by the differential illumination of the walls of the open-end boxes in which the disks were placed. In other words, the *immediate* surrounds of the test surfaces were not affected by the special illuminations, even though the observers could note the illumination cues—yet typical constancy data were obtained. Similarly, if the immediate backgrounds of standard and variable disks are made 'reduction equal' by having a blacker surface for the background which is under obviously stronger illumination, constancy effects are still found (cf. Vernon, 1937, p. 128). A similar experiment and result is reported by MacLeod (1932). (2) Certain manipulations that enhance contrast diminish constancy. If one minimizes the contour between test surface and ground, by 'fuzzing' the boundary, for example, contrast is strengthened but constancy is weakened—the loss of 'object-character' destroys the constancy effect (cf. Thouless, 1931, p. 13). (3) Although Wallach uses variations of the Gelb experiment in his own work, the fact that simply holding a small bit of white paper in the path of the concealed illumination which is making a black paper appear white, can promptly turn it back into its 'normal' appearance seems quite beyond any contrast explanation. Although the bit of high reflectance paper can serve as an illumination cue, it certainly is not sufficient in area to induce contrast.

The various *central theories* have much in common. For one thing, they all invoke some implicit standard with which any momentary input is compared. Katz (1935) refers to the general illumination of the field as its 'total insistence' and states that there is absolute memory for various degrees of it. The relative 'pronouncedness' of object surfaces in the field remains constant and is judged in terms of the brightness values these surfaces have in 'normal' illumination. Koffka (1935) draws a sharp distinction between 'whiteness' and 'brightness' (Katz's pronouncedness versus total insistence?), stating that it is the former to which constancy applies and that therefore we should speak of 'whiteness' constancy. In fact, when whiteness and brightness cannot be differentiated, as in a reduction screen, constancy is eliminated.

In its general form, Koffka's explanation of constancy goes back to the fundamental gestalt notions of cohesive and restraining forces. This can be seen most clearly in his discussion of shape constancy (1935, pp. 224-35). The orientation of surfaces in the frontal plane, although considered a special case, is the simplest case in which, dynamically, 'stimulus patterns would produce perceptual patterns according to the most simple laws.' Cohesive forces are minimal in this frontal plane, but 'to perceive a nonfrontal parallel plane would require special forces which . . . would be opposed by forces tending to pull it back into normal'—i.e. cohesive forces are created and have strength to the extent that surfaces are oriented in increasingly oblique planes. But the restraining forces established in the peripheral pattern (e.g. retinal ellipse rather than retinal circle) resist modification and supply 'new forces which will combine with the forces of orientation responsible for the stress in the field, and the final organization will be that in which all these forces are best balanced' (p. 231). Therefore, the finally perceived shape represents a compromise between the 'real' shape (e.g. that seen in the frontal plane) and the sensorily given shape.

Getting back to Koffka's discussion of brightness constancy—which is not notable for its clarity, by the way—emphasis is put on the *gradient* between intensities of various parts of the field. As we have already seen (Wallach's experiment), all gradations of whiteness can be produced by varying the brightness relations of two parts of a field which are perceived as 'belonging' to one another. Referring to Gelb's experiment, Koffka (1935, p. 245ff.) points out that the highly illuminated black disk is at the top of a 60:1 gradient with respect to the dark-room background. When the small piece of truly white paper is introduced, and perceived as

284 EXPERIMENTAL PSYCHOLOGY

'belonging to' or 'appurtenant to' the disk, the disk is now at the bottom of a 60:1 gradient with respect to the bit of paper. Why doesn't the room suddenly appear blacker-than-black? Something new must happen, says Koffka, and since it cannot be in terms of 'whiteness,' it takes the form of a 'brightness' change, the disk and the room both appearing black but the room appearing *darker*. This aspect of the theory is weak, and weak also is the handling of 'belongingness,' since no laws are given by which one determines (prior to the perceptual result) what will belong to what.

Thouless (1931) has described constancy phenomena of all kinds as 'phenomenal regression to the real object.' When the observer shows near-perfect constancy, he is perceiving in terms of how the object would appear in its normal mode of presentation. Certainly all conditions that destroy the object as a known 'thing' (blurring contours, hidden lighting, reduction screens, monocular inspection, etc.) also work against constancy. Thouless (p. 16) phrases a general law as follows: 'When two sets of sensory or perceptual cues which alone would give rise to phenomenal characteristics inconsistent with one another are presented together, the phenomenal character which is actually experienced is neither that indicated by one nor that indicated by the other set of cues but is a compromise between them.' In the special case of constancy, one set of cues is that indicating the real nature of the object and the other set is that specifying the momentary peripheral stimulation. Brunswik (1933) has given a biological, adaptive flavor to much the same point of view: the organism is pictured as striving to perceive *objects* as they are known to be through total experience. It is through active manipulation of real objects in the environment that survival is maintained. Given the mobile character of sensory data, however, these intentions of the organism can only be approximated, never fully realized.

Thouless's notion of regression toward the real object raises a significant problem. What is this 'real' object? What is the 'real' whiteness of a surface? What is the 'real' color of something? In the case of shape constancy, the answer is clear enough—the 'real' shape of a circle, square, or any other figure is that which it offers when viewed in the frontal plane. Why should this be so? It will be recalled that in discussing Ames's demonstrations of size constancy, an experimental design for arriving at 'real' size was suggested. In essence the idea was this: the 'real' size of an object is that retinal angle subtended when it is ordinarily inspected. Similarly, 'real' shape is that presented under ordinary conditions of inspection of shapes. These 'ordinary' conditions of inspection presumably develop through adjustive learning, i.e. we learn what manipulative techniques make possible the types of discriminations demanded within our biological and social setting. If we casually ask a person to compare the shapes of two objects, he will hold them in such a way that the surfaces lie in the frontal plane; if we ask him to compare the colors of several yarns, he will take them out of a dim or colored light into good daylight (which radiates almost equally in all visible wave lengths). As a provisional hypothesis, then, we might say that *the real character of an object is that stimulus pattern it presents when the keenest discriminations along the dimension concerned* (size, brightness, color, etc.) *can be made.* And 'regression' in perceptual constancy is toward this standard.

All central theories also point to some integrating and balancing mechanism in the nervous system. As Thouless's general law claims, this mechanism operates whenever peripheral cues are in conflict, not simply in constancy situations. In the apparatus for studying binocular fusion previously described (cf. p. 251), for example, the two circles, seen as one through polaroid glass, can be moved laterally toward and away from one another in the horizontal plane. This causes the eyes to alternately converge and diverge. Both retinal displacement and motor sensations provide definite cues indicating the 'real character' of a single object moving nearer and farther from the observer in space. What happens to the total perception? A single circle of light seems to move in and out, *becoming dimmer and smaller as it comes closer, and vice versa.* This perceptual integration occurs despite the fact that both brightness and size are absolutely unchanged retinally. Why does this happen? Obviously the only kind of 'real' object that could maintain a constant brightness and a constant visual angle while approaching would be one that was in fact growing dimmer and smaller. This is a rational integration of the sensory data, but the process whereby it is arrived at is entirely unconscious and immediate. At present we know nothing about the kinds of neural mechanisms mediating such integrations; presumably they involve cortical regions beyond area 17, and, possibly, cell-assemblies of the sort described by Hebb (1949)—but here even guessing stops.

Finally, to the extent that the development of constancy in perceiving involves learning, it probably fits the paradigm of *concept formation* (cf. Chap. 15). In this paradigm a group of stimuli become associated with a common mediating process which makes possible a common set of reactions. Thus, in stereotyping, the fact that a large number of individuals of quite different stimulus character are associated with a common mediating process (e.g. a particular meaning of 'Jew') makes possible a 'standard' mode of behavior. Notice that here also the observer must have sufficient cues as to the 'real' character of the object (here, cues that the person does fall in the 'Jew' category); and, to the extent that other sensory data are in conflict (uniqueness of the present person), his final behavior will represent a compromise. In perceptual constancies, a multitude of variable sensory patterns (as *signs*) must become associated with a common perceptual mediation process which adequately represents the object being dealt with (the *significate*). If the organism is to behave in terms of real objects, their various modes of appearance must have equivalent sign values. Thus the various retinal brightnesses and colors, shapes, and sizes that arise as sensory data serve the organism as signs that represent or *mean* conceptualized objects. At this level of analysis perceptual and meaningful processes become operationally indistinguishable, and it may well be that in studying one phenomenon (constancy) we can gain some insights into the nature of the other (meaning).

MOTIVATIONAL AND ATTITUDINAL DETERMINANTS

Not only do interactions of varying complexity *within* the visual system operate to determine what we perceive, but it can be shown that events quite *outside* this sensory system also contribute. Thus the deliberate manipulation of motives, attitudes, values, and meanings may measurably alter the perceived character of objects in the visual field. (Although there is no reason that such central effects should be limited to visual perception, again most of the available literature is concerned with this modality.) Whatever the neural basis of these interactions may be—as when the known value of an object influences its perceived size—it seems certain that they depend on mechanisms well beyond area 17. The general experimental procedure here is to hold peripheral visual factors constant while deliberately manipulating various central factors, measuring modifications in what is finally perceived.

Motivational State

Innumerable everyday illusions testify to the *selective* role that motives play in perceiving. An office that I pass each day is numbered 400D; inevitably, when the hour is near mealtime, I perceive this as FOOD. The car I used to drive had the euphemistic label SILVER STREAK on its dashboard; inevitably, when the hour was near mealtime, I would read this as SILVER STEAK. Phenomena of this sort illustrate the well-known, but little understood, fact that perceptual processes are readily molded to fit an individual's momentary needs. It also recalls Tolman's notion of how demands sensitize the particular means-end-readinesses and expectations with which they are associated: if each presented sensory complex is somewhat ambiguous in sign value—an 'inkblot' for which multiple meanings have varying probabilities of occurrence—then momentary needs or demands may enter to selectively enhance the probability of certain perceptual integrations at the expense of others.

One of the earliest experimental studies here was contributed by Sanford (1936). He studied the effect of hunger need upon word association and the perception of ambiguous pictures. Ten children served as subjects in natural, but controlled, conditions. With tests given both before and after meals, twice as many food-related responses were made before as after meals. In a follow-up study by the same author (1937), the time without food was more finely divided through 1 to 5 hours, and a 24-hour 'fasting' group was added. More extensive and varied tests were also used (including chain associations, drawing-completion tests, and word-completion tests). Results indicated that both 'food habit' (the acquired periodicity in food-taking) and physiological need contributed to the effects of hunger upon perception. Levine, Chein, and Murphy (1942) have obtained similar results for the effect of hunger need upon the perception of ambiguous figures.

McClelland and Atkinson (1948) have measured the effects of hunger need upon projective productions in a 'subliminal visual perception' test. After preliminary instructions, during which a very faint image was actually projected on a screen, the experimenters went through all the motions of projecting the test 'pictures,' but they were actually blanks. For most tests the experimenters made certain comments, such as 'There are three objects on a table. What are they?' In some tests no structuring of the situation was provided. Comparative estimates of the sizes of food-related and neutral objects (projected by the subjects onto the screen!) were also made. With three groups of naval trainees hungry to varied degrees (1, 4, 16 hours), the numbers of food-related responses for both structured and unstructured situations were found to increase progressively with need. Imagined food objects seemed to grow somewhat larger in relation to neutral objects as hunger increased. Food-goal-object responses (e.g. names of things to eat) did not increase, however, in frequency of occurrence, even though food-related responses (e.g. fork, plate, etc.) did. This was interpreted, along lines suggested by Sanford, as indicating an inhibition against thinking about food objects when very hungry. In other words, 'a hungry person may prefer not to think of a beefsteak at all but if he sees one it may appear larger and juicier than normal.' Also suggested in these results was a negatively accelerated function of the effect of need upon perceptual processes—although differences between 1-hour and either

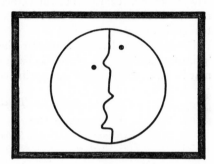

FIGURE 107. Figures used to test the influence of differential reward and punishment upon perceptual selection. Schafer and Murphy, *Journal of Experimental Psychology,* 1943, 32:337.

4- or 16-hour groups were generally significant, differences between 4- and 16-hour groups were not.

Schafer and Murphy (1943) have studied the same type of relation between a different motive and a different measure of perceptual integration. Subjects were shown four outline faces in a tachistoscope, each for $\frac{1}{3}$ sec., and required to learn the names which went with each face. Two of these faces were regularly rewarded (*S* being given 2 or 4 cents) and two were regularly punished (2 or 4 cents being taken away from *S*). The hundred training presentations included 25 of each face, but 2- and 4-cent exchanges were so manipulated that all *S*'s ended up with a small financial gain (15 cents). On the test trials the faces that had previously been seen singly were now combined into ambiguous figures, shown in Fig. 107, the same contour representing both a rewarded and a punished profile. Question: Which names would be given now, even though here no differential rewards were anticipated? The results were definite enough—the ratio of rewarded to punished names called out was $\frac{54}{13}$.

Another kind of motivational situation has been studied by Postman and Bruner (1948), one involving *frustration*. Three-word sentences, such as 'Time has healed,' were presented repeatedly one at a time in a modified Dodge tachistoscope, and subjects were instructed to report everything they saw or thought they saw. Each sentence was presented first at a flash rate of .03 sec. below each subject's previously determined threshold, then at .02 sec. below, and so on until the entire three-word sentence had been correctly recognized. Five experimental and five control subjects were treated identically for an *initial series* of nine sentences. During an interpolation period, experimental individuals were subjected to 'perceptual frustration,' a complex picture being shown at such a rate that nothing could be clearly seen, yet they were unmercifully harassed for their failures; control subjects observed this picture for 30 sec. and merely described what they had noticed. In the final *test series* of another nine sentences, this same picture was interspersed five times for both groups but with continued frustration-treatment of the experimental subjects. The following measures were secured: (1) one-, two-, and three-word *thresholds,* i.e. the minimum exposure time at which these numbers of words were correctly recognized; (2) frequency of one-, two-, and three-word *hypotheses,* i.e. the number of words guessed, regardless of correctness; and (3) the *content* of hypotheses, i.e. the occurrence of substitutions which suggested aggressive or escape tendencies.

Postman and Bruner interpret the results of this study as indicating 'primitivation' of perceptual behavior under 'perceptual frustration.' As may be seen in Table 3 by comparing columns 1 and 2 (experimental group)

TABLE 3

	EXPERIMENTAL GROUP				CONTROL GROUP			
	Exposure Time (sec.)		% Total Hypotheses		Exposure Time (sec.)		% Total Hypotheses	
	Initial	Test	Initial	Test	Initial	Test	Initial	Test
1-word	.115	.112	.47	.42	.106	.092	.24	.23
2-word	.132	.133	.24	.18	.122	.104	.23	.24
3-word	.154	.152	.19	.31	.136	.116	.43	.42
blanks			.10	.09			.10	.11
	(1)	(2)	(3)	(4)	(5)	(6)	(7)	(8)

Adapted from Postman and Bruner, *Psychological Review*, 1948, 318-19.

versus columns 5 and 6 (control group), *the frustrated subjects showed no improvement in recognition time between initial and test series, whereas the control subjects did.* But was it 'perceptual' frustration that produced this effect and was the effect necessarily upon perceptual processes? One suspects that the same results could have been obtained by frustrating these subjects with failure in other situations as well as in trying to perceive forms in a flashed picture. And it seems possible that other reactions to frustration, such as an unco-operative attitude toward the situation, interference from self-accusative thinking, and so on, could have produced the same results quite independent of changes in perceiving per se. With respect to hypotheses made, *the experimental subjects show a significant increase in the proportion of all hypotheses that involved complete three-word sentences following frustration* (column 3 to column 4). This 'increase in premature and reckless hypotheses,' as Postman and Bruner say, would hinder recognizing the correct sentence, since 'having formed a perception on the basis of a premature hypothesis, the subject must then "un-perceive" it—an act accomplished only with considerable difficulty.' But if this be the interpretation of these data, then we must also conclude that the control subjects were decidedly more reckless hypothesizers than the experimental subjects. Notice that on the initial series the control subjects gave 43 per cent three-word hypotheses as compared with only 19 per cent for the experimental subjects (who ended up, even after frustration, much less reckless). Postman and Bruner may prove right in their hunches, but there does not seem to be sufficient evidence here to show that perceptual processes themselves are made more 'primitive' by frustration.

Value

Bruner and Goodman (1947) draw a distinction between *autochthonous* and *behavioral* determinants of perception. The former 'reflect directly the *characteristic* electrochemical properties of sensory end organs and nervous tissue,' whereas the latter are 'those active, adaptive functions of the organism which lead to the governance and control of all higher-level functions' (p. 34). After reviewing the scattered literature on behavioral determinants (including studies by Ansbacher (1937) on the effect of value upon perceived numerousness of postage stamps), they set up the following hypothesis for test: *the greater the value of an object for an individual, the more it will be susceptible to organization by behavioral determinants.* Organization by behavioral determinants includes *selection* from among alternative perceptual objects, *fixation* as a perceptual response tendency, and *accentuation*. It is the latter effect in which they were interested experimentally, the effect of known value of coins upon their perceived size being studied by the classic psychophysical method of average error.

Thirty 10-year-old children of normal intelligence served as subjects, including ten rich children (drawn from a progressive school in the Boston area), ten poor children (from a settlement house in one of Boston's slum areas), and ten control children (of unspecified status). Each subject saw a circular spot of light on a ground-glass screen set in a panel just in front of him. Also on this panel was a knob which controlled the size of the light area, and each child was encouraged to explore the manipulation of this light before the experiment began. The first task for all subjects was to estimate *from memory* the sizes of a penny, a nickel, a dime, a quarter, and a half dollar in that order and then in reversed order, two judgments being made each time (one starting from the wide-open position of the diaphragm and the other from the closed position). Following this memory series, estimates were made with the actual coins present (held in the subjects' palms, about the same distance as the light), the same order of presentations being used. Control subjects were treated identically, except that medium-gray cardboard disks of the same size as coins were used. Results were expressed as per cent deviations of the size of the light spot from the actual size of the coins being estimated.

With the actual coins present, *all children significantly overestimated their sizes, the amount of overestimating increasing regularly with their value but not their real size.* In other words, although a dime is smaller than a penny, its per cent overestimation was greater (see Bruner and Goodman curve in Fig. 109). This did not hold for the largest coin (50-cent piece), and the authors suggest that the half dollar may be almost too valuable to be real to these children. These findings substantiate the hypothesis that 'socially valued objects are susceptible to behavioral determinants in proportion to their value.' Also with coins present, *poor children showed more overestimation than rich children, the difference tending to increase with value* (see Fig. 108). Bruner and Goodman make 'the reasonable assumption . . . that poor children have a greater subjective need for money than rich ones.' Certainly poor children have a greater *objective* need for money than rich ones, but do they actually have a greater *subjective* need? To argue that they must have because they showed greater overestimation of coin sizes would, of course, be entirely circular. As a matter of fact, it may well be that a subjective need for coins grows with the use

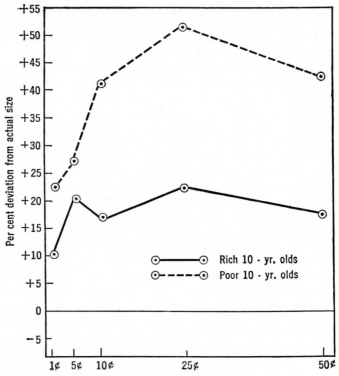

FIGURE 108. Size estimations of coins by rich and poor 10-yr. olds. Bruner and Goodman, *Journal of Abnormal and Social Psychology,* 1947, **42**:40.

of them as media of exchange for real (need-reducing) objects. Finally, *with coins absent* (i.e. estimating from memory), *poor children showed less overestimation than when coins were actually present.* Rich children showed no consistent differences here. This is very puzzling, since one would have thought that removing the autochthonous restrictions of the actual coins would give even freer rein to the poor children's needs as behavioral determinants.

After expressing skepticism with respect to these results, Carter and Schooler (1949) report a replication of this experiment—except that, unfortunately so often the case, it is not really a replication. Again estimations of size of coins was the task and both rich and poor 10-year-olds were the subjects, but conditions were quite different. Although a circular spot of light was used for estimations in part of the experiment, its brightness was much less than in the previous study. Bruner and Goodman had their subjects hold the coin in their palms *and normal to the line of regard,* but here the coins were laid flat on a piece of paper and thus probably presented eclipses rather than true circles. Bruner and Goodman used the control-group procedure, but the present investigators made each subject his own

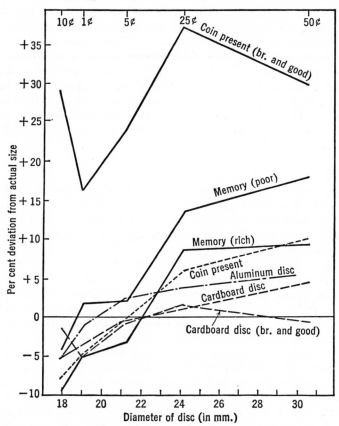

FIGURE 109. Size estimations by rich and poor 10-yr. olds, results of Carter and Schooler compared with those of Bruner and Goodman. Carter and Schooler, *Psychological Review,* 1949, **56**:204.

control. Each *S* first estimated the sizes of coins from memory with the spot of light, then matched sizes of actual coins with the spot of light; they did the same for aluminum disks cut to the right sizes, and then the same for cardboard disks. This was not all; now each *S* was shown a series of graduated aluminum disks, one at a time, and asked to decide whether each was larger or smaller than a 50-cent piece, then similarly for a 25-cent piece, and so on—one wonders how the youngsters managed it!

The results of this study might, indeed, be interpreted as justifying our hunch that the children were progressively losing interest—or perhaps that the coins and their facsimiles were losing their acquired drive value. With the spot of light, the first task was estimation from memory, the second with coins present, the third with aluminum disks, and the last with cardboard disks. The curves in Fig. 109 show a progressive decrease in over-estimation in precisely this order. Had the order of the tasks been counter-balanced, and the same results obtained, one might have drawn different conclusions. There are however two significant points to note in these data: (1) Here errors in estimation are smaller than in the Bruner and Goodman study and *vary with size rather than value*. In general, larger coins were overestimated and smaller coins were underestimated. Notice that the 10-cent piece, the smallest coin, was the most underestimated. This was in sharp contrast to the previous study. (2) *There were no significant differences between rich and poor children with coins present, but when working from memory poor children showed significantly greater overestimation than rich children.* Both findings flatly contradict those of Bruner and Goodman. Notice that these poor children overestimate *more* from memory, whereas the Boston poor children had overestimated *less* from memory. Needless to say, how value actually does affect perceived size remains to be worked out.

Meaning

Another aspect of symbolism relates to the *sign value* of what is perceived, defined as the capacity of a stimulus pattern to evoke reactions relevant to something other than itself. Bruner and Postman (1948) set up conditions for studying the effects of negative as well as positive sign value upon perceived size. The apparatus was the same as that used earlier by Bruner and Goodman: a *dollar sign* (positive sign), a *swastika* (negative sign), and an *abstract geometric design* (neutral sign) were drawn on bright pink plastic disks of identical size; the subjects' task was to match their sizes (when held in the palm of the hand) with the manipulatable spot of light, the method of average error being used with approaches from both directions. An *F*-test indicated significant variation on the basis of the symbol used. Both positive and negative signs showed greater overestimation than the neutral control. Why should the swastika be perceived as larger and not smaller? Bruner and Postman suggest that negative sign values lead to accentuation of apparent size by alerting the organism to danger or threat. This is but one of many possible hypotheses which might be applied to this result—perhaps the significant factor was simply enhanced distinctiveness.

Postman, Bruner, and McGinnies (1948) have set up the hypothesis that personal value-systems, as defined by scores on the Allport-Vernon scales (theoretical, economic, esthetic, social, political, and religious), are among the behavioral determinants of perception. Twenty-five subjects were shown 36 words, one at a time, in a modified Dodge tachistoscope. These words were chosen to represent the six values (e.g. for theoretical value, *theory, verify, science, logical, research,* and *analysis;* for social value, *loving, kindly, devoted, helpful, friendly, sociable*). Presentation order was random and the standard procedures for obtained recognition thresholds were used. According to their general thesis, as values vary, so should ease of recognizing related words. Consider a person with high social and low theoretical values, for example: his thresholds for words like 'loving' and 'devoted' should be lowered by *selective sensitization;* in the presolution period he should tend to select words covaluant with the correct word because of *value resonance;* his thresholds for words like 'verify' and 'research' should be raised because of *perceptual defense.* The results were favorable to the thesis because (1) there was a significant tendency for recognition thresholds to vary inversely with the ordering of the six values and (2) covaluant presolution hypotheses occurred significantly more frequently with high-value stimuli, whereas contravaluant hypotheses occurred significantly more frequently with low-value stimuli. The single principle of 'selective sensitization' would seem to cover these findings—'value resonance' appears to be the same notion at base, and it is doubtful whether even a highly theoretical person would erect 'perceptual defense' against an innocent social word like 'kindly'!

A final experiment, by McGinnies (1949), inquires more penetratingly into this matter of 'perceptual defense.' Threat situations have been shown to accentuate perceptual reactions (cf. Bruner and Postman's swastika) as well as inhibit recognition (cf. Postman and Bruner's effects of frustration). And the question arises: How can the threshold for inimical stimulus objects be raised or lowered *before* the observer becomes aware of their threatening character? McGinnies conjectures that autonomic reactions are aroused before conscious awareness, this emotional state being an essential part of the defensive mechanism that raises the perceptual threshold. A list of 11 neutral words and 7 critical, emotionally charged words were presented tachistoscopically and recognition thresholds determined in the usual manner. Galvanic skin responses were recorded as a measure of emotional disturbance. Eight male and eight female undergraduates served as subjects. Both *GSR* and recognition-threshold data are given in the pair of graphs in Fig. 110. Only the prerecognition trials are included in the *GSR* values. Clearly, *taboo words require longer exposures for recognition, and their prerecognition presentations are accompanied by decidedly stronger emotional reactions.* At the conclusion of the experiment all subjects were asked if they had reported their perceptions promptly and accurately—they said they had. Since the critical words here were of obvious taboo character, particularly when they had to be reported in the presence of both a male and a female experimenter, the evidence for 'perceptual defense' as a valid phenomenon looks quite compelling.

But this study has also come in for its share of criticism. Howes and Solomon (1950) have argued that it is unnecessary to appeal to 'perceptual defense' to account for McGinnies' results. They make two main points: (1) *The differences in recognition-threshold are in part due to familiarity* (frequency-of-usage). Howes and Solomon themselves (1951) have compiled extensive evidence indicating that recognition-threshold for words varies inversely with the log of their frequency-of-usage. When McGinnies' threshold values are plotted as a function of their frequency-of-usage, this same relation appears. McGinnies had argued that the actual frequencies of taboo words were much higher in *conversation* than would appear from their frequency counts in print, but Howes and Solomon have doubt 'that our conversations are as often adorned by *raped, whore, penis,* and *bitch* as by *child, clear, dance,* and *music!*' And we may add that frequency-of-conversational-usage would not affect recognizability of words as *visual* stimuli. This criticism applies with equal or even greater force to the Postman, Bruner, and McGinnies study on Allport-Vernon values—certainly, people with high theoretical values are going to read scientific materials more often and hence have a higher frequency of 'visual usage' for words like *research* and *analysis*. (2) *Emotional reactions accompany recognition of taboo words, appearing to precede recognition only because subjects inhibit reporting their perceptions.* Howes and Solomon (1950, pp. 232-3) sketch a humorous, but probably valid, picture of what might have gone through a subject's mind as he served in this experiment—that he would

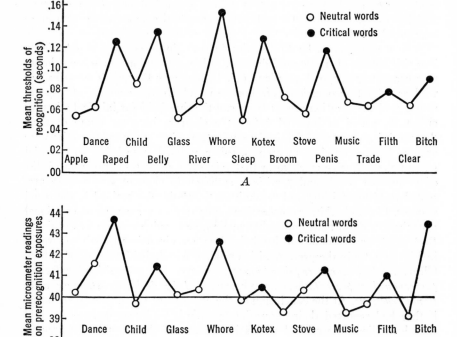

FIGURE 110. Relation between mean recognition thresholds (*A*) and mean prerecognition *GSR* readings (*B*) for experimental (solid circles) and neutral (open circles) stimulus words. McGinnies, *Psychological Review*, 1949, **56**:246-7.

have made absolutely sure the taboo words were really what they seemed before reporting them, particularly with both his professor and a member of the opposite sex present. To be sure, McGinnies' subjects said they had reported perception of all words immediately, but this is a slender thread indeed on which to hang the weighty principle of 'perceptual defense.'

Summary

This series of researches, conducted mostly by a group of psychologists at Harvard University during the past decade, appears in the philosophical framework of current functionalism, particularly that developed by Egon Brunswik in his *Wahrnehmung und Gegenstandswelt* (1934). The organism is conceived as striving to make its perceptions conform to its knowledge about real, manipulatable, approachable, and avoidable objects. With every stimulus pattern a more or less ambiguous situation, many perceptual integrations are possible, varying in their probability of occurrence. There are two general classes of determinants: autochthonous determinants tend to make what is perceived correspond to what is given sensorily and to reflect directly the neurophysiology of the sensory nervous systems; behavioral determinants tend to make what is perceived correspond to knowledge of the object and to reflect indirectly the motives, values, meanings, and attitudes of the organism toward the object. This point of view is entirely amenable to contemporary learning theory and it is also compatible with the gestalt distinction between 'cohesive' and 'restraining' forces.

Application of this functional view to human social perception has generated a number of hypotheses relating to the operation of behavioral determinants: (1) Favorable motives, values, and attitudes will *selectively sensitize* the subject's perceptual system in such a manner as to lower his threshold for recognizing relevant objects and their signs. (2) Favorable motives, values, and attitudes will *accentuate* the phenomenal characteristics (such as apparent size) of relevant objects. (3) Unfavorable motives, values, and attitudes (such as anxiety and frustration) will *desensitize* the subject's perceptual system—*perceptual defense*—and thus raise his threshold for recognizing relevant objects and their signs. Whether negative attitudes should be expected to accentuate or de-emphasize the phenomenal characteristics of objects is not clear. A number of secondary mechanisms have also been suggested: *primitivation* of perceptual processes under stress, *vigilance* under threat, and *value resonance* for the spread of effect to objects and signs of similar meaning. The experiments reported in this section were designed to test these particular hypotheses, but almost without exception the flaws in design or the lack of substantiation in repeat experiments have been such that no secure conclusions can be drawn. The value of these studies, then, lies not so much in the specific facts they have uncovered but rather in the extraordinarily fruitful research idea they have propagated: the idea that personality dynamics influence even the simplest perceptual activities and can be detected in the controlled conditions of classic experiments.

PROBLEM: NATURE OF BEHAVIORAL (CENTRAL) DETERMINANTS

The trend in these chapters has been from phenomena that are largely determined by peripheral mechanisms to phenomena that are largely determined by central mechanisms. Perhaps 'peripheral' to 'central' is not the best way to put it; it is really a trend from mechanisms inherent in the projection system (up to and including area 17) to mechanisms requiring participation of cortical regions beyond area 17. Although *contour and contrast effects* were for the most part interpretable on the basis of comparatively well-known retinal and projection processes, there were such facts as (1) abolition of contours could eliminate the included figure entirely and (2) contrast effects set up about contours are somehow transmitted to included regions quite distant from these contours. Similarly, certain aspects of *movement and space perception* could be understood in terms of projection mechanisms, but (3) the 'pure phi' phenomenon as a subjective impression of movement spans areas far beyond the lateral connections of either retina or projection system and (4) the binocular interactions underlying stereoscopic depth perception, since they involve contralateral areas 17, presuppose the involvement of at least area 18. And many other characteristics of space perception—the way in which apparent size determines perceived distance, for example—elude explanation on a 'peripheral' basis. The very nature of *constancy,* as we have said, points to (5) some remarkable integrating and balancing mechanism about which we know next to nothing. Finally, to the extent that perceptual processes per se are modified by *values, meanings, and motives,* (6) some selective 'tuning' mechanism is indicated.

In puzzling over this matter, one feels that he gets just the faintest glimmer of the Grand Design. *It seems that processes taking place about contours, as represented in area 17, serve as the sensory 'signals'; the role of integrative mechanisms* (cohesive, mediating, behavioral, or whatever they may be termed) *is to make what is perceived conform to this information.* The latency of an entire after-image conforms to the location of its contour on the retina, despite the relation between latency and distance from fovea. The perceived hue of an entire gray patch, even those portions distant from the inducing area, conforms to that produced by contrast at its borders. The subjective impression of movement when the successive appearance of two lights duplicates the cues for rapid movement in the field also represents conformity to sensory 'signals' in area 17. Why are certain portions of the visual field related and modified in the direction of consistency? We are pretty much in the dark here. One generalization can be suggested: *these integrative mechanisms operate to the extent that the observer identifies two processes, two sets of 'signals,' as representing the same real object.* The information upon which such identifications are made may be the existence of common, including contours, common size, shape, color, and so on. Various cues of this sort combine to create the identification which gives rise to perceptual constancy, i.e. the knowledge that this is such and such an object.

This leads us to the realization that what is finally perceived must also conform with sources of information other than those arising from area 17. The apparent shape of a circular disk viewed out of the frontal plane is made to conform with our knowledge of this object as well as with the elliptical sensory signal. The apparent size of this disk may be inflated in keeping with its value to us. Does this mean that visual consciousness is localized—if this unfortunate term be permitted—beyond area 17? Certainly the shape of the perceived disk in the case of constancy, or its size in the case of value, does not conform entirely to what must be the signals delivered to area 17.

What transpires beyond area 17? What other areas interact with 17 and how? We have very little information here. There is a smattering of clinical evidence (cf. Fulton, 1949, p. 350): certain visual disorganizations, such as defective spatial orientation and monocular diplopia, result from lesions in areas 18 and 19. Visual hallucinations of a highly organized nature may occur when tumors compress area 19. Failure to interpret written words, 'alexia,' may result from lesions in area 19 of the dominant hemisphere (i.e. left hemisphere of a right-handed person). Electrical stimulation of area 17 produces localized but meaningless phenomena in the visual field (such as star-points and colored flashes) ; stimulation in areas 18 and 19, on the other hand, may produce organized and meaningful hallucinations (such as the image of a friend's face or a scene). The evidence obtained with the strychninization method by Bonin, Garol, and McCulloch merely shows that area 18 displays the types of connections sufficient for complex, integrative functions, whereas area 19 displays the types of inhibitory connections with other areas sufficient for selective 'attentional' functions. This slender evidence does *not* indicate that the compromises between 'real' and retinal shapes occur in area 18; it does *not* indicate that sensitization of the religious man's threshold for perceiving religious words is accomplished by some selective operation of area 19. These remain as intriguing possibilities, as invitations to research

Part III

LEARNING

Both receptive and motivational processes bear the stamp of Darwinian principles. Selective modifications of this order result from experiences of the *species:* prolific multiplication of kind, accompanied by mutational variation in structure, and the endless competitive struggle for survival eventuate in selection according to adaptive capacity. Neural structures themselves evolve, and as they become capable of more and more complex functions, a replica of selective 'survival of the fittest' begins to appear within the behavior of individual members of species. In repeated situations of similar character, the individual organism varies and multiplies its behaviors, selection among competing responses depending upon their adaptiveness. Selective modifications of this order result from experience of the *individual.* One of the most highly evolved species, Homo sapiens, has termed this mode of selective modification *learning,* and it is uniquely significant for him.

What are to be the units for our observation and description of behavior? How is this fluid process to be segmentalized? Does behavior have its own natural units? In describing the maze behavior of a rat, for example, we might say the rat learns to 'go' to the place where food is—this would be a grossly *molar* description. Or we might conceivably detail the myriad neural impulses and muscle twitches that constitute the 'going'—this would be a minutely *molecular* description. (Of course, 'molar' and 'molecular' are always relative to the subject matter of the science in question; for the neurophysiologist electrical impulses recorded in nerve would be molar and their physiochemical substrata, molecular.) Many psychologists approach the molecular level, defining stimuli as energy changes which excite receptors (specifiable through physical measurements) and responses as muscular contractions (specifiable through physiological measurements). Yet this must be largely a matter of theoretical elegance, since these same theorists are prone to describe the 'stimulus' of a given choice point in a maze as eliciting the 'response' of turning-and-running-through-the-third-door! Actually, for the animal, the choice point comprises a compound of many thousands of stimuli thus defined, many of which are produced by the animal's own movements, and the behavior sequence initiated comprises a multitude of intricately interwoven muscular contractions.

299

Other theorists couch their descriptions in terms of 'behavior acts' which have the whole character of getting-to or getting-from specific goal situations (cf. Tolman, 1932), and thus approach, or even go beyond, the 'natural' level of observation employed by the layman. The 'natural' level specifies the association between *situations* and *acts,* both being circumscribed in concrete cases by the way in which language carves out events. Thus a 'street corner' and the 'soothing voice of a friend' become unitary stimulus situations and 'pressing the bar' and an 'expression of surprise' become unitary responses. The test for adequacy of any level of description is whether the units isolated actually function as unitary events in predictable relations. We shall find that either 'muscle movements' or 'acts' may be functional units, depending on the type of relation being studied. Therefore we shall not try to justify any one level of analysis as being *the* correct level—a procedure that would affirm the reality of arbitrary boundaries between the sciences, incidentally—but rather we shall eagerly welcome demonstration of any relation, regardless of the level of observation at which it is obtained.

Chapter 8

FUNDAMENTAL OPERATIONS IN LEARNING

The organism brings to any learning situation a fund of reflexive and previously learned behaviors. The infant, struck in the face by a bouncing ball, may blink and yell loudly for succor; the naïve rat, coming to the end of a blind alley in the maze, may sniff about the corner and rear up to claw at the wiring above. But it is characteristic of learning situations that reflexive and previously mastered responses are *not* successful. If they were, learning would not be necessary. If the organism is to adapt, the 'correct' response must occur. What defines this 'correct' response? What is the correct response for a man standing in the kitchen? What is the correct response for a rat poised on an ash heap in the city dump? In both cases 'correct' is defined in terms of the organism's motivation—digging into a garbage heap may be correct if the rat is hungry, whereas diving into a narrow hole may be correct if the rat is frightened. But in the laboratory is it not the experimenter who defines the correct response? Yes, but only indirectly—by manipulating the subject's motives and deciding what behavior will gratify them.

SELECTION

A Familiar Illustration

As an introduction to the problem of learning, we may first study a homely model, which will prove not as simple as it first seems. Suppose you wish to teach your dog the trick of lifting its paw and placing it in your hand when you say 'give me paw.' How, first of all, are you going to get this particular response to occur? Paw-lifting must somehow be made to happen before anything further can be accomplished. You find that when you pronounce the magic formula, 'give me paw,' the dumb brute wags its tail and grins in doggish fashion, or perhaps (smelling the meat) perks up its ears and barks. These are all responses, to be sure, but they are not the correct response. You want paw-lifting to occur, and you want it to occur soon after saying of 'give me paw.' It is usually said that the two fundamental 'kinds' of learning are *trial and error* and *conditioning*. We will take the position that these are merely techniques for getting the correct response to happen.

But objection will be raised at the outset that we are unduly restricting the field. How about *instruction* and *imitation* as methods for producing the correct response? We could merely tell a human subject to raise his hand, or do it ourselves and hope he would imitate. And what about *insight?* Might it not be possible that a really intelligent dog would 'understand,' from the tone of voice, the position of hand, and so on what was demanded and suddenly make the correct response insightfully? All these questions must be answered in the affirmative—these are all ways in which the correct response *can* be made to occur—but it is the fond hope and expectation of many theorists that these 'higher level' modes are analyzable into trial-and-error and/or conditioning paradigms. Whether this is actually possible, especially in the case of insight, is a question to which we will turn our full attention later (in Chap. 14).

Another common-sense objection may also be raised here: Aren't we missing the simplest and surest method of all for producing the correct response? Why not *passively* lift the dog's front leg each time we say 'give me paw'? There have been sporadic reports in the literature of successful passive conditioning, but it is doubtful that true passivity held. Miller and Konorski (1928), for example, reported that the passive lifting of a dog's foot in association with a tone resulted in conditioning, provided this combination was followed by food reward. But more recently Woodbury (1942) obtained clearly negative results. The latter investigator used a treadle on which the dog's foot was placed in a snug-fitting shoe, the treadle being lifted by the experimenter by means of an attached rope that went over a pulley. No evidence for passive conditioning appeared in a total of 350 trials. Woodbury attributes the Miller and Konorski results either to pain avoidance (since in their case a rope apparently was tied directly to the animal's ankle) or posture disruption when the leg is lifted by this method. That learning must involve mediation of the learner's own central nervous system, not the experimenter's, seems eminently reasonable.

But let us get back to the dog, which is no doubt impatiently waiting for the training to continue. How might you apply the *trial-and-error method* here? After making sure your subject was suitably motivated, here presumably by hunger, you would repeatedly say 'give me paw' and wait patiently for the correct response to occur. Because of its motivational state and the general characteristics of the total stimulus situation, the animal would emit varied responses, mostly 'errors.' If, in the course of this activity, the correct response of lifting its paw happened to occur, you would quickly reward the animal with a piece of meat. When, finally, the correct response does appear in association with the critical cue, does this mean learning is complete? Not at all. On the next trial there would be the same period of variable errors, but as trials continued you would find the correct response occurring earlier and earlier in the sequence, until saying 'give me paw' would regularly and promptly elicit paw-lifting. But suppose you, as the experimenter, give up and toss the meat to the dog as it is nuzzling your hand? Does learning fail to occur because the 'correct' response of lifting the paw hasn't been made? The point is that this response is correct in relation to the animal's motivation and is being learned—the dog can have no a priori knowledge of what is correct behavior within your private world. Needless to say, rewarded 'errors' of this sort make it more difficult to select out the 'correct' response as you have defined it.

It must be apparent at this point that trial and error is an extremely inefficient method for producing the correct response. Of course you might increase the probability of occurrence of the correct response by manipulating the external situation. You might, for example, hold the meat near the dog, but high and to the side on which you wish the paw-lifting to occur. Since the animal has previously learned to scratch at desired objects with the nearest front paw, it becomes more likely that some facsimile of 'lifting the paw' will appear as you say the magic phrase, and this speeds up the selective process. But is this still trial and error? Or are we gradually shading into what is called a different 'kind' of learning?

The essence of the *conditioning method* lies in presenting the animal with an additional stimulus which is known to regularly and unfailingly produce the desired response. The typical procedure here would be to give the new stimulus ('give me paw') and follow it promptly with shock—up comes the paw. This sequence, cue-shock-response, is repeated a sufficient number of times, whereupon it is found that merely saying 'give me paw' alone (without subsequent shock) will elicit the correct response. Of course, in order to use this conditioning procedure the dog must be harnessed in a special stall, and so on—otherwise the animal will learn to avoid the electrifiable grill and the entire situation it represents far more rapidly than paw-lifting! Is this method different from trial and error? Before trying to answer this question, we must inquire more fully into both procedures. It is certainly clear, however, that conditioning is a far more efficient method of getting the correct response to occur—if we discount the labor involved in setting up a suitable conditioning situation.

Instrumental Learning

Trial and error is one instance of the class of procedures commonly termed 'instrumental learning.' The essential characteristic defining this method is that (a) *the correct response must occur before reinforcement is given*. The paw must be lifted before the piece of meat is offered; the rat in the city dump must traverse a path to the garbage heap before food is obtained; the child must say 'please' before he can have a piece of fudge. In other words, the correct response is 'instrumental' in producing reinforcement. A number of additional supporting conditions must be met if selective modification via the instrumental mode is to be achieved: (b) the subject must be sufficiently motivated (or the emission of varied responses upon which this method depends will not occur); (c) the critical cue must occur sufficiently close in time to the correct response; (d) the correct response must be within the repertoire of the subject (indeed, speed of selection varies directly with the probability of occurrence of the correct response in any given situation); (e) reinforcement appropriate to the motivation of the subject must follow closely the occurrence of the correct response (this is a controversial matter, cf. pp. 413ff.).

The instrumental learning situation is generalized in arbitrary symbolic terms in Fig. 111. The cue stimuli (S_c) that make up the situation and the drive state (S_D) are shown as persisting through the behavior sequence constituting a single trial, and they combine to elicit varied behaviors (R's), most of which are errors. The correct response (here R_6) is shown as essential to and followed by reinforcement (R_G—goal response). Referring to the paw-lifting model, 'give me paw' and other situational stimuli (S_c) and the dog's hunger (S_D) combine to favor the emission of a variety of responses, among which occurs paw-lifting (R_6). This is followed promptly by a meat reward and subsequent eating behavior (R_G).

A large number of situations, both casual and experimental, fit the requirements of the instrumental learning paradigm. A few of the standard experimental ones will be described briefly here. In 1898 Thorndike reported a series of experiments with cats in which a hungry animal was placed in a *problem box* constructed of vertical slats through which a food reward could be both seen and smelled. The correct response was defined by the experimenter through mechanical arrangements which would cause

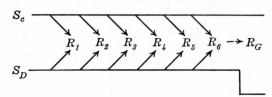

FIGURE 111. Instrumental trial and error paradigm. Combination of environmental (S_c) and motivational (S_D) stimuli evokes a series of reactions (R_1, R_2, and so on), among which may be the 'correct' reaction (R_6). The latter is defined by the dependence of reinforcement (R_G) upon its occurrence.

the door to open if the cat pressed a floor pedal, pulled a string loop, or made some other specific reaction. Usually, the hungry cat would struggle energetically to get out of the box, trying to squeeze between the slats, clawing at any movable objects, and so on, until in the course of this 'random' activity the correct response happened to be made. The time required to get out of the box usually showed a gradual and irregular decrease from trial to trial as the strength of the correct response increased. Many variants of this situation have been devised to suit the needs of different species.

Another piece of standard equipment in the animal laboratory is the *maze*. It may be composed of a series of multiple T's, with one arm of each T eventuating in a cul-de-sac or blind alley, or it may be composed of a sequence of diamond-shapes, and so on; it may be enclosed, usually with wire mesh at the top, or it may be elevated above the floor, with narrow strips of wood serving as the pathways. Mazes are often provided with valvelike doors which must be pushed open by the animal and which then close behind it to prevent retracing. Mazes vary greatly in length and complexity, but all fit the requirements of instrumental learning in that the correct responses must be made before reward is obtained. Although maze running is by no means limited to rat subjects, this species is most commonly used: rats of known genetic stock are comparatively easy to obtain; they breed rapidly in captivity, are easy to maintain in good health, and are extremely docile. The maze has a number of advantages for studying instrumental learning: errors during learning are limited in the form they can take (superficially, at least) and can be easily scored; the total performance is readily analyzable into segments (each choice point and the response made there) ; the maze situation is relatively novel to the subject and hence it is not likely to be affected by transfer from ordinary experiences.

Perhaps the simplest situation for studying instrumental learning is the *Skinner box,* developed by B. F. Skinner and described in detail in his book, *The Behavior of Organisms* (1938). The hungry subject (usually a rat) is placed in the small, soundproof, well-ventilated box shown in Fig. 112*A*. Within the box is a lever which, when pressed, activates a delivery

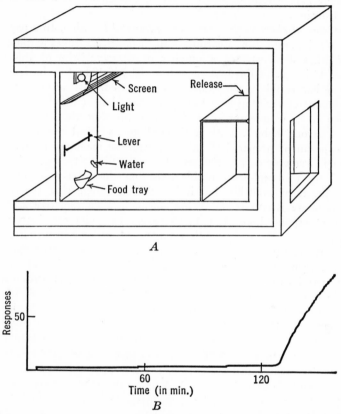

FIGURE 112. *A*. The Skinner bar-pressing apparatus. *B*. Sample cumulative record of original conditioning with every response reinforced. Skinner, *The Behavior of Organisms*, Appleton-Century-Crofts, New York, 1938, pp. 49, 67.

mechanism, and a small food pellet drops into the food tray beneath the animal's nose. This bar-pressing response is convenient for many reasons: it does not require any specific external stimulus to elicit it, being readily emitted by most subjects in the course of exploring the box; on the other hand, it does not occur so frequently without training that the course of learning is obscured (as compared with running or lifting up on the hind legs, for example) ; the response is relatively unambiguous, fairly constant in form, and easily recorded. The box serves to provide a roughly constant stimulus situation, the animal's own behavior and the release of food pellets being the only sources of variation. Since this bar-pressing activity is not directly controlled and elicited by manipulatable cues, the usual division of performance into trials cannot be made. Rather, each movement of the bar raises the arm of a recording device one step on a constantly revolving drum, thus automatically providing a cumulative record of total responses and their rate of emission. The height of the curve shown in Fig. 112*B* represents total number of pressings and the slope of the curve represents rate of responding. This gives a convenient and objective, if limited, record of behavior. Since the correct response (pressing the bar) must occur before reinforcement is given, this clearly is a case of instrumental learning.

Experimental characterization of instrumental learning. In a paper titled 'Simple Trial-and-error Learning—an Empirical Investigation,' Hull (1939 *b*) has demonstrated a number of characteristics of this type of learning. Using a modified Skinner box, in which both a horizontal and a vertical bar could be simultaneously presented, rats were first given a small amount of training at pressing one bar alone (initially weak habit) and then a large amount of training at pressing the other bar alone (initially strong habit). Both horizontal and vertical bars were present in the experiment proper, but only the response mediated by the initially weak habit was now correct and secured food pellets. This situation mimics the ordinary trial-and-error problem in that the correct response is not initially the most probable, but it has the advantage that the competing wrong response is specifiable. What phenomena characterize selection of the correct response here? (a) The stronger (wrong) reaction is the first to occur, and it is made repeatedly even though never reinforced. (b) This wrong reaction progressively weakens, shown here by the lengthening intervals between successive occurrences. (c) The weakening of the wrong reaction permits the weaker correct reaction to occur. (d) Presumably because the rate of recovery of the wrong reaction during periods when it is not being elicited (cf. *spontaneous recovery*) is more rapid than the rate of strengthening of the correct reaction, the wrong reaction often reappears after a number of correct reactions. (e) Alternation cycles between correct and incorrect reactions occur, the duration of the former increasing and of the latter decreasing until the correct reaction appears consistently.

Tolman and Krechevsky (1933) describe the trial-and-error process in somewhat different terms. When first introduced into the learning situation, the animal displays a broadly variable *means-end-readiness* (*MER*), such as 'exploratory behavior.' Within this general *MER*, the animal begins to attend to various specific features of the situation and to make certain specific responses (i.e. entering only the right-hand alleys) on the basis of certain *hypotheses* or *expectancies*. The animal may now try out still more refined hypotheses (the initial hypothesis now becoming itself an *MER*) or may revert to the general *MER* if the hypothesis is not confirmed. Once the correct hypothesis is discovered, it functions as a *docile habit,* mediating the achievement of a given end in the given situation. After numerous repetitions, this docile habit tends to become a *fixation,* and the animal finds it difficult to revert to the general *MER* if conditions are changed. Full reign is given to inferred cognitive events which are avoided in descriptions of the Hull type. The close relation of this level of analysis to phenomena of human problem-solving has been pointed out by Duncker and Krechevsky (1939).

One interesting characteristic of trial-and-error learning is the vacillation that takes place at choice points. The rat typically wavers back and forth, looking in one direction and then the other, sometimes making feints toward one place or the other. Tolman (1932) suggested that such truncated 'runnings-back-and-forth' serve to verify and strengthen the differentiation of critical cues—once the animal has crudely recognized or isolated the relevant stimuli. He relates this behavior on the part of the rat with the more purely implicit thinking in the human. Muenzinger (1938) has called this *vicarious trial and error* (*VTE*), vicarious because the animal 'goes through the motions' of trying the alternative responses without completing them. That this sampling activity facilitates learning is shown by several sources of evidence: peaks in *VTE* are usually correlated with sharp drops in error curves; any variable that increases *VTE*ing (such as administering shock in a discrimination situation) also increases learning efficiency; brain-damaged animals show less *VTE*ing and poorer learning; *VTE* usually drops out once a discrimination has been mastered, and it varies in amount with the difficulty of the discrimination. Relevant experimental literature may be found in Tolman (1938 *a*), Muenzinger (1938), Tolman and Minium (1942), Tolman and Ritchie (1943), and Tolman (1948).

In his unembellished model of the instrumental situation, Skinner has been able to describe many characteristics of this type of selection process. The bar-pressing response of the rat will show *extinction* if, after learning, conditions are changed so that pellets are no longer delivered—the rate of pressing gradually and irregularly slows until the cumulative response curve becomes essentially parallel to the base line. *Discrimination* appears as cyclic variations in the rate of response, when, for example, pellets are delivered only when a light is on but are eliminated when the animal is in darkness. The phenomenon of *disinhibition* can be shown by suddenly introducing any novel stimulus during an extinction period—the rate of responding suddenly increases. Certain phenomena observed in the Skinner box are characteristic only of that type of situation (e.g. where no specifiable stimulus complex elicits the correct response). For one thing, the animal spontaneously establishes a constant rate of responding, dependent upon such factors as the degree of motivation and the rate of reinforcement (one pellet every 3 minutes, every 6 minutes, and so on). The mechanism whereby an animal smoothly adjusts its rate of response under these conditions is unknown. Warren and Brown (1943), using apparatus in which lever-pressing produced pellets of candy, have demonstrated similar phenomena in young children.

Some common misconceptions about instrumental learning. There are many naïve assumptions about instrumental learning that the student—and his instructor in unguarded moments—is prone to make. Some of the more common ones will be considered here. (1) *That the varied responses made in the trial-and-error situation are a random sample from the animal's repertoire.* This conception has perhaps been fostered by gestalt critics of behavioristic theory in their characterization of trial-and-error learning as a 'blind' process. Actually, the behavior one observes is a narrow selection from the animal's potential activity. In the first place, the very nature of the *physical situation* restricts the behavior that can occur: the structure of a maze precludes certain responses and facilitates others. Since learning situations are never completely novel, many responses may be transferred from *previous learning* in terms of similar features: the cat in the puzzle box first tries to claw its way out and to squeeze through the slats. The nature of the animal's *motivation* also restricts potential behavior: to speed up isolation of the bar-pressing response in the Skinner box, for example, one may smear the bar with a little food. In general, the more the response required in an instrumental learning situation is compatible with the physical situation, is transferable from previous learning, and is already associated with the existing motivation, the more probable is its occurrence and hence the greater the speed of selection by this method.

(2) *That the cue stimulus is the one specified by the experimenter.* A common error on the part of both formal and informal experimenters is to assume that the cues *they* pay attention to are the only ones to which the subject is responding. For example, removal of a constant (but unessential) cue in the Skinner box, such as the 'click' made by the pellet release mechanism, may cause a temporary decline in the rate of bar-pressing. The animal subject is not telepathic and does not 'know' that any particular aspect of the total stimulus pattern is the critical one. An experiment by Kuo (1930) is interesting in this connection: cats were trained to fear rats by being shocked in a box that included one of their normal prey; after training, some cats were found to avoid rats-in-general (the 'correct' cue), others avoided only the box in which shock had been administered (showing what we might call intelligent discrimination), and yet others restricted their avoidant behavior to rats-in-boxes. Of course, many incidental stimuli fail to become associated with the response because they are variable: the illumination of a room, the chance sounds from the street, and so forth, vary from trial to trial and would not be expected to become components of the eliciting stimulus situation.

(3) *That only the correct response is strengthened by reinforcement.* When we ask, 'What is strengthened by giving the dog a piece of meat?' the pat answer is 'The response of lifting his paw.' But what sort of omniscience told the animal which response was right? Just before lifting the paw the dog had been whining—why isn't this behavior strengthened? 'Ah, well now,' replies the student, 'paw-lifting was the *last* response before reinforcement.' Was it, though? Suppose that just after lifting the paw (and before getting the food in its mouth) on trial #3, the dog happened to wag its tail; suppose that just after lifting the paw (and before getting food) on trial #7, the dog happened to flap its ears. Did the correct response go unreinforced on these trials? The answer must be 'no,' or otherwise no learning could occur since some activity is always intervening between the response we define as correct and the giving of reinforcement. We shall later describe evidence for a *gradient of reinforcement:* all responses occurring near in time to the point of reinforcement are strengthened, but to a degree varying with the temporal interval. The correct response is gradually selected from others which also occur (and are reinforced) because it is consistently followed by reinforcement, given the definition of 'correct.'

(4) *That the correct response is the same thing throughout learning.* The validity of this assumption depends upon one's level of observation and

description. When you identify the correct response of the dog as 'lifting the paw,' to be sure, some movement fitting this verbal mold must be made each time before reward is given. When Skinner specifies 'pressing the lever' as the correct response (and only observes the step-wise movements on the recording device), to be sure, some movement that effectively depresses the lever must be made if a pellet is to be released. At a more molecular level of analysis, however, the correct response can be shown to vary continuously—and the variability is lawful. The gross slashing movement with which the dog obtained reward on early trials (perhaps in attempts to scratch the meat from your hands) gradually becomes a precise, effortless lifting of the paw which is now accompanied by vigorous salivation. Rather than simple selection of an isolated response, instrumental learning involves a complex shift in total behavior within the situation, and the more elaborate an experimenter's techniques of observation, the more complicated the supposedly constant correct response.

Conditioning

It was Pavlov who, in the course of extensive studies on the physiology of the digestive glands, first described conditioning phenomena. He noted that stimuli which regularly antedated the appearance of food—the sight of the food pan, the smell of the food, and even the footsteps of the approaching experimenter—came to elicit 'psychic' secretion of the salivary glands. *Conditioned Reflexes* (1927) reported detailed observations on this salivary response, and Pavlov's work has served as the reference experiment for conditioning much as Skinner's (1938) work on the bar-pressing response was later to serve as a model for instrumental learning. Both have the advantage of an extreme simplicity (at least superficially) which highlights empirical relations. A word may be in order on the meaning of 'conditioned': in contemporary American psychology the term has become practically synonymous with 'learned'—one even reads that 'the child becomes *conditioned* to say "please" for a piece of candy.' Pavlov meant that the occurrence of the reflex to a novel cue was literally *conditional* upon certain operations, chiefly repeated association of the novel cue with an adequate stimulus.

Significantly the subtitle of Pavlov's book was 'An Investigation of the Physiological Activity of the Cerebral Cortex.' He looked upon conditioning chiefly as a *method* for studying the physiology of the brain. It was probably Watson, in his presidential address before the American Psychological Association in 1915 and later in his texts (1919, 1925), who was responsible for the introduction of 'conditioning' into American psychology. Watson had stressed philosophical materialism and scientific objectivity, and he had specified 'habit' as the psychological building block. He recognized in the conditioned reflex a yet more fundamental unit for behaviorism, and in his hands it became, not a mere method, but the *explanation* of behavior. During the 1930's, Hull (cf. 1937) was to use Pavlovian observations as a fertile *source of principles,* presumably applicable to behavior in general. Of these points of view, Pavlov's own emphasis upon conditioning as a method is perhaps the most defensible, for conditioning is certainly not *the* explanation of all behavior nor is the Pavlovian model the most representative learning situation.

The essential characteristic defining the conditioning method is that (a) *the reinforcing stimulus originally elicits the correct response:* the shock elicits lifting of the paw; food in the mouth elicits salivation. This clearly segregates conditioning from instrumental learning, in which the correct response must occur *before* reinforcement is given. A number of supporting conditions may also be mentioned. (b) The new stimulus must occur in sufficiently close temporal proximity to the reinforcing stimulus if conditioning is to occur. (c) Although elimination of incidental stimuli is not essential to this method, conditioning is definitely facilitated by minimizing such disruptive factors. The usual procedure is to restrict the general activity of the animal by placing it in a harness and to carry on the investigation in a rigidly stabilized environment (soundproof room, etc.).

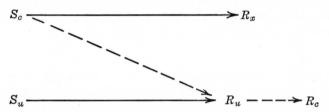

FIGURE 113. Classical conditioning paradigm. A reaction (R_u), initially elicited by unconditional stimulus (S_u) comes to be elicited by conditional stimulus (S_c), whereupon it is called a conditioned reaction (R_c). Behavior initially elicited by conditional stimulus (R_x) is usually not recorded.

(d) The 'natural' (reflexive or previously learned) responses to the to-be-conditioned signal must not be such as to interfere with the response elicited by the reinforcing stimulus: it would be difficult, for example, to use shock to one foot as a signal for flexion of the contralateral limb.

Figure 113 shows the standard conditioning paradigm, conventionally labeled. The initially inadequate stimulus or signal (S_c) is usually called the 'conditioned stimulus'; it would be more accurate to call it the *conditional stimulus,* since its capacity to evoke the desired reaction is conditional upon certain procedures. In the homely model we have been following, S_c would be the sound of 'give me paw.' The initially adequate, or reinforcing, stimulus (S_u) is usually called the 'unconditioned stimulus'; *unconditional stimulus* would be better, since its essential characteristic is that, within the given experimental situation, it regularly and unfailingly produces the desired reaction. Shock to the footpad reliably produces paw-lifting on the part of the canine subject. The varied behaviors originally elicited by S_c, that is, prior to the establishment of the new conditioned reaction, are here designated as R_x. In our example it would include such 'natural' responses to your voice as lifting the ears, looking at your face, barking, and wagging the tail. These responses are seldom recorded in conditioning experiments. The reaction to the unconditional stimulus is generally called the *unconditioned response* (R_u)—until it comes to be elicited by the new, conditional stimulus, whereupon it suddenly becomes the 'correct' *conditioned response* (R_c). Lifting the paw is initially produced by shock and is called unconditioned; after training, the 'same' response occurs at the sound of your voice, without the necessity of shock, and it is now called a conditioned response. Conditioning is often dubbed 'substitution learning,' the response made to an initially adequate stimulus being shifted to an initially inadequate stimulus. But this is an entirely naïve conception, as we soon shall see.

The range of organisms, stimuli, and reactions that have been used in conditioning experiments is practically unlimited (cf. Hilgard and Marquis, 1940, pp. 29-36). Worms, crabs, pigeons, rats, sheep, monkeys, and man have all served as subjects. The reactions elicited range from those highly involuntary (gastrointestinal, pupillary, and vasomotor), through striate muscle reflexes (flexion of leg, knee jerk, and eyelid closure), to what are usually spoken of as voluntary responses (withdrawal, swallowing, previously conditioned responses). Unconditional stimuli, of course, depend upon the reactions being conditioned (i.e. change in illumination for the pupillary reaction, patellar blow for the knee jerk, electric shock for withdrawal movements, and so on). And conditional stimuli are legion; the only limitation here is that the stimuli be manipulatable by the experimenter, at least as to their presence or absence. Despite this range of organisms, reactions, and stimuli, however, the procedural variation among experiments fitting the conditioning paradigm is less than among those fitting the instrumental paradigm, and two conditioning experiments will suffice as illustrations.

Pavlov chose to study the *salivary reaction* because this response could be easily quantified, was relatively independent of age and other such variables, and was 'high' in the hierarchy of reflexes in the sense that it is not readily inhibited by other on-going activities. By means of a minor preliminary operation, the salivary duct was transplanted to the surface of the cheek so that saliva now flowed to the outside and could be collected and measured by suitable apparatus. To eliminate the 'veritable chaos' of conflicting stimuli from the outside world, Pavlov and his assistants worked in a specially constructed building, in soundproof rooms with a partition separating experimenter and subject. (It was found that the mere presence of the experimenter, the sound of footsteps, and the like tended to vitiate experiments.) We come now to the experimental procedure itself, and it may be described in Pavlov's own words: 'The fundamental requisite is that any external stimulus which is to become the signal in a conditioned reflex must overlap in point of time with the action of an unconditioned stimulus. In the experiment which I chose as my example, the unconditioned stimulus was food. Now if the intake of food by the animal takes place simultaneously with the action of a neutral stimulus which has been hitherto in no way related to food, the neutral stimulus readily acquires the property of eliciting the same reaction in the animal as would food itself. This was the case with the dog employed in our experiment with the metronome. On several occasions this animal had been stimulated by the sound of the metronome and immediately presented with food—i.e. a stimulus which was neutral of itself had been superimposed upon the action of the inborn alimentary reflex. We observed that, after several repetitions of the combined stimulation, the sounds from the metronome had acquired the property of stimulating salivary secretion and of evoking the motor reactions characteristic of the alimentary reflex' (1927, p. 26).

A series of experiments by Hilgard (1931, 1933 a, 1933 b), Hilgard and Marquis (1935, 1936), and Hilgard and Campbell (1936) have provided precise comparative data on dogs, monkeys, and men, the reaction conditioned being the *wink reflex of the eyelid* when a sudden puff of air strikes the eye. As shown in Fig. 114, the subject's head is held rigidly in such a position that the light, stiff paper markers attached to the eyelids cast a sharp shadow on a slit past which photographic paper moves on a pendulum device (Dodge photochronograph). The same pendulum triggers both the conditional stimulus (light) and the unconditional stimulus (airpuff), the onset and duration of these stimuli being recorded on the sensitive paper along with the eye-movement response. The series of records in Fig. 115 indicate the precision obtainable by this method. Record *A* depicts

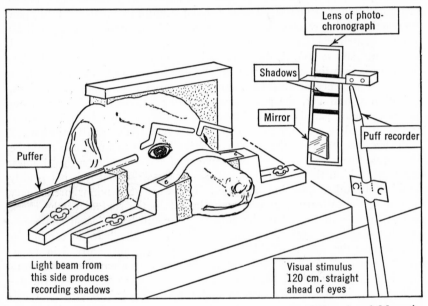

FIGURE 114. Dog subject in eyeblink conditioning apparatus. Hilgard and Marquis, *Journal of Comparative Psychology*, 1935, 19:31.

behavior characteristic of the beginning of conditioning; record *B* shows the anticipatory conditioned reflex (*CR*) to the light, followed by the response to the puff itself (*R*$_p$); record *C* shows the similar lid reflex obtained when only the light is used after sufficient training. Observe that it is not necessary to have test trials without the airpuff with this method, since the conditioned response appears previous to the airpuff as learning proceeds. The symbol *R*$_l$ indicates the slight reflexive *opening* of the eyes of this canine subject occasioned by the onset of the bright light. In man, interestingly enough, the reflexive reaction to the light is a slight *closure* of the eyelids. Another difference between species is that although the conditioned response of the dog is restricted mainly to the puffed eye, it appears also in the nonpuffed eye of both man and monkey (although with less amplitude in the case of the human).

Experimental characterization of conditioning. Most standard conditioning phenomena were described in Pavlov's original work, but later students have checked these observations and in some cases modified them. The experimental literature before 1934 is summarized by Hull (1934 *d*), and we shall add certain significant recent contributions. A number of phenomena—habit formation, extinction, spontaneous recovery, generalization, and short circuiting—will be treated separately at a later point.

We may first direct our attention to certain temporal factors. The principle of *contiguity,* long recognized by association psychologists, was also stressed by Pavlov. On the basis of research conducted in his own labora-

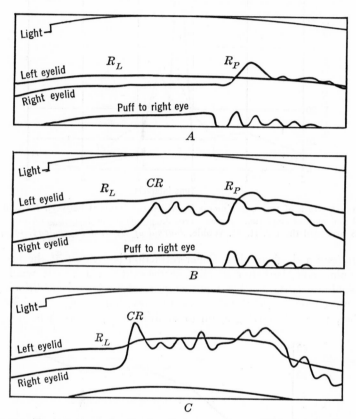

FIGURE 115. Typical stages in the development of a conditioned response of the eyelid to light: (*A*) reflexive reaction to puff; (*B*) delayed *CR* to light reinforced by puff; (*C*) prompt *CR* to light. Hilgard and Marquis, *Journal of Comparative Psychology,* 1935, 19:36.

tory, he concluded that conditioned reflexes could be formed when the conditional stimulus preceded the unconditional stimulus by a short interval or was synchronous with it, but not if the conditional stimulus came after the unconditional stimulus. In other words, he denies the possibility of 'backward conditioning.' Switzer (1930), with the eyelid reflex, and Wolfle (1930, 1932), with finger retraction to a shock stimulus, have demonstrated what appears to be 'backward conditioning,' but the phenomenon is sharply limited in time (about 1 sec. maximum) and weak in magnitude. Wolfle's 1930 data are shown in Fig. 116. Spooner and Kellogg (1947) indicate that 'backward conditioning' is an entirely different phenomenon from forward conditioning. When the percentage of conditioned reactions (finger-retractions) per presentation of the conditional stimulus (buzzer) is plotted as a function of degree of training, *the 'backward' sequence shows a decrease with trials* rather than the learning curve displayed by the forward sequence. In other words, the tendency for a buzzer

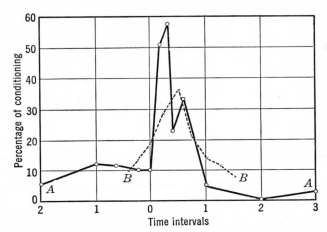

FIGURE 116. Data of two experiments in which the interval between *CS* and *US* is varied and ease of conditioning measured. At points to the left of *O* on the abscissa the *US* preceded the *CS*. H. M. Wolfle, *Journal of General Psychology*, 1932, 7:90.

that *follows* a shock to elicit finger-retraction is greatest at the beginning of training and thereafter steadily decreases (Fig. 117). It would seem that Pavlov was right—that reported cases of 'backward conditioning' are spurious, owing to *sensitization* of the reaction in all probability (cf. Grether, 1938). Referring again to Wolfle's data, it should be noted that

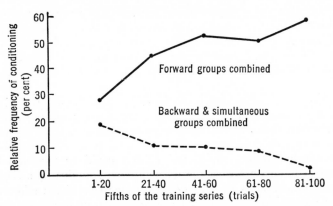

FIGURE 117. Performance curves for forward conditioning and 'backward conditioning' groups. Spooner and Kellogg, *American Journal of Psychology*, 1947, 60: 328.

conditioning occurs most readily when the conditional stimulus precedes the unconditional stimulus by a short interval (approximately .5 sec.). This is a widely reported phenomenon and probably reflects some fundamental fact about the central neurology of associational processes.

As the interval between S_c and S_u is prolonged, the delay in appearance of the CR adjusts to the size of the interval, always antedating the occurrence of S_u but less and less precisely as the length of the necessary delay increases. Since no specifiable stimuli occur during the delay interval, it is assumed that the reaction is conditioned to the trace of the conditional stimulus, hence the designation *trace conditioned reflexes*. Reynolds (1945 *a*) has shown that ease of establishing such trace reactions varies inversely with the length of the interval (beyond .450 sec.). If the conditional stimulus (e.g. a tone) persists through the delay interval, delays of many seconds can be successfully maintained, as the sample record obtained by Switzer (1934) shows (Fig. 118). This is known as a *delayed conditioned reflex*.

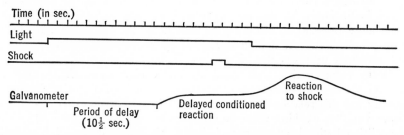

Time (in sec.)

Light

Shock

Galvanometer

Reaction to shock

Period of delay (10½ sec.)

Delayed conditioned reaction

FIGURE 118. Record of a delayed conditioned reflex. *CS* (light) antedates *US* (shock) by about 17 seconds; *CR* appears after a delay of about 10½ seconds (Hull, after data of Switzer, 1934). Murchison, *Handbook of Experimental Psychology,* Clark University Press, Worcester, Mass., 1934, p. 421.

It seemed reasonable to Pavlov to assume that the capacity of an organism to make both trace and delayed conditioned reactions depended upon some inhibitory processes: something must prevent the animal from salivating during the delay interval, since the association of salivation with the conditional stimulus has been established. Other observations substantiated this assumption. Conditioned reactions are susceptible to *external inhibition:* if, during the course of conditioning, a sudden and novel stimulus is introduced, the CR may fail to occur, and this is the reason Pavlov made such elaborate precautions to exclude incidental stimuli. What he termed *internal inhibition* (cf. *experimental extinction*) occurs when S_c is presented repeatedly without reinforcement by S_u—the CR gradually diminishes in strength until it fails entirely. Since the extinguished reaction shows partial recovery with rest (cf. *spontaneous recovery*), it would again seem that some inhibitory process is involved. For the phenomena of trace and delayed reactions, Pavlov postulates *inhibition of delay.* The presence of some active inhibitory process during such delay intervals is certainly suggested by the related phenomenon of *disinhibition:* if a novel stimulus is presented during the interval through which a dog is withholding a salivary reaction, the animal suddenly salivates copiously, i.e. the specific inhibitory process itself has been externally inhibited, releasing the positive reactive process.

Several of Pavlov's observations have not received sufficient attention from later investigators. He found, for example, that if the sound of a metronome had been strongly conditioned to salivation, a new conditional stimulus (black square) could be made a signal for salivation simply by presenting it in conjunction with the sound of the metronome—the first-order conditioned stimulus is here serving as the reinforcement for *second-order conditioning* (cf. *secondary reinforcement*). Pavlov and his associates were unable to extend this process beyond third-order conditioning. This process is certainly greatly extended in human learning, however, especially in the area of language behavior. Another relatively unexplored Pavlovian observation is that of *positive and negative induction*. Let us suppose that a tone has been conditioned to salivation, whereas a light has only been associated with the inhibition of this reaction (by being presented only during delay or extinction periods). Now if the inhibitory light is shown for a short period and is followed immediately by the excitatory tone, the flow of saliva may be as much as 100 per cent greater than normal (positive induction). Conversely, if a period of excitation with the tone is followed immediately by shining the light, the resultant inhibition proves much more resistant to disinhibition than normally (negative induction). Both processes suggest a high degree of reciprocality between excitatory and inhibitory processes that richly deserves further study.

Pavlov reported that both speed of conditioning and resistance to extinction varied with the *intensity of the unconditional stimulus,* but only recently has this relation been substantiated in systematic experimentation. Passey (1948), working with the eyelid reflex, varied the intensity of the unconditional stimulus (pressure of airpuff) through 5 degrees for as many groups of human subjects, the conditional stimulus being a tone of constant duration, frequency, and amplitude. The course of acquisition of the CR was measured through 50 paired presentations of tone and puff, and the course of extinction was followed through ten unreinforced presentations of the tone. Typical negatively accelerated learning curves were obtained for all intensities of S_u, as can be seen in Fig. 119, but both rate and final limit of conditioning increased as logarithmic functions of the intensity of the airpuff—a result in keeping with Pavlov's findings.

Some common misconceptions about conditioning. Naïveté with regard to conditioning is due in part to acceptance of the Pavlovian experiment and the theory it fostered as definitive. It is due more to the fond hope that the process would prove as simple as conventional diagrams imply. The phenomena of conditioning are actually very complicated, as analysis of the following erroneous assumptions will show.

(1) *That the unconditional stimulus must bear a reflexive relation to the correct response.* Pavlov's usage of the term 'conditioned reflex' implies that S_u must be some stimulus that elicits its response without previous learning—which may be true in some cases, as in the use of food or acid to produce salivation—but the only *requirement* is that, within the framework of a given experiment, some manipulatable stimulus reliably evoke the desired reaction. This was actually demonstrated in Pavlov's own laboratory by experiments on second-order conditioning. Finch and Culler (1934 *b*) established an avoidance CR to a 1000-cycle tone, based upon shock to the paw, and then extended this CR to a light, thence to a squirt of water on the nose, thence to an electric bell, thence to an electric fan—in each case by associating the new, neutral stimulus with the immediately previous conditional stimulus. Under these conditions (avoidance training), the transition from one S_c to the next became easier at each step. Most convincing

evidence that S_u need not bear a reflexive relation to the correct response appears in experiments in which the response is produced initially by instructions, that is, voluntarily. Thus Marquis and Porter (1939) instructed their subjects to wink when they heard a soft sound; by having a light regularly antedate the sound, the wink reaction was conditioned to the light. Notice that a soft tone such as this is not itself capable of eliciting reflexive winking; it is merely the cue for the subject to execute his voluntary wink.

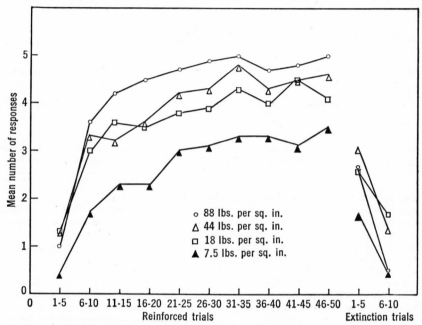

FIGURE 119. Mean number of *CR*'s during 50 reinforced and 10 unreinforced trials for groups of subjects given different intensities of *US*. Passey, *Journal of Experimental Psychology*, 1948, **38**:423.

(2) *That the unconditioned response is that specified by the experimenter.* Just as was the case in instrumental learning, complexity and variability in the 'correct' response depend upon the experimenter's techniques of observation. Pavlov measured only salivary secretion. Liddell and his co-workers (cf. 1942) have broadened the observational base. Working with salivary conditioning in the pig, for example (cf. Marcuse and Moore, 1944, 1945), they recorded head movements, general activity, respiration, and heart rate along with secretion. The sample record in Fig. 120 indicates the complexity of the response to the food stimulus (notice especially the records for general activity, respiration, and heart rate). Similar observations are reported by Liddell for reflexive avoidance of shock: lifting the leg is only a small part of the total response; complex postural adjustments, autonomic reactions (changes in skin resistance, breathing, pulse rate), and many other components make up the total reaction.

(3) *That unconditioned and conditioned reactions are identical.* The Pavlovian analysis leads one to believe that *UR* and *CR* are essentially

identical, except for the stimuli that evoke them, hence the conventional term 'substitution learning.' This view has developed in the face of facts, by arbitrary restriction of observation to isolated components of the subject's total behavior—restriction to those components (i.e. salivation) that happen to be common to unconditioned and conditioned reactions. The following description of conditioned leg flexion given by Culler (1938 a) provides a more accurate picture. 'From training scores of dogs at Illinois, we can predict, when a shock is applied to a wholly naïve animal, that its response will include many of these features: quick gasp or yelp, hasty with-

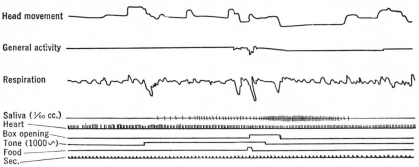

FIGURE 120. Salivary conditioned reflex in the pig. At the sounding of a tone (indicated by upstroke, third line from bottom), pig begins to secrete saliva in anticipation of food. Vertical strokes (sixth line from bottom) indicate flow of saliva in 1/60 cc. portions. Notice that anticipatory secretion of saliva increases until food drops into the box. Dropping of food (a small dog biscuit) into box is indicated by upstroke, second line from bottom. When biscuit drops, pig noses open cover of food box (shown by upstroke, fourth line from bottom). Copious secretion of saliva caused by chewing the biscuit is shown in closely packed vertical lines on secretion record. Fifth line from bottom shows heart beats, each beat giving two upstrokes of the signal magnet. Second line from top indicates general activity of the pig. Notice the almost complete absence of general movement until just before food is given. Liddell in F. A. Moss, *Comparative Psychology*, rev. ed., Prentice-Hall, Inc., New York, 1942, p. 189.

drawal of foot, adduction of tail, then whining or barking, biting or snapping at nearby objects, twisting and jerking, occasional evacuation. . . Now suppose a bell be rung just before the shock. After a few times, we witness a display of behavior (as soon as the sound begins) which seems to duplicate the actual UR; indeed, so realistic is the animal's performance that I have sometimes been misled into thinking that shock was being inadvertently applied along with bell. . . Thereafter (the UR and CR) diverge, each in accord with its own function. . . After a dog is often shocked, the same charge applied to the same place no longer yields this loose and widespread activity. It yields rather a quick, effective removal of foot, which is then slowly replaced. . . [The CR] also is changing, but its function is not to *react* to US itself, but to *get ready* for US, to make preparatory adjustments for an oncoming stimulus. . . Warner (1932) complains of his fruitless quest for a real CR in rats. To the shock (US) they would hop frantically about and breathe rapidly; to CS (bell) they would hold the breath and wait tensely' (pp. 135-6).

This conception of the conditioned response as a *preparatory adjustment* to the unconditional stimulus is a widely held view and applies reasonably to many experimental and life situations, but, as Hilgard and Marquis

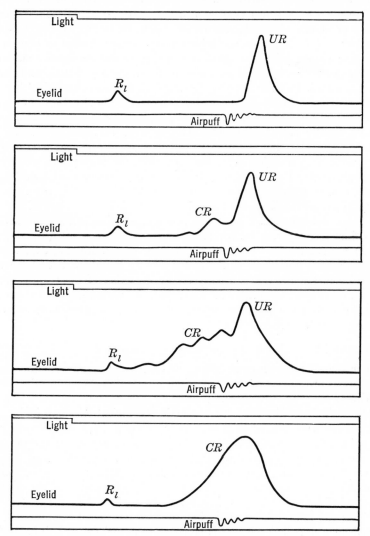

FIGURE 121. Records from a single human subject showing stages in the development of a conditioned eyelid response. Notice that at no point is the *CR* simply 'substituted' for the *UR*, nor is it completely identical to the *UR*. Hilgard and Marquis, *Conditioning and Learning*, Appleton-Century-Crofts, Inc., New York, 1940, p. 38.

(1940, p. 40) state, this is merely an evaluative description by the experimenter, and it leaves unexplained how such adaptive selection occurs. We shall return to this problem. Another common interpretation of the conditioned response, which also applies to many experimental and life situations, is that the *CR* represents *fractional components* of the total *UR*.

From the splurge of behavior initially set off by shock, only a precise poising of the paw, accompanied by a slight holding of the breath and change in heart rate, may survive in the conditioned response to the tone. The *CR* may be composed in part of new elements, reactions that never were included in the *UR*. Witness Warner's (1932) observation on the 'expectant' behavior of rats to a bell which preceded shock. Of special interest was this observation by Liddell: in conditioning leg flexion to the ticking of a metronome (shock being the *US*), it was found that the conditional stimulus elicited changes in breathing and skin resistance *before* any conditioned flexion appeared. In other words, the sound of the metronome had become a sign of 'danger' before any adjustive reaction to the situation developed.

Even where *CR* appears to be a replica of *UR,* sufficiently detailed analysis will usually reveal differences. If one were to casually observe the subject's eyelid, the final conditioned response to light (lower part of Fig. 121) would seem identical with the unconditioned response to an airpuff (upper diagram). But, as careful inspection of these records reveals, the original *UR* is a jerky, reflexive closure of the lid, whereas the eventual *CR* is a smooth gradual type of reaction. At no point does the *CR* become 'substituted' for the *UR*. Rather, the reflexive reaction persists throughout the gradual development of the anticipatory reaction. Hull (1934 *d,* pp. 427-30) has summarized data from a number of conditioning experiments to show that the amplitude of the *CR* is usually less than that of the *UR* and the latency of the *CR* is usually longer than that of the *UR*. We may conclude that the conditioned reaction is not 'the same thing as' the unconditioned reaction, and therefore any simple substitution explanation of conditioning is inadequate.

Instrumental Learning and Conditioning Compared

On the face of things, conditioning and trial and error seem to be two quite distinct processes, two different kinds of learning. What are the salient differences? (1) In instrumental learning the correct response appears *spontaneously* from the subject's available repertoire; in conditioning the correct response is *elicited* by a specifiable stimulus (S_u). Skinner (1938) has emphasized this distinction, referring to the former (spontaneous emission) as *operant behavior* and to the latter (stimulus elicited) as *respondent behavior*. In discussing operant behavior, Skinner states: 'An operant is an identifiable part of behavior of which it may be said, not that no stimulus can be found that will elicit it (there may be a respondent the response of which has the same topography), but that no correlated stimulus can be detected upon occasions when it is observed to occur' (p. 21). The critical difference thus seems to lie in the specifiability of the eliciting conditions. (2) In instrumental learning the tutor passively 'waits' for the correct response to happen, but in conditioning the tutor deliberately produces the correct response—the conditioning method is therefore more *efficient*. This difference, of course, depends on the specifiability and manipulatability of the eliciting stimuli discussed above. (3) By definition, the 'reinforcement' follows the occurrence of the correct response in instrumental learning; by definition, the stimulus which originally elicits (and therefore precedes) the correct response is the 'reinforcing agent' in conditioning. Whether or not we consider conditioning and instrumental learning to be different 'kinds' of learning comes down to whether or not these two *strengthening opera-tions* are as different fundamentally as they appear superficially.

STRENGTHENING

What are the necessary and sufficient conditions for the occurrence of that more-or-less permanent modification of behavior we call learning? All theorists agree that one necessary condition is that the correct response occur reasonably close in time to the critical cue, i.e. all theorists agree that *con-tiguity* is one necessary condition. But is this a *sufficient* condition? Is any additional operation also necessary, and if so, what is it? It is here that con-temporary theorists part company. In a subsequent chapter we shall study various contemporary theories of learning in some detail; for the present our interest lies solely in how they differ with respect to their views on strengthening.

Contiguity Sufficient (Guthrie)

Guthrie assumes that the sheer occurrence of a stimulus and a response in contiguity results in complete association between them; any subsequent failure of this stimulus to be accompanied by this response results in com-plete dissociation. The gradualness characteristic of most learning phenom-ena is explained by the variations, trial by trial, in what stimuli acquire such all-or-nothing associations with the response. Both instrumental learn-ing and conditioning are viewed as particular instances of the operation of this very general principle. In the former case the apparent efficacy of rein-forcement following an $S–R$ contingency is explained in terms of the change in stimulation this operation produces. The all-or-nothing associations are preserved, since reinforcement and the changes it produces in the subject eliminate the original stimuli, i.e. they are no longer present to become associated with any other, interfering responses. In the case of conditioning, the role of US is simply to assure that the correct response does occur con-tiguously with the critical new cues. Many problems are raised by this superficially simple theory and they will be discussed in a subsequent theo-retical chapter.

The Unconditional Stimulus as the Reinforcing Agent (Pavlov)

According to Pavlov, the necessary strengthening operation was the pairing of the CS with the $US;$ when this operation was omitted, the new learned association showed progressive weakening. But is this general or is it specific to the type of learning situation in which Pavlov happened to in-terest himself? Brogden (1939 a) has tested the generality of this strength-ening principle (and, incidentally, offered one of the rare cases in which substitution and reinforcement principles are directly compared). Using classic Pavlovian procedures, he trained dogs to make leg withdrawal re-sponses to a bell, shock being the unconditional stimulus. Each correct re-sponse was also rewarded by food. To test the efficacy of the Pavlovian prin-ciple, the shock was then omitted. The conditioned reaction was maintained for as many as 1000 trials (when tests were concluded) in the absence of shock—as long as food was regularly given. Since it cannot be argued that food-in-the-mouth is an unconditional stimulus for leg flexion, this is conclusive evidence that reinforcement in the Pavlovian sense is not necessary for maintaining the strength of an association.

Drive Reduction as Reinforcement (Hull)

In the Brogden experiment the learned association persisted as long as a food reward was given the hungry dog following each reaction. Can this type of strengthening principle be shown to be general? The most detailed attempt to rationalize the differences between instrumental learning and conditioning has been made by Hull. At the core of his theoretical system (cf. pp. 372ff.) is a 'reinforcement principle,' which may be paraphrased as follows: whenever a response process is closely contiguous to a stimulus process, and this association occurs near in time to the *reduction of a drive,* the association is strengthened. Reinforcement is defined in terms of drive reduction, drive in turn being defined in terms of physiological 'needs' of the organism. In ordinary reward training, it is clear that consuming the goal-object (e.g. food pellet) can start in motion those events which result in some reduction of a need state; in escape training, when the drive state is unpleasant in character (e.g. shock to the footpads), it is the *termination* of the pain which is reinforcing.

The applicability of the reinforcement principle to cases of instrumental learning is self-evident—instrumental learning situations are, by definition, those in which the correct response is followed by reinforcement. Conditioning is treated as a special case of instrumental learning (Hull, 1943, pp. 69-79). A dog, habituated to stand in a stock, has its foot in a soft leather moccasin with an electrifiable grid in its sole which is attached to a hinged board held down by a coil spring. The shock (S_u), which produces lifting of the paw, is regularly preceded by a buzzer (S_c), whose sound persists until the response is made. Afte.' a sufficient number of pairings, the buzzer comes to elicit foot-lifting—conditioning has occurred. Figure 122 describes Hull's analysis in his symbol system. The shock (S_u) reliably elicits the correct response (R_u), this movement being followed by drive reduction (e.g. elimination of the painful shock). We have, therefore, the necessary conditions for strengthening the new association between buzzer and paw-lifting $(S_c \rightarrow R_u)$. A similar analysis can be applied to Pavlov's classic, in which the unconditional stimulus (food powder) not only elicits the salivary reaction but is simultaneously a reinforcement (reducing hunger drive).

What is the essence of Hull's integration? He makes the assumption that every conditioning situation includes a drive state which is reduced by making the correct response. The unconditioned stimulus thus has a dual role: functioning as a cue, it reliably elicits the correct response; functioning as a drive producer, which the animal's movement can escape (e.g. shock), or as a drive reducer (e.g. food powder), it provides the necessary conditions for strengthening new associations. Hull's interpretation is bolstered by a number of studies which show that situations definable as conditioning may display relations characteristic of instrumental learning. For example, McDonald (1946) found that when human subjects were allowed to adapt to noxious stimuli (shock to finger, airpuff to eyeball) that were later to serve as unconditional stimuli in conditioning training, they yielded significantly poorer conditioning than a control group. This was true despite that fact that reflexive reactions to these stimuli were not diminished. According to this evidence, it is the capacity of the uncondi- tional stimulus to arouse a motivational state which can be reduced by the correct reaction that determines its effectiveness in learning (cf. also studies by Rogers and Bayroff, 1943, and Daniel, 1944).

From this analysis one is led to conclude that instrumental learning and conditioning differ in no fundamental respect, reinforcement being a neces- sary condition for both forms of selection. Conditioning is merely a more

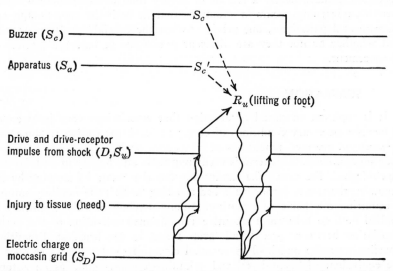

FIGURE 122. Drive reduction reinforcement interpretation of Pavlovian conditioning. Onset of the unconditional stimulus (as a cue stimulus) serves to elicit the correct reaction and its termination (as a drive stimulus) serves to strengthen preceding associations, specifically that between the conditional stimulus and the correct re- action. Hull, *Principles of Behavior*, Appleton-Century-Crofts, Inc., New York, 1943, p. 77.

efficient way of getting the correct response to occur. But do all condition- ing situations involve drive reduction? What drive is reduced in condi- tioning the eyeblink? Of course, the puff of air against the cornea may be considered an irritating and hence motivating state. Although it is ap- parently difficult to condition the knee jerk, it has been done (cf. Wendt, 1930), and one is hard put to specify what drive is initiated by the blow to the patellar tendon and reduced by the knee jerk itself. What motivation can be specified in voluntary conditioning, when the 'unconditional stimulus' is the subject's self-instruction to respond? These questions pose one of the significant problems for theory—is reinforcement necessary for learning?— which we shall consider later in Chapter 10.

Two-factor Interpretations

The views described above are monistic in that all learning phenomena are reduced to a single strengthening principle. In more recent years there has been a trend toward dualistic conceptions. Maier and Schneirla (1942), Birch and Bitterman (1949), and Mowrer (1947, 1950) have described theories that agree in the specification of two kinds of learning, though they differ in details, and the two kinds are what we have described as conditioning and instrumental learning. These writers feel that sheer contiguity may be sufficient in some cases but the additional operation of reinforcement is necessary in others. Another contemporary theorist, Tolman, is difficult to localize in this system, chiefly because he appears to have changed his views considerably in the period between his early (cf. 1932) and more recent writings (cf. 1949). The underlying nature of the strengthening operation is more nearly a matter of theory than of fact; there is agreement that learning occurs in situations that fit both the conditioning and instrumental paradigms, but precisely what the crucial operations may be and whether or not they are different paradigms at base are matters of disagreement.

SUMMATION

It is apparent to casual observation that associations vary in strength. When the necessary conditions of contiguity and (according to some) reinforcement are met, repetitions of an association increase its strength, e.g. it becomes a *habit*. This term is used frequently and loosely in both lay and psychological discourse. The family dog has the 'habit' of sleeping by the fireplace; the family father has a bad smoking 'habit'; the family youngster is acquiring the 'habit' of swearing. Among psychologists the term may be applied both to behavioral minutiae (conditioned salivation or the verbal association between 'green' and 'grass') and to the broadest dispositions (paying attention in school or personal cleanliness). It appears at once as the equivalent of 'mental set' and 'stimulus-response-bond,' as an autonomous, dynamic determinant of behavior and a passive, cognitive connection that must be energized by motives. Historically, habit came into prominence in the writing of William James (cf. his *Principles*) and those of the Functionalists of the Chicago School (Angell, Dewey, Judd, and others), all under the influence of Darwinism with its emphasis upon the adaptive character of behavior. Since the habit conception has been developed most extensively within Hull's theory, we shall follow his analysis in the main.

Logical Status of the Habit Concept

Is it necessary to have any habit conception in psychological science? Is there anything about behavior that demands this type of conceptualization? Through certain procedures we produce a modification in the behavior of a dog to the sound of a buzzer: it now lifts its leg when that stimulus is given. The first thing we observe is that this behavioral modification *persists through time;* it can be elicited a day, a week, or perhaps even a year after the original training. Another thing we observe is that this training has added a certain *consistency* to the animal's stream of behaving; on repeated occasions of a specifiable kind (a buzzer sounding in a certain laboratory room), this organism responds in ways that can be called 'the same.' Even though these consistencies in behavior which persist through time are observable only when appropriate stimulus conditions are arranged—between stimulus presentations there is nothing to be 'seen'—we infer that some *theoretically* measurable modifications in the nervous system have taken place. In other words, it is because certain consistencies in behavior persist in time that we must infer the existence of some quasipermanent change in the organism, and to this unobservable change we usually give the name 'habit.'

The habit construct thus has the scientific status of a *hypothetical construct*. Like the meson, neutron, and positron of modern physics, the habit cannot be directly observed and its quantity must therefore be *inferred* from events that can be apprehended and measured. That Hull thought of the habit as an actual entity which might conceivably be directly measured with future techniques is evident when he said (1943, p. 102), '. . . it exists as an organization as yet largely unknown, hidden within the complex structure of the nervous system.' Within the formal context of his theory, the habit-strength construct ($_sH_R$) also has the status of an *intervening variable*. It is assumed to reflect summatively the effects of certain antecedent, determining variables (such as number of reinforced repetitions, amount of reinforcement, etc.) and, in conjunction with additional intervening variables such as drive (D), to mediate reaction variables. Concepts of this order are useful in science to the extent that the functions relating them to both antecedent and subsequent conditions are specified, or, as Hull put it, to the extent that they are 'anchored' to observables. A basic equation relating these variables in Hull's theory is:

$$_sE_R = f(_sH_R) \times f(D)$$

which states that *reaction potential* is equal to some function of the *habit strength* associating a given stimulus with a given response *multiplied by* some function of *drive*. It should be noted that Hull does draw a distinction between performance and learned habit; the habit must be energized by some amount of motivation if the reaction systems of the organism are to be thrown into action.

Indices of Habit Strength

On a common-sense level, what changes in behavior do we expect to be correlated with increasing strength of a habit? For one thing, the *probability* of the correct response occurring when the critical cue is given should increase—as trials progress, the likelihood of paw-lifting to 'give me paw' becomes greater. For another thing, the *amplitude* of the correct response should increase with training. Although this would certainly hold for many conditioned reactions (such as salivation in the Pavlovian situation), it is not apparent in all learning situations. The smooth, precise movement with which the big-league catcher whips the ball to second base is certainly less amplitudinous than the sprawling attempt of the high-school girl. The problem here may be one of specifying those movements which are being learned. A third indexing correlate of habit strength is *latency*: as the dog's paw-lifting habit becomes stronger, the delay between presentation of the stimulus and occurrence of the response should decrease—the reaction should become more prompt. Another index is *extinction*. Since this is a standard procedure for weakening habits, the more extinction trials required before the subject ceases to respond, the stronger, presumably, was the original habit. This is obviously a cumbersome index and one that requires modifying habit strength in order to measure it.

$_sH_R$ cannot be measured directly; therefore if we are to determine functional relations between this construct and response variables, it becomes necessary to scale habit strength in terms of some observable *antecedent* condition specified in the theory. As can be seen by referring to Fig. 124, Hull *postulates* habit strength to be a simple growth function of the number of reinforced repetitions (N). We may therefore describe *empirical* relations between N and various reaction measures and thence infer

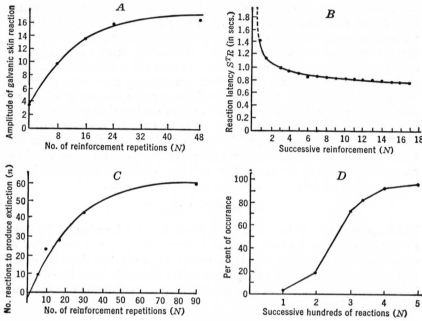

FIGURE 123. Empirical function relating various reaction variables to N, number of reinforced repetitions. *A*. Amplitude of reaction (data of Hovland, *Journal of Experimental Psychology*, 1937, 21:261-76). *B*. Latency of reaction (data of Simley, *Archives of Psychology*, 1933, #146). *C*. Number of unreinforced reactions of extinction (data of S. B. Williams, *Journal of Experimental Psychology*, 1938, 23:506-521, and Perin, *Journal of Experimental Psychology*, 1942, 30:93-113). *D*. Probability of reaction (unpublished data of Bertha I. Hull). All figures from Hull, *Principles of Behavior*, Appleton-Century-Crofts, Inc., New York, 1943, pp. 103, 105, 106, 108.

the relation of the hypothetical intervening variable, habit strength, to these reaction measures. In practice we must hold drive (D) constant while measuring these functions; since observed behavior is a direct function of $_sE_R$ rather than of $_sH_R$ (which combines multiplicatively with D), it will provide a direct index of $_sH_R$ only when the motivational component is held constant. Four sets of empirical data are shown in Fig. 123, relating amplitude of reaction A, reaction latency B, trials to extinction C, and reaction probability D to number of reinforced repetitions N.

The second step is to determine mathematical equations that best fit the obtained data points, these equations becoming then the empirical functions relating N and these reaction variables (represented by the four curves in Fig. 123). This step involves the assumption that these sample raw data are typical in form (if not in absolute magnitudes) of all such relations, but this is highly questionable. Hull points out that the determination of these functions is necessarily a trial-and-error matter, and he looked upon the present estimations as merely approximations to the 'truth.' The third step is to infer the functional relationship between the intervening variable (habit strength) and each of these reaction measures: accepting the assumption that $_sH_R$ is itself a negatively accelerated growth function of N and knowing the empirical relations between N and each reaction index, this becomes a straightforward matter of mathematical transformation. Strictly speaking, these inferred functional relationships between the intervening variable and the various reaction variables are functions of $_sE_R$, and not functions of $_sH_R$.

If these reaction measures were merely alternative indices of the 'same thing' (habit strength), we should expect them to be highly correlated when derived from the same experiment using the same subjects. This is not the case. Three sets of correlations for conditioned responses, leg flexion in the dog (Kellogg and Walker, 1938), eyelid closure in man (Campbell and Hilgard, 1936), and knee jerk in man (Campbell, 1938), are shown in Table 4. Although the correlation values are all in the predicted direction

TABLE 4

	Frequency and Amplitude	Latency and Amplitude	Latency and Frequency
Flexion (dog)	+.94	−.22	−.18
Eyelid (man)	+.63	−.15	−.54
Knee jerk (man)	+.63	−.27	−.27

After Hilgard and Marquis, *Conditioning and Learning*, Appleton-Century-Crofts, Inc., 1940, p. 138.

(latency being inversely related to both frequency and amplitude), they are not near enough 1.00 to justify the assumption that the 'same thing' is being measured. Of course it is possible that the size of these correlations is lowered because of low reliability of the individual measures. Humphreys (1943) however, using both segment-segment (first and last fourths of conditioning correlated with second and third fourths) and split-half (odd trials correlated with even trials) methods, found these measures to have satisfactory reliability. For example, the least reliable measure, latency, showed a split-half correlation of .87. Another possible explanation of these low correlations is that they are not linearly related, e.g. amplitude is a linear function of $_sE_R$ but latency is a hyperbolic function. It is probable that the correlational index *eta* would have been a more satisfactory estimate than r. Further studies are needed with this in mind.

If it turns out that quite different estimates of habit strength can be obtained by using different indices, it becomes reasonable to ask which is the *best* index of habit strength. Since we have no independent criterion here—no objective, invariant correlate of habit strength—this question cannot be answered with any degree of confidence. There are, however, other criteria that can be applied. Although latency may be somewhat less reliable (in the sense of showing greater trial-to-trial variability) than either amplitude or frequency, it offers two distinct advantages: (1) It appears to be more *sensitive* than other measures because mean latencies continue to decrease with continued training long after both amplitude and frequency have reached stable values. (2) It has considerable *generality* because it can be applied equally to conditioning, discrimination training, and instrumental situations and still yield comparable data (cf. Solomon, 1943; Zeaman, 1949), although there are conditions where it cannot be used (e.g. trace conditioning). Perhaps indicative of a trend toward the use of latency as an index is the fact that the most extensive quantitative analysis of habit strength to date, by Hull and his students (cf. Hull, Felsinger, Gladstone, and Yamaguchi, 1947), has been based upon latency as the reaction index.

Determinants of Habit Strength

By utilizing the various reaction measures described above—recognizing their fallibility and lack of equivalence—it is now possible to inquire into the antecedent conditions, or independent variables, that determine habit strength. The question is this: How does habit strength, as indexed by various reaction characteristics, vary as a function of certain manipulatable, antecedent conditions?

(1) *Number of repetitions.* An empirical law of long standing in psychology states that repetition strengthens habits, but, like most empirical laws, this one is of limited validity. Mere repetition is also a condition for weakening habits, e.g. the extinction process. Actually, repetition merely provides continued opportunities for the effective forces, whatever they may be, to operate. According to Hull's theory, the chief effective force is reinforcement, and this law must then be stated in terms of *reinforced* repetitions. *The increments from successive reinforcements summate in a manner that yields a combined habit strength ($_sH_R$) which is a simple positive growth function of the number of reinforcements* (Hull, 1943, p. 178). This postulate includes certain assumptions which should be made explicit: (a) it is assumed that the strengthening effects of successive repetitions can be added together cumulatively, despite the fact that stimulus and response processes can never be identical from trial to trial (see pp. 350-51 for discussion of this matter); (b) it assumes that the increments added by successive reinforced repetitions become progressively smaller—which follows from the fact that growth functions approach an asymptote, each increment being a constant proportion of the remaining, unrealized growth. As Hull points out, in connection with Fig. 124, this type of function is commonly observed for biological growth and decay phenomena.

It is always difficult to test a 'pure' theoretical relation of this sort, since to do so one must eliminate all complicating conditions (such as variation in motivational conditions, differences in indices used, complexities of performance learned, and so on). Siegel (1945) has tested one implication, namely, that the size of increments varies inversely with the degree of learning. One group of rats was given two forced runs to each end of a simple T-maze and another was given 40 forced runs to each side, reinforcement being given in all cases. On a subsequent learning test, with only one side of the maze reinforced, the animals with the initially weaker

habits showed a more rapid rate of learning the correct path, suggesting
that these subjects were at a point on the habit-strength curve where each
unit of differential reinforcement created a larger habit increment. This
interpretation is complicated by the possibility that the animals with the
stronger (equated) habits suffered more competition from the 'wrong'
response tendency during differential training.

Is this negatively accelerated function the 'true' form of the habit-
strength curve? Do empirical learning curves typically display this form?
When learning data for *individual subjects* are plotted as functions of *N*,
almost hopeless confusion is usually the result—extreme trial-by-trial variability obscures whatever general trends there may be. Under the assumption

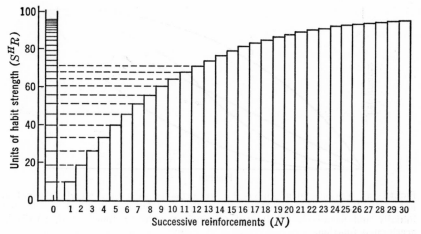

FIGURE 124. Diagrammatic representation of habit strength as a simple positive
growth function. Each increment is a constant proportion (here, ⅒) of the remaining potential habit strength as yet undeveloped. Hull, *Principles of Behavior*,
Appleton-Century-Crofts, Inc., New York, 1943, p. 116.

that these sources of individual variation are attributable to a multitude of
independent factors, and hence are normally distributed, one may average
the data for individuals and plot *mean* learning curves for groups of subjects. Since individuals vary greatly in the total time or trials required to
reach the criterion, it is common procedure to plot *Vincent curves* which
cumulate individual data on the basis of equivalent stages of mastery: each
subject's scores are divided into equal proportions, i.e. successive tenths of
his total time or trials, and the scores for the first tenth of learning, second
tenth, and so on, are averaged (see Hilgard, 1938, for details on this procedure). When individual variabilities are eliminated in this manner, does
a single 'true' function emerge? Not at all. Some smoothed curves do fit
the negatively accelerated growth function best (Fig. 125a), many prove
to be sigmoidal in form (Fig. 125b), some appear to be essentially linear
(Fig. 125c), and one occasionally obtains a positively accelerated curve
(Fig. 125d). Inspection of a sample of the empirical learning curves shown
in any text will illustrate the point. Which of these functions is the 'true'
relation between repetition and habit strength? Or is there any single 'true'
relation?

Many factors determine the shape of empirical learning curves and most of them are in the nature of artifacts attributable to particular experimental or computational procedures. (a) *Index used.* Since the intervening variable, habit strength, must be indexed by some observable reaction variable, and these reaction variables do not all bear the same functional relation to habit strength, some variation in curve form would be anticipated on this basis. Specifically, frequency (probability) of the correct response and its converse, frequency of errors, would be expected to yield sigmoidal functions, whereas amplitude, latency, and extinction measures would be expected to yield growth functions. (b) *What is repeated?* The operational meaning of N may vary from one data plot to another. If N refers to the number of

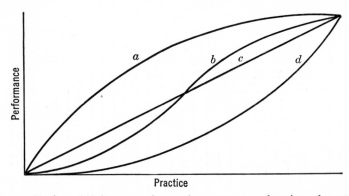

FIGURE 125. Various 'ideal' curves for performance as a function of practice; *a,* negatively accelerated growth function; *b,* sigmoidal function, positively accelerated initially and negatively accelerated terminally; *c,* linear function; *d,* positively accelerated function.

reinforced responses (i.e. each unit is an occurrence of the correct response), negatively accelerated growth functions are likely to be obtained since failures of response and errors do not appear in the record. If, on the other hand, N refers to the number of practice periods (i.e. each unit is a set number of opportunities for the correct response to appear), then positively accelerated or sigmoidal functions become more probable since the proportion of trials on which the correct reaction appears can be expected to increase slowly at first. Thus, for example, the same conditioning data can be shown to yield growth or sigmoidal functions depending on whether characteristics of successive correct responses or the per cent occurrence of the correct response are plotted.

(c) *Complexity of task.* Many performances learned in the laboratory approach the simplicity of isolated habits (e.g. conditioned reactions, individual verbal associates); many other performances are complex integrations of habits, or *skills* (e.g. developing accuracy in ball-tossing, maze-learning), which are often scored as wholes. Even though the 'true' function for isolated habits might be the negatively accelerated growth curve Hull postulates, one could still obtain quite different curves for compounded skills. Furthermore, to the extent that trial-and-error selection of the correct responses from competing errors is recorded for skills but not for isolated stimulus-response associations, the obtained curve forms will differ.

(d) *Stage of learning.* Empirical learning curves often do not represent the entire course of acquisition, from the initial selection of the correct response to the final strengthening of this response to the limits of association. If one's record of ball-tossing stops at the point where the child hits the target every trial—and does not continue to record further increases in speed and precision with practice—a positively accelerated curve may well result.

Although it is not possible to eliminate any of the four possible theoretical functions shown in Fig. 125 on empirical grounds—data fitting any of them may be obtained under appropriate conditions—it is possible to narrow the field on logical grounds. Both the linear curve *c* and the positively accelerated curve *d* imply that habits can keep on increasing in strength indefinitely if repetitions are continued, but this is simply illogical. Furthermore, we know that increasing the number of reinforced repetitions beyond a certain point is not paralleled by increases in the number of trials required for extinction (i.e. adding ten reinforced repetitions to a well-established habit may not change one whit the trials to reach extinction), indicating that the added repetitions are not increasing habit strength significantly. Observations of this sort have led psychologists to postulate a finite limit to habit strength, which is referred to as the *physiological limit.* (Just why this is a 'physiological' rather than a 'psychological' limit is not clear, since no physiological correlates of the limit have ever been demonstrated.)

Both remaining functions have been championed as the 'true' relation between *N* and habit strength. Culler's (1928) 'S-curve hypothesis,' for example, starts from the reasonable assumption that learning curves of various shapes can be obtained from a general *S*-type function, depending on the stage of practice which happens to be sampled. If one could get down to absolute zero habit strength (approximated with novel and complex performances), positive acceleration should be found; near the asymptote of strengthening, on the other hand, negative acceleration must show up. There is no real irreconcilability between this hypothesis and Hull's growth function. Hull is mainly concerned with the theoretical development of *isolated habits,* and the experimental illustrations he presents are clearly of a segmental nature; Culler, on the other hand, is more concerned with the development of *complex skills.* In learning to throw a ball accurately, for example, there are initially many interfering tendencies to be overcome and the correct response must be selected from competing responses. Once the correct skilled pattern is selected, there is a period of rapid improvement in measured performance. And there must be a final 'tapering off' as the correct habits approach their limit of strength. In developing conditioned leg flexion, on the other hand, the situation is such that the correct response must occur regularly from the beginning of association with the new cue, and learning is largely restricted to the simple strengthening of this habit.

(2) *Amount of reinforcement.* With the number of reinforced repetitions held constant, it is still possible to vary the absolute strength of a habit by manipulating other antecedent variables, such as the amount of reinforcement, the asynchronism between stimulus and response, and the delay in reinforcement. Rather than affecting the shape of the habit function, these variables are assumed to determine both the magnitude of the

increments per repetition and the maximum strength to which the growth function is asymptotic. This may be seen in Fig. 126, which illustrates the hypothetical limits set by two different amounts of reinforcement. Also suggested here by Hull is the result to be expected if, at the conclusion of 15 reinforcements with a 1-gram reward, a 6-gram reward is substituted (the shift in the habit-strength function is shown by the finely dotted line). As we shall see in a moment, this last expectation is not borne out by facts.

Supporting the general notion that the limits of habit strength vary with the amount of reinforcement are experimental results obtained by Gantt

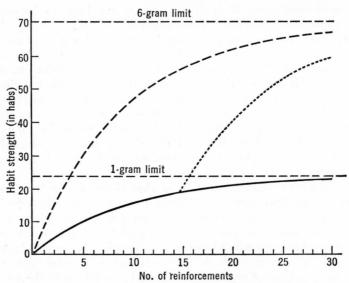

FIGURE 126. Graphic representation of the theoretical course of habit strength acquisition with a 6-gram food reinforcement (broken line) and with a 1-gram food reinforcement (solid line). Dotted curve indicates the theoretical course of habit strength acquisition on the assumption that reinforcement is abruptly shifted to six grams on the sixteenth trial of the 1-gram reinforcement curve. Hull, *Principles of Behavior,* Appleton-Century-Crofts, Inc., New York, 1943, p. 130.

(1938) with conditioned salivation in the dog and Grindley (1929-30) with the learning of an instrumental running response in the chick. Both studies show that when practice under different reward conditions is pushed to the point where performance becomes asymptotic, the absolute habit strengths of these maxima vary as negatively accelerated functions of the amount of reward.

Such a simple relation as this between amount of reinforcement, defined as drive reduction, and habit strength is seriously questioned by the recent findings of Heyer and O'Kelly (1951). They found no difference in the learning of a maze by an 11-hour water-deprivation group of rats and an 11-hour deprivation group that had also been given an injection of NaCl sufficient to produce a '36-hour' thirst. This was true despite the fact that the NaCl animals *drank significantly larger quantities of water following each trial.* In other words, here we have animals functioning under greater biological need and presumably receiving more reinforcement, yet showing no evidence of more rapid development of habit strength. This work as a whole suggested that it is not the amount of primary drive reduction per se which is the effective variable but rather the reduction in a state of 'demand,' a state of the organism more dependent upon the time through which it has been suffering deprivation than upon momentary physiological need.

This brings us to the problem of *incentive*. Extensive experiments are reported by Crespi (1942). Giving rat subjects one trial a day under constant drive conditions (22 hours hungry), he measured the running times for transversing a straight runway, the amount of incentive substance being

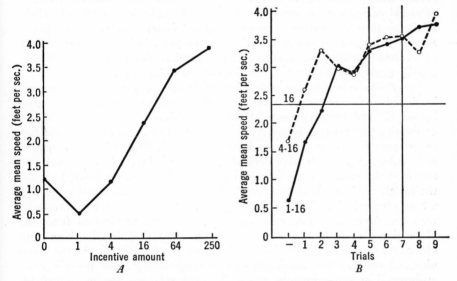

FIGURE 127. *A*. Effect of varying amount of incentive upon speed of rat traveling down a runway. *B*. Effect of abruptly shifting the amount of incentive upward upon speed of running. Crespi, *American Journal of Psychology*, 1942, **55**:488.

varied for different groups in logarithmic fashion (1, 4, 16, 64, and 256 units, where 1 unit equals one-fiftieth gram of moist Purina dog biscuit). As is shown in Fig. 127*A*, running speeds at the asymptote of performance fit the expectations from Hull theory for amounts of the incentive substance greater than 4 units. The inversion indicated for small amounts— the fact that 0 reward is more effective than 1 unit and equally as effective as 4 units—is interpreted as evidence for a frustration factor. The most significant result of this work appeared when animals trained with one amount of incentive substance to a point of stable running speed were *shifted* to another incentive amount. Shifted from 1 or 4 units *up* to 16 units, speed of running rapidly increased to a level significantly *above* the maximum of a control group kept on a 16-unit incentive. This finding is described in Fig. 127*B*. Shifted from 256 or 64 units *down* to 16 units incentive, speed of running quickly fell to a level significantly *below* that of the 16-unit control group. These results suggest that 'frustration' and 'elation' enter as variables effecting momentary 'demand' quite independent of primary needs. The same 'contrast effect,' as it has been called, is reported by Zeaman (1949) in a study similar in many respects to Crespi's.

(3) *Interval between reaction and reinforcement.* Other things being equal, both the rate and final maximum of habit strength can also be varied by manipulating the delay between occurrence of the correct reaction and the giving of reinforcement. A graph similar to Fig. 126 can be used to represent this relation, for example, putting 'limit at 10-second delay' for '6-gram limit' and 'limit at 60-second delay' for '1-gram limit.' Empirical data describing the general relation between habit strength and delay in reinforcement have been obtained by Hamilton (1929), Wolfe (1934), Anderson (1932, 1933), Perin (1943), Perkins (1947), and Grice (1948 *a*). Although all these investigators found that habit strength is inversely related to delay, the actual intervals of time over which the relation extended varied from as much as 20 minutes to as little as 5 seconds. Hull attributes these differences to confounding a *primary gradient of reinforcement* with a more extensive *goal gradient,* the latter including the operation of secondary reinforcing agents (cf. pp. 428ff.). Empirical gradients are usually negatively accelerated functions of the delay interval.

(4) *Stimulus-response asynchronism.* Stimulus-response asynchronism can be thought of as either the time intervening between the onset of a prolonged *CS* and the occurrence of response (delayed conditioned reflexes) or the time intervening between the termination of an abrupt *CS* and the occurrence of response (trace-conditioned reflexes). Rate of habit formation and maximum strength have been shown to vary inversely with both intervals. With respect to the former, Kappauf and Schlosberg (1937) varied the length of time a loud buzz persisted before being terminated by giving a reaction-producing shock. Frequency of *CR* was found to vary inversely with the duration of *CS,* according to a negatively accelerated function. Data have already been presented (see Fig. 116) that describe how conditionability varies with the interval between an abruptly terminated stimulus and the response, maximum ease of conditioning being possible with an interval of approximately .5 seconds. Both relations are interpreted by Hull (1943) as owing to change in the intensity of the stimulus trace. 'Both posterior-asynchronism gradients are tentatively regarded physiologically as increasing functions of the magnitude or intensity of the temporally contiguous afferent discharges. These in their turn are believed to be increasing functions of the frequency of impulses given off by the receptors' (p. 177). In the case of prolonged conditioned stimuli, frequency of impulses in the afferent fibers is assumed to show adaptation or equilibration, and for this there is considerable evidence. In the case of abruptly terminated stimuli, the frequency of impulses, or intensity of the trace, is assumed to diminish according to a negatively accelerated function asymptotic to zero—for this also there is some evidence, but not over the extended periods of time (30 seconds or so) that Hull assumed.

In thus relating maximum potential habit strength to intensity of afferent neural discharge at the time of conjunction with *R,* Hull was assuming that conditionability varies with intensity of *CS* or its trace. The findings of Grant and Schneider (1948, 1949) may be cited as negative evidence—when the intensity of *CS* is deliberately varied, and the *CS–R* interval is constant, no significant relation to strength of conditioning is demonstrated. This does not mean that the empirical evidence on which Hull based his assumptions is invalid. The Kappauf and Schlosberg experiment shows that conditionability does vary inversely with duration of *CS,* and Reynolds (1945 *a*) has reported evidence that conditionability varies inversely with the interval between an abruptly terminated auditory click and an eyelid reaction. These empirical relations apparently cannot be explained on the basis of intensive trace dynamics. What the actual underlying mechanism may be remains obscure. It should be said in passing that it is not necessary for a molar theory, such as Hull's purports to be, to describe the neurophysiological mechanisms mediating the postulated relations.

(5) *Strength of drive.* Hull does not consider strength of drive at the time of acquisition as one of the variables affecting habit strength per se; rather, as we have seen, strength of drive combines multiplicatively with habit strength to determine reaction potential. It seems quite conceivable, however, that the degree to which reinforcing materials are utilized physiologically could depend upon the state of need, drive strength thus entering indirectly by modulating the functional amount of reinforcement. It is difficult to subject this issue to experimentation: (a) one must keep drive constant at the time habit strength is measured (so that the differences in reaction potential will not be due to differences in contemporary motivation); (b) changes in drive strength also modify the total stimulus pattern (e.g. the stimulus may not be the same for original training and the test for habit strength); (c) it is extremely difficult to equate degrees of original learning under different degrees of motivation; (d) strongly motivated animals may learn qualitatively different habits than weakly motivated animals.

Finan (1940) trained four groups of rats, under 1, 12, 24, and 48 hours' food deprivation, respectively, in a bar-pressing habit, 30 reinforced repetitions being given each group. After 48 hours' rest and under a standard 24-hour hunger drive, all animals were extinguished to a common criterion, this being the measure of habit strength. Mean trials to extinction were 31.6, 62.0, 53.8, and 45.6, respectively. Finan suggests that a relation may hold up to some optimal level of drive (here about 12 hours), further increases in drive being disruptive in some fashion. MacDuff (1946) modified the conditions of this experiment in several important particulars: 6- and 16-unit T-maze skills were learned under both distributed and massed practice, retention after 6 weeks was used as a measure of habit strength, and during the 6-week interval all animals were maintained on the common 24-hour feeding cycle at which they were to be tested. In this case results were clearly contrary to the Hull position. With original learning to a constant criterion, rats that had acquired the skill under the 48-hour drive retained it better than those that had acquired it under the 24-hour drive, who were in turn superior to a 12-hour drive group.

Reynolds (1949) used a simple instrumental running response and trials to extinction as the measure of habit strength. Rather than varying the hours of total deprivation, a low drive group was given its usual 12-grams daily ration 24 hours before learning, but a high drive group was reduced to 3 grams for the same period. The low drive group proved significantly *more* resistant to extinction than the high drive group when both were later tested under normal maintenance conditions. This surprising outcome may be due, as Reynolds maintains, to the greater inhibitory tendencies developed during training for the high drive group (they had run more rapidly during the early trials, with less time between runs). It may also be due to the fact that the stimulus situation during extinction was less similar to the training situation for the high drive group (the low drive group was trained and extinguished under the same drive condition, which was not the case for the high drive group). In an experiment by Heyer and O'Kelly (1951) rats learned a maze under two degrees of motivation and were then tested for retention under equated motivation. Following original learning to a common criterion (which was reached in fewer trials by the more highly motivated animals), a 36-hour thirst-deprivation group showed better retention than a 12-hour deprivation group. Most of these studies indicate that strength of drive at the time of learning does affect habit strength, but the methodological difficulties listed above urge us to be cautious in our interpretations.

DECREMENT

Two Paradoxes

Let us now observe the typical behavior of a hungry rat in the Skinner box, a comparatively simple learning situation. Whenever the hungry animal, in the course of its trial-and-error activities, happens to strike the bar, there is a 'click' from the release mechanism and a pellet rolls down into the food cup—and is promptly eaten. In terms of reinforcement theory, the response of striking the bar to the stimulus of seeing the bar receives an increment in habit strength. Successive increments summate, and thus the bar-pressing habit is learned. Now, at this point, suppose we readjust the food-release mechanism so that no pellets can be delivered; the rat has no knowledge of this and, still having a strong bar-pressing habit, continues to press the bar, but without reinforcement. Shortly we note changes in the animal's behavior; it begins to act very much like a little boy faced with a cantankerous vending machine. It pauses after the first few unsuccessful presses and sniffs about the food cup. Then it may bat the bar vigorously in staccato fashion for a brief period. Then the rat rests a moment. Now it strikes the bar once or twice in normal fashion . . . bites it with its teeth . . . and wanders away within the box. Spying the bar again, the animal returns with a few more vigorous blows . . . and again pauses and sniffs about the food cup. This vacillating behavior continues for a while, with bar-pressing periods becoming shorter, and for 5 minutes or more the rat fails to make the response. At this point (if 5 minutes be the arbitrary criterion) we say the habit is *extinguished*.

Compatible with common sense this phenomenon may be, yet it is somewhat paradoxical within learning theory. Here the animal keeps on executing a habit—the stimulus keeps on eliciting the response—yet the habit seems to grow weaker. To be sure, Hull's reinforcement principle says that associations are strengthened only by *reinforced* repetitions (and no reinforcement is given here), but there is nothing in his theory saying that *un*reinforced repetitions weaken habits. Wouldn't such a postulation be the simplest and most reasonable way of handling this phenomenon? Another related paradox complicates the picture: suppose, after extinction has occurred, we take our rat out of the Skinner box and let it rest overnight in

its home cage; the next morning we put it back in the Skinner box and—
there is the habit again! This is the phenomenon of *spontaneous recovery*.
Now if we were to postulate that unreinforced repetitions weaken a habit
to the point of extinction, how would we explain this spontaneous recovery
during a rest period? In this case we should have to explain how the bar-
pressing habit is strengthened *without* reinforced repetitions and *without*
the presence of the appropriate stimulus (bar) in the home cage. Paradoxes
of this sort 'put the pressure' on theories; no theory of learning can make
any claim to adequacy without offering, within its principles, a rational
interpretation.

Experimental Information on Extinction and Spontaneous Recovery

Before discussing various points of view on the nature of response decrement it will be well to survey the major experimental facts. (1) The general
fact of extinction, as a laboratory phenomenon, is that unreinforced repetitions of an $S-R$ association are accompanied by weakening of the association. Why this should be so is the major problem for theory. (2) The
general fact of spontaneous recovery is that after extinction has been accomplished (to some arbitrary criterion), a period of rest (usually removal from
the original situation) is followed by reappearance of the same response to
the stimulus. (3) Extinction is typically a negatively accelerated function
of the number of unreinforced repetitions of the stimulus, e.g. the decremental effects develop rapidly during early nonreinforced trials, the decremental increments becoming progressively smaller and approaching an
asymptote. (4) Typically the course of spontaneous recovery through time
at rest is also negatively accelerated (Ellson, 1938), recovery occurring
rapidly at first and tapering off as rest continues. (5) Ease of obtaining
extinction varies inversely with the degree of original learning (Williams,
1938; Youtz, 1938), e.g. the stronger the original habit, the more resistant
it is to extinction. (6) For relatively short time periods, ease of obtaining
extinction varies inversely with the interval between original learning and
initiation of extinction procedures (Youtz, 1938). This presumably reflects
spontaneous recovery from inhibitions developed during the original learning process (cf. *reminiscence* in human serial learning). And (7) ease of
obtaining extinction also varies inversely with the amount of time allowed
between trials during extinction (Reynolds, 1945 *b;* Rohrer, 1947). The
more time between extinction trials, the more opportunity for decremental
processes to dissipate during the extinction procedure itself.

As we have seen, spontaneous recovery occurs following extinction.
(8) When a series of successive extinction sessions is applied, with rest
interpolated, it becomes progressively easier to obtain any given extinction
criterion. In other words, the amount of habit strength spontaneously recovered becomes less after each extinction experience. (9) Ease of obtaining
extinction varies directly with the work done, or energy expended, in making each reaction during the extinction process (Mowrer and Jones, 1943;
Solomon, 1948). More effortful reactions are easier to extinguish, at least
for gross overt behaviors. (10) It would appear that extinction can proceed 'below zero' (cf. Razran, 1939 *b*), since the portion of habit strength
recovered spontaneously with rest varies inversely with the degree of previous extinction. If animals are kept in the extinction situation after reach-

ing some arbitrary criterion of decrement (e.g. 2 minutes without a re-action), they show less spontaneous recovery than otherwise. Of course, what one considers 'zero' here is a pretty arbitrary matter.

Some of the most significant facts concern the effects of drugs and massed training. (11) Drugs, such as sodium bromide (depressants), which slow down the rate of acquisition, are found to *increase* the ease of obtaining extinction; conversely, drugs which speed up learning (excitants), such as caffeine and Benzedrine, are found to *decrease* the rate of extinction. Switzer (1935 a), for example, has demonstrated less rapid extinction of both a galvanic skin *CR* and a respiratory *CR* in human subjects given caffeine than in a control group given milk-sugar capsules. (12) In cor-responding fashion, massing of trials is found to depress the rate of learn-ing but to reliably accelerate the rate of extinction. Distribution of trials has the opposite effects.

The phenomena of extinction and spontaneous recovery are closely related to those of *inhibition of delay* and *disinhibition.* Switzer (1934), using an interval of 16 seconds between the onset of *CS* (faint light) and occur-rence of *US* (faradic current to index finger), found the latency of the anticipatory *GSR* to increase from a mean of 5 seconds during the first four trials to a mean of 10 seconds at the end of the training period, this increase in delay having a negatively accelerated course. Following a 24-hour rest, the reaction was observed to have moved back to its original latency (e.g. spontaneous recovery from inhibition of delay). Sounding a loud buzzer (disinhibitor) caused an immediate decrease in latency com-parable to that produced by a 24-hour rest. Switzer also reports that in these human subjects inhibition of delay was accompanied by decreased volume of respiration. In a further study by the same author (1935 b) it was shown that caffeine reliably reduced the latent period of delayed *CR*'s, i.e. capacity to develop inhibition of delay is affected in the same manner, administration of caffeine, as ease of obtaining extinction. Similarly, just as inhibition of delay can be 'interfered with' by a sudden extraneous stimulus (e.g. raucous buzzer), so may the course of ordinary extinction be inter-rupted, and momentary spontaneous recovery produced, by the same means (Switzer, 1933).

These facts are 'typical' and serve as a basis for comparing the effective-ness of various theories. But there are some additional facts, usually ob-tained with human subjects (but not restricted to this species), which com-plicate the picture. These will be pointed up in course.

An Explanation Based on Intrinsic Inhibition (Hull, Miller, Mowrer)

Sensations of fatigue are unpleasantly familiar. In the laboratory fatigue may be produced with an *ergograph:* a cord, passed over a pulley, connects a weight to the subject's finger or arm; the subject lifts the weight re-peatedly, and the rate and amplitude of the lifting movements are recorded on smoked or waxed paper on a drum kymograph. Although one thinks of fatigue as a physiological matter, it is possible to distinguish 'psychological' from 'physiological' fatigue. An ingenious experiment by Reid (1928) is apropos. Using an ergograph, subjects were instructed to lift the weight rhythmically; they accommodated the experimenter and persisted until (we assume) the painful sensations of fatigue became too intense. Now various additional incentives were applied, and the subjects pressed themselves yet further, finally reaching a state where they were unable voluntarily to lift the weight. At this point, the crucial condition of the experiment, the flexion muscle involved was stimulated electrically near the motor end plate of the efferent nerve. On and on went the response, with no signs of performance decrement—but presumably to the considerable discomfort of the subjects.

This experiment demonstrates the existence of two levels of fatigue: one, which may be called 'psychological,' is some form of inhibition attributable to the painful sensations of fatigue; the other, 'physiological,' represents an

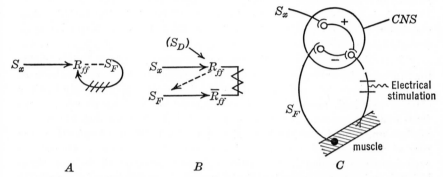

$$A \qquad\qquad B \qquad\qquad C$$

FIGURE 128. Symbolic analysis of fatigue-produced inhibition. A. Repeated elicitation of finger-flexion $(S_x \to R_{ff})$ produces fatigue stimulation which is associated with inhibition of this reaction. B. Increased motivation (S_D) permits additional reactions which, producing more fatigue, also augments incompatible inhibitory tendency (R_{ff}). C. Hypothetical neurological analysis: bombardment of motor neuron along fatigue pathways $(-)$ inhibits excitatory action $(+)$, this central inhibition being by-passed by direct electrical stimulation.

actual decrement in the capacity of the neuromuscular system to react. In a sense, 'psychological' fatigue serves as a protective cushion, preventing the organism from doing itself actual physical injury. Normally, one goes only a short way into this protective cushion before the unpleasant sensations cause him to cease responding with these muscle systems. Although we are largely in the dark concerning the actual neurophysiological basis of 'psychological' fatigue, the series of diagrams in Fig. 128 provide a possible interpretation. (A) The pattern of stimulation including instructions to preform (S_x) elicits the finger-flexion reaction (R_{ff}), and every time this reaction occurs an increment of fatigue stimulation is created (S_F). This fatigue stimulation is assumed to have an innate tendency to produce cessation of reaction in the muscles from which it arises. (B) This, then, is a situation of response competition: one pattern of stimulation (S_x) tends to elicit an excitatory reaction (R_{ff}); another (S_F) tends to elicit inhibition of the same reaction system (R_{ff}). At the point at which the subject ceases responding voluntarily, the inhibitory tendency is presumably equal to or greater than the excitatory one. Bringing additional incentives to play (S_D) temporarily upsets the balance in the excitatory direction, but since each movement further increases fatigue, new equations are inevitably reached. (C) A greatly oversimplified neurophysiological hypothesis proceeds as follows: the evocation pathway $(+)$ bombards the appropriate motor nerves at such a rate as to produce impulses in those fibers; afferent activity in 'fatigue' pathways, arising from receptors imbedded in the reacting muscle, reach the same motor system via another pathway (−). If the rate of bombardment via this indirect, inhibitory pathway is greater than that arriving via the direct excitatory pathway, the motor nerve is kept relatively refractory (or perhaps the synapse is affected chemically so as to increase its resistance to transmission). Mechanisms of this sort are discussed in the neurophysiological literature (cf. p. 168). That inhibition of this sort is central in locus is clearly shown in Reid's experiment. His application of electrical stimulation peripheral to the motor nerve effectively short-circuited the central inhibitory state.

If this is an approximation to the nature of psychological fatigue, then we should have to classify it as a *primary drive*. It arises from a state of organic need: every time a muscle reacts oxygen and other products necessary for action are used up and waste products are deposited. It is probable that fatigue afferents are excited by the presence of these end products of action. Furthermore, fatigue stimulation is associated reflexively with a class of reactions, namely, cessation of movement of those muscle systems from which the stimulation arises—and this is clearly a homeostatic type of mechanism. Now if fatigue is a drive state, then *rest is a straightforward case of reinforcement,* drive reduction in the Hullian sense. As soon as the organism ceases responding with those muscles from which fatigue stimulation is arising, the intensity of the stimulation begins spontaneously to decline. Circulation of the blood is continuously removing the chemical waste products of action and replenishing oxygen and sugar. Rest after work is certainly gratifying subjectively. We may assume that this spontaneous reduction in fatigue proceeds according to a negatively accelerated function, i.e. the rate of recovery varies with the intensity of the need state, since this function is common to homeostatic mechanisms of this kind.

What determines the intensity of fatigue drive at any given moment (and hence the potential reinforcement from rest)? Taking the simplest case in which the same reaction is repeated (as in the ergograph), at least the following factors can be indicated: (1) *Time between reactions in a sequence.* If fatigue spontaneously dissipates between reactions, the greater the time allowed between elicitations, the less should be the cumulation of fatigue. Similarly, the longer the time since the last reaction in a sequence, the less will be the intensity of fatigue. If periods between trials, or following the last trial, are sufficiently prolonged, fatigue should be reduced to zero. (2) *Number of reactions in a sequence.* Assuming that the interval between reactions permits some accumulation, successive increments of fatigue will summate. (3) *Work done in making each reaction.* Since fatigue stimulation is presumed to arise from a need state of the muscle tissues, it follows that reactions utilizing more energy will produce greater increments in fatigue. Regarding this variable, Mowrer and Jones (1943) report a study in which the weight of the bar in a Skinner-type box was varied and the effects upon extinction measured. During original training the rat subjects experienced pressing against 5-, 42.5- and 80-gram loads in irregular orders; during extinction trials the animals were divided into three groups, each being given a different loading. The rate of extinction varied directly with the weight of the bar, i.e. with the effortfulness of the task. This result has been substantiated for a jumping response, with extinction carried out under two different distances of jump, by Solomon (1948). When the work done can be shifted to alternate muscle systems, of course the total accumulation of psychologically effective fatigue is reduced. This method of 'spreading the load' can be observed in most kinds of manual labor, e.g. in carrying one's suitcase from the station. Presumably this tendency to shift from one muscle system to another in accomplishing work is learned on the basis of fatigue reduction.

We may now summarize the argument to this point: (1) Psychological fatigue is a drive state. (2) The intensity of this drive at any moment depends on the time interval separating responses, the number of responses in a sequence, and the work done in making each reaction. (3) This fatigue drive is innately associated with inhibition of the response producing it, and can become conditioned (as a stimulus) to various substitutive responses that regularly accompany fatigue reduction. (4) The greater the intensity of fatigue at any moment, the greater the tendencies to inhibit the response or shift to substitutive equivalents. (5) Rest following work is a reinforcing state of affairs. This analysis has followed in essence those presented by Miller and Dollard (1941), Mowrer and Jones (1943), and Hull (1943). Hull utilizes the following symbolic statement:

$$_s\bar{E}_R = {_sE_R} - (I_R + {_sI_R})$$

which may be read, 'The effective reaction potential $(_s\bar{E}_R)$ equals the reaction potential $(_sE_R)$ minus the summation of both innate, fatigue-produced inhibition (I_R) and conditioned inhibition $(_sI_R)$.' *

Resolution of the twin paradoxes, extinction and spontaneous recovery, follows directly from this analysis. During *learning* of the bar-pressing habit, successive increments in the association between the stimulus complex (bar, box, etc.) and the correct response (pressing) summate to yield the momentary habit strength $(_sH_R)$ which, when multiplied by some function of drive (D), gives the reaction potential $(_sE_R)$. During extinction, although habit strength is no longer increasing, the animal continues to press the bar—the combination of existing $_sH_R$ and D still yields an $_s\bar{E}_R$ which is supra-threshold. But with every subsequent repetition of the bar-pressing reaction, I_R increases. At some point the cumulative inhibition becomes great enough to bring the effective reaction potential below threshold, and the animal ceases responding temporarily. When such inhibition-produced pauses reach some arbitrarily determined length, we say the animal is extinguished. To observe the phenomenon of *spontaneous recovery* we allow the animal to rest, perhaps overnight in its home cage, and then put it back in the Skinner box for what amounts to a second extinction series. The rat again responds with bar-pressing. To explain this, we note that during this long rest period the fatigue-produced inhibition (I_R) has had ample opportunity to dissipate. Look again at Hull's symbolic statement of these relations: as I_R decreases, the effective reaction potential, $_s\bar{E}_R$, must increase equivalently, and thus the extinguished habit appears to come back 'spontaneously.'

* There are certain details of presentation omitted here (see the original source, Hull, 1943, pp. 300-302). The formulation and function of conditioned inhibition will be discussed soon.

At this point we might be inclined to terminate our deductions with a flourished Q.E.D., but hasn't this explanation of extinction and spontaneous recovery forced us into another paradox? If the only thing required to remove the effects of extinction is sufficiently prolonged rest, how can habits ever be unlearned? Having learned this bar-pressing habit in the Skinner box, it would seem that our rat could never get rid of it. Just take the rat out of the box for a while, and there is the habit again! This would mean that habits are completely irradicable; once learned, they become permanent parts of behavioral equipment. This runs contrary to common sense. It also runs contrary to the consistent experimental observation that successive extinctions are obtained more easily until spontaneous recovery disappears entirely. Evidently the animal must be *learning* not to make the response during successive extinctions, and this brings us to the matter of *conditioned inhibition* and the remaining symbol ($_sI_R$) in the equation cited above.

What does the Hullian system say must be happening whenever the animal ceases responding because of fatigue-produced inhibition? Essentially the same stimulus situation, including visual stimulation from the bar, is present, but the animal is *not* reacting by pressing, i.e. it is 'making a response of not responding.' Since it is temporarily resting those muscles from which the fatigue drive arises, we also have here a reinforcing state of affairs. We reach the inevitable conclusion that whatever stimulus-response associations occur during such periods will be strengthened. One such association is that between the same situational stimulus (bar, box, etc.) and the not-hitting-the-bar response, i.e. a learned inhibitory reaction ($_sI_R$). Since the tendency to inhibit a response is directly antagonistic to the tendency to excite it, these learned inhibitory tendencies are assumed to subtract directly from excitatory tendencies, and this represents the *permanent* unlearning of the habit being extinguished, the portion that is not subject to spontaneous recovery. In terms of Hull's symbol system, at the end of an extinction series we have

$$_s\bar{E}_R = {_sE_R} - (I_R + {_sI_R})$$

fatigue-produced and such conditioned inhibitory tendencies as have been established summating to prevent reaction; after rest, however, we have

$$_s\bar{E}_R = {_sE_R} - {_sI_R}$$

representing the permanent loss attributable to the extinction procedure, the fatigue-produced decrements having dissipated during rest. When the extinction process during a single session is prolonged, or repeated through several sessions, the amount of reaction tendency recoverable through rest decreases.

By the same token, *any* stimulus consistently associated with the extinction of a response should acquire an inhibitory association with it. Pavlov (1927) has termed such stimuli *conditioned inhibitors*. A tactile stimulus was conditioned to a salivary reaction (*US,* acid in the mouth) and the sound of a metronome was conditioned to an alimentary reaction (*US,* food in the mouth); during subsequent extinction of alimentary reaction, the sound of a whistle (originally neutral stimulus) was paired with the metronome. That the whistle had acquired inhibitory capacities—and that this inhibition transferred to another reaction—is demonstrated in Table 5.

TABLE 5

Time	Stimulus Applied during 1 Minute	Salivary Secretion in Drops during 1 Minute
3:08 P.M.	tactile	3
3:16 P.M.	tactile	8
3:25 P.M.	tactile plus whistle	less than 1 drop
3:30 P.M.	tactile	11

Pavlov, *Conditioned Reflexes*, trans. Anrep, Oxford University Press, London, 1927, 77.

Graham (1943) has extended these conclusions to the transfer of conditioned inhibition in the successive discrimination learning of two instrumental habits (running down an alley and pressing a bar). In both cases a buzzer served either as a conditioned excitor (sounding only on to-be-reinforced trials) in one group or as a conditioned inhibitor (sounding only on not-to-be-reinforced trials) in another group. Not only did the discrimination transfer from one instrumental learning situation to the other, but there was evidence that this transfer was based upon generalization of tendencies not-to-respond, i.e. generalization of the inhibition associated with either the sound of the buzzer (conditioned inhibition groups) or the *absence* of the buzzer (conditioned excitation groups). This wide generalization of inhibitory tendencies has been observed by other investigators (cf. Liberman, 1944).

Finally, we have here a mechanism whereby various substitutive, fatigue-avoiding responses can be learned. Assuming that rest is a reinforcing state of affairs, any new reactions that are made at this time are automatically strengthened. Thus, during the extinction period, the animal may rear up and sniff at the sides of the box; this new behavior is presumably being strengthened. When we shift a heavy load from one hand to the other, or change the muscle group with which a productive act is accomplished, these substitutive responses are being strengthened by fatigue reduction. And so, this analysis implies, are learned the various and sundry techniques of loafing on the job. Interesting in this connection is the fact that, according to theory at least, the fatigue-drive stimuli themselves must also become conditioned to such work-avoiding behaviors; hence, as a function of generalization, weaker and weaker intensities of fatigue should become capable of eliciting 'loafing,' once such habits have gotten a start.

An Explanation Based on Extrinsic Interference (Guthrie, Wendt)

The interference interpretation of inhibitory phenomena has not been elaborated to the same extent as the fatigue interpretation—it does not need to be. The central notion is simply that 'an activity is inhibited when some other behavior system takes its place' (Wendt, 1936). In other words, inhibitory or negative learning is the same thing as positive learning; the subject is merely learning to do something else in the same situation, and investigators have generally been misled by concentrating their observations on the behavior being extinguished rather than upon the new behavior being learned. One advantage of this view is immediately apparent—it requires no new postulates concerning 'inhibitory' states or processes. Guthrie's view of extinction is just such a straightforward interference view, one response to a set of cues being completely eliminated whenever those cues become associated with some other, incompatible response.

Drawing upon data obtained in experiments on habituation of eye movements to rotation, inhibition of food-taking responses in monkeys, and effects of immobilization of animals in the Pavlovian-type situation, Wendt (1936) has made the strongest case for an interference interpretation. In the experiments on monkeys, for example, the subjects were forced to delay their response of opening a food-drawer until a tone sounded; if opened before this tone sounded, the drawer was found to be empty. Wendt found that 'the animals achieve inhibition of response to the drawer by filling the delay period with other substitute responses *natural to the situation*' (p. 264). Opening the grill, which revealed the drawer and initiated the delay period, was generally the cue for vigorous activity: running about the cage, thumping, vocalizing, and even tearing destructively at the wooden bars of the cage with teeth and hands. As training continued, however, the nature of the interpolated activity underwent a gradual change; movements came to be more and more limited to an area close to the drawer (oftentimes being 'sublimated' in character, like pawing the air near the drawer) and behaviors interfering with listening for the tone tended to drop out entirely. Although none of the evidence cited by Wendt is directly relevant to extinction, the implication is that this form of inhibition is also in reality the substitution of interfering or competing reactions. Learning *not to* press the bar in the Skinner box is presumably learning *to* lick the paws, groom, and sniff about the enclosure.

How can dominance of the original reaction (e.g. bar-pressing) be shifted to dominance of substitute, interfering reactions (e.g. grooming)? Guthrie (1935) makes several suggestions: (1) Present the stimulus for the original, to-be-extinguished reaction at reduced intensity so that its normal response is not elicited but some other response is. This is essentially the 'reconditioning method' which has been described in connection with controlling children's fears (cf. Jersild and Holmes, 1935). (2) Repeat the original stimulus until the original reaction becomes fatigued, whereupon continued applications will result in the association of this stimulus with other reactions. This is essentially a description of the fatigue-produced inhibition theory in interference terms. (3) Combine the cue stimulus with others that elicit a reaction incompatible with the original reaction. Guthrie gives the homely illustration of training a dog not to chase chickens by tying a dead one about its neck; the avoidant reactions associated with the dead chicken interfere with previously made approach reactions to live chickens—provided the dog does not discriminate these two states of chicken existence. Wendt (1936) adds the following statements: (4) Eliminate the specific stimuli associated with the original reaction (e.g. the presence of the bar), leaving the remainder of the situation intact; (5) Enhance the stimuli, and motivation, asociated with any incompatible reaction (e.g. electrify the bar so that the rat gets shocked whenever it is touched).

Although there are few experiments in the literature directly designed to test the implications of the interference theory of response decrement, much of the data can be interpreted along its lines. This is especially true in the area of human learning and memory, where an 'interference theory of forgetting' (cf. Chaps. 12, 13) is the dominant behavioristic view. According to this view, an originally learned response to a stimulus fails to occur in a later test of retention because, during the retention interval, some other response has become more strongly associated with the same stimulus.

An Explanation in Terms of Changed Significance of Cues (Tolman)

Both theories considered so far have dealt with decrements in associations between stimuli and overt responses (S–R). In the general theory sponsored by Tolman (cf. Chap. 9) the critical associations in learning are those between stimuli (S–S), in which certain antecedent cues (signs) come to represent or signify certain subsequent stimulus situations (significates). The modifications that occur in learning are therefore changes in *cognitions* rather than movements-to-stimuli. Tolman also seems to hold to an interference theory of response decrement (cf. 1949), but it is interference among cognitive events (significances or expectations) rather than among overt response tendencies. Thus, when the dog in a conditioning experiment is no longer given food reinforcement, it develops a new, interfering expectation—that buzzer is *not* a sign of food—and therefore stops salivating.

Much of the atypical evidence on extinction and spontaneous recovery, usually obtained with human subjects, fits this view. For example, Porter (1939) varied the massing of extinction trials on conditioned eyeblink in humans from 10 seconds between trials to 180 seconds, but no consistent differences were found—as if the important factor were not rate of presentation but a shift in expectancy of airpuff which was equivalent for all groups. Ellson (1939) varied the interval between extinction and the test for spontaneous recovery with human subjects (exactly as he had done (1938) with rats, where amount of recovery varied directly with length of the interval), but recovery of the galvanic skin response in humans showed no such function, with number of reactions to the extinction criterion as the measure. Using both human and rat subjects, Humphreys (1939 *a, b;* 1940) has found that 100 per cent trials-with-reinforcement during original learning may produce a habit *less* resistant to extinction than 50 per cent trials-with-reinforcement during original learning—as if the change in significance of the critical cue were 'clearer' when contrasted with consistent reinforcement than with intermittent reinforcement. These studies of Humphreys, however, are highly controversial as to interpretation (cf. pp. 425-7). Tolman's interpretation of these data would be that after a few experiences of nonreinforcement (extinction procedure) the subject no longer expects the *US* to occur and behaves accordingly.

Evaluation of Theories of Response Decrement

An adequate discussion of Tolman's view would require both a detailed inspection of his total theory and consideration of a 'mediation hypothesis' which attempts to bridge the gap between his position and Hull's. These matters will be treated in the next chapter. The essential conclusion to be reached can be sketched as follows: The distinctive advantages of Tolman's theory, with its emphasis upon cognitive processes ('expectations') in learning, can also be achieved within a Hull-type theory if proper emphasis is given to the development of representational mediation processes. In the present context the bar initially becomes a sign of food for the hungry rat in the Skinner apparatus (e.g. as a stimulus it comes to elicit anticipatory food-taking reactions as a representational mediation process); during the extinction procedure it is this representational process that becomes extinguished (or interfered with), and there is then nothing to mediate the bar-pressing. This sort of view is compatible with the speed with which extinction can be obtained in certain cases, e.g. when repeated cycles of reinforcement and nonreinforcement are given, the subject eventually gets to the point where a single occurrence of either reinforcement or its lack will completely shift overt performance.

The mediation hypothesis (in contrast to Tolman's own view) assumes however that the same basic principles applying to gross S–R associations also apply to mediating S–r processes. Furthermore, it is assumed to hold both for developmental and decremental operations. This leads us to compare and evaluate inhibition and interference principles of decrement. The fatigue interpretation of extinction can be regarded as a special form of 'inhibition process' theory. A similar view was that held by Pavlov, who postulated a central inhibitory state which increased in concentration with evocations of a reaction and irradiated spatially through the cortex. Both views require postulation of a special class of events (inhibitory) beyond those required for excitatory learning. The interference theory is more parsimonious in that it views inhibitory phenomena as identical in character with excitatory phenomena. Does existing evidence permit issue between these positions? Or is it possible to integrate such apparently divergent interpretations?

The fatigue theory explains the permanent unlearning of a habit in terms of the subtractive effect of learning a 'response of nonresponding,' the $_sI_R$ in Hull's formulation. This behavior is by nature unobservable, being inferred from the fact that the positive response is permanently weakened. The unlearning of habit is thus circularly explained by invoking a process that is only indexible by the weakening of habit itself. The interference theory is no better off on this count; the actual behavior which does the interfering with the original response is never specified, except by inference from the fact that the original reaction fails to appear and hence 'some other activity must be taking its place.' Similarly, both theories have difficulty detailing the behavior that typically accompanies extinction and delay procedures. During extinction the animal's behavior usually first becomes agitated and then verges more and more toward behavior 'natural' to a given situation; during 'inhibition of delay,' the subject may insert vigorous substitutive responses (Wendt) or tend to depress all overt activity (Switzer). Neither theory gives an adequate account of these concomitants.

The fatigue theory runs into a number of criticisms not shared by other views. For one thing, one wonders *how it can apply to glandular and other 'light-weight' reactions*. Integral to the fatigue explanation is the assumption that the response being extinguished produced significant amounts of fatigue in its execution. Although this seems reasonable in the case of gross, overt activities, such as pressing a bar and leaping from a platform, what about such 'light' activities as secreting saliva, blinking the eyelids, and talking? It should be kept in mind, however, that I_R can be used as a mathematical construct without regard to physiological implications. One also wonders how extinction can be obtained *when successive reactions are widely separated in time.* Extinction, just like learning, can be demonstrated with intervals as long as 24 hours between trials, yet the tiny increments in fatigue (I_R) must dissipate in a small fraction of this time. It would seem that some other explanation must apply in such cases. Nor do the *phenomena of inhibition of delay and disinhibition* seem very compatible with a fatigue theory (although they fit Pavlov's conception of a central inhibitory state well enough). Although, with training, delayed reactions are made after progressively longer periods of inhibition, it is impossible to interpret the increasing delay as fatigue-produced. Furthermore, the release from inhibition following a sudden, novel stimulus (disinhibitor) is quite out of character for a fatigue-produced state.

Beyond these general criticisms, there is one difficulty within the Hull theory itself that needs clarification. It will be recalled that, following the symbolic statement, $_s\bar{E}_R = {_sE_R} - (I_R + {_sI_R})$, Hull is subtracting *both* the innate, fatigue-produced inhibition (I_R) and the conditioned inhibition ($_sI_R$) *from the reaction potential rather than from the habit strength* ($_sH_R$). Expressed in ordinary language, this seems to mean that Hull looked upon all inhibitory processes as damping *performance* rather than as subtracting from previously learned habit strength. In other words, *habits are never unlearned.* Is this paradoxical? One may envisage here a 'cluttering up of the psyche' with outmoded habits, but with our scanty knowledge of the neural nature of habit, this need not be too disturbing. Remaining within Hull's general framework, it still could be assumed that $_sI_R$, as a negative habit phenomenon, subtracts directly from $_sH_R$, a positive habit phenomenon (indeed, it seems reasonable that the tendency not to make a response should be the reciprocal of the tendency to make that response, that the strengthening of the former should be the same thing as the weakening of the latter). Fatigue-produced inhibition, I_R, would still summate algebraically with $_sE_R$, since both are performance constructs. On empirical grounds, Zeaman (1949) has reached similar conclusions.

The interference theory has also come in for its share of criticism. One line of attack has asserted that this theory cannot explain *the occurrence of spontaneous recovery* (cf. Hilgard and Marquis, 1940). If extinction is explained as the learning of a substitute response, why should the original response reappear after rest? Liberman (1944) has proposed an ingenious explanation, namely, that 'spontaneous recovery be regarded as the forgetting . . . of experimental extinction.' The various interpolated activities during the period of 'rest' serve to interfere with those responses that constitute the extinctive learning. Experimentally, it was shown that while interpolated *conditioning* of the eyeblink increased the spontaneous recovery of a previously extinguished galvanic skin response above that of a control-rest condition, interpolating *further extinction* of the eyeblink reliably decreased the amount of spontaneous recovery. Further evidence that extinction and spontaneous recovery are transfer phenomena was found: if stimuli for original and interpolated activities were similar (1000-cycle tone and a buzzer), the effects upon subsequent spontaneous recovery were greater than if the stimuli were dissimilar (1000-cycle tone and a light).

But this experiment brings up another problem: Why should interpolated activity interfere more successfully with the extinctive tendencies (thus permitting spontaneous recovery) than with the original excitatory tendencies? In other words, why should the interfering, extinctive responses be 'forgotten' more readily than the initially learned responses? Liberman's answer is that extinctive 'responses of non-responding' need not be so sharply discriminated as original 'correct' responses; hence they generalize more broadly and are more susceptible to subsequent interference. Whereas the experimenter only reinforces a specific response to a specific stimulus pattern during original learning, during extinction any manner in which the animal fails to make the response-being-extinguished is acceptable. In a test of this hypothesis (1948), rats were given equal training to traverse two distinctive runways (*A* and *B*). One group (double-extinction) was subsequently extinguished to a performance criterion on runway *A*, randomly interspersed *extinction* trials on runway *B* being given; the other group (differential-extinction) was extinguished to the same criterion on runway *A*, but the randomly interspersed trials on runway *B* were now *reinforced*. Would the necessity of discriminating to-be-extinguished activities from not-to-be-extinguished activities in the latter group serve to restrict generalization of the extinctive tendencies and thus reduce spontaneous recovery? Spontaneous recovery was significantly greater for the double-extinction animals than for the differential-extinction animals. This series of experiments makes the strongest case for an interference theory and also serves to place extinction and spontaneous recovery on a continuum with a large body of evidence on transfer and retroactive interference (cf. Chap. 12).

Another criticism of the interference theory has been based on the fact *that massing of trials slows down the rate of conditioning but speeds up the rate of extinction.* If learning and extinction are identical in nature, any such variable should affect both in similar ways. In an experiment by Rohrer (1947), intervals between acquisition trials were randomly varied between 35 and 70 seconds, yet animals extinguished with a 10-second intertrial interval reached the criterion significantly faster than those extinguished with a 90-second interval. There appears to be no case on record in which distribution of extinction trials produces a significantly *faster* rate of extinction than massing, yet this would be expected if extinction is merely the learning of another response. Another difficulty for the interference theory is its *failure to account for the effects of drugs.* As noted earlier, drugs that facilitate learning prolong extinction, but drugs that depress learning speed up extinction. Significant here also is Switzer's (1935 *b*) observation that administration of an *excitant* (caffeine) markedly *reduced* the interval over which the subject could delay a conditioned reaction; if, as Wendt claims, inhibition of delay is accomplished by the substitution of incompatible reactions, administration of an excitant should, if anything, facilitate these interfering reactions and thus prolong the delay interval. Finally, we may add that according to the interference theory, too, taken at its face value, *there is no actual unlearning.* The extinguished habit is not weakened, it is merely superseded. But if the habit-strength function is negatively accelerated, must we not eventually reach the point when the last habit in a cumulating hierarchy cannot be superseded?

Each of these two views of response decrement, considered separately, is inadequate. Can they be integrated in such a manner as to give wider coverage of the relevant phenomena? Two distinguishable processes must be dealt with: (a) *temporary inhibition* (a response may show decrement temporarily and then reappear at or near its initial strength) and (b) *permanent unlearning* (spontaneous recovery is seldom complete, and under conditions of repeated extinction responses may be completely eliminated). Both processes are visible in ordinary selective learning also, and this may provide some insights.

Suppose that after learning the bar-pressing habit, conditions are arbitrarily changed by the experimenter so that *biting* the bar now becomes the correct response. Once the rat has bitten the bar a few times and been rewarded, of course this response will be strengthened and compete successfully with the original pressing response. But before this new, interfering response can occur at all, the original pressing reaction must somehow be weakened. The fatigue theory offers one feasible mechanism whereby weakening of the original response can be accomplished: the innate tendency of fatigue stimulation to inhibit reaction of those muscles from which it arises. The interference theory offers no such direct mechanism. Rather, it must rely upon changes in the stimulus situation, such as the motivational effects of nonreward (frustration), to produce interfering responses. Now the only difference between ordinary selective learning and extinction is that in the former case the interfering response is obviously reinforced, whereas in the latter it is not. The fatigue theory has the advantage here that it provided a subtle, but immediate, reinforcement for the response of nonresponding (e.g. rest). It has the disadvantage that it is limited largely to gross overt activities.

Yet, looked at from another angle, *the fatigue process itself is nothing other than a special case of response interference,* inhibition of response being directly incompatible with elicitation. Taking our cue from this, we can make the general statement that *whatever responses in the extinction situation are reinforced will come to interfere with the original reaction.* The sources of reinforcement may be widely variable, including reductions in needs for aggression, anxiety reduction, and so on, as well as fatigue reduction.

The temporariness of large portions of response decrement may be explained either in terms of the spontaneous dissipation of fatigue (to the extent that the extinction process generated fatigue) or in terms of subsequent forgetting of the interfering responses, as Liberman (1944) has suggested. Most situations would probably involve combinations of both processes. What about permanent unlearning? In the present form of Hull's theory there is no permanent unlearning, since $_sI_R$ is subtracted from $_sE_R$, but this could easily be remedied by subtracting $_sI_R$ directly from $_sH_R$. Nor is there permanent unlearning in Wendt's version of the interference theory, decrement persisting only as long as competing responses are not themselves interfered with. Guthrie's association theory provides for the permanent elimination of the extinguished response, because stimuli associated with R_2 become completely dissociated from R_1, but to the extent that this argument is used here, Guthrie would have trouble explaining spontaneous recovery.

GENERALIZATION AND DISCRIMINATION

Generalization

The terms 'stimulus' and 'response' are used loosely and uncritically in general psychological parlance. Habits are developed, it is said, through the repetition of an association between a given S and a given R. What is this S? What is this R? The experimenter may say that *conceptually* he refers to the 'buzzer sound' by S and to 'running down the alley' by R. He would agree that the stimulus is not completely described by calling it the buzzer sound (since it includes lights and shadows in the room, effects of past movements, and so forth), any more than the response is completely described by calling it running, but conceptualization is a necessary convenience. Fair enough. But then he goes on to say that reinforced repetitions of the *same* stimulus and the *same* response summate to yield increases in habit strength. If there is one statement about the logical status of our concepts we can accept, it is this: *precisely the same stimulus or response is never repeated.* How, then, can strengthening of associations occur?

For one thing, it is apparent that the successive stimulations and respondings we call 'the same,' while never in truth identical, are also not random in character. If we had adequate techniques for measuring detailed variations in both S and R, we should anticipate a normal curve of variability when the 'same' S and R are repeated many times—operations performed by the experimenter upon the physical environment are such as to restrict the possible variations. But the basic difficulty remains: *how can summation of successive increments into habit strength occur when each member of the succession is unique?* We require a new principle here, one that will postulate a spread of effect, or transfer, for each increment to associational elements other than those specifically activated in a given occurrence. Some such conception appears in every theory of learning, with the possible exception of Guthrie's view, and it goes under a variety of labels: irradiation, equivalence, transposition, and the 'law of similarity,' to mention only a few. We shall use the term *generalization*.

This principle is of fundamental significance for behavior theory; it means that habits are not tied to the limited, specific situations in which they were learned. Think what a time-consuming process growing up would be if we had to relearn each response every time the situation was changed (especially since the same situation never repeats itself)! The child's adjustments to his kindergarten teacher would have no bearing on his behavior in first grade; learning to catch a ball thrown from a distance of 5 feet would have no carry-over for catching balls thrown from 10 feet. Fortunately, there *is* a generalization principle functioning in behavior. The child that learns to avoid one hot radiator does not have to be burned by every succeeding hot object; having learned to say 'thank you' in the home, parents can be reasonably confident their child will utilize this bit of social refinement elsewhere.

There is an important educational principle embodied here. *The more closely a training situation resembles that in which the training is to be used, the more effective will be the training.* Training infantrymen to approach an enemy position under fire is more effective if the men actually have to crawl on their bellies with bullets whistling over their heads than if they are instructed verbally while sitting in lecture hall seats. They will be less likely to 'lose their heads,' both figuratively and literally. In this connection, it is interesting to observe that the 'best trained' troops, compared with guerillas, become demoralized when forced to retreat; they haven't learned their military habits under retreat-simulating conditions. Successful educators make use of this principle. A language course designed to develop skills in speaking is handled quite differently from one designed to teach grammar. Yet how many psychologists, who piously hope their students will gain a more objective way of interpreting behavior, train them (via examinations) to recall textbook facts, but the students leave the general principles in their notebooks once the course is over.

Returning to the laboratory, let us observe a simpler case of generalization in the rat subject. Suppose the sounding of a 1000 c.p.s. tone is followed closely by administering shock to a rat standing on a grill. We continue training until, to this tone, the amplitude, latency, and so forth, of the rat's conditioned jumping response reach asymptotic value. Let us call this original training stimulus S_o and indicate the habit strength at this point on the stimulus continuum as 100 per cent. Now, using groups of subjects trained in identical fashion, we test for generalization at various other points (S_{x1}, S_{x2}, and so on) along this physically defined continuum. A 900 c.p.s. tone results in a fairly strong jumping reaction; a 700 c.p.s. tone yields a slight jump; a 500 c.p.s. tone may produce merely a tensing and quivering. The proportion of each group showing reaction is indicated by the length of the vertical bar at each point. From such a study as this it would appear that (1) generalization is a decreasing function of the difference between original and test stimuli, i.e. as shown by the broken line connecting obtained values, amount of generalization is less as the number of c.p.s. between S_o and S_x increases. Now suppose fewer training trials on S_o are given. Not only will habit strength at the point of original conditioning be less, but less also will be the generalized habit strengths at all test points along the continuum. As shown by the shaded portions of the vertical bars, (2) generalization varies directly with the degree of original learning.

The hypothetical data shown in Fig. 129 display only one wing of what is known as a *generalization gradient*. There is no reason to believe that these effects would be restricted to tones lower than 1000 c.p.s., however, and the broken lines sketch in the bidirectional gradient that would be expected if test stimuli on both sides of the 1000 c.p.s. conditioning tone were used. Even this is an arbitrary limitation. Theoretically generalization occurs simultaneously along all conceivable dimensions through which stimuli and responses can vary. Having trained a rat to jump to a 1000 c.p.s. tone, generalized reaction potential could be observed for tones varying in loudness, in timbre, in volume (if such a dimension exists), and so on. Generalization is thus to be conceived as a multidimensional affair. It may aid visualization of this to imagine a soft silk handkerchief spread out on a table; as one point near the center is lifted (original conditioning), the entire cloth is elevated, the amount of (generalized) lifting being a function of both the distance from the point picked up and the amount of elevation at this point.

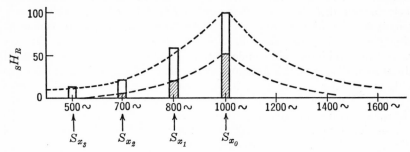

FIGURE 129. Representation of a bi-directional generalization gradient of the Hull type showing how amount of generalized habit strength ($_sH_R$) is assumed to vary with both (a) distance between training stimulus (S_o) and test stimuli (S_x) along the continuum and (b) amount of habit strength developed at the point of conditioning (cross-hatched vs. total extents of vertical bars).

Discrimination

It is not necessary that behavioral principles invariably have adjustive consequences, and certainly this applies to generalization. To be sure, this principle of behavior guarantees that successful reactions will transfer to new situations, but by the same token they will also appear in situations where they lead to failure. At an early age we learn to duck our heads at the approach of balls, blocks, and hands. Adaptively, this protective reaction generalizes to all objects that rapidly increase their visual angles on our retinas, and as adults we duck to avoid the swift flick of a released branch on the trail, to get out of the path of an errant baseball. But then there is that game of 'flinch'—quick passes are made before your eyes, and if you blink or duck, the opponent is entitled to 'bing' you on the upper arm. Here these generalized protective reactions are clearly maladaptive. Similarly, the generosity habits developed (often painfully) within the family have a way of transferring to situations outside the family, and parents find themselves touring the neighborhood recovering household goods, automobile tools, and toys that have been generously distributed by little Johnny. What is it in behavior that enters to check this overbroad generalization of response? The process is called *discrimination*. In Hull's terms, the very fact overgeneralized responses are no longer rewarded sets up the conditions under which the range of generalization is narrowed.

Let us return for a moment to the dog that had been trained to lift its paw to the command 'give me paw.' Given the inevitability of behavioral principles, generalization occurs here, and we find that this animal will execute paw-lifting in a wide variety of situations. But what happens? You are out in the field and say, 'Where's your bone?' The foolish animal lifts its paw. 'No, Rover. Where's your bone?' And again the paw is raised. But notice that no reinforcements are given in this situation. Your younger brother, who thinks this paw-lifting business is very clever but does not understand the psychological principles underlying it, catches Rover on the back steps and proceeds to elicit the response repeatedly (but without reward) until the animal extinguishes. As a result of many experiences of this order, Rover becomes a much more discriminating animal. He now will produce paw-lifting only in a limited range of situations (those including hunger sensations, the smell of food, and the voice of a known adult); the process of *differential reinforcement* has effectively reduced the range of generalization.

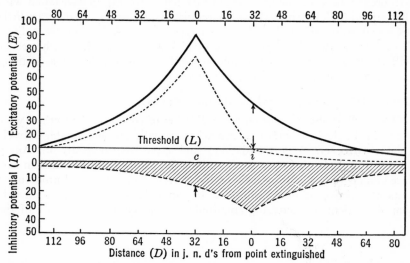

FIGURE 130. Diagrammatic representation of a primary positive generalization gradient based on 25 reinforcements and an inhibitory generalization gradient produced by experimental extinction to the reaction threshold of the generalized excitatory gradient at a point 32 j.n.d.'s from its point of reinforcement. The dotted line between shows the functional summation (effective excitatory potential, or E) of the positive and negative excitatory potentials. Hull, *Psychological Review*, 1939 a, 46:25.

The mechanism here is identical with the process of response decrement described in the preceding section, but it is now considered in terms of a continuum of situations. The response initially conditioned at S_0 generalizes to include S_{x1} and S_{x2}. With repeated and unreinforced elicitations at S_{x1} (in the field), S_{x2} (little brother on the back steps), and so on, conditioned inhibition is generated. Just as with excitatory habit strength, *this inhibitory potential is assumed to generalize.* At each point along the stimulus continuum, *these inhibitory tendencies are assumed to summate algebraically with the existing excitatory tendencies, the resultant being the effective reaction tendency.* In other words, at each point along the stimulus continuum

$$_s\bar{E}_R = {_sE_R} - {_sI_R}$$

and we have merely extended the process of response decrement to cover generalized habits. Figure 130 illustrates these processes (where c refers to point of original conditioning and i to point at which inhibitory tendencies develop). This type of discrimination is based on the development of conditioned inhibition; discrimination may also be based upon the *substitution of incompatible reactions*. The child that has learned systems of approach habits in relation with his own playful puppy may generalize this behavior to older and less amenable dogs. The avoidant tendencies developed in these latter situations, being incompatible with previous approach tendencies, interact so as to produce discrimination. The diagram in Fig. 130 is also applicable here, the general principle being that whenever a stimulus tends to evoke two or more incompatible responses, that response will occur which has the greatest effective habit strength in association with that stimulus. The child comes to restrict its approach behavior to little dogs that wag their tails. These two types of discrimination are only as distinct as the decrement processes on which they are based, and the reader will recall that conditioned inhibition itself may be considered as nothing more than a specific case of response incompatibility.

Generalization as Cortical Irradiation (Pavlov)

The earliest observations on generalization of conditioned reactions were made in Pavlov's laboratory, somewhat casually by the master himself (about 1910, cf. 1927 translation) and more systematically by Anrep (1920, 1923). In the latter study stimulation at one point on the skin surface of a dog was conditioned to a salivary reaction by the usual procedures; tests of reaction at other points on the animal's skin yielded a convexly shaped gradient of decreasing amplitude of reaction as the distance of the

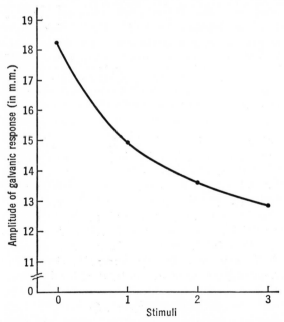

FIGURE 131. Generalization of conditioned excitatory tendency along a pitch continuum. Composite based on data of 20 subjects. Hovland, *Journal of General Psychology*, 1937 a, 17:136.

test point from the point of original conditioning increased. Pavlov interpreted his own and Anrep's findings as indicating 'irradiation' of excitatory processes in cortical tissues. Stimulation of any peripheral sensory point was assumed to be projected to an anatomically determined point in the sensory cortex, from which the excitatory neural process spread slowly and with decrement. Since all cortical elements active at the time of reaction were assumed to become associated in proportion to the intensity of their excitation, this explained the behavioral phenomenon of generalization. A similar irradiation of inhibitory processes was postulated.

Generalization as a Mathematical Construct (Hull)

While drawing heavily on Pavlov's empirical data, Hull has circumspectly avoided his neurologizing. In fact, as part of a footnote to a careful experimental check on Anrep's results (Bass and Hull, 1934), we find this statement: 'We are convinced that Pavlov's contribution to science lies in his integrity and ingenuity as an experimentalist, rather than as the elaborator of systematic theory. In the present article the writers use the term "spread," "irradiation" and "generalization" as a matter of convenience, but do not subscribe to any neurological theory whatever' (p. 47). In this experiment vibratory stimuli were applied to the skin at four points along the left side of human subjects and the galvanic skin reaction was recorded; a convex gradient of excitatory generalization much like Anrep's was obtained. Although the point is not emphasized, the gradient of inhibitory generalization obtained from the same subjects was concave in shape.

In the formal development of his theory, however, Hull (1939 a, 1943) has depended on data obtained by Hovland, who, using auditory stimuli, found *concave* gradients for both excitatory and inhibitory generalization. Since Hovland was interested in generalization along psychologically defined continua, it was first necessary, by usual psychophysical procedures, to select stimuli separated by equal numbers of j.n.d.'s. A first experiment (1937 a) studied generalization along the *pitch* continuum and a second experiment (1937 b) studied generalization along the *loudness* continuum. The procedure was to condition one of the extreme frequencies (or loudnesses) to the galvanic skin reaction and subsequently test the magnitude of this reaction to four other tones along the pitch (or loudness) continuum. In measuring generalization of *inhibitory* tendencies along the pitch continuum, equated conditioning of all four tones was given, then reaction to one of them was extinguished, and finally test of reaction to all four was made. Results for generalization of excitatory tendency along the pitch continuum, of inhibitory tendency along the pitch continuum, and of excitatory tendency along the loudness continuum are shown in Figs. 131, 132, and 133, respectively. These data represent the mean values for all subjects.

Razran (1949) has criticized this work on the ground that 'not a single of Hovland's subjects revealed a consistent gradient of CR generalization' (p. 351), basing this statement on data for individual subjects that Hovland presents (1937 a, p. 135) and a few of which are shown below:

TABLE 6

Tonal Stimuli

Subject	0	1	2	3
I	16.2	11.3	12.6	11.4
II	22.4	18.1	25.4	20.9
III	13.5	6.7	11.2	6.3
IV	15.3	6.4	3.3	7.6
V	19.2	18.5	22.8	15.3
etc.				

After data of Hovland, *Journal of General Psychology*, 1937, 17:135.

As can be seen, the data for individual subjects are highly irregular and in some cases the most remote tone tested yielded higher amplitude than the nearest tone, from which Razran concludes that the smooth function in

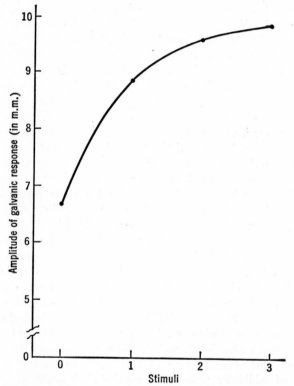

FIGURE 132. Generalization of inhibitory tendency along a pitch continuum. Experimental extinction produced at point o, following equated excitatory conditioning at all points. Composite of data from 40 subjects. Hovland, *Journal of General Psychology*, 1937 a, 17:143.

Fig. 131 is an artifact of averaging. What Razran forgets, however, is that the test stimuli for each subject were necessarily presented *in different orders* to balance extinctive effects; for individual subjects, therefore, such effects are not equated. It would have been helpful if Hovland had presented data on this progressive extinctive effect (by aligning stimuli according to order of presentation, regardless of similarity). By weighing each reaction in terms of this ordering effect, one could then answer the question Razran raises: Do individual subjects show regular and lawful generalization?

The fact that Hovland did obtain a gradient of generalization for the loudness dimension of auditory experience seems to write 'finis' to Pavlov's irradiation explanation of the phenomenon. Since there is much evidence to indicate a frequency-of-discharge basis for intensity rather than a spatial basis, and since Pavlov's irradiation notion is spatial in character, this conclusion follows. It should be observed, however, that the gradient for intensive generalization is much flatter than that for pitch (the three curves shown refer to three stages in the learning process).

Hull's formal statement of the primary generalization principle (1943, p. 199) runs as follows: *The effective habit strength $_S\bar{H}_R$ is jointly (1) a negative growth function of the strength of the habit at the point of reinforcement (S) and (2) of the magnitude of the difference (d) on the continuum of that stimulus between the afferent impulses of $\dot{s}$ and s in units of discrimination thresholds (j.n.d.'s); where d represents a qualitative difference, the slope of the negative growth function is steeper than where it represents a quantitative difference.* Or,

$$_S\bar{H}_R = {_S}H_R e - j'd$$

where d is the difference between S and $\dot{S}$ in j.n.d.'s and j' is an empirical constant of the order of .01 in the case where d is a qualitative difference but of the order of .006 where d is a quantitative difference. The adherence of this postulate to the empirical findings of Hovland is apparent. If, as observed earlier, inhibitory tendencies are assumed to generalize in the same fashion and are further assumed to summate algebraically with excitatory tendencies, then the process of discrimination becomes simply an extension of the interaction between incremental and decremental processes to include generalized reactions.

There are a large number of implications or deductions flowing from this type of analysis (cf. Hull, 1939 a), only a few of which will be stated at this point. For one thing, it becomes possible to deduce that 'a number of subliminal reinforcements conditioning the same reaction to distinct stimuli closely spaced along a stimulus continuum may yield an unbroken superthreshold zone of habit strengths extending well beyond the range of the unconditioned stimuli in question' (Hull, 1943, p. 196). This, it will be recalled, was the paradox with which we began this section. It also follows that the ease of obtaining discrimination between two stimulus situations is inversely related to the amount of generalization between them. This is true for two reasons: (a) the less the generalized reaction tendency at the point where discrimination is to be induced, the less the inhibitory tendency required to counterbalance it; (b) the further apart two stimuli, the less the inhibition generated at the negative point will generalize back to the positive point. At some high degree of generalization (behavioral similarity), the summation of excitatory and inhibitory tendencies at both positive and negative points leaves the resultant reaction potential below threshold, and the organism cannot form a discrimination.—Notice that we are now estimating the size of the *DL* by a discrimination-learning method.

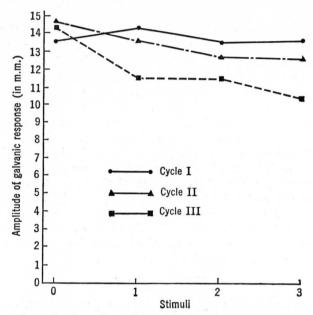

FIGURE 133. Generalization of conditioned excitatory tendency along a loudness continuum. 'Cycles' refers to three successive tests interspersed with tests at other points on the continuum. Hovland, *Journal of Genetic Psychology,* 1937 *b,* 51:286.

An Explanation in Terms of Identical Elements (Guthrie)

Guthrie's theory includes no principle of generalization. Let us suppose that stimulus elements *a, b, c, d,* and *e* have been associated with a particular response in the conditioning situation. If, during the test for generalization, stimulus elements *c, d, e, f,* and *g* are present, the probability of response will be higher than if elements *e, f, g, h,* and *i* are present. In other words, the probability of a particular response occurring in any given situation varies according to the proportion of stimulus elements that are already conditioners of that response. The greater the similarity between original and test situations, the greater should be this proportion. This aspect of Guthrie's theory contains all the advantages and disadvantages of his position in general (cf. Chap. 9). According to this view, incidentally, generalization along pitch continua should be predictable from the measured masking of one tone by another, i.e. both presumably depend upon the numbers of identical stimulus elements (auditory nerve fibers) excited by the training and test tones. This suggests a rather interesting experiment. Whether Hovland's results for pitch generalization would be interpreted as contrary to Guthrie's view would depend on whether masking can be demonstrated between a particular training tone and those 25, 50, and 75 j.n.d.'s apart. In most other conditions it would be extremely difficult to predict proportions of identical elements.

A Mediation Interpretation

A little 2-year-old learns to call his next-door playmate 'friend'; he subsequently learns to call many people 'friend,' including some of Daddy's Big People. Later still, he is shown how to shake hands with his next-door playmate. It will be observed that, in many instances and without special training, this bit of social behavior *transfers* to the other people he calls 'friend,' even to Daddy's Big People. This transfer is presumably dependent upon the prior establishment of a common mediating response (here, saying or thinking 'friend'), but it is independent of physical stimulus similarity. This process is known as *mediated generalization,* and it

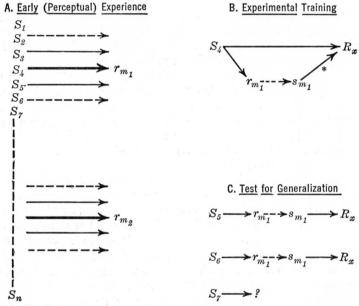

FIGURE 134. Diagrammatic exposition of a mediational theory of generalization.

has been described by Hull (1939 *a,* pp. 27-8) as a secondary mechanism that may produce pseudogeneralization effects. But Hull has not explored the possibility that *all* generalization phenomena may fit this paradigm, rendering superfluous a generalization principle per se (and hence reducing Hull's postulates by one, which is always a happy state of affairs in theory construction).

In the following argument, close attention to the diagrams in Fig. 134 will be helpful. (*A*) Let us assume that the central neural effects of physical stimulation are innately organized along continua represented by the 'dimensions of consciousness' (cf. Boring, 1933). This statement is generally in keeping with our knowledge of the structural organization of the sensory projection systems. Now the earliest *perceptual* learning of the organism involves, *we assume,* the establishment of certain distinctive mediating responses to various patterns of stimuli, which form the basis for 'recognition' of repeated patterns. (A detailed discussion of the development of mediating responses is given in the following chapter.) It is characteristic of the extra-laboratory environment, however, that 'pure' stimuli are not encountered: the warning cry of a parent is a variable stimulus, as is the crescendo of quickly applied brakes, the color of one's own baby hand, or the point of contact of thumb against lips. Nevertheless, and this is the crucial point, it is also characteristic of the stable physical environment that stimuli whose effects would be close together in terms of central continua are more likely to occur synchronously than stimuli whose effects would be far apart. Adjacent tones are more likely to be included in the same stimulus situations (warning cries, whistles, etc.) than more divergent tones; near-equal visual sizes of objects (spoons, blocks, hands, etc.) are more likely to be associated with common reactions than widely diverse visual sizes. It follows that the *probability of two stimuli being associated with the same (perceptual) mediating process varies inversely with the physical difference between them.* By the time the organism is mature enough to be experimented upon, much of the potential manifold of physical stimulation is presumably organized in terms of such perceptual behavior.

(*B*) When we come to the laboratory situation, in which we are using adult subjects and are measuring 'primary' stimulus generalization, the following can be predicted from ordinary association principles: a given stimulus of restricted character is associated with a new reaction (e.g. a tone of 1000 c.p.s. with the galvanic skin reaction). Since, as has been shown above, this stimulus is already associated with certain mediating, perceptual reactions (r_{m1} in Fig. 134*B*), these reactions will occur and their stimulus effects (s_{m1}) will also become associated with the new reaction. (*C*) In the final test for generalization, various other stimuli along the same physical continuum are presented and the magnitude of reaction to them is measured. Since the mediated stimulus (s_{m1}) is already associated with the new reaction, the magnitude of this galvanic response to the various test stimuli (900 c.p.s., 800 c.p.s., etc.) will depend upon the degree to which they are capable of evoking the same mediating reactions (r_{m1}). Having shown that the probability of two stimuli being associated with the same mediating reactions varies inversely with their nearness on physical continua, it follows that a typical 'primary generalization' gradient must be predicted, when group data are averaged.

This, it should be observed, *could* be Guthrie's interpretation of the phenomena of primary generalization, since no learning principle other than association is involved. In fact, in one place (1935, p. 88) he points out that common movement-produced cues could be the basis for generalization, particularly where a sudden stimulus elicits 'attentional' responses. But is it sufficient? There are at least three weaknesses with this view: (a) It does not account for *the original paradox.* How can necessarily unique events summate? Guthrie would not worry about this, since his theory deals with all-or-nothing associations. (b) It seems to imply an *all-or-nothing transfer* rather than the gradient usually obtained, since the mere occurrence of the appropriate mediation process should be sufficient to mediate the new reaction. Notice that this applies to individual subjects, and we have no convincing evidence that generalization gradients for individual subjects are in fact smoothly graduated. (c) This mediation explanation of generalization depends entirely on *inferred intervening proc-*

esses which cannot be independently measured at present. This makes the hypothesis very difficult to test.

Generalization and Similarity

For those of us interested in philosophy in these busy times, a relation between the principle of generalization and the ancient problem of 'the nature of similarity' seems immanent, if not exactly obvious. Suppose we ask (as has been asked in many an introductory class in philosophy), Which is more nearly similar to a red square—a green square or a red circle? The empirically oriented psychologist quickly tires of discussing matters like 'the relatedness of unique qualities' and dashes off to his laboratory to 'find out'! After setting up a reaction, any reaction, to the red square, he tests his human subject for generalization to the green square and the red circle. Does the red circle show more generalization? If so, the red circle is more nearly similar to the red square than the green circle! Does this mean that we now have an objective scale for measuring 'similarity'? *Only when we are interested in similarity as defined by the behavior of an organism.* And it must be a specific type of organism at that, since similarity scales for the rat, thus defined (or for the Australian Bushman, for that matter), would not necessarily parallel those for Western *Homo sapiens.*

This brings up a minor matter of psychological jargon that most of us take periodic cognizance of but never observe in totality. We follow the impetus of our language and say that 'there is more generalization between these two stimuli *because* they are more nearly similar,' and then (like the brash young psychologist cited above) claim that 'these two stimuli are more nearly similar *because* there is more generalization between them.' Both statements are quite valid, depending on one's definition of similarity. Using a wave-frequency analyzer, we may measure the *physical* similarity (nearness on the frequency continuum) of two tones and then measure generalization as a function of this similarity. Conversely, we may use a group of organisms as measuring instruments for the similarity of tones, as in psychophysics, which is really measuring physical continua in terms of generalization and discrimination. Observe carefully, however, that there is no guarantee that the two measures of similarity will be parallel; in fact, they seldom are. The clearest illustration of this lies in the phenomenon of *octave generalization.* For both the rat (cf. Blackwell and Schlosberg, 1943) and the human, at least, generalization of response to tones one octave apart is greater than to tones nearer on the physical frequency continuum, and they sound more nearly 'similar.' But, of course, there are those who would say that the concept of similarity is meaningful only in terms of the behavior of organisms. In this case we must be content with as many modes of similarity as there are species, and cultures within species. To define it in terms of ourselves is the rankest ego-, ethno-, and genocentrism.

Chapter 9

THEORIES OF LEARNING

Several aspects of theory in learning have already been introduced. This was necessary to provide an adequate interpretation of certain basic phenomena in the field. In this chapter we shall present a more systematic survey of learning theories, starting with what may be called the three major variants—a contiguity theory (Guthrie), a reinforcement theory (Hull), and a cognition theory (Tolman)—and concluding with a number of minor variants which have arisen out of felt insufficiencies in the major views. An attempt will be made to elaborate one of the major views (Hull's) in such a way as to take account of what seem to be its chief weaknesses.

What is the underlying theme from which these views all derive as variants? It is *associationism,* particularly as developed by the British School during the last two centuries. The British Associationists analyzed the mind in terms of one essential principle, the association of ideas by contiguity; secondary principles were also brought to bear, similarity, contrast, and (less commonly) a hedonistic pleasure-pain principle. As we have seen, all contemporary theories include contiguity as one of the necessary conditions for learning. Guthrie best retains the parental conception of a single explanatory principle, but it is stimulus element that is associated with muscle movement. Tolman best represents the parental notion that it is 'ideas' which are associated. And Hull makes full use of a kind of hedonism (his reinforcement principle), while retaining the contiguity principle, but here also it is stimuli and responses that are associated. Although these theories are not the only contenders on the contemporary scene, they are the most general in application and the most clearly formulated.

GUTHRIE: A CONTIGUITY THEORY

Although not strictly a single-principle theory, Guthrie's view employs fewer assumptions than any other contemporary position, and this is one of its scientific advantages. Partly for this reason and partly because he shares with Watson an abhorrence of mentalistic constructs, Guthrie's theory is the most frankly mechanistic in nature. We find him saying, for example: 'All that the most sophisticated man can do in any situation is to contract his muscles in some order and pattern. Sophistication consists in having developed new orders and patterns and having these dependent upon the proper signal' (1942, p. 24). Despite this emphasis, which can fairly be called atomistic, Guthrie's theory is found to apply easily to much of human learning. Indeed, no other psychological theorist's writings are so replete with illustrations from everyday life.

Nature of the Contiguity Theory

The constructs used in Guthrie's theory are essentially the same as those used by Hull (with which we are already somewhat familiar), except that there are fewer of them. Notable by their absence are many intervening variables, such as inhibition, habit strength, and reaction potential. The major unobservable in the theory is the implicit muscle movement and the distinctive proprioceptive cue it produces, but this device does yeoman's service in explicating complex behaviors, much as it did for Watson. Guthrie also makes use of the notion of 'maintaining stimuli,' roughly equivalent to both 'drive' and 'set.' His entire system can be reduced to perhaps three postulates which, through ingenious analysis, are made to cover a wide range of behavioral phenomena. Despite the consistency of interpretation in his many writings, however, Guthrie himself has never formally set forth a system. This need seems to be being met by some of his students (cf. Voeks, 1949).* But let us clarify terms before studying principles.

A *stimulus* is any change in physical energy which activates a receptor and sets up afferent impulses in the *CNS*. A *cue* is any unconditioned or previously conditioned stimulus for the response in question. Guthrie also uses the term *conditioners* to refer to stimuli which have been associated with a response. *Response* is defined as the movement of any muscle (or group of muscles) or the secretion of any gland (or glands). These muscle movements may not appear overtly, as when antagonistic muscle groups are simultaneously innervated, but such 'responses of not responding' still count in theory. *Incompatible responses* are movements that cannot be made at the same time. This distinction between compatible and incompatible responses—necessary for the theory—is easy to define but difficult to specify in concrete cases. Guthrie also draws a sharp distinction between *movements and acts:* it is movements which are associated with stimuli and which can be predicted from theory, but it is acts about which we usually talk (e.g. when we say that a boy sharpens his pencil, writes in his book, walks to the door, etc., we are speaking of the effects of his movements, not the movements themselves). This is another matter that is elegant in theory but fruitless in application, even though it is true, as Guthrie (1942) says, that 'the boy's nerves connect his sense organs with his muscles, not with his notebook, the door, or his companion' (p. 22).

* Dr. Virginia Voeks has kindly allowed me to use an unpublished (at the time of this writing) manuscript entitled 'A Formalization and Clarification of a Theory of Learning,' in which she presents Guthrie's theory as a four-postulate system and makes a number of fundamental deductions from it. The most detailed elaboration of a theory of Guthrie's type has appeared in a series of papers by Estes, published subsequent to the writing of this chapter.

The fundamental postulate in Guthrie's theory is this: *whenever a stimulus is contiguous with a response, it becomes maximally associated with that response.* This statement of single-trial association by mere contiguity is a gem for simplicity and generality, but it immediately raises a number of problems. (1) If learning is complete in one trial, why do acquisition curves usually show only gradual improvement? This brings in Guthrie's distinction between movements and acts. The particular movement (e.g. in pressing the bar) made on trial #1 is completely conditioned to the particular stimuli that were present on that trial, but on trial #2, the stimulus pattern is not identical—some elements are added and some subtracted, the animal was just turning its head as the bell was rung, a shadow had just passed overhead—and the movement which this time goes as 'correct' is not identical with that made on trial #1. The *act* of pressing the bar when the bell is heard becomes increasingly more probable (i.e. the habit is gradually learned) as more and more potential stimulus patterns and functionally equivalent movements become associated. In place of 'wearing a neural groove' as the analogy of the learning process, we have here 'setting of all the switches for the same station,' each switch being completely set in one trial. (2) Since exact contiguity is the necessary (as well as sufficient) condition for association of S and R, how can Guthrie explain the common phenomena of trace conditioning? The point is that the true conditioner in such cases is not the bell but the proprioceptive stimuli which result from movements elicited by the bell, and these *are* contiguous with the desired response. 'When the bell rings the dog responds by "listening," which is a series of movements, postural changes, turning of the head, pricking the ears, and the like. When the salivary glands begin to secrete, the accompanying stimuli are not furnished by the bell but by these responses to the bell' (1930, p. 418).

The first postulate describes the only way an association is established, and the second postulate describes the only way an association can be eliminated: *whenever a stimulus, previously associated with a given response, accompanies another response incompatible with the first, the previous association is completely eliminated.* A direct corollary of this postulate is what Voeks (1949) has termed the *principle of postremity,* namely, that what an organism does last in any situation is the most probable thing it will do the next time the same situation recurs. The specification of 'incompatible' responses in this second postulate is taken directly from Voeks. She asserts that a stimulus may continue to elicit an old response as well as a new one, provided the two responses are compatible. This makes it possible gradually to modify a response pattern under repeated presentation of slightly varying stimulus patterns, while retaining those common elements that define it as 'correct.' Guthrie himself is not clear on this. He often seems to imply that associating a stimulus with one response completely eliminates *all* other associations with that stimulus.

Both Guthrie's critics and his supporters have taken him to task for not specifying the relation between number of previously associated stimuli and occurrence of response on a given trial. How much of a previous situation must be repeated in order that the same response occurs? Voeks formally states the relation as a third postulate: *the probability of a particular response occurring at a given time is an increasing monotonic function of the* *proportion of all stimuli present that are conditioned or unconditioned cues for the response in question.** In other words, there are innumerable stimuli present at any given moment, associated with various reactions for the organism. The probability of the appearance of some specific response is assumed to vary directly with the proportion of these stimuli associated (either innately or by previous conditioning) with that response. If all the stimuli in a situation have been associated with the response, it is sure to occur; if none of them, it is sure not to occur. For proportions between 0 per cent and 100 per cent, response probability varies directly, but according to some (unspecified) monotonic function. This postulate, although clearly essential to the theory, does highlight a major difficulty. How are we to go about measuring the proportion of stimuli associated with a given response (except by observing the proportion of trials on which the response does in fact occur, which is completely circular)? The total influx of stimulation varies from moment to moment with changes in external conditions, with changes in the posture of the subject, with changes in motivational state, and so on—and we are absolutely unable to measure all this.

Guthrie's program, rather than being experimental in nature, has aimed at demonstrating through logical analysis that the fundamental principle of single-trial association by contiguity is adequate to account for all the phenomena of learning. Harassed perhaps by the insistent criticism that his theory is relatively unsupported by experimental data, he has offered one detailed analysis of behavior in an instrumental learning situation (Guthrie and Horton, 1946). As it turns out, the experiment is not so much a test of the theory as it is a demonstration that the behavior of cats in escaping from a puzzle-box can be interpreted in terms of the association principle. The situation is the familiar one originally used by Thorndike (1898): a hungry cat in a box must activate a certain mechanism in order to open the door and obtain reward. Behavior of the cats was interpreted by Thorndike as evidence for the gradual strengthening of blind connections that are followed by satisfaction. Guthrie and Horton find evidence for stereotyping the detailed movements of escape, quite independent of the presence or absence of reward as such.

Their method for obtaining data, however, represents a big improvement over earlier studies. The entire front of the puzzle-box was made of glass, the release mechanism was a pole on a rocking base so that it could be moved easily in any direction, and the release door was set into the front glass panel. In order to have the animal enter the box from approximately the same direction and position on each trial, a specially constructed, narrow starting box was attached to the rear of the puzzle-box. Since the same mechanism that opened the door also activated a camera, a detailed picture of the position of the animal at the moment it made the 'correct' response was automatically recorded. In some cases complete motion-picture records were made of entire trials, and the entire performance of one animal was taken in this manner. On a table 4 inches below the puzzle-box and outside the release door were placed small bits of salmon. Figure 135 shows part of the record for cat *G,* an animal showing unusual stereotyping. During the first 40 trials, escape was achieved by brushing the right side of the

* Slightly reworded from Voeks's own statement.

body against the pole as it aimed toward that side of the door. For trial 41, nine days later, the position of the pole was changed as shown in Fig. 135. 'Two days later the cat was given runs 42 to 60. In trial 42, immediately on entering the box, it resumed the position and movement that had released it in the first series. . . Eventual escape after seven minutes, thirty-

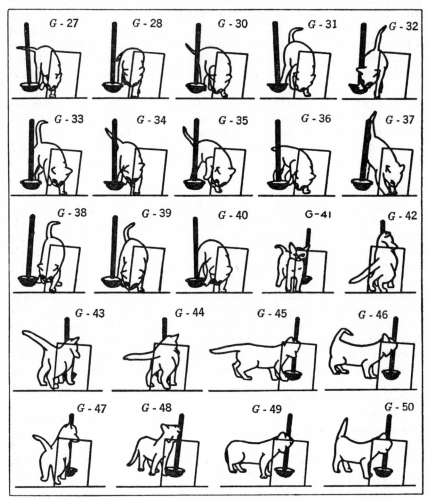

FIGURE 135. Copies of photographs showing position of cat *G* at the moment of solution for trials 27-50. Guthrie and Horton, *Cats in a Puzzle Box*, Rinehart and Company, Inc., New York, 1946, p. 51.

five seconds, was secured by turning and biting the pole. . . Every picture after this shows substantially the same position' (p. 24). Many other animals would show blocks or sets of trials in which the same escape movement was employed, shifting occasionally to different movements.

The experimenters' interpretation of their observations can best be given in their own words. 'The outstanding characteristic of the cat's behavior was its repetitiousness. . . We interpret this as due to the establishment of

one movement as a cue for the next. On the first occasion it is merely followed by the next. On the second it has the effect in occasioning the next,
rendering this following movement comparatively independent of distraction. We would not limit this to the movement-produced stimuli from proprioceptors but would include all stimulation consequent on a movement,
exteroceptive as well as interoceptive. . . But another outstanding characteristic is the special and particular repetitiousness of the end behavior,
the series of movements leading to escape. . . The reason is . . . that this
action removes the cat from the situation and hence allows no new responses
to become attached to the puzzle box situation' (pp. 38-9). In this last we
have Guthrie's explanation for the facilitative effects of reinforcement upon
performance. Giving the animal some food to eat, or merely getting out of
the box, serves to preserve intact the association last formed within the
learning situation, not because of any strengthening effect of reinforcement
per se but merely because the original cues are eliminated, and, not being
present, these critical cues cannot become connected with any other responses. An organism is therefore most likely to do what it did last in
the same situation.

Returning now to the summary: 'The third characteristic is change and
unpredictability.' How is this possible? Why isn't there perfect stereotypy?
One obvious answer is change in the stimulus situation. If the position of
the pole is shifted, if the cat happens to enter from the starting box with a
new set of movements, if an observer moves about, or if a fly lands on the
glass, there are then new stimuli present which have not been associated
with the previous sequence. But, as the authors themselves admit, 'in the
majority of cases, of course, we could not assign a cause to the failure to
repeat. It seems, however, reasonable to assume that each trial might offer
many new and distracting stimuli for such interruptions' (p. 38). This
is precisely why this experiment is a demonstration of the feasibility of
Guthrie's system without being in any sense a critical test of it. Negative
instances are attributed to unestimable changes in the stimulus situation.

Critique of the Contiguity Principle

The criticisms that can be aimed at Guthrie's theory tend to be logical
rather than experimental. (1) *Conditioned and unconditioned responses not
identical.* Evidence was presented in the preceding chapter to show that the
reactions made originally to *US* are usually not the same as those made
finally to *CS*. Does Guthrie's theory run into conflict with this observational
fact? His position is a substitution conception in this sense: any response
or response pattern that occurs must have been elicited by certain stimuli
in the situation (and those taken together constitute the *US*); once occurring, this response becomes completely associated with all other stimuli
simultaneously present (and these taken together constitute the *CS*). Since
the new stimuli cannot become conditioned to anything other than the
response made, and since they must become conditioned to all aspects of
the response, this is a straightforward substitution view. Voeks's version of
the theory, however, explicitly states that a stimulus can be simultaneously
associated with two or more responses, provided they are compatible with
one another. This would mean that, depending on successive variations in
the stimulus pattern, certain elements of the original response pattern could

368 EXPERIMENTAL PSYCHOLOGY

be eliminated and other new elements added, the only decisive factor being compatibility or incompatibility with the 'core' response regularly elicited by *US.*

But this would seem to imply a *random* variation in the response pattern about this 'core' with successive trials, whereas in fact the changes during learning are lawful. For one thing, the 'correct' response tends to become less energy-consuming, gross reactions originally evoked by *US* usually being reduced to that precise movement necessary for the response to be 'correct.' Furthermore, certain parts of the total response elicited by *US* tend to become anticipatory, not all aspects of the total response but particularly those having a 'preparatory' character. Finally, certain elements that never were part of the response to *US* are often integrated into the response to *CS:* on hearing the bell, the dog comes to look 'expectantly' at the food delivery mechanism (the unconditional response here being a vigorous plunging, grasping, and swallowing). Although Guthrie has repeatedly emphasized that responses vary continuously since stimulus patterns vary, neither he nor his students have shown how this variation can have the lawful character it displays.

(2) *Specifiable CS and the R not contiguous in conditioning.* The essence of Guthrie's theory is that events must be perfectly contiguous if associations are to be formed. Yet conditioning is most rapidly effected when the specifiable *CS* precedes the *US*-produced response by approximately half a second. As was observed earlier, Guthrie gets around this difficulty by assuming that the actual conditioners are the proprioceptive (and other) stimuli produced by the 'attentional' responses made to the specifiable *CS*— and these are precisely contiguous with the response. But why should mediated conditioning of this sort be *more* effective than actual contiguity of *CS* and *R,* i.e. where the bell *follows* the food powder at such an interval as to be coincident with the salivary reaction? Guthrie assumes that having the specifiable *CS* precede *US* by a short time serves to restrict the animal's spontaneous movements and hence create a more nearly identical stimulus for each trial. If the *CS* were synchronous with the desired response, the movements just preceding would be likely to vary more widely, thus changing the actual stimulus situation for each trial. But, in this case, shouldn't the *CS* precede *US* by even greater intervals so as to channelize behavior still more rigidly? Why a .5-second interval should be best is no more easily explained by Guthrie's theory than it is by any other existing theory.

(3) *Is it stimulus element or stimulus pattern that is associated?* Both Guthrie, in his various writings, and Voeks, in her formalization, are inconsistent in their use of stimulus (defined as energy that activates a receptor) and stimulus pattern (undefined). Thus we find Guthrie (1935, p. 33) saying, 'The stimuli present as the response occurs are the future cues for the response,' and earlier (1930, p. 420) he says, 'The "strengthening" . . . [is] . . . the result of the enlistment of increasing numbers of stimuli as conditioners.' But he also says (1930, p. 417), 'If the stimulus combination occurs, and the response is prevented by any means, the stimulus combination loses its power to elicit the response,' and later (1942, p. 23), 'A stimulus pattern that is acting at the time of response will, if it recurs, tend to produce that response.' In her own wording of the above-mentioned

postulates, Voeks uses the term 'stimulus-pattern' in postulate one and the term 'stimulus' in postulate two, and then in the third postulate she speaks of the probability of response evocation as a function of 'the proportion of . . . stimulus-patterns present for that response at that time.' Are we splitting terminological hairs here or is there a serious theoretical issue involved?

The use of the term 'pattern'—if it means anything more than mere accumulation—implies interaction among and consequent modification of the included elements, so that element *a* in pattern 1 is not identical with element *a* in pattern 2. In this way the organism can react discriminatively to *a*-1 and *a*-2 (cf. Hull's interaction principle and gestalt conceptions of field forces, Chap. 5). Guthrie does seem to indicate such a view at one point (1930, p. 416): 'The word "stimuli" need not be taken in the sense of elementary stimuli to the individual receptor cells. It seems quite probable that patterns of such elementary stimuli may act as functional units and be subject to conditioning as units, that the elementary group *ABCD* may as a group excite a group of pathways *P,* while another stimulus group, *AEFG,* excites pathway *Q*. Conditioning redirection at remote association areas would affect these stimulus groups as functional units and not as elements. The stimulus *A* would be a conditioner of one response element through *P* and a conditioner of another, possibly an antagonistic element, through the pathway *Q*.'

To the present reviewer, this acceptance of patterning or interaction seems to contradict the central theme of Guthrie's theory. One inevitable corollary of patterning is that the same pattern can never be repeated (even though many of the elements may be retained); another inevitable corollary is that all synchronous elements must affect the total pattern, to greater or lesser degrees (i.e. the entire stimulus situation contributes to the stimulus pattern of the moment). But the essence of Guthrie's system is that 'a stimulus pattern that is acting at the time of a response will, *if it recurs,* tend to produce that response.' Since patterns can never recur, learning according to Guthrie's system becomes impossible. Furthermore, how could we split up the total stimulus situation into 'the proportion of stimulus-*patterns* . . . [associated with] . . . that response,' as Voeks would have us do, if the total situation is itself the momentary pattern? We have no rules of procedure for carving up interacting patterns. Let us observe carefully, however, that these criticisms do not apply if Guthrie's theory actually deals, as most people believe it does, with associations between multitudes of stimulus elements (defined in terms of receptor units) and muscle movements.

If we conclude, however, that Guthrie's type of theory *must* deal with stimulus elements, then we run into another difficulty: How is the 'correct' response in any learning situation made to appear? The superficial answer, of course, is to enlist stimuli that are already associated with the response. If we wish the animal to lift its paw, we shock its footpad; if we want the animal to salivate, we present food powder; if we want a knee jerk, we deliver a blow to the patellar tendon. But how does the stimulation from the footpad, from the sight and smell of food, or from the pressure on the patellar become a sufficiently large proportion of the total number of stimuli acting so that it regularly and reliably elicits the desired response? Certainly, of the thousands of receptors delivering impulses at the moment any *US* is given, the proportion commanded by the *US* is infinitesimally small, yet the response reliably occurs. Similarly for learned responses, the proportion of total stimulation commanded by the noon whistle, sounded while a man is busily at work (and his synchronous movement-produced stimuli are associated with continued work responses), must be small, yet the man drops his tools. This entire question of the stimulus side of association is one which the proponents of Guthrie's theory should carefully study.

(4) *Is the theory testable?* The most serious criticism to be leveled at Guthrie's system is that it is difficult, if not impossible, to subject it to experimental test. This can best be seen by proposing several possible tests and observing their fate under Guthrian analysis. (a) *If a stimulus situation has been associated with a response, it will, on recurrence, elicit the same response.* This is, of course, the fundamental postulate, and nonoccurrence of the same response to repetition of the same stimulus situation would be evidence against the theory. When, in the Guthrie and Horton study, a cat failed on trial #32 to manipulate the pole in the same way it had on the previous trials, and there was no specifiable change in the stimulus situation, was this failure interpreted as evidence against the theory? Not at all. In such cases there was an unobservable, unspecifiable change in the stimulus situation; otherwise the response would not have changed. This argument is obviously circular. The only way the circle can be broken is by independent measurement of the stimulus—and this is impossible, in the detail demanded, with our present techniques.

(b) *Any radical change in stimulation should preserve (strengthen) the behavior preceding it.* As was pointed out in relation to the behavior of cats in the puzzle-box, Guthrie holds that it is not reward per se that strengthens preceding behavior but merely the fact that, in escaping from the box, those stimuli cannot be associated with any other responses. Similarly, the drive stimuli that contribute to the successive stimulus situations throughout the running of a maze are reduced by eating at the end, thus removing these drive stimuli and preventing their association with other responses. To critics who pointed out that the single pellet at the end of a maze does little to reduce the intensity of drive, Guthrie (1939) replies that the restless conflict behavior (which produces much proprioceptive stimulation) is eliminated, thus changing the situation sufficiently. He concludes, 'All that escape or reward does is to protect the learning from being unlearned' (p. 484).

Seward (1942) has attempted to test this hypothesis. All rat subjects were fed one pellet and then put in a bar-pressing apparatus; as soon as one correct pressing response had been made, group *A* rats were fed another pellet (reinforcement) and removed, but group *B* rats were merely removed; all animals were kept in detention boxes for 15 minutes and then returned to their home cages, one trial a day being given. As measured by both latencies during learning and response frequency during extinction, the reward group was definitely superior to the mere-removal group, yet the mere-removal group *did* learn. As Seward himself points out, these findings are not conclusively negative for Guthrie's system. The rewarded rats limited their activities more closely about the food pan and bar, reducing stimulus variation from trial to trial and therefore speeding up learning.

And, of course, there may have been more change in the stimulus situation when eating a food pellet was added than in being removed from the apparatus.

(c) *In a sequence of responses to the same stimulus situation, that one made last will be the most probable one to recur the next time the organism is in that situation.* Voeks (1948) has tested this hypothesis, which she calls the 'law of postremity,' with data obtained from human subjects learning both a multiple-T finger maze and a punchboard-stylus maze. For each trial after the first, and at each successive choice point, two 'predictions' were made: first, that the response made would be the same as that on the immediately preceding trial (postremity); second, that the response would be the same as that made most frequently on all preceding trials (frequency). These were predictions in the sense that, with all data collected, performance on a given trial was used to check both frequency and postremity expectations based on the preceding trials. Predictions based upon postremity were significantly more accurate than those based upon frequency, even when she counted only those cases where the two were in conflict (i.e. when making the same response he had made last time would mean not making the response he had made most frequently at that choice point). One would also expect that the *ratio* of 'postreme' predictions verified to 'most-frequent' predictions verified would increase steadily with the number of trials included. This is because once a given choice point is mastered, *all* succeeding correct choices will fit the postremity law, but not the frequency law until the total for correct responses at that point exceeds the total for incorrect responses. Voeks does not report any breakdown of her data in terms of successive trials. Since her subjects practiced to a criterion of three errorless trials, and she includes all trials in her data, this might help explain the superiority of 'postreme' over 'most-frequent' predictions.

Pursuing the implications of postremity yet further, O'Connor (1946) has argued that the phenomenon of delayed reward learning is critical evidence against Guthrie. Observing rat subjects in a puzzle-box, when touching a wooden pendulum was the 'correct' movement, Roberts (1930) had delayed the opening of the release door from 0 to 30 seconds with different groups. Despite the fact that there was little stereotyping of sequential movements between 'correct' response and release, learning occurred at all delay intervals and final latencies were proportional to the length of delay. Although these results are to be expected from Hull's gradient of reinforcement, they seem incompatible with Guthrie's position. Since, under conditions of delay, the 'correct' response is seldom if ever the postreme response, why isn't the connection of the stimulus situation with touching the pendulum regularly displaced by subsequent associations? Guthrie answers (1946, p. 288) that *it is!* The longer the rat remains in the puzzle-box after the correct response, the greater the *proportion* of these cues that can become associated with incompatible responses; it therefore follows that the probability of recurrence of the 'correct' response on the next trial decreases with the length of the delay interval.

This matter of postremity suggests yet another test. In a standard conditioning setup, where a dog is trained to flex its leg to a tone which precedes shock to the footpad, suppose the tone is allowed to persist until it coincides with *replacement* of the paw on the grid, the replacement movement automatically shutting off the tone. Now since replacement of the foot on the grid is clearly incompatible with the flexion movement which escapes shock, and since replacement is always the last response to the tone, wouldn't Guthrie have to predict that conditioned flexion could not be established under these conditions? But suppose conditioning *did* in fact occur (someone should do this little experiment, if it has not already been done), could Guthrie explain it? He would probably argue in this fashion: The true conditioners for flexion are not the auditory stimuli from the tone but proprioceptive cues arising from 'attentional' movements made at the onset of the tone. This distinctive proprioceptive pattern is neatly eliminated by the flexion response itself, so that these crucial stimuli are *not* present to be later associated with foot replacement. This explanation is also logically consistent with Guthrie's postulates.

It is obviously difficult to back this theory into a tight empirical corner. In the case cited above, we have in effect asked Guthrie to predict *which* of two feasible outcomes of an experiment derives from his postulates. He can apparently predict either way. Rather than being advantageous, ability to predict both ways in a situation like this is a sign that a theory is not completely satisfactory, that its constructs have not been sufficiently well defined. The very simplicity and flexibility which render this theory so readily applicable to all conceivable situations makes it hard to evaluate scientifically. *This does not mean that the theory is wrong.* No evidence disproving it has been presented, and none is likely until we are in a position to measure stimulus situations, including internal ones, with much greater accuracy and detail.

HULL: A REINFORCEMENT THEORY

The notion that organisms, including people, learn to seek pleasure and avoid pain is part of the implicit 'truth' about life held by men of all times. The little boy learns to search for hidden Easter candies *because* they are pleasant to consume; the same little boy learns to do his chores *because* failure to do so eventuates in punishment. The model pup in a previous chapter learned to lift its paw *because* this movement either gained meat or avoided shock. Within the context of formal philosophy this position is known as *hedonism,* and it was a law of life respected by both Plato and Aristotle. It was Thorndike who first clearly incorporated philosophical hedonism within a strictly psychological framework. He called it the *Law of Effect* * and phrased it as follows: 'Of several responses made to the same situation, those which are accompanied or closely followed by satisfaction to the animal will, other things being equal, be more firmly connected with the situation . . . ; those which are accompanied or closely followed by discomfort to the animal will, other things being equal, have their connections with that situation weakened. . . The greater the satisfaction or discomfort, the greater the strengthening or weakening of the bond' (1911, p. 244).

Critics were quick to point out that this should be called a law of *affect,* referring as it does to affective states of satisfaction and annoyance. Further-

---

* An excellent and detailed review of the history and present status of this law has recently been written by Postman (1947).

more, what was such a law doing in a book entitled *Animal Intelligence?* Cognizant of this difficulty, Thorndike (1911, p. 245) had tried to define these states in terms of observables, and independent of the fact of learning: 'By a satisfying state of affairs is meant one which the animal does nothing to avoid, often doing such things as to attain and preserve it. By a discomforting state of affairs is meant one which the animal avoids and abandons.' It is usually very difficult to specify when animals are 'doing things to attain or avoid,' however, other than observing whether they learn or do not learn. This underscores the ever-present danger of tautology in any effect theory. We cannot explain learning in terms of 'effects' if these consequences are themselves defined in practice by the occurrence or non-occurrence of learning.

Nature of Reinforcement Theory

In the writings of men like Spencer, Bain, and William James, direct forerunners of contemporary psychology, we find a convergence of associationism, evolutionary doctrine, and hedonism. If we now add Pavlovian conditioning as a model and investigatory tool, we have the four pillars of Hull's behaviorism. Hull's reinforcement principle (a particular kind of nonmentalistic hedonism) appears as only one of a system of interlocking postulates, but it is the core of the system. The system as a whole, with its anchoring definitions, postulates, and theorems, represents the most rigorously devised theory of general behavior presently available. Portions of this theory, particularly those relating to habit formation, inhibition, and generalization, have already been described in some detail. Our purpose here will be to provide an over-all view. The best source for a detailed description of the entire theory, of course, is Hull's own *Principles of Behavior* (1943).*

Figure 136 provides a convenient summary of the major constructs and the processes that relate them. They are ordered here according to their utilization in describing a typical instance of response elicitation. Hull conceives of the organism as a self-maintaining mechanism whose behavior is determined by the operation of a limited number of natural laws. Let us trace the sequence of events whereby environmental energy produces appropriate actions in the organism. Through the process of *reception* physical stimuli (S) become afferent neural impulses (s) in the organism's sensory systems. Afferent impulses which are simultaneously present in the nervous system are modified by the process of *interaction* into qualitatively unique impulse-patterns ($\bar{s}$). Through the process of *summation,* reinforced repetitions of the association between particular afferent and efferent events cumulate into habit strength ($_sH_R$). Since the momentary evocation stimulus on a particular trial is never identical with the central tendency of previous stimulations, the actual or generalized habit strength ($_s\bar{H}_R$) available is that remaining after the process of *generalization* is taken into account. This generalized habit strength combines multiplicatively with drive (D), ac-

* Since this writing Professor Hull has distributed a revision of his system in mimeographed form. Although the general nature of the theory is not changed, there are significant changes in details which the interested reader will want to investigate.

cording to the process of *motivation,* to yield the reaction potential $(_sE_R)$. Since biological action involves work and the consequent development of both innate (I_R) and learned $(_sI_R)$ *inhibition,* these negative effects must be subtracted from the reaction potential to yield the effective reaction potential $(_s\overline{E}_R)$. Since Hull postulates a principle of chance indeterminism, the effective reaction potential is assumed to vary from moment to moment

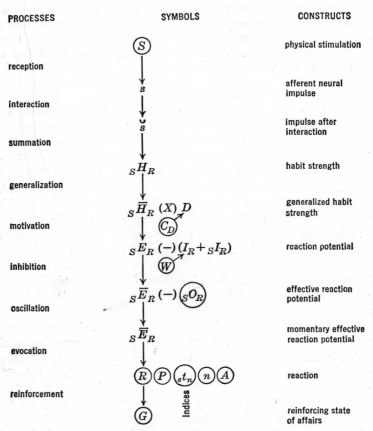

PROCESSES	SYMBOLS	CONSTRUCTS
	S	physical stimulation
reception		
	s	afferent neural impulse
interaction		
	$\overset{\smile}{s}$	impulse after interaction
summation		
	$_sH_R$	habit strength
generalization		
	$_s\overline{H}_R\ (X)\ D$ C_D	generalized habit strength
motivation		
	$_sE_R\ (-)\ (I_R + {}_sI_R)$ W	reaction potential
inhibition		
	$_s\overline{E}_R\ (-)\ (_sO_R)$	effective reaction potential
oscillation		
	$_s\dot{\overline{E}}_R$	momentary effective reaction potential
evocation		
	$R\ P\ _st_n\ n\ A$	reaction
reinforcement	Indices	
	G	reinforcing state of affairs

FIGURE 136. Summary of the major constructs, symbols, and processes involved in Hull's behavior theory. Circled symbols represent observables.

according to an *oscillation* process; the momentary effective reaction potential is that theoretically available at some particular point in time $(_s\dot{\overline{E}}_R)$. In the inferential sequence it is this construct that is directly correlated with observable reaction (R) through the process of *evocation;* the amount of $_s\dot{\overline{E}}_R$ determining R is indexed by a number of functions relating to the probability of the reaction (P), its latency $(_st_n)$, the number of unreinforced repetitions necessary to produce extinction (n), and the amplitude of reaction (A). Finally, the strengthening or weakening of this entire sequence is assumed to be dependent on its eventuation in a reinforcing state of affairs (G), which sets in motion the process of *reinforcement.*

The reader may feel compelled to remark upon the cumbersomeness and complexity of this system, but he is reminded that the behavior of organisms is not by any means simple. The system is exactly as complicated as Hull found it must be in order to render deductions of numerous phenomena of learning. Every well-authenticated behavioral phenomenon must be deducible from the set of postulates, or they must be either modified or elaborated. We have already seen how the phenomenon of generalization forces some elaboration of theory to account for spread of habit strength to situations other than those in which learning takes place; we have also seen how the phenomena of extinction and spontaneous recovery force some elaboration of theory to account for temporary decremental effects. This is not to imply that Hull or any of his students consider the present form of the theory to be perfect; it is always a provisional system, a set of postulates which are viewed as gross approximations to the 'truth.'

If the theory is to be sensitive to experimental facts, it must make explicit contact with observables. In Hull's terms, the intervening variables postulated in theory must be anchored to both antecedent and subsequent observables by clearly formulated functions. In Fig. 136 the major observables in the theory are indicated by encircling. The major dependent variable, of course, is response (R); the various observable characteristics of response, probability (P), latency $(_s t_n)$, trials to extinction (n), and amplitude (A), are linked to the terminal intervening variable in the system, momentary effective reaction potential $(_s \dot{E}_R)$, by a set of mathematical functions (cf. pp. 325-7). On the input side the major independent observable is the physical stimulation (S) which affects the organism's receptors; the actual operations whereby this input to the organism would be observed are presumably physical measurements of the environment, but this procedure is not detailed by Hull any more than it is by other theorists.

Wherever an additional source of independent variation is introduced to the system, it should have its relations to observables specified. The concept of drive (D) is such an additional source of variation, in this case the energetics of the system; drive is linked to a set of observable conditions of organismic need (C_D), admittedly insufficient in elaboration at the present time. The inhibitory inputs to the system $(I_R$ and $_s I_R)$ are another source of independent variation; they are linked directly to the amount of observable work (W) done in reacting and indirectly to other constructs in the system (e.g. habit strength, reinforcement, etc.). The oscillation function $(_s O_R)$, which modulates effective reaction potential $(_s \bar{E}_R)$ in a downward direction from its maximum, is treated as if it were an observable— this, according to Hull, is because of its presumably constant value (e.g. normal Gaussian variability). Finally, the presence or absence of reinforcement (G) is also treated as an observable; the rules of procedure here are obscure and contribute to some of the major theoretical issues in contemporary psychology. With this background we may now briefly consider the postulates in the system.

Postulate 1. Reception. The organism is coupled to the environment via its afferent nervous system, and its reception is dependent upon the neurophysiological principles governing the action of this system (cf. Chaps. 1-4 in this book). Hull makes use of certain of these principles in framing his reception postulate, as follows: * *Afferent neural impulses (s) are generated by the action of stimulus energies (S) upon receptors and are propagated toward the effectors via the brain, showing equilibration when the stimulus energy is continuous and decaying in intensity according to a negatively accelerated function of time following termination of the stimulus.* The latter part of this statement refers to the 'stimulus trace,' as it is called. This trace construct has important functions in Hull's theory, as we shall see, generating deductions of anticipatory behaviors, goal gradient phenomena, and the like. There is, however, no neurological evidence for trace effects as prolonged in time (some 30 seconds) as Hull assumes.

Postulate 2. Interaction. This is one of the most controversial of Hull's assumptions. It was formulated to take account of gestalt-like patternings of stimuli in relation to response selection, as follows: *All afferent neural impulses (s) active in the nervous system at any given instant interact with each other in such a way as to change each into something partially different (š) in a manner which varies with every concurrent associated impulse or combination of such impulses.* Hull then adds one quantitative statement to the effect that the magnitude of interaction of one impulse on another varies directly with the intensity of the first. In connection with statements about theory construction made earlier, it should be observed that interaction is an additional source of variation to the total system, yet no explicit anchoring to observables is made. This, of course, is the underlying reason why it has not proved acceptable, even to those who generally support Hull's position.

Postulate 3. Innate behavior. Any theory of behavior must make certain assumptions about what is 'given' in a species through the long process of evolution. According to Hull: *Organisms possess certain receptor-effector connections ($_sU_R$) which, under specific drive conditions, are capable of evoking a hierarchy of responses that are more likely to terminate the need than would a random selection of responses.* What this says, in effect, is that all organisms possess certain reflexes and instincts which, at birth or appearing through maturation, increase the probability of their survival. This is the fund of behavior potentiality upon which the more finely selective principles of learning operate.

Postulate 4a. Reinforcement.† This is the postulate in Hull's system that distinguishes him most clearly from other theorists. *Whenever an effector process (r) occurs in close temporal contiguity with an afferent process (s), or the perseverative trace of such a process, and this conjunction is closely associated in time with the diminution in the receptor discharge characteristic of a need, there results an increment of the tendency for that stimulus to evoke that reaction on subsequent occasions.* The two crucial conditions for learning are thus temporal contiguity and reinforcement. Observe that reinforcement is defined in terms of reduction in the intensity of a drive, this in turn being operationally defined in terms of various observable conditions

---

* I have taken the liberty of modifying the wording and arrangement of certain of these postulates. This has been done to make the system more comprehensible to students who may not have read the original. I have tried, however, to preserve Hull's essential notions.

† Hull actually combined his reinforcement and summation principles into a single postulate. What rules he followed in deciding what constituted a 'single' postulation are not clear, at least to this writer.

of need. Hull is well aware that most learning depends upon the operation of secondary drives (not primary) and has provided for the derivation of such motivating conditions in his system. He is also aware that most reinforcing states of affairs are somewhat removed in time from the *s–r* conjunctions they are assumed to effect. In accounting for this, he has described a *gradient of reinforcement* (cf. Chap. 10 for discussion).

Postulate 4b. Summation. This aspect of Hull's theory has already been discussed, but a more formal statement can be given here: *Increments from successive reinforcements summate to yield a combined habit strength ($_sH_R$) which is a simple positive growth function of the number of reinforcements (N). The upper limit (m) of this function is the product of (1) a positive growth function of the magnitude of need reduction, (2) a negative function of the delay (t) in reinforcement, and (3) a negative growth function of the degree of asynchronism of S and R.* The statement that habit strength is a function of the *delay* in reinforcement creates a problem. A number of studies by Thorndike (1933 *a, b*) and his associates (Tilton, 1939, 1945; Stephens, 1941) and others have offered evidence for what is called a *spread of effect,* in both directions from the point of reinforcement. If subjects call out numbers to a list of words, for example, and some of the responses are called 'right,' not only are these responses repeated at more than chance frequencies, but so also are nonreinforced responses bordering on *both* sides. Jenkins (1943 *a, b, c*), using rat subjects, has obtained similar results. Hull appears to accept as fact that the effects of reinforcement can spread both forward and backward, but he expresses doubt that effects subsequent to the point of reinforcement can be of much importance in selective learning (cf. 1943, p. 162). Several alternate explanations to an 'automatic' spread of reinforcement have been proposed: a set or intent to repeat (Wallach and Henle, 1941), an isolation or emphasis effect quite independent of reinforcement per se (Zirkle, 1946 *a, b*), or guessing habits for number sequences that are 'anchored' to and follow rewarded responses (Jenkins and Sheffield, 1946; Jenkins and Postman, 1948).

Postulate 5. Generalization. This principle has also been discussed earlier. *Generalized habit strength ($_s\bar{H}_R$) is jointly a negative growth function of (1) the strength of the habit at the point of reinforcement and (2) the magnitude of the difference on the continuum of that stimulus between the point of reinforcement and the evocation stimulus in units of discrimination thresholds* (j.n.d.'s). Basing his conclusion chiefly on Hovland's data (cf. pp. 355-8), Hull further postulates that the generalization gradient is steeper for qualitative (e.g. pitch) than for quantitative (e.g. loudness) continua. Hull subsequently (1949) has modified this position somewhat with respect to intensive generalization. After citing considerable evidence showing that magnitude of reaction varies directly with intensity of the eliciting stimulus (including data obtained by Hovland, 1937 *b,* and J. S. Brown, 1942), he deduces (a) that when a response is conditioned to a weak stimulus and generalizes toward stronger stimuli, the resultant gradient will be convex in shape, and (b) that when a response is conditioned to a strong stimulus and generalizes toward weaker stimuli, the resultant gradient will be concave in shape. Grice and Saltz (1950) have measured generalization along a size continuum (20, 32, 50, and 79 sq. cm.

white circles), following original training to either the smallest or largest circles. The gradients obtained fitted Hull's modified conception rather closely, provided we assume the animals were responding in terms of an intensity dimension (e.g. total brightness) rather than a size dimension per se.

Postulates 6 and 7. Motivation. In common with most other theorists, Hull attributes the energizing of behavior to conditions of biological need. The concept of drive (D) enters his system as another hypothetical construct, linked to various conditions of organic need by as many functions as there are primary need states, e.g. drive as a function of hunger (h), indexed by hours of food deprivation, drive as a function of sex hormone concentration (c), and so forth. In order to bring motivation into contact with the afferent side of behavior, drive states are assumed to produce stimuli (S_D) which have the 'triggering' character of all stimuli (i.e. can become discriminably associated with adaptive reactions). *Associated with every drive (D) is a characteristic drive stimulus (S_D) whose intensity is an increasing monotonic function of this drive.* As we have already seen, Hull assumes that learned habits combine with drive multiplicatively to produce performance of acts by organisms. *Any effective habit strength $(_S\bar{H}_R)$ is sensitized into reaction potentiality $(_SE_R)$ by all primary drives active within an organism at a given time, the magnitude of this potentiality being a product obtained by multiplying an increasing function of $_SH_R$ by an increasing function of D.* Figure 137, based on data obtained by Perin (1942), clearly illustrates the multiplicative manner in which drive (indexed by hours of food deprivation) and habit strength (indexed by number of reinforcements) combine to yield various degrees of reaction potential (indexed by the number of reactions to extinction).

Postulates 8 and 9. Whenever a reaction is evoked in an organism, there results a primary negative drive that has an innate capacity (I_R) to inhibit the reaction potentiality of that response, this innate inhibitory tendency being an increasing function of the number of reactions in a sequence and of the amount of work (W) involved in execution of the response. This reactive inhibition spontaneously dissipates as a simple negative growth function of time at rest. This postulate applies directly to the phenomena of extinction and spontaneous recovery discussed in the preceding chapter. In order to explain the permanent decrements obtained in repeated cycles of extinction, Hull postulates conditioned inhibition. *Stimuli closely associated with inhibition of response become conditioned to this inhibition and thereby generate conditioned inhibition $(_SI_R)$; conditioned inhibitions summate physiologically with innate reactive inhibition (I_R) against reaction potential just as positive habit tendencies summate with each other.* The present writer does not see why these conditions for the development of conditioned inhibition require postulation; assuming that innate inhibition is a drive state which spontaneously dissipates, and hence that rest is reinforcing, the development of conditioned inhibition in association with incident stimuli would seem to be deducible from other postulates in the system.

The remaining postulates of the system can be summarized more succinctly. *Postulate* 10 states the *oscillation principle* whereby the momentary available reaction potential is caused to vary in amount from instant to instant according to the normal law of chance; this principle provides the fluid coupling in the system, a degree of indeterminism consistent with our observations of organismic behavior. *Postulate* 11 provides a behavioral threshold: *the momentary effective reaction potential* $(_s\dot{\bar{E}}_R)$ *must exceed the reaction threshold* $(_sL_R)$ *before a stimulus will evoke a reaction.* This

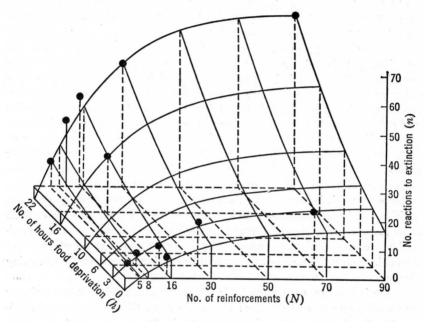

FIGURE 137. Three-dimensional graph representing the fitted 'surface' corresponding quantitatively to the combined action of the number of reinforcements (N) and the number of hours of food deprivation following satiation (h) in the joint determination of the number of unreinforced acts of the type originally conditioned that are required to produce a given degree of experimental extinction. Hull, *Principles of Behavior,* Appleton-Century-Crofts, Inc., New York, 1943, p. 229. Adapted from C. T. Perin, *Journal of Experimental Psychology,* 1942, 30:93-113.

postulation is forced by the nearly universal observation that a considerable number of training trials must be given before any measurable conditioned reaction appears. *Postulates* 12 to 15 specify the *indexing functions* whereby effective reaction potential $(_s\bar{E}_R)$ is related to probability, latency, and amplitude of response as well as to the number of trials to reach extinction. The final principle, *postulate* 16, provides the necessary statement regarding what happens when two or more reactions are in competition: *when the reaction potentials* $(_sE_R)$ *to two or more incompatible reactions occur in an organism at the same time, only the reaction whose momentary effective reaction potential* $(_s\dot{\bar{E}}_R)$ *is greatest will be evoked.* It should be emphasized that these postulates provide only the barest outline of Hull's theory; it is their combination in generating deductions of particular behavioral phenomena that gives a better picture of their explanatory power. A number of illustrations will be given throughout the remainder of this section.

Critique of Reinforcement Theory

Despite the wide potential applicability of a reinforcement principle and the support it derives from common sense—organisms certainly behave as if some such law were operative—it has been violently criticized on many grounds. The mere fact that organisms behave *as if* a law of effect were operative does not give scientific validity to the notion. Other principles could function so as to give the superficial appearance of a law of effect (e.g. Guthrie's explanation in terms of changing the stimulus situation). In this case it becomes necessary to discover or devise crucial experimental tests, and this is never an easy task. The crucial tests here concern the question, (1) *Is reinforcement necessary for learning?* Since apparently negative findings on this issue are usually explained by reinforcement theorists as owing to the presence of secondary (learned) reinforcements, a second question becomes, (2) *What is the nature of secondary motivation and reinforcement?* Both of these problems are discussed in detail in Chapter 10, 'Certain Controversial Issues in Learning Theory.' As a matter of fact, the other major issues covered in that chapter also involve Hull's theory. Much of the experimental literature in the field in recent years has been aimed either in criticism or in support of some aspect of Hull's theory; in large part this is because Hull's theory is the most explicitly worked out position and hence the most testable. These other issues are (3) *Do animals learn movements or cognitions?* and (4) *What is the nature of the discrimination process?* With the purpose of avoiding redundancy, these aspects of the critique on reinforcement theory will be considered only in the following chapter.

There is another, even more basic, difficulty which reinforcement theory shares with any 'effect' position: (5) *How can reinforcement work backward in time?* All effect theories state that behaviors are selectively strengthened or weakened on the basis of their consequences. This is true whether the consequences are conceived as satisfying states of affairs (Thorndike) or reductions in drive (Hull). If we may speak, for convenience, of 'pathways' in the central nervous system, the crucial neural event in learning is the flow of excitation from certain afferent paths into those specific efferent paths that eventuate in the correct response. This event is shown diagrammatically as happened at time-point *a* in Fig. 138. The role of reinforcement (if there is such a thing) is to strengthen selectively one direction of flow, the 'correct' one, over and against any other potential directions. But, and here's the rub, consummatory responses, satisfying and annoying states of affairs, or what have you, inevitably occur *after* the crucial neural event. What Hull terms the 'goal response' (R_G), i.e. eating the food pellets, is shown as happening at time-point *b,* somewhat delayed. And ultimate drive reduction ($S_D\daleth$) occurs at time-point *c,* an indefinite delay varying with the type of drive but probably involving many minutes in some cases (such as hunger). Since it is to this 'diminution in the receptor discharge characteristic of a need' that Hull attributes reinforcing power, we are faced with the logical paradox of retroaction: how can the facilitative effect of drive reduction search back through the myriad neural events that have already happened and selectively grace the correct one? The fact is that it can't—any conception of processes working backward in time is foreign to contemporary science.

If any effect theory is to be tenable, then, either (1) some representation of the crucial neural event must persist through time and hence be present at the time drive reduction occurs or (2) some representation of drive reduction must be present at the time the crucial neural event occurs. Utilizing the first resolution, Thorndike (1932 a) has suggested that the physiological equivalent of the connection persists in time so as to be present at the time satisfiers and annoyers occur. But so also must persist the representations of all other incorrect connections. Similarly, Troland (1928) speaks of retroflex circuits in the brain and Culler (1938 a) proposes that

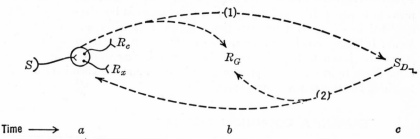

Time ⟶   a   b   c

FIGURE 138. The retroaction paradox in effect theories. The 'crucial neural events' occur at time-point *a*, followed after a variable interval by some sign of reinforcement (R_G) at time-point *b*, and followed after an even longer interval in the usual case by actual drive reduction (S_1) at time-point *c*. Either some representation of the crucial neural events must be present at the time of reinforcement or drive reduction (1) or, conversely, some representation of reinforcement or drive reduction must be present at the time of the crucial neural events (2).

just active pathways are most easily re-aroused by the new stimulation constituting reinforcement. As Postman (1947) points out in his review of the problem, 'neurologizing' of this order is quite incapable of test at the present time. Utilizing the second alternative, Carr (1925) and Hollingsworth (1928) have said that the consequence of an act, rather than working backward, works forward to change the stimulus situation on the *next* trial, i.e. after being burned, the child shuns the fire because the stimulus is now flame plus fear. Although this serves to eliminate the paradox of backward action by making the effect contiguous with the subsequent occurrence of the event, it seems quite incapable of explaining learning under conditions of delayed practice. It is a common procedure, for example, to give subjects a single trial per day. How can the effect of the trial today persist so as to modify the stimulus situation tomorrow?

Hull makes use of both possibilities. On the one hand, he postulates the *stimulus trace,* a neurological construct presumed to persist, though diminishing in intensity, through short intervals of time. From this conception he derives the gradient of primary reinforcement. In this way a representation of the crucial neural events is made contiguous with the reinforcing state of affairs, but this mechanism is sharply limited in the interval over which it can operate. On the other hand, he deduces from his theory that stimuli preceding reinforcement will become conditioned to goal responses; fractions of such goal responses can thus become anticipatory, move forward (in successive trials) in the behavior sequence, and serve as secondary re-inforcing agents. In this way a representation of the reinforcing state of affairs is brought forward and possibly made contiguous with the crucial neural events, but it is not at all clear how drive states can be reduced in anticipatory fashion.

Another fundamental question is, (6) *What is the nature of reinforce-ment?* Although it is not necessary in psychological theory that one specify the physiological nature of one's constructs, it does enhance their accepti-bility if reasonable correlates can be demonstrated. No reasonable correlates have been suggested here. Thorndike (1933 c) was reduced to talking about an 'O.K. reaction,' an unknown reaction of neurons, aroused by satisfiers, which strengthens connections. Or consider Hull's definition of reinforce-ment in terms of drive reduction: How do changes in body economy become reflected in the central nervous tissue at the right time and at the right locus? It is conceivable, of course, that, to the extent that drive and satiation states are shown to have hormonal bases, reinforcing states of affairs will come down to interactions between neural events and the chemistry of their medium, but this is again mere speculation.

TOLMAN: A COGNITION THEORY

Tolman employs terms like 'hypothesis' and 'demand' in his theorizing. This, despite his own description of his system as 'purposive behaviorism,' has led many people to think of him as antibehavioristic. On this point, Tolman himself says (1932, p. 2): 'The behaviorism here to be presented will contend that mental processes are most usefully to be conceived as but dynamic aspects, or determinants, of behavior. They are functional variables which intermediate in the causal equation between environmental stimuli and initiating physiological states or excitements, on the one side, and final overt behavior, on the other.' In other words, the raw data for Tolman, as for both Hull and Guthrie, are objectively observable physical events rather than subjectively introspectable mental events. If he refers to his intervening variables with mentalistic terms adopted from everyday lan-guage, we may think this ill-advised and confusing, but it doesn't affect the logical status of these variables—we can think of them as x's and y's, if we wish.

Tolman stresses a molar level of analysis. The natural unit of behavior is the *behavior-act,* conceived as having an emergent, 'whole' character. 'A rat running a maze . . . a man driving home to dinner . . . my friend and I telling one another our thoughts and feelings—these are behaviors (qua molar).' Behavior qua molar is characterized by its purposive nature, by the utilization of various objects in achieving these purposes, and by the tendency to select the easiest means for achieving these goals. Or, as Tolman puts it (1932, p. 12): 'Complete descriptive identification of any behavior-act per se requires descriptive statements relative to (a) the *goal-object* or objects, being got to or from; (b) the specific pattern of com-merces with *means-objects* involved in this getting to or from; and (c) the facts exhibited relative to the selective identification of routes and means-objects as involving short (easy) commerces with means-objects for thus getting to or from.' In this quotation we can see one of the reasons for dif-

THEORIES OF LEARNING 383

ficulty in understanding Tolman's position—he has a passion for originality in the use of language. Our first task, therefore, is to explore his terminology, since it is within this descriptive framework that his underlying principles must be discovered.

The chief 'immanent determinants' of behavior are *demands* and *expectations*. These are intervening variables whose existence and character are inferred from observable stimulus situations and observable behavior. In other words, demands and expectations mediate between the 'ultimate causes' (external stimuli and organic states) and overt behavior. That organisms do have demands (or purposes) is indicated by the fact that they will persist through trial and error and by the fact that behavior is selectively modifiable or *docile*. Expectations are 'bits of knowledge' concerning the nature of the goal-object, its position (direction and distance), and the natures of the means-objects and the 'commerces' which they will support. Evidence for such expectations is the fact that if any of these environmental entities are changed and hence prove *not* to be so and so, the behavior of the subject shows disruption and alteration until a new expectation is developed.

The expectation itself is a *cognitive event* having relational or gestalt properties. What is meant here seems to be this: when one pattern of stimulation (sign) is followed in time by another (significate), a relation develops between them (cognitively, centrally, perceptually), which is the knowledge or meaning that behaving in a certain manner to the sign will eventuate in its significate. Such expectations may be of a broad, orientational sort which Tolman calls *means-end-readinesses*. When, for example, an animal demands a certain type of goal-object (i.e. is motivated), a system of means-end-readinesses is energized—readiness for commerce with a certain kind of food, readiness to explore pathways, readiness to perceive food signs, and so on. These 'sets' may be innate or they may be transferred from previous experience. The more specific expectations relating to 'what leads to what' in a given situation Tolman now calls *hypotheses,* a term borrowed from Krechevsky (cf. Tolman and Krechevsky, 1933). These expectations or hypotheses are docile with respect to experience, being strengthened when confirmed (i.e. when the significates prove to be such and such) and weakened when not confirmed. Thus the animal gradually builds up a more and more refined and accurate 'cognitive map' of the situation.

Actual behavior or performance requires *behavior-supports*—it cannot proceed *in vacuo*. There must be both sensory supports or *discriminanda* (the blackness or whiteness of the walls in a discrimination box, for example) and motor supports or *manipulanda* (the run-into-ableness, climb-over-ableness, press-down-ableness, and so forth of the environment). Expectations are established concerning these discriminanda and manipulanda: after experience in a maze, the rat not only expects the goal-object to have such and such a quality and to be in such and such a place, but also expects the walls to keep on being black, the maze to smell and feel so and so, the floor to support its running movements, and the air to continue as a move-through-able medium. The existence of these expectations is also verified by the disruption and 'surprise' displayed by an organism when any significate proves not to be such and such, for example, if on the *n*th trial a strange odor is introduced or the press-down-able bar proves to be immovable.

Nature of the Cognition Theory

The most detailed statement of Tolman's theory is probably that given in his 'Determiners of Behavior at a Choice Point' (1938 *a*), originally presented as his presidential address before the American Psychological Association. The general situation envisioned is that of an animal making a choice reaction in a simple T-maze, in which the correct response is turning

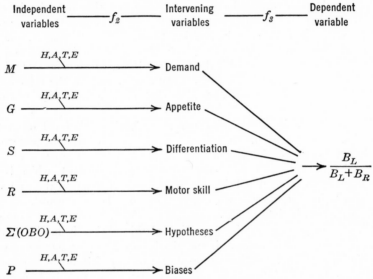

FIGURE 139. Summary of the major variables in Tolman's theory and their systematic relations. Tolman, *Psychological Review*, 1938 *a*, **45:16**.

right. Figure 139, taken from this paper, provides a convenient summary of the major constructs in his system. It will be seen that this system has the same general form as Hull's system: sets of *independent variables* are linked to a set of *intervening variables* by certain functions (f_2) and it is these variables, the 'immanent determinants,' that are linked to the *dependent variable,* behavior, by another set of functions (f_3). The difference between the two views lies mainly in the nature of these intervening variables; whereas Hull's have a materialistic tone (habit strength, drive, reaction potential, etc.), Tolman's, for the most part, have a decidedly mentalistic tone (demand, appetite, hypotheses, etc.).

The probability of left-turning behavior $[B_L/(B_L + B_R)]$, i.e. making an error, is shown to be a simultaneous function (f_3) of several intervening variables: (1) the *hypotheses* which the animal has developed in the course of previous experience $[\Sigma(OBO)]$ in this maze; (2) the *demand* which the animal's maintenance schedule (M) has produced; (3) its *appetite* for the particular food objects 'expected' in the goal-box, which depends in turn upon their 'appropriateness' (G); (4) the degree of *differentiation* which the external stimuli (S), or discriminanda, in the situation make possible; (5) the *motor skills* of the animal in relation to the types of motor response (R) required by the manipulanda in the situation; and (6) the *biases* (e.g. left-turning preferences) which have been set up by the preceding and succeeding maze units (P). These f_3 functions have not been spelled out in any detail, but the general procedure is clear enough: we need merely substitute $_sH_R$ for 'hypothesis' and probability-of-response for $B_L/(B_L + B_R)$, and the same type of procedure followed by Hull in developing his indices of habit strength would apply here. In other words, the operations whereby Tolman might work out a set of indexing functions for his intervening variables should differ in no way from those employed by other theorists.

The same statement applies to the f_2 functions relating these intervening variables to independent variables. As indicated above, 'hypotheses' depend upon the summation of previous experiences in which certain signs have eventuated in certain significates via certain behavior routes; 'demands' depend upon the physiological states engendered by certain maintenance schedules, and so on. Given the types of indexing functions described above, the effects of deliberately manipulating feeding schedules, previous experiences, stimulus situations, and so on upon the several intervening variables could be determined as the f_2 functions. That Tolman has not carried through such a program does not mean it is unfeasible.

The remaining symbols in Fig. 139, H, A, T, E, refer to individual difference variables, heredity H, age A, previous training T, and special endocrine, drug, or vitamin conditions E. These variables are assumed to influence all of the f_2 functions, i.e. special endocrine conditions may influence demand, previous training may influence hypotheses, age may influence motor skills, and so on. Hull has not paid much attention to such variables, and Tolman has done little more than to mention their importance; they form the subject matter of much of physiological psychology and the psychology of individual differences.

One difference between Tolman- and Hull-type theories, stressed by the former, should be mentioned: it concerns the manner in which intervening variables *combine* in their effects upon the terminal dependent variable, behavior. As we have seen, Hull assumes combination by simple algebraic summation (e.g. inhibitory potentials simply subtract from excitatory potentials). This reflects the underlying mechanistic model that Hull is following. Tolman (1938 *a* and elsewhere) expresses the belief that his intervening variables combine as vectors in a field and cites the model provided by Lewin (cf. 1935, 1936) as the most promising he has found. His earlier statements about the 'gestalt-like' nature of sign-significate-expectancies follow along the same line. Tolman, however, has never elaborated upon the mechanisms whereby vectors in a field become translated into movements of an organism's muscles (however, cf. 1939).

What are the postulates of Tolman's theory? Unfortunately, like Guthrie he has never given a formal statement of his principles, and it is therefore up to the reader to ferret out these things for himself—always a trepidatory procedure. Furthermore, Tolman's terminology and perhaps his principles as well have been changing during the past two decades. For these reasons the interested student will want to check the postulates given here—we find four that are directly relevant to learning itself—against his own interpretations.

(1) Motivational Principle. *Demands selectively sensitize those means-end-readinesses and hypotheses with which they are associated.* As one of the intervening variables in Tolman's system, 'demand' is itself a cognitive state of the organism, its amount and quality depending upon both the physiological state of the animal and its experience with appropriate incentives. A rat does not demand a specific type of goal-object, even though hungry, unless that object has been experienced in the environment. The sensitizing or energizing function of demands is best shown, according to Tolman (1932, p. 35), by selective responsiveness to stimuli. 'It is the hungry rat only who is responsive to food-stimuli. The satiated rat "pays no attention" to food. He even lies down and goes to sleep in its presence. . .' This relation between demands and expectancies is a docile one with respect to experience. Although 'an inexperienced rat responds to all the stimuli provided by a maze—those coming from the wire covers over the alleys, those coming from slight cracks at the corners . . . the "maze-wise" rat, on the other hand . . . becomes responsive only to such stimuli as come from the maze-alleys proper' (p. 36). It will be noted that I have lumped Tolman's 'demand' and 'appetite' variables into a single motivational principle; a more elaborate analysis might require their separation.

(2) Association Principle. *Whenever one stimulus situation* (sign) *is followed by another* (significate), *there is established a relation between them, such that on subsequent occasions the former tends to give rise to an expectation of the latter* (sign-significate-relation). In his most recent expression of this principle, Tolman (1949, p. 145) has said: 'It is my contention that when an organism is repeatedly presented on successive occasions with an environmental set-up, through which he moves and relative to which he is sensitive, he usually tends to acquire an apprehension not only of each group of immediate stimuli as it impinges upon him but he also tends to acquire a "set" such that, upon the apprehension of the first group of stimuli in the field, he becomes prepared for further "to come" groups of stimuli and also for some of the interconnections or field relationships between such groups of stimuli.' Except for the fact that Tolman's associated events are cognitive, this principle is much like Guthrie's central notion. Like Guthrie also is Tolman's recent and casual statement about unlearning: '. . . the de-acquisition of one field expectancy results from the learning of another conflicting expectancy' (1949, p. 152). Tolman, however, apparently does not hold for 100 per cent strengthening of such expectancies in a single experience, as the following strengthening principle indicates, even though White (1943), in his own interpretation of Tolman's theory, does say that a more or less permanent association results from one experience.

(3) Strengthening Principle. *Sign-significate-expectations, as relational associations, are strengthened by confirmation and weakened by nonconfirmation.* This is a very obscure aspect in Tolman's theorizing. The fact that he has been in the forefront of those attacking the 'law of effect' (both Thorndike's and Hull's versions) has led most students to believe that Tolman himself uses no effect principle. A careful reading of his works on my own part has led me to the belief that he does have a kind of effect

principle—*but the effect itself is cognitive in nature.* There are actually two implications in the principle phrased above: (a) that field expectancies, or sign-significate-expectations, do vary in strength; (b) that the strengthening operation is the confirmation of what was expected. I shall try to justify these assumptions with references to Tolman's own writings.*

(a) *That sign-significate-expectations vary in strength.* Tolman lists (1932) a number of variables governing the strength of expectations, including *frequency, recency, motivation, emphasis, and temporal relations.* Regarding the first two, he says (p. 386): '. . . the more frequently and more recently the actual sequence of sign, means-end-relation and significate have been presented, the stronger, other things being equal, this resulting sign-gestalt will tend to be.' Motivation is accepted more cautiously, and 'emphasis' is substituted for Thorndike's law of effect (cf. the Tolman *et al.* studies on the use of shock with right or wrong responses, pp. 424-5). He is not clear on how temporal relations among stimulus complexes effect the strengths of expectations—this is one of the major weaknesses of the theory. In a collaborative paper with Brunswik (1935), Tolman clearly accepts the notion that signs (local representations) are usually *equivocal* in pointing to significates (entities represented). The 'causal texture' of the environment is said to be such that a given sign may point to a number of alternative significates with varying probability (strength). If entering a lighted door has sometimes been followed by contact with food, sometimes a female, and sometimes shock, the comparative strengths of expecting food, female, or shock will vary as probability functions with the frequency of each eventuality in experience. The result of learning (repeatedly experiencing a particular sequence) under stable conditions is to strengthen one sign-gestalt at the expense of others. Brunswik (1939) did find that rats will choose right or left directions with frequencies roughly corresponding to the predetermined probabilities of food being at one place or the other, a result, of course, not at variance with other theories.

(b) *That the strengthening operation is the confirmation of what was expected.* By 'confirmation' is meant merely that the environmetnal subsequents prove to be such as were expected (e.g. that the walls prove to be black, the food object to be in such a place, of such a kind and amount, etc.); by 'nonconfirmation' is meant that things prove not to be as expected. As I have said earlier, to determine the nature of the strengthening principle employed in any theory of behavior, one must discover that operation or condition which, when present, is assumed to result in the strengthening or maintaining of an association and which, when absent, is assumed to result in the weakening and elimination of an association. In his original presentation of his systematic views (1932), Tolman repeatedly refers to the maintenance of sign-significate-expectancies when the significates 'prove in fact to be such and such' and to the 'disruption' and 'surprise' evident in the animal's behavior when the subsequent on-coming stimuli prove not to be such as were expected. In an article on 'The Acquisition of String Pulling by Rats' (1937, p. 137), he states that 'if the environment changes so that

* Although the simplest procedure might be to write to Tolman himself for a definitive statement, inclusion of his communiqué here would be the use of private information and I prefer to rely on public sources. Perhaps Tolman himself will sometime clarify his position on this matter.

the one stimulus object plus the given behavior no longer leads to the other stimulus object, then this set with its consequent behavior will under normal conditions sooner or later tend to disappear (i.e. to be unlearned again).' The term 'set' here is used synonymously with expectation. Later in the same article (p. 140) we find Tolman saying that 'mere frequency of string pulling . . . does not simply, as such, attach this string pulling to the stimulus of "string leading into box." But rather, according to my belief, it is the repetition of such occasions of induced string pulling together with the resulting further stimulus situation of "pan drawn in and food within reach" which causes a new sign-gestalt expectation to develop.' In 'Determiners of Behavior at a Choice Point' (1938 a), Tolman discusses the 'disruptions' that occur when significates prove not to be such and such in the following way: 'I believe . . . that they also are to be conceived as auxiliary, catalyzing sorts of affair which react back upon the independent variables and make the final values of the resultant behavior ratios different from what the latter originally would have been. . . The rat's disrupted behavior . . . brings about new values of the independent variables— especially G and $\Sigma(OBO)$—and thus causes a different outcome in the final behavior ratio' (pp. 171-2). It will be recalled that G and $\Sigma(OBO)$ are assumed to be functionally related to strengths of appetites and hypotheses, respectively.

(4) Action Principle. *Specific sign-significate-expectations, as cognitive events, are released by sign stimuli and, when demand is also present, mediate overt behaviors 'appropriate to' significate stimuli.* Expectations, being cognitive events, are indexible only by the overt behaviors they in turn elicit, but such overt behavior may or may not be immediately evident. The additional determinant of action is demand, itself some function of motivation. As White (1943) has put it: 'If there is a motive or "need," the goal of which is a particular object . . . and if at the same time there is available the knowledge that a particular piece of behavior is a path to that goal-object, . . . then that behavior will tend to occur' (p. 163). The knowledge or expectation elicits 'appropriate' goal-seeking movements when the organism is demanding the goal-object. This leaves us in the dark as to what 'appropriate' behaviors are and how they are organized and selected. Inherent in this action postulate are the two most distinctive aspects of Tolman's theory: (a) *It is a representational mediation theory.* Immediate environmental cues release cognitive expectations which in turn mediate overt behavior. (b) *Learning and performance are segregated.* Learning per se applies to cognitions, being reflected in overt performance only under certain additional conditions.

As might be expected, a cognition theory of this sort is readily applicable to a broad range of behavioral phenomena. The acquisition of a conditioned reaction is nothing more than the building up of a simple sign-significate-expectation, in which the conditional stimulus (bell) is the sign, the unconditional stimulus (food or shock) is the significate, and the conditioned reaction is behavior appropriate to the significate. We might say the animal learns the meaning of the bell in this situation, learns that it is a sign of coming food or shock, and then behaves so as to account for the food or shock. Tolman (1937) distinguishes between what he calls *substitute stimulus learning* and *signal learning;* in the former *CR* and *UR* are essentially the same (because the response originally made to *US* happens to be 'appropriate' when elicited by *CS*), whereas in the latter *CR* and *UR* may be quite dissimilar (e.g. holding the breath in anticipation of shock). Extinction follows a change in what is expected, a change in the meaning of the sign.

Instrumental learning is merely the temporal extension and integration of such processes. Repeatedly experiencing a behavior sequence eventuating in a demanded goal-object has two effects: first, specific sign-significate-expectations are differentiated and strengthened; second, these specific 'bits of knowledge' are integrated into what Tolman has come to call 'cognitive maps' (1948). These maps may be relatively narrow and striplike, as when an animal fixates a specific path through a maze, or they may be comparatively broad and comprehensive, as when an animal learns the general orientation of a maze pattern including the approximate location of the goal. Maps of the latter type facilitate transfer and insight; strip maps tend to be induced by brain damage, restriction of spatial cues, overlearning, and too strong motivation. How are temporal sequences integrated? Tolman (1932) suggested that '. . . the stimuli at any opening of a section of the true path will come to release not only the immediate sign-gestalt-expectation corresponding to that section per se but also a more extended, inclusive sign-gestalt-expectation corresponding to this section plus succeeding sections' (p. 147). Whether or not this integrative process proceeds backward from the goal in a manner analogous to Hull's goal gradient is not discussed by Tolman. In cases where several alternative and equally short paths are available to the same goal, the rat may display what Tolman calls 'multiple trackness,' a general expectation that any behavior-route within a variable set will eventuate in the goal (cf. Hull's 'habit-family hierarchy' notion). He cites experiments by Muenzinger (1928), Yoshioka (1929), and Dashiel (1930) as evidence that animals do vary their routes more or less by chance under such circumstances.

Critique of Cognition Theory

The major issues raised by Tolman's theory are the same as those raised by Hull's theory: (1) *Is reinforcement necessary for learning?* and (2) *Do animals learn movements or cognitions?* Tolman finds himself in opposition to Hull on both questions. He believes that reinforcement (at least, in the sense of drive reduction) is not necessary for learning per se, although it may facilitate overt performance, and he believes that learning involves the formation of cognitions rather than the association of stimuli with responses. Consideration of these issues requires evaluation of a great deal of diversified evidence and will occupy our attention in the next chapter. For the present, certain logical difficulties with Tolman's theory will be pointed up.

(3) *How are sign-significate-expectations strengthened?* In formulating the strengthening principle for this theory it is logically necessary to assume that it is the expectations which are strengthened by confirmation and not the overt behaviors they mediate. The alternative would lead to an endless regression in attempting to explain how expectations (themselves modifications of behavior) are learned. But Tolman apparently conceives of an expectation as a gestalt-like whole relating sign with significate. How does such an entity become stronger or weaker? Along what dimensions does

it vary? One can conceive of strengthening the cohesive forces binding together two stimulus events, the sign and the significate, much as the surface tension of a soap bubble might be varied. Or, sidestepping the gestalt implications (which seem only incidental to Tolman's theory), one can conceive of several physiologies for the strengthening of purely central 'whats-leading-to-whats.' Asking this question of Tolman is much like asking the reinforcement theorist to describe the precise nature of reinforcing states of affairs, and the answers are equally obscure.

Tolman, along with others, has taken the reinforcement theorist to task for indulging in fantasy by assuming that events subsequent to an association can somehow work back upon it through time. Exactly the same criticism can be aimed at Tolman himself, however, and on two counts. In the first place, signs and significates are separated by variable temporal gaps. How can the cognitive relationship between them (the expectation) be formed? Either some representation of the sign process must persist so as to be contiguous with the significate process, or some representation of the significate process must become anticipatory so as to be contiguous with the sign process on subsequent occasions. In the second place, expectations are necessarily separated from their confirmation or nonconfirmation by variable temporal gaps. How can an expectation be strengthened or weakened by an event that occurs later in time? Again, either some representation of the expectation must persist or some representation of confirmation must become anticipatory. Tolman has not criticized his own system along these lines.

(4) *How do temporal factors affect the formation of sign-significate-expectations?* Tolman appears to deal exclusively with associations in a forward direction—significates *follow* signs—and the temporal gaps between the associated events vary considerably. Nowhere, however, do we find statements about how the *degree* of temporal contiguity affects the strengths of expectations. Since it is not sensible to assume that all sequential events, regardless of their temporal separation, should become equally associated, it seems likely that Tolman will be forced to a conception much like Hull's postulation regarding stimulus-response asynchronism. This is another illustration of the way in which the nature of facts ultimately forces a confluence of theoretical principles, however diverse their origin.

(5) *Do all stimuli become both signs and significates?* Since no limiting conditions are given by Tolman, we are led to conclude that *all* antecedent stimuli, as signs, tend to become associated with *all* subsequent stimuli, as significates. In other words, each stimulus situation, such as a particular choice point in the maze or a black spot on the flooring, must serve simultaneously as one of the multitude of signs for succeeding stimulus patterns and as one of the multitude of significates of preceding stimulus patterns. But of what is the pattern of proprioceptive stimuli arising from the rat's muscles a sign? Can this pattern of muscle sensations be said to be the significate of anything that preceded it? Of what is the food object discovered in the goal-box a sign? There are no statements in Tolman's theory specifying the conditions under which certain stimulus patterns *become* signs such as to contrast with conditions under which they do not. This is a crucial difference between Tolman's type of sign-learning theory and the *mediation hypothesis* to be described later in this chapter.

(6) *How is overt behavior related to expectations?* Tolman has shown a magnificent lack of concern over the details of behaving. Having cognitions and demands, 'appropriate' behaviors just appear spontaneously. As White (1943) puts it, 'Since this behavior is not necessarily a "response" to a "stimulus," it is called simply behavior . . .' (p. 171). This lack of concern has certain advantages, chiefly that the important phenomenon of response equivalence can be accepted without explanation. It also has a serious disadvantage from the standpoint of theory, namely, that there is a gap in the inferential sequence which makes detailed predictions impossible. In other words, Tolman's f_3 functions need to be made more explicit. He has been criticized on this ground by a number of writers (Guthrie, 1935; Hilgard and Marquis, 1940; and Thorndike, 1946).

Because of this gap in the predictive sequence, one gets the impression (while reading Tolman's work) of a disembodied rat floating along the cognitive lines of its expectations, busily plotting maps of the experiential field—all quite isolated from the corporeal, behaving muscles which move it here and there. Thorndike (1946, p. 278), for example, suggests that we put the rat in a little wire car and run it repeatedly through a maze, releasing it in the food compartment and feeding it there. Will an animal treated in this fashion learn as rapidly as one that actually behaves through the sequence? We doubt it, but Tolman's theory doesn't tell us why we should. Only recently has he given any attention to the details of action, and even here only incidentally. He says (1949, pp. 153-4) : '. . . in default of other experimental theories about the learning of motor patterns I am willing to take a chance and agree with Guthrie that the conditions under which a motor pattern gets acquired may well be those in which the given movement gets the animal away from the stimuli which were present when the movement was initiated. . . A motor pattern thus gets learned without reinforcement. I would like to point out, however, that such a learning of motor patterns is of necessity always imbedded in a larger goal-directed activity—a point which is not emphasized by Guthrie.' This, of course, does not rigorously tie movements to expectations in the inferential sequence, which is the crucial issue.

(7) *How are expectations identified?* Despite Tolman's protestations that his system is a behaviorism, the central role of cognitive concepts like 'demand' and 'expectation' is likely to raise suspicions that his theory is in fact a thinly disguised mentalism. Explaining rat behavior in terms of immanent expectations is merely a sophisticated anthromorphism (instead of saying, 'If *I* were in the rat's place, I would do such and such,' we may now say, 'The rat has such and such expectations') *unless* expectations are identified in a manner independent of the overt behavior supposedly mediated. Suppose a rat has been allowed to experience that path *A* leads to water and that path *B* leads to food; suppose further that the animal is now given a 'demand' for food (as inferred from the animal's maintenance schedule). Now what Tolman says in effect is that if the rat takes path *B,* he must have expected food at the end of *B;* whereas if he does not take path *B,* he did not expect food at the end of *B* (cf. Tolman, Ritchie, and Kalish, 1946 *a,* p. 15; White, 1943, p. 175).

The only way this circle can be broken is to discover independent indices of 'expectations,' i.e. to make certain f_2 functions more explicit. In his earlier writing (1932), Tolman suggested one possible index. In connection with an experiment by Elliot in which the type of food in the goal-box was shifted and the rats, rather than eating steadily after their normal fashion, randomly searched about this box, Tolman says: 'The point we would make is that such "searching," i.e. disruption, is to be taken as the empirical evidence for, and definition of, an immanent expectation of the previously obtained bran mash' (p. 74). Generalizing, we may say that if an expectation is *not* confirmed, the animal displays 'disruption,' 'surprise,' and so forth, i.e. when the goal-object proves to be water rather than food, when the right-side alley proves not to be there, when (by some sleight of hand) the walls of the maze change color or the floor no longer supports weight. By inference, therefore, lack of 'disruption' indicates that expectations are being confirmed. Not only is this matter of observing 'disruptions' vague at best, but it links expectations to the dependent variable (behavior) rather than to any independent variables.

Tolman is not to be castigated unduly for this failure to anchor the crucial intervening variable in his system; we are in effect asking him to provide clear definition to a class of events for which our existing techniques provide no measurement. If the phenomena of behavior require the postulation of nonovert mediation processes, and much of the evidence leads one to believe that such is the case, either they must be *rigorously* linked to antecedent conditions (which has not been done in Tolman's case) or we must await the development of adequate techniques for their direct observation. Linking them only to the subsequent, dependent behavior eventuates in tautology. It is interesting that we have found evidence for circular reasoning at the core of each major contemporary theory: in many cases the presence or absence of 'reinforcement' can only be gauged by whether or not learning occurs; Guthrie's prediction that a response will or will not recur is in terms of 'changes in the stimulus situation,' which are estimable only by the fact that the response in question does or does not happen; and 'expectations' exist or fail to exist depending on whether or not the behaviors supposedly mediated occur or fail to occur.

THE MEDIATION HYPOTHESIS

Speaking before the American Psychological Association in 1946 and discussing 'reinforcement' and 'perceptual' theories of learning, Robert S. Woodworth (1947) began by saying that 'there is no obvious incompatibility of the two factors, and the thesis of this paper is that both of them are essential in any process of learning.' The gist of his position was that in both conditioning and instrumental learning the essential modifications are changes in the way the subject perceives the situation: changes in the significance of a buzzer sound in the conditioning apparatus, changes in the significance of large and small circles in an instrumental discrimination apparatus. But such changes in the meaning of cues, or in ways of perceiving them, are themselves subservient to the action of some principle of reinforcement. The overt reactions observed, lifting of the paw in the conditioning stand or approach movements in the discrimination apparatus, are old, perfectly familiar activities and do not constitute the 'new' learning in most situations. Judging from the applause and comment accorded his paper, Woodworth had again placed his finger on an issue that most psychologists vaguely sensed but had not managed to clearly formulate. In the few years since that time several attempts to integrate the apparently divergent 'perceptual' and 'reinforcement' positions have been made. The mediation hypothesis is one of these. It stems directly from certain mechanisms already available in Hull's general theory.

Short Circuiting

An inept boxer whose blows are always foreshadowed by a slight tightening of the lips, a shift of the eyes, or a telltale twitch of the shoulder is said to 'signal his punches.' These little accessory movements, originally part of the total act of delivering a hard blow, have become anticipatory and serve as reliable signs of the consummatory act. The skilled boxer, while inhibiting such signals on his own part, makes full use of the cues provided by his opponent; in fact, he makes anticipatory avoidant movements on the basis of these cues. How are we to explain this common short-circuiting phenomenon? We might say that people show 'foresight,' can anticipate coming events. But what is foresight? Is it a little man we carry about in our heads who tells us what things are about to happen? Actually, rather than serving as an explanation, foresight is itself a characteristic of behavior that very much requires explaining.

Can the humble rat show foresight? Let us turn to our furry, white test tube and see what it can tell us. An excellent demonstration apparatus has been designed by Mowrer and Miller (1942) and is pictured in Fig. 140. The large box, with its glass front for observational purposes, has an electrifiable grilled floor, a ratchet device which can be turned by the rat (shutting off the shock), and a buzzer which serves as the initially neutral cue. The plot develops as follows: the naïve rat is placed in the box and allowed a few minutes to familiarize itself with the new surroundings. Suddenly a loud buzzer sounds, lasting for 1 second; the rat's initial behavior to this sound is quite variable. Following a 5-second delay period, a strong shock is delivered through the grille, this painful stimulation persisting until the rat happens, in some manner or other, to turn the ratchet wheel. The correct response is typically stumbled upon in the course of agitated hopping, squeaking, clawing, and so on. Some rats develop a sort of waltzing behavior on their hind paws, which apparently minimizes the pain.

Certain changes in the animal's behavior begin to appear as the situation is repeated. Quite early we note that behavior to the buzzer is changing— now, at its onset, the rat may tremble and begin to lift its paws in agitated fashion, perhaps even going into its waltz—and we might say that the buzzer is acquiring a new meaning or sign-value. With further trials we observe that our furry, white organism is concentrating its activities in the area near the ratchet. Being entirely anthropomorphic about it, we comment that 'the rat seems to like this corner of the box.' The moment the shock comes on, it is promptly turned off by the animal. A final stage finds the rat largely emancipated from its bondage to the ratchet device. It roams the box freely between trials, but as soon as the buzzer sounds, it stops what it is doing, waltzes over to the ratchet (notice the 'ritualism' here), and turns it *before* the shock occurs. The rat sometimes becomes so casual that it dallies too long and receives a not-too-gentle reminder of the buzzer's significance.

Can this behavior on the part of the rat legitimately be called 'foresight'? If by the term we refer to the objective fact that an organism behaves in such a way as to 'take account of' subsequent events, then certainly the rat is showing foresight. If the term also connotes having ideas or knowledge about a coming event (i.e. the rat 'knows' that buzzer means shock), then, of course, we can say nothing about it. We have no direct way of observing ideas in rats—or, for that matter, in humans. (Other humans can use

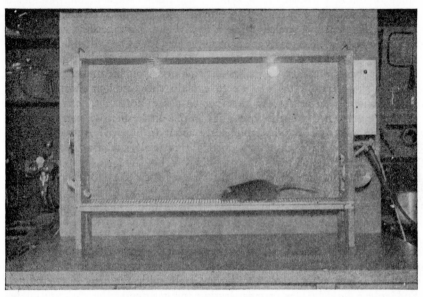

FIGURE 140. Mowrer-Miller avoidance training box. A buzzer is followed after a brief interval by electrification of the grill. Turning of ratchet device by the rat eliminates the painful stimulation. Prof. O. H. Mowrer kindly allowed the author to reproduce this photograph of the apparatus.

words to tell us that 'the buzzer sound means a shock is coming.' One *could,* presumably, train a rat to communicate its states in a limited way: to press a lever when hungry, to pull a chain when anxious, and so on, thus 'telling' the experimenter how it feels. Why doesn't some investigator produce a group of introspecting rats?) In any case, as far as the objective scientist is concerned, particularly were he the hypothetical one from Mars, the rat's behavior here is quite comparable with human sign-behavior.

The essential fact is that reactions originally elicited at one point in the behavior sequence appear to move forward in that sequence and occur in anticipatory fashion. In one of his earliest yet most forward-looking papers on learning theory, entitled 'Knowledge and Purpose as Habit Mechanisms,' Hull (1930) suggested one possible explanation: any *persisting stimulus* will become conditioned to all reactions in the sequence; since associations formed near the terminal point of reinforcement are strengthened more rapidly, the occurrence of the 'same' stimulus earlier in the sequence will tend to elicit these later reactions in antedating fashion. Hull stressed drive stimuli, such as persisting hunger tensions, in this role, thereby emphasizing this as a purposive mechanism, but any persisting or repetitive pattern of stimulation will serve as well—a continuous buzzer sound, the sights and odors in a laboratory room, or a continuous knitting of the brows. This paper of Hull's was written previous to his elaboration of the *stimulus trace hypothesis,* which offers another possible explanation of short circuiting: since the central neural effects of a brief stimulation (such as the buzzer in the example cited above) are presumed to persist through time, though diminishing in intensity, the total stimulus pattern eliciting subsequent reactions (such as the ratchet turning) must include the trace effects of the buzzer. As the traces of antedating stimuli become more strongly conditioned to subsequent reactions, these reactions will tend to occur in anticipatory fashion.

Hull's still more recent *interaction principle* complicates these explanations of short circuiting. Both the persisting stimuli and the traces of antedating intermittent stimuli will, through interaction, be modified by each successive stimulus compound in which they appear; we cannot say, therefore, that a later response conditioned to a persisting (or trace) stimulus will be made anticipatorily because the 'same' stimulation occurs early in the sequence—the stimulation is not the same. Evidently we must bring the principle of *generalization* to bear at this point: although the anxiety and ratchet-turning responses are originally conditioned to a stimulus compound which includes a heavy loading of pain (shock-produced) and only light loadings of buzzer-trace and persisting stimuli (from apparatus, etc.), these reactions will generalize to similar stimulus compounds. Compounds including more intense portions of the buzzer trace and the persisting stimuli are somewhat similar to the original eliciting compound, even though the shock-produced sensations are missing. As the habit strength at the point of original conditioning becomes stronger with successive reinforcements, generalization will spread more broadly until the habit strength of the antedating compound in association with these reactions rises above threshold. Since, by the nature of things, this antedating pattern must occur previous to the original pattern on each trial, anticipatory reactions will appear.

As is true with other behavioral mechanisms, there is no requirement that short circuiting must always lead to 'good' adjustments. To be sure, our test tube rat learned to avoid the painful shock, but the same animal will completely fail to master a maze in which similar choice points produce anticipatory errors. The human animal makes elaborate use of this mechanism in the formation of his complicated symbolic behavior, but he may find it impossible to control his anticipatory startle reaction while pulling the trigger of a gun. Nevertheless, short circuiting enters into all behavior, and its most important role lies in formation of those representational mediation processes which are our present concern.

Development of Representational Mediation Processes

In the Hull paper (1930) already referred to we find the following: 'A reflective consideration of the habit mechanisms involved in anticipatory defense reactions reveals a phenomenon of the greatest significance. This is the existence of acts whose sole function is to serve as stimuli for other acts. We shall accordingly call them *pure stimulus acts*' (p. 515). And in the summary of this paper Hull declares: 'Such behavior sequences have great biological survival significance because they enable the organism to react both to the not-here and the not-now. Incidentally it accounts for a great deal of the spontaneity manifested by organisms. The concept of the pure stimulus act appears to be the organic basis of symbolism . . .' (p. 524). For a number of reasons, chiefly the extensiveness of the research program he set for himself, Hull never did fully explore the implications of this mechanism. It will be my purpose here to elaborate this notion, using it as the basis for the mediation hypothesis.

Let us refer to those complexes of stimuli that are capable of eliciting particular instrumental sequences *without* any mediation as *stimulus-objects* ($\dot{S}$), and refer to those complexes of stimuli that come to elicit mediation processes as *signs* ($\boxed{S}$). This distinction will prove very useful later when this type of analysis is applied to a study of meaning. The reader should not be confused by the term 'object' here—'salty taste in the mouth' is as much a stimulus-object in this context as is 'rubber ball in the hand.' *Stimulus-objects typically elicit a complex pattern of reactions from the organism, some of which are dependent upon the sensory presence of the object for their occurrence and others of which can occur without the object being present.* Electric shock, as a stimulus-object, galvanizes the rat into vigorous jumping, squeaking, and running behavior—all of these activities being instrumental sequences well-established in previous experience with painful stimulation. Food objects, when contacted, elicit sequences of tasting, lip-smacking, chewing, and swallowing. A rubber ball in the hand elicits grasping movements of the fingers, perhaps certain fixational movements of the eyes, and throwing motions. Now, as the statement above indicates, certain of these reactions tend to occur only when the stimulus-object is itself stimulating the organism—agitated leaping usually occurs only to the shock itself, swallowing only to the food-in-the-mouth itself, and throwing only with the ball itself in hand. Many other reactions, initially elicited by the stimulus-object, can occur without the object's presence—autonomic 'anxiety' reactions are produced by shock and salivating reactions by food-in-the-mouth, but neither object is an essential condition for these reactions. We shall refer to the former as 'object-tied' and the latter as 'detachable' (see Fig. 141).

It is the process of short circuiting, just described, which sets up pure stimulus acts and, according to this hypothesis, makes possible mediation in general. *When other stimuli occur in conjunction with the stimulus-object, they tend to be conditioned to the total pattern of reactions elicited by the object; when later presented without support of the stimulus-object, these other stimuli elicit only the 'detachable' reactions.* The buzzer-sound, or its reverberating trace, is present at the time shock is given; originally conditioned to shock behavior in general, the buzzer alone evokes only certain reactions which may become 'detached' (e.g. anxiety). Presented in conjunction with raisins, poker chips become conditioned to many food-taking reactions, but when offered alone they may elicit only 'detachable' lip-licking and salivation. The range of cue stimuli which can, in this way, become associated with fractions of the behavior elicited by objects, and thereby serve as signs of these objects, is limited only by sequences of events in the physical world and by the sensory capacities of the organism. Although the mediation hypothesis does not force a decision on the matter, *it will be assumed here that both instrumental sequences and representational mediating reactions are selectively developed and eliminated on the basis of some reinforcement principle.*

In the process of short circuiting itself there is some reduction in the behavior elicited by a sign, as compared with that elicited by the stimulus-object. There is reason to believe that reduction continues with repetitions of the sign sequence and, furthermore, that this reduction process is lawful. *Of the total pattern of 'detachable' reactions conditioned to the sign, some fraction becomes the stable mediation process.* In other words, the final

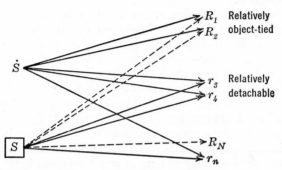

FIGURE 141. Of the total behavior elicited by a stimulus-object, some portion is relatively 'object-tied' (probability of occurrence highly dependent on presence of the object) and another portion is relatively 'detachable' (probability of occurrence largely independent of presence of the object). Signs tend to become conditioned to both types of reactions, but, when presented alone, are more likely to elicit 'detachable' reactions.

mediation process which represents the object is a further reduction in the gross behavior made to the object itself. 'Pure stimulus-act sequences present certain unique opportunities for biological economy not possessed by ordinary instrumental-act sequences . . . pure stimulus-act sequences, since they no longer have any instrumental function, may be reduced in magnitude to almost any degree consistent with the delivery of a stimulus adequate to evoke the final instrumental or goal act' (Hull, 1930, p. 518). The limit to this reduction process is implicit in Hull's quotation: *mediating reactions will tend to become as reduced as possible, while retaining their distinctive cue functions.* But what does becoming 'reduced' entail?

There are at least three principles operative here. (1) *Response interference.* Mediating reactions that interfere with goal-oriented behavior will tend to be extinguished. On trials when such interfering mediators occur the subject is delayed in obtaining reinforcement or fails entirely. If the chimpanzee persisted in looking at the vending machine in response to the poker chip, this would prevent its performing further discriminations and getting more poker chips. (2) *Energy expenditure.* The more energy expended in making a mediating reaction, the less likely it is to survive the reduction process. The vigorous jumping movements generated by shock do not survive in the final mediation sequence set in motion by the buzzer. This is due in part to the greater susceptibility of effortful reactions to extinction effects and in part to the fact that signs usually carry weaker motivational properties than stimulus-objects. It may also be true that 'light-weight' reactions (like salivating, releasing adrenalin, and slight postural adjustments) are more readily conditioned.* (3) *Discriminatory capacity.* The greater the discriminatory capacity of an organism, the more reduced and implicit can become the 'detachable' reactions finally included in the stable mediation process. The higher the organism in the evolutionary scale, the finer the discriminations it can usually make and the less gross its representing processes. Similarly, the more mature and intelligent the human individual, the less overt his symbolic processes. The hosts of fine discriminations that characterize language behavior are Nature's farthest step in this direction.

There is some evidence that responses differ in their susceptibility to conditioning, or at least their rate of conditioning. Mowrer and Lamoreaux (1942) report early experiments by Hamel (1919), Upton (1929), and Weaver (1930) as demonstrating that visceral disturbances always seem to be conditioned previous to the appearance of overt limb movements. This was also brought out clearly in experiments by Liddell and his co-workers (cf. Fig. 120); circulatory and breathing changes appeared in association with the conditional stimulus previous to occurrence of leg flexion. Mowrer and Lamoreaux also cite a personal communication from Lashley regarding early conditioning experiments he had performed in which conditioned finger withdrawal persisted only as long as respiratory and heart-rate changes to the *CS* were apparent in the records.

Whenever a reaction is made by an organism, stimulation is produced. The self-stimulation may be direct, as when the act of tightening the muscles in the hand gives rise to a distinctive pattern of proprioceptive stimuli, or it may be indirect, as when the glandular release of hormones into the blood stream causes numerous physiological changes which in turn have stimulus effects. *The mediating reactions evoked by a sign give rise to self-stimulation.* This pattern of self-stimulation, on the one hand, is assumed to be the conscious awareness of 'purposes,' 'ways of perceiving,' and 'meanings' and, on the other hand, to contribute to the elicitation of overt behavior. It is realized, of course, that the process of reduction as described here may continue to the point where the mediation process is purely cortical, i.e. this hypothesis does not presume the validity of a 'peripheral' as against a 'central' theory of consciousness, although the former is certainly easier to manipulate (cf. Chap. 15). *To the extent that this self-stimulation is distinctive, it can participate in the selection of instrumental behaviors; to the extent that it energizes the organism, this self-stimulation can have motivational and reinforcing properties.* Anticipatory food-taking reactions, or rather the self-stimulation they produce, are distinctively associated with the various overt behavior sequences which have been utilized in the attainment of food objects; this self-stimulation can also augment the organism's

---

* In conditioning a 'heavy-weight' reaction (like paw-lifting), the inhibition being generated by reacting is continually bucking the excitatory tendency being generated by successive reinforcements, thus diluting the reaction potential. This is much less true of 'light-weight' reactions (like adrenalin release). This would help explain the earlier appearance of autonomic and other 'light-weight' reactions during conditioning. This is probably a very significant fact.

motivation and its elimination can be secondarily reinforcing. In other words, certain stimulus patterns, by virtue of evoking fractional portions of the behaviors associated with drive or reinforcing states of affairs, become *signs* of these drive and reinforcing states.

Witness the hungry wild animal as it comes upon the spoor of its prey: instantly its behavior changes—trailing and stalking sequences appear, breathing is light and rapid, and the fine tremor in muscles testifies to its heightened motivation. What produces all this? The spoor of a deer is not the deer itself, but a *sign* of the deer. This particular odor has become a sign of deer because, through past associations with the deer stimulus-object, it now calls forth part of the same behavior originally elicited by the deer itself. Notice that the overt behavior sequences of the hunter are relevant to the object represented by the sign, not to the sign itself. But how are such overt skill sequences themselves organized? This is our next problem.

Development of Instrumental Sequences

At birth organisms possess a fund of reflexive adjustments to certain forms of stimulation; with growth and maturation this fund is greatly enlarged. It is upon the basis of this innately determined behavior that the complex adjustments of the mature individual are ultimately developed. There is surprisingly little information about the genesis of the sensorimotor integrations which enter into hand-eye co-ordination, visual inspection, loco- motion, vocalization, and so on. These minor instrumental skills contribute to all the behaviors we measure in learning experiments, and their organiza- tion is the continuous chore of the infant. Eye movements must be tightly wedded to visual cues if stationary objects are to be inspected and moving objects kept in view; arm, hand, and finger movements must become asso- ciated with visual and cutaneous cues if objects are to be grasped and ma- nipulated; all of the many movements concerned with maintaining posture and locomoting through space must be integrated with myriad sensory data if chairs are to be sat upon, trees climbed, and playmates chased. Learning of this kind goes on through all the long and busy days of infancy and childhood. By the time the child has matured, he has available an extensive repertoire of instrumental sequences, so well organized that they 'run them- selves' once initiated.

What little information there is here has been gathered together in Hebb's recent and stimulating book, *The Organization of Behavior* (1949, especially Chaps. 1-6). He cites evidence obtained by Senden on adult humans who, blind from birth, have their sight restored through surgery. Such individuals are immediately able to differentiate figure from ground (apparently an innate mode of sensory organization), but they require many months of laborious practice before even simple forms can be recog- nized and identified. Hebb theorizes that form perception involves the in- tegration of visual data with systems of eye-muscle movements, practice at the task resulting in stable neural organizations (cf. pp. 198-9 in this book). Correlated evidence from animal studies is also given. Eye-movement skills are only part, albeit a very important part, of the vast repertoire of instrumental behaviors that are developed in the course of exploring the environment. Presumably similar neural organizations are being formed as the infant fumblingly grasps its bottle, integrating tactual and proprioceptive data with the intricately graded muscular reactions necessary for manipulation of any object.

Although little is known about the neurological mechanisms serving to integrate systems of movements and sensory data, we can do some educated guessing about the more superficial behavioral mechanisms. Let us take for example the skill sequence involved in learning how to tie one's shoes— a surprisingly complicated skill as any parent will testify. When the experienced shoe salesman whips through the sequence, looking at *you* and conversing all the while, the speed and effortlessness of the operation defies description. So we will imagine the process as it might appear in very slow-motion film. We could also observe the fumbling and painfully slow attempts of the 5-year-old. We would observe that a fairly stable series of

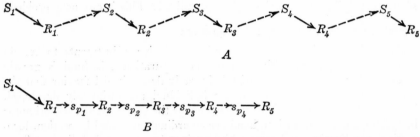

FIGURE 142. Two stages in instrumental skill development. *A*. Early stage where occurrence and sequencing of component responses depends upon presence of exteroceptive cues. *B*. Later stage where control of the behavior sequence has shifted to proprioceptive cues, e.g. each response produces the necessary cues for the next.

stimulus situations in the physical world (S_1, S_2, etc., in Fig. 142) is being paralleled by a fairly stable series of movements on the part of the organism (R_1, R_2, etc.). Let us assume that the stimulus pattern initiating shoe-tying is the sight of the loose strings. This stimulus (S_1) must be associated with the response (R_1) of grasping the strings in a certain way with both hands. Making this response changes the situation for the child; his hands appear in a new position and the strings are seen in a new relation. This second stimulus (S_2) must now be associated with the second response in the series (R_2), the movement of crossing and twisting the strings. Again, this movement changes the situation to S_3 which must in turn be associated with the third response—and so on throughout the shoe-tying sequence.

How is it that this disjointed series of isolated habits becomes a skill? Careful introspection indicates that although external cues (mainly visual) initially control and direct the sequence of acts, they lose their importance at later stages and, as in the case of the shoe salesman, the skill seems to run itself. Let us look at the stimulus pattern more closely: after a child has made the initial response of grasping the strings in a certain manner, not only has the external stimulus situation changed because of his movement, but this movement itself has produced a distinctive input of stimulation to the central nervous system. Whenever a part of the body is moved, receptors in the muscles, tendons, and joints are activated and deliver their characteristic impulse patterns to higher centers. There are many other response-produced cues, such as the changes in locus and intensity of cutaneous sensations in the present shoe-tying illustration. Now if these response-produced stimuli are present at the time the next response in the sequence is made—as they must be once the child can perform the sequence with sufficient rapidity and in the right order—then, following ordinary learning principles, they will also become conditioned to these responses. In other words, *the cues produced by preceding movements must become conditioned to succeeding movements.* When these new habits become sufficiently strengthened, *these* stimuli will elicit the movements in the sequence and, since their occurrence is immediately contingent upon each movement, there is a reduction of delay and the behavior sequence 'telescopes' in time. Once the shift-over to control by response-produced cues is accomplished, the skill sequence truly runs itself. Each movement produces the distinctive cues that initiate the next.

This behavioral analysis of the development of instrumental skills, while undoubtedly true in part, is certainly not a sufficient explanation. It relies heavily upon the sensory 'feedback' from responding muscles, and Lashley (1917) long ago pointed out that there simply isn't enough time between the components of a rapidly executed skill for signals to be relayed back and forth over the motor and sensory nerves connecting brain with periphery. He used for illustration a pianist playing a swift cadenza. It seems probable that in the final stages of skill formation cells in the central motor areas become organized in such a way (cf. Hebb, 1949) that the timing and ordering of sequential movements is determined at this locus. One of the necessary conditions for the development of such central motor organizations is probably a fairly rapid sequence of movements guided by the sensory feed-back mechanism. We need a great deal more information from the neurophysiologists on these points.

The overt behaviors of any animal—the response sequences we conveniently label 'running,' 'leaping over a barrier,' 'turning to the left,' and even 'looking at the white circle'—are actually complex skills of the sort just described. Execution of these skill sequences brings the animal repeatedly to what may be termed *behavioral choice points,* critical stimulus patterns which are not rigidly tied to further on-going movements but rather demand selection of some new skill sequence. Running down a straight alley of the maze is an overlearned skill sequence, but choice of a left or a right turning response at its end is not. It is at such behavioral choice points that the self-stimulation from representational mediators plays its most significant role; this stimulation enters the behavioral equation to 'weigh' the probabilities of shifting from skill sequence A into skill sequence F, let us say, rather than into sequences B, C, . . . N. How is selection from the vast reservoir of potential skills accomplished?

The Role of Representational Mediation Processes in Behavior

Certain stimulus patterns, as signs, are variably associated with systems of mediating reactions (e.g. a buzzer tone may signify shock, food, or a female, but with varying strengths—cf. Tolman and Brunswik's (1935) notion of the equivocality of signs) ; similarly, the self-stimulation produced by making a particular mediating reaction is variably associated with systems of skill sequences (e.g. an 'anxiety' mediation process may be associated with running, jumping, and 'waltzing' sequences, but to varying degrees).

Hull (1934 *a, b*) has termed such systems *habit-family hierarchies*. A *divergent* hierarchy is one in which a given stimulus situation is variably associated with a number of alternative reactions—the examples given above fit this case. In illustrating *convergent* hierarchies, in which a number of stimulus situations are variably associated with the same response, Hull uses a mediational example—all of the distinctive stimuli along the maze path will tend to become associated with the anticipatory goal reaction, and this common mediating process will make possible broad transfer from one type of skill sequence to another. Hull has applied this type of analysis both to the maze-learning behavior of rats and to certain gestalt-type, open-field behaviors of young children (Hull, 1931, 1938).

Many signs fall into classes based on their evocation of common mediators (e.g. convergent hierarchies). The smell of a food object, the sight of the cup in which it is usually found, and the corner around which it is usually encountered—all these stimuli as signs come to evoke fractional anticipatory food-taking reactions in common. *Stimulus patterns associated with the same stimulus-objects will acquire common mediating reactions and hence will become signs having similar significance.* Depending upon the total stimulational context, various instrumental skill sequences will be employed in behaving with respect to a particular stimulus-object. A poker chip that has been made a sign of raisins may elicit vigorous pulling-in movements (when it is spied at the end of a string), running into another room (when it is now in hand, but the raisin vendor is not), and inserting movements (when the animal is facing the vending machine). These varied instrumental sequences, a divergent hierarchy in Hull's terms, are relevant to the stimulus-object (raisins) even though they are elicited by the sign (poker chips). *The mediated self-stimulation produced by the class of signs associated with the same stimulus-object will become conditioned to the initial reactions in all of the instrumental sequences commonly employed with that stimulus-object, but to varying strengths dependent upon the frequency, proximity, and amount of reinforcement correlated with each sequence.* Since a common mediation process is associated with all of the instrumental sequences in this hierarchy, a class of overt behaviors is 'tuned up,' so to speak, and transfer within this hierarchy is facilitated. This is shown diagrammatically in Fig. 143*A*. Signs 1, 2, and 3 fall in the same class by virtue of the fact that they elicit a common mediation process, r_m; the self-stimulation arising from this mediation, s_m, is conditioned to the initial reactions in the many instrumental sequences, R_{x1}, R_{x2}, etc., involving commerce with the same stimulus-object, $\dot{S}$. Again note that these instrumental sequences themselves, as integrated patterns of behavior, are already well established at the time most experiments begin.

Signs are associated with *distinctive* mediating reactions as well as with the common mediators shared with others of their class. The placement of electrodes on the subject's finger sets up anticipatory anxiety reactions *plus* a specific tendency to withdraw the hand; placement on the subject's ear lobe also elicits the common anxiety reaction *plus* a specific tendency to move the head. *To the extent that the self-stimulation produced by mediators is distinctive and selectively associated with particular instrumental sequences, occurrence of these signs will become the condition for occurrence of these particular overt behaviors.* This represents a further and more dis-

criminative selection among potential instrumental act sequences. Figure
143*B* represents how this mechanism functions in discrimination or 'choice'
situations. Although the sight of a playmate on the other side of an open
field ($\boxed{S_1}$) and on the other side of a brook ($\boxed{S_3}$) are associated with
certain common mediation processes (anticipatory play behavior, etc.), the
former is selectively asociated with locomotion in a straight line as an instrumental act (R_{x_1}), whereas the latter is selectively associated with visual
search, detour locomotions, and so on (R_{x_3}). Figure 143*C* represents how
this mechanism may function to control and direct long sequences of instrumental acts (cf. Hull, 1930). The hunting cat runs upon somewhat 'cold'

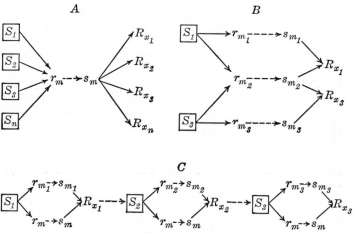

FIGURE 143. Role of representational mediation processes in behavior sequences of
various types. *A.* Association of a class of signs with a hierarchy of instrumental
sequences via representational mediation. *B.* Discrimination among instrumental
sequences by virtue of differential mediators. *C.* Maintenance of a temporal sequence of varied, but integrated, 'purposive' instrumental acts, through operation
of common and differential mediators.

spoor of its prey ($\boxed{S_1}$), which mediates rapid trailing behavior (R_{x_1});
this behavior brings it upon 'warm' spoor of its quarry ($\boxed{S_2}$), which mediates quiet stalking sequences (R_{x_2}); and this behavior in turn brings the
cat to a point in the physical world where it perceives a clump of leaves
trembling ($\boxed{S_3}$), and the mediated self-stimulation here is most strongly
associated with gathering the muscles preparatory to leaping (R_{x_3}). Notice
that all of these signs elicit in common anticipatory food-taking reactions
(r_m), which presumably gives continuity and 'purposefulness' to the entire
sequence.

The typical learning experiment employs behaviorally mature organisms
as subjects. Such organisms bring to the 'new' situation systems of representational mediating mechanisms (meanings or ways of perceiving situations) and systems of instrumental skill sequences (sensorimotor integrations of varying complexity), both types of organization acquired in previous experience. What, then, constitutes *learning? Success in the 'new'
situation may require* (a) *modification in the mediation process elicited by
a particular stimulus pattern* (e.g. the buzzer sound must come to mean

'danger'; it must be perceived in a different way) or (b) *modification in the instrumental sequence elicited by a particular mediator* (e.g. the buzzer still signifies 'danger,' but something other than running must be done). Mediational modification is indicated in Fig. 144 by a single asterisk (*) and instrumental modification by a double asterisk (**). Some learning situations may demand both modifications simultaneously. Notice that although we assume two *loci* of behavioral modification in learning, there is no implication that there are two *kinds* of learning. On the contrary, the same fundamental principles are assumed to apply both to changes in mediators and changes in instrumental acts. We may now study some of the relevant experimental evidence; additional evidence will be cited in the next chapter.

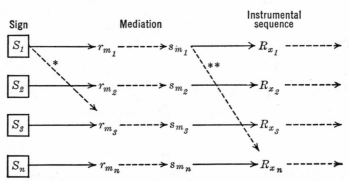

FIGURE 144. Loci of modifications in behavior (learning) of mature organism: a change in the significance of a sign (*) or a change in the instrumental sequence elicited by a mediator (**). Both types of modification may be produced in the same learning situation, e.g. trial and error.

Change in Mediation Process

A hungry, mature rat finds itself enclosed by white walls and a grid flooring. This stimulus combination (new surroundings coupled with hunger drive) is already associated with anticipatory food-taking reactions which, in this situation, mediate 'exploratory' behavior. Suddenly there is painful stimulation of the footpads: the rat runs (it happens, into the black-walled side of the compartment) and the pain ceases. After a number of experiences of this kind, the rat will run from the white to the black side of the compartment without any shock being given (cf. Miller, 1948). The instrumental response of running is *not* acquired in this situation; it is already one of the high-probability sequences in the hierarchy mediated by anxiety. What has happened is that the white walls have acquired a different meaning or sign-value than they previously had for the rat; they now elicit anxiety reactions (via short circuiting) and therefore constitute a danger signal.

Most classical conditioning situations involve a change in mediation process without any particular change in instrumental sequence. The sound of the metronome in Pavlov's laboratory certainly did not signify meat powder to the dog at the beginning of training. Being regularly associated with this stimulus-object, however, the sound of the metronome acquired some of the 'detachable' reactions elicited by meat powder and simultaneously acquired a different significance. Zener (1937) was one of the first to point out that the apparent simplicity of Pavlovian conditioning—the reason it could appear as nothing more than stimulus substitution—was due to the behavioral restrictions imposed on the subject and the observational restrictions self-imposed on the experimenter. He arranged freer conditions for behavior and observation, and his descriptions provide convincing evidence for the mediational mechanism. A dog was conditioned by usual procedures on one table in the laboratory to salivate to the *CS* (here, a moving card) ; then it was placed on another table in the room without any harness to hamper its movements. The first time this *CS* was next given, the animal promptly leaped off the second table, ran up a set of stairs onto the first table, and poised itself 'expectantly' over the food pan. This complex sequence makes sense if we view the process of conditioning as one that establishes a new *meaning* for the *CS* (e.g. it comes to signify 'meat appearing in food pan'), since appropriate instrumental acts will be transferred from previous learning; it makes no sense, is completely unexpected and unpredictable, if we view conditioning as the simple and exclusive association of a particular *CS* (moving card) with a particular reaction (salivating).

Research currently under way in our own laboratory (conducted by Mr. Jack Nygaard) is yielding further evidence for 'intelligent transfer' based upon mediational mechanisms. Rats are initially given intermittent shocks while held in a small enclosure in which the only effective response is *crouching*. The experimental animals have a buzzer sound paired with these shocks, but control animals do not (they hear the buzzer as often, but not coupled with shock). Then all animals are trained to make a *barrier-jumping escape response* to shock which cannot be anticipated and which has no signal associated with it. Once this escaping response has reached a criterion latency following the onset of shock, test trials with the buzzer are made: of the four experimental animals run so far, three have promptly leaped the barrier upon hearing the buzzer; of four control animals, only one has leaped the barrier within the 5-second interval preceding shock—and this with a long latency and attendant behavior suggesting that it was a spontaneous reaction independent of the buzzer stimulus. Since the experimental animals have never had the buzzer stimulus associated with barrier jumping, its occurrence in the test situation must be based upon the mediating anxiety reaction common to both situations. Since the anxiety mediator has been associated with both crouching and barrier leaping, and the buzzer only with crouching, as overt responses, we must consider the prompt occurrence of barrier leaping to the buzzer in the new situation a case of 'intelligent transfer' to instrumental sequences 'appropriate to' the total situational context (cf. Fig. 143B).

So far we have dealt only with cases in which a stimulus of neutral or unknown sign-value is given a specific significance by experimental operations. Is it possible to demonstrate a *change in the significance of stimuli* experimentally? Suppose a dog is given the following treatment: (1) a brief bell tone is followed by shock to the foreleg, this sequence continuing until conditioned flexion regularly antedates shock; (2) the shock is now omitted, but every conditioned reaction is promptly rewarded by a small chow biscuit (the dog is hungry). We know from Brogden's (1939 *a*) experiment that the flexion movement to the tone will continue unmodified for hundreds of trials, but what happens to the meaning of the sign? We would predict that the shift from shock to chow biscuits would be accompanied by deterioration of anxiety reactions to the bell (index of 'danger' significance) and augmentation of salivary reactions to the bell (index of 'food' significance). Brogden did report the appearance of salivation to the bell soon after food was substituted for shock, but (unfortunately, for our purposes) no autonomic records were made.

Many cases of *extinction* are better conceived as changes in the significance of signs than as decrements in instrumental response tendencies. The experiments of Humphreys (1939 *a*), Ellson (1939), and Porter (1939) on extinction and spontaneous recovery in human subjects have already been cited in connection with Tolman's explanation on an 'expectancy' basis. According to the mediation hypothesis, extinction may apply to associations between mediators and particular instrumental sequences as well as to associations between signs and particular mediators, just as learning may be effected at both loci of modification. When buzzer-produced anxiety is no longer alleviated by running but is reduced by turning a ratchet, the decrement observed in running in this situation is a case of instrumental extinction. When a bell that has been followed by shock is now followed by food (cf. Brogden experiment cited above), the decrement which *could* be observed in autonomic anxiety reactions (were appropriate recorders attached) would be a case of mediator extinction. In the latter case there would be no reason to expect that the instrumental sequences associated with anxiety mediation had been weakened—the bell simply no longer means 'danger.'

Change in the significance of signs is well illustrated in a series of experiments by Mowrer and his associates. In the first, entitled 'Time as a Determinant in Integrative Learning' (Mowrer and Ullman, 1945), a 2-second buzzer was first made a sign of food-reward by having it terminate with the delivery of a pellet in a trough. 'All animals soon learned to run to the food trough as soon as the buzzer sounded, in much the same way that a dog or cat learns to come when called.' Then the experimenters established a 'rule of rat etiquette'—it was not 'polite' for the rat to eat the pellet until 3 seconds after it had fallen into the trough, particularly since doing so resulted in a 2-second shock. The interval between 'being impolite' and getting shocked, however, was made to vary for different groups of animals, a 3-second delay for one group, a 6-second delay for another, and a 12-second delay for a third. 'Polite' behavior developed most rapidly in the 3-second group, but 'delinquent' behavior was most characteristic of the 12-second group. Solution of this problem demands a change in the significance of the buzzer. In the final 'etiquette' training, the buzzer persisted through the 3-second delay period *and,* if the rat was 'delinquent,' until the termination of its shock punishment. Thus, buzzer *sound* must become a sign of shock and buzzer *termination* a sign that 'all is clear.' The more nearly contingent shock is to buzzer-plus-sight-of-food, the more quickly the necessary change in significance develops. That a change in the sign-value of the buzzer was involved is shown by the following: when the buzzer was allowed to terminate with delivery of the pellet, as had happened in initial training, none of the animals could learn to be 'polite.'

A second experiment (Mowrer and Viek, 1948) illustrates the different consequences of controllable and uncontrollable fear. With each hungry rat standing on an electrifiable grille, a stick with some moist food on the end was stuck up through the grille directly in front of the place where the animal happened to be standing. If the rat ate the food within a 10-second period, this was counted as an *eating response;* if not, it was counted as *inhibition.* But in *either* case, a shock was applied 10 seconds later, persisting until the animal jumped into the air. An ingenious control condition was set up: each experimental rat was paired with a control rat; if a given experimental animal took 14 seconds of shock before leaping into the air, its 'twin' was also given 14 seconds of shock, *but no particular response was associated with shock termination.* In other words, the experimental rats could, in a sense, control the shock by leaping in the air, but the control rats could not, and the question was, How will the 'controllability' of a feared stimulus-object (shock) affect behavior toward the sign (food-stick)? The results were definite: in the 15 days of training (10 trials a day), the ten experimental animals inhibited eating only 16 times, whereas the ten controls inhibited eighty-five times. *Why* did the shock have less inhibitory effect on the animals that could control its termination? It is a well-authenticated observation in avoidance training that autonomic disturbance (anxiety) accompanies the trial-and-error period, but diminishes as the correct instrumental reaction is selected. Even though shock is not avoidable in the present case, it is probable that something of the same sort occurs, i.e. as the onset of shock becomes a more discriminative cue for leaping, it loses its tendency to elicit fear reactions.

Now what about the sign-value of the upthrust stick? Having by virtue of its odor and the previous experience of the rat a 'food' significance, it initially mediates food-taking reactions. With successive shock sequences, it begins to acquire a new 'danger' significance (short circuiting of fear reactions), and this mediates avoidance which, if continued for 10 seconds, is scored as 'inhibition of eating.' For the rats that could control the termination of shock, selection of leaping is accompanied by diminution in fear reaction and thence by dilution of the 'danger' value in the sign. For their 'twins,' on the other hand, no effective adjustment to the shock could be made—even though the *duration* of shock was the same as for the 'controllable' animals (and this is one of the neat points in the design of this study)—and therefore the fear reaction persists, stabilizing the 'danger' sign-value of the stick. The detailed results provide substantiation of this interpretation. Computing the number of 'inhibitions' for each group, for each third of the 15 days of training, we obtain the following:

TABLE 7

	Days 1-5	Days 6-10	Days 11-15
SHOCK CONTROLLABLE	3	9	4
SHOCK UNCONTROLLABLE	14	31	40

From data of Mowrer and Viek, *Journal of Abnormal and Social Psychology,* 1948, 43:193-200.

Whereas 'inhibitions' (an index of 'danger' sign-value for the stick) increase *and then decrease* for the experimental animals, they keep on increasing for the controls. Mowrer suggests a very plausible mechanism whereby the 'danger' significance of the stick may be reduced in the experimental animals once a successful leaping response has been selected: as soon as a fractional replica of the leaping movement (e.g. looking upward or tensing certain muscles) short-circuits and occurs upon the appearance of the stick, the anxiety *reduction* associated with this successful reaction also transfers forward and, being incompatible with anxiety *production,* reciprocally inhibits the anxiety mediator. In common-sense terms, the experimental rats can 'think about' the pain-avoiding movement at the time the sign of pain is presented—just as the sheriff can give his holster a reassuring, symbolic pat as he enters a canyon where desperadoes are in hiding.

Change in Instrumental Sequence

Our mature rat has already learned that white walls signify 'danger,' and it will run to the black side as soon as placed on the white side. Now suppose the experimenter were to insert a low barrier between the two sides of the compartment. This barrier can be leaped over but not run through. The rat would *promptly* shift from running to leaping. This is an adaptive modification of instrumental behavior, but how does it come about so promptly? In this particular case both running and leaping are *already* associated with common mediators as alternative locomotor sequences— the change in context produced by insertion of the low barrier, given the same 'danger' mediation process, is already associated with leaping behavior. But now suppose the experimenter (Miller, 1948) inserts a *wall* between the two compartments, a wall with a door that can be operated by turning a ratchet device. Placed in the white compartment, which has the same meaning as before, the rat tries to run out but cannot. In the course of the 'random' (really, broadly selective in terms of the mediator) activity which ensues, a pawing response is hit upon which happens to turn the ratchet device and open the door. Since this particular instrumental act is repeatedly reinforced (by anxiety reduction, here), it rises in the hierarchy of instrumental sequences associated with this mediator, i.e. its occurrence becomes more probable.

Observe that in the latter case the response made to the sign (ratchet turning) is not at all the same response originally made to the object signified (running). Therefore it cannot always be said that a conditioned response must represent some selection from the total behavior elicited by the unconditioned stimulus. It is the *mediation process* that must always include some portion of the behavior elicited by the unconditioned stimulus; this is what gives the sign its representing property or meaning, according to the present view. The mediation hypothesis thus has the advantage that it does not require object-elicited and sign-elicited instrumental acts to be related; there may be partial identity (e.g. salivating to a bell which precedes presentation of food) and there may not (e.g. holding the breath to a buzzer which precedes shock).

This is brought out effectively in a paper by Mowrer and Lamoreaux (1946). Using the Mowrer and Miller (1942) type of avoidance training box, the conditional stimulus (sign-to-be) was a change in illumination, from two lights above the box to a single light below the box, and the unconditional stimulus was the usual shock to the footpads. For group 1, responses to the object and the sign had to be different (leaping in the air would eliminate the shock and running would eliminate the 'dangerous' phase of the lighting) ; for group 2, responses to object and sign had to be the same (leaping in the air initially eliminated shock and subsequently also eliminated the 'dangerous' phase of the lighting) ; for group 3, no consistent response to the object was reinforced, the shock being of constant duration irrespective of the animals' behavior (no particular response eliminated shock, but leaping in the air would eliminate the 'dangerous' lighting phase). Actually, this description applies to one-half of the rats in each group; the other half had leaping and running reversed (i.e. substitute 'running' for 'leaping in the air').

The first result of significance was that all three groups developed avoidance conditioning to the *CS* via whatever instrumental act was required of them. We conclude that the sign had become associated with a new mediation process, a new meaning of 'danger,' since the change in illumination regularly antedated the shock, the common 'fear' behavior it produced, and the reinforcement of its termination. Furthermore, each particular instrumental sequence required was gradually strengthened in its association with this mediator because only this sequence terminated the 'dangerous' lighting phase and the anxiety it elicited. The second result was that group 2 ('same' response) showed the most rapid conditioning, group 3 (constant shock duration) very nearly as much, and group 1 (different response) significantly less. The superiority of group 2 would be predicted from the mediation hypothesis: as noticed earlier, signs initially tend to become conditioned to *all* the reactions produced by the stimulus-object (shock), the 'reduction' process accumulating with repetitions of the sign sequence. If the running response in the hierarchy associated with shock is strengthened by shock-termination, it will be conditioned to the traces of the sign, as well, short-circuited, and then made in anticipatory fashion to the sign itself. If running is now *also* strengthened in association with the sign, as an instrumental sequence that terminates anxiety, the process of selection from among potential instrumental acts is already accomplished. By the same argument, the relatively poorer performance of the different-response group (group 1) is understood: the short-circuited running response, continuously being built up by shock-reduction, will *interfere* and compete with occurrence of the 'correct' leaping response to the sign. We could predict that this would become less true (and groups 1 and 2 more nearly equivalent) as intensity of the shock was reduced. Mowrer's interpretation of these results, while couched in different terms, is essentially the same as given here (cf. 1950, pp. 144-8).

Instrumental sequences may shift without any new learning whatsoever. This was the case when the mature rat simply shifted from running to leaping when a low barrier was inserted between white and black compartments. Wickens (1938) has studied such *response transfer* in human subjects. With the subject's arm strapped in position, *palm down,* the middle finger was placed on an electrode and strips of metal were adjusted to both sides of this finger so that movement in either upward or downward direction (extension or flexion) could be recorded. With a buzzer as *CS* and shock as *US,* subjects were 'trained' to make anticipatory avoidance reactions which, since their palms were down, had to be *extensor* movements. To test for transfer, the hand was now turned *palm up*—most subjects immediately shifted to a *flexor* movement. Since the muscles contracted in the original conditioning here had to be reciprocally inhibited in the transfer response, it cannot be claimed that this second reaction was somehow being learned during the original conditioning. *What we have here is a change in context accompanied by transfer to those instrumental acts in the same hierarchy which have the highest habit strength in association with the new context.* With 'danger' (anticipation of shock) as a common core of mediation, each change in context (here, the sensed position of one's hand in relation to the electrodes) serves to modify the total stimulus situation and hence the prob, ability of alternative instrumental sequences.

EVALUATION OF THE MEDIATION HYPOTHESIS

In so far as its mechanics and underlying assumptions are concerned, the mediation hypothesis is an extension of Hull's theory, an extension and re-emphasis deemed necessary to account for the facts of learning. Yet the stress laid upon mediating processes and the self-stimulation produced— particularly if these processes be envisaged as implicit reactions of muscle and gland—bring this view close to Guthrie's theory, in which the subtleties of complex behavior come down to implicit movements and movement-produced stimuli. On the other hand, the impetus to elaborate such a hypothesis as this has certainly come in considerable part from Tolman's theorizing and the phenomena he has pointed up in course. The mediation hypothesis shares the advantage that Tolman's theory has in providing for independent modification of 'cognitive' (mediational) processes and performance (instrumental) processes, but it seems to make more explicit the conditions under which instrumental acts are developed, organized into flexible hierarchies, and selectively called forth by mediators. As a matter of fact, the mediation hypothesis may be viewed as a more explicit formulation (and translation into Hullian terms) of the origin, nature, and function of 'sign-gestalt-expectations.' It will not be surprising, therefore, if the supporters of each of these major theories find much in the mediation hypothesis with which they can agree. Although there are many fundamental problems remaining, as the next chapter will indicate, we seem to be approaching a point where they can be viewed within a consistent frame of reference.

We have shown that representational mediation processes of some kind must be postulated to account for the experimental and observational data available—there are many learning phenomena that cannot be incorporated on a single-stage *S–R* basis. If the postulation of mediation processes is going to prove fruitful, however, and serve as anything more than a label for ignorance, properties must be attributed to them whose natures and quantities can be inferred from antecedent and subsequent observables. What have we accomplished in this direction? Granting that stimulus-objects (as defined) do elicit various reactions, we have specified some of the conditions under which other stimuli (signs) will come to elicit portions of the same behavior. These antecedent conditions include *contiguity* between $\boxed{S}$ and $\overset{.}{S}$, *reinforcement* (probably entirely secondary), and the observable characteristics of the *behavior to* $\overset{.}{S}$ (including characteristics only observable by physiological techniques). The mechanism whereby $\boxed{S}$ acquires fractional antedating reactions has been made explicit—it is chiefly a generalization phenomenon. The *intensity* of these mediating reactions is a function of the number of reinforced repetitions, amount of reinforcement, temporal delay, S–R asynchronism, and so on, just as is assumed for overt behavior; the *nature* of these mediating reactions is dependent upon the behavior originally elicited by the stimulus-object, as modified in the combined processes of *short circuiting* (object-tied versus detachable reactions) and *reduction* (selective modification attributable to such factors as interference, energy expenditure, conditionability, and final discriminability).

All this relates to *antecedent* variables—from them we are enabled to make inferences regarding the nature of the representational mediation process developed under given conditions. What about *consequent* variables? How is observable behavior mediated by our intervening variable? Granting that mediating reactions produce self-stimulation, we may specify certain of the functions relating instrumental sequences (observable behavior) to this self-stimulation. Again the same principles that apply to single-stage associations (as developed by Hull) are assumed to apply here. The probability of any particular instrumental sequence being mediated by a particular sign process will therefore depend upon such factors as the frequency, amount, and immediacy of the reinforcement of this association in the previous history of this organism, the similarity of the mediator developed in this situation to those already associated with the instrumental activity being predicted, the existence and strength of competing instrumental acts in the same hierarchy, and so on. To the extent that the mediation processes developed in a given situation are *distinctive* (as inferable from the behaviors associated with different stimulus-objects), observable discriminatory behavior on the basis of their signs will be facilitated, including transfers of discrimination. To the extent that the mediation processes developed in a given situation include *energizing components* (perhaps emotional, hormonal reactions, also inferable from the behavior associated with stimulus-objects), they will have secondary motivating and reinforcing properties which will operate selectively upon subsequent instrumental behavior.

There are certainly weaknesses in this hypothesis, the chief one being that the unobservable nature of most representational mediation processes makes it difficult to establish functions. One of the most promising lines of research, therefore, will be to set up a few standard situations in which mediation processes *are* measurable (e.g. autonomic activity derived from shock experience, salivary activity derived from food experience, and so forth) and meticulously explore the functions relating the intervening variable to both antecedent and consequent observables. Existing information, while offering many suggestions, was not obtained with this hypothesis in mind and therefore leaves many gaps.

One of the chief advantages of this hypothesis is *the distinction it draws between the 'old' learning which the mature organism brings to any test situation and the 'new' learning which must be established in that test situation.* The mature organism, whether rat or man, has a vast fund of pre-learned mediation processes (most stimulus patterns in the ordinary environment *do* have definite significance or meaning for the organism—the momentary stimulus manifold *is* perceived in certain ways, organized in terms of certain mediators). It has an equally vast fund of pre-learned instrumental sequences, associated with both stimulus-objects and signs. (Contours of objects are explored with certain sequences of eye-muscle movements, those having reward significance are approached with certain sequences of locomotor movements, 'danger' mediators elicit varied avoidance sequences, all depending upon the total stimulating context in which they occur.)

Another advantage in this hypothesis is that *it explicitly demonstrates that the representational mediation process associated with the sign of an object must include some portion of the behavior toward the object itself.* This is the essence of the hypothesis and the reason why it so readily becomes the basis for a theory of signs. As will be shown in the final chapter of this book, the major difficulty with most attempts to deal with 'the meaning of meaning' has been their failure to offer any convincing explanation of why a particular sign refers to a particular object and not to others. The mediation hypothesis offers an excellent and very convincing reason: the sign 'means' or 'refers to' a particular object because it elicits in the organism employing it part of the same behavior which the object itself elicits. In a very real sense—since it can be shown that most 'new' learning comes down to the association of new mediation processes with old stimulus patterns or new instrumental sequences with old mediation processes—this hypothesis places the problem of *meaning* directly at the core of learning theory. Rather than implying a surrender to subjectivism, this state of affairs serves to highlight what has always been the critical problem for learning theory: to make as explicit and determinate as possible the *intervening* variables between stimulus and response.

Finally, we come back to Woodworth's expressed belief that there is no essential reason for the schism between 'reinforcement' interpretations, developed in the main by behaviorists, and 'perceptual' interpretations, developed in the main by gestaltists. There would appear to be sufficient reason as long as one group gave exclusive attention to the functional relations between stimulation and central events (viewing consequent behavior as self-evident) and the other group gave exclusive attention to the functional relations between stimulation and behavior (viewing central mediation as either self-evident or lacking). By providing for definite representational processes which intervene between stimulation and overt behavior, the present hypothesis seems to offer a basis for resolving these differences. The gestalt theorist may *prefer* to think of these mediation processes as 'ways of perceiving' situations, and the behaviorist may *prefer* to think of them as 'implicit stimulus-producing reactions'—and those interested in language behavior in humans may prefer to think of them as 'meanings'—but if the operations by which these processes are identified and manipulated are fundamentally the same, differences in preference for terms become interesting artifacts in the history of science but not legitimate causes for theoretical discord.

Chapter 10

CERTAIN CONTROVERSIAL ISSUES
IN LEARNING THEORY

Ideally, any scientific theory is sensitive to experimentation. The only defensible attitude a scientist can have toward his principles is one of constant, active distrust. This is because the only logical operation he can make is to *disprove* his hypotheses—they never can be proved valid, only becoming more and more probable with every failure to disprove. Does one negative instance disprove a hypothesis? Ideally, yes, but given the lack of rigor in both specifying experimental conditions and defining terms, most psychological facts become interpretations stemming from the individual theorist's frame of reference. One can usually discover some uncontrolled variable, some ambiguous concept, which changes the significance of this particular 'fact' for theory. Nature provides no sign posts at her crossroads. Most of the experiments described below in relation to these theoretical issues have been considered 'crucial' by their authors—in the sense that the proponents of opposing theories presumably could not explain them—but this has seldom been the case. Nevertheless, the accruing bits of evidence gradually restrict the variation that theoretical principles can have.

IS REINFORCEMENT NECESSARY FOR LEARNING?

A reinforcement principle lies at the core of Hull's theoretical system. Being the most explicitly worked out—and hence generating the most clearly testable hypotheses—it is expected that Hull's theory would be the view most often subjected to experimental attack. In the present instance, since the reinforcement principle is central to Hull's theorizing, we find the supporters of his theory aligned against most other positions, the attack coming from many directions and employing many varied weapons. The underlying procedures are either (a) to show that learning can occur without reinforcement or (b) to show that learning fails to vary as predicted from the presence, absence, or amount of reinforcement given.

Learning without Motivation (Incidental Learning)

Hull defines 'reinforcement' as the reduction of some drive state. It follows, therefore, that an organism must be motivated if there is to be any learning—some drive must exist if it is to be reduced. A bona fide case of learning without motivation would therefore constitute sufficient evidence that the reinforcement principle is not necessary. This seems to be a simple enough issue to test experimentally, but things are seldom as simple as they appear.

Critics of reinforcement theory have pointed to evidence like the following: (1) People often seem to learn things *incidentally*—a man being driven about a strange city picks up many bits of information, apparently without any motivation to do so. (2) In a more experimental vein, one group of subjects is instructed to act *as experimenters* and to read lists of 20 nonsense syllables aloud to another group of subjects who are told to learn them (J. G. Jenkins, 1933); on a recall test 24 hours later, although the intentional learners do better than the incidental learners ('experimenters'), the latter do show a significant amount of learning. (3) In certain studies animal subjects are given opportunity to experience a situation without motivation or reward and later are compared with a control group to see if they have learned anything incidentally. Buxton (1940) allowed his experimental animals to live in a 12-unit *T*-maze for several nights, but without any particular motivation being given and certainly no rewards. Later, under 48-hour hunger drive and after being given a pre-run nibble of food in the goal place, these animals were found to thread the maze with significantly fewer errors than control animals tested in the same way but lacking the opportunity for incidental learning.

Proponents of reinforcement theory answer with the following: (1) Incidental learning is the exception, not the rule. Try to recall the exact number of windows in a classroom where you have sat for many hours— and what was the instructor's eye-color? Even critics of reinforcement theory will have to agree that learning is *better* when the subjects are motivated. (2) As to the learning displayed by the 'experimenters' in Jenkins's study, how do we know they were completely lacking in motivation? As a matter of fact, Jenkins reports that many of these subjects did give themselves instructions to learn. (3) The same sort of question arises with regard to Buxton's rat subjects. There is no requirement in the reinforcement principle that the drive reduced be appropriate to the behavior being strengthened. On the basis of fatigue reduction, acquired 'curiosity' drives, or the like, could these animals have learned to eliminate many blinds in the course of their night wanderings?

The reinforcement theorist can account for such phenomena, but it requires a rather elaborate tour de force and the invocation of unspecifiable secondary motives. On the other hand, how is the critic to demonstrate the *absence* of motivation? In order to test the proposition that learning can occur without motivation, we must be able to specify absence of motivation, but this is not possible with our present techniques of measuring motives. The entire proposition appears incapable of disproof.

Latent Learning

It will be recalled that Tolman's central postulate holds that cognitive 'bits of knowledge' are formed on the basis of sheer experience of successive stimulus situations (signs and significates) without any reinforcement in the Hullian sense. Latent learning should be possible in such a case. The logic of the demonstration goes something like this: reinforcement is not essential to learning per se, but to performance; without any reinforcement subjects may learn a system of cognitive relations (e.g. 'what leads to what' in a maze), this learning only showing up in performance, however, when reward is later introduced. To demonstrate such latent learning, it is necessary to show that the *rate* of improvement, once reward is introduced, is greater for latent-learning subjects than for a control group. This experimental situation has been considered critical by many (cf. Tolman, 1938 *b*; White, 1943).

The initial experiment in a long series was contributed by Blodgett (1929). Three groups of animals were run in a 6-unit T-maze. All animals were given one trial a day and were subjected to the same motivational conditions, but group 1 (control) was fed following every trial from the beginning of training, group 2 (3-day latent) was fed on the third day and thenceforth, and group 3 (7-day latent) was fed on the seventh day and thenceforth. To test for latent learning, the greatest drop in mean errors for two successive trials for the control group (viz. between days 2 and 3) was compared with the drop in errors following introduction of reward in the two latent learning groups (viz. between days 3 and 4 for the 3-day latent and between days 7 and 8 for the 7-day latent groups). In both cases reductions in errors following latent periods were greater than at any point during continuous reinforcement. Tolman and Honzik (1930 *b*) contribute a similarly designed experiment yielding similar results.

More recently Reynolds (1945 *c*) has repeated Blodgett's conditions in all essentials, but with completely negative results. Figure 145 compares the results of the two studies for both control subjects and those reinforced on the seventh and succeeding days. Although both sets of data display the same general trends, the test for latent learning is positive in one case and negative in the other—all because of (chance?) variations in the daily error curves. This highlights a major difficulty in testing the latent learning proposition: with innumerable factors contributing to performance curves, one wonders how much of the measured variance is actually attributable to latent learning.

What are we to conclude from these studies on latent learning? In the first place, despite the use to which they have been put in this controversy, *these experiments are not relevant to the question as to whether reinforcement is necessary for learning.* Certainly learning is occurring during the unrewarded trials—the gradual but quite consistent decreases in errors during the latent periods shown in the curves in Fig. 145 is sufficient evidence, quite apart from the sudden drops when reward is introduced. But is this learning occurring without reinforcement? The situation here is no clearer than it is with unmotivated learning. Although, to be sure, no reinforcements were *deliberately* given by the experimenters, we have no guarantee that all forms of reinforcement were eliminated. We are in no better position to index precisely *absence* of reinforcement than absence of motivation. It is quite conceivable that motives were present and *were* being reduced during unrewarded trials or casual meandering. Goal-boxes similar to those used in other experiments (if the animals were maze-wise), the smell of food in the goal-box, the handling and release when an animal is taken from the goal-box (cf. Karn and Porter, 1946), all could serve as secondary reinforcing agents—and this by no means exhausts the list of possibilities. As critical tests of theory, these experiments do not refute the reinforcement principle.

What these experiments *do* demonstrate is that learning is not necessarily reflected in overt performance. The term 'latent learning' is actually a misnomer; we should speak of 'latent *performance,*' for it is not the learning that is latent but its utilization in rapidly and efficiently running the maze. The sudden drops in error and time scores that follow the introduction of rewards—and we can probably accept these drops as other than

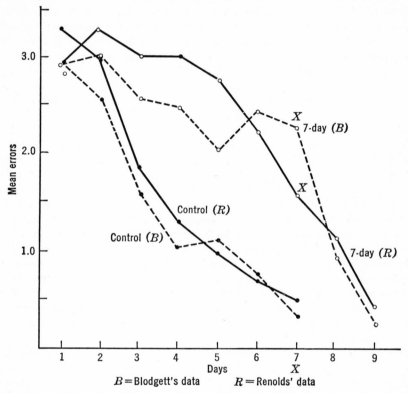

FIGURE 145. Comparison of two studies on latent learning. Experimental animals were unreinforced until the seventh day of training in both cases. Solid lines indicate Reynolds' data (*Journal of Experimental Psychology*, 1945, 35:504-516), dashed lines Blodgett's data (*University of California Publications in Psychology*, 1929, 4:113-134).

chance in trial-to-trial variations—indicate that the animal has been modified; it has learned 'what leads to what' in Tolman's terms, even though this learning does not show up immediately in performance. Notice carefully that this cognitive learning of 'what leads to what' may itself be based on the action of a reinforcement principle—there is nothing in these experiments to deny this possibility.

The real problem here is this: If reinforcement was present in these 'latent performance' situations, sufficient to learn the 'whats lead to what,' why was it not sufficient to perform? As Hilgard (1948, p. 284) says, '. . . these theories cannot have their cake and eat it too.' But perhaps they can—the mediation hypothesis offers two mechanisms whose combined effects would yield just such results as are found here. (a) Evidence has been presented to show that the 'light-weight' reactions which compose representing processes are more readily conditioned than 'heavy-weight' limb movements. Reinforcements minimal in amount and secondary in nature (such as being lifted from the end-box of a maze and replaced in the familiar home cage) could be sufficient to establish certain critical stimuli along the maze as signs of reinforcing states of affairs. (b) Once the animal has experienced a goal-object relevant to its drive state, these same critical stimuli can become associated with a short-circuited representation of this goal-object, and this mediational process has energizing (incentive) properties. Except for the assumption that reinforcement is involved in the formation of such mediation processes, there is, of course, no great difference between this interpretation and Tolman's. Both theories are able to handle this sort of phenomenon because they segregate cognitions (mediators) from overt movements (skill sequences).

Drive Discrimination Studies

The general logic of these tests runs as follows: if an organism has been allowed to experience the stimulus sequences eventuating in goal-objects appropriate to two different needs, it will be able to correctly select the path leading to the needed goal-object when later needing one of the goal-objects and not the other. This hypothesis follows directly from Tolman's theory (cf. White, 1943)—the reader will recall our postulate 4 for this theory, according to which, given the existence of cognitive sign-gestalt-expectations relating particular signs with particular significates, the co-occurrence of demand for the signified goal-object will produce behavior appropriate to that object. But can Hull's reinforcement theory handle such phenomena? There are two related problems here: (a) Can organisms discriminate among their own drive states? and (b) Can organisms associate particular behavior routes with particular goal-objects?

Hull (1933 a) trained rats to run along one path to a goal-box for food when hungry and along another path to the *same* goal-box for water when thirsty; the problem was to see whether these animals could discriminate among their own drive states. The answer was that they could, but only with great difficulty—some 25 training periods of 8 days each were required, and then the accuracy of response discrimination reached only about 80 per cent. In terms of Hull's theory, the fact that discrimination was possible is due to stimulus patterning, the pattern of choice-point cues plus hunger drive gradually becoming associated with one response tendency and the pattern of choice-point cues plus thirst drive gradually becoming associated with another response tendency. The slowness of the learning is attributed to the fact that the drive difference is only a small part of the total stimulus situation, i.e. that discrimination is a difficult one. But when looked at in relation to Tolman's sign-learning theory, isn't the slowness of discrimination here really negative evidence? Since the animals had ample opportunity to experience that path A leads to significate food and path B leads to significate water, shouldn't the rats quickly achieve perfect selective performance dependent upon the demand operative?

In a similar experiment undertaken independently, but from a Tolman point of view, Leeper (1935) also required rats to discriminate two pathways in terms of hunger or thirst demands. But here pathways *A* and *B* eventuated in two *different* goal-boxes and, rather than merely blocking the animals after a wrong choice, as Hull had done, Leeper allowed them to get to the goal-box containing the inappropriate reward. Presumably, on these wrong runs for a given day and a given motivation, the animals could learn that *that* path led to *that* specific significate, in a distinctive *place,* and this learning could be utilized on the following day when under appropriate motivation. Experience with the to-be-appropriate significate via a given path is also more recent under Leeper's conditions. These animals reached an 80 per cent level of accuracy after only *one* 8-day period of training, which is more nearly in keeping with what one would predict from Tolman's theory.

An experiment by Kendler (1946) provides further insight into this problem. During training on a single-unit T-maze, rats were run under *simultaneous* hunger and thirst, finding food in one goal-box and water in the other. Forced runs alternated with free runs to equalize experience with the two paths. The question posed was this: Although Hull's (1933 *a*) animals had been able to discriminate between their drive states when hunger and thirst were differentially associated with two responses during training, would this be possible when the same drive state (hunger *and* thirst) was present during training? Superficially, Hull's answer would seem to be 'no,' there being no discriminability in the stimulus pattern. But the rats said 'yes'—on two test trials, one under hunger and the other under thirst, these animals selected the pathways appropriate to their needs. One possible answer, according to Kendler, would be that 'only those drive stimuli which are themselves reduced become connected to a rewarded response.' This explanation, while quite outside Hull's theory, is exactly what Guthrie would predict: the eliminated stimuli preserve their association with the reward response. Another possible answer, which Kendler considers compatible with Hull's system, would be that the stimuli in the alley leading to the food box become associated with anticipatory eating responses, and the proprioceptive stimuli produced by these anticipatory responses, in turn, become associated with the correct turning response. Since the hunger drive itself is associated with these same anticipatory eating responses, through much previous experience, it is certain that these reactions will be made when the animal is only hungry, thus weighing the odds in favor of the correct response.

Kendler also observes that Tolman's sign-learning theory would fit his data very nicely, the signs at the choice point coming to signify the two alternate goal-objects through two alternate behavior routes. But what, really, is the difference between the Hull type of explanation in terms of mediating anticipatory goal reactions and Tolman's explanation in terms of mediating sign-significate-expectations? If we accept the proposition that 'pure-stimulus-acts' and 'expectations' are functionally identical intervening variables, the only difference between the two positions lies in Hull's insistence that such mediation processes are established on the basis of reinforcement. Since drives were reduced in the goal-boxes in all of these studies, there is nothing to deny the possibility that the mediators representing differential goal-objects were established via reward.

Learning under Conditions of Irrelevant Motivation and Reward

Central to Tolman's theory, according to most reviewers, is the assumption that the sheer experiencing of successive stimulus situations guarantees the formation of sign-significate-expectations. White (1943) has referred to this as the principle of 'perceptual-learning.' The experiments already cited under 'latent learning' are relevant to this hypothesis, as are those that follow. Suppose an animal is trained (by occasional forced runs) to run equally often down two paths to two goal-boxes, running only under thirst demand during this training and finding water in one goal-box (path A). Now suppose that in the other goal-box (path B) there is food available, even though the animal has no demand for it. According to Tolman's view, the sheer experiencing of path B leading to food significate (even though not at the moment food demanding) should be sufficient to establish the appropriate expectation. When the animal *is* made food demanding on later test trials, therefore, it should (a) immediately choose path B or (b) at least learn path B more rapidly than a control group for whom there was never any food in goal-box B.

Spence and Lippitt (1946) have done precisely this experiment and found no differences between food-present and control groups. On the first test trial under hunger motivation every one of the experimental subjects ran up the same alley it had learned to follow for water. To check on the possibility that the signs for the alternative choices were not sufficiently distinctive, Kendler (1947 *a*) painted right and left alleys white and black, respectively, and used a single T-maze rather than the Y-maze of Spence and Lippitt (to maximize spatial discrimination)—identical results were obtained. Both of these studies cast doubt on the proposition that merely experiencing a sign-significate sequence is a sufficient condition for acquiring an expectation.

There are several possible 'outs' for the Tolmanite here. Leeper (1948) has criticized the Spence and Lippitt study on the ground that there was no guarantee the animals actually perceived the food in goal-box B, claiming that the food pellets were 'in a hole in the floor,' whereas in his (Leeper's) study both rewards were in similar places and containers so that the animal had to perceive discriminately what each contained. Although it is not strictly true that food pellets were hidden in the Spence and Lippitt study (and in Kendler's experiment six pellets were spread about the floor of the goal-box where the rat would have great difficulty avoiding them), this is a possibility. Perhaps the temporal delays between signs and significates were too long for cognition formation? This, if anything, is a criticism of Tolman's theory, which does not specify any relationship between sign-significate intervals and expectation establishment. Perhaps the animals were overtrained, 'fixated,' on the water path to the extent that they were no longer following docile expectations but were executing a rigidly mechanical series of movements? Not knowing at what point in training fixation occurs, this possibility would be difficult to test.

By way of experimental rebuttal we have further experiments. Kendler and Mencher (1948) placed five little cups in a rack in each goal-box, one of the five in both boxes containing water but the other four containing either nothing (box A) or food pellets (box B). During training the five cups were randomly varied in relative position, so that the thirsty rats had to look into several before finding water, thus presumably guaranteeing perceptual discrimination of food. Since *both* goal-boxes contained water, it could not be claimed that need-satisfaction was lacking on the food side. But again the animals showed no evidence of having established the path B-leads-to-food expectation, only 53 per cent choosing path B on the first test trial under hunger motivation. Walker (1948) trained rats under thirst motivation to take either a long or a short path to a water goal, forced runs in both directions being given on three-fifths of the trials. In a subgoal-box halfway along the long path to water, the experimental subjects had literally to climb over a floor covered with food pellets; no food was there for the control subjects. When motivation was shifted to hunger, all animals took the old water path on the first trial, and no differences in ease of learning to choose the now direct, short path to food were found between experimental and control subjects. Grice (1948 *b*) has independently duplicated the procedures followed by Kendler and Mencher—training under thirst drive with water present at both ends of a T-maze (but with the floor of one goal-box covered with food pellets) and testing under hunger motivation—and has obtained precisely the same results. It should be observed that in all three of these studies running in both directions to approximately equal degrees was accomplished by forced runs, so it would be hard to speak of 'fixation' of the wrong path.

So far the evidence has been rather solidly against the Tolman view, but there is more recent evidence favoring it, and not wholly from research by Tolman supporters either. Tolman and Gleitman (1949) relate an experiment of somewhat different design in which hungry rats were first trained to get food rewards equally often in the two goal-boxes of a simple T-maze. These two goal-boxes, however, were made highly dissimilar. Secondly, the two goal-boxes were separated from the T-maze, placed in another room, and the rats were shocked in one but not in the other. Immediately replaced in the starting-box of the T-maze, 22 of 25 animals chose to run toward the goal-box in which they had *not* been shocked. In the original training with food in both boxes, they had apparently learned which path led to which of the two distinctive goal-boxes. Some representation of the distinctive stimuli at the ends of the maze (significates) must have become associated with the stimuli of the entrances to the two path (signs).

Spence, Bergmann, and Lippitt (1950) satiated their rats on both water and food before all trials in a simple Y-type, single-choice maze. Since preliminary exploration showed that these rats would not perform adequately under these conditions, the experimenters placed cages with other rats at the ends of the maze, using this 'social' motivation (and reinforcement) to make the animals perform. During the training trials the rats were given an opportunity to consistently experience water in one goal-box and food in the other, even though they were satiated and were not observed either to eat or to drink. Forced trials equated these goal experiences. On the first test trial the rats (now either hungry or thirsty) showed a significant tendency to choose the appropriate side, even though their motivational states had been manipulated so that this appropriate side was *not* that preferred on the free-choice trials during training. A second test trial, under reversed motivation, was in the direction predictable from Tolman's theory, but differences were not significant. The preceding reinforcement on the opposite side may, however, have confounded this second test. Essentially the same results were found by Kendler (1947 *b*) and by Meehl and Mac-Corquodale (1948).

What conclusions can be drawn from all this? In the first place, it is apparent that animals must be motivated if they are to form cognitive 'bits of knowledge' about the environment; this may simply mean that they must *perform* with respect to the environment if stimulus sequences are to be experienced. But Tolman seems to go beyond this. In his 1949 paper he explains that, although he had previously been unclear on the matter, he does believe that motivation is necessary for the formation of expectancies. Regarding the Kendler and Mencher experiment (and he might have included the Walker and Grice studies as well), he says, 'Thirsty animals apparently do not notice food, even though the experiment be rigged . . . to seem to force them to notice' (p. 150). He appears to imply here an additional assumption—that the motivation must be *appropriate* to the to-be-noticed significate. To be sure, this derives from the first postulate of his system (our version)—that demands *selectively sensitize* those specific means-end-readinesses with which they have been associated—if we grant that tendencies to perceive and recognize objects are themselves means-end-readinesses that depend upon existing demands. But will this principle operate so as to *inhibit* awareness of nondemanded objects 'right under the animal's nose'? And why, then, did the animals apparently notice, and form appropriate expectations regarding, the nondemanded goal-objects in the studies yielding positive results (Tolman and Gleitman, Spence, Bergmann and Lippitt)?

Leaving this problem for the moment, what does a Hull-type theory (as extended by the mediation hypothesis) have to say about these data? First, it must be stressed again that Hull's theory makes no requirement that the drives reduced be 'appropriate to' the habits being learned. A simple example makes this clear: hunger drive and food reinforcement have no necessary relevance to the habit of lifting the paw to the sound of a bell, yet learning occurs. Similarly here, there is no reason that stimuli arising from maze pathways should not become associated with responses to a food goal-object, even though the animal may be thirsty and receive water. Secondly, we must note that in all the experiments reviewed here, both drives *and* reinforcements were present (thirsty animals drinking in the goal-boxes, hungry animals eating, 'lonesome' animals finding cage mates, prodded animals escaping being prodded, and so on). The necessary conditions (according to Hull's theory) for learning were therefore present.

The crucial question for Hull's theory is this: What responses are being made to the irrelevant goal-objects that can be reinforced? According to the mediation hypothesis, the sights and smells of goal-objects regularly antedate the total behavior of manipulating and consuming them; therefore, these sights and smells must come to elicit, *as learned mediating habits,* fractional portions of these total goal reactions, these reactions being the reason that such stimuli signify the 'eatable,' 'drinkable,' 'get-away-from-able' character of these objects. Although the occurrence of such sights and smells without the synchronous presence of appropriate drive stimuli will not elicit these mediators as strongly or as surely as when appropriate drive stimuli are present, they will still tend to occur as learned reactions. The same argument applies to nongoal-object stimuli which are distinctive (e.g. the visually and tactually distinctive end-boxes in the Gleitman experiment); if white and black walls, or rough and smooth floorings, have been responded to differentially in previous experience, the necessary conditions were set for the establishment of differential mediation processes, or 'ways of perceiving' these environmental stimuli (cf. Lawrence experiments, pp. 451-3).

Assuming that such mediating, representational reactions are made in the goal-boxes, their associations with the traces of antedating choice-point stimuli are strengthened by reinforcement. Remember that there is no requirement for drives and reinforcements to be 'appropriate to' the habits being learned. Since the self-stimulation produced by making these reactions can only become conditioned to the right- or left-turning instrumental sequences which eventuate in the goal-object in that side of the maze, the occurrence of such mediators will become one condition for the 'correct' instrumental sequences. When a particular drive state is later created on test trials, these drive stimuli merely guarantee that the appropriate mediation process will be more probable than the inappropriate one—hunger drive stimuli are already associated with mediators representing familiar food objects. The appropriate mediation process, as a form of self-stimulation, 'weighs' the probabilities in favor of the 'correct' instrumental sequence at the choice point. A very similar analysis is given by Spence, Bergmann, and Lippitt (1950), which is not surprising since they rely upon the same mechanisms in Hull's theory (fractional anticipatory goal reactions and habit-family hierarchies) as those upon which the mediation hypothesis is built.

The really puzzling thing in both Hull and Tolman theories is the failure of effective representing processes to appear in some of these experiments (the original Spence and Lippitt experiment and those by Kendler and Mencher, Walker, and Grice). I do not see how Tolman can explain these negative instances—his notion that animals do not perceive non-demanded objects does not differentiate between the positive and the negative cases. Two possible mechanisms within mediation theory are relevant: (a) As noticed above, representations of certain goal-objects will not be called forth as strongly or reliably in the absence of appropriate drive stimuli. Therefore a considerable amount of training or a large amount of reinforcement, or both, might be necessary. (b) The necessary representing reactions may be kept from occurring by more intensely stimulated interfering reactions, e.g. if the animal is vigorously making anticipatory drinking reactions, these may interfere with making anticipatory food-taking reactions. Spence, Bergmann, and Lippitt cite this as a plausible explanation of the failures of Kendler and Mencher, Walker, and Grice to get positive results; they suggest that drinking and eating responses are incompatible (p. 550), but this seems unlikely to me. It will require a series of carefully designed parametric studies to tease out the conditions that favor and hinder the formation of effective representation processes whereby learning takes place under irrelevant drive and reward.

Learning under Irrelevant Drive and without Reinforcement

It is apparent from the arguments cited above that the basic weakness of these experiments, as a test of reinforcement theory, is that in all cases reinforcement was operative. Could an animal learn a sign-significate relation under a state of irrelevant drive (sufficient to make it perform) when no reinforcements were given? The proponents of the Hull-type theory would have to retreat if learning occurred *and these conditions were met.* I have uncovered only one experiment that attempts to meet these conditions, but there may well be more. Strange (1950) gave 22-hour *thirsty* rats 12 days of training in a modified U-maze, one leg white and the other black, in which food was present in one goal-box and nothing in the other. These animals received no water reward in the maze, nor were any of them observed to nibble at the food. Forced runs equated experience with both sides. When shifted to a 22-hour hunger drive and tested under free-choice conditions, these experimental animals were found to do significantly better than a control group which had not had the previous experience under thirst motivation. Apparently these animals had learned the location of the food objects under conditions in which no reinforcement was given.

As pointed out at the beginning of this chapter, 'facts' are curious things. Was reinforcement lacking in this experiment? At the end of each training trial the rats were 'left in the goal-box for one minute' without water. Were they then returned to their home cages where water was available? Strange does not amplify on this point—which is an important one relating to the possibilities of secondary reinforcement. Were the goal-boxes in any way similar to those in which water had been given? Did the handling of the animals constitute secondary reinforcement? This may seem like quibbling, but a broad general principle upon which the most rigorously worked-out theory available today is constructed is not something to be lightly tossed aside on the basis of a single demonstration—unless that demonstration is reproducible and can be shown to be what it pretends to be. The real onus here is on reinforcement theorists, who have not been able to make sufficiently explicit the conditions under which reinforcement is and is not present.

Another point is brought up by this experiment, although it applies to many others in this area as well. Were the rats in this experiment under an irrelevant drive, e.g. was hunger absent? In this and many other experiments training has been under thirst motivation with hunger presumably satiated. Hunger drive was assumed to be absent because the thirsty animals were supplied all the *dry* food pellets they would eat in their home cages and, furthermore, they refused to eat pellets found while traversing the maze. But do animals under thirst privation eat normal amounts of food? Do they not find it unpleasantly irritating to eat dry food without sufficient salivation? I do not know the answer to these questions, but it seems highly probable that extremely thirsty animals will also be somewhat hungry. Furthermore, the ingestion of quantities of water, by extending the stomach, does temporarily eliminate hunger pangs (irrelevant reinforcement?). To trace all the devious implications of this for the many experiments we have covered would be a space-consuming and probably profitless task, but the problem remains. These studies would be much more convincing if the irrelevant drive had been something that clearly does not interact with hunger.

Failure of Differential Learning despite Differential Reinforcement

Another line of attack on the reinforcement principle has been to design situations in which the law should operate but apparently does not. One of the first critical studies of this type was contributed by Tolman, Hall, and Bretnall (1932) and entitled in part 'a Disproof of the Law of Effect.' A metal punchboard maze was wired so that plunging through one of the holes in each of 30 pairs would deliver a buzzer sound or, under other conditions, a buzzer sound plus a shock. One group of subjects got the buzzer sound for *right* responses; a second group got the buzzer for *wrong* responses; the third group received buzzer plus shock for *right* responses; and a fourth group received both buzzer plus shock for *wrong* responses. All subjects were told what pattern to learn, i.e. learn to follow the holes which ring the buzzer, or those which do not ring the buzzer, or buzzer-shock, and so on. The results were such as to raise considerable theoretical uproar: both *buzzer-right* and *buzzer-shock-right* groups were definitely superior in learning to the other two groups; according to the authors, these stimuli served to *emphasize* (cognitively) the correct response. The *buzzer-right* group was not superior to the *buzzer-shock-right* group—addition of punishment for right responses did not weaken them. The *buzzer-shock-wrong* subjects were not superior to the *buzzer-wrong* subjects—addition of punishment for wrong responses did not facilitate performance.

An experiment by Wallach and Henle (1941) gets at the question of whether the action of rewards is automatic and independent of the subject's intent to learn. Thorndike (1933 b) presenting lists of paired words and numbers, instructed the subject to guess the number which belonged with each word and then told him immediately whether he was 'right' or 'wrong.' Responses called 'right' were found to be repeated far more often than would be expected by chance and, furthermore, there was the bidirectional spread of effect about such 'right' responses. Thorndike concluded that the effect of reward acted directly and unconsciously upon temporally contiguous connections. Wallach and Henle duplicated these procedures in all respects but one: their subjects were told that they were taking part in an experiment in extrasensory perception and hence the numbers would be paired randomly with the set of words on repeated trials. In other words, these subjects, albeit told 'right' for occasional number-responses, had no reason to expect that what was right once would be right again. Does 'reinforcement' operate in this case? Apparently not, because these investigators found that 'right' responses were not repeated at greater than chance frequencies and that there was no gradient of reward. To check on the possibilities that subjects had recalled their previous responses and intentionally inhibited them, a recall test was given but there were no differences between the retention of correct and incorrect responses.

What does the defense have to say about these findings? Referring to the experiments by Tolman and his associates on the effects of shock upon learning correct and incorrect responses, Dashiel (1938) has commented that 'we have let ourselves be surprised at this "shock-right" phenomenon; but the surprise is due to our having emphasized the word "shock" and not the word "right." ' All of the complex but powerful motives included in the phrase 'doing what is expected of us' were on the side of learning the 'right' path, and any cues that would enhance the discriminability of the 'right' path should facilitate such learning. Furthermore, according to Hull it is the *end* of punishment (drive-reduction) that is reinforcing. And what does this pain-reduction strengthen most? The responses immediately preceding the pain-reduction, which in this case were the 'right' responses. Then *why,* the reader may ask at this point, do people usually learn *not* to do things that are punished? Stimuli that antedate the punishing state of affairs become conditioned to anticipatory punishment reactions (anxiety), and avoidant responses which escape punishment are then reinforced by anxiety-reduction (cf. pp. 429-33). In the present case there is no reason to believe that the 'punishments' were such as to create strong anxiety in the subjects.

The results obtained by Wallach and Henle in their extrasensory perception study not only are embarrassing to Thorndike's conception of the law of effect, but they also seem to pose problems for Hull's reinforcement postulate. Their subjects were presumably motivated to hear the experimenter say 'right' to extrasensorily percept as many items as they could, even though they had no reason to retain any specific associations. Since Hull's principle of reinforcement is just as inevitable as Thorndike's, if the conditions for its operation exist, it seems that here again we must move toward a Tolman-like position. Overt responses are not the only ones strengthened by reinforcement; appropriate mediation processes (modes of perceiving the situation, meanings, or implicit reactions, depending on one's bias) are also capable of being strengthened or weakened. It was not the overt and specific number vocalizations that were reinforced in the Wallach and Henle study but rather the meaningfully appropriate tendency to passively call out numbers—and tendencies of this order are hard to handle rigorously in theory. Of course a reinforcement theorist could duck this entire issue by claiming that we cannot measure the reinforcement given to human subjects by saying 'right' or 'wrong,' but he should realize that in so doing he is seriously questioning the testability, and hence scientific adequacy, of his whole position.

Another necessary prediction from reinforcement theory is that, for a constant number of trials, a regularly reinforced association should become stronger than one reinforced intermittently. A considerable body of data appears to contradict this prediction. Humphreys (1939 a) compared 100 per cent reinforcement with 50 per cent reinforcement for conditioned eyelid responses in human subjects. Conditioning was equally rapid in both cases, and resistance to extinction proved to be *greater* for the 50 per cent reinforcement condition. In other experiments (1940) an instrumental response in rats was studied with essentially the same results. Related results have been obtained by Finger (1942 a, b) and Mote (1944) with rat subjects. Using a simple running response, in which the latency of the animal's leaving the starting box for a run down a 3-foot elevated runway was the measure of habit strength, these investigators found that number

of reinforcements during training was not positively correlated with resistance to extinction. In the first study by Finger, for example, animals
that were given 16 reinforced runs extinguished more easily than those
given only eight reinforced runs.

The defense here is more adequate. Mowrer and Jones (1945) question
Humphreys' notion that a single reaction constitutes the learning unit when
reinforcement is intermittent. If the subject is rewarded on every other
trial (and his response unit is therefore a pattern of two reactions),
shouldn't one measure extinction in the same units as those under which

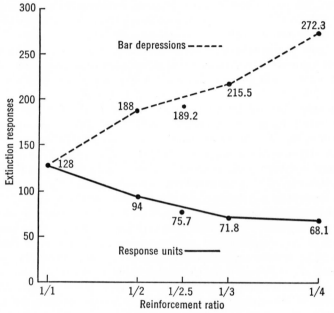

FIGURE 146. Curves showing average number of bar depressions as contrasted with
response units (reinforcement ratios of $\frac{1}{1}$ to $\frac{1}{4}$) on three days of extinction. Mowrer
and Jones, *Journal of Experimental Psychology*, 1945, 35:300.

learning occurs? In a modified Skinner box, different groups of rats were
given either one pellet per bar-press, one for two presses, one for three
presses, or one for four presses, these ratios being maintained in *regular*
sequence. A fifth group was rewarded *irregularly,* after 1, 2, 3, or 4 presses,
averaging 2.5 bar-pressing between pellets (this last group most closely
matches Humphreys' conditions). As the data in Fig. 146 show, if one
analyzes as Humphreys did (i.e. each reaction counted as a single response
unit), then resistance to extinction increases as the reinforcement ratio decreases (dashed curve). If, on the other hand, we divide the total number
of responses made during extinction trials by the response unit maintained
during training, the results confirm the reinforcement principle (solid
curve). The irregularly reinforced group falls just about where it should
in terms of the average discontinuity of reinforcement (one pellet per 2.5
pressings). This explanation applies better to Humphreys' study on rats
than those on human eyelid conditioning.

Denny (1946) offers an alternative explanation of these intermittent reinforcement findings. He suggested that there was actually reinforcement on the nonrewarded trials but that it was *secondary* in nature. By using a single-unit T-maze, one group of animals was run under the usual discrimination conditions, a white goal-box always being the correct, food-containing side and a black goal-box always being empty. The other group was run under conditions designed to minimize secondary reinforcement (e.g. the anticipatory gratification derived from merely getting into the distinctive box that sometimes contained food)—white and black boxes were used on rewarded trials, but neutral gray boxes were substituted for the nonrewarded trials. These two groups were further subdivided into 100% versus 50% reinforcement conditions. The results justified Denny's contention: there were no differences between 100% and 50% reward groups trained under the usual conditions, which encouraged the development of secondary reinforcement; with the possibility of secondary reward minimized, the 100% group did significantly better than the 50% group, which would be predicted from the reinforcement principle.

The simple running response technique used by Finger and Mote has recently been criticized by Lawrence and Miller (1947) as one yielding response conflict. To minimize handling their animals, Finger and Mote had made starting- and goal-boxes identical. After eating in one 'goal-box,' animal and box were carried around to the beginning, and that box now became 'starting-box' for the next trial. During rewarded trials, therefore, various food-seeking responses would become associated with the cues within the box; the same cues were associated with the response of leaving the box. During *training,* conflict between these responses should be minimal, since the act of eating and its sensory consequences would change the stimulus situation. During *extinction,* however, conflict should be maximal, there being no differential cues present. Eliminating this source of confusion by making starting- and goal-boxes highly distinctive and handling the animals at the end of each trial, but otherwise duplicating Finger's procedure, Lawrence and Miller found 16 reinforcement subjects more resistant to extinction than eight reinforcement subjects, a result quite in keeping with reinforcement theory.

Summary

Has the reinforcement principle been shown to be either unnecessary or insufficient? The hypothesis that learning can occur without motivation is currently untestable—we have no adequate ways of indexing the absence of motivation. The evidence on latent performance (latent learning), admittedly controversial as evidence, is not relevant to the issue, since everyone agrees that learning occurs on the 'unrewarded' trials. The fact that there are discrepancies between 'learning' and 'performance' is explained as adequately by the mediation hypothesis as by Tolman's theory. The same statements apply to the experiments cited in 'drive discrimination' and 'learning under conditions of irrelevant motivation and reward'—both drives and rewards were present in all cases and, again, the formation of relevant 'cognitions' was as readily incorporated by an extended Hull theory as by Tolman's theory. Strange's experimental demonstration of learning of effective 'cognitions' under conditions of irrelevant drive and no

428 EXPERIMENTAL PSYCHOLOGY

reinforcement is the strongest case against the reinforcement principle, but it needs confirmation. Of the several experiments cited in which degrees of learning apparently fail to correspond to degrees of reinforcement, only that by Wallach and Henle is difficult to incorporate within Hull's theory. But it is a complicated situation, 'extrasensory guessing' by human subjects, and most learning theorists will not pay much attention to it. We conclude that there is not sufficient evidence here to force us to abandon the reinforcement principle—which does not prove it to be true.

THE NATURE OF SECONDARY MOTIVATION AND REINFORCEMENT

It has been clear to psychologists for a long time that primary energizers, like hunger, thirst, and sex, are not the immediate determinants of human behavior. The graduate student slaves long hours over his books and papers, not because he is hungry nor because he relieves physical pain by these endeavors—then why? Perhaps it is for prestige and social approval, perhaps vague anxieties are eliminated when the term paper is handed in; certainly he represents to himself the monetary and other rewards of competent professional work. As a child he learned that coins and dollar bills could be traded for 'real' rewards, that parental smiles and head-pats had positive values, and eventually that even telling himself 'I'm good,' in effect, produced a pleasant glow. But if we conceive of motivation as an energizing process having roots in organismic physiology and conceive of reinforcement as a reduction in the intensity of this energizing process, we run full tilt into a puzzle: How can dollar bills, the praise of others, or saying 'I'm good' modulate the dynamic energy systems of the organism?

One easy way out of the puzzle, common in the early part of this century, was to call these secondary motives *instincts* and to assume that this explained their genesis and operation. Thus, Veblen spoke of the 'instinct of workmanship' and many post-Darwinian romanticists referred to entities such as the 'herd instinct' and the 'paternal instinct.' Holt (1931) has summarized this nonsense neatly and one can do no better than quote him: '. . . man is impelled to action, it is said, by his instincts. If he goes with his fellows, it is the "herd instinct" which activates him; if he walks alone, it is the "anti-social instinct"; if he fights, it is the "pugnacity instinct"; if he defers to another, it is the instinct of "self-abasement"; if he twiddles his thumbs, it is the thumb-twiddling instinct; if he does not twiddle his thumbs, it is the thumb-not-twiddling instinct. Thus everything is explained with the facility of magic—word magic.' There is a real danger that today we are merely substituting another label, 'secondary motivation,' for the older word 'instinct,' and assuming that because the new label fits present-day vernacular we have accomplished something by way of explanation.

Experimental Demonstrations

It will be instructive to observe the development of secondary mechanisms under simpler conditions than are offered with human materials. Both Wolfe (1936) and Cowles (1937) have reported experiments using chimpanzees as subjects. Cowles first taught his subjects to insert small 'poker chips' into a vending machine that would deliver one raisin per chip. The chimpanzees quickly learned this skill. In the second stage of the experiment the animals were presented with five discriminably different boxes in a row, in one of which would be found either a raisin (primary reinforcement) or a poker chip (secondary reinforcement). For each series of 20 discrimination trials the reward-containing box was varied. The vending machine was not immediately available, and the chimps were not allowed to 'cash in' their chips until each set of 20 trials was completed. Whereas only 20 per cent successes would have resulted on a purely chance basis, 74 per cent successes occurred when poker chips were the reward and 93 per cent successes with actual raisins. Wolfe's similar study brought out the motivating or incentive value of 'poker chips': he found that his animals, after preliminary training with the vending machine, would work strenuously at a task previously laid aside (such as pulling in a heavy weight) if visible poker chips could be secured. Secondary reinforcement based upon food rewards by no means exhausts the list, even for animal subjects. It will be recalled that a repeated 'out' for the reinforcement theorist when faced with latent learning experiments and the like was to invoke such secondary reinforcing conditions as 'curiosity,' 'being handled by the experimenter,' 'being returned to the familiar home cage,' 'the sounds and smells of fellow rats,' and so on.

The most commonly studied secondary motive of a negative sort has been anxiety, produced by shock in *avoidance training* experiments. Of many studies fitting this paradigm, an early one by Brogden, Lipman, and Culler (1938) will serve as illustration. Guinea pig subjects were placed in a revolving cage, a buzzer (*CS*) was sounded for two seconds, and this was followed by shock (*US*), causing the animals to jump and run. One group was trained according to classic Pavlovian conditioning procedures, the shock being given whether or not the subjects responded to the buzzer by running. The other animals were given avoidance training, escaping the shock entirely if they ran while the buzzer was sounding. The results of this experiment are shown in Fig. 147. By the eighth day of training, the avoidance animals were making the correct response 100 per cent of the time; nonavoidance animals never learned to make a running response consistently. A more recent experiment by Sheffield (1948), duplicating most of the Brogden, Lipman, and Culler conditions but providing for more detailed observations, showed that the avoidant running response gradually *weakens* throughout those trials where shock is avoided, until, delaying too long, the animal again gets shocked.

It is interesting to see how proponents of different theories incorporate these phenomena. Reinforcement theorists consider this a prime example of the operation of secondary reinforcement. Anxiety reactions, as part of the total response to shock, become conditioned to the onset of the buzzer via short circuiting; subsequent instrumental responses which happen to avoid the shock (e.g. running) are strengthened by anxiety reduction. Whatever responses the nonavoidance animals happen to make to the buzzer, they are interfered with by the dominant reactions to shock, hence no consistent reaction is made. Since the anxiety mediator is itself a learned reaction, continued avoidance of shock results in its gradual extinction and explains the gradual slowing down of avoidant running. Sheffield (1948) has indicated how a Guthrian contiguity theory would explain these phenomena: once running occurs to the fear-plus-buzzer, it changes the situation and its association is preserved; nonavoidant animals which stop running and crouch, jump, and so forth, to the subsequent shock are making responses incompatible with running, hence unlearning. Repeated runs without shock result in extinction of the fear response and therefore sufficient change in the stimulus situation to gradually decrease the probability of running. By way of confirmation, Sheffield found that when the response of the nonavoiding animals to shock was continued running, the animals also ran to

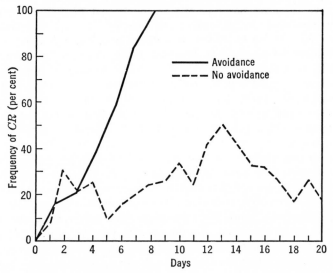

FIGURE 147. Comparison of learning under classic Pavlovian conditions with learning under avoidance training conditions. After Brogden, Lipman, and Culler, *American Journal of Psychology*, 1938, 51:110.

the buzzer on the next trial, but this was not the case for animals that made some other response to the shock on the preceding trial. Tolman's theory seems to handle avoidance training very easily: the buzzer becomes a sign of shock, so the animals behave in such a way as to avoid it. But what about the gradual weakening of the avoidance? If their expectation of nonshock via running is continually confirmed, why should the running behavior weaken? Tolman can handle this (cf. Osgood, 1950) by assuming that the demand-against-shock decreases with successful avoidance, e.g. this acquired demand depends upon the expectation that buzzer signifies shock. It can be seen that these interpretations are really quite similar at base.

Our third illustration of secondary reinforcement is drawn from Pavlov's conditioning laboratory and has already been described in a different context (Chap. 8) as 'second-order conditioning.' Frolov trained a dog to salivate to the ticking of a metronome and, once this association was well established, paired another neutral stimulus (a black square) with the sound of the metronome, no food being given (cf. Hull, 1943, p. 85). Since conditioning of the salivary reaction to the black square was demonstrated under these conditions, we must conclude that the sound of the metronome had acquired secondary reinforcing value in the course of its original association with food powder. But is it the sound of the metronome (as a stimulus) or the salivating it elicits (as a reaction) that has this reinforcing property? This brings us fully into the problem of interpretation.

Interpretation of Secondary Motivation and Reinforcement

Hull literally postulates secondary reinforcement. He amends his reinforcement principle as follows: whenever a stimulus-response connection is closely associated in time with the diminution of a need, *'or with a stimulus situation which has been closely and consistently associated with such a need diminution,'* there will result an increment . . . (1943, p. 98). This statement seems to say it is the *cue stimulus* that carries strengthening properties. We are led to believe that, somehow, a poker chip as a stimulus can strengthen behavior, to believe that, somehow, a buzzer as a pattern of auditory sensations can now modulate the organism's energy systems. This is, indeed, strong magic, stronger by far than invoking a collection of instincts. For here there is no limit whatever to the multitude of neutral situations that can become motives and rewards. And within Hull's system itself the whole thing is most mysterious. If we think of reinforcement as the reduction of some drive state, we must wonder how being stimulated with a poker chip reduces the chimp's need for food.

This statement is misleading as to Hull's actual position, as can be seen from a careful reading of the context. Discussing Cowles's experiment, for example, he says (pp. 90-91): '. . . it would be rash to conclude at once that the evocation of some fractional component of the reaction originally conditioned to the secondary reinforcing stimulus was not present at each secondary reinforcement. The principles of reinforcement learning lead *a priori* to the expectation that salivation, and probably many other hidden internal processes . . . , must have been conditioned both to the stimulus energies arising from the vending machine and to those from the food tokens.' At no point, however, does Hull elaborate the explanatory possibilities here and thereby make the process of secondary reinforcement at least a little less mysterious. The following analysis, which follows directly from the mediation hypothesis, is an attempt in that direction.

In studying the process of short circuiting we found that stimuli that regularly precede a given reaction can come to elicit that reaction in anticipatory fashion. *Goal reactions can also become anticipatory by exactly the same means.* To be sure, the animal cannot actually eat the raisin until it gets the raisin in its mouth, but it can make certain fractional parts of the total goal reaction before this ultimate event. Theoretically, any goal reaction (R_G, in Hull's terms) may be divided into two classes of events: (1) those reactions that require the goal-object for their occurrence, or at least normally occur only when the goal-object is present (e.g. squeezing the raisin between the teeth and chewing on it); and (2) those reactions that can become anticipatory and can be elicited by stimuli other than the goal-object (e.g. salivating or licking the lips). We may follow Hull's system again and represent these fractional, anticipatory components of the total goal reaction by the symbol r_G.

There is ample evidence that such fractional anticipatory goal responses do in fact occur, cases in which their overtness is an advantage to the observer, if not to the organism. Cowles reports that his chimpanzees displayed a marked tendency to place the poker chips in their mouths (although they discriminated sufficiently not to swallow them!). Wolfe reports that with his animals the chips elicited noticeable smacking of the lips and biting. Many other illustrations of such anticipatory goal reactions can be seen about us everyday in both animals and humans. The little dog sitting by the dinner table wriggles its mouth, licks its lips, and drools freely while it watches the family eat. Much of human gesture language, including facial expressions, probably has its basis in such anticipatory behavior— witness the wrinkling of the nose in disgust (anticipatory closure of the nostrils to a bad odor?) and the baring of the teeth in anger (Darwin claims this is anticipatory to biting as a rage response). Similarly, chimpanzees have been observed to develop beckoning gestures in the course of attempting to pull a fellow animal nearer to aid in a task.

In order for an initially neutral stimulus to acquire secondary motivating or reinforcement value, it must become associated with such anticipatory goal reactions. *This means it must fall within the effective range of generalization of the stimulus pattern regularly evoking the total goal response.* This will hold for stimuli that accompany the goal response. It will also be true of stimulus patterns that closely precede the goal response in time, since their traces will partake in eliciting the goal response and stronger portions of the same traces will be highly similar. Thus it is the *traces* of the buzzer in the ratchet-turning experiment, of the poker chips in Cowles's experiment, of the sound of the metronome in Frolov's experiment, that are initially conditioned to the goal reactions; through generalization, more intense portions of these traces (and hence antedating portions) come to elicit those fractional parts of the total goal responses which can be dissociated from the goal-objects. Hull assumes that the *primary* gradient of reinforcement places limits on the temporal extent of this process. It is certainly true that the capacity of neutral stimuli to acquire reinforcing properties varies inversely with their temporal displacement from the goal response, but, according to the present analysis, it is *not* because of the action of a primary gradient of reinforcement but rather because antedating and evoking stimulus patterns will be less similar, owing to greater differences in the intensity of traces and to the occurrence of intervening activities. The interpretation offered here is quite similar to that presented by Spence in a theoretical article (1947), particularly in the stress laid upon generalization as the mechanism.*

Have we managed to reduce the mystery to any extent? The essence of the argument has been that certain stimuli, originally neutral with respect to motivational properties, come to have both motivating and reinforcing values by virtue of eliciting fractional components of the total goal reaction. Is it any less mysterious that making a certain kind of reaction after a given behavior sequence should strengthen that sequence than that receiving a certain stimulus should have strengthening effects? To answer this question *we must inquire into the kind of self-stimulation produced by*

* A paper by Seward (1950) describes a closely related analysis.

making these particular kinds of mediating reactions. Most learning theorists look upon drive as a form of stimulation—witness Hull's use of S_D as a symbol for drive and Miller and Dollard's statement (1941) that any stimulus will have cue value to the extent that it is distinctive and drive value to the extent that it is intense. Although it is doubtful, in view of recent evidence for direct energizing of the central nervous system in hunger, sex, and so on (cf. Morgan's 'central motive state,' 1943), that most *primary* drives are 'stimuli' in the usual sense, it is possible that the energizing value of *acquired* drive states *is* stimulus based, and it is beginning to appear that all contemporary motivation for learning may be of this acquired sort.

The role of *anxiety* as an acquired drive and reinforcing agent provides the clearest illustration. The original shock has several stimulus functions: (1) As a distinctive, localized source of stimulation it elicits certain reflexive and learned skeletal responses (such as leaping into the air). (2) As a pain-producing stimulation it also energizes all on-going reaction systems, amplifying the vigor with which reactions are made (the rat struggles violently to climb the walls). (3) Most important in the present connection, the shock activates the animal's autonomic system: adrenalin is released into the blood stream, pulse and breathing rates increase, vegetative functions are inhibited, and so on, all serving to maintain the organism on an emergency basis. We usually refer to these autonomic changes as the emotional state of *fear*. The significant point is that such physiological reactions *in toto* give rise to a mass of intense, yet distinctive, stimulation. When, through short-circuiting mechanisms, fear becomes associated with certain antedating stimuli, such as a buzzer, and is elicited in anticipatory fashion, it is usually called *anxiety*. The physiological changes, however, are much the same (albeit perhaps less intense) and therefore the stimulation produced will be much the same. This means that the fractional, anticipatory goal reaction does reproduce part of the primary drive situation. According to the present analysis, this reaction-produced stimulation *is* the secondary drive and its reduction *is* secondary reinforcement.

Well enough for negative acquired motives like anxiety, but what about positive acquired motives like self-esteem, social approval, or even poker chips? How do the anticipatory goal reactions made to poker chips, such as lip-licking and salivating, reproduce even in part the energetics of hunger drive? In comparison with the mass of stimulation produced in anxiety, that produced by swallowing one's own saliva or by feeling oneself licking his own lips seems pale and insignificant. *Is it possible that positive motives, like hunger, also include hormonal and other autonomic reactions which, like anxiety, are conditionable?* Research by Luckhardt and Carlson (1915) and by Templeton and Quigley (1930) enlivens this possibility. It has been shown, for example, that transfusing small amounts of the blood between a hungry dog and a satiated animal can cause hunger contractions in the stomach wall of the latter; conversely, the on-going hunger contractions in the hungry dog are temporarily quieted, as if the satiated animal's blood included a 'satiation' hormone. If it could be shown that anticipatory reactions to food and other positive goal stimuli also included autonomic physiological changes, such as hormone release, the nature of positive secondary mechanisms would become much less mysterious.

Relation between Primary and Secondary Reinforcement

As the term 'secondary' implies, such energizing and reinforcing systems are assumed to depend upon primary mechanisms for their establishment and maintenance. In other words, if the associations between certain originally neutral stimuli and fractional anticipatory goal reactions are themselves learned, they should be demonstrably impermanent, susceptible to extinction. Of many experiments here, one by Grindley (1929) using baby chicks as subjects will be described. Two groups of chicks were allowed to run up an inclined plane to a plate of rice grains; one group (primary reinforcement) was allowed to peck and eat the rice grains, but the other (secondary

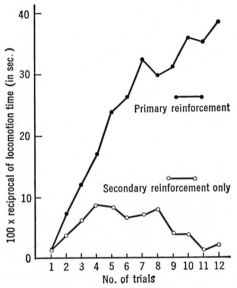

FIGURE 148. Performance of baby chicks learning to traverse a 4-foot runway under conditions of primary and secondary reinforcement. After Grindley, *British Journal of Psychology,* Cambridge University Press, London, 1929, 20:179.

reinforcement) found a piece of plate glass between them and the grains and could only look at them. Figure 148 shows the average speed of running up the inclined plane for the two groups as a function of the number of trials. The effects of secondary reinforcement are shown by the initial increases in running speed and its impermanence by the final slowing down (and we infer that anticipatory food-taking reactions at the sight of rice grains were being extinguished). This experiment is reminiscent of the fable about the little boy who crief 'wolf.' Although this is not the place to explore social implications, it is clear that to the extent that social motives are acquired they are susceptible to modification.

Estes (1949 *a, b*) has questioned this dependency relation between secondary reinforcing mechanisms and the primary drives from which they are derived. In the first study all rats were made thirsty and then given small quantities of water accompanied by a characteristic auditory stimulus. In a subsequent test—bar-pressing in a Skinner box to obtain the 'reward' of hearing the tone—one group of experimental animals was 22-hours hungry (but satiated on water) while another was 22-hours thirsty (but satiated on food). Question: Will a secondary reinforcing mechanism developed on one drive (thirst) still operate when the animal is functioning under a different drive (hunger)? Although making 25 per cent fewer pressings than animals under thirst drive, the hungry animals did do significantly more pressing than a control group which had not had the original pairing of tone with water delivery. The second experiment differed from the one cited above in one major respect: one experimental group was 23-hours hungry and another only 6-hours hungry. Question: Does the operation of this 'transferred' secondary reinforcing mechanism depend on the existence of sufficient primary motivation? The 'low-drive' group did not do significantly better than a control group which had had no pairing of tone with water delivery.

The results of the second experiment are perhaps those to be expected. Anticipatory goal reactions are learned, and Hull's theory assumes reaction potential to be a multiplicative result of habit strength *and* drive. Therefore the low-drive group would not be expected, with any surety, to either perform (press the bar very often) or make appropriate anticipatory goal reactions upon hearing the tone. But what about the nature of the anticipatory goal reactions in this case? The tone was originally associated with water delivery to *thirsty* rats; the mediating reaction in this case would have to be fractional parts of water-drinking. Since the animals were satiated on water during the test trials, it seems very unlikely that anticipatory water-drinking responses would be made to the tone or that they would have reinforcing effects in any case. But would these results be so surprising if, during the original pairings of tone with water-delivery, *these rats had also been somewhat hungry and their hunger needs were being partially reinforced by water consumption?* Although Estes's animals had been 'satiated' by having 'continuous access to dry food,' this would be a rather specious control if they failed to eat their normal amounts of dry food, a difficult procedure with parched throats, and became hungry as well as thirsty. Experiments of this sort would be more convincing if the drives involved were less liable to interaction than are hunger and thirst.

In all the experiments on secondary agents we have covered it has been necessary to associate the originally neutral stimulus with a primary reinforcing agent. It would be expected that the degree of secondary reinforcing capacity conferred upon the new stimulus would vary with the time interval between secondary and primary agents during training, assuming the amount of training to be constant. In one of the few direct tests of this prediction, Jenkins (1950) has employed a procedure very much like that of Estes. Following habituation to the Skinner box, paired presentations of a 3-second buzz with receiving food in the cup were given without any bar present to be pressed. The interval between termination of the buzz and delivery of food was varied for different groups, from 1, 3, 9, 27 to 81 seconds. On test trials the food-magazine was disconnected and a bar was inserted, each press producing a buzz (secondary reinforcement). In terms of number of bar-pressings made in a total period of 6 hours, a very regular, negatively accelerated gradient was obtained. As the interval between buzz and food is increased, the amount of secondary reinforcing capacity conferred upon the buzz as a stimulus falls off rapidly at first and then more and more gradually.

In his own theorizing Hull (cf. 1943) has drawn a sharp distinction between the *goal gradient* (a complex performance phenomenon resulting from the compounded action of many determinants, including secondary reinforcement) and the *gradient of reinforcement*. The latter is the 'pure' reflection of a primary principle that increment in habit strength varies with the time interval between an S–R association and the reinforcing state of affairs. Obviously, if one is to get at the shape of this primary gradient and measure its temporal extent, all sources of secondary reinforcement must be eliminated—and right here the experimental situation might be called ludicrous were it not for the efforts that have been expended by so many able investigators. For one can trace a series of more and more refined attempts to isolate the rat from its temporal moorings, to prevent its being stimulated by its surroundings, and with each experiment the extent of the pure gradient of reinforcement seems to become more restricted until 'poof!' it disappears altogether.

Hamilton (1929) inserted a delay chamber between the last choice point in a maze and the food box, different groups of rats being delayed 0, 1, 3, 5, and 7 minutes as a means of charting the gradient of reinforcement. Although the immediate reinforcement group was clearly superior in learning the maze, all delay groups experienced equal difficulty. This has generally been interpreted as indicating that the delay chamber, a stimulus complex always followed promptly by primary reward, had acquired equal secondary reinforcing properties for all delay groups. Working with a single-unit T-maze having distinctively different delay chambers for correct and incorrect responses, Wolfe (1934) extended the interval all the way from 0 to 20 minutes. Learning fell off sharply as delay increased up to 1 minute, then more gradually up to the 20-minute delay—and there was evidence for some learning even with the longest delay. Again, since being in the positive goal-box was always immediately followed by food-taking activity, we do not have a 'pure' gradient of primary reinforcement.

In a maze there is always a chain of external stimuli leading up to the final goal. Perin (1943 *a*, *b*), working in Hull's laboratory, arranged to have the animals kept in as constant a situation as possible during both delay and reinforcement periods. Rats learned to press a bar in a modified Skinner box under conditions of varying delay (0, 2, 5, 10, 20, or 30 seconds) between reaction and receiving the food pellet reward. Immediately following a correct response, the bar was silently withdrawn and the delay interval begun. Using reaction latency as a measure (1943 *a*), there was evidence for learning up to 10 seconds, but the 30-second group showed increasing latencies with practice, some even 'going to sleep' in the box. Using selective learning as a measure—the rat having to learn to push the bar in the nonpreferred direction (1943 *b*)—there was some evidence of learning up to 20 seconds, but the 30-second delay animals tended to extinguish before completion of the 120 training trials. These results would make it appear that the gradient of primary reinforcement is a sharply limited function in time, the much longer intervals through which goal gradients may continue to make their presence felt (e.g. 20 minutes in Wolfe's study) owing to secondary effects.

At any rate, this is Hull's conclusion. 'The conditions of Perin's experiment . . . were designed in such a way as to preclude all irrelevant secondary reinforcement as well as all irrelevant spatial orientation' (1943, p. 142). In what sense is secondary reinforcement eliminated by this design? Are there not distinctive stimuli present during the giving of primary reinforcement which are also present during the delay interval? Although the bar was withdrawn following each correct reaction, the *food cup* was present in the box throughout all delay periods, to say nothing of the other apparatus stimuli, and this cup was certainly distinctively associated with food-taking reactions for all animals. In this connection it is interesting to note Perin's report (1943 *b,* p. 48) that most of his rats seemed to be oriented toward this food cup during the delay period. But if secondary reinforcement was *not* eliminated, why the sharply limited learning function? One could argue that longer delay periods permit more extinctive inhibition of the anticipatory goal reactions to the cup, thus continually diluting the secondary reinforcement. Perin's gradient would then be a gradient of secondary reinforcement dependent upon his particular conditions.

Perkins (1947) has used a single T-maze like that employed by Wolfe. 'In order to eliminate or minimize the effectiveness of the secondary reinforcing cues normally provided by the delay compartment on the correct arm of the maze, the delay compartments were interchanged from trial to trial in a random manner . . . [and their] position was rotated 180 degrees each day' (p. 379). A control group was delayed for 45 seconds in the *same* compartment after correct choices. As expected, the control group learned more rapidly than the equivalent experimental group. When five experimental groups, having delays of 0, 5, 15, 45, and 120 seconds, were compared, the typical, negatively accelerated gradient was obtained; the height of the gradient for long delays was less, however, than it was for Wolfe's experiment. Perkins concludes that there must have been some secondary reinforcement even under these conditions, possibly from persisting proprioceptive traces set up by making the correct turning response.

By using a visual black-white discrimination situation in which the position of the positive stimulus was randomly shifted, Grice (1948 *a*) was able to eliminate proprioceptive traces as a basis for secondary reinforcement. There remains the positive cue itself—its traces can be present at the time of reinforcement and thereby become conditioned to anticipatory goal reactions, providing immediate reinforcement once short circuiting has occurred, but this would seem to be an unavoidable limitation in the test of this hypothesis. All rats had to choose between black and white entrance corridors leading into neutral gray delay boxes. For one group of rats (.5, 1.2, 2.0, 5.0, and 10.0 sec. delays), the final goal-boxes were also neutral gray; for a second group (5.0 sec. delay) the goal-boxes were black and white, corresponding to the positive and negative entrance cues; a third group (5.0 sec. delay) was forced to make differential motor responses at the time of discrimination, either twisting sharply around blocks placed in the alley or running up an inclined plane. Definite differences were produced by these treatments: although the 5.0-second-delay control group still hadn't mastered the problem after 700 trials, both secondary reinforcement groups (black-white goal-boxes or differential response) had; the animals eventuating in different goal-boxes showed the best performance, as might be expected since the critical cues were palpably present at the time of food-taking. Most significant were the results of varying the delay interval for the group that had neither differential goal-boxes nor responses, i.e. secondary reinforcement minimized. As can be seen in Fig. 149, in which Grice compares his results with those obtained by Perin, the gradient of reinforcement practically reaches its base line by 5 seconds. This means that a gradient of primary reinforcement, if such a thing exists, must be limited to at least this short a temporal extent. Grice concludes that his data are more compatible with a theory that assumes no primary delay-of-reinforcement gradient.

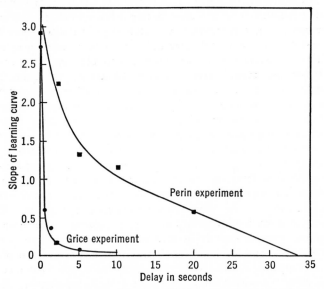

FIGURE 149. Learning rate as a function of delay of primary reinforcement in the Perin and Grice experiments. Slopes of the group learning curves are plotted against the time of delay in reward. Grice, *Journal of Experimental Psychology,* 1948, **38**:13.

Spence (1947), after reviewing all this evidence, arrives at the conclusion that 'it would not seem unreasonable to hypothesize that there is no primary gradient of reinforcement, but that all learning involving delay of the primary reward results from the action of *immediate* secondary reinforcement which develops in the situation' (p. 7). And how does this secondary reinforcement become immediate, i.e. contiguous with the association strengthened? '. . . it is the particular stimulus pattern that occurs coincidently with the food reward that acquires secondary reinforcing properties and . . . this conditioning generalizes to the stimulus patterns preceding it in time according to some gradient' (p. 5). This is the same mechanism described earlier as the basis for short circuiting.

But why, one wonders, does Spence stop here? Why does he limit the role of secondary reinforcement to learning 'involving delay of the primary reward'? Actually, there is nothing sacred about the operations by which the so-called 'primary reward' is given to the subject. The stimuli associated with smelling, tasting, and masticating a food pellet have nothing to set them apart from the sight of the food object, the food cup, and the path to the food place—*except that the former are more consistently followed by drive reduction*. Just as Grindley's baby chicks eventually ceased running to obtain the *sight* of rice grains (behind plate glass), so presumably would an animal cease learning on the basis of getting the *taste* of food pellets in its mouth—if the stimuli associated with food-in-the-mouth no longer were followed by gratification of the hunger need. But how can the taste of food in the mouth be dissociated from terminal need reduction?

Just such a dissociation has been accomplished by Hull, Livingston, Rouse, and Barker (1951). Two esophageal fistulas were produced in a dog by surgical means. When it ate in the normal fashion, the food would simply come back out of the upper fistula (sham feeding); when upper and lower fistulas were connected by a glass tube, the food could continue as usual into the stomach (real feeding). A series of tests were made on this animal: (a) When the dog was allowed to go through the activities of eating (without ingestion) until it ceased voluntarily, the amount 'eaten' dropped daily until none was consumed on the eighth day—experimental extinction of eating behavior. (b) In a simple black-white Yerkes-type discrimination box, it was found that a stable position habit could be set up on the basis of real feeding as opposed to sham feeding. (c) In the same apparatus it was shown that a stable position habit could be set up on the basis of sham feeding versus no feeding whatever—the stimuli associated with eating behavior have secondary reinforcing properties. (d) Similarly, it was shown that learning could proceed on the basis of real esophageal feeding (tube inserted in lower fistula and food put directly into the stomach) as compared with pseudoesophageal feeding (tube inserted but no food given). Stimulation from food in the mouth is not necessary for reinforcement. As Hull points out, this type of research badly needs extension, but the available data definitely suggest that the proximal stimuli associated with goal-objects (tastes, smells, etc.) themselves operate as secondary reinforcing agents.

An experiment by Sheffield and Roby (1950) may possibly be interpreted along the same lines. When given a choice between saccharin solution and ordinary water (saccharin is sweet tasting but completely nonnutritive), both hungry and food-satiated rats rapidly developed a preference for the former which persisted for 10 days—both sweetened and ordinary water was available in separate bottles in the living cages during the experiment. In a second experiment designed to test whether an instrumental approach response could be learned on the basis of saccharin-sweetened water as reward, the experimenters inserted the saccharin bottle at regular intervals in the living cages of the animals. In this case the hungry rats learned to approach and drink the solution during an 18-day period, whereas the satiated animals did not. A simple T-maze discrimination was also learned on this basis. Although the authors interpret these results as incompatible with an identification of reinforcement with 'need reduction,' the possibilities of secondary reinforcement do not seem to be eliminated. 'Sweet' taste receptors are presumably excited by the rat's ordinary diet as well as by saccharin (but not by water), and hence this stimulation can become associated with secondary reinforcing mechanisms. The fact that the sweet taste did not lose its reinforcing value throughout a long series of tests would be explained as owing to the intermittent association of the same sensations with nourishing food (the rats were fed at intervals!). Notice, however, that this provides yet further evidence that *contemporary* reinforcement for learning need not be primary.

An experiment by Kohn (1951) directly tests the notion that mouth factors, such as taste, can be involved in hunger drive reduction. Rats were first trained to make a pressing response to obtain food. They were then operated on and a plastic fistula sewed into their stomachs. After recovery from surgery, habituation to food injection, and retraining on the instrumental response, each animal was made to serve as its own control under the following conditions: (a) responding after receiving 14 cc. of enriched milk via mouth; (b) responding after receiving 14 cc. of enriched milk directly into the stomach; (c) responding after receiving 14 cc. of normal saline solution directly into the stomach. As would be expected, reductions in panel-pressing for food were much greater for both food conditions than for saline solution. The important result was that ingestion of food via the *mouth* produced significantly more satiation than direct injection of the same amount of food via the fistula. Kohn concludes (p. 420) that this '. . . probably depends on neural or neuro-humoral processes initiated by sight, smell, taste, and/or swallowing of food.' This research seems to come closer to disclosing the nature of secondary reinforcement than any other to date.

One can imagine a limited number of remote 'primary' need-reducing physiological mechanisms, each surrounded by many more-or-less standard 'avenues' of approach. These 'avenues' represent the sequences of stimuli and reactions which, once touched off, reliably eventuate in need reduction. The taste of food is almost always followed by hunger need reduction and therefore, as a stimulus, it is heavily laden with *secondary* reinforcing properties, i.e. it is a reliable *sign* of a reinforcing state of affairs. The sight of food is somewhat less reliably followed by terminal need reduction and its loading of secondary reinforcement is consequently less. Since most of these 'avenues' are established very early in the life of the organism, experiments using so-called 'primary' reinforcement are merely touching off some one of these stable sequences. The Hull *et al.* study indicates that these signs can lose their significance, but only under unusual conditions. And in studies on 'secondary' reinforcement, the operations are merely such as to add another stimulus link to one of these stable sequences—a poker chip now becomes a temporary and unstable touching-off point for the see-smell-taste-chew-swallow sequence which finally results in a change in bodily economy.

Role of Anticipatory Goal Reactions in the Behavior Sequence

Anticipatory goal reactions, or more properly the self-stimulation they release, are assumed to have *cue functions* (to the extent that they are distinctive), *drive functions* (to the extent that they are intense), and *reinforcing functions* (to the extent that their intensity is reduced or eliminated). Numerous experiments offer evidence for one or more of these functions, and many of them have already been described in connection with the mediation hypothesis. Rather than trying to give exhaustive coverage of the relevant experiments here, we shall merely cite typical illustrations.

(1) *Cue functions.* Miller (1935) trained rats to run down a straight alley to a special kind of goal-box. This box, separated from the alley by a curtain, was narrow and shaped in a abrupt right angle, so that animals were forced into a twisted, cramped posture while consuming the reward. Half of the animals twisted to the right to secure food and the other half twisted to the left to secure water. In the second stage of this experiment half of each group was shocked traumatically in the same goal-box and hence *in the same position,* but now the goal-box was separated from the straight alley and they had not just run along the alley into the goal-box. The other half of each group (control) was shocked in the same manner, but in the *other* goal-box and hence in an antagonistic position to that used during original training. When the experimental animals were replaced in the straight runway for test trials, their running speeds were sharply reduced and some even stopped part way down the alley and retreated. Control animals were largely unaffected. The beauty of this experiment is that *the only difference between the two groups was the posture in which they were shocked during stage 2.* We must assume that some representation of this posture had become associated with the cues along the alley, via short circuiting during original training. This anticipatory twisting response produced distinctive self-stimulation which, in stage 2, was associated with fear responses. When later starting their test runs down the straight alley, these cues elicited the anticipatory turning response which, *as a cue,* called forth the anxiety reaction that mediated the observed avoidant behavior.

(2) *Drive functions.* May (1948) wired a Miller-Mowrer demonstration box so that either half could be independently electrified and first trained his animals simply to run to the other side to *escape* shock. In the second phase of the study the rats were confined in a small pen with a grid floor and the last 5 seconds of a 10-second buzz were combined with shock, but no consistent response was selected. In the third phase (test trials) the rats were put back in the shuttle-box and the buzzer sounded for 10 seconds, or until an animal had made the crossing reaction. Had the pairing of the buzzer with shock in phase 2, without its connection with any consistent *instrumental* response, resulted in its acquiring drive value? The experimental subjects shuttled on about 80 per cent of the test trials. Control subjects, which in phase 2 received only shocks, buzzes, or unassociated shocks and buzzes, averaged only about 15 per cent crossings on the test trials. We conclude that the buzzer sound had acquired energizing properties for the experimental animals, e.g. had become a sign of a drive state by virtue of now eliciting part of the same behavior originally elicited by shock.

Estes (1943, 1948) has demonstrated the acquisition of motivational properties by originally neutral stimuli which are associated with positive goal-objects. A Skinner-type bar-pressing situation was used. Either *following* several experimental training periods of usual bar-pressing for food pellets (1943) or *previous to* such training (1948), the following treatment was given: rats were placed in the box with the bar withdrawn; a tone was sounded for 60 seconds followed by delivery of a pellet, this sequence being repeated ten times in each daily session. The test periods were ordinary extinction sessions, on some of which the tone was sounded. In both experiments periods when the tone was sounding were accompanied by augmented rates of bar-pressing. Since the rats were functioning under hunger drive during all sessions, these results indicate that the sound of the tone had additional, supplementary motivating properties.

(3) *Reinforcing functions.* In an experiment by Miller (1948) described earlier white walls were first made a sign of 'danger' by being associated with shock, a simple running response being all that was required for escape. When conditions were changed so that a ratchet device had to be manipulated in order to escape, this *new* instrumental response was learned solely on the basis of secondary reinforcement (anxiety reduction). Then conditions were further modified so that these animals had to give up wheel-turning and substitute bar-pressing in order to escape from the white side—this, too, was learned without further shocks. It was observed that a moderately strong initial shock level was necessary to maintain such an extended sequence of new learning on the basis of secondary anxiety effects. Brown and Jacobs (1949) report a similar experiment in which a new instrumental habit is learned on tbe hasis of turning off a buzzer sound that has previously been associated with shock. The standard *avoidance training* design is also a case in point, except that the responses finally selected are usually those originaliy included in the behavior to the shock itself. In this connection an earlier experiment by Mowrer (1940) extends our information about the reinforcing properties of mediating reactions: animals given tone-shock pairings at regular 60-second intervals (and hence able to 'relax' more completely between trials) learned the instrumental avoidant running response more rapidly and stably than either an irregularly tone-shocked group or a regular group that also had interpolated unavoidable shocks. The particular value of this experiment lies in the fact that it deliberately manipulates the *amount* of secondary reinforcement (anxiety reduction) and demonstrates that new instrumental learning varies with its amount.

Experimental demonstrations of the reinforcing function of positive secondary mechanisms are also available. An early study is that of K. A. Williams (1929). All rat subjects were regularly fed in a white-walled box before and during the experiment proper. When these animals were required to learn a maze, one group was given an actual food reward in the white-walled box at the end of the maze, a second group was merely allowed to enjoy the pleasures of entering the familiar white-walled box (secondary reinforcement), and a third group ended up in an ordinary empty box. While not learning the maze as rapidly and surely as the primary reinforcement group, the secondary reinforcement animals did show clear evidence of learning. A study by Saltzman (1949) substantiates Williams's results, both by showing that a maze (single-choice U-type) can be learned purely on the basis of secondary food reinforcement and that interpolated primary reinforcements in the distinctive goal-box facilitate such learning—presumably by preventing rapid extinction of the secondary reward value of the goal-box.

Summary

Most behavior we observe, especially in human adults, is not motivated by primary biological drives. Some additional, more flexible source of motivation is required. Instinctual explanations tend to be tautological, and principles of functional autonomy (cf. Woodworth, 1918; Allport, 1937) imply an indiscriminate transmutation of habits into drives, which simply does not occur. The behavioristic conception has two chief advantages: (a) It relates secondary mechanisms to the primary sources of organismic energy through having them depend for their origin and persistence upon primary drives. (b) The development and persistence of these secondary mechanisms is a discriminative process, since they are both learned and extinguished under specifiable conditions. In terms of the mediation theory, at least, these secondary mechanisms require no additional postulations; the stimuli that acquire such properties have merely become signs of either drive or reinforcing states of affairs, in exactly the same way that nonenergizing and nongratifying signs acquire their representational significance.

There is, however, one major difficulty in this conception. *The anticipatory goal reaction is assumed to function simultaneously as drive and as reinforcement.* It may be true that it is the *increase* in self-stimulation (from making such mediating reactions) that is supposed to motivate and the *reduction* in self-stimulation that is supposed to reinforce—but at what point in the sequence of behavior does this transition take place? The chimpanzee looks at a distant poker chip, approaches it, handles it, and finally puts it in a vending machine. At what point does reaction-produced self-stimulation begin to be reduced? As a long-distance swimmer approaches the final goal and sees the finish line, he presumably begins to make anticipatory goal reactions. Will this self-stimulation spur him on (energizing function) or will it slow him down (gratifying function)?

It has already been suggested that hormonal changes in the blood stream may underlie the shifting balance systems of drive and its reduction. Hormonal controls are definite in sexual and emotional drives and are certainly suggested by evidence on both hunger and thirst (e.g. in the latter case the antidiuretic hormone). The evidence for hunger drive, while not specifying the nature of the hormones involved, does enhance the possibility that specific hormones are associated with the satiation state as well as the hunger state. If we could assume that hormone release, via certain glandular reactions, is itself conditionable, then the following argument could be made: stimuli associated with the drive state itself become conditioned to the release of hormones which generate and maintain this state; stimuli associated with drive reduction become associated with the release of hormones which accompany the satiation state. Originally neutral stimuli which are distinctively associated with the drive state would acquire secondary motivating value (e.g. the white walls in Miller's experiment become most strongly conditioned to the glandular reactions accompanying pain drive); originally neutral stimuli which are distinctively associated with the reinforcing state of drive reduction would acquire secondary reinforcing value (e.g. the black walls in Miller's experiment become most strongly conditioned to those glandular reactions accompanying pain reduction). This hypothesis, if one can dignify such preliminary speculation with this term, involves the assumption that changes in blood chemistry are rapid and facile enough to account for the behavior observed.

THE NATURE OF DISCRIMINATION LEARNING

In Chapter 8 the nature of generalization and discrimination was discussed. Analysis of discrimination learning by means of concepts similar to Hull's has been pushed most vigorously by Spence; he has been the chief spokesman for this position in the various controversies that have developed in this area. His major assumptions (Spence, 1936) are the same as Hull's, in that (a) reinforcement strengthens reaction tendencies, (b) nonreinforcement weakens reaction tendencies, (c) the magnitudes of increments per trial are functions of the amount of habit strength at the time of reinforcement, (d) both excitatory and inhibitory tendencies generalize, (e) excitatory and inhibitory potentials at each point along any stimulus continuum summate algebraically to yield the effective reaction potential, (f) whichever of two competing reactions to the same stimulus has the greatest effective reaction potential will occur, and (g) the amplitude, probability, latency, and so on, of reaction is a function of the effective reaction potential.

Resistance to this rather mechanistic conception has come from several quarters. From the gestalt theorists, as might be expected, has come an entirely different point of view. Rather than forming isolated associations with particular stimulus elements, the subject is believed to perceive the *relations* among stimuli, to respond to 'the larger one,' 'the brighter one,' and so on. Chief spokesmen for this gestalt view of discrimination have been Köhler and Klüver. In later years a relational type of theory has been sponsored by Lashley, and it is in answer to his assertions that much of the recent research has been done.

Lashley's clearest statements of his own view are to be found in two papers (1942, 1946) that are both in the form of criticism of the neo-Pavlovian (Hull-Spence) position. With respect to generalization, the following statements are made: (1) *'The phenomena of "stimulus generalization" represent a failure of association'* (Lashley and Wade, 1946, p. 74). The initial, wide spread of reactivity in conditioning studies is not generalization at all but sensitization. As various characteristics of the stimulus situation are attended to and abstracted, response becomes differentiated along the continua defined by these abstracted characteristics. The 'gradient' thus developed is 'generalization by default,' through failure of many aspects to be noted by the subject. (2) *'The "dimensions" of a stimulus series are determined by comparison of two or more stimuli and do not exist for the organism until established by differential training.'* Lashley thus appears to deny that a generalization gradient can be generated by training on a single stimulus. The results obtained by Hovland and others cited above, with original training on a single stimulus, would presumably be due to comparisons made at the time of testing for generalization, when stimuli differing from the original along certain dimensions are presented (cf. Razran, 1949).

With respect to discrimination: (3) *'Differentiation of conditioned reflexes involves the redirection of attention to new aspects of the stimuli and the formation of new associations with these. . .'* In his earlier paper (1942), Lashley had amplified this statement by saying that this constitutes a 'set' to react to certain elements, this organization being described in part by gestalt principles of perception and in part by principles of attention. Notice that only those stimulus elements abstracted in this fashion can become associated with discriminatory reactions; aspects that are not attended by the subjects are not associated. Krechevsky (1932, 1933, 1937 c, and elsewhere) has referred to such selective abstractions as 'hypotheses'; his general point of view toward discrimination learning is much like Lashley's and he has been involved in the same controversies.

Transposition of Discrimination

Although it has been known for a long time that animals often make 'relative' choices in discrimination situations when the absolute values of the stimuli are shifted, Köhler's demonstrations of transposition behavior in hens, chimpanzees, and human children, and his use of these findings in theoretical argument, made explicit a controversy between behavioristic and gestalt positions which has always been part of the whole-part problem (Köhler, 1918; cf. Ellis, 1939). Of these experiments those on hens are the best known. These birds were trained to find grains on the darker of two gray papers; when tested on new pairs, the hens often (but not always) chose the darker of each new pair, even when the originally positive stimulus was paired with a darker paper. How could this be explained, Köhler argues, if the subject is responding to absolute properties of the stimuli, as the behaviorists claim? On the contrary, these birds must have learned to perceive the *relation* between pairs, to 'go to the darker,' to respond to the 'whole character' of the situation. In the extensive literature that has accumulated on this problem (cf. Klüver, 1933), however, the relative choice is not always observed.

Does the occurrence of relative reactions highlight a fundamental inadequacy with the behavioristic position? Spence (1937) has demonstrated how such relational discrimination transfer along a single dimension of stimulus variation can be incorporated into behavioristic theory. Referring to Fig. 150, let us assume that an organism is initially trained to react positively to 256 (the larger, brighter, louder, etc.) when this stimulus is paired with 160. Since reactions to 256 are reinforced and those to 160 are not, it follows that excitatory tendencies will be generated at the former point on the continuum and inhibitory tendencies at the latter. At the conclusion of original training it must be assumed that the effective reaction potential (algebraic summation of excitatory and inhibitory tendencies) is substantially greater at 256 than at 160—otherwise the organism would not consistently respond to 256. The generalization of both excitatory (solid lines) and inhibitory (dashed lines) tendencies along the continuum is shown in Fig. 150, and the small numbers represent the resultants of subtracting inhibitory from excitatory values. Although at this time Spence used convex gradients, in later papers (cf. 1942) he has used inflected gradients which resemble normal curves.

Inspection of this figure indicates that 'relative' choices would have to be predicted over much of the continuum. Notice however that this analysis must also predict *a breakdown of transposition for test pairs far removed from the original training pairs.* Suppose 655 is paired with 1,049—the organism will now choose the smaller stimulus, since 6.68 is greater than

2.50. Spence cites data obtained by Klüver (1933), Gulliksen (1932), and himself (1937) that clearly fit this prediction. This phenomenon gives the Spence analysis some advantage over Köhler's interpretation. It is hard to understand why or how, if an animal has learned to react to the *relation* between pairs, this relational tendency should break down. That this early Spence analysis is not sufficient for all cases of discrimination transfer has best been demonstrated by one of his own students working in his laboratory. Kuenne (1946) found that while the predicted breakdown in transposition held for preverbal children, it did not hold for older 'verbal' children. In other words, development of ability to form and apply distinctive mediators made it possible to override the more primitive mechanism described by Spence: the older children could learn to tell themselves

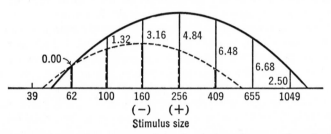

FIGURE 150. Diagrammatic representation of relations between hypothetical generalization curves, excitatory and inhibitory, after training on the stimulus combination 256 (+) and 160 (−). Small numbers indicate algebraic summation of two gradients at each point. Spence, *Psychological Review*, 1937, 44:433.

'it is the larger one' and respond accordingly regardless of the absolute stimulus magnitude.

The Continuity—Noncontinuity Controversy

At the core of the Lashley-Krechevsky interpretation of discrimination learning is the assumption that subjects selectively abstract or attend to particular aspects of the total stimulus situation, *and only those aspects being responded to at the moment are differentially affected by reinforcement or nonreinforcement.* This means that the development of discrimination should not be a continuous process; differentiation in terms of the relevant cues begins only when the subject starts attending to and responding in terms of these relevant cues. The problem is *not* whether subjects display systematic modes of behavior in the presolution period. Although Krechevsky (1932, 1937 c) refers to such systematic sequences as 'hypotheses' and Spence (1936, 1945) predicts the same sort of behavior from behavioristic principles, both have denied that this is anything other than a matter of terminology. (Nevertheless, one gets the impression that Spence does in fact have a strong distaste for terms like 'hypothesis,' when applied to the rat, and that Krechevsky does in fact think behaviorists like Spence are blind to certain obvious, humanlike cognitive processes in this animal.) There are several concrete experimental approaches to this problem.

(1) *Reversing the significance of cues.* Suppose that during the presolution period in discrimination learning S_1 is positive and S_2 is negative. Suppose further that before the beginning of solution (defined by better-than-

chance performance), the significance of these cues is reversed, S_2 becoming positive (now reinforced) and S_1 becoming negative (now unreinforced). According to the Hull-Spence view, there should be interference in learning the new discrimination, as compared with a control group, but according to the Lashley-Krechevsky view they should not be hindered (since the relevant cues have not yet been isolated and hence no differential response tendencies have been established in relation to them). The first such experiment was done by McCulloch and Pratt (1934). Rat subjects were required to discriminate between lures on the basis of their weight (a pulling-in technique being used), and three groups of animals were given different amounts of pretraining before the significance of the cues was reversed (the zero pretraining group serving as control). With both experimental groups 'reversed' before there was any sign of solution, negative transfer was observed, varying directly with the amount of pretraining. These results are certainly in keeping with the continuity position, but notice that under these conditions the subjects were forced to respond in terms of the relevant weight cues from the beginning, since they had to adjust their 'pull' to the weight of the plus or minus lures.

Krechevsky (1938 a) contributed an experiment in which difficult visual discriminanda (horizontal versus vertical rows of small black squares on white grounds) and the Lashley jumping-stand technique were used. Group 1 rats (control) had continuous training on the final discrimination; group 2 was given 2 days (20 trials) on a previous discrimination before the significance of the cues was reversed to that representing the final discrimination; group 3 was given 4 days (40 trials) on the previous discrimination before the significance of the cues was reversed. The results of the 2-day group fitted the noncontinuity position (no greater errors than the control), but those for the 4-day group did not (i.e. showed negative transfer). Krechevsky explains the latter observation by suggesting that 'four days is too long a time for the purely pre-solution period,' which, since no evidence for better-than-chance performance on the previous problem is given, merely serves to make the entire proposition untestable. The same explanation of the McCulloch and Pratt results is suggested. But how are the results for Krechevsky's group 2 to be explained by the continuity theorist? Spence (1940) says, 'From the point of view of the writer's continuity theory, the alibi is, of course, that the relevant cue aspects simply were not received at first by the subjects. They did not "see" the rows of black squares because they were fixating other aspects of the stimulus complex' (p. 281).

His contention that the relevant cues may in some cases fail to affect the animal's receptor systems differentially has been substantiated experimentally in a paper by Ehrenfreund (1948). Following the general 'reversal of cues' procedure but using the Lashley jumping stand, one group of rats was trained and tested with the relevant cues (upright versus inverted triangles) near the point on the cards at which the animals had initially been trained to jump, but for the other group the same cues were in the upper third of the cards, far from the point at which the rats jumped. The continuity prediction held in the former case (reversal of reinforcement causing interference as compared with a control group) but not in the latter.

Spence (1945) made three significant improvements in design: (a) the control group was reinforced 50 per cent of the time on *each* of the to-be-relevant cues for the same number of trials the experimental group was being trained on the previous discrimination; (b) to insure reception of the relevant cues, all runways in a Yerkes-type discrimination box were painted black and white; (c) both groups were given preliminary training (with gray runways) so as to *establish* strong position habits. This was done to predispose both groups of animals to respond on the basis of something other than the to-be-relevant (black and white) cues during previous training. Since the learning of the final discrimination by the experimental group (following reversal) was significantly slower than that of the control, 'associations apparently were being formed with the relevant stimulus cue even though the *Ss* were responding on the basis of some other hypothesis' (p. 264).

(2) *Irrelevant cues.* Lashley (1942, p. 250) states that 'if the animals are given a set to react to one aspect of a stimulus situation, large amounts of training do not establish association with other aspects, so long as the original set remains effective for reaching the food.' By way of confirmation, the following experiment is reported: four rats were trained to a criterion of 20 errorless trials in the jumping-stand apparatus to choose the larger of two circles, this training being intended to give these animals a set to react on the basis of size. At this point a large triangle was substituted for the large circle; the subjects consistently chose the triangle and were rewarded, this being continued for 200 trials. Question: During this latter training was any discrimination in terms of *form* (triangle versus circle) being established while the animals were presumably reacting on the basis of *size?* To answer this question, the experimenter then gave these rats 20 test trials with a triangle and a circle of equal size; they fell back on position habits, making 19 to 20 jumps to the same side, regardless of the positions of the two stimuli.

Blum and Blum (1949) report a repetition of Lashley's experiment, with certain minor modifications. From original training to a large circle (positive) and a small circle (negative), the rats were shifted to a large *upright* triangle versus a small *inverted* triangle. As would be expected, initial preference was for the large figure, and training was continued on this basis for 200 trials. The final test paired two equal and medium-sized triangles, one upright and the other inverted. Had these animals associated form differences while presumably responding in terms of size? Apparently so, since they now definitely favored the upright triangle. Is it possible that in both experiments the rat subjects were mainly stimulated by the lower portions of the figures? In this case there would be better definition of form under the Blum and Blum conditions than in Lashley's case. There is need for further experimentation with this design.

(3) *Discrimination after training on a single stimulus.* Another of Lashley's contentions has been that the continua along which generalization effects are measured are established in the process of actively comparing stimuli that differ in certain perceptible ways. In other words, there should be no measurable generalization when original training is restricted to a single stimulus. Using the Lashley jumping stand—when a jump at the positive stimulus results in that card falling over and admitting the rat to

food, but a jump at the negative stimulus results in a bang on the nose and a fall into a net—Lashley trained one group of animals to jump at an 8-cm. white circle opposed to a plain black card and another group to jump at a 5-cm. white circle opposed by the same black card (Lashley and Wade, 1946). A criterion of 200 errorless trials was used. The subsequent test pitted the 8-cm. circle against the 5-cm. circle for both groups, *and the* 8-*cm. circle was positive in both cases.* Surprisingly, the rats originally trained with the 5-cm. positive (which therefore had to extinguish this reaction) solved the problem faster than the rats originally trained with the 8-cm. circle positive. The reverse of this experiment is also reported—black cards originally positive and white circles negative—and here the subsequently positive 5-cm. circle was easier to learn than the subsequently negative 8-cm. circle. These results caused considerable stir, for not only are they contrary to the continuity position and the entire conception of generalization, but they are also unexpected from Lashley's own view!

Fortunately there are now available experiments by Grice (1948 *c*, 1951) that seem to clarify this anomalous situation. Lashley's procedures and materials were duplicated in all essentials, but a Yerkes-type discrimination box was used instead of the jumping stand and food reward was given for correct responses but no punishment for wrong responses. In the check on the first experiment (1948 *c*), the group originally trained on the large circle positive learned the final discrimination with the large circle also positive significantly faster than the other group; in the check on the second experiment (1951), the group for whom the negative stimulus kept on being negative learned faster than where significance was reversed. These results are quite in keeping with the continuity position. But how are we to explain Lashley's findings? Two main possibilities have been suggested: (a) The Lashley jumping stand involves considerable punishment for wrong responses. If animals had an initial tendency to make errors (i.e. jump toward the small circle in the first experiment), this habit would be weakened very rapidly and avoidance tendencies substituted. (b) Lashley used an unusual method of counting errors. Animals were allowed to keep on making repetitive errors until the correct card was struck, yet all of these wrong jumps on a single trial would be counted as one error. There is as yet no clear-cut evidence bearing on these points.

A direct test of Lashley's contention here—that training to a single stimulus should not produce any generalization—has been made by Grandine and Harlow (1948). Monkeys were trained to respond to a single stimulus and were then tested on a pair of stimuli consisting of the original item and a new item varying along either height or brightness continua. Generalization was measured in terms of errors, i.e. confusions between the original stimulus and new stimulus during test trials. Training to a single stimulus was found to produce measurable amounts of generalization.

One of Krechevsky's less frequently cited experiments (1938 *b*), while only indirectly bearing on the present issue, does seem to pose a real puzzler for behavioristic theories as presently conceived. Group 1 rats were given original training on a *difficult* discrimination: to differentiate between horizontally and vertically arranged patterns of black squares on white backgrounds, where the 'horizontal-ness' or 'vertical-ness' depended solely upon the spatial proximities of the black squares. Half of group 1 had horizontal positive and the other half vertical positive. Group 2 animals were trained on an *easier* discrimination: the same horizontal (or vertical) patterns versus a triangular pattern of squares. On the test discrimination the horizontal (or vertical) patterns that had been positive were now paired with horizontal or vertical *solid lines*. The remarkable thing about the results was this: for the difficult group, but not for the easy group, *there was marked and consistent preference for the solid lines as compared with the originally intermittent patterns.* Krechevsky interprets this result along gestalt lines: '. . . these forces (of attraction among the squares due to proximity) thus generated are of such a nature and of such a strength as to make for a perception which results in the preference of the organism for a stimulus complex where the discontinuous members do in fact coalesce as opposed to a stimulus-complex where the members are still, in some degree, discontinuous' (p. 507). He feels that the difficult discrimination forced these animals to pay attention to the relevant discriminanda. Continuity theorists take note: this seems to be a case where the originally positive stimulus is *not* preferred in a subsequent test against a novel cue. This is a striking observation which demands confirmation and extension in further research.

(4) *Successive* vs. *simultaneous discrimination training.* If differentiation along sensory continua involves the perception of relations through active comparison of stimuli, as Lashley contends, then procedures in which the stimuli to be discriminated are presented simultaneously should lead to faster learning than procedures in which they are presented successively. Grice (1949) trained two groups of rats on the same discrimination problem, a 5-cm. circle being positive and an 8-cm. circle negative. The apparatus consisted of a simple runway with stimulus doors at the far end. Under *simultaneous* conditions both stimuli appeared side by side on each trial, errors being recorded when an animal touched the negative card with its nose; under *successive* conditions a single stimulus appeared on each trial (order randomized), and errors were estimated in terms of latencies between starting down the runway and touching the door. (Having computed the median latency for each animal for successive blocks of ten trials, an error was recorded both when latency of response to the positive stimulus was *greater* than this median and when latency of response to the negative stimulus was *less* than this median.) No significant differences were found in the rates at which differential response tendencies were developed for the two groups.

Summary

Most of the contentions of the Lashley view have not been upheld experimentally. (a) The notion that only those cues selectively attended by the subject can become associated with differential reactions is not substantiated in most 'reversal-of-cues' data (McCulloch and Pratt; Krechevsky, group 3; Spence's 1945 study) or in the 'irrelevant cues' data (Blum and Blum), excepting Lashley's own rather casually reported findings. (b) The same conclusion applies to discrimination after training on a single stimulus (Grice's studies). (c) Contrary to Lashley's contention, generalization has been shown to occur in training to respond to a single stimulus (Grice's studies; Grandine and Harlow). And (d) the notion that generalization and discrimination require active comparison of stimuli by the subject—and hence that successive discrimination should be more difficult than simultaneous discrimination—has not been upheld (Grice, 1949). It is significant with respect to methodology in psychological experimentation that, almost without exception, the studies supporting the Lashley view have used the jumping stand while those supporting the continuity view have used a Yerkes-type discrimination box. Ideally these two procedures should be directly compared and their particular contributions to the problem clarified.

Selective Attending

There is one aspect of the Lashley theory, perhaps the most critical one, that has not been really tested in these experiments: the notion that animals, like humans, do pay selective attention to certain stimulus characteristics of situations and respond in their terms. This is *not* saying that only these cues become associated with responses, but rather that (through either past discriminatory learning or through innate organization of the perceptual system) certain stimulus characters are prepotent in determining choice reactions. The investigations so far considered have provided no opportunity to test this hypothesis. To do so requires an experimental design that (a) provides the subject experience with one set of cues, (b) gives discrimination training in which this and another set are equally relevant, and (c) tests for the *dominance* of the two sets of cues in determining subsequent discriminatory reactions.

Lawrence (1949, 1950) has reported experiments meeting these conditions. His underlying hypothesis was that *in learning instrumental responses in a previous discrimination situation, the relevant cues also become associated with mediating reactions which serve to make these cues more distinctive and hence facilitate any subsequent discriminations in which these cues may be involved.* The second of his studies will be described in some detail. A two-compartment discrimination box, constructed so that stiff wire 'chains' could be put at the entrances, was used throughout the sequence of training and test problems illustrated in Fig. 151. This figure actually represents the sequence of experiences for only one of four groups: those animals for whom black-white cues were relevant and black positive. The other black-white group had white positive. The two remaining groups had chains versus no-chains as relevant cues, divided in the same manner. Animals were forced to brush against these stiff wire bristles when present. Original training for all animals was on *successive discrimination*. For the animals illustrated in Fig. 151 this meant that going left if *both* sides were black was rewarded but going right if *both* compartments were white was rewarded, independent of the presence or absence of chains. Subsequent training for all groups was on *simultaneous discrimination,* both sets of cues being equally relevant. As shown in Fig. 151, a black positive (black-white) subject was rewarded for entering the black (and chains) side when simultaneously opposed to the white (no-chains) side. Other groups of animals would have other of the possible permutations of cue relations.

After 30 training trials on this simultaneous discrimination (with both sets of cues equally relevant), three different tests for cue dominance were run. I. *Opposition of cues.* If an animal had been responding to black-chains as positive and white no-chains as negative, it was now presented with two new configurations, black no-chains on one side and white-chains on the other. Notice that the two positive cues, black and chains, are now in conflict. Which cue will determine response on this dominance test? There was a statistically significant tendency for the cues originally 'attended to' in successive discrimination (here, black-white) to be dominant on this test. II. *Relearning on a single cue.* Half of the animals were now retrained on the *simultaneous discrimination,* but with only one set

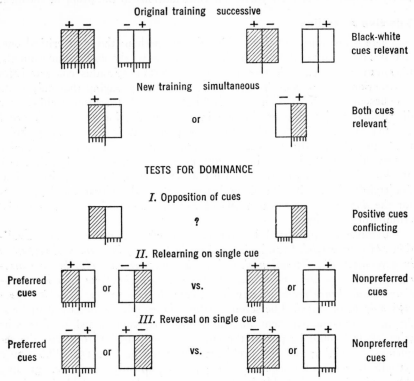

FIGURE 151. Graphic presentation of conditions involved in the sequence of training and test situations used by Lawrence in a discrimination study. Constructed from description by Lawrence, *Journal of Experimental Psychology,* 1950, **40**:175-88.

of cues being differential with respect to reward—either the originally preferred cues or the originally nonpreferred cues. For the black-white subjects (preferred cues) response to the black side was rewarded and response to white was punished, chains being either present or absent on *both* sides; or (nonpreferred cues) response to chains was rewarded and response to no-chains was punished, both sides being either black or white on various trials. As shown in Fig. 152 (under *Cues Same*), relearning in terms of the preferred, or originally attended, cues was most rapid. III. *Reversal of learning on a single cue.* The other half of the animals relearned the simultaneous discrimination exactly as shown above, but reinforcement was shifted to the originally negative cue (i.e. from black to white with the preferred cues and from chains to no-chains with the nonpreferred cues). Here again, as shown in Fig. 152 (under *Cues Reversed*), relearning was most rapid on the basis of the originally emphasized cues, *even though their significance was now reversed.*

This experiment also has several important implications. In the first place, it is apparent that the acquired distinctiveness of the preferred cues, acquired during the original successive discrimination training, maintains its facilitative effect throughout a long series of trials involving opposition and reversal in learning. Secondly, the results with reversed reinforcement (test 3 cited above) suggest that it is easier to reverse a strong habit than a weak one, since reversal was accomplished more rapidly in terms of the

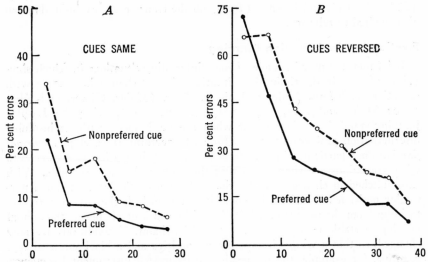

FIGURE 152. Relearning a simultaneous discrimination on the basis of a single set of cues: (*A*) when cues, either those preferred or those not preferred, have the same significance as in original learning; (*B*) when cues, either those preferred or those not preferred, have a significance opposite from that of original learning. Lawrence, *Journal of Experimental Psychology,* 1950, 40:181.

dominant cues. Flatly contrary to a single-stage $(S \rightarrow R)$ conception of learning, this finding is not necessarily opposed to a two-stage $(S \rightarrow x \rightarrow R)$ mediation theory. As Lawrence says: 'When the animals were reversed on the preferred cue, the mediating process aroused was the one appropriate to that cue. As a result that cue had an enhanced distinctiveness. In a sense the animal was paying attention to it. This enhanced distinctiveness led to a faster learning of a new habit, i.e. the reversal of the discrimination.' In other words, the mediation view makes it possible to dissociate learning (of meanings, perceptual reactions, etc.) from performance per se (the overt instrumental acts), which is precisely the essence of the Tolman and Lashley views. This mediation view is still a continuity theory, however, since the development of appropriate mediation processes is conceived to be a gradual and continuous process, quite akin to and following the same principles as the development of overt instrumental responses.

Jaynes (1950) reports an experiment similar in design to those of Lawrence which adds to our information as to the nature of the mediation process involved. It was demonstrated that varying the muscular activity initially associated with the response to a set of cues could reliably effect the amount of facilitation when these same cues were employed in other discrimination problems. He concludes that 'the results are taken as partial evidence for the hypothesis that the mediating process is some fraction of the actual response first learned to the cues, and for the law that: the effect of learning a first response to a cue upon learning a second is proportional to the magnitude of the first' (p. 408). Grice's observation (1948 a) that rats forced to make differential motor responses in the course of a black-white discrimination showed better learning in a delayed-reward situation can be interpreted along similar lines. Experiments by Wickens (1939), Walker (1942), and Kuenne (1946) on the transfer of discrimination can also be cited as relevant.

Fixation in Discrimination Learning

Brief mention may be made of some interesting situations in which sign-values of cues in discrimination situations do *not* change in keeping with objective conditions. Maier and his associates (Maier, Glaser, and Klee, 1940; Maier and Klee, 1941, 1945; Maier, 1949), using the Lashley jumping stand, have shown that when the rat is faced with an insoluble discrimination problem and yet is forced to perform, it develops *abnormal fixation* on a particular instrumental sequence, this fixation persisting even when conditions are changed so that the problem becomes solvable. With cards latched in chance order, so that neither a particular card nor a particular position is consistently rewarded or punished, the rat soon refuses to jump from the platform. When forced by shock or air blasts, the animal develops a stable response, usually a position habit. If conditions are now changed, so that a white circle is always positive and a black circle always negative, for example, the rat persists in its fixated instrumental sequence. Yet there is evidence that the animal is learning the discrimination: resistance to jumping decreases when the positive card appears on the fixated side, increases when the negative card appears there; abortive jumps (e.g. twisting so as to avoid striking the nose) decrease toward the positive stimulus and increase toward the negative one—all this despite the fact that the animal persists in leaping toward the same place! And when the rat is given manual guidance in breaking the fixation (without any cards in position), its rapid mastery of the original discrimination shows that learning had been going on.

Once the discrimination task is made soluble, even though the animal always jumps to the same place, response to the white circle is reinforced (admits to food reward), whereas response to the black circle is punished (strikes nose, etc.). The problem posed is this: Why doesn't the association between white circle and jumping response become sufficiently strong to break the fixation? To understand this situation we must recall certain information about the role of mediation processes in discrimination learning. Lawrence (1950) offered definite evidence that for *soluble* discrimination problems the relevant cues become associated with differential mediation processes (owing to differential consequences) which enhance the distinctiveness of these cues. Once the animal learned to 'pay attention' to these cues, subsequent learning on their basis was facilitated. Now in Maier's *insoluble* discrimination problem the rat is unable to attach *differential* mediators to white and black circles and therefore does not learn to 'pay attention' to this aspect of the situation. If this were all, there would be no particular problem—when the cues did become relevant, the animals would merely start from scratch. But during the 'frustration' stage the rat *is* learning something. The fear generated by frequent bumps and falls, being unrelieved through discovery of some successful instrumental sequence, short-circuits to the jumping stand, i.e. the total jumping-stand situation, including the sight of both undifferentiated cards, becomes associated with anxiety. The rat's first attempt to relieve this state is to 'leave the field'—it refuses to jump—but this is not permitted. Then, under the heightened motivation provided by shocks or air blasts, any reactions made tend to be strengthened. Contrary to Maier's notion that fixation here represents 'behavior without a goal,' any response that gets the rat off the jumping stand is strongly reinforced—the anxiety associated with being on the stand is temporarily relieved (cf. Mowrer's analysis, 1950, pp. 354-7). Much like the novice standing on a diving board and being hounded by the jibes of his audience, any response that gets him off that unprotected position, even if it leads promptly to a painful 'belly-smacker,' is gratifying. Since the rat is not 'paying attention' to the visual discriminanda, the selection of (or perhaps regression to) a position habit and its subsequent strengthening through anxiety reduction is highly probable.

Now we can understand why the rat fails to readjust when conditions are changed and visual discriminanda begin to correspond to differential consequences. The jumping-stand situation does have a definite sign-value— anxiety—but rather than being differentially associated with the visual discriminanda (white and black circles), this anxiety mediator is associated with the situation as a whole and mediates a stable instrumental position habit. The only way to *change* the sign-value is for the animal to respond differentially in terms of the visual discriminanda, experience the different consequences, and short-circuit new mediating reactions. The dominance of the anxiety mediator, which is continuously reinforced, prevents discovery of the changed significance of the visual cues. The 'guidance' technique, which both encourages a new instrumental sequence and, more importantly, reduces the anxiety associated with the jumping-stand situation, permits the animal to respond later in terms of the black and white cues and thereby learn to 'pay attention' to these cues.

DO ANIMALS LEARN MOVEMENTS OR COGNITIONS?

Whereas both Hull and Guthrie deal with the association of stimuli with responses (defined in terms of movements of muscle or reaction of glands), Tolman deals with the association of signs with significates (cognitions). Given a more or less accurate 'cognitive map' of a situation, and having a demand for something to be found within that situation, the organism will 'go' to the location of the significate with whatever movements are dictated by the physical character of the situation. We have already considered one type of evidence relevant to this issue, the learning of 'what leads to what' under conditions of irrelevant drive and reinforcement and under conditions of drive discrimination. It may be recalled that both Tolman and Hull-type theories turned out to give rather similar interpretations of these phenomena at base. Here we shall consider additional evidence—whether animals learn to 'go places' in a maze or 'make responses,' whether purely S-S associations can be formed—and we shall end up with just about the same conclusion. But let us inspect the facts.

Place Learning

Three general types of experimental situation have been designed to test Tolman's place-learning hypothesis. (1) Having learned one *spatial* route to a goal, will the animal promptly transfer to the most direct alternative route when the learned path is blocked? (2) Having learned one *behavior* route to a goal (e.g. running), will the animal immediately transfer to whatever alternative behavior route (e.g. swimming) is demanded by a change in environmental supports? (3) If conditions are arranged so that learning to go to a particular place conflicts with learning to make a particular response, will the former tendency be found dominant over the latter?

(1) *Alternate spatial routes to the same goal.* In the first of a series of studies, Tolman, Ritchie, and Kalish (1946 a) gave rats five trials running from starting point A to food box G, on the elevated maze shown in Fig. 153A. The only light in the room was located at H. On the test trial the original pathway was blocked, as shown in Fig. 153B, and a system of radiating pathways was substituted around the table-top (represented by the circle). The question was this: Would the animals choose the goal-pointing path with more than chance frequency? Percentages of animals choosing each path on the test trial are shown in Fig. 153B. A large proportion (.36) chose path #6, the most directly goal-pointing path. The very small percentages choosing paths #9 and #10, bordering on the original route, seem to indicate lack of any tendency to follow through with the originally learned movements; however, the rats had to execute a sharp turn about the 18-inch high walls of alley C in order to enter these paths. The authors conclude that their animals must have expected food at a specific location, this being shown by their selection of the most direct spatial paths to the goal when the learned path was blocked.

But now observe the results of Gentry, Brown, and Kaplan (1947) in what was essentially a replication of the above study. Here 37% of the animals chose pathways adjacent to the originally learned but now blocked path and *none* picked the direct, short-cut route to the goal. In a second study (Gentry, Brown, and Lee, 1948), with a more complicated maze interposed between the circular table-top and the goal-box and with original training to a high degree of mastery, 52% of the choices on the test trial were distributed among the two paths bordering on the originally learned route and only 5% were for the direct goal-pointing path. This suggests that a mechanical movement sequence may become 'fixated' with high degrees of original learning. This possibility is enhanced by the results of Kendler and Gasser (1948). These investigators varied the number of reinforced trials given as pretraining on an *enclosed* T-maze from 0 to 100 and found that selection of the direct goal-pointing path in a substituted radiating pattern increased through 20 reinforcements and then decreased between 20 and 100. Apparently, performance is more flexibly mediated by cognitions relating to spatial arrangements during early stages in learn-

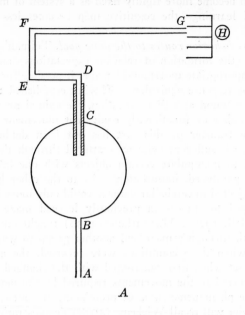

A

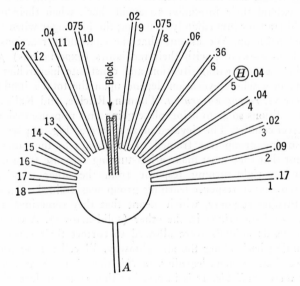

B

FIGURE 153. *A.* Training apparatus in a place-learning study; (*A–B*) starting alley; (*C*) alley bounded by 18″ high plywood walls; (*G*) goal boxes; ((*H*)) light. *B.* Test apparatus. Original pathway blocked and radiating alternate pathways leading from table-top substituted. Percentages of animals choosing various pathways indicated. Tolman, Ritchie, and Kalish, *Journal of Experimental Psychology,* 1946, **36**:16, 17.

ing and tends to become more rigidly fixed as a system of movements with high degrees of learning—the cognitive map becomes less 'fieldlike' and more 'striplike.'

(2) *Alternate behavior routes to the same goal.* Tolman's distinction between learning (the formation of relevant expectations) and performance (the release of appropriate movements) makes it possible for him to predict a high degree of response equivalence. Having established the expectation that food will be found at a given location, the animal may approach this goal via any number of functionally equivalent movement sequences. Although response transfer of this sort has not been deliberately studied extensively, there is sufficient evidence scattered through the literature. A monkey trained to manipulate certain objects with one hand will, when that member is paralyzed, immediately shift to the other hand (Lashley, 1924). Rats subjected to cerebellar damage could only move in tight circles, yet they managed to traverse a previously learned maze without error (Lashley and Ball, 1929). MacFarlane (1930) taught one group of rats to swim the path through a maze and another group to wade through the same pattern; when these conditions were reversed, the animals showed only a slight upset when first confronted with the changed conditions and promptly transferred to the movements required by the new physical supports. The same phenomenon is most prominent, of course, in human behavior. The reader will recall Wickens' (1938) demonstration that subjects trained to extend their forefinger to avoid shock when their palms were down would transfer immediately to flexing the forefinger when their hands were placed palm up. We assume that the equivalent reactions described here have been associated with their mediators (expectations) *previous* to the immediate experimental situation and constitute hierarchies of instrumental sequences whose evocation depend upon the total stimulus context.

(3) *Place* vs. *response-learning.* Tolman, Ritchie, and Kalish (1946 b) arranged conditions so as to bring place-going and response-making tendencies into direct conflict. The elevated maze shown as Fig. 154 was employed. A place-learning group was trained to go always to the same food box, which meant that they must make a left-turning response from one starting position and a right-turning response from the other starting position (dashed arrows); a response-learning group was trained to make always a specific turning response, which meant that they sometimes found food in one place and sometimes in the other (solid arrows). A correction procedure was used: animals were allowed to correct their errors by immediately running back along the straightaway. Place-learning proved to be much easier than response-learning, *in this situation where marked extra-maze cues were available.* It is interesting that response latencies (i.e. the time between being placed at a starting position and making a turn at the choice point) were about the same for both groups—as if the associations between starting-point stimuli and goal-representing mediators were equally strong (but unequally valid) for the two groups. These latency data are not discussed. The same researchers (1947), using the same setup, have extended their conclusion as to place versus response learning to the non-correction procedure—animals are prevented from correcting their errors by retracing. Some idea of the complexity of the cues to which animals may be responding in these open-field situations is provided in an experiment

by Ritchie (1947). With a setup much like that shown in Fig. 154 placed in a laboratory room, he found no differences between place-going and response-making conditions; after a long series of exploratory tests it was discovered that all the subjects were orienting themselves in terms of the odors and sounds of cage-mates that happened to be kept in a particular place in that room!

In the experiments described so far the animals have always been performing in situations in which there are marked spatial cues available. Blodgett and McCutchan (1947) trained a group of animals on an elevated T-maze moved about in a darkened, visually homogeneous dome (the experimenters being dark-adapted and the rats being introduced one by one from a lighted room); presumably these animals were pretty well

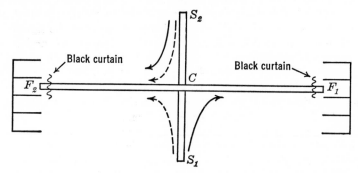

FIGURE 154. Apparatus for studying competition between place-going and response-making tendencies. Tolman, Ritchie, and Kalish, *Journal of Experimental Psychology,* 1946, **36**:223.

restricted to pure response-making. When the performance of these animals was compared with a response-making group trained in an ordinary laboratory room (i.e. duplicating the Tolman, Ritchie, and Kalish response-learning conditions), these pure-response dome-trained animals were found to do better than the room-response group. This led these investigators to the conclusion that the existence of spatial cues in ordinary rooms actually interferes with learning on a response basis.

The most simple and obvious test is contributed in another paper by Blodgett and McCutchan (1948). Rats were trained by the noncorrection method to find food at one end of a simple T-maze placed in a darkened dome. At this same end was placed a disk of light. Thus the animals *could* be learning to make a specific turning response or they *could* be learning to go to a specific place (the lighted disk), or both. To determine the relative strengths of these two possible dispositions following training, the disk was simply put at the *other* end of the T on test trials. If the animals now ran toward the disk, they must have been learning a place-going tendency; if they still ran to the same side (now non-disk), they must have been learning a response-making tendency. A control group originally learned to run to the end opposite the disk of light. On the last training trial, 6 animals made errors and 58 made correct choices; on the following test trial, with the two tendencies in conflict, 16 animals made place-going choices and 48 made response-making choices. Only systematic variation of conditions will indicate to what extent these proportions of place-going and response-making can be influenced (e.g. by varying the amount of initial training and hence 'fixation,' by varying the complexity of instrumental sequences, by varying the nature of spatial cues, and so on). This Blodgett and McCutchan design appears to be the simplest and most readily interpretable of the several proposed in this area, and therefore it should be the most useful for this purpose.

Summary

Do animals learn to 'go places' or 'make responses'? In the light of the mediation hypothesis this controversy becomes largely meaningless since it has been demonstrated that *both* mediational and instrumental modifications follow from the same general principles under appropriate conditions. The rat may establish a new meaning for a spatially localized stimulus (a disk of light may become a sign of food) and thence approach the signified goal by multiple instrumental sequences, transferring from one to another within previously established hierarchies as changes in the context demand. Or the subject may establish and 'fixate' a specific instrumental sequence to the point where its habit strength is so great in relation to other sequences in the hierarchy that transfer is hindered. If spatial signs of the goal-place are minimized, of course, a simple instrumental sequence initiated by the starting-place sign will tend to be learned. In other words, 'place-going' (modifying mediation processes) and 'response-making' (modifying instrumental sequences) tendencies are both acquirable, depending upon the stimulus conditions. The former is probably more characteristic of mature organisms and probably becomes more typical as one goes up the evolutionary scale. More studies of a parametric type are in order.

This entire controversy seems to have been largely misinterpreted. Since there is evidence that animals can learn to 'go places' under certain conditions, the real issue becomes this: *What is the nature of the mediation process which represents, for an animal, the fact that there is a certain thing in a certain place?* According to Tolman, this process is a purely cognitive association between two *stimulus* events, the sign and the significate. According to the mediation hypothesis, the representing process is a stimulus-producing *reaction* to certain stimuli (signs), although the precise nature of this reaction is not specified (e.g. whether it involves muscles and glands or may be purely cortically organized). Thus the real issue comes down to whether purely S–S associations can be formed or whether all associations are S–R relations.

Sensory Conditioning

Brogden (1939 b) reported that he had obtained evidence for 'sensory conditioning' in dogs. A bell and a light were presented simultaneously two hundred times. When one of these stimuli was later made the CS for conditioned forelimb flexion, with shock serving as US, tests with the other stimulus, which had never been paired with shock, showed that it, too, had become capable of eliciting the new response. Certain controls were applied: pretests with both stimuli showed that they did not initially elicit this reaction; animals treated identically, except for the original *pairing* of tone and light, gave no evidence of transfer. This was a highly significant experiment because it bore directly upon this fundamental issue of psychology: *Is the modification that takes place in learning a central, cognitive event (S–S) or must some behavior (S–R) be involved?* The results of this experiment made it appear that the simple contiguity in experience of purely sensory events was sufficient for learning.

Ellson (1941, 1942) found he could produce 'hallucinations' in human subjects by first pairing a light with a faint tone which gradually came above threshold and then testing with the light alone. Did the subjects actually hear the tone or was this suggestion (and what is suggestion)? Subsequently Brogden also used human subjects: in one tightly controlled experiment (1942) he failed to get sensory conditioning, and attributed the failure to the vagaries of the *GSR* which had been used as the response; in further tightly controlled experiments (Brogden, 1947; Chernikoff and Brogden, 1949) positive results were obtained, using a voluntary response (pressing a key when a light appeared, under instructions). Karn (1947) has also obtained positive results, even when a full day intervened between the original pairing of light and buzzer and the test for sensory conditioning. His subjects later reported that they felt 'there must have been *some* connection between the light and the buzzer,' and Karn attributes the phenomenon to some implicit 'set' to relate two inexplicable stimulations.

Assuming 'sensory conditioning' to be a valid phenomenon (although there is considerable doubt here), how is it to be explained? One attempt has been to 'explain it away' as *response sensitization*. During a series of conditioning trials, the reaction becomes 'tuned up' and any sudden stimulus will produce it—the preconditioning pairing is incidental. Two simple controls would take care of this: (a) testing with a third, neutral stimulus which had never been paired with the light should not yield a reaction; (b) interpolating a rest interval following conditioning, to allow for 'desensitization,' should not eliminate the transfer. Neither of these controls has been applied. The fact, however, that Brogden's control subjects, those who experienced the light and tone prior to conditioning, but never paired, did not show reaction to the tone is an equally adequate control.

Must this phenomenon be taken at its face value, as a demonstration of association between purely sensory events? The mediation hypothesis provides a feasible explanation—granted one assumption. Let us assume that the occurrence of novel stimuli (light and tone, in Brogden's original study) in an otherwise stable situation elicits a common perceptual reaction, perhaps 'attentional,' perhaps 'startle.' If one of these stimuli (light) is now deliberately conditioned to a new reaction (leg flexion via shock), the self-stimulation produced by the mediation process must also become conditioned to the new reaction; later, in the test for 'sensory conditioning,' the second stimulus (tone) elicits the common mediation process, the self-stimulation from which in turn mediates the transfer of leg flexion. This is simply a case of mediated generalization. The obvious trouble with this explanation is that we have to infer the existence of some mediation process—there is nothing particularly evident in the dog's behavior.

Fortunately there are cases in which the mediation process is specifiable with some accuracy. Shipley (1933) paired a faint light with a sudden tap on the cheek, which elicited winking; then the tap was paired with shock to the finger, eliciting withdrawal; on subsequent tests, the light flash (never paired with shock) evoked finger withdrawal. Since this did not occur unless light and tap had initially been paired, any sensitization explanation is ruled out. Now, substituting 'light-tone' (Brogden) for 'light-tap' (Shipley), it becomes evident that the only difference between this experiment and those on sensory conditioning lies in the specifiability of the mediating reaction—here, the winking movement. But did this mediating winking reaction actually occur? Lumsdaine (1939, cf. pp. 230ff. in Hilgard and Marquis, 1940) has repeated Shipley's experiment with detailed graphic recording. His records indicate that, in most cases, the light *did* elicit a winking movement which was closely followed by finger withdrawal. There were some cases, however, in which the withdrawal reaction antedated the eyelid movement, and this suggests that the winking movement may be only an overt index of the actual mediation process. This is what would be expected according to the mediation hypothesis: in the original training, the light (sign) was presumably becoming associated with the fractional anticipatory portions of the reaction to tap-on-cheek (stimulus-object), and it is this mediation process which is more or less faithfully indexed by the overt winking.

This is merely a feasible S–R interpretation of what appears superficially as a pure S–S process; there is no proof that this interpretation is correct. In any case, the really puzzling thing about these 'sensory conditioning' experiments, particularly Brogden's original dog study, is: *How does the original association, whether S–S or S–R, become established and strengthened?* The animal is merely bombarded repeatedly with a light and a tone in conjunction; the dog does nothing, at least overtly, and there is no apparent reinforcement for whatever it might do. The 'out' for the reinforcement theorist here, as usual, is to invoke secondary reinforcing mechanisms. Notice that the human subjects in Karn's experiment said 'there must have been *some* connection between the light and the buzzer.' But even assuming that some common 'attentional' reactions were established on the basis of secondary reinforcement of some obscure sort, why do these reactions not extinguish during 200 trials? Perhaps they are inhibited (dog ceases 'paying attention'), only to be abruptly disinhibited when one of the stimuli is paired with shock (dog immediately begins 'paying attention' again). But this is very tortuous reasoning, and Brogden's experiment must stand as one of the strongest cases against reinforcement theory.

IS THERE MORE THAN ONE KIND OF LEARNING?

'Conditioning' and 'trial and error' began their histories, with Pavlov and Thorndike, respectively, as independent mechanisms obeying independent laws. The general trend during the first half of this century, typified by Hull and Guthrie, has been to integrate them under a single set of principles, but in recent years there has developed increasing resistance to this brand of parsimony. This issue has been implicit in much that we have already covered—in our survey of strengthening principles, in testing whether reinforcement is necessary for learning, and, most immediately, in asking whether animals learn movements or cognitions. At this point we wish to evaluate the claims of a number of theorists who believe there are two or more 'kinds' of learning, each following different principles. As will be seen, most of the evidence they bring to bear in criticism of a single process theory is particularly relevant to the mediation hypothesis. The issue therefore becomes, in the main, whether or not the mediation hypothesis—an elaboration from a single process theory of the Hull type—is capable of incorporating these additional phenomena.

Maier and Schneirla

In the vanguard of the resistance movement have been Maier and Schneirla (1942). The essence of their position is this: in the ordinary conditioning situation, two quite different processes can be seen and must be sharply differentiated. (1) *Conditioning.* A neutral stimulus develops excitatory capacity for a response it did not initially control, simply on the basis of contiguity between *CS* and *US*. There is no necessity here for a reinforcement principle. (2) *Selective learning.* Once the *CS* does elicit the new response, subsequent modifications in the character of the response, its strengthening, depend upon the rewarding or punishing *effects,* which may be carried by the *US* or any other vehicle. But the response must antedate the *US*, i.e. must have been *conditioned* to the *CS*, before the selective effects of reinforcement can operate. Maier and Schneirla draw liberally from the conditioning literature to support their contention, and Kendler and Underwood (1948) have reanalyzed the same evidence to show that it is unnecessary to postulate 'conditioning' as a separate kind of learning.

Birch and Bitterman

These writers (1949) have taken up the cudgel for the Maier and Schneirla position, referring to the conditioning mechanism as 'sensory integration,' and we may succinctly consider the major issues in this controversy by evaluating some of the points they raise. With regard to the necessity of a reinforcement principle, they cite evidence obtained by Finch (1938 *a, b*) that salivary conditioning can be obtained with acid as the *US*, even when active salivation is prevented by injection of atropine during the training series—hence dilution of the acid cannot be the reinforcement. As Kendler and Underwood have pointed out, occurrence of the overt reaction is not necessary for association (it is the central association with appropriate efferent pathways that is significant), and we are not sufficiently familiar with the effects of acid upon the tongue to decide whether or not drive reduction (via rapid adaptation, etc.) would be involved. The Brogden, Lipman, and Culler (1938) experiment on avoidance training in the guinea pig is also cited as evidence against Hull's reinforcement principle; since the 'avoidance' animals escape the shock, drive reduction cannot explain their superior learning. For some reason or other, here and throughout their article, Birch and Bitterman make no reference to the extensive literature on the role of mediating anxiety reactions as secondary drives capable of being reduced through particular instrumental sequences. Similar interpretation is made of another experiment of Brogden's (1940) in which, having established an avoidance response to a *CS* with the shock applied at one locus, the locus of shock was shifted and only applied when the animal failed to make the anticipatory avoidance response. Rather than being a case where the conditioned response is never reinforced (as these authors claim), it is being regularly reinforced by anxiety reduction; and it is the anxiety reaction to *CS, as a motivational mediation process,* which needs occasional reinstating by shock but which is independent of the locus of shock.

The 'sensory conditioning' experiments are interpreted as incompatible with a reinforcement theory. It is true that they can only be incorporated with considerable deviousness, but there is some doubt as to the validity of the demonstrations. On the other hand, the 'sensory integration' conception is assumed to cover this phenomenon. 'In the first stage of Shipley's experiment, the light flash becomes equivalent to strike (tap-on-cheek) and in the second stage strike becomes equivalent to shock. Presentation of the light therefore results in finger-withdrawal' (p. 300). Why 'therefore'? The light flash may 'become equivalent to' the tap-on-cheek, i.e. acquire the capacity to evoke winking, but since the *light* was never contiguous with shock (and the tap-on-cheek was not 'equivalent to' shock prior to their association), how can the light elicit finger-withdrawal?

This highlights one of the fundamental weaknesses in the Maier and Schneirla (Birch and Bitterman) position. *The conditioning postulate demands that behavior made to the CS can only include reactions originally made to the US.* Subsequent applications of 'effect' may modify this behavior by strengthening or eliminating components, but the eventual reactions must have been some part of the *US*-produced activity. The same is true of the mediation process: it can only include portions of what has been the behavior to the stimulus-object, *but a wide range of instrumental acts may come to be mediated which are not included in the behavior elicited by a particular stimulus object.* The difference between these views comes out clearly in a number of the cases cited by Birch and Bitterman.

In the original Brogden, Lipman, and Culler experiment, for example, the 'nonavoidance' guinea pigs developed a pattern of behavior to the sign (buzzer) which consisted mainly in crouching and holding the breath. How could the buzzer acquire these reactions when they were not part of the behavior to shock? According to the mediation hypothesis, 'freezing' and holding the breath are sequences associated with anxiety mediators, especially when alternate, energy-expending sequences are regularly interrupted by the direct reactions to shock. A situation described by Hilgard (1948, p. 108) is also cited: if a rat is shocked on a grid in a certain place along an alley, it leaps and runs faster in the same forward direction off the grid (and these reactions to *shock* are undoubtedly being strengthened). Subsequently, while approaching the location of the grid, this animal will slow down and even back away. According to Birch and Bitterman, 'Evidently one can only account for avoidance if one assumes that stimuli contiguously related to the *onset* of shock acquire the functional properties of shock' (p. 297). But in what sense are slowing down and backing away behaviors originally elicited by shock? These *are* the instrumental sequences associated with anxiety mediation in the context (total stimulus situation) of approaching a sign which has acquired such 'danger' value (grid in floor). Of course, the terms 'functional property' and 'equivalence' could be made more explicit, but we suspect they would turn out to be indistinguishable from 'mediation process' as this construct has been developed here.

The other major weakness of the Birch and Bitterman position is *the indiscriminability of the 'sensory integration' postulate.* They invoke 'sensory integration' when it is convenient for them to do so, but have not explored the generality of its operation. Why, for example, is not 'sensory conditioning' the rule rather than the exception? Why must an animal be hungry and eat for the pairing of a neutral stimulus with food objects to be effective in establishing secondary reinforcing properties? How, in a simultaneous discrimination situation, can the animal learn to make *differential* reactions to the two stimuli, if they automatically become 'integrated' and share their 'functional properties'? The mediation hypothesis has the advantage here that it specifies those conditions under which *certain* stimulus patterns can become signs of other stimulus-objects; all stimuli do not become signs of all the other stimuli with which they happen to be temporally contiguous (cf. criticism of Tolman's theory along the same line in Chap. 9).

Mowrer

In a paper on the 'dual nature of learning' (1947) and in a recent book, *Learning Theory and Personality Dynamics* (1950), O. Hobart Mowrer has described a two-factor theory which resembles the Maier and Schneirla position in that 'conditioning' and 'problem-solving' are assumed to follow different principles, and yet it is more nearly like the conception developed here in that mediation processes with both motivational and discriminatory properties are given a critical role. Reinforcement, which is the basis for 'problem-solving,' enters the picture in two ways: (1) *primary reinforcement* determines what instrumental responses will be made to the US (stimulus-object, in our terms), e.g. whether running or jumping reactions shall be finally elicited by the shock; (2) *secondary reinforcement* determines what instrumental responses will be made to the CS (sign, in our terms), e.g. whether running or ratchet-turning shall be finally elicited by the buzzer. In the latter case reinforcement is *mediated* by the properties of the reaction made to the sign, e.g. by anxiety or fear reduction. This is all 'problem-solving' and is characterized by *response substitution*—with the stimulus situation constant, the animal must change its instrumental activity to obtain gratification.

But how does the fear reaction itself become associated with the sign? This is not a case of response substitution but *stimulus substitution:* with the (fear) response constant in quality, if not intensity, a new stimulus becomes capable of eliciting it. On the basis of certain evidence which we shall evaluate in a moment, Mowrer concludes that stimulus substitution is independent of reinforcement and depends solely upon contiguity. This is 'conditioning.' Essentially, then, signs acquire their significance through 'conditioning' on the sole basis of contiguity, whereas instrumental acts become associated with either stimulus-objects (US) or signs (CS) through 'problem-solving' on the basis of either primary or secondary reinforcement. Temporal gradients are involved in both cases; in sign-learning it is the interval between the sign and the thing signified (between CS and US), but for instrumental learning it is the interval between the correct response and the occurrence of the rewarding state of affairs.

466 EXPERIMENTAL PSYCHOLOGY

Mowrer draws a very interesting parallel between his dichotomy and the neurophysiological mechanisms subserving behavior. 'Mammals and other complex living organisms have, not *"a* nervous system," but two distinct *nervous systems.* Responses of the skeletal muscles are mediated by the *central nervous system,* whereas responses of the visceral and vascular parts of the organism are mediated by the *autonomic nervous system.* . . Without exception, the visceral and vascular responses are beyond direct voluntary control, whereas all of the skeletal responses (with the unimportant exception of a few "reflexes") are or may be brought under voluntary control' (1950, p. 238).* The contention is that only autonomic 'emotional' reactions are susceptible to conditioning, whereas the skeletal reactions mediated by the central nervous system are selected by problem-solving. 'It now seems preferable to apply the term "conditioning" to that and only that type of learning whereby emotional (visceral and vascular) responses are acquired. . . Many responses involving the skeletal musculature, which have previously been termed "conditioned responses," are, in the present conceptual scheme, not conditioned responses at all. . . If an emotion, or secondary drive, causes the skeletal musculature to be activated and if such activity results in secondary drive reduction, then the overt response thus acquired is here conceived as an instance of effect learning, not conditioning' (1950, p. 244).

One major difference between Mowrer's two-factor theory and the mediation hypothesis lies in the assumption of generality of the reinforcement principle. Whereas we have assumed some such principle to govern *all* learned modifications in behavior,† Mowrer has felt compelled to postulate two different 'kinds' of learning, one following the reinforcement principle and the other a contiguity principle. Since he has long been an ardent champion of reinforcement theory, even in extending it to more subtle situations, his change-about has special significance and we must ask why. He does not emphasize avoidance-training experiments as Birch and Bitterman have; his own earlier experiments had demonstrated how behaviors not elicited by the shock could nevertheless come to be elicited by the sign. He does refer to two experiments by Schlosberg (1934, 1936) in which it made no difference in the rate of conditioning whether the rat could escape the full duration of a .165-second shock by making the *CR* or received fixed shock independent of the *CR.* 'The results . . . seem quite unambiguous. They suggest that conditioning is a form of learning that is wholly dependent upon the paired presentation ("association") of two stimulus events . . . and that it is wholly independent of and unrelated to that form of learning which is known to be dependent upon effect' (Mowrer, 1950, p. 225). Not only is there some question about the implication of the Schlosberg studies—the rats were trussed up in such a way that the only shock-*escaping* movement was also the reflexive reaction to shock, pulling

---

* Mowrer, O. H., *Learning Theory and Personality Dynamics,* copyright 1950 by the Ronald Press Company.

† It is not that I am convinced a reinforcement principle is necessary—it may prove not to be—but I am *not* convinced by existing evidence that it is *not* necessary. However, by drawing a distinction between autonomic and *CNS* mediation, Mowrer makes the best possible case for a principle that can apply to some behavioral modifications and not to others.

the tail forward (1934) or the leg (1936)—but these are reactions of *skeletal* muscle, mediated by the *CNS* (problem-solving) and not the autonomic (conditioning).

Results obtained in Mowrer's own laboratory seem to offer the most direct refutation of reinforcement as a general law. Figures 155*A* and *B* describe the two conditions for avoidance training studied. A third condition, from one of Mowrer's earlier experiments (Mowrer and Lamoreaux, 1942), is included as Fig. 155*C* for comparison. Notice that in condition *A*

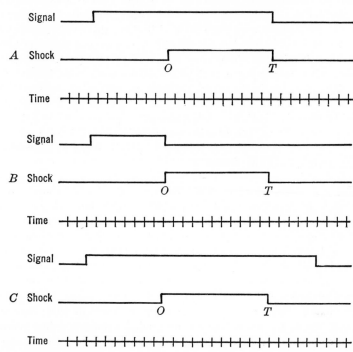

FIGURE 155. Diagrammatic summary of experimental conditions for avoidance training used by Mowrer and associates. While onset and termination of shock are constant, as is onset of signal, termination of signal occurs either coincident with termination of shock (*A*), coincident with onset of shock (*B*), or 5 seconds *after* termination of shock (*C*). *A* and *B:* Mowrer, *Learning Theory and Personality Dynamics*, The Ronald Press Co., New York, 1950; *C:* Mowrer and Lamoreaux, 1942.

the signal (flickering light) is coincident with both the onset *and the termination* of the shock; in condition *B* the signal is only coincident with the *onset* of shock. 'Our concern is to discover *where* the reinforcement involved in conditioning takes place. Hull's view is that this reinforcing state of affairs takes place when the so-called unconditioned stimulus terminates; Pavlov's view, and the one accepted here, is that all that is necessary for conditioning, properly speaking, to occur is that the conditioned stimulus coincide with (or at least approximate) the *onset* of the unconditioned stimulus' (Mowrer, 1950, p. 279). This leads directly to the contradictory predictions, from Hull's theory that condition *A* should yield superior conditioning to condition *B* and from Pavlov's (Mowrer's) theory that there should be no difference (*CS* coincides with onset of *US* in both cases). In two experiments conducted by Mowrer and his students, the Pavlovian prediction was borne out.

But now look at Fig. 155*C*. Here the signal is also coincident with the *onset* of shock, but it persists for 5 seconds *after* shock termination. In the other experiment of Mowrer's (Mowrer and Lamoreaux, 1942) conditions very similar to *A* and *C* were compared, and conditioning was *superior* for group *A*, where buzzer and shock terminated together. This, taken by itself, would certainly not favor Pavlov's theory. How can these apparently discrepant observations be put together? Mowrer suggests the answer, and in doing so shows how very close his position and the mediation hypothesis really are: 'If a *CS* is associated both with the onset and with the termination of shock, it might be thought of as having an equivocal significance: in the one case it comes to mean *both* pain (shock onset) and pleasure (shock termination), whereas in the other case it means *only* pain (shock onset). . . However, these thoughts are conjectural . . .' (1950, p. 285). When the *CS* persists *after* the shock has ceased, there is even more opportunity for its becoming associated with mediating reactions that are incompatible with production of anxiety; anxiety is being gradually *reduced* in the period following termination of the shock.

The reason this interpretation is 'conjectural' is that the response measured was the instrumental sequence of running, not the mediating 'fear' reaction which, according to both two-factor and mediation theories, is what becomes conditioned to the sign. Mowrer (1950, pp. 304-5) cites an unpublished experiment by Coppock in which a signal of short duration occurred either just before the onset of shock or just before the termination of shock. Human subjects were used and the *GSR, an index of autonomic activity,* was measured. As would be expected, conditioning was much more efficient when the signal occurred before the onset of shock. In this case we can legitimately 'put ourselves in the places of the subjects'; obviously a signal that occurs just before the *end* of a painful shock is going to come to signify 'it's almost over.' To the extent that anxiety *reduction* is being associated with the signal, it will interfere with the reciprocally antagonistic (autonomic) reactions involved in anxiety *production*. Thus, as Mowrer says above, we have here a case in which the same sign must be acquiring equivocal significance. It does not seem unreasonable that rats should develop similar mediation processes under similar conditions, and that therefore the sign should acquire 'danger' significance (emotional conditioning) to the extent that it is *distinctively* associated with shock-elicited behavior and not with after-shock behavior. If we had *one tone* (constant) just previous to the onset of shock and *another tone* (variable) just at the termination of shock, the mediation hypothesis would predict that the rate of conditioning to the constant previous tone would vary inversely with its similarity to the subsequent variable tone, i.e. the greater the similarity between the two tones, the more the antagonistic mediators would compete.

The second major difference between Mowrer's two-factor theory and the mediation hypothesis lies in his limitation of conditioning to autonomic 'emotional' reactions. We have not limited the short-circuiting process to reactions controlled by the autonomic nervous system. In fact, if the mediation hypothesis is to serve as the basis for a theory of signs (meaning), then it cannot be limited to autonomic reactions—only the connotative, attitudinal aspects of meaning would be accounted for. Mowrer seems to be aware of this difficulty since he expresses doubt as to whether his theory, 'with its emphasis upon feeling rather than upon action,' will prove adequate for a psychology of understanding or meaning (p. 272). Personal communication from R. L. Solomon is cited (p. 309) in which observations on the behavior of sympathectomized dogs are described: in keeping with both the two-factor theory and the mediation hypothesis, two phases in the development of avoidance conditioning were clearly differentiated, the avoidance stage never appearing until *after* measurable signs of the fear emotion had appeared. Contrary to Mowrer's assumptions, the dogs deprived almost completely of autonomic functioning nevertheless acquired conditioned avoidance reactions, and Solomon concludes that skeletal reactions (*CNS* mediated) can also become conditioned under classical Pavlovian procedures. To this we may add Schlosberg's evidence for *conditioning* of skeletal tail and leg movements. And the reader will recall Miller's (1935) experiment in which anticipatory *turning movements* mediated the anxiety which in turn elicited retreating behavior in a straight alley. The latter observation is particularly compelling because both experimental and control animals received shock, *but only the former in the same skeletal position* as when they had previously enjoyed food at the end of the alley.

Aside from these two disagreements, which are, to be sure, significant ones, Mowrer's two-factor theory and the mediation hypothesis are one and the same thing. Mowrer refers repeatedly to the manner in which mediating reactions (usually anxiety) serve both as cues and as secondary drives which can be reduced; so have I. He stresses the role of differential reinforcement in selecting instrumental responses in association with both stimulus-objects and signs; so have I. Perhaps I have placed more emphasis upon the pre-experimental learning of instrumental skills, which are then available to the mature animal in any new situation, but Mowrer's view does not preclude the same interpretation. He has stated that the mediation process 'conditioned' to a sign can only partake of those reactions originally elicited by the stimulus-object; so have I. But whereas he uses this as one basis for deciding there are two kinds of learning, substitution and effect, I have not. *The only reason mediating reactions to the sign are part of the behavior originally elicited by the stimulus-object, and hence make it appear like 'substitution learning,' is that presence of the stimulus-object guarantees the occurrence of certain reactions which, when short-circuited and reduced, become the mediation process.* In other words, the only essential difference between conditioning and trial and error is the *efficiency* with which a definite and predictable pattern of behavior is made to occur in the former case. Whatever behavior is produced by the stimulus-object, including instrumental *R*'s like running, automatically tends to be short-circuited, and some replica becomes the final mediation process that gives 'meaning' to the sign.

Seward

In a series of papers (1943, 1947, 1950) this author has also tried to work out a resolution among the major contemporary viewpoints. It is difficult to evaluate his position because it seems to vary somewhat from paper to paper, from a pretty wholehearted endorsement of Guthrie's associationism (1943), to an attempt to modify Hull's theory so as to make it compatible with Tolman's conceptions (1947), to an extension of Hull's secondary motivation to what is called 'tertiary motivation' (1950). There are, nevertheless, certain consistent trends throughout which, upon analysis, turn out to be similar to those found in the other dual-process theories we have reviewed. For one thing, he also denies the ubiquity of any reinforcement principle; in fact, unlike the others, he entirely eliminates reinforcement in the usual sense. Like Guthrie, he asserts that the mere association of a stimulus with a response results in an increment of conditioning. This increment varies in size, however, as a function of the time between these events (cf. 1943, p. 188; 1947, p. 86). This aspect of his position is like the conditioning by contiguity of Maier and Schneirla, and Mowrer, but the selective, response-substituting effects of reinforcement are omitted.

Seward postulates what he calls the 'surrogate response,' and this, at first sight, seems very similar to the mediation process we have been dealing with, for he says: 'This construct may be thought of as a kind of short-circuiting device interposed between an external stimulus and its explicit response. As its name implies, it stands for some phase of the original S–R connection; either certain properties of S, in which case it may be called a *perceptual response*, or certain properties of R, in which case it may be called an *implicit response*, or both' (1947, p. 87). But it turns out to be quite different in nature and development. In the formal statement of the postulate, we find: 'Each S that activates an organism's receptors evokes a *surrogate response* ($\bar{r}s$) in the neural centers capable of being conditioned as a response to concurrent S's and as a stimulus to concurrent R's . . .' (p. 88). In other words, this 'surrogate response' is some central, neural event whose character is dependent upon the *stimulus*. In latent learning experiments, for example, Seward states that the surrogate responses elicited by the goal-box will become more strongly conditioned to short-path stimuli than to long-path stimuli, as a function of the different temporal intervals between one stimulus and the other but independent of any action of reinforcement. On the trial when food is first introduced to the goal-box, the surrogate elicited by the food S becomes completely conditioned to the surrogate elicited by the goal-box S (perfect contiguity). On the next trial, the stimuli representing the short path, being more strongly associated with the goal-box surrogate, will now elicit the food surrogate (e.g. mediated by goal-box surrogate) and this augments the *drive* rather than functioning as a secondary reinforcing agent.

If these 'surrogate responses' *do* depend entirely upon the stimuli that elicit them (and there is no discussion of how the *reactions* elicited by these stimuli could influence the surrogate), then it is hard to see what is gained. In defense of this position, Seward says: 'By placing the mechanism in the central connections rather than the periphery we have simply attempted to increase its usefulness by freeing it from the restrictions governing response evocation' (pp. 87-8). He seems to forget that it is these 'restrictions governing response evocation' that make it possible to anchor intervening variables. Since 'surrogate responses' cannot be independently measured, they are useful in behavioral science only to the extent that they are tied to both antecedent and consequent observables. Otherwise we might just as well say 'entering path A gives the rat the *idea* of the goal-box' and dispense with the ponderous circumlocution, 'the stimuli at path *A* elicit *surrogate responses* in the brain which represent the goal-box.' On the side of experimentation, Seward does not present any types of evidence not already considered in relation to the mediation hypothesis.

Tolman

In a paper published in 1949 Tolman claims that 'There Is More Than One Kind of Learning.' The question is this: Can it be shown that his several 'kinds' of learning are really nothing more than phenotypes of the same underlying genotype, i.e. reducible to the general model provided by Hull's theory as extended by the mediation hypothesis? Again, it should be emphasized that in learning theory, as elsewhere in science, parsimony is desirable only when it does not do injustice to the facts.

(1) *Learning of cathexes.* By 'cathexes' is meant the attachment of specific types of goal-object, both attractive and disturbing, to basic drives via approaching, consummatory responses or avoidant, defensive responses. Tolman himself (p. 146) expresses the belief that reinforcement in the Hullian sense is the major determinant here. These basic instrumental sequences, where not reflexively elicited by appropriate goal-objects (e.g. salivation by food-in-mouth, leg flexion by shock to foot), are acquired early in the life history of the organism through the effects of differential reinforcement. The fact that the sights, smells, and sounds of goal-objects acquire *incentive* values for the organism (e.g. secondary motivating properties) is explained by the mediation hypothesis as follows: Such 'distal' aspects of goal-objects must regularly antedate the 'proximal' cues which directly evoke consummatory and avoidant reactions; therefore, via short-circuiting and reduction mechanisms, the sights, smells, and sounds of goal-objects must come to elicit fractional components of these consummatory and avoidant reactions. To the extent that these anticipatory components have energizing self-stimulational properties, their signs will 'incite' the organism to make those instrumental reactions which increase or decrease likelihood of contact with the goal-objects.

(2) *Learning of equivalence beliefs.* By 'equivalence beliefs' (a term which Tolman admits is 'shocking') is meant the capacity of stimuli other than those arising from the goal-object to acquire some of the properties of the goal-object. Tolman uses the example of subgoals, and again seems (p. 149) to accept the role of reinforcement in establishing such properties. As far as this reviewer can see, there is no essential difference between 'equivalence beliefs' and 'secondary reinforcements.' This is merely an extension of the same type of mediation mechanism (described above in relation to incentive) from distal aspects of the goal-object itself to stimuli which are associated with the goal-object but do not actually arise from it. This is a straightforward case of stimuli becoming signs of reinforcing states of affairs.

(3) *Learning of field expectancies.* 'Field expectancies' are what Tolman used to call 'sign-gestalt-expectations.' The close similarities between this construct and the representational mediation process have already been discussed. Although Tolman stresses the point that such expectancies are not stamped in by reinforcement, his arguments are those already evaluated in connection with the necessity of reinforcement for learning. Lacking critical evidence, we have assumed that some reinforcement principle operates

in the selection of mediation processes (field expectancies) as well as in the selection of instrumental skills. In connection with the role of field expectancies, Tolman speaks of 'inference abilities' as a characteristic whereby expectations relevant to aspects of the environmental field not directly experienced are formed. Part of the evidence here has been evaluated under 'Do Animals Learn Movements or Cognitions?' and the remainder will be considered in relation to insight and problem-solving (Chap. 14).

(4) *Field-cognition modes.* It is not clear what Tolman means here. As he says himself, 'This category is the one about which I am least confident. Perhaps a better name would be field lore—that is, perceptual, memorial and inferential lores' (p. 152). And later he writes, 'In a word, I am trying to summarize under this fourth category all those principles as to the structure of environmental fields which are relevant to all environmental fields, and which (whether innate or learned) are carried around by the individual and applied to each new field with which he is presented' (p. 153). In part, at least, Tolman seems to be talking about what I have referred to as the *previously learned* systems of representational mediators which can be elicited in new situations and mediate 'appropriate' behaviors. But this is certainly not a new 'kind' of learning.

(5) *Learning of drive discriminations.* There is, as Tolman asserts, evidence that animals as well as men can discriminate among their drive states, but again he gives no reasons why we should consider this a different 'kind' of learning. To the extent that drive states, either directly or indirectly, produce afferent stimulation, they can become associated with either mediational reactions (as signs of something else) or instrumental sequences. As an example of the first type, suppose a young child has been severely punished whenever caught indulging in sexual play; in later life, occurrence of sexual impulses may cause him to condemn himself verbally, to 'run away' from the situations in which these impulses were aroused, and so forth—all instrumental sequences *mediated* by an anxiety state which in turn was elicited by erotic impulses. The erotic impulses become associated with anxiety mediation, and hence become a *sign* of threat or punishment because of the childhood association of these impulses with punishment. The direct association of drive stimuli with instrumental responses has been discussed earlier in this chapter.

(6) *Learning of motor patterns.* In this category Tolman refers directly to what we have termed the development of instrumental skill sequences, and he expresses the opinion that these sensorimotor associations are learned in a single trial on the basis of sheer contiguity, after the Guthrian model. There certainly is no question but that many instrumental skills are *selected* in association with particular mediators on a differential reinforcement basis (cf. Mowrer's 'problem-solving'). But the role of reinforcement in the *development* of basic integrations like hand-eye co-ordination and vocalizing is more obscure. Young infants appear to find the mere execution of a newly discovered skilled movement, such as grasping small objects with the thumb and forefinger or vocalizing a particular syllable, *self-rewarding*—certainly they will practice such newly found skills over and over again without any obvious reinforcement. It is almost as if the establishment of new cell assemblies in the motor areas were itself a reinforcing state of affairs, but this is a running leap into complete darkness. In any case, I would agree

with Tolman that this is the least clear case of learning through reinforcement.

This survey of the contemporary views of theorists like Mowrer and Tolman has provided an opportunity to evaluate the mediation hypothesis in relation to the types of criticisms it is most likely to face. The reader is now in the best position to judge for himself how it stands up. If, as a construction built upon the foundation set by Hull, the total edifice is found reasonably sturdy and still flexible enough to encompass all the major facts, then there is no reason to build other edifices—we can all live in the same house. Of course, architects in theory are always convinced that their houses are more livable than any others, yet styles do change. When we know more about behavior, particularly about the neurophysiological substructure of learning mechanisms, which will be surveyed in the next chapter, we will be better able to interpret, evaluate, and modify the blueprints.

Chapter 11

NEUROPHYSIOLOGY OF LEARNING

It is the credo of most contemporary psychologists that the modifications in behavior that we have been studying depend upon modifications within the central nervous system. Certain questions therefore arise at this point: *What* neurological changes parallel learning and *where* in the *CNS* are they localized? To attempt exhaustive answers to these questions would be beyond the scope of this book. We shall content ourselves with a consideration of the methodology involved in obtaining answers and a brief survey of the three issues clearly relevant to the psychology of learning: (1) At what levels of the *CNS* are the processes essential for different modes of learning organized? (2) To what extent does the cortex display some mass or total function in learning? (3) What are the neural pathways essential for association? The evidence, while neither conclusive nor compelling with regard to psychological theories, is nevertheless significant for students of learning.

One reason for inconclusiveness is the bewildering complexity of the central nervous system. It has been estimated (Herrick, 1926) that there are about twelve thousand million neurons in the human brain, of which some ninety-two hundred million are in the cerebral cortex. The anatomical possibilities for interconnection are so great that the potential permutations and combinations are practically infinite. Neurologists seem pretty well agreed, however, that it is the cerebral cortex which is chiefly responsible for the plasticity which characterizes the behavior of higher organisms. In tracing the evolution of the brain in birds and mammals (two divergent trends in the vertebrate line), for example, one finds that in the birds there has been extensive development of the subcortical system (*corpus striatum*), accompanied by relative degeneration of cerebral cortex, and this is coupled with elaboration of instinctive, reflexive behaviors; in mammals, on the other hand, progressive enlargement and diversification of the cerebral cortex has been correlated with increasing capacity for flexible learning by individual members of species. Yet, and this may seem paradoxical, experimentation usually fails to reveal any unique dependence of learning upon the discrete cortical regions. Neurologists do not agree at all on how the cortex functions.

474

METHODOLOGY

The neurophysiologist uses a number of techniques in determining the pathways and regions of the *CNS* subserving various functions. Painstaking microscopic study may trace the paths of various nerve bundles through the central system. Nerve degeneration, whether initiated by disease or by artificial means, has been shown to follow functional pathways, and this provides another anatomical approach. One may stimulate portions of the superficial cortical gray matter electrically, or with certain chemicals such as strychnine, and, by observing the motor and sensory effects, draw inferences as to function. Reversing this procedure, one can make electrical recordings of impulses in nerve tissue at various levels of the *CNS* and correlate their locus and magnitude with characteristics of the stimuli applied. In studying complex, integrative processes like learning, however, the *destruction method* is most extensively employed. A portion of the brain is surgically removed (ablation) or fiber tracts are severed (lesion), and the effect upon subsequent behavior is carefully observed.

Various inferences about brain functioning may be drawn from the results of destruction experiments, depending upon the nature of the evidence. One may conclude that a particular function is *strictly localized* within a given brain area. The term 'localization' here has historical sanction, but it means merely that the region in question is *essential* to performance of a certain type of behavior. The visual cortex is essential for form discrimination, but this complex function is no more 'localized' in the visual cortex than it is in the retina of the eye. One may conclude that two areas show *replication of function,* that the neural events necessary for performance are simultaneously organized in both places. For many activities the right and left cerebral hemispheres display replication—removal of either one does not disturb behavior but elimination of both completely destroys the performance. One brain area is said to show *vicarious functioning* with respect to another if the habits lost after removal of the latter can be relearned as long as the former is intact. A given brain region (i.e. the entire cortex of the rat, the visual cortex of the monkey, etc.) is said to be *equipotential* with respect to a certain function if the losses due to extirpation of equal amounts of the region are equivalent and independent of the locus of injury. A given brain region is said to display *mass-action* if disturbance varies with the extent of injury within that region (i.e. the entire region has some general facilitative function). Since there is considerable confusion in the literature on the use of these interpretive labels, the logic behind them must be examined.

The 'ideal' destruction experiment should permit quantitative measurement of *preoperative learning* (performance in the maze, discrimination box, or other situation being studied), *postoperative retention* and, if the function being measured has been lost and retraining is possible, *postoperative relearning*. It is usually necessary to provide a control for normal forgetting, by having intact animals learn the same performance and testing them for retention and relearning over the same delay intervals used with the brain-injured subjects. If the possibilities of strict localization, equipotentiality, and mass-action are to be checked, the locus and magnitude of destruction should be deliberately varied from subject to subject. To control for spontaneous recovery of function, different animals should be tested for retention or relearning at variable times after surgery. Finally, all experimental animals should be sacrificed, their brains examined histologically, and maps prepared outlining the damaged areas. With limited numbers of subjects in most cases, with loss of animals under surgery, and with the general rigor of this type of work, it is not surprising that few experiments prove to be 'ideal,' yet clarity in interpretation varies directly with the adequacy of design.

What type of evidence is necessary to justify making each of the interpretations above? (1) *Localization of function.* To demonstrate that a given brain region is essential for a given function, habits learned prior to injury must be lost (e.g. no retention) and relearning must be shown to be impossible. (2) *Replication.* To demonstrate that a given function is simultaneously organized in regions *A* and *B,* it must be shown that performances learned prior to injury are retained as long as *either A* or *B* is intact, but are lost when both are eliminated (the last provision is necessary, since otherwise one could conclude that neither region was involved). (3) *Vicarious functioning.* Region *B* may be said to function vicariously for region *A* if, following injury of *A,* previously learned habits are *not* retained, but can be relearned as long as *B* is intact. (4) *Equipotentiality.* The various parts of a given region are equipotential with respect to a function if disturbances in retention and relearning are independent of the locus of injury within that region. Lack of *any* disturbance, regardless of the locus of injury, does not necessarily point to equipotentiality; it may merely indicate noninvolvement of the entire region. (5) *Mass-action.* A region of the brain exhibits mass-action if degree of disturbance is correlated with magnitude of lesion or ablation, *and* is independent of the locus of injury (i.e. mass-action, as a total facilitative function, implies the idea of equipotentiality, although the converse is not necessarily true).

Beyond these rules of procedure for drawing inferences from data, there are certain general warnings that need to be voiced before surveying the experimental literature. For one thing, the tasks or performances used to estimate brain functions are not simple, unitary processes; 'maze-learning,' 'brightness discrimination,' 'conditioned response,' and so forth, are complex integrative processes, and if a given type of injury does interfere with one of these performances, about all we know is that some necessary function included in the task is subserved by that brain region. If, for example, the auditory cortex is extirpated bilaterally and previously learned *CR*'s to tones are lost, we cannot (without further evidence) determine whether the reason for this loss was raising of auditory thresholds or disturbances of associational processes, or even some other function. For another thing, extending the conclusions drawn from the study of one species to other species is an extremely hazardous procedure. Much of the work on brain-functioning in learning has been done on rats. If the rat's cortex proves to be relatively equipotential with respect to problem-solving, does this conclusion apply to man? Probably not, since one of the general trends of neural development is that toward *encephalization.* Higher centers, as they increase in size and complexity, come to take over functions originally invested in lower centers, and synchronously higher centers tend to lose their generalized functions, becoming more diversified and specialized.

One of the major difficulties in interpreting the results of destruction experiments arises from the fact that some functions, initially lost after operation, show spontaneous recovery. According to Von Monakow's theory of *diaschisis* (cf. Lashley, 1933), removal of one cortical area, not essential to a certain function, may nevertheless withdraw a source of neural facilitation to other cortical or subcortical areas, thus temporarily hindering their activities. Since these other areas are assumed to recover gradually and spontaneously, these functions reappear without training. This means that to demonstrate that a given region is essential to a certain function, sufficient time must be allowed for spontaneous recovery *not* to occur. It also means that to demonstrate vicarious functioning (recovery only through retraining) control animals must be tested for retention over varying intervals without retraining.

By way of illustration of a number of these points, Marquis (1942) gives the following composite description of recovery from brain surgery in the dog: The animal learns both a conditioned response (eyeblink to a light signal) and an instrumental discriminatory reaction (discrimination between bright and dim lights for a food reward) before operation. Two days after removal of the visual areas of the cerebrum, the animal is normally healthy and active but behaves as though totally blind—neither of the previously learned habits is retained. By the fifth postoperative day, the conditioned eyeblink has recovered spontaneously. Control animals subjected to equally severe destruction of nonvisual areas had recovered this conditioned eyeblink to a light by the end of the first postoperative day, so the effect on the experimental animals was not due merely to anesthesia or other operational procedures. The instrumental brightness discrimination never shows spontaneous recovery, but it can be relearned in about as many trials as required previous to surgery. Certain of the dog's normal activities, such as locating food or avoiding objects by sight and blinking to a threatening gesture, are never recovered, either spontaneously or by training. We would conclude (a) that certain functions necessary for retaining visual *CR*'s are *replicated* in cortical and subcortical systems (additional evidence indicated that subsequent elimination of subcortical visual mechanisms completely destroyed this habit), (b) that functions necessary for learning and retaining instrumental brightness discriminations normally involve the visual cortex but other areas can take over *vicariously,* and (c) that visual orientation to objects is 'localized' in the visual cortex.

CONDITIONING

Pavlov believed the cerebral cortex essential for conditioning, and his theory of cortical action, dealing with the irradiation and concentration of excitatory and inhibitory processes in this medium, was explicitly based upon this assumption. It is now clear, however, that cortical tissue is not necessary for conditioning. In the first place, conditioned reactions can be established in invertebrates lacking typical cerebral structures, and there is no evidence that speed of simple conditioning increases with the development of those structures that characterize the vertebrate nervous system (cf.

Lashley, 1933). In the second place, incontrovertible demonstrations of conditioning in higher animals rendered decorticate by surgery are now available, with the cat (Ten Cate, 1934) and the dog (Culler and Mettler, 1934; Girden, Mettler, Finch, and Culler, 1936). Whether or not completely decorticate humans or other primates can be conditioned is not known; it is extremely difficult to keep such preparations alive, which is further testimony to the principal of functional encephalization.

Role of the Cortex in Conditioning

Does this mean that the cortex plays no role in conditioning for organisms possessing this structure? It will be recalled that avoidance conditioning of the normal dog includes at least two distinguishable stages: an early, diffuse stage in which the CR closely resembles the gross, vigorous escape movements produced by the shock itself and a later, precise stage in which the CR is a neatly adaptive raising of the paw from the grid. Girden and others (1936) found that although the diffuse stage of the CR could easily be obtained from their decorticate preparation, the final 'adaptive' selection of the correct response (and the concomitant inhibition of gross bodily reactions) never occurred. They concluded that functional cortex is necessary for such adaptive learning, but not for simple substitution. This conclusion is weakened by more recent evidence obtained by Bromiley (1948), who also trained a decorticate dog to make avoidance responses to a tone. Here clearly isolated, 'adaptive' flexion of the leg to the tone was obtained. Bromiley points out that there was more subcortical destruction in the earlier studies than in his case. It is also possible that the difference lay in the intensity of the shock stimulation used (shock was applied simultaneously to both hind paws in the former case to produce conditioning, and this procedure invariably called forth rage reactions from Bromiley's animal). Culler and Mettler (1934) found the conditioning of decorticate animals to require more trials and more intense stimuli than was the case for normal animals (the need for more intense stimuli may merely have reflected a raising of the sensory threshold).

There is other evidence, however, that the cortex functions in normal conditioning. When only limited areas of the sensory cortex are removed, previously learned CR's involving those sensory modalities are retained without modification, and the rate of acquiring new CR's does not differ from normal. Marquis and Hilgard (1936) found this to be true for conditioned eyeblink in the dog, Wing and Smith (1942) for conditioned flexion to a light, and Kryter and Ades (1943) for auditory CR's after removal of auditory cortex. Wing and Smith report further that extinction of the flexion CR proceeded much more slowly after visual cortical injury than with normal controls, suggesting that certain inhibitory functions (commonly attributed to cortical structures) had been lost. This difference between completely decorticate and visually (or acoustically) decorticate preparations seems to indicate some facilitative effect of the remaining cortex upon associational as contrasted with sensory functions (cf. evidence for mass action below).

One obvious drawback to the destruction experiment is that destroyed parts cannot be put back together again. We should like to *functionally* decorticate animals, train them in various ways, and then see what effect reassertion of cortical control has upon these behaviors. The drug *curare* offers possibilities here. Besides paralyzing somatic musculature rather completely, this drug is thought to depress cortical action without affecting subcortical tissues. The first experiment on learning under curare was contributed by Harlow and Stagner (1933). Extensive conditioning training under influence of the drug yielded no evidence of learning after the drug had worn off. Does this mean that *CR*'s cannot be established under curare or does it mean that subcortically organized *CR*'s are inhibited when the cortex resumes its normal functioning? Girden and Culler (1937) offered evidence for the second alternative: the semitendinosus muscle in the leg was dissected out and observed directly, a small but unmistakable twitch to shock (to the footpad) being discernible. Conditioning of this muscle-twitch to a bell was clearly established under curare but—and this was the interesting thing—it was lost upon recovery from the effects of the drug. Conversely, conditioning established in the normal state did not transfer to the curarized state. Similar results have been obtained on curarized monkeys (Girden, 1947). Girden and Culler conclude that conditioning under curare is subcortical in locus, being inhibited when the cortex returns to dominance; conditioning in the normal animal is cortical in locus, therefore disappearing when curare suppresses cortical activity. Girden (1940) checked this hypothesis by using animals from whom the auditory cortex had been extirpated, and in this case auditory *CR*'s established under curare did carry over to the normal state, and vice versa.

Summarizing and interpreting this evidence on the use of curare, it appears first that subcortical mechanisms function *vicariously* when cortical mechanisms are eliminated. That there is not replication of conditioning (simultaneous organization of this function) at both cortical and subcortical levels is implied by the fact that *CR*'s learned under normal conditions do *not* carry over into the curarized state. But this does not agree with the extirpation data of Marquis and Hilgard (1936), Wing and Smith (1942), and Kryter and Ades (1943), who found preoperative conditioning to be retained after ablation of restricted sensory cortex. This must mean that retention of preoperatively established *CR*'s depends upon some mass, facilitative function of the cortical tissues, i.e. elimination of restricted though appropriate sensory portions of the cortex by extirpation does not affect retention of *CR*'s, but elimination of the entire cortex by curarization does. Finally, although it is clear enough from the evidence that a normally functioning cortex suppresses associations established subcortically under curare, the mode of suppression is not apparent. It is possible that, with its cortex functioning again, the animal is more reactive to general environmental cues, which effectively changes the total stimulus situation. Fitting this interpretation is the observation that both learning and retention are *better* under curare than in the normal state (Girden and Culler, 1937; Girden, 1947). It might be remarked in passing that these curare phenomena are rather similar to the dissociation that can be set up between waking and trance states under hypnosis.

Spinal Conditioning

What is the lowest level at which conditioned reactions can be organized? Although the behavior of all protoplasmic systems is to some extent modifiable, subordinate neural systems are known to lose their generalized functions progressively as they become integrated within more and more complexly organized patterns. Shurrager and Culler (1940, 1941) have demonstrated what appears to be conditioning in spinal dogs, i.e. conditioned reflexes organized at the level of the spinal cord. The spinal cord of the experimental animals was transected at some point anterior to the third lumbar roots and the flexing, semitendinosus muscles of the hind legs were dissected out as in the curare experiments cited above. Uncontrolled movements of the spinal preparation were eliminated by piercing both femurs with a drill-rod—needless to say, these were *acute* preparations, surviving only a few days at best. With a series of shocks to the tail (sufficient to slightly curl that member) as the *CS,* a shock to the hind paw of sufficient intensity to produce contraction of the semitendinosus muscle in that leg as the *US,* and direct observation of the twitching of this muscle as a record of response, these investigators obtained reactions to *CS* in roughly half their preparations. That these responses to *CS* were true *CR*'s was shown by the following characteristics (Shurrager, 1947) : they were not elicitable by *CS* before pairing with *US;* they increased irregularly as conditioning proceeded ; they were extinguishable by omission of *US.*

Kellogg and his associates (Kellogg, Deese, Pronko, and Feinberg, 1947; Kellogg, 1947; Deese and Kellogg, 1949) have seriously questioned this interpretation, claiming that what Shurrager and Culler were observing was in truth a sensitized reflexive reaction to the *CS* rather than a conditioned response. In their first study (Kellogg *et al.* 1947) *chronic* spinal preparations were used—necessarily a much smaller number of subjects, since animals treated in this manner are extremely difficult to keep alive and experiment upon. The response was here recorded graphically from the intact muscle. No evidence of learning appeared. They concluded that this reaction is 'part of the natural or basic response to the conditioned stimulus alone . . . probably also a striped-muscle component of the startle pattern which can be produced by any abrupt tactual or electrical stimulus' (p. 116). Unfortunately, for purposes of comparison, these investigators applied the *CS* to the contralateral hind paw rather than the tail, thus inadvertently bringing in the complication of crossed-extension reflexes which may have obscured the *CR.* They also employed stronger shock for the *CS,* thus possibly creating generalized masking responses. Another difference in procedure which may have influenced the results was that while Shurrager and Culler made the *US* synchronous with *CS,* Kellogg and others had the *US* follow the *CS* by .2 seconds.

This question of whether spinal dogs can be conditioned is still being hotly debated (see discussions and comments by Shurrager, 1947, and Kellogg, 1947). Kellogg has asked how conditioning of acute spinal preparations could reach 100 per cent efficiency in as few as 20 to 40 trials, as happened in some of the Shurrager and Culler cases, when it takes from 100 to 400 trials to condition the normal, intact dog. He has also criticized the observational method of recording (as compared with his graphic method) as one yielding inaccuracies and not revealing the random character of the response. More or less by way of experimental rebuttal, Shurrager and Shurrager (1946) have presented curves for learning measured at a single synapse (again *CS* being shock to tail in a spinal preparation), and these curves are certainly regular and lawful—if they represented cumulative strength of conditioning. Deese and Kellogg (1949) have offered further negative evidence: the *CS* was here delivered to the tail of the spinal animal and was regulated in intensity as in the Shurrager and Culler experiment. An improved, more sensitive method of measuring response in the semitendinosus muscle was devised. They found that this response to the *CS* would occur in *either* hind limb, regardless of where *US* was delivered, that it was independent of reinforcement with *US,* and that its amplitude was a function of the intensity of electrical stimulation to the tail—all characteristics of a reflexive reaction to *CS* itself and not of a conditioned response. It is too early, and the data are too incomplete, to attempt any resolution of this controversy.

Summary

(1) Cortical participation is not necessary for the formation of conditioned reactions. Both subcortical brain centers and possibly spinal integrative systems have been shown capable of mediating associations of this order. (2) On the basis of existing evidence, the relationship between cortical and subcortical centers in mediating conditioned reactions is best conceived as one of *replication*. Not only is there transoperational retention of appropriate *CR*'s following ablation of visual or auditory cortex, but it has been shown further, for hearing at least (Kryter and Ades, 1943), that normal *CR*'s survive removal of *either* auditory cortex *or* inferior colliculi, but not elimination of both. The inferior colliculi are midbrain centers bypassed by some of the auditory projection fibers, and in the cat they can be removed by suction-pipette without injuring the auditory cortex. (3) Some nonspecific facilitative effect of cortex upon subcortically organized integrations is suggested by the evidence. Although completely decorticate preparations require more trials and more intense stimuli for conditioning, this is not true for partially decorticate (visual or auditory sensory cortex) preparations learning *CR*'s appropriate to the modalities involved. Similarly, injection with curare (assumed to produce complete functional decortication) eliminates *CR*'s established previously in the normal state. The fact that *CR*'s can be established while under curare presumably shows that these integrations *can* be completely subcortical in locus—notice that conditioning under curare proceeds more rapidly than with normal animals. (4) There is some indication that the cortex normally inhibits independent subcortical mechanisms. *CR*'s established under curare are inhibited in the normal state; animals lacking visual cortex extinguish visual *CR*'s more slowly than normal controls (Wing and Smith); precise, selective *CR*'s are harder to obtain in decorticate preparations, whereas the diffuse conditioned behavior appears readily (Culler and Mettler, 1934; Girden *et al.* 1936).

DISCRIMINATION LEARNING

In sharp contrast to conditioning data, where replication seems to be the rule, a large body of data on discrimination points to *vicarious functioning* of subcortical mechanisms for the cortex. Much of the evidence has been accumulated by Lashley and his associates and deals, in the main, with simple light-darkness discrimination in the rat.

Evidence for Vicarious Functioning

When rats with up to 60 per cent of the cortex removed are compared with normal animals in *ease of original learning,* no discernible deficiency can be found (Lashley, 1920, 1922, 1929). More extensive loss of cortex may retard the formation of these visual habits (cf. Lashley, 1933). Yet complete elimination of the *striate* (visual) cortex does not interfere with learning this simple discrimination (Lashley, 1926). Visual discriminations learned previous to cortical injury, however, *are not retained transoperatively,* if lesions are in the striate areas, but can be relearned in about equal time (Lashley, 1920, 1926, 1935 *b*). This is clear evidence for vicarious functioning—the visual cortex is normally utilized in the formation of simple visual discriminations, but other parts may take over when the striate areas are removed. What areas serve this vicarious function? When rats *lacking* visual cortex are trained to make simple brightness discriminations, subsequent removal of one-third of the remaining cortex, covering all remaining neocortex in different cases, does not disturb the habit (Lashley, 1922). We surmise that some subcortical visual mechanism (now thought to be the *superior colliculi,* Ghiselli and Brown, 1938) takes over this function vicariously.

Of special interest was the observation that initial learning of the light-dark discrimination by partially decorticate rats was actually *superior,* in terms of both trials and errors, to that of normal animals (Lashley, 1920, 1929). At first sight, this seems most surprising—surprising because we think of the intact animal as 'best' and any brain-injured specimen as necessarily inferior. It is probable that here the partially decorticate rats were less distractible, less susceptible to interference from incidental external and internal stimuli, i.e. they were 'best' for this simple type of learning. This does not mean, of course, that partial decortication improves learning ability in general! The true inferiority of the brain-injured subjects would undoubtedly show up in terms of fineness of discrimination, adjustment of light-dark discrimination to variations in the total situation, and so on. This finding with respect to discrimination is certainly related to the observation that conditioning under curare proceeds more rapidly than in the normal state.

Evidence for Mass-action

There is evidence for mass-action within the visual cortex of the rat on these discrimination problems, but it is of a puzzling sort. Although ease of *original* learning shows no significant correlation with extent of lesion within the striate cortex (*r*'s averaging about .10 in two studies, Lashley 1926, 1929), speed of *relearning* following striate injury is significantly related to size of lesion in the visual area (*r* of .72), and this relation is independent of locus. According to Lashley (1926, p. 46), 'The relation between cerebral mass and the efficiency of retention is interpreted as indicating a summation of the activities of different parts of the visual area. This summation takes place in spite of the cutting of any particular group of associational fibers.' In a later paper (1935 *b*, p. 60) Lashley reverses this position, citing evidence for secondary spread of degeneration to areas not directly invaded.

One might have anticipated the opposite result—that efficiency of original learning rather than degree of retention would have correlated with extent of destruction—and Ghiselli (1938) reports results pointing in this direction. A linear discrimination sequence of four light-dark choices was used. Rats operated upon previous to learning were significantly inferior in forming this sequential discrimination to normal animals, *and* degree of retardation was closely related to extent of lesion ($r = .82$). Since this relation between extent of lesion and ease of learning was independent of the locus of lesion, we have evidence for mass-action of the cortex upon original learning of a light-dark discrimination. Interestingly, complete destruction of the striate areas produced no more retardation than equivalent lesions outside this region. Another group of animals was subjected to complete destruction of the *striate* areas *after* learning this discrimination: here there was marked loss of the habit after injury, and relearning, although faster than when the habit was originally learned by operated animals, was slower than for normal animals. The last fact suggests that certain nonvisual aspects of this task were retained transoperationally. As a whole, these data are more in keeping with the findings for maze-learning (cf. below) than for simple brightness discrimination. Ghiselli interprets his results as indicating a nonspecific, nonsensory activity of the cerebral cortex in learning. Whether the differences between these results and those obtained by Lashley on light-dark discrimination are due to the sequential, mazelike character of Ghiselli's situation or to some other factors cannot be told from the existing data.

More Difficult Discriminations

As the conditions for discrimination become more difficult, results become more like those obtained by Ghiselli and less like those obtained above by Lashley. When, instead of reacting differentially to simple light and darkness, the rat is required to discriminate between two lights of near-threshold difference, *both* initial learning and relearning following postoperative amnesia are significantly retarded, and the retardations are correlated with the extent of lesion in the striate areas (Lashley, 1930). That this increased dependence of difficult discriminations upon visual cortex is a learning rather than a sensory function was shown by the fact that brightness thresholds may be normal following such striate injuries. Data on pattern discrimination indicate even greater dependence upon striate cortex. Complete removal of the rat's visual cortex produces absolute amnesia for previously learned pattern discriminations, e.g. responding differentially to upright and inverted triangles, and they cannot be relearned. On the other hand, considerable portions of the striate area can be removed without destroying previously learned discriminations (Lashley and Frank, 1934). Apparently, pattern discriminations are retained as long as there is enough cortex left to represent the relevant characteristics of the stimuli in some portion of the visual field.

Actually, our notions as to what behaviors are 'higher order' functions are not based upon reliable criteria, and this is brought out emphatically here. We would, for example, consider *transposition of discrimination* (response to relations among stimuli) a 'higher order' function. Suppose rats are trained to respond to the brighter of two lights and then are tested with a new pair of lights for which the dimmer is now equal in absolute intensity to what was originally the brighter stimulus. Will brain-injured animals fail to show transposition? Hebb (1938 b) found that both normal and brain-injured animals transposed in terms of relative brightness, and this is especially significant since lesions in most cases were such as to completely interrupt projection to the visual cortex. Similarly, we would tend to think of general spatial orientation to objects in the environment as a higher order ability. Yet Hebb (1938 a) reports that both normal and cortically injured rats 'prefer' general orientational cues (e.g. room lighting) to specific visual or other cues (a white card on food box, for example), and there were no clear differences between experimental and control animals in learning on this basis. What about the simple response of following a moving object with the eyes? Surely this is a 'lower level' function. Smith and Warkentin (1939), using graduated white strips moving against a black ground as the stimulus and the optic nystagmus as the response, found cats lacking visual cortex to have as fine acuity thresholds as normal animals—i.e. the resolving power of the subcortical visual system equals that of the cortex—but the 'simple' response of following a *single* moving stripe with the eyes was clearly disturbed.

Comparative Data

Comparative data are not extensive enough to justify any very definite conclusions. Following complete removal of visual cortex, the dog shows amnesia for previously mastered brightness discriminations, but they can be relearned in about the same number of trials (Marquis, 1934). These findings are essentially similar to those for the rat. The monkey lacking visual cortex seems to lose its capacity to respond to brightness differences, reacting rather in terms of the total light entering the eyes (Klüver, 1941). In cases in which the visual areas of the cortex in man have been accidentally destroyed, the patient is completely blind; restricted lesions in the striate cortex produce *scotomata,* sharply localized blind spots whose positions in the visual field depend precisely upon the locus of cortical injury, but no visual habits (discriminations, pattern perceptions, etc.) are lost in this case. The evidence, such as it is, points to increasing encephalization as we progress along the vertebrate series.

Summary

(1) In the mediation of simple light-dark discriminations for all mammals except the primates, subcortical visual mechanisms can function vicariously although the visual cortex is normally utilized. (2) There is evidence for mass-action (and hence equipotentiality) *in the rat* with respect to visual discrimination learning, but the evidence is not consistent: Lashley finds efficiency of *relearning* related to the amount of remaining *visual* cortex, whereas Ghiselli finds efficiency of *original learning* related to the amount of remaining *total cortex* (independent of locus). The difference here may reflect a more difficult discrimination, and hence less dependence upon visual as compared with learning functions, in Ghiselli's case. (3) With more

difficult discriminations in general, including pattern discriminations, there is evidence for more strict localization of function within the visual cortex— these performances cannot be relearned following complete extirpation of the visual areas.

Conditioning and Discrimination Situations Compared

The fact that conditioned reactions show replication of function between cortex and subcortex while simple discrimination learning shows vicarious functioning is clear enough from the experimental data, but this is an extremely puzzling state of affairs when looked at psychologically. Even the most restricted CR requires some degree of discrimination among stimuli if the reaction is to be distinctively associated with the correct cue: the light or the buzzer must be discriminated from the rest of the stimulating situation if the correct response is to occur only when that cue appears. Just what, then, is the difference between this situation and simple light-dark discrimination learning?

Wing (1946, 1947) has recently given special attention to this problem. Two hypotheses were tested experimentally: (1) that the difference between results for conditioning and discrimination studies is attributable to the type of *motivational situation* (typically shock-avoidance in CR studies and food reward in discrimination studies); (2) that the difference is attributable to what he terms the need for retention of the *significance* of two stimuli in the discrimination problem. Following the learning of hind-leg flexion to certain light stimuli, varying amounts of visual cortex were removed from different dog subjects. To test the 'motivational' hypothesis, one set of animals (1946) was trained with shock as the unconditioned stimulus and the other (1947) was trained with a food reward for correct response. To test the 'significance' hypothesis, some of the animals in each group learned to respond to the simple onset of a light stimulus as the conditional stimulus, while others were required to respond only to an increase (or decrease, with some animals) in the intensity of a continuously present light. Presumably the latter subjects had to appreciate the significance of the direction of stimulus change, beyond the mere presence or absence of light.

Because of the varied treatment given each of some 25 dogs, both surgically and experimentally, the results of this series of investigations are hard to interpret. For all animals, reactions to both onset of light and simple change in intensity were retained postoperatively, and we conclude that the differences between shock and food training conditions were not significant. Reversal tests, with the direction of intensity change altered, were given to determine whether animals had retained the significance of the stimulus relationship. Dogs that had not suffered complete removal of the visual cortex showed little disturbance of discrimination on these tests; whether there was any relation here to the extent of lesion cannot be ascertained since Wing does not report the magnitudes of the incomplete lesions. Dog #12 (shock condition) and dogs #15, #20, and #21 (food condition) suffered complete removal of visual cortex, *and all of these animals failed to retain the significance of the direction of intensity change.* Notice that in these cases the animal retains its CR to a change in intensity, but responds indiscriminately with respect to the direction of change. Since the lesions of the animals subjected to incomplete visual decortication were varied in locus, it seems probable that the visual areas are equipotential with respect to this 'significance' function. The nature of this 'significance' function remains to be elaborated (e.g. whether it is related to the representational mediation processes discussed in Chap. 9).

INSTRUMENTAL LEARNING

Manipulative Skills

Most of the discrimination situations used above are also cases of simple instrumental learning, and therefore one would expect both sets of data to fall along a continuum. Working with comparatively simple latch-box problems (Lashley, 1920, 1935 *a*), rats deprived of relatively large amounts of cortex (up to 50 per cent) covering all regions of the neopallium were found to *learn* as readily as, in fact better than, normal animals. On the other hand, postoperative *retention* of these habits was severely impaired by ablation of as little as 30 per cent of the total cortex, provided destruction was in the frontal 'motor' areas. Like much of the data on brightness discrimination, this evidence points to vicarious functioning of other regions (probably subcortical) for the frontal cortex when it is destroyed. When latch-box problems requiring more distinctive manipulative movements, such as tearing a strip of paper or pulling a chain, were used (Lashley, 1935 *a*), the results more closely resembled those obtained with difficult discrimination problems: smaller cortical lesions caused observable impairment in original learning and degree of disturbance was correlated with size of lesion independent of locus (mass-action). No test for transoperational retention of these manipulative skills, following removal of frontal cortex, was made.

Maze-learning

A still more complex, serially integrated performance is maze-running. Lashley (1929) has studied this type of behavior intensively, using three enclosed mazes of graded difficulty (1 cul-de-sac, 3 culs-de-sac, and 8 culs-de-sac). For all three mazes, *initial learning* by brain-injured rats was significantly inferior to that of normal controls—yet the same animals showed no disturbance in learning a light-dark discrimination problem given at the same time. Since tests carried out over a period of from 45 to 189 days after operation (equivalent to 7 to 15 years of human life) showed no recovery, these results cannot be attributed to operational shock or any diaschistic effect. Using the most difficult maze and another group of animals, tests for *transoperational retention* were made: for lesions exceeding 15 per cent of the cortex, irrespective of locus, there was measurable amnesia. Since *both* original learning and retention of the maze habits are disturbed by cortical lesions, we conclude that certain functions essential to maze-learning are 'localized' in the cortex. To clinch this interpretation, one would have to show that total removal of the cortex completely destroys this habit and the possibility of its relearning. In the present experiment, unfortunately, surgery involved only 80 per cent of the cortex (original learning group) and 51 per cent (retention group) as a maximum.

But in what manner is maze-learning 'localized' in the cortex of the rat? Lashley concludes that the entire cortex has some *mass-function* with respect to this performance: for both original learning and retention, degree

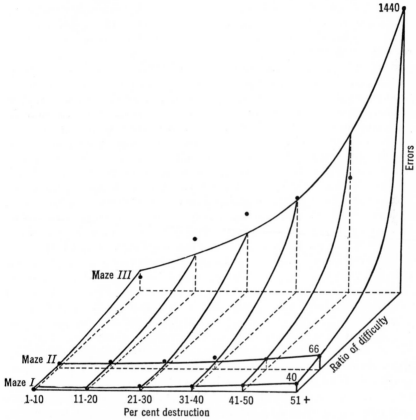

FIGURE 156. Three-dimensional graphs showing how errors in maze learning vary cumulatively with both maze complexity and amount of destruction of cerebral tissue. Lashley, *Brain Mechanisms and Intelligence,* University of Chicago Press, Chicago, 1929, p. 74.

of impairment was correlated with extent of injury but independent of its locus. Figure 156 describes this relation between size of lesion and impairment. Notice also that the degree to which impairment correlates with extent of lesion varies with the difficulty of the maze task. Lashley and Wiley (1933), although confirming the general mass-action hypothesis, have failed to obtain the relation between maze difficulty and degree of mass-functioning; however, their mazes, ranging from 4 to 16 culs-de-sac, were not of the same type used in the original Lashley study. Lashley's general conclusion (1929) is as follows: 'The learning process and the retention of habits are not dependent upon any finely localized structural changes within the cerebral cortex. . . Integration cannot be expressed in terms of connections between specific neurones. . . There is not a summation of diverse functions, but a non-specialized dynamic function of the tissue as a whole' (p. 176).

Criticism of the Mass-action Hypothesis

This conclusion applies better to the maze habit than either simple instrumental responses or light-dark discrimination, since retention of the latter is selectively impaired by lesions in frontal and occipital cortex, respectively. Furthermore, it stands in flat contradiction to a great deal of evidence favoring localization of function. From the original work of Fritsch and Hitzig in 1870 on electrical stimulation of the exposed cortex, through the detailed researches of Sherrington, Penfield, and others, there has developed imposing evidence for strict localization within the so-called 'excitable' areas. Within the motor projection areas (extending along the central sulcus, anterior to it), movements of specific groups of somatic muscles can be elicited by electrical stimulation; within the sensory projection areas (somesthetic posterior to central sulcus, auditory in the temporal regions of both hemispheres, and visual in the occipital poles), electrical stimulation induces appropriate sensory auras. There are other cortical regions, chiefly in the prefrontal and temporal lobes, where electrical stimulation fails to produce any effects—these are the so-called 'associational' areas (however, cf. recent work of Penfield and Rasmussen, 1950).

Hunter (1930) has attempted to bring Lashley's data on maze-learning into line with this body of evidence on localization, and in doing so has offered an alternative interpretation to that of mass-action. Reviewing the literature on sensory controls in maze-learning (incl. Vincent, 1915; Hunter, 1920, 1929; Dashiel, 1930), he concludes that 'the maze habit is controlled by a multiplicity of sensory cues . . . [and] in the absence of any one cue the control of the behavior shifts to those that remain' (p. 464). Now if the maze habit were controlled by discriminations within a single sensory modality (as is the light-dark habit), one might expect its retention to be impaired by lesions within a limited area (as is the case with brightness discrimination). With the maze habit controlled equivalently by many modalities (vision, touch, kinesthesis, smell, audition), Hunter assumes that lesions should interrupt increasing numbers of these equivalent pathways as a function of their extent, thus yielding Lashley's type of result. But if this were in fact the case—if the various sense modalities were equivalent—why is there any loss in retention for most lesions, which do not affect all sensory projection fields? Hunter's answer would probably be that reactive tendencies vary in proportion to the number of sensory channels preserved after injury.

The critical question here is this: Do sensory cortical fields contribute any general facilitation to learning above and beyond pure sensory control? Since sensory functions can be eliminated by destroying peripheral receptors as well as by extirpating cortex, the crucial test is to compare the effect of cortical lesions with equivalent receptor 'lesions.' Using a small number of animals Lashley (1929) found that blinding, by enucleation of the eyes after learning the maze, did not affect retention significantly; on the other hand, when *blind* animals learned the maze and were then subjected to destruction in the *visual* cortex, the habit was lost in proportion to the size of lesion, as had been the case with seeing animals. Tsang (1934) working in Lashley's laboratory, has obtained similar results: striate lesions caused greater impairment in both original learning and retention of maze habits than blinding. Animals blind from birth also showed significant impairment from lesions in the visual cortex (Tsang, 1935). Finley (1941) criticized these experiments on the ground that the lesions often went beyond the limits of the striate areas, thereby causing additional sensory disturbances. In her own experimental work, lesions in the striate cortex were found to produce no more disturbance than blinding, but in this case they were generally smaller than the visual area.

In a yet more recent investigation along these lines, Lashley (1943) has attempted to answer the criticism that lesions in the visual cortex large enough to produce significant decrement also invade nonvisual cortical areas and various subcortical areas. When rats subjected to sectioning of the posterior radiations (pathways from thalamus to visual cortex) plus damage in nonvisual cortical areas were compared with rats subjected to peripheral blinding, no significant difference in performance on mazes was found. On the other hand, total destruction of the visual cortex, admittedly including some damage to other structures, produced deterioration at least ten times as great as that following peripheral blinding. It is apparent that this test, although crucial theoretically, is difficult to execute and interpret experimentally. Even were the rat cortex shown to be highly equipotential, and to follow a principle of mass-action with respect to such complex functions as maze-learning, this would not necessarily indicate that the same degree of flexibility characterizes cortical tissue in higher organisms. Structural differentiation within the cortex increases tremendously between rat and man, and it would not be surprising to find more localization of function on this basis.

Qualitative Effects

The instrumental learning behavior of brain-injured rats also shows certain qualitative changes, one prominent characteristic being *lack of variability*. Lashley mentions this casually at several points, and Krechevsky has studied it more thoroughly. Using Dashiel's checkerboard maze, in which some 20 different paths of about equal length can be taken to the same goal (Krechevsky, 1937 *a*), rats with even minor cortical injury (10 per cent) show significantly less variability in choice of path, and reduction in variability is found to be covariant with extent of lesion and independent of locus (i.e. mass-action). If, in a choice situation, two alternate paths are equally rewarded with food but one (standard path) is constant in form while the other (variable path) is deliberately changed in form from trial to trial, cortically injured animals tend to select the stable path (1937 *b*). If, however, the stable path is made much longer than the variable path, there is no difference between brain-injured and control animals. In other words, the preference of the operated animal for a stereotyped path is reversible when the difference in goal-obtaining efficiency is gross—which is reminiscent of the results for easy versus difficult discrimination learning.

NATURE OF ASSOCIATIONS

In an earlier chapter we inquired into what is essential *psychologically* for the formation of an association. The question now is, What is essential *neurologically?* Where, in the complicated sequence of events between stimulation of receptors and movements of muscle, does the modification representing a new association occur? Nearly all the experiments designed to attack this problem have employed the conditioning paradigm—for the simple reason that this arbitrarily reduced learning situation permits more rigorous specification and manipulation of variables (*CS, US, UR, CR*). The logic of experimentation runs like this: if a given component in the associational sequence can be eliminated and conditioning still occurs, that component is not essential; if a given component is eliminated and conditioning regularly fails to occur, that component is essential.

Afferent Pathways

Direct stimulation of the receptors normally utilized by *CS* and *US* is not essential for learning. One may intercept the projection system anywhere along the pathways from receptor to cortex, if appropriate techniques are available. Loucks (1934) has devised one such method for stimulating various portions of the nervous system in intact, unanesthetized animals. A sterile, collodion-coated coil is buried beneath the skin and silver wire electrodes from the coil are placed in contact with the desired neural structures. The buried coil can then be activated by bringing it within the field of a primary coil held outside the skin (induction), faradic stimulation of the nerve tissue resulting. Loucks (1938) demonstrated that such faradic stimulation of the visual cortex of dogs could be substituted for the normal visual *CS* in the formation of conditioned leg flexion. The behavior of the animals was interesting: 'In the case of dog 1, "Sport," cortical shock (field 19) tended to elicit a blink in both eyes. After about the first ten days of training, this response became very infrequent. . . Cortical shock in the case of dog 3, "Droopy" (field 18), was followed almost invariably by a sharp turn of the animal's head, somewhat as if he were looking intently at an object in his lower quadrant of vision. This persisted through the first three weeks of training. Thereafter, it appeared only irregularly' (p. 323).

Interception of the pathways normally utilized by the *US* can be accomplished in the same manner, and similar results are obtained. Using a buzzer as *CS*, Loucks and Gantt (1938) were able to substitute faradic stimulation of afferent neurons in the spinal column for *US*. Although some animals conditioned readily, others gave no evidence of the formation of the new association until the intensity of electrical stimulation was raised greatly—this despite the fact that reflexive movements were elicited at the original intensity. The conclusion drawn was that faradization of the cord serves as an adequate *US* only when it sets up impulses in pain fibers. Carrying the *US* still higher in the central system, Brogden and Gantt (1937) have obtained conditioning when the reinforcing stimulus is electrical excitation in the lateral cerebellar lobes. From evidence such as this, we may conclude that, on the afferent side at least, the locus of the modifications necessary for association are subsequent to the peripheral receptive and projective systems.

Efferent Pathways

The status of the efferent side of association is not so clear. Several studies indicate that the mere occurrence of the motor response in conjunction with the new stimulus is *not a sufficient condition* for learning. Hilgard and Allen (1938), for example, found it impossible to condition a finger retraction movement when it was produced by electrical stimulation of the peripheral motor neurons. Loucks (1935) had found the same thing true when hind-leg movement was produced by faradic stimulation of the motor cortex (buried coil technique); no sign of conditioning to a buzzer appeared in any of three dogs in over 600 trials. But here, now, was a truly puzzling observation: if, under exactly the same stimulus conditions, each hind-leg movement was followed by a *food reward,* the buzzer-flexion association was readily formed. Why should food reinforcement *after* each electrically induced movement serve to weld buzzer sound and flexion movement together? This seems to be a case of what was earlier termed 'passive conditioning,' the correct response being produced by the experimenter rather than via the subject's own reflexive system. Loucks interprets it as a case of backward conditioning involving the proprioceptive cues caused by the leg movements. It is possible that the shock-induced movement was incidental to the actual learning process; the dog could have been selectively learning through ordinary trial-and-error procedures, the only effective trials being those on which the animal happened to react via its own sensorimotor system. To check this possibility, one would want to compare the rate of learning here with that of the same animals under ordinary trial-and-error conditions.

Although occurrence of the motor response in conjunction with the conditional stimulus may not be a sufficient condition for learning, *is it one necessary condition?* In other words, is it possible for associations to be formed *without* motor movement? This question is critical for the general controversy between 'centralists' and 'peripheralists' over whether or not purely central or cortical associations can be formed (cf. pp. 653-4). Light and Gantt (1936) eliminated the possibility of motor reaction in one hind limb by crushing the roots of its motor nerves. Training then consisted of paired presentation of buzzer (*CS*) and shock to the paw of the denervated hind limb (*US*). All dogs were carefully observed for signs of spontaneous recovery of capacity for movement of this member, and conditioning training was ended as soon as the first signs appeared. That conditioning had occurred without movement was indicated by flexion responses to *CS* alone following complete recovery of function. Kellogg, Scott, Davis, and Wolf (1940) duplicated these procedures, however, using a more careful recording method, and they showed the *CR* in this case to be a generalized avoidance pattern, involving autonomic as well as gross motor components. It is quite possible, therefore, that the specific flexion movement of the injured limb occurred after recovery either as part of an integrated avoidance pattern (established in ordinary experience previous to experiment) or was mediated by stimuli produced by these other reactions.

It is also possible to approach these problems through the use of certain drugs. When salivation is produced by injection of pilocarpine, which affects the glandular mechanism directly, conditioning of this reaction to a neutral stimulus cannot be obtained (Finch, 1938 *a*) ; when salivation is produced by injection of morphine, which acts upon central mechanisms, conditioning is readily established (Kleitman and Crisler, 1927). This evidence shows that the peripheral response is not sufficient for learning, but is it necessary? Crisler (1930) paralyzed the salivary gland with atropine and then gave conditioning training by pairing a neutral stimulus (*CS*) with injection of morphine (*US*). After recovery from the effects of atropine, conditioned salivation to the originally neutral stimulus was demonstrated. This experiment has been criticized on the same grounds as the Light and Gantt study on crushed motor roots—salivation may be part of a general nausea reaction induced by morphine. More recently, Girden (1943) has used erythroidine (a drug with effects similar to curare) to either completely or partially paralyze striated muscle, and he observed both somatic (striate muscle reaction) and autonomic (blood pressure and pulse rate) components of the response to shock. When training was in the deep-state (complete somatic paralysis), subsequent tests revealed that only autonomic reactions had been conditioned; when training was in the light-state and subsequent test for conditioning in the deep-state (but with the semitendinosus muscle isolated from the paralysis by ligature), both somatic and autonomic components showed the effects of conditioning. Girden concludes that muscular reactions must be made during training if they are to be incorporated within the learned pattern.

The reason for difference in the results of these experiments remains to be resolved in future research. Even were it demonstrated conclusively that neither peripheral sensory nor peripheral motor components are essential for the formation of associations, this should not come as any great surprise to the psychologist. One major point, seemingly glossed over by most investigators in this area, is that the conditioned reaction is seldom if ever identical with the unconditioned reaction. Another is that animals transfer readily from one type of stimulus to another and from one type of overt response to others equivalent in achieving the same goals. Psychological evidence of this sort certainly points to some mediating process as the crucial thing learned, and the neural representation of this process as the essential modification is the real problem. The burden on neurologizing is therefore a heavy one, and no simple answer would be expected.

Association Pathways

This leads one quite naturally to ask if there is any evidence for an 'association pathway' formed in learning. Indeed, we may be forced to postulate such pathways more or less through a process of elimination (cf. Hilgard and Marquis, 1940, p. 324ff.). Direct experimental evidence, however, is practically nonexistent. Culler (1938 *b*) trained a dog to flex its leg to a tone, this response being elicited by shock and observed in the semitendinosus muscle. Once conditioning was well established, the surface of the cortex contralateral to the trained leg was explored electrically. A small spot, not more than 2 mm. square, was discovered within which an electrical stimulus would produce the response. This spot was neither in auditory nor somesthetic projection areas, nor was it in the motor area for leg flexion—it was in a bordering 'association' area. Control tests showed that before conditioning this spot did not yield flexion, and it had lost its excitatory capacity after extinction. Here we have evidence for precise localization of a *learned* modification in association areas of the cortex, but it is the only evidence of this type and has only been reported in brief, abstract form.

GENERAL SUMMARY

One would like to conclude this survey of neural functions in learning with a clean-cut statement of definite principles, but the evidence does not permit. The best one can do is to express certain general impressions gathered in course. The evolution of the cortex in relation to subcortical systems is best described in terms of *the principle of encephalization:* from a relatively undifferentiated sheet of tissue displaying total, dynamogenic functions (a status approached in the rat), there has been progressive structural differentiation of cortex accompanied by increasingly strict localization of function within this medium (a status best demonstrated in primates). In line with this view, different areas of the human cortex can be clearly recognized on the basis of their microstructure but this is much less true for the rat. Even in primates, however, it is likely that equipotentiality and mass-action *within* localized regions of the cortex have been retained despite increasing differentiation of structure *between* regions. Both localized projection (and association) and mass-action can be synchronous functions of the cortex in higher organisms: the well-developed cortex is a multilayered affair, including both deeper lying projection fibers relating this structure to subcortical systems and the more superficial lying matwork of tangential 'association' fibers.

How do various types of demonstrable relation between cortex and subcortex fit this picture? (1) *Localization of function within subcortical systems accompanied by dynamogenic action of cortical tissue.* Although none of the learning functions we have studied fit this most primitive type of relation, it does apply to many reflexive activities. With regard to postural mechanisms, for example, extirpation of certain cortical areas has been shown to remove general facilitative or inhibitory neural inputs to peripheral reflexive systems and thus modify their tonus, even though these reflexive systems are organized subcortically (cf. Magoun and Rhines, 1948). (2) *Replication between cortical and subcortical systems accompanied by general dynamogenic action of cortex.* With greater differentiation of cortical tissues, functions begin to be organized within them in addition to the more primitive level of integration, i.e. two strings to the neurological bow are provided, and the dynamogenic action is preserved. This type of relation describes the data on simple conditioned reactions as obtained with both ablation and curare techniques. (3) *Vicarious functioning of subcortical for cortical systems, dynamogenic action becoming restricted to within localized cortical regions.* At this level, functions are 'normally' organized within specific regions of a more highly diversified cortex, but subcortical systems, when released from cortical 'dominance,' are still able to take over vicariously. Data for simple light-dark discrimination and relatively unskilled latch-box problems in the rat fit this picture. (4) *Localization of function in specific regions of the cortex and restriction of dynamogenesis to within these regions.* At this level of encephalization, lower centers have 'lost' their capacity to mediate certain functions, and hence the cortex is essential for their performance; the more primitive mass-action of a labile cortex now appears only within those regions whose microstructure makes possible equipotentiality. The evidence for difficult and pattern discriminations and for skilled manipulatory motor problems in the rat, brightness discrimination involving reaction to the 'significance' of stimuli in the dog, and all visual functions in the primate implies this sort of organization.

To adequately interpret the evidence, it must be kept in mind that we find different species at different stages along this evolutionary route to encephalization. With maze-learning in the rat, for example, there was evidence for both localization of function within the cortex (both original learning and retention were permanently disturbed by cortical lesions) and for mass-action of the entire cortex (degree of disturbance was shown to be independent of cortical locus). We are dealing here with the learning of a complex, serially integrated performance *by an organism whose cortical structures are relatively undifferentiated.* In this case, although the complex integrations which cortical tissues make possible are essential, these integrations are either diversely replicated throughout the cortex or these tissues function in some 'field' fashion, a situation presumably determined by the lack of differentiation within rat cortex. An analogous type of organization seems to apply to visual perception in primates: the visual cortex is essential *and* it seems to function equipotentially with respect to retention. As was pointed out earlier, performances equivalent to maze-learning in the rat have yet to be studied systematically in the primate. When this is done, one expects that equipotentiality *within* localized areas of the cortex will be demonstrated (possibly within the so-called 'association' areas). Again the reader must be cautioned that these generalizations are entirely provisional in nature.

Chapter 12

SERIAL AND TRANSFER PHENOMENA

Instrumental skill sequences are the stuff of which behavior is made. When a young man learns a new dance step, or a rat learns the path through a maze, it is not an isolated habit that is being repeated but rather a sequence of varied activities. If skill is to be attained, control must first be shifted from external to self-produced cues and thence to some 'programing' system in the higher centers. Only then can the dancer spin smoothly and effortlessly through his routine and the rat spin errorlessly through the maze. A similar situation holds for human verbal skills. In learning to say new words (viz. Constantinople) or to run through the multiplication tables, for example, various phonetic skill components become welded. Try to reel off the alphabet *backward*—it soon becomes apparent that the links are not so strong in the backward as in the forward direction. Our first task in this chapter will be to investigate the phenomena that characterize the learning of such temporally integrated skills. This is behavioral organization on a short-term basis. In the second half of this chapter we will study interactions among learned activities which occur on a long-term basis.

SERIAL LEARNING IN ANIMAL SUBJECTS

It is convenient to think of behavior sequences as driven by particular combinations of motives, composed of integrated patterns of instrumental responses, and terminated by some form of reinforcement. Such sequences vary almost infinitely in length, from the hungry-rat-sees-bar-presses-and-receives-pellet to the interminable activities that may or may not result in achieving a scientific or artistic goal. Of course, long-term sequences must be frequently punctuated by subgoals, or they are not persisted in. These subgoals become signs of the primary goal, providing both a reward for work already done and an incentive for further efforts. Investigations carried on in the laboratory are extendable to such life purposes only by analogy, their scope being necessarily more modest. The analogy, however, is compelling—to speak of one's life as a maze may be trite but it is not entirely inappropriate.

The situation in the animal laboratory that best represents serial integration of varied activities is the *maze*. As would be expected in a complex situation like this, all of the principles of any theory, such as Hull's, would be involved in one way or another. The probability of one turn at a choice point as against another will depend upon the relative strengths of competing habits, which in turn will depend upon temporal and other factors as they affect reinforcement. Generalization and discrimination factors will be introduced as similarity relations among stimulus choice points and response behaviors are manipulated. Suppose, for example, we have a simple linear maze with a succession of crossing pathways at right angles and food placed at the end of the fourth left turn. If the choice points are made as identical as possible physically, this situation proves insoluble for the rat (which cannot count); it persists in making *anticipatory errors* on the left side of the maze, even though it rapidly eliminates right-turning errors. Why? Whenever a left-turning response is made at choice point 4, it is strongly reinforced; owing to the similarity between choice points 4 and 3 and 2, the left-turning tendency generalizes to these earlier positions and causes errors. The fact that there is some discrimination based upon self-produced proprioceptive cues (e.g. the pile-up of traces from its own running movements) produces a gradient of errors on the left side, which increases for choice points nearer the correct turn. This, however, is not a typical situation.

The Goal Gradient and Maze-learning

What would happen if we purposely made the choice points as dissimilar as possible? Since discrimination would be much easier, the tendency to make anticipatory errors should be reduced. But how *would* errors be distributed? Figure 157 shows a multiple T-maze comprising four choice points. We shall assume that these choice points are sufficiently distinctive, that reinforcement is terminal (i.e. food is given only in the goal-box), and, for convenience in analysis, that the average rat takes 5 seconds to run each segment (this last assumption is actually contrary to fact, since goal gradients have been shown to affect running speed, but this will not change our analysis). We may symbolize the patterns of stimuli associated with the several choice points as S_1, S_2, S_3, and S_4 and the turning reactions as R_L and R_R, the correct sequence being *RLLR*. Now, according to reinforcement theory, the size of an increment to habit strength varies inversely with the delay in reinforcement. Thus an S–R connection made near the point of terminal reward will receive greater strengthening than one made far away. In a spatial maze situation like this, what is psychologically a 'time' difference faithfully reflects a physical 'space' difference. Since the tendency to make errors (enter blind alleys) is inversely related to the strength of correct associations, it follows that errors will be eliminated most rapidly near the goal and least rapidly near the starting point.

But too much is being taken for granted here. We cannot expect our rat subjects to *always* make the correct response at each choice point. Suppose an animal makes a right turn at S_2—since it must eventually wind up in the goal-box, this error is also reinforced. How, then, can the differentiation we call learning take place? Further analysis clarifies this situation: Whenever the rat enters a blind alley, time is used up in running in and then retracing (again, for convenience, we shall assume the full extent of the blind to be explored and that this process takes 10 seconds). This will mean that, other things being equal, an erroneous response at a choice point will be followed by reinforcement 10 seconds later than if the correct response had been made. At S_4, for example, the correct response (R_R) is followed by reinforcement after only 5 seconds, whereas the wrong response (R_L) is followed by reinforcement after 15 seconds. This is a 3/1 ratio favoring the correct response. Assuming there is some oscillation in the rat's behavior, there will be a gradual differential strengthening of the correct response

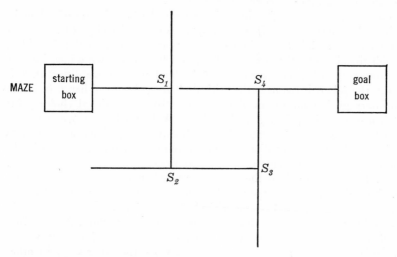

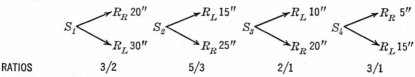

FIGURE 157. Hypothetical maze having equal distance between choice points. Middle portion of the figure gives delays in reinforcement consequent upon correct and incorrect choices, assuming that the subject fully explores the blind alley and that its subsequent choices are correct. Bottom line gives ratios of reinforcement deriving from correct as compared with incorrect choices throughout the maze.

even though several wrong reactions may be made at first (and strengthened). Notice also that magnitude of the ratio favoring the correct response must steadily decrease with distance from the goal, in the present instance from 3/1 (S_4), to 2/1 (S_3), to 5/3 (S_2), to 3/2 (S_1).

We have, then, two related reasons for expecting a backward elimination of errors in serial learning: (1) the *absolute magnitude* of the reinforcing effect decreases with distance (time) from the goal; (2) the *ratio* in strengthening correct versus erroneous reactions also decreases with distance (time) from the goal. Generalizing this analysis to serial performances of all types, it may be predicted that learning will be most effective near the point of terminal reinforcement and become progressively more difficult toward the points of origin of such behavior sequences. This is called the *goal gradient* by Hull, and the general lines of his analysis (1932 and elsewhere) have been followed here. By not taking *secondary reinforcement* into account, however, this analysis assumed a condition that probably never exists. Since principles of behavior cannot be turned on or off to suit our pleasure, various distinctive stimuli along the path to any terminal goal must acquire the properties of subgoals. The stimulus complex at S_4 will come to evoke not only a right-turning response but also anticipatory lip-licking, salivating, and so on. Similarly, choice point S_3, in its turn, will begin to acquire secondary reinforcing value. In short, serial learning includes the setting up of a sequence of subgoals.

Numerous experiments provide evidence for the functioning of subgoals, but all of them need not be cited. By way of example, Kendler (1943) compared groups X and Y (rats) in a short/long path discrimination in which, although the absolute distances for short and long paths were identical for both groups, the distances to the subgoal (final turn) were different. For group X the subgoal was near the critical choice point (and hence far from the primary goal); for group Y it was far from the critical choice point (and hence near the primary goal). Group X learned the maze with significantly greater ease. Although this result can be 'explained' ex post facto as owing to the more immediate secondary reinforcement for these animals, it would have been extremely difficult to predict this result, as Kendler realizes. Here we run into the oft-encountered difficulty of two or more competing principles, neither of which can be rigorously quantified. Whereas the nearness of the subgoal to the critical choice point for the group X subjects would facilitate differentiation (as expected and found), the fact that this subgoal was itself farther away from the point of primary reinforcement for group X than for group Y should work the other way. In other words, the secondary reinforcing values of the subgoals are themselves learned—and learned in accordance with some goal gradient function. In this particular case it seems likely that some similarity factors (generalization) between primary and subgoals were such as to override distance-time factors. Just the opposite result was obtained by Spence and Grice (1942). Although the final common path could be increased in length, thereby decreasing correct/incorrect reinforcement ratios throughout the maze, the final turn (subgoal) was at a constant distance from choice points. This time difficulty in mastering the maze increased with the distance of the primary goal, indicating that the reinforcing value of a subgoal must itself be learned according to a goal gradient function.

For most practical purposes it makes no difference in serial learning whether reinforcement is assumed to be according to a goal gradient generated at the locus of the primary goal or at various subgoals, because subgoals acquire their reinforcing properties according to their distance from the terminal goal, except in so far as similarity factors may distort the gradient. It is also true that subgoals may extend the goal gradient almost infinitely in time. After our sample maze is well learned, a new maze might be mastered on the basis of the rat's eventuating in S_1 of the original path. Anthropomorphizing, one could say that the rat likes to find itself in the friendly surroundings of the familiar, reward-signifying maze. We experience the same thing when, after stumbling about dark and unfamiliar streets, we suddenly come upon the lighted corner three blocks from home.

Utilizing the goal gradient hypothesis, Hull (1932) has made a number of predictions: (1) *Animals will tend to choose the shorter of two alternate paths to the same goal.* The response of turning into the shorter route is followed more promptly by reinforcement. (2) *Long blinds will be eliminated more readily than short ones.* Since a long blind takes longer to traverse, it constitutes a longer path to the goal. (3) *The order of elimination of blind alleys will be in a backward direction from the goal.* The basis for this prediction has already been given. (4) *Animals will move at a progressively faster pace as the goal is approached.* The association of locomotor responses with environmental cues follows the same gradient, and latency is one correlate of habit strength. Such a speed-of-locomotion gradient has been demonstrated empirically (Hull, 1934 c). If we now add to this picture the effects to be expected from conditioning of anticipatory goal reactions, it can further be predicted that (5) *animals will tend to slow down in the final sections of a maze.* The self-produced stimulation from anticipatory goal reactions is distinctively associated with eating behavior and stationary posture (the sight of a barrier approached at high speed is also a sign of painful bumps on the nose!). (6) *Blinds involving the same turning response as subsequent correct turns* (particularly the final goalward turn) *will be harder to eliminate than blinds involving other responses.* This follows from the tendency to short-circuit reinforced reactions to antedating stimuli, as already discussed. Of course, all such predictions are predicated upon the statement 'other things being equal.' Spence (1932) has demonstrated the empirical validity of many of these predictions.

The goal gradient hypothesis has come in for its share of criticism on both theoretical and empirical grounds. In many cases empirical criticism—that the results obtained with a particular maze pattern do not comply with the goal gradient hypothesis—has been predicated on the assumption that this is the *only* mechanism operating in serial-learning. We have already seen that the tendency to make anticipatory goal reactions can pile up errors in a blind that requires the same turning response as the final choice point; Spence and Shipley (1934) have shown that this latter tendency is stronger as mastery is approached (i.e. when short-circuiting mechanisms have had a chance to operate), whereas the simple goal gradient is more apparent in early trials. Another added factor is what has been called 'centrifugal swing' (Schneirla, 1929; Ballachey and Buel, 1934 a)—the inertia of body movements tends to favor certain on-going paths rather than sharp turns. There is also a tendency to orient toward the location of the goal-box (Ballachey and Buel, 1934 b), particularly with open-type mazes in which orientational cues are available. Buel (1938) has made a detailed criticism of the goal gradient hypothesis from the point of view of a Tolman-type theory.

One of the more convincing criticisms of Hull's formulation appears in experiments by Berg and Weisman (1942). In one study the distance of the goal from the final turn was constant for one group, varied at random for a second, and *used to compensate for errors* with a third group of rats (i.e. the goal-box was shifted nearer upon the occurrence of each error, keeping delay of reinforcement roughly constant). There were no significant differences between groups. In another study one group was 'rewarded' for making errors (by overcompensating with the adjustable goal-box), another group was 'punished' for making errors (by moving the goal-box even farther away), and a third group served as control. Again, there were no differences. The development of *subgoals* may provide a partial explanation. The last choice point was regularly followed by food-taking activities in the goal-box (although admittedly after varying intervals) and the distance of this subgoal was not manipulated in these studies. The amount of secondary reinforcing property generated depends upon the similarity (generalization) of secondary and primary goal situations rather than upon temporal interval per se.

Merely because primary and secondary mechanisms may combine to yield a goal gradient in serial learning does not mean they are of the same order and indistinguishable. The difference is brought out in an experiment by Epstein and Morgan (1943). Hull (1934 c) had demonstrated that the rat's speed-of-locomotion gradient is most prominent during the early trials; the terminal retardation (which he attributed to effects of short-circuited anticipatory goal reactions) appears more slowly. Epstein and Morgan compared the performance of normal rats with rats that had suffered lesions in the prefrontal cortex. The brain-injured animals displayed the typical goal gradient *but never developed any terminal retardation.* 'The experiment confirms . . . the hypothesis that the fractional goal reaction in maze behavior involves symbolic processes, and that such processes are mediated by the prefrontal cortical areas of the rat' (p. 462). It is unfortunate that other mechanisms commonly held to be dependent upon anticipatory goal reactions, such as subgoal formation, were not also studied here.

Serial Chaining of Instrumental Responses

In recent years Hull and his students began designing even more elaborate analyses of serial learning, using a situation somewhat different from the standard maze. A multiple choice straightaway was used, each segment of which consisted of an entrance and a choice point—four valves in a line, only one of which could be pushed through by the rat. In the case of *homogeneous* serial learning, the same door (e.g. #3) in each segment would be correct for a given animal; in *heterogeneous* serial learning, a different door (e.g. #2, #1, #4, #3) in each segment would be correct. Under conditions of *terminal* reinforcement, the rat would receive its pellet of food only after getting through the final valve; with *serial* reinforcement, a pellet would be received beyond each valve. All four possible combinations have been studied:

1. heterogeneous reactions with terminal reinforcement (Hull, 1947)
2. heterogeneous reactions with serial reinforcement (Hull, 1948)
3. homogeneous reactions with terminal reinforcement (Sprow, 1947)
4. homogeneous reactions with serial reinforcement (Gladstone, 1948)

Rather direct comparisons among these studies are possible since identical apparatus and identical general conditions were used.

We may first compare heterogeneous (1 and 2) with homogeneous (3 and 4) conditions. Since the four choice points were physically as identical as possible, a high degree of generalization among them would be anticipated. This should cause interference (negative transfer) when the reactions required at different points are different, but it should cause facilitation (positive transfer) when the reactions are the same throughout. Furthermore, since generalization gradients can be expected to summate more at points #2 and #3 (receiving generalized tendencies from both directions) than at points #1 and #4 (receiving generalized tendencies from only one direction), both interfering and facilitating effects should be maximal at the centers of such serial sequences. These expectations were borne out: both heterogeneous conditions yielded more total errors than the homogeneous conditions, and whereas positions #2 and #3 had relatively the *most* errors in the former conditions, they had the *least* errors in the latter conditions. This can be seen by inspection of the curves in Fig. 158 (these are idealized curves, not actual data, since the results of these studies were not reported in comparable forms—some for final one-fifth of

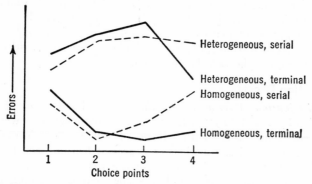

FIGURE 158. Representation of results obtained by Hull *et al.* for serial animal learning under varied conditions of response sequence and reinforcement.

learning, some for total learning, etc.). What are the effects of serial versus terminal reinforcement? Since, according to Hull's theory, a single, backward goal gradient is set up in terminal reinforcement and several summating, backward goal gradients in serial reinforcement, it would be anticipated that terminal reward would shift errors *away* from the final choice point and serial reward shift them *toward* the final choice point (there being least summation of reinforcement at this point). This expectation is also borne out in the data.

Are these results peculiar to spatial situations such as those cited above, in which the animal must locomote from choice point to choice point, or are they characteristic of all serial learning? Arnold (1947 *a, b;* 1948), also working in Hull's laboratory, used the following serial learning setup: The rat is in a small compartment. A series of panels can move successively across one wall of this compartment, each panel containing a manipulandum. The response of the rat in activating each manipulandum releases a clutch which slides in the next panel. Notice that the subject, without moving about spatially, must make a series of reactions. Habit strength was here indexed by reaction latencies. Again, the reactions required successively could be either homogeneous or heterogeneous (by making the manipulanda on the successive panels either identical or different) and the reinforcement could be either serial or terminal. Arnold's results were practically identical with those obtained on the spatial maze. Analogous results will be found for human serial learning (where reactions have always been heterogeneous), to which we now turn.

SERIAL VERBAL LEARNING IN HUMANS

Most experiments on serial learning in humans have used verbal materials. Procedures here are now so well standardized that comparisons across experiments by different investigators can be made, a situation not often reached in psychological research. Lists of 12 nonsense syllables (DOQ, MED, LUM, XOT, etc.) are learned in constant order on a memory drum by what is called the *anticipation method:* each item must be called out before it actually appears in the presentation window of the drum if the response is to be judged correct. Practice is usually continued to some criterion of mastery (e.g. two errorless trials), and, depending on the immediate problem, variations are introduced as experimental variables: the rate of presentation of items may be varied; rest periods may be inserted at certain stages of learning; degrees of similarity among the items, or their meaningfulness, may be varied; and so on.

Serial Position Effects

(1) *Distribution of errors within the series.* This was one of the problems studied by Ward (1937). Lists of 12 nonsense syllables were learned and frequencies of errors (both failures of response and intrusions combined) were computed as functions of degree of learning and locus within the list. For all degrees of learning between zero and mastery, but most marked for moderate degrees, a bow-shaped curve was obtained, items near the center of the list being harder to learn than those at either end. The peak of difficulty is usually a little past the center of the serial list. It will be remembered that this was the type of error curve found to hold for heterogeneous serial learning in rat subjects by Hull and his associates, for either terminal or serial reinforcement.

(2) *Anticipatory and perseverative errors.* Human verbal learning usually provides a clearer opportunity to study the nature of errors than animal learning, because each nonsense syllable is unique and therefore specifiable as to origin. Thus we can categorize errors both as to direction and remoteness from the stimulus syllable. When this is done (cf. Lumley, 1932; McGeoch, 1936 a), the following results are found: (a) Intrusion tendency varies inversely with remoteness in the series, i.e. the further removed one syllable from another, the less likely one is to be intruded in the place of the other, either anticipatorily or perseveratively. (b) Anticipatory errors are more frequent than perseverative ones. (c) But this must be owing to some additional factor operating upon near-anticipatory responses, since remote intrusions are roughly equal in the anticipatory and perseverative categories.

To understand these intrusion characteristics, we must recall certain mechanisms. (a) *Trace conditioning.* Since each item in a verbal series, as a stimulus, leaves a trace that persists in time, not only will the immediately following response (the correct one) become conditioned to this stimulus but so also, in decreasing degree, will more and more remote responses. This mechanism is obviously limited to the production of anticipatory errors (e.g.

each S syllable develops tendencies to elicit R syllables which *follow* the correct one) and is presumably responsible for the greater frequency of anticipatory as compared with perseverative errors. The sharp, negatively accelerated form of this trace function would account for the fact that remote items are not noticeably affected. (b) *Stimulus and response generalization.* Regardless of position in the series, the greater the similarity between items, the more errors caused by generalization. An R syllable associated correctly with a given S syllable will tend to be elicited incorrectly by a similar S syllable earlier or later in the list. This factor does not differentiate between anticipatory and perseverative intrusions.

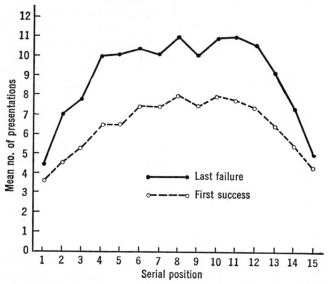

FIGURE 159. Oscillation at the threshold of recall. The gap in mean trials separating first success from last failure is greater in the central portions of a serial list. Hull *et al. Mathematico-deductive Theory of Rote Learning,* Yale University Press, New Haven, 1940, p. 73.

(3) *Oscillation at the threshold of recall.* This phenomenon was described by Hull and his associates in their monograph on rote-learning (1940). The theoretical aspects of this paper will be considered later in this chapter. If the process of learning one item in the series (viz. XOT–HAJ) is analyzed, a sequence of successes and failures such as the following would be observed: $-~-~-+--~-++-~-++++$. Between the first success and the last failure there is a period of oscillation; the strength of the habit is near the threshold of evocation and fluctuates with innumerable factors according to a Gaussian function (cf. Hull's oscillation principle, 1943). With a sufficient number of reinforcements the amount of habit strength becomes such that oscillation only rarely, if ever, will bring the momentary evocation tendency below threshold. When oscillation is measured as a function of serial position, the results shown in Fig. 159 are obtained. Notice that the oscillation range is wider in the center of the list than at either end, indicating that the *rate* of learning is slower here (i.e. increments from successive repetitions are smaller). This will be an important

fact to keep in mind throughout the following analysis of serial learning phenomena.

Similarity Relations

As the similarity between components in a verbal or motor series of acts increases, there is an increasing tendency to substitute one response for another. Since these intrusions count as errors, learning should become more difficult—as long as XOT, XOL, and XET are confused, the subject cannot reach the criterion. But despite the relevance of this homogeneity variable to theory in this field, there is surprisingly little evidence available.

(1) *All-over similarity of materials.* The greater the similarity of choice points in a maze, the greater the generalization among them with resultant anticipatory and perseverative errors. Forward and backward remote associations are the verbal counterparts of such errors, and it would be expected that they would increase with increasing over-all similarity among the items. A list made up of synonyms, therefore, should yield more remote intrusions than one composed of neutral words, but no evidence seems to be available on this problem.

(2) *Localized similarity of materials.* If several similar items are imbedded in a serial list, confusions should occur among them, elevating the error curve at those points. McGourty (1940) did this and found the typical bow shape of the error curve to be distorted in the expected direction at each of those points. Von Restorff (1933) tested the converse of this proposition, that errors are reduced by making a portion of a list less similar. A two-place number was inserted in a series of nonsense syllables, and the error curve was found to drop about its locus. Pillsbury and Raush (1943) have extended this finding: a set of eight-item lists was made up of three-place numbers (N) and nonsense syllables (S), the proportions of these two types of material varying from $1N-7S$ to $7N-1S$, including all the permutations. The most isolated material, numbers or syllables, always yielded the best recall, the advantage decreasing as the proportions approached equality. Actually, any factor serving to increase discriminability at a given point in a series should serve to reduce errors at that locus. Stagner (1933) found that inserting a slight pause in the middle of a serial list reduced errors about that point.

Temporal Relations I. Distribution of Practice

The empirical law that 'distributed practice is superior to massed practice' has been found to hold under nearly all conditions, but this is rather paradoxical on the surface. When we 'distribute' practice, periods of time-without-work are inserted and learning is facilitated; yet when we 'cease' practice and are later tested for retention, a period of time-without-work has been inserted and forgetting has occurred, How can time both facilitate and interfere with retention? It is apparent that 'time' is not an adequate concept here. We must search for differential processes working in time. Certain processes working over brief periods must facilitate performance or no improvement with distributed practice will be obtained; other processes working over longer intervals of time must interfere or no forgetting will be found. It is also important to observe that the procedures used to study distribution of practice are inextricably confounded with those yielding transfer and retroaction effects (cf. pp. 520ff.). When we compare a massed condition ($A\ A\ A\ A\ A\ A\ A$) with a distributed condition ($A\ B\ A\ B\ A\ B\ A$), the distributing activity (B) is literally interpolated between repetitions of the task being learned (A). Yet in most studies on distributed practice the character of the interpolated activity is not specified (the subject merely 'rests'), and there has been practically no attempt to investigate this variable itself (i.e. to deliberately manipulate the nature of the interpolated activity).

(1) *Between components of the task.* If the time interval between items in a serial list is increased, stimulus traces should become more attenuated and remote associations weaker, producing less interference. On the other hand, by exactly the same token, this procedure should also weaken the immediate, correct association—more, in fact, given the sharply decelerated shape of the trace function—and hence produce more interference. What is the fact of the matter? Hovland (1938 c) has compared the distribution and total magnitude of errors in the serial learning of 12 nonsense syllables under two speeds of presentation, 2 seconds versus 4 seconds between items. This apparently insignificant increase in time between items greatly reduced total errors, especially in the central portion of the list where difficulty is the greatest (compare 2-sec. massed and 4-sec. massed curves in Fig. 160). Closely similar results were obtained by Husband (1929) for human subjects learning a motor serial task: subjects allowed free time to make their choices on a Warden finger maze made fewer errors than subjects forced to make choices at every beat of a metronome (100 beats per min.), and again the improvement was most apparent in the central portion of the maze. These findings make it appear that (a) whatever factors are responsible for central portion difficulty, they are greatly minimized by slightly increasing the interval between items; (b) intruding remote associations are probably not the cause of this bow-shaped distribution of errors (since their potential competition with correct associations is increased, if anything, by lengthening the interitem interval).

(2) *Between repetitions of the task.* The term 'distribution of practice' usually refers to time interpolated between repetitions of the task as a whole, i.e. between each serial run through the list of nonsense syllables. But since we have already seen that a little time interpolated between components of the task can greatly reduce difficulty, it behooves us to compare these two kinds of distribution. Hovland (1938 c) had four groups of subjects learn the same lists of nonsense syllables: (1) 2-sec. rate of presentation, 6 seconds between trials; (2) 2-sec. rate, 2 minutes and 6 seconds between trials; (3) 4-sec. rate, 6 seconds between trials; (4) 4-sec. rate, 2 minutes and 6 seconds between trials. The groups having 2 minutes between trials (during which they named colors presented in the memory drum to prevent rehearsal) had 'distributed practice,' in the usual sense of the term, but those with only 6 seconds between trials had 'massed practice.' Results are summarized in Fig. 160. *Within-trial distribution* (2-sec. massed vs. 4-sec. massed) *is far more effective in reducing errors than between-trial distribution* (2-sec. massed vs. 2-sec. distributed). A very small amount of 'relaxation' between items more than compensates for a relatively large amount between trials. As a matter of fact, if a little extra time is allowed between items, distributing trials yield practically no improve-

ment over massing trials (compare 4-sec. massed with 4-sec. distributed). Again it should be observed that improvements due to distribution are most apparent in the central portions of the lists.

When the component items within a task are compressed in time (i.e. when the subject is under pressure), nearly all investigators have found inter-trial distribution beneficial, but the important practical and theoretical problem is, *how much distribution is most facilitative?* Lorge (1930) compared massed practice at several tasks (mirror-drawing, mirror-reading, and code-substitution) with 1-minute and 1-day distributed practice. The significant finding was that intervals of only 1 minute were very nearly as

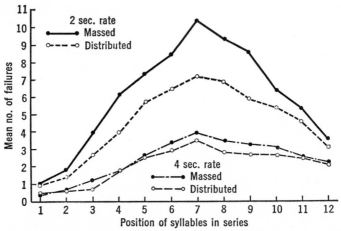

FIGURE 160. Comparison of *massed* (6 sec. between trials) and *distributed* (2 min. 6 sec. between trials) practice under two rates of presentation (2 vs. 4 sec. between items). Notice that time between items is relatively more effective than time between trials. Hovland, *Journal of Experimental Psychology*, 1938, **23**:178.

beneficial as intervals of 1 day. The facilitative processes that function through time-after-practice appear to be short-lived. Actually, of course, the 'most beneficial interval' might have lain anywhere between 1 minute and 1 day—no other intervals were tested by Lorge. One way of checking this would be to see if there is a regular curve of facilitation, leveling off at about 1 minute.

Kientzle (1946) has done just such a study. Subjects printed the alphabet upside down in such a fashion that when the paper is turned through an 180° angle, the alphabet can be read in the usual manner. Trials were uniformly of 1-minute duration, the subjects accomplishing as much as they could in that time. The intervals inserted between trials ranged, as may be seen in Fig. 161, from 0 to 90 seconds, with one group receiving one trial every 7 days. Results are expressed in terms of the average gains between trial #1 and trial #10 in number of inverted letters written. Two important facts are expressed here: (a) the amount of facilitation in learning attributable to inter-trial distribution is a negatively accelerated function of the length of the interval, and (b) the leveling-off point of the function occurs by approximately 45 seconds, slightly less than 1 minute. The fact that the 7-day interval between trials does not yield significantly poorer results than the 1-minute interval is surprising. It presumably indicates that there is practically no interference from interpolated activities upon this type of learning.

Combining the results obtained by Lorge with those of Kientzle, we may conclude that the beneficial effects of interpolated rest periods increase sharply within short time intervals and are maximal at about 1 minute. Although the interval of maximal benefit would probably increase with effortfulness of the task (cf. Kimble and Horenstein, 1948), there is no reason to expect that the negatively accelerated shape of the function would

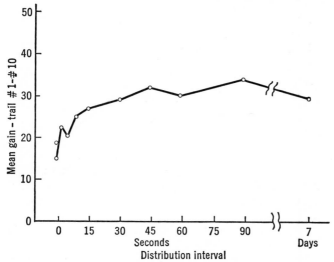

FIGURE 161. Mean gain in performance on mirror-writing task between first and tenth practice trials, with varying amounts of distribution between trials. After Kientzle, *Journal of Experimental Psychology,* 1946, **36**:194.

change. Related findings have been obtained in the development of conditioned reactions (Humphreys, 1940; Cole, Woodbury, and Philleo, 1942).

(3) *Between blocks of trials (rest periods).* The length of each rest period may be constant, but the amount of work before rest may be varied. Jost (1897) distributed 24 repetitions of a list of nonsense syllables in this manner and found that the amount learned in this constant number of trials decreased as the number of trials in each block-before-rest increased from two to eight. Similarly, with motor performance, Travis (1939), has shown that longer practice periods (blocks of trials) require longer rest intervals for most efficient learning. The problem as to the most favorable point of inserting rest periods within the total course of learning has received considerable attention, but conflicting results have been obtained. McGeoch (1942, pp. 122-4) summarizes a number of studies in this area. Many complicating factors are involved and, as is only too often the case, uncontrolled variation in methods and materials makes comparisons between experiments impossible.

(4) *Between learning and the test for retention.* Most theories designed to account for the superiority of distributed over massed practice postulate some interfering or inhibitory process that dissipates rapidly with rest.

Thus distribution during learning is superior to massing because these inhibitory processes are continually being reduced, and rest periods permit the same reduction in inhibition. These explanations lead inevitably to the prediction that material learned by massed practice should be better retained over long intervals. Since massed learning is temporarily 'damped' by interfering effects, spontaneous improvement through time should reflect itself in higher recall scores. The important variable to be controlled here is the criterion of mastery used. Superior retention under massed practice would be expected only when materials are learned to the *same criterion of mastery* (i.e. one perfect repetition) by both methods.

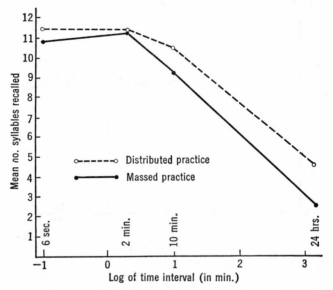

FIGURE 162. Mean number of syllables recalled at various intervals following massed and distributed practice to a criterion of one perfect recitation. Notice that the rate of forgetting is greater following massed practice. Hovland, *Journal of Experimental Psychology,* 1940, 26:575.

Hovland (1940 *a*) tested the prediction under the necessary conditions. His results, shown in Fig. 162, cover retention intervals from 6 seconds to 24 hours, a logarithmic scale being used. After massed practice recall is found to improve somewhat during the first 2 minutes (reminiscence), but beyond this point recall is approximately a linear function of log time for both massed and distributed conditions. The *slope* of the curve for retention following distributed practice is flatter, however, and recall is therefore superior for all intervals beyond the first few minutes. Cain and Willey (1939), using similar conditions and materials, have extended the same conclusion to longer retention intervals. The theoretical expectation is not verified—distribution not only facilitates learning but also leads to better retention—and this, as we shall see, provides one of the main problems for theory.

(5) *Similarity of components and effects of distribution.* There is very little direct evidence here. One might expect, however, that relatively homogeneous tasks (composed of similar part activities) would benefit more

from distributed practice. Garrett (1940) presents data remotely relevant to this hypothesis: he found that simple, repetitious tasks, like code-learning, benefited more from distribution of trials than did complex, difficult tasks, such as learning an artificial language. If we may consider relatively meaningless materials like nonsense syllables and three-place digits to be more homogeneous (i.e. less well differentiated) than meaningful and logically related materials like prose and poetry, then a number of additional studies would testify to the importance of this variable. Lyon (1914), for example, found the learning of nonsense syllables and digits to be facilitated by distribution of practice, but the learning of prose and poetry was not. There are a considerable number of empirical gaps that need filling even in this well-trodden area.

Temporal Relations II. Reminiscence (the Ward-Hovland Phenomenon)

In everyday language, when we say a man 'reminisces' we mean that he reviews experiences of the past, usually the distant past. There are two technical uses of the term in psychology, neither of which corresponds to this one. *The Ward-Hovland Phenomenon* refers to a temporary improvement in performance, without practice, appearing over short intervals, between 2 and 5 minutes. *The Ballard-Williams Phenomenon,* also known as reminiscence, is similar in that it refers to improvement in performance without practice, but it is different in that the temporal interval over which it appears is much longer, favorable delays being as great as 2 or more days. We will consider this phenomenon in Chap. 13.

The gross fact that learning occurs, that performance improves from trial to trial on the average, means that facilitation over short temporal intervals must be operative. That trial #4 is better than trial #3, trial #8 better than #7, and so on, means that some facilitative effects are carried over from one trial to another. Experimentation on reminiscence may be viewed as an attempt to plot the temporal course of this facilitative effect and to determine the interval for which it is maximum. The term 'reminiscence' refers to the objective fact of improved performance; the *cause* of the improvement may be simple positive 'growth' (Snoddy, 1935), dissipation of inhibitions during rest (Hull *et al.* 1940), differential weakening of remote associations (McGeoch, 1942), consolidation of memory traces (Müller and Pilzecker, 1900), or recovery from a performance decrement (McClelland, 1942 *a*).

Some Methodological Considerations. The phenomenon of reminiscence is also confounded with that of retroaction. When subjects learn one task (A), interpolate another (B), and then recall or relearn the first (A), the extent and character of the interpolated activity variably effects retention of the original task. In the procedure designed to measure reminiscence, experimental subjects practice to a certain degree of mastery (A), rest or partake in a specified activity such as color naming (B), and then return to recall and complete the learning of the original materials (A). It is clear that obtained reminiscence may reflect retroactive facilitation, whereas failure to obtain it may merely indicate the presence of retroactive interference. The two phenomena are not operationally separable.

Any valid demonstration of the occurrence of reminiscence requires strict adherence to adequate experimental design (see Buxton, 1943, for an excellent discussion of this). Obviously if the subject rehearses (practices implicitly) during the rest period, measured reminiscence is an artifact. There are no procedures that can absolutely guarantee the absence of implicit practice during rest. Techniques used to minimize it have included asking subjects not to indulge, forcing them to name colors vigorously through the interval (thus inadvertently varying retroactive effects), and eliminating subjects who admit rehearsal in a subsequent interview. Adequate design also requires a *control condition* in which no rest is given, but the ordinary rate of learning is continued. Of several feasible designs, the most commonly used is that of having both experimental and control subjects practice to a point at which about 75 per cent of the items are mastered, whereupon the control group continues without rest and the experimental group rests before continuing. The *recall measure* of reminiscence

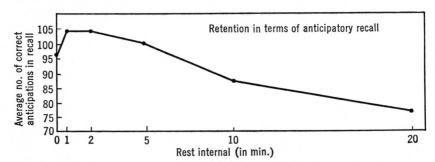

FIGURE 163. Reminiscence as a function of the rest interval between termination of practice and a recall trial, as measured by average number of correct anticipations at recall. Ward, *Psychological Monographs,* 1937, 49, #220:17.

compares the first trial after rest for the experimental group with the first trial after reaching the 75 per cent criterion for the control group; *the relearning measure* compares the number of trials beyond the 75 per cent level required by both groups to reach the same criterion of final mastery.

Experimental characterization. The classic study here is that of Ward (1937). After learning a 12-unit list of nonsense syllables to a criterion of seven correct anticipations, one group of subjects continued to complete mastery without rest and four groups of experimental subjects rested for ½, 2, 5, 10, or 20 minutes before continuing learning. The interpolated 'rest' activity in this experiment was the reading of jokes. Mean recall scores immediately following 'rest' intervals of varying length are shown in Fig. 163, the phenomenon of reminiscence being indicated by the superior recall of the short-interval subjects. With intervals as long as 10 minutes, no reminiscence was present, but rather decrements in recall as compared with the control group. Ward also measured the number of trials required to reach mastery and reaction latencies, both yielding essentially the same results as the recall measure. Hovland (1938 *a, b*) followed Ward's general procedures (with one or two exceptions to be observed later) and obtained substantiating results.

Reminiscence is by no means limited to the learning of serial verbal lists. It has been obtained, for example, in the learning of motor skills (cf. Melton, 1941; Buxton, 1943), and a more recent study of this type by Kimble and Horenstein (1948) may be described. Subjects were given ten trials on a pursuit rotor (keeping a stylus on a contact point that rotates on a turntable), each trial lasting 50 seconds with 10 seconds being allowed between trials. After the tenth trial, subjects rested for various intervals and were then given two test trials as measures of reminiscence. When mean gains for the test trials over trial #10 were plotted as a function of the length of the rest interval, the negatively accelerated curve showed in Fig. 164 was obtained. Improvement with rest increased for about 600 seconds (10 minutes). The fact that the most beneficial rest interval here was longer than that for verbal materials probably reflects the greater effortfulness of this motor task.

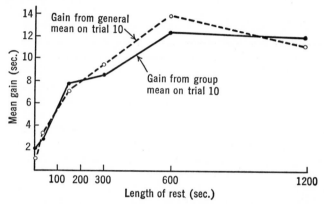

FIGURE 164. Reminiscence in a motor task (pursuit rotor) as a function of the length of interpolated rest period. Kimble and Horenstein, *Journal of Experimental Psychology*, 1948, 38:242.

Variables affecting reminiscence. Reminiscence is by no means a dependable phenomenon. Although some studies obtain it in significant quantities, others which apparently fit the necessary design do not (e.g. Shipley, 1939; Melton and Stone, 1942). This lack of dependability shows that the relevant conditions have not been isolated. The variables affecting reminiscence, in so far as they have been isolated, fall into two categories, those relating to the magnitude and course of the phenomenon when it is obtained and those relating to the presence or absence of it.

Variables determining magnitude may be summarized briefly: (1) Reminiscence is maximal after brief rest intervals, the most effective interval depending on the type of task but being limited to a few minutes. (2) Learning to a moderate degree of mastery (about 75 per cent) yields more reminiscence than learning to either a low or a high degree (Hovland, 1938 *a, b*). The phenomenon, however, may occur at both high and low degrees (Hovland, 1938 *a;* Ward, 1937). (3) Conditions that 'force' the subject, such as increasing the presentation rate of items or decreasing the inter-trial interval, facilitate reminiscence and the effect is greatest in the central portions of serial lists (Hovland, 1938 *a, b*). (4) The greater the number of items in a serial list, the greater the magnitude of reminiscence. This is suggested in Shipley's experiment (1939); although no absolute improvement in performance over the control group was obtained, recall after rest improved steadily as the length of the list was increased.

Factors relating to the presence or absence of reminiscence require more extensive discussion. (1) *Type of learning procedure.* All of the verbal studies considered so far have used serial learning, and the question arises as to whether reminiscence is specific to this procedure. Hovland (1939) compared serial with paired-associate learning, the order of pairs being randomized from trial to trial. No evidence of reminiscence with the paired-associate method was found. This experiment was inconclusive, however, since the interval varied for the two methods. Whereas one response every 2 seconds was required on serial learning, only one response every 4 seconds was required with the paired associates (i.e. the stimulus members of the pairs served solely as cues). The cause of the obtained difference in reminiscence might be the method of learning, the difference in response rate, or even the factor of randomization.

McClelland (1942 a), attacking the problem from a different angle, used a discrimination method of learning. Subjects were presented with 20 pairs of adjectives, one word in each pair always being 'correct' (saying such 'correct' words was rewarded by the ringing of a bell). The pairs to be discriminated were presented in randomized order on successive trials. The control subjects learned continuously to mastery, but the experimental group 'rested' (took a steadiness test) for 2 minutes after reaching the criterion of 15/20 items; 2- and 4-second rates of presentation were compared. No significant differences were found for the 4-second rate (checking with Hovland's findings for serial learning), and whether or not one considers reminiscence to have been demonstrated in the 2-second group depends upon the criterion used. In terms of recall (actually differential recognition here), no differences appeared; in terms of relearning to mastery, the experimental group was significantly superior. McClelland interprets this as evidence that reminiscence is not limited to the serial form of learning, yet the use of relearning scores as a measure of reminiscences is a debated issue [see Buxton's (1943) review].

(2) *Correction* vs. *noncorrection procedures.* Ward (1937) used the noncorrection procedure, subjects being instructed merely to anticipate, whereas Hovland (1938 a, etc.) used the correction procedure, subjects being required to both anticipate and pronounce each item as it appeared— both studies revealed reminiscence. Melton and Stone (1942) duplicated Hovland's general procedures, with the single exception that they followed Ward's noncorrection procedure. With unrelated meaningful adjectives as material, no evidence for reminiscence was obtained. This was true even when the rate of presentation was increased from 2 seconds to 1.45 seconds. These investigators do not believe their failure to obtain reminiscence was due to the use of meaningful rather than nonsense materials, but rather that it was somehow a function of the experimental procedures, perhaps the use of the noncorrection method or the vigor with which colors were named during rest (retroactive interference). The latter explanation seems the more likely, since both Ward and Hovland found reminiscence with different correction techniques.

(3) *Similarity of materials.* Another feasible explanation of the Melton and Stone failure to obtain reminiscence could be phrased in terms of the

homogeneity of materials. All the studies we have surveyed point to the importance of interference or response conflict in producing reminiscence; whereas nonsense syllables (Ward and Hovland) are initially undifferentiated and much confusion is produced, unrelated meaningful adjectives (Melton and Stone) are initially well differentiated through previous experience with them.

(4) *Amount of retroactive interference*. Since the paradigm for measuring reminiscence is confounded with that for producing retroactive effects, it seems quite possible that, depending on the nature of the interpolated 'rest' activities, reminiscence may or may not be obtained. There is a little scattered evidence. Ward (1937) showed that interpolated color naming resulted in more reminiscence than interpolated reading. Shipley (1939) found that interpolated manipulations with a mechanical toy interfered less with reminiscence for nonsense syllables than did reading *College Humor*. So much for a shy phenomenon.

Number of Components in the Serial Task

A number of studies indicate that for both verbal and motor serial learning difficulty increases *disproportionately* with the number of components (Lyon, 1917; Robinson and Heron, 1922; Scott and Henninger, 1933; and others). Figure 165 compares the results obtained by Robinson and Heron for lists of nonsense syllables (*A*) with those obtained by Scott and Henninger for learning finger mazes having varying numbers of blind alleys (*B*). Whereas a 9-item list requires approximately 100 units of learning time, an 18-item list requires about 300 units; whereas a 5-blind maze takes about 200 units of time, a 10-blind maze takes 900 units. Hovland (1940 *b*) has shown that errors in the central portions of serial lists increase more rapidly with increasing length than do errors at either end, the bow shape thus becoming sharper. This indicates that the specific inhibitory processes associated with serial learning increase with the length of list. This being the case, it would be expected that *distributed practice* would become increasingly beneficial as length is increased. This expectation is borne out. Lyon (1914) compared learning times for massed and distributed practice of lists of nonsense syllables varying in length from 8 to 72 items (by learning time is meant the total time spent at work, not including rest intervals). Although total time increased under both methods, the relative superiority of distributed practice became greater as the lists became progressively longer. Hovland (1940 *b*) obtained identical results over the narrower range from 8 to 14 items.

Initial Habit Strength of Component Associations

To the extent that indiscriminability, based upon stimulus and response similarities within the list, is responsible for errors in learning, *pretraining* on the component associations later to be combined in a series should improve ultimate performance. The difficulties specifically related to trace conditioning and the forms of inhibition presumably produced thereby, on the other hand, should be largely unaffected by pretraining on components. An experiment by Lyon (1914) offers suggestive evidence: allowing one trial a day, the amount of time spent learning serial lists of 200 nonsense syllables was 93 minutes, 200 digits was 85 minutes, and 200 words of meaningful prose only 24 minutes. The nonsense materials were novel to the subjects and obviously unrelated serially, the digits were familiar but previously linked in series not necessarily like those in the experiment, and the meaningful prose certainly contained many sequences that had previously been

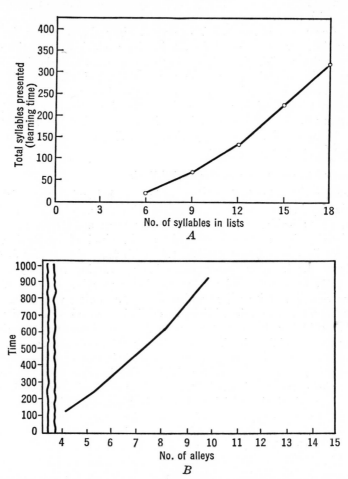

FIGURE 165. Relation between ease of learning and amount of material: (*A*) for lists of nonsense syllables (Robinson and Heron, *Journal of Experimental Psychology*, 1922, 5:442); (*B*) for x-type finger mazes varying in number of *culs de sac* (Scott and Henninger, *Journal of Experimental Psychology*, 1933, 16:671).

practiced to varying degrees. In a rough way, then, Lyon's data support the hypothesis. An unpublished minor study from my own laboratory (conducted by Miss Sievers) yielded further substantiating evidence: when varying degrees of pretraining on the syllables later to be linked in series were given, *as paired associates in random order,* ease of learning the final serial list varied concomitantly. Although the bow-shaped distribution was not affected, there was some evidence that maximum occurrence of anticipatory errors was progressively moved toward later trials with increased pretraining. There seems to be no further evidence here.

INTERPRETATIONS OF SERIAL LEARNING PHENOMENA

It has become increasingly evident to the reader that the various phenomena we have been studying are interrelated to a high degree. Both distributed practice and reminiscence make their effects felt most strongly in the central portions of serial lists, where difficulty is greatest. If a little extra time is allowed between component items in a series, both distribution between trials and the rest pause used to produce reminiscence fail to have their usual beneficial effect. If learning proceeds by distributed practice, reminiscence cannot be obtained. Any satisfactory theory must cover all of these interlocking effects as well as those attributable to similarity factors.

Rehearsal

The possibility of implicit practice by subjects during short rest intervals must be checked. Such unmeasured practice would explain the general superiority of distributed practice as well as the reminiscence phenomenon. But there is much this homely hypothesis fails to explain. (1) In many carefully controlled experiments interpolated 'rest' periods have been filled with specifiable activity (cf. Hovland's technique of naming colors), yet typical phenomena are found. (2) Improved performance following short rest intervals (reminiscence) persists for only 5 minutes or so, yet there is opportunity for rehearsal over the longer periods. (3) Distributed practice is not superior to massed when the inter-item interval is increased from 2 to 4 seconds (Hovland, 1938 c), despite the added opportunity for rehearsal. And there are many other points that might be scored against this explanation.

Fatigue

Following the relations between fatigue and inhibition explored earlier (Chap. 8), it might be thought that this factor would operate here as well. When dealing with activities that produce significant amounts of fatigue, it undoubtedly is a factor, but in most of the behaviors with which this chapter has been concerned (viz. reciting lists of nonsense syllables and tracing finger mazes) the amount of fatigue produced is minimal. In any case, (1) it would not account for the bow-shaped distribution of errors in serial learning. (2) It would not account for the fact that distribution of practice reduces errors mainly in the central portion of a serial list. (3) It would not explain the superior retention of materials learned by the distribution method, since fatigue-produced inhibition is assumed to dissipate spontaneously with time.

Perseveration (Consolidation)

Müller and Pilzecker, in 1900, proposed a theory designed to cover many of the phenomena of remembering. In essence the theory stated that the neural processes initiated in learning perseverate through time and become more firmly fixed because of this persisting activity. This type of theory has more recently been sponsored by Woodworth (1938) under the term 'consolidation.' This theory does, to be sure, predict the general advantage of distributed practice and the phenomenon of reminiscence, rest periods not interfering with the 'setting in' process (assuming that when 'resting' the organism is in a neural vacuum!). (1) It does not, however, account for the distribution of errors in serial learning; in fact, since each succeeding item should interfere with the consolidation of all preceding items, one would have to predict maximum difficulty at the beginning of the list and continuous improvement toward the end. (2) It will not explain the fact that an *inter-item* interval of 4 seconds is maximally effective, but an *inter-trial* interval of nearer 1 minute is maximally effective. (3) On general grounds, without added assumptions governing the relation of similarity of materials to their interfering capacity, the theory can predict nothing since some neural processes are always present.

Differential Diminution of Excitatory and Inhibitory Tendencies

The most comprehensive attempt to incorporate the varied phenomena in this area has been made by Hull and his associates (Hovland, Ross, Hall, Perkins, and Fitch) in a monograph entitled 'The Mathematico-deductive Theory of Rote Learning' (1940). Regardless of the ultimate validity of the approach, this work stands as a monumental demonstration of the rigor with which theory can be applied to a restricted problem. Only a brief and necessarily inadequate summary can be presented here; sufficiently intrepid readers are referred to the original. We shall first present the major postulates of the theory, then the deductions it renders, and finally the difficulties it encounters.

Postulates. (1) *Each item in a series, as a stimulus, creates a trace that diminishes in intensity progressively through time.* Thus ZAP (item 1) generates stimulus effects which persist through the remainder of the series (KEM, XOT, WUJ, etc.), similarly KEM, and so forth. It therefore follows that the actual stimulus evoking any response is a compound of the traces of all preceding stimuli. (2) *Every presentation of the series generates an increment of excitatory tendency for each item to evoke the succeeding (correct) item.* These excitatory increments are assumed to summate from trial to trial and to be equal for all associations in the series. (3) Simultaneously *each presentation of the series generates an increment of inhibitory tendency between each item and the succeeding (correct) item.* This requires a little elaboration. Following a hypothesis originally phrased by Lepley (1934), we can state that each item as a stimulus is kept from evoking remote items (as trace conditioned reactions) by *inhibition of delay* (cf. p. 315). Since the trace of each preceding stimulus is present in the compound evoking a given response, but has an inhibitory loading which subtracts from the excitatory tendency at this point, the resultant reaction potential is diminished. The greater the distance between items, the less this inhibitory contribution. (4) *Both excitatory and inhibitory tendencies associated with the same reaction diminish through time according to negatively accelerated functions, the inhibitory tendencies diminishing at a faster rate.* Algebraic summation of these competing tendencies yields the effective habit strength ($\bar{E}$ in Fig. 166) which must first increase and then decrease as shown. There are many other subsidiary postulates in the system, but these contain the essence of the theory.

Sample deductions. (1) *The bow-shaped distribution of errors.* Since the number of traces from preceding items increases through a series, the inhibitory tendencies associated with these traces must also increase. On the other hand, the number of items requiring delay decreases as the end of the series is approached and therefore the more a given stimulus compound is associated with excitation than with inhibition. Given these opposing trends in the development of inhibition, the typical distributon of errors is obtained. (2) *Distribution favors serial learning.* Since inhibitory tendencies are assumed to diminish more rapidly in time than excitatory tendencies, short rest intervals will facilitate learning. (3) *Reminiscence.* Similarly, a rest interval after learning (by massed practice) will allow the inhibitory

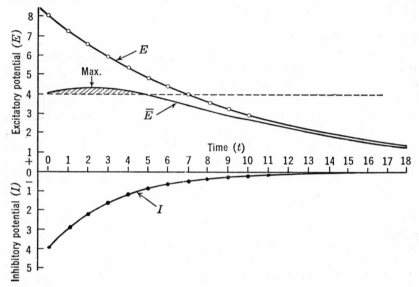

FIGURE 166. Diagram showing the major constructs and their functional properties in Hull's theory of rote learning. Differential decay of excitatory (*E*) and inhibitory (*I*) potentials during rest following practice permits temporary increase in effective excitatory potential ($\bar{E}$). Hull *et al. Mathematico-deductive Theory of Rote Learning,* Yale University Press, New Haven, 1940, p. 121.

tendencies to dissipate, thus producing temporary improvement in performance. (4) *The effects of both distribution and reminiscence will be most apparent in the central portion of a serial list.* Since the most inhibition is generated in the center of a list, anything that reduces inhibition will show up most clearly at this locus. (5) *The facilitative effects of both distribution and reminiscence will be limited in the time over which they operate.* Improvement in performance will persist only as long as the faster rate of reduction in inhibitory potential overcompensates for the slower, but continuous, reduction in excitatory potential.

Difficulties encountered. This theory leaves several questions unanswered, the import being that it offers an insufficient explanation, not an erroneous one. (1) *Explanation of forgetting.* This theory merely postulates that excitatory tendencies diminish through time. No account is given of the variables governing the rate of forgetting, its amount under various conditions, and so forth. (2) *Similarities within and between practiced and intervening materials.* Despite the existence at the time the theory was formulated of some evidence on the effects of similarity of materials upon serial learning and distribution of practice, no account of this variable is offered. Given the characteristics of Hull's general theory of behavior (1943), however, extensions could be made to cover this criticism. (3) *The superior retention of materials learned by distributed practice.* As is often the case, a worker from within the fold is able to make the most cogent criticisms of a theory. Hovland (1940 a) demonstrated that this theory (and most others) inevitably leads to the prediction that massed learning should result in better retention over long intervals than distributed learning, if practice is to the same criterion. He then conducted an experiment which gave clearly contrary evidence.

Performance Decrement

McClelland (1942 a, b, 1943 a) has proposed that it is conflict among the responses involved in any task that causes performance to lag behind actual learning, especially when the subject is under pressure. During rest periods this decrement is overcome and performance 'catches up' with true learning. The exact nature of this decrement and the manner in which it is overcome is not clarified. This is a common-sense hypothesis that fits many of the phenomena in this field. It covers reminiscence for any kind of learned activity, the superiority of distributed practice, and even the effects of similarity—if we assume amount of conflict to increase with the similarity among items. But is this interpretation really different at base from Hull's? McClelland, to be sure, has used a discrimination type of learning situation (the subject must learn to call out the 'correct' one of each pair of words, pairs being presented in random order) and has obtained some evidence for reminiscence. Although this is not a serial situation, and hence we cannot speak of inhibition of *delay* in trace conditioning, the essence of Hull's view is that the stimulus compound evoking each reaction becomes associated wtih both excitatory and inhibitory tendencies, regardless of the source of the inhibition. In McClelland's situation, inhibition of vocalizing the 'wrong' word in each pair is compounded with excitatory tendencies toward vocalizing the 'correct' word. As a matter of fact, there is evidence in McClelland's studies that the 'wrong' words were being actively inhibited (i.e. when later paired with novel words, these originally 'wrong' responses were called out more often than chance).

Differential Forgetting of Immediate and Remote Associations

McGeoch (1942) has sketched the outline of an interference theory which relates the phenomena of serial learning to those of transfer and retroaction. The early syllables in a series tend to transfer as errors to later positions, whereas the later items in turn tend to retroactively affect earlier ones. Remote perseverative and anticipatory errors in serial learning bear witness to the presence of such interference, and its amount increases with inter-item similarities in the list. This theory thus incorporates the similarity variable directly, a major omission of the theory of Hull et al. In order to explain the phenomena of reminiscence and distribution of practice, McGeoch (p. 143) must assume that 'since the conflicting associations . . . [are] . . . less well fixated than the right ones, they should be forgotten sooner during the rest intervals. . .' The more rapid disappearance of remote, interfering associations allows performance to improve after an interval has elapsed.

In an early test of this hypothesis, McGeoch (1936 *a*) had subjects learn serial lists of adjectives to a criterion and then associate the first word that occurred to them when items from the list were called out in random order. The latencies of both immediate (correct) associations and either anticipatory or perseverative errors of varying degrees of remoteness were recorded. The shorter latency for immediate associations in the forward direction demanded by the theory was *not* obtained. Wilson (1943) has also designed an experiment to test this prediction. After equated learning of a series of 16 adjectives, four groups of subjects were given tests for associations after delays of ½, 2, 5, or 20 minutes, items of the original list being presented as stimuli in random order. To satisfy McGeoch's hypothesis, the frequency of remote associations should drop at a faster rate than the frequency of immediate, correct associations. The results were largely negative. The basic assumption underlying both studies—that remote associations are initially weaker than the correct ones they replace— seems entirely unjustified. *The mere fact that an intruding, remote association can successfully displace the correct response must mean that it is at least equal in strength at that moment.* If two response tendencies are of equal strength at the beginning of a rest interval, they should weaken through time at equivalent rates unless we assume a differential rate of dissipation, which is the essence of Hull's position.

The failure of this aspect of the theory does not vitiate the portions that relate to the similarity variable. Based on stimulus and response generalization, the greater the similarity within the primary activities being learned or between these and intervening activities, the greater the resultant interference, expressed in overt or implicit intrusions. The reduction of such errors during learning reflects the development of discriminations within the list. This generalization-discrimination hypothesis meets most insufficiencies of the theory advanced by Hull and his associates. (1) It accounts for the existence of perseverative errors and the variation in total errors with changes in the similarity of materials. (2) Through its direct relation to transfer and retroaction phenomena (cf. below), it will account more adequately for the general loss in retention over long temporal intervals. (4) The puzzling fact that materials learned by massed practice show poorer retention than those learned by distributed practice to the same criterion might also be incorporated: since a greater variety of activities is present in distributed learning (i.e. the 'rest' activities), the primary materials can become discriminated from many potential sources of interference. The use of specific delimited activities during distribution periods, as in the experiments by Hovland (1938 *c*) and others, casts doubt however on this interpretation.

Summary

The phenomena of serial learning, reminiscence and distribution of practice, have been shown by experiment to be interrelated. None of the theories we have evaluated, in itself, is capable of covering all the facts. The evidence as a whole points to the operation of two independent factors. (1) *A short-term temporal factor.* The succession of activities through time is accompanied by trace conditioning and the resultant development of a form of inhibition. This inhibition is maximal in the central portion of a list learned serially. It dissipates rapidly (within a few minutes), giving rise to the phenomenon of reminiscence and producing the superiority of distributed practice. This factor is the one explored in theory and experiment by Hull and his associates. (2) *An interference factor.* Depending upon the degrees of similarity *within* the materials being learned, interference is produced among them, resulting in both overt and implicit anticipatory and perseverative intrusions. Depending upon the degrees of similarity *between* the primary and intervening activities, there is interference between them, resulting in cumulative loss in retention of the learned materials through time. This interference factor will be studied in detail in the remainder of this chapter. Finally, it is necessary to assume that dissipation of the inhibition characteristic of factor I occurs at a more rapid rate than the loss in retention attributable to factor II.

TRANSFER AND RETROACTION

Behavior is a continuous, fluid process, and activities learned in the laboratory are as much a part of it as a trip to the county fair. The segments that an experimenter arbitrarily selects for analysis are inextricably imbedded in this expanding matrix and are interpretable only in terms of interactions within it. Experiments on transfer and retroaction are explicit attempts to gauge these interactions. It is common procedure to study transfer of training under the general topic of learning and as somehow separable from retroaction, which is usually subsumed under the general topic of forgetting. They will be treated here as a single problem. The essential identities among the phenomena to which these terms refer and the common theories that apply to them will justify this approach.

Some Methodological Considerations

Transfer refers to the effect of a *preceding* activity upon the learning of a given task; retroaction refers to the effect of an *interpolated* (intervening) activity upon the retention of a task previously learned. Both effects may vary in degree and direction: facilitative transfer is called *positive transfer* and interfering transfer is called *negative transfer*. Although *retroactive facilitation* is commonly and acceptably used for positive retroaction, the term 'retroactive inhibition' has unfortunately been applied when negative retroaction is found. What is referred to here is simply an observed decrement in performance, not a process—the decrement may or may not be due to some inhibitory process—so henceforth we shall use the more neutral term, *retroactive interference.*

Suppose subjects practice one finger maze for five trials and then learn a second finger maze—can any inferences be drawn as to the transfer from maze *A* to maze *B?* Suppose they then return to maze *A* for a test of retention—can any inferences be drawn as to the interpolation effect of maze *B* upon recall of maze *A?* Obviously not; we would not know how well they would have done on *B without* the pretraining on *A* (transfer) or how well they would have remembered *A without* the interpolation of *B.* In both cases it is generally believed necessary to have a *control condition* in which the specific pretraining or interpolation is not given. Differences between the scores of experimental and control groups on learning the test task (transfer) or recalling the original task (retroaction) would then be interpreted as evidence for facilitative or interfering effects of the specific experimental activity. Typical transfer and retroaction paradigms are shown

TRANSFER PARADIGM

EXPERIMENTAL	learn A	learn B	(or)	$S_1 \rightarrow R_1$	$S_2 \rightarrow R_2$
CONTROL	(rest)	learn B	(or)	$S_x \rightarrow R_x$	$S_2 \rightarrow R_2$

RETROACTION PARADIGM

EXPERIMENTAL	learn A	learn B	test A	(or)	$S_1 \rightarrow R_1$	$S_2 \rightarrow R_2$	$S_1 \rightarrow R_1$
CONTROL	learn A	(rest)	test A	(or)	$S_1 \rightarrow R_1$	$S_x \rightarrow R_x$	$S_1 \rightarrow R_1$

here. The use of $S_x \rightarrow R_x$ serves to make explicit the fact that merely because a subject is said to 'rest' does not mean that he is suspended in a behavioral vacuum. There are several variations in the design of transfer and retroaction experiments (cf. Woodworth, 1938; McGeoch, 1942; Gagné, Foster, and Crowley, 1948) ; those shown here are perhaps the most common.

These experimental designs are sometimes employed without a clear understanding of their underlying assumptions. First, with regard to the transfer paradigm, what is the purpose of the design? Ultimately we wish to compare the performance of subjects on a given task after they've had a certain type of pretraining with *how they would have performed* without such pretraining. What does the paradigm actually measure? *It actually compares the transfer effects of a specific preceding activity* $(S_1 \rightarrow R_1)$ *with those of a nonspecific preceding activity* $(S_x \rightarrow R_x)$. In interpreting the results obtained with this design, then, one assumption is made : the pretest behavior of the control subjects is equivalent to that in which the experimental subjects would have indulged had they not been learning the first task. It sometimes happens that, in his zeal for exercising rigid control over miscellaneous variables, an experimenter will make all of his control subjects vigorously learn lists of numbers or do mechanical puzzles for the same amount of time the experimental subjects are learning the first task. And what is being measured in this case? The specific first-task transfer effects are being compared with the specific transfer effects of learning number lists or doing mechanical puzzles, which was not at all the purpose of the design.

With regard to the retroaction paradigm, the traditional procedure—having a control group that rests for the same temporal interval that the experimental group practices the interpolated materials—seems to reflect a stage in theory when time itself was considered a cause of forgetting. Thus, the effects of interpolated 'work' had to be evaluated against the effects of a 'rest' period or pure time itself. As was pointed out above, however, during a rest period the subject is not in a vacuum ; the so-called 'rest' condition is actually a kind of work conditioned in which the activities are seldom specified and almost never measured.* The practical justification given for using 'rest' as a control condition is generally that it renders the

* Irion (1948), however, has gathered together a number of results from experiments in the literature in which 'rest' decrements could be computed, and in all cases decrements were found.

results of different experiments comparable. This implies that the effects of interpolated 'rest' will always be equivalent, which appears most unlikely since the character of these periods depends entirely upon the whims of individual investigators, some requiring their subjects to read *College Humor,* others having them name colors, and yet others having their subjects do jigsaw puzzles. Since the reference level (performance of the control group) from which the amount and direction of retroaction is computed will vary freely with the quality and intensity of the 'rest' activity, it is hard to see how different experiments are thus rendered comparable.

Since we are primarily interested in the relative facilitation or interference produced by the specific interpolated activity, a more justifiable method of control would be to use performance at the conclusion of the original learning (task A) as a reference level. Any variation from this level would represent some change due to *all* intervening events, and the experimenter's job would be to submit as many of them as possible to quantitative control. Thus, if a subject had learned ten items at the conclusion of his original training, the fact that he can recall only six after interpolation represents retroaction interference regardless of what 'control' subjects do; the problem is to specify the reason for this loss. The traditional procedure has been given priority here since nearly all research in the field has followed it.

Similarity Relations I. Locus Unspecifiable

The phenomena of transfer and retroaction have been most frequently and adequately studied in relation to the similarity variable. In many studies the exact locus of the similarity relations is not specifiable, the subject merely learns one maze and then another maze. In others, especially the more recent investigations in the field, the experimental designs have been such that it has been possible to specify more exactly the locus and degree of similarity, and these provide more fruitful insights into the processes at work, as we shall see.

It is a common procedure in learning experiments to give subjects preliminary practice on the type of task they are later to be tested on in order to eliminate any 'practice effects' in the final results. In serial verbal learning, for example, the subject may learn several 'buffer' lists before working on the experimental materials. If his performance is recorded, he will typically show *cumulative positive transfer,* i.e. his performance will improve consistently from list to list. Figure 167, from Ward's (1937) monograph on serial learning, illustrates this type of transfer. These results are typical in that the amount of positive transfer from list to list is shown to be a *negatively accelerated function of the number of similar tasks* (cf. Fernberger, 1916; Melton and Von Lackum, 1941; Bunch, 1944). Cumulative positive transfer has also been obtained with animal subjects, as when a series of practice mazes are learned (Marx, 1944). This type of positive transfer might be described by saying that the human subjects 'learn how to learn lists of nonsense syllables' and that the rats 'learn how to learn mazes.' Although it is apparent that there is considerable all-over similarity between the materials successively practiced in these cases, the exact locus is not specifiable.

What is found when retention of the first task is measured after varying numbers of similar interpolated tasks? The typical result is *cumulative retroactive interference*. The larger the number of similar interpolated

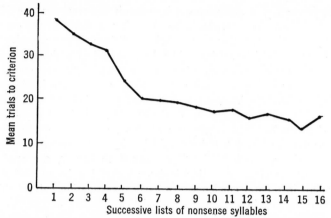

FIGURE 167. Cumulative positive transfer in learning successive lists of nonsense syllables. Ward, *Psychological Monographs*, 1937, **49**, #220:13.

activities, the greater the decrement in recalling or relearning the original task. Twining (1940) measured the average recall of a list of eight nonsense syllables after an interval of 30 minutes, the successive learning of 1, 2, 3, 4, or 5 other eight-syllable lists being interpolated during this

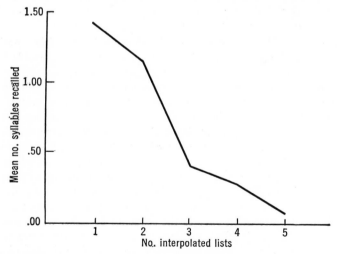

FIGURE 168. Mean number of original nonsense syllables recalled after interpolated learning of 1, 2, 3, 4, or 5 other lists. Original learning with criterion of one perfect repetition, i.e. 8 syllables correct. After data of Twining, *Journal of Experimental Psychology*, 1940, 26:493.

interval. His results are shown in Fig. 168. Because the materials and procedures were quite similar, we may compare these results with those obtained by Ward (1937) on transfer. Roughly both curves have a negatively accelerated form, indicating that the factors which produce facilitative transfer and those which produce interfering retroaction both reach saturation levels.

The limiting case of over-all similarity, of course, is *ordinary learning* of any performance. Here the successive stimuli and responses are 'identical,' and the mere fact that learning does occur is testimony to the existence of cumulative positive transfer under such conditions. The successive practice of similar tasks, which we have just been studying, although less homogeneous than continuous repetition of the same task, represents a high degree of similarity, and positive transfer is also obtained. What results will appear when the successively practiced tasks become still less homogeneous? This question brings us to the classic educational problem known as *formal discipline*. The champions of this doctrine have long held that certain studies are 'good for the mind,' i.e. have high transfer value. The study of Latin or mathematics is presumed to benefit the student, *not* because of any specific utilization in later work, but because of a general improvement in mental efficiency. An early investigation calling this entire proposition into question was that undertaken by Thorndike and Woodworth (1901). Subjects were trained in a variety of tasks, such as estimating the sizes of figures, cancellation of letters and words, and so forth, and then were tested for transfer to other related tasks. Transfer was found to be highly variable in direction and generally small in magnitude. A large number of experiments on a wide range of materials have been done (cf. Woodworth, 1938), and results are quite inconsistent. About the only conclusion to be drawn is that under such complex conditions the important variables are not revealed and hence the findings are of little value practically or scientifically. One cannot even conclude, and be confident about it, that the doctrine of formal discipline is invalid.

We see that under complex, unanalyzable conditions either positive or negative transfer may be obtained. What appears to be responsible for positive transfer when it does appear? Referring again to Fig. 167 we notice that the course of cumulative positive transfer in a series of similar tasks is negatively accelerated. This is the curve form we might expect if a habit were being learned from trial to trial. Is the subject learning certain behaviors and strengthening (transferring) them from task to task? Such a hypothesis is borne out in a number of studies (cf. McGeoch, 1942, p. 421ff.) whose combined import is that positive transfer occurs when general principles, techniques, or modes of attack apply equally to the tasks successively practiced. This analysis renders rather nebulous any distinction between transfer and ordinary learning, at least under these complex conditions. If we pay attention *only* to the sequence of tasks, which are not, to be sure, identical, then it appears as though positive transfer were occurring from one to the other. If, more reasonably, we attend to the learning situation as a whole, we observe that certain common adjustive skills are being learned *and retained* from task to task. But how is one to explain the fact that retroactive interference of the first task in a series is observed under these same conditions? Although the series of tasks (e.g. lists of nonsense syllables) are generally similar, the specific items included in each are different. Positive transfer is attributable to the general task homogeneities, whereas negative retroaction is attributable to the heterogeneities within the materials. In other words, while the subject is 'learning how to learn lists of nonsense syllables' (positive transfer), he is also 'forgetting the details of the first list' (retroactive interference).

Similarity Relations II. Locus Specifiable

The studies surveyed so far have not revealed the basic variables determining either direction or degree of effect, and the reason seems to be insufficient analysis of the relations among successively practiced activities. Do the similarities existing among stimulus situations or among responsive behaviors affect transfer and retroaction? The answer to this question will be found to be clearly affirmative, but by no means uncomplicated. An early law supposedly governing these relations was that voiced by Müller and Schumann (1894): once any two items have been associated, it becomes more difficult to associate either of them with a third item. This has become known as the law of *associative inhibition* and, as we shall see, it is not generally valid. Its main value lay in bringing the analytic problem into focus.

(1) *Stimulus variation* $(S_1 \rightarrow R_1 ; S_2 \rightarrow R_1 ; S_1 \rightarrow R_1)$.

The experimental conditions subsumed under this paradigm are those in which the subject first practices the association between one stimulus and a given response, or a set of such associations, and is then either (a) tested for transfer of the same response to a new stimulus or (b) finally tested for retention of the first association following such interpolation. The transfer part of this paradigm will be recognized as the exact procedure used in measuring *stimulus generalization*. As will be recalled from our discussion in Chap. 8, *the greater the similarity between practice and test stimuli, the greater the amount of positive transfer* (generalization). This statement holds over a broad range of materials and conditions and it is, of course, in direct contradiction to the Müller-Schumann law of associative inhibition. McKinney (1933) required subjects to respond with a correct letter upon seeing each of four geometrical designs. After this original training, the subjects were tested for transfer of the same response to alterations of these visual designs. The greater the alteration (the less the stimulus similarity), the less frequent the transfer of response. Substantiating results have been found by E. J. Gibson (1939), with a vibratory stimulus applied to the back; Yum (1931), with visually presented nonsense syllable stimuli; and Hamilton (1943), with visually presented geometrical forms.

While the retroactive data derived from this paradigm are not as extensive, the available evidence shows that *retroactive facilitation* is obtained. Hamilton (1943) had subjects learn lists of paired associates in which the stimuli were geometrical forms and the responses were nonsense syllables. Before the experiment proper the degree of generalization among the stimulus forms was determined independently as an index of similarity. Then lists were arranged so that in condition I original and interpolated stimuli were identical (100% generalization), in conditions II and III there were 41% and 10% average stimulus generalization, respectively, and in condition IV (control) there was 0% generalization—response nonsense syllables were always identical on both original and interpolated lists. The magnitude of retroactive facilitation was found to decrease regularly as similarity among the stimulus members decreased, becoming approximately zero with neutral stimuli. These results are shown by the dashed line in Fig. 170. We may now state the empirical law for this paradigm: *when stimuli are varied and responses are functionally identical, positive transfer and retroactive facilitation are obtained, the magnitude of both increasing as the similarity among the stimulus members increases.*

(2) *Response variation* $(S_1 \rightarrow R_1; S_1 \rightarrow R_2; S_1 \rightarrow R_1)$.

The condition in which stimuli are constant and responses are varied is the standard associative and reproductive interference paradigm, and, as might be expected, a large number of experiments (e.g. Bruce, 1933; Gibson, 1941; Underwood, 1945) testify to the fact that interference is produced. But there is also a large body of evidence indicating positive transfer under what appear to be the same conditions. Much of the latter can be discounted because the so-called transferred response can be shown to have been *learned previous to the experimental situation.* In discussing the mediation hypothesis it will be recalled that numerous examples were given of transfer to alternate 'behavior routes' when contextual conditions were changed. The point was that these alternatives were not learned in the contemporary situation but were part of the subject's repertoire of instrumental skill hierarchies. Thus a maze path learned with one hand may 'transfer' readily to the other hand, and the rat may 'transfer' from running to leaping. Many other cases of apparent positive transfer with this paradigm are *attributable to 'practice effects.'* The subject has learned 'how to learn nonsense syllables' and this general skill more than compensates for the interference inherent in the design. Whenever this is true, the positive transfer is *not* paralleled by retroactive facilitation, as is normally the case.

This is brought out clearly in an experiment by Underwood (1945), who compared transfer and retroaction effects when stimulus members are constant and responses are varied. The materials consisted of lists of ten pairs of adjectives, identical lists being used to measure both transfer and retroaction. In measuring transfer, subjects learned 0, 2, 4, or 6 lists *prior to* learning a test list, then rested for 25 minutes and were tested for recall of the test list. To measure retroactive effects, subjects had 0, 2, 4, or 6 lists interpolated *after* the original learning of the test list and were finally tested for recall of the test list. (a) The number of trials required to learn the test list decreased regularly with the number of *preceding* lists. Underwood interprets this as attributable to 'practice effects' which obscured actual negative transfer (cf. also Siipola, 1941; Bugelski, 1942). (b) Yet when the test list (learned after varying numbers of previous lists) was *recalled* after 25 minutes, recall decreased regularly with the number of previous lists. Since zero previous lists is the control, this clearly indicates negative transfer. (c) What about the retroactive effects attributable to the interpolation of a varying number of lists having the same stimuli but different responses? Retroactive interference was obtained, varying directly in magnitude with the number of interpolated lists.

These experiments on response variations have dealt only with the raw fact of difference among responses. What about the *degree of similarity* among the varied responses? Perhaps because of difficulty in defining response similarity, there is little data here. In a study by Osgood (1946), original learning of a set of paired associates (such as *c.m.-elated*) was followed by three types of interpolated items, in which the stimulus members were always identical and the response members were varied through three degrees of similarity (such as *c.m.-high, c.m.-left* or *c.m.-low*), as defined by judges. Each subject was made to serve as his own control by learning an equal number of items in each similarity relation. Although retroactive interference was obtained under all conditions, it was significantly *less* for similar meaningful relations. In other words, although the learning of different responses to the same stimulus is always accompanied by some interference, the more nearly similar the two responses, the less

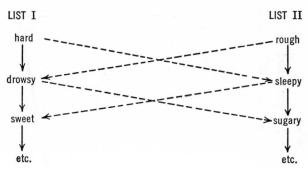

LIST I   LIST II

FIGURE 169. Habit systems generated in the successive learning of serial lists where items having the same ordinal positions are similar. Solid arrows indicate correct, reinforced habits and dashed arrows indicate generalized habits. In this case generalization contributes to errors.

difficulty experienced. We may now state the empirical law for this paradigm: *when stimuli are functionally identical and responses are varied, negative transfer and retroactive interference are obtained, the magnitude of both decreasing as similarity between the responses increases.*

> (3) *Stimuli and responses simultaneously varied*
> $(S_1 \rightarrow R_1; S_2 \rightarrow R_2; S_1 \rightarrow R_1)$.

When lists of material are learned in constant serial order, and similarities are between items having the same serial positions on successive lists, the paradigm cited above is generated. This is the procedure that follows most readily from use of the traditional memory drum, and perhaps for this reason there are many investigations in which this relationship may be analyzed (viz. McGeoch and McDonald, 1931; Johnson, 1933; Melton and Von Lackum, 1941). Figure 169 describes the direct (solid arrows) and generalized (dashed arrows) habit tendencies that are formed under these conditions. Because of the high degree of *stimulus* generalization, for example, between 'drowsy' and 'sleepy,' there will be a tendency for 'sleepy' as a stimulus on the second list to evoke 'sweet' as a response in place of 'sugary.' Similarly, because of the high degree of *response* generalization between 'drowsy' and 'sleepy,' there will be a strong tendency to substitute 'drowsy' as a response to 'rough' during the learning of list II. In other words, both stimulus and response generalization occur here as under the preceding conditions, *but intrusive errors are produced* and hence increasing similarity should yield increased negative transfer and retroactive interference.

These theoretical expectations are clearly verified in the literature. McGeoch and McDonald (1931), in a classic study relating meaningful similarity and interference in learning, used serial lists. Interpolated materials were lists of synonyms of the adjectives learned on the original list,

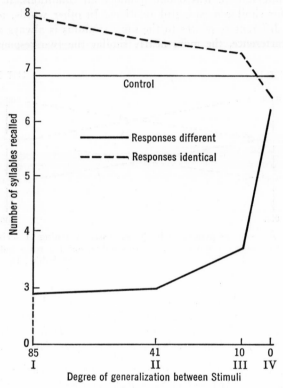

FIGURE 170. Comparison of direction and magnitude of retroactive effect when responses are different and neutral (Gibson's data) and when they are identical (Hamilton's data). Stimuli varied through measured degrees of similarity. Other conditions the same for both studies. Hamilton, *Journal of Experimental Psychology*, 1943, 32:370.

varying through three degrees of synonymity (as ranked by judges). Retroactive interference was found to increase as similarity increased, being maximum with the closest synonyms. Johnson (1933) followed the same procedure with meaningful nouns and obtained the same results; both Johnson (1933) and McGeoch (1937) have showed that negative transfer also appears under these conditions. Melton and Von Lackum (1941) found identical results when nonsense syllables, varying in degrees of similarity, are learned in serial lists.

It is not to be thought, however, that the serial method of learning is essential to these results: any arrangement that creates the same paradigm (both stimuli and responses simultaneously varied) yields the same outcome. An important experiment by E. J. Gibson (1941) illustrates this: her materials and procedures were identical with those reported above for Hamilton (1943)—the Gibson experiment was actually the first of the series—with visual stimulus forms being varied through independently measured degrees of generalization. But here the response members (nonsense syllables) were different and neutral. The solid line in Fig. 170 indicates that retroactive interference was obtained under these conditions increasing in magnitude with increasing similarity. Similar results were found for transfer. These two studies provide a very interesting comparison. The only variation between them is in terms of the identity (Hamilton) or difference (Gibson) among the response members. With identical responses facilitative transfer and retroaction result, but with different responses negative transfer and retroaction result. And notice especially that when the stimulus members are neutral, the relationship among the responses becomes inconsequential, effects of approximately zero magnitude being obtained in both experiments. We may now state the empirical law for the present paradigm: *when both stimulus and response members are simultaneously varied, negative transfer and retroactive interference are obtained, the magnitude of both increasing as the stimulus similarity increases.*

There are a considerable number of substantiating studies which have not been cited here, but if the writer's survey of the literature has been adequate, *there are no exceptions to the above-mentioned empirical laws.* The question may arise, however, as to why these relations have not been phrased in quantitative form. Unfortunately it is comparatively rare in psychology that a group of relations are systematically explored and related by the same investigator under the same conditions and using the same materials. With the number of uncontrolled and even unknown variables at work, it is literally impossible to make cross comparisons in quantitative terms.

One exception to this dictum may be cited. Bruce (1933), using training and test lists of paired nonsense syllables, systematically varied relations among stimuli and responses and measured the amounts of transfer from the first to the second lists. Table 8 gives the relationship studied, a sample

TABLE 8

| | Paradigm | Sample | Degree of Learning Original List | | | |
			0	2	6	12
(a)	S's identical; R's identical	req-kiv req-kiv	(not measured)			
(c)	S's similar; R's identical	req-kiv reb-kiv	100	84	64	44
	S's different; R's identical	req-kiv zaf-kiv	100	115	83	63
(b)	S's different; R's different	req-kiv zaf-yor	100	100	108	84
(e)	S's similar; R's different	req-kiv reb-yor	(not measured)			
	S's different; R's similar	req-kiv zaf-kib	(not measured)			
(d)	S's identical; R's similar	req-kiv req-kib	100	102	101	80
	S's identical; R's different	req-kiv req-yor	100	117	116	109

From data of Bruce, *Journal of Experimental Psychology*, 1933, 347-53.

item, and the number of trials required to learn the test list as a percentage of the number required with no repetition of the first list. The results for the control condition, zero repetitions (100 per cent), are compared with those for 2, 6, and 12 repetitions of the original list. Despite considerable variations within the same condition for different degrees of practice on the training list, certain general conclusions, substantiating our earlier findings, are shown. (a) The condition in which the same items are simply learned further (*S*'s identical; *R*'s identical) was not measured, but we should expect maximum facilitation, i.e. a very low percentage. (b) The condition in which both stimuli and responses are different and neutral (req-kiv zaf-yor) is really the *control condition* here and it reflects the 'practice effect.' Thus for the 12-trial group, we should consider 84 per cent the neutral point. (c) Stimulus variations yield facilitation, the magnitude increasing with stimulus similarity. (d) Response variations tend to yield interference. The case in which responses are similar is clearly superior to that in which they are neutral. (e) Unfortunately conditions in which *both* stimuli and responses are different but degrees of similarity within each are systematically varied are not covered in this study.

The Similarity Paradox

The classic statement of the relation between similarity and interference in human learning, which is found in most textbooks in psychology, is that 'the greater the similarity, the greater the interference.' Although this law is traceable mainly to the work of McGeoch and his associates (McGeoch and McDonald, 1931; Johnson, 1933; McGeoch and McGeoch, 1937), many other experiments appear superficially to substantiate it. When carried to its logical conclusions, however, this law leads to an impossible state of affairs. The highest degree of similarity of both stimulus and response in the materials successively practiced is that in which any simple habit or *S–R* association is learned. The stimulus situation can never be precisely identical from trial to trial, nor can the response, but they are maximally similar—and here the greatest facilitation (ordinary learning) is obtained. *Ordinary learning is at once the theoretical condition for maximal interference but obviously the practical condition for maximal facilitation.* This is the fundamental paradox, and it shows that something is radically wrong with our formulations.

A series of attempts to integrate the facts of transfer and retroaction can be traced in the history of this problem. As early as 1919 Wylie made a distinction between stimulus and response activities, stating that the transfer effect is positive when an 'old' response is associated with a new stimulus but negative when an 'old' stimulus must be associated with a new response. This principle is valid, of course, within the limits of its gross differentiation, but it fails to account for degrees of either stimulus or response similarity. Robinson was one of the first to perceive clearly the paradox, and in 1927 he offered what is now known as the *Skaggs-Robinson Hypothesis* as a resolution. As shown in Fig. 171, facilitation is supposed to be greatest when successively practiced materials are identical (point *A*); it is least, and hence interference is greatest, with some moderate degree of similarity (point *B*); facilitation increases again as we move toward complete neutrality (point *C*), but never attains the original level. Notice that while point *A* defines maximum similarity and point *C* defines minimum similarity, point *B* actually specifies no degree of similarity at all but merely shows that somewhere there is a low point in the facilitation curve. Several experiments (Robinson, 1927; Cheng, 1929; Harden, 1929; Kennelly, 1941) combine to give rough validation to this poorly defined hypothesis, especially the *A–B* sector of it.

The series of studies by McGeoch and his associates ran into direct conflict with this hypothesis and the experimental evidence supporting it, for they had found interference to increase steadily with increasing similarity, no upturn being obtained for even closest synonyms. In the *Psychology of Human Learning* (1942), McGeoch offered two alternative *rapprochements:* (1) He distinguished 'similarity of meaning' and 'degrees of identity' as two different dimensions of similarity, each having a different interference function. Some of the experiments supporting the Skaggs-Robinson Hypothesis had employed numeral and letter combinations with similarity

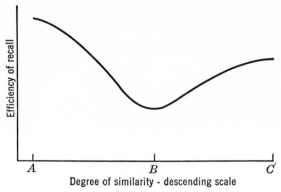

Degree of similarity - descending scale

FIGURE 171. Skaggs-Robinson Hypothesis: point *A* specifies maximum similarity (identity) and point *C* minimum similarity (neutrality) among successively practiced materials; point *B* merely indicates the low point for efficiency of recall. Robinson, *American Journal of Psychology*, 1927, 39:299.

indexed by the number of identical elements. But other substantiating studies had used materials in which identical elements were no more specifiable than with meaningful words: Dreis (1933) used code-substitution and Watson (1938) used card-sorting. (2) At a later point he suggested that his results applied only to the portion of the Robinson curve between *B* and *C*, i.e. that the maximum similarity of his meaningful materials only reached point *B*. Given the multidirectional shape of this theoretical function, however, and the fact that point *B* defines no degree of similarity, *any* obtained data could be fitted to some portion of it. And there is clear experimental evidence against either of McGeoch's resolutions in the experiment by Osgood (1946) previously cited. Meaningful materials were also used here and in the traditional retroaction paradigm, but interference was found to *decrease* as meaningful similarity among the response members increased. Not only would these results fit 'degree of identity' as the functioning dimension, despite the meaningful character of the materials, but they fall within the *A–B* sector of the theoretical curve!

One of the most recent attempts to integrate these data has been made by E. J. Gibson (1940). She followed Wylie's lead in differentiating between stimulus variation and response variation, and she added to this picture the refinement of stimulus generalization, derived from Pavlovian conditioning principles. Her two theoretical laws were these: (1) if responses are *identical*, facilitation is obtained, its magnitude increasing with stimulus generalization (similarity); (2) if responses are *different*, interference is obtained, its magnitude increasing with stimulus generalization (similarity). These hypotheses fit much of the data in the field and further serve to integrate the phenomena of human learning with those of the animal laboratory. But they are insufficient. (a) No account is given of the *degree* of response similarity, and this is one of the relevant variables. (b) The fundamental paradox remains: responses can never be truly identical, yet ordinary learning does occur.

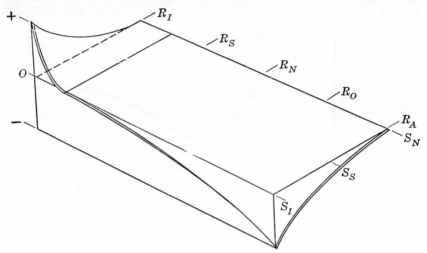

FIGURE 172. Transfer and retroaction surface: medial plane represents effects of zero magnitude; response relations distributed along length of solid and stimulus relations along width. Osgood, *Psychological Review*, 1949, **56**:140.

Osgood (1949) has shown that a resolution of this paradox can be literally constructed from existing empirical data. The three empirical laws described in the preceding section sharply limit the possible theoretical models that can be generated. Integration of these laws yields the three-dimensional model described as Fig. 172 (for details, see the original article), which has been called *the transfer and retroaction surface*. Direction and degree of both transfer and retroaction are represented by the vertical dimension of this model; degrees of stimulus similarity are distributed along the width of the solid and degrees of response similarity along the length of the solid. The medial plane of the model represents effects of zero magnitude. Notice that where the stimuli in successively practiced tasks are completely unrelated (S_N—the rear edge of the surface), it makes no difference how the responses are related; effects of zero magnitude are obtained (cf. results of Gibson, 1941, and Hamilton, 1943, with stimuli neutral). As the stimuli in successively practiced tasks are made more nearly similar, the directional effects of response relations become increasingly significant, until with stimuli 'identical' (front edge of model) a sharply inflected function is obtained, highly similar responses (R_I) yielding facilitation and different responses (R_S to R_A) yielding increasing amounts of interference.

All available empirical evidence can be referred to some series of points on the theoretical surface which intersects the medial plane between functionally 'identical' responses (R_I) and different but similar responses (R_S). The transfer (generalization) data of Hovland (1937 a) and the retroaction data of Hamilton (1943) were obtained under conditions in which stimulus relations were varied and responses were constant—the upper edge of this surface, between S_I and S_N (for R_I) represents the generalization gradient obtained. Maximum facilitation is shown to occur when both stimuli and responses are functionally identical (ordinary learning). Gibson (1941) varied stimulus relations while keeping responses different and *neutral*. A series of points placed along the plane defined by R_N would represent the fact that she found increasing interference as stimuli approached identity under these conditions. Osgood (1946) kept stimuli identical, varying response relations through similarity to opposition in meaning. His data are satisfactorily represented by a series of points along the frontal edge (S_I) of this surface from R_S to R_O. Although no empirical evidence is available for directly antagonistic reactions, there is reason to believe that this would be the response condition for maximal interference, when stimuli are identical (cf. Osgood, 1948). Even the apparently anomalous data obtained by McGeoch and his associates fit this surface: since he simultaneously increased the similarity of *both* stimuli and responses from neutrality to high similarity (but not identity), a series of points representing his conditions would have to run downward (increasing interference) from the medial plane at R_N, S_N to the point on the surface defined by R_S, S_S.

This transfer and retroaction surface was constructed on a qualitative basis, because the essential empirical data, obtained by different investigators using different materials and procedures, cannot be combined quantitatively. There is need, therefore, for an extensive *quantitative check* on this surface, by one investigator using equivalent subjects, materials, and procedures. It should be noticed that this surface *predicts* certain relations which have not yet been checked—particularly (a) the effects of response antagonism and (b) the fact that for some high degree of response similarity zero transfer and retroaction should be obtained regardless of the relations among stimuli (e.g. the series of points representing the intersection of the surface and the medial plane). Beyond resolving the fundamental paradox with which this section began, this hypothesis has the advantage that both transfer and retroaction data are integrated within a single framework. It also removes the need for distinguishing between meaningful and nonsense materials or between meaningful similarity and degrees of identity; data fitting this surface have been described under all these conditions.

Temporal Relations I. Transfer

After a training task has been practiced to a criterion, an interval of varying length may be inserted before the test task is given. In a certain sense the amount of transfer from the first task to the second is a measure of the *retention* of the first—the weaker the first-task habits have become, the less effectively they can interfere with (or facilitate) learning of the second. If the previous task is gradually forgotten, its transfer to a subsequent task should also decrease. A number of experiments (Bunch, 1936;

Bunch and McCraven, 1938; Bunch and Lang, 1939; and others) have failed to verify this prediction. Bunch (1936), using human subjects, compared amounts of transfer over varying intervals (learning of new task) with retention over the same intervals (relearning of original task). The results, shown in Fig. 173, indicate a lack of correspondence between retention of an activity and its transfer capacity. Although retention shows loss through time, the amount of transfer effect is roughly constant over this 90-day period. On the face of it, this is a very puzzling finding. It appears that an activity, itself gradually forgotten, can nevertheless maintain its transfer effects upon similar performances that occur later. It may be that

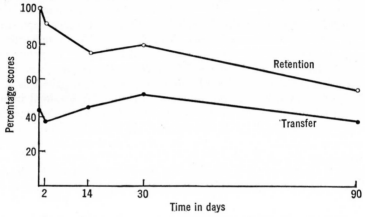

FIGURE 173. Curves for retention and transfer over identical intervals and under the same general conditions. Bunch, *Journal of Comparative Psychology,* 1936, 22:333.

the loss in retention was primarily for specific associations, whereas the transfer was due to more stable 'practice effects'—while forgetting particular items, the subjects may have remembered 'how to learn' this type of task.

But this is not the whole picture. In the case of negative transfer there is also a *discrimination factor* involved. The better the previous activity is itself discriminated (within-material and extra-material confusions eliminated through practice), the less it will be confused with the test activity. In the present connection this means that as the time interval between previous and test tasks is increased, negative transfer should first increase and then decrease. Ray (1945) reasoned in this manner and his experimental results bore him out. Paired associates (with stimuli constant and responses varied in prior and test lists) were learned to a criterion of two perfect repetitions by five groups of subjects, each having a different interval between the two lists. As shown in Fig. 174, maximum negative transfer occurred with a 2-day interval. Although the differences between the points on this curve were not significant statistically, the trend is apparent. Bunch and Rogers (1936) obtained a trend roughly corresponding to this.

How are we to reconcile these conflicting results? One group of studies finds no relation between time interval and transfer, but another group finds a definite relation, and both have certain theoretical justification. (1) Regardless of whether the paradigms in various experiments are designed to yield positive or negative transfer, 'practice effects' are undoubtedly present, their magnitudes being difficult to assay. (2) In some studies the locus of homogeneities is not specifiable, and hence it is difficult to know what transfer effects, if any, to expect. (3) The criterion of mastery for original learning is especially important. Ray's (1945) results are undoubtedly in part a function of his use of a strict criterion (two perfect repetitions), thus bringing into play the discrimination factor. (4) Another important factor is the measure of transfer used. In some cases the measurement has been based on the first fifth of the learning and in others it has been based on the number of trials to reach mastery. Yet Underwood (1945) has shown

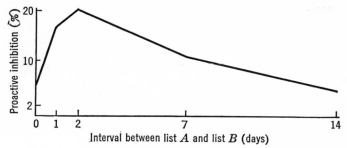

FIGURE 174. Proactive inhibition (measured by correct anticipations at end of first fifth of learning) as a function of the time interval between lists *A* and *B*. Ray, *American Journal of Psychology*, 1945, 58:523.

that transfer effects are largely restricted to the first few trials on the test materials. These and many other factors may enter in to obscure the actual relations.

Temporal Relations II. Retroaction

Both direction and degree of retroactive effect have been found to depend upon the similarity between original and interpolated materials. Is the temporal point of interpolation itself an effective factor? Ray's (1945) results suggest that interpolation should be most effective at that point where the original habits have been reduced to moderate strength, i.e. not immediately after original learning nor yet after too long an interval, but somewhere *in the middle of the retention period*. Many of the early workers, following Müller and Pilzecker (1900), believed that interpolating the specific interfering activity *immediately after original learning* should produce the most interference—disturbing the consolidation of memory traces. Robinson's monograph (1920) on retroaction concludes that *the degree of interference is independent of interpolation*. Both Whitely (1927) and McGeoch (1933) found the effect to be greatest if the specific interpolated activity were inserted *just before relearning*. Minami and Dallenbach (1946) and Postman and Alper (1946) have agreed in finding at least two points of maximal interference, *both closely following original learning and closely preceding relearning*. Every possibility has its supporters!

The Minami and Dallenbach study (1946) made ingenious use of the common cockroach as subject. The original learning involved running back and forth along a lighted runway, avoiding entering a darkened area in which they were shocked. The interpolated activity was forced running while held over a specially devised moving belt. Poorest retention occurred when the forced activity was given immediately after original learning or just before relearning. The authors interpret these results as indicating the existence of two factors, 'anticonsolidation' and 'irritability,' the latter being attributable to the after-effects of forced activity upon relearning. We shall reconsider these factors in the final theoretical section. The condition of forced activity used here is quite dissimilar to the types of interpolated behaviors used with human subjects, of course, and the 'irritability' factor may not apply in most studies.

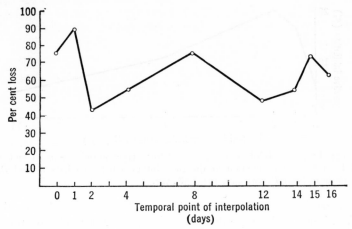

FIGURE 175. Per cent retention loss as a function of temporal point of interpolating *B* between original learning and recall of *A*. Postman and Alper, *American Journal of Psychology,* 1946, 59:444.

A more typical study was that by Postman and Alper (1946). Subjects first learned 20 pairs of monosyllabic words (*A–B*) and then had interpolated 20 new pairs having the same stimuli but different responses (*A–K*). Nine groups of subjects, seven individuals in each, learned these interpolated materials at various points in a total retention period of 16 days; immediately after original learning, after 1, 2, 4, 8, 12, 14, and 15 days, and just before recall of the original materials. Exactly five trials were given on both the original and interpolated lists. The results are shown in Fig. 175 and are reported in terms of per cent loss at recall, i.e. 100 per cent loss would mean that no items were recalled; 50 per cent loss would mean that half as many items were recalled as were present on the last trial of the original learning. Although there is a rough correspondence shown here with other findings, two surprising phenomena appear: (a) maximal interference shows up a full day after original learning and a full day before relearning rather than immediately following and preceding, and (b) there is a third point of maximal effect, exactly in the middle of the temporal interval.

Using punchboard mazes, Bunch (1946) compared the retroactive effect produced by interpolating a highly similar task either immediately after original learning or after the long interval of 120 days. Notice that here the experimental variable is the length of the delay interval between original and interpolated learning, relearning commencing immediately after interpolation in both cases. Two 'rest' control conditions are necessary here, one being tested for retention after 20 minutes (the time taken for interpolated work in the first experimental group) and the other being tested for retention after 120 days. Whereas immediate interpolation produced retroactive interference, interpolation after a long period produced definite facilitation, the experimental group relearning the original maze more easily than the control group. Assuming that the amount of interpolation was actually equivalent, this experiment indicates that the facilitative 'practice effect' of doing a similar interpolated problem after a long interval more than compensates for the minimal confusion it causes.

Although both the point at which interpolated material is inserted and the length of the retention interval are shown to be important variables, exactly how they function is not clear. Unspecifiable variations among experiments in terms of both materials and procedures are again responsible. Looming large is the *criterion of interpolated learning* employed. If subjects are given an equal *number* of trials (cf. Postman and Alper, 1946), there is inadequate control over the actual degree of learning. If learning is to the same *criterion of mastery* (cf. Bunch, 1946), then amount of interpolated activity probably varies with the amount of forgetting that has occurred. Other factors, such as the similarity of original and interpolated materials used in different experiments, are also confounded with the temporal factor. Until such procedural difficulties are ironed out, little conclusive evidence can be expected.

Degree of Learning

At the simplest level, it has been shown that the magnitude of generalization (Hovland, 1937 c) first increases *and then decreases* as the number of reinforced trials on the original training increases. Although Bruce (1933) found positive transfer to continue increasing up to 12 trials on the original materials, it is possible that this number was not sufficient to reveal the final decrease indicated by Hovland's results. Working with a paradigm designed to yield negative transfer, Siipola and Israel (1933) found its magnitude first to increase and then decrease with increasing amounts of original training, the sign of the transfer becoming positive with a sufficient number of trials. This final shift from negative to positive probably indicates that the diminution of negative effects permitted 'practice effects' to make their existence felt. Razran's (1940) study on configural conditioning of the salivary reaction and E. J. Gibson's (1942) study on within-list interference (in paired-associate learning) both indicate that generalization first increases, causing confusion, and then decreases as a function of the degree of learning.

Gagné and Foster (1949) contribute a significant study here. The test task was a complex motor skill, requiring the subject to make differential switch-closing reactions to patterns of four lights. Matched subgroups were given 0 (control), 10, 30, or 50 preliminary trials *on a component of the total task*. Both reaction time and error scores were obtained. As may be seen in Fig. 176, 30 or 50 trials on a component yielded immediate transfer to the learning of the total task. Total errors made while learning the final, complex skill are shown in Fig. 177 to first increase and then decrease as the degree of pretraining on a component is increased, thus justifying Gibson's (1940) and Gagné's hypothesis that generalization first increases and then decreases as a function of the degree of learning. Careful inspection of the reaction-time curves shown in Fig. 176 reveals another interesting phenomenon: each curve shows a *plateau* during which continued practice is not accompanied by further improvement (the 50-trial group

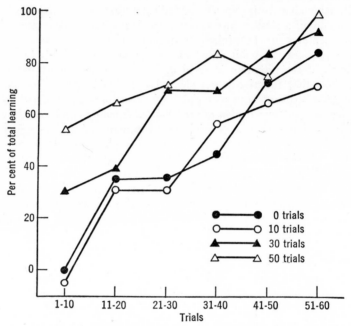

FIGURE 176. Per cent of total learning of a motor skill after varying numbers of preliminary training trials on components of the skill. Gagné and Foster, *Journal of Experimental Psychology*, 1949, **39**: 57.

even showing a temporary drop in performance), and we notice that the stage in learning the total skill at which these plateaus occur is progressively delayed as the degree of practice on a component is increased. One possible interpretation is that, other things being equal (i.e. similarity factor), maximum confusion and mutual blocking between competing responses occur when they are of roughly equal habit strength. This point would be reached at progressively later stages in the learning of the total skill as pretraining on a component is increased—the potential competitors must themselves become stronger in order to exert maximum effect. Just such a relation between equality of habit strength and degree of motor conflict has been found by Sears and Hovland (1941).

The same phenomenon, increasing and then decreasing interference, has been found with some regularity in retroaction studies in which the *degree of interpolated learning* has been systematically varied. Melton and Irwin (1940) varied the number of trials on an interpolated list having the same number of items as the original list; maximum interference appeared where the number of interpolated trials was approximately double those given in original learning (see total *RI* curve in Fig. 179). Osgood (1948) varied the number of *correct responses* on the interpolated items, and although interference increased regularly with degree of interpolation, the function was negatively accelerated, the leveling-off point occurring at about double the degree of original learning. Thune and Underwood (1943) obtained the same negatively accelerated curve, again with a leveling-off point at about double the degree of practice given on original learning. If we can

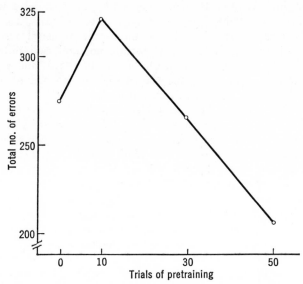

FIGURE 177. Generalization following various amounts of pretraining on components of a motor skill, as estimated from number of errors during final practice on total task. Gagné and Foster, *Journal of Experimental Psychology,* 1949, **39**:60.

assume that, in order to reach equal habit strength, the interpolated responses must be given approximately double practice—to counteract negative transfer effects from the original to the interpolated learning—then we have evidence that is in essential agreement with Sears and Hovland (1941) and Gagné and Foster (1949), response confusion and blocking being maximal when competing habits are roughly equal in strength.

We have here common findings for both transfer and retroaction. As the amount of practice on the preceding material is increased toward high degrees of mastery, *both facilitative and interfering effects appear to reach a maximum and then decrease in magnitude.* That some discrimination process develops with high degrees of learning on specific materials has been suggested by a number of writers (cf. Underwood, 1945). With increasing practice there is increasing differentiation of the preceding materials, and as they become better differentiated they are less likely to be confused with the test activities. According to this point of view, discrimination between two sets of material is minimal, and interference therefore maximal, when both are learned to approximately equal but moderate degrees.

Whole vs. Part Methods of Learning

Like so many psychological problems, the question as to the comparative values of repeating the entire task 'globally' on each trial or dividing it 'piecemeal' into more manageable parts had its origin in the schoolroom, and here the dictum was usually 'divide and conquer.' Yet most of the earlier experimenters found the whole method superior, and they used school-type materials, like short selections of prose or poetry. Superiority of the whole method has also been found when the materials were not organized (Seibert, 1932, with paired English and French vocabulary words), not meaningful (Warner Brown, 1924, with paired stimulus words and response nonsense syllables), and not even verbal (Crafts, 1929, with a card-sorting task). But this is by no means the universal result: many investigators have been able to demonstrate no significant difference between methods (Winch, 1924; G. O. McGeoch, 1931), and at least one recent study (Orbison, 1944) has shown the part method to become increasingly superior as amount of material is increased.

The learning of mazes by both animals and humans, the maze being a serial task like a poem, might be expected to show superiority of the whole method. Using sophisticated maze-runners, some investigators (e.g. Hanawalt, 1931, 1934) have obtained this result; others (e.g. Pechstein, 1917, 1921, and Barton, 1921) have found part methods superior; and another student (Cook, 1936, 1937) obtained no significant differences. Extensive reviews of an inconclusive literature on this problem may be found in Woodworth (1938) and McGeoch (1942). Actually, 'whole' and 'part' methods refer more accurately to arbitrary distinctions made by experimenters than to different behaviors of their subjects: one 'part' of a 16-line poem is usually four lines that are learned as a 'whole' before one proceeds with other 'parts'; in learning by the 'whole' method, the subject typically concentrates upon certain 'parts' at any given stage of learning before incorporating them with other 'parts.'

There are sufficient reasons for confusion in this area. The whole-part problem is a high-level issue resting upon many simpler but variable factors, all complexly interrelated. In many experiments in which serial learning is used for both wholes and parts, first-position items in one part are likely to interfere with first-position items in other parts, and so forth. Differences between massed and distributed practice are involved—since repetitions of each item are necessarily more 'massed' in the part than in the whole method, distribution would seem to favor the latter. Both positive and negative transfer and retroaction are simultaneously operative, obviously in the part method and more subtly in the whole method. Referring again to Gagné's (1949) work in which it was shown that both positive and negative transfer vary with the *degree of learning,* it may be seen that this factor will be fluctuating in the part method and relatively more stable for the whole method, but exactly how ease of learning by the two techniques would be affected is difficult to predict.

A theoretical analysis of at least part of the problem has been made by McGeoch (1942, pp. 188-95) and utilized by Orbison (1944) in his experimental work. Let Tw represent the time required to learn a given set of materials by the whole method and Tp represent that required to learn the same materials by the part method. Let us assume, for simplicity's sake, that the material is divided into two parts of equal length; the time for learning the two parts can be expressed as Tp_1 and Tp_2. Now since we know that the total time required to learn a list of materials increases *disproportionately* with the length of the list, it follows that one list of 16 items will take longer than two lists of 8 items each, i.e. that Tw will be greater than Tp_1 plus Tp_2. Does this mean that the part method should always be superior to the whole method? Not at all. The separately mastered parts must finally be *combined* into the whole, and this also takes time. If we let Tc represent the time required to combine the parts, then Tp equals Tp_1 plus Tp_2 plus Tc. If we let D represent the gross difference

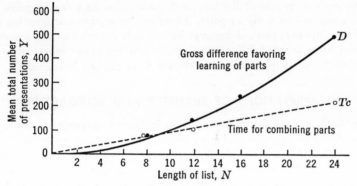

FIGURE 178. Data showing increasing superiority of part over whole methods of learning as amount of material to be learned increases. Time for combining parts (dashed curve) rises more slowly than the gross difference favoring the learning of parts. W. D. Orbison, Unpublished Ph.D. thesis, Yale University, 1944.

in time between learning by the whole method (Tw) and learning the separate parts (Tp_1 plus Tp_2), then the relative efficiencies of the whole and part methods will depend upon the magnitudes of D and Tc. In other words, if the time required to combine the parts, once they have been separately mastered, is greater than the saving obtained by learning short parts rather than the long whole, then the whole method will be superior—and vice versa. It becomes apparent from this analysis that the most important variables for the whole-part problem will be those that differentially alter the magnitude of Tc and D.

By making certain additional assumptions concerning inter-item generalization and discrimination, both within and between parts, Orbison has been able to predict that *the part method should become superior as the amount of material learned increases.* The essence of the argument is this: since items become increasingly well discriminated (from possible sources of interference) as the lists in which they appear are lengthened, the time to combine parts (Tc) should increase at a slower rate than the saving in learning short parts over longer wholes (D); this assumes that the size of the parts varies (and the number of parts stays constant) as the length of the whole increases. To test this prediction, Orbison had different groups of matched subjects learn sets of 8, 12, and 24 paired associates by both whole and part methods, word-nonsense syllable pairs being presented *randomly* to avoid serial effects. When learning was by the whole method, the entire set of pairs was presented on each trial, practice continuing until a criterion of one perfect repetition was attained. When learning was by the part method, two parts were each practiced separately to a criterion of one perfect repetition, then the pairs in both parts were combined and practice continued until the same criterion for the total list was reached. The major results are shown in Fig. 178 and they clearly substantiate the prediction: time for combining the parts (dashed line) rises more slowly with increasing length than the gross difference favoring the learning of the separate parts over the whole (solid line). The actual values for complete learning by whole and part methods are not shown directly in this figure, but they may be derived from the curves; the per cent that Tp was of Tw for the various lengths of list was 99.6 for 8 pairs, 82.4 for 12 pairs, 81.5 for 16 pairs and 65.5 for 24 pairs. These results answer one question quite decisively: the part method becomes increasingly superior as the amount of material to be learned is increased. But there are many other factors influencing the whole-part issue that remain to be studied intensively.

INTERPRETATIONS OF TRANSFER AND RETROACTION

The fields of transfer and retroaction in human learning are among the best explored in experimental psychology. From this survey it has become apparent that the two sets of phenomena are intimately related, sufficiently so that the major variables one can isolate are found to affect them in equivalent ways. An adequate theory then must incorporate both. An attempt to clarify the similarity paradox was made in an earlier theoretical section, and the crucial theoretical question remaining is this: *What are the underlying causes of transfer and retroaction?* Why do the measured facilitative and interfering effects occur?

Perseveration and Anticonsolidation

Müller and Pilzecker, in 1900, advanced a pseudoneurological theory to explain retroactive interference. They argued that the neural correlates of learning persist through time after active practice has ceased, this perseveration serving to strengthen or consolidate the associations formed. If, therefore, other activity is introduced immediately after learning, the consolidation process is interfered with and loss in retention results. This general type of theory, it will be recalled, was also proposed as an explanation of reminiscence and the beneficial effects of distributed practice. According to this hypothesis, interpolation should become progressively less detrimental as the specific interfering activities are inserted after increasing intervals of time, and disappear entirely after a sufficiently long (undefinable by the theory) interval. The evidence here is conflicting, as we have seen. In many studies retroactive interference has been shown when the specific activity is given after many days or even weeks. On general grounds the perseveration theory falls down because it has nothing specific to say about the role of the similarity factor, degrees of similarity between original and interpolated materials having been revealed as perhaps the most important single variable. Finally, and perhaps most critically, the theory will not account for facilitative transfer or retroaction. How can certain types of interpolated activities increase the consolidation process?

These arguments show quite conclusively that the perseveration construct is not sufficient, but it could still be one factor in the total picture. Minami and Dallenbach (1946) have referred to this type of interfering process as an anticonsolidation factor, the subsequent activity being assumed to prevent fixation of the original associations. It is tempting to relate the evidence for perseveration with the phenomenon of *reminiscence*. In this case the anticonsolidating effect of immediate interpolation would be due to interference with reminiscence, i.e. with dissipation of inhibitory tendencies, following original learning. This possibility is readily testable—immediate interpolation should not produce greater forgetting if the original learning proceeded under conditions of distributed practice, since there would be no inhibition with whose dissipation the interpolated activity could interfere. Should this relation appear, it also would help explain the conflicting results on the temporal point of inserting the interpolated activity.

Competition-of-response Theory

The phenomena of transfer, retroaction, and forgetting are clearly placed on the same continuum in the competition-of-response theory, which, as its label indicates, is a straightforward interference point of view. Sponsored most vigorously by McGeoch and his associates (see McGeoch, 1942, pp. 488-95), this theory originates in the experimental evidence relating transfer and retroaction to the similarity of materials. *Associative inhibition* (negative transfer) is due to the overt or implicit intrusion of responses from the training materials during the learning of the test materials; *reproductive inhibition* (retroactive interference) is due to the overt or implicit intrusion of interpolated responses at the time of recalling the original materials. Stated most succinctly, the response of saying B to stimulus A is inhibited because another response, K, takes its place, and the frequent appearance of such intrusions is direct positive evidence. McKinney and McGeoch (1935) estimated that about 25 per cent of the total retroaction might be due to overt intrusions, the remainder presumably being attributed to implicit competition. Gibson (1940), following the general outlines of Hull's behavioral system, has applied the principles of conditioning to these phenomena of verbal learning. Her analysis was mainly concerned with elaborating the effects of *stimulus generalization*. The more difficult it is to discriminate the stimulus members, the greater become the confusion among the responses. Rather than contradicting the competition-of-response theory, Gibson's generalization hypothesis renders more specific and predictable the conditions under which more or less response competition will occur.

The bulk of the data can be fitted into this theory, but is competition among responses the sole factor determining transfer and retroaction? Before attempting to answer this question, one must look carefully at the indices employed to reveal the functioning of this or other possible factors. The mere occurrence or nonoccurrence of the correct response during recall, although generally used to measure total retroactive interference, gives no indication of *why* the correct reactions fail to appear. What other data does the experimenter have available in his records that can give him clues as to the cause of interference? (a) *Overt interlist intrusions.* Here the subject substitutes a response that had appeared on the interpolated list. This intrusion may have been associated with the same or a similar stimulus on the interpolated list, in which case we are dealing directly with interlist response competition. (b) *Overt intralist intrusions.* The subject intrudes one of the other responses within the same set of materials he is practicing or recalling. Such intrusions reflect indiscriminability within the list. (c) *Blanks.* Simple failures of response may represent just that—some inhibitory process—or they may frequently reflect *implicit intrusions,* e.g.

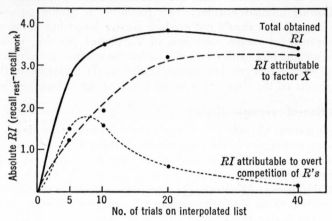

FIGURE 179. Relation of total *RI* to competition index as number of trials on interpolated material varies. Factor *X* is determined by subtracting *RI* attributable to competition from total *RI*. Melton and Irwin, *American Journal of Psychology,* 1940, **53**: 198.

the subject thinks of the interpolated intrusive response, recognized it as wrong in the present recall context, and hence remains silent. (d) *Latency of response.* The speed with which either correct or intrusive responses are given is yet another useful measure. As we have already seen in an earlier chapter, latency is one measure of habit strength, and hence strong associations should yield faster response times than weak associations.

If competition-of-response were the sole cause of retroactive interference, total interference should always be correlated with the number of overt *interlist* intrusions, the most direct index of the competition factor. The frequency of such overt intrusions is only an index, not an accurate measure, since much of the competition can be assumed to be implicit, resulting in blanks being recorded. Melton and Irwin (1940) have made such a test and obtained negative results. After equated learning of one list of nonsense syllables, different groups of subjects were given varying amounts of practice on the interpolated list, o trials (control rest condition), 5, 10, 20, and 40 trials; finally, all subjects recalled and relearned the original list of materials. Figure 179 shows their results as a function of the amount of interpolated learning. Although total interference increases with amount of interpolation through 20 trials (falling off slightly with 40 interpolated trials), the amount of *RI* attributable to response competition decreases consistently after five interpolated trials. In other words, *the indexed amount of response competition does not parallel the variations in total interference.* Melton and Irwin therefore reasoned that some other factor (or factors), which they labeled 'Factor X,' must also be operating to produce loss in retention. They tentatively identified this factor as *unlearning during interpolation,* e.g. the original-list responses that occur during interpolation are wrong in that context and hence are unlearned. The dashed line in Fig. 179, representing 'Factor X,' was obtained by subtracting the amount of RI attributable to competition from the total measured RI.

Two-factor Theory of Retroactive Interference

Competition and unlearning factors have been combined into what is now known as the two-factor theory. Total interference is attributed to (a) competition of original and interpolated responses at the point of recall and (b) unlearning of the original responses during interpolation. Since, as Underwood (1945) has pointed out, the effect of unlearning is to reduce the effectiveness with which the original responses can compete at the time of recall, total RI is still due to interference of the interpolated responses during the attempted recall of the original materials—this is still an interference theory of forgetting. There have appeared recently several experimental checks of predictions from this theory. Since proactive interference involves only the competition factor, whereas retroactive interference includes unlearning decrements as well, retroaction should be of greater magnitude than proaction for the same materials. McGeoch and Underwood (1943) verified this prediction with the $A-B$; $A-K$; $A-B$ paradigm. Another implication of the two-factor theory is this: the appearance and unlearning of original responses during interpolation produces *negative transfer* (proactive interference); since the process producing negative transfer is thus presumably the same as that which increases retroaction (e.g. unlearning), and since negative transfer has been shown to be of brief duration (lasting for only the first few trials of interpolation), one may predict that the difference between proactive and retroactive interference should be constant after the first few trials. This prediction has been verified by Underwood (1945).

Is the two-factor theory adequate? Does it cover all relevant facts? The answer appears to be that it is not adequate. First, in just the same sense that frequency of overt interlist intrusions during recall is an index of the competition factor, *so the frequency of overt intrusions of original responses during interpolation is an index of the unlearning factor.* That is, in order that an original response be 'punished' and unlearned, it must occur either overtly or implicitly. In Melton and Irwin's own data (1940), the frequencies of these intrusions varied irregularly with the degree of interpolated learning, not fitting the 'Factor X' function. Other experimenters (Thune and Underwood, 1943; Osgood, 1948) have found frequencies of such intrusions to be insignificantly small. Either the unlearning factor is of limited importance or the use of overt intrusions is an invalid index of it (cf. Underwood, 1945).

Most direct evidence against the adequacy of the two-factor theory is to be found in a previously cited experiment by Osgood (1946). Using the paradigm designed to maximize interference effects, $A-B$; $A-K$; $A-B$, the responses were meaningful adjectives varying in similarity between members on the two lists. Significantly *less* interference occurred for similar responses than for either neutral responses or those opposed in meaning. Now if this difference in total *RI* were due to the competition factor, overt intrusion of interpolated items during recall should have been least frequent for the similar condition (to explain the minimal interference here). But *more* of these intrusions occurred for the similar condition than for any other. If, on the other hand, this difference in total *RI* were due to the unlearning factor, then overt intrusions of original responses during interpolation should occur least frequently in the similar condition (to explain their lesser unlearning). But significantly *more* intrusions of original responses during interpolation occurred in the similar condition than in either of the others. Neither the competition factor nor the unlearning factor, as indexed by intrusions, is able to account for the data of this experiment.

Reciprocal Inhibition of Antagonistic Responses

The fact that none of the factors considered so far can explain the above-mentioned results implies the existence of yet another factor (or factors). Despite the conventional use of the term 'retroactive *inhibition*' in this field,

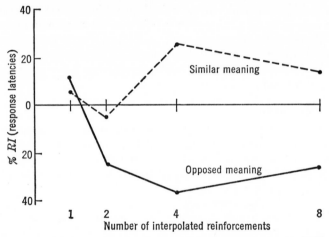

FIGURE 180. Comparative amounts of retroactive interference or facilitation, as measured by speed of responding on the first relearning trial, for words *similar* or *opposed* in meaning to the interpolated responses. Results for 1, 2, 4, and 8 degrees of interpolated reinforcement are shown. Osgood, *Journal of Experimental Psychology*, 1948, 38:142.

none of the explanations discussed so far actually utilizes any conception of an inhibitory psychological process. The competition theory merely assumes that the response of saying *B* to stimulus *A* fails to occur because another response, *K*, takes its place. Osgood (1948) interpreted the results of his experiments as indicating the existence of an *actual inhibitory process*, the nature of which was revealed in the characteristics of successively learning meaningfully *opposed* responses. These characteristics were: (1) increased latency (slowing) of responses in both transfer and retroaction situations, (2) persistence of blanks (failures of response) through the course of relearning the original materials, and (3) both latency of response and persistence of blanks increasing with the degree of interpolated learning, according to a negatively accelerated function. The average latencies of response for similar and opposed meaningful materials on the first recall trial are shown in Fig. 180 as a function of the degree of interpolated learning. Whereas the speed of responding for similar materials tends actually to increase as the amount of interpolated learning is increased, opposed responses are made progressively more slowly. Since it has been demonstrated that response latency varies inversely with habit strength, it would appear that a selective weakening of habits occurs when responses of opposed meaning are interpolated.

The hypothesis proposed to account for these phenomena was that *simultaneous with the learning of any positive habit there is generated equal inhibitory tendency in the association of the same stimulus with the directly antagonistic reaction.* These inhibitory tendencies were assumed to generalize in the same manner as excitatory tendencies. Thus the generalized inhibitory tendencies developed during the interpolation of meaningfully opposed materials subtract directly from the excitatory tendencies produced during original learning, this weakened habit strength being reflected in decreased speed of responding at recall. Such reciprocal inhibition has been explored only in terms of meaningful verbal materials, and even here several assumptions are made. One assumption is that the meanings of verbal opposites, such as 'tense-relaxed,' are based upon reciprocally antagonistic mediating reactions (cf. Chap. 9). Another is that these inhibitory characteristics are specific to antagonistic reactions and are not found in the successive learning of neutral materials.

An Irritation Factor

Minami and Dallenbach (1946), using cockroach subjects, found that forced activity produced maximum interference if interpolated immediately after original learning or immediately before relearning. They interpret these results as indicating the existence of two factors: (a) an 'anticonsolidation factor,' which has already been discussed, and (b) an 'irritability factor,' which is attributed to the after-effects of activity upon relearning. The choice of the term 'irritability' to describe this factor was based upon the fact that 'after being transferred from the treadmill to the learning box, S shows a marked restlessness and runs immediately in the dark compartment. After receiving a shock it turns back to the illuminated part of the box with such speed that it often bumps into the end wall. This violent response is repeated many times almost without pause . . . defecation and urination were often observed. They also become very sensitive to external stimuli such as light touches or accidental air-currents' (pp. 15-16). It seems doubtful that such a factor would apply to all retroactive phenomena; it is probably limited to the conditions of this type of experiment and the organism used as subject. A fatigue explanation is ruled out by Minami and Dallenbach because the cockroaches showed increased vigor of activity after the treadmill workout; however, if the cockroach can rest satisfactorily only in the darkness, then the effects of fatigue would be to increase motivation toward getting into the dark. In other words, in this experiment the effect of the interpolated activity may be one of increasing the drive behind the wrong response (running into the dark compartment where they are shocked).

Summary on Causes of Retroactive Interference

An evaluation of current theories of transfer and retroaction makes it clear that no single theory and no single factor is sufficient. Several relevant factors have been isolated and more will probably be discovered. Exactly which factors are responsible for the loss in retention in a given investigation depends upon the materials used and the procedures followed. Nevertheless, on the basis of existing evidence, one may sketch the causes at work to produce interference (or facilitation) in most situations.

The most pervasive cause of interference in learning, whether it be negative transfer or retroactive interference, is undoubtedly competition among responses in the successive materials. If the paradigm employed is one in which stimulus and response generalization leads to errors, then the magnitude of response competition increases with the similarity of materials, with resultant increase in measured negative transfer or retroaction. If, on the other hand, the paradigm is one in which the same stimulus and response generalization strengthens the correct associations, measured facilitative transfer and retroaction increases with the similarity of materials. For a more detailed discussion of these homogeneity relations the reader is referred to the discussion of the similarity paradox. The frequency of overt interlist intrusions is a direct index of the magnitude of the competition factor in a given situation.

Beyond this general cause of interference in learning there are several specific causes whose presence or absence depends upon the precise nature of the materials and procedures. Active unlearning of the original materials because of their erroneous intrusions during interpolation is a reasonable factor—indeed, it is merely another locus (proactive) of response competition—but recent studies indicate that it plays a minor role. It is presumably dependent upon the degree of original learning, low degrees increasing the importance of this factor. Whether anticonsolidation of perseverative traces is a valid conception in itself, or whether it merely reflects lessened discriminability between lists when interpolation immediately follows original learning, is still a moot question. The fact that increased interference is also obtained when interpolation immediately precedes recall recommends the latter possibility. Reciprocal inhibition, to the extent that it is a valid phenomenon, is clearly limited to the opposed materials for which it operates.

Chapter 13

RETENTION

WHY DO WE FORGET?

Why do we forget what we have learned? It is one of the most pertinent facts of existence that we do. The carefully organized lecture notes that we studied the night before are recalled somewhat spottily the next morning. The details of that glorious adolescent summer—we swore never to forget a single precious moment—have gradually faded away. Even the things we know well by virtue of steady repetition, a friend's name or our own telephone number, are sometimes briefly obscured. Why do we forget?

The Layman's Point of View

The layman has his theory for this, born as usual in the implications of linguistic metaphor. We forget, he says, because impressions fade with time. Just as we learn, strengthen behavior, by using it, so we forget, weaken behavior, by not using it. This is *the theory of disuse*. Some psychologists have attempted to bolster such a theory by postulating the existence of neural grooves or pathways, organic correlates of behavior which are presumed to persist in time, though steadily deteriorating. We are offered a picture of the mind as a sort of sandy plain; learning deepens the pathways, whereas the mere passage of time and disuse gradually obliterate these signs of the past.

Just about everything is wrong with this theory. (1) In the process of *extinction* an activity is used (the stimulus-response association is practiced), yet the habit weakens and is forgotten. (2) The phenomena of *spontaneous recovery* and *reminiscence* are both cases where disuse is accompanied by improvement of performance. (3) On general scientific grounds, the entire notion that time itself is a variable is indefensible. An iron bar left out in the elements rusts through time. But does the iron bar rust *because of time?* No, we would agree that iron rusts because of processes occurring *in* time. Time merely provides an opportunity for the effective variables to operate. This was brought out clearly in investigations on retroactive interference; forgetting was a function, not of time itself, but of the nature of the interpolated activity happening in time.

549

An Interference Theory (Behavioristic)

Just exactly what, in behavioral terms, is a memory? Is it a vague, formless essence, an idea, that is tucked away in some one of the innumerable 'cells' in the brain? This is the layman's notion; he even speaks of 'cudgeling one's brains' in striving to recall some elusive fact, as if by exerting sufficient pressure the shy idea could be squeezed out of its cell! *Behaviorally, a memory is nothing more than a response produced by a stimulus.* If, at a social function, I am introduced to Mr. P. H. Doe, and later the same face appears and I say 'Hullo, Doe,' one would say that I *remember;* if two weeks later on the avenue the same face appears and I fail to make the correct labeling response, one would say that I had *forgotten* his name. When the stimulus is presented on the tenth trial of learning and the correct response is made, one does not usually call this 'remembering,' yet the only difference between this situation and the usual test for retention is the amount of time that intervenes between one trial and another. Following this reasoning, if a memory is merely the maintained association of a response with a stimulus over an interval of time, the question of 'why we forget' comes down to this: *what are the conditions under which stimuli lose their capacity to evoke previously associated responses?* In other words, the problem of forgetting is identical with the causes of response decrement, and we are already familiar with some of the relevant conditions.

When a stimulus-response association is forced repeatedly but no reinforcement is given, response decrement or forgetting occurs. Will this extinction process account for all of human forgetting? No, it will not. The adequate conditions for extinction—repeated evocation of the association—are seldom met. If, however, one follows the interference theory of extinction, then it becomes merely one specific instance of a general interference theory of forgetting. The extinction paradigm is the same as that for retroactive interference; extinction of R_1 is the genesis and substitution of R_2 for the same stimulus. Another cause of response decrement is *modification of the eliciting stimulus.* There are many illustrations from everyday life. A well-dressed gentleman standing in the theater line smiles and says hello to you. You return a timid smile and spend most of your time in the theater trying to remember who that person was. And how do you go about trying to recall? You probably set the problem-face successively into a series of contexts, the faculty members at the university, the people in the bank, clerks in various stores, and so forth. Finally it comes to you— he's the man at the meat market! And why couldn't you remember? Because he usually appears in a white coat and an old straw hat—the stimulus situation had been sufficiently modified.

The basic constructs of the interference theory of forgetting are the stimulus and the response, and interpretations can be made with clarity only where these constructs and their relationships are specifiable. The fundamental condition for forgetting is this: *forgetting is a direct function of the degree to which substitute responses are associated with the original stimuli during the retention interval.* This will be recognized as a definition of retroactive interference, hence the interference theory must specify the variables which determine the direction and degree of retroaction. Summarizing the conclusions reached in Chapter 12, we may say that identity between responses in original and interpolated activities yields facilitation, whereas difference between responses yields interference (forgetting), and the magnitude of either facilitation or interference is a function of the stimulus similarities between original and interpolated activities. These are empirical laws, not principles.

What *are* the behavioristic principles underlying these laws? (1) *Habit formation.* Successive increments generated through repetitions of an association summate to yield the strength of a habit. (2) *Response competition.* Whenever the same stimulus tends to evoke two or more incompatible reactions, that one having the strongest habit strength in association with the stimulus will occur. (3) *Stimulus generalization.* Responses associated with a given stimulus generalize to other stimuli to an extent dependent upon the original habit strength and the similarity between the stimuli. (4) *Response generalization.* Tendencies for a stimulus to evoke a given response generalize to other responses to an extent dependent upon the original habit strength and the similarity among the responses. These are merely the most obvious principles functioning in this area; actually all behavioristic principles apply, as well as many theoretical elaborations, such as the development of discrimination, mediating reactions, and so forth.

Two preliminary comments on this theory must be made. First, it is commonly stated that 'retroactive interference is the *cause* of forgetting.' This is only a half-truth. Retroactive interference is itself only a measured decrement in performance; it is not an explanation but an observed fact. What is really meant is this: all those processes that eventuate in measured retroactive interference (e.g. response competition, unlearning, reciprocal inhibition, and the like) together account for forgetting. Secondly, in cases of everyday forgetting the presence of interpolated interference is simply *inferred* from analogy with retroaction experiments—the hypothetical interfering events are never directly measured.

A Memory Trace Theory (Gestalt)

The layman's conception of 'impressions that fade with time' finds its modern psychological expression in the gestalt theory of memory and forgetting. But here the conception is far more sophisticated. Rather than being merely a passive etching which is gradually obscured, for gestalt theorists like Köhler, Koffka, and Lewin the memory trace is a *dynamic* affair, existing in fields of stress set up by conditions of perception and motivation. As is the case with other extensions of the gestalt point of view, the basic principles are those discovered and tested in the study of *perception.* Although the conception was not original with psychologists of the Gestalt School nor its use limited to them (cf. Bartlett, 1932), there is no question but that they have handled the memory trace most elaborately and effectively.

Despite the vivid connotations of the term 'trace,' as used in this theory it is as much a purely hypothetical construct as is the behaviorist's 'habit.' The essence of the gestalt theory of memory can be expressed as follows: *the temporal (mnemonic) dimension of experience is transformed into spatial dimensions within the brain field and is thereby rendered interpretable by the same principles that apply to perception.* Chapter 10 in Koffka's *Principles of Gestalt Psychology* (1935) is a detailed presentation of this transformation. Koffka illustrates the transformation in this manner. When two taps are heard in succession they appear perceptually *as a pair,* the perception of the second being modified by the pre-existence of the first. The excitation processes of the second communicate with the trace of the first tap. How does this communication take place within the brain field? Across the trace of the interval that separates them (just as two simultaneous visual patches affect one another across the ground between them). Koffka argues that the two 'tap' experiences cannot have the same locus in the brain field; otherwise there would be no discrimination between them and thus no awareness of temporality. What happens with a continuous excitation? Keeping in mind that each successive unit of excitation affects a slightly different locus within the brain field, 'the whole deposit unit consists of dead traces except for its "tip" where it is just being *made* by an excitation. . . Change of excitation . . . [is] . . . accompanied by change of deposits, segregat[ing] these pieces from each other, in perfect analogy to spatial organization' (p. 447). The moving finger of excitation writes by leaving a spatial trace within the brain field; when the quality of the excitation changes, another line is begun at another locus.

How does retention or memory enter the picture? So far we have merely 'deposits' of traces—lines on the brain field. But these 'lines' exist within a dynamic field and hence are within a system of forces. In the first place, the traces themselves have form and, having form, include internal, *autonomous* forces. In other words, 'the shape of the original process distribution must also be preserved in a dynamical shape of the trace. Traces of spatial units, then, are systems under stress . . .' (p. 443). If the original excitation was in the form of a slightly distorted circle, the trace in the brain field drawn by this excitation will include the same dynamics, i.e. a continuing tendency toward a 'good' circle. In the second place, the trace process is affected by *external influences.* Similar traces tend to be *assimilated* (fused together, losing individual identity) and new excitations may communicate with an old trace and hence modify it. In sum, we have two sources of change in memory traces, autonomous and externally induced changes.

The first dynamism appears at the point of original perception itself. The better articulated the materials to be learned and retained, i.e. the more certain parts stand out as 'figures' from the 'ground,' the more likely is survival of their traces. Out of the chaotic manifold of peripheral, sensory events, not all contenders have an equal chance of persisting in memory. (1) *Organized, well-structured materials lay down more stable memory traces.* A single number in a mass of nonsense syllables is both easier to learn and, presumably, better retained. According to Koffka, 'If any perceived form is a product of organization . . . [it] is sustained by real forces. . . . . . in cases of very irregular patterns the internal forces of organization will . . . be in conflict with the external ones; the perceived forms will be under stress. Therefore, if the trace retains the dynamic pattern of the original excitation, it will be under stress too, and the changes which occur within it will be such as to reduce those internal stresses' (1935, p. 496). (2) *The dynamic stresses present in original perception are preserved in the memory trace where, freed from restrictive peripheral stimulation, a gradual resolution of the stresses occurs.* Suppose subjects are shown a sharply etched circle with a slight gap in the circumference: during the retention interval, a gradual and progressive filling in of the gap should occur, the same effect that can be obtained with the after-image of this figure, in brief tachistoscopic presentation, or under low illumination.

How is the fate of the trace determined by external influences? Individual memory traces exist in a total, interacting field. They are affected by other traces, tending to merge with similar ones, and by the continuous flux of new perceptual activity. Thus the traces of a group of nonsense syllables will tend to form an undifferentiated mass, whereas a single number amongst them remains isolated. (3) *Memory traces tend toward assimilation with others simultaneously present in the trace field, the degree of assimilation varying as a function of similarity.* This law may be used to explain the common phenomenon termed *object-assimilation:* the memory image of a distinctive pine tree, with just this angle to its boughs and just that massing of its foliage, becomes more and more typical of its class with the passage of time.

So far we have been dealing with individual memory traces. How is the whole field organized? The whole is divided into certain major regions which in turn are subdivided into numerous *sub-systems.* The spatial organization of these sub-systems is also a function of similarity, e.g. 'neighboring' regions are affected by excitations of similar quality (cf. the gestalt notion of *isomorphism*). At the center of this field is that region termed the *Ego.* The nearer a given event is to the Ego, the more it is charged with real as opposed to quasi needs, the former being stronger and more permanent. How does all this relate to memory? (4) *The greater the tension within the region where a memory trace exists, the more it will resist autonomous disintegration or assimilation with other traces.* This is partly because increased tension within a sub-system renders its boundaries less permeable to interactions between regions. This conception leads to several hypotheses concerning the relation between ego-involvement and memory which will be tested at a later point in this chapter.

Memory traces are not themselves conscious. Their effect upon behavior is through 'communication with' present excitations. Which of the multitude of available traces are 'communicated with' by a particular momentary excitation again depends upon similarity. 'A process should, *certeris paribus,* communicate with a trace system which possesses the same whole character. This must be a trace system which had been produced by a process of the same whole character, because we assumed that the trace retained the dynamic character of the process in the form of tensions or stresses' (Koffka, 1935, p. 463). Forgetting, according to this view, represents the failure of present excitation to 'come into communication with' an older trace or trace system. Under what conditions are memory traces unavailable? (a) *Autonomous disintegration.* Koffka speaks of 'the low survival value of chaotic units.' (b) *Assimilation.* This process, whereby memory traces lose their individuality, has already been discussed. (c) *Low tension in the trace system.* The further the locus of a trace from the Ego, the more susceptible it will be to the destructive processes cited above. (d) *Simple failure of communication.* Koffka (p. 527) is not clear on this, but it seems that the probability of 'communication' would depend upon the similarity between the present excitation and the memory trace. This would seem to be identical with the behaviorist's notion that a previously learned response may fail to occur because the eliciting stimulus is changed sufficiently.

The Repression Sequence (Freud)

Although it does not pretend to be a general theory of forgetting, mention should be made of Freud's concept of repression and the motivated forgetting to which it is assumed to lead. Such forgetting is certainly a valid observation in the clinic and probably would be verified in the laboratory were adequate conditions designed to reveal it. At a later point we shall review the attempts which have been made to test this hypothesis—that under special conditions where strong ego-anxiety is produced, the materials that give rise to this state are more susceptible to forgetting. Any theory that *does* presume generality (e.g. the gestalt and behavioristic views) must however be able to incorporate these facts. How adequately this can be done will be seen at a later point. Our purpose throughout the remainder of this chapter will be to present the major sources of evidence on remembering and forgetting and to evaluate it in terms of these theoretical positions.

RETENTION CURVES AND THEIR DETERMINANTS

The Classic Curve of Forgetting

It is high time, in a chapter devoted mainly to human learning and memory, that we consider the important contributions of Ebbinghaus. Among his pioneering studies on memory (1885), that in which he delineated an empirical curve of forgetting is the best known. There are many reasons for this: it represented one of the first attempts to gauge a highly subjective, mental characteristic by objective measurement; it inaugurated the use of nonsense materials; and it represented an extreme of painstaking, selfless labor. Ebbinghaus himself was his only subject. Learning and later relearning a total of over 1200 lists of 13 nonsense syllables, in groups of eight lists at a sitting, he gradually etched in his forgetting curve. His measure of retention was the saving, in total time or number of trials, of the relearning over the original learning. The dashed-line curve in Fig. 181 represents Ebbinghaus's classic results.

Numerous investigators since Ebbinghaus's time have roughly duplicated his procedures, and, despite considerable variations in details, essentially the same sharp, negatively accelerated curve has been found (e.g. Finkenbinder, 1913; Luh, 1922; Van Ormer, 1932; Boreas, 1930). Forgetting occurs with great rapidity during the first hour (only 44 per cent saving found by Ebbinghaus after this interval), thereupon leveling out, very little loss occurring between 2- and 6-day periods. Results obtained by Boreas (1930) are included for comparison. Why is the curve found by Boreas consistently higher than that obtained by Ebbinghaus? The latter learned eight lists in rapid succession, whereas Boreas' subjects learned only one 15-item list for each interval; the difference probably reflects interlist interferences (both negative transfer and retroactive interference) for Ebbinghaus.

These classical forgetting curves fit a *logarithmic function of time* quite accurately. That is, when retention is plotted as a function of log time in minutes, a fairly straight-line relation is found. This may be seen from Fig. 182 in which Boreas' data have been plotted in that manner. A

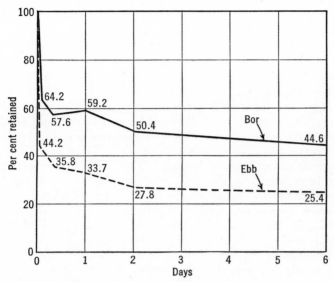

FIGURE 181. Retention curves for lists of nonsense syllables, as determined by the saving method. Ebbinghaus curve is from one subject about 40 years old, who learned and relearned over 1200 13-syllable lists. Boreas curve gives the average for 20 students, each learning one 15-syllable list for each interval. Woodworth, *Experimental Psychology*, Henry Holt and Co., Inc., New York, 1938, p. 53. Data of Ebbinghaus, 1885, and Boreas, 1930.

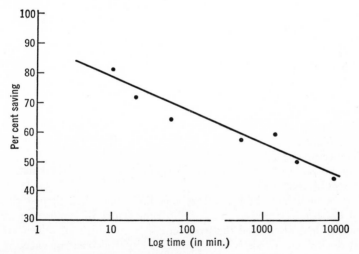

FIGURE 182. Retention expressed in logarithmic time units. Each data point based on 20 subjects relearning one 15-syllable list of nonsense material (data from Boreas, 1930).

practical advantage of using log time as the unit is that the long period of little change is collapsed into manageable dimensions for graphic presentation. But this logarithmic function also offers suggestions as to the nature of forgetting: *whatever the determining factors may be, their effect is proportional to the amount retained at any given moment.* Soon after learning there is a large amount of material remembered but the rate of loss is rapid; after several days there is little retained and the rate of loss is infinitesimal. It has been shown that both the rate of forgetting and the terminal level can be influenced by the *degree of original learning.* Ebbinghaus (1885) and more recently Krueger (1929) have inquired into this question. To meet a 100% overlearning criterion, Krueger's subjects were given double the number of trials required for one perfect repetition (the level of zero overlearning) and for a 50% overlearning criterion they were given half that many. The materials were monosyllabic nouns, and both recall (first relearning trial) and total relearning were measured over varying intervals. Although curves of the same form were obtained, the rate constants became less as amount of overlearning increased. The effects of overlearning were shown to be negatively accelerated—100% overlearning does not improve retention much beyond that obtained with 50% overlearning.

The *interference theory* would interpret the negatively accelerated curve of forgetting in this manner: The more material being retained at a given moment, the more possibilities exist for interference from the variety of normal activities of the individual. The fact that the *rate* of forgetting decreases merely indicates that the sources of interference are being exhausted—intervening activities sufficiently similar to the residual materials do not occur with sufficient frequency. In other words, by the same token that certain items survive the early retroactive effects, they are less likely to be affected by later activities. The effects of overlearning are readily explained in terms of the relative strength of competing habits; if the original habits are overlearned (stronger), intervening activities must either be more highly reinforced or function over longer periods to have the same effect.

The *gestalt trace theory* also faces no great difficulty with these data. Koffka (1935) has stated that the traces of chaotic and unorganized materials (such as nonsense syllables or lists of unrelated words) are unstable and either fade or are assimilated with other traces if not repeatedly reinforced. Those items that resist this fate are presumably well organized. The effects of overlearning are merely such as to increase the strength of a memory trace without changing its other characteristics. It is surprising that the proponents of neither theory appear to have analyzed the *nature of the residual items* which seem to have been either (a) unsusceptible to interference or (b) better organized. If the residual items for different subjects turned out to be only random samples from the original list, neither theory would receive any support.

In many textbooks in psychology one finds the Ebbinghaus-type curve labeled *the* curve of forgetting, as if by some stroke of genius or pure luck that master had discovered the 'true' curve from which all others are artifactual deviations. There is here perhaps a slight element of ancestor worship within the psychological family; or perhaps there is the feeling that the use of nonsense syllables somehow 'purified' the curve. Without intending to minimize Ebbinghaus's contributions in the least, it is nevertheless true that his curve is as artifactual as any other. What we propose to undertake at this point is an exploration of some of the more important variables that affect the character of forgetting curves.

Methods of Measurement

The interference theory assumes that at any given moment after original learning there are a certain number of the original habits remaining above the response threshold—something specific is retained. Similarly, the trace theory assumes that certain memory traces, because of their isolation, organization, or some other factor, persist into a given moment—again something specific is retained. But if 'retention' is of a specific something, then we certainly have to conclude that the performances by which it is indexed yield highly varying estimates. For, depending upon the method of measurement selected, estimates of retention can vary by as much as 79 per cent.

Various *quantitative methods* of measuring retention may be briefly described. In *unaided recall* the subject is asked to reproduce spontaneously as many items as he can. Lacking cues, this method not only yields low estimates, but its freedom does not permit analysis of the causes of errors in memory. In *aided recall* the subject is given the same stimuli as on original learning and must make the correct responses. The usual measure in this case is exact correctness of the response, although latencies may also be measured. When the *savings method* is used, the subject relearns the materials to the same criterion of mastery as originally, and the percentage saving over original learning is measured; if ten trials were necessary for original learning and only two for relearning, saving is 80 per cent. Since the first relearning trial is simultaneously a measure of aided recall, the most common procedure is to report both values.

The task for the subject is quite different in the *recognition method*. On the basis of what is retained of the original impression or learning, he must recognize the original materials when they are imbedded among other items of the same class. There are two sources of invalidity in this method which are not always recognized: (a) a certain number of 'correct' choices will be due to pure chance, and hence this must be accounted for statistically, and (b) the accuracy of recognition depends heavily upon the homogeneity of the samples in the test (cf. G. H. Seward, 1928). If the original item was a picture of a red apple and the 'wrong' samples are other red apples differing only in shade, recognition is bound to be poor. This means that the comparability of recognition as a measure from experiment to experiment is practically nil. *Reconstruction* technically means rearranging the parts of an original task, presented randomly, in the original order. But more generally, given a minimal cue (such as remembering a 'squarish figure'), the subject 'reconstructs' such a figure not so much on the basis of memory as on the basis of his general knowledge of 'squarish figures.'

When these methods are applied to the same original learning materials, do identical curves of forgetting appear? The most comprehensive answer to this question was contributed by Luh (1922). All subjects learned lists of 12 nonsense syllables by the usual anticipation method to a criterion of one perfect repetition, and retention was measured after the various intervals shown in Fig. 183. What is here termed 'written reproduction' is what was termed 'unaided recall' cited above; 'anticipation' was what we labeled 'aided recall.' (1) The different methods vary mainly in the amount of apparent retention (i.e. the over-all altitude of the curves), recall being the most difficult performance and recognition the easiest. (2) Although nearly all curves have a negatively accelerated form, that for relearning is the sharpest, i.e. retention as measured in this manner decreases very rapidly at first and then levels out.

Is retention 'a specific something' that is variously estimated by different measures? If this were the case we should have to conclude that *recognition* is the best estimate, the best estimate, that is, of the suprathreshold responses or the state of the memory traces. Recognition yields the highest estimate of retention and therefore 'the specific something' retained must be at least that much. But this interpretation is rather farcical. It is not 'a specific something' (retention) that is variously estimated, *but rather each method*

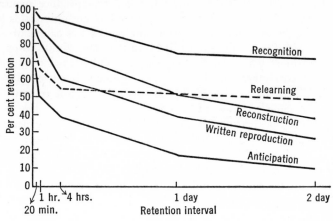

FIGURE 183. Comparison of several indices of retention obtained from the same subjects over the same intervals. Luh, *Psychological Monographs*, 1922, 31, #142:22.

is measuring something different. The *savings method* measures not only the availability of specific responses (or traces) but also retention of general procedures and 'tricks of the trade.' The *recall method,* on the other hand, demands production of the specific items originally learned and allows only one chance to do it. In the *recognition method,* finally, there is no demand that specific items be available; the original stimuli are presented to the subject, among others, and if any one of the many aspects of the total stimulus complex representing a given item is sufficient to reactivate any one of the complex reactions originally made to it, then this serves as a basis for discrimination. From this analysis we may conclude that a complex pattern of behavior is evolved in learning, only part of which is tapped by any single method of measuring retention.

There are also *qualitative methods* of studying memory which perhaps approach more closely the conditions of everyday life. Bartlett's stimulating book, *Remembering,** explores some of these methods fully, and they justify themselves by the richness of insights made possible. One such method was that of *repeated reproduction.* Bartlett had subjects read a North American folk tale twice to themselves. Fifteen minutes later the first free reproduction was obtained, and subsequent reproductions by the same individuals

* Bartlett, *Remembering,* Cambridge University Press, 1932.

were obtained over a wide range of intervals. Let us trace the fate of the story in one subject's memory. The original ran as follows.

THE WAR OF THE GHOSTS

One night two young men from Egulac went down to the river to hunt seals, and while they were there it became foggy and calm. Then they heard war-cries, and they thought: "Maybe this is a war-party." They escaped to the shore, and hid behind a log. Now canoes came up, and they heard the noise of paddles, and saw one canoe coming up to them. There were five men in the canoe, and they said:
"What do you think? We wish to take you along. We are going up the river to make war on the people."
One of the young men said: "I have no arrows."
"Arrows are in the canoe," they said.
"I will not go along. I might be killed. My relatives do not know where I have gone. But you," he said, turning to the other, "may go with them."
So one of the young men went, but the other returned home.
And the warriors went on up the river to a town on the other side of Kalama. The people came down to the water, and they began to fight, and many were killed. But presently the young man heard one of the warriors say: "Quick, let us go home: that Indian has been hit." Now he thought: "Oh, they are ghosts." He did not feel sick, but they said he had been shot.
So the canoes went back to Egulac, and the young man went ashore to his house, and made a fire. And he told everybody and said: "Behold I accompanied the ghosts, and we went to fight. Many of our fellows were killed, and many of those who attacked us were killed. They said I was hit, and I did not feel sick."
He told it all, and then he became quiet. When the sun rose he fell down. Something black came out of his mouth. His face became contorted. The people jumped up and cried.
He was dead.

This story makes exceptionally good material because it has a style quite different from our own, it deals with the supernatural, and many of the meaningful sequences are foreign to our culture, such as '. . . then he became quiet. When the sun rose he fell down.' Here is the first reproduction (15 minutes after reading) of subject P.

THE WAR OF THE GHOSTS

Two youths were standing by a river about to start seal-catching, when a boat appeared with five men in it. They were all armed for war.
The youths were at first frightened, but they were asked by the men to come and help them fight some enemies on the other bank. One youth said he could not come as his relations would be anxious about him; the other said he would go, and entered the boat.
In the evening he returned to his hut, and told his friends that he had been in a battle. A great many had been slain, and he had

been wounded by an arrow; he had not felt any pain, he said. They told him that he must have been fighting in a battle of ghosts. Then he remembered that it had been queer and he became very excited.

In the morning, however, he became ill, and his friends gathered round; he fell down and his face became very pale. Then he writhed and shrieked and his friends were filled with terror. At last he became calm. Something hard and black came out of his mouth, and he lay contorted and dead.

Even in the immediate reproduction we note many modifications and intrusions to fit our own cultural norms. 'He had been wounded by an *arrow*' refutes the supernaturalism of the original, as does *'they told him* he must have been fighting a battle of ghosts.' Emotionally exciting elements are not only remembered well but elaborated upon, as is the final death scene. Yet the central portion of the original drops out completely. Let us look at a reproduction made by the same subject after two months had elapsed.

The War of the Ghosts

Two youths went down to the river to hunt for seals. They were hiding behind a rock when a boat with some warriors in it came up to them. The warriors, however, said they were friends, and invited them to help them to fight an enemy over the river. The elder one said he could not go because his relations would be so anxious if he didn't return home. So the younger one went with the warriors in the boat.

In the evening he returned and told his friends that he had been fighting in a great battle, and that many were slain on both sides.

After lighting a fire he retired to sleep. In the morning, when the sun rose, he fell ill, and his neighbors came to see him. He had told them that he had been wounded in the battle but he had felt no pain then. But soon he became worse. He writhed and shrieked and fell to the ground dead. Something black came out of his mouth.

The neighbors said he must have been at war with the ghosts.

Still further adjustments to fit a civilized Western frame of reference have occurred. Now the two young men have become the elder and the younger. Now he 'retires to sleep'—to explain how he spent the time until the morning sun rose. The ghost aspects have largely disappeared. A reproduction obtained from the same subject after two and a half years runs as follows:

Some warriors went to wage war against the ghosts. They fought all day and one of their number was wounded.

They returned home in the evening, bearing their sick comrade. As the day drew to a close, he became rapidly worse and the villagers came round him. At sunset he sighed; something black came out of his mouth. He was dead.

At last the warriors are fighting against the ghosts, which is certainly more fitting. And they bear home a sick comrade who, conveniently and picturesquely, dies just *at sunset*. One striking detail remains practically unaltered throughout—something black coming out of the dying man's mouth.

From a careful inspection of serial reproductions by a considerable number of subjects, Bartlett synthesizes certain general tendencies, among which are the following: (a) The general form of a subject's first reproduction is preserved throughout his own series (this is undoubtedly due to some extent to the reinforcement of repeated practice). (b) There is a strong tendency to rationalize unconnected or disturbing elements, i.e. making the young man sleep through an unexplained interval or changing the 'something black' to 'foamed at the mouth,' as one subject had it. (c) Certain dominant elements may serve as focal points of organization, about which reasonable details are embellished. (d) Various inventions, in tune with the subject's frame of reference, are worked into the reproduction. What is remembered is an emotionally oriented, meaningful core (the schemata) about which is reconstructed a fitting cloak of half-recalled and half-invented detail. The entire personality of the individual, his emotions, his attitudes, his cultural frame of reference, contribute to what he 'remembers.'

Nature of the Materials Learned

Bartlett criticized the methods developed by Ebbinghaus as being *artificial* in the extreme. Nonsense syllables create an atmosphere not at all characteristic of human memory in everyday life. Is the classic curve of forgetting simply an artifact of the nonsense materials used? Many would point to the apparent resistance of motor skills to the effects of forgetting or to the apparently superior retention of meaningfully organized materials as evidence. A man may show a great deal of savings for the skills of tennis learned 20 years ago or for a long poem learned in childhood.

It is a widespread popular notion *that motor skills are better retained than verbal ones.* There is a considerable experimental literature here, but it serves little purpose other than to suggest the nature of some of the methodological difficulties in testing this proposition. (1) *How does one index the degree of 'motorness' or 'verbalness' in tasks?* True, different muscles are employed in reciting a list of words or a poem than in typing or swimming, but this is scarcely a difference in kind. For example, Freeman and Abernethy (1930) compared the retention of typing from a large diagram with that for translating the same passage into number symbols, there being one number-symbol substitution for each stroke in typing. There was somewhat better retention for typing, but which is the more 'verbal' task? Waters and Poole (1933) and Van Tilborg (1936) find no difference in retention between stylus and mental mazes—but for the human to what extent is learning a stylus maze also a 'verbal' task? (2) *How does one equate learning for dissimilar tasks?* McGeoch and Melton (1929) compared the retention of nonsense syllable lists and finger mazes of varying difficulty. The only significant difference was in terms of savings in trials to reach the criterion of one perfect execution, and nonsense syllable retention was superior! But whereas a subject might happen to make a perfect run through a finger maze early in learning by chance alone (there being only two alternatives at each choice point), this would be extremely unlikely for lists of nonsense syllables. So the nonsense syllables may have been better learned. The occurrence of *reminiscence* for some activities also makes it difficult to equate original learning; Leavitt and Schlosberg (1944) found that subjects trained on the pursuit-rotor did *better* at the end of a 7-day retention period than they had at the conclusion of original training, but this was not the case for verbal materials given the same amount of practice. There remained some superiority for the motor task after the effects of reminiscence had been accounted for, and Leavitt and Schlosberg suggest that it was because verbal activities are more subject to retroactive interference than motor activities. Although this seems to be an entirely gratuitous assumption (has anyone compared the frequencies with which we waggle our tongues as against wiggle our arms and fingers?), it does set another methodological problem: (3) *How can we estimate the amounts of retroactive interference encountered by motor and verbal activities?*

It is also taken more or less for granted that meaningful materials are both more easily learned and better retained than nonsense materials. As to *learning,* Lyon (1914) did find that 200 meaningful items required only about one fourth as much time to learn as 200 nonsense syllables. Why? The usual explanation is that meaningful associations are already partially learned. Sheffield (1946) has questioned this explanation and substituted another: *meaningful materials are more easily learned because, as stimuli, they are already discriminated from each other by virtue of being associated with distinctive implicit reactions.* When he gave subjects pretraining with the individual nonsense syllables later to be combined in pairs, associating distinctive reactions with each (e.g. making a punch in a card for ZIB, crossing out a letter for RUL and so on), the difference between ease of learning these nonsense materials and meaningful words was eliminated. This was true for syllables later used as stimuli but not for those later used as responses. In a sense, what Sheffield did was to make these nonsense materials meaningful. As to the *retention* of meaningful as compared with nonsense materials, surprisingly enough there seems to be no direct information. McGeoch (1942), on a priori grounds, concluded that 'the higher retention values of meaningful materials are to be expected from the relatively low susceptibility of these materials to interference from interpolated learning' (p. 367). Compare Leavitt and Schlosberg's conclusion given above. On the contrary (on a priori grounds), it would seem to this writer that nonsense syllables should be least susceptible to interpolated interference. How often, in everyday experience, does one encounter other nonsense syllables? In fact, if it were clearly demonstrated that nonsense materials are less well retained than meaningful words, it would constitute presumptive evidence against the retroaction theory of forgetting which McGeoch held.

Change of 'Set' and 'Warm-up' Effects

The fact that so-called 'rest' control groups show loss in retention has already been noted in connection with the logic of transfer and retroaction experiments. The interference theory of forgetting attributes this to incidental and unspecified sources of interference: some of the stimuli become associated with conflicted responses during the interval. As a matter of fact, since the competing responses, which are assumed to cause forgetting in ordinary experience, are never specifiable (but simply inferred from retroaction experiments), what goes on in the 'rest' condition is closest to real-life forgetting. Irion (1948) has questioned this interpretation: he points out that (1) the competing responses learned in this 'incidental' fashion should be relatively weak in strength and (2) the stimuli with which these competing responses are associated should be quite dissimilar from those eliciting the correct responses (e.g. the test materials are absent).

Both Ammons (1947) and Irion (1948) suggest another explanation of the loss in retention for 'rest' groups: during the time interval there is a *loss of the set* to perform the task. No matter what the task may be, learning pairs of nonsense syllables, tracing finger mazes, or following the contact point on a pursuit-rotor, certain postural, receptor, and attitudinal adjustments favor performance. The subject must look at the right place and at the right time, he must impress a certain optimal pace on his activities, and he must pay attention to those particular cues that are crucial in enforcing alternations in instrumental sequences. All of these activities serve to create a particular background of self-stimulation, *and this is a major part of the total stimulus situation to which the task responses are conditioned.* During a rest period, particularly if dissimilar activities are indulged in, this set is lost, the total stimulus situation is modified, and the probability of the correct responses being made during the first trials of relearning is reduced. Notice how nicely this fits the standard observation that retroactive decrements are rapidly dissipated as relearning proceeds. Notice also how neatly this analysis would follow from Guthrie's type of learning theory.

If this interpretation is valid, one would predict that *a brief warm-up* on a similar task just before relearning should serve to reinstate the original pattern of self-stimulation and hence erase that portion of the decrement attributable to loss of set. Irion (1949 *b*) has verified this prediction: The learning materials were 15 paired associates (adjectives) presented on a memory drum in the usual manner. After a 24-hour interpolated rest, one group was given a single warm-up trial (color naming) before relearning but another was not. The remarkable thing about the result was not that the warm-up subjects showed better retention than the rest-without-warm-up subjects—although this would be significant in itself—*but the fact that these subjects actually showed no forgetting over 24 hours, even improving slightly!* It would appear that, in this case, all of the forgetting was attributable to a change in set and none to interpolated interference per se. In another experiment, using the Koerth pursuit-rotor, the same investigator (1949 *a*) has shown that amount of warm-up effect is a function of both the amount of pre-rest original practice (i.e. depends on how definite a set is established) and the length of the rest interval (i.e. depends on how much the set has deteriorated).

A number of implications from this analysis are drawn (Irion, 1948, p. 340) which give rise to a host of intriguing, if complicated, problems. For example, it follows that retention following a rest period should be better if it is filled with activities similar to the task than with activities dissimilar to the task—the set will be better maintained. But what about all the other evidence on retroactive interference? There is ample evidence that interpolating the learning of another list of paired associates causes more loss than simply resting, yet learning the second list is more nearly like resting and certainly maintains the set. Furthermore, the warm-up

564 EXPERIMENTAL PSYCHOLOGY

should be effective in proportion to its nearness in time and similarity in kind to the relearning activity, yet these are also ways in which maximum interference can be produced. In order to resolve this superficial conflict in the evidence, we must distinguish between two general classes of task behavior. On the one hand, there are the nonspecific activities that characterize *any* instance of the task in question (e.g. memory drum work— seated posture, attention on window in panel, anticipatory reactions to a certain rate of events, etc.); these activities contribute largely to what is called the 'practice effect' and are mainly responsible for the savings found even after long retention periods. On the other hand, there are the specific activities that characterize this *particular* instance of the task (e.g. that 'brazen' must be responded to with 'musty,' 'toxic' with 'noonday,' etc.); these specific habits *can* be interfered with by interpolation of appropriate materials.

Set and warm-up phenomena are generally subsumable under the laws of transfer and retroaction. The changed stimulus situation that accompanies the loss of set, or rather *is* the loss of set, is relatively less strongly associated with the correct responses than with competing responses. The warm-up procedure probably has two effects: (1) It causes the subject to make again the types of orientational responses originally made to the task situation, thereby re-creating the stimulus situation originally associated with the correct responses. (2) It also serves as *retroactive facilitation,* i.e. there is positive transfer from the warm-up activity to the relearning activity (cf. Bunch, 1946). Although the similarity relations have not been worked out as yet, we would predict that the magnitude and direction of the 'warm-up' effect could be made to vary continuously by manipulating the stimulus and response relations between 'warm-up' and task behaviors, and this variation should be predictable from the 'transfer and retroaction surface.' The most impressive finding here is that measured forgetting can be just about entirely eliminated by the warm-up procedure. If repeated experiments continue to yield this result, it will mean that most of what we usually call 'forgetting' is really loss of set—that in the ordinary course of life activities (e.g. 'rest' from the particular task) very little loss occurs from interpolated interference.

Reminiscence—The Ballard-Williams Phenomenon

The term 'reminiscence' has already been encountered in what is known as the Ward-Hovland Phenomenon. The Ballard-Williams Phenomenon also refers to enhancement of recall, but here the similarity ends: this phenomenon makes its appearance after much longer intervals, usually about 2 days; rather than applying to serial lists of nonsense syllables, it is typically found for well-organized, meaningful materials. The retention curves obtained are quite distinct from classic curves; whereas the classic form shows negatively accelerated loss, the Ballard-Williams retention curve rises through the first few days before forgetting appears. To call this 'retention' is actually erroneous; no more can be 'retained' than was present at the point of original learning. What we have here is facilitation of performance where it would seem forgetting should occur.

In Ballard's pioneer study (1913) children about 12 years of age partially learned a fairly long poem, were tested for immediate recall, and, in separate groups, were again tested after varying intervals of time. The results are shown in Fig. 184. Poem *A,* 'The Wreck of the Hesperus,' showed the most reminiscence, and Ballard notes that this one was the most interesting to the children. All materials showed the general effect, however, and the resulting curves are certainly not 'classic' ones. Two points of technique must be noted: (a) original learning is necessarily not to com-

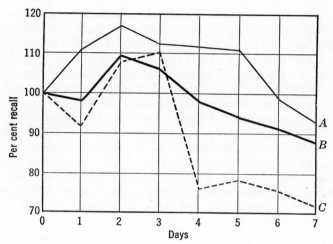

FIGURE 184. Retention curves for 12-yr. old children on (*A*) selections from 'The Wreck of the Hesperus,' (*B*) selections from 'The Ancient Mariner,' and (*C*) nonsense verses. Ballard, *British Journal of Psychology,* Monograph Supplement, Cambridge University Press, New York, 1913, 1, #2:5.

plete mastery, since that would leave no room at the top for reminiscence to appear; (b) one recall test is given immediately to measure the original level of mastery and a second test is given after a varying delay period.

Possible variables. Since this phenomenon obviously doesn't characterize all cases of remembering, we immediately want to know what special conditions lead to this special effect. (1) *Meaningful organization of the materials.* Williams (1926) compared retention of a partially memorized poem with that for partially learned lists of abstract words; the poem showed the effect but the unrelated words did not. Reminiscence also ap-

TABLE 9. IMMEDIATE AND DELAYED RECALL OF A POEM BY SUBJECTS
OF VARIOUS AGES

Average Age	Immediate Recall	Delayed Recall
9.7 years	4.95 items	5.38 items
12.7 years	8.68 items	8.61 items
16.2 years	12.28 items	11.42 items
College students	15.37 items	12.67 items

From data of Williams, *Journal of Experimental Psychology,* 1926, 9:368-87.

pears for the meaning of paragraphs but not for recognition of sentences taken verbatim from them (Edwards and English, 1939). Another important variable seems to be (2) *the age of the subjects.* Williams systematically varied the age of his subjects as shown in Table 9. The only group to show reminiscence was the youngest, averaging 9.7 years of age; the other age groups showing ordinary forgetting. A final variable to mention is (3) *the degree of motivation.* Ballard noted that the poem on which the most reminiscence was obtained was the one in which his children showed the most interest. Another investigator (Nicolai, 1922) found reminiscence for recalling toys hidden in a box.

Explanations of the phenomenon. (1) In order to explain his own findings, Ballard (1913) postulated a *process opposite to forgetting* which he termed 'reminiscence.' It was conceived as a facilitative, strengthening effect upon memory traces, and as such is quite similar to the statements made by gestalt theorists. Koffka (1935), Katona (1940), and others have stated that the traces of well-organized, meaningful—and especially ego-involved—materials are more stable and resistant to interference. Whether they become stronger is another matter. (2) The fact that young children seem more prone to the effect leads to another obvious possibility, that of *rehearsal.* G. O. McGeoch (1935) directly checked on this possibility, asking the children before the delayed test if they had reviewed and telling them that it was quite in order to have done so. She found that the subjects who denied rehearsing showed just as much reminiscence as those who admitted it. Although we may hesitate to question the word of little children, there is nevertheless no real control here over rehearsal, especially when the youngsters were led to believe that it was 'good' to have practiced on their own. (3) Is the Ballard-Williams effect due to *the facilitating effects of the immediate recall upon the delayed recall?* Warner Brown (1923) offered a very sober and reasonable explanation: in the first recall certain items appear and are further strengthened; in the second recall certain new items appear above the threshold and are added to the strengthened items from the first recall; measured reminiscence results. In one of his experiments Brown asked students to write down the names of as many states as they could in 5 minutes; they got an average of 36.4. After half an hour they were given a second opportunity and averaged 34.4 of the original items *plus* 5.3 new states, yielding a total of 39.7—reminiscence (cf. also Gray, 1940). But if this be the explanation, why is the effect typical of young children? Why does it seem to vary with motivation? With the meaningful organization of materials? The Ballard-Williams Phenomenon is probably the fortuitous result of some combination of such factors as these.

Organization of Materials

There would be little disagreement with the statement that organization facilitates *learning,* especially if organization be considered equivalent to initial discriminability. But it will be recalled that the *gestalt theory of memory* also states that memory traces established in original learning are more stable and resistant to assimilation and interference if the materials are well structured, i.e. that *retention* is facilitated by perceptual organization. This is another proposition entirely and its demonstration requires that degrees of original learning be carefully equated. Original learning can be measured by an *immediate* recall; then the effects of a variable upon retention per se can be estimated by another *delayed* recall after a nonpractice interval of any desired length. Unfortunately in most studies on this problem there has been no control for differences in degree of original learning, and we are therefore unable to determine to what extent it is retention itself that is affected.

A series of studies by H. von Restorff (1933) provide evidence that relatively 'isolated' items in experience are better retained than relatively 'massed' items. In one study five types of material (nonsense syllables, figures, numbers, letters, and colors) were arranged in serial lists of paired associates so that each list contained four pairs of one kind of material and one pair each of the other materials. When recalled after two or three readings, all types of material showed better retention when 'isolated' than when 'massed,' and on each list the four different items, as a group, did better than the four items of the same kind. Behaviorists would attribute these results to intraserial interference. In a second study designed to determine whether the superiority of the 'isolated' items was due to their distinctiveness or to agglutination of the 'massed' items, recall of a heterogeneous list (ten items of different kind, including one number and one syllable) was compared with that for two homogeneous lists (either nine nonsense syllables and one number or the reverse). The critical items (either number or nonsense syllable) were recalled about 40 per cent of the time when appearing in the heterogeneous list but about 70 per cent of the time when in otherwise homogeneous lists. Since the critical item was equally unique in both cases, the difference must be due to the agglutinization (indiscriminability) of the 'massed' items. The third study was a retroaction experiment with degree of similarity between original and interpolated items as the independent variable. The type of material in the homogeneous interpolated lists determined which items on the original heterogeneous lists were most interfered with—which can also be interpreted from either gestalt or behavioristic positions. Since degrees of original learning were not measured in any of these cases, nothing can be said about the effects of 'isolation' and 'massing' upon retention per se.

In an experiment by Siegel (1943), we find a much more adequate use of experimental controls. One of the major difficulties with von Restorff's original work was that she not only varied the degree of isolation of materials, but also the number of massed items was always greater. This made it possible to interpret the results in terms of increased intraserial interference for such homogeneous materials. Siegel used lists of combined nonsense syllables and numbers arranged in the form shown in Table 10. The perceptual analogy shows that for the experimental group the arrangement is such that two crucial items (3 and 13) are relatively isolated from others of the same kind while two others (6 and 16) are imbedded in a set of three similar ones. By giving one half of the experimental group a list that exactly reverses syllables and numbers, any special differences between materials are accounted for, and the control group learns a list in which the homogeneities are balanced (XOXOXO, etc.). As can be seen from the mean recall values, relatively isolated (**) items are recalled much better than relatively massed (*) items. Unfortunately, Siegel failed to measure *delayed recall* as well. His procedure was to show each item once in the order given and to have the subjects recall as many as they could immediately after the last item. It is therefore impossible to differentiate between learning and retention. If the gestalt theory holds, a delayed recall should

TABLE 10

Posi-tion	EXPERIMENTAL GROUP				CONTROL GROUP	
	Perceptual Analogy	Series I	Series II	Mean Recall	Perceptual Analogy	Mean Recall
1	X	gub	341	28.0	X	29.5
2	X	kev	258	25.0	O	29.5
3	O	406	sih	39.0 **	X	22.5
4	X	dac	179	13.5	O	16.0
5	X	rul	417	13.0	X	12.0
6	X	hof	562	5.0 *	O	10.0
7	O	763	fip	20.5	X	8.0
8	X	vom	738	10.5	O	6.5
9	O	581	ter	21.5	X	9.0
10	X	waj	269	14.0	O	10.0
11	O	341	gub	25.0	X	10.0
12	O	258	kev	21.0	O	7.0
13	X	sih	406	42.0 **	X	4.0
14	O	179	dac	13.5	O	7.0
15	O	417	rul	10.5	X	6.5
16	O	562	hof	5.0 *	O	7.5
17	X	fip	763	14.0	X	13.0
18	O	738	vom	14.5	O	9.5
19	X	ter	581	19.0	X	21.0
20	O	269	waj	20.0	O	21.0

After Siegel, *Journal of Experimental Psychology*, 1943, 33:314.

show even greater differences between isolated and massed items, since the isolating and assimilating forces would have longer to operate.

Saul and Osgood (1950) have checked this inadequacy by having not only an immediate recall but also two delayed recalls, the first after 1 hour and the second after 1 day. Otherwise Siegel's materials and organizational procedures were duplicated. No substantiation of the gestalt hypothesis was obtained in this study: differences in retention between isolated and massed items were not significant on either delayed recall test, this being true for both absolute scores and for deviations from the immediate recall level (measure of original learning). The same conclusion came when *all* items (not just the starred ones in Table 10) were analyzed in terms of their *degrees* of isolation from other materials of the same type. Even on the immediate recall, which was identical with Siegel's measurement, differences of much smaller magnitude were obtained—the reason for this discrepancy is not clear. In any case, Siegel himself states that 'Gibson's analysis of memory (1940) employing $S-R$ constructs, very nicely generates Von Restorff's original results . . . [and] . . . it is conceivable that with some slight extension, the results here might be similarly deduced' (p. 315). All of which leads one to the conclusion that there is little to choose between the two theories on this problem. The evidence has proved interpretable from either position.

Method of Learning

Katona (1940) has drawn a sharp distinction between meaningful and nonsense methods of learning. Nonsense methods are equated with simple conditioning and the formation of rigid 'connections,' whereas meaningful methods are equated with 'apprehension of relations' and 'insight into situations.' Different principles are said to apply to each. In one experiment it was shown that *grouping materials according to a principle facilitates both learning and retention,* as compared with pure memorizing. Subjects were shown the following numbers on the blackboard:

$$2\ 9\ 3\ 3\ 3\ 6\ 4\ 0\ 4\ 3\ 4\ 7$$
$$5\ 8\ 1\ 2\ 1\ 5\ 1\ 9\ 2\ 2\ 2\ 6$$

One group was given 3 minutes to discover the principle involved and another spent the same time memorizing the numbers in rhythmic groups of three. Both were given an immediate test and a delayed test 3 weeks later. The results were certainly clear-cut. On the immediate test 38% of the principle seekers made perfect reproductions and 33% of the memorizers; after 3 weeks 23% of the principle seekers still made perfect reproductions, but *none* of the memorizers could do it. What was the principle? Simply that (starting with the bottom row) *5* plus *3* is 8 plus *4* is 12 plus *3* is 15 plus *4* is 19, and so on adding *3* and then *4*. Here at last we have some direct evidence on retention itself, and there is no question but that the effects of memorization are more rapidly forgotten than the effects of learning a principle. But is a memory trace conception of the gestalt type essential to the explanation? Before trying to answer this question, let us look at another of Katona's experiments.

A variety of match-stick problems was used; the subject had to move a limited number of sticks to create a new, prescribed pattern. Actually, solutions were drawn on paper. Some subjects were given sheer memorization training on the moves that solved two problems and other subjects were trained to understand the basic principle—here, to look for sticks that were doing double duty, serving simultaneously as sides for two squares, and to move them so that they functioned as the side of only one square. A control group was given no instruction. Immediately after training, all subjects were tested on four new problems (measure of immediate transfer). A month later they were all tested on (a) the two original training problems (retention), (b) two of the earlier test problems (retention), and (c) two new problems (delayed transfer). On both immediate and delayed transfer tests the principle-learning subjects did significantly better than the memorization subjects; on retention tests there were no clear-cut differences.

Although, from a practical point of view, these results are those to be expected—subjects trained to understand the basic principle of a type of task show that they can generalize their training to many instances of that task—there are certain confusions of design which make interpretation difficult. On the delayed test, for example, each subject was given all six tasks at one sitting and in the same order. Task eight (an original training problem) was always third in order, following tasks six (previous test problem) and five (a new task). Is not the measured 'retention' of task eight a function in part of transfer from doing task five? Is not performance on task five in part a function of retention of old task six, which precedes it? In other words, transfer and retention effects are confounded with each other and both with cumulative practice effects during the testing. There is also some question as to whether those who had learned the general principle would have been more prone to rehearse and apply it during the month's interval. In any case, Katona (1940, pp. 115ff.) concludes that the 'structural' traces set up by meaningful, organized methods of learning are more adaptable and persist longer, whereas rote memorization establishes chaotic 'individual' traces which are relatively rigid and which vanish quickly if not reinforced. Hence meaningful methods yield better retention and broader transfer.

An alternative explanation can be phrased in terms of *what* is learned and *how much* must be retained under 'memorization' and 'principle' methods. In memorizing, a specific set of sequential responses is practiced—an instrumental skill. In principle learning, a new way of perceiving the situation is developed, particular aspects of the stick configurations acquire new significance, and the mediational mechanisms here can selectively call forth whatever movements are appropriate. Katona states (p. 118) that the memorizing group, when presented with new tasks, immediately grasped their pencils and began drawing their mechanical solution, whereas the principle groups began by scrutinizing the figures without using their pencils. To the extent that the rote habits of the memorizers interfere with solutions of new problems, negative transfer will occur. In this experiment the memorizers actually did a little poorer on transfer tests than the control group that received no instruction. What about the greatly superior retention displayed by the principle-seeking group in the first experiment? There is a very simple and obvious answer. The absolute amount of forgetting varies with how much must be retained. All that the subjects who learned the principle had to retain was 'start with the bottom line of numbers, add 3, then 4, then 3, and so on,' and the remainder of the reproduction was not retention but *reconstruction*. The memorizing subjects, on the other hand, must try to recall 24 separate numbers and their locations. That none of them succeeded in making perfect reproductions after 3 weeks is not surprising.

MOTIVATION AND MEMORY

One of the earliest systematic attempts to relate affective and mnemonic variables was undertaken by Bartlett in his book, *Remembering* (1932), already referred to. The essence of his view was that the core of memory in lifelike situations is an emotional attitude which, at the time of reproduction, serves to organize and transmute that which is recalled. More recently Rapaport (1942, 1943) has detailed many phenomena observed in the clinic and the psychiatrist's office that are clearly relevant to theories of memory. There is, for example, the severe form of selective forgetting known as *fugue,* involving loss of all memories that would bring the individual back into a pain-producing situation—his name, his address, his associates, and so on. Everyday forgetting of particular names and places, motivated slips of the tongue and pen, and motivated 'accidental' movements, such as breaking an unwanted gift, are richly substantiated in the observations of Freud (cf. 1914) and other psychoanalysts. In the area of social psychology it is often said that people remember best that which agrees with their personal mores and beliefs, conveniently forgetting facts that contradict them. Methodologically, here as in studying the relation between perceptual organization and memory, the critical experimental problem is to segregate retention from learning. No one denies that learning is affected by motivation. But does motivation affect memory itself? Are unpleasant experiences forgotten at a faster rate than pleasant experiences? Does ego-involvement in a task at the time of learning slow down the rate at which it is forgotten?

Ego-involvement I. Forgetting of the Unpleasant

The concept of repression lies at the core of Freudian theory. Briefly, it is a barrier flung between the conscious and unconscious minds, defended by repressive forces originating in the Super ego, representing the dictates of society, and under constant attack from expressive forces originating in the Id, representing the sum total of blind, selfish, and primitive urges. What must be repressed? The systems of ideas associated with aggressive and sexual strivings and those that threaten the security of the individual's ego-ideal (his idealized picture of himself). In sum, all ideas and behaviors that produce *ego-anxiety* tend to be pushed out of the conscious mind into the unconscious. When such material is repressed, it does not lose its psychic energy (libidinal charge). It exerts continuous pressure upon the repressive barrier toward becoming conscious, occasionally breaking through the barrier in disguised forms as symptoms. Motivated forgetting itself is one of the major symptoms of underlying repression. Materials which may be themselves innocuous but which have become associated with repressed strivings suffer the same fate. Since they would tend through free association to draw painful ideas into consciousness, the repressive blanket must be extended to include them, and the person forgets.

This is admittedly a very superficial presentation of the Freudian theory of repression, and certainly a very uncritical one, but a more adequate offering would go far beyond the bounds of this book. The Freudian analysis as a whole leads directly to the prediction that individuals should forget unpleasant materials more quickly than pleasant materials, but many experimental defenders of traditional psychology were quick to prove Freud wrong—to their own satisfaction.

Judged vs. *felt affect.* Most of the earlier investigators failed to distinguish between two different facets of the problem. Subjects may *judge* certain external stimuli (words, colors, and the like) to be either pleasant or unpleasant without *feeling* any emotional affect; conversely, unpleasant emotional affect may be aroused in certain subjects by many things they would judge as pleasant, for example words like 'kiss,' 'kitten,' or 'succeed.' There is the neurotic lass whose sexual anxieties are liberated by the word 'kiss'; there is the lad who recalls having tortured young animals when he hears 'kitten'; and there are many people with strong inferiority feelings to be aroused by the word 'succeed.' The Freudian proposition applies to felt affect, not mere judgment on an intellectual or even esthetic basis. More specifically, *Freudian theory would predict repression only for those materials that evoke anxiety.*

Experiments in which materials have been divided according to judged pleasantness or unpleasantness have yielded inconsistent results. One technique has been to have children or college students evaluate their experiences during a vacation and later try to recall these experiences. Then measurement was made of the relative proportions of pleasant or unpleasant experiences recalled. Positive results have been obtained, i.e. fewer unpleasant experiences recalled (Meltzer, 1930; Jersild, 1931; Stagner, 1931, for example), negative results (cf. Cason, 1932; Menzies, 1935; Waters and Leeper, 1936), and even mixed results within the same experiment (Thomson, 1930). Several difficulties with this procedure are immediately apparent. The repressive sequences demanded by Freud are probably well under way before the initial record and judgment of experience is obtained; in other words, experiences producing strong anxiety seldom appear in such experiments. There is no guarantee that ego-involvements of any sort are involved. It is even possible that highly pleasant experiences are actively rehearsed during the retention interval, in which case the obtained results indicate not repression of the unpleasant but rather practice of the pleasant.

Another technique has brought the problem into the confines of the laboratory. Ratliff (1938) had subjects learn lists of paired associates in which the stimulus members were odors, sounds, or colors—all carefully rated in terms of pleasantness or unpleasantness—and the responses were numbers. After learning to a criterion of three correct repetitions, recall tests were made both immediately and after 5- or 10-minute delays. Differences were in no case significant, pleasant colors and sounds being somewhat better recalled than unpleasant, but the opposite being true for odors. Consistent differences would not be expected from the Freudian theorem in this or in other experiments of the same nature; there is absolutely no control over the felt affect and probably no ego-involvement in any case.

The most common experimental technique has been to use meaningful words that are judged by the subjects to be pleasant or unpleasant; some investigators (viz. Barrett, 1938) have gone farther to require their subjects to produce relevant associations to the words. These materials are then generally learned, either intentionally or incidentally, with recall or recognition being tested after a varying interval. Here again results are conflicting (positive, Thomson, 1930; Barrett, 1938; negative, Balken, 1933). An experimental attempt to index the presence of felt affect has been to measure psychogalvanic reactions to various words before testing their retention (Jones, 1929; Lynch, 1932). Words yielding high PGR values generally show better retention, but just what this means in relation to the problem is not clear since PGR measures merely the presence of emotional excitement, not its quality. A general survey of studies utilizing the judgmental criterion (cf. Meltzer, 1930, for work previous to 1930; Barrett, 1938) does show a preponderance of positive results—experiences or materials judged to be unpleasant tend to be less well recalled or recognized than those judged as pleasant—but there is no real test of the Freudian hypothesis here.

Intensity of the affect. A number of investigators have recognized the importance of producing real ego-anxiety in testing the Freudian hypothesis and this has appeared explicitly in the design of their experiments. But yet another variable is involved: if the repressive sequence is to be initiated, the anxiety must be sufficiently intense. Clinical observations on repressive mechanisms are obtained from patients suffering violent emotional conflicts. Can ego-involvement of sufficient intensity to initiate repression be produced under conditions that can be controlled experimentally? One of the earliest experiments on retention appearing to involve real ego-involvement was that of Koch (1930). Grades received on 10 true-false quizzes served as the test material, the students being required to rate their feelings upon receiving each grade. Five weeks after the last grade was received, a test for recall was given: high (pleasant) grades were remembered best and poor (unpleasant) grades worst. Although the investigator does not interpret these results in terms of the Freudian hypothesis, they seem to substantiate it. In the competitive struggle for academic prestige, receiving a poor grade is a cue for the arousal of ego-anxiety; there is presumably a strong wish to forget one's personal failures. Whether the anxiety created was sufficiently intense is another matter, of course. An alternative explanation of this experiment would be that the high grades were better learned,

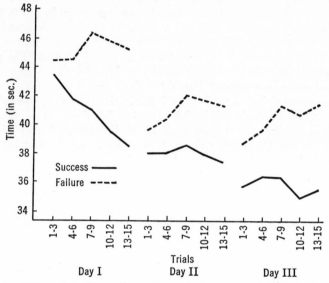

FIGURE 185. Differential effects of experimentally induced success and failure upon performance in card-sorting. Average time scores for trials on three successive days. R. R. Sears, *Journal of Experimental Psychology*, 1937, 20:575.

i.e. they were reviewed and 'gloated over' by the subjects while the low grades were consciously avoided.

As observed earlier, to demonstrate poorer *retention* of anxiety-producing materials, care must be taken to insure equal original learning. This is especially difficult, of course, because the same affect that theoretically leads to repression may also be expected to hinder original learning. An experiment by Sears (1937), although not directly on the problem of retention, does bear on the matter of original learning. Each subject had three experimental sessions following this pattern: (1) learn one list of nonsense syllables, (2) fifteen trials at card-sorting, (3) learn another list of nonsense syllables. Half of the subjects were made to fail in the card-sorting by being given fake time scores by stop watch and by receiving subtle, derogatory remarks from the experimenter; the other subjects were given exaggerated success by similar methods. No success-failure treatment was given in the verbal learning. The differential effects of felt success and felt failure on the true card-sorting times are shown in Fig. 185. The failure group shows a cumulative decrement within each day's work, recovery occurring at the beginning of each new day (indicating that skill actually was increasing). The effects of failure also spread or generalized to the other task, learning nonsense syllables; in trials required to learn the failure group showed an average decrease of only 3.5 per cent as compared with a reduction of 25.9 per cent for the success group. This experiment makes it clear that motivational conditions involving ego-anxiety may cause measurable decrement in the original learning of a task, regardless of what effects may be produced upon retention itself. This enormously complicates the interpretation of much evidence supposedly demonstrating the more rapidly forgetting of unpleasant materials.

Perhaps the closest approach in the laboratory to the condition demanded by the Freudian contention is to be found in an experiment by Sharp (1938). She used both normal subjects and a group of psychoneurotic and mildly psychotic patients, who learned lists of word-pairs to a criterion of one perfect repetition, recall being tested after 2, 9, and 16 days. The pairs of words were taken directly from clinical case histories of the abnormal patients and were incorporated into three lists, one of acceptable materials ('acting-generously'), one of neutral materials ('carrying-baskets'), and one of anxiety-producing materials ('feeling-inferior'). The assumption made here is that verbal cues such as 'feeling-inferior' will give rise, especially in the abnormal patients, to a series of unpleasant associations along with their attendant anxiety. The anxiety-producing materials proved to be both less well recalled and harder to relearn. But there were no differences between neurotics (from whose case histories the materials were taken) and normal controls. This suggests another possible explanation. Possibly 'anxiety-producing' materials were merely more unusual words or perhaps less tritely paired than the others—in any case, simply harder to learn. The design of this experiment is weak in that it is impossible to disentangle the affective variable from others linked with the use of different materials in the three conditions.

The use of hypnosis as a technique. One of the most common phenomena reported in connection with hypnosis, indeed considered its essence by some, is restriction of the field of awareness with a correlated minimization of external interferences. To this is related *posthypnotic amnesia* for what has transpired during the period of hypnosis, especially where this is suggested to the subject before being brought out of his trance state. If one set of materials were learned in the waking state and another set in the trance state, and there were dissociation between them, transfer and retroaction effects should be minimal. This opens what appears to be an ideal method for inquiring into the natures of both hypnosis and interference in learning, and the results obtained so far bear on motivational dynamics.

The general procedure used by Nagge (1935) was to have his ten male subjects both learn and recall an original list of nonsense syllables in either a waking or a trance state; interpolated activity was also in either a waking or a trance state, being light reading ('rest') or learning another list of syllables. Various combinations of these conditions yield the comparisons shown in Table 11, where differences in percentage savings greater than 12 may be considered fairly significant (Woodworth, 1938). Comparison 1 merely indicates that fairly significant amounts of retroactive interference

TABLE 11. RETROACTIVE INTERFERENCE IN RELATION TO WAKING AND TRANCE STATES

Original Learning and Recall	Interpolation		% Saving	
1. waking	waking activity		38	
waking	waking rest		49	
trance	trance activity		48	
trance	trance rest		64	
2. waking	waking activity		38	
waking	trance activity		50	
trance	trance activity		48	
trance	waking activity		64	
3. waking	waking rest		49	
waking	trance rest		63	
trance	trance rest		64	
trance	waking rest		78	
4. waking	waking activity	waking rest		
waking	trance activity (and)	trance rest (averaged)	44	56
trance	trance activity	trance rest		
trance	waking activity (and)	waking rest (averaged)	56	71

Data of Nagge, *Journal of Experimental Psychology*, 1935, 663-82.

are produced by interpolating another list of nonsense syllables as compared with reading light literature (rest), this being true for both waking and trance states. Comparison 2 shows that less interference occurs when original and interpolated tasks are learned in different states; this checks the hypothesis that waking and trance states are dissociated from one another. Interestingly enough, in comparison 3 we find that interpolated 'rest' also produces less interference when it occurs in a different state than original learning. This seems to bear out an opinion voiced earlier that the so-called rest condition is not a satisfactory control in retroaction studies. Comparison 4 shows that for either interpolated activity or interpolated rest occurring in either waking or trance states, material learned originally under hypnosis is better retained than that learned in the waking state. Prentice (1943) has utilized this aspect of Nagge's data as evidence in favor of the gestalt memory trace theory, arguing that hypnosis serves to 'insulate' the traces established in original learning from subsequent interference.

But then one runs up against a nearly identical experiment yielding absolutely contrary results. Mitchell (1932) used 3-place numbers rather than nonsense syllables. Original learning was in either waking or trance states, interpolated learning in either, and recall was measured in the same state as original learning—identical with Nagge's procedures. The experiment was not so extensive as Nagge's, however, only two subjects being employed and fewer conditions. Both subjects are reported to have readily achieved a deep trance state, and the instructions for posthypnotic amnesia were also given. Direct comparisons with Nagge's data are given in Table 12. Notice that point for point there exists direct refutation. Since no rest conditions were used in this experiment, most other comparisons cannot be

TABLE 12. COMPARISON OF MITCHELL'S DATA * WITH DATA OF NAGGE

Original Learning and Recall	Interpolation	% Saving Mitchell	Nagge
waking	waking activity	46	38
waking	trance activity	21	50
trance	trance activity	30	48
trance	waking activity	7	64

* *Journal of General Psychology*, 1932, 7:343-59.

made. One observes, however, that here learning in the trance condition, regardless of the interpolation state, tends to yield *poorer* retention, directly contradicting Nagge's finding as well as Prentice's (1943) interpretation in terms of the 'insulation' of memory traces.

It does not seem reasonable to explain the differences between these two studies on the basis of the use of nonsense syllables in one case and numbers in the other, or in terms of the depth of trance obtained, or even in terms of the number of subjects employed (although Nagge's results would seem the more reliable on this basis). It seems more probable that some gross difference existed in the reactions of the two sets of subjects to the experience of hypnosis itself. Possibly the two subjects used by Mitchell were seasoned veterans and took the experiment as a rather routine matter, whereas Nagge's subjects were far more ego-involved in their performance. Lest the reader think this is pure wool-gathering on the writer's part, I hasten to one of the more recent investigations on this problem, one in which the role of ego-involvement is especially evident.

Rosenthal (1944) undertook to clarify the nature of hypnotic hypermnesia by varying the materials (nonsense versus meaningful) and the degree of ego-anxiety present. The basic procedure in the series of experiments to be described was to have all subjects learn or solve tasks in the waking state and then to be tested for recall either in the waking state (control) or under trance (experimental). Two significant controls were added: (1) Each of the 13 subjects was made to serve as his own control by recalling equated materials under both states. (2) Both experimental and control subjects were first tested for recall in the waking state (Recall I) while the second recall (Recall II) was under hypnosis for the experimental group. This makes it possible to estimate how equivalent the original learning and retention of the two groups was before the differential hypnotic treatment was given.

Table 13 presents the results obtained in the various experiments in terms of mean recall values and levels of significance of differences between experimental (trance) and control (waking) groups. First, as to nonsense versus meaningful material, recall in hypnotic trance yields superior recall of poetry (experiment 4) but not of nonsense syllables (experiment 1). As to the effects of anxiety, results for the failure items in experiments 3 and 7 indicate clearly that hypnotic recall of anxiety-producing materials is superior to ordinary waking recall. But what about the negative results in experiment 5? Rosenthal believes that they were due to the low level of original learning of the ten short poems used and to the inter-poem con-

TABLE 13. RECALL UNDER TRANCE AND WAKING STATES FOR VARIOUS TYPES OF MATERIAL

Material	Experimental Group		Control Group		Confidence Level Diff. I and II
	Recall I	Recall II	Recall I	Recall II	
1. NS syllables	8.76	8.84	8.39	8.57	80% *
2. Innocuous words in NS lists	9.47	9.69	8.92	9.22	n.s.
3. Same as #2, plus Anxiety production					
(a) Success items	4.9	5.0	5.0	5.2	60%
(b) Failure items	3.3	4.8	3.1	3.3	1%
4. Poetry (N words)	46.3	61.3	48.3	52.4	1%
5. Poetry (1 reading) Anxiety production					
(a) Success poems	44.4	45.0	45.3	47.1	n.s.
(b) Failure poems	45.5	46.0	46.6	47.3	n.s.
6. Lists of profane	8.4	8.5	8.6	8.7	n.s.
vs. innocuous pairs (of NS syllables)	7.8	7.8	7.9	7.9	n.s.
7. Performance tasks Anxiety production					
(a) Success tasks	7.46	7.54	7.92	8.25	40%
(b) Failure tasks	5.76	7.23	5.92	6.31	1%

* Levels of confidence: % equals times in 100 that difference of given magnitude could have occurred by chance, i.e. the lower the values, the greater the significance; n.s. indicates level not computed by experimenter, but obviously not significant.

From data of Rosenthal, 1944.

fusions. But why were negative findings obtained in experiment 6? Here profane-sounding items were produced by pairing nonsense syllables and recall was compared with that for innocuous pairs: Rosenthal explains the negative results in this case as owing to failure of the profane or obscene items to produce the desired effect: 'The relationship between subjects and experimenter was not stilted or formal . . . , [the profane items] . . . were happily and gleefully recalled.' Justification for this interpretation exists in the recall result for this experiment: by both experimental and control groups the profane items were better recalled than the innocuous items.

The results obtained with hypnosis have not proved as conclusive as one might have hoped. (1) It seems probable that hypnosis serves to minimize interference between materials successively practiced (despite Mitchell's negative results) and hence facilitates recall under certain conditions. (2) It seems to be materials that cause ego-anxiety that show hypermnesia. In other words, it appears that the repressive effects produced by anxiety are specifically counteracted by hypnosis. Notice in Rosenthal's investigation that it was only where the items presumed to produce anxiety *actually yielded poorer recall for both experimental and control groups* that hypermnesia was obtained. This is about the best experimental evidence available that the kind of motivated forgetting postulated by Freud does occur. The weight of clinical evidence favoring the Freudian repression hypothesis leads one to accept it as valid despite the lack of experimental verification.

Most experiments we have surveyed have not been designed in such a way as to provide fair tests of it.

Ego-involvement II. Enhancement of Memory under Positive Motivation

In a description of the gestalt theory of memory it was pointed out that the stability of memory traces is assumed to vary directly with the amount of tension in the region where they exist. Since the ego is a region of high psychic tension, according to this theory, it follows that memory traces of ego-involved tasks or experiences will be more stable and will resist assimilation with other traces. This leads to the prediction that ego-involved performances will be recalled more accurately and over longer periods of time than performances in which the subject is not ego-involved. It is clear that degrees of original learning must be equated if this notion is to be tested.

Degree of original learning. An experiment by Biel and Force (1943) illustrates the importance of this variable. Lists of nonsense syllables were prepared in six different styles of type. An *intentional learning* group was instructed to learn the lists, but an *incidental learning* group was told it was merely helping to evaluate the legibility of the different type styles. The intentional learning group required 6 repetitions of the list and the incidental group 12 to reach the same criterion of mastery. The equal values for immediate recall (Table 14) show that original learning had actually

TABLE 14

	Intentional	Incidental	Critical Ratio
Immediate recall	6.08	6.08	0.35
19-day recall	1.92	2.08	0.70
19-day recognition	7.88	8.52	2.21

From data of Biel and Force, *Journal of Experimental Psychology*, 1943, 32:52-63.

been equated. After a 19-day retention interval no significant differences appear. If anything, the incidental group is superior. Intentional learning does not appear to yield superior retention if degree of original learning is constant.

Relating the gestalt thesis directly to retroactive interference, Prentice (1943) has offered the following statement: 'Increased ego-involvement in any learning situation has the effect of maintaining for a longer time a high degree of organization in the resulting trace systems, with the consequence that similar traces have a reduced destructive influence and retroactive inhibition is thereby diminished' (p. 284). In one of several tests, Prentice compared the effects of intentional versus incidental learning upon retroactive interference. All four groups of subjects used were read an original list of ten familiar words twice. Groups 1 and 2 were merely to classify these words as parts of speech; groups 3 and 4 were to both classify and learn the words. For interpolated activity, group 1 and group 3 counted *C*'s on a mimeographed sheet while groups 2 and 4 were given another list of ten words. Average recall values for the four groups are shown in Table 15. That intentional *learning* is superior to incidental *learning* is shown by the

TABLE 15. COMPARATIVE RETROACTIVE INTERFERENCE WITH INTENTIONAL
AND INCIDENTAL LEARNING

Group	Mean Recall
Group 1 (incidental—'rest')	6.3
Group 2 (incidental—activity)	2.7
Group 3 (intentional—'rest')	7.9
Group 4 (intentional—activity)	5.2

From data of Prentice, *American Journal of Psychology*, 1943, 56:283-92.

higher recall scores for group 3 (7.9) as compared with group 1 (6.3). Presumably the same difference in degree of original learning existed for groups 2 and 4, yet here the difference is even greater than that between groups 1 and 3. Prentice concludes that intentional learning in group 4 minimized the interference effects of retroaction, thereby permitting higher recall after interpolated activity than in group 2. Another possibility is that the difference in retroaction could be a function of the degree of original learning, quite apart from 'intention' as such. In the preceding chapter it was shown that retroactive effects decrease with high degrees of original learning, so it may be that the higher degree of original learning 'insulated the traces' rather than intent to learn.

Studies in which ego-involvement is the experimental variable. In neither of the above-mentioned investigations has ego-involvement per se been the experimental variable, unless one assumes that all intentional learning is ego-involved. An experiment by Heyer and O'Kelly (1949) gave two groups of subjects an equal number of trials on learning a list of 20 nonsense syllables. One group was told, 'Your grade on this exercise will *count a full* 10 *per cent of your quarter's grade,'* a reasonable explanation being included; the other group was told only that they were helping to standardize the materials. At the end of five presentations of the list, subjects wrote down as many items as they could (Recall I—measure of original learning). After a week's interval, with no indications there might be any further testing, they were again asked to recall as many as they could (Recall II—measure of retention). Surprising was the result that there were no *significant* differences in original learning between the two groups (although the ego-involved group was somewhat superior); differences in retention after one week were significant and favored the ego-involved group. Taken at face value, these results substantiate the hypothesis that ego-involvement, as a form of motivation, does facilitate *retention.* (a) The two groups, however, were not strictly equated on original learning; (b) it is possible that the performance of the ego-involved group was 'damped' by anxiety over their grades (see Alper experiment below); and (c) the possibility of differential rehearsal during the retention interval is not entirely eliminated.

Many experiments in the field of social psychology demonstrate a tendency for materials that coincide with a person's frame of reference (system of evaluation) to be better learned and retained than those which contradict his position. Watson and Hartmann (1939), for example, compared the recall by theistic and atheistic students of controversial materials, finding retention better in both cases where the individual's evaluative framework was supported. Edwards (1941) read a 10-minute speech to a group of college students, some of whom favored the New Deal, some of whom were neutral and some of whom were anti-New Deal. There was a consistent tendency for the relative amount forgotten to be related to the degree of conflict between the read material and the frame of reference of the subject.

Levine and Murphy (1943) designed a study in which the *rates* of both learning and forgetting controversial materials could be observed. The material dealt with the Soviet Union, one group of subjects being decidedly procommunist and the other equally anticommunist in their social philosophies. One pro- and one anticommunist paragraph were read over twice, in

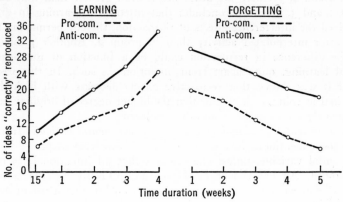

FIGURE 186. Learning and forgetting curves for pro- and anti-communist students reading an anti-communist selection. Levine and Murphy, *Journal of Abnormal and Social Psychology,* 1943, **38**:513.

varying orders for different subjects, and reproduced several times during each weekly session. Four weekly sessions constituted the learning period and five further weekly tests were made of retention only. The results for the anti-Soviet passage are shown in Fig. 186. The procommunist subjects learned this passage more slowly—that is clear enough. But that the rate of forgetting materials which conflict with one's frame of reference is more rapid is barely suggested by the slight tendency for the discrepancy between pro- and anticommunist curves to increase during the retention period. Certainly the major factor, in this study at least, is the ease of learning. Similar results were found for the pro-Soviet selection.

Ego-orientation vs. *task-orientation.* An investigation by Alper (1946) approximates ideal conditions for the study of ego-involvement. The materials for learning consisted of a series of 20 items (ten nonsense syllables and ten 3-place numbers). Twenty of the total 40 subjects were *ego-oriented,* by being told that the task was a special short-form intelligence test developed by the Harvard Psychological Clinic, and the remainder were *task-oriented,* mainly by establishing an impersonal, routine work atmosphere. Alper explicitly avoids the terms 'ego-involvement' and 'task-involvement,' stating very reasonably that the experimenter, by his instructions, can orient the subject toward task or ego goals but cannot guarantee any specific kind of involvement. The subjects in each orientation group were further subdivided into incidental and intentional learning groups, by having ten subjects in each serve as experimenters (not told they were to learn the materials) and the other ten serve as their subjects (told to learn). After going through the serial list twice on day 1 (experimenter-subjects presenting the cards to the subject-subjects), immediate recall was measured for all subjects; all were requested to return 'for another experiment' the following day, at which time a measure of delayed recall was obtained. Alper's main purpose was to show that the classic law of forgetting—that immediate recall is superior to delayed recall—holds only under conditions of task-orientation, not ego-orientation. When each subject's immediate recall was compared with his own delayed recall (i.e. each subject serving as his own control), *task-oriented subjects did show a significant loss in retention while ego-oriented subjects did not,* and this held for all conditions.

It is on the interpretation of these results that one may find reason for disagreement. Alper believes that the results as a whole substantiate a trace theory of learning and memory. 'Traces established under conditions of ego-orientation would seem to be available both for immediate and for delayed recall. Ego-orientated traces, therefore, seem to be more stable, less likely merely to sink or to assimilate with the general mass of memory traces, than are task-orientated traces' (p. 246). But if this is the case, why was ego-orientated learning (day 1) not superior to task-orientated learning? Alper answers that the ego-orientation instructions aroused the subjects' anxieties, these reactions temporarily inhibiting performance on day 1 but dissipating over the 24-hour interval. Actually, this suggestion, if followed through, leads to an alternative explanation which does not contradict the classic law of forgetting. If such anxiety-produced inhibition existed, then the 'true' learning of the ego-oriented group is not reflected in their immediate recall scores on day 1—they had actually learned more than their measured performance showed. *Ergo,* they may have forgotten relatively as much as the task-oriented subjects, and the classical law of forgetting still holds.

Another interesting fact reveals itself in these data: the experimenter-subjects in the ego-orientation group actually recalled more items on day 11 than they had apparently learned on day 1. How can more be recalled than is originally learned? There was no control in this experiment over *rehearsal during the retention interval.* If ego-motivated subjects are more predisposed to rehearse the task whenever the general experimental situation reoccurs to them, their superior performance on day 11 is readily explained without any recourse to stability of memory traces. Although evidence on rehearsal was not reported in Alper's original (1946) article, the following appeared in a subsequent report (1948) based upon identically the same experiment: 'When asked at the end of the experiment on day 11 whether they had tended to rehearse the series during the 24-hour interval between reproduction and recall, 15 of the 20 ego-oriented Ss answered "Yes"; five answered "No." Task-oriented Ss, on the other hand, were evenly divided in their tendency to rehearse: 10 said "Yes" and 10 said "No"' (p. 231, 1948). Since further statistical analysis in this second report shows that the ego-oriented subjects who rehearsed did better on day 11 than those who did not, the conclusions reached in the original report are considerably weakened.

The Zeigarnik Effect

Now we turn to a technique in which either or both positive and negative ego-involvements may be present, a technique that was developed to check another prediction arising from the gestalt conception of motivation, namely, that interrupted tasks should be better recalled than completed ones. If an individual is motivated toward success in a task, a specific tension system is assumed to be generated, which persists through manipulation of the task and is resolved by completion of it. If the task is interrupted, the goal tension persists, leading to (1) a tendency to perseverate organization of the memory traces relating to the task and hence its better recall and (2) a tendency to resume the interrupted task or one similar to it. The earliest attempt to verify these hypotheses is to be found in an investigation by Zeigarnik (1927).

Zeigarnik gave her subjects a series of 18 to 22 brief and varied tasks, half of which were completed and half were interrupted by the experimenter on a plausible pretext. Immediately following completion of the last task in the series, subjects were asked to recall the names of as many as they could. A higher proportion of interrupted tasks was recalled, verifying the gestalt prediction. The introduction of several variable conditions, such as having 'guests' try various tasks while on a 'tour' of the laboratory, seemed to isolate the essential role of ego-involvement in producing the effect. Attesting to the general validity of the phenomenon are a number of other studies. Brown (1933) not only checked Zeigarnik's conclusion but extended information on it by showing that the effect varies directly with the degree of motivation toward the tasks. Rosenzweig (1933) substantiated Brown's work, finding further that with low degrees of motivation completed tasks tended to be recalled better. Under more carefully controlled conditions (interruption procedures standardized, the length of interrupted and completed tasks equated, orders of presentation systematically randomized), Marrow (1938) also obtained the Zeigarnik effect.

Critical studies designed to isolate relevant variables. The history of the Zeigarnik effect parallels that of other novel psychological phenomena in this respect: early investigations demonstrate the existence of the phenomenon and later ones attempt to shake loose its determining conditions, without spectacular success, however, in the present instance. As a first step in this process we have a study by Freeman (1930). This investigator was interested in that aspect of the gestalt theory which states that *psychological tensions* are created by a task and resolved by its completion. Is this construct, psychological tension, objectively measurable? Freeman measured *motor tension* and found it to increase at the beginning of a task, gradually reduce during manipulation, and to be definitely augmented by interruption. To a certain extent, then, measures of motor tension may offer an independent index of psychological tension states—the importance of this direction of research will soon become apparent.

Boguslavsky and Guthrie (1941) have asked this question: Is the effect really due to a task's 'being interrupted' or perhaps rather to its 'interrupting' another task, with resulting increase in annoyance and tension? Twenty pencil-and-paper tasks, with written instructions, were presented in an order so randomized that *each task* was (a) completed following a completed task, (b) completed after interrupting the preceding task, (c) interrupted following a completed task, and (d) interrupted after interrupting the preceding task. Each task occurred an equal number of times in each of these conditions, making it possible to use each task as its own control. The results are shown in Table 16. Although the difference be-

TABLE 16

Condition	Frequency of Recall
a. Task completed, following completed	108
b. Task completed, following interrupted	120
c. Task interrupted, following completed	94
d. Task interrupted, following interrupted	116

From unpublished paper of Boguslavsky, 1941.

tween the recall scores for completed (*a* and *b*) and interrupted (*c* and *d*) tasks was not highly significant, the direction of the result is clearly contrary to those reported above—the Zeigarnik effect does not appear. This investigator offers no explanation of why the completed tasks are recalled somewhat better than the interrupted ones. It is possible that motivation to complete the tasks was too low, since subjects were told they would be interrupted on some of the tasks. Zeigarnik reports that she had almost to fight with some of her subjects to interrupt them!

On the other hand, tasks which *interrupted* preceding ones (*b* and *d*) were recalled significantly better than those which did not (*a* and *c*). Bogoslavsky interprets this as substantiating his contention that it is not the tension produced by interruption per se which leads to better recall but rather the tension present during the execution of a task. Why should this be so? Following Guthrie's associationistic theory, it is assumed that since recall is the evocation of a response by a given set of stimuli, the more common components there are in both the original task situation and the recall situation, the more probable will be recall. Since tasks that interrupt others proceed under higher degrees of motor tension (cf. Freeman, 1930) and the direction 'to recall as many tasks as you can' also creates motor tension, more 'interrupting' tasks are remembered. Unfortunately no actual measures of motor tension were made in this investigation; the basic assumption (that tension at recall is more nearly like that present during interrupting tasks) is not tested.

Another suggestion as to why the effect may show up in some experiments but not in others is contained in research done by Rosenzweig (1943). Following the usual procedure of interrupting half of the tasks and allowing the others to be completed, one group of college students, the 'informal group,' was told they were only helping the experimenter standardize a set of jigsaw puzzles, while another 'formal group' was told they were taking an intelligence test. The 'informal' group displayed the Zeigarnik effect, whereas the 'formal' group showed the opposite trend, completed tasks being better recalled. Rosenzweig believes that the 'informal' subjects were motivated mainly by *need-persistence* (i.e. unresolved tension set up by the incompleted tasks), whereas the 'formal' subjects were motivated also by *ego-defense* (i.e. anxiety over failure leading to repression of incompleted tasks).

A comparison of Alper's (1946) findings reported above with these obtained by Rosenzweig might be fruitful. In both cases one group of subjects was ego-oriented by being told they were taking an intelligence test, whereas the other group was task-oriented. Whereas Rosenzweig attributes the increased recall of incompleted tasks in the *task-oriented* group to need-persistence, Alper finds decreased recall; whereas Rosenzweig attributes decreased recall of incompleted tasks in the *ego-oriented* group to ego-defense (repression), Alper attributes the increased recall for her equivalent 'intelligence test' group to their ego-involvement. By what subtle metamorphosis does the ego-involvement aroused by 'taking an intelligence test' lead to forgetting in one case and to improved recall in the other? Is the interruption technique the essential difference? This is a possibility we shall investigate in just a moment. Another explanation may lie in the fact that Rosenzweig's groups were not strictly equivalent: the 'informal' subjects were secured and paid by the Student Employment Bureau, but the 'formal' subjects were freshmen advisees of the Harvard Psychological Clinic. It seems likely that the general motivational patterns of these two groups would have differed considerably.

Yet another significant variable is *the similarity of tasks*. According to the gestalt theory, when tension exists within one specific sub-system, it tends to spread into neighboring sub-systems. This results in a search for substitute goals if the primary goal is blocked. Conversely, reduction of tension within one system tends to reduce tension in neighboring systems, making it possible to attain satisfaction through substitute activities. The degree of spread of tension is a function, largely, of the permeability of barriers between systems and their 'nearness.' Nearness in gestalt topological space is equivalent to similarity, and this conception of 'spread' is equivalent to generalization in the behaviorist's system. If all the tasks in a series were highly similar in nature, the Zeigarnik effect should be washed out entirely. Tension increases produced by interruption of some tasks and tension decreases produced by completion of others would presumably spread through permeable barriers (generalize) and thus counteract each other. On the other hand, if all the interrupted tasks were highly similar to one another, but quite different from the group of completed tasks, the Zeigarnik effect should be maximized. This variable has not been checked experimentally (however, cf. Cartwright, 1942, for related information).

Related to the Zeigarnik effect upon recall is the effect of interruption upon *the resumption of tasks*. The same hypothetical tension whose persistence leads to improved recall also manifests itself in a tendency to resume the interrupted task or one similar to it. Although this has been shown to occur for interrupted as compared with completed tasks (Ovsiankina, 1928), the nature of the motivational situation created by the interruption appears to be the crucial factor. Nowlis (1941) accompanied some interruptions with success-provoking statements and others with failure-provoking statements. Interrupted 'success' tasks tended to be resumed but interrupted 'failure' tasks did not, a result checking with Rosenzweig's (1943) findings for recall under similar conditions.

Prentice (1943) has predicted that the increased tension generated by interruption of tasks should stabilize the traces of these activities and hence render them less susceptible to retroactive interference. To test this prediction, four groups of subjects were employed: group 1 was given an original set of 16 tasks, all of them being either completed or interrupted (for different individuals), read an interesting book (rest) for 18 minutes, and was finally tested for recall of the names of the 16 tasks. Group 2 was handled as group 1, with the exception that these subjects had interpolated a new set of eight tasks instead of reading; group 3 had half its original tasks interrupted, otherwise serving as a 'rest' group like group 1; group 4 had half its original tasks interrupted and also learned the eight interpolated tasks. Of the total 16 original tasks, the average number recalled after this differential treatment was group 1, control—rest, 12.3; group 2, control—activity, 8.1; group 3, interrupted—rest, 13.2; and group 4, interrupted—activity, 10.5.

Groups 1 and 2 were included as a control condition for the Zeigarnik effect itself since Prentice had found earlier that when all 16 tasks were completed or all interrupted, no difference in recall was found. Although this fact is not discussed further, it seems to be a relevant bit of information. Why do the tensions presumably created by interruption fail to improve recall when all tasks are treated in this manner? Why isn't the effect even maximized? The fact that group 1 recalls less than group 3 (uniform *vs.* one-half interruption) suggests that the effect appears when half the tasks are interrupted. Of special interest to Prentice was the finding that group 4 (interrupted plus interpolated activity) showed less retroactive interference than group 2 (uniform plus interpolated activity), and he concluded that the tensions set up by interruption of half the tasks stabilized the memory traces and hence minimized interference. It would be interesting to see if, as the gestalt thesis implies, those original tasks for group 4 which were interrupted were those most frequently recalled, but no data on this point are given.

A series of experiments by H. B. Lewis (Lewis, 1944; Lewis and Franklin, 1944) serves ideally to lay bare the basic difficulty in this area of research. *Experiment CW* (co-operative work) was conducted in the following manner: a planted co-worker brought in each subject ostensibly to 'help her do some work for' the author; the investigator was not present during the work, this being performed by each subject and the co-worker in a friendly, informal atmosphere. The planted co-worker casually interrupted half the tasks *and finished them herself,* allowing the subject to complete the other half alone. The question is this: Will the objective completion of interrupted tasks by the partner successfully resolve the tensions produced by interruption? The results were positive, an average ratio of only 0.88 indicating lack of any Zeigarnik effect. A clear-cut conclusion that objective completion of tasks by another person resolves the tensions produced by interruption is shaken by the results of *experiment III.* Here the interrupted tasks were immediately, and before the subject's gaze, *completed by the experimenter.* Does 'objective completion' resolve tensions in this case? An average ratio of 1.20 was obtained which, although not a large difference, shows significantly more Zeigarnik effect than in the first experiment. Does this mean that the important variable is 'co-operative task-orientation' rather than 'objective completion'? In *experiment II,* as in experiment CW, the subject and a planted co-worker co-operated in a 'friendly, informal work-atmosphere,' but here the experimenter presented the tasks and interrupted half of them. A ratio of 1.50 appeared, substantial evidence for the Zeigarnik effect! Apparently neither 'co-operative task-orientation' nor 'objective completion' explains the results of experiment CW.

This problem of identifying causative factors is most sharply etched in *experiment I* and the interpretation of its results. The experiment was designed to compare the effects of *task-orientation* and *ego-orientation* when subjects work individually with the experimenter. The differences between these two kinds of orientation hinged upon a slight difference in the instructions:

> *Experiment I* (task-orientation). 'I am planning some experiments for next semester, and would much appreciate your help in finding out something about the materials I want to use. You are a kind of preliminary guinea pig who will tell me something about these materials. Just do the tasks I have prepared so that I can find out about them. You see, of course, that this isn't at all a test of you. It's a test of the tasks. You are in no sense on the spot.'
>
> *Experiment IA* (ego-orientation). 'I have some tasks here which I should like to have you do. Please work any way you like. This is in preparation for some experiments I want to perform next semester. This is a kind of preliminary.'

Lewis says that these instructions accentuated variations in attitude. In any case, the results were startlingly different for the two groups: experiment I showed a marked Zeigarnik effect (I/C ratio of 1.75), whereas IA showed the reverse effect (ratio of 0.625). These results are interpreted in this manner: '. . . for the Ss in Experiment I tension systems were aroused to complete the tasks. Interruption left unresolved some of these task-completion tension systems. . . For the Ss in Experiment IA . . . interruption meant, primarily, a loss of ego-status, and only secondarily a suspension of the tension-system of task completion' (pp. 198-199). Such insights as these may approximate the truth, but *how* correct they are depends upon the validity of Lewis's clinical judgments about the changing ego-states of her subjects. It is to obviate the necessity for just such *post hoc* intuitions that experimentation should be designed.

This series of experiments illustrates the basic difficulty here—circularity of explanation. They illustrate it because the conflicting results within the same series using the same general methods gave rise to alternative explanatory devices. Certain subjects are said to recall completed tasks better *because* they derived 'ego-enhancement' from them. How do we know the subjects felt 'ego-enhancement'? Why, because they recalled more completed tasks! With the Zeigarnik problem one can select his own hyphenated catch phrase to suit the results: 'ego-defense,' 'task-orientation,' 'ego-enhancement,' and many others wait like bonnets in a young lady's wardrobe for use when the suitable occasion arises. Circularity is practically unavoidable here *because the supposedly independent variable (ego-state) is not independently measurable.* How does one know that the subjects in experiment IA felt ego-enhancement when they completed tasks? How does one know that subjective resolution of tension occurred when the co-worker completed a task in the co-operative situation? Lewis is unable to measure these ego-states directly and is thus forced to draw inferences from introspections of the subjects, their facial expressions, and the like—and the validity of the whole demonstration depends upon the clinical intuitiveness of the investigator. What is needed in this field is painstaking preliminary work designed to isolate those observable signs or measures that indicate the existence and intensity of various ego-states. This may prove difficult, perhaps impossible at present, but until one can assess the motivational state of his subject *independent of* the way he performs a learning or recall task, little in the way of conclusive evidence on the effects of ego-involvement can be expected.

Summary on the Effects of Positive Ego-involvement

In evaluating these propositions which have derived from the gestalt theory it is necessary to distinguish sharply between practical and theoretical laws. On a practical level there is no doubt that we remember better those things in which we are personally involved. Many of the studies reviewed here show that this is the case, and many more could have been brought to bear. But 'remembering better' as a statement of practical fact merely says that there is a difference at the time of recall. The gestalt theory postulates certain dynamisms operating *upon memory traces during the retention interval,* influencing their stability and longevity. To justify this notion, as a part of general psychological theory, it is necessary to eliminate all factors other than mnemonic. This has not been done satisfactorily as yet. In some cases there has not been adequate control over original learning (if ego-involved subjects learned their tasks better, there is no need to postulate additional mnemonic effects); in other cases there has been evidence for differential rehearsal (if ego-involved subjects are more prone to practice the task during the retention interval, there is no need to postulate additional mnemonic effects); and finally, investigators have often specified the presence and nature of the independent variable (ego-state) solely in terms of the dependent variable (performance at recall), rendering the entire proposition untestable.

THE CRITICAL THEORETICAL ISSUE

Contrary to superficial appearances, trace and interference theories do not differ to any great extent in the explanatory principles they employ. The gestalt principles of assimilation and isolation duplicate the behavioristic principles of generalization and discrimination; tension systems and drives are roughly equivalent motivational conceptualizations. True, there are differences here in terminology, but these are matters for semantic rather than experimental analysis. Nor does the real distinction lie in the variables stressed; both theories deal with the homogeneity of materials and their temporal relations.

The critical difference lies in the trace notion itself. *The gestalt theory postulates an active process that persists in and spontaneously changes during time; the behavioristic theory postulates an association that is only modified at those points in time when members of the association are utilized—no changes occur between these points.* Imagine a stage that is empty except for two large cubes, one made of ice (trace) and the other made of wood (association); after a certain interval, pieces are cut from both cubes (assimilation or interpolated activity); after a longer interval these cubes are measured. Whereas all of the modification in the wooden cube is attributable to external, interpolated events, modification of the cube of ice is attributable to both external and autonomous (melting) events. This analogy leads directly to the chief differential implication of the two theories. The trace theory necessarily implies that autonomous changes will occur within the memory trace. The interference theory necessarily implies that there are no autonomous changes. The interesting thing about these completely opposed positions is this: to demonstrate successfully the validity of *either* theory, all sources of external (interpolated) influence must be either eliminated or controlled. Keeping this basic differential in mind, let us turn to the evidence.

That Autonomous Mnemonic Changes Do Occur (Gestalt)

The most fruitful source of information relevant to this hypothesis is data on *memory for visual forms*. Since gestalt principles originated in the

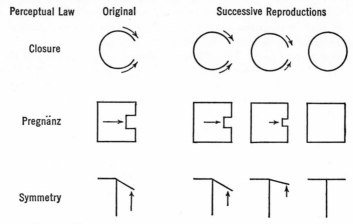

FIGURE 187. Figures illustrating the two major predictions about memory for forms deriving from the gestalt theory: changes should be in those *directions* which resolve forces in the perceptual field (indicated by arrows) and should be *progressive over-time* in the same direction.

field of visual perception, and its dynamisms can be most definitely indicated there, this is not surprising. When a subject observes a series of figures like those shown in Fig. 187 and is asked to recall them after an interval, numerous errors are bound to occur. The important question concerns the nature of such errors. The gestalt theory (cf. Koffka, 1935) must make two predictions: (1) *The modifications within the memory trace for visual forms must be in the direction of reducing the stresses present in the original perception.* In other words, the predicted autonomous changes in memory follow from the laws of perception. Sample laws are illustrated in Fig. 187. Figures having gaps will tend to become closed (closure); deviations from 'good' figures will tend to be corrected (pregnänz); unbalanced figures will tend to become balanced (symmetry). The direction of application of the theoretical forces in original perception is shown by the arrows in the original forms. (2) *The changes in reproduced figures must be progressively in the same direction.* In others words, the dynamic stresses set up in the original perception can work only toward their own resolution; they cannot be reversed or shifted in direction in mid-course except by external influences. When existing in memory traces and therefore relatively free from the influence of peripheral restraining forces, these perceptual dynamisms are presumably freer to operate.

The direction of changes. The first experiment to definitely utilize the gestalt interpretation was one by Wulf (1922). A number of simple patterns were exposed for brief periods, no strict serial order being followed and some time being inserted between patterns. Subjects were told to observe them carefully since they would be asked to reproduce them at a later time. Reproductions were called for immediately (30 seconds), after 24 hours, and after a week. Wulf concluded that 'with the exception of 8 out of 400 [reproductions] . . . the comparison of the reproductions with the original reveals *throughout a clear deviation of the former from the latter in the direction of either sharpening or leveling.*' Wulf's figures contained marked asymmetries. Later investigators, using figures more adequately designed to reveal autonomous changes within the memory traces, have in some cases substantiated the gestalt position. Allport (1930) found a clear tendency for a figure that was symmetrical to remain so and for one that was not to shift toward better balance, although this trend did not necessarily apply to all subjects. Perkins (1932) concluded that 'all changes were in the direction of some balanced or symmetrical patterns.'

A rather different technique was used by J. J. Gibson (1929). A large number of figures were exposed in quick succession, and immediately after seeing the last one the subject was to draw as many as he could from memory. Practice was continued until all figures could be reproduced with reasonable correctness. Delayed reproductions were requested 5 weeks later and after a year. As might be anticipated from the method employed, a large proportion of the errors could be attributed to intraserial confusions (16% of changes). Another major source of error was 'object-assimilation' (14%), reproduced figures shifting toward the class type. A finding of considerable theoretical interest was that 57% of the reproductions showed no definite change, and this despite the fact that most of Gibson's figures were clearly 'stressful.' In an experiment by Warner Brown (1935) each figure was exposed separately and reproduced after 30 seconds, 5 minutes, and unexpectedly after 14 to 17 days. This researcher, after admitting some difficulty in being objective about his classifications, reported 21% 'regularized' (toward more symmetrical form), 10% 'normalized' (typical of class), and 3% 'accented' (overemphasis of some characteristic). These trends agree with Wulf's formulation. But 27% of the changes were 'irregularized,' 'reduced,' or 'increased' and the 39% which were 'correct' (i.e. remained unstable).

Progressiveness of changes. Even though it may be difficult to avoid subjectivity in judging the direction of changes, it certainly should be possible to be objective about progressiveness. Wulf (1922) published 20 individual series, presumably his clearest, as evidence for progressiveness. Woodworth (1938), in reviewing this report, states that 'in the present writer's opinion,

590 EXPERIMENTAL PSYCHOLOGY

only one of these 20 shows an unequivocal progression; 10 show progression in some respect along with non-progressive changes in some other respect, while the remaining 9 are unequivocally non-progressive' (p. 89). Apparently progressiveness is not as objective a matter as one might think. Gibson (1929) cautiously reported progressiveness when the direction was toward either 'object-assimilation' or 'completion.' Allport (1930) noted some tendency for asymmetrical figures to show progressive changes and Perkins (1932) wholeheartedly embraces the gestalt position. Hanawalt (1937) showed more sophistication in method: when successive reproductions by the same individual were compared with reproductions at different intervals by different subjects, there was no evidence for progressiveness in either case. It would be hard to predict, however, what changes to expect in his figures. He also demonstrated that a large part of the change usually attributed to trace dynamics was often present in a direct copy made with the diagram in front of the subject. Following Hanawalt's lead, Goldmeier (1941) used the subject's own original copy as a criterion from which to estimate changes; no evidence for progressiveness was obtained. Also following Hanawalt's lead, Seidenfeld (1938) used *recognition* as a measure, the subject having to select the original from a series of similar drawings; there were frequent reversals in direction of errors rather than the progressiveness demanded by theory.

Critique on methodology. In such a state of conclusive inconclusiveness as this a critical evaluation of methodology is in order. (1) *What changes test the theory?* The gestalt position is that the stresses set up in original perception persist in the memory trace and are responsible for both the direction and progressiveness of changes. Obviously, then, one should use forms for which the perceptual dynamics are known. There are many methods for estimating such dynamics, changes in after-images, modifications in dim illumination, and so forth (cf. Chap. 5). In not a single case has this control been exerted over the choice of materials. (2) *What is the best index of the state of a trace?* Most investigators have used reproduction as an index of the state of a trace, yet Hanawalt (1937) has shown that subjects get significantly more figures correct when recognition is the measure. But recognition itself presents difficulties: here we allow present perceptual dynamics (created in the process of comparing figures) to confuse the measurement. (3) *Why permit serial confusions?* In nearly all the studies considered so far a considerable number of different figures have been presented to the subject for simultaneous retention. Bartlett (1932) and Gibson (1929) offer perfectly unambiguous evidence that under such conditions intraserial intrusions account for a large proportion of errors. Ideally, a single subject should be required to retain only a single figure. (4) *Perceptual* vs. *memory trace dynamics.* Very few psychologists would question the fact that dynamic forces operate upon perception. For that very reason it is important to keep this source of changes segregated from possible mnemonic sources. Yet, by the use of the original presented figure as the criterion from which to measure divergence rather than the subject's own first reproduction, the two dynamisms are confused (cf. Hanawalt, 1937; Goldmeier, 1941).

Lastly, we have the most critical issue of all. (5) *Should the same or different subjects be used in successive tests?* The gestalt theorist argues, very reasonably, that both the direction of change and its rate probably vary from person to person, so how can the course of a trace be plotted except within the single individual by successive testings? The critic replies, also very reasonably and patiently, that in that case the proposition isn't being tested at all; both direction and occasional progressiveness may be due to cumulative constant errors that are random in origin, i.e. each successive reproduction 'jiggles' the subject a little farther in one direction or another. Is this paradox insoluble? (a) If an original figure having a *single, dominant stress* were used and sufficiently large subgroups were tested only once but after varying intervals, the gestalt prediction should reveal itself in a progressively shifting average discrepancy. (b) Work on hypnosis presented previously in this chapter suggests that *dissociation* between waking and trance states may be fairly complete under some conditions. Would it be possible to present a figure in the waking state, but to have all successive tests (on the same individual) occur in a trance state, with instructions for posthypnotic amnesia? Would this 'isolate' the original memory trace from interference with the successive tests? These stand at present as moot questions.

Critical studies. Irwin and Seidenfeld (1937), recognizing the difficulties in both reproduction and recognition techniques, used an ingenious method wherein *successive comparison of the same figure* is the measure of the state of the trace. Subjects were shown various unstable figures for 5 seconds and then, after 3 minutes, were shown the same figure again and asked such questions as, 'Is the gap in this circle larger or smaller than in the one previously shown?' In this case approximately two-thirds of the subjects reported gaps in the original as smaller, thus indicating the trace had undergone dynamic changes. These experimenters found that such modifications as they observed were strictly limited to the most immediate (3 minutes) comparison; repeated comparisons at a 10-minute interval and after a week showed no further changes. This suggests that we are dealing with perceptual rather than mnemonic dynamics, for the 'true' limit of the change might be as short as a few seconds.

The most adequately designed investigation in this field is reported by Hebb and Foord (1945). These authors used only two figures, both having clearly predictable dynamic directions. Different groups of subjects were used at 5-minute and 24-hour intervals, and recognition rather than reproduction was employed as the measure of the state of the trace. Objectivity in scoring was obtained by scaling figures on the recognition tests (see Fig. 188), and each subject's deviation could thus be measured in terms of the number-of-units displacement from the original he had been shown. Entirely negative results were found; changes were neither consistent in direction nor progressive in magnitude. Could this be explained by arguing that opposing 'directions' (viz. opening versus closing the gap) were progressive in different individuals and hence canceled each other out? If this were the case, the error curves should display an increasing bimodality, but essentially normal, chance curves of error appeared at both delay intervals. Hebb and Foord interpret these results as conclusive evidence against the occurrence of dynamic autonomous activity within the memory trace.

Verbal mediation. One possibility remains to be explored. Following Bartlett's (1932) notion that memory for forms is essentially *reconstruction* about a core of meaning, we could identify this remembered core as a verbal response. In other words, when a subject is asked after a delay to 'reproduce the figures he was shown earlier,' what he actually recalls are *words* such as 'a circle with a hole in it,' 'a square with a dent,' and so on. And his reproduction is really a reconstruction governed by the precision of his verbal self-stimulation. There is much incidental evidence to favor this interpretation. Granit (1921), for example, reports that young children depended almost exclusively upon labeling the forms; they had to know

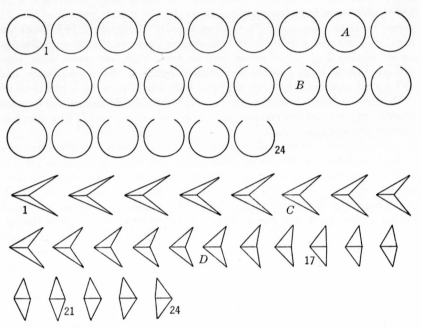

FIGURE 188. Graded stimulus series used to measure mnemonic dynamics. Different groups of subjects were initially shown *A* or *B* and *C* or *D*. In a subsequent test, subjects indicated which form they thought they had seen originally. Hebb and Foord, *Journal of Experimental Psychology*, 1945, 35:344.

'what the diagram was a picture of,' and presumably this influenced their retention. Or in Koffka's (1935) discussion of Wulf's experiment we find this: 'One subject, however, reproduced this figure with a progressive flattening. The reason for this effect is clear from the reports. Whereas the other subjects perceived this pattern as a zigzag or something similar, this one subject saw it as a "broken line," i.e. as a modification of a straight line. Naturally, it is the form as perceived, and not as a mere geometric drawing —which is no gestalt at all—that is under stress and therefore determines the successive changes' (p. 499). Or we might say that what a subject labels a geometric drawing determines how he later reconstructs it.

Fortunately we have a classic investigation of this problem available. Carmichael, Hogan, and Walter (1932) labeled ambiguous figures for their subjects at the time of original presentation and measured immediate reproduction at the conclusion of the series. The neat turn in the experimental procedure was that half of the subjects were given one verbal label (e.g. 'curtains in a window' for the first design in Fig. 189) and the others were given a different meaning for the same design (e.g. 'diamond in a rectangle'). Many of the reproductions displayed obvious influence of the verbal label, as may be seen in Fig. 189. There are, however, two limitations on the interpretation of this experiment. (a) There was no condition of *delayed* reproduction, and it is here actually that one would anticipate maximal effects of verbal mediation. (b) The figures chosen did not generally include *definable perceptual stresses,* and hence the gestalt problem isn't really tested.

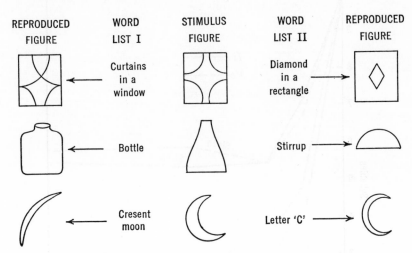

REPRODUCED FIGURE	WORD LIST I	STIMULUS FIGURE	WORD LIST II	REPRODUCED FIGURE
	Curtains in a window		Diamond in a rectangle	
	Bottle		Stirrup	
	Cresent moon		Letter 'C'	

FIGURE 189. Effect of verbal labels upon immediate reproduction of ambiguous visual forms. Carmichael, Hogan, and Walter, *Journal of Experimental Psychology,* 1932, 15:76.

By implication, then, many of the spontaneous modifications observed in all the preceding experiments could have been due to such verbal mediation. Differences between subjects in the *direction* of their errors would depend upon what characteristics their labels had emphasized, for example, 'a squarish figure' yielding pregnänz in Fig. 187, 'a square with a laughing mouth' yielding sharpening. The *progressiveness* of errors would reflect simplification of the verbal label itself. Although a subject may recall 'a square with an even dent' after 10 minutes, it may become 'a square with a dent' after a week, and be reduced to 'a square' after a month. Bartlett (1932) offers a great deal of evidence for this sort of process. This verbal mechanism would not, however, require perfectly progressive changes for all subjects on all figures.

That Autonomous Mnemonic Changes Do Not Occur (Behavioristic)

The essence of the behavioristic interpretation of forgetting is that the originally learned responses to certain cues are interfered with by the same stimuli becoming associated with other interpolated responses. It follows, then, that retention should be perfect in the absence of all interpolated activity. This corollary of the interference position is readily stated in theory but practically impossible to test in practice. How are we going to completely eliminate interpolated activity? No one has yet devised a method for putting the subject into a state of suspended animation immediately after learning. But there have been attempts in this direction and they are worth studying.

Studies with human subjects. Nagge's (1935) use of hypnosis was one approach. Yet even when subjects rested in a trance between original learning and recall, saving was only 68 per cent. Of course all activity is not

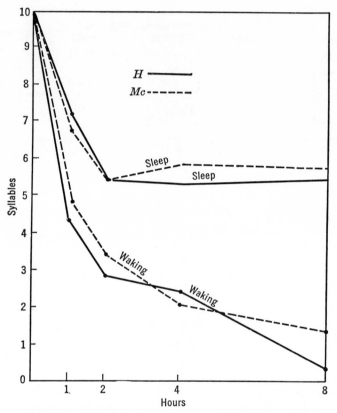

FIGURE 190. Comparison of retention over the same intervals filled with either sleep or waking activities. *H* and *Mc* were the two subjects employed. McGeoch, *Psychology of Human Learning,* Longmans, Green and Co., New York, 1942, p. 475. After data of Jenkins and Dallenbach, *American Journal of Psychology,* 1924, **35:** 609.

lacking in the trance state. Jenkins and Dallenbach (1924) compared retention over intervals occupied with sleep or waking activities. Two well-trained subjects, each serving as his own control, worked and slept in the laboratory. For the 'sleep' tests, the subject was awakened after the various intervals shown in Fig. 190, however, only one interval being tested on a single night. The results fit the general format of the interference theory, but they do not test its corollary. There was about 50 per cent loss even in the sleep condition. As the authors point out, however, sleep could not be achieved immediately after learning; it is not a state of complete inactivity, and subjects dream.

Studies with animal subjects. What is practically impossible with the human subject might be quite feasible with animal subjects, and this line of attack has been vigorously pushed, but without spectacular success. Hunter (1932) used cockroaches for subjects, these animals being rendered inactive by cold, and he found that animals treated in this manner showed *poorer* retention than those that merely rested. But is it possible that the

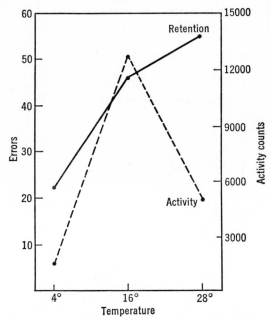

FIGURE 191. Comparison of retention scores for fish subjects with their gross activity during the retention period. J. W. French, *Journal of Experimental Psychology,* 1942, 31:85.

cold temperature had deleterious physiological effects upon the cockroaches quite apart from any effects upon retention? Russell and Hunter (1937) produced interpolated inactivity in rats by injecting sodium amytal and found no significant differences between these and control animals in relearning a maze. Similar studies on various types of organisms with drug and temperature conditions have yielded conflicting results (cf. Minami and Dallenbach, 1946), but retention effects were regularly confounded with possible physiological ones.

A recent investigation by French (1942) on maze-learning by the goldfish casts light upon the methodological difficulties here. After equated original learning of a water maze kept at 22°, one group of fish was kept in cold 4° water for 24 hours, another in cool 16° water, and a third group at 28° Centigrade. Relearning of the water maze was at the original 22° temperature. Saving in relearning, as measured by errors, was greatest for the 4° fish and least for the 28° fish, a result fitting the interference theory. But now for the methodological problems. (a) *Deleterious effects upon learning capacity.* French used a control group in which varying temperature treatments were administered before original learning, and the 4° fish proved to be significantly slower. This will not explain the main result, however, since the 4° fish showed superior retention. (b) *Interpolated activity.* The whole point in varying temperature during the interpolation interval is to control degree of activity, not to freeze the fish. How, then, does temperature relate to activity in this experiment? French ingeniously inserted a series of celluloid fins in the bottles with the fish, movement of these making and breaking electrical contacts and hence providing a continuous record of activity during the retention interval. Figure 191 compares gross activity scores with retention scores for the three temperature

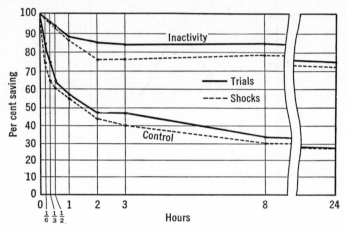

FIGURE 192. Comparative retention over the same intervals of cockroaches kept immobile with those under control 'rest' conditions. Solid lines indicate number of trials required to relearn to a criterion of mastery. Dashed lines indicate number of shocks received for making errors during relearning. Minimi and Dallenbach, *American Journal of Psychology,* 1946, **59**: 52.

groups. The group showing maximum interpolated activity (16°) does *not* show the poorest retention, and this constitutes negative evidence for the interference theory. The corollary of the theory, however, is not really tested in this experiment either—the 4° fish were in no sense inactive.

The most recent investigation on this problem is that by Minami and Dallenbach (1946), some details of which have been given earlier. Essentially, either vigorous, forced activity (running a treadmill) or nearly complete immobilization (obtained by inducing the roaches to crawl into a small, dark resting-box filled with tissue paper) was interpolated between the original learning and the retention of a darkness-avoiding running response. Control animals were merely placed in a circular cage, also in darkness. Retroactive interference was found to increase markedly with increasing amounts of interpolated activity and to decrease significantly with amount of time spent immobilized. Both results clearly fit an interference theory of forgetting, and there is no reason here to suspect any deleterious physiological effects from resting in a tissue-lined box. The curves in Fig. 192 show the magnitude of the difference in retention for control and immobilized animals, expressed in savings scores. The immobilized roaches save nearly 80 per cent over intervals as long as 24 hours. *But why not* 100 *per cent?* This discrepancy between fact and theory may merely reflect excusable inadequacies of the experimental technique—the cockroaches were alive during the interval!—or it may indicate the presence of some autonomous factors. Incidentally, one would like to know what effect a brief 'warm-up' would have had.

Additional Implications of the Interference Theory

We have already seen that retention varies with *the nature of the interpolated activity;* this is essentially a function of similarity relations, and the transfer and retroaction surface provides a concise summary of the empirical evidence. Another implication of a 'pure' interference theory is that amount of forgetting should be *independent of the temporal point of interpolation.* As we have seen, the evidence here is conflicting. It is a difficult proposition to test without running into numerous complicating factors. The theory also implies that retention should vary with *the degree of interpolated activity.* This follows since the interference theory deals with competition among correct (original) and incorrect (interpolated) responses; the stronger the interpolated responses, the better they can compete. Although generally positive evidence has been found, with high degrees of interpolated learning there tends to be a leveling off or even a reduction of interference. The leveling off may be simply a reflection of the fact that habits have asymptotes; Underwood (1945) has interpreted reductions in interference with high degrees of interpolated learning as owing to some discrimination factor.

Another interesting implication of the interference theory has not been considered as yet: interference should vary directly with *the amount of interpolated material.* Oddly enough, most investigations have varied the degree of learning a limited set of materials rather than the number of interpolated events, yet the latter is clearly more relevant to theories of forgetting. The reason is that the interference theory postulates a multitude of independent events occurring in the interval after original learning, which interfere to the extent that corresponds to the similarities involved but summates to yield the traditional curve of forgetting. Twining (1940), using human subjects and varying numbers of interpolated lists of nonsense syllables, and Marx (1944), using rat subjects and varying numbers of interpolated mazes, both obtained evidence generally in favor of this prediction. Underwood (1945) has directly compared the retroactive effects produced by varying the *degree* of interpolation with those produced by varying the *amount* of interpolation. With degree of original learning constant, one group of subjects had 0, 8, 16, or 24 trials on a single interpolated list, whereas the other group had four trials each on 0, 2, 4, or 6 different interpolated lists, the total number of interpolated trials thus being equated. Figure 193 gives the results for the first (recall) trial on the relearning of the original materials. Whereas the interference produced by varying the degree of interpolation is sharp, negatively accelerated (24 trials on one list interfering little more than 8 trials), that produced by varying the amount of interpolation increases almost linearly (cf. also McGeoch, 1936 *b*). Any particular, restricted set of interpolated materials represents only a portion of the potential sources of interference, and it therefore can have only limited interfering effect.

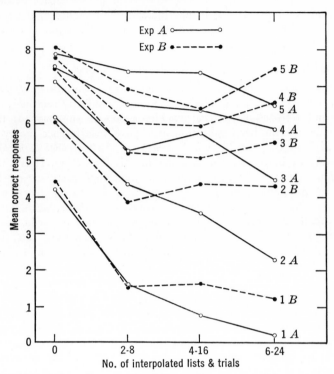

FIGURE 193. Retroactive effects produced by varying *amount* of interpolated learning (Experiment *A*) compared with varying *degree* (Experiment B) of interpolated learning, when total number of repetitions is held constant. Numbers 1-5 refer to results for successive relearning trials on original list. Underwood, *Psychological Monographs*, 1945, #273:19.

SUMMARY ON THEORIES OF FORGETTING

Why do we forget? According to the gestalt theory experiences leave traces that are under stress to the extent that the perceptions producing them contained unresolved tensions. The unique corollary of this theory—that autonomous changes in memory do occur—has not been adequately tested, although the best designed experiments to date yield negative results. According to the behavioristic theory, forgetting is entirely attributable to the interference of interpolated events during the retention interval (decrements due to changes in the eliciting stimulus situation, or 'set,' are not really forgetting but inadequate estimates). The unique corollary here—that autonomous changes in memory do *not* occur—is probably untestable, but the closer the ideal conditions for making this test are approached, the nearer retention approaches perfection.

What about the generality of these two theories? (1) *Details of transfer and retroaction.* There is little to choose between gestalt and behavioristic interpretations of these phenomena. The reason is that the gestalt conceptions of isolation and assimilation yield about the same predictions as the behavioristic conceptions of generalization and discrimination. Perhaps the behavioristic view does better in predicting details of these phenomena, the direction and degree of facilitation and interference and the occurrence of specific types of intrusive and omissive errors. (2) *Effects of motivation upon retention.* Although experiments to date have failed to satisfactorily demonstrate enhancement of *memory* (as apart from learning) under conditions of positive ego-involvement, would positive evidence be necessarily incompatible with an interference theory? Each occurrence of a potentially interfering event during the retention interval is a competition situation. If the subject is highly motivated with respect to the originally learned materials (e.g. sets of numbers supposed to be a measure of his intelligence), these original responses are more likely to occur in such competition situations and constitute further practice. In other words, the same motivational conditions that lead to better original learning are likely to turn many potential interference situations into opportunities for further practice (rehearsal). (3) *The Freudian type of negative ego-involvement.* Is this a case in which tension is created in specific sub-systems of the Ego, yet memory traces are disrupted rather than being stabilized? This writer is not sufficiently agile in gestalt theory to attempt an analysis of this phenomenon along its lines. Behaviorists have tackled this problem (cf. Sears, 1943; Mowrer, 1950; Dollard and Miller, 1950). The essence of the analysis is that 'repression into the unconscious' can be translated into 'substitution of an interfering response.' If the original association $(S_1:R_1)$ produces an anxiety state, any subsequent response made to the same situation $(S_1:R_2)$ that *reduces* this anxiety will be directly reinforced. In other words, anxiety sets up conditions that increase the probability of learning substitute responses to the same stimulus. There is no space here to elaborate this behavioral conception of repression.

In summary, then, neither the gestalt trace theory nor the behavioristic interference theory has been satisfactorily tested as yet. While the gestalt workers have shown brilliance and breadth in theorizing, there has been decided weakness in the design of experiments supposedly substantiating their position. The interference theory still stands as an elaborate analogy from retroaction experiments, and there is need for further clarification of the underlying causes of retroactive interference itself. The interference theory seems, however, to have the advantage of greater precision in its experimental evidence.

Part IV

SYMBOLIC PROCESSES

A hungry young chimpanzee is in a large outdoor enclosure and a bunch of bananas is placed just beyond its reach. This animal has already mastered the use of sticks as tools, but no sticks are available at the moment. There is, however, a dead bush in the enclosure. Were a human placed in this same situation, he would probably look at the dead bush, think or verbalize 'dead bush . . . branch . . . stick!' and be on his way to a prompt solution of the problem. But language symbols are beyond the ken of the chimpanzee, and its solution is long in appearing. What are the conditions under which it finally does solve the problem? In the course of much random activity, the animal happens to *grasp* one of the branches of the dead bush, perhaps in momentary rage; instantly, all randomness disappears from its behavior. Glancing swiftly at the bananas and then back at the branch, it tears the branch off with one wrench and is already off toward the fruit.

The human animal stimulated himself with spoken or implicit words. The chimpanzee had to stimulate itself in some overt manner, here by the same grasping reaction that had been used in previous 'stick' situations. But isn't there a common element in the behavior of both subjects? The overt, problem-solving responses are initiated and directed by some form of mediating self-stimulation. By placing its hand about the branch, the chimpanzee is providing itself with a distinctive pattern of stimulation which is quite analogous to saying 'stick.' In general terms, *the association between the observable situation and the observable response is mediated by a symbolic process.* The mediating response of the chimpanzee happens to be overt and easily observable itself, helping us to trace the sequence, but most symbolic processes in humans are implicit and hence difficult to index.

Symbolic processes go under a variety of labels in psychology—thoughts, ideas, images, perceptions, meanings, representative factors, and many others. The essential equivalence of these concepts can be seen when they are successively substituted in the same explanatory role. The chimpanzee has a sudden flash of insight into the problem because grasping the stick gives rise to the *thought* or the *idea* of 'stick-tool'; the position of the hand creates the *image* of a stick being held; it suddenly *perceives* the bush-part as a stick; this hand position produces the *meaning* of stick or *represents* stick. These statements can be used quite interchangeably, although theorists of certain schools tend to favor certain modes of expression over others. All of these concepts refer to processes having a mediating role, processes usually classed as 'mental' events.

The notion of mediation is not a new one to the reader. It has been referred to repeatedly in previous sections of this book. In Chapter 9 a theory of learning was described which had the mediation process as its core construct. No attempt was made at that time, however, to inquire into the nature of such processes. In the present section of this book we shall both survey many classes of phenomena which require some such notion for their interpretation and carefully scrutinize experimental attempts that have been made to reveal their underlying nature. This survey will include investigations of problem-solving and insight (Chap. 14), of thinking in humans and animals (Chap. 15), and of language behavior (Chap. 16). These topics have often been omitted from textbooks in the past—perhaps because of some subtle aura of 'mentalism.' Historically, of course, thought and meaning were the central problems for psychology. The wide circle that American psychologists have been making through behaviorism seems to be bringing them back again to the same core of the science, but perhaps they are returning with more precise techniques and a more objective point of view than would otherwise have been attained.

Chapter 14

PROBLEM-SOLVING AND INSIGHT

A pebble dropped in a quiet pool gives rise to an intricate pattern of ripples; a quirk of fate in human affairs may have analogous consequences. It is doubtful whether, in the ordinary course of events, Wolfgang Köhler would have interested himself with the problem of animal-learning. He had done his early work in the field of perception in Germany. But it just so happened that Köhler was visiting the anthropoid station established by the Prussian Academy of Sciences on the island of Tenerife at precisely the time when the First World War began. Since he was a German citizen and this island was under British control, Köhler was marooned for several years on this spot in the middle of nowhere. Here there was no laboratory for studying the phi phenomenon or color contrast. There was, however, a colony of chimpanzees, and Köhler applied himself to the material at hand. The book that resulted from these labors, *The Mentality of Apes* (1925), has been one of the most important pieces of psychological writing in this century, comprising not only a mine of vividly detailed observations on problem-solving behavior but also a creative application of gestalt theory to the field of learning.

Although there had been interest in animal learning prior to the turn of the present century, most available evidence was anecdotal in form and it generally credited animals with reasoning powers. Lloyd Morgan (1894), in phrasing his famous canon and marshaling evidence to support it, was among the first to decry this prevalent notion. His credo was that animal behavior should be explained on the simplest possible level, and he believed his own observations warranted the limitation of animal-learning to the trial-and-error mode. The behavior of his own fox terrier as well as that of baby chicks and other animals he observed could be explained on the basis of a gradual elimination of errors and a gradual strengthening of the correct response through repetition, or so he believed. Another early British investigator came to somewhat more liberal conclusions. In 1901 Hobhouse reported some informal but brilliantly conceived experiments on his own dogs and some zoo animals. One of the simplest situations required the dog to pull a piece of meat down from a shelf by means of an attached string; in other cases a dummy string (unattached) was added; in a more complex setup, the dog observed Hobhouse attach meat to one of three strings, was then held for a period without seeing the strings, and finally released. Hobhouse was here anticipating the delayed reaction technique which was to be extensively explored by later students. He concluded that animals were capable of learning from simple attention to a sequence of events, that they were capable of what he termed 'practical ideas,' defined as 'a combination of efforts to effect a definite change in the perceived object.'

Whereas Hobhouse's work had considerable effect upon technique, the studies on problem-solving by Thorndike, summarized in his book, *Animal Intelligence* (1911), established the theoretical position originally taken by Lloyd Morgan. Thorndike felt himself forced to conclude from his experimental results that animals are incapable of higher mental processes such as reasoning and insight—that they are limited to the 'stamping in' and 'stamping out' mode of trial and error. With rare exceptions his animal subjects showed only a gradual and irregular elimination of errors. But what were the problem situations he posed? The puzzle-box was typical. A hungry cat was put in a barred box; the correct response was to press upon a certain button which, through mechanical contrivance, automatically opened the door to a food reward outside. Or the correct response in another experiment was to have the cat lick itself, and even here the animals gradually reduced the time required to get out of the box—the licking response becoming reduced, however, to a mere symbolic vestige in the final trials.

But are such situations as these adequate tests of animal problem-solving ability? Köhler and other gestalt psychologists definitely thought not. Köhler (1925) criticized Thorndike's approach on several grounds that seem quite valid today. (1) *Unnaturalness of the correct response.* The solution of Thorndike's problems demanded behaviors that were quite beyond the animal's normal repertoire. Cats do not get out of boxes by pressing buttons or by washing themselves; rather, they try to squeeze through narrow openings or scratch at the barriers, and Thorndike's animals were observed attempting just such solutions as part of their early trial and error. In other words, the correct response in a situation like Thorndike's could *only* be hit upon by sheer, blind chance. (2) *Necessary components for solution hidden.* The cat cannot see the mechanical contrivance that connects the button and the door and, in any case, would be unable to understand it. Köhler decided to set problems for his animal subjects wherein all of the elements necessary for solution would be available and where the required acts would be within the normal repertoire of the animal. Yet the situations had to pose real problems for the subject. As Köhler puts it (p. 4), '. . . we do not speak of behavior as being intelligent when human beings or animals attain their objective by a direct unquestionable route which clearly arises naturally out of their organization. But we tend to speak of "intelligence" when, circumstances having blocked the obvious course, the human being or animal takes a roundabout path, so meeting the situation.' All of Köhler's problem situations were designed to meet these criteria, many of them being borrowed from Hobhouse's earlier work.

Köhler found his chimpanzee subjects capable of intelligent solutions. Drawing upon concepts originating in the field of perception, gestalt psychologists have explained such intelligent problem-solving in terms of the emergent principle of insight. In contrast, early behaviorists (like Thorndike) have utilized the analytic principle of trial and error, whereas modern behaviorists (like Hull) make use of analytic principles drawn from the phenomena of conditioning. We shall have opportunity to compare these theoretical positions later in this chapter. Köhler's original portrayal of his chimpanzee subjects stands as a classic of descriptive psychology as well as a detailed application of gestalt thinking to problems of behavior.

A GESTALT INTERPRETATION OF PROBLEM-SOLVING

Gestalt writings are typically phenomenological in character. This does not mean that gestalt psychologists have no theory. On the contrary, the works of Koffka, Köhler, and Lewin are pregnant with general principles. These are not presented with attendant definitions and indexing correlations, to be sure, but rather are implicit in the consistent interpretations made. Köhler's work on the chimpanzee serves as more than a mere temporal bridge between the earlier work on perception and the more recent studies on personality by Lewin and others. We find Köhler using many ideas that are common to both areas of investigation. For example, where investigators of perceptual processes had utilized the notion of 'cohesive forces in the visual field,' Köhler's apes show evidence of 'tensions being set up by the objective.' By carefully reading between the lines of Köhler's *Mentality of Apes* it has seemed possible to tease out at least the essence of his theory of problem-solving. The results of this search will follow (after one informative illustration of problem-solving), in the form of five principles and the major variables that limit their action. Of course, it is dangerous to attempt a formulation of someone else's theory, but the effort is made here so that gestalt and behavioristic positions may be contrasted.

An example of insightful solution: the double-stick problem. This situation was one of the most difficult Köhler used, and as such it illustrates many of the mechanisms in which we shall be interested. The 'path' to a desired goal in this case can only be covered by an implement, but the implement itself must first be constructed. 'This time Sultan is the subject of the experiment. His sticks are two hollow, but firm, bamboo rods. . . One is so much smaller than the other, that it can be pushed in at either end of the other quite easily. Beyond the bars lies the objective, just so far away that the animal cannot reach it with either rod. . . Nevertheless, he takes great pains to try to reach it with one stick or the other, even pushing his right shoulder through the bars. When everything proves futile, Sultan commits a "bad error," or, more clearly, a great stupidity. . . He pulls a box from the back of the room towards the bars; true, he pushes it away again at once as it is useless, or rather, actually in the way. Immediately afterwards, he does something which, although practically useless, must be counted among the "good errors": he pushes one of the sticks out as far as it will go, then takes the second, and with it pokes the first one cautiously towards the objective . . . he pushes very gently, watches the movements of the stick that is lying on the ground, and actually touches the objective with its tip. Thus, all of a sudden, for the first time, the contact "animal-objective" has been established, and Sultan visibly feels (we humans can sympathize) a certain satisfaction in having even so much power over the fruit that he can touch it and slightly move it by pushing the stick' (p. 125).

This experiment has lasted about an hour, and Köhler leaves the scene to Sultan and a keeper, whose report runs as follows: 'Sultan first of all squats indifferently on the box, which has been left standing a little back from the railings; then he gets up, picks up the two sticks, sits down again on the box and plays carelessly with them. While doing this, it happens that he finds himself holding one rod in either hand in such a way that they lie in a straight line; he pushes the thinner one a little way into the opening of the thicker, jumps up and is already on the run towards the railings, to which he has up to now half turned his back, and begins to draw a banana towards him with the double stick. I call the master: meanwhile, one of the animal's rods has fallen out of the other, as he pushed one of them only a little way in the other; whereupon he connects them again' (p. 127). With this example in mind, we may now present what seem to be the underlying notions Köhler is employing in his interpretations.

I. *Organisms tend to approach a goal by the most direct path.*

In all the demonstrations with chimpanzee subjects it was observed that the animals first attempted to obtain the goal by a direct locomotor or reaching movement. 'When any of those higher animals, which make use of vision, notice food (or any other objective) somewhere in their field of vision, they tend—so long as no complications arise—to go after it in a straight line. We may assume that this conduct is determined without any previous experience, provided only that their nerves and muscles are mature enough to carry it out' (p. 11). This most direct path, of course, need not be conceived only in terms of spatial, locomotor movement; the direct path to an annoying flea in Sultan's hide may be to scratch with the right hand, but if the hands are otherwise occupied he may take the roundabout 'path' via rubbing his back against the bars of his cage. Notice that Köhler does not consider the direct paths to have been formed by learning but rather to have been 'determined without any previous experience.'

II. *Tension is generated in the psychological field whenever an obstruction intervenes between an organism and a goal in the geographical field.*

The geographical field refers to the real world of physical objects and events, whereas the psychological field refers to the fluid patterns of perceptual processes wherein psychological dynamics transpire. This distinction is clarified and extended in later works by Köhler (1929) and by Koffka (1935). The geographical field helps determine the momentary state of the psychological field (cf. notion of 'restraining forces,' in perception theory). Tension, of course, is the direct paralog of drive, and this principle states that tension is increased by blocking the direct path to a goal. Köhler's chimpanzees typically showed increased agitation when the usual approaches to a goal failed.

The amount of tension generated in any situation seems to vary with two major factors, desire for an objective and the amount of attention paid to it. Köhler often reports that the subject seems disinterested in the bananas or, conversely, that the subject has been for a long period without fruit and is therefore more actively interested in it. He also refers frequently to the fact that the experimenter brought the animal's attention to the objective by touching it, moving it slightly nearer, or by adding another banana. *Tension in the psychological field varies* (a) *with the need for the goal and* (b) *with the figure quality of the goal-object.* By figure quality of the goal-object is meant the degree to which it stands out from the background, its distinctiveness and contrast with the rest of the environment. Making a hanging banana swing enhances its figure quality, as does pointing to it or touching it.

III. *Unresolved tension in the psychological field distributes itself in a pattern, the form of which is determined simultaneously by the conductive force of the goal and the restraining characteristics of the geographical field.*

The conductive force of the goal is equivalent to cohesive forces in visual perception and to Lewin's conception of goal valence; the geographical field exerts stable 'restraining forces,' i.e. Lewin's 'barriers.' Picturing the subject as an iron filing in a system of magnets, we can see how behavior is shaped by the momentary forces being exerted. Thus the animal tends to gravitate about a point by the bars of the cage directly opposite the objective, and will repeatedly look and reach along the path (conductive forces) toward the objective. 'It follows that, under the influence of strong, unsatisfied emotion, the animal must do something in the spatial direction in which the object of his emotion is situated. He must somehow get into touch with this objective, even if not practically, must *do* something, even if it is only to hurl the movables in his cage towards it' (p. 89). We recall Sultan pushing his hopeless half-stick along the path to the unobtainable goal.

There are two variables, at least, which Köhler associates with the functioning of this principle. (1) *The conductive force of the goal-object increases with psychological nearness of the organism to the goal.* That it is nearness in the psychological field and not the geographical field is shown by numerous illustrations. The animals were observed to cease incidental activities suddenly when they happened to glance at the goal-object; conversely, their general tension decreased if they turned their eyes away or, better, turned their backs on it. Köhler gives the example of the dog that had easily shown insight into running around a fence to get food. 'It is worth noting that when, on repeating this experiment, the food was not thrown far out, but was dropped just outside the fence, so that it lay directly in front of her, separated only by the wire, she stood seemingly helpless, as if the very nearness of the object and her concentration upon it (brought about by her sense of smell) blocked the "idea" of the wide circle round the fence; she pushed again and again with her nose at the wire fence, and did not budge from the spot' (p. 14). (2) *The entire pattern of conductive and restraining forces varies with the position of the organism in the geographical field.* The perceived barrier quality of a fence varies with the point from which it is observed, and if a subject, in changing his position in the field, comes close enough to the corner of the fence, the pattern of forces changes. Similarly, moving into such a position that a stick is seen simultaneously with viewing the goal changes the pattern, or, as happened with Sultan and double-stick problem, holding by chance two sticks so that they make a continuous straight line increases the likelihood of solving the problem.

IV. *The unstable, fluctuating pattern of tensions in the psychological field tends to be minimized through sudden reorganizations, involving the perception of new paths to the goal.*

This sudden reorganization of forces in the psychological field is the occurrence of *insight*. It appears in gestalt theory as an irreducible postulate, at once the theory's major tenet and its major weakness. Nowhere is the nature of this process, or how it occurs, explained—it just happens. Köhler clearly delineates this core of intelligent solutions: 'Suddenly Tschego leaps to her feet, seizes a stick, and quite adroitly, pulls the bananas . . . , but all of a sudden [Sultan's] behavior changes completely . . . , [Sultan] pushes the thinner one a little way into the opening of the thicker, jumps up and is already on the run towards the railings. . .' There is, of course, nothing in this principle requiring that all reorganizations lead to success; in fact, the behavior of the animals presents the picture of a series of reorganizations preceding the correct one—Köhler calls these 'good errors.' Witness Sultan pushing the half-stick into contact with the objective. Köhler's 'bad errors' are also reorganizations of the psychological field, as when Sultan brings over a useless box in the double-stick problem.

If the gestalt theory leaves one in the dark as far as the nature of insight is concerned (and indeed, it can be utilized as a postulate without being explained), it does offer several variables that govern the probability of such reorganization occurring. Two factors were suggested under the preceding principle. (1) *Insight is more likely to occur if the goal tension is moderate than when it is excessive.* (2) *To the extent that the animal varies its position in the geographical field, the process of reorganization is facilitated.*

To these we may add several more. (3) *The likelihood of new paths or new tools being utilized in insightful reorganization varies with the degree to which they fit into the momentary existing pattern of forces in the field.* The combination of conductive (goal) tensions and those generated by the geographical field sets up a certain pattern of forces—in a sense, a vacuum which strongly needs filling. Now if one tool (long stick) near the chimpanzee corresponds in shape to this 'need-space,' it is likely to be utilized. On the other hand, a square box or a round pillow, fitting this need-space less well, is less likely to be seized upon as a tool. Witness the 'good errors' of a sickly little ape by the name of Koko, in a situation where no stick was available. 'Some days after he employed a large piece of stiff cardboard, a rose-branch, the brim of an old straw hat, and a piece of wire. All objects, especially of a long or oval shape, such as appear to be movable, become "sticks" in the purely functional sense of "grasping-tool" in these circumstances and tend in Koko's hands to wander to the critical spot. . . Long-shaped and movable objects are no longer beheld with strict and static impartiality, but always with a "vector" or a "drive" towards the critical point' (p. 35). Köhler employs the concepts 'path' and 'tool' as equivalents. In just the sense that a path is a locomotory extension of the organism in the direction of goal, so a tool is another method of extending the organism along the path to the goal. 'The objective was at a distance of over one meter from the bars of the cage, and a soft straw was tied to it, lying across the intervening space, which was otherwise empty, right up to the bars. Nueva had hardly seen the objective before she seized the straw and carefully pulled the prize toward her' (p. 26). Thus the animal makes an immediate transfer from actual bodily extension toward the goal to a substitute extension through the medium of a clearly delineated tool.

(4) *The less distance between the goal and a tool, or the more direct a path toward a goal, in the psychological field, the more likely is insightful reorganization.* '. . . sticks . . . seem to lose all their functional or in-

strumental value, if they are at some distance from the critical point. More precisely: if the experimenter takes care that the stick is not visible to the animal when gazing directly at the objective—and that, vice versa, a direct look at the stick excludes the whole region of the objective from the field of vision—then, generally speaking, recourse to this instrument is either prevented or, at least, greatly retarded, even when it has already been frequently used' (p. 37). Similarly, if the initial locomotions required for a new path take the animal temporarily away from the goal, the problem will be more difficult than if the initial locomotions lead toward the general

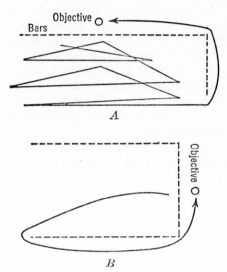

FIGURE 194. Typical detour pathways followed by (*A*) a hen, and (*B*) a dog, in reaching a lure behind a barrier. Köhler, *The Mentality of Apes,* Harcourt, Brace and Company, Inc., New York, 1925, p. 15.

vicinity of the goal. Given the perceptual orientation of gestalt psychologists, it would be expected that the figure-quality of tools and paths would affect their utilization. (5) *The greater the figure quality of a tool or a path, the more likely it is to be utilized in insightful reorganizations.* In earlier examples Köhler pointed out how the straw connecting the objective lay in *an otherwise empty ground,* or how a stick that is touched or moved by the experimenter is more likely to be seized and used.

Finally, (6) *the likelihood of insightful reorganization occurring in a given problem situation varies with the phylogenetic level of the organism.* The figure above contrasts the chance solution of a chicken with the insightful one of a dog, for a similar spatial problem. Notice the random path of the chicken as compared with the smooth, continuous path of the dog in circuiting the fence. Köhler attributes the differences between species to at least two factors: (a) the degree of cortical development—presumably capacity for reorganization of the psychological field depends upon the amount and complexity of the cortex; and (b) the structure of the organism's effectors—the flexible hand of the chimp facilitates solving certain problems that are insurmountable for the dog.

610 EXPERIMENTAL PSYCHOLOGY

V. *Whenever a given reorganization of the psychological field occurs, it exerts cohesive force over its parts and resists modification.*

This integration of 'part-processes' into a new whole and the consequent persistence of this structure has previously been encountered under perception as *closure*. 'Sultan grabs at objects behind the bars and cannot reach them with his arm; he thereupon walks about searchingly, finally turns to a shoe-scraper, made of iron bars in a wooden frame, and manipulates it until he has pulled out one of the iron bars; with this he runs immediately to his real objective, at a distance of about ten metres, and draws it toward him' (p. 101). Sultan's tearing away at the iron bar seems foolish by itself. This part-process achieves meaning only when considered in relation to the whole solution pattern. The whole exerts organization over its parts. On the other hand, the same directive force of a given organization of the field may, if unworkable, tend to persist and block any further reorganization. When box-piling problems were first presented, for example, the chimpanzees who had previously used sticks would often seize one and futilely try to knock down the hanging fruit. The same organization appeared to direct the animals in a fruitless search for longer sticks, this behavior blocking occurrence of the correct insight.

THE CHARACTERISTICS OF INSIGHT AS A MODE OF PROBLEM-SOLVING

The gestalt psychologist utilizes insight as an emergent principle of behavior. The behaviorist, as we shall see, attempts to deduce the phenomena that characterize insightful problem-solving from his own lower level postulates. What are the phenomena that distinctively characterize insight as a mode of problem-solving? What observations lead the experimenter to call a given bit of activity insightful? Many criteria have been suggested (cf. Pechstein and Brown, 1939); some of these, such as 'response to the situation as a whole,' or 'response to the meaningful relationships in a situation,' really refer to the presumed nature of the process and are of no use whatever in objectively specifying when it (insight) does or does not occur.

(1) *Suddenness.* Perhaps the most obvious criterion of an insightful solution is the suddenness with which it occurs. Ordinary learning, in either the trial-and-error or conditioning mode, typically displays a gradual and irregular accretion. Insightful solutions, on the other hand, occur with dramatic suddenness and, once the insight has occurred, usually persist as permanent acquisitions. Both the chimpanzee and the human may fumble about and scratch their heads for a long period, but then, suddenly, the solution appears—the box is brought up underneath the objective or the two sticks are assembled—and from this point on repetitions of the problem are solved immediately. This, it must be emphasized, represents only the typical case; insightful solutions may occur through a process of gradual partial insights, and trial-and-error solutions may show a sudden shift to the correct response under certain conditions. Even some of Thorndike's cats (1898) produced learning curves with sudden drops in time required for solution, and, conversely, many experiments on insightful behavior in animals and humans (cf. Ruger, 1910; Durkin, 1937; Pechstein and Brown, 1939) reveal the role of chance discoveries.

(2) *Smoothness.* Another characteristic of insightful solutions is the smoothness with which the solution sequence is executed. Köhler repeatedly points this out—the animal races over to the wall, grabs the tool, and is already smoothly curving back toward the objective; again, the dog traces a continuous, smooth course around the fence, as contrasted with the irregular, jerky course followed by the chicken. The gestalt explanation of smoothness is that since the organism is in a field of continuously varying forces, any change of position in the field results in a concomitant change in the direction of the forces, yielding a smooth and continuous course of movement (cf. Lewin, 1936). Here again this characteristic by itself does not serve to index the occurrence of an insight. A given sequence of activity in trial and error may also be executed smoothly, as a well-learned skill. Similarly, a succession of partial insights may display the jerky character more typical of ordinary trial and error.

(3) *Point in behavior sequence where solution occurs.* In the typical trial-and-error situation, as exemplified by Thorndike's puzzle-box, the solution of the problem *follows* the occurrence of the correct response. To anthropomorphize for a moment, we might say that the cat happens to strike the button (correct response) and then, lo! and behold, the door is open. In typical insightful situations, on the other hand, the solution of the problem *precedes* the behaviors that execute it. The chimpanzee happens to look at the stick, looks back at the banana, and 'is already' on his way through the solution. It is apparent, according to Köhler, that the animal has mentally solved the problem before it initiates the actual behavior. This is perhaps the essential characteristic of insight; implicit recognition and understanding of the solution precedes its execution. Of course, we can only infer the previous occurrence of the solution from overt behavior of the animal (pauses, visual survey of the field, and so forth) or from introspective reports of human subjects.

(4) *Novelty of the solution.* If the situation in which a sudden, smooth solution occurs is one in which the animal has had considerable previous experience, we attribute it to mere habit, the effects of previous learning. If, on the other hand, the situation is a novel one, we are likely to attribute a sudden, smooth solution to insight. Novelty is however a matter of degree. In none of the illustrations of insight given above has the solution involved completely novel situations or responses. The chimpanzees were familiar with handling sticklike objects, strings, and the like; the novelty lay in the selection necessary for the particular situation. Indeed, one of Köhler's main criticisms of Thorndike's work was that the situations set for the subjects were completely beyond their normal repertoire.

BEHAVIORISTIC INTERPRETATION OF PROBLEM-SOLVING

Having Thorndike's early and crude conception of 'stamping in' and 'stamping out' in mind, no doubt, many people have thought of trial and error as a blind and senseless process. The animal or person is supposed to merely 'do things' with his body until, by pure chance, a movement is followed by success. Under rare conditions this may be the case: the first time a primitive encountered the phenomenon of a photoelectric cell opening a door, he would not understand it and would be limited to merely narrowing

down the locus of movements which happened to open the door; Thorndike's puzzle-boxes limited his subjects to this level of adjustment. But this
is a naïve conception of the trial-and-error process as it generally occurs, and
no present-day behaviorist would subscribe to it. Trial-and-error learning is
a far more subtle process of selection, with many mechanisms contributing
to the overt product.

The Goal Gradient

Both in connection with maze-learning (1932) and, more relevantly, in
connection with certain of Lewin's 'field-force' problems in young children
(1938), Hull has developed the notion of a goal gradient and the role it
may play in complex behaviors (cf. pp. 497-9). One of the direct deductions from this hypothesis was that *animals will tend to choose the shorter
of two paths to the same goal.* Coupled with the habit-family hierarchy
mechanism (cf. below), which indicates how such preferences will become
part of the permanent equipment of the animal, this appears strictly equivalent to Köhler's notion that organisms tend to approach a goal by the most
direct path. And for both theorists, problem situations arise when such
direct paths are blocked.

When locomotor behavior is taking place under conditions in which the
field of vision is unobstructed (as was typical of Köhler's problems for
chimpanzees and Lewin's problems for young children), visual characteristics of the goal-object, such as its texture and the angle subtended on the
retina, will vary with distance of the organism from the goal. *These* stimulus patterns (rather than those arising from the walls of a maze) will
become associated with approach movements according to a goal gradient
principle. If long and short paths to the goal are available, there will be a
differential favoring the shorter, as we have already seen. But now suppose
the shorter, direct path is blocked? Whereas a sophisticated organism will
have available in its pre-established habit-family hierarchy alternate sequences via roundabout paths, a naïve organism will first expend energy
striving to follow the direct path—this nonadjustive behavior serving to
inhibit the direct tendency and thus make possible alternative sequences
which can then be included in the hierarchy. Since the ratio favoring the
short over the long path increases with nearness to the goal, *the nearer the
goal-object to the organism and the stronger its motivation, the more difficult will be selection of the longer path* (i.e. solution). Motivation has its
effect here through elevating the entire goal gradient. This analysis applies
to situations like that in which a piece of meat is thrown directly under a
dog's nose—but on the other side of a fence. Again coupling the goal gradient
hypothesis with the habit-family hierarchy conception, it can be deduced
that *the probability of a circuitous route being taken* (and solution achieved
thereby) *will vary inversely with the angle between the direct and roundabout paths.*

The Habit-family Hierarchy

Apart from its combination with the goal gradient, this mechanism has
its own contributions to an understanding of problem-solving behavior. As
indicated diagrammatically in Fig. 195, any instigatory situation is variably
associated with a number of behavior sequences eventuating in the same

goal. Thorndike's cats first tried to squeeze through the bars; Köhler's chimpanzees first tried to reach the objective with their hands. Because of the regularity with which such direct paths have been reinforced in the past history of the organism, they are most likely to occur in the present. Hull's development of this conception has already been described. The basic notion is that the instigatory situation (including both environmental and motivational cues) is differentially associated with a hierarchy of instrumental behaviors, all designed to achieve the same goal but all varying in their probability of occurrence.

Several deductions concerning problem-solving arise from this conception. (1) *The position in the hierarchy, and hence the probability of occurrence, of a given response will vary with the degree to which it has previously been reinforced in similar situations.* What Köhler terms 'direct

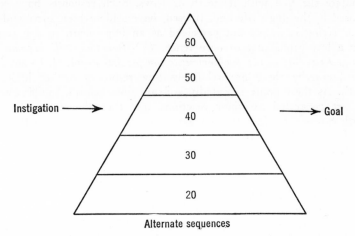

Alternate sequences

FIGURE 195. Diagrammatic representation of a habit-family hierarchy.

routes' are high probability reactions in this sense. Although the use of sticks as implements was initially low in the response hierarchy, as evidenced by the delays in achieving insightful solutions, this behavior rapidly became strengthened as rewards were secured in this manner. In fact, the chimpanzee subjects frequently showed *fixation* of the stick-using response, i.e. this behavior became sufficiently strong to block other responses which were 'correct' in later problems.

Köhler assumed that insightful use of a stick as an implement arose directly from the momentary organization of the field, quite independent of the previous experience of the animal, but he actually did not know the life history of his subjects. Birch (1945) has recently made a direct test of this assumption, using as subjects six young chimpanzees brought up under nearly continuous observation in the Yerkes Laboratories of Primate Biology at Orange Park, Florida. Previous to the experiment proper, only one of these naïve animals, Jojo by name, had been observed using a stick regularly as a tool. On a preliminary test with a simple stick problem, Jojo was the only subject to solve it directly and smoothly within a 30-minute work period. After this preliminary test, all of the animals were allowed 3 days of spontaneous play with short, straight sticks, which were placed in their enclosure. The use of sticks as poking, shoveling, and prying instruments was seen to develop gradually during this period, appearing first as accidental accompaniments of various arm movements made when a stick happened to be held in the hand. On the second test, all subjects solved stick problems smoothly and quickly, the slowest animal taking only 20 seconds for the original problem. The conclusion seems inescapable that past experience played a role in the insightful solution of problems, both in preparing the animals to perceive sticks as tools and in refining the skill with which they used them.

(2) *An organism's structure will determine in part the locus of specific responses in the hierarchy and hence its normal modes of problem-solving.* Whereas a primate can readily seize a string or stick, a dog might well starve in a situation demanding the use of such a tool, even though it *could* manipulate the tool with its teeth or paws. Such responses have seldom been used in the dog's life and, if used, have seldom been successful—the stick or string is simply not perceived as an implement, such a response having a low probability of occurrence. (3) *Behavior will become more varied and random as the problem situation persists unsolved.* In any habit-family hierarchy there are relatively few responses having high habit strength. As these occur repeatedly and are unsuccessful, inhibitory tendencies are generated for these reactions, and those having weaker habit strength can occur. Since the number of responses associated with the situation is assumed to increase as habit-strength level decreases, the behavior observed becomes more varied. If the correct response is buried somewhere in the hierarchy (as is necessarily the case in a problem situation), it can only occur after the prepotent reactions have been weakened.

(4) *The relative strengths of responses within any hierarchy vary with successive presentations of the situation.* The fact that a response of relatively low probability does ultimately occur and is reinforced makes it more likely that this response will occur next time. But there is no guarantee in the behaviorist's system that a single success will produce complete learning. When a chimpanzee has obtained the objective by means of a stick, this mode of solution gains in probability of occurrence, but on the next presentation of a similar situation the animal may again first try reaching for the banana directly, though more quickly shifting to the new approach. The phenomenon of spontaneous recovery would also lead one to predict reinsertion of initially prepotent responses. Thus the behaviorist must predict a somewhat gradual selection, whereas the gestalt theorist predicts an abrupt and complete appearance of the correct reaction. Although this would seem to be a clear-cut and empirically testable distinction, actually most insightful solutions in animals are either not described in terms of successive trials or ambiguous on this point.

Implicit Trial and Error

Judging from the introspections of human subjects, much trial-and-error exploration within the habit-family hierarchy is implicit in nature. The act of reaching for a distant goal is represented symbolically and eliminated symbolically, no overt 'trial' being made. When the human individual has a problem—as the financially vacuous student who has a date with a girl who likes nothing but the best—he doesn't break into a rash of random behaving. He doesn't suddenly twist a doorknob, then spout a line of Wordsworth, and then poise with left foot against knee of right leg. He may, however, look through the pockets of his other suits (error—change in stimulus situation); he may visualize the last page in his checkbook (error—change in stimulus situation); he may think about borrowing money from John and then recall that he already owes him $10 (error—change in stimulus situation); and he may finally stumble into thinking about Little Albert, who never refuses anyone anything—and our subject 'is already' on his way down the hall. Most of the trial and error here has been implicit; an observer would probably have noticed little more than a generalized increase in tension. Can the same process be attributed to lower primates? Köhler reports that his apes would often cease their gross activity, look about the field searchingly, and scratch their heads in very humanoid puzzlement. Although one could interpret these periods as evidence for implicit trial and error, they could not have much status as a scientific explanation of insight.

Generalization

A man has just about finished making a minor repair on a small table radio and is putting in the last screws that hold the grill-like back on the set when one of the small screws slips down into the bowels of the set. Holding the radio there, looking down through the grillwork at the lost screw, and feeling highly frustrated, insight suddenly occurs. A clear recollection of a similar situation—fishing coins from sidewalk ventilators with gum and yardstick as a child—flashes through his mind, and he 'is already' on his way toward sticky substance and pencil for retrieving the lost screw. The novelty of situations demanding insightful solutions is a relative matter; to be sure, this man had never dropped a screw inside a table radio before, but the stimulus provided by looking down through the grillwork was adequate to evoke a generalized response originally learned in childhood. Many illustrations of the role of generalization can be found in Köhler's detailed observations. In one case Sultan, who had already solved many problems by means of a climbing pole, was in a situation in which no long stick was at hand. 'Presently the keeper passed by crossing the room beneath the objective; Sultan walked quickly up to him, took his hand, pulled him in the direction of the fruit . . . and made unmistakable efforts to climb onto his shoulders' (p. 48). The response originally made in terms of a certain stimulus-object (a climbing pole) is transferred to another stimulus (a man's form).

Far more significant for insightful problem-solving than primary stimulus generalization is the process of *mediated generalization* (cf. pp. 359-60). In the introduction to this section on symbolic processes use was made of the situation in which only a dead bush is available within an enclosure and a desired object lies outside. The human subject says to himself, 'I need a *stick* to reach that fruit.' Looking searchingly around, he may first glance past the bush, but returns to it again, thinking, 'Look at that long *branch* on the bush.' Immediately he starts for the bush and tears off the branch. The problem is solved the moment an appropriate mediation process occurs. Here mediation is based upon semantic generalization, but lower animals do not share the advantage of a prolific elaboration of discriminative language symbols. The chimpanzee also might view the dead bush, but it makes (we assume) reactions to the bush as a whole—bushes have not been used as sticks. But if the animal, in the course of its random behavior, happens to grasp a branch, it is very likely to show the sudden redirection of behavior we call insight. Why? Because the response of grasping the branch is essentially similar to the response of grasping any stick, and this act thereby serves to mediate the remainder of the sequence. The overt grasping movement of the chimpanzee is functionally identical to the implicit verbalization of 'branch is a stick' by the human. This, as we shall see, is perhaps the most important basis for human insights. The thing to observe here is this: all the acts essential for solution of the problem have previously been learned; the occurrence of insight waits upon the self-production of a mediating stimulus (verbal or otherwise) that will set off the correct sequence. The execution of the solution is a pedestrian matter.

Movement-produced Stimuli—Skills

One of the major characteristics of insightful solutions is the smoothness with which the sequence of acts is executed once the correct pattern is initiated. When the lure is dropped in front of the dog, on the other side of the fence, the animal hesitates a moment, turns, and starts around the fence, running and turning movements being firmly integrated in a smooth pattern. The nature of skill formation was discussed earlier. In a lifetime of experience, a dog has overlearned not only running sequences in general but also running-around-corner sequences in particular. Once such a skill is initiated—once the dog starts moving along the fence—the behavior carries itself along. Similarly, once the chimpanzee has grasped an appropriate tool, the sequence of movements necessary to execute the solution (running to the bars, reaching out, and pulling in the fruit) appear smoothly because they are all overlearned skills.

The Assembly of Behavior Segments

Many problem situations require the subject to put together several segments of activity in a certain order. Sultan, for example, had first to get a box, then place it under the lure, and finally mount it. In another situation he had to retreat from the goal-object, carefully pry loose a footscraper to use as a tool, and then return to the bars. What is it that binds together these discrete activities and gives coherence to the sequence? N. R. F. Maier (1929, 1932) has described a number of experiments purporting to show intelligent assembly of segments ('reasoning') in the white rat, and Hull (1935) has attempted a rigorous deduction of Maier's results from his own behavioristic principles. Since the heart of the controversy between gestalt and behavioristic theorists is revealed in this analysis, we will trace the alternative explanations in some detail.

Although the situations set by Maier for his rats varied in detail, they had in common the following: the animals were given training on segments of the final solution and then tested to see whether they could put these parts together in a logical manner. The situation given in Fig. 196 is a conventionalized form of Maier's reasoning situations used by Hull in making his analysis. The four goal-boxes are set up on tables in the laboratory and connected by identical raised runways. The boxes themselves are made highly distinctive, both in shape and in flooring (rats having very sensitive footpads). The sequence of training events is as follows: (1) R to X for food reward; (2) U to X for food reward; (3) R to U for water reward; (4) R to H for water reward. We may assume for simplicity that these segmental habits are made strong and equal. It is also important that during the training on each segment all other pathways be blocked. We may further assume that previous to the test for reasoning the rats are placed *thirsty* at R with both U and H paths open, and that they do run each way 50 per cent of the time. In the test situation each animal is placed *hungry* at R and the direct, previously learned path to X is blocked; both R–U and R–H are open, and the question is whether the rat subjects will

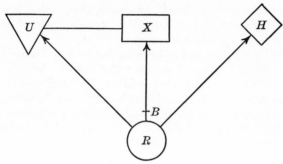

FIGURE 196. Series of locomotor paths representing a conventionalized form of Maier's 'reasoning' experiment with rats. Pathways would be enclosed, as would be areas R, X, U, and H. The floor of X might be of soft, flossy silk; that of U, cold metal with rough, sharp points; that of H, polished warm metal; and that of R, several layers of thin rubber dam. While training was taking place on one path, all others would be closed. Hull, *Psychological Review*, 1935, 42:222.

run toward U (and hence around to X) more frequently than toward H. The empirical fact is that they do—but why? Maier would argue that the rat *reasons* as follows: 'I have previously been from U to X and found food there; I have never gone from H to X for food; therefore, since I am hungry now, I shall run first to U and from there on to X and get food.' Of course, Maier does not imply that rats use language but rather that equivalent implicit processes are employed, i.e. that the rat, while at R, can somehow represent the completed path via U. One could also say the rats show *insight* here.

The behaviorist (here, Hull) wants to explain the same phenomenon without taking recourse to higher level mental processes. The crux of his problem is to demonstrate that the stimulus pattern at R is more strongly associated with the response of running toward U than with the response of running toward H at the time the crucial test is made. The analysis hinges on the role of mediating reactions (here, anticipatory food-taking reactions). (a) While running from U to X for food when hungry, fractional parts of the total goal reaction become conditioned to the traces of the distinctive U stimuli, become short-circuited, and hence occur when the animal is in box U. The stimuli produced by this mediation process become conditioned to running U to X. (b) Subsequently, while running from R to U for water when thirsty, the stimuli at U elicit these anticipatory food-taking reactions as a learned habit, and this representing process is regularly reinforced by drinking. (*Note:* There is no requirement in Hull's theory that the drive reduced be appropriate to the association reinforced.) By the same mechanism of short-circuiting, this distinctive representational process comes to be elicited by the distinctive stimuli at R. The representational processes associated with drinking behavior are equally associated with running both to U and to H and hence are not discriminative. (c) On the test trial the rats are placed *hungry* in R with the R to X path blocked. Hunger drive stimuli guarantee the occurrence of anticipatory food-taking reactions and since the self-stimulation arising from this representational process is already differentially associated with running to U rather than to H, this weights the balance in favor of the 'insightful' reaction. Once the animal reaches U, of course, the problem is solved. Hull must predict that speed of running will increase sharply when the animal reaches U, evidence for which has been observed.

This deduction may be rather devious, but it does follow from Hull's principles. It should be pointed out that this analysis depends upon a certain sequence of experiences during training. The anticipatory food-taking reactions must already be associated with box U when the animals run there from R for water. If training followed a different sequence—if the two water runs, from R to U and from R to H, *preceded* the training on U to X for food—the behaviorist would have to predict purely chance choices on the final test trial since there would be no way in which food-taking reactions and their stimuli could be associated distinctively with running toward U. Would the rats still do better than chance? If so, and other variables were carefully controlled, it would appear that rats can reason. This would seem to be a crucial test between gestalt and behavioristic positions, but, as far as this writer is aware, the experiment remains to be done.

An experiment performed by Tolman and Honzik (1930 *a*) seems to display the assembly of behavior segments or reasoning or insight in rats under conditions in which the Hull type of analysis would not be applicable. The ground plan of the elevated maze employed is shown in Fig. 197. With all pathways open, rats readily learned to take the direct, short path to the food box. When a block was inserted at A, the animals could take either path 2 or 3 but rapidly learned to choose path 2. (The gate in path 2 allows the animals to go through and then closes behind them so as to prevent entering path 2 from path 1.) The test situation in this experiment was provided by inserting a block at point B rather than at A. Will the subjects, after encountering this new block and retracing to the initial choice point, show the effects of learning and choose path 2 (which eventuates in the same blocked common path) or show insight and choose path 3 (which circumvents the new block)? Of the 15 rats used, 14 chose path 3, much as if they had said to themselves, 'It won't do me any good to go around through the gate this time, since it would bring me right back behind the barrier, so I'll take the long way around.'

This result has been checked by Dove and Thompson (1943). In their first experiment the maze plan and conditions used by Tolman and Honzik were duplicated with one exception: hinged cellophane doors replaced the blocks and these were sometimes left unlocked, so that the animals couldn't tell when path 1 would be available. This change eliminated the need for forcing the animals to try path 1 every time, which had been the case in the Tolman and Honzik study. Yet on the 'insight' test runs only two of the 11 rats avoided path 2 (showed insight) on the first trial, nine on the

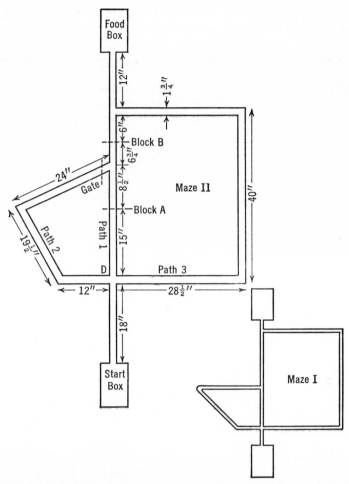

FIGURE 197. Mazes used to study insight in rats. Maze *I* is that used by Tolman and Honzik (1930) and Maze *II* is the modification introduced by Dove and Thompson. Dove and Thompson, *Journal of Genetic Psychology*, 1943, **63**:236.

second trial, and all 11 on the third trial. The results are not as clear-cut as the above; they might be interpreted as evidence for insight or as evidence for rapid learning. In a second experiment the maze plan was changed slightly so that the upper limb of path 2 converged with path 1 at a 45° angle and at a point immediately behind block *B*. This change in maze design is shown by the dashed line in Fig. 197. In this case none of the 26 animals showed insight on the first test trial, only ten choosing path 3 on the third trial. It appears that the blocked anticipatory left-turning responses had contributed largely to the 'insightful' choice of path 3 in the original Tolman and Honzik study. In a final experiment Dove and Thompson eliminated the need for retracing entirely by using blocks with heavily painted parallel lines which the rats could see from the choice point. Under these conditions the insightful choice of path 3 was never made by any animal on any of the three test trials. A companion study reported by the original authors (Tolman and Honzik, 1930 a) revealed no evidence for insight when side walls were added to the pathways.

COMPARISON OF GESTALT AND BEHAVIORISTIC THEORIES

By way of summary on insight in animals, let us borrow one final illustration from Köhler's work and apply both theories to it. 'Sultan is squatting at the bars, but cannot reach the fruit, which lies outside, by means

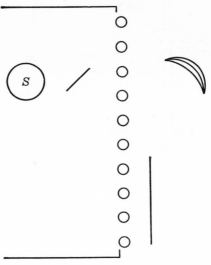

FIGURE 198. Diagrammatical representation of short-and-long-stick problem. The chimpanzee subject (*S*) must use the short stick to obtain the long stick which can then be used to secure the banana.

of his only available short stick. A longer stick is deposited outside the bars, about two meters on one side of the objective, and parallel with the grating. It can not be grasped with the hand, but it can be pulled within reach by means of the small stick [see Fig. 198]. Sultan tries to reach the fruit with the smaller of the two sticks. Not succeeding, he tears at a piece of wire that projects from the netting of his cage, but that, too, is in vain. Then he gazes about him; (there are always in the course of these tests some long pauses, during which the animals scrutinize the whole visible area). He suddenly picks up the little stick once more, goes with it to the point opposite to the long stick, scratches it towards him with the "auxiliary," seizes it, and goes with it to the point opposite the objective, which he secures' (1925, p. 174).

Gestalt analysis. The initial efforts with the short stick, as well as the subsequent attempt to tear away the fence, would probably be termed 'good errors,' i.e. the pattern of conductive forces set up by the objective and the given geographical situation direct activity along the line toward the goal—reaching toward it and trying to remove the barrier. During the scrutiny of the field (the need-space being a long line toward the objective), the long stick is spied. Since this object fits the need-space perceptually, reorganization of the psychological field (insight) is facilitated, and Sultan starts toward this subgoal. The smoothness with which the long stick is secured and then used to secure the objective is due to the fact that the segmental acts are part of the unified whole, i.e. parts of the new organization of the psychological field, which exerts cohesive force upon its parts.

Behavioristic analysis. Sultan has already had considerable experience using sticks as tools. The response of extending the available stick is therefore high in the habit-family hierarchy and likely to occur. So too are responses designed to remove a barrier (i.e. Sultan has frequently been reinforced by getting objective when he knocks down or pushes aside a branch, a box, or another chimpanzee). But both of these responses are unsuccessful in the present situation and hence are temporarily inhibited. The cessation of direct approaches and 'scrutiny' of the situation makes it possible for Sultan to perceive the long stick outside the bars. Since such long tools have in the past experience of this animal been associated with food goal-objects, this stimulus is assumed to evoke fractional anticipatory goal reactions. This new pattern of stimulation is already associated with the skill sequence of extending the short stick and securing such an objective (here the long stick is functioning as a subgoal). Once the long stick is grasped, its stimulation, in conjunction with traces of the primary goal stimulation and the hunger motivation, leads directly to the final segment. The smoothness of execution here is due to the fact that each segment is an overlearned, well-integrated serial skill.

Which Is the Better Explanation?

Behavioristic principles originated in the conditioning area and are generally applied to 'simpler' aspects of behavior, like maze-learning and transfer; gestalt principles originated in the area of human perception and are generally applied to more 'complex' aspects of behavior. The phenomenon of insight, especially as observed in animals, lies within the areas of fruitful application of both theories, and they meet head-on—yet the sense of concussion is not pronounced. Perhaps the two theories have been traveling along a more nearly parallel course than the proponents of either have realized. Which is the better explanation? This question cannot be answered satisfactorily from our present level of understanding.

To explain behavior in terms of the dynamics of the psychological field and its reorganizations (insights) becomes circular unless these dynamic properties can be indexed independently of the behavior they are supposed to explain. Similarly, to explain insightful behavior in terms of fluctuations within a habit-family hierarchy, of secondary generalization and anticipatory reactions, becomes circular unless these mechanisms can be indexed by some means other than the fact that insight occurs. Both theories employ these unobservable hypothetical constructs, and they serve the same function, that of mediating overt behavior. This last point makes one ask if the differences here are more apparent than real. If the behaviorist explains insight essentially as a change in the *meaning* of a situation (assuming, of course, that meaning is reducible to patterns of implicit 'reactions') and the gestaltist explains it as a change in the *perception* of a situation, the two theories can be distinct only as meaningful and perceptual processes can be segregated—and a defensible differentiation here would be difficult indeed. This integrative point of view will appear even more clearly in human problem-solving, to which we now turn our attention.

PROBLEM-SOLVING IN HUMAN SUBJECTS

Clean, precise thinking has been the cause of wonderment and respect ever since man has been the object of his own study. The intellectual feats of men such as Milton and Einstein fill us at once with a feeling of awe and a sense of the inadequacy of psychological science. Most attempts to understand creative thinking do strike one as rather feeble and barren. The proliferation of chains of ideas, via the laws of association, seem to miss the essential element of creativeness. Formal logic, to be sure, provides rules of procedure by which the truth or falsity of conclusions can be tested, but it does not in itself establish the validity of its premises nor does it help the thinker select the crucial content for its molds. The gestalt psychologists, more than any other group, have attempted to bring the problem of creative human thinking into focus as an experimental task, their more flexible concepts being perhaps more readily applicable to such complex events.

At the forefront of the gestalt attack on human problem-solving has been Max Wertheimer. Although his own stimulating book, *Productive Thinking,* has appeared only recently and posthumously (1945), his investigations on creative thinking go back to the early years of this century and his influence upon others through his teaching has been tremendous. One finds, for example, important studies by Duncker (1935, trans. Lees, 1945) in Germany and by Luchins (1942) and others in America dedicated to Wertheimer as the source of their inspiration. Even Köhler, whose work on the chimpanzee was the direct stimulus for studies on human thinking by many American psychologists (e.g. Alpert, 1928; Brainard, 1930; Matheson, 1931; Richardson, 1932; and others), was himself strongly influenced by Wertheimer during his formative years in Germany. It is only fitting, therefore, that our consideration of human problem-solving begin with a presentation of Wertheimer's views.

Wertheimer on Productive Thinking

Professor Wertheimer is visiting a public school classroom. The teacher reviews with the pupils the method for finding the area of a rectangle. The students all know that 'the area of a rectangle is equal to the product of the two sides.' 'Now,' says the teacher, 'we shall go on.' He draws a parallelogram on the board and labels the corners *a, b, c,* and *d* (see Fig. 199). He then drops two perpendiculars from the upper corners, extends the base line, labels the two new points *e* and *f,* and proceeds with the usual proof of the theorem that the area of a parallelogram is equal to the product of the base by the altitude. The page in the text where this ritual is to be found is then pointed out, and the young students are admonished to repeat the lesson carefully so they will know it well. On the next day Professor Wertheimer is again a guest observer in the same class-room. A student is called upon to demonstrate the proof learned the previous day and performs it neatly. The teacher whispers to Wertheimer, 'He is not the best of my pupils.' But Wertheimer is disquieted: have they done any thinking at all? do they understand *why* just these steps are made? have they grasped the issue here, or are they blindly repeating? The good professor, asking permission of the teacher, draws the parallelogram shown as *B* in Fig. 199. The students are taken aback: one complains that they haven't had that yet; others draw the lines as they were taught and then sit back bewildered; others state firmly that 'the area of a parallelogram is equal to the base times the altitude' but become perplexed when asked to show why it is true in this case; a few students smile suddenly and, rotating their papers through 45°, solve it (Wertheimer, 1945, pp. 14-17).

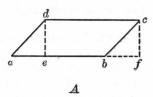 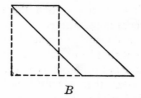

A   *B*

FIGURE 199. Parallelogram problem: (*A*) as given in classroom demonstration by teacher; (*B*) as given by Wertheimer to test students' understanding of the solution. After Wertheimer, *Productive Thinking,* Harper and Brothers, New York, 1945, pp. 15, 16.

Since Wertheimer's figure was identical with the teacher's original, but for the rotation, it becomes apparent that most of the pupils have merely learned a rote procedure, have failed to understand *what* was accomplished in abstract terms. A child that really understood the solution could generalize, or, in gestalt terms, transpose his solution to situations in no direct way similar to the training situation.

In a series of informal experiments with young children, Wertheimer first helped them to understand how the usual method for determining the area of a rectangle arises from the essential nature of that figure. If the height of a rectangle can be expressed as so many little squares, then the area will equal the total number of vertical columns of little squares included; $a \times b$ thus comes down to seeing how many columns of squares of a certain height are included in the rectangle. This, according to Wertheimer, is *productive* thinking because (a) it starts with a desire to get at the inner relatedness of form and size, (b) there is structuralization of sub-wholes in relation to the whole figure and the specific problem, and (c) the entire process is one consistent line of thinking throughout, not an aggregate of piecemeal operations. Armed with such an understanding of how the size of a rectangle is determined, the children were then given the problem of finding the area of the parallelogram; nothing further was said and Wertheimer simply waited to see what they would say or do.

Real thinking could be observed in many cases. One subject asked for a folding ruler and demonstrated that a rectangle having sides of the same length as the parallelogram could be formed, but he was shown that the area changed in the process. A five-and-a-half-year-old child performed as follows: 'I certainly don't know how to do *that*.' Then after a moment of silence she said: 'This is *no good here*,' pointing to the region at the left end; *'and no good here*,' pointing to the region at the right. 'It's troublesome, here and there.' Suddenly she cried out, 'May I have a scissors? What is bad here is just what is needed here. It fits.' She made a vertical cut through the parallelogram and moved the left half around and fitted it onto the right edge, making a rectangle which could then be treated in the usual manner (pp. 40-49). The child's problem-solving behavior is intelligent we would all agree; she realizes that the vertical columns of little squares cannot be fitted against diagonal lines; she understands that the figure must somehow be transformed into a rectangle, and her sudden solution happens to be correct. But should we judge the 'solution' attempted by another child, with the folding ruler, as less intelligent because it was incorrect? At any rate, how much cleaner and more 'understandingful' are these attempts than the blind, rote procedures of the pupils in the classroom noted above.

How do such insightful solutions arise in the human thinker? It is apparent that he must somehow grasp the essentials of the problem, but how is this accomplished? Wertheimer's interpretation is in keeping with general gestalt theory. Solutions arise not from blind recall of past experience or blind trial and error but rather from the (perceptual) requirements of the problem. 'Such a process is not just a sum of several steps, not an aggregate of several operations, but the growth of one line of thinking out of the gaps in the situation, out of the structural troubles and the desire to remedy them, to straighten out what is bad, to get at the good inner relatedness' (p. 50). Or again, 'When the problem is realized, [the problem situation] contains structural strains and stresses that are resolved in [the solution-situation]. The thesis is that the very character of the steps, of the operations, of the changes . . . springs from the nature of the vectors set up in these structural troubles in the direction of helping the situation, of straightening it out structurally' (p. 193).

The educational implications of Wertheimer's work are immense. His thesis is that we cannot expect forceful, productive thinking in problem situations from people who are trained by blind, rote methods. The practical weakness in Wertheimer's position is that he does not clearly specify *how* we may educate people to think. After all, did not his special subjects learn a rote method of thinking about rectangles? To be sure, conceiving the area of a rectangle as made up of columns of little squares may be more generally applicable than the notion of $a \times b$, since it leads to searching for a way to make the novel parallelograms into rectangles, but is what is learned different in kind? Although rich in theoretical implications, Wertheimer's book actually includes no tests of theory. The informal observations are pointed up as illustrating the dynamics of gestalt principles, but the same observations might conceivably be interpreted in terms of modern behavioristic principles as well—though, perhaps, not so attractively.

One underlying reason for disagreement between behavioristically and gestalt-trained students appears clearly in Wertheimer's book and is worth mentioning. The two groups of psychologists speak subtly different languages. It is apparent in *Productive Thinking* that terms such as 'inner structure,' 'centering,' 'sensible,' and 'relatedness' involve rich connotations for Wertheimer and other gestalt psychologists that are not shared by their behavioristic brethren. These are good terms, set in opposition to bad terms such as 'blind,' 'random,' 'rote,' and 'senseless.' The modern behaviorist might understandably take some offense at the ridiculous straw version of himself he finds even in recent gestalt works like this one. At one point we find this: 'It is not the teachers who are at fault. Many are somehow deeply dissatisfied with the emphasis on mechanical associations, on blind drill. Many rely on them because they seem to them to be in line with scientific psychology—by which they mean the psychology of learning rote syllable series, and of conditioning' (Wertheimer, 1945, p. 114). Similar naïveté is found when modern behaviorists criticize gestalt views. Both tend to select the most primitive and philosophically unsophisticated expressions of the opposing theory for attack, not with deliberate intent to mislead but simply because they have been unable to keep abreast of the rapidly expanding forefront of the other theory. Köhler would have just about as much difficulty in really understanding Hull's *Principles of Behavior* as Hull would have really understanding Köhler's recent discussions of the figural after-effect. Both presuppose a long process of 'aging' within a given theoretical mold.

The Experimental Characterization of Human Problem-solving

(1) *Developmental level and the probability of insight.* One of the clearest studies on this aspect of the problem is that of Richardson (1932). Using the Gesell normative group of children at the Yale Clinic of Child Development, she presented simple string problems, previously used by Köhler, to infants of varying ages. In the typical situation a brightly painted toy was placed beyond the child's reach; a string, connected to the toy, lay within reach. In some tests a grill (to prevent crawling approaches) was also employed. Infants under 7 months of age displayed various chance solutions—while playing with the string, the toy might happen to be drawn within reach, for example; much activity was directed toward their own hands or the bars of the grill. The insightful solution required that the child actually watch the objective while manipulating the string, thus using the string as a tool, and this type of behavior was clearly shown to be dependent upon processes developing between 7 and 10 months in the human infant. There is here, of course, no specification of the relative importance of maturation or learning; both are presumably involved. Kreezer and Dallenbach (1929) studied the ability of young children, 5 to 7½ years of age, to handle the abstract concept of opposition. The children were asked such questions as, 'What is the opposite of "good"?' 'What is the opposite of "up"?' The percentages of children giving correct answers increased with age. If a child once made a correct response, all subsequent questions tended to be answered correctly. The experimenters concluded from this that the concept of opposition was acquired through the sudden process of insight rather than through trial and error.

(2) *The search.* Insightful solutions of problem situations are usually preceded by a period of exploration of the field. One of the earliest studies in this area, that of Ruger (1910), brings out the importance of interplay between motor and verbal search. Subjects were given various mechanical

puzzles to untangle, such as the familiar twisted nails or the 'heart and bow' puzzle. Detailed data were kept on both the time required for each trial and the verbal commentaries (introspections) of the subjects. Certain of Ruger's conclusions are well worth noting: (a) *Locus analysis.* Subjects quickly noticed the crucial area and temporal point in a puzzle that demanded careful inspection: 'Hm . . . it's got to go through this small loop somehow . . .'—more or less in the manner that Thorndike's cats restricted their activity about the critical mechanism. (b) *Analysis after the fact.* Subjects would suddenly find the puzzle solved, the pieces apart in their hands, and would then make a quick *verbal* review of the movements they had just made: 'Well! . . . there it is, but . . . just had 'em pointed this way. . .' (c) *Stages of analysis.* After mastery of the basic principle of a puzzle, the subject would often analyze the details, striving thereby to increase his speed of solution.

Duncker (1935, transl. 1945) has made an exciting and penetrating analysis of human problem-solving at the complex rational and verbal level we would most like to understand. Students were given tough technical problems with the request that they think aloud, even the seemingly foolish notions that occurred to them, and they were free to ask any questions they wished. One problem ran as follows: given a human being with an inoperable stomach tumor, and rays that destroy organic tissues at sufficient intensity, by what procedure can one free him of the tumor by these rays and at the same time avoid destroying the healthy tissue which surrounds it? A sample sequence of proposals by one subject ran as follows:

> (1) Send rays through the esophagus. (2) Desensitize the healthy tissues by means of a chemical injection. (3) Expose the tumor by operating. (4) One ought to decrease the intensity of the rays on their way; for example—would this work?—turn the rays on at full strength only after the tumor has been reached. (Experimenter: False analogy; no injection is in question.) (5) One should swallow something inorganic (which would not allow passage of rays) to protect the healthy stomach-walls. (E.: It is not merely the stomach-walls which are to be protected.) (6) Either the rays must enter the body or the tumor must come out. Perhaps one could alter the location of the tumor—but how? Through pressure? No. . . (9) Move the tumor toward the exterior. (The E. repeats the problem and emphasizes, '. . . which destroys *at sufficient intensity.*') (10) The intensity ought to be variable. (Compare 4.) (11) Adaptation of the healthy tissues by previous weak application of the rays. (E.: How can it be brought about that the rays destroy only the region of the tumor?) (12) Reply: I see no more than two possibilities: either to protect the body or to make the rays harmless. (E.: How could one decrease the intensity of the rays en route?) (13) Reply: Somehow divert . . . diffuse rays . . . disperse . . . stop! Send a broad and weak bundle of rays through a lens in such a way that the tumor lies at the focal point and thus receives intensive radiation. (Total duration about half an hour.) *

* Duncker, *Psychological Monographs,* 1945, #270, 58: pp. 2-3.

Actually, since the rays in question cannot be deflected by ordinary lenses, the 'best' solution is the crossing of several weak bundles of rays at the tumor so that the intensity necessary for destruction is reached only there.

What general conclusions does Duncker draw concerning the search process? (a) *Proposed solutions are not blind attempts.* The subject's suggestion that rays be sent down the esophagus, impractical though it may be, is guided by one possible solution-theory: to get the rays at the tumor through some opening without touching any healthy tissues. Of course, all proposals appear within the general frame of reference of the modern European; the subject does not, as Duncker points out, think of appropriate magic formulas or action at other places; his solution attempts are relevant to the material relations between rays, tissues, and tumor. (b) *Each proposal serves to reformulate the problem.* When the subject suggests to himself 'move the tumor toward the exterior,' this sets up an entirely new process of evaluation. The problem suddenly appears in a new light and a new set of practical hypotheses is tried out. Presumably the effectiveness with which a human subject can solve abstract problems of this sort depends upon the flexibility with which he can shift his formulations. (c) *The effectiveness of concrete proposals depends upon their functional value.* A variety of practical hypotheses may have equivalent functional value, i.e. that of weakening the rays as they pass through healthy tissues or that of getting the tumor moved to an approachable locus. According to Duncker, it is this understanding of the general functional value of a proposal that is indispensable in evaluating it as a solution. (d) *Solutions are transposable to the extent that their functional values are grasped.* Wertheimer stated that children who grasp the 'inner structure' of the parallelogram solution can readily transpose it to a wide variety of situations. Conversely, a 'blind' solution is restricted to the specific problem on which it happened to work; the ritualistic practice of bleeding the patient in primitive medicine might have worked successfully in certain cases, but failure to understand its functional value limited its transposability.

A related process in problem-solving is the use of *search models.* The subject's search for a material or verbal tool is directed by the perceptual or meaningful requirements of the situation. Selz (1922) used the concept of anticipatory 'schema' or frames in thinking: given the task to 'name opposites,' for example, the subject is guided by a conceptual pattern of opposition, which he might even diagram. The earlier term 'set' or *aufgabe* expresses much the same notion. Köhler (1925) clearly had the same view of guided search: the pattern of forces set up by the objective within the psychological field serves to outline a definite need-space, and this form guides the chimpanzee in its exploration of the geographical field. The jigsaw puzzle is a neat example of the use of search models (cf. Johnson, 1944). The puzzler's exploration of the available pieces is clearly guided by inferred characteristics of the space that needs filling—its color, the lines that run through it, the distinctive shape, and so on. One observes, introspectively, the use of mediating verbal cues in this procedure, such as 'a sharply pointed, half-blue-sky piece,' as well as feelings of perceptual 'cohesion' when the right piece is spotted.

(3) *The role of experience.* A frequently encountered criticism of the gestalt view of problem-solving is that it makes no use of the previous his-

tory or experience of the subject. This is another straw-man argument. Although the modern gestalt theorist emphasizes forces in the immediate perceptual situation, he does not deny the role of relevant past experience. The difference lies in how experience is supposed to be utilized by the subject. The gestalt psychologist believes that *specific aspects of past experience are selected dynamically by the structural requirements of the situation.* Is the distinction here a real one? Before attempting to answer this question, let us look at some of the evidence.

Wertheimer, noting that one bright child had spontaneously asked for scissors and used them insightfully (see pp. 623-4), asks himself this ques-

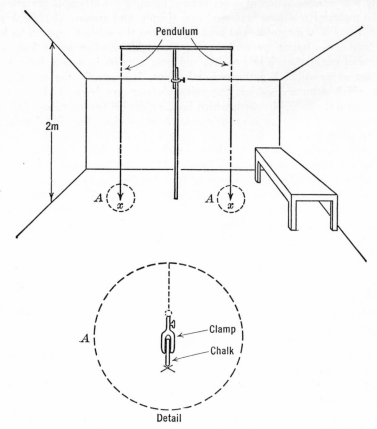

FIGURE 200. Diagram showing situation and solution of 'double pendulum' problem. Inset shows how lab clamp and chalk were attached. N. R. F. Maier, *Journal of Comparative Psychology,* 1930, 10:123.

tion: Does the passive recall of scissors lead to solution or does the structural requirement of the problem situation call forth this bit of past experience? He goes about answering it in this manner (1945, p. 59): 'I put the scissors on the table at the beginning of the experiment or even have the child cut some paper. Sometimes it helps (e.g. if I bring the scissors after some deliberation by the child, after some remarks showing that the structural requirement is felt). But there are cases in which it does not help.

The child looks at the scissors, then looks again at the figure. Seeing the two he is clearly troubled but nothing happens. I increase the "help." "Don't you want to take the scissors and cut the figure?" The reaction is sometimes a blank stare; the child obviously does not know what I want. . . We see that furnishing the scissors, and its common use, does not in itself help; it may result in entirely blind and foolish actions . . . it does seem to help if the structural requirement is already felt or if it is elicited by the scissors. . .' In other words, the crucial thing is that the subject stimulate himself (e.g. feel the structural requirement) with 'I've got to make a rectangle out of this figure,' 'I've got to remove the diagonal parts,' or something equivalent.

Among a number of experiments upon problem-solving in humans conducted by N. R. F. Maier, there are two that relate directly to the use of past experience. In his earliest (1930) the question posed was this: Is selection of and practice on the necessary components of a solution sufficient, or must the subject also have the right 'direction' to unify these elements of past experience? College students were given clamps, rods, cord, and so on, as shown in Fig. 200, the room being otherwise bare, and their task was to produce the double pendulum shown already assembled in the figure. All students were given practice on the part-responses necessary for the solution (i.e. how to make a plumb line out of a cord, a clamp, and a pencil; how to clamp two rods together), but only one group was then given the right 'direction': 'Observe how easy the solution would be if you could only hang the pendulums from two nails in the ceiling.' Although eight of the 22 subjects in the 'directions' group solved the problem, only one of the 62 subjects without direction solved it, both groups having had equivalent experience. Similarly, those of Wertheimer's children who had insight into the nature of the parallelogram problem could utilize the scissors effectively, whereas those who were 'blind' to its nature could not. But one child, it will be recalled, *asked for* the scissors when they were not present in the problem situation at all. Is this a higher level utilization of past experience? Will it prove harder to restructure a problem situation when the relevant cues are not available in the present situation?

A more recent study by Maier (1945) gets at this problem. The student subjects were to construct a 'hatrack' in a certain spot in an open room, the only equipment being two boards and a 3-inch C clamp (see Fig. 201). Both sets of experimental subjects (groups 1 and 2) had previously helped the experimenter construct a piece of apparatus in which four 'supports' were made, each essentially identical with the 'hatrack' in Fig. 201. In the test situation the four 'supports' were left standing while subjects in group 1 tried to construct a 'hatrack,' but they were removed for group 2. Group 3 subjects had no previous experience with the construction materials. While 72 per cent of the group 1 subjects (relevant cues perceptually available) solved the problem, only 48 per cent of the group 2 subjects (relevant cues available only in recall) solved it; 24 per cent of the control subjects were successful. If we can hypothesize the probable sequence of events here, the setting of the problem (build a 'hatrack') initiates a *search* in the sense discussed earlier; since the subjects are limited to the two boards and a clamp, they are likely to 'look at,' either directly (in group 1) or in retrospect (in group 2), previous constructions with similar materials; the crucial problem is whether the screw part of the clamp will be perceived as 'something to hang a hat on.' From the evidence here we would conclude that having the relevant cue available in the immediate situation facilitates solving this problem in much the same way that having scissors available would help children hit upon cutting as a solution of the parallelogram problem. In both cases the distinctive cue serves to initiate the appropriate mediation process.

The critical issue is whether these 'mediation processes' appear as learned reactions (via primary or mediated generalization) or as spontaneous reorganizations of the problem-field (via perceptual stresses and their resolution). The issue is *not* whether students have had experience in clamping

FIGURE 201. Solution of 'hatrack' problem. Having had experience with the same construction, but with a different function (support), subject must come to perceive lab clamp as 'hook' rather than as 'handle.' N. R. F. Maier, *Journal of Experimental Psychology*, 1945, **35**:352.

boards together or children have had experience using scissors. Certainly the pretraining Wertheimer gave children in 'understanding' the usual method of figuring the area of a rectangle developed processes that would help mediate solution of the parallelogram problem. Certainly the 'out-jutting' of the clamp-handle, especially when directly looked at, could evoke the learned mediating reaction of saying 'hook . . . aha! hatrack,' especially in students who have hung their hats on hooks and nails. Is the mediation process dependent upon learning or upon the dynamics of the present perceptual field? These experiments yield no answer, if indeed anything more than terminology is involved.

(4) *Role of Representational Processes in Problem-solving.* It is clear that both gestalt and behavioristic theories resort to implicit intervening mechanisms. This being the case, *the mediation hypothesis* described earlier might be expected to offer something in the way of a model for studying

problem-solving. Figure 202 is analogous to Fig. 144, which described in general terms how behavioral modification may take place on either mediational or instrumental levels. If a subject is shown a STICK and asked to state its properties as they occur to him, he might respond as follows: 'long, wooden, hard, flexible, round . . . ,' later responses having longer latencies, i.e. being less readily available. In other words, subjects have hierarchies of ways of perceiving objects—a STICK, being more readily perceived as *long* rather than *thick,* is more likely to be utilized as a probing tool than as a wedge to separate objects. If we provide the subject with the meaning of *wooden* and ask him to state various potential functions, he might respond

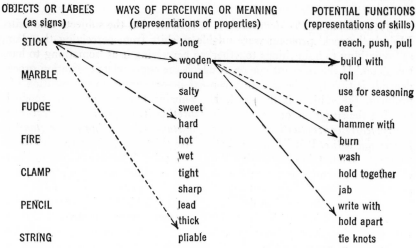

OBJECTS OR LABELS (as signs)	WAYS OF PERCEIVING OR MEANING (representations of properties)	POTENTIAL FUNCTIONS (representations of skills)
STICK	long	reach, push, pull
	wooden	build with
MARBLE	round	roll
	salty	use for seasoning
FUDGE	sweet	eat
	hard	hammer with
FIRE	hot	burn
	wet	wash
CLAMP	tight	hold together
	sharp	jab
PENCIL	lead	write with
	thick	hold apart
STRING	pliable	tie knots

FIGURE 202. Mediational model of problem-solving. Objects (or labels of objects) as signs are associated with hierarchies of representational mediators (ways of perceiving objects or their significance) which in turn elicit readiness for executing a hierarchy of instrumental skills.

as follows: 'build things, burn, strike, nail. . .' Again, evidence for a hierarchy of potential functions would be obtained. Incidentally, we note that our language conveniently provides adjectives for categorizing properties and verbs for categorizing functions.

Figure 202 treats objects such as STICK and FUDGE as if they were signs. In discussing the constancy phenomenon in perception as well as the incentive value of food objects it was pointed out that the various modes of appearance of objects are themselves signs of the 'real' object, as something to be handled, approached, avoided, and otherwise behaved toward. Similarly, dispositions toward the various skill sequences employed with the *class* of objects having certain properties in common (e.g. *stickiness, flexibility*) become associated with such perceived properties. For illustration, the meaning of 'flexibility' is associated with anticipated switching movements, tying movements, and so on; a particular object, such as a PIECE OF ROPE, which is perceived as flexible, will readily elicit such tying and switching skill sequences.

Now suppose we ask subjects to first list properties of certain objects and later various potential functions. We would predict a correlation between the hierarchies of perceived properties and anticipated functions. A subject for whom perceived *woodenness* of PENCIL is relatively available should be more likely to think of 'burning' as a potential function—and he should be more likely to survive in a problem situation in which using pencils for kindling is the correct solution. Suppose we use labels rather than actual objects as stimuli (which would be akin to Maier's group 2 above for whom the previous constructions were no longer present). If the response hierarchies for both object and label stimuli were the same, there would be no difference in problem-solving behavior, but this does not seem to be the case (cf. Karwoski, Gramlich, and Arnott study, pp. 711-12). Numerous experimental implications can be derived from this model; however, only a few have been studied as yet.

(5) *Fixation in Problem-solving.* It is likely that the subjects who failed Maier's 'hatrack' problem were unable to shift from perceiving the clamp as 'something to hold things together' to perceiving it as 'something to hang things on.' If the relevant cue upon which the appropriate mediation process depends is tightly imbedded in a context inappropriate to the solution of a problem, the subject is hindered. He remains fixated upon one mode of viewing the situation, one mode of interpreting it. *Objects and object-labels are typically conceptualized in terms of a standard meaning and a standard functional value.* Pencils in the abstract are things to write with. Books are things to read. Cigarettes are things to smoke. The association between object and potential function has become automatic, not mediated by perceived properties of the object as such.

Such standardization has definite value in thinking and problem-solving. The human subject looks at a dead bush and says, 'branch . . . stick,' thereby solving the problem; Maier's subjects look at the out-jutting handle of the clamp, conceptualize it as 'hook,' and solve their problem. But this same standardizing process may also restrict the flexibility with which one can search and hence utilize his environment. A pencil can function as a prying tool, as a wedge for maintaining space between things, as kindling for a fire, or even as a teething substitute for babies, yet most of us, when searching for something to serve *these* functions, will pass by the humble pencil because 'it is something to write with.' Actually, all objects are multifunctional to some degree, but experience and language combine to delimit the range of their utilization. There are at least two conditions, however, that tend to break down these functional barriers: Where sufficient physical similarity exists between the available object and the one needed, the former may be utilized despite any awareness of its functional significance. This is merely a case of *primary stimulus generalization,* of course, and is perhaps most probable under high degrees of motivation—the enraged young woman, lacking a dagger or stickpin, may grasp a pencil and strike at her adversary. Secondly, a new functional value or meaning for an object may be literally manufactured through the process of *mediation,* usually verbal in the human subject: nails are to be driven in but there is no hammer available, so the subject explores his situation, mumbling 'something heavy and hard . . . heavy and hard . . . ,' until he happens to look at his own shoes with their solid leather heels, and the problem is solved.

This second mechanism is lucidly revealed in another of Maier's studies (1931). In the experimental room two lightweight strings were hung from the ceiling at such a distance apart that, while holding one, the subject could not reach the other. The only available piece of equipment was a pair of pliers. The correct solution was for the subject to tie the pliers pendulum-wise to one string and swing it, catching it again while holding the other string. The critical aspect of the experiment was this: if the subject had not spontaneously solved the problem within 10 minutes, Maier supplied him with a hint; he would 'accidentally' brush against one of the strings, causing it to swing gently. Of those who solved the problem after this hint, the average interval between hint and solution was only 42 seconds, demonstrating that this distinctive cue immediately set off an appropriate process which mediated the solution. Given this 'realization of the inner structure' (Wertheimer) or 'direction' (Maier), the execution of the solution became a pedestrian matter. In regard to the functional value of the pliers, it can be seen that this depended on and varied with the mediation process involved. Another interesting finding in this experiment was that most of those subjects who solved the problem immediately after the hint did so without any realization that they had been given one. The 'idea' of making a pendulum with the pliers seemed to arise spontaneously. This supplies us with further insight into the nature of insight. The apparent spontaneity of solutions may be attributable to the occurrence of distinctive cues even though neither the subject nor (usually) the experimenter can isolate them.

Some of the most suggestive studies to date on human problem-solving have been reported by Duncker (1945), working directly within this framework. His basic procedure was as follows: Various everyday objects lay in confusion upon a laboratory table. With the experimental subjects, the critical object was first used in an inconspicuous and usual manner (function I), and later the subjects were placed in a problem situation in which only the critical object could be effectively utilized, but in a novel manner (function II). Control subjects were placed in the problem situation without out the previous, normal use of the object. The question was this: Will the preliminary use of an object serve to 'fix' its function and thus hinder the subject's use of it in a novel, problem-solving manner? A sample test situation (p. 86):

> The 'weight problem': A pendulum, consisting of a cord and a weight, is to be hung from a nail ('for experiments on motion'). To this end, the nail must be driven into the wall. On the table lies, among other things, the crucial object: a weight. *Solution:* with this weight (as 'hammer'), the nail is driven into the wall. In the pre-utilization situation the weight is given expressly as pendulum-weight (with the string already tied to it); in the control situation, a joint serves as pendulum weight. Thus for the experimental subjects, the weight functions first as 'pendulum-weight' (function I) and then as 'hammer' (function II).

The results were clear-cut. Whereas nearly 100 per cent of the control subjects utilized the critical object in the novel way, only about 50 per cent of the experimental subjects for whom this object had been fixed in function did so. Duncker also found that the availability of an object for a novel function depended upon its 'imbeddedness' in various contexts. If, for example, the critical object were a cork bottle stopper and it was seen in the test situation only in this imbedded way, inserted in an *empty* ink bottle, it would be more firmly fixed and unavailable than if it were lying openly on the table. On the other hand, if the same stopper had to be used during the test, i.e. removed from a *full* ink bottle, the solution was relatively facilitated. In general terms, we may say that the meaning, and hence the functional value, of objects varies with the contexts in which they appear.

Many human problem situations require manipulation of verbal symbols rather than physical objects, yet effects similar to those observed above would be anticipated—fixation upon a narrow meaning of the words employed in thinking should restrict problem-solving performance in much the same manner that fixation upon a given way of perceiving objects does. Perhaps the restriction would be even greater since the subject would be unable to 'walk around' the symbolic object and be stimulated by its various aspects. Duncker (1945) offers a neat illustration of this (p. 56):

> On a mountain trip, on which descent was by the same path as had been the ascent of the previous day, I asked myself whether there must be a spot en route at which I must find myself at exactly the same time on the descent as on the ascent. It was of course assumed that ascent and descent took place at about the same time of day, say from five to twelve o'clock.—But without further probing, I could arrive at no conclusive insight. . . Let the reader himself ponder a bit.—Certainly there exist several approaches to an evident solution. But probably none is, I might almost say, more drastically evident than the following view of the situation: let ascent and descent be divided between *two* persons on the *same* day. They must *meet*. Ergo . . . With this, from an unclear, dim condition not easily surveyable, the situation has suddenly been brought into full daylight.

Although Duncker uses this as an illustration of the difference between situations in which a conclusion is not directly evident and those in which it is self-evident, it is simultaneously a case of semantic fixation. Why is 'one person meeting himself at some spot on two different days' not self-evident? Because the meaning of 'one person' or 'oneself' does not readily include the aspect of 'meeting.' One does not 'meet himself' except in metaphor. Nor do things 'meet' at different times. Yet insight into this problem requires the thinker to manipulate symbols in such a way that these things are conceived as occurring. On the other hand, *two* people do *meet* at the *same time,* especially when they start simultaneously from different ends of the same path. Once the problem is recast in these terms, a firm meaningful coherence is obtained and the conclusion *is* self-evident.

(6) *Fixation in method.* A group of children in a geometry class have been taught how to get the area of a trapezoid by drawing auxiliary lines and using the formula $[(a + b)/2] h$. The teacher now refers to a picture on the wall of the classroom (see Fig. 203), gives the values for the inner and outer sides of the frame, and then asks the children to compute the total area of the picture frame. Most of the dutiful children busily set to work computing the area of the separate trapezoids, but a few smiled wisely and, merely multiplying a by b and then c by d and subtracting the former

result from the latter (i.e. subtracting the inner *rectangle* from the outer one), solved the problem quickly (Wertheimer, 1945, p. 77). Most of the children are fixated upon the plodding, mechanical method they have just been taught. Sultan showed similar fixation in method when, after a series

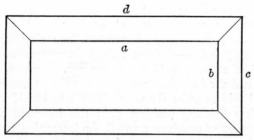

FIGURE 203. Picture frame problem.

of 'stick' problems, he was faced with a problem requiring building with boxes. The boxes were disregarded while Sultan searched for sticks or stick substitutes.

The most extensive study on fixation in human problem-solving presently available has been conducted by one of Wertheimer's students. Luchins (1942) gave subjects the series of computational problems shown in Table 17. The first solution was demonstrated on the blackboard; the 3-unit jar

TABLE 17

PROBLEM	GIVEN: the following empty jars as measures			OBTAIN: the following amount of water
1.	29	3		20
2. E	21	127	3	100
3. E	14	163	25	99
4. E	18	43	10	5
5. E	9	42	6	21
6. E	20	59	4	31
7. C	23	49	3	20
8. C	15	39	3	18
9.	28	76	3	25
10. C	18	48	4	22
11. C	14	36	8	6

Luchins, *Psychology Monographs*, 1942, 54:1, 248.

is emptied from the 29-unit jar three times, leaving 20 units in the larger jar. The second problem was written on the board and the subjects given 2½ minutes to solve it, whereupon this was also demonstrated: the 21-unit jar is emptied from the 127-unit one (leaving 106 units) and then the smallest 3-unit jar is emptied twice, leaving the required amount. Then the remaining problems were presented in order with no further instructions. It will be noted that problems 1 through 6 (the *Einstellung* or 'set' problems) are all solvable by the same method, filling the largest container and successively subtracting the smaller ones. Problems 7, 8, 10, and 11 (the *Critical* problems) can be solved in the 'set' way if the subject is persistent in repetitive subtracting, but they can be solved much more rapidly by manipulating only the two smaller jars; problem 9 can only be solved by the direct use of the two smaller jars. Luchins's general question is, Does the successful use of-a given method serve to fixate the subject and blind him to other possible approaches?

The answer to this question was obviously affirmative. Even a group of graduate students and college instructors kept plodding mechanically through problems 7 and 8—without a single exception—and when shown the direct method at the conclusion of the experiment, exclaimed, 'How stupid of me!' and the like. As a procedural variation, some subjects were taken aside and told to write the words 'Don't be blind!' on their papers immediately after finishing problem #6; this increased the number of 'intelligent' solutions of problems 7 and 8. An interesting exception to these results occurred in the younger public school children. Here the 'Don't be blind!' instructions were ineffective, apparently because typical school procedures had led them to do as they were taught, blindly; when asked what 'Don't be blind!' meant, some of the children gave such answers as 'Just do what you did before' or 'Don't be blind to the rule which solves all the problems'!

These experiments have greater practical than theoretical relevance. While the gestalt worker points to the rigidity of organization established by rote, mechanical practice, the behaviorist invokes the concept of the 'habit-family hierarchy,' the mechanical method being strengthened by a series of successes with it and hence persisting as the strongest habit within the hierarchy. Luchins tried a number of variations in procedure the results of which also fit either theory. For example, (a) when problems solvable by several methods were inserted before the fixation E tasks, no great improvement on the critical tasks was found—the final mechanical successes serve to produce a rigid organization or elevate that method in the hierarchy. (b) On the other hand, when E problems and problems unsolvable by this method (such as #9) are alternated preceding the critical tests, little evidence of fixation appeared; this could mean a flexible orientation to the problem situation or that alternative sequences in the habit-family hierarchy were of roughly equal strength. (c) When subjects were forced to work with a short time limit, i.e. under pressure, the degree of fixation or mechanization increased in every case. Rather than surveying each problem first, subjects immediately initiated the 'set' sequence of subtractions, literally an automatic skill sequence even though not the most effective one in this case.

Practical Suggestions for Effective Problem-solving

Regardless of the theoretical position one happens to favor—and the evidence certainly suggests that differences here are largely terminological—several practical suggestions toward more effective human thinking are embodied in this chapter. (1) *Moderate motivation.* Extreme motivation or emotional involvement in a problem situation clearly hinders productive thinking, this having been shown for both animals and man. It is probably best to drop a problem temporarily and return to it when in a calmer state. On the other hand, motivation must be sufficient or no persistence is shown.

(2) *Vary 'position' in the field.* The probability of getting a hunch is greater if the person moves about (in a spatial problem) or 'looks at it from different angles' (in nonspatial problems). This is presumably because a wider range of aspects of the problem are encountered in this manner. In the verbal problems that typically confront the human individual, this probably comes down to trying out various hypotheses—does it have something to do with the air supply? with the shape of the parts? with the kind of material . . . ? (3) *Active manipulation.* This is, of course, similar to the preceding point, but here we refer more specifically to producing planned changes in the situation. Maier's subjects could have given themselves the 'hint' by manipulating the strings; solution of Duncker's tumor problem might have been aided by drawing diagrams. (4) *Shift functional properties (meanings) of objects.* This is much more easily stated than executed. Perhaps it is best accomplished by verbalizing the characteristics of the needed object (word, plan, act, etc.) and then evaluating the environment in these terms. Being locked out of my car but seeing a small opening in one window, I say, 'I need something long and flexible, with a hook of some kind on the end . . . coat hanger? . . . belt? . . .' Shifting the functional values of abstract notions is a much more difficult process, yet this was probably essential to Einstein's thinking out the problem of relativity (see Wertheimer, 1945). (5) *Avoid fixation.* This again is easily offered advice, but hard to follow. Presumably we could, when blocked in solving a problem, stimulate ourselves with 'Don't be blind!' Here too, leaving the problem temporarily is a practical suggestion.

But how do we *train* young people to think productively, to be flexible in their approach rather than blindly mechanical? This is a practical educational problem of the highest order, yet psychologists so far have little to offer. For one thing, we need a criterion of productive thinking; perhaps a graduated scale of problems of the sort developed by Wertheimer and Duncker and others could be devised and the effectiveness of training techniques evaluated against it. There is no question but that the various practical suggestions arising in this chapter and listed above would be among the aims of such training and should serve as general principles to guide the thinker, but just how one trains a child to 'shift the function values of objects' or 'avoid fixation' is something else again. Perhaps deliberate training with multifunctional objects, such as a cube and a flexible wire, would help. Perhaps children who grow up in families where there are frequent, facile plays-on-words are being better trained to think productively. And here we are, back at the core of a classic psychological problem—transfer of training—for of what avail is such training in productive thinking if it is specific to the training materials?

Chapter 15

THINKING

What is the nature of thought? In the preceding chapter we studied many of the conditions that surround productive thinking by humans as it relates to the solving of problems, but little was uncovered concerning the fundamental nature of the thought process itself. The term 'thought,' as it is used in everyday language, connotes vague, immaterial stuff, activity that takes place in the brain but is not strictly part of it. It falls in the same category as ideas and images, mentalistic constructs that Watson, as an early and forceful behaviorist, ejected from psychological science as 'ghosts.' Although we cannot deny that some processes warranting these labels exist, we must follow Watson in denying that they partake of something other than the material world. Otherwise we should be unable to investigate them at all with scientific methods.

The major difficulty here is the lack of adequate techniques of observation. Thoughts, ideas, and images are, more or less by definition, implicit activities and as such not directly observable. How can the presence or nature of an idea be measured? Of a thought? If a person pauses before answering a question, we may say he is giving a 'thoughtful answer.' Similarly, the chimpanzee pauses and appears to survey the problem-field, and we may infer that he is also thinking. If the student in his seat nods sagely from time to time, or better, shakes his head and frowns occasionally, the naïve professor may attribute productive thought to him. Are there not any *direct* measures? Every year or so an article appears in the national press stating that 'Scientists Read Minds with Brain Waves.' The electroencephalogram is, to be sure, a record of changes in electrical potentials in the brain. Gross distortions in the rhythm of waves or their form may indicate epilepsy, the locus of distortions may isolate a brain tumor, and other relations are constantly being discovered. But to use electroencephalography as a fine index of the nature of thoughts, as a means of discriminating the qualities of images and meanings, would be like trying to measure the sharpness of razor blades with a yardstick.

What techniques have been brought to bear on this problem? The method having historical primacy—and still serving as the ultimate criterion of the presence and nature of thought—is *introspection*. The human subject reports, as best he can within his limited language system, what seems to be going on during the thinking process. Another group of techniques employs *animal subjects*. If it be accepted that animals think and have ideas, then one is able to perform many precise experimental operations not permissible with humans. Finally, we will consider in detail the implications of experiments recording *peripheral motor activity* in human subjects during thinking and imagining, for these studies bear directly upon the major theoretical controversy in this area. And what is this controversy? Many investigators believe that thought is a purely central process, involving complex interactions in an admittedly complex brain. This is known as the *central theory*. Other investigators believe thinking is nothing more than minimal responses in the peripheral effectors, the brain for all its complexity serving only as a relay station. This is the *peripheral* (motor) *theory*. Although the evidence will not allow any final decisions, careful study of these two theories will prove a profitable exercise in the nature of scientific thinking.

THE INTROSPECTIVE METHOD

Let us first 'look into our own minds,' a method for investigating the nature of thought that is immediately available to everyone. We all indulge in introspection regularly, and certainly most of the creative inspirations and hunches of the rigorous experimentalist, who often shuns this method formally, have their origin here. Settling off to sleep, I suddenly find myself thinking that my cleaning bill is due. Where did that come from? I trace it back: bill . . . money . . . brown pocketbook (image) . . . leather . . . skin . . . cow (image) . . . chewing on grass . . . BLANK. Whence 'chewing on grass'? This idea seems to have appeared without antecedent, full-blown like Athena from the forehead of Zeus; yet if we hold to a deterministic position, *some* causal precedent must have eventuated in 'chewing on grass'—which serves to illustrate one of the difficulties with this method. But what inferences can be drawn from such casual introspections as these? For one thing, we observe *associations,* series of relatively unitary thoughts that appear as if strung beadlike through time. More penetrating analysis of introspective samples would reveal certain laws which these associations seem to follow. A basic principle of *contiguity* appears to tie associations together, 'skin' arising quite reasonably from 'cow' and 'pocketbook' from 'leather.' *Similarity* plays a role, 'sun' often leading to 'star' or to 'light,' as does *contrast,* for example, 'black' strongly beckoning to 'white.' For many of us, the thought process would appear as chains of *images* rather than of 'pure' verbal thoughts, the sensory quality of this imagery varying from person to person. All of these superficial characteristics of thinking had been observed by Aristotle certainly, and probably, in pensive moments, by the shaggy cave dweller as well.

But scientific utilization of this method is another matter entirely. Psychology developed as that facet of philosophy devoted to the study of the mind, and its constructs were therefore the elements of mind—sensations, images, feelings, and ideas. Philosophical dualism is implicit in this approach, of course, the physiologist being expected to deal with the material body and the psychologist being expected to tout in the mental arena. But psychologists differed among themselves as to how the mental sphere should be analyzed. Were all images and ideas and feelings reducible to elementary sensations as the fundamental building blocks? Can ideas exist independent of imagery? How many dimensions of feeling are there? Ordinary self-observation was clearly not equal to this analytic task. It required carefully trained introspectionists, carefully trained to give purely descriptive accounts of momentary sensations, carefully trained to avoid what Titchener called 'the stimulus error' (confounding the objects thought about with the sensory content itself).

Certain primitive assumptions underlie this approach just as other primitive assumptions underlie present-day approaches. It was necessarily assumed that language is a faithful mirror of conscious experience, for the sum total of raw data for psychological science became the words produced by self-observers. It was also assumed that the human mind is essentially the same from individual to individual, for a few highly trained introspectionists were the only subjects. Man was looked upon as a purely rational animal; all the processes that make up mind must be available to conscious self-observation or the method is inadequate. These and other assumptions predicate the introspective method, and many of them would be seriously questioned today.

The Role of Imagery in Thought

The Greek philosophers had a great deal to say about images and ideas. In fact, they used the two terms more or less interchangeably. Plato, for example, argued that since an image looks just like the original object, but is smaller since it resides within the head, it must be a tiny replica of the original that enters the head through the eyes. Puerile as this notion may seem today, it must be remembered that the Greeks knew little about the nervous system. The organism was dealt with as a sort of hollow shell, with a few assorted fluids like black bile, blood, and phlegm included, to be sure—and this despite the fact that men spilled their brains much as they do today. The Greeks were never strong on empiricism. But isn't there a real problem here? An image is a pattern of activity in nerve fibers.—How can it 'look just like' an object? This problem is actually more apparent than real. What, after all, is the original *perception* of an object but a pattern of activity in nerve fibers? The fact that one nervous process 'looks just like' another is not quite so surprising.

As a matter of fact, images are seldom exact duplicates of original impressions. What appears to be a perfectly recalled image proves, upon careful analysis, to be lacking in detail. Images are also reported as being less clear and less stable as well as less saturated than perceptions. The image of a brilliant sunset is a rather jaded affair in comparison with its origin; the exact locations of farmhouses and stone walls on a New England hillside, as recalled, are usually not very clear. The major variable along which perceptions and various types of images range, however, seems to be that of *intensity*. This was brought out neatly in an experiment by Perky (1910). Subjects were asked to imagine seeing a banana, for example, against a screen in the laboratory while, unknown to the subject, an assistant projected the actual picture of one faintly on the same spot. Without exception, 27 adults mistook the picture for their own imaginal production. Although the projection was actually very faint (in terms of the normal intensity of perceived objects), it was judged to be a very strong, clear image. On the other hand, while under anesthetic, in a state of delirium or under the influence of certain drugs, images may become so intense as to rival perceptions. The hallucinations of the alcoholic are reacted to as real, and the colored parrots or circus clowns that parade through a nightmare are only too vivid. The effects of a Mexican drug, mescal, are especially interesting in that it seems to intensify visual imagery per se (Klüver, 1926). Karwoski (1936) tried to determine whether the absolute thresholds for visual hue and brightness were affected by mescal; unfortunately, the same intoxicating effect that enhanced visual imagery also incapacitated the observer, as far as the accuracy of the psychophysical measurements was concerned. He was chiefly occupied with a private visual revelry that obscured the experimental test patches! Little if anything is known in regard to how toxic conditions and certain drugs can intensify those neural processes that subserve imagery.

Some individuals, particularly young children, possess what is known as *eidetic imagery*. If the child is shown a picture for a few moments and then looks at a gray surface, a memory image is projected so clearly that he can literally count the number of spokes on a wheel or even read forward or backward the letters in an unfamiliar word. These eidetic images are not ordinary visual after-images; the child freely moves his eyes about exploring the object during the original impression rather than rigidly fixing a given point. One especially interesting characteristic of the eidetic image is that the individual appears able at will to focus upon any detail and make it gradually become clearer, the rest of the picture remaining obscure (Klüver, 1930). Another point worth noting, which relates this form of imagery to ego-involvement and other personality factors, is that the probability of the child's producing an eidetic image seems to depend upon the degree of interest in the picture (Allport, 1924). Despite the amount of work that has been done on the problem, however (see Jaensch, 1930, and Klüver, 1932, for reviews), the basic nature of eidetic imagery is unknown.

There are marked *individual differences in imagery*. People differ in both the general vividness of their imagery and the modality in which they are most proficient. Beethoven was able to create magnificent symphonic works after he had gone deaf, relying on the richness of his auditory imagery. The writings of Emile Zola are pregnant with olfactory imagery which he enjoyed to the fullest extent. Even psychologists vary among themselves in the form of imagery most vividly experienced, and these differences have helped mold their theories on the matter. Stricker (1880), for example, relied heavily upon kinesthetic imagery himself and assumed that this was true of all people. He was unable to imagine words like 'bubble' and 'mutter' while he held his mouth open; unfortunately for his theory, most other psychologists could. Galton (1883), a psychologist with clear visual imagery, was astonished to discover that many scientists seemed to have no visual imagery at all. In attempting to explain how his men of science could have ideas without visual images, Galton anticipated the motor theory of thought, saying that 'the missing faculty seems to be replaced so serviceably by other modes of conception, chiefly, I believe, connected with the incipient motor sense, not of the eyeballs only but of the muscles generally. . .'

Since Galton's time a number of objective studies of imagery have been undertaken, most of them designed to segregate people into imagery 'types' (cf. Woodworth, 1938, pp. 41-4). (a) *Association method*. Subjects are asked to name as many objects as they can having characteristic colors, producing characteristic sounds, and so on, in a limited amount of time. (b) *Learning method*. Subjects learn material presented either orally or visually, the assumption being that one's type of imagery will determine the ease with which learning proceeds under each type of presentation. (c) *Distraction method*. While learning a set of materials, the subject is distracted by auditory stimuli in some cases, visual stimuli in others, and by having to hold his tongue between his teeth in yet others, the assumption being that if he is utilizing a given type of imagery in learning, he will suffer more from distractions within the same modality. The entire proposition that there are distinct 'types' of people emphasizing one form of imagery at the expense of other forms is rendered most dubious by results obtained by Betts (1909). Extending Galton's type of questionnaire to include other forms of imagery, ratings of vividness for the various modalities were found to be highly intercorrelated, a subject expressing vivid visual imagery generally claiming vivid olfactory and auditory imagery as well. A type theory would demand that visualizers be relatively poor in other modalities. One doubts, however, the validity of this questionnaire method.

Synesthetic Thinking

A complex and highly rational form of imagery appears in *synesthesia,* defined by Warren in his *Dictionary of Psychology* as 'a phenomenon characterizing the experiences of certain individuals, in which certain sensations belonging to one sense or mode attach to certain sensations of another group and appear regularly whenever a stimulus of the latter type occurs.' This definition implies a sort of 'sensory short circuiting' present in only a few abnormal people, and this proves to be an inadequate view. The classic studies in this area (see monograph by Karwoski and Odbert, 1938, for review) gave credence to this point of view by reporting occasional 'freak' cases. Here was a girl who associates colors with the notes of bird calls; another subject reports pressure sensations about the teeth and cheeks whenever cold spots on his arm are stimulated (Dallenbach, 1926); a girl associates certain specific colors with specific notes on the musical scale, two tests of her chromesthesia seven and one-half years apart showing nearly perfect consistency (Langfeld, 1914). Such rigidity in associations across modalities suggested a neurophysiological basis for the phenomenon. But here is a man who imagines number 1 as yellow, 2 as blue, 3 as red, 4 as purple, 5 as orange . . . and of course 8 as black; anyone who has played pool will recognize these colors as those on billiard balls having these numbers—what modalities are crossed here? A little girl recalls her friends as having pink faces and her enemies as having purple faces—what modalities are crossed here?

Recent studies of synesthesia by Karwoski and Odbert (1938) clearly relate the phenomenon to *meaning* and thus to thinking in general. Various experiential continua are made parallel and translations are made from one to the other, as synesthetic associations or language metaphors. Thus, fast, exciting music may be pictured by the synesthete as sharply etched, bright red forms, whereas his less imaginative brother merely agrees that terms like 'red-hot,' 'bright,' 'fiery,' as verbal metaphors, adequately describe the music. Conversely, a slow, melancholic selection is visualized as heavy, slow-moving 'blobs' of somber hue and is adequately described in metaphor as 'heavy,' 'blue,' and 'dark.' A happy man is said to feel 'high,' a sad man feels 'low'; the pianist travels 'up' and 'down' the scale from treble to bass; souls travel 'up' to the good place and 'down' to the bad place; hope is 'white' and despair is 'black.'

Rather than being a rare phenomenon, Karwoski and Odbert found that as many as 13 per cent of Dartmouth College students regularly indulged in color-music synesthesia, often as a means of enriching their enjoyment of classical music. Although these subjects, called *photistic visualizers,* differed from one another in the general mode of their translation from sound to vision and were individually consistent in their mode, they were found quite flexible in the specific associations made. A given note in isolation might be reported as a 'teardrop of blue-violet,' whereas it might become a 'bright exploding star' when imbedded within a spritely musical context. Some visualizers typically imagined the whole visual field as being uniformly colored, hues verging into one another as the mood of the music changed. Others reported multiplex bands of color that kept moving across the field as the music progressed, the timbre of instruments often being reflected in the color of various horizontal layers of the band. Certain consistent relations were found in most subjects: fast music generated sharp and angular figures, but slow music produced large, rounded ones; joyous music was typically bright in color, but sad music was dark; treble notes were usually light in color and small in size, bass notes were larger and darker. One interesting subject regularly created meaningful scenes to go with the musical selections—a rolling and descending phrase in the reeds might be pictured as a herd of wild ponies charging down over a rolling slope—yet, aside from the fact that his photisms were always meaningful rather than abstract, he displayed the same general relations between musical qualities and the forms and colors he employed as did the other subjects. Many of these complex visualizers could pin down their first synesthetic experience, often a somewhat traumatic experience in childhood, such as seeing a loud brass band at the circus as a shimmering yellow. Some could recall a gradual process of elaboration and systematization in the development of their modes of translation. These synesthetic experiences, although internally consistent, were in no sense rigidly automatic; they could be produced if desired and avoided when the subject was otherwise occupied.

Responses to complex selections of music are themselves too complex for analysis of the specific relations between auditory-mood variables and color-form responses. In a later experiment (Karwoski, Odbert, and Osgood, 1942) simple melodic lines recorded by a single instrument (clarinet) served as the stimuli. Subjects in the first part of the study were typical photistic visualizers and they drew their photisms after hearing each short selection in a darkened room. The simplest stimulus was the combination of crescendo and diminuendo on a single note—the sound merely grew louder and then faded away. A sample of responses made to this simple auditory stimulus is shown in Fig. 204. Subject *a* indicates loudness by making the center of his line *heavier;* subject *b* represents loudness by increasing *vibra-*

tion in the center. Subjects *e, f,* and *g* parallel loudness with the *thickness* of a solid form, and subject *j* shows relaxed dispersion for softness and concentrated *focusing* for loudness. Subject *i* represents variations in loudness by means of a little car that travels rapidly toward his eyes and then away again as the tone dies away. These are functionally or meaningfully *equivalent responses* to the same auditory stimulation.

Are these photistic visualizers exercising a 'rare' capacity, or are they merely expressing overtly modes of translation that are implicit in the language of our culture? Subsequent portions of this study produced evidence

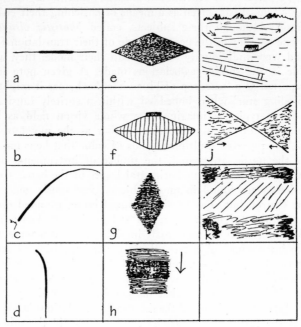

FIGURE 204. Drawings by photistic visualizers to represent a clarinet tone that grows louder and then softer, i.e. crescendo and diminuendo. Karwoski, Odbert, and Osgood, *Journal of General Psychology,* 1942, 26: 202.

favoring the latter view. A second group of subjects, who had never even thought of 'seeing things' when they heard music, were played the same simple melodic lines and instructed to 'force themselves to draw something to represent what they heard.' They produced the same types of forms as the photistic visualizers and in approximately the same relative frequencies. A group of 100 unselected students was given a *meaning-polarity test,* each item of which appeared in the following form: LARGE–small; SOFT–LOUD, with instructions to circle the word of the second pair that 'seems most clearly related' to the capitalized word of the first pair. Here again, on a purely verbal level, the same relations between music-mood and color-form variables discovered among sensitive synesthetes were linked meaningfully on the polarity test. For example, LARGE was linked to LOUD by 92 per cent of these subjects, NEAR with FAST by 86 per cent, BRIGHT with HAPPY by 96 per cent, and TREBLE with UP by 98 per cent. These results suggest that synesthetes, in developing their own systematic translation systems, draw heavily upon the meaningful relations among descriptive qualities that already exist as verbal metaphors in their culture.

Further evidence substantiating the same conclusion was found in a third study in this series (Odbert, Karwoski, and Eckerson, 1942) in which the interrelationships among music, color, and mood were studied. A group of 243 college students first listened to ten short excerpts from classical scores and indicated the dominant mood of each selection by checking one

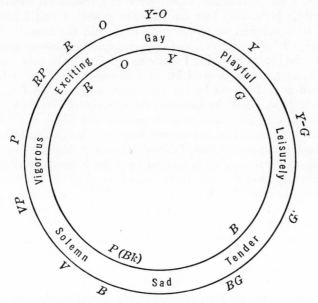

FIGURE 205. Relation of color to mood in testing the effects of theatrical stage-lighting gelatins (*inner letters*—Ross, 1938) and in response to musical selections (*outer letters*). Odbert, Karwoski, and Eckerson, *Journal of General Psychology*, 1942, 26:170.

of eight groups of descriptive adjectives arranged in a *mood circle,* devised earlier by Hevner (1936). The outline of this mood circle is shown in Fig. 205. Upon hearing the same selections again, the subjects stated what colors they associated with each musical excerpt and specified the vividness of their color experience. As shown by the position of the letters *inside* the mood circle, color associations made to classical music tended to follow the mood created. A portion of Delius's 'On Hearing the First Cuckoo in Spring' was judged leisurely in mood and preponderantly green in color; a portion of Wagner's *Rienzi Overture* was judged exciting or vigorous in mood and preponderantly red in color. When another group of 105 subjects was merely shown the groups of mood adjectives and asked to indicate which color best suited each mood group (with no musical stimulation whatever), even *more* consistent relations were obtained, suggesting that the unique characteristics of the music had, if anything, confused the purely verbal or metaphorical relations between color and mood. The color letters *outside* the circle describe results obtained by Ross (1938) on the relation between colors used in stage lighting and the reported moods produced in subjects, a close parallel with the present study being shown.

The Imageless Thought Controversy

Is the sensory, imaginal aspect of synesthesia separable from its meaningful aspects? Can thought occur without the presence in consciousness of sensations, images, or feelings? Can one think 'in the abstract,' or does all such activity involve concrete, particular sensory content? In 1710 Berkeley had said, 'Whether others have this wonderful faculty of abstracting their ideas, they best can tell. For myself, I find I have indeed a faculty of imagining, or representing to myself, the idea of those *particular* things I have perceived, and of variously compounding and dividing them . . . the idea of man that I frame to myself must be either of a white, or a black, or a tawny, a straight, or a crooked, a tall, or a low, or a middle-sized man. I cannot by any effort of thought conceive the *abstract* idea.' About 1900, when the imageless thought controversy took shape, the general thesis was the same, that all images and ideas and feeling are compounds of elemental sensations and hence no thought could be present without such conscious content. Galton's discovery that the vast majority of scientific thinkers apparently had no need for images started this theoretical structure shaking, and the experiments of the Würzburg School of psychologists created a major rift. Of all the problems attacked by the introspective method, this controversy over the existence of imageless thought bears most closely on the fundamental nature of thinking.

The so-called 'thought experiments' were rather simple affairs considering the theoretical weight they bore. A subject was asked to perform a brief mental task and then immediately to introspect on his states of consciousness during that period. Following the usual criteria of introspection, the subject was a completely passive observer, describing his experiences in detail (that often required many minutes for a few seconds' experience) and leaving all inferences to the experimenter. These introspections included a share of sensations, images, and feelings, but—and this was the crucial issue—much conscious content was reported as entirely 'empty' imageless thought. In reaching an understanding of a paradoxical aphorism, such as 'One must be both pitiful and cruel in order really to be either,' for example, the subject might experience a brief period of 'nil' followed by a sudden, complete flash of understanding, *after which* the verbal explanation unfolded (Bühler, 1907; after Woodworth, 1938). Titchener (1909) criticized these experiments because although the observers were supposed to describe merely their conscious experience, here they often allowed meanings to creep into their reports, stating that they thought *about* this or that.

At this point in the controversy it will be well to insert a reanalysis of the nature of the problem. Is the question whether or not thought can occur without *any* sensory content? If so, it comes down to whether awareness must be sensory in nature, for we are aware of thoughts. Woodworth, for example, says, 'If meanings are ruled out as non-existent and non-occurrent, then no imageless thoughts will be found, for the imageless thoughts are simply the meanings which Os report with such ease and certainty' (1938, p. 788). *But just what is the nature of meaning?* This, perhaps, is the real problem. Do meanings, attitudes, 'sets,' and the like have sensory content and, if so, what is its nature? What the experiments on 'imageless thought' really demonstrate is that thought can proceed simply as a sequence of meanings, bereft of identifiable images or silent speech.

When all other content was avoided but meaningful thought was still present in consciousness, what sensory experience could the acute observer report? The answer most often given in introspective studies on the problem was *kinesthetic sensations*. Comstock (1921) reported organic and kinesthetic sensations as present in so-called imageless thought; Marbe (1901) and others, in studying the process of judgment, had come across conscious states difficult to reduce to accepted categories of experience, but readily labeled 'hesitation,' 'expectancy,' and the like. Washburn (1916) incorporated these conscious attitudes into her general motor theory as being based on kinesthetic sensations, the feeling of 'hesitation,' for example, being the kinesthetic input resulting from simultaneous but antagonistic reaction tendencies. Clark (1911) and Crosland (1921) both reported introspective studies yielding evidence for kinesthetic sensations during thought.

And this is about as far as the introspective method will go. The human self-observer, when pushed to the limits of critical analysis, reports vague muscular and organic tensions as being present during thought. Do these sensations constitute thought itself, or are they merely a background of bodily tonus? Why are we ordinarily unaware of the muscular quality of thought if that is its nature? These questions are not answerable by the introspective method. Of course, we are not ordinarily aware of muscular sensations while executing a skilled act. When tying a shoe or dealing a pack of cards, we are mainly aware of the external effects of the activity, not of the internal proprioceptive effects. Similarly, assuming this view of thought to be valid, we are aware of attitudes and ideas as 'mental' acts, not as patterns of kinesthetic sensations. Only the highly trained self-observer, practiced in paying precise attention to *sensory* events, can detect the kinesthetic quality of thought, if indeed it has that quality.

Critique on the Introspective Technique

Although the introspective method is the only feasible one for a psychology founded on mentalistic constructs, it presents several serious defects from the point of view of science. (1) *The data it yields are patently unverifiable.* Boring (1946) reports a humorous illustration of this: '. . . there is always to be remembered that famous session of the Society of Experimental Psychologists in which Titchener, after a hot debate with Holt, exclaimed: "You can see that green is neither yellowish nor bluish!" And Holt replied: "On the contrary, it is obvious that a green is that yellow-blue which is just exactly as blue as it is yellow." That impasse was an ominous portent of the fate of introspection. When two distinguished experts could disagree vis-à-vis about so basic a matter as the nature of hue, some other method of approach was needed' (p. 176). (2) *Many relevant data are unavailable to the method.* Many of the important events determining the course of behavior and thought are not conscious, yet the introspective method can handle only conscious materials. Freud's contributions, stressing the unconscious determinants of action, make this clear. (3) *Language is not a mirror of thought.* Language is only as fine a tool as the discriminations it contains; it can only report observations that have previously been made by members of the culture and formulated in words. Thus we find the introspective method giving rise to a science of verbal metaphor. Pleasantness is sensed as X sensations and called *'bright pressure'*; unpleasantness is sensed as Y sensations and called *'dull pressure.'* (4) *Only the effects of thought, not the process itelf, can be oberved.* A man cannot lift himself up by his own bootstraps; neither can he observe that which is doing the observing. The brain is remarkably free of receptors. What is observed are the *effects* of thought, not the thought process itself. A young philosopher, after considerable pondering upon this problem of 'observing what is doing the observing,' once asked what it would be like if one were to watch his own brain in action via a system of mirrors, the skull being removed. Certainly one would not see words or pictures written on the surface of the gray matter!

MOTOR ACTIVITY DURING THOUGHT IN HUMAN SUBJECTS

Experimentalists picked up the problem at precisely the point at which the introspectionists had per force dropped it—was it possible that sensitive apparatus could record these minimal motor activities that eluded conscious analysis? It was Watson, in *Behavior: An Introduction to Comparative Psychology* (1914), who first made a comprehensive defense of the thesis that thoughts, ideas, and images are merely implicit verbal responses. As the most vigorous sponsor of a nascent behaviorism, he was crusading against mentalism in psychology, and such concepts as 'thought' and 'image' are certainly mentalistic in connotation. This materialistic position was not original with Watson; many thinkers before him had stated its essence. Bain, for example, had said, 'Thinking is restrained speaking and acting.' But Watson's statements were made at a time when experimental psychology was taking root, and the proposition—*thought is implicit speech*—was an open invitation to the gadgeteer.

Most of the early experimental work on the problem may be criticized on several grounds. For one thing, it was often naïvely assumed that 'thought movements' had to be localized in the vocal apparatus itself—a literal interpretation of Watson's dictum. Experiments yielding *positive* results often based this conclusion on the gross occurrence of any type of movement of the complex vocal apparatus during directed thinking activity. They did not take into account the possibilities of suggestion or annoyance arising from the presence of grotesque instruments in their subjects' mouths—one experimenter had subjects read poetry silently while their tongues were stuck into flattened glass cups! Investigations yielding *negative* results often based this conclusion upon evidence obtained with insensitive apparatus, whereas the proposition demands maximum sensitivity in recording.

One of the more carefully planned and executed investigations will serve as an illustration of early approaches to this problem. Thorson (1925) used an elaborate system of levers to transfer the movements of a small metal suction cup, attached to the tongue, to a recording surface, smoked paper on a revolving kymograph. This apparatus magnified tongue movements about three and one-half times and recorded both vertical and horizontal movement simultaneously. Subjects both spoke certain test words softly and merely thought them, the problem being to determine whether any similarity existed between the overt responses and those occurring during equivalent thought. No observable correlation was found. Is there any necessary reason to expect one? The hypothesis does not require that movements made in thought must be little *replicas* of overt speech movements. Thorson also tried to test the proposal that implicit thought may be 'shifted over' to alternative muscle systems. She had some subjects think 'experimental psychology' (!) over and over while both holding a sung note and tapping with the fingers. The idea was to 'drive' the representing process into the tongue by eliminating other systems, but there was no increase in the similarity of tongue-movement patterns to those made in overt speech.

The Electrical Recording of Motor Nerve Potentials

Electrodes placed near the motor end plates of efferent fibers can pick up minute changes in potential and these will cause deflections in a sensitive string galvanometer. These energy changes can be fed through a vacuum tube amplifier, magnified many thousands of times, and recorded on photographic film. Potential changes as small as one millionth of a volt are recorded in this manner. The independent work of Jacobson (summarized, 1932) and Max (summarized, 1935, 1937) represents a detailed application of this new technique and offers the basic evidence for what has come to be known as the motor theory of consciousness. It is interesting that no further direct research on this problem has appeared in the succeeding decade. Perhaps the new technique served to reveal the true nature of the problem without offering any way of solving it.

Jacobson's earlier work (1929) had demonstrated to his satisfaction a general correlation between motor and mental activity. Through progressive relaxation of the peripheral musculature, all conscious mental processes could be eliminated. In his later electrophysiological studies, Jacobson used subjects who had been trained in progressive relaxation; in this way the 'background level' of motor activity could be minimized and the experimentally induced action given prominence.

The general procedure was to have the relaxed subject do various 'thought' tasks, starting at one click of a telegraph key and stopping at another. When subjects were instructed to *imagine* lifting the right arm, records like those shown in Fig. 206 were obtained. Imagining tasks normally accomplished by flexion of the right arm, such as pulling up one's socks or lifting a cigarette to the lips, also yielded positive records in 97.5 per cent of the cases. When subjects imagined looking up the Eiffel Towel, from base to tip, recordings from eye muscles yielded records correlating well with those made when actually moving the eyes upward. Various repetitive acts, such as hitting a tack with a hammer, were imagined and produced discrete bursts of potential changes. Two such records are shown in Fig. 206. In a check on Thorson's data, electrodes were attached to the tongue and lips while subjects imagined counting, telling the date, and so forth. The records were similar to those obtained for faintly speaking the same materials, in the sense that temporal bursts of activity were correlated but not in terms of a close correspondence in details. Complete introspective reports were kept and, according to the investigator, these made possible both control observations (i.e. recorded periods when the thought process in question was *not* in progress) and accurate localization of the relevant motor activity (i.e. when it did not appear in the expected muscle system). We may observe, therefore, that introspective reports served as the ultimate criterion of the presence and nature of the thought processes being studied.

What controls are needed in this type of experiment? In the first place, it is possible that the potential changes recorded at the periphery merely represent a *general overflow* of motor tension during mental work. To check this Jacobson recorded from the right arm while the subject imagined lifting the *left* arm. These records generally gave no evidence of increased motor potential (Fig. 206, panel #2) indicating that the implicit activity was restricted to the relevant muscle system. A second question relates to the

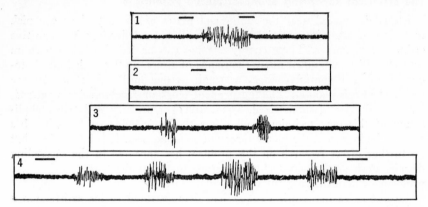

FIGURE 206. Record of motor potentials from biceps in right arm during mental activity: (1) imagining lifting the right arm; (2) imagining lifting the left arm; (3) imagining striking a nail twice with a hammer in right; (4) imagining another rhythmical act. Jacobson, *American Journal of Psychology*, 1932, 44:683.

necessity of the motor activity. Potential changes at the periphery may represent *specific overflow* and not be necessary for thought. In an attempt to check on this possibility Jacobson designed a mechanical lever which would magnify arm movements eightyfold. Imagining lifting a weight with that arm was accompanied by 'microscopic' flexion movements, and Jacobson reports that subjects could not simultaneously imagine this act and remain completely relaxed, as shown by the lever records combined with introspective reports. Of course, 'simultaneity' here rests upon the reliability and validity of the subjects' introspections. Finally, what about the *negative instances?* Occasionally subjects would report 'imagining lifting a cigarette to the lips,' for example, yet no activity would be recorded in the arm. Is this valid evidence against the theory? In the example given, the subject reported having a visual image of the act and, sure enough, when the electrodes were shifted to the eye muscles positive records were obtained. In other words, Jacobson suggests that if a given mental event is not measurable at *a,* it must be happening at *x.* This is a most difficult hypothesis to test.

Max (1935, 1937) instituted a different and very ingenious type of control. He used *deaf-mutes as experimental subjects* and compared them with normal individuals. Since deaf-mutes 'talk' with their fingers, their mental activities should be reflected in more motor activity at this locus than with normal controls. The amplifying and recording apparatus used was essentially similar to Jacobson's. (a) *Sleeping* vs. *dreaming* (1935). Nineteen deaf-mutes were trained to sleep with the electrodes in position. The process of 'falling asleep' was paralleled by a progressive diminution in the amplitude of action potential from the finger muscles, recordable activity disappearing entirely in many cases. During sleep occasional, prolonged bursts of activity (2½ minutes or more in length) occurred. Of 33 instances where deaf-mutes were awaked during such bursts, 30 reported dreams. Of 62 occasions on which these subjects were awaked during quiescent periods, 52 reported they had not been dreaming. On the other hand, of 33 tests made with normal subjects when there was no motor activity in the fingers, 10 reported dreams. (b) *Abstract problems* (1937). Both deaf-mutes and normal subjects were given a variety of problems to solve 'in their heads.' These included arithmetic (multiplying $7 \times 9 \times 3 \times 12$, for example), mentally repeating words, judging the truth or falsity of jumbled sentences, and many items from the standard intelligence tests. Although 84 per cent of the tests on deaf-mutes were positive, only 31 per cent of the tests on normal subjects were positive. The average amplitude of response in positive cases was 3.41 microvolts for the deaf-mutes and only .80 for normals. When problems that lent themselves to kinesthetic representation with the fingers were given (such as imagining holding a live fish or telegraphing an SOS signal), no such extreme differences were found: 88 per cent of the tests with deaf-mutes were positive and 73 per cent were positive with normal controls.

Certain incidental findings are of interest here. Below a certain microvoltage (amplitude), varying with the individual, subjects could report no sensations of feeble muscle contractions even though they were measurably present. Max (1937, p. 307) suggests that this may cut the foundation from the presuppositions underlying the imageless thought controversy —'muscular activity might actually be present throughout a given thought experience without being introspectively detectable.' One wonders, following a motor theory, what the nature of thought might be if such states of awareness are devoid of even kinesthetic sensations. It seems more likely that whatever thought was present during these measurements had its origins in other muscle systems than those under scrutiny and hence was not reported as kinesthetic by the subjects. Finally, correlations between the average microvoltage for individual subjects doing mental problems and their scores on several intelligence tests were all negative, ranging from −.22 to −.92. The consistent negative trend suggests that the more intelligent an individual, the less overt his symbolic processes.

Muscular Tonus and Mental Efficiency

There is another way of looking at the relation between motor activity and thought. Whereas the Jacobson and Max experiments were concerned with the muscular mediation of specific thoughts, ideas, and images, it may be that motor tonus merely serves as a facilitative agent for mental activity in general. This point of view has been most vigorously pressed by G. L. Freeman (cf. 1931, 1933, and 1937). By way of incidental evidence, he observes that motor tension (as measured in his own quadriceps at half-hour intervals) parallels mental efficiency, being lowest at waking, rising rapidly during the early morning, declining again in the afternoon, and reaching a new peak in the evening. To this we may add the common observation that people working under conditions of high motivation show more general bodily tension than when poorly motivated (cf. Leuba, 1930).

There is no lack of experimental evidence for this view. Jacobson and Carlson (1925) found that the knee jerk could be abolished by sufficient relaxation. Freeman himself demonstrated that motor tension increases during the execution of a task and diminishes when it is completed, that motor tension must be higher under fatigue or distraction conditions in order to maintain a normal level of mental work. Considerable attention has been paid to the relation between motor tension and learning. Bills (1927) found that a moderate degree of constant pressure on a hand dynamometer facilitated the learning of lists of nonsense syllables and paired associates. Stroud (1931) obtained similar results for the learning of stylus mazes while holding with one hand a 14-pound weight against a pulley. McTeer (1933) found that increasing rates of learning mirror-tracing, accomplished by giving electric shock for errors, were accompanied by increased tension in the inactive hand. Freeman (1931) had also suggested that tension would become disruptive in its effects upon mental activity if increased beyond a certain point, and this has been verified by an experiment. Courts (1939) induced varying motor tension in his subjects by having them press a hand dynamometer to different fractions of their maximum grip; learning scores for a set of nonsense materials first rose above and then fell below the normal performance level as pressure increased. The evidence is not all positive. Block (1936), for example, made repeated observations on the same subjects, finding little consistency in the degree of tension, if any, that was maximally effective. Zartman and Cason (1934) also obtained inconsistent results.

How does tension in the musculature facilitate mental activity? Freeman (1931, 1933) has offered a feasible mechanism. The cortical centers predominantly involved in mental activity are assumed to have relatively high excitation-thresholds. Irradiation of impulses from the lower centers, especially those involved in muscular contraction, serves to lower the excitation-thresholds of the higher centers, i.e. the steady bombardment of cortical neurons by impulses acts to 'tune up' these higher centers and increase their 'vigilance' (a term originally used by the British neurologist, Henry Head, 1923). Although a certain rate of motor bombardment facilitates response of the cortical neurons to exteroceptive stimulation, a too rapid frequency inhibits response. Lack of motor bombardment (as in deep sleep) permits elevation at cortical thresholds to a point where external stimulation of ordinary intensity cannot elicit any activity. This conception receives support from the study of similar facilitative and inhibitory processes in the retina, which, it will be recalled, functions much like a higher nervous center. Freeman also gives as evidence the reported mental lassitude of patients suffering from cord-transection; in these cases cortical stimulation from the proprioceptive system is greatly reduced. In an interesting experiment by M. Miller (1926), whose subjects reacted to electrical shock during extreme muscular relaxation as compared with a normal state of motor readiness, both the amplitude and speed of reaction were markedly reduced by muscular relaxation *and the subjects reported an apparent diminution in the intensity of the shock sensation.* In other words, an external stimulus of constant objective intensity varies in subjective intensity with the degree of cortical 'vigilance.' One is reminded of the 'far away' quality of external events while in that drowsy state between sleep and full wakefulness.

There is much to be said in favor of this motor-facilitation hypothesis and little in the way of contrary experimental evidence. There are, however, certain methodological or logical difficulties which the theory faces. In the first place, none of the casual or experimental observations on the relation between motor tension and mental efficiency specify the causal sequence. Does reduction in muscular tension *cause* a relaxation in mental 'vigilance' (as the theory supposes), or does a relaxation in mental 'vigilance' cause reduction in motor tension? Much of the evidence merely demonstrates a parallelism between two measures of human activity. The term 'mental efficiency' itself is a very loosely defined notion as it is used in this context; it sometimes refers to 'responsiveness to external stimulation,' sometimes to 'degree of wakefulness,' and sometimes to 'effectiveness in learning.' The theory assumes that all these things reflect a general 'mental efficiency,' which is defined in terms of the (unobservable) excitation-threshold of cortical neurons. With regard to the central-peripheral controversy, this motor-facilitation hypothesis is actually noncommittal: the playback from muscle systems could have the *general* function of facilitating all cortical activities and the *specific* function of mediating distinctive symbolic processes.

An Evaluation of Central vs. Peripheral Theories

Nearly all psychologists today would agree that mediation processes are necessary for thinking, reasoning, imagining, and the like; the disagreement lies in the postulated *locus* of these intervening activities. Behavioristically inclined theorists generally favor a peripheral locus. Nurtured on an *S–R* diet, it is satisfying for them to describe mediation as an implicit *response* which yields a distinctive cue. Most others, including field theorists and laymen, favor a central theory—field theorists are accustomed to speaking in terms of cortical interactions and the layman considers the brain to be the seat of the mind. Although the fundamental philosophical question of materialism may divide people on this problem, it is actually not relevant. A vigorous materialist could support either the peripheral or the central position; both conceive of material nerve fibers in action. The real issue is the locus of the critical nervous activity, and the chief difficulty has lain in assembling crucial evidence.

According to *the peripheral theory,* the initiating stimulus, whether external or internal, evokes certain implicit responses within the organism, these responses producing distinctive patterns of stimulation. This (proprioceptive) stimulation arises to the sensory cortex. And what is the role of the brain in the peripheral theory? It has two functions: first, it serves as a *relay station,* transmitting impulses from receptors to effectors and from movement-produced reception to yet other effectors; second, the sensory cortex is the *locus of awareness* of thought, the patterns of proprioceptive and other sensations arising from implicit responses constituting the momentary states of awareness. Thought is thus conceived to be just as much a behavioral matter as running a maze, the difference being only the degree of skeletal involvement. We observe that although the locus of awareness of thought is central, necessary conditions for thought are peripheral.

According to *the central theory,* all interactions necessary and sufficient for thought occur in the brain; incoming patterns of stimulation are routed to (or change the total pattern of activity in) other central areas, giving rise to ideas, images, and the like. But beyond this gross, affirmative statement, there is nothing more the central theory can accomplish. This is not to be construed as a criticism of the theory itself but rather as a judgment of the present status of our knowledge about cortical mechanisms. Although the architecture of the brain is certainly adequate for complex interactions, neurophysiologists can tell us little in detail about what goes on here. Everything is feasible; little is precisely measurable.

Given our limitations of technique, the central theory cannot be tested. On the other hand, the peripheral theory does give rise to some potentially testable hypotheses. We have, then, two competing theories and only one of them is testable. What is the only scientific procedure in such a case? Since scientific methods cannot prove a theory to be correct, we cannot rule out the central theory by validating peripheral implications. *The only possible procedure is to render the testable (peripheral) theory untenable.* If this were done, the central theory would remain the only tenable contemporary position—by default. But this has not been done; if anything, the available evidence has strengthened the peripheral position, without, of course, being able to prove it. When introspectionists are pushed to the limits of their self-observation, they find vague kinesthetic sensations. There is a generally consistent correlation between introspectively indexed mental activity and electrically indexed motor nerve activity.

But is motor feedback *sufficient?* An oft-heard criticism is that it cannot explain non-motor imagery. How can one have a *motor* image of white sails in the sunset? We recall that Perky's (1910) subjects confused faint projections of an object with their image of it, which certainly makes it appear that the neural processes underlying both experiences are very similar. Is motor feedback *necessary?* Can thought occur without muscular activity? Jacobson's report—that his subjects could not simultaneously maintain relaxation and imagine lifting their arms—rests upon the validity of introspective judgments, but this does not exhaust the possible sources of evidence. Could we create predictable 'thoughts' in relaxed subjects by electrically stimulating their motor nerves (running the theory backward, so to speak)? If a subject is forced to *imagine* lifting his arm over and over again, will motor and imaginal components 'extinguish' together? Can one imagine complex manipulations with an arm or leg that has 'gone to sleep'? I have tried this little experiment, but find it difficult to differentiate between 'thought' about movements and visual representations of movement. These read like questions from another era, but perhaps we should reconsider them.

On the basis of the available evidence one may take an extreme peripheral position, but in this case the complex interactions of which the brain is capable are not fully utilized. If, on the other hand, one takes the extreme central position, he should wonder at the uneconomical overflow of activity along motor pathways in the generally economical organism. And this position does not yield any empirical predictions that the experimentalist can get his fingers into. Perhaps the most reasonable view is a compromise: the *development* of symbolic processes may require peripheral mediation, which becomes telescoped to a largely central representation in the mature individual. This view would fit much of the evidence. Young humans make more use of overt mediation than adults, and adults tend to regress to more overt levels when under stress. Less intelligent individuals show higher amplitude of motor potentials during thought and imagination than their more intelligent brethren. And in the following section we shall find a decreasing dependence upon overt motor-representing mechanisms in animal subjects as we move up the phylogenetic scale. This compromise point of view has the advantage that while it recognizes certain inadequacies with a purely peripheral theory, it does encourage further research.

ANIMAL EXPERIMENTATION

Is It Legitimate to Study 'Thought' in Animals?

The classic tradition draws a clean distinction between Homo sapiens, the 'rational' being, and all other living organisms. It attributed a soul only to man, and both the soul and the mind were conceived as interrelated and opposed to the physical aspects of the cosmos. To have ideas animals would have to have minds, and this would mean allowing them some of the non-material 'stuff' that constitutes mind. With complete disregard for the academician, but for no better reasons, laymen have always believed that higher animals do think and have ideas. Remarkable tales are told about animal friends—how the faithful dog mourns over the grave of his master and will eat only when his master's shoes are placed near his plate. And do not animals dream, twitching and growling as they fight imaginary battles? Anecdotal evidence of this sort is seldom consistent. We are also told that the cow, when lamenting over a dead calf and presented with the stuffed skin of its offspring, will lick it in 'motherly' devotion until the hay stuffing protrudes, and then calmly continue to eat the hay. Worker wasps are known, when other food is lacking, to bite off part of one end of the larva's body and offer it to the other end to be eaten (Washburn, 1936).

Lloyd Morgan's canon—that the behavior of animals should not be explained in terms of human attributes if it can be explained on a lower level—was designed to counteract the common tendency to put oneself in an animal's place and explain its actions in terms of what we would do in that situation. The introductory student in psychology often says 'the rat turns the wheel because it *knows* this will shut off the shock.' Regardless of the validity of the statement, it does not constitute an adequate explanation of the rat's behavior; it leaves unexplained how the rat, or the human, in the rat's situation, would *know* shock was coming. It is interesting that through the behavioristic phase in which American psychology has been moving, Lloyd Morgan's canon has been subtly inverted. Many present-day psychologists are loath to attribute to *humans* any characteristics that cannot be demonstrated in lower animals. Animals are being used as test tubes for the laws of human behavior.

Is it legitimate to study thought in animals? Only when 'thought' can be *objectively indexed*. In other words, ideation should be attributed to lower animals only where it is necessary to postulate some implicit, symbolic process to explain their behavior. Ordinary learning situations, in which the distinctive cues are available in the immediate environment, do not necessitate any assumptions about symbolic activities—although such processes may, of course, occur. Clear evidence for 'thought' in animals will be obtained *in situations in which the relevant cues are not available in the external environment at the time the correct response is required, but must be supplied by the organism itself.* Several situations that meet this criterion have been devised and extensively studied. Two of the earliest animal experimentalists, Lloyd Morgan (1900) and Thorndike (1911), did conclude that animals are incapable of higher mental processes, have no ideas or thoughts as such. More recent investigators have refuted this position, yet, and this is an interesting bow to the classic tradition, they have cautiously referred to 'representative factors' rather than to 'thought' when describing symbolic processes in animal subjects.

Experimental Evidence for 'Representative Factors' in Animals

The delayed reaction. In an early approach to this question, Hunter (1913) tested the ability of both rats and human children to make delayed reactions. The rats were first trained to run to whichever of three doors was lighted. After this habit was well established, a delay interval was inserted between flashing a light over one of the doors (distinctive cue) and releasing the animal, the rat being held in a glass-sided box throughout this period. With the children, an attractive toy was dropped into one of three boxes and, after a delay interval, the child was allowed to look into one of three boxes for the toy. In both cases the distinctive cue is not available at the time the correct response must be made; to the extent that correct responses are made beyond chance frequencies, some symbolic, representative processes must be functioning. Hunter found that the maximal delay for the rat was about 10 seconds and even then success seemed to depend upon the animal's maintaining bodily orientation toward the correct door. Children, on the other hand, were not only capable of much longer delays but could respond successfully without maintaining any specific overt orientation. That the actual length of delay for the rat depends upon specific experimental procedures is shown by the results of other investigators. Honzik (1931) allowed his animals to run toward the relevant cue before it was removed, thus insuring that the rat actually received the stimulus, and he obtained delays of 45 seconds or more. McCord (1939) found rats capable of delays of 4 or more minutes. He used a square enclosure with distinctive cards on each of the four sides, the rats being required to jump from a central stool at the form under which the experimenter had previously held and withdrawn a food cup. The fact that the four alternative cues were separated by 90° angles in this case, thus minimizing the likelihood of interference from conflicting response tendencies during the delay period, probably facilitated the maintenance of the correct set.

Other species have been used as subjects in delayed reaction experiments, and maximum delays are highly variable. The cat has been found capable of delays of from 3 to 17 hours (Adams, 1929), the monkey 15 to 20 hours (Tinklepaugh, 1928), and the chimpanzee as long as 48 hours (Yerkes and Yerkes, 1928). These values can only be considered suggestive since experimental procedures varied widely. Nevertheless, a certain trend in the data is apparent: *the length of the delay interval increases with the phylogenetic level of the organism.* Another general conclusion seems warranted as well. Hunter (1913) had observed that his rats could delay successfully only if they maintained bodily orientation toward the correct door; McCord (1939) increased the discriminability of the alternative cues and obtained longer delays; the capacity of both human children and adults to make delayed reactions is known to depend upon the character of the intervening activity. *The length of the delay interval varies with the nature of the interpolated activity.* We shall return to this point again.

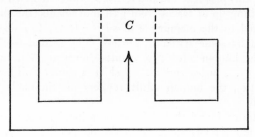

FIGURE 207. Apparatus for studying delayed and double alternation performances. In delayed alternation, animal is held for various intervals at point C before being allowed to respond. In double alternation, animal must make two turns in one direction before shifting (LLRRLLRR).

Delayed alternation. A similar technique for investigating implicit activity in animals is the delayed alternation. The animal is first trained to alternate his response in an objectively constant situation. In the apparatus shown in Fig. 207 the animal first turns left at the choice point C and upon the second approach must turn right, and so forth (LRLRLR). Rats easily master such alternation habits, each response producing the distinctive cues for the next. If the animal is delayed after the execution of one response, however, the distinctive cue for making the next (alternating) response must be maintained or produced by the animal itself. The major difference between this technique and the delayed reaction is that in the latter case the relevant cue is generally visual and produced by the experimenter, whereas here the relevant cue is primarily motor and produced by the animal's own preceding behavior. Although no direct comparison has been made, it appears that rats (Loucks, 1931) and raccoons (Elder and Nissen, 1933) can delay longer under these conditions than with the usual delayed reaction technique. Since, with the delayed alternation method, reception of the relevant cue is guaranteed by the animal's making the correct preceding reaction and since this cue is also relatively constant, this longer delay might be expected. On the other hand, Jacobsen and Nissen (1937), using monkeys as subjects and a somewhat different alternation procedure, directly compared delayed reaction with delayed alternation and found longer delay intervals under the former method. They interpret this as owing to their subjects' being dominantly visual animals.

Double alternation. In the procedures so far discussed a delay period has been used to separate the relevant external cue and the correct response. The double alternation technique accomplishes the same end without requiring any delay period and hence eliminates the possibility of unspecifiable interference. Using the same temporal maze shown in Fig. 207, for example, the animal is now required to go *twice* to the right and then *twice* to the left, and so forth (RRLLRRLL). This is a very different matter from single alternation. Here the cues produced by each response must at one point evoke the repetition of that response and at the next point evoke the alternate response, i.e. $S_L \rightarrow R_L$ and then $S_L \rightarrow R_R$. Since differential reactions cannot be discriminatively associated with identical stimuli and the external situation is constant, the animal itself must supply some additional distinctive cue if the problem is to be mastered. One of the earliest investigators of this problem (Hunter, 1920) suggested two feasible mechanisms: (1) a piling up of traces from past movements, the shift in response being conditioned to the magnitude of such effects; (2) distinctive stimulation produced by some symbolic process. The second mode is obviously employed by the human adult; he counts, 'once around, *twice* . . . now the other way . . . once, *twice* . . . shift again. . .' Through his own symbolic activities, the human adult renders discriminable that which is not so externally.

Actually, Hunter found that only an occasional rat was capable of mastering the simplest RRLL sequence in the temporal maze described above, and then only after very extensive training. Similar results were obtained by other investigators. A more recent study by Schlosberg and Katz (1943) demonstrated that fairly stable double alternation sequences could be established in the rat, one animal maintaining an errorless series as long as 35 RRLL sequences. However, an entirely different type of apparatus was used. A lever was arranged with electrical contacts and stepping relays so that when moved twice in one direction and then twice in the other a small amount of dry food powder would be delivered to the rat. The investigators conclude that 'the performance is relatively easy for the rat because all four responses are made rapidly and without intervening behavior. Thus the effects of all stimuli and responses can persist throughout the whole sequence, and serve to fuse the individual responses into a single pattern of behavior' (p. 282). In other words, the rats learn a sequential skill under these conditions, which fits Hunter's first suggested mechanism cited above. There seems no reason for postulating symbolic processes in such a case. Higher organisms than the rat have been shown to master double alternation in the temporal maze and in similar situations that seem to require symbolic mediation. Raccoons (Hunter, 1928), cats (Karn, 1938), and dogs (Karn and Malamud, 1939) manage a single RRLL sequence but not beyond. Monkeys execute the RRLL series in the temporal maze and when two boxes loaded in double alternation with food reward are used instead of a maze, they can extend their mastery to as many as 16 RRLL sequences (Gellerman, 1931). Again we have evidence of variation in representing capacity along the phylogenetic scale.

Observational learning. When an observer (human or animal) watches another individual solve a problem one or more times and then, *without the demonstrator's being present and without ever having previously made the*

correct responses, solves the same problem more readily, some implicit mediation process must be functioning. The observer must somehow be able
to represent what has previously been passively observed. Can animals
profit from the experience of others in this manner? The evidence is somewhat controversial. Thorndike (1898), on the basis of experiments with
chicks, cats, and dogs, reached negative conclusions, but it seems likely that
the problems he used were both unnatural and too difficult for his subjects.
Yerkes (1927) and Köhler (1925), on the other hand, report numerous
casual observations of such learning among subhuman primates, and Warden and Jackson (1939) obtained positive experimental results with rhesus
monkeys. Is the capacity for observational learning, and the complex form
of representational process it probably requires, restricted to primates?

Herbert and Harsh (1944) studied such learning in cats under conditions that permitted quantitative measurement of both performance on the
initial trial after observation (immediate imitation) and effort necessary
for learning (continued effects of observation). The five problems used
varied in difficulty from *turn-table,* which merely required persistent clawing movements at a revolving platform, to *pedal-door,* which involved both
a hidden mechanism and a detour between tool and goal. On each problem
certain animals were *original learners* (given 30 training trials), others
were 30-*trial observers* (placed in cages adjoining the work cage during all
30 demonstration trials), and yet others were 15-*trial observers* (observing
only the *last* 15 trials by the demonstrator); all observers were hungry
while watching the performance and food-attainment of the demonstrator.
The mean solution time on each problem for both the first trial and the
average of the first ten trials is shown in Table 18. The five problems are

TABLE 18. MEAN TIME IN SECONDS FOR SOLUTION OF PROBLEMS BY ORIGINAL
LEARNERS, 15-TRIAL OBSERVERS AND 30-TRIAL OBSERVERS (CATS)

Problem	Original Learners		15-Trial Observers		30-Trial Observers	
Trials →	(1)	(1-10)	(1)	(1-10)	(1)	(1-10)
Turn–table	62.3	18.0	56.5	21.8	15.8	7.8
Lever–cart	86.3	21.4	28.5	10.2	10.0	6.7
String–pull	112.0	36.4	48.5	30.3	22.8	7.4
Pull–door	140.2	18.8	141.5	25.8	31.0	7.6
Pedal–door	135.7	26.9	All failed		33.0	7.3

Computed from data of Herbert and Harsh, *Journal of Comparative Psychology,* 1944,
37:90.

ordered in terms of their difficulty as indexed by the average time for the
original learners. Although the number of subjects on the various problems
in this experiment was apparently too small to warrant statistical analysis,
the magnitudes of the mean differences appear to justify the following conclusions: (1) Both the initial performance and the ease of learning a new
problem are facilitated by observation. (2) Cats that observe only the last
(and facile) 15 trials by the demonstrator show (a) less facilitation than
those observing all 30 trials and (b) no facilitation on the most difficult
problems. Whether these differences are attributable to the need for observing the elimination of errors, the 'slow-motion' early trials, or are due
merely to the total amount of observing done cannot be judged from this
study; no animals observed only the *first* 15 trials.

What does the observing animal carry over to its own performance? Crawford and Spence (1939) have suggested that observation helps the animal discriminate the relevant aspects of the situation: it learns 'to scratch in this corner of the cage' or 'to extend the paw through the grill.' Herbert and Harsh believe that more than this is involved, since both the 15-trial and the 30-trial observers behaved in a manner indicating that the relevant aspects of the situation had been isolated; they suggest that the 30-trial observers learned to persist in manipulation of the relevant objects. In many cases, however—certainly with primates and in several instances with these cats—the observer performs the new act smoothly and rapidly on the first trial, indicating that some quite specific representations of the demonstrator's behavior must be functioning. In man, of course, we would speak of 'images' or 'ideas' or 'memories' of how the demonstrator did it, and the human subject would probably help us by verbalizing the process; just how the cat mediates from quiet observation to active performance is not known.

Dependence of Symbolic Processes upon the Prefrontal Cortex

When a century ago Phineas Gage suffered the misfortune of having a crowbar driven through his head, contemporary neurologists had the good fortune of observing the effects of frontal lesions upon behavior. Since that time the role of these so-called 'association areas' has been studied with great interest. Brickner (1936), for example, has analyzed clinically the case of a man who underwent extensive bilateral frontal lobectomy. The postoperative behavior of this individual was characterized on the one hand by inability to inhibit reaction, ready distractibility, and freeness of emotional expression and on the other hand by a permanent deterioration in those higher capacities we call conceptual reasoning. Whereas the patient had been comparatively mild, unassuming, and self-controlled prior to his operation, he became markedly aggressive, boastful, and sexual in his speech. While immediate memory was fallible, his memory for remote events seemed largely unimpaired. With the parallel development of surgical techniques and animal research it would be expected that the frontal areas would be studied in connection with 'representative factors' in animals, and this has been the case.

Jacobsen's studies. A series of classic studies on the cerebral localization of behavioral functions has been made by Jacobsen and his associates, using primates as subjects. The general experimental procedure is as follows: (a) the animal's performance capacity at a given task is determined prior to operation; (b) unilateral ablation of a portion of the brain (in the present instance, the frontal lobes) is made, time is allowed for recovery from the operation, and postoperational tests of performance capacity are run; (c) the remaining (contralateral) portion of that area is then removed and, after recovery, final tests are run. It is thus possible to compare preoperational behavior with that in which either unilateral or bilateral lesions are involved, each animal serving as his own control. This method does pose one technical problem: it is possible in some cases that actual loss in capacity may be obscured by practice effects; and certain of Jacobsen's data show evidence of these effects.

In one experiment (1935) Jacobsen compared the effects of frontal lobectomy upon three types of problems: *visual discrimination, problem-boxes* (manipulation of various locks, cranks, and levers to open boxes containing food rewards), and *delayed reaction* (animal observes food being hidden under one of two identical cups and, after a delay, is allowed to choose). Neither unilateral nor bilateral lesions produced significant deterioration in visual discrimination or problem-box performance. In both tasks, it should be observed, the relevant cues for solution are present at the time the response must be made. Results on the delayed reaction were strikingly different. Although the performance of animals with unilateral lesions was if anything superior to the preoperative level (presumably owing to practice effects), bilateral lesions severely restricted the interval over which the animal could delay, in most cases completely eliminating this capacity. Even when many times the amount of practice given preoperatively was allowed, no improvement appeared in the animals with bilateral lesions. Equivalent or even larger lesions made in areas other than the prefrontal failed to affect this performance.

Jacobsen and Nissen (1937) have used the same general procedures in studying *delayed alternation,* which, it will be recalled, differs from the delayed reaction mainly in that motor rather than visual cues are involved. Here again, while unilateral lesions produced little disturbance, bilateral lesions resulted in permanent loss of this performance capacity. Utilizing problems reminiscent of those originated by Köhler in his studies on the mentality of apes, Jacobsen, Wolfe, and Jackson (1935) have been able to extend their conclusions to *reasoning and insightful behavior.* The simplest problem merely required the animal to use a stick to draw a food reward into its cage; prefrontal lesions did not hinder this performance. A more complex setup (Fig. 208A) required the animal to first use a small stick to reach a larger and more distant one, which in turn could be used to reach another, and so forth; again neither unilateral nor bilateral lesions hindered solution, and it should be observed that although the problem is a complex, serial affair, all the elements necessary for solution are in the immediate perceptual field of the animal. A third test involved two platforms (Fig. 208B), a goal-object being placed beyond reach on one and the necessary tool on the other; although unilateral lesions had no effect, bilateral lesions severely interfered with solution. A final test (Fig. 208C) required the animal to obtain one stick from one platform, which could be used to reach a larger stick on the other platform, which in turn could be used to reach a still larger stick on the first platform, and so forth—in short, a 'shuttle' problem. Here again unilateral lesions had no effect, whereas bilateral lesions resulted in clear failures.

Are the two frontal lobes completely equipotential? Jacobsen's data are consistent in demonstrating no measurable decrement when unilateral lesions are made. This seems to mean that the symbolic processes studied are simultaneously organized in both hemispheres *if* the symbolic processes are 'localized' in these frontal areas. Results obtained by Warden, Barrera, and Galt (1942) indicate certain limitations on equipotentiality of the two frontal lobes. Using visual discrimination and platform problems of varying complexity, but similar in type to those employed by Jacobsen, these investigators found that although unilateral lesions had no effect upon the retention of simpler problems, the more complex performances were disturbed. A finding of special interest concerned recovery of performance with re-training. An animal that had had complete bilateral frontal lobectomy in *one* stage showed complete recovery of even the most complex platform tests 20 weeks after operation. Because post-mortem autopsy showed that this animal had suffered as extensive lesions as the others, this questions the validity of the entire hypothesis that symbolic processes are 'localized' in the frontal areas. Is the difference here owing to removal of the lobes in a single rather than two sequential operations? It doesn't seem likely.

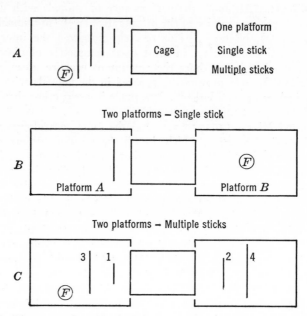

FIGURE 208. Diagrams of problem-solving situations to which chimpanzee subjects were submitted. Animal was always in cage, food reward was at *F,* and tool place-ments were as shown. Jacobsen, Wolfe, and Jackson, *Journal of Nervous and Mental Disease,* 1935, 82:4.

Evidence from studies using rat subjects. Results of experiments on rat subjects are confusing. Maier (1932), using one of his 'reasoning' situa-tions, found that cortical injury had decremental effects when the amount of tissue removed was greater than 18 per cent, but the effect was inde-pendent of locus. Hunter and Hall (1941) and Andrews and Hunter (1943) found that bilateral removal of equivalent amounts of cortical tissue from central and occipital areas reduced performance on a double alternation-type problem just as effectively as bilateral removal of frontal cortex, which is also indicative of nonspecific involvement of frontal areas in the rat. One wonders, however, to what extent representative factors were essential to the performance in this case; furthermore, the number of animals used was very small. In flat contradiction to these studies are the results of Morgan and Wood (1943). Relatively small lesions in the fron-tal cortex, but not elsewhere, completely abolished delayed alternation in their rat subjects. Similar conclusions are reached by Stellar, Morgan, and

Yarosh (1942). Using a method previously described by Crutchfield (1939), in which the animal must learn to run a constant distance along a linear maze despite the jumbling of exteroceptive cues from trial to trial, they found that relatively small lesions within the frontal areas produced marked disturbance, whereas large lesions elsewhere produced little decrement. These experimenters themselves, however, are not too confident that this performance requires symbolic, representing mechanisms. If anything can be concluded from these sketchy data, it is that we have been unable to specify with any certainty what types of performance (in the rat) require 'representative factors.' Until this can be done, hypotheses concerning the localization of such factors within the rat cortex are patently untestable.

Nature of 'Representative Factors'

Animals can perform delayed reactions and double alternations successfully and they can learn through observation and insight; all these activities seem to share a dependence upon certain symbolic processes, termed 'representative factors.' Since the relevant cue is not present at the time the correct response is made, the animal must supply itself with some distinctive cue, some mode of representing what is lacking in the present external environment. The frontal lobes have been shown to play an important role in such performances—whether as the locus of mediation processes or merely as a facilitative agent is not yet clear. From introspective reports we are led to believe that the human animal stimulates himself with distinctive verbal cues in situations of this sort. By what process does the subhuman organism mediate between past and present experiences?

Overt motor orientation. A simple explanation, attributing little in the way of higher level capacities to subhuman species, is that the animal maintains an overt muscular 'set' toward the relevant cue until the correct response can be made. Hunter (1913) believed that rats and dogs were limited to this level of performance. These animals 'pointed' toward the light which flashed and held this motor orientation until released. Forcing them to change position resulted in failures. Although this is undoubtedly one method of bridging a temporal interval, it is clearly not the only possibility for an animal. Raccoons and preverbal children did not need to maintain a motor 'set,' and even the humble rat may be able to perform delayed reactions when their motor orientations are disturbed (Honzik, 1931). Furthermore, this explanation would not explain successes in double alternation, observational learning, and insightful problem-solving.

Implicit motor orientation. There is, of course, no reason why a mediating motor 'set' should be either overt or obviously related to the goal-object in question. When the human adult thinks 'it's behind the *third* door,' the observer cannot see the response, and there is no essential relation between thinking 'third' and the actual goal-place beyond the representing relation itself. The animal might conceivably maintain an increased tension in the muscles about the left eye after a light has flashed on that side, the stimulation from this response serving as the distinctive cue once the delay interval is over (cf. Hull's 'pure-stimulus-act,' 1930). Such a hypothesis, attractive though it may be, is practically untestable. Where in the organism are we to look for the specific muscle system being used for mediation? In any case, what meager evidence exists is in the negative:

Loucks (1931) administered a general anesthetic during the delay period and found his rat subjects still capable of successful delayed reactions.

Representation and retention. Is it actually necessary that any activity persist through the delay interval in order that successful mediation occur? The only requirement is that some distinctive cue be given *at the time the correct response must be made.* If our human subject learns to say 'it's behind the third door' at the time of original presentation, he does not need to keep repeating the phrase during the retention interval; all he must do in order to demonstrate a delayed reaction hours or even days later is to *recall* 'it's behind the third door' when again brought into the test situation. Similarly, the rat does not have to maintain tension in the muscles about the left eye throughout the delay period; it merely has to 'remember' to make this response at the time of release and thus provide itself with the distinctive cue. This interpretation clearly places 'representative factors' on a continuum with ordinary retention. Are there any differences? There appear to be two salient ones: (1) Only a single trial is provided for original impression (except for whatever implicit repetitions are made by the organism during the interval). (2) The stimulus in the test situation is not identical with that during original learning (the relevant cue is missing). The latter difference between original and test situations is probably bridged through generalization.

If the retention interpretation is valid, capacity to delay will vary with fixation of the original impression. Finan (1942), after duplicating Jacobsen's results on delayed reaction with two monkeys whose frontal lobes were surgically removed, found that if just before the delay period the animals were given a bite of food from the cup under which it was to be hidden, they could make better-than-chance successes over intervals as long as 15 seconds. This pre-delay reinforcement presumably served both to clearly delineate the relevant cue and to immediately reinforce this attentional response. Similar results and conclusions are offered by Campbell and Harlow (1945), who also used monkeys as subjects. Certain other observations made by these authors are of interest: Two experimental animals, after bilateral frontal lobectomy, made scores comparable with those of the best normal controls, especially when the technique of pre-delay reinforcement was used. The longer the interval between operation and testing, the better the performance, suggesting some recovery of these functions although not specifying the basis for recovery. The operated animals showed marked hyperactivity, distractibility, and rapid loss of motivation, which made experimentation difficult and probably contributed to their poor performance.

This interpretation also places a premium upon the character of the delay period interpolated between original impression and the test for retention. The availability of the 'representative factor' at the end of the delay period should depend upon the degree to which it has suffered *retroactive interference* during that period. This hypothesis has been directly tested by Malmo (1942). Using the type of delayed reaction procedure developed by Jacobsen, Malmo found that monkeys lacking both frontal lobes were capable of successful performance if they were kept in darkness during the delay interval. Apparently monkeys without frontal cortex are more susceptible to interference during the delay period; remove the major sources of interference by darkening the cage and their performance becomes normal.

Many of the data from experiments with rats also fit this interpretation. McCord (1939) found rats capable of longer delays when he used a method that minimized interference from alternative responses; Loucks's (1931) technique of anesthetizing his animals during the delay period would be expected to improve performance, if anything, since it reduced interpolated interference (assuming that no deleterious physiological affects were produced). Although only unspecifiable sources of interference have been studied to date, it would be feasible to specify experimentally the nature of the interfering activities introduced during the delay period and thus directly test the implications of a retroactive interference hypothesis.

What may we conclude as to the role of the frontal lobes? The fact that, under appropriate conditions (Malmo, 1942; Finan, 1942; Campbell and Harlow, 1945), primates can utilize 'representative factors' after the frontal cortex has been extirpated bilaterally indicates that these mediation processes cannot be 'localized' in this area. This is also forcefully emphasized by the fact that occasional lobectomized animals can perform these behaviors under ordinary conditions (Warden, Barrera, and Galt, 1942; Campbell and Harlow, 1945). There is also to be considered the repeated observation that the two frontal lobes are largely equipotential, i.e. whatever their function may be, it is a generalized one. *The types of mediation processes known as 'representative factors' are not localized in the frontal lobes* (indeed, they may vary in locus with the type of problem, the sensory modalities involved, and so forth), *but these cortical areas exercise a general function of inhibiting reactions to incidental stimuli and hence facilitate performances requiring recent memory.*

This conclusion is certainly justified by the characteristic behavior of subjects lacking frontal cortex. Their susceptibility to distraction (and thus interference) from incidental stimuli has been noted by numerous investigators (cf. Jacobsen, 1935; Finan, 1942; Campbell and Harlow, 1945). Jacobsen, for example, states that '. . . the momentary distraction of attention by incidental noises reduced the score to a mere chance value . . . the defect in the mechanism for delayed reaction . . . appears . . . to be a specific impairment of recent memory existing in the face of the normal adjustments made to other situations' (1935, p. 561). Actually all the performances to which the label 'representative factors' is applicable— those in which bilateral frontal lobectomy causes marked disturbance—are basically tests of recent memory. The animal must 'keep an idea in its head,' maintain a 'set' of some kind. Brickner's human subject, we recall, showed marked loss in recent memory: he would forget the name of a doctor he'd just met, forget that he'd just finished lunch; if interrupted momentarily in a story, to tie his shoe or light a cigarette, he would ask, 'What was I talking about?' What eliminates these recent memories? Presumably the subject without frontal lobes is less capable of inhibiting normal adjustive reactions to the host of incidental stimuli about him, and these interpolated reactions interfere with retention. But what *are* 'representative factors' themselves? Animal research to date has failed to reveal their essential nature. Although this approach has shown that higher animals are capable of thought, objectively indexed, it has not provided any understanding of the underlying nature of thought.

CONCEPT FORMATION AND ABSTRACTING ABILITY

When human beings think, they use concepts. These concepts may be quite concrete (e.g. TREE) or quite abstract (e.g. GRAVITY). Of course, concept formation is intimately tied up with language and meaning and might be taken up in the next chapter as well as here—chapter boundaries are rather arbitrary matters. Just what, in everyday language, is a concept? It is a common response (usually verbal) made to a class of phenomena the members of which display certain common characteristics. When the child can discriminatively use the label 'kitty' in response to situations having fur, four legs, and a 'meow' in common, we generally concede that he has learned that concept. There is no requirement that the child be able to make explicit these common characteristics—indeed, adults use many concepts more or less accurately that they find hard to define. This common-sense definition of a concept does not, however, distinguish between simple discriminative labeling and abstract conceptualization. The mere fact that the child vocalizes 'kitty' when cats are present does not guarantee he 'has' the abstract concept of cat as a zoological category— he might come forth with 'kitty' when looking at a dog, a bird, or even a bouncing ball. Nor does this common-sense definition specify the nature of the 'common characteristics' upon which concepts are formed, the problem to which we now turn our attention.

Experimental Studies of Concept Formation

Experimental approaches to the problem of concept formation have been divided in terms of how that question—what are the common characteristics upon which concepts are based?—is answered. To one group of investigators the common characteristics are *identical elements* carried like tags by each member of the class. Some books are red and some brown, some are thick and others thin, but they all have covers, pages, and letters in common. To other investigators the common characteristics are *relations among the parts* (gestalts, configurations) of each member of the class. Although the moon, a penny, and a ball have no identical elements, they all display circularity of contour and hence may be related by the concept 'circle.' Perhaps, in the final analysis, the only essential common characteristic is that a group of discrete situations be associated through learning with the *same mediating or symbolic reaction.* Beets, pole beans, and spinach would certainly be classed as 'vegetables,' yet there are neither any identical elements nor any common perceptual relations.

Identical elements. Hull's classic study (1920) began with the assumption that concepts are formed through the abstracting of common elements. As an illustration of the process in everyday life, he offered the following: 'A young child finds himself in a certain situation, reacts to it by approach, say, and hears it called "dog." After an indeterminate intervening period he finds himself in a somewhat different situation, and hears that called "dog." . . The "dog" experiences appear at irregular intervals. The appearances are thus unanticipated. They appear with no obvious label as to their essential nature. . . At length the time arrives when the child has a "meaning" for the word dog' (1920, p. 5). Hull patterned the materials and procedures of his experiment directly upon this presumed nature of concepts. Subjects were shown a series of 12 packs of cards, each card bearing a complex Chinese character. Each pack of cards included one instance of each 'concept' and was practiced to a criterion before the next pack was begun. Thus, each pack contained a character with a checkmark-like element which was to be called 'oo.' The subjects were not told to look for the common elements (any more than the child is told to look for the common characteristics of dogs), but they were encouraged to anticipate the correct label as soon as they could, being prompted by the experimenter after a short delay interval. Hull found the development of concepts to be typical of ordinary discrimination learning.

But was Hull actually studying *concept* formation? The subjects were required to discriminate the characteristic common to a certain group of stimulus situations and associate a specific vocal reaction with it. The response of saying 'oo' was found to generalize to other stimulus patterns causing errors, the response gradually becoming restricted to those patterns having checkmark-like elements. Is this in any way different from the learning of any habit? When a dog is conditioned to flex its leg to a specific cue, such as the sound of a buzzer, the relevant cue must also be discriminated from the manifold of stimulating events about the animal. It would seem that Hull was here studying the development of *labeling;* the fact that he found this to be typical of other learned behaviors would be anticipated— the combined processes of generalization and discrimination in terms of physical similarities work in all such cases. Goldstein and Scheerer (1941) have criticized this investigation along the same lines: 'What Hull has justly termed "the child has a meaning for the word 'dog' " indicates however an entirely different level of activity than these former concrete stages of situational speech. Now the child has shifted his approach; he is now able to *detach* the word from the concrete situations and use it outside of these situations in the abstract . . .' (p. 27).

Actually, Hull's conception would include all learning under concept formation, thus making it rather a useless term. We should certainly have to agree, in this case, that most animals can form concepts. Fields (1932) even titled a paper 'The Development of the Concept of Triangularity by the White Rat.' Patterning his work directly on Hull's approach, he showed that rats could learn to jump toward a triangular form, when paired with other forms in a discrimination situation, despite large variations in size, shading, position, amount of outline, and so forth. Yet, should we conclude that the rat can understand the *abstract* concept of triangularity? Would the rat respond positively to three dots in a triangular arrangement versus four dots arranged in a square? Or react positively to three people, three places on a map, a three-cornered block, as 'triangles'? As Goldstein points out, the abstract level of using concepts is quite distinct from simple transposition in terms of stimulus similarities.

Common relations. Are there really any identical stimulus *elements* between a Pomeranian and a great Dane, between a ball and a penny, between a rose and a buttercup? Another school of thought says *no*—there are no identical elements as such among these stimulating events, but there are common perceptual relations. Smoke (1932) provides us with an experimental demonstration of this approach. He defined a concept as a common symbolic reaction made to a class of stimuli having no necessary physical identities but displaying common perceptual organization or pattern. Among the experimental materials were a 'dax' (circle and two dots, one being within and the other without the boundary), a 'mib' (a triangle and a line extending at right angles from its shortest side). Sample 'daxes' and 'mibs' are shown in Fig. 209 and it may be seen that, although a common, verbalizable relation exists among all instances of a given concept, the actual figures vary widely and it would be hard to specify 'identical elements.' Since subjects did develop correct concepts under these conditions, we may conclude that the existence of identical elements among the members of a class being conceptualized is not necessary. Smoke also reports that subjects could often learn to make the correct labeling reactions

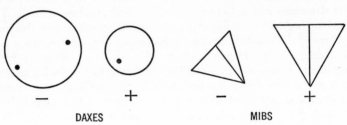

DAXES   MIBS

FIGURE 209. Sample materials used in an experiment on concept formation. Instances of the concept in question ($+$) and those which do not fit the concept ($-$). After Smoke, *Psychological Monographs*, 1932, 42, #191:13.

without being able to verbalize the relevant characteristics—they could pick out the 'mibs' without being able to define 'mibness.'

Common mediation process. But are common perceptual relations any more essential to concept formation than identical elements? Must there be any similarity at all in the external stimulations? What perceptual commonness exists among mittens, hats, and neckties (they are all 'clothing')? Among crawl, swim, and fly (they are all 'locomotions')? Among France, Japan, and Russia (they are all 'nations')? It would seem that the only *essential* condition for concept formation is the learning of a common mediating response (which is the meaning of the concept) for a group of objects or situations, identical elements and common perceptual relations merely facilitating the establishment of such mediators. Several recent experiments on concept formation fit this view.

Reed (1946 *a, b, c*) has studied the learning and retention of concepts, defining a concept as any word or idea that stands for any one of a group of things. Subjects were shown cards containing four English words (e.g. 'club'—'picnic'—'reaches'—'beet'), one of which was an instance of a given concept, such as BEP, this being written on the back of the card and spoken by the experimenter after a short interval. All BEP cards included some vegetable; all KUN cards contained some animal; all DAX cards some color name; and so forth. A sample of these cards, with the relevant words underlined, is shown in Fig. 210. What is the learning process here? There are two separable tasks for the subject: (a) He must first discriminate which of the four words on each card is the relevant one; this is equivalent to isolating the crucial aspect of a complex visual figure, as required in the experiments previously surveyed. Once the relevant word has been isolated, the conceptualizing process (thinking of a beet as a 'vegetable') demands little additional effort—this has been learned previous to the experimental situation. (b) The second task is to associate this mediation process, saying or thinking 'vegetable,' with the correct nonsense syllable, BEP, as an overt response. This latter process is common to all members of the class and is merely a new substitutive vocalization for 'vegetable.' The conceptualizing paradigm suggested here is shown in the lower portion of Fig. 210. Do the results fit this hypothesis?

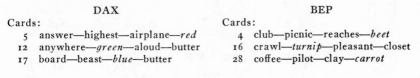

DAX		BEP	
Cards:		Cards:	
5	answer—highest—airplane—*red*	4	club—picnic—reaches—*beet*
12	anywhere—*green*—aloud—butter	16	crawl—*turnip*—pleasant—closet
17	board—beast—*blue*—butter	28	coffee—pilot—clay—*carrot*

LEARNING PARADIGM

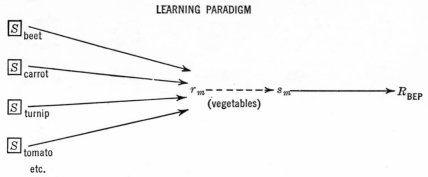

FIGURE 210. Sample materials in an experiment on concept formation (Reed, 1946) and a mediational model suggested as the learning paradigm involved.

The measure of learning and retention used by Reed was the number of promptings required by the subjects. (1) Subjects who were given a 'set' to look for general concepts (i.e. told that each nonsense syllable represented a definite class of things) clearly showed superior learning and retention as compared with subjects who were merely instructed to learn the correct nonsense syllable for each card—the former were actively trying out various conceptual mediators. (2) The rates of forgetting consistent (correct) concepts, inconsistent (incorrect) concepts, and ordinary nonsense syllables (from data of Ebbinghaus) were compared. Consistent concepts showed practically no loss over as long a period as 40 days. (3) When the number of cards (and hence the number of instances of each class) was increased, only a slight increase in effort was required for learning consistent concepts. This is to be contrasted with the general findings on amount of material (e.g. the data obtained by Lyon, 1914), where effort increases disproportionately with amount of material.

Although Reed attributes the facility with which concepts are learned and retained to such factors as increased motivation, lessened retroactive inhibition, logical relations, and the like (and indeed these factors may be involved), a large proportion of the effect would seem to lie directly in the learning paradigm. Once a subject has discovered the correct mediating process (the correct concept, 'vegetable'), the inclusion of new members (such as spinach and string beans) requires a minimum of effort, these associations being based upon much pre-experimental learning. With regard to retention, instead of retaining each specific association, the subject merely has to remember that 'vegetables are called BEP'; this means that he need retain only six associations between mediating concepts and their appropriate nonsense labels as compared with 42 unique associations between

FIGURE 211. Materials used in Heidbreder's experiments on concept formation. Heidbreder, *Journal of General Psychology*, 1946, 35:182.

each card and its label. Once the correct mediation process and its association with the nonsense label is mastered, increasing the number of instances of each class causes only a slight increase in difficulty in learning; what additional difficulty there is lies in discriminating which of the four words on each new card is the relevant one. Finally, the mediation hypothesis leads to the prediction that there would be no differences in degree of retention as the number of cards for each concept is increased. This is borne out neatly in Reed's data: the number of promptings per concept during relearning was .38 for the 24-card list, .91 for the 42-card list, and only .36 for the 60-card list, none of these differences being significant.

In a recent and intensive study, Heidbreder (1946 *a, b;* 1947) * has investigated the attainment of *various types of concepts*. She defined a concept as a 'logical construct which, through signs or symbols or both, is transferable from situation to situation and communicable from person to person.' Using a method reminiscent of Hull's, she showed her subjects 16 series of drawings on a memory drum, each series including instances of nine concepts; they were instructed to anticipate the nonsense names where possible, the experimenter prompting where necessary. Each series was learned to a criterion of two perfect trials. The materials, shown in Fig. 211, were reminiscent of those used by Smoke in that the members of each conceptual class did not have identical elements but they did have a common verbalizable meaning. All 'faces' were to be called RELKS, all 'circle' objects were FARDS, all groups of six units were MANKS, and so forth. The learning procedure in this experiment also fits the general paradigm shown in Fig. 210. Again there are two steps in learning: (a) the correct mediation process ('face,' 'circle,' 'six,' etc.) must be associated with each individual drawing and (b) the overt response (nonsense label) appropriate for each class must be learned. Actually, of course, before a concept was attained, much of the learning would be in terms of isolated associations between specific drawings and specific nonsense syllables.

Two measures of concept attainment were employed in this experiment; first, the number of the series in which the first correct anticipation of the nonsense label appeared; second, the number of the series on which the subject began to label correctly all instances of a given concept. Thus, the specific face on series 2 might be correctly called RELK without prompts (first measure), yet it might not be until series 5 that faces-in-general began to be consistently called RELKS (second measure). The range between these two points in the set of 16 series is equivalent to Hull's (1940) oscillation function and indicates the *rate* at which a given concept is being learned. Table 19 gives the average series number on which each concept

TABLE 19

Concrete Objects		Spatial Forms		Abstract Numbers	
Face (RELK)	3.35	O (FARD)	4.46	2 (LING)	6.14
Building (LETH)	3.48	✕ (PRAN)	5.05	6 (MANK)	8.76
Tree (MULP)	3.94	∝ (STOD)	5.19	5 (DILT)	10.22

After Heidbreder, *Journal of General Psychology*, 1946, 35:192.

was attained (second measure). In terms of their ease of attainment, the concepts may be seen to fall into three rational groups: concrete objects, spatial forms, and abstract numbers. The differences between these classes were highly significant, and two supplementary experiments with different materials yielded the same results. Heidbreder discusses and dismisses many possible explanations of this order of difficulty, such as *familiarity* or having a *conventional name* (two of the spatial forms were less familiar than the numbers and had no conventional names), *simplicity, goodness or uni-*

* Further experiments in this series have appeared since this writing.

formity of drawings (informal inspection of the drawings seemed to reveal no consistent differences on these bases), and *trial and error* or *insight* (which might be involved in concept formation but which would not explain the obtained order). It is obvious that the obtained order varies with the 'abstractness' of the concepts, but there is no agreement among psychologists as to what this means.

Heidbreder's own hypothesis, deriving from her general theory of cognition (cf. Heidbreder, 1945), is that in human beings 'the perception of concrete objects is the dominant mode of cognitive reaction—i.e. likely to occur promptly and vigorously in ordinary conditions of stimulation.' The perception of pure spatial forms, being non-objects, is assumed to be a more primitive type of cognition and not dominant in humans. Purely abstract, symbolic perceptions, such as number groups, are even less likely in human perceiving, requiring more than mere perception. In other words, when presented with two red cubes on a table, the human organism's dominant tendency is to perceive manipulatable objects rather than 'rectilinearity' or 'redness' or the more purely symbolic 'twoness.' The applicability of this hypothesis to the data of the experiment is obvious.

It is perhaps possible to formulate an explanation of the order of difficulty that does not require such assumptions about human nature. The explanation would emphasize two factors: (1) the comparative *availability* of the correct mediation processes and (2) the comparative degree of *interference* among potential mediators. One way of checking directly on the comparative availability of mediators would have been to present each picture to a group of subjects instructed to give the first label that came to mind. In doing this informally, this writer found that while the concrete objects frequently yielded the 'correct' concept (i.e. the faces often evoked 'face' as a label, although sometimes 'boy' or 'man,' and the trees almost always produced 'tree,' except for 'palm'), the numbers scarcely ever were called 'two' or 'six' but rather were labeled in terms of the objects represented, such as 'stockings' for the upper-left item in Fig. 211. The novel forms, of course, would have zero availability. But if this explains the easier attainment of concrete object concepts, why weren't the numbers easier than the novel spatial forms? Assuming that the subjects *did* tend to apply the wrong labels to the number representations in the beginning (i.e. calling a *two* concept 'stockings'), this would undoubtedly cause interference with learning the correct mediation process. There is suggestive evidence for this in the oscillation data (range between first success and last failure): the three concrete objects and the circle had very narrow ranges, indicating that the main difficulty here lay in learning the correct nonsense label; the oscillation ranges for the two nameless forms and the number concepts were much broader, suggesting that here the subjects had either to gradually discover a serviceable mediation process (nameless forms) or eliminate erroneous ones (number concepts). It is possible that what we have termed availability of mediators is equivalent to Heidbreder's notion of dominant modes of human perceiving; she states that in the stages of developing concepts 'successively less thing-like aspects of the presented instances became the critical perceptual and situational determinants of the overt naming reactions.'

A Nonexperimental Approach

Another important source of evidence on the nature of concept formation is the work of Piaget (1928, 1930, 1932). His penetrating observations on the spontaneous language behavior of children provide a richer insight into the development of concepts than is usually obtained within the compass of the laboratory. In *The Child's Conception of Physical Causality* (1930), for example, Piaget reports detailed observations on the changes that occur in the child's conception of physical forces with increasing age. A series of simple demonstrations of physical forces were shown each child, who was asked to explain them. The following are samples: By expanding and compressing cupped hands, the experimenter makes puffs of air against the child's cheek. 'Where does the air come from?—*Through the window.*—Is it open?—*No, shut.*—And yet the air could get through?—*Yes.*—Where?— . . .' (p. 6). This four-year-old child does not conceive of air as being in the room; air is identified with wind, which is outside and hence must get into the room and thus into the hands. What causes the wind, according to an eight-year-old? It is caused by the very bodies (clouds, trees, etc.) we think of as being moved by the wind. 'DELESD (8): Is there any air outside?—*Yes.*—There's a lot today. Why is that?—*Because there's a wind.*—What is it?—*It's the trees moving. It blows.*—Where does the wind come from?—*Because it blows.*—But how is it that it blows?—*Because if you go by* [past] *a tree that is moving, it makes air.*—Why?—*Because it is moving . . .'* (p. 40).

How does Piaget explain the conceptualizations of the child? 'During the early stages the world and the self are one; neither term is distinguished from the other. But when they become distinct, these two terms begin by remaining very close to each other: the world is still conscious and full of intentions, the self is still material, so to speak, and only slightly interiorized . . . there is never complete objectivity: at every stage there remain in the conception of nature what we might call "adherences," fragments of internal experience which still cling to the external world' (p. 244). The sun and moon move because *we* move, they follow us; later they move because *they* want to, they are endowed with our projected intentions; later still they move because of forces, but these forces are themselves analogous to our own muscular force. The child's concepts are first concrete and tied to his own perceptual experiences: it is outdoors that he feels the wind against his face, it is from outside that he feels the wind blowing into the house—and his early conceptions of air and wind depend upon this immediate experience. Only by a process of high abstraction does a pebble become heavy (in terms of its density) in relation to a lake. Paralleling this development of objectivity toward the world is the development of subjectivity toward the self and thought: during early stages the child believes that thoughts are in words themselves (adults never quite lose this reference); later, thought and self move into the central cavities of the body, and only much later are localized in the head. This brief review of Piaget's work is intended to give only its flavor, not its substance.

674 EXPERIMENTAL PSYCHOLOGY

Concrete and Abstract Behavior

Some of the most stimulating information on conceptual thinking in recent years has come from the field of abnormal behavior. At the close of the First World War two German neuropsychiatrists, Goldstein and Gelb (1918, 1924), were studying the intellectual impairment of soldiers suffering traumatic lesions in the frontal areas. They were particularly struck by the loss of ability to think conceptually. When such individuals were given a box of varicolored yarns (Holmgren Woolens) and asked to sort them according to certain classes, they showed a restricted, concrete level of performance—although they could pick a few yarns closely resembling a given test color, they could not generalize widely or shift from one basis of classification to another. Subsequent investigations have justified the conclusion that individuals with brain injuries, especially in the frontal areas, suffer loss of *abstracting ability*. As will be seen, the test situations designed to reveal the presence or absence of abstracting ability in mental patients are equally tests of ability to form concepts.

Goldstein postulates two distinct levels of functioning capacity for the individual, abstract and concrete. The patient with frontal lobe pathology is considered to be capable of functioning only on the concrete level; the normal adult can function equally well on both. In a recent monograph (1941), Goldstein and Scheerer present many illustrations of concrete behavior in mental patients. The patient is *unable to manipulate objects in the abstract, as members of a class.* 'Patient F. is asked to take a comb from a table and bring it to the examiner. She cannot do this without combing her hair ("forced responsiveness")' (p. 4). 'Another patient cannot demonstrate how to drink out of an empty glass whereas he can drink out of a full glass' (p. 7). The patient is *unable to use abstract concepts accurately.* 'A patient is able to throw balls into three boxes which are located at different distances from him. He never misses. Asked which box is further and which nearer, he is unable to give any account or to make a statement concerning his procedure in aiming' (p. 5). 'A patient can count numbers on his fingers and by various roundabout methods; in this fashion he can even obtain the results which look like subtraction and addition, but he is entirely unable to state whether 7 or 4 is more and he has no concept of the value of numbers whatsoever' (p. 7). The patient *cannot isolate and verbalize the common characteristics of a group of discrete things.* Although the patient may utilize a generic term, such as 'flower' or 'animal,' he is merely using it to replace a forgotten concrete word, for he may say immediately thereafter, 'I grow flowers and roses in my garden.'

A large number of tests of abstracting ability have been designed and used by various investigators, including such varied activities as copying block and stick designs (Goldstein and Scheerer, 1941), sorting colored yarns (Goldstein and Gelb, 1925), classifying common objects (Weigl, 1927; Goldstein and Scheerer, 1941), and sorting blocks of various shapes, colors, and sizes (Hanfmann and Kasanin, 1937). Two of these tests will be described in some detail.

The *G.G.W.S. object sorting test* (Goldstein and Scheerer, 1941) presents the subject with a set of objects that are common in his environment. The male form of this test, for example, includes hammer, knife, spoon, ball, chocolate, cigar, candle, pipe, matches, apple, pincers, and so forth. The subject is requested to (1) group the objects with one which he has selected himself; then group them with an article selected by the examiner. (2) Group *all* the articles as he thinks they belong together. (3) Group them yet another way. There are varied possibilities for classification: function (tools, eating), color, material, and so forth. The normal subject can readily classify the objects in terms of use and then shift to a classification in terms of materials, but not the patient with frontal pathology.

FIGURE 212. Materials for Hanfmann-Kasanin performance test on abstracting ability. Hanfmann and Kasanin, *Journal of Psychology,* 1937, 3:523. Used with permission of H. Stoelting and Company.

Hanfmann and Kasanin (1937), extending a technique developed by Ach (1921), have developed a test in which wooden blocks of various colors, shapes, heights and top-surface areas must be classified accordingly into four groups. The blocks are presented to the subject in jumbled arrangement in the middle of a board, as shown in Fig. 212. The subject is told that there are four different kinds of blocks, each with a different name (written on the under surface), and he must sort them into the four corners of the board. The examiner then turns over one of the blocks, indicating its name, and places it in one corner, suggesting that the subject begin by selecting all the blocks he thinks might belong with that one. The correct classification disregards both color and shape, the large tall objects being *lags,* the large flat ones being *biks,* the small tall ones being *murs,* and the small flat ones being cevs. After sorting is made, the experimenter turns over the wrongly placed blocks, and the subject must discover for himself the conceptual basis for classification. Normal and abnormal subjects differ markedly on this test. The former try out various verbally maintained hypotheses—'all the triangles go together, the squares . . . no . . . all the tall red ones are *lags* . . .' and so forth. The mental patient may respond to identical elements of color or shape, grouping all red ones together or all circular pieces, but he cannot combine two concepts (tall and large) or shift readily from one basis to another.

Factors determining abstracting ability. Many analytic investigations have been carried out in this fertile field for research and many others are under way. Weigl (1927) compared patients with organic brain disease with both normal children and normal adults on an object classification test similar to the G.G.W.S. described above. The children performed more concretely than the normal adults but were flexible in their approach, continuously shifting their conceptual bases for classification. On the other hand, the patients with brain pathology were not only restricted to a simple, concrete level of performance but also unable to shift easily from one basis to another. Nadel (1938) directly tested the hypothesis previously implied by many clinicians that pathology in the frontal areas is responsible for losses in abstracting ability. Fifteen cases diagnosed by competent neurologists as having frontal damage were compared on a variety of tests of abstraction with a control group having brain injuries in areas other than the frontal. Patients with frontal lobe pathology consistently showed more concrete performances. Using a battery of psychological tests, including those on abstracting ability, Rylander (1939) compared the postoperative performance of patients undergoing unilateral frontal lobectomy (for the removal of brain tumors) with a group of normal controls, carefully matched with the patients in terms of age, socioeconomic status, and occupation. The patients gave significantly poorer performance on the specific abstracting tests as well as upon other tests that appeared to involve concept-forming ability. Notice that *unilateral* lobectomy with the human subject appears to produce significant decrement in abstracting performance, in contradiction to studies by Jacobsen on symbolic processes in monkeys.

The study of *conceptual thinking in schizophrenia* has pointed up some of the underlying problems in this area, especially the question of 'levels' of conceptualizing. Although this disorder has generally been considered functional rather than organic in nature, the schizophrenic usually performs at a concrete level in tests of abstracting ability. Two groups of investigators, psychoanalysts and gestalt theorists (cf. Storch, 1924; White, 1926; Birenbaum and Zeigarnik, 1935; Werner, 1940), have concluded that schizophrenia represents *regression* to more infantile levels of adjustment, the analysts stressing affective-adjustmental regression of the libido and the gestalt theorists stressing the lesser permeability of barriers between systems in the child and the schizophrenic. The fact that such patients do show loss in ability to form abstract concepts (typical of young children) appears superficially to substantiate this position. But (a) the performance of the schizophrenic is not qualitatively like that of the child and (b) there is serious question as to whether the schizophrenic is capable, because of his personality disorder, of fully co-operating in the test situation.

The pioneer work on schizophrenic thinking was done by Vygotski (1934 *a, b*), a Russian psychologist. He also believed the essence of schizophrenic thinking to be a regression to that level where the individual 'thinks in complexes,' objects being grouped in terms of their concrete, physical similarities or associations. The modern classic in this area is the monograph by Hanfmann and Kasanin (1942). The testing procedure used by these investigators, employing variously colored, shaped, and sized blocks with nonsense indicators on their bottom sides, has already been described. The performances of 62 schizophrenics, 24 patients with organic brain disease, and 95 normal controls, both of college and noncollege levels, were studied.

Hanfmann and Kasanin found it necessary to postulate three levels of performance: the *primitive level* is characterized by a trial-and-error approach, the solution being achieved mechanically and not being reproducible. At the *intermediate level,* although solution may be accompanied by partial insight, reproduction of the correct sorting proceeds with many errors and hesitations. The *conceptual level* is characterized by active search for the unknown basis of classification, solutions being accompanied by verbalizable insight which makes possible smooth and immediate reproduction. (1) *Are there 'levels' of conceptual thinking?* Hanfmann and Kasanin report an extremely wide variation in performance among both normals and psychotics, and there is certainly no evidence here for Goldstein's 'either-or' abstract versus concrete levels. (2) *Do normal subjects always perform at the 'conceptual level'?* The answer here is definitely negative. Only the college-educated group as a whole performed consistently at this level. The noncollege group varied widely, mean performance being intermediate. (3) *Do schizophrenics show loss in conceptual ability?* Although the mean performance of schizophrenics was inferior to that of normal controls of their own educational level, the range here was also broad. Many college-educated schizophrenics were superior to most noncollege normals, some performing consistently at the highest level; yet one third of the college-educated schizophrenics performed at a primitive level. The organic patients were more consistently primitive in level than the schizophrenics.

In direct contrast, Cameron (1938, 1939) concludes that personality disorganization is the prime factor, the measured decrement in conceptualization being a direct reflection of this rather than a specific deterioration in capacity to generalize. He reports that his subjects tended to intrude personal, emotionally colored materials into the test situation, which obscured the immediate task. One schizophrenic, for example, refused to put yellow blocks with white ones because no Chinese were working with white people in the hospital! Although this may show severe disorientation of the personality, it also seems to represent a rather high degree of abstracting ability. He also found his schizophrenics unwilling to remain within the bounds of the test; they wanted to 'change the rules of the game' freely. There was further discrepancy noted between the performance and verbal levels of schizophrenic patients: a subject might sort blocks into a rational, conceptual order and then be unable to verbalize the classification.

Is the schizophrenic's conceptualizing difficulty attributable to his personality disorganization, or is his disorganized personality largely attributable to a specific intellectual (conceptual) deficit? The bulk of the evidence seems to favor the latter position, but the issue is by no means closed.

Does the schizophrenic's performance resemble that of children (and hence represent a functional regression), or does it resemble more nearly that of organic patients (and hence represent itself an organic disorder, perhaps in the frontal areas)? Hanfmann and Kasanin (1942) seem to favor the organic view, but what about the schizophrenics who do function on the highest conceptual level? Either the organic interpretation must be modified or the psychiatric classification of certain patients as 'schizophrenic' is invalid.

Concept Formation, Abstracting Ability, and 'Representative Factors'

The type of behavioral performance required of subjects by Hull (1920)—discriminating the common identical elements within complex stimulus patterns and setting up specific vocal reactions to them—is more reasonably to be considered *labeling* than concept formation. Such reactions, based upon generalization among physically similar stimuli, are typical of what Goldstein (1941) has termed a *concrete performance level*. The patient with frontal pathology can say 'red' when any object of that color is shown. He can pick out red yarns if they are sufficiently similar physically to the sample color. He can respond to the direction, 'Give me the comb,' and his reaction of running it through his hair is a discriminative one to such a stimulus; he will make the same response to red combs and green ones, to long ones and short ones, to combs with either narrow or wide spacings. But the patient *cannot* tell you what combs-in-general are for or show you (without a comb in his hand) how to use one. He has no abstract concept of comb.

On the other hand, the type of performance demanded by Reed (1946) and Heidbreder (1946, 1947)—making a common symbolic response to a class of stimuli that are not necessarily similar physically—represents a form of behavior distinct from ordinary discriminative habits and hence justifies the use of a distinctive term, *conceptual behavior*. Such reactions are typical of what Goldstein has termed an *abstract performance level*. The normal adult taking an abstraction test typically guides himself with such mediating verbal cues as 'tall, flat ones' or 'things used to eat with' and so forth. The overt sorting or labeling behaviors are based, not upon physical identities or common configurations among the stimuli, but upon common cues resulting from the subject's own symbolic processes which guide his sorting and labeling activities.

The fact that individuals who have organic brain pathology in the *frontal* areas are the ones who typically suffer loss in abstracting ability further suggests that this ability is related to what have been termed 'representative factors' in higher animals. It will be remembered that surgical removal of frontal cortex in primates and other animals often disrupted symbolic activities like the delayed reaction. The most probable role of the frontal cortex seemed to be that of inhibiting reactions to incidental cues, thus facilitating retention of the symbolic process. The importance of this recent memory factor also appears in clinical case studies of human subjects who have undergone surgical removal of the frontal lobes. Will this help explain the concrete performance of organic and schizophrenic patients? It is true that both seem less able to avoid responding to the immediate stimulus characteristics of the test materials than do normal subjects. To the extent that these 'forced' reactions interfere with symbolic processes and prevent the maintenance of a set, a performance rated as 'concrete' might well result. In any case, it seems highly probable that continuing research in this general area will reveal close relationships among the phenomena of concept formation, abstracting ability, and representative factors in animal subjects.

Chapter 16

LANGUAGE BEHAVIOR

It is only in comparatively recent times that scientists have begun to study language by objective methods. There have been two major hindrances to objectivity here. The first of these is the *philosophical dualism* inherent in our own language itself. We divide our universe into the physical and the mental. This is not entirely a matter of choice or rational decision on our part; it is borne in upon us by the very words we have to use and their connotations. Nor is the Man in the Ivory Tower immune to the implications of his own language. As Whorf (1941) puts it, 'Monistic, holistic, and relativistic views of reality appeal to philosophers and some scientists, but they are badly handicapped for appealing to the "common sense" of the Western average man. This is not because nature herself refutes them (if she did, philosophers could have discovered this much) but because they must be talked about in what amounts to a new language' (p. 88). Even such a renowned psychologist as Wilhelm Wundt defined language as 'the medium for the expression of images and ideas,' implying that these mental events are primary and by some elaborate system managed to express themselves in speech.

The second hindrance to objectivity is the ubiquitous *tendency to reify the word,* to assume the word itself somehow carries its own meaning. The infant randomly produces the noise 'ma-ma' and that fond parent exclaims, 'Why, the little darling, he knows me!' The word is produced and therefore the child must have the idea behind it. Malinowski aptly dubbed this naïve conception the 'bucket theory' of meaning—words like little buckets are assumed to pick up their loads of meaning in one mind, carry them across intervening space, and dump them in another mind. 'This attitude in which the word is regarded as a real entity, containing its meaning as a Soul-box contains the spiritual part of a person or thing, is shown to be derived from the primitive, magical uses of language and to reach right into the most important and influential systems of metaphysics. Meaning, the real "essence" of a word, achieves thus Real Existence in Plato's realm of Ideas . . .' (Malinowski, 1938, p. 308). Among some primitives a man never reveals his real name; it may be inscribed on a piece of wood or stone and hidden in some secret and sacred place, because if an ill-wisher were to discover the real name and practice magic upon it, its owner might become ill and die. Piaget has amply demonstrated that for the child names appear to 'adhere' to the things signified; they seem to be as much parts of objects as do colors and shapes—after all, it has always been sufficient to merely look at something to know its name. Of course, civilized adults, except when they are being exceptionally self-critical, reify words just as primitives and young children do.

Having decided to be objective, we may first survey the problem in a manner brutishly materialistic. Heard language, the swift conversational flow of words and phrases, is nothing more than pressures on the eardrums or, as far as the awareness of the hearer is concerned, patterns of nervous activity in the auditory cortex—this is physical enough. Spoken language, the equally swift flow of vocalizations, is nothing more than a complexly integrated series of skilled movements of the diaphragm, vocal cords, jaws, lips, and tongue, with air being driven through the varied openings at appropriate moments and pressures—this is physical enough. What of the selective association of noises made with situations being experienced? Just as the organism learns to flex its arm or clasp a bar in response to a pattern of cues, so it may learn to produce certain vocal reactions in certain situations. But what lies behind all this expelling of air through conformations of the vocal apparatus? What is lacking in this mechanical monstrosity? Meaning must be brought into the picture somehow, and here's the rub— meaning has no accepted material correlate. If we are to hold to our materialistic moorings, we must *postulate material events for meaning* and then investigate the theoretical consequences of this postulation. Since this problem is the crucial one, the larger portion of this chapter will be devoted to it.

Language in Animals

We may begin before the beginning and briefly consider the question of language in lower animals. (1) *Animals can respond to quasilinguistic cues.* Long ago Thorndike observed that his cats could learn to leap upon their feeding boxes when he said 'Time to eat' or something equivalent. This is nothing more than ordinary conditioning, of course, in which the distinctive cues happen to be verbal and have meaning to the human observer. Thorndike found that his cats would also learn to make the same response when he regularly said 'Today is Tuesday.' (2) *Some animals can produce humanoid noises.* The parrot, for example, can reproduce sounds that clearly approximate human speech and, through conditioning, can make these responses in appropriate situations. Mowrer (1950) has reported an intensive study of the development of speech in this species. Here again it would seem that we are dealing with conditioning, with emphasis upon characteristics of the response. (3) *Animals display symbolic processes.* We have already seen that higher animals make use of 'representative factors' in delayed reaction situations and the like (cf. Chap. 15). It can also be shown that some animals can represent to themselves different objects discriminatively. For example, Tinklepaugh (1928) first trained a monkey to wait blindfolded through a delay period and then choose that one of two cups under which a food reward had previously been hidden by the experimenter. Occasionally, when the monkey was blindfolded, the experimenter would substitute a piece of lettuce for the piece of banana he had hidden while the animal watched. When released, the monkey would turn over the correct cup, extend her hand for the food, but then not touch it; instead, she would search about the cup, giving unmistakable signs of irritation, and reject the less preferred lettuce entirely. That the lettuce was still appetizing to her, however, was shown by the fact that she would eat it when it was the 'expected' food on subsequent trials. (4) *Animals communicate with one another.* Colonies of howler monkeys utilize a considerable variety of signals in their natural habitat (Carpenter, 1934); certain cries by 'lookouts' produce flight, others approach. In such cases it appears that the sounds are not made with any intent to communicate, but rather they represent momentary emotional states of the speaker. The listening animal responds in terms of the state expressed, perhaps through identi- fication (the sound quality being similar to that produced by the listening animal itself when in the same states).

If all these things be true of animals, why is it that only the human species has developed language as such? The chimpanzee is capable of vocalizations almost as elaborate as man's. Yerkes and Learned (1925) have identified as many as 32 different speech sounds in this animal. The chimpanzee is also capable of distinctively representing objects in its environment; it can learn by observation and insight. Yet none of the various attempts to teach these animals to speak has been very successful. Why is man the only talking animal? We can only guess at the reasons: the development of language requires (a) a sufficiently elaborate vocalizing mechanism, (b) sufficient complexity of cortical development (intelligence) to establish and maintain a multitude of fine discriminations, *and* (c) *cultural standardization, transmission and elaboration of specific, distinctive symbolic reactions.* If the human organism had not developed stable cultural organizations in which the products of one generation could be adopted by another, it is doubtful whether human speech would have developed much above the sympathetic communication of emotional states displayed in other primates.

Speculations on the Origin of Language

How did the first apelike men, or manlike apes, begin to communicate? This is a question that has intrigued speculative philosophers of all ages, and the question is as purely speculative as one could hope since there seems little likelihood that any of the hypotheses will ever be put to experimental test. There are three time-honored theories. (1) *The 'ding-dong'* (mystical) *theory* assumes that certain objects have the power to evoke certain sounds from man. Once these sounds have been made in association with experiencing the object, the sounds come to mean the objects. Given the commonness of men, communication results. One wonders why communication is so imperfect in this case! (2) *The 'bow-wow'* (imitative) *theory* assumes that the beginnings of communication lay in imitating the sounds made by animals and things. Drawing heavily upon onomatopoeic words, such as 'buzz,' 'rumble,' and 'bark,' the theory states that given the idea of thunder, say, and the wish to communicate this idea, the primitive man-ape points skyward and mouths 'rumble, rumble.' With this as a starter, man goes on elaborating, and his products are standardized by cultural mechanisms. Various linguistic processes like shortening, combining, prefixing, and suffixing explain why most of our words are no longer onomatopoeic in nature. (3) *The 'pooh-pooh'* (interjectional) *theory* assumes that various unlearned, emotional vocal responses tended to occur in stereotyped situations: when a bad taste or smell was experienced, 'ugh!'; when a sudden pain, 'ow!'; when pleasant tastes were being enjoyed, 'mmm!' Again, this just serves to initiate communication.

Sir Richard Paget (1944) has offered a theory that stresses the utility of speech for a social animal, and it has been dubbed the 'yum-yum' theory. Parts of the total behavior toward objects are assumed to be mouth and throat movements. Thus, part of the anticipatory behavior toward a juicy food-object involves mouth-smacking. When air happens to be blown through the smacking mouth, 'yum, yum, yum' is produced. Language thus occurs rather accidentally from an elaborate system of gestures. Why should the vocal aspect be selected for symbolism and communication? This brings up the utility notion. Suppose two man-apes are busily digging grubs with their hands and wish to communicate the fact that they taste good; to be sure, they could stop digging and rub their tummies, but this would mean missing a few grubs; better, they could 'yum, yum, yum' between bites. In other words, the vocal apparatus is less likely to be occupied with daily chores than the hands, and hence communication becomes restricted to this area.

After reviewing the above theories, Thorndike (1943) presents one of his own, dubbing it alternatively the 'babble-babble' or 'lucky-chucky' theory. We take as given the pre-existence of social grouping among prehumans and the presence of various natural objects, tools, and playthings in the environment. We further assume that at an early age our man-apes develop memory images, ideas, and expectations (X's) concerning people and objects about them. Let us finally assume that these man-apes play with their vocal apparatus much as the young infant spontaneously produces noises. Now suppose by chance an intelligent man-ape produces 'uk!' when he spies a clam. The making of this 'uk' noise will become associated, through the ordinary laws of learning, with the X which accompanies clam experiences. Our intelligent man-ape gathers some clams and comes back to the cave, calling 'uk, uk, uk!' and displays his catch; other less intelligent members of the group imitate the sound while observing and eating the clams. This theory has the advantage that the selection of noises to represent objects is no longer restricted to imitation of natural sounds or emotional ejaculations. Of course, the 'bowwow' and 'pooh-pooh' mechanisms might give an initial advantage to noises of these types.

DEVELOPMENT OF LANGUAGE IN HUMANS

Elaboration of Vocal Mechanisms

(1) *The birth cry.* Since there seems little chance that infants vocalize before birth, we may begin with the birth cry by which most infants greet the extrauterine world. There has been a great deal of nonsense written about the meaning of this reflexive response. A well-known psychoanalyst (who will be left unnamed) had this to say: 'The birth cry is an expression of the infant's overwhelming sense of inferiority on thus suddenly being confronted with reality, without ever having had to deal with its

problems.' What is the simplest explanation of this cry? When the umbilical cord is severed, the infant's oxygen supply is cut off; the increase in carbon dioxide in the blood initiates reflexive expansion of the lung cavity, with a result that air is drawn rapidly over the vocal cords; and, depending on the chance position of the vocal cords, noise is produced. A large proportion of the early vocalizations of the infant is crying and screaming of a similar reflexive nature.

(2) *The first 4-5 months.* Equally random and reflexive are the spontaneous vocalizations of a noncrying nature that occur during the first few months of life. The vocal apparatus is a muscular system, and activity here partakes of the gross, mass activity of the total organism. Just as arms and legs are randomly moved about, so the jaws, lips, tongue, and vocal cords are randomly exercised, and when air happens to be pushed through the oral cavity, varying patterns of sound are produced. Many of the earlier investigators, attempting to bring order to this chaos, listened to these noises and reported the order of appearance of the various speech sounds (phonemes), implying that in the course of maturation the infant successively 'becomes capable' of making more and more complex speech sounds. The labial consonants (p, b, m) and velars ($k, g, x,$ etc.), for example, are usually said to be the first to appear after the crying noises, which are largely vowel in character. The large, but not too consistent, literature on this topic is surveyed by McCarthy (1933, 1946) and Esper (1935). The inadequate recording methods employed in most of the early studies make the data of dubious validity. The typical procedure was merely to listen to the spontaneous vocalizations of an infant and write down what was heard. The selective factor of auditory perception—listeners 'hear' most readily those sounds that correspond to the phonemes of their own language—was not considered. Another difficulty with this informal method is that the data are not reproducible; from the total splurge of sounds made by an actively vocal infant, only the small sample that happens to strike the observer is recorded at all, and no opportunity is given to go back and check the observations.

Actual transcription (via microphone and tape or records) of infant vocalizations solves many of these difficulties. This method was used by the writer in a study on the development of vocalization in a single infant during the first year of life.* Approximately 10 minutes of vocal activity were recorded each week, partly of spontaneous vocalization and partly of responses to standard stimulus situations. The first observation of note was that within the data for the first two months of life may be found all of the speech sounds that the human vocal system can produce, including French vowels and trills, German umlaut and guttural sounds, and many that are only describable in phonetic symbols. This is in flat contradiction to the notion that the infant gradually 'becomes capable' of making various sounds. A more accurate statement would be that the comparative *frequencies* of various speech sounds change as development proceeds; owing to a number of anatomical factors, there is variation in the *probability* of

---

* The complete set of recordings described here is on file at the Clinic of Child Development of Yale University. Detailed phonetic analysis of these data by a trained phoneticist has not as yet been made, and the findings presented here should be taken as suggestive only.

given combinations of jaw, lip, and tongue positions being assumed (and hence the probability of various sounds being produced).

Rather than bearing any direct relation to external stimulus situations, the character of the infant's vocalization seemed to depend upon his momentary physiological state. During and after feeding, for example, soft, open vowels predominate; the same sounds may be produced at other times by softly stroking the cheeks or drawing a piece of soft tissue over the lips—these sounds are accompanied by bodily quiescence and correspond to what may be characterized as a passive, 'pleasant' physiological state. Conversely, when the nipple is abruptly withdrawn while the infant is still hungry, a rising crescendo of vocal activity, starting with vigorous grunts and ending in full-scale crying, is regularly recorded. The speech sounds here are explosive and hard in quality, such as '. . . erh! . . . errâh! . . . argurh! . . . erh! erh! erh! . . . errâh! errâh! . . .' These sounds are accompanied by rapidly increasing vigor of general bodily movement and correspond to what may be characterized as an active, 'unpleasant' physiological state. The same sequence can be obtained by holding a hand over the infant's eyes or preventing arm or head movement; later, removing a toy from the infant's hand would produce the same effect. It seems likely that the same efferent neural patterns that produce relaxation of the gross bodily musculature also serve to relax the muscles that participate in vocalizing, whereas increasing tension in the bodily musculature is paralleled by increasing tension in the vocal muscles.

In these recordings it was possible to trace the development of *control* over various aspects of the vocalizing process. No intention on the part of the infant is implied by 'control' here; rather, it is operationally defined as the repeated production of a particular vocalic act, i.e. nonrandom recurrence. From the completely random vocal behavior that characterizes the first few weeks of life, the first aspect of speech to achieve control seems to be *volume of sound*. Within the second month there appear in the recordings more and more frequently cases in which the volume is 'deliberately' varied. Much as if a new game had been discovered, the infant explores all the ramifications of this skill—whatever vocal cord and lip-tongue-jaw position happens to be present, the volume of the sound is systematically varied. The control here presumably depends upon discriminative innervation of the muscles of the diaphragm. Within the third and fourth months (in the case of this infant) control is extended to the vocal cord muscles and hence over *pitch*. It is only about the fifth month that control extends to the complicated systems of muscles that determine the *quality of the speech sounds,* the muscles controlling movements of the tongue, the jaw, and the lips. This point coincides with the beginning of the babbling. Rather than appearing in cleanly separated steps, continuous overlapping of these 'stages' was apparent in the recordings.

Although all speech sounds *can* be made by the young infant, the actual frequencies of different sounds vary as development proceeds. Figure 213 compares the *relative frequency patterns* for normal infants of varying ages with those for American adults, the data being taken from investigations by O. C. Irwin (1948, 1952). The infant pattern gradually becomes more like that of the speech he hears about him, elements foreign to the culture into which he is born dropping out and those indigenous to it becoming

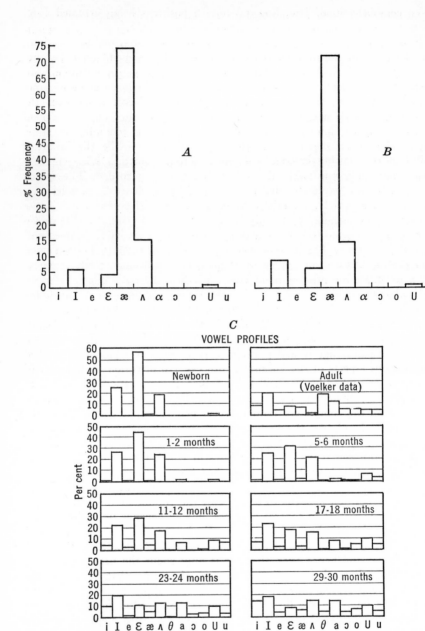

FIGURE 213. Vowel phoneme frequency profiles: (*A* and *B*) comparison of newborn white and Negro infants (Irwin, *Journal of Speech and Hearing Disorders,* 1952, 17:272); (*C*) gradual shift of phoneme distribution toward a pattern typical of adults in the infant's environment (O. C. Irwin, *Journal of Speech and Hearing Disorders,* 1948, 13:32).

more prominent. Since a large part of this 'acculturation' occurs before the child can actually be said to speak, it appears that the infant in its babbling is differentially reinforced for making parentlike sounds. The phonetic frequency patterns for feeble-minded infants show a much more gradual modification (Irwin, 1942). Irwin and Chen (1946) have studied the rate at which the infant's repertoire of speech sounds develop, finding it to be a negatively accelerated function of age during the first $2\frac{1}{2}$ years of life. The method of securing data was to visit infants in their homes (95 subjects being used) and take down in the International Phonetic Alphabet the sounds uttered during 30 breaths, this constituting the sample for each infant on each visit. From this it can be seen that only the more prominent (frequent) phonemes were likely to be included. Results demonstrate a regularly increasing *diversity* in the speech sounds of young children. Although boys and girls are found to start with the same speech-sound diversity, girls develop at a slightly faster rate, this finding being quite consistent with a great deal of other evidence on sex differences in speech. The ratio of consonants to vowels also increases regularly during this period, from about $1/5$ to about $1/1$, which approximates the adult ratio.

(3) *Syllabic babbling.* From about 5 months on, the infant's vocalization becomes more and more syllabic in nature, although still incomprehensible. Shirley (1933) observed creations such as 'uggle-uggle,' 'erdaherdah,' 'oddle-oddle,' 'a-bah-bah,' 'hey-hey,' 'bup-bup-bup,' 'aduh-duhdeh-duhe-ooh,' 'adhu-ajuh,' 'awooh-awah,' and 'lul-lul-lah.' These syllabic sounds are clearly languagelike. 'Awooh-awah' is a fair facsimile of 'Are you awake?' and any of these sound patterns *could* be meaningful in our speech. Much of this babbling has a clear social reference, as has been observed by both Bean (1932) and Shirley (1933). Babbling in isolation probably has a pseudosocial reference as well, the infant presumably making no clear distinction between self-stimulation with sounds and stimulation from adults. Another characteristic of babbling reported by Shirley, Bean, and others is the way in which infants seem to select certain syllables for practice during a given period, then shifting to another, and so on. As elsewhere in the development of language, one gets the impression that the mere discovery of a skilled movement is sufficient reinforcement for its own practice, and syllabic babbling has the important function of providing the child with practice on the part-processes that are later to be utilized in communicative speech.

The repetitiousness of syllabic babbling has been overemphasized because of its theoretical implications. It is true, of course, that during this period many sounds are immediately repeated, often many times over, but a larger proportion of babbling is not repetitious. This emphasis can probably be traced to Floyd Allport's influential treatment of language development in his *Social Psychology* (1924). Allport made explicit use of E. B. Holt's circular reflex hypothesis. According to this hypothesis the excitation threshold for a reaction is temporarily lowered through its own occurrence. Since the auditory stimuli produced by any vocal reaction are present as traces when the response is reactivated, they become conditioned to that vocal reaction. The fact that deaf children do not babble has been interpreted as favoring this hypothesis, and also the fact that speech sounds that have been spontaneously babbled can most easily be evoked 'imitatively' by the speech of others.

Actually, the failure of deaf children to babble is evidence *against* the Holt theory: vocal reactions produce other forms of self-stimulation than auditory; for example, there is the complex of proprioceptive sensations. Why are these response-produced stimuli not circularly conditioned to vocal reactions in the deaf child? This evidence really favors a theory that emphasizes the social reinforcement from vocalizing. Since the deaf child cannot create a parent-substitute by its own babbling, i.e. sounds like those made by the parents who fondle and care for him, there is little reinforcement for this activity. Another important point against the reflex aspect of Holt's theory is that all speech sounds are not repeated. Why should a reflexive arrangement function in such a way that only certain sounds, especially those resembling the language forms heard in infant's social environment, are selectively babbled? The value of the Holt view is that it provides a mechanism whereby speech sounds can become conditioned to the muscular reactions which produce them, and this sets the stage for the later development of labeling. Any mechanism whereby serial repetition of speech sounds is guaranteed would, however, serve the same function.

(4) *Imitation of speech sounds.* The elaborate practice provided by babbling serves both to develop and stabilize those complex skill sequences that are required for speech and to associate auditory sounds (self-produced) with the motor reactions that produce them. This primary association between self-produced sound and vocal response is shown diagrammatically as Fig. 214(1). For the child to imitate speech sounds made by other people about him, the response must *generalize* from self-produced cues originally established in stage (1) to a similar cue produced by others. Stage (2) in Fig. 214 adds another face (e.g. the mother) and describes this substitution of cues. That generalization is involved here is shown convincingly by the fact that persons with high-pitched voices like the child (mothers) are more readily imitated than persons with low-pitched voices (fathers). This is, of course, an oversimplified picture of this stage in language development: (a) It is frequently a question of who imitates whom—often fond parents hear the little one produce 'da-da' and happily imitate the child. (b) Imitation is seldom accurate duplication. The child's capacity to imitate speech sounds is in part limited by the spontaneous babbling practice it has had. There are also differences between speech sounds originally babbled by the child and those he hears from adults. (c) Imitation is not an automatic phenomenon once a given developmental stage has been reached. Although it occurs with sufficient frequency to play an important role in language development, there are more occasions in which the child fails to imitate.

(5) *Labeling.* Given a repertoire of syllabic vocalizations as well-practiced skills and a readiness to imitate, the acquisition of object labels is a straightforward learning phenomenon. Referring again to Fig. 214(3), the adult holds up or points to a doll within the child's field of vision and says 'doll'; the child (ideally) makes an imitative approximation, vocalizing 'da,' and reaches for the object; the parent feels very much pleased with this and immediately applies social rewards. In theoretical terms the visual cues from the object are being conditioned to the vocal response. The

final step in labeling, as shown in Fig. 214(4), is making the correct vocal response to the object as a stimulus without needing an adult model. *Labeling is thus the discriminative association of a specific vocal reaction pattern with a given stimulus situation.* This picture is, of course, a highly simplified theoretical paradigm.

All of the fundamental principles of learning operate here. While learning to say 'da-da' to the appropriate father-object, the child *generalizes* the

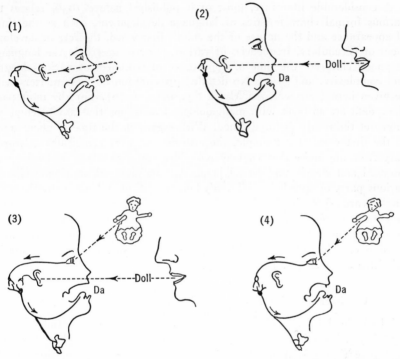

FIGURE 214. Stage (1): random articulation of syllables with fixation by circular reflex. Stage (2): evocation of the same articulate elements by speech sounds of others. Stage (3): conditioning of the articulate elements (evoked by others) by objects. Stage (4): sight of the doll alone is now sufficient to evoke its name ('da' being as close as the baby can come to the pronunciation of 'doll'). F. H. Allport, *Social Psychology,* Houghton Mifflin Co., Boston, 1924, p. 184.

response widely and often embarrassingly to large individuals of all shapes, sizes, ages, and colors; anything from a bird to a horse as well as the household cat may briefly be known as a 'kikki.' With differential reinforcement and resultant *discrimination,* vocal responses become narrowed to appropriate objects. Children usually display various forms of baby talk which is equivalent to the fumbling, awkward movements made in the learning of any complex motor skill. Many parents, thinking it cute, *reinforce* these fumbling vocal movements, strengthening them to a point where they become difficult to eradicate, much to the same parents' later discomfort. Children sometimes learn novel labels for objects and situations, yet the same laws of learning are functioning. The writer's daughter, when asked, 'What do you say?' as she was given a toy that had been dropped, replied 'dagum' neatly and clearly; the same response occurred soon after when she was given a cooky, and within a few days this noise had become her standard response in 'thank you' situations. This phenomenon of creating novel label systems is often found among twins; presumably a variety of spontaneously produced sounds becomes standardized within the social environment twins provide one another. The development of such 'little languages,' as Jesperson (1922) has called them, offers an unusual opportunity to study the psychology of language.

A considerable literature, most of it published before 1930, relates to various formal characteristics of language development, such as the time of appearance and the nature of the child's first word, the rate of development of vocabulary, frequencies of various parts of speech in the language of young children, the time of appearance of sentences of various length and complexity, and so on. No detailed presentation of these matters will be given here (however, see McCarthy, 1933, 1946). For the most part these data are so beset with methodological questions that any attempt to interpret the results is foredoomed. With regard to the time of appearance of the first word, for example, the criteria for what constitutes a 'word' vary from any noise that vaguely resembles adult speech to a clearly pronounced and clearly understood label. All the material on frequencies of various parts of speech in children's language is of dubious value because single words serve in multiple grammatical roles for the child. 'Mommy' may mean *mother, come!* or *mother is there* or even *look what I've done!* depending upon the situational and gestural context. Single words thus serve as complete phrases, as is also true of the adult language of certain primitive cultures (cf. Latif, 1934).

CONCEPTIONS OF THE SIGN-PROCESS

The little child whose language development we have been studying may say 'kitty' when stimulated by that furry, four-legged object, but this is no guarantee that this noise represents anything to her. Now suppose the child's mother asks, 'Where is Kitty?' and she immediately begins searching—in the sunny corner of the porch, by the cat's dinner plate. Does 'kitty' now have meaning? Is it functioning as a sign? It would seem that such is the case: the child is responding to a stimulus that is not the object (to the *word* 'kitty') in a manner that is relevant to the object signified; the child's behavior is apparently organized and directed by some implicit process initiated by the word. We may even hear her repeating 'where's kitty' to herself while she hunts. Similarly, it will be recalled that the patient restricted to a concrete level of performance could label objects correctly, could respond directly to them as stimuli, but could not guide his own behavior by means of abstract symbols of these objects.

The Defining Problem

It would appear, then, that not all stimuli are meaningful. Not all stimuli signify something other than themselves. The shock that galvanizes the rat into vigorous escape movements does not usually stand for something else nor does the pellet of food found at the end of a maze nor a hammer in one's hand nor a shoe on one's foot. The defining problem is simply to differentiate the conditions under which a pattern of stimulation is a sign of something else from those conditions where it is not. This certainly does not seem difficult, yet it has troubled philosophers for centuries.

We may now go at the problem somewhat formally and in doing so compare several theories of the sign-process that have been offered. Certain terms already introduced in connection with the mediation hypothesis will be useful here as well: *

$\dot{S}$ = object = any pattern of stimulation which evokes reactions on the part of an organism;

$\boxed{S}$ = sign = any pattern of stimulation which is not $\dot{S}$ and yet evokes reactions relevant to $\dot{S}$ (conditions under which this holds not stated as yet).

The definition of $\dot{S}$ is broad enough to include any response of the organism to stimulation. This is necessary since, although one usually thinks of 'objects' as being the things denoted by signs, actually any and all patterns of stimulation—a gust of cold, northerly wind against the face, the mass of sensations we call a 'bellyache,' the pattern of sensations that accompany being rained upon—may be 'objects' at this level of discourse. In fact, one sign may be the 'object' represented by another sign, e.g. when the picture of an apple is called a DAX in certain experiments or when we learn that 'nexus' means 'link.' The definition of $\boxed{S}$ is purposely left incomplete at this point since it varies with one's hypothesis concerning the nature of the sign-process. In simplest terms, then, the question is: *Under what conditions does something which is not an object become a sign of that object?* The pattern of stimulation which is the sign is never identical with the pattern of stimulation which is the object—the word HAMMER is not the same stimulus as the object hammer, yet the sign does elicit behavior that is in some manner relevant to the object, a characteristic not shared by an infinite number of other stimulus patterns which are *not* signs of that object.

Mentalistic View

According to this view the relation between signs and their objects is established through the mediation of ideas. The 'idea' is the essence of meaning. The word HAMMER gives rise to the idea of that object in the mind; conversely, perception of the object hammer gives rise to the same idea which can be 'expressed' in appropriate signs. In terms of our symbol system:

$$\boxed{S} \rightarrow \text{'idea'} \rightarrow \dot{S}$$

(or)

$$\dot{S} \rightarrow \text{'idea'} \rightarrow \boxed{S}$$

* No attempt will be made to follow the terminology that has been developed in semiotic. For this material the reader may consult Morris (1946) and other references he cites. Rather, we shall use where possible the psychological terms already incorporated within this book, only adding new concepts where existing terms fail to achieve necessary distinctions.

Dualism is, of course, inherent in this view; objects and signs, as material events, achieve their signifying relation by being tied to the same mentalistic ideas. The ideas, via some unspecified mind-matter transfer system, are able to express themselves in signs. The major difficulty with this theory from the point of view of science is that it is completely untestable. Actually, it merely substitutes a word (idea) for an explanation; in order to explain the sign-process we must first explain the nature of ideas.

Substitution Theory

Naïve application of Pavlovian conditioning principles by early behaviorists such as Watson leads to the theory that signs achieve their meaning simply by being conditioned to the same reactions originally made to objects. An object evokes certain behavior from the organism; if any other stimulus pattern is consistently paired with the original object, it becomes conditioned to the same responses and thus gets its meaning. The object is the unconditioned stimulus and the sign is the conditioned stimulus, the latter being merely substituted for the former. In symbolic terms:

and the definition of sign-process would be that *whenever something which is not the object evokes in an organism the same reaction evoked by the object, it is a sign of that object.* The very simplicity of this theory highlights its inadequacy. Signs almost never evoke the same responses as do the objects they represent. The word FIRE has meaning for the reader without sending him into wild flight; the word APPLE has meaning without eliciting chewing movements. It will be remembered that the simple substitution theory of learning on which this view of sign-processes is based has itself been shown to be insufficient: the response to the conditioned stimulus is seldom if ever identical with the response to the unconditioned stimulus. Nevertheless, this substitution theory represents a first step toward a behavioral interpretation of the sign-process.

The Sign-process as a 'Set'

In a paper entitled 'Foundations of the Theory of Signs' (1938), Charles Morris, a semiotician working in the philosophical tradition established by Peirce and other American pragmatists, proposed a formula for the sign-process that avoids the pitfall of substitution theory. He stated in essence that signs achieve their meanings by eliciting reactions that 'take account of' the objects signified. The sign HAMMER may evoke different responses than those evoked by the object, but they must have the character of being relevant to the object. In symbolic terms:

$$\dot{S} \longrightarrow R$$

$$\boxed{S} \dashrightarrow R_x \text{ ('taking account of' } \dot{S})$$

As Morris puts it, the response made to the sign, called the 'interpretant,' mediately takes account of the object signified. This may eliminate the substitution problem, but it seems a step backward toward the mentalistic position as well. It is precisely this 'taking account of' that needs explaining.

During the period intervening between this paper and his recent book, *Signs, Language and Behavior* (1946), Morris studied with two prominent behavior theorists, Tolman and Hull. The effects of this immersion in learning theory are evident in his book, which is a pioneer attempt to reduce semiology to an objective behavioral basis, but one can still find faint traces of mentalism in his position. He states that 'if anything, A, is a preparatory-stimulus which in the absence of stimulus-objects initiating response-sequences of a certain behavior-family causes a disposition in some organism to respond under certain conditions by response-sequences of this behavior-family, then A is a sign' (p. 10). Reduced to its essentials and translated into the terms we have been using, this becomes: *any pattern of stimulation which is not the object becomes a sign of the object if it produces in an organism a 'disposition' to make any of the responses previously elicited by the object.* Symbolically:

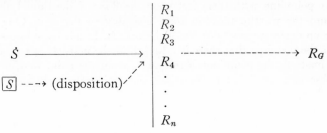

In other words, HAMMER is a sign of that object because it 'disposes' certain human organisms to make responses which have previously been made to the hammer itself. There is no requirement that the *overt* reactions originally elicited by the object be made to the sign; the sign merely creates a disposition or set to make such reactions, actual occurrence depending upon the concurrence of supporting conditions.

Regarding the crucial term here, Morris says, 'A *disposition to respond* to something in a certain way is a state of an organism at a given time which is such that under certain additional conditions the response in question takes place.' Morris can be forgiven for vagueness here; 'disposition' is one of those terms that materialistically inclined writers find hard to define. But rules for identifying 'dispositions' must be formulated or there is more than a trace of mentalism in the system. Morris discusses this problem (pp. 12-15): *complete identification* can be obtained by placing the organism in an adequate situation and observing whether the response-sequences in question do in fact occur (e.g. place a rat on a grill and observe whether it will run when the buzzer sounds—but will this work with all signs?); *segments of complete response-sequences* may serve to identify dispositions (e.g. the chimpanzee salivates upon seeing a poker chip which has been associated with raisins—Morris doesn't explore this possibility fully); ideally, some objectively measurable state may be discovered as an *invariant correlate* of 'disposition' (e.g. brain waves); finally, there are the *introspections* of sign-using and verbalizing organisms (the pitfalls here being fully appreciated by Morris).

Beyond the fundamental danger that 'dispositions' may serve as mere surrogates for 'ideas' in this theory, there are certain other difficulties. For one thing, Morris seems to have revived the substitution notion, except that it is no longer 'simple' substitution. As the position is stated, the sign disposes the organism to *make response-sequences of the same behavior-family originally elicited by the object signified.* But is this the case? Is my response to the word APPLE (e.g. free-associating another sign, PEACH) any part of the behavior-family elicited by the object apple? Is my response to the symbol X in an equation any part of the behavior-family associated with the 'pounds of butter' which X signifies? Behavior toward signs is functionally independent of behavior toward the objects signified; *it is the disposition itself that is dependent upon original object-tied behavior.* The second difficulty with Morris's formulation is that it fails to differentiate sign-behavior from many instinctive reactions and from ordinary conditioning. To appreciate this difficulty will require a brief digression.

When a breach is made in a termite nest, the worker-termites set up a distinctive pounding with their feet upon the floor of the tunnel about the breach, and the warrior-termites come charging to the spot. Once there, they take up defensive positions about the breach. Is this pounding stimulus a sign for the warriors that there is a breach in the nest? It is true that the response made to the pounding is relevant (from the point of view of the human observer, certainly) to something other than itself. But is this sufficient? It happens that this behavior on the part of the warrior-termites is purely instinctive; they do not have to learn that this pounding is followed by enemies entering the nest in order to behave this way. Most students of sign-behavior would wish to exclude such purely reflexive reactions, believing that signs must achieve their meanings through learning.

But is learning itself an adequate criterion? Are all stimuli that become conditioned to responses automatically signs? The pupillary contractile response can be conditioned to a tone by pairing this stimulus with a bright light, the response in this case being quite involuntary, i.e. the subject being unaware of his reaction. Does the tone now mean bright light to the subject? In developing any skill, such as tying the shoes, the proprioceptive stimuli produced by one response are conditioned to the succeeding response, but of what are these proprioceptive stimuli signs? With repeated experience on an electrifiable grill a rat will learn to rear up on its hind paws and alternatively lift them, this behavior reducing the total intensity of pain. The shock stimulus thus is conditioned to a new response, but of what is the shock a sign? In none of these cases would we say that the stimuli concerned have come to represent anything other than themselves, hence it is apparent that stimuli can be conditioned to reactions without simultaneously becoming signs.

If all sign-processes must be learned, but not all learned stimulus-response connections confer sign properties upon their eliciting stimuli, we must discover some reasonable distinction *within* the class of learned behaviors. Let us look for a moment at some common instances of sign-behavior in humans. When one human hears another say, 'Bring me the *hammer,* please' and responds appropriately by fetching that object, there is no question but that 'hammer,' as a pattern of auditory stimuli, is functioning as a sign. When one savage, traveling along a forest trail, spies a *bent twig* and thereupon changes course, either toward or away from that previously taken by another savage, we would also refer to sign-behavior—the response made to the bent twig is clearly relevant to something else, the other savage. The professor comes out upon his doorstep one morning and, looking up, sees dark rain-laden clouds; he ducks back into his house and forearms himself with rubbers and umbrella before setting out for the campus. Are the *dark clouds* a sign of rain? The response made to them as a stimulus is again relevant to something else, and we may legitimately say that the dark clouds signify or mean rain.

No difficulties have been encountered so far, but we have been dealing with human sign-behavior. Can sign-behavior be observed in lower animals? In an experiment discussed earlier, chimpanzees learned that *poker chips* could be 'traded in' for raisins; thereafter these animals would master difficult discrimination problems to obtain them as rewards, would hoard them and steal them from other chimpanzees. Have the poker chips become signs of raisins? All behavioral indications were positive: the chimpanzees would salivate over the poker chips, put them to their mouths—all responses were relevant, not to the chips themselves, but to the raisins they represent. In another experiment with the white rat as subject, a buzzer was followed in 5 seconds by electric shock, wheel-turning by the rat being the response that eliminated the painful stimulus. Does the *buzzer* become a sign of shock for the rat? After a number of trials the rat responded to the buzzer stimulus in such a way as to 'take account of' the shock. If we accept the idea that dark clouds are a sign of rain for the professor, then we must also agree that the buzzer is a sign of shock for the rat—the behavioral processes are objectively the same.

What is it that is common to the learning situations that involve sign-processes and yet lacking in those situations that do not? *The distinguishing condition is the presence or absence of a representational mediation process in association with the stimulus.* The buzzer elicits an 'anxiety' reaction—part of the 'fear' response originally made to the shock—and it is by virtue of this fact that it means or represents shock. It is this response that mediates wheel-turning or any number of other avoidant responses, given adequate contexts. Similarly, it is because the poker chips now produce mediating 'food-taking' reactions that they signify raisins. At the human level such mediating reactions (assuming they *are* 'reactions') are not readily observable. We cannot see anticipatory shivering when the professor looks at dark clouds or anticipatory grasping, pounding movements when a man understands the meaning of the word 'hammer,' although we might observe one savage glance in the direction taken by the other and perhaps mutter his name upon spying the bent twig.

The Mediation Hypothesis

Whereas Morris links sign and object through partial identity of object-produced and disposition-*produced* behavior, we shall link sign and object through partial identity of the 'disposition' *itself* with the behavior elicited by the object. Words represent things because they produce some replica of the actual behavior toward these things. This is the crucial identification, the mechanism that ties signs to particular stimulus-objects and not to

696 EXPERIMENTAL PSYCHOLOGY

others. Stating the proposition formally, we may say: *a pattern of stimulation which is not the object is a sign of the object if it evokes in an organism a mediating reaction, this* (a) *being some fractional part of the total behavior elicited by the object and* (b) *producing distinctive self-stimulation that mediates responses which would not occur without the previous association of nonobject and object patterns of stimulation.* All of these limiting conditions seem necessary. The mediation process must include part of the same behavior made to the object if the sign is to have its representing property. What we have done here, in a sense, is to make explicit what may be implicit in Morris's term 'disposition.' The last stipulation adds the learning requirement lacking in Morris's formulation. The response of warrior-termites to pounding on the tunnel floor is ruled out because it does not depend upon previous association of pounding with a breach in the nest. Notice, however, that there is no requirement here that the overt responses to the sign be in any way related to those made to the object; this is in direct contrast to Morris's position.

This conception of the sign-process is not concocted solely to meet the needs of semantics; it is the application of a general theory of learning to this particular class of phenomena. The mediation theory has been described in detail in an earlier chapter. At this point we shall be content to trace and illustrate the development of certain sign-processes as they apply to the problem of meaning. Paradigm A in Fig. 215 gives an abbreviated symbolic account of the development of a *sign* ($\boxed{S}$) via direct association with the stimulus-object signified. Paradigm B gives a similar account, necessarily somewhat more elaborate, of the development of an *assign* ($/S/$), which achieves its meaning indirectly through association with other signs rather than through direct association with stimulus-objects.

As an illustration of a largely *connotative sign* we may use the word SPIDER. This has special reference to the writer, who as a 9-year-old was badly frightened by these stimulus-objects—his tent-mates at a boys' camp, in ordinary youthful callousness, told him they had put a nest of large gray spiders in his bunk, and he lay awake all night awaiting the first crawly contact! The stimulus-object ($\dot{S}$), the actual visual pattern of hairy-legged insect body, elicits a pattern of behavior (R_T), *which in this case includes a heavy loading of autonomic 'fear' activity.* Through short circuiting, 'detachable' portions of this total behavior to the spider-object (particularly 'anxiety') become conditioned to the sign, the word SPIDER. With repetitions of the sign-process, the magnitude of the representational mediation process becomes reduced to some minimally effortful and minimally interfering replica—but still includes the release of those autonomic reactions which literally confer the unpleasant, connotative meaning of threat upon this word. This mediating reaction (r_m) produces a distinctive pattern of self-stimulation (s_m) which can elicit a variety of overt behaviors (R_X)—shivering and saying 'ugh!', running out of a room when someone says, 'There's a spider in here.' Another interesting phenomenon may be observed here: the overt behavior elicited by a sign may gradually operate to change its meaning, by exactly the same short-circuiting mechanism. In the present case, the writer, in his teens, deliberately tried manipulating the spider-object, first at the end of a long stick and later even by holding it with his hand by its own strand. This repeated manipulatory behavior gradually diluted the 'anxiety' meaning of the sign.

The word HAMMER will serve as an example of a largely *denotative sign*. The stimulus-object, a heavy thing having certain visual characteristics and certain tactual and proprioceptive effects, elicits in the young child, usually under instructions or imitation of some adult, a total pattern of behavior, including grasping and pounding movements. According to the

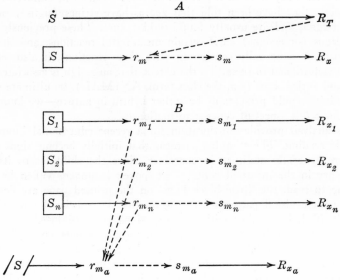

FIGURE 215. *A.* Development of a *sign*. A minimal but distinctive portion of the total behavior (R_T) originally elicited by an object $(\dot{S})$ comes to be elicited by another pattern of stimulation ($\boxed{S}$) as a representational mediation process (r_m), the self-stimulation (s_m) from which mediates various instrumental sequences (R_x). This representational mediation process is the meaning of the sign. *B.* Development of an *assign*. Portions of the representational behaviors $(r_{m_1} - r_{m_n})$ associated with a set of signs $(S_1 - S_n)$ transfer to a new pattern of stimulation, the assign $(/S/)$, as a 'distilled' representational process (r_{m_a}), which becomes the meaning of this assign.

mediation hypothesis, anticipatory portions of this behavior become short-circuited to the sign HAMMER. The process of reduction is especially important in the case of denotative signs—obviously, overt movements of the hands will interfere with other on-going instrumental behaviors and therefore tend to be extinguished. A young child, however, may actually be observed to clench his hand and move it up and down when asked for 'hammer.'

Just what the representational processes may be that ultimately become associated with denotative signs in adult humans is entirely unknown. We have been treating mediation processes *as if* they involved actual (though minimal) muscular and glandular reactions, i.e. as if the Jacobson and Max peripheral theory of consciousness were valid. It is convenient to think of it this way, and hypotheses of testable nature can be generated—but the mediation notion does not *require* that mediators be peripheral. If we keep in mind that the representational mediation process is a hypothetical construct, there is little danger in this approach; it could be entirely cortical without invalidating behavioral implications.

A very large proportion of the verbal signs used in communication are what we have termed *assigns*—their meaning is literally 'assigned' to them via association, not with the objects represented but with other *signs*. Consider for example the word ZEBRA: This word is probably understood by most 5-year-olds, yet few of them have ever reacted in any way to the object itself. They have seen pictures of these animals in children's books (symbols); they have been told that zebras have stripes (signs), run like horses (sign), and are usually found wild (sign). These previously established signs (or assigns) elicit certain meaningful reactions, and since the new assign is temporally contiguous with these reactions, it also tends to become conditioned to them. To the extent that an assign is associated with many and varied signs (e.g. the class term, ANIMAL), its ultimate mediation activity would presumably be rather hybrid in nature—we know very little about this aspect of concept formation.

This analysis provides justification for a recent educational innovation, phonetic reading. The stimulus patterns that initially become signs of objects are generally auditory in character, since the child learns its basic vocabulary in the informal contexts of spoken language. When he starts learning to read, the 'little black bugs' on the printed page are definitely *assigns;* these visual patterns are seldom directly associated with the objects signified, but rather with auditory signs (created by the child and teacher as they verbalize) and occasional visual symbols (pictorial representations of objects). Obviously, then, the more quickly the child can learn to make the right sound for the visual stimulus, the more quickly these new, visual assigns will acquire significance for him. The child already has meanings for 'house,' 'dog,' and even 'typewriter' as *heard* stimulus patterns, but these mediating processes must be assigned to *seen* stimulus patterns. Our stereotyped notions of social reality are similarly derived. An 'alien' is not something directly contacted with the senses. This label has acquired its unsavory significance through association with assigns which have themselves only a mediate connection with objects and experiences. 'We don't want any enemy ALIENS poisoning our country.' 'That troublemaker is an ALIEN and ought to be shipped back where he came from.' This class of signs could appropriately be termed *sign-assigns* (e.g. signs-of-assigns), they are that far removed from direct contact with the objects they are supposed to represent.

Multiple Semantic Relations

Semiotic is the science of signs. When analyzed psychologically, it resolves into several distinct behavioral relations. (1) *The representing relation* is that between the mediation process elicited by the sign (r_m) and the total behavior elicited by the object represented (R_T). It is by virtue of the fact that the mediation process does include a fractional part of the behavior made to the object that the sign has its distinctive representing character. As the term has been used in semiology, this is the *semantic* relation, i.e. the relation between signs and their referents. (2) *The mediating relation* is that between the mediation process as a form of self-stimulation (s_m) and the response sequences (R_x) elicited. This relation is composed of hierarchies of habits associating intervening variables with overt behavior; the relative strengths of such habits depend upon momentary contextual conditions and pervasive cultural factors which have influenced the reward systems in a particular society. (3) *The 'empathic' relation* is that between the response made to a sign (R_X) and that made to the object represented (R_T). At one extreme R_X is practically identical with R_T and 'empathy' is maximal—the individual responds to the sign exactly as he would to the object. The little girl listening to a ghost story hears 'a hairy hand crept for her throat' and lets out a shrill scream. At the other extreme R_X bears no relation to R_T and 'empathy' is minimal. The fact that X in a mathematical formula happens to refer to so many horses does not influence the computations. Whereas poetic language is designed to have high empathic values, scientific language is designed to have low empathic values, to convince by logical analysis and numeration. Both of the above-mentioned relations are part of what is known as the *pragmatic* dimension of semiotic, the relation between signs and their users or the effect of signs upon their users. (4) *The communicating relation* is that between mediation processes ($r_m \rightarrow s_m$) and particular classes of instrumental skill sequences (R_V), usually vocalic or gestural, which have the property of interpersonal communality. Given certain 'intentions,' one individual may selectively produce temporally ordered and coded vocalizations that are equally coded signs for another individual. From the point of view of general communication theory, this relation is the *encoding* process; in the classic terminology of semiotic, this relation concerns the *syntactical* dimension of language. This brief categorization, although sufficient for the purposes of this book, merely touches on a host of research problems that are only beginning to be investigated.

THE PROBLEM OF MEASURING MEANING

Whether the process essential to meaning be called a 'representative factor,' a 'disposition,' an 'expectancy,' a 'mediating reaction,' or any other name, some intervening process is being referred to. There is sufficient experimental evidence available to show that the phenomena of sign behavior demand this kind of conception, but measurement of such intervening processes has always been the most difficult task for psychologists. In this section we shall review some of the attempts that have been made in this direction. Ideally we should like to discover some direct physiological correlates of meaning; this approach has not been outstandingly successful, as we shall see. Since meanings develop through learning, we might expect some relations here; there are relations, but they do not provide much in the way of measurement. Association and scaling methods will be found to provide the most encouraging results to date.

Physiological Indices

(1) *Action potentials in the striated musculature.* If the representational mediators we have postulated as essential to meaning do in fact involve the peripheral musculature, i.e. if they are 'reactions' in the usual sense, then it might be expected that sensitive electrical recordings from the voluntary muscles would yield significant correlations. The major research here has

been contributed by Max (1935) and Jacobson (1932), and we have already studied their findings in connection with the nature of thinking. Their records certainly revealed a convincing correlation between ideas, as introspectively indexed, and motor activity, as electrically indexed—but does this index provide a measure of the presence or absence of meaning, its degree and quality? This is an attractive possibility, but the index is a crude one. There is no way of 'reading' the meaning of a sign to a subject from these records of his implicit muscular activity. The ultimate criterion of meaning in these studies is still introspection by the subject; he verbalizes meaning while the experimenter scurries about his periphery trying to pick it up on instruments. And there has been no crucial demonstration of the *necessity* of the motor component; meaning may be present without motor activity, or the relevant activity may be taking place at some other locus. The same criticism applies with equal force to other physiological correlates of meaning that have been proposed.

(2) *Glandular reactions.* Another pioneer investigation into the organic correlates of meaning was that of Razran (1936). Meaningfulness of a series of signs was the independent variable and amount of salivation was the dependent variable. The stimuli were words for 'saliva' in various languages. That the actual meanings here were complex affairs and varied in more than intensity from language to language for Razran (who was his own subject) is shown by his detailed introspections. While viewing the Russian word *slyuna,* he reported 'visual imagery of babies, cribs, drooling, herring, raw pork'; English *saliva* included 'visual imagery of microscope, epithelial cells, steak, cotton, mint, pretzels, kiss.' Salivation was greatest in his childhood tongue (Russian), next in his most proficient one (English), and still less in three slightly known languages (French, Spanish, and Polish). Control conditions (the Gaelic *smugaid* and the nonsense syllables QER SUH) showed no differences among themselves, despite the fact that Razran 'knew' the Gaelic word meant *saliva.* Introspections in the latter case included 'verbal image of *smugaid* localized cortically . . . attitude of "don't, don't, you're not to do this," of coldness and objectivity,' which may explain the inhibition of salivation in this case. Although this experiment demonstrates a rough correlation between the magnitude of a glandular reaction and the degree of meaningfulness—and therefore provides another feasible physiological index of meaning, albeit a limited one— again we must ask whether salivation is *necessary* here. Can a person think of 'steak' or 'chocolate sundae' without salivation, if he has just eaten to satiation?

(3) *The psychogalvanic skin response.* There are a large number of studies employing psychogalvanic response (*PGR*) measurements of autonomic disturbance remotely related to the problem of meaning: the *PGR* is readily elicited by any warning or preparatory stimulus that precedes shock (Darrow and Heath, 1932; Switzer, 1933; Mowrer, 1938), and this response may be an indication that the preparatory stimulus has become a sign of shock. In connection with the free association technique, the *PGR* has been found a good indicator of the emotional effect of stimulus words (Smith, 1922; Jones and Wechsler, 1928). It is unfortunate that the most pertinent experiment in this area leaves much to be desired in the way of methodological finesse. Bingham (1943) measured the *PGR* to 72 words

selected from educational and philosophical writings. The highly abstract level of these words is evident from the following sample, obtained by selecting every seventh item in Bingham's list: *perfection, knowledge, individual, power, spiritual, children, act, situation, come, materials.* After the *PGR* measurements, the 50 student subjects rated the words in terms of their personal meaningfulness, significance, and importance (*MSI*), and finally introspected on the sensory content included in the meaning of each word. Words having the highest judged *MSI* yielded the greatest average change in skin resistance. A breakdown of the data in terms of introspected sensory content showed that the high *MSI* words had more frequent 'organic' sensory content (the high 'organic' content words were *intellectual, freedom, God, truth* and *love,* in this order!). On a priori grounds one might expect that words having high personal affect should produce 'organic' sensations (stomach-tightening, rapid breathing, and *perspiring*) and hence be reflected in large *PGR* deflections. For some reason no data are presented on this relation between type of sensory content and magnitude of *PGR*. Much remains to be done in this direction. It is not inconceivable that the descriptive, denotative aspects of meaning are mediated through the peripheral musculature (and measurable as action potentials here), whereas the affective, connotative aspects of meaning are mediated by the autonomic system (and measurable by the *PGR* and related methods).

Semantic Generalization

(1) *From object to sign.* In the experiments to be described here, some reaction is conditioned to a nonverbal stimulus (blue-colored light, for example) and then tests are made for generalization of the response to verbal signs which represent the original stimulus (the word BLUE). The precise nature of the reaction conditioned is unimportant—all the standard *CR*'s have been used, salivation, *PGR,* finger-retraction, the pupillary reflex, and so on. It must be assumed that a meaningful mediation process is operative *during the original conditioning of the reaction to the nonverbal stimulus* in these experiments; it is this mediation process that is simultaneously conditioned to the new reaction and thereby mediates the 'generalized' reaction to the word. There is considerable evidence here and it is all positive. Russian investigators, applying Pavlovian methods, were the first to explore this area, but, unfortunately, most of their published work is available to American scientists only in the form of brief abstracts.

Kapustnik (1930) set up conditioned salivary reactions to visual and auditory stimuli, transfer to verbal signs for the original cues being tested, and obtained significant amounts of generalization. Smolenskaya (1934) established discriminative *CR*'s to patterns of colored lights; substitution of color words for the visual stimuli yielded measurable amounts of generalization in one half of the subjects. Kotliarevsky (1935) employed a cardiovasomotor reflex (the Aschner Phenomenon in which the pulse is retarded when the eyeball is pressed); with a special pneumatic apparatus fitted on the eyeball to apply pressure, the sound of a bell was conditioned to the pulse retardation, and generalization to the word BELL was clearly demonstrated. Metzner (1942) has obtained similar results with the eyelid closure reflex. Some idea of the complexity of semantic conditioning is revealed in further Russian experiments. Traugott (1934) established a positive CR to the sound of a bell and a negative CR to the bell plus a blue light, the blue light thus serving as a conditioned inhibitor. Substitution of the words BLUE, BLUE was found to inhibit the response in 70 per cent of the cases; actual red light inhibited the response in 60 per cent; the words RED, RED produced inhibition in 40 per cent and neutral words in only 20 per cent of the cases. If measured generalization be accepted as an index of meaningful similarity, it follows that the words BLUE, BLUE are semantically more nearly similar to blue light than is an actual red light. Another interesting phenomenon observed by Traugott was that the inhibitory effects of the words BLUE, BLUE generalized more broadly to *other* previously conditioned reflexes than did the effects of actual blue light. One is reminded of the pervasive spread of the parental 'no, no!' Conditioning and free association techniques were combined in a study by Traugott and Fadeyeva (1934). With excitatory CR's established to a bell-whistle-light pattern and inhibitory CR's to a whistle-touch pattern, free associations to the verbal signs of these stimuli were obtained along with the latencies with which associations were made. Free associations to the words representing conditioned excitors were made with greater speed than those to the signs of conditioned inhibitors. Interestingly enough, after extinction of the excitatory CR's, free associations became slower *and* generically older, i.e. associations now referred to pre-experimental situations.

(2) *From sign to sign*. When a response is initially conditioned to one sign and generalization to another sign is measured, the role of meaningful mediation is merely more obvious than in the preceding situation. Razran (1939 *a*) extended his conditioned salivation technique to this problem. Words and short sentences were flashed on a screen in random order at 2-minute intervals while six adults were consuming food. Conditioning developed rapidly, and on the second session tests of transfer to new words and sentences were made. The conditioning sentences consisted of three words, including a subject, a copula, and a predicate, and the test sentences varied certain of these parts. Generalization from the original (e.g. POVERTY IS DEGRADING) to statements having total agreement in meaning was greatest; however, when the copulas were reversed (e.g. POVERTY IS NOT UPLIFTING), there was less generalization than when the entire meaning was shifted. Apparently, distinctive elements like 'uplifting' in the stimulus compound are more effective than commonly used elements such as 'not.' With single words, generalization was found to be greater to semantically similar words (e.g. STYLE to FASHION) than to phonetically similar homonyms (e.g. STYLE to STILE). This finding, indicating dominance of semantic over physical similarities, agrees with Traugott's (1934) results discussed above and data obtained by Riess (1940) using the galvanic skin response as a measure.

In another study Riess (1946) has related the characteristics of semantic conditioning to stages in genetic development. Four groups of subjects, varying in mean age from 7 years 9 months to 18 years 6 months, were conditioned to give the galvanic skin response to selected verbal stimuli, these being associated with a moderately loud buzzer while neutral words were not so reinforced. After this pretraining, tests for transfer to synonyms, antonyms, and homonyms of the originally conditioned words were run. The values shown in Table 20 represent mean differences in measured

TABLE 20. GENERALIZATION AS A FUNCTION OF AGE AND RELATION BETWEEN SIGNS

	Mean Age in Years and Months			
Relations Compared	7:9	10:8	14:0	18:6
Original–synonym	92.09	166.78	132.96	132.50
	(.01)	(.01)	(.01)	(.01)
Original–antonym	82.42	129.41	165.76	177.92
	(.01)	(.01)	(.01)	(.01)
Original–homonym	62.95	161.46	182.50	228.84
	(.01)	(.01)	(.01)	(.01)
Synonym–antonym	−9.67	−37.37	32.80	45.42
	(.20)	(.01)	(.02)	(.20)
Synonym–homonym	−29.14	−5.22	49.84	96.34
	(.01)	(.70)	(.01)	(.01)
Antonym–homonym	−19.47	32.05	17.04	50.92
	(.02)	(.01)	(.30)	(.20)

Riess, *Journal of Experimental Psychology*, 1946, 36:147.

galvanic skin response between the two relations at the left (in terms of gain over preliminary test); the values for the original words were the magnitudes of response to these stimuli at the conclusion of initial conditioning. Significance levels are indicated in parentheses. The comparisons between original and various test stimuli, given in the first three rows, merely demonstrate that reactions to originally conditioned stimuli are stronger than reactions to any other stimuli. Tracing the bottom three lines of data in this table, one finds certain general relations between semantic generalization and individual development: meaningful or semantic similarities (synonyms) increase in importance as the individual matures, whereas the importance of physical similarities (homonyms) decreases. The course of opposed meaningful relations (antonyms) is not so clear: generalization among synonyms becomes greater than among antonyms, whereas generalization among antonyms seems to become greater than among homonyms, but neither of these trends is definite in terms of significance levels. One methodological difficulty should be mentioned: the original and test words used with subjects of different age levels varied and therefore these differences are confounded with those attributable to age.

All of the evidence encountered so far has been positive in the sense that generalization occurs among semantically related signs. A slightly discordant note is sounded by Keller (1943). After conditioning the *PGR* to a *picture* of a boy scout hat, tests for generalization to the picture of a fireman's hat and the word HAT were made, control items being pictures and words for DUCK and BALL. Although significant amounts of generalization occurred to the picture of the fireman's hat, no transfer to the word HAT occurred. Keller argues quite reasonably that if generalization between the two pictures of hats was based upon a common mediating process, it could not have been saying or thinking 'hat' or the printed word should have shown the same effect. Perhaps generalization here was solely in terms of physical similarity—which doesn't tell us why this was true here and not elsewhere.

(3) There are several other semantic relations that could be studied, but little evidence is available. For example, one would expect generalization to occur *from verbal sign to the object represented,* even though this seems to reverse the sequence of events in the development of sign processes. Thus, conditioned *PGR* to the word BLUE should generalize to objects of that color. Kapustnik (1930) demonstrated that salivary reactions conditioned to verbal signs representing visual and auditory stimuli transferred to these stimuli themselves. This dimension of semantic generalization is undoubtedly of great social importance. The aggressive reactions associated with NAZI and JAP on a verbal level certainly transferred to the social objects represented under appropriate conditions. Similarly, prejudicial behaviors established while reading about a member of a social class can transfer to the class as a whole—and minority group prejudices certainly transfer to individual members of these groups. Finally, mention should be made of *generalization from object to object via semantic mediation.* The reverential care with which an adolescent boy handles a certain handkerchief, a certain lock of blond hair, and a certain lipstick-printed napkin certainly has nothing to do with physical similarities among these objects themselves; the conserving and collecting approach of the miser to miscellaneous objects is certainly not due to any similarities among the objects themselves. 'Inferiority feelings' render a wide range of social situations equivalent in meaning and reaction for the individual who suffers with them (cf. G. W. Allport's (1937) trait hypothesis).

Nature of semantic generalization. It is obvious that something more than mere primary stimulus generalization is functioning in the various experiments described above. Primary generalization is assumed to occur along dimensions of *physical* similarity, and there is no such external similarity between words like STYLE and FASHION or between blue light and the word BLUE. Rather, the meaningful similarity of verbal and other signs depends upon previous learning. Cofer and Foley (1942) have given yeoman's service by relating the various studies on semantic conditioning to the theoretical mediation process. They state that semantic generalization 'thus presupposes and depends upon the pre-experimental formation of conditioned responses or associations, i.e. *the gradient of generalization is a gradient along a dimension of conditioned stimulus functions.* The stimuli need be similar only in so far as they have been previously conditioned to the same (or similar) response' (p. 520). This is identical with the analysis of mediated generalization given in Chapter 8.

It is doubtful, however, whether this explanation is sufficient. It demands that the *same* mediating reaction be made to both original and test signs, i.e. that they be synonymous in meaning rather than merely similar. This is because Cofer and Foley provide no mechanism for degrees of similarity among mediation processes (although they do recognize the problem by their parenthetical 'or similar' in the quotation cited above). It would seem that we must also postulate gradients of *primary generalization,* either among mediating reactions, the self-stimulation they produce, or (more likely) both. In other words, having conditioned the *PGR* to the word

HAPPY, we assume that the self-stimulation produced by HAPPY (e.g. via the representational mediation process associated with this sign) also becomes conditioned to *PGR*. Since this habit strength generalizes, other patterns of self-stimulation (produced by ELATED, HIGH, etc.) will acquire capacity to elicit *PGR* in proportion to their physical similarity to the original pattern. It follows, therefore, that the greater the similarity *in meaning* between original and test signs, the greater the probability of obtaining a generalized response. This extended interpretation fits the available evidence—that magnitude of semantic generalization varies with the *degree* of meaningful similarity.

Transfer and Interference Methods of Studying Meaning

Although a great many learning experiments involve the use of meaningful materials, very few of them have utilized meaning itself as a variable, and even here it has usually been the effects upon learning that have been of interest. A *transfer method* has been used by Cofer and Foley and their associates in testing their mediated generalization hypothesis. The general procedure was as follows: first a single repetition on a *buffer list* of numbers (spelled out) was given as practice; then an *equating list* of proper names was presented once and scored immediately, subjects being assigned to the various experimental conditions on the basis of their performance here; each subject was then given *four* unscored repetitions on either a *reinforcement list* or a *control list;* all subjects were finally tested for recall of a *test list* of words immediately after a single presentation. The actual materials used in the first experiment (Foley and Cofer, 1943) are shown in Table 21. Notice that although homonym reinforcement lists I

TABLE 21. MATERIALS FOR AN EXPERIMENT ON MEDIATED TRANSFER

REINFORCEMENT LISTS

CONTROL LIST	*Homo- nym I*	*Homo- nym II*	*Synonym I*	*Synonym II*	TEST LIST
palm	cent	scent	dispatched	killed	sent
set	vain	vane	vessel	ship	vein
reed	pare	pair	fruit	result	pear
very	sew	so	plant	factory	sōw
numb	rain	rein	rule	principle	reign
me	seas	seize	looks	appearance	sees
day	write	rite	just	barely	right
snap	noes	nose	apprehends	arrests	knows
rope	meat	mete	join	enlist	meet
spire	dō	doe	batter	bruise	dough

Foley and Cofer, *Journal of Experimental Psychology*, 1943, 32:170.

and II are essentially equivalent to one another in containing words of similar sound to those on the test list, synonym lists I and II are in no sense equivalent. The words on synonym list I are close synonyms of those on the test list, but the words on II actually bear no semantic relation whatever to the test words (e.g. *arrests—knows*), being synonyms of the words on list I (e.g. *apprehends—arrests*). As for results, the mean numbers of words on the test list recalled after its single presentation were following homonym list I, 6.72 words; following homonym II, 5.64; following synonym I, 5.88; synonym list II, 5.24; and following the control list, 4.80 words.

There are several curious points in these results. In the first place, the best homonym list shows more generalization to the test list than does synonym list I, which included close synonyms of the test words. This is in flat contradiction to many other data in this field; Traugott (1934), Razran (1939 a), and Riess (1940, 1946) agree in finding generalization among synonyms to be greater than among homonyms, at least for adult subjects. Secondly, one wonders why the difference between the two homonym lists should be greater than that between the two 'synonym' lists; the former are equivalent but the latter clearly are not. Thirdly, although recall after reinforcement with synonym list II was not significantly superior to that after the control list, it is surprising that there should be any difference at all, since the words on synonym list II bear no relation to the test words—witness *killed–sent, ship–vein, result–pear, factory–sōw*, and so on. The investigators' assumption was that the words on synonym list II mediated those on synonym list I which in turn provided mediated reinforcement of the test words. In searching for an explanation of these points, a flaw in design was discovered that renders the entire technique suspect. Since all the words on a given reinforcement list bore the same relation to those on the test list, all a subject had to do was to 'catch on' to this relation and then proceed to literally manufacture the test list rather than recall it. The subject is given four trials on the reinforcement list and presumably learns most of it. If, after the single presentation of the test list, he realizes that the new words are *homonyms* of those he already knows, then recalling *cent, vain,* and *pare,* he can easily manufacture *sent, vein,* and *pear,* checking them through recognition. Realizing that the new words are *synonyms* of those he already knows and then recalling *dispatched, vessel,* and *fruit,* he can manufacture *sent, vein,* and *pear.* The obtained differences between homonym and synonym lists could be due to the fact there are fewer alternatives in the former case.

This loophole in design is even more apparent in later experiments of this series. In a study on *antonym gradients* (Cofer, Janis, and Rowell, 1943), the authors themselves point out that of the 28 subjects given the antonym reinforcement list, 19 clearly recognized the antonym relation *and* showed better recall than those who did not. In a third study (Foley and Mathews, 1943), the reinforcement list was made up of Spanish words and the test list of their English equivalents. Two groups of subjects were tested before and after a month's interval, the experimental group receiving training in a Spanish course throughout this time. The experimental group showed a significant increase in 'transfer' to the test list after the training interval, but the control group did not. Having learned the meanings of the Spanish words (e.g. *ciudad* means 'city'), the subjects were literally practicing the English test-list words during their four reinforcement trials. It is unfortunate that this flaw in design is present in these experiments; the underlying mediation conception which Cofer and Foley have described in theory is certainly an important contribution. Flaws of this type are the most difficult methodological errors to catch when designing research—the experimenter, intent on the relevance of his technique to theory and on the elimination of subtle variables, is very likely to forget that the naïve subject will follow what is to him the most obvious route to the goal.

In a series of investigations by Osgood (1946, 1948) nonsense letters served as stimuli and meaningful adjectives as responses in the standard retroactive interference paradigm. Since words of similar meaning were assumed to be mediated by similar implicit reactions, the original learning of one such reaction should facilitate the interpolated learning of a similar reaction through generalization of excitatory tendency. Words of opposed meaning were assumed to be mediated by antagonistic implicit reactions,

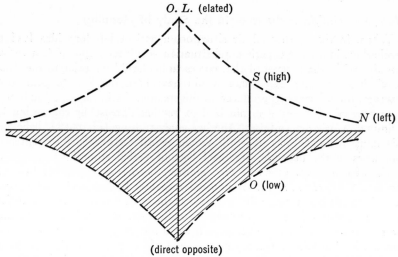

FIGURE 216. Theoretical situation at the conclusion of original learning (*O.L.*) of an associate, *c.m.* → *elated*. Generalized excitatory tendency has developed between *c.m.* and a meaningfully similar response, *high,* generalized inhibitory tendency for a meaningfully opposed response, *low,* maximum reciprocal inhibition for the directly antagonistic response, *dejected,* and presumably no associative tendency toward a neutral response, *left.* Osgood, *Journal of Experimental Psychology,* 1946, 36:285.

and the original learning of one reaction here should interfere with the interpolated learning of the opposed reaction, through generalization of inhibitory tendency. Consider one of the items for illustration: after all subjects had learned *c.m.* = *elated* as one of 15 original paired associates, some would have interpolated *c.m.* = *high* (similar meaning), some *c.m.* = *left* (neutral), and others *c.m.* = *low* (opposed meaning), all subjects having to recall and relearn *c.m.* = *elated* as a measure of retroaction. The materials learned by each subject included five items in each of the three meaningful relations, thus making it impossible for the subject to establish the type of set for a given relation which troubled the Cofer and Foley studies.

The theoretical situation at the conclusion of original learning is shown in Fig. 216. The original learning of *elated* has generated excitatory tendency toward *high,* but generalized inhibitory tendency toward *low;* the word *left* is assumed to be beyond the generalization gradients. The results for both transfer and retroactive interferences point to the following general conclusion: *when a sign or an assign is conditioned to a mediator, it will also tend to elicit other mediators in proportion to their similarity to the original reaction; it will tend to inhibit other mediators in proportion to the directness of their antagonism to the original reaction.* In everyday terms, signs that develop a certain meaning through direct training readily elicit similar meanings, but resist being associated with opposed meanings. If the sign RUSSIAN means *bad* to the conservative college student, he easily accepts substitution of *dirty, unfair* and *cruel,* but it is difficult for him to think of Russians as being *clean, fair* and *kind* (cf. Stagner and Osgood, 1946).

Word Association Techniques in the Study of Meaning

When, in the psychoanalytic situation, a patient lets 'one idea lead to another' or, in a more experimental situation, a subject responds to a verbal stimulus with 'the first word that comes to his head,' we refer to the 'free' association technique. As Freud would have been the first to point out, however, the associations produced in this manner are in no sense random—'eating ice cream cones' does not lead to 'mother's breast' by chance but by definite semantic determinism. Another analyst, Jung (cf. 1918), believing that unusual associations to words would reveal the existence of repressed complexes in the neurotic, arranged lists of verbal stimuli calculated to touch off complexes (such as *kiss, mother, touch*) among neutral words (such as *door, chair, leaf*). As unusual responses he included rare associations, long reaction times, failure to repeat the same response on a repetition of the list, blushing and other complex indicators. Jung also assumed that the nature of a patient's response to a word indicated the meaning of that sign to him, but what meanings are unusual? If a neurotic patient responds to FATHER by saying *fate,* does this indicate that the mediation process elicited by this sign in this subject is unusual? Kent and Rosanoff (1910) obtained responses to 100 common English nouns and adjectives from 1000 normal subjects comprising a fairly random sample of the population. For most of these stimuli a large proportion of the responses was restricted to a small number of verbal associates—712 of the 1000 responses to NEEDLE, for example, are included in the words *thread, pin(s), sharp, sew(s),* and *sewing.* From norms like these, the 'unusualness' of a subject's response can be indexed by the frequency of occurrence of that word in the normative sample; *sharp* can be expected to occur as a response to NEEDLE 152 times per 1000, but *weapon* occurs only one time per 1000.

Not all 'free' associations to verbal stimuli, however, are attributable to semantic determinants. The verbal response is not necessarily mediated by the *meaning* of the stimulus word. As shown in the hypothetical analysis of free association in Fig. 217, the subject may make a 'clang' reaction, producing a word that sounds like the stimulus (i.e. MAN = *pan*), or some other mechanical response. For semantically determined associations, which constitute the gross majority of responses, the sign-process elicited by the stimulus word mediates the verbal association. All semantically determined associates are *similar* in some way to the stimulus word, similar in *meaning* (NEEDLE = *pin, sharp, point, pricks, pointed*), similar in *context* (NEEDLE = *thread, sew, eye, thimble, cotton, cloth*), or similar in the sense of *hierarchical relations* (NEEDLE = *steel, instrument, implement, tool, metal*). Actually, approximately 950 of the 1000 responses to NEEDLE are semantically determined associations in this sense. As Karwoski and Schacter (1948), after an extensive analysis of the problem of classifying free associations, point out, nearly all responses can be categorized as some form of either similarity or contrast.

But what about contrast responses? In free association tests, such as the Kent-Rosanoff, the direct opposite of the stimulus word is often the single most frequent reaction. In the case diagrammed, WOMAN is actually the single most frequent association made to MAN—is this not a semantically determined response? Is not WOMAN in a sense similar in meaning to

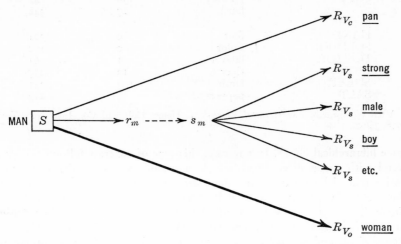

FIGURE 217. Suggested model of 'free' association process. Most associates are mediated by an intervening process ($r_m \rightarrow s_m$) and are *similar* in some respect to the stimulus word. So-called 'clang' reactions occur occasionally, and the most common single response, as in this case, may be the direct opposite.

MAN? As shown in Fig. 216, the directly opposite response is not here attributed to semantic mediation but rather to the overlearning of purely verbal habits in the culture. The free association of common opposites like LIGHT–DARK, GOOD–BAD, and MAN–WOMAN is of the same *nonsemantic* order as the frequent association of words like APPLE–CART, FOOT–BALL, and WASTE–BASKET. The stimulus words APPLE, FOOT, and WASTE do not elicit CART, BALL, and BASKET through their meanings as signs but rather through the frequent association of these vocal reactions as vocimotor skills, and the same explanation is assumed to apply to common verbal opposites. Is there any evidence supporting this rather novel interpretation? For one thing, the tendency to free-associate direct opposites increases with age, children favoring similar, contextual responses. This may be seen in the upper portion of Table 22, taken from Woodworth's review of this problem (1938) and utilizing responses to the Kent-Rosanoff list by 1000 children between 9 and 12 years of age (Woodrow and Lowell, 1916) and by 1000 adult men in industry (O'Connor, 1928). It is difficult to decide whether the co-ordinate associates shown in the lower portion of this table should be considered functional opposites or functional similars (in the sense of falling within the

TABLE 22

Stimulus	Response	1000 Children	1000 Men in Industry
DARK	night	421	162
	light	38	626
MAN	work	168	17
	woman	8	561
DEEP	hole	257	20
	shallow	6	296
SOFT	pillow	138	42
	hard	27	548
HAND	foot	0	321
SOLDIER	sailor	0	102
DOCTOR	lawyer	1	161
LION	tiger	13	237
SHEEP	lamb	108	241
SALT	pepper	29	213

After Woodworth, *Experimental Psychology*, Henry Holt and Co., Inc., New York, 1938, 346-7.

same hierarchical class). In any case, this type of contrast follows the same trend with age as direct opposites. As a second form of evidence, we may notice that although there are many *different* similar associations made to the same stimulus on the Kent-Rosanoff lists, there is usually only the *single* direct opposite. Why, of all the possible words opposed in meaning to SOFT is *hard* the only one frequently given? Why not *tough, firm, stony, rigid,* and so on? A count of the number of *different* similar responses with a frequency of 50 or more versus the number of *different* opposed responses with a frequency of 50 or more, for the same 20 stimulus items which typically yield opposites, shows an average of 6.11 similar variations per item versus only 2.05 opposed variations per item. This difference is highly significant. Whereas there is a general (semantic) tendency to free-associate meaningfully similar responses, there is only a specific (nonsemantic) tendency to associate opposed responses.

There appears to be only one experiment that directly studies similarity and opposition in free association. Karwoski and Schachter (1948) measured the reaction times of associations made to 70 common words taken from Thorndike's (1932) list of the first 500 words acquired by children. The subjects here were 50 college students. Responses were classified as *General Identification,* including essential similarity (LARGE–big, STORY–tale), *Functional Identification* (LAWYER–case, GIRL–dress), and *General Identification* (CABBAGE–vegetable, DARK–color), *Specific Identification* (OCEAN–Pacific, FRIEND–Tom), *Contingent Relation* (LAKE–boat, HILL–ski), and *Essential Contrast* (BLACK–white, LOVE–hate). It may be seen that all the 'identification' categories presume an equivalence between stimulus and response that is mediated by the sign-process (meaning) elicited by the stimulus. Table 23 reveals two very significant facts: (1) Direct opposites, as free associations, are made with much shorter *RT*'s than any of the similar classifications. This fact is compatible with the view that opposites are direct verbal associates and

TABLE 23

	Essential Contrast	General Identifica- tion	Specific Identifica- tion	Con- tingent Relation
Mean *RT* (seconds)	1.104	1.344	1.516	1.442
Total responses	1133	822	77	624
Number of different words	125	240	52	391
Concentration	9.06	3.43	1.48	1.61

After Karwoski and Schachter, *Journal of Social Psychology*, 1948, 28:105.

do not require any meaningful mediation process (thus taking less time for response). (2) Opposed reactions are less variable than similar reactions. Although there were more opposed reactions than any other single category, there were relatively fewer *different* words, i.e. subjects showed more agreement in their choice of opposed associations than in their similar associations. Again, this may be taken as evidence for the cultural standardization of common verbal opposites.

Stimuli other than words can be used to elicit free associations. Dorcus (1932) gave subjects bits of actual color as stimuli rather than color words. Whereas co-ordinate and contrast responses are most common to color words (WHITE–black, RED–blue), responses to actual colors were typically the names of objects (BLUE–ribbons, RED–finger nails). More recently, Karwoski, Gramlich, and Arnott (1944) have compared associations to objects, pictures of these objects, and labels of these objects in terms of both type of response and reaction time. We have here three degrees of 'abstraction': the pattern of stimulation received from the object is the concrete 'object' itself; the pictorial representation is a sign of the object but is itself physically similar to the object in certain respects; and the label is yet further abstracted. The technique used in this experiment merits brief description: a revolving stage, divided into quadrants, was fitted tightly into a window between two rooms, the subject being in one (darkened) and the experimenter in the other. An object, picture, or printed word stimulus was placed in a quadrant and, after a ready-signal, was swung into position facing the subject. A switch that illuminated this stage also started a time clock, and the subject's vocal reaction activated a voice-key, stopping the clock and providing a measure of the reaction time. The objects (and hence pictures and labels) were such everyday things as *light bulb, screw driver, pipe, leaf, shoe, dollar, hammer,* and *pistol.* Eight of the 25 items yielded marked differences between the modes of presentation, some of these being shown in Table 24. The common verbal response to the word *fork* is, of course, *knife*—on both pictorial and object levels *eat* is the more common reaction. Where differences did appear, like those shown in this table, the dividing line was usually between the verbal level and the other two modes of presentation. Reaction times were also shortest for the verbal level, and the authors suggest that both object and pictorial stimuli required an intermediary symbol before a verbal response to them could be made. It is also probable that for both object and pictorial presentations the dominant tendency to label them interfered with other possible verbal responses. Both the Dorcus experiment and this one agree in showing that

TABLE 24

Stimulus	Verbal		Pictorial		Object	
DOLLAR	bill	13	bill	28	bill	1
	money	10	money	18	money	28
FORK	knife	20	knife	7	knife	8
	eat	6	eat	17	eat	12
KETTLE	pot	10	pot	0	pot	0
	water	2	water	11	water	14
BASKET	ball	11	ball	0	ball	1
	carry	1	carry	8	carry	8

From Karwoski, Gramlich, and Arnott, *Journal of Social Psychology*, 1944, 20:238.

free associations to signs are not necessarily the same as those to the objects signified, and this follows directly from the postulated nature of the sign-process.

Scaling Methods

Considering the number of traits, abilities, and attitudes that psychologists have measured by scaling methods, it is significant that there has been little attempt to measure meaning this way. Since many psychologists must have thought about the problem at one time or another, this probably reflects the general belief that meanings are too complicated, too unique, or both. There have been attempts to scale the meaningfulness of verbal materials used in learning experiments, the 'association values' of nonsense syllables (Glaze, 1928; Hull, 1933 *b;* Witmer, 1935) and the degrees of synonymity, vividness, familiarity, and association between adjectives (Haagen, 1949). In the latter case these aspects of the meaning of adjectives were always measured in comparison with a 'standard' word, which varied from set to set. This did not apply to the vividness scale, and this measurement does presumably tap some general dimension of meaning.

Mosier (1941) made the most direct application of scaling methods to the study of meaning itself. College subjects rated some 300 adjectives on an 11-point scale in terms of their favorableness-unfavorableness. Frequency distributions for approximately 200 of them were essentially linear when plotted against probability paper, indicating normal distribution of judgments; many items showed a 'precipice effect' at one side or the other of the midpoint of the scales, indicating that subjects agreed better on the direction (favorable or unfavorable) of the evaluation than on the intensity. From these data Mosier concluded that 'first, . . . the meaning of a word may be considered *as if* it consisted of two parts, one constant and representative of the usual meaning of the word, and one variable, representative of individual interpretation in usage and associated context and general usage; second, that the frequency with which any particular meaning is evoked is describable by the Gaussian Law.' Although Mosier demonstrated the feasibility of scaling certain aspects of meaning, his limitation of the procedure to a single dimension of meaning (evaluation) was insufficient. If there is one thing we can accept at the outset, it is that meanings vary in a considerable, but unknown, number of dimensions, and we must frame our methodology accordingly.

A combination of scaling and association procedures which takes into account this multidimensionality of meaning has been described by Osgood (1952). Earlier research on synesthesia (cf. pp. 642-5) and on the measurement of social stereotypes (Stagner and Osgood, 1946) gave rise to the following assumptions: (1) *The process of description or judgment can be conceived as the allocation of a concept to an experiential continuum defined by a pair of polar terms.* As a working hypothesis we assume that these 'experiential continua' will turn out to be reflections (in language) of the sensory differentiations made possible by the human nervous system. Discriminations in meaning, which is itself a state of awareness, cannot be any finer or involve any more variables than are made possible by the sensory system (cf. Boring, *The Physical Dimensions of Consciousness,* 1933). (2) *Many different experiential continua, or ways in which meanings vary, are essentially equivalent and hence may be represented by a single dimension.* It was this fact that was borne in on us in the synesthesia and stereotype studies. In the latter, for example, the descriptive scales *fair-unfair, high-low, kind-cruel, valuable-worthless, Christian-anti-Christian* and *honest-dishonest* were all found to be intercorrelated .90 or better, as used in judging social concepts. It is this fact about language and thinking that makes the development of a quantitative measuring instrument feasible. If the plethora of descriptive terms we utilize were in truth unique and independent of one another—as most philosophers of meaning seem to have supposed—then quantitative measurement would be impossible. (3) *A limited number of such continua can be used to define a semantic space within which the meaning of any concept can be specified.* This indicates factor analysis as the methodology to be employed. If it can be shown that a limited number of factors accounts for most of the variance in meaning of a large and randomly selected sample of concepts—and if the technique meets the usual criteria of measurement (objectivity, validity, reliability, sensitivity, and comparability)—then such an instrument *is* an objective measure of meaning.

We may look upon the procedures followed in obtaining such a measure of a concept for a particular subject as an operational definition of the meaning of that concept to him, in the same sense that the procedures followed in obtaining an I.Q. score provide an operational definition of intelligence. In the present instance the operations are explicit: they involve the subject's allocation of a concept within a standard system of descriptive scales by means of a series of independent associative judgments. Presented with a pair of descriptive polar terms (e.g. *rough-smooth*) and a concept (e.g. LADY), the subject merely indicates the direction of his association (e.g. LADY–*smooth*) and its intensity by either the extremeness of his checkmark on a graphic scale or the speed of his reaction in a reaction-time device. The distribution of his judgments on a standardized series of such scales serves to differentiate the meaning of this concept from others; for this reason this measuring instrument has been called a 'semantic differential.' The profiles in Fig. 218, using a preliminary set of scales, provides an illustration of the method. The data are taken from a larger study. Each

point on each scale represents the median of 20 subjects. The upper portion
of this figure compares the differentiations of the *same* concept, POLITE,
by two groups of subjects—the high degree of correspondence between the
two profiles gives some evidence for the reliability of the method. The lower
portion compares the differentiations of two *different,* but somewhat similar,

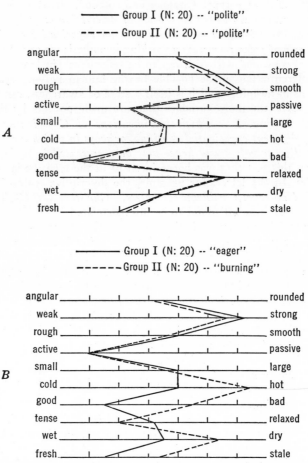

FIGURE 218. Application of a preliminary form of the 'semantic differential' to
measurement of the connotative meaning of certain adjectives; (*A*) medians for
two groups of 20 subjects differentiating 'polite'; (*B*) medians for same subjects
differentiating 'eager' and 'burning.' Osgood, *Psychological Bulletin,* 1952, **49**:229.

concepts, EAGER and BURNING. The scales that differentiate these two
concepts are just those which would be expected if the method were valid—
EAGER is relatively *good*(er), *fresher,* and more *relaxed* than BURN-
ING, whereas BURNING is relatively *hotter* and *drier* than EAGER.
The factor analytic work here, basic to selecting the scales to be used in the
semantic differential, has only begun, and the various checks on reliability,
sensitivity, and so on, remain to be made. It is therefore too early to evaluate
this approach. Its chief claim for promise lies in the fact that it does take
into account the multidimensionality of the meaning-space.

THE STATISTICAL STRUCTURE OF LANGUAGE BEHAVIOR

It is convenient to view the language process within the individual as a more or less continuous interaction between two parallel systems of behavioral organization: sequences of *central events* (e.g. 'ideas' or representational mediation processes) and sequences of *instrumental skills,* vocalic, gestural, or orthographic, which create the communicative product. Execution of sequences of communicative skills brings the talker repeatedly to 'choice points'—points where the next overt sequence is not highly predictable from the preceding product itself. It is at these points that determinants within the semantic, mediational system enter to effectively 'load' the transitional probabilities. Once the communicative product is 'on the air' or 'in print,' so to speak, the lawfulness of its sequences can be studied as objective physical events largely independent of either speakers or hearers. This is traditionally the field of the *linguist.* For the most part, however, linguists have not been statistically oriented, being content to describe the structures of languages in terms of what forms can or cannot occur in certain positions. Only recently have linguists and psychologists begun counting the frequencies of recurrent events as a means of studying the structure of languages.

Statistical Structure of Messages

Samples from the continuous flow of spoken or written language can be analyzed into various categories; then these part-processes can be counted and their comparative frequencies of occurrence determined. This level of analysis, lying in the borderland between psychology and linguistics, has been called *dynamic philology,* which 'views speech-production as a natural psychological and biological phenomenon to be investigated in the objective spirit of the exact sciences . . . our chief method of procedure (being) the application of statistical principles to the observable phenomena of the stream of speech' (Zipf, 1935, p. 3). When, for example, words appearing in a large sample of newspaper English are classified and ranked according to length, it is found that frequency of their usage bears an inverse relation to their length. The individual language behavior of John Doe does not appear in the data, yet the lawfulness of this relation presumably stems from certain principles governing the behavior of many John Does.

(1) *Relations exemplifying the principle of least effort.* In the past two decades George Kingsley Zipf has compiled an impressive series of demonstrations of the lawfulness of language phenomena. His earlier work is summarized in *The Psychobiology of Language* (1935) and his later studies, including a comprehensive theoretical analysis, are presented in a volume entitled *Human Behavior and the Principle of Least Effort* (1949). Space permits only a brief and necessarily inadequate survey of this work. Employing frequency counts of large samples of colloquial Peiping Chinese, Plautine Latin (four of Plautus' plays) and American newspaper English, he finds that (a) *the frequency of occurrence of words is inversely related to their length,* i.e. there is a tendency (common to all these languages) for individuals to use short words more often than long ones. Zipf adduces convincing evidence that frequency of usage is what causes the shortening of

words, rather than the reverse—the reduction of 'gasoline' to 'gas' and of 'moving pictures' to 'movies' are familiar examples. As a corollary of this relation, (b) *the lower the rank order in frequency, the more different words are found at that rank,* i.e. although there are many different words that occur *once* in a sample of 1000, there are very few words that occur as frequently as 40 times per 1000. Figure 219 represents a plot of this relation on double logarithmic paper. As Zipf points out, this lawfulness in

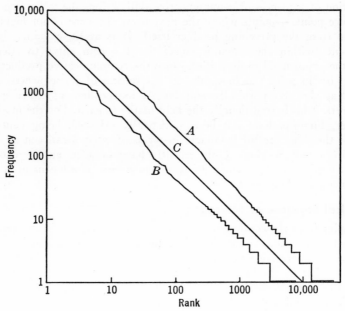

FIGURE 219. Double log rank-frequency distributions for two sets of empirical data, James Joyce's 'Ulysses' (*A*) and Eldridge's samples of newspaper English (*B*), compared with an ideal slope of negative unity (*C*). Zipf, *Human Behavior and the Principle of Least Effort,* Addison-Wesley Press, Inc., Cambridge, Mass., 1949, p. 25.

the stream of speech is especially interesting when one considers that speakers and writers pay little if any attention to the size or frequency of the words they use.

When the elementary speech sounds of language are ordered according to their complexity or difficulty—and Zipf feels this is in terms of the energy required to produce them vocally—he finds that (c) *the more 'effortful' a sound, the less frequent its occurrence tends to be.* This law suggests one possible explanation of the apparently spontaneous phonetic changes in language. Zipf gives the example of how the *d* of Old High German, preserved in the English 'do,' becomes *tun* in Modern German, as part of a general *d* to *t* phonetic shift. Unfortunately for Zipf's general thesis, we also find that the medial *t* in American English is shifting to *d* (e.g. witness pronunciations of 'traitor' and 'bottle'). It would be difficult to argue that *d* tends to shift toward *t* because the latter is less effortful. Applying the same logic, he finds that (d) *accent gravitates away from the more frequently used elements of speech,* i.e. it requires more energy to accent elements in the stream of speech. Among the prefixes of Modern German, the four most frequently used (*ge-, be-, ver-,* and *er-*) are never accented, whereas most prefixes of comparatively lower frequency are usually accented. We may also look upon accent as an *attention-calling device* in encoding, bring the listener's attention to what would otherwise be an unexpected signal—more frequently used signals do not require special attention on the part of the decoder.

Sampling from James Joyce's *Ulysses,* Zipf (1945 *a*) has demonstrated that (e) *the size of intervals* (in pages) *between the successive occurrences of the same word is inversely related to the number of such intervals,* i.e. the lawfulness in the stream of speech is such that short time intervals between

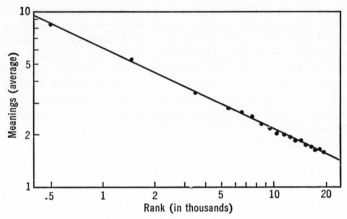

FIGURE 220. Average number of meanings per word of the 20,000 most frequently used English words, when ranked in order of decreasing frequency of usage. Zipf, *Journal of General Psychology,* 1945, 33:253.

the use of a word predominate over long intervals, this being independent of the absolute frequency of occurrence. Further analysis shows that (f) *intervals of varying size tend to be evenly distributed through time.* The frequency of recurrence of intervals of a particular size depends upon the number of such size intervals. Again, we have evidence for a grand harmony or balance in language behavior.

In another investigation (1945 *b*), employing data from Thorndike's list of 20,000 most frequent words (1932 *b*) in conjunction with the number of different meanings of these words as given in the *Thorndike-Century Senior Dictionary* (1941), Zipf has found that (g) *the average number of different meanings per word is proportional to its frequency of occurrence.* This relation may be seen in Fig. 220. A necessary corollary of this function is that short words would tend to have a higher multiplicity of meanings than long ones. Words such as *bar, case,* and *let* are more variable in meaning (i.e. depend more upon context) than words like *dictionary, antelope,* and *motivate.* In interpreting this relation, Zipf postulates two opposed 'drives': the speaker's drive for economy of effort, which would ultimately lead to a single word with infinite meanings, and the hearer's drive for comprehension, which would ultimately lead to an infinite number of different words with unique meanings. The above-mentioned relation represents the balancing of these opposed tendencies. Of course, 'speaker' and 'hearer' are abstract entities here, like the 'economic man'; individual humans do not have these motives, and, further, individual humans function both as speakers and hearers.

As a preliminary description of his general theory (cf. 1945 a), Zipf uses the following analogy: Imagine a skilled artisan working at a long tool bench having a production space at one end; his tools vary in the effort required to use them and are laid out along this lengthy bench. As each one becomes necessary, he must travel up to its location and back to his production space. We assume that this skilled artisan can improvise on his equipment, invent new tools and modify old ones, and that his motivation is to accomplish maximum work with the least effort. Now it is apparent that our workman will tend to use the least effortful tools as much as he can (relation a cited above—short words used more often than long ones). The most frequently used tools will be small in number and varied in use, but the less frequently used will be large in number and more specialized in use (relations b and g cited above—the number of different words used increases as the rank order of frequency decreases; short and frequent words tend to have more different meanings than long and infrequent ones). If a tool requiring considerable effort comes to be used more frequently, the artisan will try to modify it in order to make it less effortful to use (relations c and d cited above—effortful sounds occur less frequently and are modified when their frequency of use increases; effortful stress or accent tends to gravitate away from the most frequently used elements). Finally, our worker will place the most frequently used tools near at hand on the linear bench so that his effortful traveling up and down will be minimized; this means that he will make relatively more short trips than long ones, and he will tend to balance the tiring long trips against a series of shorter ones (relations e and f cited above—there are more short intervals between successive occurrences of the same word than long ones; intervals of varying size are evenly distributed through time).

This is an entirely delightful analogy, and all the relations it contains stem from a single fundamental postulate, the *principle of least effort*. But where in individual behavior does this principle have its moorings? There is no question but that these complex social phenomena of language are lawful because the behavior of individual human beings is lawful, but at what point can these two levels of discourse be linked? To find the answers to this question it will be necessary to study these relations within the language behavior of individuals. For one thing, it is certain that we are dealing with both convergent and divergent hierarchies of instrumental skills. Each linguistic unit (phoneme, morpheme, word, or phrase) is both preceded and followed by a variety of other units, but these transitional dependencies are of variable frequency of occurrence and hence habit strength. Competition among such hierarchies would be expected. It might be possible to demonstrate shifts in speech sounds when the individual is under stress; similar demonstrations might be made for the accent relations. Analysis of the typical errors made by individuals in the pronunciation and accent of words might provide a picture of the dynamics at work in language change and hence the direction that changes will take. In any case, it is likely that the psychological substratum of Zipf's linguistic laws will prove to be extremely complicated.

(2) *The adjective-verb quotient.* In 1925 a German investigator, Busemann, recorded spontaneous stories on various subjects told by children and analyzed these language data into relative frequencies of *qualitative descriptions* (adjectives, nouns, and participles) and *active expressions* (all verbs except auxiliaries). By dividing the former into the latter (action/description) he obtained what he called the *action quotient* and claimed that this ratio varied with rhythmical changes in emotionality during development. The importance of Busemann's work, however, lies not in the validity of this hypothesis but in the suggestion of a new method for studying language as it relates to personality, writing style, and so on. Boder (1940), reporting work actually done in 1927, has studied the dependence of the adjective-verb ratio upon the *content* of written language, i.e. what is written about. The *adjective-verb quotient* (*Avq.*) was the number of adjectives per 100 verbs (adjective/verb $\times$ 100). Taking selections of 300 to 350 words as samples, the descriptive, qualifying character of writing was found to be lowest for drama (mean *Avq.* 11.2), somewhat higher for legal writing (*Avq.* 20.0), still higher for fiction (*Avq.* 35.2), and highest for scientific writing (*Avq.* 75.5). The difference between drama and fiction probably reflects the greater action content of the former, as well as the substitution of scenery and gesture for descriptive adjectives. Although the precision of legal statutes is achieved mainly through choice of verbs, precision in science is achieved through choice of qualifying adjectives.

(3) *The type-token ratio* (*TTR*). This measure is the ratio of the number of different words (types) to the total number of words (tokens) in a given language sample. When the size of samples taken from different individuals is constant, this ratio provides an index of the flexibility or variability in their speech (cf. Carroll, 1938, 1944; Johnson, 1944). Some interesting individual differences have appeared from the application of this measure. Fairbanks (1944) took samples of *spoken* language from ten schizophrenics and ten college freshmen. Dividing each sample into 30 consecutive 100-word segments and computing *TTR*'s for each independently, the internal consistency of the measure proved to be quite high. The *TTR* for schizophrenics (.57) proved to be significantly lower than that for college freshmen (.64), and we may infer that this measure is valid in the sense that it differentiates between the language samples of two groups in a manner to be expected on a priori grounds. College freshmen are more successful than schizophrenics in introducing variety into their spoken language. Mann (1944) contributes a parallel study on the *written* language of schizophrenics and college freshmen. Essentially similar results were obtained. Although numerous comparisons are made between the spoken and written samples in these two studies, they are of somewhat dubious significance since the content of the messages was quite different—discussing proverbs such as 'Let sleeping dogs lie' (Fairbanks) versus 'Write a story of your life' (Mann).

Figure 221 provides interesting comparisons among telephone-conversation language (data from French, Carter, and Koenig, 1930), schizophrenic speech, normal speech, and written materials (data from Dewey, 1923) in terms of the proportions of total words that are accounted for by the five most frequent words used, ten most frequent, and so on. The 100 most frequent words in schizophrenic speech account for nearly 70 per cent of their total production, approaching the stereotyped, repetitious level of telephone conversations. For college freshmen the 100 most frequent words account for 63 per cent of total speech, nearer the more varied and flexible level of written language. Notice also that for both telephone conversations and schizophrenic speech only about 30 different words make up 50 per cent of all utterances.

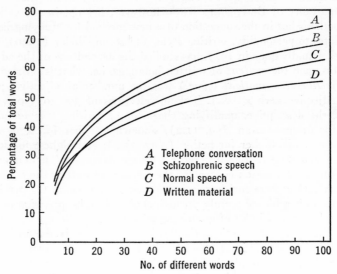

FIGURE 221. Curves showing cumulative percentages of total words accounted for by the 100 most frequently used words, for the sample types listed in the figure. H. Fairbanks, *Psychological Monographs*, 1944, **57**, #255:33.

An extensive methodological analysis of TTR is contributed by Chotlos (1944). Each of 1000 children between 8 and 18 years of age submitted a 3000-word language sample, following the instructions, 'You are to write about anything you want to write about. Just make it up as you go along. . .' An experimental group of 108 subjects was selected from this pool so as to conform to a factorial design, from the analysis of which the variance attributable to I.Q., age, location (city, town, rural), and sex could be determined. As measured by the number of types (different words) and the magnitude of the type-token ratio (number of different words/total words), diversity of written language was found to increase with both I.Q. and age but to be largely independent of location and sex. When equivalent analyses of nouns, adjectives, verbs, and adverbs were made (i.e. the type-token for nouns being the number of different nouns divided by the total number of nouns), the frequencies of both nouns and adjectives were found to increase with I.Q. and age, and a disproportionately frequent use of verbs characterized the low I.Q. and younger children. In other words, language is not only more diversified with older and more intelligent individuals but also more finely qualified and discriminative. The latter portion of Chotlos's report contains a detailed analysis of the relation between the number of different words used (types) and the size of the sample (tokens). Although space does not permit complete coverage of this material, Fig. 222 described a portion of the data. It may be seen that the number of *different* words increases as a negatively accelerated function of the size of the sample, the number of *new* words added with each increase in size of the sample becoming progressively smaller and theoretically reaching zero when the subject's vocabulary is exhausted. From the difference in slope of these

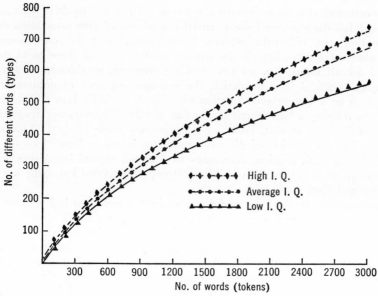

FIGURE 222. Cumulative type-token ratios for subjects having high, average, or low I.Q. Chotlos, *Psychological Monographs*, 1944, **57**, #255:105.

functions for high and low I.Q. subjects we infer that the size of the total vocabulary varies with intelligence—which is exactly what most designers of intelligence tests have long assumed.

Associational Structure

The overt communicative product or message has been shown to have a remarkably stable statistical structure. Although we are as yet unable to specify in any detail the dependence of this structure upon the habit systems of individual communicators, there undoubtedly are such relations. In this case we are dealing with convergent and divergent hierarchies of *instrumental skill sequences*—the behaviors of individuals which immediately precede and determine the series of physical events we call messages. If the events that comprise *semantic or mediational sequences* are also systems of habits arranged in hierarchies, we should expect this level of language behavior to also display a stable statistical structure. In other words, 'idea' *A* should be variably associated with 'ideas' *B, C, D* ⋯ *N* as a divergent hierarchy; similarly, various 'ideas' should tend to elicit *A* as the response in a convergent hierarchy with different probabilities. The techniques of word association provide us with a tool for investigating the statistical structure of associations at the semantic level.

(1) *The hierarchical structure of associations.* At an earlier point in this chapter the typical phenomena of free association were described. We may look upon each stimulus word in this method as tapping a 'pool' of potential associates. Is selection from this pool a random matter or is it lawfully determined by the comparative habit strengths of associates arranged in a response hierarchy? The evidence favors the latter view. For one thing, the frequency patterns for various responses to the same stimulus words obtained by Kent and Rosanoff have been closely duplicated by other investigators, demonstrating that these frequency patterns are not due to chance. Skinner (1937) has demonstrated the essential lawfulness of free association data in another way. When the responses to each stimulus on the Kent-Rosanoff test are *ranked* according to frequency of occurrence and these ranks combined for all items (i.e. all first ranking responses combined, all second ranking combined, and so forth), the average frequency of occurrence is found to be a logarithmic function of rank (cf. Zipf's Law). The fact that the relation is logarithmic means that the drop in frequency from rank to rank is sharp at first, becoming progressively more gradual. This also means that the number of different associates increases logarithmically as the habit strength required decreases—in the 'pool' tapped by a given stimulus word there are very few responses strongly associated but many having weak association.

An ingenious method for studying a variety of problems in language behavior, including the present one, has also been designed by Skinner (1936). Called the *verbal summator,* it is a device for repeating samples of meaningless speech sounds obtained by permuting and combining elemental speech sounds, a sort of verbal ink-blot. Upon hearing such a sound pattern repeated several times, the subject may himself supply a meaningful form, the readiness and frequency with which various meaningful forms occur indexing their relative verbalization strengths. According to Skinner, the verbal summator 'evokes latent verbal responses through summation with imitative responses to skeletal samples of speech.' In actual experimentation each sample was repeated softly until the subject could make a meaningful 'projection,' this being written down along with the number of repetitions required. The same logarithmic relation demonstrated above for free associations was found to apply here: when words (in these verbalizations) are ranked according to their frequency of occurrence in a sample of 1000, i.e. fifty times per thousand, ten per thousand, one per thousand, etc., the number of different words in each rank is found to vary logarithmically with the rank. A relatively small number of words are used frequently, but a large number of words occur only once or twice. This is again in keeping with Zipf's Law.

In the methods so far considered, the strength of associations has been inferred from group data—the total sample of 1000 responses has not been obtained by repeated testing of the same individual. Is there any basis for expecting the same laws to apply to the availability of associations *within the single individual?* Thumb and Marbe (1901) obtained a logarithmic relation between individual reaction times for free associations and the frequency of occurrence of these responses in a population. This has come to be known as Marbe's Law and has been substantiated by a number of other investigators (cf. Woodworth, 1938). Cason and Cason (1925) report similar findings for words taken from the Kent-Rosanoff list. Accepting reaction time (latency) as a measure of habit strength, we have here a clean-cut relation between the frequency of occurrence of a given association in the population and the strength of that association within individuals drawn from that population. But if this be the case, shouldn't the most frequent response be the only response to a given stimulus? Shouldn't the response having the strongest association with the stimulus always be made by every individual? There are several reasons for variability: the habit strengths of the potential responses presumably show continuous oscillation (cf. Hull, 1943); the actual stimulus is a compound affair varying with the momentary context; and there remain real individual differences in the nature of mediation processes that have been established for the same signs.

A method of obtaining repeated associations from the same individual has been devised by Bousfield and Sedgewick (1944). The subject is given a limiting set, to name as many cities in the United States as he can, to give the names of as many makes of cars as he can, and, while writing down his list, he draws demarcation lines every 2 minutes at a signal given by the experimenter. Sample results from a subject instructed to name quadruped animals were as follows: *horse, cow, pig, raccoon, mink, sheep, beaver, cat, dog, bear, donkey, woodchuck, tiger, lion, giraffe, leopard, wildcat, deer, goat—/2/—mule, squirrel, chipmunk, rabbit, bear, elk, seal, lynx, antelope, coyote—/4/—gopher, rat, oxen, wolf, whale, water buffalo, bison—/6/—ape, gorilla, chimpanzee, prairie dog—/8/—zebra, kangaroo, panther—/10/—otter, mole—/12/—muskrat—/14/—*. With the instructions serving to restrict the 'pool' of available associates (much as the stimulus word functions in the ordinary free association method), the rate at which responses are drawn from the 'pool' is rapid at first, while the readily available responses are being made, the rate progressively slowing down as responses of weaker strength must be drawn.

Data obtained in this manner also fit a logarithmic function closely, which the investigators interpret as meaning that the rate of production is a function of the number of remaining associations; all curves approach an asymptote, a value presumably indexing the total number of responses available in the 'pool.' To obtain a graphic record of individual performance, a telegraph key was pressed every time a new word was produced; this activated a heated stylus which made a cumulative record on waxed paper. A sample record for a single subject is shown in Fig. 223. Bousfield (1944) reports similar results with subjects instructed to produce sequences of pleasant or unpleasant associates; here, interestingly enough, rate and asymptote for pleasant associates was higher, justifying the commonly held notion that the 'pool' for pleasant associates is larger than that for unpleasant associates. Bousfield and Barclay (1950) have demonstrated that the order of appearance of particular associates in the sequential series *for an individual* is related to the frequency of usage of these associates in the group as a whole. In other words, the common, strong associates (like *horse, cat,* and *dog*) occur both more frequently among different subjects and earlier in the sequence for each individual subject; rare and weaker associates (like *bison, lynx,* and *armadillo*), being at the bottom of the 'pool,' occur both later and less frequently. This is again a function that would be predicted from the

habit-family hierarchy conception—probability and latency are both functions of habit strength.

(2) *Contextual determinants of association.* Bousfield and Sedgewick
noted irregularities on the production curves for individual subjects. Inspection of Fig. 223 shows that associations tend to come in 'bursts' or
'clusters,' and this can also be seen in the detailed sample of responses for
quadruped animals cited above—the word *tiger* is followed by a group of
related associates, *lion, giraffe,* and *leopard,* all inhabitants of the jungle
scene. It is also likely that these associates were written down in rapid succession. This phenomenon indicates that the stimulus situation eliciting

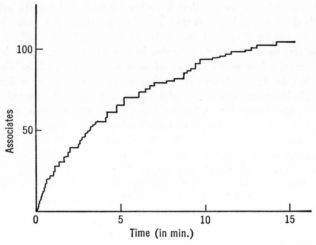

FIGURE 223. Kymographic record of the cumulative responses of a single subject
instructed to name cities of the U. S. Notice that clusters of associates are separated
by relatively long periods of latency. Bousfield and Sedgewick, *Journal of General
Psychology,* 1944, **30**:160.

responses from the general 'pool' is actually not a constant; rather, the
occurrence of each successive response, as a self-stimulational 'feedback,'
subtly modifies the context. Unpublished research by both Bousfield and
the present writer indicates that the transitional probabilities between particular associates (as determined by group data) are higher when the
latencies between successive items are shorter, i.e. these 'clusters' are composed of relatively high probability associates to the particular stimulus
context created by the first item in the cluster.

This, of course, is only a special instance of the effects of context upon
the responses made to signs. *Any and all stimulations that combine with the
patterns of stimulation directly elicited by signs are parts of the context and
function in greater or lesser degree to determine the mediational and instrumental reactions made.* The sign DUCK! when accompanied by the
self-stimulations of the speaker's own vocalic responses, does not produce
the vigorous avoidant behavior it does in the hearer; the same objective
sign DUCK elicits quite different mediational processes when heard in the
environmental context of a baseball game than when heard in the context
of a farmyard. Context phenomena can also be treated in terms of the

statistical structure of language behavior; the transitions from one response to another in either mediational or instrumental sequences can be handled as dependent probabilities—dependent upon the total momentary context and the existing habit hierarchies with which such contexts are associated.

It is a matter of common observation that a man's moods, emotions, and motives influence the character of his verbalizations. An angry man tends to select short, common words. These emotional and motivational states constitute the *internal nonverbal context*. In one of the few relevant studies, Bousfield and Barry (1937) had subjects first rate their own moods on a scale from +5 to −5, +5 meaning 'feeling as well as possible' and −5 'as badly as possible,' and then write down as many pleasant and unpleasant associations as they could. A total of 3 minutes divided into two periods was allowed for each type of association. The ratio of pleasant to unpleasant associations was found to vary consistently with rated euphoria, 'happy' subjects producing relatively more pleasant associations than 'sad' subjects. It should be possible to induce various internal states experimentally, such as frustration and elation, and then determine their effects upon free association and verbal 'projection' (e.g. Skinner's verbal summator technique), but no information is available here. There have been some attempts to differentiate forms of mental disorder on the basis of free associations (cf. Murphy, 1923; Martin, 1945), but the data are not consistent.

There is also the *internal verbal context*. The response an individual makes to a given sign often depends upon the implicit verbalization that sign elicits, i.e. upon his attitude toward the object signified. By way of illustration, one study (Foley and MacMillan, 1943) may be described briefly. Five groups of subjects, first-year law students, second-year law, first-year medical, second-year medical, and a control group of nonprofessional students, were asked to write down associations to 40 stimulus words, 20 of which were homophones interpretable in legal, medical, or nonprofessional senses (e.g. *binding, administer, discharge,* and so forth). Significant differences between groups were obtained, the consistency of 'professional interpretation' increasing with amount of professional training. Generalizing from these data, it would be expected that any attitude, as a persistent pattern of self-stimulation, would affect verbal as well as nonverbal behavior.

Despite, or perhaps because of, the obvious importance of the *external nonverbal context* in determining the momentary meaning of signs, little work has been done. The external nonverbal context includes the facial expressions of the speaker, his gestures, the objects present, and the activities under way—in short, the total situational matrix within which signs are produced. The word 'fine!' may even imply its own opposite, as when spoken in the presence of a deflated tire. Think of the phrase 'he was caught stealing home' without its baseball situational context, or of how meaningless a movie script would be if heard without the accompanying action. Either the free association or verbal summator technique could be applied here to demonstrate that selection from the 'pool' of potential responses depends in part upon the momentary situational context.

Some attention has recently been given to the effects of the *external verbal context*. Again, it is obvious that the meaning of a verbal sign depends upon the pattern of other language signs within which it is imbedded. Howes and Osgood (1953) studied one aspect of this problem from the point of view of behavior theory, using a modified free association technique. A sequence of four spoken words made up each item, the first three serving as the 'context' and the fourth, spoken with greater emphasis, serving as the actual stimulus for word association by the subjects. One experiment got at the effects of varying the *consistency* or *emphasis* of verbal context: one group of subjects heard three context-stimuli of very similar meaning (*sinister, devil, evil*–DARK), a second group had one neutral word added (*eat, devil, evil*–DARK), a third had two miscellaneous words added (*eat, basic, evil*–DARK), and a fourth group, as control, included none of the influencing words. When the frequencies of response-words related to the particular context (e.g. *night, thief, mystery, dead,* etc.) were plotted as a function of the density in the context of such influence, the number of influenced associations turned out to be a simple multiple of the number of relevant words in the context. Frequency of the most common associate (DARK–*light*) decreased as the number of interrelated influencing words in the context increased, confirming the notion that the meaning of a word is made more specific by its context.

In the second experiment three influencing words of relatively independent meaning were used as 'context,' and the question was how *temporal proximity* affects word association. With an item like *feminine, strong, young*–MAN, the responses clearly relevant to each contextual stimulus could be isolated (*woman, girl* vs. *hard, work* vs. *boy, child,* for example). Then the frequency of occurrence of such related responses was plotted as a function of the order of presentation of their contextual stimuli (e.g. frequencies of *woman* and *girl* when *feminine* is in third place, nearest MAN; second place; and first place, most remote from MAN). The results indicated that the degree of influence of a contextual stimulus upon the meaning of a sign is a sharply negatively accelerated function of the temporal interval between them. In other words, the influence of one word upon another falls off rapidly as the amount of intervening material increases. The function, incidentally, was remarkably similar to that for the stimulus trace, as derived by Hull from conditioning data. A third experiment got at the matter of *familiarity*. With two of the contextual stimuli constant, one group heard a third word very common in usage (e.g. bright, gay, *calm*–GREEN) and the other a third word synonymous in meaning but relatively rare (e.g. bright, gay, *quiescent*–GREEN). As anticipated, contextual words were found to have effect in proportion to their familiarity. Many other characteristics of context could be studied with the same general technique.

SUMMARY

In looking back over this final chapter one is impressed first, perhaps, with the great breadth of the area covered by language behavior. It includes the descriptive analysis of messages by linguists, analytic study of the encoding and decoding processes by psycholinguists (phoneticians, psychoacousticians, learning theorists), and the study of speakers and hearers, their intentions, meanings, attitudes, and motives, by psychologists, anthropologists, and other social scientists. In terms of content, study of language behavior runs the gamut from neurophysiology of speech mechanisms and aphasia, through comparative, experimental, developmental, and social psychology, into cultural anthropology and the philosophy of science. One also gets the impression that there are empirical gaps of considerable magnitude in this area, which is not surprising because its range is so great. Nevertheless, the first toddling steps of the science of language behavior are provocative.

One of the healthiest things about this infant science is the relative ease with which its data can be quantified and subjected to statistical analysis. This is certainly true for the communicative products (messages) themselves and generally true for the instrumental and reception skills by which these products are encoded and decoded. In this connection co-operation between linguists and psychologists is now beginning to take place. The situation with respect to the semantic or mediational level of communication behavior is less satisfactory, yet even here steps toward quantitative measurement are being taken. A final impression one gets is this: language behavior is clearly a learned activity—as a matter of fact it is by all odds the most complex product of learning mechanisms to be found. Language behavior is also composed of units whose quantities and interrelations are readily described in mathematical terms. It is to be anticipated, therefore, that one of the most fruitful developments in this field is going to be a fusion of learning theories with techniques of mathematical statistics. In terms of its central relevance to general psychological theory and its potential applicability to complex social problems, no other area of experimental psychology so greatly demands attention as language behavior—and in the past has received so little.

Bibliography and Author Index

This reference section has been arranged to maximize its usefulness to both student and investigator. The form of citation is that established by the American Psychological Association for use in its journals. Each reference is to be found under the name of the first author and is numbered. Names of second authors appear in appropriate alphabetical position, the location of the citation being indicated by reference number. Names used without specification of particular books or papers appear without reference number. The bracketed numbers at the end of each citation or name refer the reader to pages in this book on which that material or person is discussed.

Abernethy, E. M. (*See* No. 317)

1. Abrahams, H., Krakauer, D., & Dallenbach, K. M. Gustatory adaptation to salt. *Amer. J. Psychol.*, 1937, **49**, 462-9. [78, 81]
2. Ach, N. Über die Begriffsbildung. *Untersuchungen zur Psychol. und Philos.*, 1921, Vol. 3. [675]
3. Adams, D. K. Experimental studies of adaptive behavior in cats. *Comp. Psychol. Monogr.*, 1929, **6**, No. 27. [657]
4. Ades, H. W., Mettler, F. A., & Culler, E. Functional organization of the medial geniculate bodies in the cat. *Amer. J. Physiol.*, 1938, **123**, 1-2. [111]

Ades, H. W. (*See* No. 697)

5. Adrian, E. D. *The basis of sensation.* London: Christophers, 1928. [12, 66, 80, 104]
6. Adrian, E. D. *The mechanism of nervous action. Electrical studies of the neurone.* Philadelphia: Univ. of Penn. Press, 1932. [14]
7. Adrian, E. D. Electric responses of the human eye. *J. Physiol.*, 1945, **104**, 84-104. [154, 184, 185]
8. Adrian, E. D. Rod and cone components in the electric response of the eye. *J. Physiol.*, 1946, **105**, 24-37. [137, 152, 154, 188]
9. Adrian, E. D., & Matthews, R. Action of light on the eye: I. The discharge of impulses in the optic nerve and its relation to electric changes in the retina. *J. Physiol.*, 1927, **63**, 378-404. [68, 150, 151, 166]
10. Adrian, E. D., & Matthews, R. Action of light on the eye: III. The interaction of retinal neurons. *J. Physiol.*, 1928, **65**, 273-98. [146, 167]
11. Allen, F. On reflex visual sensations. *J. Opt. Soc. Amer.*, 1923, **7**, 583-626. [82]
12. Allen, F., & Hollenberg, A. On the tactile sensory reflex. *Quart. J. exper. Physiol.*, 1924, **14**, 351-78. [82]
13. Allen, F., & Weinberg, M. The gustatory sensory reflex. *Quart. J. exper. Physiol.*, 1925, **15**, 385-420. [82]

Allen, M. K. (*See* No. 495)

14. Allport, F. H. *Social psychology.* Boston: Houghton Mifflin, 1924. [687-9]
15. Allport, G. W. Eidetic imagery. *Brit. J. Psychol.*, 1924, **15**, 99-120. [641]
16. Allport, G. W. Change and decay in the visual memory image. *Brit. J. Psychol.*, 1930, **21**, 133-48. [589-90]
17. Allport, G. W. *Personality: a psychological interpretation.* New York: Holt, 1937. [443, 704]
18. Alper, T. G. Task-orientation vs. ego-orientation in learning and retention. *Amer. J. Psychol.*, 1946, **59**, 236-48. [579, 580-81, 584]

19. Alper, T. G. Task-orientation and ego-orientation as factors in reminiscence. *J. exp. Psychol.*, 1948, 38, 224-38. [581]

Alper, T. G. (*See* No. 942)

20. Alpert, A. The solving of problem-situations by pre-school children: an analysis. *Teach. Coll. Contrib. Educ.*, 1928, No. 323. [622]
21. Alrutz, S. Omförnimmelsen 'hett.' *Uppsala Läkfören*, 1897, Förh. 2, ser. 2, 340-59. [18]
22. Ames, A. *Nature and origin of perceptions* (preliminary laboratory manual). Hanover, N. H.: The Hanover Institute, 1949. [263-6, 271]
23. Ames, A., Ogle, K. N., & Gliddon, G. H. Corresponding retinal points, the horopter and size and shape of ocular images. *J. Opt. Soc. Amer.*, 1932, 22, 538-631. [256]
24. Ammons, R. B. Acquisition of motor skill: I. Quantitative analysis and theoretical formulation. *Psychol. Rev.*, 1947, 54, 263-81. [563]
25. Anderson, A. C. Time discrimination in the white rat. *J. Comp. Psychol.*, 1932, 13, 27-55. [324]
26. Anderson, A. C. Runway time and the goal gradient. *J. exp. Psychol.*, 1933, 16, 423-8. [324]
27. Anderson, E. E., & Weymouth, F. W. Visual perception and the retinal mosaic. *Amer. J. Physiol.*, 1923, 64, 561-84. [164]
28. Andrews, R. C., & Hunter, W. S. Double alternation by a maze-bright strain of rats, with some data on brain lesions. *Amer. J. Psychol.*, 1943, 56, 87-94. [662]

Angell, F. [324]

29. Anrep, G. V. Pitch discrimination in the dog. *J. Physiol.*, 1920, 53, 367-85. [354]
30. Anrep, G. V. The irradiation of conditioned reflexes. *Proc. roy. Soc.*, 1923, B94, 404-25. [354]
31. Ansbacher, H. Perception of number as affected by the monetary value of the objects. *Arch. Psychol., N. Y.*, 1937, No. 215. [289]

Aristotle [372]

32. Arnold, W. J. Simple reaction chains and their integration: I. Homogeneous chaining with terminal reinforcement. *J. comp. physiol. Psychol.*, 1947a, 40, 349-64. [501]
33. Arnold, W. J. Simple reaction chains and their integration: II. Heterogeneous chaining with terminal reinforcement. *J. comp. physiol. Psychol.*, 1947b, 40, 427-40. [501]
34. Arnold, W. J. Simple reaction chains and their integration: III. Heterogeneous chaining with serial reinforcement. *J. comp. physiol. Psychol.*, 1948, 41, 1-10. [501]

Arnott, P. (*See* No. 630)

35. Aronoff, S., & Dallenbach, K. M. Minor studies from the Psychological Laboratory of Cornell University: LXXXI. Adaptation of warm spots under continuous and intermittent stimulation. *Amer. J. Psychol.*, 1936, 48, 485-90. [80]
36. Arrer, M. von. Über die Bedeutung der Convergenz- und Accommodationsbewegungen für die Tiefenwahrnehmung. *Philos. Stud.*, 1898, 13, 116-61, 222-304. [267]

Atkinson, J. W. (*See* No. 820)

37. Bain, A. [373, 648]
38. Baird, J. W. The influence of accommodation and convergence upon the perception of depth. *Amer. J. Psychol.*, 1903, 14, 150-200. [267]
39. Balken, E. R. Affective, volitional and galvanic factors in learning. *J. exp. Psychol.*, 1933, 16, 115-28. [572]

Ball, J. (*See* No. 717)

40. Ballachey, E. L., & Buel, J. Centrifugal swing as a determinant of choice-point behavior in the maze running of the white rat. *J. comp. Psychol.*, 1934a, 17, 201-23. [499]
41. Ballachey, E. L., & Buel, J. Centrifugal swing as a factor determining the distribution of errors in the maze running of the rat. *J. genet. Psychol.*, 1934b, 45, 358-70. [499]
42. Ballard, P. B. Obliviscence and reminiscence. *Brit. J. Psychol.*, 1913, *Monogr. Suppl.*, 1, No. 2. [564-6]
43. Bappert, J. Neue Untersuchungen zum Problem des Verhältnisses von Akkommodation und Konvergenz zur Wahrnehmung der Tiefe. *Z. Psychol.*, 1922, 90, 167-203. [268]

Barclay, W. D. (*See* No. 108)

Barker, A. N. (*See* No. 551)

Barrera, S. E. (*See* No. 1191)

44. Barrett, D. M. Memory in relation to hedonic tone. *Arch. Psychol., N. Y.,* 1938, **31**, No. 223. [572]

Barry, H., Jr. (*See* No. 109)

45. Bartlett, F. C. *Remembering: A study in experimental and social psychology.* Cambridge: Cambridge Univ. Press, 1932. [551, 558-61, 570, 590-93]

Bartlett, N. (*See* No. 383)

46. Bartley, S. H. Action potentials of the optic cortex under the influence of strychnine. *Amer. J. Physiol.,* 1933, **103**, 203-12. [153]
47. Bartley, S. H. Relation of intensity and duration of brief retinal stimulation by light to the electrical response of the optic cortex of the rabbit. *Amer. J. Physiol.,* 1934, **108**, 397-408. [154]
48. Bartley, S. H. The time of the occurrence of the cortical response as determined by the area of the stimulus object. *Amer. J. Physiol.,* 1935, **110**, 666-74. [154]
49. Bartley, S. H. Subjective flicker rate with relation to critical flicker frequency. *J. exp. Psychol.,* 1938, **22**, 338-49. [145, 146]
50. Bartley, S. H. Some factors in brightness discrimination. *Psychol. Rev.,* 1939, **46**, 337-58. [149]
51. Bartley, S. H. *Vision: A study of its basis.* New York: Van Nostrand, 1941. [133, 135, 136, 146, 151, 153, 230]
52. Bartley, S. H., & Bishop, G. H. Optic nerve response to retinal stimulation in the rabbit. *Proc. Soc. exp. Biol., N. Y.,* 1940, **44**, 39-41. [150, 151, 196]

Bartley, S. H. (*See* No. 332)

53. Barton, J. W. Smaller vs. larger units in learning the maze. *J. exp. Psychol.,* 1921, **4**, 418-29. [540]
54. Bass, M. J., & Hull, C. L. The irradiation of a tactile conditioned reflex in man. *J. comp. Psychol.,* 1934, **17**, 47-65. [354]

Bayroff, A. G. (*See* No. 984)

55. Bazett, H. C., & McGlone, B. Studies in sensation: III. Chemical factor in the stimulation of end organ giving temperature sensations. *Arch. Neurol. and Psychiat.,* 1932, **28**, 71-91. [16]
56. Bazett, H. C., McGlone, B., Williams, R. G., & Lufkin, H. M. Sensation: I. Depth, distribution and probable identification in the prepuce of sensory end-organs concerned in sensations of temperature and touch; thermometric conductivity. *Arch. Neurol. Psychiat., Chicago,* 1932, **27**, 489-517. [7]
57. Bean, C. H. An unusual opportunity to investigate the psychology of language. *J. genet. Psychol.,* 1932, **40**, 181-202. [687]
58. Beck, L. H. Unpublished manuscript. 1949. [21, 26-9]
59. Beck, L. H. Osmics: Theory and problems related to the initial events in olfaction. In O. Glasser (ed.), *Medical physics.* Chicago: The Year Book Publishers, 1950. Vol. II.
60. Beck, L. H., & Miles, W. R. Some theoretical and experimental relationships between infra-red absorption and olfaction. *Science,* 1947, **106**, 511. [26]

Beethoven, L. van. [641]

61. Beitel, R. J. Spatial summation of subliminal stimuli in the human retina. *J. gen. Psychol.,* 1934, **10**, 311-27. [167]
62. Beitel, R. J. Inhibition of threshold excitation in the human eye. *J. gen. Psychol.,* 1936, **14**, 31-61. [168]
63. Békésy, G. von. Zur Theorie des Hörens. Über die eben merkbare Amplituden- und Frequenzänderung eines Tones. Die Theorie der Schwebungen. *Physik. Z.,* 1929, **30**, 721-45. [115]
64. Békésy, G. von. Über das Fechnersche Gesetz und seine Bedeutung für die Theorie der akustischen Beobachtungsfehler und die Theorie des Hörens. *Ann. Physik,* 1930, **7**, 329-59. [59, 61]
65. Békésy, G. von. Variation of phase along the basilar membrane with sinusoidal vibrations. *J. acoust. Soc. Amer.,* 1947, **19**, 452-60. [92]
66. Békésy, G. von. On the resonance curve and the decay period at various points on the cochlear partition. *J. acoust. Soc. Amer.,* 1949, **21**, 245-54. [121]

Békésy, G. von. [95, 96, 102]

67. Bell, Charles. On the nervous circle which connects the voluntary muscles with the brain. *Phil. Trans. roy. Soc., London,* 1826, **2**, 163-73. [29]

Bentley, M. [20]

68. Benussi, V. Versuche zur Analyse taktil erweckter Scheinbewegungen. *Arch. ges. Psychol.,* 1916, **36**, 59-135. [244]

Benussi, V. [235]

69. Berg, I. A., & Weisman, R. L. The goal gradient in a maze of variable path length. *J. Psychol.,* 1942, **14**, 307-15. [499]

Bergmann, G. (*See* No. 1067)

70. Berkeley, G. *An essay toward a new theory of vision.* Dublin, 1709. [29, 248-9, 267]
71. Berkeley, G. *A treatise concerning the principles of human knowledge.* Dublin, 1710. [646]
72. Betts, G. H. *The distribution and functions of mental imagery.* New York: Teachers College, Columbia Univ., 1909. [642]
73. Beryl, R. Über die Grössenauffassung bei Kindern. *Z. Psychol.,* 1926, **100**, 344-71. [279]

Biddulph, R. (*See* No. 1035)

74. Bidwell, S. Some curiosities of vision. *Proc. Roy. Instit. Great Britain,* 1898, XV, No. 91, 354-65. [185]
75. Biel, W. C., & Force, R. C. Retention of nonsense syllables in intentional and incidental learning. *J. exp. Psychol.,* 1943, **32**, 52-63. [578]
76. Bills, A. G. The influence of muscular tension on the efficiency of mental work. *Amer. J. Psychol.,* 1927, **38**, 227-51. [652]
77. Bingham, W. E., Jr. A study of the relations which the galvanic skin response and sensory reference bear to judgments of the meaningfulness, significance, and importance of 72 words. *J. Psychol.,* 1943, **16**, 21-34. [700-701]
78. Birch, H. G. The relation of previous experience to insightful problem-solving. *J. comp. Psychol.,* 1945, **38**, 367-83. [613-14]
79. Birch, H. G., & Bitterman, M. E. Reinforcement and learning: the process of sensory integration. *Psychol. Rev.,* 1949, **56**, 292-308. [323-4, 463-5, 466]
80. Birenbaum, G., & Zeigarnik, B. A dynamic analysis of thought disturbances. *Sov. Neuropath., psychiat. Psycho-hygiene,* 1935, **4**, No. 6. [676]
81. Bishop, G. H. Fiber groups in the optic nerve. *Amer. J. Physiol.,* 1933, **106**, 460-74. [187]
82. Bishop, G. H. The peripheral unit for pain. *J. Neurophysiol.,* 1944, **7**, 71-80. [11]
83. Bishop, G. H. Neural mechanisms of cutaneous sense. *Physiol. Rev.,* 1946, **26**, 77-102. [11]
84. Bishop, G. H., & O'Leary, J. L. Potential records from the optic cortex of the cat. *J. Neurophysiol.,* 1938, **1**, 391-401. [154, 188]

Bishop, G. H. (*See* No. 52)

Bitterman, M. E. (*See* No. 79)

85. Blackwell, H. R., & Schlosberg, H. Octave generalization, pitch discrimination, and loudness thresholds in the white rat. *J. exp. Psychol.,* 1943, **33**, 407-19. [361]
86. Bliss, A. F. The chemistry of daylight vision. *J. gen. Physiol.,* 1946, **29**, 277-97. [148]

Blix, M. [4, 5]

87. Block, H. Influence of muscular exertion upon mental performance. *Arch. Psychol., N. Y.,* 1936, No. 202. [652]
88. Blodgett, H. C. The effect of the introduction of reward upon the maze performance of rats. *Univ. Calif. Publ. Psychol.,* 1929, **4**, 113-34. [415]
89. Blodgett, H. C., & McCutchan, K. Place versus response learning in the simple T-maze. *J. exp. Psychol.,* 1947, **37**, 412-22. [459]
90. Blodgett, H. C., & McCutchan, K. Relative strength of place and response learning in the T maze. *J. comp. Physiol. Psychol.,* 1948, **41**, 17-24. [459-60]

Blum, J. S. (*See* No. 91)

91. Blum, R. A., & Blum, J. S. Factual issues in the 'continuity' controversy. *Psychol. Rev.,* 1949, **56**, 33-50. [448, 450]
92. Boder, D. P. The adjective-verb quotient; a contribution to the psychology of language, *Psychol. Rec.,* 1940, **3**, 309-44. [719]

93. Boguslavsky, G. W., & Guthrie, E. R. The recall of completed and interrupted activities: an investigation of Zeigarnik's experiment. *Psychol. Bull.*, 1941, **38**, 575-6. (Abstract.) [582-3]

Boll, F. [147]

94. Bonin, G. V., Garol, H. W., & McCulloch, W. S. The functional organization of the occipital lobe. In Klüver, H., *Visual mechanisms*. Lancaster, Pa.: Jacques Cattell, 1942. Pp. 165-92. [199, 260, 297]
95. Boreas, Th. Experimental studies on memory: II. The rate of forgetting. *Praktika de l'Acad. d'Athènes*, 1930, **5**, 382ff. [554-5]
96. Boring, E. G. The control of attitude in psychophysical experiments. *Psychol. Rev.*, 1920, **27**, 440-52. [49]
97. Boring, E. G. A new system for the classification of odors. *Amer. J. Psychol.*, 1928, **40**, 345-9. [28, 29]
98. Boring, E. G. *A history of experimental psychology*. New York: Appleton-Century, 1929. [77]
99. Boring, E. G. A new ambiguous figure. *Amer. J. Psychol.*, 1930, **42**, 444-5. [207]
100. Boring, E. G. *The physical dimensions of consciousness*. New York: Appleton-Century, 1933. [33, 39, 359, 713]
101. Boring, E. G. Intensity. In Boring, Langfeld, and Weld, *Psychology*. New York: Wiley and Sons, 1935. [72]
102. Boring, E. G. *Sensation and perception in the history of experimental psychology*. New York: Appleton-Century-Crofts, 1942. [6, 20, 21, 25, 29, 95, 201, 275]
103. Boring, E. G. The moon illusion. *Amer. J. Physics*, 1943, **11**, 55-60. [248]
104. Boring, E. G. Mind and mechanism. *Amer. J. Psychol.*, 1946, **59**, 173-92. [647]
105. Boring, E. G., & Stevens, S. S. The nature of tonal brightness. *Proc. nat. Acad. Sci., Wash.*, 1936, **22**, 514-21. [126]

Boring, E. G. (*See* No. 508)

106. Bourdon, B. *La perception visuelle de l'espace*. Paris: Librairie C. Reinwald, 1902. [268]
107. Bousfield, W. A. An empirical study of the production of affectively toned items. *J. gen. Psychol.*, 1944, **30**, 205-15. [723]
108. Bousfield, W. A., & Barclay, W. D. The relationship between order and frequency of occurrence of restricted associative responses. *J. exp. Psychol.*, 1950, **40**, 643-7. [723]
109. Bousfield, W. A., & Barry, H., Jr. Quantitative correlates of euphoria. *J. exp. Psychol.*, 1937, **21**, 218-22. [725]
110. Bousfield, W. A., & Sedgewick, C. H. W. An analysis of sequences of restricted associative responses. *J. gen. Psychol.*, 1944, **30**, 149-65. [723, 724]
111. Brainard, P. P. The mentality of a child compared with that of apes. *J. genet. Psychol.*, 1930, **37**, 268-93. [622]

Bray, C. W. (*See* No. 1225, 1226, 1227, 1228)

Bretnall, E. P. (*See* No. 1141)

Breuer, J. [32]

112. Brickner, R. M. *The intellectual functions of the frontal lobes*. New York: Macmillan, 1936. [660]

Brickwedde, F. G. (*See* No. 948)

113. Brogden, W. J. Unconditioned stimulus substitution in the conditioning process. *Amer. J. Psychol.*, 1939a, **52**, 46-55. [321-2, 405-6]
114. Brogden, W. J. Sensory pre-conditioning. *J. exp. Psychol.*, 1939b, **25**, 323-32. [460, 461, 462]
115. Brogden, W. J. Conditioned flexion responses in dogs re-established and maintained with change of locus in the application of the unconditioned stimulus. *J. exp. Psychol.*, 1940, **27**, 583-600. [463]
116. Brogden, W. J. Tests of sensory pre-conditioning with human subjects. *J. exp. Psychol.*, 1942, **31**, 505-17. [461]
117. Brogden, W. J. Sensory pre-conditioning of human subjects. *J. exp. Psychol.*, 1947, **37**, 527-40. [461]
118. Brogden, W. J., & Gantt, W. H. Cerebellar conditioned reflexes. *Amer. J. Physiol.*, 1937, **119**, 277-8. [490]
119. Brogden, W. J., Lipman, E. A., & Culler, E. The role of incentive in conditioning and extinction. *Amer. J. Psychol.*, 1938, **51**, 109-17. [429, 430, 463, 464]

Brogden, W. J. (*See* No. 182)

120. Bromley, R. B. The development of conditioned responses in cats after unilateral decortication. *J. comp. physiol. Psychol.*, 1948, 41, 155-64. [478]

Brown, C. W. (*See* No. 352)

Brown, F. D. (*See* No. 920)

121. Brown, H. C. The relation of flicker to stimulus area in peripheral vision. *Arch. Psychol., N. Y.*, 1945, No. 298. [162, 167]
122. Brown, J. F. Über die dymamischen Eigenschaften der Realitäts- und Irrealitätsschichten. Untersuchungen zur Handlungs- und Affektpsychologie XIV. *Psychol. Forsch.*, 1933, 18, 2-26. [582]
123. Brown, J. F., & Voth, A. C. The path of seen movement as a function of the vector-field. *Amer. J. Psychol.*, 1937, 49, 543-63. [200, 202-8, 225, 246-7]
124. Brown, J. S. The generalization of approach responses as a function of stimulus intensity and strength of motivation. *J. comp. Psychol.*, 1942, 33, 209-26. [377]
125. Brown, J. S., & Jacobs, A. The role of fear in the motivation and acquisition of responses. *J. exp. Psychol.*, 1949, 39, 747-59. [442]

Brown, R. H. (*See* No. 384, 1194)

126. Brown, W. *The judgment of difference.* (Univ. of Calif. Stud.) Berkeley: Univ. Press, 1910. [49, 64]
127. Brown, W. The judgment of very weak sensory stimuli with special reference to the absolute threshold of sensation for common salt. *Univ. Calif. Publ. in Psychol.*, 1914, 1, 199-268. [64]
128. Brown, W. To what extent is memory measured by a single recall? *J. exp. Psychol.*, 1923, 49, 191-6. [566]
129. Brown, W. Whole and part methods in learning. *J. educ. Psychol.*, 1924, 15, 229-33. [540]
130. Brown, W. Growth of 'memory images.' *Amer. J. Psychol.*, 1935, 47, 90-102. [589]

Brown, W. L. (*See* No. 349, 350)

131. Bruce, R. W. Conditions of transfer of training. *J. exp. Psychol.*, 1933, 16, 343-61. [526, 529-30, 537]
132. Brükner, A. Die Raumschwelle bei Simultanreizung. *Z. Psychol.*, 1901, 26, 36-60. [68]
133. Bruner, J. S., & Goodman, C. C. Value and need as organizing factors in perception. *J. abnorm. soc. Psychol.*, 1947, 42, 33-44. [289-92]
134. Bruner, J. S., & Postman, L. Symbolic value as an organizing factor in perception. *J. soc. Psychol.*, 1948, 27, 203-8. [292]

Bruner, J. S. (*See* No. 943, 944)

135. Brunswik, E. Zur Entwicklung der Albedowahrnehmung. *Z. Psychol.*, 1929, 109, 40-115. [274]
136. Brunswik, E. Die Zugänglichkeit von gegenständen für die wahrnehmung. *Arch. ges. Psychol.*, 1933, 88, 377-418. [284]
137. Brunswik, E. *Wahrnehmung und Gegenstandswelt.* (Perception and the world of objects.) Leipzig: Deuticke, 1934. [294-5]
138. Brunswik, E. Probability as a determiner of rat behavior. *J. exp. Psychol.*, 1939, 25, 175-97. [387]
139. Brunswik, E. Thing constancy as measured by correlation coefficients. *Psychol. Rev.*, 1940, 47, 69-78. [275, 276]

Brunswik, E. (*See* No. 1139)

140. Buel, J. A criticism of Hull's goal gradient hypothesis. *Psychol. Rev.*, 1938, 45, 395-413. [499]

Buel, J. (*See* No. 40, 41)

141. Bugelski, B. R. Interference with recall of original responses after learning new responses to old stimuli. *J. exp. Psychol.*, 1942, 30, 368-79. [526]
142. Bühler, K. Tatsachen und Probleme zu einer Psychologie der Denkvorgänge. *Arch. ges. Psychol.*, 1907, 9, 297-365. [646]

Bunch, L. L. (*See* No. 411)

143. Bunch, M. E. The amount of transfer in rational learning as a function of time. *J. comp. Psychol.*, 1936, 22, 325-37. [533, 534]
144. Bunch, M. E. Cumulative transfer of training under different temporal conditions. *J. comp. Psychol.*, 1944, 37, 265-72. [522]
145. Bunch, M. E. Retroactive inhibition or facilitation from interpolated learning as a function of time. *J. comp. Psychol.*, 1946, 39, 287-91. [536-7, 564]

146. Bunch, M. E., & Lang, E. S. The amount of transfer of training from partial learning after varying intervals of time. *J. comp. Psychol.,* 1939, **27**, 449-59. [534]
147. Bunch, M. E., & McCraven, V. G. The temporal course of transfer in the learning of memory material. *J. comp. Psychol.,* 1938, **25**, 481-96. [534]
148. Bunch, M. E., & Rogers, M. The relationship between transfer and the length of the interval separating the mastery of the two problems. *J. comp. Psychol.,* 1936, **21**, 37-52. [534]
149. Burian, H. M. Fusional movements. Role of peripheral retinal stimuli. *Arch. Ophthal., Chicago,* 1939, **21**, 486-91. [252]
150. Burkamp, W. Versuche über das farbenwiedererkennen der Fische. *Zeit. Psychol. Physiol. Sinnesorg,* 1923, **55**, 133-70. [279]
151. Burns, M., & Dallenbach, K. M. The adaptation of cutaneous pain. *Amer. J. Psychol.,* 1933, **45**, 111-17. [80]
152. Burzlaff, W. Methodologische Beiträge zum Problem der Farbenkonstanz. *Z. Psychol.,* 1931, **119**, 177-235. [277-80]
153. Busemann, A. *Die Sprache der Jugend als Ausdruck der Entwichlungsrhytmik.* Jena: Fisher, 1925. [719]
154. Buxton, C. E. Latent learning and the goal gradient hypothesis. *Contr. psychol. Theor.,* 1940, **2**, No. 2. [414]
155. Buxton, C. E. The status of research in reminiscence. *Psychol. Bull.,* 1943, **40**, 313-40. [509, 510, 512]
156. Buytendijk, F. J. J. On the negative variation of the nervus acusticus caused by a sound. *Akad. Wettensch. Amsterdam,* Proc. Sect. Sci., 1910, **13**, 649-52. [93]
157. Cain, L. I., & Willey, R. de. The effect of spaced learning in the curve of retention. *J. exp. Psychol.,* 1939, **25**, 209-14. [508]
158. Cameron, N. Reasoning, regression, and communication in schizophrenics. *Psychol. Monogr.,* 1938, **50**, No. 1. [677]
159. Cameron, N. A study of thinking in senile deterioration and schizophrenic disorganization. *Amer. J. Psychol.,* 1939, **51**, 650-64. [677]
160. Campbell, A. A. The interrelations of two measures of conditioning in man. *J. exp. Psychol.,* 1938, **22**, 225-43. [327]
161. Campbell, A. A., & Hilgard, E. R. Individual differences in ease of conditioning. *J. exp. Psychol.,* 1936, **19**, 561-71. [327]

Campbell, A. A. (*See* No. 496)

Campbell, C. J. (*See* No. 313)

162. Campbell, R. J., & Harlow, H. F. Problem solution by monkeys following bilateral removal of the prefrontal areas: V. Spatial delayed reactions. *J. exp. Psychol.,* 1945, **35**, 110-26. [664, 665]
163. Cannon, W. B., & Rosenblueth, A. *Autonomic neuro-effector systems.* New York: Macmillan, 1937. [201]

Carlson, A. J. (*See* No. 583, 766)

164. Carmichael, L., Hogan, H. P., & Walter, A. A. An experimental study of the effect of language on the reproduction of visually perceived form. *J. exp. Psychol.,* 1932, **15**, 73-86. [592-3]
165. Carpenter, C. R. A field study of the behavior and social relations of howling monkeys. *Comp. Psychol. Monogr.,* 1934, **10** (2). [682]
166. Carr, H. A. *Psychology, a study of mental activity.* New York: Longmans, Green, 1925. [381]
167. Carr, H. A. *An introduction to space perception.* New York: Longmans, Green, 1935. [249, 254, 268-9]
168. Carroll, J. B. Diversity of vocabulary and the harmonic series law of word-frequency distribution. *Psychol. Rec.,* 1938, **2**, 379-86. [719]
169. Carroll, J. B. The analysis of verbal behavior. *Psychol. Rev.,* 1944, **51**, 102-19. [719]

Carter, C. W. (*See* No. 323)

170. Carter, L. F., & Schooler, K. Value, need and other factors in perception. *Psychol. Rev.,* 1949, **56**, 200-207. [290-92]
171. Cartwright, D. Relation of decision-time to the categories of response. *Amer. J. Psychol.,* 1941, **54**, 174-96. [51]
172. Cartwright, D. The effect of interruption, completion, and failure upon the attractiveness of activities. *J. exp. Psychol.,* 1942, **31**, 1-16. [584]

Cason, E. B. (*See* No. 174)

173. Cason, H. The learning and retention of pleasant and unpleasant activities. *Arch. Psychol., N. Y.,* 1932, 21, No. 134. [572]
174. Cason, H., & Cason, E. B. Association tendencies and learning ability. *J. exp. Psychol.,* 1925, 8, 167-89. [722]

Cason, H. (*See* No. 1277)

175. Cate, J. ten. Akustische und optische Reaktionen der Katzen nach teilweisen und totalen Exterpationen des Neopalliums. *Arch. neerl. de Physiol.,* 1934, 19, 191-264. [478]
176. Chapanis, A. Spectral saturation and its relation to color-vision defects. *J. exp. Psychol.,* 1944, 34, 24-44. [142, 144, 182]
177. Chapanis, A. Night vision—a review of general principles. *Air Surg. Bull.,* 1945, 2, 279-84. [137, 160]
178. Chapanis, A. The dark adaptation of the color anomalous. *Amer. J. Physiol.,* 1946, 146, 689-701. [183]
179. Chapanis, A. The dark adaptation of the color anomalous measured with lights of different hues. *J. gen. Physiol.,* 1947, 30, 423-37. [183]
180. Chase, A. M. An accessory photosensitive substance in visual purple regeneration. *Science,* 1937, 85, 484. [148]

Chase, A. M. (*See* No. 464)

Chein, I. (*See* No. 737)

Chen, H. P. (*See* No. 575, 576)

181. Cheng, N. Y. Retroactive effect and degree of similarity. *J. exp. Psychol.,* 1929, 12, 444-9. [530]
182. Chernikoff, R., & Brogden, W. J. The effect of irstructions upon sensory preconditioning of human subjects. *J. exp. Psychol.,* 1949, 39, 200-207. [461]
183. Chotlos, J. W. Studies in language behavior: IV. A statistical and comparative analysis of individual written language samples. *Psychol. Monogr.,* 1944, 56, 75-111. [720-21]
184. Churcher, B. G. A loudness scale for industrial noise measurements. *J. acoust. Soc. Amer.,* 1935, 6, 216-26. [115, 118]

Clark, A. (*See* No. 1183)

185. Clark, H. M. Conscious attitudes. *Amer. J. Psychol.,* 1911, 22, 214-49. [647]
186. Clark, W. E. LeG. The visual centers of the brain and their connexions. *Physiol. Rev.,* 1942, 22, 205-32. [260]
187. Clark, W. E. LeG. Anatomical patterns as the essential basis of sensory discrimination. 49th Boyle Lecture, Oxford Univ. Jun. Sci. Club, 1947. [33, 36, 37, 189]

Coakley, J. D. (*See* No. 230)

189. Cofer, C. N., & Foley, J. P. Mediated generalization and the interpretation of verbal behavior: I. Prolegomena. *Psychol. Rev.,* 1942, 49, 513-40. [704-7]
190. Cofer, C. N., Janis, M. G., & Rowell, M. M. Mediated generalization and the interpretation of verbal behavior: III. Experimental study of antonym gradients. *J. exp. Psychol.,* 1943, 32, 266-9. [706]

Cofer, C. N. (*See* No. 310)

191. Cohen, J. Color adaptation of the human eye. *Amer. J. Psychol.,* 1946a, 59, 84-110. [181, 186, 188]
192. Cohen, J. Color adaptation to 1945. *Psychol. Bull.,* 1946b, 43, 121-40. [181]
193. Cohen, J. Apparatus for colorimetry: I. Multichromatic colorimeters. *Trans. Illum. Eng. Soc.,* 1953, in press. [142]

Cohen, J. [188, 235]

194. Cole, L. E., Woodbury, C. B., & Philleo, C. The effect of order and rate of presentation of stimuli upon the establishment of a conditioned discrimination. *J. gen. Psychol.,* 1942, 26, 35-49. [507]
195. Committee on Colorimetry. The psychophysics of color. *J. opt. Soc. Amer.,* 1944, 34, 245-66. [137, 140]

Compton, B. (*See* No. 1208)

196. Comstock, C. On the relevancy of imagery to the processes of thought. *Amer. J. Psychol.,* 1921, 32, 196-230. [647]

Cook, C. (*See* No. 385)

197. Cook, T. W. Binocular and monocular relations in foveal dark adaptation. *Psychol. Monogr.,* 1934, 45 (3). [158]

198. Cook, T. W. Factors in whole and part learning a visually perceived maze. *J. genet. Psychol.*, 1936, **49**, 3-31. [540]
199. Cook, T. W. Whole versus part learning the spider maze. *J. exp. Psychol.*, 1937, **20**, 477-94. [540]

Coppée, G. (*See* No. 647, 648)

Coppock, H. W. [468]

200. Courts, F. A. Relations between experimentally produced muscular tension and memorization. *J. exp. Psychol.*, 1939, **25**, 235-56. [652]
201. Cowles, J. T. Food-tokens as incentives for learning by chimpanzees. *Comp. Psychol. Monogr.*, 1937, **14**, 1-96. [428-9, 432]
202. Crafts, L. W. Whole and part methods with non-serial reactions. *Amer. J. Psychol.*, 1929, **41**, 543-63. [540]
203. Craik, K. J. W. Physiology of colour vision. *Nature, Lond.*, 1943, **151**, 727. [184]
204. Craik, K. J. W., & Vernon, M. D. The nature of dark adaptation. *Brit. J. Psychol.*, 1941, **32**, 62-81. [80, 82]
205. Craik, K. J. W., & Zangwill, O. L. Observations relating to the threshold of a small figure within the contour of a closed-line figure. *Brit. J. Psychol.*, 1939, **30**, 139-50. [220]
206. Cramer, T. Über die Beziehung des Zwischenmediums zu den Transformations- und Kontrasterscheinungen. *Zeit. Psychol.*, 1923, **54**, 215-42. [275]
207. Crawford, H. P., & Spence, K. W. Observational learning of discrimination problems by chimpanzees. *J. comp. Psychol.*, 1939, **27**, 133-47. [660]
208. Creed, R. S., Denny-Brown, D., Sherrington, C. S., Eccles, J. C., & Liddell, E. G. T. *Reflex activity of the spinal cord.* Oxford: Clarendon Press, 1932. [168]
209. Creed, R. S., & Granit, R. On the latency of negative after-images following stimulation of different areas of the retina. *J. Physiol.*, 1928, **66**, 281-98. [230]
210. Creed, R. S., & Granit, R. Observations on the retinal action potential with especial reference to the response to intermittent stimulation. *J. Physiol.*, 1933, **78**, 419-42. [146]
211. Crespi, L. P. Quantitative variation of incentive and performance in the white rat. *Amer. J. Psychol.*, 1942, **55**, 467-517. [333]
212. Crisler, G. Salivation is unnecessary for the establishment of the salivary conditioned reflex induced by morphine. *Amer. J. Physiol.*, 1930, **94**, 553-6. [492]

Crisler, G. (*See* No. 660)

213. Crocker, F. C., & Henderson, L. F. Analysis and classification of odors. *Amer. Perfum.*, 1927, **22**, 325-7. [28]

Crook, M. N. (*See* No. 629)

214. Crosland, H. R. A qualitative analysis of the process of forgetting. *Psychol. Monogr.*, 1921, **29**, No. 130. [647]
215. Crowe, S. J., Guild, S. R., & Polvogt, L. M. Observations on the pathology of high-tone deafness. *Johns Hopk. Hosp. Bull.*, 1934, **54**, 315-79. [114, 121]

Crowe, S. J. (*See* No. 411)

Crowley, M. E. (*See* No. 335)

216. Crozier, W. J. Chemoreception. In C. Murchison (ed.), *Handbook of general experimental psychology.* Worcester: Clark Univ. Press, 1934. Pp. 987-1036. [22, 24, 80]
217. Crozier, W. J. The theory of the visual threshold: I. Time and intensity. *Proc. nat. Acad. Sci.*, 1940a, **26**, 54-60. [69]
218. Crozier, W. J. The theory of the visual threshold: II. On the kinetics of adaptation. *Proc. nat. Acad. Sci.*, 1940b., **26**, 334-9. [69]
219. Crozier, W. J. On the law for minimal discrimination of intensities: IV. ΔI as a function of intensity. *Proc. nat. Acad. Sci.*, 1940c, **26**, 382-9. [69-72]

Crozier, W. J. [74-6, 80, 121, 122]

220. Crozier, W. J., & Wolf, E. On the duplexity theory of visual response in vertebrates: II. *Proc. nat. Acad. Sci., Wash.*, 1938, **24**, 538-41. [137]
221. Crozier, W. J., & Wolf, E. Theory and measurement of visual mechanisms. *J. gen. Physiol.*, 1941, **24**, 635-54. [163]

Crozier, W. J. (*See* No. 509, 510)

222. Crutchfield, R. S. Psychological distance as a function of psychological need. *J. comp. Psychol.*, 1939, **28**, 447-69. [663]

223. Cruze, W. W. Maturation and learning in chicks. *J. comp. Psychol.*, 1935, 19, 371-409. [226]
224. Culler, E. A. Thermal discrimination and Weber's Law. *Arch. Psychol.*, 1926a, 13, No. 81. [78, 80]
225. Culler, E. A. Studies in psychometric theory. *Psychol. Monogr.*, 1926b, 35, No. 163, 56-137. [49]
226. Culler, E. A. Nature of the learning curve. *Psychol. Bull.*, 1928, 25, 143-4. [331]
227. Culler, E. A. An experimental study of tonal localization in the cochlea of the guinea pig. *Ann. Otol., etc., St. Louis*, 1935, 44, 807-13. [101]
228. Culler, E. A. Recent advances in some concepts of conditioning. *Psychol. Rev.*, 1938a, 45, 134-53. [318, 381]
229. Culler, E. A. Observations on direct cortical stimulation in the dog. *Psychol. Bull.*, 1938b, 35, 687-8. [492]
230. Culler, E. A., Coakley, J. D., Lowy, K., & Gross, N. A revised frequency-map of the guinea-pig cochlea. *Amer. J. Psychol.*, 1943, 56, 475-500. [102, 121]
231. Culler, E. A., & Mettler, F. A. Conditioned behavior in a decorticate dog. *J. comp. Psychol.*, 1934, 18, 291-303. [478, 481]

Culler, E. A. (*See* No. 4, 119, 299, 300, 367, 368, 1037, 1038)

232. Curtis, H. J. Intercortical connections of corpus callosum as indicated by evoked potentials. *J. Neurophysiol.*, 1940, 3, 407-13. [260]
233. Dallenbach, K. M. Synaesthesis: 'Pressury' cold. *Amer. J. Psychol.*, 1926, 37, 571-7. [642]
234. Dallenbach, K. M. The temperature spots and end-organs. *Amer. J. Psychol.*, 1927, 39, 402-27. [5]

Dallenbach, K. M. (*See* No. 1, 35, 151, 589, 687, 695, 735, 857, 1093, 1094)

235. Dandy, W. E. Effects on hearing after sub-total section of the cochlear branch of the auditory nerve. *Johns Hopk. Hosp. Bull.*, 1934, 55, 240-43. [106]
236. Daniel, W. J. Conditioning a systematic searching response. *J. comp. Psychol.*, 1944, 37, 251-63. [323]
237. Darrow, C. W., & Heath, L. L. Reaction tendencies relating to personality. In C. P. Stone, C. W. Darrow, C. Landis, and L. L. Heath, *Studies in the dynamics of behavior*. Chicago: Univ. of Chicago Press, 1932. [700]

Darwin, C. [299, 432]

Darwin, E. [32]

238. Dashiell, J. F. Direction orientation in maze running by the white rat. *Comp. Psychol. Monogr.*, 1930, 7, No. 2 [389, 488, 489]
239. Dashiell, J. F. Part V of symposium on the law of effect. *Psychol. Rev.*, 1938, 45, 212-14. [425]

da Vinci, Leonardo [248, 254]

240. Davis, H. The electrical phenomena of the cochlea and the auditory nerve. *J. acoust. Soc. Amer.*, 1935, 6, 205-15. [110]
241. Davis, H., Derbyshire, A. J., Kemp, E. H., Lurie, M. H., & Upton, M. Functional and histological changes in the cochlea of the guinea pig resulting from prolonged stimulation. *J. gen. Psychol.*, 1935, 12, 251-78. [100]
242. Davis, H., Derbyshire, A. J., Lurie, M. H., & Saul, L. J. The electric response of the cochlea. *Amer. J. Physiol.*, 1934, 107, 311-32. [93]
243. Davis, H., Morgan, C. T., Galambos, R., & Smith, F. W. Temporary deafness following exposure to loud tones and noise. *Laryngoscope*, 1946, 56, 19-21. [113]
244. Davis, H., & Saul, L. J. Action currents in the auditory tracts of the mid-brain of the cat. *Science*, 1931, 74, 205-6. [93]
245. Davis, H., Silverman, S. R., & McAuliffe, D. R. Some observations on pitch and frequency. *J. acoust. Soc. Amer.*, 1951, 23, 40-41. [99]

Davis, H. (*See* No. 249, 336, 337, 898, 1085, 1086, 1087)

Davis, R. C. (*See* No. 645)

Davis, W. A. (*See* No. 396)

246. DeCillis, O. E. Absolute thresholds for the perception of tactual movements. *Arch. Psychol., N. Y.*, 1944, No. 294. [62]
247. Deese, J., & Kellogg, W. N. Some new data on the nature of 'spinal conditioning.' *J. comp. physiol. Psychol.*, 1949, 42, 157-60. [480, 481]

Deese, J. (*See* No. 644)

248. Denny, M. R. The role of secondary reinforcement in a partial reinforcement learning situation. *J. exp. Psychol.*, 1946, **36**, 373-89. [427]

Denny-Brown, D. (*See* No. 208)

249. Derbyshire, A. J., & Davis, H. The action potentials of the auditory nerve. *Amer. J. Physiol.*, 1935, **113**, 476-504. [93, 103, 104]

Derbyshire, A. J. (*See* No. 241, 242)

Descartes, R. [31, 34, 248, 266]

250. De Silva, H. R. An analysis of the visual perception of movement. *Brit. J. Psychol.*, 1929, **19**, 268-305. [244]
251. De Silva, H. R. The perception of movement. In Boring, Langfeld, and Weld, *Psychology*. New York: Wiley and Sons, 1935. [244]
252. Dewey, G. Relative frequency of English speech sounds. *Harvard Stud. Educ.*, 1923, **4**. [719]

Dewey, J. [324]

253. Dieter, W. Über die subjektiven Farbenempfindungen bei angeborenen Störungen des Farbensinnes. *Z. Sinnesphysiol.*, 1927, **58**, 73. [176]

Dieterici, C. (*See* No. 684)

254. Dimmick, F. L. The investigation of the olfactory qualities. *Psychol. Rev.*, 1927, **34**, 321-35. [28]
255. Dixon, E. T. On the relation of accommodation and convergence to our sense of depth. *Mind,* 1895, **4**, 195-212. [267]
256. Dollard, J., & Miller, N. E. *Personality and psychotherapy.* New York: McGraw-Hill, 1950. [599]

Dollard, J. (*See* No. 855)

Donaldson, H. H. [4, 5]

257. Dorcus, R. M. Habitual word associations to colors as a possible factor in advertising. *J. appl. Psychol.*, 1932, **16**, 277-87. [711]
258. Doughty, J. M., & Garner, W. R. Pitch characteristics of short tones: I. Two kinds of pitch threshold. *J. exp. Psychol.*, 1947, **37**, 351-65. [123]
259. Dove, C. C., & Thompson, M. E. Some studies on 'insight' in white rats. *J. genet. Psychol.*, 1943, **63**, 235-45. [618-20]
260. Dove, H. A. Die Combination der Eindrücke beider Ohren und beider Augen zu einem Eindruck. *Ber. preuss. Akad. Wiss.*, 1841, 251ff. [270]
261. Dreis, T. A. Two studies in retroaction: I. Influence of partial identity. II. Susceptibility to retroaction at various grade levels. *J. gen. Psychol.*, 1933, **8**, 157-71. [531]
262. Duncker, K. On problem-solving. (Translated by L. S. Lees from the 1935 original.) *Psychol. Monogr.*, 1945, **58**, No. 270. [622, 626-7, 633-4, 637]
263. Duncker, K., & Krechevsky, I. On solution-achievement. *Psychol. Rev.*, 1939, **46**, 176-85. [307]
264. Durkin, H. E. Trial-and-error, gradual analysis, and sudden reorganization: An experimental study of problem solving. *Arch. Psychol., N. Y.,* 1937, **30**, No. 210. [610]
265. Dusser de Barenne, J. G. The labyrinthine and postural mechanism. In C. Murchison (ed.), *Handbook of general experimental psychology*. Worcester: Clark Univ. Press, 1934. Pp. 204-46. [32]
266. Ebbinghaus, H. Über das Gedächtnis: Untersuchungen zur experimentellen Psychologie. Leipzig: Duncker and Humblot, 1885. (Translated as *Memory: A contribution to experimental psychology,* by H. A. Ruger & C. E. Bussenius. Columbia Univ. Coll. Educ. Reprints, No. 3. New York: Teachers College, Columbia Univ., 1913.) [554-6, 669]
267. Ebbinghaus, H. *Grundzüge der Psychologie*. Leipzig: 1902. [130]

Eccles, J. C. (*See* No. 208)

Eckerson, A. B. (*See* No. 904)

268. Edwards, A. L. Political frames of reference as a factor influencing recognition. *J. abnorm. soc. Psychol.*, 1941, **36**, 34-50. [580]
269. Edwards, A. L., & English, H. B. Reminiscence in relation to differential difficulty. *J. exp. Psychol.*, 1939, **25**, 100-108. [565]

Egan, J. P. (*See* No. 1088)

270. Ehrenfreund, D. An experimental test of the continuity theory of discrimination with pattern vision. *J. comp. Psychol.*, 1948, **41**, 408-22. [447]

271. Ehrenstein, W. Untersuchungen über Figur-Grund Fragen. *Z. Psychol.*, 1930, 117, 339-412. [218, 225]

Einstein, A. [147, 622]

272. Elder, J. H., & Nissen, H. W. Delayed alternation in raccoons. *J. comp. Psychol.*, 1933, 16, 117-35. [657]

273. Ellis, W. D. *A source book of gestalt psychology.* New York: Harcourt, Brace, 1939. [445]

274. Ellson, D. G. Quantitative studies of the interaction of simple habits: I. Recovery from specific and generalized effects of extinction. *J. exp. Psychol.*, 1938, 23, 339-58. [337, 345]

275. Ellson, D. G. Spontaneous recovery of the galvanic skin response as a function of the recovery interval. *J. exp. Psychol.*, 1939, 25, 586-600. [345, 406]

276. Ellson, D. G. Hallucinations produced by sensory conditioning. *J. exp. Psychol.*, 1941, 28, 1-20. [461]

277. Ellson, D. G. Critical conditions influencing sensory conditioning. *J. exp. Psychol.*, 1942, 31, 333-8. [461]

278. Elsberg, C. A. The sense of smell: VIII. Olfactory fatigue. IX. A. Monorhinal, birhinal and bisynchronorhinal smell. B. Some facts regarding the psychophysiology of the olfactory sense. *Bull. neurol. Inst., N. Y.,* 1935, 4, 479-99. [26]

279. Elsberg, C. A., & Levy, I. A new and simple method of quantitative olfactometry. *Bull. neurol. Inst., N. Y.,* 1935, 4, 5-19. [25]

280. Elsberg, C. A., & Spotnitz, H. The sense of vision: II. The reciprocal relation of area and light intensity and its significance for the localization of tumors of the brain by functional visual tests. *Bull. neurol. Inst., N. Y.,* 1937, 6, 243-52. [156]

281. Elsberg, C. A., & Spotnitz, H. A theory of retinocerebral function with formulae for threshold vision and light and dark adaptation at the fovea. *Amer. J. Physiol.,* 1938, 121, 454-64. [156]

Emery, D. A. (*See* No. 680)

English, H. B. (*See* No. 269)

282. Epstein, M. A., & Morgan, C. T. Cortical localization of symbolic processes in the rat: III. Impairment of anticipatory functions in prefrontal lobectomy in rats. *J. exp. Psychol.,* 1943, 32, 453-63. [500]

283. Erlanger, J., & Gasser, H. S. *Electrical signs of nervous activity.* Philadelphia: Univ. of Pennsylvania Press, 1937. [10, 12]

284. Esper, E. A. Language. In Murchison (ed.), *A handbook of social psychology.* Worcester: Clark Univ. Press, 1935. Pp. 417-60. [684]

285. Estes, W. K. Discriminative conditioning: I. A discriminative property of conditioned anticipation. *J. exp. Psychol.,* 1943, 32, 150-55. [441-2]

286. Estes, W. K. Discriminative conditioning: II. Effects of a Pavlovian conditioned stimulus upon a subsequently conditioned operant response. *J. exp. Psychol.,* 1948, 38, 173-7. [441-2]

287. Estes, W. K. A study of motivating conditions necessary for secondary reinforcement. *J. exp. Psychol.,* 1949a, 39, 306-10. [434-5]

288. Estes, W. K. Generalization of secondary reinforcement from the primary drive. *J. comp. physiol. Psychol.,* 1949b, 42, 286-95. [434-5]

Estes, W. K. [363]

Euclid [248]

Fadeyeva, V. K. (*See* No. 1151)

289. Fairbanks, H. Studies in language behavior: II. The quantitative differentiation of samples of spoken language. *Psychol. Monogr.,* 1944, 56, No. 2. 19-38. [719, 720]

290. Fechner, G. T. *Elemente der Psychophysik.* Leipzig: Breitkopf und Hartel, 1860. [43]

Fechner, G. T. [42, 76-7]

Feinberg, M. (*See* No. 644)

Felsinger, J. M. (*See* No. 549)

291. Fernberger, S. W. The effects of practice in its initial stages in lifted weight experiments and its bearing upon anthropometric measurements. *Amer. J. Psychol.,* 1916, 27, 261-72. [522]

292. Fernberger, S. W. Instructions and the psychophysical limen. *Amer. J. Psychol.,* 1931, 43, 361-76. [48, 58]

293. Fick, A. Die Lehre von der Lichtempfindung. In L. Herman, *Handbuch der Physiologie.* Leipzig, 1879. iii, Part I. [175]

294. Fields, P. E. Studies in concept formation: I. The development of the concept of trangularity by the white rat. *Comp. Psychol., Monogr.*, 1932, **9**, No. 2. [667]

295. Finan, J. L. Quantitative studies in motivation: I. Strength of conditioning in rats under varying degrees of hunger. *J. comp. Psychol.*, 1940, **29**, 119-34. [335]

296. Finan, J. L. Delayed response with pre-delay re-enforcement in monkeys after the removal of the frontal lobes. *Amer. J. Psychol.*, 1942, **55**, 202-14. [664, 665]

297. Finch, G. Salivary conditioning in atropinized dogs. *Amer. J. Physiol.*, 1938*a*, **124**, 136-41. [463, 492]

298. Finch, G. Hunger as a determinant of conditional and unconditional salivary response magnitude. *Amer. J. Physiol.*, 1938*b*, **123**, 379-82. [463]

299. Finch, G., & Culler, E. Effects of protracted exposure to a loud tone. *Science*, 1934*a*, **80**, 41-2. [100]

300. Finch, G., & Culler, E. Higher order conditioning with constant motivation. *Amer. J. Psychol.*, 1934*b*, **46**, 596-602. [316]

Finch, G. (*See* No. 368)

301. Findley, A. E. Further studies of Henning's system of olfactory qualities. *Amer. J. Psychol.*, 1924, **35**, 436-45. [28]

302. Finger, F. W. The effect of varying conditions of reinforcement upon a simple running response. *J. exp. Psychol.*, 1942*a*, **30**, 53-68. [425, 427]

303. Finger, F. W. Retention and subsequent extinction of a simple running response following varying conditions of reinforcement. *J. exp. Psychol.*, 1942*b*, **31**, 120-33. [425, 427]

304. Finkenbinder, E. O. The curve of forgetting. *Amer. J. Psychol.*, 1913, **24**, 8-32. [554]

305. Finley, C. B. Equivalent losses in accuracy of response after central and after peripheral sense deprivation. *J. comp. Neurol.*, 1941, **74**, 203-37. [489]

306. Fisichelli, V. R. Reversible perspective in Lissajous figures; some theoretical considerations. *Amer. J. Psychol.*, 1947, **60**, 240-49. [221]

Fisichelli, V. R. (*See* No. 931)

Fitch, F. B. (*See* No. 550)

307. Fletcher, H. *Speech and hearing*. New York: Van Nostrand, 1929. [118]

308. Fletcher, H., & Munson, W. A. Loudness, its definition, measurement, and calculation. *J. acoust. Soc. Amer.*, 1933, **5**, 82-108. [115, 118]

Flourens, P. [32]

309. Flynn, B. M. Pitch discrimination: the form of the psychometric function and simple reaction time to liminal differences. *Arch. Psychol., N. Y.*, 1943, No. 280. [61, 62]

310. Foley, J. P., & Cofer, C. N. Mediated generalization and the interpretation of verbal behavior: II. Experimental study of certain homophone and synonym gradients. *J. exp. Psychol.*, 1943, **32**, 169-75. [705-6]

311. Foley, J. P., & MacMillan, Z. L. Mediated generalization and the interpretation of verbal behavior: V. Free association as related to differences in professional training. *J. exp. Psychol.*, 1943, **33**, 299-310. [725]

312. Foley, J. P., and Mathews, M. Mediated generalization and the interpretation of verbal behavior: IV. Experimental study of the development of inter-linguistic synonym gradients. *J. exp. Psychol.*, 1943, **33**, 188-200. [706]

Foley, J. P. (*See* No. 189)

Foord, E. N. (*See* No. 457)

313. Forbes, A., Campbell, C. J., & Williams, H. B. Electrical records of afferent nerve impulses from muscular receptors. *Amer. J. Physiol.*, 1924, **69**, 282-303. [66]

314. Forbes, A., & Gregg, A. Electrical studies in mammalian reflexes: the correlation between strength of stimuli and direct and reflex nerve response. *Amer. J. Physiol.*, 1915, **39**, 172-235. [66]

315. Forbes, A., Miller, R. H., & O'Connor, J. Electric responses to acoustic stimuli in the decerebrate animal. *Amer. J. Physiol.*, 1927, **80**, 363-80. [93]

Forbes, T. W. (*See* No. 316)

Force, R. C. (*See* No. 75)

Foster, H. (*See* No. 334, 335)

316. Fowler, E. P., Jr., & Forbes, T. W. Depression of the cochlear response in order of frequency. *Amer. J. Physiol.*, 1936, **116**, 51-2. [101]

Frank, M. (*See* No. 718)

Franklin, M. (*See* No. 742)

317. Freeman, F. N., & Abernethy, E. M. Comparative retention of typewriting and of substitution with analogous material. *J. educ. Psychol.*, 1930, **21**, 639-47. [561]
318. Freeman, G. L. Changes in tonus during completed and interrupted mental work. *J. gen. Psychol.*, 1930, **4**, 309-33. [582, 583]
319. Freeman, G. L. Mental activity and the muscular processes. *Psychol. Rev.*, 1931, **38**, 428-47. [651-3]
320. Freeman, G. L. The facilitative and inhibitory effects of muscular tension upon performance. *Amer. J. Psychol.*, 1933, **45**, 17-52. [651-3]
321. Freeman, G. L. The optimal locus of 'anticipatory tensions' in muscular work. *J. exp. Psychol.*, 1937, **21**, 554-64. [651]
322. French, J. W. The effect of temperature on the retention of a maze habit in fish. *J. exp. Psychol.*, 1942, **31**, 79-87. [595-6]
323. French, N. R., Carter, C. W., & Koenig, W. The words and sounds of telephone conversations. *Bell Syst. tech. J.*, 1930, **9**, 290-324. [719-20]
324. Freud, S. *Psychopathology of everyday life.* New York: Macmillan, 1914. [570]

Freud, S. [554, 570-77, 599, 647, 708]

325. Frey, M. von. Untersuchungen über die Sinnesfunctionen der menschlichen Haut: Druckempfindung und Schmerz. *Abhandl. sächs. Gesell. Wiss.*, math-phys. Cl., 1896, **23**, 175-266. [4]
326. Frey, M. von. *Vorlesungen über physiologie.* Berlin: 1904. [18]

Frey, M. von. [7, 12, 14]

327. Frey, M. von, & Goldman, E. Der zeitliche Verlauf der Einstellung bei den Druckempfindungen. *Zeit. Biol.*, 1915, **65**, 163-82. [79]
328. Fritsch, G., & Hitzig, G. Über die elektrische Erregbarkeit des Grosshirns. *Arch. Anat. Physiol.*, 1870, 300-332. [488]
329. Frölich, F. W. Untersuchungen über periodische Nachbilder. *Z. f. Sinnesphysiol.*, 1921, **52**, 60-88. [185]
330. Frölich, F. W. Über der Hell- und Dunkeladaptation auf den Verlauf der periodischen Nachbilder. *Z. f. Sinnesphysiol.*, 1922, **53**, 88-104. [185]

Frolov, Dr. [430, 432]

331. Fry, G. A. Photoreceptor mechanism for the modulation theory of color vision. *J. opt. Soc. Amer.*, 1945, **35**, 114-35. [169]
332. Fry, G. A., & Bartley, S. H. The effect of one border in the visual field upon the threshold of another. *Amer. J. Physiol.*, 1935, **112**, 414-21. [230, 232, 245]
333. Fulton, J. F. *Physiology of the nervous system.* New York: Oxford Univ. Press, 1949. [168, 233, 296]

Fulton, J. F. (*See* No. 996)

334. Gagné, R. M., & Foster, H. Transfer of training from practice on components in a motor skill. *J. exp. Psychol.*, 1949, **39**, 47-68. [537-9, 540]
335. Gagné, R. M., Foster, H., & Crowley, M. E. The measurement of transfer of training. *Psychol. Bull.*, 1948, **45**, 97-130. [521]
336. Galambos, R., & Davis, H. The response of single auditory-nerve fibers to acoustic stimulation. *J. Neurophysiol.*, 1943, **6**, 39-58. [103, 118, 127]
337. Galambos, R., & Davis, H. Inhibition of activity in single auditory nerve fibers by acoustic stimulation. *J. Neurophysiol.*, 1944, **7**, 286-303. [103, 118, 127]

Galambos, R. (*See* No. 243)

Galen [248]

Galloway, A. (*See* No. 1187)

Galt, W. (*See* No. 1191)

338. Galton, F. *Inquiries into human faculty and its development.* London: 1883. [641-2, 646]
339. Gantt, W. H. The nervous secretion of saliva: The relation of the conditioned reflex to the intensity of the unconditioned stimulus. *Proc. Amer. Physiol. Soc., Amer. J. Physiol.*, 1938, **123**, 74. [332]

Gantt, W. H. (*See* No. 118, 750, 762)

340. Garner, W. R. Auditory thresholds of short tones as a function of repetition rates. *J. acoust. Soc. Amer.*, 1947, 19, 600-608. [123]
341. Garner, W. R., & Miller, G. A. Differential sensitivity to intensity as a function of the duration of the comparison tone. *J. exp. Psychol.*, 1944, 34, 450-63. [123]
342. Garner, W. R., & Miller, G. A. The masked threshold of pure tones as a function of duration. *J. exp. Psychol.*, 1947, 37, 293-303. [123]

Garner, W. R. (*See* No. 258, 851)

Garol, H. W. (*See* No. 94)

343. Garret, H. E. Variability in learning under massed and spaced practice. *J. exp. Psychol.*, 1940, 26, 547-67. [509]
344. Gasser, H. S. Conduction in nerves in relation to fiber types. *Res. Publ. Ass. nerv. ment. Dis.*, 1935, 15, 35-59. [10]

Gasser, H. S. (*See* No. 283)

Gasser, W. P. (*See* No. 653)

345. Gelb, A. Die 'Farbenkonstanz' der Sehdinge. *Handbuch norm. und pathol. Physiologie,* her. von Bethe, W. A., 1929, 12, 1, 594-678. [274, 283]
346. Gelb, A., & Granit, R. Die Bedeutung von 'Figur' und 'Grund' für die Farbenschwelle. *Z. Psychol.*, 1923, 93, 83-118. [219]

Gelb, A. (*See* No. 374, 375)

347. Gellerman, L. W. The double alternation problem. *J. genet. Psychol.*, 1931, 39, 50-72, 197-226, 359-92. [658]
348. Gengerelli, J. A. Apparent movement in relation to homonymous and heteronymous stimulation of the cerebral hemispheres. *J. exp. Psychol.*, 1948, 38, 592-9. [247, 259]
349. Gentry, G., Brown, W. L., & Kaplan, S. J. An experimental analysis of the spatial location hypothesis in learning. *J. comp. physiol. Psychol.*, 1947, 40, 309-22. [456]
350. Gentry, G., Brown, W. L., & Lee, H. Spatial location in the learning of a multiple T maze. *J. comp. physiol. Psychol.*, 1948, 41, 312-18. [456]

German, W. J. (*See* No. 996)

351. Ghiselli, E. E. Mass action and equipotentiality of the cerebral cortex in brightness discrimination. *J. comp. Psychol.*, 1938, 25, 273-90. [483, 484]
352. Ghiselli, E. E., & Brown, C. W. Subcortical mechanisms in learning: III. Brightness discrimination. *J. comp. Psychol.*, 1938, 26, 93-107. [482]
353. Gibson, E. J. Sensory generalization with voluntary reactions. *J. exp. Psychol.*, 1939, 24, 237-53. [525]
354. Gibson, E. J. A systematic application of the concepts of generalization and differentiation to verbal learning. *Psychol. Rev.*, 1940, 47, 196-229. [531, 538, 543, 568]
355. Gibson, E. J. Retroactive inhibition as a function of degree of generalization between tasks. *J. exp. Psychol.*, 1941, 28, 93-115. [526, 528-9, 532, 533]
356. Gibson, E. J. Intra-list generalization as a factor in verbal learning. *J. exp. Psychol.*, 1942, 30, 185-200. [537]
357. Gibson, J. J. The reproduction of visually perceived forms. *J. exp. Psychol.*, 1929, 12, 1-39. [589-90]
358. Gibson, J. J. Adaptation, after-effect, and contrast in the perception of curved lines. *J. exp. Psychol.*, 1933, 16, 1-31. [236]
359. Gibson, J. J. Adaptation, after-effect, and contrast in the perception of tilted lines: II. Simultaneous contrast and the areal restriction of the after-effect. *J. exp. Psychol.*, 1937, 20, 553-69. [236]
360. Gibson, J. J. The perception of visual surfaces. *Amer. J. Psychol.*, 1950, 63, 367-84. [262]
361. Gibson, J. J., & Mowrer, O. H. Determinants of the perceived vertical and horizontal. *Psychol. Rev.*, 1938, 45, 300-323. [236]
362. Gibson, J. J., & Radner, M. Adaptation, after-effect, and contrast in the perception of tilted lines: I. Quantitative studies. *J. exp. Psychol.*, 1937, 20, 453-67. [236]

Gibson, W. A. [188]

363. Gilmer, B. v. H. The glomus body as a receptor of cutaneous pressure and vibration. *Psychol. Bull.*, 1942, 39, 73-93. [12]
364. Girden, E. Cerebral mechanisms in conditioning under curare. *Amer. J. Psychol.*, 1940, 53, 397-406. [479]

365. Girden, E. Role of the response mechanism in learning and in excited emotion. *Amer. J. Psychol.*, 1943, 56, 1-20. [492]
366. Girden, E. Conditioned responses in curarized monkeys. *Amer. J. Psychol.*, 1947, 60, 571-87. [479]
367. Girden, E., & Culler, E. Conditioned responses in curarized striate muscle in dogs. *J. comp. Psychol.*, 1937, 23, 261-74. [479]
368. Girden, E., Mettler, F. A., Finch, G., & Culler, E. Conditioned responses in a decorticate dog to acoustic, thermal, and tactile stimulation. *J. comp. Psychol.*, 1936, 21, 367-85. [478, 481]
369. Gladstone, A. E. Reactively homogeneous compound trial-and-error learning with distributed trials and serial reinforcement. *J. exp. Psychol.*, 1948, 38, 289-97. [500]

Gladstone, A. I. (*See* No. 549)

370. Glanville, H. D. The psychological significance of the horopter. *Amer. J. Psychol.*, 1933, 45, 592-627. [256]

Glaser, N. M. (*See* No. 787)

371. Glaze, J. A. The association value of nonsense syllables. *J. genet. Psychol.*, 1928, 35, 255-67. [712]

Gleitman, H. (*See* No. 1140)

Gliddon, G. H. (*See* No. 23)

Goldman, E. (*See* No. 327)

372. Goldmeier, E. Progressive changes in memory traces. *Amer. J. Psychol.*, 1941, 54, 490-503. [590]
373. Goldscheider, A. Neue Thatsachen über die Hautsinnesnerven. *Arch. Physiol.*, Leipzig, 1885, Suppl. Bd., 1-110 (Ges. Abhardl., I, 107-218). [4, 5]

Goldscheider, A. [13, 14]

374. Goldstein, K., & Gelb, A. Zur Psychologie des optischen Wahrnehmungs und Erkennungs-vor-ganges. *Z. ges. Neurol. und Psychiatrie*, 1918, 41, 1. [674]
375. Goldstein, K., & Gelb, A. Über Farbenanmesie. *Psychol. Forsch.*, 1924, 6, 127-99. [674]
376. Goldstein, K., & Scheerer, M. Abstract and concrete behavior; an experimental study with special tests. *Psychol. Monogr.*, 1941, 53, No. 2. [667, 674-5, 677, 678]

Goodman, C. C. (*See* No. 133)

377. Gordon, D. A. The relation between the thresholds of form, motion and displacement in parafoveal and peripheral vision at a scotopic level of illumination. *Amer. J. Psychol.*, 1947, 60, 202-25. [137, 160]
378. Göthlin, G. F. Inhibitory processes underlying color vision and their bearing on three-component theories. *Amer. J. Psychol.*, 1943, 56, 537-50. [186-8]
379. Göthlin, G. F. Excitatory and inhibitory processes in the synthesis of the sensations of color and of white. *J. Physiol.*, 1944, 103. [176]
380. Gottschaldt, K. Über den Einfluss der Erfahrung auf die Wahrnehmung von Figuren. *Psychol. Forsch.*, 1926, 8, 261-317. [216, 217]
381. Götz, W. Expermentelle Untersuchungen zum Problem der Sehgrössen Konstanz beim Haushuhn. *Z. Psychol.*, 1926, 99, 247-60. [279]
382. Graham, C. H. The relation of nerve response and retinal potential to number of sense cells illuminated in an eye lacking lateral connections. *J. cell. comp. Physiol.*, 1932, 2, 295-310. [167]
383. Graham, C. H., & Bartlett, N. The relation of size of stimulus and intensity in the human eye: III. The influence of area on foveal intensity discrimination. *J. exp. Psychol.*, 1940, 27, 149-59. [162]
384. Graham, C. H., Brown, R. H., & Mote, I. A., Jr. The relation of size of stimulus and intensity in the human eye: I. Intensity thresholds for white light. *J. exp. Psychol.*, 1939, 24, 555-73. [156, 157]
385. Graham, C. H., & Cook, C. Minor studies from the Psychological Laboratory of Clark University XXXII. Visual acuity as a function of intensity and exposure-time. *Amer. J. Psychol.*, 1937, 49, 654-61. [164]
386. Graham, C. H., & Granit, R. Comparative studies on the peripheral and central retina: VI. Inhibition, summation, and synchronization of impulses in the retina. *Amer. J. Physiol.*, 1931, 98, 664-73. [167, 168]
387. Graham, C. H., & Kemp, E. H. Brightness discrimination as a function of the duration of the increment in intensity. *J. gen. Physiol.*, 1938, 21, 635-50. [162]

388. Graham, C. H., & Margaria, R. Area and the intensity-time relation in the peripheral retina. *Amer. J. Physiol.*, 1935, 113, 299-305. [156, 166]

Graham, C. H. (*See* No. 443, 978)

389. Graham, F. K. Conditioned inhibition and conditioned excitation in transfer of discrimination. *J. exp. Psychol.*, 1943, 33, 351-68. [343]

Gramlich, F. W. (*See* No. 630)

Granath, L. P. (*See* No. 483, 484)

390. Grandine, L., & Harlow, H. F. Generalization of the characteristics of a single learned stimulus by monkeys. *J. comp. physiol. Psychol.*, 1948, 41, 327-38. [449, 450]

391. Granit, A. R. A study on the perception of form. *Brit. J. of Psychol.*, 1921, 12, 223-47. [225, 592]

392. Granit, R. Comparative studies on the peripheral and central retina: I. On interaction between distant areas in the human eye. *Amer. J. Physiol.*, 1930, 94, 41-50. [167]

393. Granit, R. The components of the retinal action potentials in mammals and their relation to the discharge in the optic nerve. *J. Physiol.*, 1933, 77, 207-39. [149]

394. Granit, R. The retinal mechanism of color reception. *J. opt. Soc. Amer.*, 1941, 31, 570-80. [179]

395. Granit, R. *Sensory mechanisms of the retina.* New York: Oxford Univ. Press, 1947. [137, 148, 149, 158, 161, 178-80, 181, 183, 184, 185, 186, 187, 188]

396. Granit, R., & Davis W. A. Comparative studies on the peripheral and central retina: IV. Temporal summation of subliminal visual stimuli and the time course of the excitatory after-effect. *Amer. J. Physiol.* 931, 98, 644-53. [166]

397. Granit, R., & Harper, P. Comparative studies on the peripheral and central retina: II. Synaptic reactions in the eye. *Amer. J. Physiol.*, 1930, 95, 211-28. [162, 165, 167]

Granit, R. (*See* No. 209, 210, 346, 386)

398. Grant, D. A., & Schneider, D. E. Intensity of the conditioned stimulus and strength of conditioning: I. The conditioned eyelid response to light. *J. exp. Psychol.*, 1948, 38, 690-96. [334]

399. Grant, D. A., & Schneider, D. E. Intensity of the conditioned stimulus and strength of conditioning: II. The conditioned galvanic skin response to an auditory stimulus. *J. exp. Psychol.*, 1949, 39, 35-40. [334]

400. Grant, V. W. Accommodation and convergence in visual space perception. *J. exp. Psychol.*, 1942, 31, 89-104. [269]

401. Gra,;, A. A. On a modification of the Helmholtz theory of hearing. *J. Anat. Physiol.*, 1900, 34, 324-50. [96]

402. Gray, S. The influence of methodology upon the measurement of reminiscence. *J. exp. Psychol.*, 1940, 27, 37-44. [566]

Gregg, A. (*See* No. 314)

403. Grether, W. F. Pseudo-conditioning without paired stimulation encountered in attempted backward conditioning. *J. comp. Psychol.*, 1938, 25, 91-6. [314]

404. Grice, G. R. The relation of secondary reinforcement to delayed reward in visual discrimination learning. *J. exp. Psychol.*, 1948a, 38, 1-16. [437-8, 454]

405. Grice, G. R. An experimental test of the expectation theory of learning. *J. comp. physiol. Psychol.*, 1948b, 41, 137-43. [420, 421]

406. Grice, G. R. The acquisition of a visual discrimination habit following response to a single stimulus. *J. exp. Psychol.*, 1948c, 38, 633-42. [449, 450]

407. Grice, G. R. Visual discrimination learning with simultaneous and successive presentation of stimuli. *J. comp. physiol. Psychol.*, 1949, 42, 365-73. [450, 451]

408. Grice, G. R. The acquisition of a visual discrimination habit following extinction of response to one stimulus. *J. comp. physiol. Psychol.*, 1951, 44, 149-53. [449, 450]

409. Grice, G. R., & Saltz, E. The generalization of an instrumental response to stimuli varying in the size dimension. *J. exp. Psychol.*, 1950, 40, 702-8. [377]

Grice, G. R. (*See* No. 1068)

410. Grindley, G. C. Experiments on the influence of the amount of reward in learning of young chickens. *Brit. J. Psychol.*, 1929-30, 20, 173-80. [332, 434, 439]

Gross, N. (*See* No. 230)

411. Guild, S. R., Crowe, S. J., Bunch, L. L., & Polvogt, L. M. Correlations of differences in the density of innervation of the organ of Corti with differences

in the acuity of hearing, including evidence as to the location in the human cochlea of the receptors for certain tones. *Acta. Oto-Laryngol.*, 1931, 15, 269-308. [121]

Guild, S. R. (*See* No. 215, 522)

412. Guilford, J. P. *Psychometric methods*. New York: McGraw-Hill, 1936. [48]
413. Guilford, J. P., & Park, O. G. The effect of interpolated weights upon comparative judgments. *Amer. J. Psychol.*, 1931, 43, 589-99. [55]
414. Gulliksen, H. Studies of transfer of response: I. Relative versus absolute factors in the discrimination of size by the white rat. *J. genet. Psychol.*, 1932, 40, 37-51. [446]
415. Guthrie, E. R. Conditioning as a principle of learning. *Psychol. Rev.*, 1930, 37, 412-28. [364, 368, 369]
416. Guthrie, E. R. *The psychology of learning*. New York: Harper, 1935. [344, 360, 368, 391]
417. Guthrie, E. R. The effect of outcome on learning. *Psychol. Rev.*, 1939, 46, 480-85. [370]
418. Guthrie, E. R. Conditioning: A theory of learning in terms of stimulus, response, and association. In National Society for the Study of Education, *The forty-first yearbook*. Bloomington, Ill.: Public School Publ. Co., 1942. [363, 368]
419. Guthrie, E. R. Recency or effect? Reply to V. J. O'Connor. *Harvard Ed. R.*, 1946, 16, 286-9. [371]

Guthrie, E. R. [321, 344, 349, 362-72, 380, 410, 455, 462, 469-70, 562]

420. Guthrie, E. R., & Horton, G. P. *Cats in a puzzle box*. New York: Rinehart, 1946. [365-7, 370]

Guthrie, E. R. (*See* No. 93)

Gutmann, E. (*See* No. 1205)

Guttmann, L. (*See* No. 1205)

421. Haagen, C. H. Synonymity, vividness, familiarity, and association value ratings of 400 pairs of common adjectives. *J. Psychol.*, 1949, 27, 453-63. [712]
422. Hahn, H. Die psycho-physischen Konstanten und Variablen des Temperatursinnes: II. Die Umstimmung der Erregbarkeit der Temperaturnerven. *Z. Sinnesphysiol.*, 1930, 60, 198-232. [78]

Haig, C. (*See* No. 464, 465)

Hall, B. E. (*See* No. 565)

Hall, C. S. (*See* No. 1141)

Hall, M. (*See* No. 550)

423. Hallpike, C. S., & Rawdon-Smith, A. F. The 'Wever and Bray phenomenon.' A study of the electrical response in the cochlea with especial reference to its origin. *J. Physiol.*, 1934a, 81, 395-408. [101]
424. Hallpike, C. S., & Rawdon-Smith, A. F. The origin of the Wever and Bray phenomenon. *J. Physiol.*, 1934b, 83, 243-54. [101]
425. Halverson, H. M. Tonal volume as a function of intensity. *Amer. J. Psychol.*, 1924, 35, 360-67. [125]
426. Hamel, I. A. A study and analysis of the conditioned reflex. *Psychol. Monogr.*, 1919, 27, No. 118. [398]
427. Hamilton, E. L. The effect of delayed incentive on the hunger drive in the white rat. *Genet. Psychol. Monogr.*, 1929, 5, 133-207. [334, 436]
428. Hamilton, R. J. Retroactive facilitation as a function of degree of generalization between tasks. *J. exp. Psychol.*, 1943, 32, 363-76. [525, 529, 532, 533]

Hamilton, W. F. (*See* No. 724)

429. Hammer, E. R. Temporal factors in figural after-effects. *Amer. J. Psychol.*, 1949, 62, 337-54. [241-2]
430. Hanawalt, E. M. Whole and part methods in trial and error learning. *Comp. Psychol. Monogr.*, 1931, 7, No. 35. [540]
431. Hanawalt, E. M. Whole and part methods in trial and error learning: Human maze learning. *J. exp. Psychol.*, 1934, 17, 691-708. [540]
432. Hanawalt, N. G. Memory trace for figures in recall and recognition. *Arch. Psychol., N. Y.*, 1937, 31, No. 216. [590]
433. Hanfmann, E., & Kasanin, J. A method for the study of concept formation. *J. Psychol.*, 1937, 3, 521-40. [674-6]
434. Hanfmann, E., & Kasanin, J. Conceptual thinking in schizophrenia. *Nerv. ment. Dis. Monogr.*, 1942, No. 67. [677, 678]

435. Harden, L. M. A quantitative study of the similarity factor in retroactive inhibition. *J. gen. Psychol.*, 1929, **2**, 421-32. [530]

Hardy, J. D. (*See* No. 483, 484)

436. Harlow, H. F., & Stagner, R. Effect of complete striate muscle paralysis upon the learning process. *J. exp. Psychol.*, 1933, **16**, 283-94. [479]

Harlow, H. F. (*See* No. 162, 390)

Harper, P. (*See* No. 397)

Harpman, J. A. (*See* No. 1262)

Harriman, A. E. (*See* No. 991)

437. Harris, J. D. Pitch-discrimination under masking. *Amer. J. Psychol.*, 1948, **61**, 194-204. [119]
438. Harrower, M. R. Changes in figure-ground perception in patients with cortical lesions. *Brit. J. Psychol.*, 1939, **30**, 47-51. [221]

Harsh, C. M. (*See* No. 482)

439. Hartline, H. K. Intensity and duration in the excitation of single photoreceptor units. *J. cell. comp. Physiol.*, 1934, **5**, 229-47. [165, 166]
440. Hartline, H. K. The response of single optic nerve fibers of the vertebrate eye to illumination of the retina. *Amer. J. Physiol.*, 1938, **121**, 400-415. [152]
441. Hartline, H. K. The receptive fields of optic nerve fibers. *Amer. J. Physiol.*, 1940, **130**, 690-99. [167]
442. Hartline, H. K. The neural mechanisms of vision. *The Harvey Lect.*, 1941, The Harvey Society, N. Y., series 37. [152]
443. Hartline, H. K., & Graham, C. H. Nerve impulses from single receptors in the eye. *J. cell. comp. Physiol.*, 1932, **1**, 277-95. [152]

Hartmann, G. W. (*See* No. 1203)

444. Hartmann, L. Neue Verschmelzungsprobleme. *Psychol. Forsch.*, 1923, **3**, 319-96. [219]
445. Hartridge, H. Physiology of colour vision. *Nature, Lond.*, 1944, **152**, 190-91. [184]
446. Hartridge, H. The change from trichromatic to dichromatic vision in the human retina. *Nature, Lond.*, 1945a, **155**, 657-62. [184]
447. Hartridge, H. The importance of taste and smell in nutrition. *J. Physiol.*, 1945b, **103**, 34-5. [24]
448. Hartridge, H. Colour receptors of the human fovea. *Nature, Lond.*, 1946a, **158**, 97-8. [177, 178]
449. Hartridge, H. Fixation area in the human eye. *Nature, Lond.*, 1946b, **158**, 303. [177, 178]
450. Hartridge, H. Response curve of the yellow receptors of the human fovea. *Nature, Lond.*, 1946c, **158**, 946-8. [177, 178]
451. Head, H. The conception of nervous and mental energy. *Brit. J. Psychol.*, 1923, **24**, 277-99. [652]

Heath, L. L. (*See* No. 237)

452. Hebb, D. O. The innate organization of visual activity: I. Perception of figures by rats reared in total darkness. *J. genet. Psychol.*, 1937a, **51**, 101-26. [226]
453. Hebb, D. O. The innate organization of visual activity: II. Transfer of response in the discrimination of brightness and size by rats reared in total darkness. *J. comp. Psychol.*, 1937b, **24**, 277-99. [226]
454. Hebb, D. O. Studies of the organization of behavior: I. Behavior of the rat in a field orientation. *J. comp. Psychol.*, 1938a, **25**, 333-53. [484]
455. Hebb, D. O. The innate organization of visual activity: III. Discrimination of brightness after removal of the striate cortex in the rat. *J. comp. Psychol.*, 1938b, **25**, 427-37. [484]
456. Hebb, D. O. *The organization of behavior. A neuropsychological theory.* New York: Wiley, 1949. [194, 198-200, 215, 222, 225-8, 248, 285, 399, 401]
457. Hebb, D. O., & Foord, E. N. Errors of visual recognition and the nature of the trace. *J. exp. Psychol.*, 1945, **35**, 335-48. [591-2]
458. Hecht, S. On the binocular fusion of colors and its relation to theories of color vision. *Proc. nat. Acad. Sci., Wash.*, 1928, **14**, 237-41. [177]
459. Hecht, S. The development of Thomas Young's theory of color vision. *J. opt. Soc. Amer.*, 1930, **20**, 231-70. [170-72, 175-7, 186]
460. Hecht, S. Vision II. The nature of the photoreceptor process. In C. Murchison

(ed.), *Handbook of general experimental psychology*. Worcester: Clark Univ. Press, 1934. [69, 74, 78, 144, 156, 158, 164, 166, 175, 183]

461. Hecht, S. A theory of visual intensity discrimination. *J. gen. Physiol.*, 1935, **18**, 767-89. [69]

462. Hecht, S. Energy and vision. *Amer. Scientist*, 1944, **32**, 159-77. [147, 155]

463. Hecht, S. Sunlight harms night vision. *Air Surgeon's Bull.*, 1945, **2**, 45. [161]

Hecht, S. [75, 80, 179, 188]

464. Hecht, S., Haig, C., & Chase, A. M. The influence of light adaptation on subsequent dark adaptation of the eye. *J. gen. Physiol.*, 1937, **20**, 831-51. [159, 160]

465. Hecht, S., Haig, C., & Wald, G. Dark adaptation of retinal fields of different size and location. *J. gen. Physiol.*, 1935, **19**, 321-37. [160]

466. Hecht, S., & Hsia, Y. Dark adaptation following light adaptation to red and white lights. *J. opt. Soc. Amer.*, 1945, **35**, 261-7. [160]

467. Hecht, S., & Mandelbaum, J. Rod-cone dark adaptation and vitamin A. *Science*, 1938, **88**, 219-21. [149, 161]

468. Hecht, S., & Mintz, E. U. The visibility of single lines at various illuminations and the retinal basis of visual resolution. *J. gen. Physiol.*, 1939, **22**, 593-612. [163, 164]

469. Hecht, S., Peskin, J. C., & Patt, M. Intensity discrimination in the human eye: II. The relation between $\Delta I/I$ and intensity for various parts of the spectrum. *J. gen. Physiol.*, 1938, **22**, 7-19. [163]

470. Hecht, S., Ross, S., & Mueller, C. G. The visibility of lines and squares at high brightness. *J. opt. Soc. Amer.*, 1947, **37**, 500-507. [164]

471. Heidbreder, E. Toward a dynamic psychology of cognition. *Psychol. Rev.*, 1945, **52**, 1-22. [672]

472. Heidbreder, E. The attainment of concepts: I. Terminology and methodology. *J. gen. Psychol.*, 1946a, **35**, 173-89. [671-2, 678]

473. Heidbreder, E. The attainment of concepts: II. The problem. *J. gen. Psychol.*, 1946b, **35**, 191-223. [671-2, 678]

474. Heidbreder, E. The attainment of concepts: III. The process. *J. gen. Psychol.*, 1947, **24**, 93-138. [671-2, 678]

475. Helmholtz, H. von. *Physiological optics*. (Translated by J. P. C. Southall from the 3rd German edition.) Optical Society of America, 1924. Vol. I, II, III. [170]

Helmholtz, H. von. [36, 95, 169, 170, 171, 177, 243, 248, 257]

476. Helson, H. The effects of direct stimulation of the blind spot. *Amer. J. Psychol.*, 1929, **41**, 345-97. [135]

477. Helson, H. How do we see in the blind spot? *J. exp. Psychol.*, 1934, **17**, 763-72. [135]

478. Helson, H., & Judd, D. B. A study of photopic adaptation. *J. exp. Psychol.*, 1932, **15**, 380-98. [275]

Hempstead [223]

Henderson, L. F. (*See* No. 213)

Henle, M. (*See* No. 1188)

479. Henneman, R. H. A photometric study of the perception of object color. *Arch. Psychol., N. Y.*, 1935, No. 179. [278]

480. Henning, H. Der Geruch: I. *Z. Psychol.*, 1915, **73**, 161-257. [28]

Henninger, L. L. (*See* No. 1014)

481. Hensen, V. Studien über das Gehörorgan der Decapoden. *Z. wiss. Zool.*, 1863, **13**, 319-412. [96]

Hensen, V. [95]

Herbart, J. F. [43]

482. Herbert, M. J., & Harsh, C. M. Observational learning by cats. *J. comp. Psychol.*, 1944, **37**, 81-95. [659-60]

483. Herget, C. M., Granath, L. P., & Hardy, J. D. Thermal sensation and discrimination in relation to intensity of stimulus. *Amer. J. Physiol.*, 1941a, **134**, 645-55. [17, 19, 82-3]

484. Herget, C. M., Granath, L. P., & Hardy, J. D. Warmth sense in relation to skin area stimulated. *Amer. J. Physiol.*, 1941b, **135**, 20-26. [68, 74]

485. Hering, E. *Grundzüge der Lehre vom Lichtsinn*. Berlin: Springer, 1920. [173]

Hering, E. [177-9, 280]

Heron, W. T. (*See* No. 983)

486. Herrick, C. J. *Brains of rats and men.* Chicago: Univ. of Chicago Press, 1926. [474]
487. Hevner, K. Experimental studies of the elements of expression in music. *Amer. J. Psychol.,* 1936, **48,** 246-68. [645]
488. Heyer, A. W., Jr., & O'Kelly, L. I. Studies in motivation and retention: II. Retention of nonsense syllables learned under different degrees of motivation. *J. Psychol.,* 1949, **27,** 143-52. [579]
489. Heyer, A. W., & O'Kelly, L. I. Studies in motivation and retention: III-VII. *Comp. Psychol. Monogr.,* in press.

Heyer, A. W. (*See* No. 912)

490. Hilgard, E. R. The conditioned eyelid reactions to a light stimulus based on the reflex wink to sound. *Psychol. Monogr.,* 1931, **41,** No. 1. [311]
491. Hilgard, E. R. Reinforcement and inhibition of eyelid reflexes. *J. gen. Psychol.* 1933*a,* **8,** 85-113. [311]
492. Hilgard, E. R. Modification of reflexes and conditioned reactions. *J. gen. Psychol.,* 1933*b,* **9,** 210-15. [311]
493. Hilgard, E. R. A summary and evaluation of alternative procedures for the construction of Vincent curves. *Psychol. Bull.,* 1938, **35,** 282-97. [329]
494. Hilgard, E. R. *Theories of learning.* New York: Appleton-Century-Crofts, 1948. [416, 464]
495. Hilgard, E. R., & Allen, M. K. An attempt to condition finger reactions based on motor point stimulation. *J. gen. Psychol.,* 1938, **18,** 203-7. [491]
496. Hilgard, E. R., & Campbell, A. A. The course of acquisition and retention of conditioned eyelid responses in man. *J. exp. Psychol.,* 1936, **19,** 227-47. [311]
497. Hilgard, E. R., & Marquis, D. G. Acquisition, extinction, and retention of conditioned lid responses to light in dogs. *J. comp. Psychol.,* 1935, **19,** 29-58. [311-13]
498. Hilgard, E. R., & Marquis, D. G. Conditioned eyelid responses in monkeys, with a comparison of dog, monkey, and man. *Psychol. Monogr.,* 1936, **47,** 186-98. [311]
499. Hilgard, E. R., & Marquis, D. G. *Conditioning and learning.* New York: Appleton-Century-Crofts, 1940. [311, 319, 327, 347, 391, 462, 492]

Hilgard, E. R. (*See* No. 161, 800)

500. Hillebrand, F. Das Verhältnis von Accommodation und Konvergenz zur Tiefenlokalisation. *Z. Psychol.,* 1894, **7,** 97-151. [267]
501. Hirsh, I. J. Binaural summation—a century of investigation. *Psychol. Bull.,* 1948*a,* **45,** 193-206. [115]
502. Hirsh, I. J. Binaural summation and interaural inhibition as a function of the level of masking noise. *Amer. J. Psychol.,* 1948*b,* **61,** 205-13. [119]

Hitzig, G. (*See* No. 328)

503. Hoagland, H. The Weber-Fechner law and the all-or-none theory. *J. gen. Psychol.,* 1930, **3,** 351-73. [70]
504. Hobhouse, L. T. *Mind in evolution.* New York: Macmillan, 1901. [603-4]

Hogan, H. P. (*See* No. 164)

Hollenberg, A. (*See* No. 12)

505. Hollingsworth, H. L. *The inaccuracy of movement.* (Archives of Psychology, No. 13) New York: The Science Press, 1909. [56]
506. Hollingsworth, H. L. *Psychology, its facts and principles.* New York: Appleton, 1928. [381]

Holmes, F. B. (*See* No. 611)

507. Holt, E. B. *Animal drive and the learning process, an essay toward radical empiricism.* Vol. 1. New York: Holt, 1931. [428, 687-8]
508. Holway, A. H., & Boring, E. G. Determinants of apparent visual size with distance variant. *Amer. J. Psychol.,* 1941, **54,** 21-37. [262]
509. Holway, A. H., & Crozier, W. J. Differential sensitivity for somesthetic pressure. *Psychol. Rec.,* 1937*a,* **1,** 170-76. [13]
510. Holway, A. H., & Crozier, W. J. The significance of area for differential sensitivity in somesthetic pressure. *Psychol. Rec.,* 1937*b,* **1,** 178-84. [13]
511. Honzik, C. H. Delayed reaction in rats. *Univ. Calif. Publ. Psychol.,* 1931, **4,** 307-18. [656, 663]

Honzik, C. H. (*See* No. 1142, 1143)

Horenstein, B. R. (*See* No. 659)

Horton, G. P. (*See* No. 420)

512. Hovland, C. I. The generalization of conditioned responses: I. The sensory generalization of conditioned responses with varying frequencies of tone. *J. gen. Psychol.*, 1937a, 17, 125-48. [355-8, 377, 533]
513. Hovland, C. I. The generalization of conditioned responses: II. The sensory generalization of conditioned responses with varying intensities of tone. *J. genet. Psychol.*, 1937b, 51, 279-91. [355-8, 377]
514. Hovland, C. I. The generalization of conditioned responses: IV. The effects of varying amounts of reinforcement upon the degree of generalization of conditioned responses. *J. exp. Psychol.*, 1937c, 21, 261-76. [537]
515. Hovland, C. I. Experimental studies in rote-learning theory: I. Reminiscence following learning by massed and by distributed practice. *J. exp. Psychol.*, 1938a, 22, 201, 224. [510, 511, 512]
516. Hovland, C. I. Experimental studies in rote-learning theory: II. Reminiscence with varying speeds of syllable presentation. *J. exp. Psychol.*, 1938b, 22, 338-53. [510, 511]
517. Hovland, C. I. Experimental studies in rote-learning theory: III. Distribution of practice with varying speeds of syllable presentation. *J. exp. Psychol.*, 1938c, 23, 172-90. [505, 506, 515, 519]
518. Hovland, C. I. Experimental studies in rote-learning theory: IV. Comparison of reminiscence in serial and paired-associate learning. *J. exp. Psychol.*, 1939, 24, 466-84. [512]
519. Hovland, C. I. Experimental studies in rote-learning theory: VI. Comparison of retention following learning to same criterion by massed and distributed practice. *J. exp. Psychol.*, 1940a, 26, 568-87. [508, 518]
520. Hovland, C. I. Experimental studies in rote-learning theory: VII. Distribution of practice with varying lengths of list. *J. exp. Psychol.*, 1940b, 27, 271-84. [513]

Hovland, C. I. [444, 515]

Hovland, C. I. (*See* No. 550, 1017)

521. Howe, H. A. The relation of the organ of Corti to audioelectric phenomena in deaf albino cats. *Amer. J. Physiol.*, 1935, 111, 187-91. [94]
522. Howe, H. A., & Guild, S. R. Absence of the organ of Corti and its possible relation to electrical auditory nerve responses. *Anat. Rec.*, 1932-3, 55, 20. [94]
523. Howes, D. H. The loudness of multicomponent tones. *Amer. J. Psychol.*, 1950, 63, 1-30. [118]
524. Howes, D. H., & Osgood, C. E. On the combination of associative probabilities in linguistic contexts. In press. [725-6]
525. Howes, D. H., & Solomon, R. L. A note on McGinnies' 'Emotionality and perceptual defense.' *Psychol. Rev.*, 1950, 57, 229-34. [293-4]
526. Howes, D. H., & Solomon, R. L. Visual duration thresholds as a function of word-probability. *J. exp. Psychol.*, 1951, 41, 401-10. [293]
527. Hsia, Y. Whiteness constancy as a function of difference in illumination. *Arch. Psychol., N. Y.*, 1943, No. 284. [274, 276-7, 282]

Hsia, Y. (*See* No. 466)

528. Hughson, W., Thompson, E., & Witting, E. G. Tone localization in the cochlea. *Ann. Otol., etc., St. Louis*, 1935, 44, 777-92. [101]
529. Hull, C. L. Quantitative aspects of the evolution of concepts. *Psychol. Monogr.*, 1920, No. 123. [666-7, 671, 678]
530. Hull, C. L. Knowledge and purpose as habit mechanisms. *Psychol. Rev.*, 1930, 37, 511-25. [394-7, 403, 663]
531. Hull, C. L. Goal attraction and directing ideas conceived as habit phenomena. *Psychol. Rev.*, 1931, 38, 487-506. [402]
532. Hull, C. L. The goal gradient hypothesis and maze learning. *Psychol. Rev.*, 1932, 39, 25-43. [497, 499, 612]
533. Hull, C. L. Differential habituation to internal stimuli in the albino rat. *J. comp. Psychol.*, 1933a, 16, 255-73. [417, 418]
534. Hull, C. L. The meaningfulness of 320 selected nonsense syllables. *Amer. J. Psychol.*, 1933b, 45, 730-34. [712]
535. Hull, C. L. The concept of the habit-family-hierarchy and maze learning: Part I. *Psychol. Rev.*, 1934a, 41, 33-54. [402, 612-14]
536. Hull, C. L. The concept of the habit-family hierarchy and maze learning: Part II. *Psychol. Rev.*, 1934b, 41, 134-52. [402, 612-14]
537. Hull, C. L. The rat's speed-of-locomotion gradient in approach to food. *J. comp. Psychol.*, 1934c, 17, 393-422. [499, 500]
538. Hull, C. L. Learning: II. The factor of the conditioned reflex. In C. Murchison (ed.), *Handbook of general experimental psychology*. Worcester: Clark Univ. Press, 1934d. Pp. 382-455. [312, 315, 320]

539. Hull, C. L. The mechanism of the assembly of behavior segments in novel combinations suitable for problem solution. *Psychol. Rev.*, 1935, 42, 219-45. [616-18]

540. Hull, C. L. Mind, mechanism and adaptive behavior. *Psychol. Rev.*, 1937, 44, 1-32. [309]

541. Hull, C. L. The goal-gradient hypothesis applied to some 'field force' problems in the behavior of young children. *Psychol. Rev.*, 1938, 45, 271-300. [402, 612]

542. Hull, C. L. The problem of stimulus equivalence in behavior theory. *Psychol. Rev.*, 1939a, 46, 9-30. [353, 355, 357, 359]

543. Hull, C. L. Simple trial-and-error learning—an empirical investigation. *J. comp. Psychol.*, 1939b, 27, 233-58. [306]

544. Hull, C. L. *Principles of behavior. An introduction to behavior theory.* New York: Appleton-Century-Crofts, 1943. [209-12, 215, 216, 322-3, 325-36, 341-2, 346, 347, 355, 356, 357, 373-9, 430, 431-3, 436-8, 503, 518, 625, 723]

545. Hull C. L. The discrimination of stimulus configurations and the hypothesis of afferent neural interaction. *Psychol. Rev.*, 1945, 52, 133-42. [211]

546. Hull, C. L. Reactively heterogeneous compound trial-and-error learning with distributed trials and terminal reinforcement. *J. exp. Psychol.*, 1947, 37, 118-35. [500]

547. Hull, C. L. Reactively heterogeneous compound trial-and-error learning with distributed trials and serial reinforcement. *J. exp. Psychol.*, 1948, 38, 17-28. [500]

548. Hull, C. L. Stimulus intensity dynamism (V) and stimulus generalization. *Psychol. Rev.*, 1949, 56, 67-76. [377]

Hull, C. L. [194, 322, 362, 363, 372-382, 384, 385, 393, 410, 413, 418, 421, 425, 444, 455, 462, 467, 470, 473, 496, 502, 605, 693, 726]

549. Hull, C. L., Felsinger, J. M., Gladstone, A. I., & Yamaguchi, H. G. A proposed quantification of habit strength. *Psychol. Rev.*, 1947, 54, 237-54. [328]

550. Hull, C. L., Hovland, C. I., Ross, R. T., Hall, M., Perkins, D. T., & Fitch, F. B. *Mathematico-deductive theory of rote learning.* New Haven: Yale Univ. Press, 1940. [503, 509, 516-19, 671]

551. Hull, C. L., Livingston, J. R., Rouse, R. O., & Barker, A. N. True, sham, and esophageal feeding as reinforcements. *J. comp. physiol. Psychol.*, 1951, 44, 236-45. [439, 440]

Hull, C. L. (*See* No. 54)

552. Humphrey, G. *The nature of learning.* New York: Harcourt, Brace, 1933. [210]

553. Humphreys, L. G. The effect of random alternation of reinforcement on the acquisition and extinction of conditioned eyelid reactions. *J. exp. Psychol.*, 1939a, 25, 141-58. [345, 406, 425, 426]

554. Humphreys, L. G. Generalization as a function of method of reinforcement. *J. exp. Psychol.*, 1939b, 25, 361-72. [345]

555. Humphreys, L. G. Extinction of conditioned psychogalvanic responses following two conditions of reinforcement. *J. exp. Psychol.*, 1940, 27, 71-5. [345, 425, 426, 507]

556. Humphreys, L. G. Measures of strength of conditioned eyelid responses. *J. gen. Psychol.*, 1943, 29, 101-11. [327]

557. Hunt, W. A. Anchoring effects in judgment. *Amer. J. Psychol.*, 1941, 54, 395-403. [50]

558. Hunt, W. A., & Volkmann, J. The anchoring of an affective scale. *Amer. J. Psychol.*, 1937, 49, 88-92. [50]

559. Hunter, W. S. The delayed reaction in animals and children. *Animal Behav. Monogr.*, 1913, 2, No. 1. [656, 657, 663]

560. Hunter, W. S. The temporal maze and kinaesthetic sensory processes in the white rat. *Psychobiol.*, 1920, 2, 1-18. [488, 658]

561. Hunter, W. S. The behavior of raccoons in a double alternation temporal maze. *J. genet. Psychol.*, 1928, 35, 374-88. [658]

562. Hunter, W. S. The sensory control of the maze habit in the white rat. *J. genet. Psychol.*, 1929, 36, 505-37. [488]

563. Hunter, W. S. A consideration of Lashley's theory of the equipotentiality of cerebral action. *J. gen. Psychol.*, 1930, 3, 455-68. [488]

564. Hunter, W. S. The effect of inactivity produced by cold upon learning and retention in the cockroach, *blatella germanica. J. genet. Psychol.*, 1932, 41, 253-65. [595]

565. Hunter, W. S., & Hall, B. E. Double alternation behavior of the white rat in a spatial maze. *J. comp. Psychol.*, 1941, 32, 253-66. [662]

Hunter, W. S. (*See* No. 28, 998)

566. Husband, R. W. A note on maze learning with the time factor constant. *J. gen. Psychol.*, 1929, **2**, 366-9. [505]
567. Ipsen, G. Über Gestaltanffassung (Erörterung des Sanderschen Parallelo-gramms). *Neue psychol. Stud.*, 1926, **1**, 167-279. [56]
568. Irion, A. L. The relation of 'set' to retention. *Psychol. Rev.*, 1948, **55**, 336-41. [521, 563-4]
569. Irion, A. L. Retention and warming-up effects in paired-associate learning. *J. exp. Psychol.*, 1949*a*, **39**, 669-75. [563]
570. Irion, A. L. Retention as a function of amount of pre-recall warming up. *Amer. Psychologist*, 1949*b*, **4**, 219-20. (Abstract.) [563]
571. Irwin, F. W., & Seidenfeld, M. A. The application of the method of com-parison to the problem of memory changes. *J. exp. Psychol.*, 1937, **21**, 363-81. [591]

Irwin, J. McQ. (*See* No. 842)

572. Irwin, O. C. The developmental status of speech sounds of ten feeble-minded children. *Child Develpm.*, 1942, **13**, 29-39. [687]
573. Irwin, O. C. Infant speech: development of vowel sounds. *J. Speech Hearing Disorders*, 1948, **13**, 31-4. [685-6]
574. Irwin, O. C. Speech development in the young child: 2. Some factors related to the speech development of the infant and young child. *J. Speech Hearing Disorders*, 1952, **17**, 269-79. [685-6]
575. Irwin, O. C., & Chen, H. P. A reliability study of speech sounds observed in the crying of newborn infants. *Child Develpm.*, 1941, **12**, 351-68. [687]
576. Irwin, O. C., & Chen, H. P. Development of speech during infancy: curve of phonemic types. *J. exp. Psychol.*, 1946, **36**, 431-6. [687]

Israel, H. E. (*See* No. 1043)

577. Ives, H. E. The transformation of color mixture equations from one system to another: II. Graphical aids. *J. Franklin Inst.*, 1923, **195**, 23-44. [170]

Jackson, T. A. (*See* No. 580, 1192)

Jacobs, A. (*See* No. 125)

578. Jacobsen, C. F. Functions of the frontal association areas in primates. *Arch. Neurol. Psychiat., Chicago*, 1935, **33**, 558-69. [660-63, 664, 665]
579. Jacobsen, C. F., & Nissen, H. W. Studies of cerebral function in primates: IV. The effects of frontal lobe lesions on the delayed alternation habit in monkeys. *J. comp. Psychol.*, 1937, **23**, 101-12. [657, 661]
580. Jacobsen, C. F., Wolfe, J. B., & Jackson, T. A. An experimental analysis of the functions of the frontal association areas in primates. *J. nerv. ment. Dis.*, 1935, **82**, 1-14. [661-2]
581. Jacobson, E. *Progressive relaxation*. Chicago: Univ. of Chicago Press, 1929. [649]
582. Jacobson, E. Electrophysiology of mental activities. *Amer. J. Psychol.*, 1932, **44**, 677-94. [649-51, 654, 697, 700]
583. Jacobson, E., & Carlson, A. J. The influence of relaxation upon the knee jerk. *Amer. J. Physiol.*, 1925, **73**, 324-8. [652]
584. Jaensch, E. R. *Eidetic Imagery*. New York: Harcourt, Brace, 1930. [641]
585. Jaensch, E. R., & Müller, E. A. Über die Wahrnehmung farbloser Hellig-keiten und den Helligkeitkontrast. *Z. Psychol.*, 1920, **83**, 266-341. [280]
586. Jahn, T. L. Color vision and color blindness: A mechanism in terms of modern evidence. *J. opt. Soc. Amer.*, 1946, **36**, 595-7. [183]

James, W. [32, 125, 193, 324, 373]

Janis, M. G. (*See* No. 190)

587. Jaynes, J. Learning a second response to a cue as a function of the magnitude of the first. *J. comp. physiol. Psychol.*, 1950, **43**, 398-408. [453-4]
588. Jenkins, J. G. Instruction as a factor in 'incidental' learning. *Amer. J. Psychol.*, 1933, **45**, 471-7. [414]
589. Jenkins, J. G., & Dallenbach, K. M. Obliviscence during sleep and waking. *Amer. J. Psychol.*, 1924, **35**, 605-12. [594]
590. Jenkins, W. L. Studies in thermal sensitivity: I. Adaptation with a series of small circular stimulators. *J. exp. Psychol.*, 1937, **21**, 670-77. [16, 80, 82]
591. Jenkins, W. L. Studies in thermal sensitivity: II. Adaptation with a series of small rectangular stimulators. *J. exp. Psychol.*, 1938*a*, **22**, 84-9. [16]
592. Jenkins, W. L. Studies in thermal sensitivity: III. Adaptation with a series of small annular stimulators. *J. exp. Psychol.*, 1938*b*, **22**, 164-77. [15, 16]
593. Jenkins, W. L. Studies in thermal sensitivity: IV. Minor contributions. *J. exp. Psychol.*, 1938*c*, **22**, 178-85. [16]

594. Jenkins, W. L. Studies in thermal sensitivity: V. The reactions of untrained subjects to simultaneous warm and cold stimulation. *J. exp. Psychol.*, 1938*d*, 22, 451-61. [16]

595. Jenkins, W. L. Studies in thermal sensitivity: VI. The reactions of untrained subjects to simultaneous warm and cold and electric shock. *J. exp. Psychol.*, 1938*e*, 22, 564-72. [19]

596. Jenkins, W. L. Studies in thermal sensitivity: VII. Further synthetic evidence against the Alrutz theory. *J. exp. Psychol.*, 1938*f*, 23, 411-16. [19]

597. Jenkins, W. L. Studies in thermal sensitivity: IX. The reliability of seriatim cold-mapping with untrained subjects. *J. exp. Psychol.*, 1939*a*, 24, 278-93. [15]

598. Jenkins, W. L. Studies in thermal sensitivity: X. The reliability of seriatim warm-mapping with untrained subjects. *J. exp. Psychol.*, 1939*b*, 24, 439-49. [15]

599. Jenkins, W. L. Studies in thermal sensitivity: XI. Effects of stimulator size in seriatim cold-mapping. *J. exp. Psychol.*, 1939*c*, 25, 302-6. [15]

600. Jenkins, W. L. Studies in thermal sensitivity: XII. Part-whole relations in seriatim cold-mapping. *J. exp. Psychol.*, 1939*d*, 25, 373-88. [15]

601. Jenkins, W. L., & Stone, L. J. Recent research in cutaneous sensitivity: II. Touch and the neural basis of the skin senses. *Psychol. Bull.*, 1941, 38, 69-91. [10, 13]

Jenkins, W. L. (*See* No. 1095)

602. Jenkins, W. O. Studies in the spread of effect: I. The bidirectional gradient in the performance of white rats on a linear maze. *J. comp. Psychol.*, 1943*a*, 35, 41-56. [377]

603. Jenkins, W. O. Studies in the spread of effect: II. The effect of increased motivation upon the bidirectional gradient. *J. comp. Psychol.*, 1943*b*, 35, 57-63. [377]

604. Jenkins, W. O. Studies in the spread of effect: III. The effect of increased incentive upon the bidirectional gradient. *J. comp. Psychol.*, 1943*c*, 35, 65-72. [377]

605. Jenkins, W. O. A temporal gradient of derived reinforcement. *Amer. J. Psychol.*, 1950, 63, 237-43. [435]

606. Jenkins, W. O., & Postman, L. Isolation and 'spread of effect' in serial learning. *Amer. J. Psychol.*, 1948, 61, 214-21. [377]

607. Jenkins, W. O., & Sheffield, F. D. Rehearsal and guessing habits as sources of the 'spread of effect.' *J. exp. Psychol.*, 1946, 36, 316-30. [377]

608. Jerome, E. A. Olfactory thresholds measured in terms of stimulus pressure and volume. *Arch. Psychol., N. Y.*, 1942, 39, No. 274. [25]

609. Jerome, E. A. Olfactory thresholds measured in terms of stimulus pressure and volume. *Arch. Psychol., N. Y.*, 1943, No. 274. [61]

610. Jersild, A. T. Memory for the pleasant as compared with the unpleasant. *J. exp. Psychol.*, 1931, 14, 284-8. [572]

611. Jersild, A. T., & Holmes, F. B. Methods of overcoming children's fears. *J. Psychol.*, 1935, 1, 75-104. [344]

612. Jesperson, O. *Language: its nature, development and origin.* London: G. Allen & Unwin, Ltd., 1922. [690]

613. Johnson, D. M. A modern account of problem solving. *Psychol. Bull.*, 1944, 41, 201-29. [627]

614. Johnson, L. M. Similarity of meaning as a factor in retroactive inhibition. *J. gen. Psychol.*, 1933, 9, 377-88. [527, 528, 530]

615. Johnson, W. Studies in language behavior: I. A program of research. *Psychol. Monogr.*, 1944, No. 255, 1-15. [719]

616. Jones, H. E. Emotional factors in learning. *J. gen. Psychol.*, 1929, 2, 263-72. [572]

617. Jones, H. E., & Wechsler, D. Galvanometric technique in studies of association. *Amer. J. Psychol.*, 1928, 40, 607-12. [700]

Jones, H. M. (*See* No. 872, 873)

618. Jones, L. A. The fundamental scale of pure hue and retinal sensibility to hue differences. *J. opt. Soc. Amer.*, 1917, 1, 63-77. [144]

619. Jost, A. Die Assoziationsfesfestigkeit in ihrer Abhängigkeit von der Verteilung der Wiederholungen. *Z. Psychol.*, 1897, 14, 436-72. [507]

Judd, C. H. [324]

620. Judd, D. B. Facts of color-blindness. *J. opt. Soc. Amer.*, 1943, 33, 294. [182]

Judd, D. B. (*See* No. 478)

621. Jung, C. G. *Studies in word-association*. London: William Heinemann, 1918. [708]

Kalish, D. (*See* No. 1147, 1148, 1149)

Kant [248]

Kaplan, S. J. (*See* No. 349)

622. Kappauf, W. E., & Schlosberg, H. Conditioned responses in the white rat: III. Conditioning as a function of the length of the period of delay. *J. genet. Psychol.*, 1937, 50, 27-45. [334]
623. Kapustnik, O. P. The interrelation between direct conditioned stimuli and their verbal symbols (trans. from Russian title). *Psychol. Abstracts,* 1930, 8, No. 152. [701, 704]
624. Karn, H. W. The behavior of cats on the double alternation problem in the temporal maze. *J. comp. Psychol.*, 1938, 26, 201-8. [658]
625. Karn, H. W. Sensory pre-conditioning and incidental learning in human subjects. *J. exp. Psychol.*, 1947, 37, 540-45. [461, 462]
626. Karn, H. W., & Malamud, H. R. The behavior of dogs on the double alternation problem in the temporal maze. *J. comp. Psychol.*, 1939, 27, 461-6. [658]
627. Karn, H. W., & Porter, J. M. The effects of certain pretraining procedures upon maze performance and their significance for the concept of latent learning. *J. exp. Psychol.*, 1946, 36, 461-9. [415]
628. Karwoski, T. F. Psychophysics and mescal intoxication. *J. gen. Psychol.*, 1936, 15, 212-20. [641]
629. Karwoski, T. F., & Crook, M. N. Studies in the peripheral retina: I. The Parkinje after-image. *J. gen. Psychol.*, 1937, 16, 323-56. [185]
630. Karwoski, T. F., Gramlick, F. W., & Arnott, P. Psychological studies in semantics: I. Free association reactions to words, drawings, and objects. *J. soc. Psychol.*, 1944, 20, 233-47. [632, 711-12]
631. Karwoski, T. F., & Odbert, H. S. Color-music. *Psychol. Monogr.*, 1938, 50, No. 2. [642-3]
632. Karwoski, T. F., Odbert, H. S., & Osgood, C. E. Studies in synesthetic thinking: II. The role of form in visual responses to music. *J. gen. Psychol.*, 1942, 26, 199-222. [643-4]
633. Karwoski, T. F., & Schacter, J. Psychological studies in semantics: III. Reaction times for similarity and difference. *J. soc. Psychol.*, 1948, 28, 103-20. [709, 710-11]
634. Karwoski, T. F., & Warrener, H. Studies in the peripheral retina: II. The Purkinje after-image in the near foveal area of the retina. *J. gen. Psychol.*, 1942, 26, 129-51. [185, 223]

Karwoski, T. F. (*See* No. 904)

Kasanin, J. (*See* No. 433, 434)

635. Katona, G. *Organizing and memorizing*. New York: Columbia Univ. Press, 1940. [566, 569-70]

Katz, A. (*See* No. 1010)

636. Katz, D. Die Erscheinungsweisen der Farben. *Z. Psychol.*, 1911, Ergbd. 7. [128, 272-3]
637. Katz, D. *The world of color*. London: Kegan Paul, Trench, Trubner, 1935. (Translation of *Der Aufbau der Farbwelt*. Leipzig: Barth.) [128, 271, 283]
638. Katz, D., & Revesz, G. Experimentelle Studien zur vergleichenden Psychologie. Versüche mit Huhnern. *Z. ang. Psychol.*, 1921, 18, 307-20. [279]
639. Keller, M. Mediated generalization: the generalization of a conditioned galvanic skin response established to a pictured object. *Amer. J. Psychol.*, 1943, 56, 438-48. [703-4]
640. Kellogg, W. N. An experimental comparison of psychophysical methods. *Arch. Psychol.*, 1929, 17, No. 106, 1-86. [58]
641. Kellogg, W. N. An experimental evaluation of equality judgements in psychophysics. *Arch. Psychol.*, 1930, 17, No. 112. [49, 50]
642. Kellogg, W. N. The time of judgment in psychometric measures. *Amer. J. Psychol.*, 1931, 43, 65-86. [51]
643. Kellogg, W. N. Is 'spinal conditioning' conditioning? Reply to 'A comment.' *J. exp. Psychol.*, 1947, 37, 264-5. [480]
644. Kellogg, W. N., Deese, J., Pronko, N. H., & Feinberg, M. An attempt to condition the chronic spinal dog. *J. exp. Psychol.*, 1947, 37, 99-117. [480]
645. Kellogg, W. N., Scott, V. B., Davis, R. C., & Wolf, I. S. Is movement necessary for learning? *J. comp. Psychol.*, 1940, 29, 43-74. [491]

646. Kellogg, W. N., & Walker, E. L. An analysis of the bilateral transfer of conditioning in dogs, in terms of the frequency, amplitude and latency of the responses. *J. gen. Psychol.*, 1938, 18, 253-65. [327]

Kellogg, W. N. (*See* No. 247, 1071)

647. Kemp, E. H., & Coppée, G. The latency of electric responses in the auditory tracts of the brain stem. *Amer. J. Physiol.*, 1936, 116, 91-2. [103]
648. Kemp, E. H., Coppée, G. E., & Robinson, E. H. Electric responses of the brain stem to unilateral auditory stimulation. *Amer. J. Physiol.*, 1937, 120, 304-15. [103, 110]

Kemp, E. H. (*See* No. 241, 387)

649. Kendler, H. H. The influence of a sub-goal on maze behavior. *J. comp. Psychol.*, 1943, 36, 67-73. [498]
650. Kendler, H. H. The influence of simultaneous hunger and thirst drives upon the learning of two opposed spatial responses of the white rat. *J. exp. Psychol.*, 1946, 36, 212-20. [418]
651. Kendler, H. H. An investigation of latent learning in a T-maze. *J. comp. physiol. Psychol.*, 1947a, 40, 265-70. [419]
652. Kendler, H. H. A comparison of learning under motivated and satiated conditions in the white rat. *J. exp. Psychol.*, 1947b, 37, 545-9. [421]
653. Kendler, H. H., & Gasser, W. P. Variables in spatial learning: I. Number of reinforcements during training. *J. comp. physiol. Psychol.*, 1948, 41, 178-87. [456]
654. Kendler, H. H., & Mencher, H. C. The ability of rats to learn the location of food when motivated by thirst—an experimental reply to Leeper. *J. exp. Psychol.*, 1948, 38, 82-8. [419-20, 421]
655. Kendler, H. H., & Underwood, B. J. The role of reward in conditioning theory. *Psychol. Rev.*, 1948, 55, 209-15. [463]
656. Kennelly, T. W. The role of similarity in retroactive inhibition. *Arch. Psychol., N. Y.*, 1941, 37, No. 260. [530-31]
657. Kent, G. H., & Rosanoff, A. J. A study of association in insanity. *Amer. J. Insanity*, 1910, 67, 37-96. [708, 709, 710, 722, 723]

Kepler [248]

658. Kientzle, M. J. Properties of learning curves under varied distributions of practice. *J. exp. Psychol.*, 1946, 36, 187-211. [506-7]
659. Kimble, G. A., & Horenstein, B. R. Reminiscence in motor learning as a function of length of interpolated rest. *J. exp. Psychol.*, 1948, 38, 239-44. [507, 510-11]

Klee, J. B. (*See* No. 787, 788, 789)

660. Kleitman, N., & Crisler, G. A quantitative study of a salivary conditioned reflex. *Amer. J. Physiol.*, 1927, 80, 311-26. [492]
661. Klüver, H. An experimental study of the eidetic type. *Genet. Psychol. Monogr.*, 1926, 1, No. 2, 69-230. [641]
662. Klüver, H. Fragmentary eidetic imagery. *Psychol. Rev.*, 1930, 37, 441-58. [641]
663. Klüver, H. *Behavior mechanisms in monkeys*. Chicago: Univ. of Chicago Press, 1933. [445, 446]
664. Klüver, H. Visual functions after removal of the occipital lobes. *J. Psychol.*, 1941, 11, 23-45. [484]

Klüver, H. [444]

Konorski, J. (*See* No. 856)

665. Knox, G. W. Investigations of flicker and fusion: I. The effect of practice, under the influence of various attitudes, on the CFF. *J. gen. Psychol.*, 1945a, 33, 121-9. [146]
666. Knox, G. W. Investigations of flicker and fusion: II. The effect of the stimulus pattern on the CFF. *J. gen. Psychol.*, 1945b, 33, 131-7. [146, 219]
667. Knox, G. W. Investigations of flicker and fusion: III. The effect of auditory stimulation on the visual CFF. *J. gen. Psychol.*, 1945c, 33, 139-43. [146]
668. Knox, G. W. Investigations of flicker and fusion: IV. The effect of auditory flicker on the pronouncedness of visual flicker. *J. gen. Psychol.*, 1945d, 33, 145-54. [146]
669. Koch, H. L. The influence of some affective factors upon recall. *J. gen. Psychol.*, 1930, 4, 171-90. [572]

Koenig, W. (*See* No. 323)

670. Koester, T., & Schoenfeld, W. N. The effect of context upon judgments of pitch differences. *J. exp. Psychol.,* 1946, **36**, 417-30. [56, 121]
671. Koffka, K. Some problems of space perception. In *Psychologies of* 1930. Worcester: Clark Univ. Press, 1930. Pp. 161-87. [248, 255-8]
672. Koffka, K. *Principles of gestalt psychology.* New York: Harcourt, Brace, 1935. [55, 200-204, 216-19, 235, 256-7, 283, 551-4, 556, 566, 588, 592, 605, 606]
673. Köhler, W. Aus der Anthropoidenstation auf Teneriffa. IV. Nachweis einfacher strukturfunktionen beim Schimpansen und beim Haushuhn: Über eine neue Methode zur Untersuchung des bunten Farbensystems. *Abh. preuss. Akad. Wiss.,* Berlin, 1918, 1-101. [279, 445, 446]
674. Köhler, W. Zur Theorie des Sukzessivvergleichs und der Zeitfehler. *Psychol. Forsch.,* 1923, **4**, 115-75. [55]
675. Köhler, W. *The mentality of apes.* New York: Harcourt, Brace, 1925. [603-10, 611, 612, 613, 615, 620, 622, 627, 659]
676. Köhler, W. *Gestalt psychology.* New York: Liveright, 1929. [606]
677. Köhler, W. Some tasks of gestalt psychology. In *Psychologies of* 1930. Worcester: Clark Univ. Press, 1930. [202]
678. Köhler, W. The place of value in a world of facts. New York: Liveright, 1938. [200]
679. Köhler, W. *Dynamics in psychology.* New York: Liveright, 1940. [200, 201, 202, 206, 207, 219, 221, 222, 236, 248]

Köhler, W. [194, 209, 444, 551, 625]

680. Köhler, W., & Emery, D. A. Figural after-effects in the third dimension of visual space. *Amer. J. Psychol.,* 1947, **60**, 159-201. [240-41]
681. Köhler, W., & Wallach, H. Figural after-effects. *Proc. Amer. phil. Soc.,* 1944, **88**, 269-357. [201, 236-43]
682. Kohn, M. Satiation of hunger from food injected directly into the stomach versus food ingested by mouth. *J. comp. physiol. Psychol.,* 1951, **44**, 412-22. [440]
683. König, A. Über 'Blaublindheit.' Sitzungsber. Akad. Wissensch., Berlin, 1897. [176]
684. König, A., & Dieterici, C. Die Grundempfindungen in normalen und anomalen Farbensystemen und ihre Intensitälsverteilung im Spectrum. *Z. Psychol.,* 1892, **4**, 241. [170, 171]
685. Korte, A. Kinematoscopische Untersuchungen. *Z. Psychol.,* 1915, **72**, 193-206. [244]
686. Kotliarevsky, L. I. Cardio-vascular conditioned reflexes to direct and to verbal stimuli (trans. from Russian title). *Psychol. Abstracts,* 1935, **13**, No. 4046. [701]
687. Krakauer, D., & Dallenbach, K. M. Gustatory adaptation to sweet, sour, and bitter. *Amer. J. Psychol.,* 1937, **49**, 469-75. [81]

Krakauer, D. (*See* No. 1)

688. Krechevsky, I. 'Hypotheses' in rats. *Psychol. Rev.,* 1932, **39**, 516-32. [445, 446]
689. Krechevsky, I. Hereditary nature of 'hypotheses.' *J. comp. Psychol.,* 1933, **16**, 99-116. [445]
690. Krechevsky, I. Brain mechanisms and variability: I. Variability within a means-end-readiness. *J. comp. Psychol.,* 1937a, **23**, 121-38. [489]
691. Krechevsky, I. Brain mechanisms and variability: II. Variability where no learning is involved. *J. comp. Psychol.,* 1937b, **23**, 139-63. [489]
692. Krechevsky, I. A note concerning 'the nature of discrimination learning in animals.' *Psychol. Rev.,* 1937c, **44**, 97-104. [445, 446]
693. Krechevsky, I. A study of the continuity of the problem-solving process. *Psychol. Rev.,* 1938a, **45**, 107-33. [447, 450]
694. Krechevsky, I. An experimental investigation of the principle of proximity in the visual perception of the rat. *J. exp. Psychol.,* 1938b, **22**, 497-523. [211, 449-50]

Krechevsky, I. (*See* No. 263, 1144)

695. Kreezer, G., & Dallenbach, K. M. Learning the relation of opposition. *Amer. J. Psychol.,* 1929, **41**, 432-41. [625]
696. Krueger, W. C. F. The effect of overlearning on retention. *J. exp. Psychol.,* 1929, **12**, 71-8. [556]
697. Kryter, K. D., & Ades, H. W. Studies on the function of the higher acoustic nervous centers in the cat. *Amer. J. Psychol.,* 1943, **56**, 501-36. [110, 478, 479, 481]

Kryter, K. D. (*See* No. 748)

698. Kuenne, M. R. Experimental investigation of the relation of language to transposition behavior in young children. *J. exp. Psychol.*, 1946, **36**, 471-90. [446, 454]

Kühne, W. [147]

699. Kuo, Z. Y. Genesis of the cat's responses toward the rat. *J. comp. Psychol.*, 1930, **11**, 1-36. [308]
700. Ladd-Franklin, C. *Colour and colour theories.* New York: Harcourt, Brace, 1929. [136, 173-5, 177]

Lambert [248]

Lamoreaux, R. R. (*See* No. 874, 875)

Lane, C. E. (*See* No. 1206)

Lang, E. S. (*See* No. 146)

701. Langfeld, H. S. Note on a case of chromaesthesia. *Psychol. Bull.*, 1914, **11**, 113-14. [642]
702. Lanier, L. H. An experimental study of cutaneous innervation. *Proc. Ass. Res. nerv. ment. Dis.*, 1935, **15**, 437-56. [11]
703. Lasareff, P. Studien über das Weber-Fechner'sche Gesetz. Einfluss der Grösse des Gesichtsfeldes auf den Schwellenwert der Gesichtsempfindung. *Arch. ges. Physiol.* (Pflüger), 1911, **142**, 235-40. [162]
704. Lasareff, P. Theorie ionique de l'excitation des tissus vivants. *Coll. Monogr. scient. étrang*, 1928. [24, 78]
705. Lashley, K. S. The accuracy of movement in the absence of excitation from the moving organ. *Amer. J. Physiol.*, 1917, **43**, 169-94. [401]
706. Lashley, K. S. Cerebral function in learning. *Psychobiol.*, 1920, **2**, 55-136. [482, 486]
707. Lashley, K. S. Studies of cerebral function in learning: IV. Vicarious function after destruction of the visual areas. *Amer. J. Physiol.*, 1922, **59**, 44-71. [482]
708. Lashley, K. S. Studies of cerebral function in learning: V. The retention of motor habits after destruction of the so-called motor areas in primates. *Arch. Neur. & Psychiat.*, 1924, **12**, 249-76. [458]
709. Lashley, K. S. Studies of cerebral function in learning: VII. The relation between cerebral mass, learning, and retention. *J. comp. Neurol.*, 1926, **41**, 1-58. [482]
710. Lashley, K. S. *Brain mechanisms and intelligence.* Chicago: Univ. Chicago Press, 1929. [482, 486-8]
711. Lashley, K. S. The mechanism of vision: II. The influence of cerebral lesions upon the threshold of discrimination for brightness in the rat. *J. genet. Psychol.*, 1930, **37**, 461-80. [483]
712. Lashley, K. S. Integrative functions of the cerebral cortex. *Physiol. Revs.*, 1933, **13**, 1-43. [477, 478, 482]
713. Lashley, K. S. Studies of cerebral function in learning: XI. The behavior of the rat in latch box situations. *Comp. Psychol. Monogr.*, 1935a, **11**, No. 52, 5-42. [486]
714. Lashley, K. S. Studies of cerebral function in learning: XII. Nervous structures concerned in the acquisition and retention of habits based on reactions to light. *Comp. Psychol. Monogr.*, 1935b, **11**, No. 52, 43-79. [482]
715. Lashley, K. S. An examination of the 'continuity theory' as applied to discrimination learning. *J. gen. Psychol.*, 1942, **26**, 241-65. [444, 448-9, 451]
716. Lashley, K. S. Studies of cerebral function in learning: XII. Loss of the maze habit after occipital lesion in blind rats. *J. comp. Neurol.*, 1943, **79**, 431-62. [489]

Lashley, K. S. [398, 446, 482-9]

717. Lashley, K. S., & Ball, J. Spinal conduction and kinesthetic sensitivity in the maze habit. *J. comp. Psychol.*, 1929, **9**, 71-105. [458]
718. Lashley, K. S., & Frank, M. The mechanism of vision: X. Postoperative disturbances of habits based on detail vision in the rat after lesions in the cerebral visual areas. *J. comp. Psychol.*, 1934, **17**, 355-91. [483]
719. Lashley, K. S., & Russell, J. T. The mechanism of vision: XI. A preliminary test of innate organization. *J. genet. Psychol.*, 1934, **45**, 136-44. [226]
720. Lashley, K. S., & Wade, M. The Pavlovian theory of generalization. *Psychol. Rev.*, 1946, **53**, 72-87. [444-5, 449, 450]
721. Lashley, K. S., & Wiley, L. E. Studies of cerebral function in learning: IX. Mass action in relation to the number of elements in the problem to be learned. *J. comp. Neurol.*, 1933, **57**, 3-55. [487]

722. Latif, I. The physiological basis of linguistic development and of the ontogeny of meaning. *Psychol. Rev.*, 1934, **41**, 55-85. [690]

723. Lauenstein, O. Ansatz zu einer physiologischen Theorie des Vergleichs und der Zeitfehler. *Psychol. Forsch.*, 1933, **17**, 130-77. [55, 56]

724. Laurens, H., & Hamilton, W. F. The sensibility of the eye to differences in wave-length. *Amer. J. Physiol.*, 1923, **65**, 547-68. [144, 172]

725. Lawrence, D. H. Acquired distinctiveness of cues: I. Transfer between discriminations on the basis of familiarity with the stimulus. *J. exp. Psychol.*, 1949, **39**, 770-84. [422, 451]

726. Lawrence, D. H. Acquired distinctiveness of cues: II. Selective association in a constant stimulus situation. *J. exp. Psychol.*, 1950, **40**, 175-88. [211, 422, 451-3, 454]

727. Lawrence, D. H., & Miller, N. E. A positive relationship between reinforcement and resistance to extinction produced by removing a source of confusion from a technique that had produced the opposite results. *J. exp. Psychol.*, 1947, **37**, 494-509. [427]

Learned, B. W. (*See* No. 1271)

728. Leavitt, H. J., & Schlosberg, H. The retention of verbal and of motor skills. *J. exp. Psychol.*, 1944, **34**, 404-17. [562]

Lee, H. (*See* No. 350)

729. Leeper, R. A study of a neglected portion of the field of learning—the development of sensory organization. *J. genet. Psychol.*, 1935*a*, **46**, 41-75. [227]

730. Leeper, R. The role of motivation in learning: A study of the phenomenon of differential motivational control of the utilization of habits. *J. genet. Psychol.*, 1935*b*, **46**, 3-40. [418]

731. Leeper, R. Dr. Hull's Principles of Behavior. *J. genet. Psychol.*, 1944, **65**, 3-52. [209]

732. Leeper, R. The experiments by Spence and Lippitt and by Kendler on the sign-gestalt theory of learning. *J. exp. Psychol.*, 1948, **38**, 102-6. [419]

Leeper, R. (*See* No. 1197)

Leibnitz, G. W. [43]

733. Lepley, W. M. Serial reactions considered as conditioned reactions. *Psychol. Monogr.*, 1934, **46**, No. 205. [516]

734. Leuba, C. J. A preliminary analysis of the nature and effects of incentives. *Psychol. Rev.*, 1930, **37**, 429-40. [652]

735. Levine, H. A., & Dallenbach, K. M. Adaptation of cold spots under continuous and intermittent stimulation. *Amer. J. Psychol.*, 1936, **48**, 490-97. [80]

736. Levine, J. M., & Murphy, G. The learning and forgetting of controversial material. *J. abnorm. soc. Psychol.*, 1943, **38**, 507-17. [580]

737. Levine, R., Chein, I., & Murphy, G. The relation of the intensity of a need to the amount of perceptual distortion: a preliminary report. *J. Psychol.*, 1942, **13**, 283-93. [286]

Levy, I. (*See* No. 279)

738. Lewin, K. *A dynamic theory of personality.* (Trans. by D. K. Adams & K. E. Zener.) New York: McGraw-Hill, 1935. [385, 605]

739. Lewin, K. *Principles of topological psychology.* New York: McGraw-Hill, 1936. [385, 551, 605, 607, 611, 612]

740. Lewis, D., & Reger, S. N. An experimental study of the role of tympanic membrane and ossicles in the hearing of certain subjective tones. *J. Acous. Soc. Amer.*, 1933, **5**, 153-8. [124]

741. Lewis, H. B. An experimental study of the role of the ego in work: I. The role of the ego in cooperative work. *J. exp. Psychol.*, 1944, **34**, 113-26. [585-7]

742. Lewis, H. B., & Franklin, M. An experimental study of the role of the ego in work: II. The significance of task-orientation in work. *J. exp. Psychol.*, 1944, **34**, 195-215. [585-7]

743. Lewis, T. *The blood vessels of the skin and their responses.* London: Shaw & Sons, 1927. [15, 16]

744. Lewis, T. *Pain.* New York: Macmillan, 1942. [11]

745. Liberman, A. M. The effect of interpolated activity on spontaneous recovery from experimental extinction. *J. exp. Psychol.*, 1944, **34**, 282-301. [343, 347-8, 349]

746. Liberman, A. M. The effect of differential extinction on spontaneous recovery. *J. exp. Psychol.*, 1948, **38**, 722-33. [348]

747. Licklider, J. C. R. An electrical investigation of frequency localization in the auditory cortex of the cat. Doctor's dissertation, Univ. of Rochester, 1942. [111]

748. Licklider, J. C. R., & Kryter, K. D. Frequency localization in the auditory cortex of the monkey. *Fed. Proc. Amer. Soc. exp. Biol.*, 1942, **1**, No. 1, Part II, 51. Abstract. [111]

Liddell, E. G. T. (*See* No. 208)

749. Liddell, H. S. The conditioned reflex. In Moss, *Comparative psychology*. New York: Prentice-Hall, 1942. Ch. 8. [317, 318, 320, 398]
750. Light, J. S., & Gantt, W. H. Essential part of reflex arc for establishment of conditioned reflex. Formation of conditioned reflex after exclusion of motor peripheral end. *J. comp. Psychol.*, 1936, **21**, 19-36. [491, 492]

Lindemann [224]

751. Linke, P. Die Stroboskopischen Täuschungen und das Problem des Sehens von Bewegungen. *Psychol. Stud.*, 1907, **3**, 393-545. [248]
752. Lipman, E. A. Comparative exploration of the auditory cortex in the dog by conditioning and electrical methods. *Psychol. Bull.*, 1940, **37**, 497. Abstract. [111]

Lipman, E. A. (*See* No. 119)

Lippitt, R. (*See* No. 1067, 1069)

Livingston, J. R. (*See* No. 551)

753. Locke, N. M. Color constancy in the rhesus monkey and in man. *Arch. Psychol., N. Y.*, 1935, No. 193. [279]
754. Locke, N. M. A comparative study of size constancy. *J. genet. Psychol.*, 1937, **51**, 255-65. [279]
755. Lorente de Nó, R. Anatomy of the eighth nerve. The central projection of the nerve endings of the internal ear. *Laryngoscope*, 1933, **43**, 1-38. [92]
756. Lorente de Nó, R. Analysis of the activity of the chains of internuncial neurons. *J. Neurophysiol.*, 1938, **1**, 207-44. [196, 209]
757. Lorge, I. Influence of regularly interpolated time intervals upon subsequent learning. *Teach. Coll. Contr. Educ.*, 1930, No. 438. [506]
758. Loucks, R. B. Efficiency of the rat's motor cortex in delayed alternation. *J. comp. Neurol.*, 1931, **53**, 511-67. [657, 664, 665]
759. Loucks, R. B. Preliminary report of a technique for stimulation or destruction of tissues beneath the integument and the establishing of conditioned reactions with faradization of the cerebral cortex. *J. comp. Psychol.*, 1934, **16**, 439-44. [490]
760. Loucks, R. B. The experimental delimitation of neural structures essential for learning: The attempt to condition striped muscle responses with faradization of the sigmoid gyri. *J. Psychol.*, 1935, **1**, 5-44. [491]
761. Loucks, R. B. Studies of neural structures essential for learning: II. The conditioning of salivary and striped muscle responses to faradization of cortical sensory elements, and the action of sleep upon such mechanisms. *J. comp. Psychol.*, 1938, **25**, 315-32. [490]
762. Loucks, R. B., & Gantt, W. H. The conditioning of striped muscle responses based upon faradic stimulation of dorsal roots and dorsal columns of the spinal cord. *J. comp. Psychol.*, 1938, **25**, 415-26. [490]
763. Low, F. N. The development of peripheral visual acuity during the process of dark adaptation. *Amer. J. Physiol.*, 1946, **146**, 622-9. [160]

Lowell, F. (*See* No. 1258)

Lowy, K. (*See* No. 230)

764. Lucas, K. *The conduction of the nervous impulse*. Revised by E. D. Adrian. London: Longmans, Green, 1917. [66]
765. Luchins, A. S. Mechanization in problem solving: The effect of Einstellung. *Psychol. Monogr.*, 1942, **54**, No. 248. [622, 635-6]
766. Luckhardt, A. B., & Carlson, A. J. Contributions to the physiology of the stomach: XVII. On the chemical control of the gastric hunger mechanism. *Amer. J. Physiol.*, 1915, **36**, 37-46. [433]

Lufkin, H. M. (*See* No. 56)

767. Luh, C. W. The conditions of retention. *Psychol. Monogr.*, 1922, **31**, No. 142. [554, 557-8]
768. Lumley, F. H. Anticipation as a factor in serial and maze learning. *J. exp. Psychol.*, 1932, **15**, 331-42. [502]
769. Lumsdaine, A. A. Conditioned eyelid responses as mediating generalized finger reactions. *Psychol. Bull.*, 1939, **36**, 650. [462]

Lurie, M. H. (*See* No. 241, 242, 1087)

770. Lynch, C. A. The memory values of certain alleged emotionally toned words. *J. exp. Psychol.,* 1932, **15,** 298-315. [572]
771. Lyon, D. O. The relation of length of material to time taken for learning and the optimum distribution of time. *J. educ. Psychol.,* 1914, **5,** 1-9, 85-91, 155-63. [509, 513, 562, 669]
772. Lyon, D. O. *Memory and the learning process.* Baltimore: Warwick and York, 1917. [513]
773. Lythgoe, R. J. The absorption spectra of visual purple and of indicator yellow. *J. Physiol.,* 1937, **89,** 331-58. [148]
774. Lythgoe, R. J. The mechanism of dark adaptation: a critical résumé. *Brit. J. Ophthal.,* 1940, **24,** 21-43. [148]

MacCorquodale, K. (*See* No. 840)

775. MacDonald, A. The effect of adaptation to the unconditioned stimulus upon the formation of conditioned avoidance responses. *J. exp. Psychol.,* 1946, **36,** 1-12. [322]
776. MacDonald, M. K. An experimental study of Henning's system of olfactory qualities. *Amer. J. Psychol.,* 1922, **33,** 535-54. [28]
777. MacDuff, M. M. The effect on retention of varying degrees of motivation during learning in rats. *J. comp. Psychol.,* 1946, **39,** 207-40. [335]
778. MacFarlane, D. A. The role of kinesthesis in maze learning. *Univ. Calif. Publ. in Psychol.,* 1930, **4,** 277-305. [458]
779. MacLeod, R. B. An experimental investigation of brightness constancy. *Arch. Psychol.,* 1932, No. 135. [282]

MacMillan, Z. L. (*See* No. 311)

780. Magoun, H. W., & Rhines, R. Spasticity, the stretch-reflex and extrapyramidal systems. *Amer. Lect. Series,* 1948, No. 9. Springfield, Ill.: Charles C. Thomas. [493]
781. Maier, N. R. F. Reasoning in white rats. *Comp. Psychol. Monogr.,* 1929, **6,** No. 29. [616-17]
782. Maier, N. R. F. Reasoning in humans: I. On direction. *J. comp. Psychol.,* 1930, **10,** 115-43. [628-9]
783. Maier, N. R. F. Reasoning in humans: II. The solution of a problem and its appearance in consciousness. *J. comp. Psychol.,* 1931, **12,** 181-94. [632-3, 637]
784. Maier, N. R. F. The effect of cerebral destruction on reasoning and learning in rats. *J. comp. Neurol.,* 1932, **54,** 45-75. [616-17, 662]
785. Maier, N. R. F. Reasoning in humans: III. The mechanisms of equivalent stimuli and of reasoning. *J. exp. Psychol.,* 1945, **35,** 349-60. [629-30, 632]
786. Maier, N. R. F. *Frustration, the study of behavior without a goal.* New York: McGraw-Hill, 1949. [454-5]
787. Maier, N. R. F., Glaser, N. M., & Klee, J. B. Studies of abnormal behavior in the rat: III. The development of behavior fixations through frustration. *J. exp. Psychol.,* 1940, **26,** 521-46. [454-5]
788. Maier, N. R. F., & Klee, J. B. Studies of abnormal behavior in the rat: VII. The permanent nature of abnormal fixations and their relation to convulsive tendencies. *J. exp. Psychol.,* 1941, **29,** 380-89. [454-5]
789. Maier, N. R. F., & Klee, J. B. Studies of abnormal behavior in the rat: XVII. Guidance versus trial and error in the alteration of habits and fixations. *J. Psychol.,* 1945, **19,** 133-63. [454-5]
790. Maier, N. R. F., & Schneirla, T. C. Mechanisms in conditioning. *Psychol. Rev.,* 1942, **49,** 117-33. [323-4, 462-5, 470]

Malamud, H. R. (*See* No. 626)

791. Malinowski, B. The problem of learning in primitive languages. Supplement in Ogden, C. K., & Richards, I. A., *The meaning of meaning.* New York: Harcourt, Brace, 1938. [680]
792. Melmo, R. B. Interference factors in delayed response in monkeys after removal of frontal lobes. *J. Neurophysiol.,* 1942, **5,** 295-308. [664-5]

Mandelbaum, J. (*See* No. 467)

793. Mann, M. B. Studies in language behavior: III. The quantitative differentiation of samples of written language. *Psychol. Monogr.,* 1944, **56,** No. 2, 41-74. [719]
794. Marbe, K. *Experimentell-psychologische Untersuchungen über das Urteil.* Leipzig: Engelmann, 1901. [647]

Marbe, K. (*See* No. 1125)

795. Marchetti, P. V. Time-errors in judgments of visual extents. *J. exp. Psychol.,* 1942, **30,** 257-61. [56]

796. Marcuse, F. L., & Moore, A. U. Tantrum behavior in the pig. *J. comp. Psychol.*, 1944, **37**, 235-41. [317]

Marcuse, F. L. (*See* No. 859)

Margaria, R. (*See* No. 388)

797. Marks, M. R. Some phenomena attendant on long fixation. *Amer. J. Psychol.*, 1949, **62**, 392-8. [236]

798. Marquis, D. G. Effects of removal of the visual cortex in mammals with observations on the retention of light discrimination in dogs. *Res. Publ. Ass. nerv. ment. Dis.*, 1934, **13**, 558-92. [484]

799. Marquis, D. G. The neurology of learning. In Moss, *Comparative psychology*. New York: Prentice-Hall, 1942. Ch. 7. [477]

800. Marquis, D. G., & Hilgard, E. R. Conditioned lid responses to light in dogs after removal of the visual cortex. *J. comp. Psychol.*, 1936, **22**, 157-78. [478, 479]

801. Marquis, D. G., & Porter, J. M. Differential characteristics of conditioned eyelid responses established in reflex and voluntary reinforcement. *J. exp. Psychol.*, 1939, **24**, 347-65. [317]

Marquis, D. G. (*See* No. 497, 498, 499)

802. Marrow, A. J. Goal tensions and recall: I, II. *J. gen. Psychol.*, 1938, **19**, 3-35, 37-64. [582]

803. Marshall, W. H., & Talbot, S. A. Recent evidence for neural mechanisms in vision leading to a general theory of sensory acuity. In H. Klüver (ed.), *Visual mechanisms.* Lancaster, Pa.: Cattell, 1942. Pp. 117-64. [164, 196-7, 199, 214, 229, 237-43, 244, 252, 259]

Marshall, W. H. (*See* No. 1107)

804. Martin, A. A study of types of word-association in dementia praecox and manic-depressives. *J. gen. Psychol.*, 1945, **33**, 257-64. [725]

805. Martin, L. J., & Müller, G. E. *Zur Analyse der Unterschiedsempfindlichkeit.* Leipzig: Barth, 1899. [54]

806. Martin, T. M., & Pickford, R. W. The effect of veiling glare on apparent size relations. *Brit. J. Psychol.*, 1938, **29**, 92-103. [262]

807. Martius, G. Über die scheinbare Grösse der Gegenstände und ihre Beziehung zur Grösse der Netzhautbilder. *Phil. Stud.*, 1889, **5**, 601-17. [275, 278]

808. Marx, M. H. The effects of cumulative training upon retroactive inhibition and transfer. *Comp. Psychol. Monogr.*, 1944, **18**, No. 2. [522, 597]

809. Matheson, E. A study of problem solving behavior in pre-school children. *Child Develpm.*, 1931, **2**, 242-62. [622]

Mathews, M. (*See* No. 312)

810. Matthews, B. H. C. The response of a muscle spindle during active contraction of a muscle. *J. Physiol.*, 1931, **72**, 153-74. [30, 70]

Matthews, R. (*See* No. 9, 10)

811. Max, L. W. An experimental study of the motor theory of consciousness: III. Action-current responses in deaf-mutes during sleep, sensory stimulation, and dreams. *J. comp. Psychol.*, 1935, **19**, 469-86. [649-51, 697, 700]

812. Max, L. W. An experimental study of the motor theory of consciousness: IV. Action-current responses in the deaf during awakening, kinaesthetic imagery, and abstract thinking. *J. comp. Psychol.*, 1937, **24**, 301-44. [649-51, 697, 700]

813. May, M. A. Experimentally acquired drives. *J. exp. Psychol.*, 1948, **38**, 66-77. [441]

McAuliffe, D. R. (*See* No. 245)

814. McCarthy, D. Language development. In C. Murchison (ed.), *Handbook of child psychology.* Worcester: Clark Univ. Press, 1933. [684, 690]

815. McCarthy, D. Language development in children. In L. Carmichael (ed.), *Manual of child psychology.* New York: Wiley, 1946. Pp. 476-581. [684, 690]

816. McClelland, D. C. Studies in serial verbal discrimination learning: I. Reminiscence with two speeds of pair presentation. *J. exp. Psychol.*, 1942a, **31**, 44-56. [509, 512, 518]

817. McClelland, D. C. Studies in serial verbal discrimination learning: II. Retention of responses to right and wrong words in a transfer situation. *J. exp. Psychol.*, 1942b, **31**, 149-62. [518]

818. McClelland, D. C. Studies in serial verbal discrimination learning: IV. Habit reversal after two degrees of learning. *J. exp. Psychol.*, 1943a, **33**, 457-70. [518]

819. McClelland, D. C. Factors influencing the time error in judgments of visual extent. *J. exp. Psychol.*, 1943*b*, 33, 81-95. [55-7]
820. McClelland, D. C., & Atkinson, J. W. The projective expression of needs: I. The effect of different intensities of the hunger drive on perception. *J. Psychol.*, 1948, 25, 205-22. [286-7]
821. McCord, F. The delayed reaction and memory in rats: I. Length of delay. *J. comp. Psychol.*, 1939, 27, 1-37. [656, 657, 665]

McCraven, V. G. (*See* No. 147)

822. McCulloch, T. C., & Pratt, J. C. A study of the pre-solution period in weight discrimination by white rats. *J. comp. Psychol.*, 1934, 18, 271-90. [447, 450]

McCulloch, W. S. (*See* No. 94)

McCutchan, K. (*See* No. 89, 90)

McDonald, W. T. (*See* No. 831)

823. McDougall, W. The sensations excited by a single momentary stimulation of the eye. *Brit. J. Psychol.*, 1904, 1, 78-113. [185]
824. McGarvey, H. R. Anchoring effects in the absolute judgment of verbal materials. *Arch. Psychol., N. Y.*, 1943, No. 281. [50]
825. McGeoch, G. O. The intelligence quotient as a factor in the whole-part problem. *J. exp. Psychol.*, 1931, 14, 333-58. [540]
826. McGeoch, G. O. The conditions of reminiscence. *Amer. J. Psychol.*, 1935, 47, 65-89. [566]

McGeoch, G. O. (*See* No. 832)

827. McGeoch, J. A. Studies in retroactive inhibition: II. Relationships between temporal point of interpolation, length of interval, and amount of retroactive inhibition. *J. gen. Psychol.*, 1933, 9, 44-57. [535]
828. McGeoch, J. A. The direction and extent of intraserial associations at recall. *Amer. J. Psychol.*, 1936*a*, 48, 221-45. [502, 519]
829. McGeoch, J. A. Studies in retroactive inhibition: VII. Retroactive inhibition as a function of the length and frequency of presentation of the interpolated lists. *J. exp. Psychol.*, 1936*b*, 19, 674-93. [597]
830. McGeoch, J. A. *The psychology of human learning.* New York: Longmans, Green, 1942. [507, 509, 518-19, 521, 524, 531, 540, 543, 562]
831. McGeoch, J. A., & McDonald, W. T. Meaningful relation and retroactive inhibition. *Amer. J. Psychol.*, 1931, 43, 579-88. [527, 528, 530]
832. McGeoch, J. A., & McGeoch, G. O. Studies in retroactive inhibition: X. The influence of similarity of meaning between lists of paired associates. *J. exp. Psychol.*, 1937, 21, 320-29. [528, 530]
833. McGeoch, J. A., & Melton, A. W. The comparative retention values of maze habits and of nonsense syllables. *J. exp. Psychol.*, 1929, 12, 392-414. [561]
834. McGeoch, J. A., & Underwood, B. J. Tests of the two-factor theory of retroactive inhibition. *J. exp. Psychol.*, 1943, 32, 1-16. [545]

McGeoch, J. A. (*See* No. 838)

835. McGinnies, E. Emotionality and perceptual defense. *Psychol. Rev.*, 1949, 56, 244-51. [293-4]

McGinnies, E. (*See* No. 944)

McGlone, B. (*See* No. 55, 56)

836. McGourty, M. C. Serial position effects in learning as a function of interfering. Master's thesis, State Univ. of Iowa, 1940. [504]
837. McKinney, F. Quantitative and qualitative essential elements of transfer. *J. exp. Psychol.*, 1933, 16, 854-64. [525]
838. McKinney, F., & McGeoch, J. A. The character and extent of transfer in retroactive inhibition: disparate serial lists. *Amer. J. Psychol.*, 1935, 47, 409-23. [543]
839. McTeer, W. Changes in grip tension following electric shock in mirror tracing. *J. exp. Psychol.*, 1933, 16, 735-42. [652]
840. Meehl, P. E., & MacCorquodale, K. A further study of latent learning in the T-maze. *J. comp. physiol. Psychol.*, 1948, 41, 372-96. [421]
841. Melton, A. W. The effect of rest pauses on the acquisition of the pursuitmeter habit. *Psychol. Bull.*, 1941, 38, 719. (Abstract.) [510]
842. Melton, A. W., & Irwin, J. McQ. The influence of degree of interpolated learning on retroactive inhibition and the overt transfer of specific responses. *Amer. J. Psychol.*, 1940, 53, 173-203. [538-9, 545]
843. Melton, A. W., & Stone, G. R. The retention of serial lists of adjectives over

short time-intervals with varying rates of presentation. *J. exp. Psychol.,* 1942, 30, 295-310. [511, 512-13]

844. Melton, A. W., & Von Lackum, W. J. Retroactive and proactive inhibition in retention: evidence for a two-factor theory of retroactive inhibition. *Amer. J. Psychol.,* 1941, 54, 157-73. [522, 527, 528]

Melton, A. W. (*See* No. 833)

845. Meltzer, H. Individual differences in forgetting pleasant and unpleasant experiences. *J. educ. Psychol.,* 1930, 21, 399-409. [572]

Mencher, H. C. (*See* No. 654)

846. Menzies, R. The comparative memory values of pleasant, unpleasant and indifferent experiences. *J. exp. Psychol.,* 1935, 18, 267-79. [572]

Mettler, F. A. (*See* No. 4, 231, 368)

847. Metzner, C. A. The influence of preliminary stimulation upon human eyelid responses during conditioning and during subsequent heteromodal generalization. *Summ. doct. Diss. Univ. Wis.,* 1942, 7, 152-4. [701]

848. Meyer, M. An introduction to the mechanics of the inner ear. *Univ. Missouri Studies, Sci. Ser.,* 1907, 2, No. 1. [97]

849. Miles, W. R. Movement interpretations of the silhouette of a revolving fan. *Amer. J. Psychol.,* 1931, 43, 392-405. [221]

850. Miles, W. R. Red goggles for producing dark adaptation. *Fed. Proc. Amer. Soc. exp. Biol.,* 1943, 2, 109-15. [160]

Miles, W. R. (*See* No. 60)

851. Miller, G. A., & Garner, W. R. Effect of random presentation on the psychometric function: implications for a quantal theory of discrimination. *Amer. J. Psychol.,* 1944, 57, 451-67. [64]

Miller, G. A. (*See* No. 341, 342)

852. Miller, M. Changes in the response to electric shock produced by varying muscular conditions. *J. exp. Psychol.,* 1926, 9, 26-44. [652]

853. Miller, N. E. A reply to 'sign-Gestalt or conditioned reflex?' *Psychol. Rev.,* 1935, 42, 280-92. [441, 469]

854. Miller, N. E. Studies of fear as an acquirable drive: I. Fear as motivation and fear-reduction as reinforcement in the learning of new responses. *J. exp. Psychol.,* 1948, 38, 89-101. [404, 408, 442, 443]

855. Miller, N. E., & Dollard, J. *Social learning and imitation.* New Haven: Yale Univ. Press, 1941. [341, 433]

Miller, N. E. (*See* No. 256, 727, 876)

Miller, R. H. (*See* No. 315)

856. Miller, S., & Konorski, J. Sur une forme particulière des reflexes conditionnels. *C. R. Soc. Biol., Paris,* 1928, 99, 1155-57. [302]

Milton, J. [622]

857. Minami, H., & Dallenbach, K. M. The effect of activity upon learning and retention in the cockroach. *Amer. J. Psychol.,* 1946, 59, 1-58. [535, 536, 542, 547, 595, 596-7]

Minium, E. (*See* No. 1145)

Mintz, E. U. (*See* No. 468)

858. Mitchell, M. B. Retroactive inhibition and hypnosis. *J. gen. Psychol.,* 1932, 7, 343-59. [575-7]

859. Moore, A. U., & Marcuse, F. L. Salivary, cardiac and motor indices of conditioning in two sows. *J. comp. Psychol.,* 1945, 38, 1-16. [317]

Moore, A. U. (*See* No. 796)

860. Morgan, C. Lloyd. *An introduction to comparative psychology.* London: W. Scott, 1894. [603-4]

861. Morgan, C. Lloyd. *Animal behavior.* London: E. Arnold, 1900. [655, 656]

862. Morgan, C. T. *Physiological psychology.* New York: McGraw-Hill, 1943. [12, 14, 22, 119, 433]

863. Morgan, C. T., & Wood, W. M. Cortical localization of symbolic processes in the rat: II. Effect of cortical lesions upon delayed alternation in the rat. *J. Neurophysiol.,* 1943, 6, 173-80. [662]

Morgan, C. T. (*See* No. 243, 282, 1078, 1080)

864. Morris, C. W. Foundations of the theory of signs. *Int. Encyl. unif. Sci.*, 1938, No. 1, 63-75. [692]
865. Morris, C. W. *Signs, language and behavior*. New York: Prentice-Hall, 1946. [691, 693-6]
866. Mosier, C. L. A psychometric study of meaning. *J. soc. Psychol.*, 1941, 13, 123-40. [712]
867. Mote, F. A. The effect of different amounts of reinforcement upon the acquisition and extinction of a simple running response. *J. exp. Psychol.*, 1944, 34, 216-26. [425, 427]

Mote, F. A. (*See* No. 384)

868. Mowrer, O. H. Preparatory set (expectance)—a determinant in motivation and learning. *Psychol. Rev.*, 1938, 45, 62-91. [700]
869. Mowrer, O. H. Anxiety-reduction and learning. *J. exp. Psychol.*, 1940, 27, 497-516. [442]
870. Mowrer, O. H. On the dual nature of learning—a reinterpretation of 'conditioning' and 'problem solving.' *Harv. educ. Rev.*, 1947, 17, 102-48. [323-4, 465-9, 470, 472, 473]
871. Mowrer, O. H. *Learning theory and personality dynamics*. New York: The Ronald Press, 1950. [323-4, 409, 455, 465-9, 599, 681]
872. Mowrer, O. H., & Jones, H. M. Extinction and behavior variability as functions of effortfulness of task. *J. exp. Psychol.*, 1943, 33, 369-86. [337, 340, 341]
873. Mowrer, O. H., & Jones, H. M. Habit strength as a function of pattern of reinforcement. *J. exp. Psychol.*, 1945, 35, 293-311. [426]
874. Mowrer, O. H., & Lamoreaux, R. R. Avoidance conditioning and sign duration—a study of secondary motivation and reward. *Psychol. Monogr.*, 1942, 54, No. 5. [398, 467-8]
875. Mowrer, O. H., & Lamoreaux, R. R. Fear as an intervening variable in avoidance conditioning. *J. comp. physiol. Psychol.*, 1946, 39, 29-50. [408-9]
876. Mowrer, O. H., & Miller, N. E. A multi-purpose learning demonstration apparatus. *J. exp. Psychol.*, 1942, 31, 163-70. [393-4, 408]
877. Mowrer, O. H., & Ullman, A. D. Time as a determinant in integrative learning. *Psychol. Rev.*, 1945, 52, 61-90. [406]
878. Mowrer, O. H., & Viek, P. An experimental analogue of fear from a sense of helplessness. *J. abnorm. soc. Psychol.*, 1948, 43, 193-200. [407-8]

Mowrer, O. H. (*See* No. 361)

Mueller, C. G. (*See* No. 470)

879. Muenzinger, K. F. Plasticity and mechanization of the problem box habit in guinea pigs. *J. comp. Psychol.*, 1928, 8, 45-69. [389]
880. Muenzinger, K. F. Vicarious trial and error at a point of choice: I. A general survey of its relation to learning efficiency. *J. genet. Psychol.*, 1938, 53, 75-86. [307]

Müller, E. A. (*See* No. 585)

881. Müller, G. E., & Pilzecker, A. Experimentelle Beiträge zur Lehre vom Gedächtniss. *Z. Psychol.*, Ergbd., 1900, 1, 1-288. [509, 515, 535, 542]
882. Müller, G. E., & Schumann, F. Über die psychologischen Grundlagen der Vergleichung gehobene Gewichte. *Arch. ges. Physiol.*, 1889, 45, 37-112. [56]
883. Müller, G. E., & Schumann, F. Experimentelle Beiträge zur Untersuchung des Gedächtnisses. *Z. Psychol.*, 1894, 6, 81-190. [525]

Müller, G. E. (*See* No. 805)

Müller, Johannes [5, 12, 95]

Munson, W. A. (*See* No. 308)

884. Murphy, G. Types of word-association in dementia-praecox, manic-depressives, and normal persons. *Am. J. Psychiat.*, 1923, 79, 539-72. [725]

Murphy, G. (*See* No. 736, 737, 1007)

885. Murray, E. Binocular fusion and the locus of 'yellow.' *Amer. J. Psychol.*, 1939, 52, 117-21. [177]
886. Nadel, A. B. A qualitative analysis of behavior following cerebral lesions diagnosed as primarily affecting the frontal lobes. *Arch. Psychol.*, N. Y., 1938, No. 224. [676]
887. Nafe, J. P. The pressure, pain, and temperature senses. In C. Murchison (ed.), *A handbook of general experimental psychology*. Worcester: Clark Univ. Press, 1934. Pp. 1037-87. [14, 15, 16, 17]
888. Nafe, J. P. Dr. W. L. Jenkins on the vascular theory of warmth and cold. *Amer. J. Psychol.*, 1938, 51, 763-9. [16]

889. Nafe, J. P., & Wagoner, K. S. I. The experiences of warmth, cold and heat. *J. Psychol.*, 1936*a*, 2, 421-31. [16]
890. Nafe, J. P., & Wagoner, K. S. II. The sensitivity of the cornea of the eye. *J. Psychol.*, 1936*b*., 2, 433-9. [16]
891. Nafe, J. P., & Wagoner, K. S. V. The effect of thermal stimulation upon dilation and constriction of the blood vessels of the skin of a contralateral hand. *J. Psychol.*, 1936*c*, 2, 461-77. [17]
892. Nagge, J. W. An experimental test of the theory of associative interference. *J. exp. Psychol.*, 1935, 18, 663-82. [574-6, 594]
893. Needham, J. G. Rate of presentation in the method of single stimuli. *Amer. J. Psychol.*, 1935*a*, 47, 275-84. [55]
894. Needham, J. G. The effect of the time interval upon the time-error at different intensity levels. *J. exp. Psychol.*, 1935*b*, 18, 530-43. [56]
895. Neff, W. D. The effects of partial section of the auditory nerve. *J. comp. physiol. Psychol.*, 1947, 40, 203-15. [106-10, 114, 127]

Neff, W. D. (*See* No. 1229)

896. Neff, W. S. A critical investigation of the visual apprehension of movement. *Amer. J. Psychol.*, 1936, 48, 1-42. [244, 248]
897. Neuhaus, W. Experimentelle Untersuchung der Scheinbewegung. *Arch. ges. Psychol.*, 1930, 75, 315-458. [244]
898. Newman, E. B., Stevens, S. S., & Davis, H. Factors in the production of aural harmonics and combination tones. *J. acoust. Soc. Amer.*, 1937, 9, 107-18. [123]
899. Newman, E. B., Volkmann, J., & Stevens, S. S. On the method of bisection and its relation to a loudness scale. *Amer. J. Psychol.*, 1937, 49, 134-7. [115]

Newman, E. B. (*See* No. 1092)

Newton, Sir Isaac [142, 169]

900. Nicolai, F. Experimentelle Untersuchung über das Haften von Gesichtsein-drücken und dessen zeitlichen Verlauf. *Arch. ges. Psychol.*, 1922, 42, 132-49. [566]

Nissen, H. W. (*See* No. 272, 579)

901. Nowlis, H. H. The influence of success and failure on the resumption of an interrupted task. *J. exp. Psychol.*, 1941, 28, 304-25. [584]

Nygaard, J. [405]

902. O'Connor, J. *Born that way*. Baltimore: Williams & Wilkins, 1928. [709-10]

O'Connor, J. (*See* No. 315)

903. O'Connor, V. J. Recency or effect? A critical analysis of Guthrie's theory of learning. *Harvard educ. Rev.*, 1946, 16, 194-206. [371]
904. Odbert, H. S., Karwoski, T. F., & Eckerson, A. B. Studies in synesthetic think-ing: I. Musical and verbal association of color and mood. *J. gen. Psychol.*, 1942, 26, 153-73. [645-6]

Odbert, H. S. (*See* No. 631, 632)

Ogle, K. N. (*See* No. 23)

O'Kelly, L. I. (*See* No. 488, 489)

O'Leary, J. L. (*See* No. 84)

905. Orbison, W. D. Shape as a function of the vector field. *Amer. J. Psychol.*, 1939, 52, 31-45. [203, 206]
906. Orbison, W. D. The relative efficiency of whole and part methods of learning paired-associates as a function of the length of list. Doctor's dissertation, Yale Univ., 1944. [540-42]
907. Osgood, C. E. Meaningful similarity and interference in learning. *J. exp. Psychol.*, 1946, 36, 277-301. [526-7, 531, 533, 545, 707-8]
908. Osgood, C. E. An investigation into the causes of retroactive interference. *J. exp. Psychol.*, 1948, 38, 132-54. [533, 539, 545, 546-7, 707-8]
909. Osgood, C. E. The similarity paradox in human learning: A resolution. *Psychol. Rev.*, 1949, 56, 132-43. [532-3]
910. Osgood, C. E. Can Tolman's theory of learning handle avoidance training? *Psychol. Rev.*, 1950, 57, 133-7. [430]
911. Osgood, C. E. The nature and measurement of meaning. *Psychol. Bull.*, 1952, 49, 197-237. [713-14]
912. Osgood, C. E., & Heyer, A. W. A new interpretation of figural after-effects. *Psychol. Rev.*, 1951, 59, 98-118. [236-43]

Osgood, C. E. (*See* No. 524, 632, 1006, 1075)

913. Østerberg, G. Topography of the layer of rods and cones in the human retina. *Acta Ophthal. Suppl.,* 1935, **61**, 1-102. [136, 137]
914. Ovsiankina, M. Die Wiederaufnahme unterbrochener Handlungen. *Psychol. Forsch.,* 1928, **11**, 302-79. [584]
915. Paget, R. A. The origin of language. *Science,* 1944, **99**, 14-15. [683]

Patt, M. (*See* No. 469)

Park, O. G. (*See* No. 413)

916. Passey, G. E. The influence of intensity of unconditioned stimulus upon acquisition of a conditioned response. *J. exp. Psychol.,* 1948, **38**, 420-28. [316, 317]
917. Pavlov, I. P. *Conditioned reflexes.* (Trans. by G. V. Anrep.) London: Oxford Univ. Press, 1927. [309-14, 316, 317, 321, 322, 342, 343, 346, 347, 354, 373, 430, 462, 467-8, 477]
918. Pechstein, L. A. Whole vs. part methods in motor learning. A comparative study. *Psychol. Monogr.,* 1917, **23**, No. 2. [540]
919. Pechstein, L. A. Massed vs. distributed effort in learning. *J. educ. Psychol.,* 1921, **12**, 92-7. [540]
920. Pechstein, L. A., & Brown, F. D. An experimental analysis of the alleged criteria of insight learning. *J. educ. Psychol.,* 1939, **30**, 38-52. [610]
921. Peckham, R. H. An objective study of binocular vision. *Amer. J. Psychol.,* 1936, **48**, 474-9. [256]

Peirce, C. S. [693]

922. Penfield, W., & Rasmussen, T. *The cerebral cortex of man; a clinical study of localization of function.* New York: Macmillan, 1950. [34, 488]
923. Perin, C. T. Behavior potentiality as a joint function of the amount of training and degree of hunger at the time of extinction. *J. exp. Psychol.,* 1942, **30**, 93-113. [378-9]
924. Perin, C. T. A quantitative investigation of the delay-of-reinforcement gradient. *J. exp. Psychol.,* 1943*a*, **32**, 37-51. [324, 436-7]
925. Perin, C. T. The effect of delayed reinforcement upon the differentiation of bar responses in white rats. *J. exp. Psychol.,* 1943*b*, **32**, 95-109. [324, 436-7]
926. Perkins, C. C. The relation of secondary reward to gradients of reinforcement. *J. exp. Psychol.,* 1947, **37**, 377-92. [324, 437]

Perkins, D. T. (*See* No. 550)

927. Perkins, F. T. Symmetry in visual recall. *Amer. J. Psychol.,* 1932, **44**, 473-90. [589-90]
928. Perky, C. W. An experimental study of imagination. *Amer. J. Psychol.,* 1910, **21**, 422-52. [640-41, 654]

Peskin, J. C. (*See* No. 469)

929. Peter, R. Untersuchungen über die Beziehungen zwischen primären und sekundären Faktoren der Teifenwahrnehmung. *Arch. ges. Psychol.,* 1915, **34**, 515-64. [268]
930. Pfaffman, C. Gustatory afferent impulses. *J. cell. comp. Physiol.,* 1941, **17**, 243-58. [22]
931. Philip, B. R., & Fisichelli, V. R. Effect of speed of rotation and complexity of pattern on the reversals of apparent movement in Lissajon figures. *Amer. J. Psychol.,* 1945, **58**, 530-39. [221]

Philleo, C. (*See* No. 194)

932. Piaget, J. *Judgment and reasoning in the child.* New York: Harcourt, Brace, 1928. [673, 681]
933. Piaget, J. *The child's conception of physical causality.* New York: Harcourt, Brace, 1930. [673-81]
934. Piaget, J. *The moral judgment of the child.* New York: Harcourt, Brace, 1932. [673, 681]
935. Pickford, R. W. Binocular colour combinations. *Nature, Lond.,* 1947, **159**, 268-9. [177]

Pickford, R. W. (*See* No. 806)

936. Pieron, H. Les temps de réaction au chroma en excitation isolumineuse. *C. R. Soc. Biol., Paris,* 1932, **3**, 380-82. [184, 185]
937. Pillsbury, W. B., & Rausch, H. L. An extension of the Köhler-Restorff inhibition phenomenon. *Amer. J. Psychol.,* 1943, **56**, 293-8. [504]

Pilzecker, A. (*See* No. 881)

Plato [372, 640]

Polvogt, L. M. (*See* No. 215, 411)

938. Polyak, S. L. *The retina*. Chicago: Univ. Chicago Press, 1941. [134, 135, 167, 179, 180, 183, 259]

Poole, G. B. (*See* No. 1198)

939. Porter, J. M., Jr. Experimental extinction as a function of the interval between successive non-reinforced elicitations. *J. gen. Psychol.*, 1939, 21, 109-34. [345, 406]

Porter, J. M. (*See* No. 627, 801)

Post, D. (*See* No. 1209)

940. Postman, L. The time-error in auditory perception. *Amer. J. Psychol.*, 1946, 59, 193-219. [121]

941. Postman, L. The history and present status of the law of effect. *Psychol. Bull.*, 1947, 6, 489-563. [372, 381]

942. Postman, L., & Alper, T. G. Retroactive inhibition as a function of the time of interpolation of the inhibitor between learning and recall. *Amer. J. Psychol.*, 1946, 59, 439-49. [535-6, 537]

943. Postman, L., & Bruner, J. S. Perception under stress. *Psychol. Rev.*, 1948, 55, 314-24. [287-8]

944. Postman, L., Bruner, J. S., & McGinnies, E. Personal values as selective factors in perception. *J. abnorm. soc. Psychol.*, 1948, 43, 142-54. [292-4]

Postman, L. (*See* No. 134, 606)

945. Pratt, C. C. Time-errors in the method of single stimuli. *J. exp. Psychol.*, 1933, 16, 798-814. [56]

Pratt, J. C. (*See* No. 822)

946. Prentice, W. C. H. Retroactive inhibition and the motivation of learning. *Amer. J. Psychol.*, 1943, 56, 283-92. [575, 576, 578-9, 584-5]

947. Prentice, W. C. H. New observations of 'binocular yellow.' *J. exp. Psychol.*, 1948, 38, 284-8. [177]

948. Priest, I. G., & Brickwedde, F. G. The minimum perceptible colorimetric purity as a function of dominant wave length with sunlight as neutral standard. *J. opt. Soc. Amer.*, 1926, 13; Natl. Bur. Standards, RP1099. [145, 172]

Pronko, N. H. (*See* No. 644)

Ptolemy [248]

949. Purdy, D. M. The structure of the visual world: I. Space-perception and the perception of wholes. *Psychol. Rev.*, 1935a, 42, 399-424. [249]

950. Purdy, D. M. The structure of the visual world: II. The action of motor impulses on sensory excitations. *Psychol. Rev.*, 1935b, 42, 528-36. [249]

951. Purdy, D. M. The structure of the visual world: III. The tendency towards simplification of the visual field. *Psychol. Rev.*, 1936, 43, 59-82. [224, 249]

Purkinje, J. E. [32]

Quigley, J. P. (*See* No. 1108)

Radner, M. (*See* No. 362)

952. Rapaport, D. *Emotions and memory*. Baltimore: Williams & Wilkins, 1942. [570]

953. Rapaport, D. Emotions and memory. *Psychol. Rev.*, 1943, 50, 234-43. [570]

Rasmussen, T. (*See* No. 922)

954. Ratliff, M. M. The varying function of affectively toned olfactory, visual and auditory cues in recall. *Amer. J. Psychol.*, 1938, 51, 695-701. [572]

Raush, H. L. (*See* No. 937)

Rawdon-Smith, A. F. (*See* No. 423, 424)

955. Ray, W. S. Proactive inhibition: A function of time-interval. *Amer. J. Psychol.*, 1945, 58, 519-29. [534-5]

956. Razran, G. H. S. Salivating and thinking in different languages. *J. Psychol.*, 1936, 1, 145-51. [700]

957. Razran, G. H. S. A quantitative study of meaning by a conditioned salivary technique (semantic conditioning). *Science*, 1939a, 90, 89-90. [702, 706]

958. Razran, G. H. S. The nature of the extinctive process. *Psychol. Rev.*, 1939b, 46, 264-97. [337]

959. Razran, G. H. S. Studies in configurational conditioning: V. Generalization and transposition. *J. genet. Psychol.*, 1940, **56**, 3-11. [537]
960. Razran, G. H. S. Stimulus generalization of conditioned responses. *Psychol. Bull.*, 1949, **46**, 337-65. [355, 444]
961. Reed, H. B. Factors influencing the learning and retention of concepts: I. The influence of set. *J. exp. Psychol.*, 1946a, **36**, 71-87. [668-70, 678]
962. Reed, H. B. The learning and retention of concepts: II. The influence of length of series. III. The origin of concepts. *J. exp. Psychol.*, 1946b, **36**, 166-79. [668-70, 678]
963. Reed, H. B. The learning and retention of concepts: IV. The influence of complexity of the stimuli. *J. exp. Psychol.*, 1946c, **36**, 252-61. [668-70, 678]

Reger, S. N. (*See* No. 740)

964. Reid, C. Mechanism of muscular fatigue. *Quart. J. exper. Physiol.*, 1928, **19**, 17-42. [338-40]
965. Restorff, H. von. I. Über die Wirkung von Bereichsbildungen im Spurenfeld. (In W. Köhler & H. von Restorff, Analyse von Vorgängen im Spurenfeld.) *Psychol. Forsch.*, 1933, **18**, 299-342. [504, 567]

Revesz, G. (*See* No. 638)

966. Reynolds, B. The acquisition of a trace conditioned response as a function of the magnitude of the stimulus trace. *J. exp. Psychol.*, 1945a, **35**, 15-30. [315, 335]
967. Reynolds, B. Extinction of trace conditioned responses as a function of the spacing of trials during the acquisition and extinction series. *J. exp. Psychol.*, 1945b, **35**, 81-95. [337]
968. Reynolds, B. A repetition of the Blodgett experiment on 'latent learning.' *J. exp. Psychol.*, 1945c, **35**, 504-16. [415-16]
969. Reynolds, B. The relationship between the strength of a habit and the degree of drive present during acquisition. *J. exp. Psychol.*, 1949, **39**, 296-305. [335]

Rhines, R. (*See* No. 780)

970. Rich, G. J. A preliminary study of tonal volume. *J. exp. Psychol.*, 1916, **1**, 13-22. [125]
971. Rich, G. J. A study of tonal attributes. *Amer. J. Psychol.*, 1919, **30**, 121-64. [126]
972. Richardson, H. M. The growth of adaptive behavior in infants: an experimental study at seven age levels. *Genet. Psychol. Monogr.*, 1932, **12**, 195-359. [215, 622, 625]
973. Riesen, A. H. The development of visual perception in man and chimpanzee. *Science*, 1947, **106**, 107-8. [225, 226, 227]
974. Riess, B. F. Semantic conditioning involving the galvanic skin reflex. *J. exp. Psychol.*, 1940, **26**, 238-40. [702, 706]
975. Riess, B. F. Genetic changes in semantic conditioning. *J. exp. Psychol.*, 1946, **36**, 143-52. [702-3, 706]
976. Riesz, R. R. Differential intensity sensitivity of the ear for pure tones. *Phys. Rev.*, 1928, **31**, 867-75. [120, 122]
977. Riggs, L. A. Dark adaptation in the frog eye as determined by the electrical response of the retina. *J. cell. comp. Physiol.*, 1937, **9**, 491-510. [161]
978. Riggs, L. A., & Graham, C. H. Some aspects of light adaptation in a single photoreceptor unit. *J. cell. comp. Physiol.*, 1940, **16**, 15-23. [161]
979. Ritchie, B. F. Studies in spatial learning: III. Two paths to the same location and two paths to two different locations. *J. exp. Psychol.*, 1947, **37**, 25-38. [459]

Ritchie, B. F. (*See* No. 1146, 1147, 1148, 1149)

980. Roberts, W. H. The effect of delayed feeding on white rats in a problem cage. *J. genet. Psychol.*, 1930, **37**, 35-58. [371]

Robinson, E. H. (*See* No. 648)

981. Robinson, E. S. Some factors determining the degree of retroactive inhibition. *Psychol. Monogr.*, 1920, **28**, No. 128. [535]
982. Robinson, E. S. The similarity factor in retroaction. *Amer. J. Psychol.*, 1927, **39**, 297-312. [530-31]
983. Robinson, E. S., & Heron, W. T. Result of variations in length of memorized material. *J. exp. Psychol.*, 1922, **5**, 428-48. [513-14]

Roby, T. B. (*See* No. 1031)

Rogers, M. (*See* No. 148)

984. Rogers, R. C., & Bayroff, A. G. Response errors in conditioned discrimination. *J. comp. Psychol.,* 1943, **35**, 317-26. [323]
985. Rogers, S. The anchoring of absolute judgments. *Arch. Psychol., N. Y.,* 1941, No. 261. [50]
986. Rohrer, J. H. Experimental extinction as a function of the distribution of extinction trials and response strength. *J. exp. Psychol.,* 1947, **37**, 473-93. [337, 348]

Rosanoff, A. J. (*See* No. 657)

Rosenblueth, A. (*See* No. 163)

987. Rosenthal, B. G. Hypnotic recall of material learned under anxiety and non-anxiety producing conditions. *J. exp. Psychol.,* 1944, **34**, 369-89. [576-7]
988. Rosenzweig, S. Preferences in the repetition of successful and unsuccessful activities as a function of age and personality. *J. genet. Psychol.,* 1933, **42**, 423-40. [582]
989. Rosenzweig, S. An experimental study of 'repression' with special reference to need-persistive and ego-defensive reactions to frustration. *J. exp. Psychol.,* 1943, **32**, 64-74. [583-4]
990. Ross, R. T. Studies in the psychology of the theater. *Psychol. Rec.,* 1938, **2**, 127-90. [645-6]

Ross, R. T. (*See* No. 550)

991. Ross, S., & Harriman, A. E. A preliminary study of the Crocker-Henderson odor-classification system. *Amer. J. Psychol.,* 1949, **62**, 399-404. [28, 29]

Ross, S. (*See* No. 470)

992. Rothschild, H. Über den Einfluss der Gestalt auf das negative Nachbild ruhendervisueller Figuren. *Arch. Ophthalm.,* 1923, **112**, 1-24. [222-3]

Rouse, R. O. (*See* No. 551)

Rowell, M. M. (*See* No. 190)

993. Rubin, E. *Synsoplevede Figurer.* Kobenhavn: 1915. [218]
994. Rubin, E. *Visuell wahrgenommene Figuren.* Kobenhavn: 1921. [218]
995. Ruch, T. C. Cortical localization of somatic sensibility. The effect of precentral, postcentral and posterior parietal lesions upon the performance of monkeys trained to discriminate weights. *Res. Publ. Ass. nerv. ment. Dis.,* 1935, **15**, 289-330. [30]
996. Ruch, T. C., Fulton, J. F., & German, W. J. Sensory discrimination in monkey, chimpanzee and man after lesions of the parietal lobe. *Arch. Neurol. Psychiat., Chicago,* 1938, **39**, 919-37. [30]
997. Ruger, H. A. The psychology of efficiency: An experimental study of the process involved in the solution of mechanical puzzles and in the acquisition of skill in their manipulation. *Arch. Psychol., N. Y.,* 1910, **2**, No. 15. [610, 625-6]

Russell, J. T. (*See* No. 719)

998. Russell, R. W., & Hunter, W. S. The effects of inactivity produced by sodium amytal on the retention of the maze habit in the albino rat. *J. exp. Psychol.,* 1937, **20**, 426-36. [595]
999. Rutherford, W. The sense of hearing. *J. Anat. Physiol.,* 1886, **21**, 166-8. [97]
1000. Rylander, G. Personality changes after operations on the frontal lobes. *Acta Psychiat., Kbh.,* 1939, Suppl. 20. [676]

Saltz, E. (*See* No. 409)

1001. Saltzman, I. J. Maze learning in the absence of primary reinforcement: A study of secondary reinforcement. *J. comp. physiol. Psychol.,* 1949, **42**, 161-73. [442]
1002. Sander, F. Experimentelle Ergebnisse der Gestalt-psychologie. *Ber. ü. d.,* 10, *Kongr. exp. Psychol.,* Bonn, 1928, 23-88. [252]
1003. Sanders, F. K. Special senses, cutaneous sensation. *Annu. Rev. Physiol.,* 1947, **9**, 553-68. [10, 13]
1004. Sanford, R. H. The effects of abstinence from food upon imaginal processes: a preliminary experiment. *J. Psychol.,* 1936, **2**, 129-36. [286]
1005. Sanford, R. H. The effects of abstinence from food upon imaginal processes: a further experiment. *J. Psychol.,* 1937, **3**, 145-59. [286-7]
1006. Saul, E. V., & Osgood, C. E. Perceptual organization of materials as a factor influencing ease of learning and degree of retention. *J. exp. Psychol.,* 1950, **40**, 372-9. [568]

Saul, L. J. (*See* No. 242, 244)

Schacter, J. (*See* No. 633)

1007. Schafer, R., & Murphy, G. The role of autism in a visual figure-ground relationship. *J. exp. Psychol.*, 1943, 32, 335-43. [221, 287]

Scheerer, M. (*See* No. 376)

1008. Schlosberg, H. Conditioned responses in the white rat. *J. genet. Psychol.*, 1934, 45, 303-35. [466-7, 469]
1009. Schlosberg, H. II. Conditioned responses based upon shock to the foreleg. *J. genet. Psychol.*, 1936, 49, 107-38. [466-7, 469]
1010. Schlosberg, H., & Katz, A. Double alternation lever-pressing in the white rat. *Amer. J. Psychol.*, 1943, 56, 274-82. [658]

Schlosberg, H. (*See* No. 85, 622, 728)

Schneider, D. E. (*See* No. 398, 399)

1011. Schneirla, T. C. Learning and orientation in ants. *Comp. Psychol. Monogr.*, 1929, 6, No. 30, 1-143. [499]

Schneirla, T. C. (*See* No. 790)

Schoenfeld, W. N. (*See* No. 670)

Schooler, K. (*See* No. 170)

1012. Schriever, H. Über den Wärmeschmerz. *Z. Biol.*, 1926, 85, 67-84. [17]
1013. Schumann, F. Beiträge zur Analyse der Gesichtswahrnehmungen. *Z. Psychol.*, 1900, 23, 1-32; 24, 1-33. [212-213]

Schumann, F. (*See* No. 882, 883)

1014. Scott, T. C., & Henninger, L. L. The relation between length and difficulty in motor learning; a comparison with verbal learning. *J. exp. Psychol.*, 1933, 16, 657-78. [513-14]

Scott, V. B. (*See* No. 645)

1015. Sears, R. R. Initiation of the repression sequence by experienced failure. *J. exp. Psychol.*, 1937, 20, 570-80. [573-4]
1016. Sears, R. R. Survey of objective studies of psychoanalytic concepts. *Soc. Sci. Res. Coun. Bull.*, 1943, No. 51. [599]
1017. Sears, R. R., & Hovland, C. I. Experiments on motor conflict: II. Determination of mode of resolution by comparative strengths of conflicting responses. *J. exp. Psychol.*, 1941, 28, 280-86. [538, 539]

Sedgewick, C. H. W. (*See* No. 110)

1018. Seibert, L. C. A series of experiments on the learning of French vocabulary. *Johns Hopk. Univ. Stud. Educ.*, 1932, No. 18. [540]
1019. Seidenfeld, M. A. Time as a factor in the recognition of visually perceived figures. *Amer. J. Psychol.*, 1938, 51, 64-82. [590]

Seidenfeld, M. A. (*See* No. 571)

1020. Selz, O. *Zur Psychologie des produktiven Denkens und des Irrtums.* Bonn: Cohen, 1922. [627]
1021. Senden, M. von. *Raum- und Gestaltauffassung bei operierten Blindgeborenen vor und nach der Operation.* Leipzig: Barth, 1932. [225, 227, 399]
1022. Senders, V. L. The physiological basis of visual acuity. *Psychol. Bull.*, 1948, 45, 465-90. [164]
1023. Seward, G. H. Recognition time as a measure of confidence. *Arch. Psychol.*, 1928, 16, No. 99, 1-54. [557]
1024. Seward, J. P. An experimental study of Guthrie's theory of reinforcement. *J. exp. Psychol.*, 1942, 30, 247-56. [370]
1025. Seward, J. P. Reinforcement in terms of association. *Psychol. Rev.*, 1943, 50, 187-202. [469-70]
1026. Seward, J. P. A theoretical derivation of latent learning. *Psychol. Rev.*, 1947, 54, 83-98. [469-70]
1027. Seward, J. P. Secondary reinforcement as tertiary motivation: a revision of Hull's revision. *Psychol. Rev.*, 1950, 57, 362-74. [432, 469-70]
1028. Sharp, A. A. An experimental test of Freud's doctrine of the relation of hedonic tone to memory revival. *J. exp. Psychol.*, 1938, 22, 395-418. [574]
1029. Sheffield, F. D. The role of meaningfulness of stimulus and response in verbal learning. Doctor's dissertation, Yale Univ., 1946. [562]
1030. Sheffield, F. D. Avoidance training and the contiguity principle. *J. comp. physiol. Psychol.*, 1948, 41, 165-77. [429, 430]

1031. Sheffield, F. D., & Roby, T. B. Reward value of a non-nutritive sweet taste. *J. comp. physiol. Psychol.*, 1950, **43**, 471-81. [439-40]

Sheffield, F. D. (*See* No. 607)

Sherrington, C. S. [488]

Sherrington, C. S. (*See* No. 208)

1032. Shipley, W. C. An apparent transfer of conditioning. *Psychol. Bull.*, 1933, **30**, 541. [461-2, 464]
1033. Shipley, W. C. The effect of a short rest pause on retention in rote series of different lengths. *J. gen. Psychol.*, 1939, **21**, 99-117. [511, 513]

Shipley, W. C. (*See* No. 1070)

1034. Shirley, M. *The first two years: III. Personality manifestations*. Minneapolis: Univ. of Minnesota Press, 1933. [687]
1035. Shower, E. G., & Biddulph, R. Differential pitch sensitivity of the ear. *J. acoust. Soc. Amer.*, 1931, **3**, 275-87. [121, 122]

Shurrager, H. C. (*See* No. 1039)

1036. Shurrager, P. S. A comment on 'an attempt to condition the chronic spinal dog.' *J. exp. Psychol.*, 1947, **37**, 261-3. [480]
1037. Shurrager, P. S., & Culler, E. A. Conditioning in the spinal dog. *J. exp. Psychol.*, 1940, **26**, 133-59. [480, 481]
1038. Shurrager, P. S., & Culler, E. A. Conditioned extinction of a reflex in the spinal dog. *J. exp. Psychol.*, 1941, **28**, 287-303. [480]
1039. Shurrager, P. S., & Shurrager, H. C. The rate of learning measured at a single synapse. *J. exp. Psychol.*, 1946, **36**, 347-54. [480]
1040. Siegel, P. S. Structure effects within a memory series. *J. exp. Psychol.*, 1943, **33**, 311-16. [567-8]
1041. Siegel, P. S. The role of absolute initial response in simple trial-and-error learning. *J. exp. Psychol.*, 1945, **35**, 199-205. [328]

Sievers, D. [514]

1042. Siipola, E. M. The relation of transfer to similarity in habit-structure. *J. exp. Psychol.*, 1941, **28**, 233-61. [526]
1043. Siipola, E. M., & Israel, H. E. Habit-interference as dependent upon stage of training. *Amer. J. Psychol.*, 1933, **45**, 205-27. [537]

Silverman, S. R. (*See* No. 245)

1044. Skinner, B. F. The verbal summator and a method for the study of latent speech. *J. Psychol.*, 1936, **2**, 71-107. [722, 725]
1045. Skinner, B. F. The distribution of associated words. *Psychol. Rec.*, 1937, **1**, 71-6. [722]
1046. Skinner, B. F. *The behavior of organisms. An experimental analysis*. New York: Appleton-Century-Crofts, 1938. [305-6, 307-9, 320]
1047. Sloan, L. L. Rate of dark adaptation and regional threshold gradient of the dark-adapted eye: physiologic and clinical studies. *Amer. J. Ophthal.*, 1947, **30**, 705-20. [136]

Smith, F. W. (*See* No. 243)

1048. Smith, K. R. The problem of stimulation deafness: II. Histological changes in the cochlea as a function of tonal frequency. *J. exp. Psychol.*, 1947, **37**, 304-17. [100, 102]
1049. Smith, K. R. Visual apparent movement in the absence of neural interaction. *Amer. J. Psychol.*, 1948, **61**, 73-8. [247, 259]

Smith, K. R. (*See* No. 1230)

1050. Smith, K. U., & Warkentin, J. The central neural organization of optic functions related to minimum visible acuity. *J. genet. Psychol.*, 1939, **55**, 177-95. [484]

Smith, K. U. (*See* No. 1248)

1051. Smith, S. The essential stimuli in stereoscopic depth perception. *J. exp. Psychol.*, 1946, **36**, 518-21. [270-71]
1052. Smith, S. A further reduction of sensory factors in stereoscopic depth perception. *J. exp. Psychol.*, 1949, **39**, 393-4. [270-71]
1053. Smith, W. W. *The measurement of emotion*. New York: Harcourt, Brace, 1922. [700]
1054. Smoke, K. L. An objective study of concept formation. *Psychol. Monogr.*, 1932, **42**, No. 191. [667-8]

1055. Smolenskaya, E. P. Verbal symbols of conditioned and differentiated stimuli. (Trans. from Russian.) *Na Putyakh k Izuch. rysshykh Form Neirodin*, 1934, 304-15. [701]

1056. Snoddy, G. *Evidence for two opposed processes in mental growth.* Lancaster: Science, 1935. [509]

1057. Snow, W. B. Change of pitch with loudness at low frequencies. *J. acoust. Soc. Amer.*, 1936, 8, 14-19. [120]

1058. Solomon, R. L. Latency of response as a measure of learning in a 'single-door' discrimination. *Amer. J. Psychol.*, 1943, 56, 422-32. [328]

1059. Solomon, R. L. Effort and extinction rate: A confirmation. *J. comp. physiol. Psychol.*, 1948, 41, 93-101. [337, 341]

Solomon, R. L. [469]

Solomon, R. L. (*See* No. 525, 526)

1060. Spence, K. W. The order of eliminating blinds in maze learning by the rat. *J. comp. Psychol.*, 1932, 14, 9-27. [499]

1061. Spence, K. W. The nature of discrimination learning in animals. *Psychol. Rev.*, 1936, 43, 427-49. [444, 446]

1062. Spence, K. W. The differential response in animals to stimuli varying within a single dimension. *Psychol. Rev.*, 1937, 44, 430-44. [445-6]

1063. Spence, K. W. Continuous versus non-continuous interpretations of discrimination learning. *Psychol. Rev.*, 1940, 47, 271-88. [447]

1064. Spence, K. W. The basis of solution by chimpanzees of the intermediate size problem. *J. exp. Psychol.*, 1942, 31, 257-71. [445]

1065. Spence, K. W. An experimental test of the continuity and non-continuity theories of discrimination learning. *J. exp. Psychol.*, 1945, 35, 253-66. [446, 448, 450]

1066. Spence, K. W. The role of secondary reinforcement in delayed reward learning. *Psychol. Rev.*, 1947, 54, 1-8. [432, 438]

1067. Spence, K. W., Bergmann, G., & Lippitt, R. A study of simple learning under irrelevant motivational reward conditions. *J. exp. Psychol.*, 1950, 40, 539-51. [420, 421, 422]

1068. Spence, K. W., & Grice, G. R. The role of final and sub-goals in distance discrimination by the white rat. *J. comp. Psychol.*, 1942, 34, 179-84. [498]

1069. Spence, K. W., & Lippitt, R. O. An experimental test of the sign-Gestalt theory of trial-and-error learning. *J. exp. Psychol.*, 1946, 36, 491-502. [419]

1070. Spence, K. W., & Shipley, W. C. The factors determining the difficulty of blind alleys in maze learning by the white rat. *J. comp. Psychol.*, 1934, 17, 423-36. [499]

Spence, K. W. (*See* No. 207)

Spencer, H. [373]

1071. Spooner, A., & Kellogg, W. N. The backward conditioning curve. *Amer. J. Psychol.*, 1947, 60, 321-34. [313-14]

Spotnitz, H. (*See* No. 280, 281)

1072. Sprow, A. J. Reactively homogeneous compound trial-and-error learning with distributed trials and terminal reinforcement. *J. exp. Psychol.*, 1947, 37, 197-213. [500]

1073. Stagner, R. The redintegration of pleasant and unpleasant experiences. *Amer. J. Psychol.*, 1931, 43, 463-8. [572]

1074. Stagner, R. Factors influencing the memory value of words in a series. *J. exp. Psychol.*, 1933, 16, 129-37. [504]

1075. Stagner, R., & Osgood, C. E. Impact of war on a nationalistic frame of reference: I. Changes in general approval and qualitative patterning of certain stereotypes. *J. soc. Psychol.*, 1946, 24, 187-215. [708, 713]

Stagner, R. (*See* No. 436)

1076. Steindler, O. *Die Farbenempfindlichkeit des normalen und farbenblinden Auges.* Wien: Holder, 1906. [144]

1077. Steinhardt, J. Intensity discrimination in the human eye: I. The relation of $\Delta I/I$ to intensity. *J. gen. Physiol.*, 1936, 20, 185-209. [162]

1078. Stellar, E., Morgan, C. T., & Yarosh, M. Cortical localization of symbolic processes in the rat. *J. comp. Psychol.*, 1942, 34, 107-26. [662-3]

1079. Stephens, J. M. The influence of symbolic punishment and reward upon strong and upon weak association. *J. gen. Psychol.*, 1941, 25, 177-85. [377]

1080. Stevens, S. S. The volume and intensity of tones. *Amer. J. Psychol.*, 1934a, 46, 397-408. [125]

1081. Stevens, S. S. The attributes of tones. *Proc. nat. Acad. Sci., Wash.*, 1934b, 20, 457-9. [125]

1082. Stevens, S. S. Tonal density. *J. exp. Psychol.*, 1934c, **17**, 585-92. [125]
1083. Stevens, S. S. The relation of pitch to intensity. *J. acoust. Soc. Amer.*, 1935, **6**, 150-54. [119]
1084. Stevens, S. S. On the problem of scales for the measurement of psychological magnitudes. *J. Unif. Sci.*, 1939, **9**, 94-9. [121]
1085. Stevens, S. S., & Davis, H. Psychophysiological acoustics: pitch and loudness. *J. acoust. Soc. Amer.*, 1936, **8**, 1-13. [93]
1086. Stevens, S. S., & Davis, H. *Hearing: Its psychology and physiology.* New York: Wiley, 1938. [60, 86, 96, 103, 106, 111, 115, 124, 126]
1087. Stevens, S. S., Davis, H., & Lurie, M. H. The localization of pitch perception on the basilar membrane. *J. gen. Psychol.*, 1935, **13**, 297-315. [101, 102, 114, 121]
1088. Stevens, S. S., & Egan, J. P. Diplacusis in 'normal' ears. (Abstract) *Psychol. Bull.*, 1941, **38**, 548. [112, 113]
1089. Stevens, S. S., Morgan, C. T., & Volkmann, J. Theory of the neural quantum in the discrimination of loudness and pitch. *Amer. J. Psychol.*, 1941, **54**, 315-35. [59-65]
1090. Stevens, S. S., & Volkmann, J. The quantum of sensory discrimination. *Science*, 1940a, **92**, 583-5. [64]
1091. Stevens, S. S., & Volkmann, J. The relation of pitch to frequency: A revised scale. *Amer. J. Psychol.*, 1940b, **53**, 329-53. [113]
1092. Stevens, S. S., Volkmann, J., & Newman, E. B. A scale for the measurement of the psychological magnitude, pitch. *J. acoust. Soc. Amer.*, 1937, **8**, 185-90. [111, 112]

Stevens, S. S. (*See* No. 105, 898, 899)

Stone, G. R. (*See* No. 843)

1093. Stone, L. J., & Dallenbach, K. M. Adaptation to the pain of radiant heat. *Amer. J. Psychol.*, 1934, **46**, 229-42. [14]
1094. Stone, L. J., & Dallenbach, K. M. The adaptation of areal pain. *Amer. J. Psychol.*, 1936, **48**, 117-25. [80]
1095. Stone, L. J., & Jenkins, W. L. Recent research in cutaneous sensitivity: I. Pain and temperature. *Psychol. Bull.*, 1940, **37**, 285-311. [13, 15]

Stone, L. J. (*See* No. 601)

1096. Storch, A. Erlebnisanalyse und Sprachwissenschaft. *Z. Psychol.*, 1924, **94**, 146-52. [676]
1097. Strange, J. R. Latent learning under conditions of high motivation. *J. comp. physiol. Psychol.*, 1950, **43**, 194-7. [423, 427]
1098. Strauss, H. H., & Uhlman, R. F. Adaptation of superficial pain. *Amer. J. Psychol.*, 1919, **30**, 422-4. [80, 81]
1099. Stricker, S. *Studien über die Sprachvorstellungen.* Wien, 1880. [641]
1100. Stroud, J. B. Apparatus for measuring muscular tensions. *J. exp. Psychol.*, 1931, **14**, 184-5. [652]

Stumpf, C. [125]

1101. Swenson, H. A. The relative influence of accommodation and convergence in the judgment of distance. *J. gen. Psychol.*, 1932, **7**, 360-80. [268-9]
1102. Switzer, St. C. A. Backward conditioning of the lid reflex. *J. exp. Psychol.*, 1930, **13**, 76-97. [313]
1103. Switzer, St. C. A. Disinhibition of the conditioned galvanic skin response. *J. gen. Psychol.*, 1933, **9**, 77-100. [338, 700]
1104. Switzer, St. C. A. Anticipatory and inhibitory characteristics of delayed conditioned reactions. *J. exp. Psychol.*, 1934, **17**, 603-20. [315, 338, 346]
1105. Switzer, St. C. A. The effect of caffeine on experimental extinction of conditioned reactions. *J. gen. Psychol.*, 1935a, **12**, 78-92. [338]
1106. Switzer, St. C. A. The influence of caffeine upon 'inhibition of delay.' *J. comp. Psychol.*, 1935b, **19**, 155-75. [338, 348]
1107. Talbot, S. A., & Marshall, W. H. Physiological studies on neural mechanisms of visual localization and discrimination. *Amer. J. Ophthal.*, 1941, **24**, 1255-64. [259]

Talbot, S. A. (*See* No. 803)

1108. Templeton, R. D., & Quigley, J. P. The action of insulin on motility of the gastro-intestinal tract. II. *Amer. J. Physiol.*, 1930, **91**, 467-74. [433]

Thompson, E. (*See* No. 528)

Thompson, M. E. (*See* No. 259)

1109. Thomson, G. H. A new point of view in the interpretation of threshold measurements in psychophysics. *Psychol. Rev.*, 1920, **27**, 300-307. [49]

1110. Thomson, R. H. An experimental study of memory as influenced by feeling tone. *J. exp. Psychol.,* 1930, **13**, 462-7. [572]

1111. Thorndike, E. L. Animal intelligence: An experimental study of the associative processes in animals. *Psychol. Rev., Monogr. Supplements,* 1898, **2**, No. 4 (whole No. 8). [304, 462, 610, 611, 612, 613, 659, 681)

1112. Thorndike, E. L. Animal intelligence. *Experimental Studies.* New York: Macmillan, 1911. [372-3, 380, 604, 611, 656]

1113. Thorndike, E. L., et al. *The fundamentals of learning.* New York: Teachers College, Columbia Univ., 1932*a*. [381]

1114. Thorndike, E. L. *A teachers' word book of the twenty thousand words found most frequently and widely in general reading for children and young people.* New York: Teachers College, Columbia Univ., 1932*b*. [717]

1115. Thorndike, E. L. An experimental study of rewards. *Teach. Coll. Contr. Educ.,* 1933*a*, No. 580. [377]

1116. Thorndike, E. L. A proof of the law of effect. *Science,* 1933*b*, **77**, 173-5. [377, 424]

1117. Thorndike, E. L. A theory of the action of the after-effects of a connection upon it. *Psychol. Rev.,* 1933*c*, **40**, 434-9. [382]

1118. Thorndike, E. L. *The Thorndike-Century senior dictionary.* New York: Appleton-Century-Crofts, 1941. [717]

1119. Thorndike, E. L. The origin of language. *Science,* 1943, **98**, 1-6. [683]

1120. Thorndike, E. L. Expectation. *Psychol. Rev.,* 1946, **53**, 277-81. [391]

1121. Thorndike, E. L., & Woodworth, R. S. The influence of improvement in one mental function upon the efficiency of other functions. (I) ; II. The estimation of magnitudes; III. Functions involving attention, observation and discrimination. *Psychol. Rev.,* 1901, **8**, 247-61, 384-95, 553-64. [524]

1122. Thorson, A. M. The relation of tongue movements to internal speech. *J. exp. Psychol.,* 1925, **8**, 1-32. [648-9]

1123. Thouless, R. H. Phenomenal regression to the real object. I. *Brit. J. Psychol.,* 1931, 21, 339-59; II. 22, 1-30. [274, 276, 278, 280, 283-5]

1124. Thouless, R. H. Individual differences in phenomenal regression. *Brit. J. Psychol.,* 1932, 22, 216-41. [278-9]

1125. Thumb, A., & Marbe, K. *Experimentelle Untersuchungen über die psychologischen Grundlagen der sprachlichen Analogiebildung.* Leipzig: W. Engelmann, 1901. [722]

1126. Thune, L. E., & Underwood, B. J. Retroactive inhibition as a function of degree of interpolated learning. *J. exp. Psychol.,* 1943, **32**, 185-200. [539, 545]

1127. Thurlow, W. R. Studies in auditory theory: II. The distribution of distortion in the inner ear. *J. exp. Psychol.,* 1943, **32**, 344-50. [120]

1128. Tilton, J. W. The effect of 'right' and 'wrong' upon the learning of nonsense syllables in multiple choice arrangement. *J. educ. Psychol.,* 1939, **30**, 95-115. [377]

1129. Tilton, J. W. Gradients of effect. *J. genet. Psychol.,* 1945, **66**, 3-19. [377]

1130. Tinklepaugh, O. An experimental study of representative factors in monkeys. *J. comp. Psychol.,* 1928, **8**, 197-236. [657, 681]

1131. Titchener, E. B. *Lectures on the experimental psychology of the thought processes.* New York: Macmillan, 1909. [646]

1132. Tolman, E. C. *Purposive behavior in animals and man.* New York: Appleton-Century-Crofts, 1932. [300, 307, 324, 382-3, 386, 387, 389, 392]

1133. Tolman, E. C. The acquisition of string-pulling by rats—conditioned response or sign-Gestalt? *Psychol. Rev.,* 1937, **44**, 195-211. [387, 388]

1134. Tolman, E. C. The determiners of behavior at a choice-point. *Psychol. Rev.,* 1938*a*, **45**, 1-41. [307, 384-5, 388]

1135. Tolman, E. C. The law of effect: A roundtable discussion. II. *Psychol. Rev.,* 1938*b*, **45**, 200-203. [415]

1136. Tolman, E. C. Prediction of vicarious trial-and-error by means of the schematic sow-bug. *Psychol. Rev.,* 1939, **46**, 318-36. [385]

1137. Tolman, E. C. Cognitive maps in rats and men. *Psychol. Rev.,* 1948, **55**, 189-208. [307, 389]

1138. Tolman, E. C. There is more than one kind of learning. *Psychol. Rev.,* 1949, **56**, 144-55. [324, 345, 386, 391, 421, 471-3]

Tolman, E. C. [286, 345, 346, 362, 382-92, 406, 410, 414, 417, 418, 419, 427, 455, 460, 465, 470, 693]

1139. Tolman, E. C., & Brunswik, E. The organism and the causal texture of the environment. *Psychol. Rev.,* 1935, **42**, 43-77. [387, 401]

1140. Tolman, E. C., & Gleitman, H. Studies in learning and motivation: I. Equal reinforcements in both end-boxes followed by shock in one end-box. *J. exp. Psychol.,* 1949, **39**, 810-19. [420, 421]

1141. Tolman, E. C., Hall, C. S., & Bretnall, E. P. A disproof of the law of effect and a substitution of the laws of emphasis, motivation and disruption. *J. exp. Psychol.*, 1932, **15**, 601-14. [424]

1142. Tolman, E. C., & Honzik, C. H. 'Insight' in rats. *Univ. Calif. Publ. Psychol.*, 1930a, **4**, 215-32. [618-20]

1143. Tolman, E. C., & Honzik, C. H. Introduction and removal of reward and maze performance in rats. *Univ. Calif. Publ. Psychol.*, 1930b, **4**, 257-75. [415]

1144. Tolman, E. C., & Krechevsky, I. Means-end readiness and hypothesis. A contribution to comparative psychology. *Psychol. Rev.*, 1933, **40**, 60-70. [306, 383]

1145. Tolman, E. C., & Minium, E. VTE in rats: overlearning and difficulty of discrimination. *J. comp. Psychol.*, 1942, **34**, 301-6. [307]

1146. Tolman, E. C., & Ritchie, B. F. Correlation between VTE's on a maze and on a visual discrimination apparatus. *J. comp. Psychol.*, 1943, **36**, 91-8. [307]

1147. Tolman, E. C., Ritchie, B. F., & Kalish, D. Studies in spatial learning: I. Orientation and the short-cut. *J. exp. Psychol.*, 1946a, **36**, 13-24. [391, 456-7]

1148. Tolman, E. C., Ritchie, B. F., & Kalish, D. Studies in spatial learning: II. Place learning versus response learning. *J. exp. Psychol.*, 1946b, **36**, 221-9. [458-9]

1149. Tolman, E. C., Ritchie, B. F., & Kalish, D. Studies in spatial learning: V. Response learning versus place learning by the non-correction method. *J. exp. Psychol.*, 1947, **37**, 285-92. [458]

1150. Traugott, N. N. The interrelations of immediate and symbolic projections in the process of the formation of conditioned inhibition. (Trans. from Russian title.) *Psychol. Abstracts*, 1934, **9**, No. 1166. [702, 706]

1151. Traugott, N. N., & Fadeyeva, V. K. The effect of difficult extinction of food-procuring conditioned reflexes upon the general and speech behavior of children. (Trans. from Russian title.) *Psychol. Abstracts*, 1934, **9**, No. 1167. [702]

1152. Travis, R. C. Length of the practice period and efficiency in motor learning. *J. exp. Psychol.*, 1939, **24**, 339-45. [507]

1153. Tresselt, M. E. Time errors in successive comparison of simple visual objects. *Amer. J. Psychol.*, 1944, **57**, 555-8. [57]

1154. Troland, L. T. The enigma of color vision. *Amer. J. physiol. Opt.*, 1921, **2**, 23-48. [169]

1155. Troland, L. T. *The fundamentals of human motivation.* New York: Van Nostrand, 1928. [381]

1156. Troland, L. T. The psychophysiology of auditory qualities and attributes. *J. gen. Psychol.*, 1929, **2**, 28-58. [97]

1157. Troland, L. T. *The principles of psycho-physiology,* Vol. 2. New York: Van Nostrand, 1930. [181, 195, 196]

1158. Troland, L. T. Vision I. Visual phenomena and their visual correlates. In C. Murchison (ed.), *Handbook of general experimental psychology.* Worcester: Clark Univ. Press, 1934. [157, 169]

1159. Tsang, Y. C. The functions of the visual areas of the cerebral cortex of the rat in the learning and retention of the maze. I. *Comp. Psychol. Monogr.*, 1934, **10**, No. 50. [489]

1160. Tsang, Y. C. The functions of the visual areas of the cerebral cortex of the rat in the learning and retention of the maze. II. *Comp. Psychol. Monogr.*, 1935, **12**. [489]

1161. Tunturi, A. R. Audio frequency localization in the acoustic cortex of the dog. *Amer. J. Physiol.*, 1944, **141**, 397-403. [111]

1162. Tunturi, A. R. Further afferent connections to the acoustic cortex of the dog. *Amer. J. Physiol.*, 1945, **144**, 389-94. [111]

1163. Tunturi, A. R. A study on the pathway from the medial geniculate body to the acoustic cortex in the dog. *Amer. J. Physiol.*, 1946, **147**, 311-19. [111]

1164. Turnbull, W. W. Pitch discrimination and tonal duration. *J. exp. Psychol.*, 1944, **34**, 302-16. [123]

1165. Twining, P. E. The relative importance of intervening activity and lapse of time in the production of forgetting. *J. exp. Psychol.*, 1940, **26**, 483-501. [523, 597]

Uhlman, R. F. (*See* No. 1098)

Ullman, A. D. (*See* No. 877)

1166. Underwood, B. J. The effect of successive interpolations on retroactive and proactive inhibition. *Psychol. Monogr.*, 1945, **59**, No. 3. [526, 535, 539, 545, 597-8]

Underwood, B. J. (*See* No. 655, 834, 1126)

1167. Upton, M. The auditory sensitivity of guinea pigs. *Amer. J. Psychol.*, 1929, 41, 412-21. [398]

Upton, M. (*See* No. 241)

1168. Van Ormer, E. B. Retention after intervals of sleep and waking. *Arch. Psychol., N. Y.*, 1932, 21, No. 137. [554]

1169. Van Tilborg, P. W. The retention of mental and finger maze habits. *J. exp. Psychol.*, 1936, 19, 334-41. [561]

Veblen, T. [428]

Viek, P. (*See* No. 878)

1170. Verhoeff, F. W. A theory of binocular perspective. *Amer. J. physiol. Opt.*, 1925, 6, 416-48. [236]

1171. Vernon, M. D. *Visual perception.* New York: Macmillan, 1937. [280, 282]

1172. Vernon, M. D. The perception of distance. *Brit. J. Psychol.*, 1937-8, 28, 1-11, 115-49. [248]

Vernon, M. D. (*See* No. 204)

1173. Vincent, S. B. The white rat and the maze problem. *J. Animal Behav.*, 1915, 5, 1-24, 140-57, 175-84, 367-74. [488]

1174. Voeks, V. W. Postremity, recency, and frequency as basis for prediction in the maze situation. *J. exp. Psychol.*, 1948, 38, 495-510. [371]

1175. Voeks, V. W. A formalization and clarification of a theory of learning. Unpublished manuscript, 1949. [363-5, 367, 368-9]

1176. Volkmann, J. Evidence for the quantal discrimination of visual size. *Amer. Psychologist,* 1946, 1, 271. Abstract. [63]

Volkmann, J. (*See* No. 558, 899, 1089, 1090, 1091, 1092)

1177. Von Karpinska, L. Experimentelle Beiträge zur Analyse der Tiefenwahrnehmung. *Z. Psychol.*, 1910, 57, 1-88. [270]

Von Lackum, W. J. (*See* No. 844)

Von Monakow [477]

Voth, A. C. (*See* No. 123)

1178. Vygotski, L. S. Thought in schizophrenia. (Trans. by J. Kasanin.) *Arch. Neurol. Psychiat., Chicago,* 1934, 31, 1063-77. [676-7]

1179. Wada, Y. Der Zeitfehler beim Suk zessivvergleich der Tonhöhe. *Jap. J. Psychol.*, 1932, 7, 505-38. [55]

Wade, M. (*See* No. 720)

Wagoner, K. S. (*See* No. 889, 890, 891)

1180. Wald, G. Carotenoids in the visual cycle. *J. gen. Physiol.*, 1935, 19, 351-73. [148]

1181. Wald, G. Bleaching of visual purple in solution. *Nature, Lond.*, 1937, 139, 587-8. [148]

1182. Wald, G. The chemistry of rod vision. *Science,* 1950, 113, 287-91. [148]

1183. Wald, G., & Clark, A. Visual adaptation and chemistry of the rods. *J. gen. Physiol.*, 1937, 21, 93-105. [158]

Wald, G. (*See* No. 465)

1184. Walker, E. L. Drive specificity and learning. *J. exp. Psychol.*, 1948, 38, 39-49. [420, 421]

Walker, E. L. (*See* No. 646)

1185. Walker, K. C. The effect of a discriminative stimulus transferred to a previously unassociated response. *J. exp. Psychol.*, 1942, 31, 312-21. [454]

1186. Wallach, H. Brightness constancy and the nature of achromatic colors. *J. exp. Psychol.*, 1948, 38, 310-24. [281-3]

1187. Wallach, H., & Galloway, A. The constancy of colored objects in colored illumination. *J. exp. Psychol.*, 1946, 36, 119-26. [280-83]

1188. Wallach, H., & Henle, M. An experimental analysis of the law of effect. *J. exp. Psychol.*, 1941, 28, 340-49. [377, 424-5, 428]

Wallach, H. (*See* No. 681)

1189. Walls, G. L. Human rods and cones. The state of knowledge. *Arch. Opthal., Chicago,* 1934, 12, 914-30. [136]

Walter, A. A. (*See* No. 164)

Walzl, E. M. (*See* No. 1263)

1190. Ward, L. B. Reminiscence and rote learning. *Psychol. Monogr.*, 1937, **49**, No. 220. [502, 510, 511, 512, 513, 522-3]

1191. Warden, C. J., Barrera, S. E., & Galt, W. The effect of unilateral and bilateral frontal lobe extirpation on the behavior of monkeys. *J. comp. Psychol.*, 1942, **34**, 149-71. [661-2, 665]

1192. Warden, C. J., & Jackson, T. A. Imitative behavior in the rhesus monkey. *J. comp. Psychol.*, 1939, **27**, 133-47. [659]

Warkentin, J. (*See* No. 1050)

1193. Warner, L. H. An experimental search for the 'conditioned response.' *J. genet. Psychol.*, 1932, **41**, 91-115. [318, 320]

1194. Warren, A. B., & Brown, R. H. Conditioned operant response phenomena in children. *J. gen. Psychol.*, 1943, **28**, 181-207. [307]

Warrener, H. (*See* No. 634)

1195. Washburn, M. *Movement and mental imagery.* Boston: Houghton Mifflin, 1916. [647]

1196. Washburn, M. *The animal mind.* New York: Macmillan, 1936. [655]

1197. Waters, R. H., & Leeper, R. The relation of affective tone to the retention of experiences of daily life. *J. exp. Psychol.*, 1936, **19**, 203-15. [572]

1198. Waters, R. H., & Poole, G. B. The relative retention values of stylus and mental maze habits. *J. exp. Psychol.*, 1933, **16**, 429-34. [561]

1199. Watson, B. The similarity factor in transfer and inhibition. *J. educ. Psychol.*, 1938, **29**, 145-57. [531]

1200. Watson, J. B. *Behavior: An introduction to comparative psychology.* New York: Holt, 1914. [648]

1201. Watson, J. B. *Psychology from the standpoint of a behaviorist.* Philadelphia: Lippincott, 1919. [309]

1202. Watson, J. B. *Behaviorism.* New York: The People's Institute, 1925. [309]

Watson, J. B. [362, 363, 692]

1203. Watson, W. S., & Hartmann, G. W. The rigidity of a basic attitudinal frame. *J. abnorm. soc. Psychol.*, 1939, **34**, 314-35. [579]

1204. Weaver, J. B. Upper limit of hearing in the cat. *J. comp. Psychol.*, 1930, **10**, 221-33. [398]

Weber, E. H. [75]

Wechsler, D. (*See* No. 617)

1205. Weddell, G., Guttmann, L., & Gutmann, E. *J. neurol. Psychiat.*, 1941, **3**, 206-25. [7]

Weddell, G. (*See* No. 1262)

1206. Wegel, R. L., & Lane, C. E. The auditory masking of one pure tone by another and its probable relation to the dynamics of the inner ear. *Phys. Rev.*, 1924, **23**, 266-85. [118]

1207. Weigl, E. Zur Psychologie sogenannter Abstraktionsprozesse: I. Untersuchungen über das 'Ordnen.' *Z. Psychol.*, 1927, **103**, 1-45. [674, 676]

Weinberg, M. (*See* No. 13)

Weisman, R. L. (*See* No. 69)

1208. Weitz, J., & Compton, B. A further stereoscopic study of figural after-effects. *Amer. J. Psychol.*, 1950, **63**, 78-83. [236]

1209. Weitz, J., & Post, D. A stereoscopic study of figural after-effects. *Amer. J. Psychol.*, 1948, **61**, 59-65. [236]

1210. Wendt, G. R. An analytic study of the conditioned knee-jerk. *Arch. Psychol.*, 1930, No. 123. [323]

1211. Wendt, G. R. An interpretation of inhibition of conditioned reflexes as competition between reaction systems. *Psychol. Rev.*, 1936, **43**, 258-81. [343-4, 346, 349]

1212. Wendt, G. R. Methods of recording action. *Arch. Psychol., N. Y.*, 1938, **32**, No. 228. [7]

1213. Weenzel, B. M. Techniques in olfactometry: a critical review of the last one hundred years. *Psychol. Bull.*, 1948, **45**, 231-47. [25]

1214. Werner, H. Studies on contour: I. Qualitative analyses. *Amer. J. Psychol.*, 1935, **47**, 40-64. [231-2, 245]

1215. Werner, H. Dynamics in binocular depth perception. *Psychol. Monogr.*, 1937, **49**, No. 2. [258]

1216. Werner, H. *Comparative psychology of mental development.* (Trans. by E. B. Garside.) New York: Harper, 1940. [676]

1217. Werner, H., & Zeitz, K. Über die dynamische Struktur der Bewegung (Studien über Strukturgesetze, VIII). *Z. Psychol.*, 1928, **105**, 226-49. [244]

Werner, H. (*See* No. 1280)

1218. Wertheimer, M. Experimentelle Studien über das Sehen von Bewegung. *Z. Psychol.*, 1912, **61**, 161-265. [243-4, 247]

1219. Wertheimer, M. Untersuchungen zur Lehre von der Gestalt. II. *Psychol. Forsch*, 1923, **4**, 301-50. [213]

1220. Wertheimer, M. *Productive thinking*. New York: Harper, 1945. [622-5, 628, 630, 633, 634-5, 637]

Wertheimer, M. [235]

1221. Wever, E. G. Figure and ground in the visual perception of form. *Amer. J. Psychol.*, 1927, **38**, 194-226. [218]

1222. Wever, E. G. Beats and related phenomena resulting from the simultaneous sounding of two tones. *Psychol. Rev.*, 1929, **36**, 402-18, 512-23. [124]

1223. Wever, E. G. The electrical responses of the ear. *Psychol. Bull.*, 1939, **36**, 143-87. [94, 95, 101]

1224. Wever, E. G. *Theory of hearing*. New York: Wiley, 1949. [94, 96, 99, 102, 106, 112, 120, 121]

1225. Wever, E. G., & Bray, C. W. The nature of bone conduction as shown by the electrical response of the cochlea. *Ann. Otol., etc., St. Louis*, 1936, **45**, 822-30. [90]

1226. Wever, E. G., & Bray, C. W. The perception of low tones and the resonance-volley theory. *J. Psychol.*, 1937a, **3**, 101-14. [94]

1227. Wever, E. G., & Bray, C. W. The effects of sodium chloride upon the electrical responses of the cochlea. *Psychol. Bull.*, 1937b, **34**, 519-20. [101]

1228. Wever, E. G., Bray, C. W., & Willey, C. F. The response of the cochlea to tones of low frequency. *J. exp. Psychol.*, 1937, **20**, 336-49. [94]

1229. Wever, E. G., & Neff, W. D. A further study of the effects of partial section of the auditory nerve. *J. comp. physiol. Psychol.*, 1947, **40**, 217-26. [106]

1230. Wever, E. G., & Smith, K. R. The problem of stimulation deafness: I. Cochlear impairment as a function of tonal frequency. *J. exp. Psychol.*, 1944, **34**, 239-45. [100]

Weymouth, F. W. (*See* No. 27)

1231. Wheatstone, C. Contributions to the physiology of vision. *Phil. Trans. roy. Soc. London*, 1838, **128**, 371-94. [254]

1232. White, R. K. The case for the Tolman-Lewin interpretation of learning. *Psychol. Rev.*, 1943, **50**, 157-86. [386, 388, 391, 415, 417, 419]

1233. White, W. A. The language of schizophrenia. *Arch. Neur. & Psychiat.*, 1926, **16**, 395-413. [676]

1234. Whitely, P. L. The dependence of learning and recall upon prior intellectual activities. *J. exp. Psychol.*, 1927, **10**, 489-508. [535]

1235. Whorf, B. L. The relation of habitual thought and behavior to language. In Spier, L., Hallowell, A. I., & Newman, S. S. (eds.), *Language, culture, and personality: essays in memory of Edward Sapir*. Menasha, Wis.: Sapir Memorial Publ. Fund, 1941. Pp. 75-93. [680]

1236. Wickens, D. D. The transference of conditioned excitation and conditioned inhibition from one muscle group to the antagonistic muscle group. *J. exp. Psychol.*, 1938, **22**, 101-23. [409-10, 458]

1237. Wickens, D. D. The simultaneous transfer of conditioned excitation and conditioned inhibition. *J. exp. Psychol.*, 1939, **24**, 332-8. [454]

Wiley, L. E. (*See* No. 721)

Willey, C. F. (*See* No. 1228)

Willey, R. de (*See* No. 157)

Williams, H. B. (*See* No. 313)

1238. Williams, K. A. The reward value of a conditioned stimulus. *Univ. Calif. Publ. Psychol.*, 1929, **4**, 31-55. [442]

1239. Williams, O. A study of the phenomenon of reminiscence. *J. exp. Psychol.*, 1926, **9**, 368-87. [565]

Williams, R. G. (*See* No. 56)

1240. Williams, S. B. Resistance to extinction as a function of number of reinforcements. *J. exp. Psychol.*, 1938, **23**, 506-22. [337]

1241. Willmer, E. N. Colour of small objects. *Nature, Lond.*, 1944, **153**, 774-5. [184]

1242. Willmer, E. N. *Retinal structure and colour vision: a restatement and an hypothesis.* Cambridge, Eng.: Cambridge Univ. Press, 1946. [183-6, 189]
1243. Willmer, E. N., & Wright, W. D. Colour sensitivity of the fovea centralis. *Nature, Lond.,* 1945, 156, 119-21. [184]
1244. Wilson, J. T. Remote associations as a function of the length of interval between learning and recall. *J. exp. Psychol.,* 1943, 33, 40-49. [519]
1245. Winch, W. H. Should poems be learnt by school-children as 'wholes' or in 'parts'? *Brit. J. Psychol.,* 1924, 15, 64-79. [540]
1246. Wing, K. G. The role of the optic cortex of the dog in the retention of learned responses to light: Conditioning with light and shock. *Amer. J. Psychol.,* 1946, 59, 583-612. [485-6]
1247. Wing, K. G. The role of the optic cortex of the dog in the retention of learned responses to light: Conditioning with light and food. *Amer. J. Psychol.,* 1947, 60, 30-67. [485-6]
1248. Wing, K. G., & Smith, K. U. The role of the optic cortex in the dog in the determination of the functional properties of conditioned reactions to light. *J. exp. Psychol.,* 1942, 31, 478-96. [478, 479, 481]
1249. Witmer, L. R. The association value of three-place consonant syllables. *J. genet. Psychol.,* 1935, 47, 337-60. [712]

Witting, E. G. (*See* No. 528)

Wohlfahrt [223]

Wolf, E. (*See* No. 220, 221)

Wolf, I. S. (*See* No. 645)

1250. Wolfe, J. B. The effect of delayed reward upon learning in the white rat. *J. comp. Psychol.,* 1934, 17, 1-21. [324, 436, 437]
1251. Wolfe, J. B. Effectiveness of token-rewards for chimpanzees. *Comp. Psychol. Monogr.,* 1936, 12, 1-72. [428-9, 432]

Wolfe, J. B. (*See* No. 580)

1252. Wolfle, H. M. Time factors in conditioning finger-withdrawal. *J. gen. Psychol.,* 1930, 4, 372-8. [313-14]
1253. Wolfle, H. M. Conditioning as a function of the interval between the conditioned and the original stimulus. *J. gen. Psychol.,* 1932, 7, 80-103. [313]

Wood, W. M. (*See* No. 863)

1254. Woodburne, L. S. The effect of a constant visual angle upon the binocular discrimination of depth differences. *Amer. J. Psychol.,* 1934, 46, 273-86. [262]
1255. Woodbury, C. A note on 'passive' conditioning. *J. gen. Psychol.,* 1942, 27, 359-61. [302]
1256. Woodbury, C. B. The learning of stimulus patterns by dogs. *J. comp. Psychol.,* 1943, 35, 29-40. [210-11]

Woodbury, C. B. (*See* No. 194)

1257. Woodrow, H. Weight discrimination with a varying standard. *Amer. J. Psychol.,* 1933, 45, 391-416. [56]
1258. Woodrow, H., & Lowell, F. Children's association frequency tests. *Psychol. Monogr.,* 1916, 22, No. 5. [709-10]
1259. Woodworth, R. S. *Dynamic psychology.* New York: Columbia Univ. Press, 1918. [443]
1260. Woodworth, R. S. *Experimental psychology.* New York: Holt, 1938. [28, 48, 49, 77, 115, 185, 515, 521, 524, 540, 574, 589-90, 642, 646, 709, 710, 722]
1261. Woodworth, R. S. Reënforcement of perception. *Amer. J. Psychol.,* 1947, 60, 119-24. [392, 412]

Woodworth, R. S. (*See* No. 1121)

1262. Woolard, H. H., Weddell, G., & Harpman, J. A. Observations on the neuro-histological basis of cutaneous pain. *J. Anat., Lond.,* 1940, 74, 413-40. [14]
1263. Woolsey, C. N., & Walzl, E. M. Topical projection of nerve fibers from local regions of the cochlea to the cerebral cortex of the cat. *Johns Hopkins Hosp. Bull.,* 1942, 71, 315-44. [111]
1264. Wright, W. D. A re-determination of the trichromatic coefficients of the spectral colours. *Trans. Opt. Soc.,* 1928-9, 30, 141-64. [140, 141, 187]
1265. Wright, W. D. The measurement and analysis of colour adaptation phenomena. *Proc. roy. Soc.,* 1934, B115, 49. [158]
1266. Wright, W. D. *Researches on normal and defective colour vision.* London: Kimpton, 1946; St. Louis: C. V. Mosby, 1947. [142]

Wright, W. D. (*See* No. 1243)

1267. Wulf, F. Über die Veränderung von Vorstellungen (Gedachtnis und Gestalt). *Psychol. Forsch.*, 1922, 1, 333-73. [589-90]
1268. Wundt, W. *Beiträge zur Theorie der Sinneswahrnehmung.* Leipzig und Heidelberg: C. F. Winter'sche Verlagshandlung, 1862. [267]

Wundt, W. [235, 680]

1269. Wylie, H. H. An experimental study of transfer of response in the white rat. *Behav. Monogr.*, 1919, 3, No. 16. [530-31]

Yamaguchi, H. G. (*See* No. 549)

Yarosh, M. (*See* No. 1078)

Yerkes, D. N. (*See* No. 1272)

1270. Yerkes, R. M. The mind of a gorilla. *Genet. Psychol. Monogr.*, 1927, 2, No. 142. [659]
1271. Yerkes, R. M., & Learned, B. W. *Chimpanzee intelligence and its vocal expressions.* Baltimore: Williams & Wilkins, 1925. [682]
1272. Yerkes, R. M., & Yerkes, D. N. Concerning memory in the chimpanzee. *J. comp. Psychol.*, 1928, 8, 237-71. [657]
1273. Yoshioka, J. G. A note on a right or left going position habit with rats. *J. comp. Psychol.*, 1928, 8, 429-34. [389]
1274. Young, T. On the mechanism of the eye. *Phil. Trans. roy. Soc. London,* 1801, 91, Part 1, 23-88. [169]
1275. Youtz, R. E. P. Reinforcement, extinction and spontaneous recovery in a non-Pavlovian reaction. *J. exp. Psychol.*, 1938, 22, 305-18. [337]
1276. Yum, K. S. An experimental test of the law of assimilation. *J. exp. Psychol.*, 1931, 14, 68-82. [525]

Zangwill, O. L. (*See* No. 205)

1277. Zartman, E. N., & Cason, H. The influence of an increase in muscular tension on mental efficiency. *J. exp. Psychol.*, 1934, 17, 671-9. [652]
1278. Zeaman, D. Response latency as a function of the amount of reinforcement. *J. exp. Psychol.*, 1949, 39, 466-83. [328, 333, 347]
1279. Zeigarnik, B. III. Das Behalten erledigter und unerledigter Handlungen. In K. Lewin (ed.), Untersuchungen zur Handlungs- und Affektpsychologie. *Psychol. Forsch.*, 1927, 9, 1-85. [582-7]

Zeigarnik, B. (*See* No. 80)

1280. Zeitz, K., & Werner, H. Über die dynamische Struktur der Bewegung. *Z. Psychol.*, 1927, 105, 226-48. [244]

Zeitz, K. (*See* No. 1217)

1281. Zener, K. The significance of behavior accompanying conditioned salivary secretion for theories of the conditioned response. *Amer. J. Psychol.*, 1937, 50, 384-403. [405]
1282. Zigler, M. J. Touch and kinesthesis. *Psychol. Bull.*, 1932, 29, 260-78. [80, 81, 82]
1283. Zipf, G. K. *The psycho-biology of language.* Boston: Houghton Mifflin, 1935. [715-18]
1284. Zipf, G. K. The repetition of words, time-perspective, and semantic balance. *J. gen. Psychol.*, 1945a, 32, 127-48. [717, 718]
1285. Zipf, G. K. The meaning-frequency relationship of words. *J. gen. Psychol.*, 1945b, 33, 251-6. [717]
1286. Zipf, G. K. *Human behavior and the principle of least effort.* Cambridge, Mass.: Addison-Wesley, 1949. [715-18, 722]
1287. Zirkle, G. A. Success and failure in serial learning: I. The Thorndike effect. *J. exp. Psychol.*, 1946a, 36, 230-36. [377]
1288. Zirkle, G. A. Success and failure in serial learning: II. Isolation and the Thorndike effect. *J. exp. Psychol.*, 1946b, 36, 302-15. [377]

Zola, E. [641]

1289. Zoll, P. M. The relation of tonal volume, intensity, and pitch. *Amer. J. Psychol.*, 1934, 46, 99-106. [125]
1290. Zwaardemaker, H. *Die Physiologie des Geruchs.* Leipzig, 1895. [78]

Zwaardemaker, H. [25]

Subject Index

In order to facilitate finding materials through use of this index, certain major topical headings have been capitalized: FORGETTING, HEARING, LANGUAGE, LEARNING, MEMORY, PERCEPTION, SENSORY PROCESSES, SYMBOLIC PROCESSES, VISION, and THEORIES. Under each of these headings will be found listings of the general topics in that area, each of which in turn offers a finer break-down of relevant content. This organization is added to the usual alphabetical collection of subjects. Cross-references are employed to guide the reader to related topics, and double listings are often given of the same content to increase the probability of finding the desired material via different approaches. Where page numbers follow a major topic as well as following sub-topics, the former refer to the most directly relevant material.

Absolute threshold (AL)
  limit on sensitivity as, 42
  unit as, 43-4
  see also Thresholds, sensory
Abstracting, 674-9
  concept formation and, 678-9
  factors determining, 676
  Goldstein's views, 674
  imageless thought and, 646
  levels of performance, 677
  representative processes and, 678-9
  schizophrenia in, 676-8
  tests of, 674-5
Accentuation, perceptual, 289-92, 295
Accommodation
  distance perception in, 266-71
  image clarity and, 133
Achromatic interval, 181
Action potentials, muscle, 649-51, 699-700
Action principle, Tolman, 388-9
Adaptation, 77-82
  area of stimulus and, 82
  chromatic, 181-2
  Crozier's theory, 80
  differential, pain and other, 13-14
  figural after-effects in, 238
  Hecht's theory, 80
  impulse frequency and, 67
  intensity of stimulus and, 80-82
  limit on sensitivity as, 42
  methodology, 78
  olfactory, 78-82
  pain, 78-82
  pressure, 78-82
  reflexive enchancement, 82
  reflexive, thermal, 17-18
  taste, 25, 78-82

Adaptation (Cont.)
  temporal course of, 78-80
  terminology, 78
  thermal, 14, 16, 18, 78-82
  visual, dark, 158-61
  visual, light, 158
  weights hefted and, 48
Adjective-verb quotient, 719
Aerial perspective, 261
Afferent neural impulse, Hull, 376
After-image
  'Bidwell's Ghosts,' 185
  complementary, Göthlin, 187
  Hering, 185
  movement of, 243
  perceptual organization, study, 222-3
  phenomena, 185
  Purkinje, 185
Albedo, 272-4
Alexia, 296
All-or-none Law (neural), 33
Alpha rhythm, 153
Amacrine cells, 134, 135, 167
Ambiguous figures
  gestalt theory and, 206-8
  interpretations, 221-2
  probability systems as, 220-21
  stimulus arrangement and, 220
Ames's demonstrations, 263-6
Amplifier, sound, 87
Amplitude, reaction, 325-8
Amplitude, sound, 84, 88
Annulospiral endings, 30
Anoxia, 161
Anticipatory errors, 496-501, 502-3
Anticipatory responses
  avoidance training in, 429-30

Anticipatory responses (Cont.)
  cue functions, 441
  drive discrimination in, 421-2
  drive functions, 441
  effect retroaction and, 381-2
  formation of, 431-2
  problem-solving in, 617-20
  reinforcing functions, 442
  secondary drive and reinforcement, 431-3
  short circuiting and, 394-5
Antonyms
  generalization among, 702-5
  mediated transfer and, 706
  word association in, 709-11
Anxiety
  avoidance training in, 429-30, 442
  fixation and, 455
  forgetting and, 571-7
  secondary drive as, 433
Apparent movement
  contour formation related, 232
  gestalt theory and, 204-6
  perceptual organization and, 225
Aqueous humor, 133
Areal summation
  numbers of fibers and, 68
  thresholds and, 74
Arpeggio paradox, 210, 216
Artificial pupil, 143
Assembly of behavior segments, 616-20
Assigns, 696-8
Assimilation
  memory traces, 552, 553
  time error and, 55-6
Association
  afferent pathways, 490-91
  association pathways, 492-3
  chaining of, introspection, 639
  classic and modern theories, 362
  efferent pathways, 491-2
  neurophysiology of, 490-93
  principle, Guthrie, 364
  principle, Hull, 376
  principle, Tolman, 386
  problem-solving in, 622
  see also Word association
Associative inhibition, 525, 543
Asynchronism, stimulus-response, 334-5
Attention, discrimination learning, 444-5, 451-4
Attenuator, 87
Attitude
  imageless thought and, 646-7
  perception and, 285-95
  perception and, summary, 294-5
  retention and, 579-80
Audition, see Hearing
Auditory nerve, 92; see also VIIIth nerve
Autochthonous determinants, 289, 295
Autonomic nervous system, 318, 466-9
Avoidance training
  mediation theory in, 393-4
  secondary drive and reinforcement, 429-30, 442
Awareness
  environment of, 1-2
  inferential process as, 1-2, 40

Awareness (Cont.)
  intensive, 42
  neural basis, 2, 33-41
  see also Sensory quality

b

'Babble-babble' theory, language, 683
'Backward conditioning,' 313-14
Barriers, problem-solving, 606-8
Basilar membrane
  anatomy of, 91-2
  function, theory, 95-6
Basket cells, 6-7, 12
Beats, sound, 86, 123-4
Behavior
  innate, Hull theory, 376
  molar and molecular, 299
  units of, 299-300
Behavioral determinants, perceptual, 289-95
Behavioristic view of perception, 208-12
  difficulties with, 208-9
  Hull theory and, 209-12
  interaction principle, 209-12
  learning of perceptions, 208-9
  stimulus patterning, 210-11
Behavioristic theory of memory, 550-51, 587-8, 593-9
Behavioristic theory of problem-solving
  assembly of behavior segments, 616-20
  generalization in, 615-16
  gestalt theory compared, 620-22
  goal gradient in, 612
  habit-family hierarchy in, 612-14
  implicit trial and error in, 614-15
  skills, role in, 616
Bel, 88
Beta rhythm, 154
Binocular disparity
  corresponding points and, 256
  fusion, peripheral, 252
  geometrical analysis, 254-5
  gestalt analysis, 255-8
  'statistical' theory of, 257-8
Binocular fusion
  central determinants, 252-4
  color of, 177
  dynamics of, 257-8
  neurological paradox, 258-60
  peripheral determination, 252
Binocular rivalry, 177
Bipolar cells, 134
Birth cry, 683-4
Bisection, method of scaling, 112-15
Blind spot, 135
'Bow-wow' theory, language, 682-3
Brightness
  AL, f. area, 155-6
  AL, f. duration, 156
  AL, f. retinal locus, 156-7
  AL, f. wave length, 157
  AL, minimum, 155
  color blind in, 182
  constancy and, 272-5
  contrast and summation, 233-4
  definition, 137
  dimension of experience, 129
  DL, f. intensity, 162-3

Brightness (Cont.)
DL, f. time and area, 162-4
DL, methods of study, 161-2
functions, color theory, 183
physical correlates, 130, 141-2
wave length, f. of, 143
whiteness, distinguished, 283
Brunswik ratio, 274, 276
Bunsen-Roscoe Law, 156

C

Cancellation, sound, 86
Cathexes, Tolman, 471
Cathode ray oscillograph, 9-10, 88
Central dynamics, perception, 261-97
Brunswik's views, 294-5
constancy, 271-85
distance perception, 261-71
identity recognition in, 296
integration beyond area 17, 296
motivation, attitude, 285-95
nature of, summary, 295-7
sensory 'signals,' area 17, 296
Central nervous system
complexity of, 474
learning, two-factor theory, 466-9
Centrifugal swing, 499
Chemical senses, 21-9
adequate stimuli, 24-9
common chemical sense, 22
gustation, 21-9
olfaction, 21-9
receptors, 22-4
Choroid layer, 133
Chromaticity, 137
Circular reflex, Holt, 687-8
Closure
perceptual organization, 214
problem-solving, 610
Coaxial electrode, 8
Cochlea
anatomy of, 91-2
destruction, effects, 99-101
drugs, injection, 101
electrical mapping of, 101-3
electrical recording from, 101
functioning of, 92
hydraulic system as, 96
microdestruction, 101
Cochlear microphonic
auditory nerve potentials and, 93
discovery of, 93
nature of, 93-4
source of, 94
Cognition
change in, inhibition, 345
discrimination learning in, 444, 446
field structure, 471-2
formation, motivation and, 421-2
movement *vs.* learning, 455-62
sensory conditioning and, 460-62
sign-significate expectation, 383
strengthening of, 389-90
see also Expectancy
Cognitive maps, Tolman, 383, 389
Cohesive forces, gestalt
constancies in, 283-4
depth perception in, 257-8

Cohesive forces (Cont.)
nature, laws governing, 202-3
problem-solving in, 605, 607-9
Color
adaptation, 181-2
classification, 129
constancy, 275, 280-81
contrast and summation, 233-5
dimensions of, 129
experience, varieties, 128
quantitative measurement, 139
solid (model), 129
surface, constancy, 271
synesthesia, 643, 645-6
word associations to, 711
Color blindness, 173-5
dark adaptation in, 183
experience in, 174
Ladd-Franklin theory and, 173-5
luminosity functions in, 182
neutral points, 176-7
perimetry measurements and, 173-5
saturation functions in, 182-3
varieties of, 174
Young-Helmholtz theory and, 174
Colorimeter, 132
Colorimetry, 139-41
Color mixture
data, 141
inhibitory processes in, 187-8
laws of, 130-32
methods, 130
Color receptors, evidence
binocular fusion of yellow, 177
color blind, neutral points, 176-7
electrophysiological, 178-81
latency data, 184
microstimulation, 177-8
thresholds, 176
Color theories
Göthlin, 186-8
Granit, 178-81
Hering, 173
Ladd-Franklin, 173-6
Willmer, 183-6
Young-Helmholtz, 169-73
Color vision, *see* Visual quality
Color wheel
color mixture in, 130, 132
constancy studies in, 272-4
Communication, 682, 699; *see also* Language
Concept formation, 666-73, 678-9
abstracting and, 678-9
children in, 673
constancy and, 285
identical element basis, 666-7
identity recognition and, 227
mediational basis, 668-72
paradigm for, 669
perceptual relations basis, 667-8
perceptual theory of, 672
Piaget's approach, 673
rat in, 667
representative processes and, 678-9
transposition and, 215
Concrete behavior, 674-9
Conditioned inhibitor, 342-3

Conditioned response
    definition, 310
    fractional components as, 319-20
    preparatory adjustment as, 319-20
Conditioning, 309-21
    autonomic components, 318
    cortex, role of, 478-9
    CR, UR relations, 317-20
    curare and, 479
    decorticate preparations, 478
    definition, 310
    drugs, use of, 492
    examples of, 311-12
    experimental characterization, 313-16
    instrumental learning and, 320, 323
    'kind' of learning, 301, 320
    intensity of CS, f. of, 334-5
    intensity of US, f. of, 316-17
    meanings of, 309
    mediation theory of, 405
    misconceptions, 316-20
    neurophysiology of, 477-81
    paradigm for, 310-11
    passive, 302
    Pavlov's work, 309, 311
    spinal, 479-81
    subcortical, 477-9
    reflexive nature, 316-17
    two-factor theories in, 463, 469
    UR, nature of, 317
    voluntary, 317
    see also Substitution learning
Cones
    anatomy, 135-6
    data on, 136
    electroretinogram and, 150
    numbers of, 136
    photochemistry of, 148-9
    retinal connections, 134
Confirmation, Tolman, 387-8, 392
Consciousness, central theory, 653-5
Consciousness, peripheral theory, 653-5
Consolidation, traces
    retroaction, 536, 542-3
    serial learning, 515-16
Constancy, 271-85
    absolute stimulus difference, f. of, 276-7
    artists in, 278
    attitude and, 278-9
    biological significance, 271, 284
    brightness, 272-5
    central theories, 283-5
    children in, 277-80
    color, 275, 280-81
    comparative data, 279-80
    concept formation and, 285
    contrast phenomenon as, 280-83
    discrimination and, 284
    gestalt theory of, 283-4
    identity recognition and, 277-8
    interpretations of, 280-85
    measurement of, 272-74
    phenomenal regression, 284-5
    ratios, 274
    'real object,' nature, 284
    shape, 275-6
    size, 275
    size, distance perception, 266
    transposition and, 215

Context effects, association, 724-6
Contiguity
    association in, 639
    conditioning in, 313-14
    Guthrie theory in, 368
    Hull theory in, 376
    necessary condition, learning, 321
    Tolman theory in, 390
Continuity, 214
Continuity-noncontinuity controversy, 446-51
    irrelevant cues, 448
    pattern discrimination, 449-50
    reversal of cues, 446-8, 452-4
    successive vs. simultaneous comparison, 450
Contour formation, 229-32
    apparent movement, related, 232
    contrast effects and, 234
    inhibitory processes in, 230-32
    'ironing out' process, 230
    'statistical' theory of, 229-30
    subjective, 232
Contour localization, subjective, 238-40
Contrast, 232-6
    association in, 639
    brightness, 233-6
    central factors, 235-6
    color, 233-5
    constancy and, 280-83
    contour and, 234
    'ironing out' process, 235-6
    lateral interaction hypothesis, 233-4
    simultaneous, interaction principle, 209
    vertical meridian and, 259
Convergence, 266-71
Cornea, 132-3
    thermal sense and, 16-17
Corpus callosum, 258-60
Corresponding points, retinal, 250-54, 256
'Correct' response, definition, 301
Cortex
    after-effects in, 238
    auditory experience and, 94-5
    auditory, lesions in, 110
    auditory, recording from, 36
    awareness and, 1-2, 653-5
    conditioning, role of in, 477-9
    differentiation, man and rat, 494
    electrical recording from, 475
    electrical stimulation of, 2, 475
    frontal, symbolic processes, 660-65, 678-9
    plasticity of, 474
    sensory, direct stimulation, 2, 34
    sensory, spontaneous firing, 36
    vigilance, motor tonus and, 652-3
    visual, direct stimulation, 153-4
    visual, discrimination learning, 482
    visual, electrical activity, 153-4
    visual, lesion vs. blinding, 488-9
    visual, pattern discrimination, 483
    visual, projection and, 196
    visual, quality localization, 36-7
    visual, response as f. wave length, 154
Cribiform plate, 23-4
Crista, 31-2
Curare, conditioning, 479

d

Damping, 86
Dark adaptation, 158-61
  color blind in, 183
  form perception and, 160
  individual differences in, 161
  neurophysiology of, 161
  pre-adapting light, f. of, 159
  pupil size, 158
  red goggles and, 160
  rod and cone components, 158-9
  retinal locus, f. of, 160
  wave length, f. of, 159-60
  vitamin A and, 161
Deaf mutes, 650-51
Deafness
  aging, selective, 114
  children, language development, 687-8
  stimulational, 100-101
  tonal lacunae, 114
  transmission, 114
Decibel, 88
Defense, perceptual, 292-5
Delayed alternation, 657, 661
Delayed reaction, 315, 656-7, 661
Delay of reinforcement
  habit strength and, 334-5
  maze learning in, 497-501
  see also Gradient of primary rein-
    forcement
Demand, Tolman, 383, 384
Depth perception, 248-60
  binocular disparity, 254-8
  cohesive forces in, 257-8
  factors in, 254
  fixation point, relation to, 250-54
  history of, 248-9
  paradox of, 248-9
  'statistical' theory of, 251-3
Destruction method, neurophysiology,
  475-7
Deuteranopic dichromatism, 174
Development of language, 683-90
  birth cry, 683-4
  generalization in, 688-9
  imitation in, 688
  labeling, 688-90
  speech skills, 684-7
  syllabic babbling, 687-8
Diaschisis, 477
Difference threshold (DL)
  Crozier's theory, 70-72, 83
  definition, 51
  limitation of sensitivity as, 42
  unit as, 43-4
  see also Thresholds, sensory
Difference tones, 123-4
'Ding-dong' theory, language, 682
Diplacusis, 112-13
Diplopia, 296
Discriminanda, Tolman, 383
Discrimination, 350-61
  complex, neurophysiology, 483-4
  concept formation and, 667
  constancy and, 284
  continuity-noncontinuity controversy,
    446-50
  controversies, 444-55
  differential reinforcement and, 353

Discrimination (Cont.)
  drive states of, 417-19
  examples of, 352-3
  fixation in, 454-5
  language labeling in, 689-90
  generalization and, 352-3
  Hull-Spence view, 444
  inhibition and, 353-4
  Lashley-Krechevsky view, 444-5
  mass-action in, 482-3
  mediation view, 453-4
  method, reminiscence, 518
  neurophysiology of, 481-5
  relational, Köhler, 445-6
  response interference and, 354
  patterns, cortex, 483
  perceptual patterning and, 210-11
  psychophysics in, 51
  selective attending, 444-5, 451-4
  serial learning in, 504, 519
  Skinner box in, 307
  transfer and, 534, 539
  transposition controversy, 445-6
  verbal cues, role, 446
Disinhibition
  experimental data, 338
  nature of, 315
  Skinner box in, 307
Displacement, contours, 237-42
Disposition, sign-process, 693-4
Distance perception, 261-71
  absolute, Ames's demonstrations, 265-6
  absolute, and motor theory of thought,
    269
  absolute, critical experiments, 270-71
  absolute, motor cues, 266-71
  absolute, size cues, 265-6
  learning of, 265-6
  relative, Ames's demonstrations, 263-4
  relative, factors, 261-2
  relative, size cues, 262
  subjects blind from birth in, 226
Distribution of practice, 504-9
  components of task between, 505
  Hull theory and, 517
  learning and retention between, 507-8
  number of components and, 513
  repetitions of task between, 505-7
  rest periods, 507
  retroaction, relation to, 504-5
  similarity and, 508-9
Dominators, vision, 178-80
Double alternation, 658
Double images, 261
Drive
  discrimination, studies, 417-19, 472
  habit strength and, 335-6
  habit strength, multiplicative relation,
    325, 378-9
  hunger and thirst interaction, 423-4,
    435
  irrelevant, learning under, 419-24
  principle, Hull, 378-9
  reduction, problems, 380-82
  reduction, strengthening, 322
  psychological tension and, 606
  secondary, 428-43
  specificity, reinforcement, 418, 421-2
  see also Motivation

Dualism
  Fechner, psychophysics, 42
  introspective method and, 639-40
  language study in, 680-81
  sensory quality and, 34-5
Duplexity Law
  brightness, DL functions, 162
  rods and cones, 136-7
Dynamogenesis, 493-4

e

Ear
  anatomy of, 88-92
  inner, 90-92
  mechanical characteristics, 88-90
  middle, 89-90
  outer, 89
  sensitivity of, 88-9
Effect
  law of, 372-3
  law, disproof, 424-5
  nature of, 380-82
  principle, Tolman, 386-8
  retroaction paradox, 380-82
  spread of, 377, 424-5
Ego
  region in psychological field, 553
  tension systems in, 578
Ego-involvement
  negative, 571-7
  positive, 578-87
  retention and, summary, 587
  Zeigarnik effect, 582-7
Eidetic imagery, 641-2
Electrical recording
  auditory cortex, 111
  auditory fibers, isolated, 103-4
  auditory nerve, 92-4
  cortex, 475
  cutaneous nerves, 11
  motor nerves, thinking, 649-51
  vision, cortex, 153-4
  vision, individual fibers, 152-3
  vision, optic nerve, 150-52
  vision, retina, 149-50
Electrical stimulation
  area 17, 297
  areas 18, 19, 20, 297
  cortex, 2, 475
  faradic, cortex, 490
  localization studies, 488
  muscle contraction, fatigue, 339
  skin, 4
Electroencephalography (EEG), 8, 153
Electrophysiological methods, 7-10
  electroencephalography, 8
  isolated fibers, 12, 103-4, 152-3
  pick-up systems, 7-8
  recording systems, 9-10
  skin senses in, 10-12
  transmission systems, 8
Electroretinogram (ERG), 149-50
  component analysis, 149-50
  flicker-fusion and, 150
  inhibitory processes in, 187
  rod and cone contributions, 150
  wave length variation, 184
Empathy, 699

Encephalization, 476-7, 493-4
Endolymph, 31, 91
Entoptic light, 133
Environment and nervous system, 2-3
Equal-appearing intervals, method, 115
Equal loudness contours, 113-14
Equal pitch contours, 119-20
Equilibration, 104-5
Equipotentiality, neurophysiological
  frontal lobes, 661-2
  logical requirements, 475-6
Equivalence beliefs, Tolman, 471
Ergograph, 338
Eustacian tube, 89
Evolution
  learning and, 299
  senses in general, 3
  skin senses, 20
Expectancy
  identification of, 391-2
  language origin and, 683
  perceptual dynamics and, 286
  pure-stimulus-acts and, 418
  trial and error and, 306
  see also Cognitions
Extensity, sensory dimension, 33
External meatus, 89
Extinction
  atypical human data, 345
  cyclical, 346
  experimental data, 337-8
  fatigue theory explanation, 338-43
  forgetting and, 549-50
  index of habit strength, 325-8
  interference explanation, 344-5
  massing, drugs, effects, 338, 348-9
  mediation theory in, 406
  ordinary learning compared, 349
  paradox of, 336-7
  Pavlovian theory, 346, 355-6
  repetitions, f. of, 326-7
  secondary mechanisms of, 434-5
  Skinner box in, 307
Eye
  accommodation, 133
  anatomy of, 132-3
  light reception, 133
  movements, 132
Eyelid conditioning, 311-12
Eye movements
  contour resolution and, 197
  fixational, 250-54
  form perception, 199
  sensations, orientation, 249

f

'Factor X,' retroaction, 544-6
Faradic stimulation, 490
Fatigue
  ambiguous figures in, 221
  drive as, 340-41
  inhibition and, 338-43
  physiological and psychological, 339
  serial learning in, 515
Fechner's Law, 77, 274
Fiber types
  conduction rate, 10
  cutaneous, 10

Fiber types (Cont.)
  myelination, 10
  'on-off' after-effects, 238
  'on-off' contours, 229-30
  optic nerve in, 153
  sensory experience, correlates, 11-12
  sensory quality and, 36
  size, 10
  visual quality, analysis, 36-7
  visual, rod and cone, 154, 187-8
Field cognition modes, Tolman, 472
Field expectancies, Tolman, 471-2
Figural after-effects, 236-43
  distance paradox, 239-40
  field theory of, 236-7
  inspection and delay time, f. of, 241-2
  'statistical' theory of, 237-8
  summary, 243
  third dimension in, 240-41
  typical phenomena, 236-7
Figure-ground organization, 217-20
  energy differential between, 219-20
  grouping, laws and, 217-18
  phenomenology, 218-19
  problem, 217
  problem-solving in, 606-9
'Filling in' phenomenon
  contour formation and, 232
  perceptual organization and, 223-4
Filter, light, 142
Filter, sound, 87
Fixation, eyes
  binocular problems, 259-60
  determinants, 250-54
Fixation, learning
  discrimination in, 454-5
  habit of, 306
  mediation view, 455
  problem-solving in, 610, 613, 632-6
Flicker-fusion method (CFF), 145-6
  adaptation and, 77-8
  alpha rhythm and, 146
  animal preparations in, 146
  auditory flicker and, 146
  brightness DL as, 162-3
  electroretinogram and, 150
  functions, 146
  psychophysical method, 50
  subjective flicker, 145-6
  Talbot-Plateau Law, 145
  thermal sense in, 17
Flower-spray endings, 30
FORGETTING
  behavioristic theory of memory, 550-51
  gestalt theory of memory, 551-4
  interference theory, forgetting, 587-99
  memory for visual forms, 588-93
  motivated forgetting, 571-7
  repression, 554
  retention, 549-99
  retroaction, 520-48
  theories, forgetting, 549-54, 587-99
  of the unpleasant, 571-7
  see also Memory, Memory trace
Formal discipline, 524
Fovea
  blue-blind of, 184
  location, 135
Fractionation, method of scaling, 115

Frame of reference, 50, 56
Free nerve endings
  chemical senses, 22
  olfaction, 24
  pain, 13
  pressure, 12
  thermal sense, 15
Frequency-of-usage, words
  meanings and, 717-18
  recognition thresholds, and, 293-4
  Zipf's Law, 717-18
Frequency, sound, 84-8
Frustration, perception in, 287-9
Fugue, 570
Functional autonomy, Allport, 443

g

Galvanic skin response (GSR)
  meaning, measurement, 700-701
  perception studies, 293-4
Generalization
  anticipatory responses and, 432
  cortical irradiation (Pavlov), 354
  experimental characterization, 355-8
  gradients, shape of, 377-8
  habit strength, f. of, 351-2
  identical elements (Guthrie), 358
  inhibition of, 353-4
  language development in, 688-9
  Lashley view, 444, 448-9
  logical problem, 350
  mathematical construct (Hull), 354-5
  mediation interpretation, 359-61
  philosophical problem, 361
  positive transfer and, 525-6
  practical significance, 350-51
  principle, Hull, 356, 377-8
  problem-solving in, 615-16
  semantic, 701-5
  serial learning in, 503, 519
  short circuiting and, 395
  similarity and, 361
  stimulus difference, f. of, 351-2
  transfer and, 538-9, 543
Geniculate bodies, 196
Geographical field (gestalt), 606-8
Gestalt view of perception, 200-208
  cohesive and restraining forces, 202-3
  cohesive forces, laws, 202-3
  isomorphism, 201-2
  neurological notions, 200-201
  persistence of organization, 206-8
  resolution of forces, phenomena, 203-6
  visual field, nature, 200-201
Gestalt theory of memory, 551-4, 587-92,
    598-9; see also Trace theory, mem-
    ory
Gestalt theory of problem-solving, 605-
    10
  behavioristic theory, compared, 620-22
  educational implications, 624
  humans, 622-5
  principles, 606-10
Gesture, language, 683
Glomus bodies, 12
Goal gradient
  criticism of, 499-500
  deductions from, 499

Goal gradient (Cont.)
  maze learning in, 496-501
  problem-solving in, 612
  secondary reinforcement and, 436
Golgi tendon organs, 30
Göthlin's color theory, 186-8
Gradient of primary reinforcement
  temporal extent of, 436-8
  trial and error in, 308
Granit's color theory, 178-81
  brightness functions, 183
  critique, 179-80
  luminosity in, 178-9
  nature, general, 178-9
Grouping, perceptual, 213-15
Gustation, 21-9
  adequate stimuli, 24-5
  chemical theory, 24-5
  receptors, 22
Guthrie, contiguity theory, 362-72
  avoidance training and, 429-30
  critique, 367-72
  experimental evidence, 365-7
  nature of, 363-5
  principles, 364-5
  stimulus elements *vs.* patterns, 368-70
  testability of, 370-72

h

Habit, 324-5
Habit-family hierarchy
  mediation theory in, 402-3
  problem-solving in, 612-14
  statistical structure of language, 718, 722
Habit strength
  amount of reinforcement, f. of, 331-3
  asynchronism, S-R, f. of, 334-5
  delay of reinforcement, f. of 334
  determinants, 328-36
  drive, multiplicative relation, 325, 378-9
  function, shape of, 329-31
  growth function as, 328-9
  indices, 325-8
  indices, correlation among, 327
  principle, Hull, 377
  repetitions, f. of, 326, 328-31
  strength of drive, f. of, 335-6
  Tolman theory in, 387
Hair cells
  anatomical arrangement, 91-2
  innervation, 92
  resonators as, 96-7
Hallucinations
  alcoholic, visual, 641
  area 19, stimulation, 296
  mescal, 641
  sensory conditioning and, 461
Harmonic series, 84-5
HEARING
  cochlear microphonic, 93-4
  frequency theories, 97-9
  Helmholtz's theory, 95-6
  neurophysiology of, 99-111
  nonresonance place theory, 96-7
  psychophysics of, 111-23
  resonance place theory, 95-6

HEARING (Cont.)
  resonance-volley theory, 99
  'subjective' experiences, 123-4
  thresholds and innervation density, 122
  tonal attributes, 124-6
  Wever-Bray effect, 92-3
'Heat,' experience of, 18-20
Hedonism, 372-3
Helicotrema, 91
Henning's smell prism, 28
Hering's color theory, 173
Histology
  brain, 476
  skin receptors, 6-7
Homeostatic mechanisms, temperature, 15
Homonyms, 702-6
Horopter, 254, 256
Hue
  complementary, 131
  dimension of experience, 129
  discrimination, f. wave length, 143-4
  matching, colorimetry, 141
  physical correlates, 130, 141-2
Hull, reinforcement theory, 372-82
  anchoring to observables, 375
  avoidance training and, 429-30
  constructs, processes, and symbols, 373-4
  critique, 380-82
  effect theory as, 372-3
  nature of, 373-5
  principles, 375-9
Hypnosis
  memory, study of, 574-8
  retention period during, 594
Hypnotic hypermnesia, 576-7
Hypotheses
  discrimination learning in, 445-6
  perceptual, 288
  Tolman theory in, 383, 385
  trial and error and, 306

i

Idealistic monism, 34-5
Identical elements
  concept formation in, 666-7
  generalization and, 358
  retroaction and, 531
Identity recognition
  constancy and, 272, 277-8
  perceptual organization in, 227-8
  phi phenomenon in, 248
  relative distance perception in, 263
Illusion
  deceleration of, 194-5
  geometric, gestalt theory, 206
  orientation of, 1, 249
  size-distance relation, 285
Imageless thought, 646-7, 651
Imagery
  association in, 639
  drug induced, 641
  eidetic, 641
  individual differences, 641-2
  intensity of, 640-41
  methods of study, 642
  motor theory and, 649-50

Imagery (Cont.)
 perception and, 640-41
 visual, and motor theory, 654
Imitation
 language development in, 688
 language origin and, 682
 selection of response, mode of, 302
Incentive, 333, 471
Incidental learning, 413-14, 578-9
Incompatible responses
 Guthrie theory in, 363, 364
 Hull theory in, 379
 mediation theory in, 397
Incus, 89-90
Induction, Pavlov, 316
Inferior colliculi, 110, 481
Inhibition, 336-50
 associative, law of, 525, 543
 auditory masking in, 119
 change in significance as, 345
 color vision in, 186-8
 conditioned, 341-3, 378
 constancy in, 282
 delay of, 338
 eating, rats, 407
 external, 315
 external, interference theory, 343-5
 fatigue theory, critique, 346-7
 frontal cortex and, 665, 678-9
 generalization of, 343, 348
 Hull statement, 341-2
 interference theory, critique, 347-8
 internal, extinction, 315
 intrinsic, fatigue-produced, 338-43
 lateral, contour formation, 229-32
 lateral, contrast effects, 233-4
 lateral, movement perception, 245-6
 neural, retina, 167-8
 principle, Hull, 378
 reciprocal, 546-7
 reproductive, 543
 retina, theory of, 168
 retroactive, 520, 546
 semantic, perception, 287
 serial learning in, 516-18
 theories of, evaluation, 345-50
Inhibition of delay, 315
Ink-writing polygraph, 9
Insight
 characteristics of, 610-11
 children in, 625
 frontal lobectomy and, 661-2
 habit-family hierarchy, probability of, 613
 motivation and, 607-8, 612
 phylogenetic level and, 609
 postulation of, 607
 in rats, 616-20
 restructuring of field as, 607-10
 selection of response, mode, 302
 see also Problem-solving
Instincts, 428
Instruction method, 302
Instrumental learning, 303-9
 conditioning, compared, 320-23
 definition, 303
 examples of, 304-6
 experimental characterization, 306-7
 misconceptions, 307-9

Instrumental learning (Cont.)
 neurophysiology, maze learning, 486-8
 neurophysiology, skills, 486
 neurophysiology, qualitative effects, 489
 paradigm for, 303-4
 two-factor theories in, 463, 469
 see also Trial and error
Intelligence, 651, 721-2
Interaction principle
 critique, 211-12
 gestalt laws and, 212
 perception, 209-12
 short circuiting and, 395
 statement of, 376
Interference theory, forgetting
 factor, serial learning, 520
 generality of, 598-9
 implications of, 593-8
 inactivity corollary, 593-7
 inhibition, 343-5
 nature, general, 550-51
 principle, 550-51
 retention curve and, 556
 trace theory compared, 587-8
Intertones, 123-4
Interval of uncertainty, 48-9
Introspection
 assumptions underlying, 640
 critique of, 647-8
 data obtained, 639
 in rats, 394
Intrusions, types, 544
Iodopsin, 148
Iris, 133
'Ironing out' process
 contours within, 230
 contrast in, 235-6
Irritability, 536, 547-8
Isomorphism
 depth perception and, 258-9
 gestalt theory in, 201-2, 553
 transposition and, 216

k

Kapper's Law of Neurobiotaxis, 198
Kent-Rosanoff lists, 708-10, 722
Kinds of learning, 462-73
 Birch and Bitterman, 463-5
 Maier and Schneirla, 463-4
 Mowrer, 465-9
 Seward, 469-71
 Tolman, 471-3
 two-factor theories, 463-9
Kinephantoscope, 221
Kinesthesis, 29-33
 associated phenomena, 32-3
 bodily movement sense, 30-32
 bodily position sense, 30-32
 distance perception in, 266-71
 imageless thought and, 647
 motor theory of thought in, 651, 654
 see also Proprioception
Knowledge of results, 51
Korte's Laws, 244
Krause's end bulbs, 6-7, 14-15
Kymograph, 9

I

Labeling, 688-9
Labyrinth, 30-32, 90-91
Ladd-Franklin color theory, 173-6
 color blindness and, 173-5
 evolutionary nature, 174-5
 perimetry measurement and, 173-5
LANGUAGE
 animals in, 681-2
 animal vs. human, 682
 concept formation and, 666-73
 context effects, 724-6
 development of, 683-90
 introspection in, 647-8
 measurement of meaning, 699-714
 objectivity in the study of, 680-81
 origins of, 682-3
 semantic generalization, 701-5
 sign-process, 690-99
 statistical structure, 715-26
 summary, 726-7
Lashley jumping stand, 447-51, 454-5
Latency
 index of habit strength, 325-8
 measure, transfer and retroaction,
 repetition, f. of, 326-7
 sensitivity of, 328
Latent learning, 414-17
LEARNING
 curves, types of, 329-31
 decrement, inhibition, 336-50
 discrimination, 444-55
 generalization, 350-61
 Guthrie, contiguity theory, 362-72
 habit strength, summation, 324-36
 Hull, reinforcement theory, 372-82
 kinds of, 462-73
 mediation theory, 392-412
 motor tonus and, 652-3
 movement vs. cognition, 455-62
 neurophysiology of, 474-94
 reinforcement controversy, 413-28
 secondary drive and reinforcement,
  428-43
 selection process in, 301-21
 serial, 495-520
 strengthening operations, 321-4
 Tolman, cognition theory, 382-92
 transfer and retroaction, 520-48
 whole vs. part, 540-42
Least effort, principle, 715-19
Lens, eye, 133
Lepley Hypothesis, 516-17
Liebmann effect, 202
Light, 137-40
 colorimetry, 139-41
 composition, 142
 definition, 137
 illumination engineering, 137-8
 photometry, 138-9
 quanta and sensitivity, 155
 units of measurement, 138
 visible spectrum, 137
Limen, see Absolute threshold, Difference
 threshold
Limulus, 152, 165
Lissajous figures, 221-2
Lloyd Morgan's Canon, 603, 655
Lobectomy, frontal, 660-62

Localization of function
 cortical, 493-4
 electrical stimulation data, 488
 logical requirements, 475-6
 maze learning of, 486
 subcortical, 493
Loudness
 discrimination, f. duration, 123
 discrimination, f. frequency, 120-23
 frequency, f. of, 113-14
 generalization of, 355-8
 intensity, f. of, 115-16
 masking and, 118
 neural basis of, 116, 118
Loudspeaker, 87
Luminance, 137-8
Luminosity functions
 color blind in, 182
 cone, 143, 178
 constancy studies in, 273-4
 foveal, 178
 rod, 143
 single fibers for, 178-9

m

Maculae, 31-2
Macular region, retina, 134, 135, 199
Malleus, 89
Manipulanda, Tolman, 383
Marbe's Law, 722-3
Masking, auditory, 116-19
 characteristics, 117-18
 explanations, 118-19
 neural correlate, 118-19
Masking, distance cue, 261, 263-4
Massed practice
 extinction and, 338, 348-9
 serial learning, 504-5
Mass-action, neurophysiology
 critique, 488
 discrimination learning in, 482-3
 instrumental learning in, 487-9
 lesion vs. blinding, 488-9
 logical requirements, 475-6
 maze learning in, 487-8
Materialistic monism
 awareness, nature of and, 38-41
 Boring's view, 39-40
 sensory quality and, 34-5
Maze, 304, 495-502
Meaning
 constancies and, 285
 imageless thought and, 646-7
 measurement of, 699-714
 memory and, 561
 Mowrer's theory in, 468-9
 object perception and, 292
 perception and, relation, 194-5, 621-2
 perceptual dynamics and, 286
 perceptual grouping and, 214
 polarity test of, 644-5, 713
 problem-solving and, 630-34
 synesthesia and, 642-6
 word recognition and, 293-4
Meaning of perception, 192-5
 characteristics, 193
 definition, 194
 habit and, 194
 meaning and, 194-5

Meaning of perception (Cont.)
  motor processes and, 194
  sensation and, 193
  symbolic process as, 192
Meaning measurement, 699-714
  physiological indices, 699-701
  scaling methods, 712-14
  semantic differential, 713-14
  semantic generalization, 701-5
  transfer and interference, 705-8
  word association, 708-12
Meaningful materials
  reminiscence with, 512, 565-6
  retroaction and, 531-3
  serial learning of, 509
Means-end-readiness, Tolman, 306, 383
Mediated generalization
  Cofer and Foley studies, 705-6
  nature of, 359-61
  problem-solving, role in, 615-16
  semantic, meaning, 701-5
  see also Semantic generalization
Mediation process
  concept formation basis, 668-72
  cortical injury and, 486
  nature of, 697-8
  problem-solving, role in, 630-32
  see also Sign process
Mediation theory, 392-412
  advantages, 411-12
  anchoring to observables, 410-12
  change in mediation, 404-8
  change in instrumentation, 408-10
  conditioning and, 405
  discrimination in, 398
  energy expenditure and, 397-8
  evaluation of, 410-12
  extinction in, 406
  inhibition and, 345-6
  instrumental skills, development, 399-
    401
  meaning and, 412
  Mowrer's view, compared, 466-9
  new learning in, 403-4
  other theories, relations, 410
  perception and, 412
  perception dilemma and, 194
  perceptual and reinforcement views,
    392-3
  reduction mechanisms in, 397-8
  reinforcement, role in, 397
  representational processes, develop-
    ment, 395-9
  representational processes, role of,
    401-4
  sign-process of, 695-8
  two-process theories and, 464, 469
Mediators
  choice situations, role in, 403
  differential reinforcement of, 402
  discrimination learning in, 446, 453-4
  irrelevant drive studies and, 421-2
  latent learning and, 416-17
  place learning and, 460
  purposive sequences, role, 403
  secondary drive and reinforcement,
    431-3
  sensory conditioning in, 461-2
Meissner's corpuscles, 6-7, 12

Mel (unit of pitch), 112
Memory
  ego-involvement and, 578-87
  forgetting, critical issue, 587-98
  forgetting, viewpoints, 549-54
  forms, visual for, 588-93
  motivated forgetting, 571-7
  motivation and, 570-87
  retention curves and determinants,
    554-70
  summary, 598-9
  see also FORGETTING, Retention
Memory drum, 502
Memory trace
  excitation, relation to, 553-4
  gestalt construct as, 551-3
  visual forms of, 588-93
  see also Trace theory, Memory
Memory for visual forms, 588-93
  critique on methodology, 590-91
  direction of changes, 589
  gestalt predictions, 588-9
  progressiveness of changes, 589-90
  verbal mediation, 591-3
Mental efficiency, 651-3
Merkel disks, 12
Mescal, imagery and, 641
Metaphor
  introspection in, 648
  synesthesia and, 642-6
Microphone, 87
Mind-body problem, 33-41
Modiolus, 121
Modulators, vision, 178-80
Monaural-binaural equations, 115
Monochromatism, 174
Monochrometer, 142-3
Mood circle, Hevner, 645
Mood, synesthesia, 645-6
Motivated forgetting, 571-7
  hypnotic technique, 574-8
  intensity of affect, 572-4
  judged vs. felt affect, 571-2
  repression sequence in, 571
Motivation
  acquired, 428-43
  Hull theory in, 378-9
  learning and, 413-14
  memory and, 571-87
  motor tonus and, 652
  perception and, 286-9
  perception and, summary, 294-5
  problem-solving in, 607-8, 612
  psychophysics in, 51
  Skinner box in, 307
  Tolman theory in, 386
  see also Drive
Motor theory of thought, 648-55
  deaf mute controls, 650-51
  distance perception and, 269
  Galton's notions, 641
  individual differences, 651
  meaning and, 699-700
  mediation theory and, 398
  proprioception and, 33
Motor tonus, 651-3
  learning and, 652-3
  mental efficiency and, 651-3
  motivation and, 652

Movement perception, 243-8
  contour formation and, 244-5
  perceptual organization, study, 225
  'pure phi,' 243-4, 246-8
  real movement, 245-6
  'statistical' theory of, 245-6
  stroboscopic, 243-6
  variables, 244
Movements *vs.* cognitions, learning, 455-62
  place learning, 456-60
  sensory conditioning, 460-62
Multiple trackness, Tolman, 389
Muscle spindle, 30
Myelination, 10

n

Nativism *vs.* empiricism, 225
Nearness, perceptual, 213
'Neurograms,' 196
Neurophysiology of hearing, 99-111
  cochlear destruction, 99-101
  cochlear mapping, 101-3
  cochlear microdestruction, 101
  higher centers, 110-11
  innervation density, cochlea, 121-3
  isolated fibers, recording, 103-4
  VIIIth nerve trunk, 104-10
  VIIIth nerve sectioning, 106-10
Neurophysiology of learning, 474-95
  association, nature of, 490-93
  conditioning, 477-81
  conditioning, discrimination, compared, 485-6
  conditioning, summary, 481
  discrimination, 481-5
  discrimination, summary, 484-5
  instrumental learning, 586-9
  logic of interpreting data, 475-7
  methodology, 475-7
  summary, 493-4
Neurophysiology of vision, 146-55
  cortical activity, 153-4
  electroretinogram, 149-50
  Granit, microelectrode work, 178-9
  optic nerve discharge, 150-52
  photochemistry of retina, 147-9
  retinal interactions, 165-8
  summary, 154-5
Nonsense syllables, 502, 712
Nystagmus
  physiological, 199, 230, 259
  postrotational, 249
  optic, brain-injured, 484

o

Object-assimilation, 553
Observational learning, 658-60
Octave
  generalization, 361
  size, subjective and objective, 112
Olfaction
  adequate stimuli, 25-9
  chemical view, 25-6
  classification systems, 27-9
  Henning's prism, 28
  odor mixture, 29
  odorous substances, chemistry, 27-8

Olfaction (Cont.)
  osmics, descriptive, 21
  perfume chemistry and, 21
  physical view, 26-7
  radiation theory, 26-7
  receptors, 23-4
  sensitivity, menstruation, 26
  sensitivity, pigmentation, 26
Olfactometer, 25
Olfactory bulb, 23-4, 37
Olfactory epithelium, 23
Operant behavior, 320
Optic chiasma, 195, 259
Optic nerve
  electrical activity in, 150-52
  fiber types, 153
  ganglion cells, 134
  'giant' ganglion cells, 135
  isolated fibers, study, 152-3
  methods of study, 150
  'midget' ganglion cells, 135
  perception, projection system, 195
  rod and cone contributions, 151-2
Optic radians, 196
Organization of materials, retention, 566-8
Organs of Corti, 91-2
Orientation
  area 17 lesions and, 296
  illusions of, 1, 249
  inferences about, 249
Oscillation
  principle, Hull, 378-9
  serial learning in, 503-4
Oscillator, beat-frequency, 87
Oval window, middle-ear, 90
Overtones, 123-4

p

Pacinian corpuscles, 30
Pain sensitivity, 13-14
  absolute threshold, 74
  adequate stimuli, 13-14
  chemical theory, 13
  gradient theory, 13
  receptors, 13
  specificity of, 13-14
  stimulators, 4
Paradoxical sensory quality, 5, 17, 18
Parallax
  binocular, 254
  head movement, 254
Partial reinforcement
  extinction and, 345
  reinforcement controversy in, 425-7
  Skinner box in, 307
PERCEPTION
  behavioristic view, 208-12
  central dynamics, 261-97
  constancy, 271-85
  contour formation, 229-32
  contrast, 232-6
  depth, 248-60
  distance perception, 261-71
  figural after-effects, 236-43
  gestalt view, 200-208
  imagery and, 640-1
  meaning of, 192-5
  motivation, attitude, 285-95

PERCEPTION (Cont.)
  movement, 243-8
  perceptual organization, 212-28
  physiological view, 195-200
  projection dynamics, 229-60
Perceptual learning, mediated generali-
    zation, 359-60
Perceptual organization, 212-28
  ambiguous figures, 220-22
  figure-ground, 217-22
  grouping, interpretations, 214-15
  grouping, laws of, 212-15
  identity recognition in, 227-8
  innate or acquired, 225-8
  maximizing cohesive forces, 222-5
  stimulus patterning in, 215
  subjects blind from birth in, 225-6
  summary, 228
  transposition, 215-16
  unum and duo, 216-17
Performance
  latent learning and, 414-17
  learning vs., 388-9, 391
Perilymph, 91
Perimetry measurements, 173-5
Perseverative errors, verbal learning,
    502-3
Perseveration theory
  reminiscence and, 543
  serial learning, 515-16
  transfer and retroaction, 542-3
Phenomenology of vision, 128-32
  color classification, 129-30
  color experience, dimensions, 129-30
  color experience, varieties of, 128
  color mixture, 130-32
  form and color, 128
  spatial organization, 128
Phi phenomenon, 243-8
  cohesive forces and, 202-3
  critical studies, 247
  gestalt theory and, 246-7
  interpretations, 247-8
  nature of, 243-4
  vertical meridian and, 259
Phonetic reading, 698
Photistic visualizers, 643
Photochemical equivalence, law of, 147
Photochemistry
  cones, 148-9
  pigmentation of retina, 134
  regenerative mechanisms, 148
  rhodopsin, 147-9
  rods, 147-8
  temporal summation and, 166
Photochronograph, Dodge, 312
Photometry, 138-9
  heterochromatic, 139
  psychophysics and, 138-9
Physiological limit (habit), 331
Physiological view of perception, 195-200
  areas, 17, 18, 19, relations, 198-9
  Hebb's analysis, 198-200
  nature of, 195
  neural mechanisms, 196-200
  projection system, 195-8
  'statistical' theory, 196-8
Physiological zero, 78
Piezoelectric effect, 94

Pinna, 89
Piper's Law, 156
Pitch
  discrimination, f. duration, 123
  discrimination, f. frequency, 120-23
  frequency, f. of, 111-13
  generalization of, 355-7
  intensity, f. of, 119-20
  speech development and, 685
Place learning, 456-60
  alternate behavior routes, 458
  alternate spatial routes, 456-8
  response learning vs., 458-60
Place principle, audition
  nature of, 96-7
  volleying, interpretation, 106
'Pooh-pooh' theory, language, 683
Posthypnotic amnesia, 574
Postremity, 364, 371-2
Practice effect
  positive transfer as, 522
  psychophysics in, 51
  transfer and, 526, 535
Pragmatics, 699
Prägnanz
  grouping and, 215
  law of, 204
  unit formation in, 216-17
Pressure sensitivity, 12-13
  absolute threshold, 74
  adequate stimuli, 12-13
  chemical theory, 13
  gradient theory, 13
  receptors, 12
  stimulators, 4
Pressure waves, 84-6
Primitivization, perceptual, 288-9, 295
Probability
  choice points at, 384-5, 401
  Guthrie theory in, 364-5
  index of habit strength, 325-8
  repetitions, f. of, 326-7
Problem-solving, animal, 603-22
  behavioristic view, 611-20
  gestalt, behavioristic views compared,
    620-22
  gestalt view, Köhler, 605-10
  historical background, 603-4
  Köhler's critique, 604
  past experience and, 613-14
  trial and error as, 603-4
  see also Insight
Problem-solving, human, 622-37
  developmental level and, 625
  Duncker's views, 626-7, 633-4
  experimental characterization, 625-36
  fixation in, 632-6
  Maier's studies, 628-30, 632-3
  mediation processes, role in, 630-32
  past experience, role of, 627-30
  practical suggestions, summary, 636-7
  search process in, 625-7
  verbal problems, 626, 634
  Wertheimer's views, 622-5
  see also Insight
Productive thinking, 622-5, 637
Progressive relaxation, 649
Projection dynamics, perception, 229-60
  contour and contrast, 229-36

Projection dynamics (Cont.)
  depth and solidity, 248-60
  figural after-effects, 236-43
  movement perception, 243-8
  nature of, 196-8
Projection system
  binocular problems raised, 258-9
  isomorphism and, 201
  sensory quality and, 36-7
  'statistical' theory of, 196-8
Proprioception, 29-33
  discrimination in, 30
  higher mental processes and, 30
  receptors, 30
  see also Kinesthesis
Protanopic dichromatism, 174
Protensity, sensory dimension, 33
Psychological field (gestalt), 606-9
Psychophysical methods, 43-59
  absolute comparison, 50
  adjustment methods, 44-6
  assumptions underlying, evaluation, 51-4
  average error, method of, 44-5
  comparison methods, 47-50
  constant stimuli, method of, 47-50
  discrimination learning method, 51
  evaluation of methods, 58-9
  flicker-fusion method, 50
  history of, 43
  instructions in, 48-9
  methodological problems, 58-9
  reaction time method, 51
  serial exploration, method of, 45-6
  single stimuli, method of, 50
  standard deviation, unit, 49-50
  three category comparison, 48-9
  two category comparison, 49-50
Psychophysics of hearing, 111-23
  discrimination, f. duration, 123
  discrimination, f. frequency, 120-23
  loudness, f. frequency, 113-14
  loudness, f. intensity, 115-16
  masking, 116-19
  pitch, f. frequency, 111-13
  pitch, f. intensity, 119-20
  scaling attributes, 111-12, 115-16
Psychophysics of vision, 137-46
  brightness, f. wave length, 143
  colorimetry, 139-41
  color mixture, 141
  flicker-fusion method, 145-6
  hue discrimination, f. wave length, 143-4
  photometry, 138-9
  saturation, f. wave length, 144-5
  spectral systems, 141-3
  see also Luminosity functions
Pure stimulus act, 395-6
Pure tone experience, 96
Purkinje shift, 136, 180
Puzzle (problem) box
  Guthrie, analysis, 365-7
  instrumental learning as, 304
  problem-solving in, 604

q

Quantal hypothesis, 59-65
  classical data and, 64-5

Quantal hypothesis (Cont.)
  nature of, 60-61, 65
  predictions and tests, 61-4
  variability, sources of, 59-60

r

Rat, experimental subject as, 304-5
Reasoning
  in rats, 616-20
  see also Thinking
Recall method, 557-8
Recent memory, 660, 665
Reciprocal inhibition
  mediators among, meaning, 708
  retroaction, factor, 546-7
Recognition method, 557-8
Recognition thresholds
  Allport-Vernon values and, 292-4
  frustration and, 288
  perceptual defense and, 294-5
Reconstruction method, 557-8
Recording methods
  cathode ray oscillograph, 9-10
  ink-writing polygraph, 9
  kymograph, 9
  optical transmission systems, 8
  spark-gap recordograph, 9
  vacuum tube amplifier, 8-9
  waxed paper recordograph, 9
Reduction screen, constancy, 272-4
Refractory Law (neural)
  Crozier's theory and, 70-72
  impulse frequency and, 66-7
  sensory quality and, 34
Regression
  phenomenal, perception, 284-5
  schizophrenia in, 676-7
Rehearsal, learning, 515
Reification, words, 680-81
Reinforcement
  conditioning in, 322-3
  'contrast effects,' 333-4
  differential, 353, 424-7
  Guthrie theory in, 367, 370
  habit strength and, 331-3
  language labeling in, 689-90
  mediation theory in, 397
  nature of, 380-82
  partial, 307, 345, 425-7
  principle, Hull, 376
  retroaction paradox, 380-82
  secondary, 428-43
  sensory conditioning in, 462
  serial, 500-501
  skill formation in, 472-3
  terminal, 500-501
  two-factor theories in, 463, 469
Reinforcement controversy, 413-28
  differential reinforcement, failure, 424-7
  drive discrimination studies, 417-19
  incidental learning, 413-14
  irrelevant drive and reward, 419-23
  irrelevant drive, no reward, 423-4
  latent learning, 414-17
  summary, 427-8
Reissner's membrane, 91
Reminiscence, Ballard-Williams, 564-6
  Ward-Hovland, compared, 509

Reminiscence, Ward-Hovland, 509-13
  experimental findings, 510-11
  forgetting and, 549-50
  Hull theory of, 517
  interpretations of, 509
  methodological considerations, 509-10
  motor skills for, 510-11
  perseveration and, 543
  retroaction and, 509, 513
  variables, magnitude, 511-12
  variables, occurrence, 512-13
Remote associations, 502, 518-19
Repetition, habit strength and, 326-30
Replication of function, neurophysiology
  conditioning in, 481
  cortex and subcortex, 493
  logical requirements, 475-6
Representational processes in animals,
    655-65
  abstracting and, 678-9
  concept formation and, 678-9
  delayed alternation, 657
  delayed reaction, 656-7
  double alternation, 658
  frontal cortex, role of, 660-65
  Jacobsen's studies, 660-62
  nature of, 663-5
  observational learning, 658-60
  in rats, 662-3
  retention and, 664-5
  retroaction in, 657, 664-5
  see also Thinking in animals
Repression, 554, 571-7
Reproductive inhibition, 543
Resonance, 86
Resonance-place theory (hearing), 95-6
Resonance-volley theory (hearing), 99
Respondent behavior, 320
Response-produced stimuli
  Guthrie theory in, 363
  mediation theory in, 398-9
  problem-solving in, 616
  secondary drive and reinforcement in,
    432-4
  skill formation in, 400-401
Rest
  control condition as, 521-2
  reinforcement as, 340
Rest periods, 507
Restraining forces (gestalt), 202
Restructuring (gestalt), 607-10, 624, 627
Retention, 549-99
  amount of interpolated material and,
    597-8
  attitudes and, 579-80
  curves and determinants, 554-70
  degree of original learning and, 556
  distributed vs. massed practice, 507-8,
    518-19
  Ebbinghaus's work, 554-6
  enhancement, ego-involvement, 578-87
  ego- vs. task-orientation, 584-7
  inactivity during, 593-7
  intentional vs. incidental, 578-9
  log f. time as, 554-6
  materials, types of, 561-2
  meaning and, Bartlett, 558-61
  meaningful vs. nonsense, 562
  measurement, methods, 557-61

Retention (Cont.)
  method of learning and, 568-70
  organization of materials and, 566-8
  reminiscence, Ballard-Williams, 564-5
  symbolic processes and, 664-5
  transfer and, same intervals, 533-4
  verbal vs. motor, 561-2
  warm-up effect and, 562-4
  Zeigarnik effect, 582-7
  see also FORGETTING, Memory
Retina, 133-7
  anatomy, fine, 134-5
  anatomy, gross, 133-5
  integrative functions, 165-8
  location in eye, 133
  microstimulation of, 177-8
  neural connections in, 133-5
  perception, projection system, 195, 259
  pigmentation of, 134
  rods and cones, 135-7
  units of measurement on, 135
Retinene, 148-9
Retroaction
  cause of forgetting as, 551
  degree of learning and, 538-9
  ego-involvement under, 578-9
  facilitative, stimulus variation, 525-6
  interfering, response variation, 526-7
  interfering, stimulus and response var-
    iation, 527-9
  paradigm for, 521
  symbolic processes and, 657, 664-5
  similarity paradox and, 530-33
  temporal relations, 535-7
  Zeigarnik effect and, 584-5
Retroactive inhibition, 520, 546
Rhodopsin
  absorption spectrum, 147
  decomposition of, 147-8
Ricco's Law, 156
Rods
  anatomy, 135-6
  blue modulators as, 184-6, 188
  color vision, role in, 183-6
  cone-like, adaptation, 161
  cone-like, color theory, 186
  data on, 136
  electroretinogram and, 150
  numbers of, 136
  photochemistry of, 147-8
  retinal connections, 134
  sensitivity of, 155
  types of, 137
  visual purple and, 135-6
Rods of Corti, 95
Round window, middle ear, 90
Ruffini cylinders, 6-7

S

Saccule, 31
Salivary reaction
  meaning, measurement, 700
  Pavlovian conditioning, 311
'Satiation,' figural process, 237
Saturation
  color blind in, 182-3
  colorimetry in, 141
  color mixture in, 131

Saturation (Cont.)
  color theories and, 181
  dimension of experience, 129
  intensity, f. of, 181
  physical correlates, 130, 141-2
  wave length, f. of, 144-5
Savings method, 557-8
Scala media, 91
Scala tympani, 91
Scala vestibuli, 91
Schizophrenia, 719-20
Sclerotic coat, eye, 132
Scotoma, 484
S-curve hypothesis, 331
Secondary drive and reinforcement, 428-
    43
  experimental demonstrations, 428-31
  extinction of, 434-5
  hormonal conditioning, 433, 443
  instincts and, 428
  interpretations, 431-3
  maze learning in, 497-8
  mediation theory in, 398-9
  primary reinforcement and, 434-40
  role in behavior, 440-42
  short circuiting and, 438-9
  sign behavior as, 440
  summary, 442-3
Second-order conditioning, 315-16, 430-
    31
Selection process, learning, 301-21
  conditioning, 309-20
  conditioning and instrumental learn-
    ing, compared, 320-21
  instrumental learning, 301-9
Semantic differential, 713-14
Semantic generalization, 701-5
  age levels and, 702-3
  nature of, 704-5
  object to sign, 701-2
  object to object, 704
  sign to object, 704
  sign to sign, 702-4
  see also Mediated generalization
Semantics
  psychological relations subsumed, 698-
    9
  sign-process, conceptions, 690-99
Semi-circular canals, 31-2, 91
Semitendinosus muscle, 479-81
Sensation
  Fechner's Law and, 77
  measurement of, problem, 43-4, 54
  perception and, 192-4
Sensitization, reaction
  'backward conditioning' in, 314
  sensory conditioning in, 461
Sensitization, perceptual, 292-5
Sensory conditioning, 460-62
Sensory integration, 464-5
Sensory intensity, 65-83
  adaptation phenomena, 72-82
  Crozier's neural theory, 69-72
  frequency and number integration, 68
  frequency of impulses and, 66-7
  Hecht's chemical theory, 68-9
  neural basis of, 65-72
  number of fibers and, 67-8
  quality and, integration, 82-3

Sensory intensity (Cont.)
  refractory law and, 66-7
  threshold data, 72-7
SENSORY PROCESSES
  adaptation, 77-82
  audition, 84-127
  chemical senses, 21-9
  hearing, 84-127
  kinesthesis, 29-33
  methods of investigation, 3-12
  neural basis, intensity, 65-72
  neural basis, quality, 33-41
  quality and intensity, integration, 82-3
  quantal hypothesis, 59-65
  relations studied, 3-4
  psychophysical methods, 43-59
  skin senses, 3-21
  threshold data, 72-7
  vision, 128-89
Sensory quality, 33-41
  all-or-none law and, 33
  Boring's analysis, 39-40
  essential identity law, 33-4
  inferences, development of, 40
  intensity, integration, 82-3
  language and, 40
  modalities between, 36
  modalities within, 36-7
  neural correlates of, 35-8
  peripheral selection, 38
  philosophical positions, 34-5
  philosophical problems, 38-40
  physiological variables, 33-4
  psychological variables, 33
Serial learning, 495-520
  animal subjects in, 495-502
  differential forgetting explanation,
    518-19
  distribution of practice, 504-9
  fatigue explanation, 515
  goal gradient in, 496-501
  habit strength of components, 513-14
  heterogeneous responses, 500-501
  homogeneous responses, 500-501
  Hull theory of, 516-18
  human, verbal, 502-14
  interpretations of, 515-20
  interpretations, summary, 519-20
  maze, 495-502
  number components in task, 513
  performance decrement explanation,
    518
  perseveration explanation, 515-16
  position effects in, 502-4
  rehearsal explanation, 515
  reminiscence, Ward-Hovland in, 509-
    13
  similarity relations, 504
Set
  imageless thought and, 646-7
  retention and, 562-4
  problem-solving in, 627, 634-6
  theory, sign-process, 692-4
Shading, depth cue, 254
Short circuiting
  analysis of, 394-5
  foresight and, 393-4
  mediation theory in, 393-5
Sign-assign, 698

Sign-process, 690-99
  critical illustrations, 694-5
  defining problems, 690-91
  learning criterion, 694-5
  mediation theory of, 695-8
  mentalistic view, 691-2
  multiple semantic relations, 698-9
  paradigm for, 697
  'set' theory of, 692-4
  substitution theory of, 692
  Tolman theory in, 390
  see also Mediation process
Signs
  changing significance of, 405-8
  classes of, 402
  connotative, 696
  drive and reinforcing states, of, 440
  denotative, 697
  development of, paradigm, 696-7
  generalization among, 701-5
  learning, Mowrer studies, 406-8
  learning of, mediation, 395-9
  mediation theory and, 396
  theories of, 690-99
Similarity
  assimilation and, 553
  association in, 639
  distribution of practice and, 508-9
  generalization and, 361
  mediators, meaning measurement, 707-
  8
  paradox, human learning, 530-33
  perceptual grouping and, 213-14
  recall (gestalt) and, 553
  reminiscence and, 512-13
  tasks, among, Zeigarnik effect, 584
  variable, serial learning, 504
  variable, transfer and retroaction, 522-
  30
  word association and, 708-10
Sine wave, 84-5
Size
  absolute distance perception and, 265-
  6
  apparent, 262
  constancy, 275
  'normal,' how inferred, 266
  visual angle, distance, 262
Skaggs-Robinson Hypothesis, 530-31
Skills
  central organization of, 401
  mediation theory in, 399-401
  motor feedback in, 400-401
  reinforcement and, 472-3
  Tolman's theory in, 385, 472-3
  transfer in learning of, 537-9
Skin senses
  electrophysiology of, 10-12
  cutaneous blends, 20
  histological analysis, 6-7
  methods of investigation, 3-12
  pain, 13-14
  paradoxical quality, 5, 17
  punctate nature, 4-6
  stability of 'spots,' 5
  summary, 20-21
  thermal, 14-20
  touch, 12-13
Skinner box, 305

Slant, relative distance cue, 262
Sleep
  dreaming, motor activity, 651
  motor tonus and, 652-3
  retention and, 594
Smell, see Olfaction
Sone (unit of loudness), 115-16
Sound
  amplitude, 84-5, 88
  apparatus, 86-8
  cancellation, 86
  frequency, 84-6, 88
  measurement of, 88
  physics of, 84-8
  pressure wave, characteristics, 84-5
  summation, 85-6
Spark-gap recordograph, 9
Specific energies
  auditory theory and, 95, 108-9
  bodily rotation in, 32
  cutaneous fiber types and, 10-12
  gustation and, 22
  Hering's color theory and, 173
  law of, Müller, 5
  sensory quality and, 35-6
  thermal sense and, 18
  Young-Helmholtz theory in, 169
Spectrum, visual, 137
Speech skills
  development of, 684-7
  frequency patterns (phonemes), 685-7
Spinal conditioning, 479-81
Spiral ganglia, 92
Spontaneous recovery
  atypical human data, 345
  experimental evidence, 337-8
  fatigue theory explanation, 338-43
  forgetting and, 549-50
  interference theory and, 347-8
  paradox of, 336-7
Spread of effect, 377, 424-5
Standing waves, 86
Stapedius muscle, 89
Stapes, 89
Statistical structure of language
  adjective-verb quotient, 719
  associations, 721-6
  contextual factors, 724-6
  frequency-of-usage counts, 717-18
  habit-family hierarchy and, 718, 722
  sequential association method, 723-5
  type-token ratio, 719-21
  Zipf's contributions, 715-19
'Statistical' theory, projection system
  binocular disparity and, 257-8
  contour formation, 197, 229-30
  depth and solidity, 251-3
  figural after-effects, 237-43
  movement perception, 245-6
  nature, 196-8
  visual acuity and, 164, 197
Stereoscope, 254, 268-9
Stimulus, defined, 12
Stimulus error, 640
Stimulus-object, mediation theory, 396
Stimulus trace
  effect retroaction paradox and, 381-2
  perceptual interaction and, 209
  postulation of, 376

Stimulus trace (Cont.)
  short circuiting and, 395
  serial learning, role in, 516-17
Strengthening of association
  contiguity (Guthrie), 321
  reinforcement (Hull), 322-3
  substitution (Pavlov), 321-2
  two-factor views, 323-4
Stretch afferents, 30
Stroboscope, 231-2, 243-6
Subgoals, learning, 495-500
Substitution learning
  criticism, 320, 321-2
  meaning of, 692
  paradigm for, 310-11
  see also Conditioning
Summation
  amplitude, sound, 85-6
  areal, acuity and, 165
  areal, retina, 166-7
  areal, single fiber in, 167
  chromatic, 181
  color, 234
  constancy and, 282
  habit strength into, 324-6
  retinal, contrast, 233-4
  principle, habit, Hull, 377
  temporal, Hecht's theory, 166
  temporal, vision, 165-6
  vertical meridian and, 259
Summation tones, 123-4
Superior colliculi, 482
Surrogate response, Seward, 470
SYMBOLIC PROCESSES
  abstracting, 666-79
  concept formation, 666-79
  development of language, 683-90
  frontal cortex and, 660-65
  language, 680-726
  measurement of meaning, 699-714
  problem-solving, animal, 603-22
  problem-solving, human, 622-37
  sign-process, 690-99
  statistical structure of language, 714-25
  thinking, animal, 655-65
  thinking, human, 638-55
Synchronization, impulses
  auditory, higher centers, 110
  retina, 167
  VIIIth nerve trunk, 104
Synesthesia, 642-6
  color, music, mood, 643, 645-6
  individual differences, 642-4
  semantic differential and, 713
  tonal attributes and, 124-5
Synonyms
  generalization among, 702-5
  mediated transfer, 705-6
  scaling of, 712
Syntactics, 699

t

Tachistoscope
  ambiguous figures, perception, 287-8, 292
  perceptual organization, study, 224-5
  recognition threshold measurement, 288, 292-5

Taste
  'blindness,' 24
  buds, 23-4
  cells, 23-4
  qualities, 22
  see also Gustation
Temporal summation
  Hecht's theory, chemical, 166
  thresholds and, 75
  vision in, 165-6
Tension
  memory and, 553, 578, 582
  problem-solving and, 606-8
  visual field in, 203-4
Tensor tympani, 89
Termites, signs in, 694
Texture, visual, 262
THEORIES
  brightness summation and inhibition, 165-8
  central dynamics, perception, 294-7
  color vision, 168-89
  constancy, 280-85
  contrast, 233-6
  depth perception, 257-60
  discrimination, 444-55
  distance perception, 266, 269-71
  figural after-effects, 236-8
  forgetting, 549-54, 587-99
  hearing, 94-9, 127
  inhibition, 345-50
  learning, 362-412, 462-73
  olfaction, 25-7
  perception, 195-212
  problem-solving, 605-20
  quantal, sensation, 59-65
  secondary drive and reinforcement, 439-40, 443
  sensory intensity, 65-72
  sensory quality, 33-41
  serial learning, 515-20
  sign-process, 690-99
  similarity and learning, 530-33
  thermal sensitivity, 14-20
  thought, 653-5
  transfer and retroaction, 542-8
Thermal sensitivity
  adequate stimuli, 14
  chemical theory, 15-16
  differential sensitivity, 17, 19-20, 82-3
  evaluation of theories, 16-18
  gradient theory, 14
  'heat,' nature of experience, 18-20
  Jenkins's theory, 15-17
  Nafe's theory, 15
  reaction time, receptors, 17
  receptors, 14-18
  smooth muscle, role in, 15, 16
  stimulators, 5
  Von Frey's theory, 14-15
Thinking, animal, 655-65
  anecdotal evidence, 655
  criterion for, 656
  legitimacy of study, 655-6
  see also Representational processes in animals
Thinking, human, 638-65
  abstracting ability, 674-9
  central vs. peripheral theories of consciousness, 653-5

Thinking (Cont.)
concept formation, 666-73
imagery, role of, 640-42
imageless thought controversy, 646-7
implicit speech as, 648
introspective method, 639-48
Max and Jacobson studies, 649-51
motor activity in, 648-55
problem-solving as, 622-37
synesthetic, 642-6
Thouless ratio, 274, 278
Threshold, reaction, 379
Thresholds, sensory, 72-7
area of stimulus and, 74
correlation, AL and DL, 73
Crozier's theory, 74-6
duration of stimulus and, 75
Hecht's theory, 75-6
receptor density and, 73-4
sizes of, modalities, 72-3
units of measurement, 72
Weber's law of, DL, 75-7
Timbre, 85
Time error, 54-8
adaptation explanation, 57
central tendency effect, 56-7
context explanation, 56-7
pitch *vs.* loudness in, 121
psychophysical methods in, 54
summary, 57-8
terminology, 55
trace explanation, 55-6
weights, hefted, 48
Würzburg School and, 54
Tolman, cognition theory, 382-92
avoidance training and, 430
conditioning, 388-9
critique, 389-92
individual differences in, 384-5
instrumental learning in, 389, 391
gestalt aspects, 385, 389-90
mediation theory as, 388
nature of, 384-5
principles of, 385-9
terminology, 382-4
Tonal attributes, 124-6
Tone and noise, 85
Touch sensitivity, *see* Pressure sensitivity
Trace conditioning
delay phenomena, 315
serial learning in, 502-3, 516-17
Trace theory, memory
generality of, 598-9
interference theory, compared, 587-8
memory for forms, 588-93
nature of, 551-4
retention curve and, 556
Transfer
degrees of learning and, 537-9
discrimination and, 534
'intelligent,' rat, 405
mediated equivalence and, 526
meaning and, 705-6
negative, response variation, 526-,
negative, stimulus and response variation, 527-9
ordinary learning and, 524-5
paradigm for, 521

Transfer (Cont.)
positive, and generalization, 525-6
positive, stimulus variation, 525-6
response, mediated, 408-10
response, place learning, 458-60
retention and, same intervals, 533-4
temporal relations, 533-5
Transfer and retroaction, 520-48
competition-of-response theory, 543-5
degree of learning and, 537-9
interpretations of, 542-8
irritability factor, 547-8
mediators among, meaning, 707-8
methodological considerations, 520-22
perseveration theory, 542-3
reciprocal inhibition and, 546-7
response similarity and, 526-7
rest condition, as control, 521-2
similarity, locus specified, 525-30
similarity, locus unspecified, 522-5
similarity paradox, 530-33
stimulus and response variation with, 527-9
stimulus variation with, 525-6
surface, similarity relations, 532-3
summary, 548
temporal relations, 533-7
terminology, 520
time error in, 57
two-factor theory of, 545-6
warm-up effect and, 563-4
'Transient orange,' 148-9
Transient tones, 86
Transposition
brain-injured, in, 483-4
discrimination learning in, 445-6
perceptual organization in, 215-16
Spence analysis, 445-6
subjects blind from birth in, 226-8
Trial and error
'blind,' in problem-solving, 611-12
'correct' response in, 308-9
cues in, 308
efficiency of, 320
implicit, problem-solving, 614-15
'kind' of learning, 301, 320
randomness of, 307-8
strengthening in, 308
see also Instrumental learning
Trichromatic coefficients, 139-40
Trichromatism, 174
Tritanopia, 174
Tuning fork, 84-5
Twins, language development, 690
Two-factor theories
learning, 463-9
retroaction, 545-6
Tympanic membrane, 89
Type-token ratio, 719-22

U

Unconditioned response, 310, 317
Unconscious inference, Helmholtz
constancy in, 279
depth perception in, 248-9
movement perception in, 243, 248
Unum and duo, 216-17
Utricle, 31

V

Vacuum tube amplifier, 8-9
Value, perception and, 289-95
Verbal summator, 722-3
Vertical meridian, 259-60
Vestibule, ear, 91
Vicarious functioning, neurophysiology
    cortex and subcortex, 493
    discrimination learning in, 481-4
    logical requirements, 475-6
Vicarious trial and error (VTE), 307
'Vigilance,' 652-3
VIIIth nerve
    amplitude f. frequency in, 104-6
    anatomy, 92
    electrical recording from, 104-6
    non-auditory segment, 30-31
    partial sectioning of, 106-10
Vincent curves, 329
VISION
    color, see Visual quality
    eye, the, 132-7
    intensity functions, 155-68
    neurophysiology of, 146-55
    phenomenology of, 128-32
    psychophysics, 137-46
    quality (color), 168-88
    retina, 133-7
    rods and cones, 135-7
Visual acuity
    areal summation and, 165
    brightness DL as, 162-3
    illumination and, 164
    retinal mosaic and, 164
    'statistical' theory of, 164
Visual intensity
    absolute thresholds, 155-8
    adaptation, 158-61
    Crozier's neural theory, 69-72
    difference thresholds, 161-5
    Hecht's chemical theory, 68-9
Visual purple
    dark adaptation and, 158-9
    regeneration of, 148-9
    rod function and, 135-6
    rod thresholds and, 156
Visual quality (color), 168-88
    brightness relations, 181-3
    color blindness, 173-5
    Granit's theory, 178-81
    Hering's theory, 173
    inhibitory processes, 186-8
    Ladd-Franklin theory, 173-6
    receptor types, 176-81
    rods, role of, 183-6
    theory, limitations, 168-9
    theory, summary, 188-9
    Young-Helmholtz theory, 169-73
Vitamin A
    dark adaptation and, 161
    visual chemistry in, 148-9
Vitreous humor, 133
Volley principle
    criticism, 98-9

Volley principle (Cont.)
    evidence for, 104-6
    nature of, 97-9
    Wever-Bray effect and, 93
Voltmeter, 87-8
Volume
    attribute of sound, 124-6
    speech development in, 685
Voluntary conditioning, 323

W

Warm-up effect (retention), 562-4
Wave analyser, 88
Wave length, light, 137
Waxed paper recordograph, 9
Weber's Law, 75-7
    brightness DL and, 162
    Crozier's theory and, 70-72, 77
    evaluation, 76-7
    Fechner's contributions, 75-7
Wedge photometer, 44-5, 46
Weight
    judgments, psychophysics, 47-50
    time error in, judgments, 48
'Wetness,' synthesis of, 20
Wever-Bray effect, 92-3
'White noise,' 85
Whole vs. part learning, 540-42
Willmer's color theory, 183-6
Word association, 708-12
    classification of, 708-9
    context and, 725-6
    Freud and Jung views, 708
    Kent-Rosanoff data, 708-10
    mode of sign and, 711-12
    opposites in, role, 709-11
    paradigm for, 708-9
    statistical structure of, 721-6
Würzburg School
    imageless thought, 646
    time error, 54

Y

Yerkes discrimination box, 448-51
Young-Helmholtz theory, color vision,
        169-73
    brightness functions in, 183
    color blindness, 174, 175
    color mixture and, 170-71
    excitation curves for, 170-71
    Granit's data and, 180-81
    Hecht's contributions, 171-3
    history, 169
    hue discrimination in, 170-72
    luminosity and, functions, 170-72
    nature, general, 169-70
    saturation in, 170-72
'Yum-yum' theory, language, 683

Z

Zeigarnik effect, 582-7
Zipf's Law, 716, 722